THE INDIANA FACTBOOK

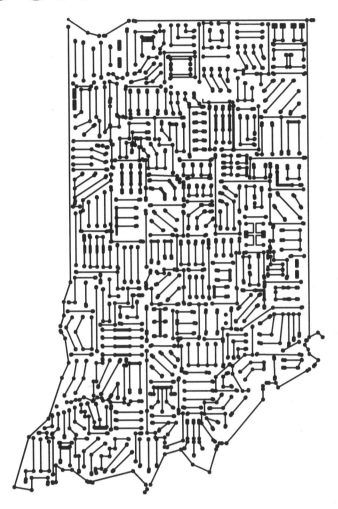

1998-99

Created and Developed By:

Terry Creeth
Editor

Bethany Sprague
Information Specialist

Christine Fisk
Database Coordinator

Morton J. Marcus
Director

http://www.iupui.edu/it/ibrc

Published for the
Indiana Department of Commerce and the
Indiana University, Kelley School of Business
Indiana Business Research Center
by Indiana University Press
Bloomington and Indianapolis

Indiana University, Kelley School of Business

Dan R. Dalton
Dean
R. Jeffery Green
Associate Dean for Research & Operations
John G. Helmkamp
Associate Dean-Indianapolis Programs
Bruce L. Jaffee
Associate Dean for Academics

Indiana Business Research Center

Morton J. Marcus

Jo Basey
Terry Creeth
Hui Mei Chuang
Mary Belle Davis
Matt Dye
Christine Fisk
Elaine Goodwin
Debbie Hoke
Nikki Livingston
Victoria Nelson
Joan Rainey
Carol. O. Rogers
Bethany Sprague

Additional copies of the *Indiana Factbook* are available from IU Press — 1-800-842-6796

Indiana Factbook **Sponsored by:**
Northern Indiana Public Service Company
Hoosier Energy Rural Electric Cooperative, Inc.
CINERGY/PSI

The paper used in this publication meets the minimum requirements of American National Standard for Information Sciences—Permanence of Paper for Printed Library Materials, ANSI Z39.348-1984.

Manufactured in the United States of America

ISSN 0886-330X

1 2 3 4 5 03 02 01 00 99 98

Introduction

Why do we continue to publish a book of numbers in a world moving rapidly toward electronic transmission of information? The answer is simple: many modes may exist simultaneously to satisfy consumer wants.

Fast food restaurants have eliminated neither formal dining nor family picnics. Television has driven neither books nor radio into extinction. Walking, bicycling, and riding in a car are three very different ways of getting somewhere and each provides distinctive advantages for exploring our environment.

A volume of statistics is necessarily different from a series of web pages. It allows the user to roam and to learn in a way different from watching pixels proliferate on a screen. In a world of rapidly changing relationships, or when precision is required for a decision, a dynamic data base (which is not often found as yet on the web) may be best. But most economic and demographic relationships do not change very rapidly. Quantities (the specific population of a county) may change, but relationships (the ranking of that county in the state) may be very stable over time.

This *Factbook*, in this and its previous four editions, has been dedicated to adding value, through rankings and other calculations, to the basic data presented. As such, it may be out-of-date instantly, yet retain extraordinary timeliness and utility for its users.

This fifth edition of the *Indiana Factbook* should be very familiar to those who have used earlier editions. We have attempted to update all tables where new data are available, but have kept those tables where no new data will be ready until after the Census of 2000. New graphics have been added to highlight trends and give visual representation to more data.

The only deletion from earlier editions is the directories section. There are two good reasons for dropping the directories:

■ The organizations which maintain the directories from which we took listings, do not keep them as up-to-date as users of this *Factbook* might desire. Therefore, we found ourselves publishing incorrect names, addresses, and telephone numbers. In addition to the embarrassment of inaccurate listings, we felt it is a disservice to our users to provide them with inferior information.

■ The wide and growing use of the web makes it easier to access directory information than it had been previously. Efficiency in the use of resources requires that we examine carefully each entry in this publication. If we are to provide directory services, links to the originating organizations on our own web-site may be the best place to do so.

Each time this *Factbook* is issued, we are impressed by our dependency on the agencies which compile and issue the data we publish. To the federal and state organizations which provide data, we extend our sincere appreciation and our sympathy. Many of these agencies are battling rising costs with falling real budgets. They endure legislative indifference to the importance of their efforts. They suffer high turnover of personnel because they are not permitted to pay competitive wages. That they perform so well is a tribute to their long-term, dedicated employees.

We would like to give special thanks, therefore to the people at the . . .

> **U.S. Bureau of Economic Analysis**
> **U.S. Bureau of the Census**
> **Indiana Department of Workforce Development**
> **Health Professionals Bureau**
> **Indiana Department of Revenue**
> **Indiana Board of Tax Commissioners**
> **Indiana State Department of Health**
> **Indiana Department of Higher Education**
> **Indiana Bureau of Motor Vehicles**
> **Indiana Department of Health and Human Services**
> **Indiana Secretary of State**
> **Indiana State Police**

and others who have contributed, without intending to do so, to this *Factbook*.

This work is part of the continuing, daily activities of the Indiana Business Research Center (IBRC) in the Kelley School of Business at Indiana University. It is not feasible to separate credit for the *Factbook* from the honors accruing to those who maintain and support the data base of the IBRC.

At the risk of leaving out a few names, let us recognize the continuing efforts of Marybelle Davis, Vickie Nelson, Debbie Hoke, and Christine Fisk whose routine dedication is extraordinary.

Carol Rogers has been instrumental in providing vision and guidance for this volume. But the heaviest responsibilities for placing this volume in your hands has fallen on Terry Creeth and Bethany Sprague. They have attended to the accuracy and appearance of each column and each row on each page. They have labored to make each graphic an example of clarity. And to them, for their tenacity, their concern, and their sustained good cheer, each user of this volume is indebted.

Those who purchase this volume are direct beneficiaries of the continuing support from three Indiana firms. The price of each copy of this *Factbook* has been reduced by $10 through the generous contributions of **Northern Indiana Public Service Company, Hoosier Energy Rural Electric Cooperative, Inc.,** and **CINERGY/PSI**. We are delighted to pass along the entire amount of their gifts to the people of Indiana.

It is also fitting to give credit to the **Indiana Department of Commerce** which funds part of the work of this *Factbook*. Few government agencies are willing to support an activity of this nature without some editorial review. Yet, at no time has any member of that Department ever suggested that we exclude certain numbers which do not put Indiana in a good light. At no time have we been asked to direct our efforts to support positions or policies of that agency in any way.

Finally, we wish to acknowledge what may seem obvious, but which deserves notice nonetheless: the support of **Indiana University** and the **Kelley School of Business**. In these times of profit centers and the encouragement of academic entrepreneurs, we have been fortunate to sustain the support of both a university and a professional school which continue to see value in services provided to our state. We appreciate an environment where responsibility still coexists harmoniously with revenue generation.

Morton J. Marcus, Director
May 1998

Glossary

Age—Age data are needed to interpret most social and economic characteristics and are used to plan and examine many programs and policies.

African-American—Many Americans of African descent use this term of identification. As used in this book, it is synonymous with the descriptor "Black" used by the U.S. Bureau of the Census. *For more detail, see Race.*

AFDC—Aid to Families with Dependent Children, a program providing cash assistance to very low-income families with children—maximum benefit levels are determined by individual states.

Asian-American—People with Asian or Pacific Island origins. *For more detail, see Race.*

Average Earnings Per Job—A statistical measurment calculated by dividing total earnings by the number of jobs.

Birth Rate—Generally, the number of births per 1,000 population in a given year *(births / total population x 1000).*

Contract Rent—Contract rent is the monthly rent agreed to or contracted for, regardless of any furnishings, utilities, fees, meals, or services that may be included.

Commuting—These data from the census show the county of destination for work, based on the census question "where did you work last week." Commuting patterns will be affected by the type of job—for example, people in sales and construction work in many different counties and states.

Death Rate—The number of deaths per 1,000 population in a given year *(deaths / total population x 1000).*

Disposable Personal Income—Disposable personal income is personal income less personal tax and nontax payments. It is the income available to persons for spending or saving.

Earnings—This income measure is the sum of wage and salary disbursements, other labor income, and proprietors' income. It is often used in regional economic analysis to serve as a proxy for income generated from participation in current production. The measure "net earnings" is earnings less personal contributions for social insurance. These contributions are included in earnings by type and industry, but they are not included in personal income; therefore, they are subtracted from earnings in the computation of personal income as the sum of earnings, plus dividends, interest, and rent, plus transfer payments.

Educational Attainment—Data on educational attainment were derived from a sample of persons in the 1990 Census and are presented here for persons 25 years and older. Persons are classified according to the highest level of school completed or the highest degree received. The question included response categories which allowed persons to report completing the 12th grade without receiving a high school diploma, and which instructed respondents to report as "high school graduate(s)" persons who received either a high school diploma or the equivalent (for example the G.E.D.), and did not attend college.

High School Graduate or Higher—Includes persons whose highest degree was a high school diploma or its equivalent, persons who attended college or professional school, and persons who received a college, university, or professional degree. Persons who reported completing the 12th grade but not receiving a diploma are not included.

Employment—There are many sources for employment numbers. Those from the decennial census count the number of people with jobs at the time of enumeration. The Bureau of Labor Statistics estimates people working (employed) or looking for work (unemployed) and estimates the number of jobs by industry based on covered employment. The Bureau of Economic Analysis estimates the number of jobs by industry (by place of work) and also includes sole proprietors (which BLS does not). Caution is urged when "mixing" sources, since each agency uses different estimation methods and therefore have somewhat different numbers.

Food Stamp Program—A federal program designed to raise the nutritional level of low-income households by providing coupons for food items.

Hispanic Origin—Persons of Hispanic origin are those who classified themselves in one of the specific Hispanic origin categories listed on the questionnaire—"Mexican," "Puerto Rican," or "Cuban"—as well as those who indicated that they were of "other Spanish/Hispanic" origin—from Spain, the Spanish-speaking countries of Central or South America, or the Dominican Republic.

Group Quarters—All persons not living in households. Two general categories of group quarters are recognized: (1) institutionalized persons under formally authorized, supervised care or custody in institutions such as correctional institutions and nursing homes at the time of enumeration, and (2) other persons in group quarters which includes all persons who live in group quarters other than institutions or persons who live in living quarters when there are 10 or more unrelated persons living in the unit.

Household Types and Relationships:
Household—A household includes all the persons who occupy a housing unit. In 100-percent tabulations, the count of households or householders always equals the count of occupied housing units. In sample tabulations, the numbers may differ as a result of the weighting process.

Family—A family consists of a householder and one or more other persons living in the same household who are related to the householder by birth, marriage, or adoption. All persons in a household who are related to the householder are regarded as members of his or her family. Families are classified by type as either a "married-couple family" or "other family" according to the sex of the householder and the presence of relatives.

Married-Couple Family—A family in which the householder and his or her spouse are enumerated as members of the same household.

Other Family:
> *Male Householder, No Wife Present*—A family with a male householder and no spouse of householder present; with or without children.

> *Female Householder, No Husband Present*—A family with a female householder and no spouse of householder present; with or without children.

Child—Includes a son or daughter by birth, a stepchild, or adopted child of the householder, regardless of the child's age or marital status. The category excludes sons-in-law, daughters-in-law, and foster children.

Natural-Born or Adopted Son/Daughter—A son or daughter of the householder by birth, regardless of the age of the child. Also, this category includes sons or daughters of the householder by legal adoption, regardless of the age of the child. If the stepson/stepdaughter of the householder has been legally adopted by the householder, the child is still classified as a stepchild.

Stepson/Stepdaughter—A son or daughter of the householder through marriage but not by birth, regardless of the age of the child. If the stepson/stepdaughter of the householder has been legally adopted by the householder, the child is still classified as a stepchild.

Own Child—A never-married child under 18 years who is a son or daughter by birth, a stepchild, or an adopted child of the householder. In certain tabulations, own children are further classified as living with two parents or with one parent only. Own children of the householder living with two parents are by definition found only in married-couple families.

"Related children"—in a family include own children and all other persons under 18 years of age in the household, regardless of marital status, who are related to the householder, except the spouse of the householder. Foster children are not included.

Non-relatives—Includes any household member, including foster children not related to the householder by birth, marriage or adoption. Examples are roomer, boarder, foster child, housemate or roomate, or unmarried partner.

Householder—Includes the person or one of the persons in whose name the home is owned, being bought or rented, and who is listed in column 1 of the census questionnaire.

Housing Unit—A house, apartment, mobile home or trailer, a group of rooms or a single room occupied or intended to be occupied as separate living quarters.

Income of Households—Includes the income of the householder and all other persons 15 years old and over in the household, whether related to the householder or not. Because many households consist of only one person, average household income is usually less than average family income.

Median Income—The median divides the income distribution into two equal parts, one having incomes above the median and the other having incomes below the median. For households and families, the median income is based on the distribution of the total number of units, including those with no income.

Mean Income—The mean is obtained by dividing total household income by the total number of households.

Manufacturing—This industry group includes (1) durable goods such as lumber and wood, furniture and fixtures, primary metal, fabricated metal, machinery, electric and electronic equipment, transportation equipment, motor vehicles and equipment, stone, clay, and glass, and instruments and (2) non durable goods such as food, textile mills, apparel, paper, chemicals, petroleum, rubber and plastics.

Marital Status—The marital status classification refers to the status at the time of enumeration for persons 15 years old and over. Couples who live together (unmarried persons, persons in common-law marriages) were allowed to report the marital status they considered the most appropriate.

    Never Married—Includes all persons who have never been married, including persons whose only marriage(s) was annulled.

    Ever Married—Includes persons married at the time of enumeration (including those separated), widowed, or divorced.

    Now Married, Except Separated—Includes persons whose current marriage has not ended through widowhood, divorce, or separation (regardless of previous marital history). The category may also include couples who live together or persons in common-law marriages if they consider this category the most appropriate.

    Separated—Includes persons legally separated or otherwise absent from their spouse because of marital discord. Included are persons who have been deserted or who no longer live together but have not obtained a divorce.

    Widowed—Includes widows and widowers who have not remarried.

    Divorced—Includes persons who are legally divorced and who have not remarried.

Mean—This measure represents an arithmetic average of a set of values. It is derived by dividing the sum of a group of numerical items (or aggregate) by the total number of items. Aggregates are used in computing mean values. For example, mean family income is obtained by dividing the aggregate of all income reported by persons in families by the total number of families.

Median Age—This measure divides the age distribution into two equal parts: one-half of the cases falling below the median value and one-half above the value.

Money Income—The Bureau of the Census uses a "money income" concept as the basis for its per capita income estimate. Money income is the sum of all sources of cash income including wages and salaries, income earned through self employment and farming, interest, dividends, and rental income, social security payments, disability payments, pensions, alimony and child support, winnings from gambling, and other cash income sources.

Other Labor Income—This component of personal income consists of employer payments to privately administered pension and profit-sharing plans, private group health and life insurance plans, privately administered workers' compensation plans, supplemental unemployment benefit plans, corporate directors' fees, and several minor categories of employee compensation, including judicial fees to jurors and witnesses and compensation of prisoners.

Natural Increase—A component of population change that occurs when the number of births is larger than the number of deaths. When the opposite occurs, it is called natural decrease.

Per Capita Money Income—The total money income for all persons within a geographic location is divided by the total number of persons in that location to produce a per capita income estimate. In order to be consistent with the decennial census, the Census Bureau compiles income estimates for the prior calendar year and divides by the present year's estimated mid-year population.

Per Capita Personal Income—This income measure is the total personal income of the residents of a given area divided by the resident population of the area. Per capita personal income is often used as an indicator of the quality of consumer markets and of the economic well-being of the residents of an area.

Personal Contributions for Social Insurance—These include the following programs: old-age, survivors, and disability insurance (social security); hospital insurance and supplemental medical insurance (medicare); state unemployment insurance; government employee retirement; railroad retirement; veterans life insurance; and temporary disability insurance.

Personal Dividend Income—This component of personal income consists of payments in cash or other assets, excluding stock, by corporations organized for profit to noncorporate stockholders who are U.S. residents. For the state and local area estimates, this component is combined with personal interest income and rental income of persons.

Personal Income—Personal income is the income received by persons from all sources—that is, from participation in production, from both government and business transfer payments, and from government interest. Personal income is measured as the sum of wage and salary disbursements, other labor income, proprietors' income, rental income of persons, personal dividend income, personal interest income, and transfer payments, less personal contributions for social insurance. See also Persons, Wages and salaries, Other labor income, Proprietors' income, Rental income of persons, Personal dividend income, Personal interest income, Transfer payments, and Personal contributions for social insurance.

Personal Interest Income—This component of personal income is the interest income of persons from all sources. In addition to monetary interest, personal interest income includes imputed interest, which is paid by corporate financial business. The imputed interest paid by life insurance carriers and noninsured pension plans credits their investment income to persons in the year in which it is earned. The imputed interest paid by financial intermediaries other than life insurance carriers and private noninsured pension plans represents the value to persons of financial services for which they are not explicitly charged. For the state and local area estimates, it is combined with personal dividend income and rental income of persons.

Population Density—Population per unit of land area *(total population / land area)*.

Population Projections—Cohort-component methodology was used to project the population of Indiana's 92 counties. For each five year period, the population is projected for individual age/sex cohorts and separately by the components of change—mortality, migration, and fertility. The cohort-component method is based on the traditional demographic accounting system:

$$P1 = P0 + B - D + NM$$
where
P1 = population at the end of the period
P0 = population at the beginning of the period
B = births during the period
D = deaths during the period
NM = net migration during the period

This model uses birth, death, and migration data, with the 1990 Census as the *jump-off* population. The population is projected to a July 1 date.

Projections of Income and Employment—Produced by the U.S. Bureau of Economic Analysis, two series are presented in this book: projections of income and employment for the 50 States and projections for Indiana counties. Each series uses a different methodology and were produced at different points in time. It is suggested that the choice of which Indiana projection to be used be determined by whether one is comparing states or counties.

Proprietors' Income—This component is the current-production income of sole proprietorships and partnerships and of tax-exempt cooperatives. The imputed net rental income of owner-occupants of farm dwellings is included.

Race—The concept of race as used by the Census Bureau reflects self-identification; it does not denote any clear-cut scientific definition of biological stock. The data for race represent self-classification by people according to the race with which they most closely identify. The racial classification used generally adheres to the guidelines issued by the U.S. Office of Management and Budget, which provides standards for statistical reporting to be used by all Federal agencies. The 1990 census categories are provided below.

White—Includes persons who indicated their race as "White" or reported entries such as Canadian, German, Italian, Lebanese, Near Easterner, Arab, or Polish.

Black—Includes persons who indicated their race as "Black or Negro" or reported entries such as African American, Afro-American, Black Puerto Rican, Jamaican, Nigerian, West Indian, or Haitian. (The *Factbook* opted for the now more widely used African-American).

American Indian, Eskimo, or Aleut—Includes persons who classified themselves as such in one of the specific race categories relating to Native Americans. (The *Factbook* opted for the now more widely used Native American).

Asian or Pacific Islander—Includes persons who reported in one of the Asian or Pacific Islander groups listed on the questionnaire or who provided write-in responses such as Thai, Nepali, or Tongan. (The *Factbook* opted for the more widely used Asian-American).

Other Race—Includes all other persons not included in the "White," "Black," "American Indian, Eskimo, or Aleut," and the "Asian or Pacific Islander" race categories described above. Persons reporting in the "Other race" category and providing write-in entries such as multiracial, multiethnic, mixed, interracial, or a Spanish/Hispanic origin group (such as Mexican, Cuban, or Puerto Rican) are in this category.

Real Dollars—In reference to financial or income items, it denotes the adjustment for inflation. The *Factbook* used the personal consumption deflator in its calculations. Real percent change is calculated using the following formula:

$$R\$ = (N - (O / (P/C))) / (O / (P/C)) * 100$$
where
R$ = real dollars
N = current year value
O = past year value
C = Implicit price deflator, personal consumption expeditures, current year
P = Implicit price deflator, personal consumption expeditures, past year

Residence (place of)—Income is recorded either by place of work or by place of residence. By definition, personal income is a measure of income where received, and the state and local area estimates of total personal income reflect the residence of the recipient.

Resident—In the context of measuring personal income, resident refers to individuals. Individuals actually residing in a county are counted as residents. Military personnel are considered residents of the county in which they are stationed (or of an adjacent county if they commute daily), even though they may consider themselves permanent residents of another county. Wages that workers earn during short temporary assignments away from their usual places of work are assigned to their usual places of residence. Similarly, tourists or others in such a temporary status are not counted as residents. Seasonal migrant workers are considered residents of the area in which their work is performed, with wages assigned to the county where a worker lives while earning the wages. Persons located abroad and foreign citizens employed by international organizations and by foreign embassies and consulates in the U.S. are not counted as residents of any county, and their income is excluded from personal income. The concept of residence as it relates to personal income refers to the location where the income to be measured is received rather than to usual, permanent, or legal residence. This treatment differs from that of the Census Bureau, which counts many seasonal and short-term workers at their usual place of residence, even if they are living and working elsewhere at the time the information is gathered.

Residence Adjustment—This adjustment is made to wages and salaries, other labor income, and personal contributions for social insurance (with minor exceptions) to place them on a place-of-residence (where-received) basis. The adjustment is necessary because these components of personal income are estimated from data that are reported by place of work (where earned).

Rural—Territory and population not classified as urban constitute rural, generally places of less than 2,500 persons *(for more detail, see **Urban**)*.

Standard Industrial Classification (SIC)—This system is used in the classification of establishments by the type of activity in which they are engaged. An establishment is defined as an economic unit, generally at a single physical location, where business is conducted or where services or industrial operations are performed. The SIC is designed to cover all economic activity, public as well as private. Its structure consists of the following: Divisions (e.g., manufacturing); major groups, or two-digit levels (e.g., food and kindred products); three-digit levels (e.g., meat products); and four-digit levels (e.g., meat packing plants). Each establishment is assigned an industry code on the basis of its primary activity. The SIC, which is revised from time to time to reflect the changing industrial structure of the economy, is published by the Office of Management and Budget in the *Standard Industrial Classification Manual.*

Transfer Payments—This component of personal income consists of income payments to persons for which no current services are performed. These are payments by government and business to individuals and nonprofit institutions. Generally, they are paid in monetary form; major exceptions are food stamps and medical vendor payments. Government transfer payments to nonprofit institutions exclude payments for work under research and development contracts.

Units in Structure—A structure is a separate building that either has open spaces on all sides or is separated from other structures by dividing walls that extend from ground to roof. Census of Housing data exclude stores and office space.

Urban—Places of 2,500 or more persons in incorporated places (cities and towns), but excluding the rural portions or "extended cities" and Census designated places of 2,500 or more persons (e.g. Granger, Indiana).

Wages and Salaries—This component of personal income is defined as the monetary remuneration of employees; this remuneration includes the compensation of corporate officers; commissions, tips, and bonuses; voluntary employee contributions to certain deferred compensation plans such as 401(k) plans; and receipts in kind, or pay-in-kind, that represent income. Wage and salary disbursements are measured before deductions, such as social security contributions and union dues, and they reflect the amount of wages and salaries disbursed, but not necessarily earned, during the year.

Specified Housing Units—Includes only one-family houses on less than 10 acres without a business or medical office on the property. The data for "specified" units exclude mobile homes, houses with a business or medical office, houses on 10 or more acres, and housing units in multi-unit buildings.

Tenure—An indicator of whether a housing unit is owner-occupied or renter-occupied.

Value—Value is the respondent's estimate of how much the property (house and lot, mobile home and lot, or condominium unit) would sell for if it were for sale (at time of enumeration). If the house or mobile home was owned or being bought, but the land on which it sits was not, the respondent was asked to estimate the combined value of the house or mobile home and the land.

Table of Contents

Section 1— *Indiana in Perspective: U. S. & 50 States*

Section 3 - *Counties in Profile: Indiana and 92 Counties*

Sources for the Indiana Counties in Profile

SECTION 1

Indiana in Perspective:
U.S. and 50 States

Population

1.1 Population Counts and Estimates 1950 to 1997 *(000)*

	Census					Estimates					
	1950	1960	1970	1980	1990	1992	1993	1994	1995	1996	1997
United States	151,326	179,323	203,302	226,546	248,710	255,002	257,753	260,292	262,761	265,179	267,636
Alabama	3,062	3,267	3,444	3,894	4,041	4,138	4,193	4,232	4,262	4,287	4,319
Alaska	129	226	303	402	550	587	597	601	602	605	609
Arizona	750	1,302	1,775	2,718	3,665	3,868	3,994	4,149	4,308	4,434	4,555
Arkansas	1,910	1,786	1,923	2,286	2,351	2,394	2,424	2,451	2,481	2,506	2,523
California	10,586	15,717	19,971	23,668	29,760	30,892	31,183	31,369	31,558	31,858	32,268
Colorado	1,325	1,754	2,210	2,890	3,294	3,462	3,563	3,657	3,742	3,816	3,893
Connecticut	2,007	2,535	3,032	3,108	3,287	3,277	3,273	3,270	3,267	3,267	3,270
Delaware	318	446	548	594	666	689	698	706	716	723	732
Dist. Of Col.	802	764	757	638	607	585	577	566	552	539	529
Florida	2,771	4,952	6,791	9,746	12,938	13,501	13,712	13,956	14,181	14,419	14,654
Georgia	3,445	3,943	4,588	5,463	6,478	6,761	6,896	7,049	7,192	7,334	7,486
Hawaii	500	633	770	965	1,108	1,150	1,160	1,173	1,179	1,183	1,187
Idaho	589	667	713	944	1,007	1,066	1,101	1,135	1,165	1,188	1,210
Illinois	*8,712*	*10,081*	*11,110*	*11,427*	*11,431*	*11,601*	*11,675*	*11,737*	*11,795*	*11,845*	*11,896*
Indiana	3,934	4,662	5,195	5,490	5,544	5,648	5,700	5,742	5,788	5,828	5,864
Percent U.S.	2.60	2.60	2.56	2.42	2.23	2.21	2.21	2.21	2.20	2.20	2.19
Rank	12	11	11	12	14	14	14	14	14	14	14
Iowa	2,621	2,758	2,825	2,914	2,777	2,807	2,820	2,829	2,841	2,848	2,852
Kansas	1,905	2,179	2,249	2,364	2,478	2,516	2,535	2,554	2,570	2,579	2,595
Kentucky	*2,945*	*3,038*	*3,221*	*3,661*	*3,685*	*3,752*	*3,793*	*3,824*	*3,856*	*3,882*	*3,908*
Louisiana	2,684	3,257	3,645	4,206	4,220	4,271	4,285	4,307	4,329	4,341	4,352
Maine	914	969	994	1,125	1,228	1,235	1,237	1,236	1,234	1,239	1,242
Maryland	2,343	3,101	3,924	4,217	4,781	4,904	4,945	4,989	5,027	5,060	5,094
Massachusetts	4,691	5,149	5,689	5,737	6,016	5,991	6,008	6,029	6,061	6,085	6,118
Michigan	*6,372*	*7,823*	*8,882*	*9,262*	*9,295*	*9,466*	*9,524*	*9,580*	*9,655*	*9,731*	*9,774*
Minnesota	2,982	3,414	3,806	4,076	4,375	4,472	4,524	4,567	4,607	4,649	4,686
Mississippi	2,179	2,178	2,217	2,521	2,573	2,610	2,635	2,663	2,691	2,711	2,731
Missouri	3,955	4,320	4,678	4,917	5,117	5,194	5,238	5,281	5,325	5,364	5,402
Montana	591	675	694	787	799	823	840	855	869	877	879
Nebraska	1,326	1,411	1,485	1,570	1,578	1,603	1,613	1,623	1,636	1,649	1,657
Nevada	160	285	489	800	1,202	1,333	1,382	1,459	1,530	1,601	1,677
New Hampshire	533	607	738	921	1,109	1,113	1,122	1,134	1,146	1,160	1,173
New Jersey	4,835	6,067	7,171	7,365	7,730	7,824	7,869	7,911	7,956	8,002	8,053
New Mexico	681	951	1,017	1,303	1,515	1,582	1,617	1,656	1,686	1,711	1,730
New York	14,830	16,782	18,241	17,558	17,990	18,080	18,139	18,154	18,146	18,134	18,137
North Carolina	4,062	4,556	5,084	5,882	6,629	6,833	6,948	7,062	7,187	7,309	7,425
North Dakota	620	632	618	653	639	635	637	640	641	643	641
Ohio	*7,947*	*9,706*	*10,657*	*10,798*	*10,847*	*11,000*	*11,058*	*11,095*	*11,133*	*11,163*	*11,186*
Oklahoma	2,233	2,328	2,559	3,025	3,146	3,204	3,229	3,248	3,271	3,295	3,317
Oregon	1,521	1,769	2,092	2,633	2,842	2,975	3,036	3,089	3,143	3,196	3,243
Pennsylvania	10,498	11,319	11,801	11,864	11,882	11,981	12,022	12,043	12,046	12,040	12,020
Rhode Island	792	859	950	947	1,003	1,001	998	994	990	988	987
South Carolina	2,117	2,383	2,591	3,122	3,487	3,593	3,625	3,654	3,683	3,717	3,760
South Dakota	653	681	666	691	696	715	723	730	735	738	738
Tennessee	3,292	3,567	3,926	4,591	4,877	5,013	5,083	5,158	5,235	5,307	5,368
Texas	7,711	9,580	11,199	14,229	16,987	17,680	18,035	18,385	18,738	19,091	19,439
Utah	689	891	1,059	1,461	1,723	1,821	1,875	1,929	1,974	2,018	2,059
Vermont	378	390	445	511	563	570	574	579	583	586	589
Virginia	3,319	3,967	4,651	5,347	6,187	6,383	6,465	6,538	6,601	6,666	6,734
Washington	2,379	2,853	3,413	4,132	4,867	5,144	5,250	5,339	5,436	5,520	5,610
West Virginia	2,006	1,860	1,744	1,950	1,793	1,806	1,816	1,819	1,822	1,820	1,816
Wisconsin	3,435	3,952	4,418	4,706	4,892	4,991	5,038	5,075	5,113	5,146	5,170
Wyoming	291	330	332	470	454	464	469	475	479	480	480

Population Index 1990 - 1997
1990 = 100

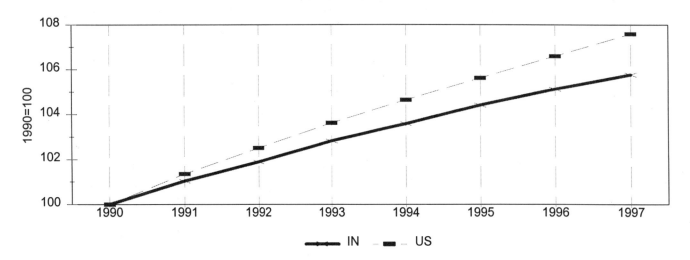

Source: U.S. Bureau of the Census
EDIN table(s): POPU, POPE

1.2 Population by Age Groups: Percentages 1996

	Under 5 Years	5 to 14 Years	15 to 24 Years	25 to 34 Years	35 to 44 Years	45 to 54 Years	55 to 64 Years	65 Years and Over
United States	7.3	14.5	13.7	15.2	16.4	12.2	8.1	12.8
Alabama	6.9	13.8	14.7	14.7	15.7	12.4	8.8	13.0
Alaska	8.2	17.4	15.6	14.1	19.3	13.6	6.7	5.2
Arizona	7.7	14.1	13.8	15.3	15.9	11.8	8.1	13.2
Arkansas	7.0	14.6	14.6	13.6	14.7	12.1	9.0	14.4
California	8.6	15.2	13.5	16.9	16.5	11.4	6.9	11.0
Colorado	7.1	14.7	13.6	14.7	18.2	13.6	8.1	10.1
Connecticut	6.8	13.8	11.7	15.4	17.0	12.8	8.1	14.3
Delaware	6.9	13.5	12.9	16.8	16.9	12.2	8.1	12.8
Dist. Of Col.	6.3	11.1	11.3	20.3	16.4	12.3	8.4	13.9
Florida	6.6	13.4	11.8	13.9	15.3	11.6	8.9	18.5
Georgia	7.5	14.6	14.4	16.6	16.9	12.5	7.6	9.9
Hawaii	7.7	14.2	13.8	14.2	16.7	12.6	7.9	12.9
Idaho	7.6	16.2	16.5	12.6	15.6	12.0	8.1	11.4
Illinois	*7.7*	*14.6*	*13.6*	*15.2*	*16.3*	*12.0*	*8.0*	*12.5*
Indiana	**7.0**	**14.1**	**14.3**	**14.9**	**16.3**	**12.4**	**8.4**	**12.6**
Rank	**18**	**32**	**20**	**22**	**26**	**23**	**15**	**27**
Iowa	6.4	14.1	14.2	13.5	15.7	12.1	8.8	15.2
Kansas	7.0	15.0	14.2	14.1	16.2	11.7	7.9	13.7
Kentucky	*6.7*	*13.7*	*14.8*	*14.6*	*16.1*	*12.7*	*8.8*	*12.6*
Louisiana	7.5	15.8	15.6	14.1	15.6	11.8	8.1	11.4
Maine	5.7	14.1	13.3	14.2	17.4	13.1	8.3	13.9
Maryland	7.1	14.4	12.3	16.5	17.7	12.9	7.7	11.4
Massachusetts	6.4	13.3	12.1	17.2	16.7	12.5	7.8	14.1
Michigan	*7.0*	*14.9*	*13.9*	*14.8*	*16.5*	*12.4*	*8.0*	*12.4*
Minnesota	6.8	15.3	13.7	14.9	17.1	12.1	7.7	12.4
Mississippi	7.5	15.3	16.1	14.2	15.0	11.4	8.2	12.3
Missouri	6.8	14.7	13.8	14.4	16.0	12.0	8.5	13.8
Montana	6.3	15.2	14.7	11.5	16.6	13.4	9.0	13.2
Nebraska	6.9	15.1	14.6	13.6	16.0	11.8	8.1	13.8
Nevada	7.7	14.4	12.3	15.9	16.6	12.8	8.8	11.4
New Hampshire	6.5	14.8	12.3	16.2	18.5	12.5	7.2	12.0
New Jersey	7.2	13.8	12.2	15.0	16.9	12.8	8.4	13.8
New Mexico	7.9	16.4	14.9	13.5	16.2	12.0	8.1	11.0
New York	7.3	13.8	12.7	15.7	16.2	12.5	8.5	13.4
North Carolina	7.0	14.0	13.7	15.8	16.1	12.4	8.5	12.5
North Dakota	6.4	14.9	15.1	13.6	15.8	11.4	8.2	14.5
Ohio	*6.8*	*14.3*	*13.8*	*14.6*	*16.3*	*12.3*	*8.4*	*13.4*
Oklahoma	6.9	15.1	14.7	13.5	15.3	12.2	8.9	13.5
Oregon	6.6	14.2	13.4	13.7	16.9	13.5	8.2	13.4
Pennsylvania	6.3	13.6	12.7	14.2	16.2	12.4	8.7	15.9
Rhode Island	6.4	13.6	12.4	16.2	16.4	11.8	7.5	15.8
South Carolina	6.9	14.1	14.6	15.4	16.0	12.5	8.4	12.1
South Dakota	7.0	15.7	15.2	12.9	15.6	11.2	8.1	14.4
Tennessee	6.8	13.7	13.9	15.1	16.2	12.9	8.8	12.5
Texas	8.3	15.6	14.9	15.3	16.4	11.7	7.5	10.2
Utah	9.4	18.3	19.3	14.4	13.8	9.7	6.3	8.8
Vermont	6.0	14.6	13.2	15.0	17.8	13.5	7.8	12.1
Virginia	6.8	13.7	13.7	16.7	17.1	12.9	7.9	11.2
Washington	7.0	14.6	13.6	15.1	17.6	13.0	7.6	11.6
West Virginia	5.8	12.7	14.8	12.7	15.6	13.4	9.8	15.2
Wisconsin	6.5	14.9	14.0	14.5	16.6	12.1	8.1	13.3
Wyoming	6.5	15.7	16.1	11.7	17.1	13.2	8.4	11.2

Population by Age Groups
Percentages 1996

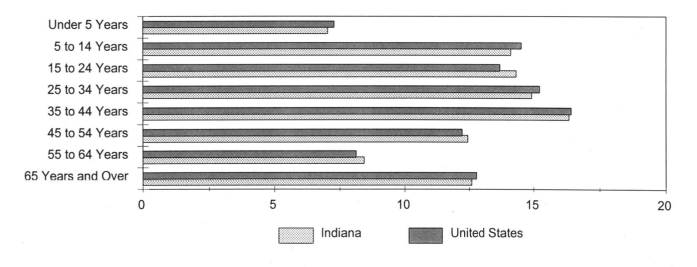

Source: U.S. Bureau of the Census
EDIN table(s): PAGE

1.3 Selected Population Characteristics 1996

	Total Population	1986 to 1996 Change	Percent Change	Male	Female	Median Age	Percent Under 19 Years	Percent 65 Years and Over
United States	265,283,783	25,150,942	10.5	129,810,215	135,473,568	35	28.8	12.8
Alabama	4,273,084	281,522	7.1	2,054,281	2,218,803	35	28.2	13.0
Alaska	607,007	62,738	11.5	319,298	287,709	32	33.7	5.2
Arizona	4,428,068	1,119,806	33.8	2,192,581	2,235,487	34	28.8	13.2
Arkansas	2,509,793	177,803	7.6	1,214,148	1,295,645	35	29.3	14.4
California	31,878,234	4,775,993	17.6	15,963,923	15,914,311	33	30.5	11.0
Colorado	3,822,676	585,229	18.1	1,896,268	1,926,408	35	28.9	10.1
Connecticut	3,274,238	50,501	1.6	1,591,547	1,682,691	36	26.7	14.3
Delaware	724,842	97,285	15.5	353,257	371,585	35	26.9	12.8
Dist. Of Col.	543,213	-95,065	-14.9	254,383	288,830	36	22.2	13.9
Florida	14,399,985	2,732,481	23.4	6,993,990	7,405,995	38	26.1	18.5
Georgia	7,353,225	1,268,565	20.8	3,583,009	3,770,216	33	29.4	9.9
Hawaii	1,183,723	131,964	12.5	597,342	586,381	35	28.7	12.9
Idaho	1,189,251	199,025	20.1	594,604	594,647	33	32.9	11.4
Illinois	*11,846,544*	*459,286*	*4.0*	*5,784,530*	*6,062,014*	*34*	*29.4*	*12.5*
Indiana	5,840,528	386,414	7.1	2,846,191	2,994,337	35	28.6	12.6
Percent U.S.	*2.20*	*1.54*	*—*	*2.19*	*2.21*	*—*	*—*	*—*
Rank	*14*	*19*	*27*	*14*	*14*	*14*	*27*	*27*
Iowa	2,851,792	59,826	2.1	1,389,670	1,462,122	36	28.2	15.2
Kansas	2,572,150	139,534	5.7	1,266,212	1,305,938	35	29.7	13.7
Kentucky	*3,883,723*	*195,910*	*5.3*	*1,886,869*	*1,996,854*	*35*	*28.0*	*12.6*
Louisiana	4,350,579	-56,339	-1.3	2,097,558	2,253,021	33	31.6	11.4
Maine	1,243,316	73,195	6.3	607,220	636,096	37	26.8	13.9
Maryland	5,071,604	584,647	13.0	2,469,575	2,602,029	35	27.8	11.4
Massachusetts	6,092,352	189,670	3.2	2,940,798	3,151,554	36	25.7	14.1
Michigan	*9,594,350*	*466,574*	*5.1*	*4,676,908*	*4,917,442*	*35*	*29.3*	*12.4*
Minnesota	4,657,758	452,550	10.8	2,298,010	2,359,748	35	29.6	12.4
Mississippi	2,716,115	122,519	4.7	1,304,446	1,411,669	33	31.2	12.3
Missouri	5,358,692	335,624	6.7	2,597,463	2,761,229	35	28.8	13.8
Montana	879,372	65,624	8.1	438,111	441,261	37	29.6	13.2
Nebraska	1,652,093	77,757	4.9	809,208	842,885	35	29.8	13.8
Nevada	1,603,163	622,510	63.5	817,422	785,741	35	28.4	11.4
New Hampshire	1,162,481	137,426	13.4	572,415	590,066	35	27.9	12.0
New Jersey	7,987,933	365,783	4.8	3,875,876	4,112,057	36	27.3	13.8
New Mexico	1,713,407	250,680	17.1	845,621	867,786	33	32.4	11.0
New York	18,184,774	351,355	2.0	8,760,858	9,423,916	35	27.5	13.4
North Carolina	7,322,870	1,001,288	15.8	3,558,460	3,764,410	35	27.7	12.5
North Dakota	643,539	-25,950	-3.9	321,408	322,131	35	29.4	14.5
Ohio	*11,172,782*	*442,514*	*4.1*	*5,409,219*	*5,763,563*	*35*	*28.3*	*13.4*
Oklahoma	3,300,902	48,171	1.5	1,615,192	1,685,710	35	29.7	13.5
Oregon	3,203,735	520,204	19.4	1,583,503	1,620,232	36	28.0	13.4
Pennsylvania	12,056,112	273,367	2.3	5,804,443	6,251,669	37	26.6	15.9
Rhode Island	990,225	12,882	1.3	476,535	513,690	36	26.2	15.8
South Carolina	3,698,746	355,977	10.6	1,786,976	1,911,770	34	28.3	12.1
South Dakota	732,405	36,425	5.2	361,074	371,331	35	31.1	14.4
Tennessee	5,319,654	580,941	12.3	2,572,358	2,747,296	35	27.7	12.5
Texas	19,128,261	2,567,149	15.5	9,450,785	9,677,476	33	31.5	10.2
Utah	2,000,494	337,656	20.3	996,638	1,003,856	27	38.1	8.8
Vermont	588,654	54,599	10.2	290,010	298,644	36	27.6	12.1
Virginia	6,675,451	863,760	14.9	3,271,690	3,403,761	35	27.2	11.2
Washington	5,532,939	1,080,217	24.3	2,756,056	2,776,883	35	28.7	11.6
West Virginia	1,825,754	-56,596	-3.0	881,249	944,505	38	26.2	15.2
Wisconsin	5,159,795	404,170	8.5	2,538,652	2,621,143	35	28.9	13.3
Wyoming	481,400	-14,224	-2.9	242,375	239,025	35	31.1	11.2

Percent Change in Population
1986 to 1996

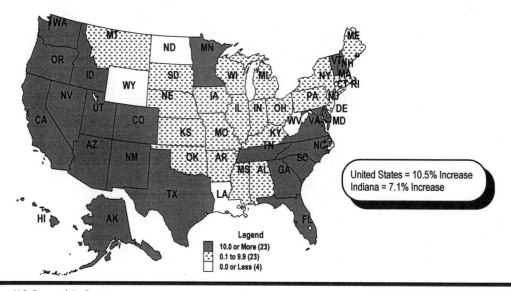

United States = 10.5% Increase
Indiana = 7.1% Increase

Legend
■ 10.0 or More (23)
⠿ 0.1 to 9.9 (23)
□ 0.0 or Less (4)

Source: U.S. Bureau of the Census
EDIN table(s): PAGE, PAMF
Note: The 1996 population shown here differs from Table 1.1 due to Census Bureau methodology and release dates.

1.4 Race and Hispanic Origin 1994

	Total Population	White	Percent Total	Black	Percent Total	American Indian Eskimo, Aleut	Percent Total	Asian and Pacific Islander	Hispanic Origin (Can Be Of Any Race)	Percent Total
United States	260,340,990	216,469,870	83.1	32,672,162	12.5	2,209,664	0.8	8,989,294	26,076,799	10.0
Alabama	4,218,792	3,096,302	73.4	1,078,822	25.6	16,501	0.4	27,167	30,972	0.7
Alaska	606,276	462,871	76.3	25,452	4.2	93,642	15.4	24,311	21,762	3.6
Arizona	4,075,052	3,623,149	88.9	138,631	3.4	238,473	5.9	74,799	823,589	20.2
Arkansas	2,452,671	2,034,457	82.9	389,050	15.9	13,542	0.6	15,622	26,746	1.1
California	31,430,697	25,210,268	80.2	2,415,189	7.7	301,647	1.0	3,503,593	8,939,200	28.4
Colorado	3,655,647	3,387,181	92.7	157,716	4.3	34,059	0.9	76,691	492,094	13.5
Connecticut	3,275,251	2,909,890	88.8	294,850	9.0	7,625	0.2	62,886	239,103	7.3
Delaware	706,351	563,166	79.7	128,848	18.2	2,235	0.3	12,102	19,266	2.7
Dist. Of Col.	570,175	185,198	32.5	365,942	64.2	1,533	0.3	17,502	39,347	6.9
Florida	13,952,714	11,672,983	83.7	2,025,713	14.5	44,583	0.3	209,435	1,872,370	13.4
Georgia	7,055,336	4,968,243	70.4	1,966,121	27.9	15,589	0.2	105,383	140,640	2.0
Hawaii	1,178,564	394,569	33.5	28,774	2.4	6,526	0.6	748,695	97,432	8.30
Idaho	1,133,034	1,100,715	97.1	5,081	0.4	15,558	1.4	11,680	65,961	5.8
Illinois	*11,751,774*	*9,587,479*	*81.6*	*1,794,674*	*15.3*	*25,295*	*0.2*	*344,326*	*1,050,730*	*8.9*
Indiana	**5,752,073**	**5,228,644**	**90.9**	**464,434**	**8.1**	**13,394**	**0.2**	**45,601**	**115,433**	**2.0**
Percent U.S.	*2.21*	*2.42*	—	*1.42*	—	*0.61*	—	*0.51*	*0.51*	—
Rank	*14*	*12*	*20*	*20*	*23*	*35*	*39*	*26*	*26*	*32*
Iowa	2,829,252	2,735,877	96.7	54,192	1.9	7,921	0.3	31,262	43,369	1.5
Kansas	2,554,047	2,337,552	91.5	154,315	6.0	23,037	0.9	39,143	108,828	4.3
Kentucky	*3,826,794*	*3,527,035*	*92.2*	*271,951*	*7.1*	*5,886*	*0.2*	*21,922*	*26,225*	*0.7*
Louisiana	4,315,085	2,882,433	66.8	1,364,138	31.6	18,563	0.4	49,951	101,560	2.4
Maine	1,240,209	1,221,604	98.5	4,767	0.4	5,874	0.5	7,964	7,243	0.6
Maryland	5,006,265	3,492,503	69.8	1,321,294	26.4	14,427	0.3	178,041	162,778	3.3
Massachusetts	6,041,123	5,485,198	90.8	364,296	6.0	13,586	0.2	178,043	338,676	5.6
Michigan	*9,496,147*	*7,948,460*	*83.7*	*1,363,728*	*14.4*	*57,766*	*0.6*	*126,193*	*226,778*	*2.4*
Minnesota	4,567,267	4,290,182	93.9	121,709	2.7	55,141	1.2	100,235	71,596	1.6
Mississippi	2,669,111	1,686,906	63.2	957,845	35.9	8,822	0.3	15,538	19,127	0.7
Missouri	5,277,640	4,623,678	87.6	581,877	11.0	20,450	0.4	51,635	71,323	1.4
Montana	856,047	797,105	93.1	2,789	0.3	50,998	6.0	5,155	14,637	1.7
Nebraska	1,622,858	1,531,264	94.4	62,174	3.8	13,223	0.8	16,197	48,463	3.0
Nevada	1,457,028	1,272,719	87.4	103,227	7.1	25,584	1.8	55,498	175,650	12.1
New Hampshire	1,136,820	1,116,895	98.2	7,144	0.6	2,069	0.2	10,712	13,097	1.2
New Jersey	7,903,925	6,397,735	80.9	1,134,263	14.4	19,080	0.2	352,847	867,964	11.0
New Mexico	1,653,521	1,445,456	87.4	40,237	2.4	147,769	8.9	20,059	645,788	39.1
New York	18,169,051	14,082,630	77.5	3,178,868	17.5	69,034	0.4	838,519	2,498,136	13.7
North Carolina	7,069,836	5,344,431	75.6	1,568,136	22.2	87,493	1.2	69,776	95,667	1.4
North Dakota	637,988	602,386	94.4	3,670	0.6	27,325	4.3	4,607	5,179	0.8
Ohio	*11,102,198*	*9,738,139*	*87.7*	*1,234,638*	*11.1*	*21,332*	*0.2*	*108,089*	*157,376*	*1.4*
Oklahoma	3,258,069	2,703,063	83.0	251,096	7.7	262,577	8.1	41,333	101,581	3.1
Oregon	3,086,188	2,900,052	94.0	54,900	1.8	43,525	1.4	87,711	141,865	4.6
Pennsylvania	12,052,367	10,708,528	88.8	1,156,843	9.6	16,377	0.1	170,619	269,951	2.2
Rhode Island	996,757	924,158	92.7	47,288	4.7	4,468	0.4	20,843	57,570	5.8
South Carolina	3,663,984	2,525,976	68.9	1,102,186	30.1	8,564	0.2	27,258	36,376	1.0
South Dakota	721,164	660,056	91.5	3,546	0.5	53,514	7.4	4,048	6,386	0.9
Tennessee	5,175,240	4,284,189	82.8	838,651	16.2	11,035	0.2	41,365	43,382	0.8
Texas	18,378,185	15,630,973	85.1	2,235,278	12.2	81,661	0.4	430,273	5,022,636	27.3
Utah	1,907,936	1,820,319	95.4	15,366	0.8	28,692	1.5	43,559	104,760	5.5
Vermont	580,209	571,982	98.6	2,343	0.4	1,641	0.3	4,243	3,961	0.7
Virginia	6,551,522	5,054,916	77.2	1,276,978	19.5	17,643	0.3	201,985	196,672	3.0
Washington	5,343,090	4,795,366	89.7	176,095	3.3	97,713	1.8	273,916	268,896	5.0
West Virginia	1,822,021	1,753,187	96.2	57,661	3.2	2,425	0.1	8,748	9,561	0.5
Wisconsin	5,081,658	4,693,063	92.4	275,682	5.4	44,073	0.9	68,840	111,632	2.2
Wyoming	475,981	458,739	96.4	3,694	0.8	10,174	2.1	3,374	27,465	5.8

Population by Race Percentages 1994

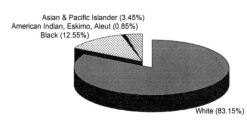

Indiana

Asian & Pacific Islander (0.79%)
American Indian, Eskimo, Aleut (0.23%)
Black (8.07%)
White (90.90%)

United States

Asian & Pacific Islander (3.45%)
American Indian, Eskimo, Aleut (0.85%)
Black (12.55%)
White (83.15%)

Hispanic Origin 1994

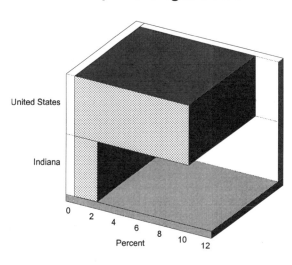

United States

Indiana

Percent: 0, 2, 4, 6, 8, 10, 12

Source: U.S. Bureau of the Census
EDIN table(s): PORE

1.5 Components of Population Change 1990 to 1997 *(000)*

	Population Change			Births			Deaths			Net Migration		
	1990 -1993	1990 -1995	1990 -1997	1990 -1993	1990 -1995	1990 -1997	1990 -1993	1990 -1995	1990 -1997	1990 -1993	1990 -1995	1990 -1997
United States	8,987	13,995	18,870	13,303	21,201	29,016	7,062	11,630	16,296	2,746	4,423	6,151
Alabama	152	221	278	203	324	446	130	214	300	79	111	132
Alaska	46	51	59	37	59	79	7	12	17	16	4	-2
Arizona	328	642	889	223	364	515	98	166	240	204	445	615
Arkansas	73	130	172	114	184	256	82	135	188	40	81	104
California	1,397	1,772	2,482	1,965	3,104	4,192	697	1,143	1,592	129	-188	-118
Colorado	268	447	598	176	284	395	73	121	173	165	284	375
Connecticut	-13	-20	-17	157	248	337	91	150	210	-80	-119	-144
Delaware	32	49	65	35	56	76	19	31	44	15	25	33
Dist. Of Col.	-29	-54	-77	35	55	72	22	35	49	-43	-74	-101
Florida	773	1,243	1,715	629	1,010	1,392	441	730	1,040	585	963	1,363
Georgia	418	714	1,008	360	582	810	173	287	407	231	419	605
Hawaii	52	70	78	64	102	139	22	37	52	10	5	-9
Idaho	94	158	203	55	90	127	25	42	59	63	109	135
Illinois	*244*	*364*	*465*	*628*	*1,005*	*1,373*	*336*	*551*	*767*	*-47*	*-89*	*-140*
Indiana	**156**	**243**	**319**	**277**	**443**	**609**	**163**	**269**	**376**	**42**	**70**	**86**
Rank	*17*	*18*	*17*	*14*	*14*	*14*	*14*	*14*	*14*	*21*	*22*	*22*
Iowa	43	63	75	126	200	275	88	143	200	4	6	1
Kansas	57	92	117	123	198	271	72	119	168	6	13	13
Kentucky	*105*	*169*	*221*	*174*	*280*	*386*	*115*	*190*	*264*	*46*	*78*	*100*
Louisiana	63	106	129	230	365	497	123	203	282	-43	-55	-84
Maine	8	6	14	53	82	110	36	59	83	-8	-16	-12
Maryland	163	246	313	255	403	546	126	208	293	34	51	60
Massachusetts	-8	44	101	288	455	617	174	285	397	-122	-125	-118
Michigan	*228*	*360*	*478*	*480*	*754*	*1,020*	*259*	*426*	*595*	*8*	*32*	*53*
Minnesota	148	231	309	217	345	472	114	188	264	45	73	101
Mississippi	59	115	155	138	222	304	83	137	190	4	30	41
Missouri	120	207	285	252	399	547	166	274	383	34	82	120
Montana	40	69	79	37	59	81	23	37	53	26	47	51
Nebraska	34	57	78	77	123	170	47	78	109	4	12	17
Nevada	180	327	475	71	118	170	32	55	81	141	264	386
New Hampshire	12	37	63	53	83	113	27	45	64	-13	0	15
New Jersey	120	208	305	394	628	852	231	378	525	-42	-41	-21
New Mexico	101	171	214	90	145	200	36	60	85	47	86	100
New York	148	155	146	947	1,502	2,044	543	882	1,216	-256	-465	-681
North Carolina	315	554	792	335	538	746	193	320	452	173	337	499
North Dakota	-1	2	2	28	46	62	18	30	42	-12	-13	-18
Ohio	*211*	*285*	*339*	*534*	*846*	*1,152*	*325*	*534*	*747*	*1*	*-25*	*-65*
Oklahoma	83	125	171	154	246	338	99	164	230	28	44	63
Oregon	193	300	401	138	222	309	83	138	197	138	216	289
Pennsylvania	139	163	136	541	853	1,150	400	654	912	-1	-35	-101
Rhode Island	-5	-13	-16	46	72	98	21	40	60	-29	-45	-53
South Carolina	138	197	273	184	288	391	99	165	233	53	73	115
South Dakota	26	38	41	35	56	77	21	35	49	12	17	13
Tennessee	205	358	490	240	387	534	152	253	357	117	225	313
Texas	1,048	1,751	2,453	1,035	1,680	2,344	415	688	969	428	759	1,078
Utah	151	251	336	119	196	279	31	52	74	63	107	131
Vermont	11	20	26	25	40	53	15	25	34	0	4	7
Virginia	276	411	544	315	502	686	160	264	370	120	173	228
Washington	383	569	743	259	415	570	123	203	289	247	358	462
West Virginia	22	28	22	72	115	157	64	104	145	14	17	10
Wisconsin	146	221	277	233	370	504	139	229	321	52	80	94
Wyoming	15	24	26	22	34	47	10	17	25	3	7	3

Net Migration 1990 - 1997

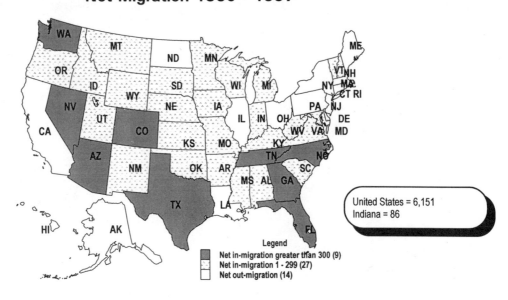

United States = 6,151
Indiana = 86

Legend
- Net in-migration greater than 300 (9)
- Net in-migration 1 - 299 (27)
- Net out-migration (14)

Source: U.S. Bureau of the Census
EDIN table(s): POCH

1.6 Population Projections 2000 to 2020 *(000)*

	2000	2005	Change 2000 to 2005	Percent Change 2000 to 2005	2010	Change 2000 to 2010	Percent Change 2000 to 2010	2015	Change 2000 to 2015	Percent Change 2000 to 2015	2020	Change 2000 to 2020	Percent Change 2000 to 2020
United States	274,634	285,981	11,347	4.1	297,716	23,082	8.4	310,133	35,499	12.9	322,742	48,108	17.5
Alabama	4,451	4,631	180	4.0	4,798	347	7.8	4,956	505	11.3	5,100	649	14.6
Alaska	653	700	47	7.2	745	92	14.1	791	138	21.1	838	185	28.3
Arizona	4,798	5,230	432	9.0	5,522	724	15.1	5,808	1,010	21.1	6,111	1,313	27.4
Arkansas	2,631	2,750	119	4.5	2,840	209	7.9	2,922	291	11.1	2,997	366	13.9
California	32,521	34,441	1,920	5.9	37,644	5,123	15.8	41,373	8,852	27.2	45,278	12,757	39.2
Colorado	4,168	4,468	300	7.2	4,658	490	11.8	4,833	665	16.0	5,012	844	20.2
Connecticut	3,284	3,317	33	1.0	3,400	116	3.5	3,506	222	6.8	3,621	337	10.3
Delaware	768	800	32	4.2	817	49	6.4	832	64	8.3	847	79	10.3
Dist. Of Col.	523	529	6	1.1	560	37	7.1	594	71	13.6	625	102	19.5
Florida	15,233	16,279	1,046	6.9	17,363	2,130	14.0	18,497	3,264	21.4	19,634	4,401	28.9
Georgia	7,875	8,413	538	6.8	8,824	949	12.1	9,200	1,325	16.8	9,552	1,677	21.3
Hawaii	1,257	1,342	85	6.8	1,440	183	14.6	1,553	296	23.5	1,677	420	33.4
Idaho	1,347	1,480	133	9.9	1,557	210	15.6	1,622	275	20.4	1,683	336	24.9
Illinois	*12,051*	*12,266*	*215*	*1.8*	*12,515*	*464*	*3.9*	*12,808*	*757*	*6.3*	*13,121*	*1,070*	*8.9*
Indiana	6,045	6,215	170	2.8	6,318	273	4.5	6,404	359	6	6,481	436	7.2
Percent U.S.	2.20	2.17	—	—	2.12	—	—	2.06	—	—	2.01	—	—
Rank	14	15	21	35	15	22	39	15	26	44	16	26	44
Iowa	2,900	2,941	41	1.4	2,968	68	2.3	2,994	94	3.2	3,019	119	4.1
Kansas	2,668	2,761	93	3.5	2,849	181	6.8	2,939	271	10.2	3,026	358	13.4
Kentucky	*3,995*	*4,098*	*103*	*2.6*	*4,170*	*175*	*4.4*	*4,231*	*236*	*5.9*	*4,281*	*286*	*7.2*
Louisiana	4,425	4,535	110	2.5	4,683	258	5.8	4,840	415	9.4	4,991	566	12.8
Maine	1,259	1,285	26	2.1	1,323	64	5.1	1,362	103	8.2	1,396	137	10.9
Maryland	5,275	5,467	192	3.6	5,657	382	7.2	5,862	587	11.1	6,071	796	15.1
Massachusetts	6,199	6,310	111	1.8	6,431	232	3.7	6,574	375	6.0	6,734	535	8.6
Michigan	*9,679*	*9,763*	*84*	*0.9*	*9,836*	*157*	*1.6*	*9,917*	*238*	*2.5*	*10,002*	*323*	*3.3*
Minnesota	4,830	5,005	175	3.6	5,147	317	6.6	5,283	453	9.4	5,406	576	11.9
Mississippi	2,816	2,908	92	3.3	2,974	158	5.6	3,035	219	7.8	3,093	277	9.8
Missouri	5,540	5,718	178	3.2	5,864	324	5.8	6,005	465	8.4	6,137	597	10.8
Montana	950	1,006	56	5.9	1,040	90	9.5	1,069	119	12.5	1,097	147	15.5
Nebraska	1,705	1,761	56	3.3	1,806	101	5.9	1,850	145	8.5	1,892	187	11.0
Nevada	1,871	2,070	199	10.6	2,131	260	13.9	2,179	308	16.5	2,241	370	19.8
New Hampshire	1,224	1,281	57	4.7	1,329	105	8.6	1,372	148	12.1	1,410	186	15.2
New Jersey	8,178	8,392	214	2.6	8,638	460	5.6	8,924	746	9.1	9,238	1,060	13.0
New Mexico	1,860	2,016	156	8.4	2,155	295	15.9	2,300	440	23.7	2,454	594	31.9
New York	18,146	18,250	104	0.6	18,530	384	2.1	18,916	770	4.2	19,359	1,213	6.7
North Carolina	7,777	8,227	450	5.8	8,552	775	10.0	8,840	1,063	13.7	9,111	1,334	17.2
North Dakota	662	677	15	2.3	690	28	4.2	704	42	6.3	717	55	8.3
Ohio	*11,319*	*11,428*	*109*	*1.0*	*11,505*	*186*	*1.6*	*11,588*	*269*	*2.4*	*11,671*	*352*	*3.1*
Oklahoma	3,373	3,491	118	3.5	3,639	266	7.9	3,789	416	12.3	3,930	557	16.5
Oregon	3,397	3,613	216	6.4	3,803	406	12.0	3,992	595	17.5	4,177	780	23.0
Pennsylvania	12,202	12,281	79	0.6	12,352	150	1.2	12,449	247	2.0	12,567	365	3.0
Rhode Island	998	1,012	14	1.4	1,038	40	4.0	1,070	72	7.2	1,105	107	10.7
South Carolina	3,858	4,033	175	4.5	4,205	347	9.0	4,369	511	13.2	4,517	659	17.1
South Dakota	777	810	33	4.2	826	49	6.3	840	63	8.1	853	76	9.8
Tennessee	5,657	5,966	309	5.5	6,180	523	9.2	6,365	708	12.5	6,529	872	15.4
Texas	20,119	21,487	1,368	6.8	22,857	2,738	13.6	24,280	4,161	20.7	25,729	5,610	27.9
Utah	2,207	2,411	204	9.2	2,551	344	15.6	2,670	463	21.0	2,781	574	26.0
Vermont	617	638	21	3.4	651	34	5.5	662	45	7.3	671	54	8.8
Virginia	6,997	7,324	327	4.7	7,627	630	9.0	7,921	924	13.2	8,204	1,207	17.3
Washington	5,858	6,258	400	6.8	6,658	800	13.7	7,058	1,200	20.5	7,446	1,588	27.1
West Virginia	1,841	1,849	8	0.4	1,851	10	0.5	1,851	10	0.5	1,850	9	0.5
Wisconsin	5,326	5,479	153	2.9	5,590	264	5.0	5,693	367	6.9	5,788	462	8.7
Wyoming	525	568	43	8.2	607	82	15.6	641	116	22.1	670	145	27.6

Percent Change in Projected Population
2000 to 2020

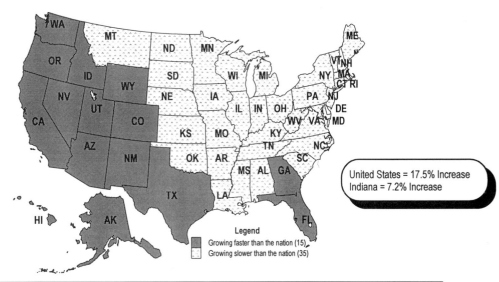

United States = 17.5% Increase
Indiana = 7.2% Increase

Legend
Growing faster than the nation (15)
Growing slower than the nation (35)

Source: U.S. Bureau of the Census
EDIN table(s): PPST

1.7 Households by Type 1990 - Part I

	Total Households	Family Households	Married Couple Families	Percent of Total Households	Male Householder	Female Householder	Non-family Households	Percent of Total Households
United States	91,947,410	64,517,947	50,708,322	55.1	3,143,582	10,666,043	27,429,463	29.8
Alabama	1,506,790	1,103,835	858,327	57.0	44,288	201,220	402,955	26.7
Alaska	188,915	132,837	106,079	56.2	8,529	18,229	56,078	29.7
Arizona	1,368,843	940,106	747,806	54.6	49,980	142,320	428,737	31.3
Arkansas	891,179	651,555	527,358	59.2	25,273	98,924	239,624	26.9
California	10,381,206	7,139,394	5,469,522	52.7	477,692	1,192,180	3,241,812	31.2
Colorado	1,282,489	854,214	690,292	53.8	39,353	124,569	428,275	33.4
Connecticut	1,230,479	864,493	684,660	55.6	39,448	140,385	365,986	29.7
Delaware	247,497	175,867	137,983	55.8	8,565	29,319	71,630	28.9
Dist. Of Col.	249,634	122,087	63,110	25.3	10,402	48,575	127,547	51.1
Florida	5,134,869	3,511,825	2,791,734	54.4	171,535	548,556	1,623,044	31.6
Georgia	2,366,615	1,713,072	1,306,756	55.2	76,675	329,641	653,543	27.6
Hawaii	356,267	263,456	210,468	59.1	15,579	37,409	92,811	26.1
Idaho	360,723	263,194	224,198	62.2	10,113	28,883	97,529	27.0
Illinois	*4,202,240*	*2,924,880*	*2,271,962*	*54.1*	*147,173*	*505,745*	*1,277,360*	*30.4*
Indiana	**2,065,355**	**1,480,351**	**1,202,020**	**58.2**	**60,703**	**217,628**	**585,004**	**28.3**
Percent U.S.	*2.25*	*2.29*	*2.37*	*—*	*1.93*	*2.04*	*2.13*	*—*
Rank	*14*	*14*	*13*	*13*	*15*	*17*	*16*	*36*
Iowa	1,064,325	740,819	629,893	59.2	25,785	85,141	323,506	30.4
Kansas	944,726	658,600	552,495	58.5	24,672	81,433	286,126	30.3
Kentucky	*1,379,782*	*1,015,998*	*816,732*	*59.2*	*39,606*	*159,660*	*363,784*	*26.4*
Louisiana	1,499,269	1,089,882	803,282	53.6	52,471	234,129	409,387	27.3
Maine	465,312	328,685	270,565	58.1	13,760	44,360	136,627	29.4
Maryland	1,748,991	1,245,814	948,563	54.2	65,362	231,889	503,177	28.8
Massachusetts	2,247,110	1,514,746	1,170,275	52.1	73,548	270,923	732,364	32.6
Michigan	*3,419,331*	*2,439,171*	*1,883,143*	*55.1*	*113,789*	*442,239*	*980,160*	*28.7*
Minnesota	1,647,853	1,130,683	942,524	57.2	46,605	141,554	517,170	31.4
Mississippi	911,374	674,378	498,240	54.7	30,917	145,221	236,996	26.0
Missouri	1,961,206	1,368,334	1,104,723	56.3	55,436	208,175	592,872	30.2
Montana	306,163	211,666	176,526	57.7	8,743	26,397	94,497	30.9
Nebraska	602,363	415,427	350,514	58.2	14,738	50,175	186,936	31.0
Nevada	466,297	307,400	239,573	51.4	20,318	47,509	158,897	34.1
New Hampshire	411,186	292,601	245,307	59.7	12,517	34,777	118,585	28.8
New Jersey	2,794,711	2,021,346	1,578,702	56.5	104,189	338,455	773,365	27.7
New Mexico	542,709	391,487	303,789	56.0	23,143	64,555	151,222	27.9
New York	6,639,322	4,489,312	3,315,845	49.9	254,201	919,266	2,150,010	32.4
North Carolina	2,517,026	1,812,053	1,424,206	56.6	77,971	309,876	704,973	28.0
North Dakota	240,878	166,270	142,374	59.1	6,373	17,523	74,608	31.0
Ohio	*4,087,546*	*2,895,223*	*2,294,111*	*56.1*	*123,042*	*478,070*	*1,192,323*	*29.2*
Oklahoma	1,206,135	855,321	695,961	57.7	33,891	125,469	350,814	29.1
Oregon	1,103,313	750,844	613,297	55.6	35,785	101,762	352,469	31.9
Pennsylvania	4,495,966	3,155,989	2,502,072	55.7	146,909	507,008	1,339,977	29.8
Rhode Island	377,977	258,886	202,283	53.5	12,261	44,342	119,091	31.5
South Carolina	1,258,044	928,206	710,089	56.4	41,913	176,204	329,838	26.2
South Dakota	259,034	180,306	152,519	58.9	7,076	20,711	78,728	30.4
Tennessee	1,853,725	1,348,019	1,059,569	57.2	55,751	232,699	505,706	27.3
Texas	6,070,937	4,343,878	3,435,540	56.6	206,512	701,826	1,727,059	28.4
Utah	537,273	410,862	348,029	64.8	13,756	49,077	126,411	23.5
Vermont	210,650	144,895	118,905	56.4	6,630	19,360	65,755	31.2
Virginia	2,291,830	1,629,490	1,302,219	56.8	72,165	255,106	662,340	28.9
Washington	1,872,431	1,264,934	1,029,267	55.0	60,145	175,522	607,497	32.4
West Virginia	688,557	500,259	406,105	59.0	20,627	73,527	188,298	27.3
Wisconsin	1,822,118	1,275,172	1,048,010	57.5	52,632	174,530	546,946	30.0
Wyoming	168,839	119,825	100,800	59.7	5,035	13,990	49,014	29.0

Family Householders by Type
Percentages 1990

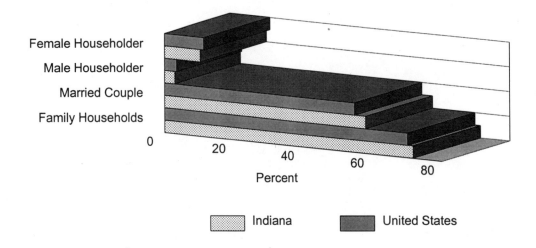

Indiana   United States

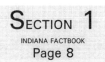
SOURCE: U.S. Bureau of the Census
EDIN table(s): PC90

1.8 Households by Type 1990 - Part II

	Total Non-family Households	Non-family Households — Householder Living Alone	Non-family Households — Householder 65 Years and over	Persons Living in Households	Persons per Household	Group Quarters — Total	Group Quarters — Institutionalized	Group Quarters — Other
United States	27,429,463	22,580,420	8,824,845	242,012,129	2.63	6,697,744	3,334,018	3,363,726
Alabama	402,955	358,078	154,191	3,948,185	2.62	92,402	51,583	40,819
Alaska	56,078	41,826	5,737	529,342	2.80	20,701	4,574	16,127
Arizona	428,737	337,681	119,287	3,584,545	2.62	80,683	41,508	39,175
Arkansas	239,624	213,778	103,386	2,292,393	2.57	58,332	34,223	24,109
California	3,241,812	2,429,867	818,520	29,008,161	2.79	751,860	376,374	375,486
Colorado	428,275	340,962	95,849	3,214,922	2.51	79,472	35,976	43,496
Connecticut	365,986	297,161	121,918	3,185,949	2.59	101,167	48,424	52,743
Delaware	71,630	57,451	21,566	646,097	2.61	20,071	8,662	11,409
Dist. Of Col.	127,547	103,626	27,237	565,183	2.26	41,717	14,070	27,647
Florida	1,623,044	1,309,954	591,468	12,630,465	2.46	307,461	173,637	133,824
Georgia	653,543	537,702	185,027	6,304,583	2.66	173,633	87,266	86,367
Hawaii	92,811	68,985	20,933	1,070,597	3.01	37,632	7,805	29,827
Idaho	97,529	80,800	32,939	985,259	2.73	21,490	10,478	11,012
Illinois	*1,277,360*	*1,081,113*	*423,740*	*11,143,646*	*2.65*	*286,956*	*149,842*	*137,114*
Indiana	585,004	496,841	208,437	5,382,167	2.61	161,992	81,686	80,306
Percent U.S.	*2.13*	*2.20*	*2.36*	*2.22*	*99.24*	*2.42*	*2.45*	*2.39*
Rank	*16*	*15*	*13*	*14*	*21*	*14*	*14*	*13*
Iowa	323,506	275,466	130,964	2,677,235	2.52	99,520	47,841	51,679
Kansas	286,126	245,156	104,297	2,394,809	2.53	82,765	42,896	39,869
Kentucky	*363,784*	*321,247*	*142,045*	*3,584,120*	*2.60*	*101,176*	*47,609*	*53,567*
Louisiana	409,387	356,060	137,596	4,107,395	2.74	112,578	67,276	45,302
Maine	136,627	108,474	48,257	1,190,759	2.56	37,169	14,136	23,033
Maryland	503,177	394,572	135,318	4,667,612	2.67	113,856	62,760	51,096
Massachusetts	732,364	580,774	243,334	5,802,118	2.58	214,307	84,345	129,962
Michigan	*980,160*	*809,449*	*317,659*	*9,083,605*	*2.66*	*211,692*	*112,903*	*98,789*
Minnesota	517,170	413,531	167,001	4,257,478	2.58	117,621	63,279	54,342
Mississippi	236,996	212,949	98,180	2,503,499	2.75	69,717	29,733	39,984
Missouri	592,872	510,684	221,516	4,971,676	2.54	145,397	80,854	64,543
Montana	94,497	80,491	32,208	775,318	2.53	23,747	11,125	12,622
Nebraska	186,936	159,671	69,640	1,530,832	2.54	47,553	25,620	21,933
Nevada	158,897	119,627	33,244	1,177,633	2.53	24,200	13,550	10,650
New Hampshire	118,585	90,364	34,522	1,077,101	2.62	32,151	11,466	20,685
New Jersey	773,365	646,171	273,736	7,558,820	2.70	171,368	92,670	78,698
New Mexico	151,222	124,883	42,964	1,486,262	2.74	28,807	14,024	14,783
New York	2,150,010	1,806,263	700,016	17,445,190	2.63	545,265	267,122	278,143
North Carolina	704,973	596,959	226,384	6,404,167	2.54	224,470	83,400	141,070
North Dakota	74,608	63,953	28,021	614,566	2.55	24,234	10,574	13,660
Ohio	*1,192,323*	*1,020,450*	*416,352*	*10,585,664*	*2.59*	*261,451*	*152,331*	*109,120*
Oklahoma	350,814	309,369	131,237	3,051,908	2.53	93,677	51,211	42,466
Oregon	352,469	278,716	108,579	2,776,116	2.52	66,205	33,378	32,827
Pennsylvania	1,339,977	1,150,694	526,264	11,533,219	2.57	348,424	174,210	174,214
Rhode Island	119,091	99,111	44,627	964,869	2.55	38,595	14,801	23,794
South Carolina	329,838	281,347	109,012	3,370,160	2.68	116,543	44,134	72,409
South Dakota	78,728	68,308	31,560	670,163	2.59	25,841	13,305	12,536
Tennessee	505,706	442,129	178,077	4,748,056	2.56	129,129	65,389	63,740
Texas	1,727,059	1,452,936	472,029	16,593,063	2.73	393,447	221,272	172,175
Utah	126,411	101,640	38,320	1,693,802	3.15	29,048	12,739	16,309
Vermont	65,755	49,366	19,648	541,116	2.57	21,642	6,161	15,481
Virginia	662,340	523,770	178,575	5,978,058	2.61	209,300	84,292	125,008
Washington	607,497	476,320	162,520	4,746,161	2.53	120,531	55,313	65,218
West Virginia	188,298	168,735	84,405	1,756,566	2.55	36,911	19,469	17,442
Wisconsin	546,946	443,673	192,072	4,758,171	2.61	133,598	71,288	62,310
Wyoming	49,014	41,287	14,431	443,348	2.63	10,240	5,434	4,806

Nonfamily Households by Type
Percentages 1990

Group Quarters:

Group Quarters Other
Group Quarters Institutionalized
Group Quarters Total

Nonfamily:

Householder 65 Years and Over
Householder Living Alone

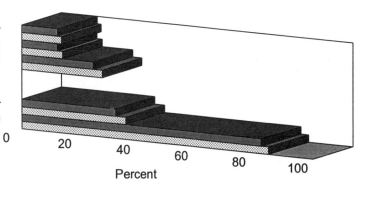

Percent

▨ Indiana   ■ United States

Source: U.S. Bureau of the Census
EDIN table(s): PC90

Vital Statistics
1.9 Births, Deaths and Marriages 1994 to 1996

	Births						Deaths						Marriages					
	1994		1995		1996		1994		1995		1996		1994		1995		1996	
	Number	Rate	Number	Rate	Number	Rate	Number	Rate	Number	Rate	Number	Rate	Number	Rate	Number	Rate	Number	Rate
United States	3,979,000	15.3	3,892,000	14.8	3,899,000	14.7	2,286,000	8.8	2,309,000	8.8	2,311,000	8.7	2,362,000	9.1	2,336,000	8.9	2,344,000	8.8
Alabama	60,745	14.4	61,182	14.4	61,514	14.4	42,092	10.0	42,254	10.0	42,668	10.0	40,179	9.5	42,006	9.9	47,367	11.1
Alaska	12,079	20.1	10,081	16.7	10,176	16.8	2,443	4.1	2,450	4.1	2,562	4.2	5,560	9.3	5,461	9.1	5,425	8.9
Arizona	66,143	16.2	68,434	15.9	79,530	18.0	34,643	8.5	33,633	7.8	39,005	8.8	36,711	9.0	38,949	9.0	39,223	8.9
Arkansas	34,571	14.1	34,340	13.8	35,876	14.3	26,627	10.8	25,960	10.4	25,666	10.2	38,169	15.5	36,626	14.7	36,232	14.4
California	581,763	18.5	564,156	17.9	543,832	17.1	224,039	7.1	223,521	7.1	232,266	7.3	202,827	6.5	199,609	6.3	219,039	6.9
Colorado	54,144	14.8	49,938	13.3	47,610	12.5	24,437	6.7	24,852	6.6	25,853	6.8	34,367	9.4	34,295	9.2	34,453	9.0
Connecticut	42,108	12.9	45,180	13.8	44,011	13.4	28,552	8.7	28,956	8.9	29,183	8.9	21,888	6.7	22,581	6.9	21,426	6.5
Delaware	10,361	14.6	10,013	14.0	10,142	14.0	6,185	8.7	6,151	8.6	6,443	8.9	5,066	7.2	5,355	7.5	5,198	7.2
Dist. Of Col.	9,669	17.0	8,943	16.1	8,240	15.2	6,921	12.2	6,653	12.0	6,317	11.6	3,616	6.4	3,535	6.4	3,360	6.2
Florida	191,003	13.7	188,098	13.3	189,369	13.2	148,414	10.6	153,588	10.8	153,746	10.7	144,548	10.4	144,341	10.2	149,941	10.4
Georgia	108,908	15.4	113,196	15.7	114,603	15.6	56,377	8.0	58,230	8.1	58,802	8.0	62,879	8.9	61,451	8.5	60,092	8.2
Hawaii	19,244	16.4	18,388	15.6	18,345	15.5	7,219	6.2	7,527	6.4	7,861	6.6	17,927	15.3	18,760	15.9	19,478	16.5
Idaho	17,358	15.3	17,735	15.2	18,868	15.9	8,559	7.5	8,488	7.3	8,685	7.3	15,234	13.4	15,479	13.3	14,970	12.6
Illinois	*189,228*	*16.1*	*185,442*	*15.7*	*184,526*	*15.6*	*107,685*	*9.2*	*108,735*	*9.2*	*106,355*	*9.0*	*92,719*	*7.9*	*83,218*	*7.1*	*90,178*	*7.6*
Indiana	**83,381**	**14.5**	**84,188**	**14.5**	**83,417**	**14.3**	**53,284**	**9.3**	**52,514**	**9.1**	**54,321**	**9.3**	**50,282**	**8.7**	**50,426**	**8.7**	**49,198**	**8.4**
Percent U.S.	2.10	—	2.16	—	2.14	—	2.33	—	2.27	—	2.35	—	2.13	—	2.16	—	2.10	—
Rank	14	25	14	13	13	20	15	17	15	23	13	16	16	23	15	21	15	23
Iowa	35,926	12.7	36,399	12.8	34,838	12.2	26,364	9.3	25,897	9.1	26,315	9.2	22,732	8.0	22,049	7.8	23,832	8.4
Kansas	33,272	13.0	37,205	14.5	40,243	15.6	23,494	9.2	23,653	9.2	23,868	9.3	20,914	8.2	22,108	8.6	20,601	8.0
Kentucky	*51,926*	*13.6*	*51,015*	*13.2*	*52,545*	*13.5*	*37,438*	*9.8*	*38,319*	*9.9*	*37,550*	*9.7*	*47,322*	*12.4*	*47,576*	*12.3*	*43,290*	*11.1*
Louisiana	68,454	15.9	67,376	15.5	66,291	15.2	40,447	9.4	39,348	9.1	40,460	9.3	41,750	9.7	40,840	9.4	38,932	8.9
Maine	14,320	11.6	14,006	11.3	13,718	11.0	11,386	9.2	11,625	9.4	11,035	8.9	10,872	8.8	10,757	8.7	NA	NA
Maryland	71,553	14.3	72,198	14.3	71,042	14.0	40,600	8.1	41,004	8.1	41,965	8.3	43,385	8.7	42,808	8.5	41,781	8.2
Massachusetts	83,449	13.8	85,045	14.0	80,165	13.2	54,558	9.0	55,965	9.2	55,328	9.1	49,695	8.2	43,593	7.2	40,584	6.7
Michigan	*139,931*	*14.8*	*132,783*	*13.9*	*137,518*	*14.3*	*83,320*	*8.8*	*83,394*	*8.7*	*83,972*	*8.8*	*70,751*	*7.5*	*70,963*	*7.4*	*69,091*	*7.2*
Minnesota	64,681	14.1	62,752	13.6	63,657	13.7	36,436	8.0	37,028	8.0	36,804	7.9	32,510	7.1	32,782	7.1	33,185	7.1
Mississippi	43,382	16.3	37,198	13.8	41,442	15.3	26,924	10.1	27,189	10.1	26,756	9.9	22,360	8.4	21,528	8.0	21,340	7.9
Missouri	75,366	14.3	74,946	14.1	73,132	13.6	56,010	10.6	55,599	10.5	53,697	10.0	44,223	8.4	44,879	8.4	46,102	8.6
Montana	11,032	12.9	11,230	12.9	10,797	12.3	7,357	8.6	7,646	8.8	7,710	8.8	6,895	8.0	6,645	7.6	6,626	7.5
Nebraska	23,032	14.2	23,159	14.1	23,355	14.1	14,742	9.1	15,284	9.3	15,472	9.4	12,347	7.6	12,125	7.4	12,762	7.7
Nevada	21,511	14.7	21,324	13.9	23,439	14.6	11,738	8.0	12,191	8.0	12,897	8.0	140,325	95.9	134,785	87.9	141,228	88.1
New Hampshire	14,605	12.9	15,069	13.1	14,125	12.2	8,907	7.8	9,244	8.1	9,114	7.8	9,818	8.7	9,631	8.4	9,720	8.4
New Jersey	117,289	14.8	115,116	14.5	113,713	14.2	72,575	9.2	74,974	9.4	71,895	9.0	52,776	6.7	52,397	6.6	51,688	6.5
New Mexico	27,981	16.9	27,142	16.1	27,173	15.9	12,279	7.4	12,475	7.4	12,325	7.2	12,159	7.3	15,094	8.9	16,026	9.4
New York	279,187	15.3	264,253	14.5	271,569	14.9	167,977	9.2	168,140	9.2	162,875	9.0	149,615	8.2	147,405	8.1	152,263	8.4
North Carolina	101,911	14.4	102,165	14.2	106,261	14.5	64,512	9.1	65,132	9.0	66,357	9.1	51,934	7.3	61,644	8.6	61,902	8.5
North Dakota	8,639	13.5	8,719	13.6	8,396	13.0	6,134	9.6	6,099	9.5	5,753	8.9	4,791	7.5	4,597	7.2	5,029	7.8
Ohio	*162,059*	*14.6*	*155,568*	*14.0*	*152,233*	*13.6*	*105,623*	*9.5*	*105,799*	*9.5*	*105,213*	*9.4*	*92,797*	*8.4*	*90,125*	*8.1*	*82,844*	*7.4*
Oklahoma	45,682	14.0	45,894	14.0	45,151	13.7	32,473	10.0	32,852	10.0	33,224	10.1	29,297	9.0	28,546	8.7	26,675	8.1
Oregon	42,276	13.7	42,953	13.6	43,798	13.7	27,317	8.8	28,011	8.9	28,293	8.8	25,186	8.1	25,688	8.2	25,568	8.0
Pennsylvania	157,060	13.0	151,754	12.6	149,911	12.4	128,164	10.6	128,078	10.6	129,463	10.7	75,512	6.3	75,803	6.3	70,173	5.8
Rhode Island	13,440	13.5	12,695	12.8	12,601	12.7	9,333	9.4	9,640	9.7	9,574	9.7	6,976	7.0	7,385	7.4	7,828	7.9
South Carolina	50,907	14.0	49,841	13.6	50,568	13.7	31,570	8.7	32,570	8.9	34,603	9.4	50,872	14.0	44,619	12.2	43,136	11.7
South Dakota	10,615	14.7	10,574	14.5	10,081	13.8	6,858	9.5	6,901	9.5	6,314	8.6	7,451	10.3	7,281	10.0	6,728	9.2
Tennessee	75,688	14.6	73,892	14.1	73,658	13.8	49,665	9.6	50,658	9.7	49,934	9.4	80,030	15.5	82,335	15.7	82,064	15.4
Texas	322,268	17.5	333,155	17.7	315,755	16.5	137,608	7.5	141,635	7.5	136,593	7.1	190,798	10.4	188,522	10.0	179,693	9.4
Utah	38,808	20.3	38,870	19.9	41,214	20.6	10,524	5.5	10,814	5.5	11,077	5.5	20,325	10.6	21,639	11.1	22,048	11.0
Vermont	7,158	12.3	6,780	11.6	6,773	11.5	4,573	7.9	5,031	8.6	4,885	8.3	5,831	10.0	6,051	10.3	5,923	10.1
Virginia	95,865	14.6	89,948	13.6	89,149	13.4	53,829	8.2	52,989	8.0	52,847	7.9	69,256	10.6	67,938	10.3	65,406	9.8
Washington	79,296	14.8	78,160	14.3	79,808	14.4	39,642	7.4	40,582	7.4	39,493	7.1	43,557	8.1	42,030	7.7	39,194	7.1
West Virginia	21,554	11.8	20,954	11.5	19,621	10.7	20,221	11.1	19,887	10.9	19,106	10.5	10,946	6.0	11,205	6.1	11,068	6.1
Wisconsin	68,856	13.5	67,064	13.1	66,761	12.9	44,697	8.8	44,768	8.7	45,047	8.7	36,368	7.2	36,300	7.1	36,247	7.0
Wyoming	6,385	13.4	6,293	13.1	6,198	12.9	3,522	7.4	3,781	7.9	3,610	7.5	4,825	10.1	5,153	10.8	4,897	10.2

Marriage, Death and Birth Rates
1996

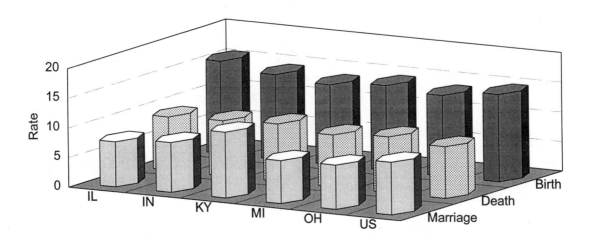

Footnote: Rates per 1,000 population.
Source: U.S. Department of Health and Human Services
EDIN table(s): VITS

1.10 Death by Cause 1995

	Total Deaths	Heart Disease	Percent Total	Malignant Neoplasms	Percent Total	Cerebro-vascular Diseases	Percent Total	Accidents and Adverse Effects	Percent Total	Motor Vehicle Accidents	Percent Total	Suicide	Percent Total
United States	2,312,132	737,563	31.9	538,455	23.3	157,991	6.8	93,320	4.0	43,363	1.9	31,284	1.4
Alabama	42,362	13,361	31.5	9,414	22.2	2,774	6.5	2,234	5.3	1,139	2.7	563	1.3
Alaska	2,553	547	21.4	574	22.5	145	5.7	339	13.3	97	3.8	103	4.0
Arizona	35,342	10,234	29.0	8,020	22.7	2,185	6.2	1,984	5.6	990	2.8	805	2.3
Arkansas	26,702	8,440	31.6	6,079	22.8	2,272	8.5	1,213	4.5	652	2.4	360	1.3
California	224,213	68,329	30.5	51,423	22.9	16,239	7.2	9,253	4.1	4,439	2.0	3,694	1.6
Colorado	25,011	6,448	25.8	5,467	21.9	1,600	6.4	1,491	6.0	696	2.8	654	2.6
Connecticut	29,457	9,787	33.2	7,060	24.0	1,873	6.4	1,077	3.7	349	1.2	323	1.1
Delaware	6,282	1,980	31.5	1,630	25.9	343	5.5	266	4.2	126	2.0	80	1.3
Dist. Of Col.	6,896	1,676	24.3	1,481	21.5	370	5.4	193	2.8	68	1.0	39	0.6
Florida	153,176	49,804	32.5	37,321	24.4	9,895	6.5	5,398	3.5	2,806	1.8	2,165	1.4
Georgia	58,387	17,452	29.9	12,765	21.9	4,044	6.9	2,963	5.1	1,539	2.6	825	1.4
Hawaii	7,633	2,326	30.5	1,856	24.3	611	8.0	327	4.3	142	1.9	142	1.9
Idaho	8,516	2,470	29.0	2,006	23.6	637	7.5	526	6.2	264	3.1	186	2.2
Illinois	*108,469*	*36,010*	*33.2*	*25,100*	*23.1*	*7,488*	*6.9*	*4,013*	*3.7*	*1,737*	*1.6*	*1,118*	*1.0*
Indiana	53,287	17,082	32.1	12,554	23.6	3,996	7.5	2,206	4.1	995	1.9	698	1.3
Percent U.S.	*2.30*	*2.32*	—	*2.33*	—	*2.53*	—	*2.36*	—	*2.29*	—	*2.23*	—
Rank	*14*	*13*	*20*	*14*	*19*	*13*	*16*	*16*	*30*	*14*	*27*	*15*	*28*
Iowa	28,021	9,436	33.7	6,226	22.2	2,201	7.9	1,168	4.2	547	2.0	335	1.2
Kansas	23,935	7,638	31.9	5,283	22.1	1,811	7.6	993	4.1	451	1.9	291	1.2
Kentucky	*37,201*	*12,190*	*32.8*	*8,847*	*23.8*	*2,467*	*6.6*	*1,707*	*4.6*	*851*	*2.3*	*480*	*1.3*
Louisiana	39,705	12,131	30.6	9,304	23.4	2,544	6.4	1,841	4.6	910	2.3	544	1.4
Maine	11,754	3,648	31.0	3,015	25.7	744	6.3	399	3.4	182	1.5	161	1.4
Maryland	41,842	11,922	28.5	10,181	24.3	2,645	6.3	1,393	3.3	679	1.6	509	1.2
Massachusetts	55,476	16,750	30.2	14,083	25.4	3,459	6.2	1,218	2.2	487	0.9	489	0.9
Michigan	*83,661*	*28,153*	*33.7*	*19,430*	*23.2*	*5,865*	*7.0*	*3,168*	*3.8*	*1,623*	*1.9*	*980*	*1.2*
Minnesota	37,507	10,381	27.7	8,693	23.2	3,125	8.3	1,666	4.4	664	1.8	520	1.4
Mississippi	27,026	9,603	35.5	5,748	21.3	1,870	6.9	1,608	5.9	904	3.3	319	1.2
Missouri	54,402	18,380	33.8	12,282	22.6	3,883	7.1	2,315	4.3	1,098	2.0	721	1.3
Montana	7,629	2,004	26.3	1,770	23.2	594	7.8	380	5.0	195	2.6	201	2.6
Nebraska	15,267	5,108	33.5	3,375	22.1	1,165	7.6	576	3.8	254	1.7	187	1.2
Nevada	12,526	3,778	30.2	2,976	23.8	710	5.7	551	4.4	305	2.4	395	3.2
New Hampshire	9,227	2,950	32.0	2,356	25.5	634	6.9	287	3.1	135	1.5	137	1.5
New Jersey	74,087	24,102	32.5	18,427	24.9	4,244	5.7	2,316	3.1	842	1.1	578	0.8
New Mexico	12,545	3,305	26.3	2,689	21.4	719	5.7	920	7.3	450	3.6	297	2.4
New York	*168,382*	*63,518*	*37.7*	*38,684*	*23.0*	*8,119*	*4.8*	*4,989*	*3.0*	*1,798*	*1.1*	*1,370*	*0.8*
North Carolina	64,918	19,390	29.9	14,879	22.9	5,204	8.0	2,951	4.5	1,490	2.3	908	1.4
North Dakota	5,975	1,952	32.7	1,375	23.0	496	8.3	210	3.5	84	1.4	94	1.6
Ohio	*105,940*	*35,391*	*33.4*	*25,208*	*23.8*	*6,688*	*6.3*	*3,250*	*3.1*	*1,387*	*1.3*	*1,077*	*1.0*
Oklahoma	32,853	11,157	34.0	7,142	21.7	2,377	7.2	1,473	4.5	725	2.2	502	1.5
Oregon	28,214	7,539	26.7	6,744	23.9	2,440	8.6	1,366	4.8	593	2.1	497	1.8
Pennsylvania	127,866	43,419	34.0	30,267	23.7	8,287	6.5	4,266	3.3	1,578	1.2	1,459	1.1
Rhode Island	9,657	3,307	34.2	2,478	25.7	641	6.6	217	2.2	80	0.8	89	0.9
South Carolina	33,527	10,197	30.4	7,416	22.1	2,761	8.2	1,635	4.9	849	2.5	436	1.3
South Dakota	6,915	2,277	32.9	1,564	22.6	534	7.7	324	4.7	161	2.3	86	1.2
Tennessee	51,302	16,197	31.6	11,611	22.6	4,193	8.2	2,485	4.8	1,288	2.5	681	1.3
Texas	137,821	41,730	30.3	31,622	22.9	9,802	7.1	6,431	4.7	3,328	2.4	2,234	1.6
Utah	10,940	2,891	26.4	2,119	19.4	778	7.1	633	5.8	335	3.1	288	2.6
Vermont	4,951	1,627	32.9	1,163	23.5	334	6.7	192	3.9	94	1.9	76	1.5
Virginia	52,940	15,896	30.0	12,600	23.8	3,803	7.2	2,212	4.2	922	1.7	827	1.6
Washington	40,788	11,330	27.8	9,938	24.4	3,294	8.1	1,894	4.6	743	1.8	781	1.9
West Virginia	20,238	6,927	34.2	4,743	23.4	1,242	6.1	739	3.7	387	1.9	276	1.4
Wisconsin	45,088	14,417	32.0	10,571	23.4	3,578	7.9	1,824	4.0	775	1.7	622	1.4
Wyoming	3,720	976	26.2	896	24.1	268	7.2	240	6.5	130	3.5	82	2.2

Deaths by Cause
1995

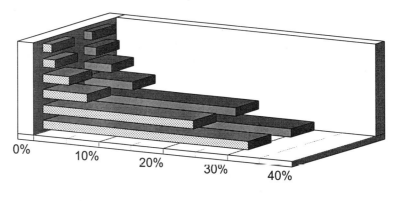

Suicide
Motor vehicle accidents
Accidents and adverse effects
Cerebrovascular diseases
Malignant neoplasms
Diseases of heart

0%   10%   20%   30%   40%

▨ Indiana   ▨ United States

Source: U.S. Department of Health and Human Services
EDIN table(s): VITD

Education
1.11 Selected Statistics for Public Schools 1993 to 1994

	Average Daily Attendance		Current Expenditures ($000)				Number of High School Graduates		SAT Scores			
			1993	Per A.D.A. ($)	1994	Per A.D.A. ($)			1993		1994	
	1993	1994					1993	1994	Verbal	Math	Verbal	Math
United States	39,570,462	40,146,393	220,948,052	5,584	231,521,500	5,767	2,233,241	2,221,098	424	478	423	479
Alabama	694,078	696,071	2,610,514	3,761	2,809,713	4,037	36,007	34,447	480	526	482	529
Alaska	110,797	112,869	967,765	8,735	1,002,515	8,882	5,535	5,747	438	477	434	477
Arizona	610,558	631,450	2,753,504	4,510	2,911,304	4,611	31,747	31,799	444	497	443	496
Arkansas	413,076	416,479	1,703,621	4,124	1,782,645	4,280	25,655	24,990	478	519	477	518
California	5,066,708	5,108,907	24,219,792	4,780	25,140,639	4,921	249,320	253,083	415	484	413	482
Colorado	568,158	579,682	2,919,916	5,139	2,954,793	5,097	31,839	31,867	454	509	456	513
Connecticut	468,992	465,487	3,739,497	7,973	3,943,894	8,473	26,799	26,330	430	474	426	472
Delaware	95,660	97,247	600,161	6,274	643,915	6,621	5,492	5,230	429	465	428	464
Dist. Of Col.	71,201	70,079	670,677	9,419	713,427	10,180	3,136	3,207	405	441	406	443
Florida	1,818,011	1,873,199	9,661,012	5,314	10,331,896	5,516	89,428	88,032	416	466	413	466
Georgia	1,125,385	1,148,319	5,273,143	4,686	5,643,843	4,915	57,602	56,356	399	445	398	446
Hawaii	165,851	169,779	946,074	5,704	998,143	5,879	8,854	9,369	401	478	401	480
Idaho	217,933	223,489	804,231	3,690	859,088	3,844	12,974	13,281	465	507	461	508
Illinois	*1,685,678*	*1,709,915*	*9,942,737*	*5,898*	*10,076,889*	*5,893*	*103,628*	*102,126*	*475*	*541*	*478*	*546*
Indiana	**897,799**	**899,585**	**4,797,946**	**5,344**	**5,064,685**	**5,630**	**57,559**	**54,650**	**409**	**460**	**410**	**466**
Percent U.S.	*2.27*	*2.24*	*2.17*	*95.70*	*2.19*	*97.62*	*2.58*	*2.46*	*96.46*	*96.23*	*96.93*	*97.29*
Rank	*13*	*13*	*15*	*26*	*15*	*26*	*12*	*13*	*46*	*46*	*46*	*42*
Iowa	467,788	477,916	2,459,141	5,257	2,527,434	5,288	30,677	30,247	520	583	506	574
Kansas	408,689	410,862	2,224,080	5,442	2,325,247	5,659	24,720	25,319	494	548	494	550
Kentucky	*579,446*	*578,020*	*2,823,134*	*4,872*	*2,952,119*	*5,107*	*36,361*	*38,454*	*476*	*522*	*474*	*523*
Louisiana	722,626	732,202	3,199,919	4,428	3,309,020	4,519	33,682	34,822	481	527	481	530
Maine	200,462	199,125	1,217,418	6,073	1,208,411	6,069	12,103	11,633	422	463	420	463
Maryland	668,778	687,455	4,556,266	6,813	4,783,023	6,958	39,523	39,091	431	478	429	479
Massachusetts	796,897	810,028	5,281,067	6,627	5,637,337	6,959	48,321	47,453	427	476	426	475
Michigan	*1,467,900*	*1,474,413*	*9,532,994*	*6,494*	*9,816,830*	*6,658*	*85,302*	*83,385*	*469*	*528*	*472*	*537*
Minnesota	744,567	756,725	4,135,284	5,554	4,328,093	5,720	48,002	47,514	489	556	495	562
Mississippi	473,262	471,367	1,600,752	3,382	1,725,386	3,660	23,597	23,379	481	521	485	528
Missouri	759,529	778,605	3,710,426	4,885	3,981,614	5,114	46,864	46,566	481	532	485	537
Montana	144,718	146,849	785,159	5,425	822,015	5,598	9,389	9,601	459	516	463	523
Nebraska	267,975	267,931	1,430,039	5,336	1,513,971	5,651	17,569	17,072	479	544	482	543
Nevada	204,440	217,681	1,035,623	5,066	1,099,058	5,049	9,042	9,485	432	488	429	484
New Hampshire	172,376	175,968	972,963	5,644	1,007,129	5,723	10,065	9,933	442	487	438	486
New Jersey	1,053,135	1,079,653	9,915,482	9,415	10,448,096	9,677	67,134	66,125	419	473	418	475
New Mexico	304,661	310,610	1,240,310	4,071	1,323,459	4,261	15,172	14,892	478	525	475	528
New York	2,347,468	2,404,426	20,898,267	8,902	22,059,949	9,175	132,963	132,708	416	471	416	472
North Carolina	1,035,258	1,051,295	4,930,823	4,763	5,145,420	4,894	60,460	57,738	406	453	405	455
North Dakota	111,174	111,770	511,095	4,597	522,377	4,674	7,310	7,522	518	583	497	559
Ohio	*1,594,191*	*1,609,855*	*9,173,393*	*5,754*	*9,612,678*	*5,971*	*109,200*	*107,700*	*454*	*505*	*456*	*510*
Oklahoma	560,744	566,155	2,442,320	4,355	2,659,460	4,697	30,542	31,872	482	530	482	537
Oregon	452,509	455,492	2,849,009	6,296	2,852,723	6,263	26,301	26,338	441	492	436	491
Pennsylvania	1,588,514	1,609,125	10,944,392	6,890	11,236,417	6,983	103,715	101,958	418	460	417	462
Rhode Island	134,736	135,016	934,815	6,938	990,094	7,333	7,640	7,450	419	464	420	462
South Carolina	581,775	586,178	2,690,009	4,624	2,790,878	4,761	31,297	30,603	396	442	395	443
South Dakota	126,916	127,550	553,005	4,357	584,894	4,586	7,952	8,442	502	558	483	548
Tennessee	786,146	796,744	3,139,223	3,993	3,305,579	4,149	44,166	40,643	486	531	488	535
Texas	3,237,958	3,306,297	15,121,655	4,670	16,193,722	4,898	160,546	163,191	413	472	412	474
Utah	432,781	439,484	1,376,319	3,180	1,511,205	3,439	24,197	26,407	500	549	509	558
Vermont	96,121	97,550	616,212	6,411	643,828	6,600	5,215	5,414	426	467	427	472
Virginia	1,049,901	1,065,071	5,228,326	4,980	5,441,388	5,109	56,948	56,140	425	469	424	469
Washington	833,641	850,813	4,679,698	5,614	4,892,690	5,751	45,262	47,235	435	486	434	488
West Virginia	294,202	291,238	1,626,005	5,527	1,663,868	5,713	20,228	19,884	439	485	439	482
Wisconsin	765,184	769,711	4,954,900	6,475	5,170,343	6,717	50,027	48,371	485	551	487	557
Wyoming	94,109	94,650	547,938	5,822	558,353	5,899	6,174	5,997	463	507	459	521

Current Expenditures Per Pupil A.D.A
1994

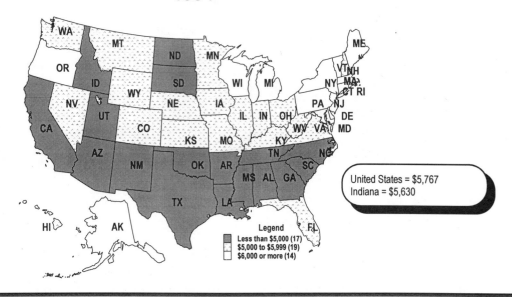

United States = $5,767
Indiana = $5,630

Legend
- Less than $5,000 (17)
- $5,000 to $5,999 (19)
- $6,000 or more (14)

SOURCE: U.S. Department of Education, Digest of Education Statistics
EDIN table(s): EDPU, EDSA

1.12 Number of Public Schools and Average Annual Teachers Salary 1994 and 1995

	Number of Schools 1994				Avg. Annual Teachers Salary 1994 (Current $)	Number of Schools 1995				Avg. Annual Teachers Salary 1995 (Current $)
	Elem. Grades Only	Secondary Grades Only	Elem. & Second.	Unclassified		Elem. Grades Only	Secondary Grades Only	Elem. & Second.	Unclassified	
United States	60,052	20,059	2,674	2,608	35,819	60,808	20,282	2,764	2,367	36,802
Alabama	849	289	156	0	28,705	859	290	160	0	31,144
Alaska	190	89	204	13	47,512	185	87	206	20	47,951
Arizona	829	261	13	30	31,800	818	250	20	48	32,175
Arkansas	646	416	8	0	28,098	647	414	10	2	28,934
California	5,588	1,882	173	91	40,264	5,695	1,863	183	80	41,078
Colorado	1,005	341	15	58	33,826	1,031	343	22	64	34,571
Connecticut	764	204	16	16	49,769	784	206	48	7	50,045
Delaware	118	41	18	0	37,469	121	42	19	0	39,076
Dist. Of Col.	117	39	6	11	42,543	120	37	4	14	43,700
Florida	1,824	415	317	59	31,944	1,906	471	350	6	32,588
Georgia	1,364	319	72	0	30,712	1,382	316	69	0	32,633
Hawaii	184	47	10	0	36,564	182	47	13	0	38,518
Idaho	378	202	15	8	27,756	380	202	19	7	29,783
Illinois	*3,095*	*890*	*27*	*183*	*39,387*	*3,054*	*876*	*28*	*237*	*39,431*
Indiana	1,397	423	35	57	35,712	1,390	430	33	59	36,785
Percent U.S.	*2.33*	*2.11*	*1.31*	*2.19*	—	*2.29*	*2.12*	*1.19*	*2.49*	—
Rank	*14*	*15*	*16*	*15*	*19*	*14*	*15*	*18*	*14*	*18*
Iowa	1,075	451	22	8	30,760	1,078	446	22	8	31,511
Kansas	1,042	430	7	3	33,919	1,046	427	14	4	34,652
Kentucky	*991*	*319*	*23*	*39*	*31,625*	*991*	*338*	*2*	*43*	*32,257*
Louisiana	983	313	113	50	26,285	999	315	119	26	26,461
Maine	555	133	14	4	30,996	552	130	16	35	31,972
Maryland	1,016	211	18	26	39,453	1,029	214	15	5	40,661
Massachusetts	1,416	332	30	13	40,852	1,437	335	27	32	42,174
Michigan	*2,304*	*688*	*67*	*297*	*45,186*	*2,496*	*776*	*67*	*93*	*47,360*
Minnesota	1,126	624	84	249	36,146	1,166	655	87	192	35,948
Mississippi	565	230	79	135	25,153	569	229	79	141	26,818
Missouri	1,413	587	29	188	30,310	1,432	574	33	195	31,189
Montana	541	358	1	0	28,200	537	362	0	0	28,785
Nebraska	1,018	363	25	21	29,564	1,012	363	21	23	30,922
Nevada	303	90	8	6	33,955	314	93	9	5	34,836
New Hampshire	357	103	1	0	34,121	355	99	4	0	34,720
New Jersey	1,778	388	4	117	44,693	1,786	387	5	117	46,087
New Mexico	521	170	9	9	27,922	533	169	4	9	28,491
New York	2,926	911	153	92	45,772	2,948	935	147	100	47,612
North Carolina	1,504	400	32	22	29,728	1,513	397	39	19	30,793
North Dakota	369	223	9	39	25,506	356	219	8	40	26,327
Ohio	*2,667*	*879*	*125*	*147*	*35,678*	*2,696*	*869*	*119*	*128*	*36,802*
Oklahoma	1,200	613	1	6	27,009	1,210	606	0	8	28,172
Oregon	893	273	40	13	37,590	904	261	39	9	38,590
Pennsylvania	2,364	711	29	89	42,411	2,362	712	30	86	44,510
Rhode Island	242	61	3	5	39,261	242	59	2	5	40,729
South Carolina	788	248	11	47	29,566	793	248	10	43	30,279
South Dakota	455	299	0	23	25,259	511	299	0	17	25,994
Tennessee	1,108	323	52	40	30,514	1,117	324	55	58	32,477
Texas	4,408	1,510	406	0	30,519	4,448	1,616	401	0	31,223
Utah	469	215	14	20	27,706	473	222	12	21	29,082
Vermont	302	55	18	25	34,517	297	55	17	25	35,406
Virginia	1,352	344	15	117	33,009	1,372	339	22	118	33,998
Washington	1,256	505	99	170	35,863	1,290	516	101	157	36,151
West Virginia	633	196	24	54	30,549	626	180	25	52	31,944
Wisconsin	1,481	527	24	0	35,990	1,480	521	29	0	37,746
Wyoming	283	118	0	8	30,952	284	118	0	9	31,285

Average Annual Teachers Salary
1995

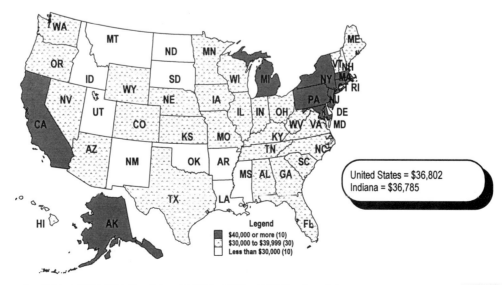

United States = $36,802
Indiana = $36,785

Legend
■ $40,000 or more (10)
▨ $30,000 to $39,999 (30)
□ Less than $30,000 (10)

Source: U.S. Department of Education, Digest of Education Statistics
EDIN table(s): EDUN, EDEA

1.13 Educational Attainment 1990

	Total Persons Age 25 & Older	Less Than 9th Grade	9th to 12th, No Diploma	High School Graduate	Some College, No Degree	Associate Degree	Bachelor's Degree	Graduate Or Professional Degree	% High School Graduate or Higher	Percent Bachelor's Degree or Higher
United States	158,868,436	16,502,211	22,841,507	47,642,763	29,779,777	9,791,925	20,832,567	11,477,686	75.2	20.3
Alabama	2,545,969	348,848	494,790	749,591	427,062	126,450	258,231	140,997	66.9	15.7
Alaska	323,429	16,621	26,623	92,925	89,319	23,444	48,617	25,880	86.6	23.0
Arizona	2,301,177	207,509	283,571	601,440	584,328	157,456	306,554	160,319	78.7	20.3
Arkansas	1,496,150	227,633	275,848	489,570	249,100	54,695	132,712	66,592	66.3	13.3
California	18,695,499	2,085,905	2,364,623	4,167,897	4,225,911	1,484,489	2,858,107	1,508,567	76.2	23.4
Colorado	2,107,072	118,252	209,804	558,312	506,037	146,411	379,150	189,106	84.4	27.0
Connecticut	2,198,963	185,213	271,995	648,366	350,418	145,278	356,289	241,404	79.2	27.2
Delaware	428,499	31,009	65,463	140,030	72,620	27,655	58,615	33,107	77.5	21.4
Dist. Of Col.	409,131	39,107	70,759	86,756	63,677	12,547	65,892	70,393	73.1	33.3
Florida	8,887,168	842,811	1,428,263	2,679,285	1,723,385	589,019	1,062,649	561,756	74.4	18.3
Georgia	4,023,420	483,755	686,060	1,192,935	684,109	199,403	519,613	257,545	70.9	19.3
Hawaii	709,820	71,806	69,700	203,893	142,881	59,116	111,837	50,587	80.1	22.9
Idaho	601,292	44,219	77,568	182,892	145,291	45,187	74,443	31,692	79.7	17.7
Illinois	*7,293,930*	*750,932*	*984,857*	*2,187,342*	*1,414,555*	*421,248*	*989,808*	*545,188*	*76.2*	*21.0*
Indiana	**3,489,470**	**297,423**	**552,591**	**1,333,093**	**578,705**	**184,717**	**321,278**	**221,663**	**75.6**	**15.6**
Percent U.S.	*2.20*	*1.80*	*2.42*	*2.80*	*1.94*	*1.89*	*1.54*	*1.93*	—	—
Rank	*14*	*19*	*12*	*10*	*18*	*17*	*22*	*16*	*31*	*46*
Iowa	1,776,798	163,335	190,465	684,368	302,600	136,638	207,269	92,123	80.1	16.9
Kansas	1,565,936	120,951	172,321	514,177	342,964	85,146	221,016	109,361	81.3	21.1
Kentucky	*2,333,833*	*442,579*	*383,278*	*741,012*	*354,227*	*94,610*	*189,539*	*128,588*	*64.6*	*13.6*
Louisiana	2,536,994	372,913	430,959	803,328	437,622	83,049	267,055	142,068	68.3	16.1
Maine	795,613	70,153	98,307	295,074	127,799	54,928	100,788	48,564	78.8	18.8
Maryland	3,122,665	246,505	427,427	878,432	580,833	163,304	486,695	339,469	78.4	26.5
Massachusetts	3,962,223	317,943	474,714	1,178,509	624,944	287,114	657,161	421,838	80.0	27.2
Michigan	*5,842,642*	*452,893*	*903,866*	*1,887,449*	*1,191,518*	*392,869*	*638,267*	*375,780*	*76.8*	*17.4*
Minnesota	2,770,562	239,322	249,443	913,265	526,792	237,156	431,381	173,203	82.4	21.8
Mississippi	1,538,997	240,267	309,418	423,624	259,477	79,264	149,109	77,838	64.3	14.7
Missouri	3,291,579	380,613	477,755	1,090,940	607,163	149,347	383,678	202,083	73.9	17.8
Montana	507,851	41,144	55,325	170,070	112,236	28,555	71,610	28,911	81.0	19.8
Nebraska	996,049	79,925	101,147	345,778	209,872	70,665	130,172	58,490	81.8	18.9
Nevada	789,638	47,771	119,857	248,968	203,599	48,803	79,693	40,947	78.8	15.3
New Hampshire	713,894	47,691	79,732	226,267	128,695	57,568	117,260	56,681	82.2	24.4
New Jersey	5,166,233	486,210	718,996	1,606,555	801,791	268,664	826,887	457,130	76.7	24.9
New Mexico	922,590	105,362	124,612	264,943	192,835	46,502	111,957	76,379	75.1	20.4
New York	11,818,569	1,200,827	1,776,777	3,485,686	1,851,182	770,268	1,561,719	1,172,110	74.8	23.1
North Carolina	4,253,494	539,974	737,773	1,232,868	713,713	290,117	510,003	229,046	70.0	17.4
North Dakota	396,550	59,354	33,073	111,215	81,467	39,802	53,637	18,002	76.7	18.1
Ohio	*6,924,764*	*546,954*	*1,137,934*	*2,515,987*	*1,179,409*	*369,144*	*767,845*	*407,491*	*75.7*	*17.0*
Oklahoma	1,995,424	195,015	311,946	607,903	425,225	100,366	236,112	118,857	74.6	17.8
Oregon	1,855,369	114,724	228,885	536,687	464,420	128,482	252,626	129,545	81.5	20.6
Pennsylvania	7,872,932	741,167	1,253,111	3,035,080	1,017,897	412,931	890,660	522,086	74.7	17.9
Rhode Island	658,956	72,842	111,502	194,064	99,092	41,296	88,634	51,526	72.0	21.3
South Carolina	2,167,590	295,167	392,093	639,358	342,965	137,174	243,161	117,672	68.3	16.6
South Dakota	430,500	57,707	41,013	144,990	80,944	31,955	52,773	21,118	77.1	17.2
Tennessee	3,139,066	500,929	532,985	942,865	531,012	130,284	330,742	170,249	67.1	16.0
Texas	10,310,605	1,387,528	1,485,031	2,640,162	2,171,439	531,540	1,428,031	666,874	72.1	20.3
Utah	897,321	30,379	102,936	244,132	250,406	69,715	138,534	61,219	85.1	22.3
Vermont	357,245	30,945	37,692	123,430	52,594	25,730	55,120	31,734	80.8	24.3
Virginia	3,974,814	443,668	543,535	1,059,199	736,007	219,511	612,679	360,215	75.2	24.5
Washington	3,126,390	171,311	334,472	873,150	782,010	248,478	496,866	220,103	83.8	22.9
West Virginia	1,171,766	196,319	202,208	429,123	155,089	44,509	88,136	56,382	66.0	12.3
Wisconsin	3,094,226	294,862	367,210	1,147,697	515,310	220,177	375,603	173,367	78.6	17.7
Wyoming	277,769	15,919	31,194	92,081	67,231	19,149	36,354	15,841	83.0	18.8

Percent Bachelor's Degree or Higher
1990

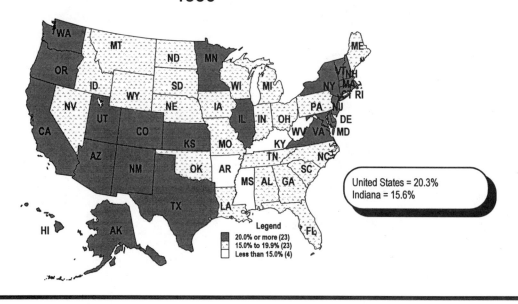

United States = 20.3%
Indiana = 15.6%

Legend
■ 20.0% or more (23)
· 15.0% to 19.9% (23)
□ Less than 15.0% (4)

Source: U.S. Bureau of the Census
EDIN table(s): EDAT

1.14 Higher Education: Enrollment 1994

	Total	Under-Graduate	Percent of Total	Enrollment — First Profes-sional	Percent of Total	Graduate	Attendance Status — Full-Time	Part-Time	Sex of Student — Male	Female	Control of Institution — Public	Private
United States	14,278,790	12,262,608	85.9	294,713	2.1	1,721,469	8,137,776	6,141,014	6,371,898	7,906,892	11,133,680	3,145,110
Alabama	229,511	202,408	88.2	3,834	1.7	23,269	151,890	77,621	102,275	127,236	206,546	22,965
Alaska	28,798	27,189	94.4	NA	NA	1,609	12,456	16,342	11,829	16,969	27,631	1,167
Arizona	274,932	241,290	87.8	1,549	0.6	32,093	127,710	147,222	124,470	150,462	252,184	22,748
Arkansas	96,294	87,197	90.6	1,705	1.8	7,392	66,973	29,321	41,354	54,940	85,601	10,693
California	1,835,791	1,624,924	88.5	35,340	1.9	175,527	863,630	972,161	833,864	1,001,927	1,582,837	252,954
Colorado	241,295	201,110	83.3	3,206	1.3	36,979	128,356	112,939	111,728	129,567	209,717	31,578
Connecticut	159,990	125,939	78.7	3,394	2.1	30,657	81,910	78,080	69,427	90,563	102,450	57,540
Delaware	44,197	38,296	86.6	1,333	3.0	4,568	25,932	18,265	19,054	25,143	36,322	7,875
Dist. Of Col.	77,705	43,667	56.2	8,819	11.3	25,219	49,246	28,459	35,473	42,232	11,048	66,657
Florida	634,237	562,961	88.8	8,653	1.4	62,623	302,139	332,098	279,398	354,839	528,024	106,213
Georgia	308,587	263,604	85.4	9,595	3.1	35,388	202,819	105,768	135,080	173,507	243,855	64,732
Hawaii	64,322	55,850	86.8	495	0.8	7,977	35,230	29,092	28,932	35,390	51,646	12,676
Idaho	60,393	51,783	85.7	559	0.9	8,051	40,358	20,035	27,163	33,230	48,994	11,399
Illinois	*731,420*	*617,549*	*84.4*	*17,173*	*2.3*	*96,698*	*372,431*	*358,989*	*324,236*	*407,184*	*545,958*	*185,462*
Indiana	**292,276**	**252,801**	**86.5**	**5,513**	**1.9**	**33,962**	**190,024**	**102,252**	**133,152**	**159,124**	**228,270**	**64,006**
Percent U.S.	*2.05*	*2.06*	*100.70*	*1.87*	*90.48*	*1.97*	*2.34*	*1.67*	*2.09*	*2.01*	*2.05*	*2.04*
Rank	*16*	*16*	*30*	*20*	*21*	*17*	*13*	*21*	*15*	*16*	*16*	*14*
Iowa	172,450	149,331	86.6	6,650	3.9	16,469	120,621	51,829	78,379	94,071	122,017	50,433
Kansas	170,603	148,046	86.8	2,075	1.2	20,482	97,928	72,675	76,127	94,476	152,798	17,805
Kentucky	*182,577*	*158,177*	*86.6*	*4,512*	*2.5*	*19,888*	*119,369*	*63,208*	*75,940*	*106,637*	*151,575*	*31,002*
Louisiana	203,567	172,561	84.8	6,102	3.0	24,904	144,368	59,199	86,630	116,937	175,112	28,455
Maine	56,724	50,274	88.6	667	1.2	5,783	32,049	24,675	23,046	33,678	39,188	17,536
Maryland	266,214	220,535	82.8	4,173	1.6	41,506	124,659	141,555	112,424	153,790	223,692	42,522
Massachusetts	416,505	323,868	77.8	13,283	3.2	79,354	261,261	155,244	183,986	232,519	179,799	236,706
Michigan	*551,307*	*474,357*	*86.0*	*10,681*	*1.9*	*66,269*	*278,545*	*272,762*	*242,966*	*308,341*	*466,758*	*84,549*
Minnesota	289,300	251,649	87.0	5,838	2.0	31,813	161,645	127,655	131,048	158,252	227,015	62,285
Mississippi	120,884	108,003	89.3	1,895	1.6	10,986	90,464	30,420	52,219	68,665	108,398	12,486
Missouri	293,810	247,484	84.2	10,208	3.5	36,118	167,080	126,730	130,006	163,804	191,859	101,951
Montana	40,095	36,414	90.8	235	0.6	3,446	30,754	9,341	19,044	21,051	34,927	5,168
Nebraska	116,000	100,482	86.6	3,219	2.8	12,299	66,661	49,339	52,059	63,941	95,877	20,123
Nevada	64,085	57,103	89.1	218	0.3	6,764	21,197	42,888	28,230	35,855	63,271	814
New Hampshire	62,847	53,154	84.6	724	1.2	8,969	39,889	22,958	26,846	36,001	34,988	27,859
New Jersey	335,480	286,020	85.3	6,588	2.0	42,872	172,614	162,866	146,950	188,530	272,420	63,060
New Mexico	101,881	88,643	87.0	625	0.6	12,613	51,380	50,501	43,759	58,122	97,073	4,808
New York	1,057,841	856,719	81.0	27,707	2.6	173,415	675,233	382,608	456,000	601,841	604,433	453,408
North Carolina	369,386	327,812	88.7	6,525	1.8	35,049	235,233	134,153	159,083	210,303	303,649	65,737
North Dakota	40,184	37,016	92.1	483	1.2	2,685	31,865	8,319	20,011	20,173	36,639	3,545
Ohio	*549,304*	*471,266*	*85.8*	*12,321*	*2.2*	*65,717*	*342,044*	*207,260*	*248,155*	*301,149*	*417,566*	*131,738*
Oklahoma	185,174	159,288	86.0	3,582	1.9	22,304	110,197	74,977	83,869	101,305	161,748	23,426
Oregon	164,447	144,583	87.9	3,559	2.2	16,305	92,428	72,019	77,043	87,404	141,027	23,420
Pennsylvania	611,174	513,257	84.0	15,462	2.5	82,455	386,419	224,755	278,456	332,718	342,565	268,609
Rhode Island	74,718	64,743	86.6	655	0.9	9,320	47,017	27,701	33,566	41,152	39,376	35,342
South Carolina	173,070	148,120	85.6	2,369	1.4	22,581	107,486	65,584	73,510	99,560	148,514	24,556
South Dakota	37,764	33,281	88.1	512	1.4	3,971	27,488	10,276	16,667	21,097	30,980	6,784
Tennessee	242,966	211,374	87.0	5,766	2.4	25,826	156,017	86,949	107,624	135,342	191,425	51,541
Texas	954,495	832,145	87.2	19,194	2.0	103,156	514,460	440,035	443,460	511,035	843,002	111,493
Utah	146,196	132,211	90.4	1,250	0.9	12,735	95,847	50,349	73,368	72,828	108,593	37,603
Vermont	35,409	30,459	86.0	898	2.5	4,052	23,895	11,514	15,118	20,291	20,505	14,904
Virginia	354,149	300,598	84.9	6,419	1.8	47,132	199,428	154,721	155,497	198,652	293,165	60,984
Washington	284,662	257,746	90.5	3,307	1.2	23,609	172,399	112,263	127,163	157,499	244,772	39,890
West Virginia	87,741	74,844	85.3	1,384	1.6	11,513	60,588	27,153	38,754	48,987	76,120	11,621
Wisconsin	303,861	269,548	88.7	3,568	1.2	30,745	180,963	122,898	134,317	169,544	250,246	53,615
Wyoming	30,682	27,771	90.5	232	0.8	2,679	17,555	13,127	13,462	17,220	30,015	667

Enrollment by Attendance Status
1994

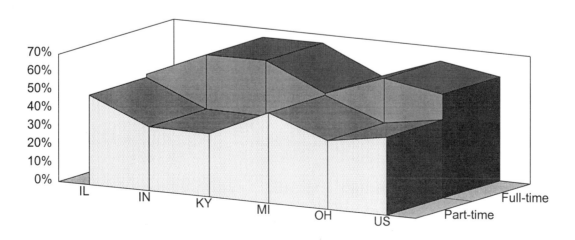

Source: U.S. Department of Education, Digest of Educational Statistics
EDIN table(s): EDHI

1.15 Higher Education: Residence and Migration of All New Students 1994 (Fall)

	Enrolled in Institutions Located in the State	Attending College in any State	Attending College in Home State	Ratio Remaining to Students Enrolled	Ratio Remaining to Student Residents	Migration of Students Out of	Migration of Students Into	Migration of Students Net
United States	1,441,705	1,418,338	1,145,571	0.79	0.81	272,767	296,134	23,367
Alabama	28,927	24,757	22,554	0.78	0.91	2,203	6,373	4,170
Alaska	1,198	2,227	997	0.83	0.45	1,230	201	-1,029
Arizona	17,850	15,160	13,002	0.73	0.86	2,158	4,848	2,690
Arkansas	12,734	12,535	10,689	0.84	0.85	1,846	2,045	199
California	167,374	168,803	153,097	0.91	0.91	15,706	14,277	-1,429
Colorado	18,410	17,435	12,773	0.69	0.73	4,662	5,637	975
Connecticut	15,055	19,120	9,011	0.60	0.47	10,109	6,044	-4,065
Delaware	5,504	4,343	2,818	0.51	0.65	1,525	2,686	1,161
Dist. Of Col.	8,476	3,039	1,758	0.21	0.58	1,281	6,718	5,437
Florida	48,583	48,192	39,134	0.81	0.81	9,058	9,449	391
Georgia	38,246	36,797	30,746	0.80	0.84	6,051	7,500	1,449
Hawaii	5,944	6,943	5,188	0.87	0.75	1,755	756	-999
Idaho	7,316	6,545	4,860	0.66	0.74	1,685	2,456	771
Illinois	*64,861*	*74,362*	*58,504*	*0.90*	*0.79*	*15,858*	*6,357*	*-9,501*
Indiana	**37,514**	**32,316**	**27,758**	**0.74**	**0.86**	**4,558**	**9,756**	**5,198**
Percent U.S.	*2.60*	*2.28*	*2.42*	*—*	*—*	*1.67*	*3.29*	*—*
Rank	*12*	*13*	*11*	*28*	*10*	*19*	*8*	*5*
Iowa	24,063	20,978	17,769	0.74	0.85	3,209	6,294	3,085
Kansas	16,910	15,429	13,397	0.79	0.87	2,032	3,513	1,481
Kentucky	*21,823*	*20,454*	*17,985*	*0.82*	*0.88*	*2,469*	*3,838*	*1,369*
Louisiana	24,550	22,766	19,584	0.80	0.86	3,182	4,966	1,784
Maine	5,913	6,831	3,863	0.65	0.57	2,968	2,050	-918
Maryland	21,803	24,700	15,285	0.70	0.62	9,415	6,518	-2,897
Massachusetts	46,209	37,740	26,154	0.57	0.69	11,586	20,055	8,469
Michigan	*54,817*	*55,492*	*49,170*	*0.90*	*0.89*	*6,322*	*5,647*	*-675*
Minnesota	25,651	26,790	19,359	0.75	0.72	7,431	6,292	-1,139
Mississippi	19,922	18,713	16,821	0.84	0.90	1,892	3,101	1,209
Missouri	28,430	26,645	21,875	0.77	0.82	4,770	6,555	1,785
Montana	5,031	5,399	3,707	0.74	0.69	1,692	1,324	-368
Nebraska	11,532	11,463	9,234	0.80	0.81	2,229	2,298	69
Nevada	3,282	3,807	2,425	0.74	0.64	1,382	857	-525
New Hampshire	8,148	6,481	3,464	0.43	0.53	3,017	4,684	1,667
New Jersey	30,524	49,681	27,486	0.90	0.55	22,195	3,038	-19,157
New Mexico	7,693	8,522	6,379	0.83	0.75	2,143	1,314	-829
New York	106,847	110,750	87,169	0.82	0.79	23,581	19,678	-3,903
North Carolina	39,418	30,960	28,285	0.72	0.91	2,675	11,133	8,458
North Dakota	6,609	5,353	4,309	0.65	0.80	1,044	2,300	1,256
Ohio	*61,777*	*61,673*	*51,983*	*0.84*	*0.84*	*9,690*	*9,794*	*104*
Oklahoma	16,516	16,482	14,221	0.86	0.86	2,261	2,295	34
Oregon	16,487	16,103	12,766	0.77	0.79	3,337	3,721	384
Pennsylvania	74,938	68,581	55,543	0.74	0.81	13,038	19,395	6,357
Rhode Island	10,344	5,795	3,644	0.35	0.63	2,151	6,700	4,549
South Carolina	20,994	19,271	16,594	0.79	0.86	2,677	4,400	1,723
South Dakota	4,786	4,342	3,067	0.64	0.71	1,275	1,719	444
Tennessee	26,527	24,407	20,227	0.76	0.83	4,180	6,300	2,120
Texas	86,748	86,586	78,262	0.90	0.90	8,324	8,486	162
Utah	19,420	15,072	13,994	0.72	0.93	1,078	5,426	4,348
Vermont	4,802	3,306	1,573	0.33	0.48	1,733	3,229	1,496
Virginia	35,769	32,385	25,141	0.70	0.78	7,244	10,628	3,384
Washington	28,578	28,617	24,425	0.85	0.85	4,192	4,153	-39
West Virginia	12,162	10,183	8,561	0.70	0.84	1,622	3,601	1,979
Wisconsin	31,404	32,013	26,627	0.85	0.83	5,386	4,777	-609
Wyoming	3,286	3,173	2,334	0.71	0.74	839	952	113

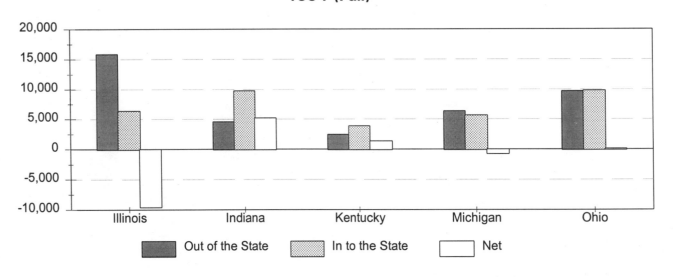

Migration of All New Students
1994 (Fall)

Out of the State · In to the State · Net

Source: U.S. Department of Education, Digest of Educational Statistics
EDIN table(s): EDRM

Housing

1.16 Housing: Occupancy and Tenure 1990

	Occupied Housing Units			Vacant Housing Units				Persons Per Occupied Unit		Units with Over One Person per Room
	Total	Owner Occupied	Percent of Total	Total	For Seasonal, Recreational or Occasional Use	Homeowner Vacancy Rate	Rental Vacancy Rate	Owner Occupied	Renter Occupied	
United States	91,947,410	59,024,811	64.2	10,316,268	3,081,923	2.1	8.5	2.8	2.4	4,548,799
Alabama	1,506,790	1,061,897	70.5	163,589	35,609	1.8	9.3	2.7	2.4	52,927
Alaska	188,915	105,989	56.1	43,693	16,991	4.5	8.5	3.0	2.6	16,201
Arizona	1,368,843	878,561	64.2	290,587	96,104	3.6	15.3	2.7	2.5	101,636
Arkansas	891,179	619,938	69.6	109,488	18,224	2.4	10.4	2.6	2.5	33,197
California	10,381,206	5,773,943	55.6	801,676	195,385	2.0	5.9	2.8	2.7	1,275,377
Colorado	1,282,489	798,277	62.2	194,860	63,814	3.3	11.4	2.7	2.3	38,139
Connecticut	1,230,479	807,481	65.6	90,371	20,428	1.9	6.9	2.7	2.3	28,237
Delaware	247,497	173,813	70.2	42,422	19,328	2.3	7.8	2.7	2.4	5,624
Dist. Of Col.	249,634	97,108	38.9	28,855	1,575	3.1	7.9	2.5	2.1	20,587
Florida	5,134,869	3,452,160	67.2	965,393	417,670	3.4	12.4	2.5	2.4	297,557
Georgia	2,366,615	1,536,759	64.9	271,803	33,637	2.5	12.2	2.8	2.5	95,828
Hawaii	356,267	191,911	53.9	33,543	12,806	0.8	5.4	3.2	2.8	56,708
Idaho	360,723	252,734	70.1	52,604	24,252	2.0	7.3	2.8	2.5	15,199
Illinois	*4,202,240*	*2,699,182*	*64.2*	*304,035*	*25,056*	*1.5*	*8.0*	*2.8*	*2.4*	*166,805*
Indiana	**2,065,355**	**1,450,898**	**70.2**	**180,691**	**36,945**	**1.5**	**8.3**	**2.7**	**2.3**	**45,376**
Percent U.S.	*2.25*	*2.46*	*—*	*1.75*	*1.20*	*—*	*—*	*—*	*—*	*1.00*
Rank	*14*	*13*	*8*	*21*	*23*	*40*	*26*	*22*	*28*	*24*
Iowa	1,064,325	745,377	70.0	79,344	14,644	1.5	6.4	2.6	2.3	16,009
Kansas	944,726	641,762	67.9	99,386	7,336	2.3	11.1	2.6	2.3	23,690
Kentucky	*1,379,782*	*960,469*	*69.6*	*127,063*	*20,962*	*1.6*	*8.2*	*2.7*	*2.4*	*35,873*
Louisiana	1,499,269	987,919	65.9	216,972	30,333	2.7	12.5	2.8	2.6	89,268
Maine	465,312	327,888	70.5	121,733	88,039	1.8	8.4	2.7	2.2	7,998
Maryland	1,748,991	1,137,296	65.0	142,936	42,268	1.6	6.8	2.8	2.5	53,139
Massachusetts	2,247,110	1,331,493	59.3	225,601	90,367	1.7	6.9	2.8	2.2	56,700
Michigan	*3,419,331*	*2,427,643*	*71.0*	*428,595*	*223,549*	*1.3*	*7.2*	*2.8*	*2.3*	*90,551*
Minnesota	1,647,853	1,183,673	71.8	200,592	105,122	1.5	7.9	2.8	2.1	34,126
Mississippi	911,374	651,587	71.5	99,049	16,000	1.9	9.5	2.8	2.7	52,890
Missouri	1,961,206	1,348,746	68.8	237,923	55,492	2.2	10.7	2.7	2.2	48,264
Montana	306,163	205,899	67.3	54,992	20,481	2.9	9.6	2.7	2.3	8,886
Nebraska	602,363	400,394	66.5	58,258	10,978	1.7	7.7	2.7	2.3	10,512
Nevada	466,297	255,388	54.8	52,561	11,258	2.3	9.1	2.7	2.4	29,890
New Hampshire	411,186	280,372	68.2	92,718	57,135	2.7	11.8	2.8	2.2	6,610
New Jersey	2,794,711	1,813,381	64.9	280,599	100,591	2.5	7.4	2.9	2.4	108,771
New Mexico	542,709	365,965	67.4	89,349	21,862	2.3	11.4	2.9	2.5	42,810
New York	6,639,322	3,464,436	52.2	587,569	212,625	1.9	4.9	2.9	2.4	431,733
North Carolina	2,517,026	1,711,817	68.0	301,167	98,714	1.8	9.2	2.6	2.4	72,635
North Dakota	240,878	157,950	65.6	35,462	7,236	2.8	9.0	2.7	2.2	4,762
Ohio	*4,087,546*	*2,758,149*	*67.5*	*284,399*	*37,324*	*1.3*	*7.5*	*2.7*	*2.3*	*71,771*
Oklahoma	1,206,135	821,188	68.1	200,364	25,169	3.7	14.7	2.6	2.4	39,941
Oregon	1,103,313	695,957	63.1	90,254	30,200	1.4	5.3	2.6	2.3	40,135
Pennsylvania	4,495,966	3,176,121	70.6	442,174	144,359	1.5	7.2	2.7	2.2	82,518
Rhode Island	377,977	224,792	59.5	36,595	12,037	1.5	7.9	2.8	2.2	8,676
South Carolina	1,258,044	878,704	69.8	166,111	49,843	1.7	11.5	2.8	2.5	51,061
South Dakota	259,034	171,161	66.1	33,402	8,391	1.8	7.3	2.7	2.3	7,660
Tennessee	1,853,725	1,261,118	68.0	172,342	23,389	2.1	9.6	2.7	2.4	50,767
Texas	6,070,937	3,695,115	60.9	938,062	151,919	3.2	13.0	2.9	2.6	494,578
Utah	537,273	365,979	68.1	61,115	21,023	2.4	8.6	3.4	2.7	29,577
Vermont	210,650	145,368	69.0	60,564	45,405	2.1	7.5	2.7	2.2	3,595
Virginia	2,291,830	1,519,521	66.3	204,504	41,742	2.1	8.1	2.7	2.4	65,042
Washington	1,872,431	1,171,580	62.6	159,947	55,832	1.3	5.8	2.7	2.3	72,798
West Virginia	688,557	510,058	74.1	92,738	22,403	2.2	10.1	2.6	2.3	13,123
Wisconsin	1,822,118	1,215,350	66.7	233,656	150,601	1.2	4.7	2.8	2.3	38,340
Wyoming	168,839	114,544	67.8	34,572	9,468	3.9	14.4	2.7	2.4	4,702

Overcrowding — 1990
Percent of Units with Over One Person Per Room

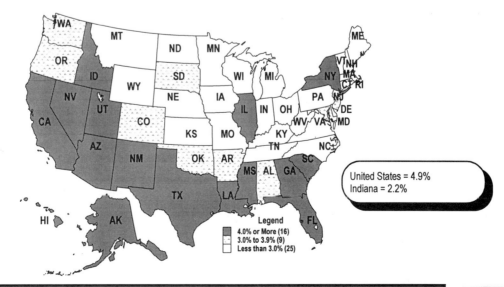

United States = 4.9%
Indiana = 2.2%

Legend
■ 4.0% or More (16)
▨ 3.0% to 3.9% (9)
□ Less than 3.0% (25)

Source: U.S. Bureau of the Census
EDIN table(s): HC90

1.17 Housing: Units in Structure 1990

	1 Unit — Detached	1 Unit — Attached	Percent Total	2 to 4 Units	Percent Total	5 to 9 Units	Percent Total	10 or More	Percent Total	Mobile Home, Trailer, Other	Percent Total
United States	60,383,409	5,378,243	64.3	9,876,407	9.7	4,935,841	4.8	13,168,769	12.9	8,521,009	8.3
Alabama	1,133,927	31,943	69.8	96,104	5.8	66,413	4.0	102,462	6.1	239,530	14.3
Alaska	124,185	15,963	60.3	30,358	13.1	16,171	7.0	21,229	9.1	24,702	10.6
Arizona	867,884	109,989	58.9	88,371	5.3	61,111	3.7	257,208	15.5	274,867	16.6
Arkansas	708,751	18,175	72.6	60,820	6.1	27,024	2.7	44,454	4.4	141,443	14.1
California	6,119,265	811,684	62.0	966,355	8.6	705,704	6.3	1,899,934	17.0	679,940	6.1
Colorado	884,431	87,437	65.8	89,997	6.1	63,855	4.3	249,360	16.9	102,269	6.9
Connecticut	748,626	66,681	61.7	243,600	18.4	75,497	5.7	155,492	11.8	30,954	2.3
Delaware	156,013	40,161	67.7	13,919	4.8	10,148	3.5	32,612	11.2	37,066	12.8
Dist. Of Col.	34,602	71,321	38.0	30,699	11.0	20,783	7.5	118,237	42.5	2,847	1.0
Florida	3,032,769	335,798	55.2	462,438	7.6	320,580	5.3	1,127,629	18.5	821,048	13.5
Georgia	1,638,847	73,412	64.9	198,036	7.5	167,552	6.4	232,683	8.8	327,888	12.4
Hawaii	202,990	34,041	60.8	24,182	6.2	22,258	5.7	100,238	25.7	6,101	1.6
Idaho	285,885	9,102	71.4	29,151	7.1	11,701	2.8	17,242	4.2	60,246	14.6
Illinois	*2,557,169*	*157,771*	*60.2*	*648,275*	*14.4*	*290,519*	*6.4*	*663,448*	*14.7*	*189,093*	*4.2*
Indiana	1,574,160	57,445	72.6	170,801	7.6	99,836	4.4	167,718	7.5	176,086	7.8
Percent U.S.	2.61	1.07	—	1.73	—	2.02	—	1.27	—	2.07	—
Rank	12	21	6	16	22	15	25	20	34	20	30
Iowa	852,993	17,735	76.1	86,956	7.6	40,745	3.6	76,761	6.7	68,479	6.0
Kansas	747,318	34,868	74.9	74,100	7.1	34,720	3.3	74,710	7.2	78,396	7.5
Kentucky	*1,010,860*	*25,285*	*68.8*	*109,291*	*7.3*	*65,348*	*4.3*	*96,494*	*6.4*	*199,567*	*13.2*
Louisiana	1,083,921	79,002	67.8	152,060	8.9	58,819	3.4	124,916	7.3	217,523	12.7
Maine	378,413	11,753	66.5	74,077	12.6	28,553	4.9	26,230	4.5	68,019	11.6
Maryland	938,514	393,185	70.4	104,332	5.5	105,530	5.6	294,364	15.6	55,992	3.0
Massachusetts	1,237,786	88,746	53.6	597,143	24.1	159,332	6.4	338,585	13.7	51,119	2.1
Michigan	*2,673,184*	*130,583*	*72.9*	*267,767*	*7.0*	*150,831*	*3.9*	*336,721*	*8.8*	*288,840*	*7.5*
Minnesota	1,230,561	69,267	70.3	115,347	6.2	45,190	2.4	276,475	15.0	111,605	6.0
Mississippi	710,298	17,060	72.0	56,813	5.6	35,675	3.5	41,322	4.1	149,255	14.8
Missouri	1,489,661	57,345	70.3	212,483	9.7	85,323	3.9	172,360	7.8	181,957	8.3
Montana	237,533	8,432	68.1	29,327	8.1	10,376	2.9	16,931	4.7	58,556	16.2
Nebraska	479,124	15,767	74.9	39,656	6.0	24,959	3.8	59,058	8.9	42,057	6.4
Nevada	235,912	26,819	50.6	49,889	9.6	40,757	7.9	89,864	17.3	75,617	14.6
New Hampshire	297,777	23,072	63.7	68,105	13.5	26,985	5.4	46,022	9.1	41,943	8.3
New Jersey	1,637,129	234,829	60.9	526,997	17.1	146,396	4.8	453,254	14.7	76,705	2.5
New Mexico	387,830	28,352	65.8	38,833	6.1	16,434	2.6	48,239	7.6	112,370	17.8
New York	2,929,333	301,794	44.7	1,320,073	18.3	374,858	5.2	1,998,074	27.6	302,759	4.2
North Carolina	1,830,229	74,318	67.6	177,700	6.3	130,801	4.6	150,986	5.4	454,159	16.1
North Dakota	172,938	10,286	66.3	21,127	7.6	12,011	4.3	30,362	11.0	29,616	10.7
Ohio	*2,896,826*	*147,651*	*69.6*	*461,286*	*10.6*	*204,074*	*4.7*	*415,589*	*9.5*	*246,519*	*5.6*
Oklahoma	1,005,020	32,851	73.8	69,010	4.9	56,306	4.0	99,611	7.1	143,701	10.2
Oregon	764,258	32,355	66.7	86,371	7.2	46,847	3.9	118,592	9.9	145,144	12.2
Pennsylvania	2,636,631	909,676	71.8	507,488	10.3	171,041	3.5	393,091	8.0	320,213	6.5
Rhode Island	218,776	11,188	55.5	109,460	26.4	23,024	5.6	43,280	10.4	8,844	2.1
South Carolina	898,161	33,891	65.4	91,572	6.4	67,091	4.7	80,065	5.6	253,375	17.8
South Dakota	202,166	5,249	70.9	19,166	6.6	10,003	3.4	21,642	7.4	34,210	11.7
Tennessee	1,358,124	55,399	69.8	145,992	7.2	92,936	4.6	166,172	8.2	207,444	10.2
Texas	4,388,813	215,201	65.7	390,675	5.6	343,049	4.9	1,040,600	14.8	630,661	9.0
Utah	393,374	23,702	69.7	57,715	9.6	20,503	3.4	62,050	10.4	41,044	6.9
Vermont	168,272	9,367	65.5	40,864	15.1	13,742	5.1	10,376	3.8	28,593	10.5
Virginia	1,531,857	216,199	70.0	143,530	5.7	135,833	5.4	286,815	11.5	182,100	7.3
Washington	1,272,721	48,086	65.0	138,785	6.8	91,003	4.5	274,586	13.5	207,197	10.2
West Virginia	546,165	11,415	71.4	46,445	5.9	20,179	2.6	28,923	3.7	128,168	16.4
Wisconsin	1,342,230	50,380	67.7	277,221	13.5	81,331	4.0	175,285	8.5	129,327	6.3
Wyoming	129,197	6,212	66.6	15,645	7.7	6,084	3.0	10,418	5.1	35,855	17.6

Mobile Homes as a Percent of All Homes
1990

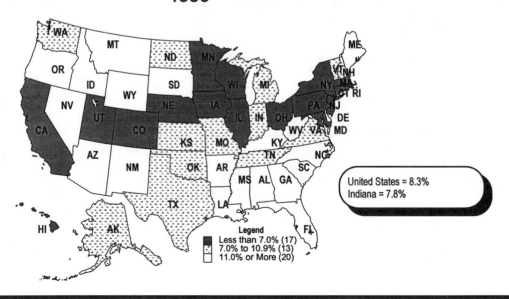

United States = 8.3%
Indiana = 7.8%

Legend
Less than 7.0% (17)
7.0% to 10.9% (13)
11.0% or More (20)

Source: U.S. Bureau of the Census
EDIN table(s): HC90

1.18 Housing: Value Owner Occupied 1990

	Total Units Owner Occupied	Median Value ($)	Units Less Than $50,000	$50,000 to $99,999	$100,000 to $149,999	$150,000 to $199,999	$200,000 to $299,999	$300,000 or More
					Percent of Total			
United States	44,918,000	79,100	25.4	37.8	15.1	8.9	7.5	5.3
Alabama	753,827	53,700	45.6	41.2	8.3	2.7	1.5	0.7
Alaska	77,527	94,400	14.2	41.1	29.7	9.7	4.1	1.2
Arizona	668,718	80,100	14.8	55.7	17.8	6.1	3.6	2.1
Arkansas	427,676	46,300	55.1	36.7	5.5	1.6	0.8	0.4
California	4,690,264	195,500	2.5	13.6	17.3	18.2	24.5	23.9
Colorado	637,629	82,700	13.2	56.9	19.3	5.9	3.1	1.6
Connecticut	643,500	177,800	0.7	5.7	25.7	29.2	23.4	15.3
Delaware	137,526	100,100	8.6	41.3	28.0	11.4	7.6	3.1
Dist. Of Col.	71,532	123,900	2.3	35.3	21.0	9.6	11.7	20.1
Florida	2,378,207	77,100	18.2	52.1	16.1	6.4	4.2	3.0
Georgia	1,138,775	71,300	27.6	46.6	14.3	5.9	3.5	2.0
Hawaii	144,431	245,300	2.3	9.1	11.6	14.6	27.5	34.9
Idaho	177,333	58,200	37.7	50.4	8.0	2.1	1.1	0.7
Illinois	*2,084,708*	*80,900*	*25.2*	*37.7*	*19.3*	*8.8*	*5.5*	*3.4*
Indiana	**1,137,766**	**53,900**	**45.2**	**42.5**	**8.2**	**2.4**	**1.2**	**0.5**
Percent U.S.	*2.53*	*68.14*	—	—	—	—	—	—
Rank	*13*	*40*	*12*	*24*	*38*	*39*	*39*	*40*
Iowa	566,559	45,900	56.1	37.0	4.9	1.2	0.6	0.2
Kansas	500,628	52,200	47.5	39.9	8.2	2.5	1.3	0.6
Kentucky	*662,174*	*50,500*	*49.4*	*39.3*	*7.2*	*2.4*	*1.2*	*0.5*
Louisiana	733,914	58,500	39.4	46.9	8.6	2.7	1.6	0.8
Maine	214,663	87,400	17.5	44.3	23.0	8.4	4.7	2.2
Maryland	970,864	116,500	9.0	31.0	28.2	14.4	10.6	6.8
Massachusetts	1,004,573	162,800	0.9	9.3	30.9	29.7	19.5	9.6
Michigan	*1,916,143*	*60,600*	*38.5*	*42.5*	*11.4*	*4.1*	*2.4*	*1.0*
Minnesota	894,345	74,000	22.9	53.9	15.5	4.3	2.4	1.0
Mississippi	441,821	45,600	56.4	35.3	5.5	1.6	0.8	0.4
Missouri	1,005,407	59,800	38.3	45.0	10.1	3.3	2.0	1.2
Montana	132,419	56,600	39.5	51.6	6.3	1.6	0.8	0.2
Nebraska	314,363	50,400	49.4	42.1	5.9	1.5	0.8	0.3
Nevada	183,816	95,700	4.6	50.8	27.9	8.7	5.0	3.0
New Hampshire	199,358	129,400	3.1	22.9	40.1	20.0	10.6	3.3
New Jersey	1,466,270	162,300	3.1	16.5	23.8	25.0	20.6	11.0
New Mexico	262,309	70,100	28.0	48.9	14.2	4.9	2.7	1.3
New York	2,387,606	131,600	10.2	28.2	18.1	18.4	16.0	9.1
North Carolina	1,217,975	65,800	31.4	47.3	12.7	4.6	2.7	1.2
North Dakota	103,702	50,800	48.8	44.7	4.9	1.0	0.5	0.1
Ohio	*2,241,277*	*63,500*	*32.7*	*49.2*	*11.6*	*3.6*	*1.9*	*0.9*
Oklahoma	616,290	48,100	52.5	38.2	6.0	1.8	1.0	0.5
Oregon	511,829	67,100	26.0	54.9	12.2	3.8	2.0	0.9
Pennsylvania	2,581,261	69,700	32.1	39.4	15.3	7.0	4.2	1.9
Rhode Island	176,494	133,500	1.7	17.6	44.4	20.1	11.0	5.1
South Carolina	615,434	61,100	36.7	45.5	10.3	3.9	2.4	1.2
South Dakota	113,057	45,200	56.8	37.5	4.1	0.9	0.5	0.2
Tennessee	938,366	58,400	39.6	44.4	9.8	3.4	1.9	0.9
Texas	2,949,089	59,600	39.0	42.8	10.7	3.8	2.3	1.5
Utah	303,724	68,900	20.1	62.1	11.6	3.5	1.9	0.8
Vermont	89,157	95,500	8.8	46.3	28.7	9.4	4.9	1.9
Virginia	1,192,077	91,000	17.3	39.1	17.1	11.1	9.8	5.5
Washington	896,436	93,400	13.8	41.4	21.5	11.3	7.6	4.4
West Virginia	350,059	47,900	52.9	39.1	5.4	1.5	0.8	0.3
Wisconsin	916,708	62,500	31.3	53.7	10.4	2.7	1.3	0.6
Wyoming	78,414	61,600	33.0	55.9	8.0	1.9	0.9	0.5

Median Value of Owner Occupied Housing
1990

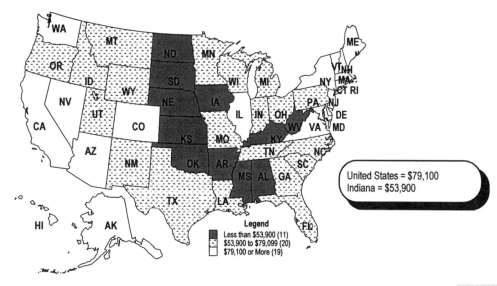

United States = $79,100
Indiana = $53,900

Legend
Less than $53,900 (11)
$53,900 to $79,099 (20)
$79,100 or More (19)

Source: U.S. Bureau of the Census
EDIN table(s): HC90

1.19 Housing: Contract Rent 1990

	Total Units, Renter Occupied Paying Cash Rent	Median Contract Rent ($)	Less Than $250	Percent of Total	$250 to $499	$500 to $749	$750 to $999	$1,000 or More	Percent of Total
United States	30,490,535	374	7,478,207	24.5	14,371,897	6,188,367	1,626,608	825,456	2.7
Alabama	386,179	229	214,363	55.5	155,027	14,380	1,594	815	0.2
Alaska	70,579	503	5,785	8.2	29,167	23,750	8,455	3,422	4.8
Arizona	456,937	370	73,866	16.2	290,538	76,518	10,461	5,554	1.2
Arkansas	227,643	230	129,535	56.9	90,452	6,204	895	557	0.2
California	4,400,105	561	330,342	7.5	1,385,031	1,692,456	668,470	323,824	7.4
Colorado	452,881	362	88,745	19.6	271,347	76,533	10,937	5,319	1.2
Connecticut	401,254	510	56,694	14.1	135,109	152,144	38,238	19,069	4.8
Delaware	68,249	425	12,669	18.6	36,047	16,687	1,835	1,011	1.5
Dist. Of Col.	148,553	441	23,897	16.1	65,510	37,629	12,668	8,849	6.0
Florida	1,591,461	402	261,349	16.4	892,383	355,636	49,428	32,665	2.1
Georgia	759,499	344	251,826	33.2	361,984	127,415	13,143	5,131	0.7
Hawaii	139,266	599	15,119	10.9	36,779	43,763	25,164	18,441	13.2
Idaho	92,907	261	42,967	46.2	44,092	4,599	938	311	0.3
Illinois	*1,416,273*	*369*	*352,318*	*24.9*	*703,816*	*283,237*	*53,525*	*23,377*	*1.7*
Indiana	**554,678**	**291**	**204,414**	**36.9**	**310,071**	**33,448**	**4,434**	**2,311**	**0.4**
Percent U.S.	*1.82*	*—*	*2.73*	*—*	*2.16*	*0.54*	*0.27*	*0.28*	*—*
Rank	*17*	*32*	*15*	*20*	*14*	*28*	*29*	*26*	*33*
Iowa	268,439	261	125,112	46.6	129,124	12,343	1,287	573	0.2
Kansas	270,761	285	108,024	39.9	135,967	22,396	2,744	1,630	0.6
Kentucky	*351,165*	*250*	*175,280*	*49.9*	*160,392*	*12,875*	*1,499*	*1,119*	*0.3*
Louisiana	452,077	260	211,769	46.8	213,862	21,781	3,209	1,456	0.3
Maine	122,972	358	30,198	24.6	68,579	21,448	1,902	845	0.7
Maryland	574,109	473	88,093	15.3	223,038	196,835	50,950	15,193	2.6
Massachusetts	879,173	506	164,904	18.8	265,621	308,154	98,604	41,890	4.8
Michigan	*925,304*	*343*	*232,954*	*25.2*	*536,905*	*128,873*	*17,827*	*8,745*	*0.9*
Minnesota	431,301	384	103,986	24.1	217,401	93,630	12,804	3,480	0.8
Mississippi	214,289	215	126,942	59.2	80,106	6,222	588	431	0.2
Missouri	548,587	282	223,902	40.8	275,787	40,831	5,290	2,777	0.5
Montana	85,542	251	42,446	49.6	40,278	2,389	199	230	0.3
Nebraska	174,052	282	69,594	40.0	91,576	10,966	1,188	728	0.4
Nevada	202,782	445	19,063	9.4	111,139	62,940	7,587	2,053	1.0
New Hampshire	121,779	479	14,724	12.1	51,960	45,058	7,804	2,233	1.8
New Jersey	942,141	521	106,627	11.3	321,775	381,923	92,517	39,299	4.2
New Mexico	157,095	312	49,767	31.7	88,292	16,096	1,951	989	0.6
New York	3,059,911	428	529,128	17.3	1,387,210	764,656	223,110	155,807	5.1
North Carolina	709,716	284	288,186	40.6	360,735	52,038	4,888	3,869	0.5
North Dakota	69,800	266	31,355	44.9	35,647	2,476	227	95	0.1
Ohio	*1,231,515*	*296*	*431,181*	*35.0*	*692,202*	*87,843*	*11,495*	*8,794*	*0.7*
Oklahoma	341,131	259	159,710	46.8	162,583	15,568	2,037	1,233	0.4
Oregon	378,482	344	82,356	21.8	241,786	44,473	6,444	3,423	0.9
Pennsylvania	1,216,440	322	397,012	32.6	601,609	174,432	28,834	14,553	1.2
Rhode Island	146,347	416	30,696	21.0	69,365	38,510	5,709	2,067	1.4
South Carolina	332,473	276	145,105	43.6	161,649	21,732	2,691	1,296	0.4
South Dakota	72,810	242	38,086	52.3	31,425	2,955	270	74	0.1
Tennessee	524,172	273	228,983	43.7	260,056	29,370	3,742	2,021	0.4
Texas	2,192,550	328	573,792	26.2	1,321,160	239,984	36,426	21,188	1.0
Utah	161,608	300	46,261	28.6	101,235	11,278	2,144	690	0.4
Vermont	57,846	378	11,239	19.4	34,117	10,390	1,495	605	1.0
Virginia	698,751	411	150,635	21.6	297,353	165,383	60,428	24,952	3.6
Washington	655,701	383	122,103	18.6	373,552	130,901	21,321	7,824	1.2
West Virginia	146,057	221	88,872	60.8	53,411	3,312	267	195	0.1
Wisconsin	560,465	331	146,221	26.1	343,580	61,539	6,780	2,345	0.4
Wyoming	46,728	270	20,012	42.8	24,085	2,368	165	98	0.2

Median Contract Rent
1990

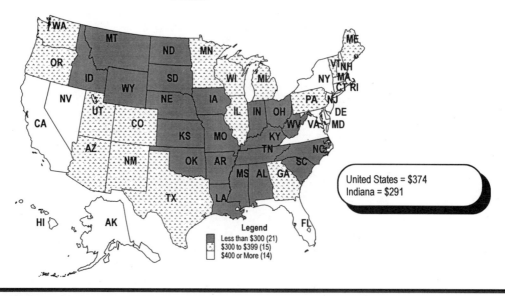

United States = $374
Indiana = $291

Legend
Less than $300 (21)
$300 to $399 (15)
$400 or More (14)

Source: U.S. Bureau of the Census
EDIN table(s): HC90

1.20 Housing: Year Structure Built for Year Round Units 1990

	Total Units	Before 1950	Percent of Total	1950 to 1959	1960 to 1969	Year Built 1970 to 1979	1980 to 1984	1985 to 1988	1989 to March 1990	Percent of Total
United States	102,263,678	27,508,653	26.9	14,831,071	16,506,410	22,291,826	9,931,917	9,024,365	2,169,436	2.1
Alabama	1,670,379	298,303	17.9	244,389	309,318	426,594	177,403	176,555	37,817	2.3
Alaska	232,608	16,248	7.0	19,407	32,373	76,124	57,295	27,636	3,525	1.5
Arizona	1,659,430	110,746	6.7	171,456	240,042	509,539	300,928	280,928	45,791	2.8
Arkansas	1,000,667	176,662	17.7	123,123	180,597	278,379	121,714	99,652	20,540	2.1
California	11,182,882	2,211,243	19.8	1,931,706	2,059,742	2,424,359	1,017,889	1,194,025	343,018	3.1
Colorado	1,477,349	270,562	18.3	186,792	228,043	426,405	219,302	128,898	17,347	1.2
Connecticut	1,320,850	462,808	35.0	227,124	216,631	206,852	80,441	107,740	19,254	1.5
Delaware	289,919	64,704	22.3	45,243	50,889	58,679	27,195	33,945	9,264	3.2
Dist. Of Col.	278,489	155,194	55.7	43,176	41,412	23,279	9,048	4,731	1,649	0.6
Florida	6,100,262	472,481	7.7	715,247	992,958	1,786,497	1,003,017	911,095	218,967	3.6
Georgia	2,638,418	381,827	14.5	309,335	453,853	646,094	349,315	405,556	92,438	3.5
Hawaii	389,810	52,347	13.4	54,048	83,455	118,872	39,178	31,692	10,218	2.6
Idaho	413,327	100,738	24.4	50,074	53,944	134,117	43,739	23,630	7,085	1.7
Illinois	*4,506,275*	*1,662,888*	*36.9*	*737,211*	*746,181*	*830,606*	*237,016*	*226,422*	*65,951*	*1.5*
Indiana	**2,246,046**	**756,843**	**33.7**	**332,135**	**377,084**	**453,736**	**146,959**	**142,830**	**36,459**	**2**
Percent U.S.	*2.20*	*2.75*	—	*2.24*	*2.28*	*2.04*	*1.48*	*1.58*	*1.68*	—
Rank	*14*	*11*	*17*	*12*	*14*	*17*	*24*	*22*	*24*	*30*
Iowa	1,143,669	490,394	42.9	147,913	159,930	230,514	66,202	36,834	11,882	1.0
Kansas	1,044,112	345,564	33.1	165,656	144,371	211,563	90,379	72,923	13,656	1.3
Kentucky	*1,506,845*	*364,678*	*24.2*	*206,673*	*257,980*	*375,996*	*144,327*	*122,778*	*34,413*	*2.3*
Louisiana	1,716,241	333,965	19.5	258,594	311,647	433,427	245,598	116,130	16,880	1.0
Maine	587,045	242,858	41.4	48,543	58,059	116,337	46,389	60,512	14,347	2.4
Maryland	1,891,917	473,984	25.1	295,122	343,386	371,343	162,369	195,513	50,200	2.7
Massachusetts	2,472,711	1,157,737	46.8	309,360	316,129	348,860	135,907	166,154	38,564	1.6
Michigan	*3,847,926*	*1,228,635*	*31.9*	*688,994*	*622,650*	*785,613*	*214,435*	*232,299*	*75,300*	*2.0*
Minnesota	1,848,445	585,539	31.7	247,915	263,833	408,531	152,653	153,344	36,630	2.0
Mississippi	1,010,423	167,685	16.6	130,727	190,715	277,874	120,220	100,768	22,434	2.2
Missouri	2,199,129	629,868	28.6	311,888	380,427	473,517	173,598	187,762	42,069	1.9
Montana	361,155	108,805	30.1	45,209	48,031	95,926	39,734	19,632	3,818	1.1
Nebraska	660,621	249,631	37.8	79,797	100,105	145,834	45,457	30,858	8,939	1.4
Nevada	518,858	31,044	6.0	38,749	82,533	158,366	82,573	82,864	42,729	8.2
New Hampshire	503,904	162,201	32.2	41,061	57,736	103,476	51,765	75,194	12,471	2.5
New Jersey	3,075,310	1,082,121	35.2	537,409	539,742	459,597	182,183	228,704	45,594	1.5
New Mexico	632,058	97,750	15.5	95,473	97,605	167,391	89,454	71,275	13,110	2.1
New York	7,226,891	3,401,416	47.1	1,187,957	1,097,623	861,496	278,465	321,086	78,848	1.1
North Carolina	2,818,193	494,675	17.6	360,172	470,484	686,179	352,115	374,055	80,513	2.9
North Dakota	276,340	85,128	30.8	32,526	39,213	73,634	28,520	14,427	2,892	1.0
Ohio	*4,371,945*	*1,561,695*	*35.7*	*737,513*	*725,770*	*813,367*	*238,892*	*228,004*	*66,704*	*1.5*
Oklahoma	1,406,499	298,347	21.2	203,335	236,731	356,828	212,820	86,324	12,114	0.9
Oregon	1,193,567	316,648	26.5	149,093	186,453	342,967	104,443	66,681	27,282	2.3
Pennsylvania	4,938,140	2,213,386	44.8	720,956	612,604	778,612	266,690	271,938	73,954	1.5
Rhode Island	414,572	181,215	43.7	55,061	54,854	61,044	24,741	30,205	7,452	1.8
South Carolina	1,424,155	218,781	15.4	183,553	233,689	374,599	191,803	182,148	39,582	2.8
South Dakota	292,436	107,374	36.7	33,683	36,275	71,813	23,774	15,558	3,959	1.4
Tennessee	2,026,067	380,068	18.8	285,521	367,101	503,402	206,607	226,188	57,180	2.8
Texas	7,008,999	1,008,475	14.4	964,539	1,136,548	1,818,149	1,295,101	696,179	90,008	1.3
Utah	598,388	127,266	21.3	74,474	82,603	168,147	80,250	56,664	8,984	1.5
Vermont	271,214	109,780	40.5	16,149	31,386	53,157	25,417	27,058	8,267	3.0
Virginia	2,496,334	481,679	19.3	334,512	433,857	589,187	262,524	312,631	81,944	3.3
Washington	2,032,378	500,808	24.6	248,403	314,535	500,161	217,263	186,504	64,704	3.2
West Virginia	781,295	270,441	34.6	100,964	93,433	178,183	74,101	50,814	13,359	1.7
Wisconsin	2,055,774	757,204	36.8	277,876	288,716	433,401	141,608	119,036	37,933	1.8
Wyoming	203,411	48,254	23.7	25,235	23,134	63,203	33,101	9,086	1,398	0.7

Percent of All Houses Built Before 1950
As Reported in 1990

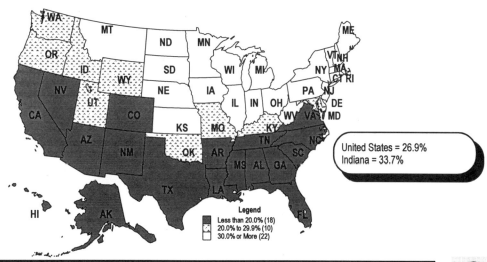

United States = 26.9%
Indiana = 33.7%

Legend
Less than 20.0% (18)
20.0% to 29.9% (10)
30.0% or More (22)

Source: U.S. Bureau of the Census
EDIN table(s): HSYR

1.21 Housing: Race and Hispanic Origin of Householder 1990

	Total Occupied Housing Units	White	African-American	Percent Total	Native American	Percent Total	Asian American	Percent Total	Other Races	Hispanic Origin	Percent Total
United States	91,947,410	76,880,105	9,976,161	10.8	591,372	0.6	2,013,735	2.2	2,486,037	6,001,718	6.5
Alabama	1,506,790	1,159,263	334,513	22.2	5,288	0.4	6,077	0.4	1,649	7,373	0.5
Alaska	188,915	153,215	6,927	3.7	22,305	11.8	4,674	2.5	1,794	4,671	2.5
Arizona	1,368,843	1,177,349	37,140	2.7	49,894	3.6	15,934	1.2	88,526	184,942	13.5
Arkansas	891,179	760,287	121,338	13.6	4,539	0.5	3,228	0.4	1,787	5,350	0.6
California	10,381,206	7,871,635	751,563	7.2	78,848	0.8	777,913	7.5	901,247	1,836,989	17.7
Colorado	1,282,489	1,154,983	49,255	3.8	8,959	0.7	17,099	1.3	52,193	130,704	10.2
Connecticut	1,230,479	1,096,812	90,882	7.4	2,383	0.2	13,558	1.1	26,844	61,580	5.0
Delaware	247,497	204,968	37,229	15.0	773	0.3	2,538	1.0	1,989	4,497	1.8
Dist. Of Col.	249,634	88,295	152,356	61.0	612	0.2	4,070	1.6	4,301	10,455	4.2
Florida	5,134,869	4,457,493	553,561	10.8	13,088	0.3	42,895	0.8	67,832	510,849	9.9
Georgia	2,366,615	1,756,916	574,113	24.3	4,812	0.2	20,279	0.9	10,495	29,873	1.3
Hawaii	356,267	138,425	7,787	2.2	1,586	0.4	202,518	56.8	5,951	20,176	5.7
Idaho	360,723	345,484	1,095	0.3	4,082	1.1	2,602	0.7	7,460	13,464	3.7
Illinois	*4,202,240*	*3,447,865*	*550,311*	*13.1*	*7,438*	*0.2*	*80,671*	*1.9*	*115,955*	*229,993*	*5.5*
Indiana	2,065,355	1,889,853	149,055	7.2	4,519	0.2	10,853	0.5	11,075	27,571	1.3
Percent U.S.	2.25	2.46	1.49	—	0.76	—	0.54	—	0.45	0.46	—
Rank	14	12	21	23	32	36	25	36	22	22	31
Iowa	1,064,325	1,036,774	15,741	1.5	2,157	0.2	6,287	0.6	3,366	8,926	0.8
Kansas	944,726	867,644	48,365	5.1	6,974	0.7	8,357	0.9	13,386	25,606	2.7
Kentucky	*1,379,782*	*1,278,806*	*92,639*	*6.7*	*2,108*	*0.2*	*4,634*	*0.3*	*1,595*	*6,220*	*0.5*
Louisiana	1,499,269	1,069,650	406,880	27.1	5,686	0.4	10,404	0.7	6,649	29,990	2.0
Maine	465,312	460,110	1,458	0.3	1,860	0.4	1,503	0.3	381	1,880	0.4
Maryland	1,748,991	1,293,894	401,460	23.0	4,406	0.3	38,062	2.2	11,169	34,404	2.0
Massachusetts	2,247,110	2,061,948	99,402	4.4	4,208	0.2	38,728	1.7	42,824	81,649	3.6
Michigan	*3,419,331*	*2,907,741*	*441,984*	*12.9*	*17,709*	*0.5*	*28,204*	*0.8*	*23,693*	*55,798*	*1.6*
Minnesota	1,647,853	1,579,722	31,201	1.9	14,168	0.9	17,198	1.0	5,564	14,039	0.9
Mississippi	911,374	623,470	281,515	30.9	2,329	0.3	3,203	0.4	857	4,745	0.5
Missouri	1,961,206	1,747,422	188,853	9.6	7,298	0.4	11,584	0.6	6,049	18,444	0.9
Montana	306,163	290,030	760	0.2	13,230	4.3	1,040	0.3	1,103	3,374	1.1
Nebraska	602,363	571,603	19,720	3.3	3,342	0.6	3,264	0.5	4,434	10,517	1.7
Nevada	466,297	407,859	26,485	5.7	6,564	1.4	10,875	2.3	14,514	35,658	7.6
New Hampshire	411,186	404,832	2,322	0.6	764	0.2	2,421	0.6	847	3,255	0.8
New Jersey	2,794,711	2,307,810	333,782	11.9	5,105	0.2	73,840	2.6	74,174	215,526	7.7
New Mexico	542,709	435,810	10,377	1.9	33,489	6.2	3,733	0.7	59,300	178,709	32.9
New York	6,639,322	5,184,827	947,597	14.3	20,375	0.3	201,644	3.0	284,879	665,079	10.0
North Carolina	2,517,026	1,977,594	492,214	19.6	25,528	1.0	13,706	0.5	7,984	21,533	0.9
North Dakota	240,878	231,488	1,077	0.4	6,998	2.9	879	0.4	436	1,138	0.5
Ohio	*4,087,546*	*3,621,244*	*415,670*	*10.2*	*7,688*	*0.2*	*26,824*	*0.7*	*16,120*	*41,119*	*1.0*
Oklahoma	1,206,135	1,027,966	79,203	6.6	77,846	6.5	9,439	0.8	11,681	23,481	1.9
Oregon	1,103,313	1,043,711	15,385	1.4	11,923	1.1	20,008	1.8	12,286	28,204	2.6
Pennsylvania	4,495,966	4,045,430	376,034	8.4	5,353	0.1	37,362	0.8	31,787	65,338	1.5
Rhode Island	377,977	352,749	12,445	3.3	1,339	0.4	4,471	1.2	6,973	13,092	3.5
South Carolina	1,258,044	923,440	323,878	25.7	2,747	0.2	5,599	0.4	2,380	8,586	0.7
South Dakota	259,034	244,847	987	0.4	12,053	4.7	712	0.3	435	1,321	0.5
Tennessee	1,853,725	1,576,161	262,505	14.2	3,771	0.2	8,797	0.5	2,491	9,649	0.5
Texas	6,070,937	4,800,925	684,255	11.3	23,482	0.4	91,141	1.5	471,134	1,158,010	19.1
Utah	537,273	508,404	3,770	0.7	5,841	1.1	8,582	1.6	10,676	22,720	4.2
Vermont	210,650	208,607	557	0.3	591	0.3	718	0.3	177	1,147	0.5
Virginia	2,291,830	1,839,325	391,280	17.1	5,505	0.2	41,199	1.8	14,521	43,756	1.9
Washington	1,872,431	1,708,223	51,645	2.8	24,699	1.3	59,205	3.2	28,659	55,706	3.0
West Virginia	688,557	664,100	20,941	3.0	965	0.1	2,147	0.3	404	2,785	0.4
Wisconsin	1,822,118	1,712,217	75,441	4.1	11,515	0.6	12,284	0.7	10,661	24,165	1.3
Wyoming	168,839	160,879	1,208	0.7	2,630	1.6	772	0.5	3,350	7,662	4.5

Housing Units Per 1,000 Persons
1990

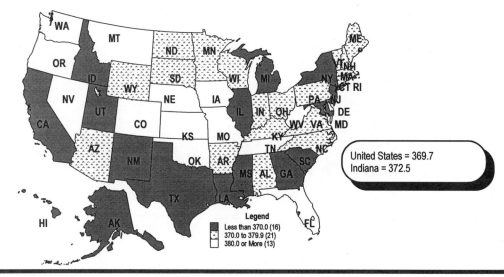

United States = 369.7
Indiana = 372.5

Legend
- Less than 370.0 (16)
- 370.0 to 379.9 (21)
- 380.0 or More (13)

Source: U.S. Bureau of the Census
EDIN table(s): HC90

Income

1.22 Median Money Income of Households 1989 to 1995 *(Constant 92 Dollars)*

	1989	Standard Error	1990	Standard Error	1991	Standard Error	1992	Standard Error	1993	Standard Error	1994	Standard Error	1995	Standard Error
United States	33,685	185	33,105	169	31,962	153	30,636	145	31,241	146	32,264	146	34,076	197
Alabama	24,803	1,247	25,823	1,146	25,830	1,133	27,261	1,118	26,453	1,147	27,967	1,603	25,991	1,266
Alaska	41,959	1,606	43,447	1,799	43,087	1,933	44,156	1,221	45,278	1,721	46,653	1,536	47,954	2,008
Arizona	33,272	1,410	32,310	1,261	32,610	952	31,011	1,149	32,178	1,181	32,180	795	30,863	1,360
Arkansas	24,976	1,066	25,192	1,085	24,863	831	25,227	1,477	24,299	891	26,290	971	25,814	999
California	38,466	720	36,805	625	35,715	727	36,868	664	35,936	686	36,332	637	37,009	723
Colorado	31,238	1,629	33,978	1,002	33,419	1,321	34,313	1,554	36,373	1,605	38,905	1,487	40,706	1,552
Connecticut	49,318	1,855	42,974	2,318	44,723	2,062	43,141	2,083	41,676	1,751	42,262	1,640	40,243	2,269
Delaware	37,370	1,320	34,056	1,231	34,571	1,179	37,687	1,471	38,036	895	36,890	1,225	34,928	1,848
Dist. Of Col.	31,175	1,183	30,284	1,727	31,706	2,019	31,950	1,187	28,797	1,820	30,969	1,138	30,748	1,182
Florida	30,397	554	29,503	502	28,913	504	28,889	558	30,111	745	30,124	650	29,745	612
Georgia	32,095	1,190	30,471	1,311	28,870	1,154	30,419	1,297	33,394	1,342	32,359	1,273	34,099	897
Hawaii	40,827	1,548	43,030	1,563	39,516	1,729	44,484	1,516	44,994	1,855	43,453	2,492	42,851	1,292
Idaho	28,730	1,111	27,977	1,078	27,708	1,092	29,264	923	32,705	1,384	32,430	1,314	32,676	1,116
Illinois	*36,475*	*726*	*35,978*	*800*	*33,827*	*758*	*33,328*	*794*	*34,653*	*854*	*36,075*	*822*	*38,071*	*875*
Indiana	**30,180**	**1,191**	**29,771**	**1,215**	**28,740**	**978**	**30,136**	**1,389**	**31,086**	**1,435**	**28,647**	**1,061**	**33,385**	**1,444**
Rank	*36*	*27*	*36*	*22*	*37*	*35*	*33*	*16*	*30*	*11*	*42*	*37*	*28*	*10*
Iowa	30,607	923	30,169	1,090	30,293	1,074	30,361	1,027	30,230	1,330	34,016	1,316	35,519	942
Kansas	31,303	1,058	33,076	1,303	31,080	991	32,055	1,201	31,398	1,211	29,125	1,094	30,341	921
Kentucky	*27,132*	*1,405*	*27,396*	*1,341*	*25,212*	*1,110*	*24,807*	*1,330*	*25,709*	*1,151*	*27,349*	*1,057*	*29,810*	*1,149*
Louisiana	26,640	2,164	24,771	1,747	26,841	1,226	26,871	1,206	27,751	1,228	26,404	1,544	27,949	1,090
Maine	32,887	1,619	30,364	1,738	29,566	1,329	31,285	1,084	28,938	1,207	31,175	1,581	33,858	1,088
Maryland	41,970	1,383	42,960	1,765	39,204	1,503	39,298	1,718	42,123	1,352	40,309	1,440	41,041	1,627
Massachusetts	42,052	820	40,074	915	37,890	838	38,406	780	39,090	1,003	41,648	1,090	38,574	1,475
Michigan	*35,863*	*921*	*33,098*	*733*	*34,074*	*731*	*34,084*	*804*	*34,448*	*719*	*36,284*	*704*	*36,426*	*994*
Minnesota	35,175	1,489	34,787	1,137	31,275	1,216	32,725	1,370	35,523	1,342	34,597	1,399	37,933	1,848
Mississippi	23,210	1,104	22,308	887	20,662	1,117	21,728	1,134	23,404	1,296	26,120	773	26,538	1,028
Missouri	30,878	869	30,218	1,541	29,628	1,501	28,902	1,533	30,250	1,545	31,046	1,483	34,825	1,373
Montana	27,609	1,528	25,843	1,087	26,340	944	26,019	769	27,917	1,017	28,414	1,281	27,757	1,105
Nebraska	30,670	1,772	30,384	1,247	31,350	1,068	31,740	1,131	32,703	879	32,695	1,148	32,929	1,155
Nevada	34,191	1,105	35,404	1,303	34,944	1,659	33,705	841	37,772	1,137	36,888	1,577	36,084	1,314
New Hampshire	43,737	1,598	45,113	1,452	38,228	1,421	41,657	2,030	40,040	1,709	36,244	1,889	39,171	1,556
New Jersey	45,587	1,105	42,824	955	42,490	1,096	41,196	888	42,714	1,043	43,478	1,094	43,924	1,400
New Mexico	26,339	1,199	27,683	1,159	28,157	1,268	27,316	1,423	28,221	900	27,667	1,421	25,991	1,100
New York	36,703	528	34,927	565	33,732	571	32,799	559	33,430	586	32,803	491	33,028	716
North Carolina	30,772	602	29,109	615	28,489	541	29,335	651	30,396	689	30,967	689	31,979	888
North Dakota	29,400	1,052	27,931	1,109	27,470	989	28,477	952	29,655	838	29,079	1,147	29,089	1,217
Ohio	*33,819*	*763*	*33,182*	*796*	*31,605*	*805*	*33,172*	*620*	*32,995*	*694*	*32,758*	*601*	*34,941*	*988*
Oklahoma	27,580	1,440	26,959	1,154	27,014	1,145	26,708	1,136	27,696	1,574	27,756	1,247	26,311	880
Oregon	33,245	1,672	32,373	1,068	32,030	1,153	33,725	2,154	34,950	1,207	32,347	1,160	36,374	970
Pennsylvania	33,433	797	32,067	761	32,218	651	31,565	705	32,690	731	32,975	673	34,524	683
Rhode Island	35,104	1,578	35,343	1,299	32,715	1,157	32,146	1,514	35,341	1,632	32,833	1,358	35,359	1,373
South Carolina	27,732	1,234	31,769	1,529	29,137	1,206	29,131	1,515	27,477	1,012	30,692	1,171	29,071	1,400
South Dakota	28,094	1,164	27,165	949	26,141	828	27,738	707	29,253	1,106	30,576	1,219	29,578	1,610
Tennessee	26,349	1,521	24,977	961	25,943	971	25,687	964	26,474	876	29,451	1,057	29,015	1,268
Texas	30,166	651	31,208	792	29,423	664	29,527	670	30,298	647	31,627	674	32,039	634
Utah	35,795	1,182	33,325	1,125	29,723	1,442	36,180	1,209	37,742	1,310	36,728	1,071	36,480	919
Vermont	36,469	1,324	34,381	1,472	30,932	1,296	34,599	1,408	32,763	1,008	36,817	1,960	33,824	1,242
Virginia	39,758	1,404	38,776	1,159	38,339	1,417	40,349	1,436	38,425	1,463	38,714	1,574	36,222	1,391
Washington	37,245	1,715	35,503	1,370	36,040	1,257	35,809	1,317	37,604	1,172	34,483	1,224	35,568	1,252
West Virginia	25,261	982	24,474	1,263	24,558	974	21,412	942	23,647	1,035	24,232	1,251	24,880	870
Wisconsin	33,938	1,445	33,954	992	33,030	1,080	35,184	1,159	33,503	1,413	36,391	1,308	40,955	1,318
Wyoming	34,402	1,502	32,571	1,096	30,820	1,466	31,910	1,500	31,052	1,231	34,079	1,900	31,529	1,136

Median Money Income of Households
1989 to 1995 ($)

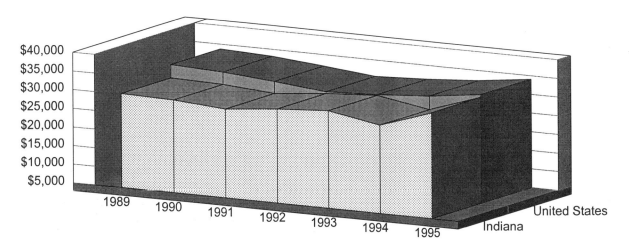

Source: U.S. Bureau of the Census
EDIN table(s): MEDI

1.23 Annual Estimates of Personal Income 1991 and 1996

	1991 Total Personal Income ($MIL)	1991 Per Capita ($)	1996 Total Personal Income ($MIL)	1996 Per Capita ($)	Percent U.S.	Percent Change Total Personal Income	Percent Change Per Capita ($)
United States	4,963,545	19,689	6,479,914	24,426	100.0	30.6	24.1
Alabama	65,166	15,946	86,021	20,131	82.4	32.0	26.2
Alaska	12,250	21,517	14,810	24,398	99.9	20.9	13.4
Arizona	64,094	17,104	94,596	21,363	87.5	47.6	24.9
Arkansas	35,093	14,799	47,584	18,959	77.6	35.6	28.1
California	655,102	21,552	807,975	25,346	103.8	23.3	17.6
Colorado	67,918	20,159	98,258	25,704	105.2	44.7	27.5
Connecticut	88,181	26,810	110,916	33,875	138.7	25.8	26.4
Delaware	15,214	22,368	20,095	27,724	113.5	32.1	23.9
Dist. Of Col.	16,115	27,091	18,539	34,129	139.7	15.0	26.0
Florida	260,004	19,563	348,849	24,226	99.2	34.2	23.8
Georgia	119,065	17,973	168,959	22,977	94.1	41.9	27.8
Hawaii	25,168	22,279	30,072	25,404	104.0	19.5	14.0
Idaho	16,312	15,698	23,591	19,837	81.2	44.6	26.4
Illinois	*242,666*	*21,072*	*318,061*	*26,848*	*109.9*	*31.1*	*27.4*
Indiana	98,978	17,666	132,001	22,601	92.5	33.4	27.9
Percent U.S.	*1.99*	*—*	*2.04*	*—*	*—*	*—*	*—*
Rank	*16*	*32*	*16*	*29*	*29*	*20*	*12*
Iowa	48,404	17,340	63,613	22,306	91.3	31.4	28.6
Kansas	46,253	18,564	59,585	23,165	94.8	28.8	24.8
Kentucky	*58,567*	*15,765*	*76,885*	*19,797*	*81.1*	*31.3*	*25.6*
Louisiana	66,284	15,630	85,548	19,664	80.5	29.1	25.8
Maine	21,440	17,352	26,124	21,011	86.0	21.9	21.1
Maryland	111,424	22,930	140,068	27,618	113.1	25.7	20.4
Massachusetts	141,926	23,657	181,505	29,792	122.0	27.9	25.9
Michigan	*179,174*	*19,130*	*239,330*	*24,945*	*102.1*	*33.6*	*30.4*
Minnesota	88,126	19,898	119,530	25,663	105.1	35.6	29.0
Mississippi	34,738	13,402	47,735	17,575	72.0	37.4	31.1
Missouri	94,748	18,373	123,366	23,022	94.3	30.2	25.3
Montana	12,922	15,988	16,896	19,214	78.7	30.8	20.2
Nebraska	28,729	18,051	37,862	22,917	93.8	31.8	27.0
Nevada	26,553	20,654	41,699	26,011	106.5	57.0	25.9
New Hampshire	23,765	21,455	30,939	26,615	109.0	30.2	24.1
New Jersey	197,837	25,471	250,295	31,334	128.3	26.5	23.0
New Mexico	23,375	15,096	32,217	18,803	77.0	37.8	24.6
New York	426,850	23,665	530,655	29,181	119.5	24.3	23.3
North Carolina	115,821	17,149	162,602	22,205	90.9	40.4	29.5
North Dakota	9,830	15,503	13,159	20,448	83.7	33.9	31.9
Ohio	*203,861*	*18,653*	*262,077*	*23,457*	*96.0*	*28.6*	*25.8*
Oklahoma	51,102	16,132	64,514	19,544	80.0	26.3	21.2
Oregon	52,389	17,936	73,922	23,074	94.5	41.1	28.7
Pennsylvania	239,478	20,047	299,031	24,803	101.5	24.9	23.7
Rhode Island	20,119	20,028	24,331	24,572	100.6	20.9	22.7
South Carolina	56,047	15,767	73,890	19,977	81.8	31.8	26.7
South Dakota	11,356	16,174	15,303	20,895	85.5	34.8	29.2
Tennessee	84,136	17,005	116,760	21,949	89.9	38.8	29.1
Texas	312,747	18,008	426,212	22,282	91.2	36.3	23.7
Utah	26,364	14,910	39,199	19,595	80.2	48.7	31.4
Vermont	10,195	17,949	13,227	22,470	92.0	29.7	25.2
Virginia	129,238	20,560	168,300	25,212	103.2	30.2	22.6
Washington	102,644	20,456	139,356	25,187	103.1	35.8	23.1
West Virginia	26,711	14,848	33,155	18,160	74.4	24.1	22.3
Wisconsin	90,625	18,315	120,325	23,320	95.5	32.8	27.3
Wyoming	8,438	18,426	10,371	21,544	88.2	22.9	16.9

Per Capita Personal Income
1996

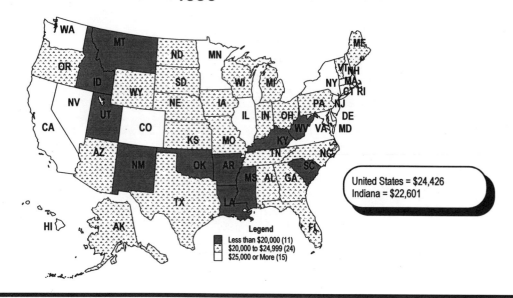

United States = $24,426
Indiana = $22,601

Legend
- Less than $20,000 (11)
- $20,000 to $24,999 (24)
- $25,000 or More (15)

Source: U.S. Bureau of Economic Analysis
EDIN table(s): PITX

1.24 Personal Income 1996 *($MIL)*

	Total Earnings by Place of Work	Net Earnings by Place of Work	Plus Residence Adjustment	Net Earnings by Place of Residence	Plus Dividends, Interest, and Rent	Plus Transfer Payments	Personal Income by Place of Residence
United States	4,548,138	4,242,296	-3,395	4,238,901	1,173,114	1,067,899	6,479,914
Alabama	59,680	55,380	687	56,067	12,622	17,332	86,021
Alaska	11,586	10,804	-758	10,047	2,059	2,705	14,810
Arizona	65,124	60,597	248	60,845	17,405	16,345	94,595
Arkansas	33,278	31,041	-322	30,719	6,972	9,893	47,584
California	570,329	531,562	-728	530,834	151,522	125,620	807,975
Colorado	71,866	67,247	64	67,312	18,227	12,719	98,257
Connecticut	74,877	70,112	3,927	74,039	22,024	14,853	110,916
Delaware	15,446	14,495	-1,219	13,277	3,948	2,871	20,095
Dist. Of Col.	34,298	32,100	-20,637	11,464	3,247	3,829	18,539
Florida	207,974	193,821	512	194,333	89,138	65,378	348,849
Georgia	126,017	117,859	-194	117,666	26,510	24,782	168,958
Hawaii	21,243	19,876	0	19,877	5,321	4,874	30,071
Idaho	16,714	15,560	220	15,781	4,068	3,742	23,591
Illinois	*227,762*	*212,630*	*-573*	*212,057*	*60,854*	*45,150*	*318,060*
Indiana	**94,929**	**88,596**	**2,334**	**90,930**	**21,410**	**19,661**	**132,000**
Percent U.S.	*2.09*	*2.09*	*—*	*2.15*	*1.83*	*1.84*	*2.04*
Rank	*15*	*15*	*6*	*16*	*19*	*18*	*16*
Iowa	44,805	41,669	311	41,980	11,619	10,015	63,613
Kansas	40,976	38,081	1,045	39,126	11,410	9,049	59,584
Kentucky	*53,736*	*49,952*	*-327*	*49,625*	*11,992*	*15,268*	*76,885*
Louisiana	58,225	54,469	-146	54,323	12,838	18,388	85,548
Maine	17,012	15,808	225	16,034	4,778	5,311	26,123
Maryland	85,910	80,051	13,579	93,630	25,365	21,073	140,067
Massachusetts	130,454	122,162	-3,071	119,091	34,468	27,945	181,504
Michigan	*170,930*	*159,720*	*741*	*160,462*	*41,939*	*36,929*	*239,329*
Minnesota	88,849	82,560	-726	81,834	21,054	16,642	119,529
Mississippi	32,085	29,706	1,055	30,761	6,139	10,835	47,734
Missouri	87,683	81,738	-3,184	78,554	23,969	20,843	123,365
Montana	10,832	9,967	-10	9,957	3,570	3,369	16,896
Nebraska	27,911	25,948	-513	25,435	6,901	5,525	37,861
Nevada	30,802	28,984	-614	28,370	7,628	5,702	41,699
New Hampshire	19,781	18,411	2,471	20,882	6,009	4,047	30,939
New Jersey	162,872	151,623	14,200	165,824	50,688	33,784	250,295
New Mexico	22,057	20,445	83	20,528	5,225	6,465	32,216
New York	375,519	351,032	-18,980	332,053	97,198	101,404	530,654
North Carolina	119,692	111,319	-823	110,496	25,123	26,983	162,602
North Dakota	9,352	8,665	-276	8,390	2,414	2,356	13,159
Ohio	*185,451*	*172,864*	*-1,547*	*171,317*	*44,244*	*46,515*	*262,076*
Oklahoma	43,300	40,242	735	40,978	10,475	13,061	64,513
Oregon	52,780	49,031	-1,368	47,663	14,208	12,050	73,922
Pennsylvania	199,478	185,656	1,446	187,102	55,148	56,781	299,030
Rhode Island	15,243	14,044	969	15,013	4,433	4,885	24,331
South Carolina	51,787	48,059	718	48,777	11,161	13,951	73,889
South Dakota	10,830	10,071	-157	9,914	2,783	2,606	15,303
Tennessee	85,929	80,363	-1,063	79,300	16,523	20,938	116,760
Texas	319,149	299,091	-848	298,244	64,196	63,772	426,212
Utah	30,300	28,311	0	28,312	5,462	5,426	39,199
Vermont	8,917	8,310	76	8,386	2,770	2,071	13,227
Virginia	115,007	107,332	5,645	112,978	31,285	24,037	168,299
Washington	97,384	90,466	1,426	91,892	25,559	21,905	139,356
West Virginia	20,947	19,376	170	19,546	5,116	8,493	33,155
Wisconsin	84,118	78,640	1,823	80,464	21,788	18,073	120,324
Wyoming	6,911	6,430	-17	6,413	2,309	1,650	10,371

Transfer Payments as a Percent of Personal Income by Place of Residence — 1996

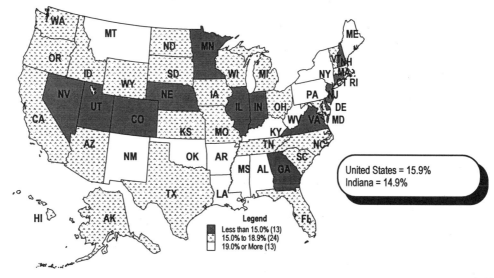

United States = 15.9%
Indiana = 14.9%

Legend
- Less than 15.0% (13)
- 15.0% to 18.9% (24)
- 19.0% or More (13)

Source: Bureau of Economic Analysis
EDIN table(s): PIRE

1.25 Selected Calculations of Personal Income 1986 and 1996

	\<--Percent of Personal Income Received From-->						Per Capita Personal Income % Chg. 1986-96
	Earnings		Dividends, Interest and Rent		Transfer Payments		
	1986	1996	1986	1996	1986	1996	
United States	66.9	65.4	18.9	18.1	14.2	16.5	60.9
Alabama	68.1	65.2	14.8	14.7	17.2	20.1	70.9
Alaska	75.6	67.8	11.6	13.9	12.7	18.3	31.9
Arizona	65.2	64.3	20.7	18.4	14.2	17.3	51.8
Arkansas	63.4	64.6	17.8	14.7	18.8	20.8	65.6
California	68.1	65.7	18.8	18.8	13.1	15.5	46.2
Colorado	69.5	68.5	18.9	18.6	11.6	12.9	64.3
Connecticut	69.1	66.8	20.4	19.9	10.5	13.4	69.7
Delaware	69.5	66.1	18.4	19.6	12.1	14.3	69.1
Dist. Of Col.	63.4	61.8	16.8	17.5	19.9	20.7	84.8
Florida	57.4	55.7	26.8	25.6	15.7	18.7	58.8
Georgia	71.6	69.6	15.7	15.7	12.7	14.7	66.2
Hawaii	69.5	66.1	17.0	17.7	13.5	16.2	65.0
Idaho	65.6	66.9	19.0	17.2	15.3	15.9	69.4
Illinois	*67.3*	*66.7*	*19.6*	*19.1*	*13.2*	*14.2*	*65.8*
Indiana	**68.3**	**68.9**	**18.0**	**16.2**	**13.7**	**14.9**	**66.6**
Rank	*16*	*4*	*33*	*36*	*30*	*39*	*14*
Iowa	62.8	66.0	22.2	18.3	14.9	15.7	62.3
Kansas	65.9	65.7	20.5	19.1	13.6	15.2	57.0
Kentucky	*65.7*	*64.5*	*17.2*	*15.6*	*17.0*	*19.9*	*68.4*
Louisiana	65.4	63.5	17.5	15.0	17.1	21.5	66.0
Maine	64.5	61.4	18.5	18.3	17.0	20.3	57.3
Maryland	69.6	66.8	17.7	18.1	12.7	15.0	57.4
Massachusetts	68.0	65.6	18.8	19.0	13.2	15.4	63.7
Michigan	*68.0*	*67.0*	*17.5*	*17.5*	*14.5*	*15.4*	*61.9*
Minnesota	68.1	68.5	18.6	17.6	13.3	13.9	64.6
Mississippi	65.2	64.4	15.1	12.9	19.7	22.7	77.0
Missouri	64.8	63.7	20.8	19.4	14.4	16.9	59.2
Montana	58.9	58.9	23.3	21.1	17.7	19.9	58.0
Nebraska	66.0	67.2	20.5	18.2	13.5	14.6	64.5
Nevada	68.2	68.0	18.5	18.3	13.3	13.7	65.5
New Hampshire	70.1	67.5	19.6	19.4	10.3	13.1	55.3
New Jersey	68.1	66.3	20.5	20.3	11.4	13.5	64.8
New Mexico	65.8	63.7	18.5	16.2	15.7	20.1	58.4
New York	65.3	62.6	19.2	18.3	15.4	19.1	63.8
North Carolina	70.7	68.0	15.8	15.5	13.5	16.6	71.3
North Dakota	61.7	63.8	22.1	18.3	16.2	17.9	61.7
Ohio	*66.4*	*65.4*	*17.7*	*16.9*	*15.9*	*17.7*	*61.4*
Oklahoma	66.1	63.5	18.3	16.2	15.6	20.2	50.8
Oregon	63.8	64.5	20.4	19.2	15.8	16.3	68.1
Pennsylvania	63.4	62.6	19.3	18.4	17.3	19.0	66.1
Rhode Island	64.4	61.7	19.1	18.2	16.5	20.1	59.4
South Carolina	69.4	66.0	15.2	15.1	15.3	18.9	69.0
South Dakota	62.0	64.8	22.0	18.2	16.0	17.0	73.4
Tennessee	69.3	67.9	15.4	14.2	15.3	17.9	73.3
Texas	70.5	70.0	17.8	15.1	11.8	15.0	58.9
Utah	71.3	72.2	15.5	13.9	13.2	13.8	71.5
Vermont	66.1	63.4	20.0	20.9	14.0	15.7	63.1
Virginia	69.4	67.1	18.1	18.6	12.5	14.3	58.4
Washington	65.9	65.9	18.9	18.3	15.2	15.7	64.4
West Virginia	60.8	59.0	16.7	15.4	22.5	25.6	61.9
Wisconsin	65.8	66.9	19.2	18.1	15.1	15.0	62.4
Wyoming	68.4	61.8	19.1	22.3	12.6	15.9	59.2

Personal Income by Source
Percentages 1996

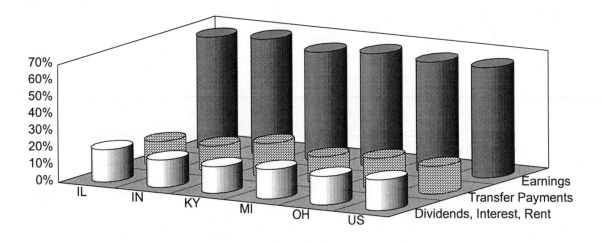

Source: Bureau of Economic Analysis
EDIN table(s): PIRE

1.26 Transfer Payments 1991 and 1996 *($000)*

	Indiana 1991	Indiana 1996	Percent Change 1991-96	Percent Of U.S.	United States 1991	United States 1996	Percent Change 1991-96	Percent Distribution Indiana	Percent Distribution U.S.
Total Payments	14,632	19,661	34.4	1.8	769,806	1,067,899	38.7		
Govt. Payments to Individuals	13,863	18,628	34.4	1.8	734,890	1,021,431	39.0	94.8	95.7
Retirement & Disability Insurance Benefit	7,919	9,949	25.6	2.0	387,613	506,895	30.8	50.6	47.5
Old Age, Survivors, & Disability Ins.	6,487	8,085	24.6	2.4	264,099	342,050	29.5	41.1	32.0
Railroad, Retirement & Disability	205	228	11.2	2.8	7,513	8,086	7.6	1.2	0.8
Federal Civilian Employee Retirement	434	523	20.5	1.3	33,746	40,462	19.9	2.7	3.8
Military Retirement	218	274	25.7	0.9	23,785	29,174	22.7	1.4	2.7
State & Local Govt. Employee Retirement	513	777	51.5	1.1	44,702	72,903	63.1	4.0	6.8
Worker's Comp. (Fed. & State)	23	24	4.3	0.2	9,330	10,459	12.1	0.1	1.0
Other	39	38	-2.6	1.0	4,438	3,761	-15.3	0.2	0.4
Medical Payments	4,360	6,585	51.0	1.8	223,524	361,259	61.6	33.5	33.8
Medicare Payments	2,372	3,877	63.4	2.0	118,190	195,583	65.5	19.7	18.3
Public Assistance Medical Care	1,953	2,685	37.5	1.6	102,116	163,612	60.2	13.7	15.3
CHAMPUS	34	22	-35.3	1.1	3,218	2,064	-35.9	0.1	0.2
Income Maintenance Benefits	910	1,271	39.7	1.3	69,515	98,060	41.1	6.5	9.2
Supplemental Security Income (SSI)	207	375	81.2	1.3	18,611	29,148	56.6	1.9	2.7
Aid to Families with Dependent Children (AFDC)	213	139	-34.7	0.6	21,974	21,691	-1.3	0.7	2.0
Food Stamps	315	321	1.9	1.5	18,248	21,934	20.2	1.6	2.1
Other	175	436	149.1	1.7	10,682	25,287	136.7	2.2	2.4
Unemployment Insurance Compensation	214	274	28.0	1.2	27,095	22,366	-17.5	1.4	2.1
State	206	264	28.2	1.2	26,226	21,492	-18.1	1.3	2.0
Federal Civilian Employment (UCFE)	2	2	0.0	0.6	429	337	-21.4	0.0	0.0
Railroad Employment	4	3	-25.0	3.8	88	80	-9.1	0.0	0.0
Veterans (UCV)	2	2	0.0	0.8	186	261	40.3	0.0	0.0
Other	1	2	100.0	1.0	166	196	18.1	0.0	0.0
Veterans Benefits	293	332	13.3	1.6	18,131	21,335	17.7	2.0	2.0
Compensation	260	280	7.7	1.6	15,696	17,977	14.5	1.8	1.7
Education Assistance to Veterans, Dependents & Survivors	6	22	266.7	1.7	521	1,315	152.4	0.0	0.1
Life Insurance	27	30	11.1	1.5	1,873	1,997	6.6	0.2	0.2
Other	1	1	0.0	2.2	41	46	12.2	0.0	0.0
Federal Education & Training Assistance (Excluding Veterans)	159	199	25.2	2.1	7,199	9,408	30.7	1.0	0.9
Other	8	18	125.0	0.9	1,813	2,108	16.3	0.1	0.2
Payments to Nonprofit Institutions	432	627	45.1	2.2	18,831	28,117	49.3	3.0	2.6
Federal Government	104	137	31.7	2.2	4,675	6,175	32.1	0.7	0.6
State and Local Government	221	321	45.2	2.2	9,393	14,288	52.1	1.6	1.3
Business	106	169	59.4	2.2	4,763	7,654	60.7	0.9	0.7
Business Payments to Individuals	337	406	20.5	2.2	16,085	18,351	14.1	2.1	25.2

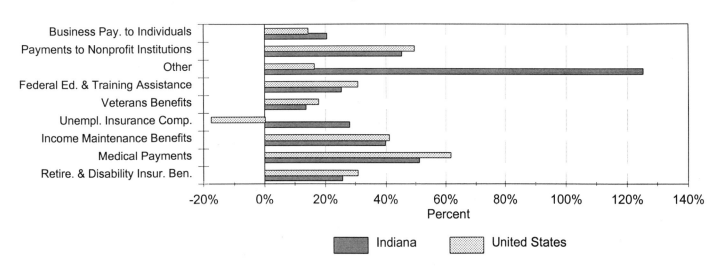

Transfer Payments
Percent Change 1991 to 1996

Legend: ▨ Indiana   ▨ United States

1.27 Projections of Population (000) and Per Capita Income (1987 Dollars) 1998 to 2045

	Population						Per Capita Income					
	1998	2000	2005	2010	2025	2045	1998	2000	2005	2010	2025	2045
United States	270,721	276,241	288,286	300,431	338,338	381,779	17,356	17,718	18,752	19,696	22,003	26,157
Alabama	4,332	4,383	4,516	4,668	5,211	5,899	14,463	14,745	15,708	16,594	18,849	22,658
Alaska	640	657	694	727	815	919	18,800	19,116	20,047	20,991	23,619	27,896
Arizona	4,365	4,526	4,881	5,217	6,192	7,219	15,263	15,562	16,542	17,445	19,683	23,564
Arkansas	2,532	2,567	2,655	2,749	3,078	3,461	13,464	13,720	14,537	15,295	17,240	20,622
California	33,398	34,470	36,657	38,710	44,372	50,731	18,043	18,517	19,575	20,551	22,930	27,167
Colorado	3,879	3,996	4,273	4,538	5,287	6,140	17,913	18,338	19,408	20,386	22,657	26,840
Connecticut	3,378	3,434	3,564	3,702	4,160	4,694	23,323	23,833	25,165	26,330	28,818	33,902
Delaware	739	757	793	830	945	1,065	18,152	18,530	19,564	20,470	22,514	26,682
Dist. Of Col.	562	559	554	555	577	617	24,991	25,531	26,881	28,016	31,080	36,480
Florida	15,047	15,642	16,900	18,127	21,860	25,498	17,331	17,690	18,748	19,708	22,022	26,278
Georgia	7,412	7,602	8,033	8,464	9,711	11,213	16,218	16,597	17,671	18,656	21,100	25,279
Hawaii	1,245	1,281	1,354	1,427	1,648	1,874	19,300	19,798	20,813	21,723	23,864	28,037
Idaho	1,186	1,216	1,277	1,335	1,514	1,725	14,639	14,993	15,933	16,809	18,841	22,514
Illinois	*12,087*	*12,260*	*12,677*	*13,098*	*14,475*	*16,140*	*18,799*	*19,143*	*20,221*	*21,200*	*23,522*	*27,905*
Indiana	**5,890**	**5,962**	**6,133**	**6,325**	**6,993**	**7,844**	**16,215**	**16,509**	**17,543**	**18,473**	**20,713**	**24,748**
Percent U.S.	*2.18*	*2.16*	*2.13*	*2.11*	*2.07*	*2.05*	*93.43*	*93.18*	*93.55*	*93.79*	*94.14*	*94.61*
Rank	*14*	*14*	*15*	*15*	*15*	*15*	*30*	*30*	*30*	*30*	*30*	*30*
Iowa	2,869	2,893	2,949	3,014	3,269	3,586	15,835	16,013	17,036	17,952	20,095	24,003
Kansas	2,639	2,684	2,772	2,863	3,165	3,498	16,749	17,106	18,180	19,146	21,414	25,506
Kentucky	*3,917*	*3,967*	*4,086*	*4,219*	*4,666*	*5,217*	*14,244*	*14,563*	*15,445*	*16,260*	*18,415*	*22,035*
Louisiana	4,421	4,478	4,611	4,749	5,221	5,751	13,969	14,247	15,133	15,971	18,208	21,855
Maine	1,280	1,302	1,352	1,405	1,577	1,775	15,713	16,083	17,030	17,911	20,217	24,149
Maryland	5,228	5,347	5,598	5,847	6,589	7,451	19,858	20,258	21,329	22,308	24,659	29,114
Massachusetts	6,219	6,301	6,523	6,760	7,550	8,474	20,320	20,758	21,885	22,893	25,267	29,811
Michigan	*9,656*	*9,741*	*9,927*	*10,150*	*11,026*	*12,236*	*17,309*	*17,511*	*18,525*	*19,456*	*21,761*	*25,919*
Minnesota	4,733	4,816	4,998	5,177	5,732	6,395	17,764	18,015	19,069	20,012	22,191	26,334
Mississippi	2,721	2,750	2,819	2,897	3,180	3,524	12,554	12,745	13,576	14,361	16,497	19,905
Missouri	5,444	5,531	5,728	5,933	6,602	7,386	16,437	16,716	17,698	18,600	20,830	24,845
Montana	898	920	968	1,014	1,143	1,277	14,370	14,732	15,604	16,416	18,549	22,225
Nebraska	1,671	1,696	1,747	1,799	1,971	2,171	16,576	17,026	18,127	19,111	21,373	25,521
Nevada	1,595	1,664	1,839	2,005	2,462	2,942	18,924	19,291	20,309	21,248	23,584	27,918
New Hampshire	1,191	1,218	1,276	1,335	1,511	1,716	18,552	18,951	20,024	20,988	23,238	27,520
New Jersey	8,182	8,334	8,638	8,950	9,960	11,117	22,219	22,674	23,881	24,930	27,252	31,938
New Mexico	1,742	1,788	1,895	1,998	2,305	2,637	13,659	13,979	14,864	15,696	17,826	21,339
New York	18,358	18,472	18,654	18,895	19,970	21,508	20,542	20,984	22,176	23,268	26,008	30,850
North Carolina	7,422	7,610	8,006	8,414	9,664	11,070	15,733	16,113	17,094	17,993	20,263	24,257
North Dakota	646	651	661	674	725	784	14,716	15,007	16,010	16,905	19,131	22,943
Ohio	*11,353*	*11,432*	*11,677*	*11,961*	*13,050*	*14,431*	*16,625*	*16,844*	*17,870*	*18,808*	*21,085*	*25,160*
Oklahoma	3,355	3,406	3,517	3,634	4,036	4,484	14,225	14,549	15,409	16,205	18,281	21,805
Oregon	3,234	3,314	3,493	3,665	4,191	4,806	16,355	16,681	17,674	18,583	20,819	24,845
Pennsylvania	12,277	12,413	12,682	13,010	14,319	15,820	17,693	18,041	19,078	20,019	22,313	26,520
Rhode Island	1,021	1,037	1,070	1,106	1,240	1,393	17,692	18,082	19,120	20,077	22,365	26,562
South Carolina	3,828	3,919	4,116	4,314	4,912	5,568	14,218	14,577	15,526	16,399	18,587	22,277
South Dakota	749	763	794	824	922	1,033	15,370	15,587	16,554	17,450	19,595	23,421
Tennessee	5,397	5,521	5,771	6,026	6,784	7,686	15,560	15,906	16,910	17,823	20,104	24,029
Texas	19,263	19,724	20,734	21,703	24,514	27,635	16,019	16,422	17,428	18,362	20,688	24,712
Utah	2,063	2,147	2,336	2,509	2,984	3,518	13,665	13,943	14,832	15,666	17,653	21,067
Vermont	605	619	647	676	759	858	16,070	16,489	17,474	18,354	20,539	24,472
Virginia	6,810	6,953	7,284	7,630	8,708	9,939	17,917	18,260	19,287	20,221	22,513	26,708
Washington	5,663	5,833	6,237	6,625	7,719	8,898	17,970	18,394	19,406	20,335	22,672	26,868
West Virginia	1,843	1,858	1,884	1,925	2,108	2,325	13,512	13,756	14,588	15,386	17,747	21,427
Wisconsin	5,242	5,327	5,518	5,716	6,371	7,166	16,746	17,040	18,089	19,039	21,310	25,407
Wyoming	492	501	520	538	598	664	16,452	16,935	17,912	18,868	21,213	25,275

Per Capita Income Index 1998 to 2045

Population Projections Index 1998 to 2045

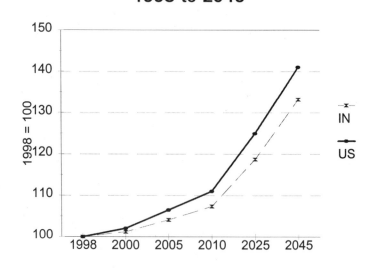

Footnote: BEA population projections were developed as a component of the BEA personal income, earnings, and employment projections. Therefore, these population projections should be used only within this context.
Source: OBERS Regional Projections, U.S. Bureau of Economic Analysis
EDIN table(s): PPOP, PPIR

Labor Force

1.28 Annual Average Employment and Unemployment 1990 and 1995 *(000)*

	1990 Labor Force	1990 Employed	1990 Unemployed Number	1990 Unemployed Rate	1995 Labor Force	1995 Employed	1995 Unemployed Number	1995 Unemployed Rate	Percent Change 1990 to 1995 Labor Force	Percent Change 1990 to 1995 Employed	Percent Change 1990 to 1995 Unemployed
United States	125,840	118,793	7,047	5.6	132,304	124,900	7,404	5.6	5.1	5.1	5.1
Alabama	1,889	1,759	130	6.9	2,060	1,931	129	6.3	9.1	9.7	-0.2
Alaska	270	251	19	7.0	304	282	22	7.3	12.4	12.0	16.8
Arizona	1,800	1,701	99	5.5	2,207	2,095	112	5.1	22.6	23.1	13.6
Arkansas	1,126	1,048	78	7.0	1,222	1,163	59	4.9	8.5	11.0	-24.1
California	15,193	14,319	874	5.8	15,427	14,217	1,211	7.8	1.5	-0.7	38.5
Colorado	1,764	1,675	89	5.0	2,091	2,004	88	4.2	18.5	19.6	-1.6
Connecticut	1,833	1,739	95	5.2	1,713	1,618	94	5.5	-6.6	-6.9	-0.1
Delaware	359	340	19	5.2	383	366	17	4.3	6.6	7.6	-11.2
Dist. Of Col.	329	307	22	6.6	286	260	25	8.9	-13.3	-15.4	16.5
Florida	6,468	6,078	390	6.0	6,849	6,473	376	5.5	5.9	6.5	-3.6
Georgia	3,300	3,118	182	5.5	3,627	3,450	177	4.9	9.9	10.6	-2.9
Hawaii	550	534	16	2.9	577	543	34	5.9	5.0	1.8	111.3
Idaho	493	464	29	5.9	601	569	32	5.4	22.0	22.7	11.3
Illinois	*5,916*	*5,547*	*369*	*6.2*	*6,055*	*5,743*	*312*	*5.2*	*2.3*	*3.5*	*-15.4*
Indiana	2,794	2,645	149	5.3	3,131	2,985	146	4.7	12.0	12.8	-2.2
Percent U.S.	2.22	2.23	2.11	—	2.37	2.39	1.97	—	—	—	—
Rank	14	14	13	28	14	14	15	36	8	7	28
Iowa	1,448	1,386	62	4.3	1,561	1,507	55	3.5	7.8	8.7	-11.7
Kansas	1,276	1,219	57	4.5	1,333	1,274	59	4.4	4.5	4.5	3.7
Kentucky	*1,767*	*1,662*	*104*	*5.9*	*1,861*	*1,760*	*100*	*5.4*	*5.3*	*5.9*	*-3.9*
Louisiana	1,837	1,721	117	6.3	1,957	1,822	135	6.9	6.5	5.9	15.5
Maine	635	602	33	5.2	642	605	37	5.7	1.2	0.5	12.2
Maryland	2,609	2,487	122	4.7	2,721	2,582	139	5.1	4.3	3.8	13.4
Massachusetts	3,228	3,033	195	6.0	3,176	3,006	170	5.4	-1.6	-0.9	-12.5
Michigan	*4,596*	*4,246*	*350*	*7.6*	*4,734*	*4,480*	*253*	*5.3*	*3.0*	*5.5*	*-27.7*
Minnesota	2,386	2,269	117	4.9	2,599	2,502	96	3.7	8.9	10.3	-17.8
Mississippi	1,184	1,094	90	7.6	1,260	1,182	77	6.1	6.4	8.1	-14.4
Missouri	2,594	2,443	151	5.8	2,828	2,693	135	4.8	9.0	10.2	-10.4
Montana	401	377	24	6.0	438	412	26	5.9	9.1	9.2	7.9
Nebraska	815	796	18	2.2	900	876	24	2.6	10.4	10.0	31.5
Nevada	665	633	33	4.9	804	761	43	5.4	20.9	20.3	32.7
New Hampshire	628	592	36	5.7	634	609	25	4.0	1.0	2.8	-29.2
New Jersey	4,067	3,861	206	5.1	4,067	3,806	261	6.4	0.0	-1.4	26.6
New Mexico	708	662	46	6.5	792	743	50	6.3	12.0	12.3	8.0
New York	8,843	8,375	467	5.3	8,537	7,996	541	6.3	-3.5	-4.5	15.7
North Carolina	3,468	3,324	144	4.2	3,640	3,482	158	4.3	4.9	4.7	9.3
North Dakota	318	305	13	4.0	336	325	11	3.3	5.5	6.3	-14.1
Ohio	*5,409*	*5,099*	*310*	*5.7*	*5,583*	*5,317*	*266*	*4.8*	*3.2*	*4.3*	*-14.1*
Oklahoma	1,514	1,428	86	5.7	1,548	1,475	73	4.7	2.2	3.3	-15.4
Oregon	1,491	1,407	83	5.6	1,656	1,576	80	4.8	11.1	12.0	-3.4
Pennsylvania	5,791	5,476	315	5.4	5,842	5,499	343	5.9	0.9	0.4	9.1
Rhode Island	519	484	35	6.8	488	454	34	7.0	-6.0	-6.1	-3.7
South Carolina	1,739	1,656	83	4.8	1,858	1,764	94	5.1	6.9	6.5	14.0
South Dakota	347	334	14	3.9	384	373	11	2.9	10.5	11.6	-17.0
Tennessee	2,387	2,262	126	5.3	2,708	2,567	141	5.2	13.4	13.5	11.6
Texas	8,616	8,071	545	6.3	9,613	9,034	579	6.0	11.6	11.9	6.3
Utah	816	781	35	4.3	974	940	35	3.6	19.4	20.3	-1.4
Vermont	305	289	15	5.0	320	306	14	4.2	4.9	5.8	-11.1
Virginia	3,239	3,098	141	4.3	3,491	3,333	157	4.5	7.8	7.6	11.9
Washington	2,538	2,413	125	4.9	2,817	2,637	180	6.4	11.0	9.3	43.5
West Virginia	761	697	64	8.4	787	725	62	7.9	3.5	4.1	-3.3
Wisconsin	2,581	2,467	115	4.4	2,851	2,745	106	3.7	10.4	11.3	-7.8
Wyoming	236	223	13	5.5	256	244	12	4.8	8.5	9.3	-6.2

Percent Change in Average Annual Employment
1990 to 1995

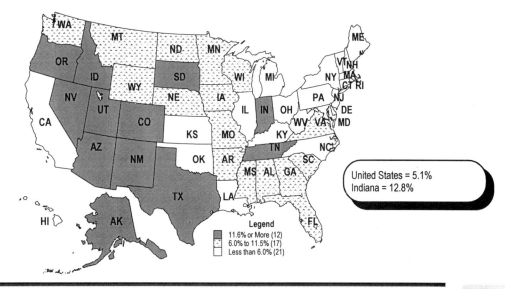

United States = 5.1%
Indiana = 12.8%

Legend
11.6% or More (12)
6.0% to 11.5% (17)
Less than 6.0% (21)

Source: U.S. Department of Labor
EDIN table(s): LFAS

1.29 Number of Establishments Reporting Employment in 1995

	Total Private	Ag., Forestry, & Fishing	Mining	Construction	Manufacturing	Transport. & Public Utilities	Wholesale Trade	Retail Trade	Finance, Insurance & Real Estate	Services
United States	6,801,869	183,282	28,597	671,997	397,053	282,618	635,927	1,438,938	595,352	2,514,876
Alabama	96,433	1,928	337	9,602	7,043	4,467	9,940	23,233	8,069	31,815
Alaska	16,387	262	221	1,883	620	1,404	1,089	3,509	1,071	6,184
Arizona	101,734	3,031	224	10,659	4,831	3,909	10,730	19,667	10,158	38,141
Arkansas	63,263	1,943	317	6,371	4,450	3,741	6,045	15,371	5,063	19,899
California	939,285	37,804	1,175	70,072	56,014	28,607	66,438	162,755	75,290	428,936
Colorado	118,161	2,670	1,159	13,202	5,691	4,593	11,273	23,858	11,904	43,406
Connecticut	100,605	2,436	79	10,475	6,069	3,387	9,885	20,229	8,792	38,159
Delaware	19,777	421	6	2,266	642	763	1,820	4,154	3,334	6,373
Dist. Of Col.	24,756	56	24	663	705	800	627	3,560	2,156	15,888
Florida	380,018	12,059	198	34,908	15,107	14,672	35,944	76,835	34,376	142,610
Georgia	182,008	3,807	195	18,140	10,517	7,692	22,350	38,965	15,915	63,093
Hawaii	31,324	706	10	2,801	1,002	1,554	2,508	7,345	4,027	11,002
Idaho	36,069	1,774	147	5,343	2,177	1,977	3,399	7,552	3,025	10,666
Illinois	*280,100*	*4,997*	*765*	*28,190*	*20,203*	*12,622*	*28,467*	*56,615*	*25,753*	*102,141*
Indiana	140,452	2,935	406	16,181	9,758	6,561	14,462	32,606	12,653	44,694
Percent U.S.	*2.06*	*1.60*	*1.42*	*2.41*	*2.46*	*2.32*	*2.27*	*2.27*	*2.13*	*1.78*
Rank	*16*	*18*	*16*	*14*	*13*	*15*	*14*	*14*	*16*	*17*
Iowa	80,580	2,030	199	7,747	4,241	4,408	9,290	19,779	7,484	25,402
Kansas	71,158	1,776	1,110	6,824	3,313	3,583	8,176	16,110	6,745	23,521
Kentucky	*88,030*	*1,714*	*1,018*	*9,300*	*4,799*	*4,674*	*8,150*	*21,505*	*7,193*	*28,737*
Louisiana	98,532	1,981	1,843	8,195	4,416	5,501	9,488	22,258	8,915	35,401
Maine	37,164	882	31	4,337	2,416	2,011	3,018	9,123	2,491	12,782
Maryland	134,971	2,650	68	16,155	3,874	5,173	10,875	27,537	10,696	56,614
Massachusetts	162,589	3,554	89	14,850	9,405	5,909	15,628	36,919	12,968	63,269
Michigan	*212,042*	*4,901*	*456*	*23,323*	*16,823*	*7,572*	*19,647*	*47,839*	*16,340*	*72,977*
Minnesota	125,869	2,761	192	12,074	8,542	5,810	14,145	27,174	12,598	42,574
Mississippi	56,452	1,771	417	5,124	4,086	3,478	5,007	13,724	5,270	17,572
Missouri	141,169	2,983	329	15,764	8,579	7,424	15,030	30,660	13,350	47,050
Montana	30,637	850	369	3,739	1,544	1,684	2,390	7,155	2,497	10,353
Nebraska	44,713	1,637	151	4,953	2,017	2,437	5,003	10,290	4,112	14,114
Nevada	39,296	791	323	4,443	1,725	1,695	3,440	7,843	4,590	14,191
New Hampshire	37,402	720	57	3,672	2,528	1,398	4,396	8,341	2,745	13,304
New Jersey	223,104	5,217	90	23,628	12,033	10,114	24,396	47,176	15,964	81,735
New Mexico	43,600	1,154	742	5,667	1,815	1,815	3,753	9,465	3,627	15,511
New York	485,890	7,399	380	40,186	26,005	18,345	46,516	105,229	52,659	180,978
North Carolina	174,483	4,477	179	21,163	11,474	6,641	18,263	42,356	13,968	55,964
North Dakota	20,531	582	273	2,285	780	1,489	2,609	4,785	1,980	5,748
Ohio	*253,880*	*4,953*	*936*	*26,785*	*18,875*	*9,778*	*23,729*	*58,519*	*21,055*	*87,716*
Oklahoma	78,436	1,501	2,419	6,690	4,771	3,903	6,938	17,967	7,384	26,552
Oregon	96,170	3,631	147	11,717	6,990	4,120	8,917	18,467	8,509	32,934
Pennsylvania	267,912	5,148	1,010	27,902	18,139	10,137	24,772	62,732	20,534	97,539
Rhode Island	30,410	749	18	3,465	2,904	952	3,037	6,362	1,989	10,566
South Carolina	87,887	1,942	99	10,562	5,104	3,304	7,031	22,523	7,049	29,472
South Dakota	23,349	532	76	2,633	976	1,633	2,629	5,563	2,264	7,044
Tennessee	114,273	1,969	230	10,979	7,936	5,072	11,907	26,063	9,392	40,272
Texas	414,526	14,284	7,049	33,337	22,922	19,390	41,501	86,520	39,638	149,589
Utah	49,516	855	352	7,242	2,975	2,066	4,869	10,229	4,655	16,240
Vermont	20,634	504	57	2,538	1,425	898	1,566	4,957	1,435	7,256
Virginia	166,360	3,472	399	19,980	6,545	6,917	13,479	34,916	14,615	64,127
Washington	172,087	13,318	208	21,715	9,025	6,284	14,093	29,790	13,487	64,168
West Virginia	42,600	542	1,073	5,496	1,990	2,502	3,709	10,366	3,221	13,694
Wisconsin	128,007	2,768	169	14,485	10,684	6,716	12,339	28,660	10,998	41,161
Wyoming	17,241	462	783	2,288	552	1,043	1,220	3,787	1,357	5,750

Number of Establishments Reporting Employment 1995

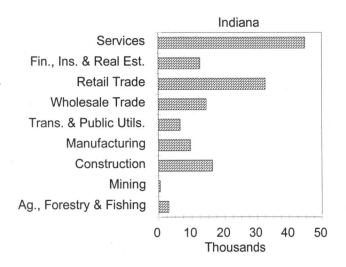

Indiana

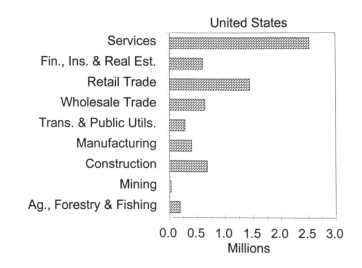

United States

Footnote: Reporting units are individual establishments. An establishment generally is defined as a single physical location at which one type of economic activity is carried on.
Source: U.S. Bureau Of Labor Statistics
EDIN table(s): EMM1, EMM2

1.30 Average Annual Employment: Distribution of Employment by Industry 1995

	Total Private	Percent of Total								
		Ag., Forestry, & Fishing	Mining	Construction	Manufacturing	Transport. & Public Utilities	Wholesale Trade	Retail Trade	Finance, Insurance & Real Estate	Services
United States	96,885,982	1.7	0.6	5.3	19.1	6.0	6.6	21.9	6.8	31.9
Alabama	1,437,083	1.3	0.8	6.0	27.3	5.9	6.4	22.1	5.1	25.1
Alaska	187,316	0.7	5.2	6.9	9.1	12.2	4.6	24.3	5.6	31.0
Arizona	1,511,147	2.7	0.9	7.9	12.8	5.7	6.2	23.2	7.1	33.4
Arkansas	878,555	1.7	0.4	5.0	29.4	6.8	5.6	22.0	4.6	24.4
California	10,724,739	4.3	0.3	4.5	16.6	5.7	6.9	20.5	6.8	33.9
Colorado	1,519,166	1.6	1.0	6.7	12.6	7.4	6.3	23.6	7.2	33.5
Connecticut	1,344,015	1.0	0.1	3.8	20.8	5.2	5.8	19.6	9.9	33.7
Delaware	310,295	1.0	0.0	6.1	19.9	4.6	4.5	22.0	13.1	28.7
Dist. Of Col.	372,900	0.1	0.0	2.4	3.5	4.6	1.5	12.5	7.4	68.0
Florida	5,103,476	3.0	0.1	5.9	9.4	5.8	6.2	24.1	7.3	37.5
Georgia	2,794,886	1.3	0.3	5.4	21.0	7.5	8.2	22.5	6.2	27.6
Hawaii	427,992	2.4	0.1	6.1	4.0	9.5	5.0	26.7	8.7	37.5
Idaho	388,274	5.0	0.7	7.6	18.3	5.4	7.2	24.1	5.3	26.5
Illinois	*4,720,877*	*0.9*	*0.3*	*4.6*	*20.4*	*6.4*	*7.5*	*20.4*	*7.9*	*31.7*
Indiana	2,354,746	1.0	0.3	5.5	29.0	5.7	5.8	22.6	5.5	24.7
Percent U.S.	2.43	—	—	—	—	—	—	—	—	—
Rank	14	29	24	25	4	29	35	27	37	48
Iowa	1,107,212	1.1	0.2	5.0	22.5	5.2	7.5	23.3	6.9	28.2
Kansas	948,231	1.4	0.8	5.4	20.2	6.5	7.7	23.4	6.1	28.5
Kentucky	*1,327,402*	*1.0*	*1.9*	*5.5*	*23.7*	*6.6*	*6.0*	*23.7*	*4.9*	*26.7*
Louisiana	1,382,734	1.0	3.3	7.7	13.6	7.5	6.6	23.4	5.5	31.1
Maine	439,583	1.3	0.0	4.9	20.7	4.9	5.7	25.5	5.7	31.2
Maryland	1,738,035	1.1	0.1	7.3	10.1	5.8	6.1	24.2	7.4	37.7
Massachusetts	2,537,781	0.7	0.1	3.5	17.5	4.9	6.5	20.6	7.9	38.3
Michigan	*3,609,786*	*1.1*	*0.2*	*4.2*	*27.2*	*4.4*	*5.9*	*21.8*	*5.4*	*29.6*
Minnesota	1,969,907	1.0	0.4	4.2	21.6	5.6	7.1	22.0	6.9	31.1
Mississippi	852,068	1.9	0.6	5.3	30.2	5.8	5.2	21.6	4.6	24.8
Missouri	2,081,125	1.0	0.2	5.4	20.3	7.2	6.9	22.1	6.8	30.1
Montana	270,937	1.5	2.0	6.0	8.6	6.5	6.6	28.7	5.6	34.4
Nebraska	650,549	1.6	0.2	5.3	17.2	6.0	8.2	23.4	7.8	30.2
Nevada	689,274	1.0	1.9	9.0	5.3	5.7	4.4	18.4	5.2	48.9
New Hampshire	458,108	0.9	0.1	4.2	22.3	4.3	5.7	25.2	6.0	31.2
New Jersey	2,972,129	0.9	0.1	4.1	16.8	8.2	8.9	19.6	7.4	33.9
New Mexico	521,016	2.9	3.1	8.6	8.7	5.6	5.3	26.0	5.6	34.1
New York	6,408,821	0.7	0.1	3.9	14.6	6.1	6.7	18.4	11.2	37.9
North Carolina	2,898,285	1.4	0.1	6.0	29.8	5.6	6.2	21.3	5.0	24.5
North Dakota	229,465	1.3	1.7	5.9	9.5	7.3	9.1	25.4	5.9	34.0
Ohio	*4,412,900*	*0.9*	*0.3*	*4.7*	*25.0*	*4.9*	*6.3*	*22.6*	*5.9*	*29.4*
Oklahoma	1,017,059	1.2	3.2	4.7	16.7	7.1	6.4	24.3	6.0	30.4
Oregon	1,191,796	3.4	0.1	5.7	19.1	5.7	7.5	22.5	6.2	29.5
Pennsylvania	4,425,779	0.9	0.4	4.5	21.3	5.8	6.0	21.0	6.8	33.2
Rhode Island	373,874	0.7	0.0	3.6	22.8	3.9	5.1	21.0	6.3	36.4
South Carolina	1,339,413	1.2	0.1	6.5	28.2	5.2	4.8	24.0	5.0	24.7
South Dakota	269,470	1.0	0.9	5.2	17.2	5.7	7.3	25.2	6.9	30.5
Tennessee	2,082,718	0.8	0.2	5.2	25.8	6.4	6.7	21.4	5.1	28.3
Texas	6,473,546	1.7	2.4	6.3	15.9	7.1	7.2	22.8	6.5	30.1
Utah	722,300	0.9	1.1	7.6	17.0	6.8	6.3	23.9	6.6	29.7
Vermont	222,860	1.3	0.3	5.6	20.2	5.0	5.9	23.0	5.3	33.5
Virginia	2,436,307	1.2	0.5	6.9	16.5	6.0	5.8	22.9	6.5	33.5
Washington	1,919,182	4.5	0.2	6.0	17.1	5.9	7.2	22.5	6.2	30.5
West Virginia	526,472	0.8	5.2	6.2	15.6	7.0	5.7	24.4	4.8	30.3
Wisconsin	2,145,159	1.0	0.1	4.6	28.0	5.3	5.9	21.5	6.3	27.1
Wyoming	159,234	1.9	10.6	8.9	6.1	7.1	4.7	27.8	4.9	28.0

Rank in Employment by Industry
1995

Sector or Industry	ILLINOIS	INDIANA	KENTUCKY	MICHIGAN	OHIO
Total	5	14	27	8	7
Ag., Forestry, & Fishing	6	17	32	11	12
Mining	12	24	6	18	11
Construction	5	12	26	10	6
Manufacturing	5	9	22	4	2
Transport. & Public Utilities	4	15	23	11	8
Wholesale Trade	4	18	27	10	6
Retail Trade	6	13	26	8	5
Finance, Insur., Real Estate	4	18	29	10	7
Services	5	20	26	8	7

Source: U.S. Bureau of Labor Statistics
EDIN table(s): EMM1, EMM2

1.31 Average Annual Wages 1995

	Total Private ($Mil)	Ag., Forestry, & Fishing	Mining	Construction	Manufacturing	Transport. & Public Utilities	Wholesale Trade	Retail Trade	Finance, Insurance & Real Estate	Services
United States	2,658,527.2	26,368.7	26,364.7	148,707.5	642,042.3	205,264.5	229,900.5	312,240.	255,286.5	808,706.4
Alabama	34,086.7	294.8	479.1	2,041.7	10,774.3	2,848.8	2,784.4	4,207.6	2,157.4	8,498.5
Alaska	5,688.6	35.7	758.9	589.5	507.9	908.6	289.8	818.2	321.5	1,449.0
Arizona	37,598.0	594.9	554.4	3,119.3	6,905.9	2,787.5	3,034.7	5,324.5	3,426.2	11,836.5
Arkansas	18,565.6	269.3	104.0	984.2	6,154.0	1,760.5	1,359.4	2,616.6	1,061.4	4,255.0
California	321,969.6	6,815.8	1,530.5	15,641.9	68,510.5	23,081.4	27,792.4	37,157.8	29,386.5	110,854.6
Colorado	40,666.3	430.6	755.6	2,901.6	6,709.7	4,246.4	3,450.1	5,343.4	3,676.4	13,138.6
Connecticut	46,958.4	302.9	36.0	1,842.3	12,476.6	2,836.3	3,735.3	4,600.5	6,998.5	14,031.5
Delaware	8,977.7	61.5	2.8	538.7	2,895.0	479.5	481.5	976.7	1,356.7	2,185.4
Dist. Of Col.	14,181.0	6.3	6.2	290.2	654.6	925.0	270.9	741.8	1,360.9	9,911.4
Florida	122,989.2	2,310.0	254.3	7,634.3	14,910.5	9,541.4	10,876.9	18,555.9	12,257.6	45,958.2
Georgia	73,891.8	603.6	293.5	3,987.9	16,950.6	8,027.2	8,636.2	8,999.2	6,200.1	20,101.0
Hawaii	11,090.4	233.7	18.2	1,080.7	494.7	1,348.9	668.4	1,898.5	1,165.5	4,165.3
Idaho	8,783.3	294.3	96.1	773.9	2,307.6	581.4	693.9	1,238.5	535.7	2,261.1
Illinois	*141,446.1*	*806.2*	*589.0*	*7,876.2*	*35,703.4*	*11,164.3*	*13,939.3*	*14,634.3*	*15,814.7*	*40,879.6*
Indiana	59,891.0	389.9	255.8	3,762.8	23,836.9	4,079.1	4,371.4	6,875.6	3,695.9	12,614.4
Percent U.S.	2.25	1.48	0.97	2.53	3.71	1.99	1.90	2.20	1.45	1.56
Rank	14	19	22	14	9	17	18	14	20	21
Iowa	24,769.5	214.0	61.1	1,491.7	7,665.1	1,652.3	2,325.5	3,098.7	2,235.0	6,026.1
Kansas	22,390.1	239.2	238.0	1,327.4	5,953.3	1,933.1	2,328.0	2,889.0	1,654.8	5,827.2
Kentucky	*30,733.6*	*221.0*	*964.8*	*1,783.5*	*9,437.4*	*2,663.9*	*2,330.0*	*4,007.9*	*1,831.9*	*7,452.0*
Louisiana	33,182.9	222.6	1,975.8	2,689.5	6,379.0	3,331.3	2,706.3	4,204.7	2,181.4	9,457.1
Maine	9,882.9	98.4	2.4	523.6	2,671.7	618.6	729.3	1,542.8	772.6	2,918.3
Maryland	48,332.8	355.5	40.4	3,788.5	6,417.5	3,616.4	4,016.8	6,705.3	4,658.7	18,681.3
Massachusetts	81,599.7	390.2	47.4	3,202.2	18,129.1	4,526.7	7,126.7	8,382.7	9,468.6	30,326.1
Michigan	*109,901.7*	*649.3*	*326.8*	*4,949.2*	*44,291.6*	*5,805.4*	*8,590.6*	*11,060.3*	*6,372.2*	*27,686.5*
Minnesota	53,286.5	362.8	335.2	2,767.7	15,021.8	3,741.5	5,248.9	6,043.9	5,105.7	14,658.9
Mississippi	17,666.5	260.4	146.8	1,002.3	6,001.1	1,471.5	1,207.0	2,276.1	1,022.7	4,278.7
Missouri	53,285.3	344.4	178.3	3,367.5	13,951.6	4,925.5	4,873.1	6,366.2	4,499.5	14,779.2
Montana	5,293.0	61.9	221.8	402.7	600.7	509.6	462.5	942.5	375.2	1,714.1
Nebraska	14,216.4	183.7	33.4	902.8	3,116.2	1,174.3	1,405.8	1,832.7	1,471.9	4,095.6
Nevada	17,789.2	127.6	610.3	1,962.3	1,100.9	1,224.5	1,001.2	2,130.1	1,097.4	8,511.4
New Hampshire	12,131.5	72.9	14.8	549.2	3,533.0	627.5	1,096.7	1,735.6	927.1	3,557.9
New Jersey	100,726.5	543.2	85.7	4,580.1	21,001.3	10,144.9	11,525.9	10,371.6	10,031.1	32,179.5
New Mexico	11,361.9	175.4	585.6	1,024.7	1,274.1	886.7	747.8	1,813.1	741.9	4,109.6
New York	222,176.5	812.8	210.5	8,893.3	37,146.5	15,747.9	18,134.9	19,403.9	47,292.4	74,080.3
North Carolina	69,911.7	688.9	132.1	4,203.1	23,929.4	5,456.6	5,974.9	8,623.1	4,804.0	16,099.8
North Dakota	4,581.1	53.8	141.3	337.3	554.9	489.7	544.8	666.8	337.5	1,455.1
Ohio	*117,213.4*	*645.4*	*493.0*	*6,067.8*	*40,994.8*	*7,070.8*	*9,779.0*	*13,590.4*	*8,163.3*	*30,298.8*
Oklahoma	22,648.0	187.0	1,309.1	1,079.3	4,902.2	2,341.9	1,812.9	3,121.3	1,587.2	6,293.5
Oregon	30,003.8	650.6	57.4	2,117.8	7,571.2	2,221.9	3,104.8	4,062.6	2,237.6	7,948.0
Pennsylvania	121,000.0	743.1	761.4	6,123.1	32,747.7	9,039.9	9,359.3	13,170.5	10,580.5	38,474.5
Rhode Island	9,449.2	51.3	5.0	405.5	2,555.4	464.2	649.0	1,123.5	796.9	3,376.1
South Carolina	30,723.8	261.7	59.8	2,128.1	10,955.3	2,146.3	1,964.1	4,309.4	1,845.7	7,000.6
South Dakota	5,185.6	45.7	85.3	319.8	1,089.2	389.6	489.0	781.5	451.5	1,534.0
Tennessee	51,544.6	253.4	160.4	2,860.9	15,610.3	4,248.9	4,501.9	6,440.3	3,387.4	14,041.7
Texas	175,736.0	1,609.0	8,373.2	11,243.7	35,712.2	16,212.0	16,888.4	21,953.6	14,313.0	49,409.7
Utah	16,725.5	94.1	339.2	1,342.6	3,529.1	1,574.3	1,368.4	2,354.9	1,317.2	4,803.5
Vermont	5,153.0	46.7	15.2	304.3	1,422.7	336.3	388.9	699.6	355.5	1,583.8
Virginia	63,599.8	491.6	436.0	4,336.1	12,348.7	5,197.9	5,172.7	8,010.0	5,286.4	22,234.4
Washington	51,250.6	1,244.5	134.9	3,398.2	12,276.1	3,966.1	4,601.1	6,701.2	3,837.8	15,090.7
West Virginia	12,184.7	58.5	1,220.9	814.7	2,681.7	1,179.9	843.5	1,546.6	593.7	3,244.9
Wisconsin	52,650.7	413.1	87.2	3,014.3	19,419.2	3,355.5	4,016.7	5,757.6	4,036.6	12,548.7
Wyoming	3,455.3	45.4	740.1	337.9	258.2	355.0	199.4	531.1	199.6	788.7

Private Industry Average Annual Wages
1995

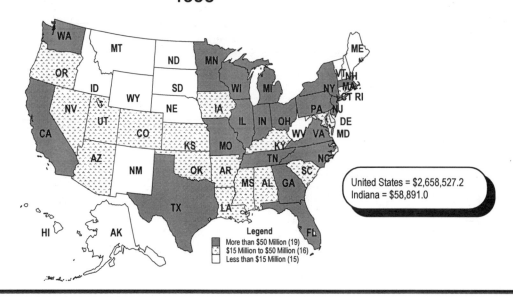

United States = $2,658,527.2
Indiana = $58,891.0

Legend
More than $50 Million (19)
$15 Million to $50 Million (16)
Less than $15 Million (15)

Source: U.S. Bureau of Labor Statistics
EDIN table(s): EMM1, EMM2

1.32 Average Annual Weekly Wage 1995 *($)*

	Total Private	Ag., Forestry, & Fishing	Mining	Construction	Manufacturing	Transport. & Public Utilities	Wholesale Trade	Retail Trade	Finance, Insurance & Real Estate	Services
United States	528	309	871	562	668	674	692	284	742	503
Alabama	456	316	847	453	528	642	581	255	562	453
Alaska	584	505	1,487	872	573	763	645	346	586	480
Arizona	478	277	823	501	687	627	622	292	610	450
Arkansas	406	339	575	429	458	570	528	260	509	381
California	577	283	1,007	621	741	721	724	325	771	586
Colorado	515	335	975	547	673	729	693	286	647	496
Connecticut	672	417	962	701	859	784	914	335	1,017	597
Delaware	556	364	622	545	901	652	667	275	640	472
Dist. Of Col.	731	468	2,128	634	973	1,037	911	307	952	752
Florida	463	292	712	484	596	623	657	291	634	462
Georgia	508	322	734	508	555	737	729	275	693	501
Hawaii	498	436	977	802	561	638	597	320	605	500
Idaho	435	293	678	502	625	535	479	255	505	423
Illinois	*576*	*369*	*828*	*699*	*715*	*710*	*760*	*292*	*815*	*526*
Indiana	**489**	**328**	**770**	**558**	**671**	**589**	**613**	**248**	**552**	**418**
Percent U.S.	*92.61*	*106.15*	*88.40*	*99.29*	*100.45*	*87.39*	*88.58*	*87.32*	*74.39*	*83.10*
Rank	*24*	*22*	*22*	*21*	*16*	*38*	*29*	*40*	*37*	*35*
Iowa	430	324	557	522	591	553	535	231	560	371
Kansas	454	357	572	495	598	607	612	250	554	414
Kentucky	*445*	*327*	*739*	*467*	*578*	*587*	*564*	*245*	*547*	*405*
Louisiana	462	295	821	488	651	618	568	250	550	422
Maine	432	324	423	464	564	553	564	265	594	409
Maryland	535	361	692	573	703	685	723	306	697	548
Massachusetts	618	418	676	689	785	703	828	309	904	600
Michigan	*585*	*322*	*747*	*624*	*869*	*703*	*776*	*270*	*628*	*498*
Minnesota	520	343	826	644	680	650	719	268	719	460
Mississippi	399	311	577	424	448	572	523	238	501	390
Missouri	492	316	702	579	637	636	648	266	611	453
Montana	376	289	807	480	494	557	495	233	472	353
Nebraska	420	330	504	501	535	576	507	232	560	401
Nevada	496	354	890	608	579	595	637	323	592	485
New Hampshire	509	336	615	548	666	616	809	289	646	478
New Jersey	652	387	839	718	811	803	840	343	874	615
New Mexico	419	223	702	440	539	580	524	257	493	444
New York	667	372	847	685	761	770	818	316	1,262	586
North Carolina	464	316	697	464	534	647	635	268	638	436
North Dakota	384	346	712	478	490	561	504	220	481	359
Ohio	*511*	*324*	*684*	*569*	*716*	*623*	*677*	*262*	*601*	*449*
Oklahoma	428	302	785	433	553	626	534	243	502	392
Oregon	484	307	653	595	639	627	665	291	581	435
Pennsylvania	526	352	748	590	669	672	676	272	675	504
Rhode Island	486	360	570	584	578	613	659	275	651	477
South Carolina	441	310	626	471	559	592	586	257	530	406
South Dakota	370	320	703	435	451	491	475	222	465	359
Tennessee	476	306	671	505	559	612	620	277	614	459
Texas	522	289	1,033	529	666	682	695	286	654	488
Utah	445	279	804	471	552	617	575	262	531	430
Vermont	445	310	525	469	609	576	570	262	580	408
Virginia	502	321	736	497	589	679	702	276	643	524
Washington	514	279	784	569	721	671	636	299	618	496
West Virginia	445	279	863	477	627	618	538	232	449	391
Wisconsin	472	356	676	584	621	563	606	240	577	415
Wyoming	417	296	840	458	511	608	515	231	489	340

Average Weekly Wage by Industry
1995

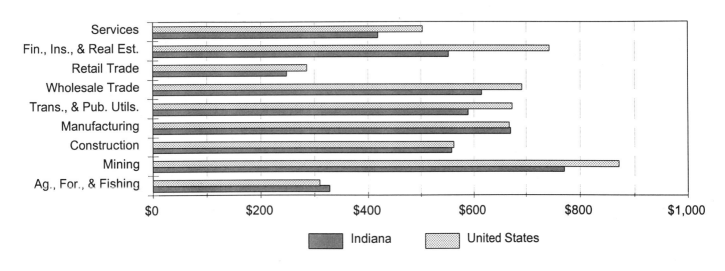

Indiana   United States

Source: U.S. Bureau of Labor Statistics
EDIN table(s): EMM1, EMM2

1.33 Non-Farm Wage and Salary Employment by Industry 1996 *(000)*

	Total Non-farm	Ag. Services, Forestry, Fisheries	Mining	Construction	Manufacturing	Transport. and Public Utilities	Wholesale Trade	Retail Trade	Services	Finance, Insurance, & Real Estate	Government
United States	149,383	1,883	880	8,118	19,234	7,209	7,013	25,705	46,365	11,283	21,693
Alabama	2,218	25	12	141	396	105	101	389	559	110	381
Alaska	370	13	11	19	19	27	10	59	99	19	94
Arizona	2,376	43	17	160	212	106	111	434	768	190	335
Arkansas	1,343	19	7	83	263	76	53	242	338	65	197
California	17,286	390	46	804	1,964	760	832	2,801	5,915	1,384	2,391
Colorado	2,496	31	25	164	211	136	109	452	811	202	354
Connecticut	1,977	21	2	94	285	83	88	316	671	188	229
Delaware	447	4	0	28	59	17	15	79	127	54	63
Dist. Of Col.	716	10	0	10	14	22	5	49	309	36	260
Florida	7,674	149	14	455	514	366	364	1,462	2,678	641	1,032
Georgia	4,286	45	9	250	600	247	251	755	1,184	283	662
Hawaii	730	9	0	33	20	46	25	138	229	63	167
Idaho	655	18	4	50	80	29	32	124	178	37	105
Illinois	*6,852*	*58*	*24*	*326*	*992*	*373*	*362*	*1,115*	*2,126*	*608*	*868*
Indiana	**3,363**	**28**	**10**	**195**	**688**	**162**	**148**	**636**	**881**	**201**	**413**
Percent U.S.	*2.25*	*1.49*	*1.14*	*2.40*	*3.58*	*2.25*	*2.11*	*2.47*	*1.90*	*1.78*	*1.90*
Rank	*14*	*21*	*21*	*12*	*9*	*15*	*18*	*13*	*18*	*21*	*17*
Iowa	1,701	24	3	94	256	77	89	319	486	111	243
Kansas	1,559	19	23	85	203	80	81	281	426	92	271
Kentucky	*2,024*	*24*	*27*	*122*	*321*	*108*	*87*	*378*	*538*	*96*	*323*
Louisiana	2,210	25	59	152	196	123	98	385	654	117	400
Maine	718	15	0	47	98	29	29	138	217	42	102
Maryland	2,806	30	3	177	183	125	116	486	955	230	503
Massachusetts	3,807	36	2	176	463	153	180	610	1,444	310	432
Michigan	*5,211*	*46*	*14*	*253*	*995*	*194*	*235*	*936*	*1,531*	*356*	*651*
Minnesota	2,978	26	9	142	446	142	160	524	920	232	377
Mississippi	1,343	15	9	76	254	62	48	227	336	65	252
Missouri	3,154	30	7	180	432	186	157	557	944	222	439
Montana	497	9	7	32	29	26	20	103	157	31	84
Nebraska	1,055	16	2	56	117	59	56	194	313	79	162
Nevada	1,025	11	16	91	42	47	36	163	439	68	112
New Hampshire	709	8	1	44	111	25	30	140	224	48	79
New Jersey	4,376	35	4	188	497	278	285	669	1,419	421	581
New Mexico	887	12	20	59	53	37	31	165	268	54	188
New York	9,693	68	9	379	961	476	457	1,395	3,466	1,076	1,406
North Carolina	4,377	51	5	284	866	190	193	749	1,093	256	691
North Dakota	395	5	5	23	23	23	23	75	121	25	73
Ohio	*6,370*	*54*	*24*	*327*	*1,123*	*274*	*305*	*1,175*	*1,838*	*452*	*798*
Oklahoma	1,760	22	62	91	184	91	71	316	510	103	311
Oregon	1,865	37	3	111	254	85	97	341	564	122	251
Pennsylvania	6,480	56	27	330	965	316	283	1,126	2,112	498	768
Rhode Island	549	6	0	24	85	18	20	92	189	41	74
South Carolina	2,053	21	2	132	375	83	73	387	505	122	354
South Dakota	450	7	3	25	50	21	21	88	133	34	69
Tennessee	3,117	28	7	187	534	166	152	546	879	213	405
Texas	10,539	130	263	657	1,107	562	519	1,824	3,070	794	1,613
Utah	1,206	11	9	86	137	59	53	217	361	92	181
Vermont	369	5	1	25	52	15	14	65	121	22	49
Virginia	3,945	40	13	245	414	183	154	661	1,175	272	788
Washington	3,142	58	5	180	368	141	158	552	927	232	521
West Virginia	832	6	31	51	86	45	32	156	236	40	148
Wisconsin	3,095	30	4	154	621	140	139	559	845	217	387
Wyoming	297	5	18	21	13	16	8	58	77	19	62

Non-Farm Wage and Salary Employment by Industry
Percent Distribution — 1996

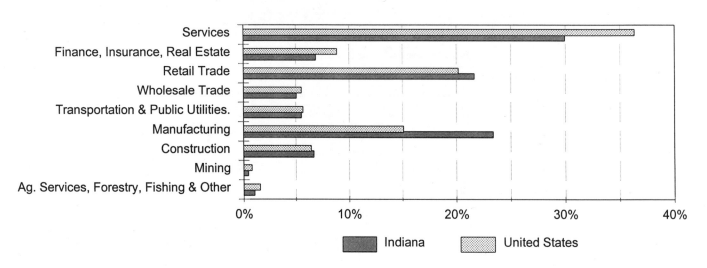

Legend: Indiana | United States

Source: Bureau of Economic Analysis
EDIN table(s): EMPT

1.34 Percent Change in Non-Farm Wage and Salary Employment by Industry 1986 to 1996

	Total Non-farm	Ag. Services, Forestry, Fisheries	Mining	Construction	Manufacturing	Transport. And Public Utilities	Wholesale Trade	Retail Trade	Services	Finance, Insurance, & Real Estate	Government
United States	20.9	57.3	-23.8	19.6	-1.3	21.5	13.7	24.3	42.7	12.0	10.6
Alabama	23.1	66.8	-12.3	35.6	6.3	27.8	20.1	35.7	47.3	-0.9	7.8
Alaska	19.2	-13.2	5.8	-1.3	37.1	38.4	15.9	42.2	52.3	-22.2	1.3
Arizona	40.5	81.6	19.6	14.7	11.0	57.7	65.4	46.4	70.4	6.8	27.1
Arkansas	28.6	72.4	-38.4	35.2	20.9	28.6	21.7	39.4	45.9	-1.2	16.3
California	18.9	54.6	-21.7	11.6	-7.1	18.9	12.3	20.4	42.9	3.9	7.8
Colorado	32.7	65.3	-34.5	40.2	8.9	41.3	30.7	42.4	59.7	4.9	12.6
Connecticut	2.1	42.7	-37.1	-8.2	-29.4	10.1	-8.5	2.1	32.7	-6.4	1.9
Delaware	22.0	68.4	-28.3	9.4	-16.5	16.2	31.8	27.3	45.6	54.2	11.1
Dist. Of Col.	-2.3	56.5	-27.7	-36.0	-14.0	-16.6	-41.1	-15.3	16.7	-32.6	-7.7
Florida	28.7	36.5	-11.4	-0.4	-4.2	28.7	27.2	29.6	57.7	4.8	23.3
Georgia	30.6	70.8	-6.9	16.7	3.5	34.2	18.4	38.9	67.3	15.7	18.6
Hawaii	21.3	81.5	96.0	39.9	-21.0	23.3	19.4	26.1	43.4	7.3	3.0
Idaho	49.9	86.7	5.8	96.8	41.7	32.4	47.8	62.0	67.9	12.9	24.9
Illinois	*18.3*	*85.2*	*-43.1*	*29.7*	*2.2*	*20.9*	*-1.1*	*18.1*	*34.1*	*24.9*	*7.8*
Indiana	**26.3**	**75.9**	**-27.0**	**43.6**	**12.2**	**19.9**	**26.6**	**33.6**	**44.1**	**14.9**	**12.1**
Rank	*20*	*20*	*34*	*12*	*21*	*28*	*15*	*19*	*29*	*23*	*20*
Iowa	25.4	81.8	4.9	58.2	23.8	18.7	15.8	28.0	36.7	4.0	9.9
Kansas	20.8	78.7	-43.7	24.0	12.9	11.1	14.7	31.9	39.4	-4.8	15.5
Kentucky	*26.0*	*65.4*	*-43.8*	*38.3*	*23.0*	*31.0*	*29.6*	*32.9*	*44.4*	*-9.4*	*14.4*
Louisiana	16.9	66.7	-26.0	25.7	15.4	4.6	11.5	17.1	40.5	-12.2	7.8
Maine	15.5	11.0	-15.4	8.9	-10.8	16.8	10.3	25.6	41.7	14.5	-1.1
Maryland	16.1	45.0	-22.2	1.0	-15.2	18.4	4.0	12.5	37.2	23.3	6.8
Massachusetts	5.3	21.6	-22.2	-2.8	-27.1	9.2	-0.1	1.5	30.2	3.0	-0.3
Michigan	*21.7*	*85.2*	*-9.5*	*48.1*	*-1.2*	*18.1*	*27.3*	*26.1*	*40.0*	*30.7*	*7.1*
Minnesota	29.2	52.3	15.4	25.9	16.2	25.3	28.5	27.9	47.0	23.9	16.8
Mississippi	25.2	56.8	-32.7	40.8	9.1	30.6	11.6	30.4	60.1	4.9	10.9
Missouri	17.7	52.6	-8.1	21.7	-0.7	14.7	14.9	22.7	29.6	7.2	15.5
Montana	33.5	66.6	-0.5	58.0	23.6	5.1	23.3	44.1	53.6	16.2	11.2
Nebraska	27.7	82.5	-27.7	38.9	28.3	17.0	15.4	31.6	49.1	12.4	4.3
Nevada	79.5	178.7	131.8	160.6	81.3	65.2	100.2	84.5	76.1	63.1	47.3
New Hampshire	15.1	58.4	-12.3	-18.1	-11.3	21.7	14.2	21.0	44.5	10.0	11.7
New Jersey	6.0	20.7	-50.3	-10.3	-29.7	11.0	-1.3	3.1	28.3	34.7	2.3
New Mexico	33.5	101.9	3.7	29.7	33.6	13.1	30.8	38.0	55.4	15.4	18.3
New York	3.0	27.5	-46.2	-9.2	-25.8	5.4	-11.7	3.4	20.6	6.3	-1.4
North Carolina	28.8	75.9	-16.2	27.5	1.4	26.2	26.4	35.1	65.3	24.7	22.7
North Dakota	24.7	85.4	-11.3	27.9	40.0	22.4	10.5	27.8	42.2	25.3	1.4
Ohio	*20.0*	*79.6*	*-32.6*	*39.8*	*0.0*	*18.3*	*19.0*	*24.6*	*35.2*	*21.5*	*10.5*
Oklahoma	16.7	95.3	-38.2	25.0	11.0	21.5	9.3	24.6	44.7	-8.0	3.4
Oregon	37.7	39.0	19.2	84.9	20.1	27.7	35.2	41.2	61.0	12.6	16.7
Pennsylvania	13.4	53.7	-38.2	13.8	-9.9	15.6	3.1	14.1	32.4	22.5	3.9
Rhode Island	1.9	0.0	12.0	-4.6	-30.9	9.3	-15.5	2.9	29.2	17.5	0.5
South Carolina	23.1	55.5	21.3	14.4	0.6	31.9	17.7	39.8	54.5	20.8	5.4
South Dakota	38.9	85.2	-4.5	50.0	67.9	31.6	20.8	42.8	55.2	38.6	4.5
Tennessee	31.3	90.8	-19.2	39.4	6.3	44.5	21.5	37.7	58.5	27.7	13.9
Texas	26.9	84.5	-19.2	16.8	13.7	32.7	15.6	27.7	52.4	7.5	22.5
Utah	53.6	121.6	2.4	86.2	42.9	47.3	39.9	62.2	78.1	56.4	16.1
Vermont	21.9	99.3	12.1	3.0	-6.3	24.1	15.2	28.5	45.0	6.1	19.8
Virginia	21.0	66.9	-31.6	8.4	-4.8	19.5	20.4	27.4	48.2	12.8	8.9
Washington	37.2	41.6	21.9	45.3	15.9	30.3	38.8	42.4	58.3	23.7	23.7
West Virginia	17.2	79.3	-27.1	44.9	-5.3	8.3	3.2	20.5	43.6	8.6	10.3
Wisconsin	27.5	62.6	0.7	49.2	18.4	28.6	29.9	26.6	41.1	23.6	11.8
Wyoming	17.8	70.2	-19.3	-3.8	45.7	-1.7	-7.6	34.4	42.8	29.7	4.7

Non-Farm Wage and Salary Employment by Industry
Percent Change — 1986 to 1996

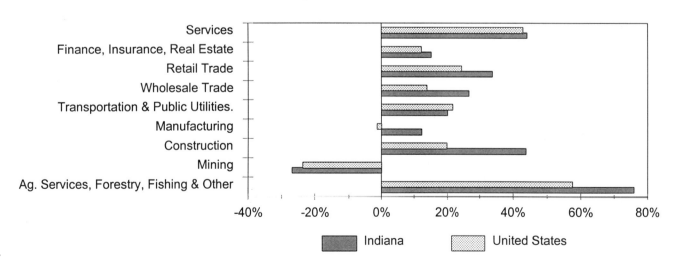

1.35 Employment by Industry: Agriculture and Construction 1996

	Ag. Serv., Forestry, Fisheries and Other	Ag. Services	Forestry, Fisheries, and Other	Forestry	Fisheries	Other	Construction	General Building Contractors	Heavy Construction Contractors	Special Trade Contractors
United States	1,883,000	1,731,100	151,900	52,200	80,700	19,000	8,118,000	1,713,300	906,200	5,498,500
Alabama	24,753	21,353	3,400	2,380	1,020	0	141,175	32,212	17,328	91,635
Alaska	13,207	2,332	10,875	161	10,714	0	19,352	4,765	3,464	11,123
Arizona	43,351	42,748	603	390	213	0	160,435	29,259	16,104	115,072
Arkansas	18,582	16,825	1,757	1,440	317	0	83,002	16,808	11,155	55,039
California	390,147	379,821	10,326	3,807	5,892	627	803,780	189,804	71,847	542,129
Colorado	31,407	30,714	693	290	403	0	163,953	32,246	16,549	115,158
Connecticut	21,124	20,391	733	291	442	0	94,017	15,748	7,847	70,422
Delaware	4,285	4,118	167	31	136	0	27,910	6,463	3,207	18,240
Dist. Of Col.	9,795	513	9,282	6	4	9,272	10,356	3,478	1,616	5,262
Florida	148,763	140,323	8,440	1,992	6,353	95	454,723	85,603	47,773	321,347
Georgia	44,711	41,165	3,546	2,702	844	0	249,601	51,161	26,986	171,454
Hawaii	9,471	7,718	1,753	NA	NA	0	32,666	9,048	3,368	20,250
Idaho	17,509	16,121	1,388	1,064	324	0	50,174	10,739	6,595	32,840
Illinois	*58,145*	*56,719*	*1,426*	*701*	*421*	*304*	*326,298*	*69,381*	*24,494*	*232,423*
Indiana	28,024	27,458	566	388	178	0	195,479	48,422	18,821	128,236
Percent U.S.	1.49	1.59	0.37	0.74	0.22	0.00	2.41	2.83	2.08	2.33
Rank	22	19	39	31	39	9	12	13	13	14
Iowa	23,586	23,113	473	NA	NA	0	93,649	19,518	10,974	63,157
Kansas	19,005	18,731	274	NA	NA	0	84,694	16,527	12,140	56,027
Kentucky	*24,148*	*23,580*	*568*	*320*	*248*	*0*	*121,630*	*23,905*	*15,125*	*82,600*
Louisiana	24,828	17,732	7,096	1,290	5,616	190	151,699	23,272	47,147	81,280
Maine	14,824	8,425	6,399	1,305	5,094	0	47,267	8,707	5,418	33,142
Maryland	30,079	27,751	2,328	451	1,877	0	176,742	39,815	16,088	120,839
Massachusetts	36,422	30,362	6,060	476	5,584	0	175,718	31,311	13,805	130,602
Michigan	*46,471*	*43,984*	*2,487*	*1,904*	*583*	*0*	*253,185*	*55,129*	*15,563*	*182,493*
Minnesota	25,610	24,199	1,411	886	525	0	141,890	27,357	14,603	99,930
Mississippi	15,128	12,274	2,854	1,873	981	0	76,129	18,216	12,914	44,999
Missouri	30,164	29,532	632	427	205	0	180,110	40,052	17,025	123,033
Montana	8,901	7,883	1,018	636	382	0	32,092	8,016	5,218	18,858
Nebraska	16,007	15,782	225	137	88	0	56,206	12,050	7,145	37,011
Nevada	10,965	10,714	251	NA	NA	0	90,690	17,718	9,753	63,219
New Hampshire	7,809	7,103	706	427	279	0	43,779	8,953	3,321	31,505
New Jersey	35,187	33,883	1,304	310	994	0	187,975	40,089	15,130	132,756
New Mexico	12,330	12,039	291	195	96	0	59,093	16,304	9,024	33,765
New York	67,600	57,110	10,490	1,167	1,096	8,227	379,286	73,193	28,189	277,904
North Carolina	50,875	45,808	5,067	2,317	2,750	0	283,796	64,145	31,972	187,679
North Dakota	5,353	5,220	133	NA	NA	0	22,855	4,873	4,215	13,767
Ohio	*54,172*	*52,935*	*1,237*	*850*	*387*	*0*	*326,853*	*68,364*	*28,475*	*230,014*
Oklahoma	21,525	20,998	527	323	204	0	91,294	15,425	12,587	63,282
Oregon	36,539	26,955	9,584	6,474	3,110	0	111,173	27,117	11,807	72,249
Pennsylvania	55,520	53,487	2,033	1,636	302	95	330,282	74,461	29,000	226,821
Rhode Island	5,832	4,341	1,491	52	1,439	0	23,891	5,358	1,448	17,085
South Carolina	21,003	18,536	2,467	1,792	675	0	132,323	33,993	13,111	85,219
South Dakota	6,611	6,335	276	144	132	0	24,559	5,928	3,693	14,938
Tennessee	28,409	27,227	1,182	696	486	0	187,244	42,847	18,335	126,062
Texas	130,220	123,023	7,197	1,879	5,128	190	656,840	105,141	127,413	424,286
Utah	10,974	10,359	615	93	522	0	85,596	20,609	7,833	57,154
Vermont	5,485	5,039	446	398	48	0	25,084	5,932	1,990	17,162
Virginia	40,096	36,896	3,200	1,287	1,913	0	244,835	51,648	30,816	162,371
Washington	57,665	43,969	13,696	4,219	9,477	0	180,348	49,433	21,458	109,457
West Virginia	6,024	5,674	350	302	48	0	50,845	13,512	9,279	28,054
Wisconsin	29,504	27,260	2,244	1,607	637	0	154,294	34,605	11,944	107,745
Wyoming	4,855	4,522	333	154	179	0	21,133	4,640	5,088	11,405

Percent Change in Agriculture and Construction Employment 1990 to 1996

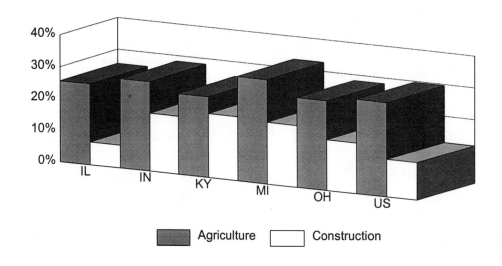

Agriculture ■ Construction □

Source: U.S. Bureau of Economic Analysis
EDIN table(s): EMAG, EMCO

1.36 Employment by Industry: Manufacturing - Nondurable Goods 1996

	Total Manufacturing	Non-Durable Goods	Food and Kindred	Textile Mill	Apparel and Other Textile	Paper	Printing and Publishing	Chemical	Petroleum and Coal	Tobacco Manufacturer	Rubber and Misc. Plastics	Leather and Leather Goods
United States	19,233,500	7,995,000	1,728,200	634,800	920,600	689,600	1,711,000	1,040,800	139,800	41,800	982,100	106,300
Alabama	396,211	192,310	37,814	40,407	44,550	21,242	16,560	12,017	1,461	648	17,369	242
Alaska	18,794	14,225	10,608	NA	185	NA	2,039	NA	NA	3	40	54
Arizona	212,188	53,965	11,647	1,208	3,502	2,444	20,865	5,898	145	3	7,689	564
Arkansas	262,962	123,253	57,012	4,117	9,408	15,044	11,957	7,168	1,009	6	13,893	3,639
California	1,963,727	764,252	183,480	20,951	168,570	40,175	178,768	71,281	19,537	31	73,540	7,919
Colorado	211,326	80,659	26,589	449	5,170	3,134	30,830	4,386	713	0	7,616	1,772
Connecticut	285,115	85,390	9,114	2,128	4,927	7,987	28,257	20,036	1,128	416	10,552	845
Delaware	58,900	44,528	9,875	NA	1,160	2,079	2,718	23,765	NA	8	NA	NA
Dist. Of Col.	14,168	12,067	372	28	50	77	11,245	253	37	NA	NA	3
Florida	514,294	208,471	42,578	4,280	27,843	14,645	70,654	20,151	1,648	1,812	21,020	3,840
Georgia	600,117	353,251	70,146	108,962	42,415	34,385	46,837	21,010	822	2,992	24,698	984
Hawaii	20,020	14,838	6,577	NA	2,713	NA	3,873	NA	641	6	233	NA
Idaho	79,757	30,671	17,797	57	694	2,203	5,831	2,524	24	6	1,218	317
Illinois	*992,129*	*397,854*	*96,817*	*3,202*	*14,044*	*35,395*	*110,582*	*62,279*	*10,004*	*341*	*60,959*	*4,231*
Indiana	688,242	195,233	34,437	1,345	9,385	15,458	43,919	29,077	3,795	52	55,800	1,965
Percent U.S.	*3.58*	*2.44*	*1.99*	*0.21*	*1.02*	*2.24*	*2.57*	*2.79*	*2.71*	*0.12*	*5.68*	*1.85*
Rank	*9*	*16*	*22*	*27*	*22*	*19*	*15*	*13*	*9*	*15*	*5*	*18*
Iowa	255,645	109,053	50,785	549	5,190	6,007	22,450	7,292	221	0	15,169	1,390
Kansas	202,626	85,840	31,790	187	3,837	4,672	23,929	6,070	2,279	0	12,768	308
Kentucky	*321,397*	*138,230*	*24,836*	*8,537*	*25,988*	*11,772*	*23,230*	*14,884*	*3,273*	*4,305*	*19,768*	*1,637*
Louisiana	196,099	105,585	21,564	4,935	9,022	12,401	10,821	30,182	11,097	17	5,428	118
Maine	98,284	48,956	6,828	4,791	2,513	14,679	6,916	1,695	335	0	2,939	8,260
Maryland	183,073	93,598	21,684	NA	6,820	7,582	30,837	13,872	NA	8	9,286	1,009
Massachusetts	462,557	175,796	22,240	14,967	16,215	19,520	54,405	16,866	1,598	6	25,571	4,408
Michigan	*994,554*	*252,200*	*45,392*	*679*	*20,301*	*21,712*	*48,282*	*43,289*	*1,877*	*6*	*66,487*	*4,175*
Minnesota	446,342	188,628	55,588	1,782	5,362	31,564	59,270	10,918	2,227	0	19,715	2,202
Mississippi	253,808	101,617	30,492	4,137	25,800	10,288	8,445	6,956	2,480	6	12,610	401
Missouri	432,308	185,214	51,436	616	20,025	13,881	45,548	27,627	1,789	28	18,810	5,454
Montana	29,452	10,428	2,776	22	985	817	3,650	604	962	6	350	256
Nebraska	117,353	60,909	36,404	329	1,846	2,038	10,517	2,711	120	0	6,503	441
Nevada	42,199	16,015	3,196	61	1,205	379	6,410	1,005	105	NA	3,485	NA
New Hampshire	111,074	34,973	2,745	3,683	2,364	4,510	8,976	1,382	139	0	9,124	2,050
New Jersey	497,070	298,430	38,907	9,966	27,547	21,567	62,548	98,866	6,783	NA	29,067	NA
New Mexico	52,747	17,263	5,172	603	2,226	436	5,519	819	711	17	1,469	291
New York	961,385	455,528	61,857	18,104	90,447	33,375	149,022	55,755	3,761	1,336	33,950	7,921
North Carolina	866,354	472,692	57,445	185,521	58,037	24,934	36,105	49,332	771	17,586	40,559	2,402
North Dakota	23,403	10,200	5,392	NA	366	NA	2,997	188	235	3	820	69
Ohio	*1,122,923*	*367,182*	*61,385*	*4,496*	*14,891*	*36,555*	*81,766*	*66,307*	*6,913*	*11*	*92,269*	*2,589*
Oklahoma	183,807	66,902	17,688	930	7,713	4,568	13,056	3,749	4,696	2	13,674	826
Oregon	254,156	71,266	26,876	1,551	3,703	8,459	18,935	3,324	NA	NA	7,320	676
Pennsylvania	965,133	411,264	86,963	22,726	45,053	36,868	89,425	67,445	9,627	1,006	46,565	5,586
Rhode Island	85,211	30,743	2,977	7,841	1,007	2,359	6,566	2,650	17	3	6,008	1,315
South Carolina	374,701	225,264	18,130	81,950	29,588	17,779	14,306	39,137	397	74	23,800	103
South Dakota	49,965	16,858	8,768	NA	1,634	NA	3,613	200	0	6	1,695	84
Tennessee	534,145	238,481	35,890	19,655	43,759	21,620	39,500	37,520	1,034	1,173	33,674	4,656
Texas	1,107,392	461,771	102,180	3,899	66,650	30,205	86,362	84,707	27,112	94	51,852	8,710
Utah	137,015	45,257	13,152	549	4,688	2,294	13,130	6,019	1,163	0	3,862	400
Vermont	51,688	17,905	4,871	602	1,462	2,244	6,104	676	90	0	1,802	54
Virginia	413,597	208,765	40,758	35,963	20,400	17,747	40,669	20,625	511	9,472	21,358	1,262
Washington	368,236	117,582	43,352	1,131	9,561	16,994	28,749	5,782	2,239	0	8,683	1,091
West Virginia	86,064	34,663	5,142	1,131	2,278	1,328	5,630	15,241	547	210	2,457	699
Wisconsin	620,682	242,246	67,588	3,012	7,231	52,489	56,442	14,209	351	11	35,355	5,558
Wyoming	13,103	6,729	1,088	12	270	22	1,935	2,176	811	0	243	172

Percent Change in Nondurable Manufacturing Employment 1990 to 1996

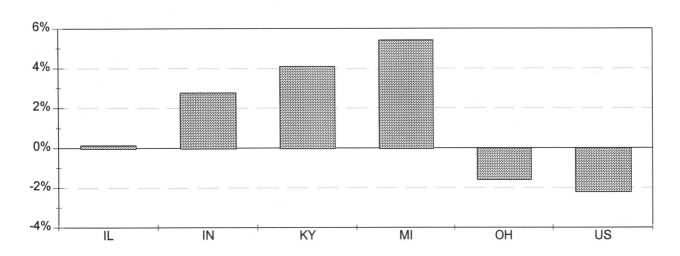

Source: U.S. Bureau of Economic Analysis
EDIN table(s): EMMA

1.37 Employment by Industry: Manufacturing - Durable Goods 1996

	Durable Goods	Lumber and Wood	Furniture and Fixtures	Primary Metal Industries	Fabricated Metal	Machinery Except Electrical	Electric and Electronic Equip.	Transport. Eq. Except Motor Vehicles	Motor Vehicles and Equip.	Stone, Clay, and Glass	Instruments and Related Products
United States	11,238,500	914,500	533,800	711,500	1,501,600	2,171,200	1,686,000	828,700	967,800	580,300	855,800
Alabama	203,901	42,378	12,253	26,101	23,590	30,965	22,558	13,953	12,672	9,808	3,268
Alaska	4,569	2,449	109	13	469	192	53	269	7	500	43
Arizona	158,223	10,176	5,187	7,806	13,600	14,255	46,419	27,047	5,903	9,153	12,232
Arkansas	139,709	26,851	10,567	10,557	18,900	19,501	21,408	6,031	10,066	5,938	5,104
California	1,199,475	60,871	55,088	35,036	128,124	222,458	249,438	128,952	33,719	50,247	174,398
Colorado	130,667	6,819	5,549	2,887	13,790	31,919	19,622	9,253	2,629	10,406	20,512
Connecticut	199,725	3,180	2,578	9,163	34,859	36,437	28,723	47,601	3,074	3,281	22,905
Delaware	14,372	528	517	1,475	1,991	1,466	NA	NA	3,399	835	3,262
Dist. Of Col.	2,101	33	77	32	47	120	NA	NA	36	122	41
Florida	305,823	23,995	14,221	6,195	33,663	38,967	63,212	43,725	8,214	23,520	36,789
Georgia	246,866	43,668	11,669	14,339	25,028	36,235	33,709	27,190	15,918	20,192	10,701
Hawaii	5,182	644	454	8	552	229	101	521	18	1,300	44
Idaho	49,086	16,913	1,427	258	3,404	10,619	10,135	1,534	943	1,691	518
Illinois	*594,275*	*14,905*	*16,394*	*45,735*	*110,336*	*155,734*	*119,800*	*12,584*	*37,186*	*22,587*	*33,652*
Indiana	**493,009**	**31,448**	**25,873**	**67,392**	**62,958**	**76,019**	**65,020**	**23,482**	**89,799**	**19,097**	**19,194**
Percent U.S.	4.39	3.44	4.85	9.47	4.19	3.50	3.86	2.83	9.28	3.29	2.24
Rank	8	12	6	3	8	9	7	13	3	11	13
Iowa	146,592	11,699	6,355	8,281	18,952	44,482	26,318	NA	11,825	7,185	NA
Kansas	116,786	5,507	1,921	3,692	10,463	24,049	8,906	40,256	8,876	6,576	4,142
Kentucky	*183,167*	*17,698*	*5,397*	*17,558*	*23,012*	*36,625*	*26,384*	*4,567*	*30,460*	*11,734*	*4,122*
Louisiana	90,514	16,135	899	2,846	14,552	15,729	5,402	19,870	3,398	6,618	1,504
Maine	49,328	15,441	1,550	519	3,568	4,616	7,657	11,048	368	1,739	1,041
Maryland	89,475	4,709	3,624	8,069	8,855	16,869	13,107	5,141	4,975	6,979	14,281
Massachusetts	286,761	5,341	5,088	10,176	37,599	66,252	62,015	17,393	1,619	9,081	53,652
Michigan	*742,354*	*21,583*	*38,343*	*36,765*	*130,070*	*136,922*	*33,806*	*10,516*	*285,600*	*19,554*	*17,951*
Minnesota	257,714	23,714	7,404	7,212	36,111	75,546	33,839	7,783	6,388	10,304	38,643
Mississippi	152,191	32,158	26,960	4,523	13,761	18,781	22,871	14,951	7,316	5,699	1,687
Missouri	247,094	16,228	14,693	12,730	36,224	39,184	31,936	30,548	33,616	12,039	9,767
Montana	19,024	9,450	672	1,068	1,073	1,907	277	295	216	1,291	427
Nebraska	56,444	NA	3,411	1,781	8,451	13,399	10,717	NA	3,752	3,123	5,256
Nevada	26,184	1,945	909	1,152	3,859	3,159	2,991	725	318	3,661	2,358
New Hampshire	76,101	6,403	1,194	4,484	8,696	19,065	18,878	844	421	2,106	11,259
New Jersey	198,640	4,170	6,254	11,676	32,495	35,869	34,158	3,614	6,981	17,492	30,371
New Mexico	35,484	2,518	931	1,487	2,125	2,448	11,334	1,765	1,169	3,688	3,187
New York	505,857	18,097	16,830	19,799	55,830	100,410	84,436	10,204	32,099	26,487	97,034
North Carolina	393,662	47,079	78,341	16,863	34,450	71,639	62,372	5,205	28,574	23,974	14,917
North Dakota	13,203	NA	NA	NA	1,421	4,739	1,212	540	1,533	789	NA
Ohio	*755,741*	*32,844*	*16,832*	*95,453*	*133,239*	*168,905*	*76,636*	*26,196*	*113,204*	*44,896*	*27,312*
Oklahoma	116,905	5,563	3,042	5,298	22,402	32,493	10,656	7,123	11,930	9,567	4,464
Oregon	182,892	57,951	4,346	11,074	15,291	23,246	31,534	7,573	8,294	5,875	10,578
Pennsylvania	553,869	40,194	17,823	74,502	87,229	107,596	76,055	32,419	18,065	39,927	36,185
Rhode Island	54,468	914	1,936	4,958	7,232	4,532	5,795	2,474	453	1,400	5,229
South Carolina	149,437	17,078	4,991	8,699	18,570	38,796	24,926	3,838	13,630	9,797	4,844
South Dakota	33,107	3,426	NA	NA	2,012	13,764	4,164	158	1,639	1,316	1,949
Tennessee	295,664	26,459	29,594	16,656	45,036	44,282	40,742	10,522	41,071	17,197	10,609
Texas	645,621	49,038	20,015	29,858	99,890	139,703	121,631	58,924	16,880	42,010	42,552
Utah	91,758	5,785	4,162	6,986	9,537	12,949	8,249	10,057	7,591	5,254	10,114
Vermont	33,783	5,674	2,463	916	2,645	4,286	9,466	1,869	563	2,532	1,455
Virginia	204,832	28,876	21,456	10,201	19,145	27,294	31,760	26,369	12,198	12,921	10,187
Washington	250,654	41,234	4,891	11,512	14,893	25,650	15,793	95,528	5,305	10,404	13,664
West Virginia	51,401	11,682	857	12,367	6,187	5,757	1,824	2,512	731	6,479	1,777
Wisconsin	378,436	36,889	17,183	24,059	64,775	113,792	46,457	8,910	23,092	11,060	18,341
Wyoming	6,374	1,900	193	337	639	1,349	239	274	67	869	131

Percent Change in Durable Manufacturing Employment
1990 to 1996

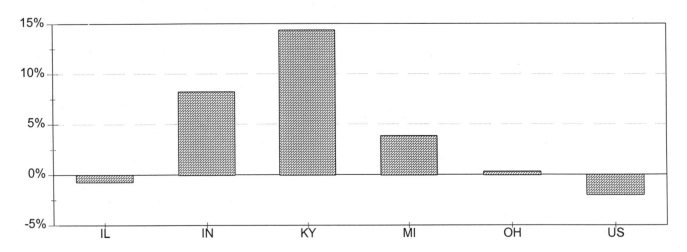

Source: U.S. Bureau of Economic Analysis
EDIN table(s): EMMA

1.38 Employment by Industry: Transportation and Public Utilities 1996

	Total	←—————————————————————————————— Transportation —————————————————————————————→							←— Public Utilities —→	
		Railroad Trans.	Trucking and Warehousing	Water Transport.	Other Transport.	Local and Inter-urban Passenger	Air Transport.	Pipelines Except Natural Gas	Transport. Services	Communication	Electric Gas and Sanitary
United States	7,209,300	224,000	2,195,900	186,500	2,241,100	551,000	1,140,100	14,000	536,000	1,438,300	923,500
Alabama	104,553	3,758	43,819	NA	NA	NA	6,846	68	3,524	22,179	17,501
Alaska	27,405	0	4,145	2,249	13,707	2,515	8,086	978	2,128	4,033	3,271
Arizona	105,518	2,245	27,469	325	39,951	6,463	25,323	192	7,973	22,500	13,028
Arkansas	76,124	3,986	40,119	625	10,571	2,088	5,989	220	2,274	10,730	10,093
California	759,886	13,640	210,718	20,292	269,046	51,742	134,692	1,386	81,226	162,195	83,995
Colorado	136,124	4,483	31,597	199	39,277	6,522	23,337	119	9,299	43,756	16,812
Connecticut	83,025	NA	16,741	2,272	NA	13,566	9,579	NA	7,489	19,096	13,628
Delaware	17,292	NA	5,565	808	NA	2,110	1,370	NA	866	2,282	3,164
Dist. Of Col.	22,123	NA	1,282	229	NA	2,773	1,020	NA	1,874	9,170	3,607
Florida	366,215	7,841	89,088	21,987	133,133	20,767	70,753	124	41,489	78,344	35,822
Georgia	247,475	6,778	69,718	3,656	76,498	8,270	51,108	441	16,679	65,808	25,017
Hawaii	45,862	0	4,402	4,085	26,913	7,081	12,213	0	7,619	6,700	3,762
Idaho	29,186	1,804	13,067	243	5,853	1,481	2,809	21	1,542	4,027	4,192
Illinois	*373,017*	*17,372*	*106,731*	*4,248*	*137,114*	*30,731*	*69,845*	*508*	*36,030*	*61,855*	*45,697*
Indiana	162,382	6,424	76,182	2,362	33,422	7,819	19,232	262	6,109	21,816	22,176
Percent U.S.	*2.25*	*2.87*	*3.47*	*1.27*	*1.49*	*1.42*	*1.69*	*1.87*	*1.14*	*1.52*	*2.40*
Rank	*15*	*13*	*8*	*19*	*20*	*21*	*21*	*12*	*26*	*22*	*13*
Iowa	76,907	3,604	37,837	583	11,948	2,519	6,027	130	3,272	12,705	10,230
Kansas	79,536	7,130	27,407	98	15,458	3,874	6,820	630	4,134	17,683	11,760
Kentucky	*108,393*	*4,560*	*36,070*	*3,366*	*35,269*	*4,089*	*26,858*	*81*	*4,241*	*13,930*	*15,198*
Louisiana	123,061	3,450	32,131	25,015	23,688	8,229	8,414	764	6,281	18,953	19,824
Maine	29,131	NA	11,326	NA	NA	2,267	2,147	NA	1,369	5,115	4,983
Maryland	125,467	NA	34,308	4,562	NA	13,865	14,555	NA	8,407	31,900	15,297
Massachusetts	152,584	2,739	31,982	NA	NA	24,034	22,190	NA	13,924	31,245	23,414
Michigan	*193,796*	*5,769*	*59,970*	*2,377*	*57,307*	*9,286*	*29,579*	*260*	*18,182*	*32,998*	*35,375*
Minnesota	142,068	6,001	42,433	1,134	54,233	13,814	29,408	310	10,701	21,925	16,342
Mississippi	61,854	1,739	26,546	2,558	9,390	1,860	5,422	188	1,920	11,250	10,371
Missouri	186,476	7,925	66,364	2,144	48,097	11,728	25,040	164	11,165	40,407	21,539
Montana	25,552	2,954	8,729	68	5,583	1,672	2,395	87	1,429	3,917	4,301
Nebraska	58,633	10,340	26,712	67	9,116	2,236	4,416	80	2,384	9,206	3,192
Nevada	47,173	799	9,011	NA	NA	8,038	9,337	NA	3,431	8,187	7,943
New Hampshire	24,916	393	6,936	NA	NA	3,150	2,875	NA	1,553	4,827	4,866
New Jersey	277,685	1,949	73,048	9,535	98,220	36,739	39,637	136	21,708	68,598	26,335
New Mexico	37,081	1,843	9,858	66	10,329	3,284	5,083	169	1,793	7,304	7,681
New York	475,550	7,397	86,166	9,067	203,872	85,978	77,989	100	39,805	112,458	56,590
North Carolina	189,650	2,636	75,084	1,805	47,509	6,187	31,481	101	9,740	35,673	26,943
North Dakota	23,023	1,929	8,575	26	4,325	1,355	1,387	83	1,500	3,516	4,652
Ohio	*274,393*	*9,008*	*106,097*	*3,701*	*68,705*	*14,133*	*35,299*	*531*	*18,742*	*46,511*	*40,371*
Oklahoma	90,555	1,736	32,450	382	23,722	1,845	17,815	971	3,091	17,649	14,616
Oregon	85,387	2,728	33,245	NA	NA	5,431	11,152	NA	6,703	13,899	9,828
Pennsylvania	315,659	13,732	93,110	4,333	99,600	36,851	45,132	600	17,017	52,966	51,918
Rhode Island	17,957	228	4,707	668	6,023	2,753	1,897	0	1,373	3,604	2,727
South Carolina	82,796	1,878	31,671	3,289	15,429	NA	7,524	NA	5,164	15,708	14,821
South Dakota	21,285	699	10,179	76	3,955	1,427	1,740	45	743	3,745	2,631
Tennessee	165,774	4,853	69,315	NA	NA	8,054	41,586	NA	8,024	22,674	8,873
Texas	561,586	15,151	165,019	16,544	173,388	23,640	104,483	3,483	41,782	116,966	74,518
Utah	59,349	2,076	21,068	80	17,899	1,651	12,686	56	3,506	9,529	8,697
Vermont	14,664	205	5,133	220	3,704	1,500	1,274	0	930	2,878	2,524
Virginia	183,348	7,414	50,098	6,059	51,751	12,151	27,647	77	11,876	47,119	20,907
Washington	140,743	4,670	40,397	10,115	45,744	7,239	23,591	93	14,821	29,556	10,261
West Virginia	44,848	3,607	15,368	1,106	4,757	1,612	2,127	25	993	8,625	11,385
Wisconsin	139,833	4,244	61,846	1,153	36,792	17,420	11,802	100	7,470	18,475	17,323
Wyoming	16,400	3,017	5,061	61	2,654	674	1,083	192	705	2,108	3,499

Percent Change in Transportation and Public Utilities Employment 1990 to 1996

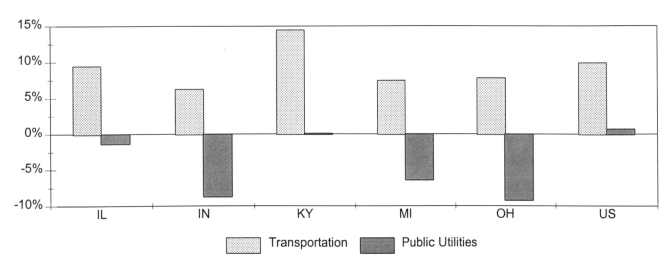

Transportation   Public Utilities

Source: U.S. Bureau of Economic Analysis
EDIN table(s): EMTR

1.39 Employment by Industry: Wholesale and Retail 1996

	Wholesale	Retail Total	Building Materials & Farm Eq.	General Merchandise Stores	Food Stores	Auto Dealers & Service Stations	Apparel & Accessory Stores	Furniture & Home Furnishings	Eating & Drinking Places	Misc. Retail
United States	7,013,200	25,704,900	1,022,700	2,815,700	3,736,900	2,548,100	1,281,900	1,133,900	8,084,800	5,080,900
Alabama	100,813	389,006	16,509	47,995	58,411	47,719	20,276	15,669	114,798	67,629
Alaska	9,881	58,846	2,242	8,095	7,693	5,758	1,706	1,864	16,914	14,574
Arizona	111,309	434,194	15,519	42,621	58,305	47,770	15,942	22,750	145,102	86,185
Arkansas	53,047	242,231	10,652	44,713	33,516	27,841	8,770	8,782	67,272	40,685
California	832,188	2,801,315	93,644	260,032	354,499	251,304	157,104	143,494	930,125	611,113
Colorado	108,676	452,084	18,552	42,191	52,648	40,829	17,789	20,109	156,246	103,720
Connecticut	87,811	316,465	12,347	30,249	55,826	29,406	19,988	14,613	83,005	71,031
Delaware	15,073	78,974	3,377	8,829	11,079	7,443	3,971	3,763	24,586	15,926
Dist. Of Col.	5,446	49,058	690	1,821	5,340	1,338	3,508	1,075	26,871	8,415
Florida	363,866	1,461,640	55,784	158,215	252,336	139,145	75,879	68,586	462,939	248,756
Georgia	250,867	755,365	32,796	86,267	111,416	77,057	39,299	35,131	252,470	120,929
Hawaii	25,300	137,891	2,668	13,267	15,546	9,553	10,534	4,017	49,822	32,484
Idaho	31,594	123,510	6,849	11,110	18,587	13,876	3,993	5,622	36,995	26,478
Illinois	361,790	1,115,213	49,428	133,950	145,766	99,821	60,092	50,353	360,761	215,042
Indiana	148,460	635,935	29,489	81,595	76,036	67,217	22,931	23,398	206,364	128,905
Percent U.S.	2.12	2.47	2.88	2.90	2.03	2.64	1.79	2.06	2.55	2.54
Rank	18	13	11	11	16	13	18	17	11	12
Iowa	88,692	318,655	15,803	34,004	46,382	39,140	12,737	12,254	94,267	64,068
Kansas	80,507	280,805	12,137	32,610	37,227	29,350	12,475	11,861	87,226	57,919
Kentucky	86,764	378,178	16,871	47,220	57,990	42,652	14,526	15,554	118,876	64,489
Louisiana	98,424	385,419	15,075	47,294	63,482	41,457	17,380	13,971	124,755	62,005
Maine	28,753	138,257	5,859	12,696	22,073	14,363	5,641	4,080	38,063	35,482
Maryland	115,533	485,742	20,332	48,477	71,480	47,541	24,757	24,575	148,524	100,056
Massachusetts	180,113	610,329	19,934	46,594	101,548	48,238	41,894	25,750	196,855	129,516
Michigan	235,243	935,551	40,640	133,451	115,349	93,464	40,343	38,300	300,374	173,630
Minnesota	159,780	523,568	21,702	64,769	64,438	55,024	20,843	24,405	158,610	113,777
Mississippi	47,895	226,525	10,615	33,284	36,933	28,882	9,603	8,597	63,203	35,408
Missouri	156,786	556,763	23,614	69,358	66,975	67,436	23,148	21,573	181,939	102,720
Montana	19,922	102,596	5,050	9,352	11,997	12,880	3,012	4,136	34,346	21,823
Nebraska	56,387	193,889	8,542	20,267	26,474	20,856	7,269	8,145	57,856	44,480
Nevada	35,610	162,695	5,801	16,661	20,524	17,709	8,387	7,340	52,507	33,766
New Hampshire	29,948	139,598	5,929	15,034	22,680	13,950	6,861	5,999	38,026	31,119
New Jersey	284,779	668,543	22,795	67,811	120,417	60,815	52,198	33,620	176,151	134,736
New Mexico	31,153	165,417	6,716	16,003	19,766	19,502	6,049	7,016	56,626	33,739
New York	456,779	1,394,910	48,660	134,463	240,543	103,029	103,531	62,216	411,551	290,917
North Carolina	192,841	748,552	37,327	83,857	115,203	76,248	34,711	37,466	234,105	129,635
North Dakota	22,550	74,886	3,543	8,090	8,698	10,001	2,524	2,739	23,197	16,094
Ohio	304,759	1,174,810	46,369	131,842	172,607	114,381	48,314	48,319	382,915	230,063
Oklahoma	70,647	316,404	12,038	35,275	41,819	36,912	13,198	13,109	100,313	63,740
Oregon	96,612	340,930	14,414	36,262	44,890	37,046	15,216	13,422	110,440	69,240
Pennsylvania	283,377	1,125,962	44,454	127,361	191,215	108,295	57,599	43,132	322,611	231,295
Rhode Island	20,133	91,619	2,539	7,189	16,460	7,770	4,245	2,533	30,540	20,343
South Carolina	72,741	386,722	17,062	40,128	66,734	38,895	18,475	16,869	126,122	62,437
South Dakota	21,278	87,504	4,326	8,752	10,776	11,369	2,709	3,302	26,537	19,733
Tennessee	151,924	545,921	22,319	65,803	77,808	59,948	27,126	22,013	170,028	100,876
Texas	518,583	1,824,404	64,134	215,645	272,227	183,985	89,071	79,369	579,541	340,432
Utah	52,991	217,368	9,354	22,669	29,790	23,288	9,223	12,202	64,514	46,328
Vermont	14,045	64,957	2,922	3,664	11,155	6,977	2,760	2,134	18,433	16,912
Virginia	153,684	660,810	25,305	73,332	96,382	70,815	31,123	36,235	200,376	127,242
Washington	157,988	552,121	24,946	48,599	76,934	51,925	26,754	24,165	175,434	123,364
West Virginia	32,324	156,407	7,136	18,944	26,280	19,699	5,130	5,915	46,250	27,053
Wisconsin	139,274	558,623	25,649	62,595	68,690	59,655	19,318	20,500	180,537	121,679
Wyoming	8,260	57,733	2,242	5,395	5,950	8,526	1,968	1,858	18,882	12,912

Percent Change in Retail and Wholesale Employment 1990 to 1996

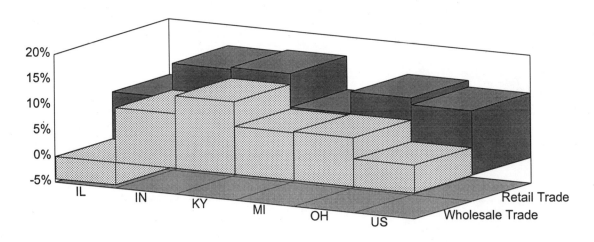

Source: U.S. Bureau of Economic Analysis
EDIN table(s): EMRT

1.40 Employment by Industry: Finance, Insurance, and Real Estate 1996

	Total Finance, Insurance & Real Estate	←————Finance————			←———Insurance——→		←————Real Estate————→	
		Banking and Credit	Other Finance, Insurance & Real Estate	Security & Commodity Brokers	Carriers	Agents, Brokers & Services	Real Estate	Holding, Other Investment Companies
United States	11,282,900	2,557,900	8,725,000	695,300	1,503,000	1,388,800	3,914,400	1,223,500
Alabama	109,724	36,177	73,547	2,792	15,671	16,174	28,969	9,941
Alaska	18,776	4,468	14,308	435	949	1,876	5,753	5,295
Arizona	189,517	49,631	139,886	7,500	19,530	23,384	64,618	24,854
Arkansas	65,163	18,576	46,587	2,732	6,349	11,654	19,004	6,848
California	1,383,768	277,154	1,106,614	74,110	133,221	161,848	564,590	172,845
Colorado	202,408	38,183	164,225	11,868	24,718	22,467	64,978	40,194
Connecticut	187,774	32,205	155,569	11,483	60,894	19,751	38,714	24,727
Delaware	54,332	28,952	25,380	1,834	5,513	2,921	7,513	7,599
Dist. Of Col.	35,633	8,203	27,430	2,897	4,002	1,319	12,530	6,682
Florida	640,893	136,338	504,555	31,754	75,001	82,209	262,204	53,387
Georgia	282,745	71,880	210,865	9,949	39,378	39,680	97,821	24,037
Hawaii	62,653	12,976	49,677	1,040	4,509	6,491	30,261	7,376
Idaho	36,688	9,332	27,356	1,153	3,753	5,968	12,090	4,392
Illinois	*607,667*	*140,080*	*467,587*	*61,374*	*102,409*	*67,501*	*171,751*	*64,552*
Indiana	200,926	56,839	144,087	6,225	33,402	28,686	65,617	10,157
Percent U.S.	*1.78*	*2.22*	*1.65*	*0.90*	*2.22*	*2.07*	*1.68*	*0.83*
Rank	*21*	*14*	*22*	*23*	*15*	*16*	*19*	*29*
Iowa	111,447	29,680	81,767	3,596	27,770	21,996	20,307	8,098
Kansas	91,624	23,814	67,810	3,628	13,471	18,875	21,611	10,225
Kentucky	*95,846*	*31,601*	*64,245*	*4,682*	*10,209*	*17,017*	*25,684*	*6,653*
Louisiana	117,355	36,214	81,141	3,287	13,528	25,216	27,403	11,707
Maine	41,958	10,973	30,985	1,114	7,659	6,039	14,297	1,876
Maryland	229,722	47,677	182,045	11,497	26,629	23,264	97,077	23,578
Massachusetts	310,215	65,824	244,391	42,699	50,755	34,050	92,046	24,841
Michigan	*355,907*	*84,087*	*271,820*	*11,222*	*43,956*	*42,174*	*127,607*	*46,861*
Minnesota	232,168	46,103	186,065	16,907	41,004	30,443	76,207	21,504
Mississippi	65,468	21,149	44,319	1,366	6,911	12,407	18,939	4,696
Missouri	221,758	56,274	165,484	18,382	31,083	30,952	68,383	16,684
Montana	31,168	7,049	24,119	1,270	2,228	5,405	11,999	3,217
Nebraska	79,352	18,876	60,476	3,018	17,018	15,175	19,328	5,937
Nevada	68,085	13,949	54,136	1,704	5,103	7,172	27,792	12,365
New Hampshire	48,288	8,161	40,127	1,806	9,802	6,218	18,641	3,660
New Jersey	420,663	68,957	351,706	37,873	59,533	42,639	165,678	45,983
New Mexico	53,507	13,718	39,789	1,534	4,225	7,077	20,907	6,046
New York	1,076,088	226,171	849,917	178,850	120,951	91,666	339,690	118,760
North Carolina	255,838	71,847	183,991	8,336	30,490	32,916	94,712	17,537
North Dakota	24,502	6,695	17,807	864	3,068	5,165	7,683	1,027
Ohio	*452,498*	*108,142*	*344,356*	*15,901*	*67,727*	*55,074*	*162,080*	*43,574*
Oklahoma	103,283	27,294	75,989	2,730	11,671	18,037	30,089	13,462
Oregon	122,369	29,321	93,048	4,524	16,310	16,356	43,139	12,719
Pennsylvania	498,068	117,074	380,994	21,580	95,322	58,911	150,901	54,280
Rhode Island	40,909	8,974	31,935	1,356	6,973	4,533	15,231	3,842
South Carolina	121,747	29,509	92,238	2,466	14,875	16,330	48,496	10,071
South Dakota	33,781	11,972	21,809	995	2,516	6,588	8,915	2,795
Tennessee	212,589	49,549	163,040	6,299	24,007	25,779	89,765	17,190
Texas	793,746	155,772	637,974	27,570	90,157	109,310	292,233	118,704
Utah	91,887	24,427	67,460	2,460	8,359	12,149	27,164	17,328
Vermont	21,704	5,313	16,391	595	2,604	2,949	8,611	1,632
Virginia	272,062	71,823	200,239	9,112	30,277	27,679	108,685	24,486
Washington	232,453	45,085	187,368	9,157	26,927	25,376	101,514	24,394
West Virginia	40,130	12,333	27,797	858	3,838	7,112	13,113	2,876
Wisconsin	217,241	48,129	169,112	8,386	45,402	32,375	65,359	17,590
Wyoming	18,807	3,370	15,437	530	1,343	2,447	6,701	4,416

Percent Change in Finance, Insurance and Real Estate Employment 1990 to 1996

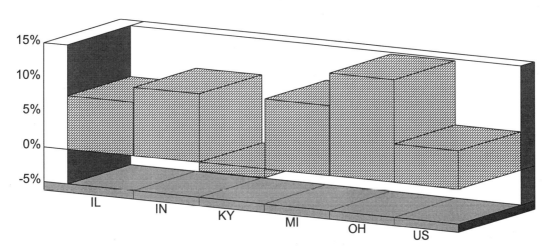

Source: U.S. Bureau of Economic Analysis
EDIN table(s): EMFI

1.41 Employment by Industry: Services 1996

	Total	Hotels and Other Lodging	Personal Services	Private Households	Business Services	Auto Repair and Garages	Misc. Repair Services	Amusement, Recreation & Motion Pictures	Health Services	Legal Services	Education Services	Social Services	Other Misc. Services
United States	46,364,800	1,927,200	2,814,400	1,246,000	9,732,600	1,684,100	730,700	3,081,700	10,788,000	1,465,700	2,682,000	2,535,000	7,677,400
Alabama	558,953	16,503	41,198	23,246	108,041	24,746	12,283	25,423	141,802	17,771	24,374	24,016	99,550
Alaska	98,750	8,254	5,985	1,706	15,083	4,237	2,366	8,024	16,497	2,685	3,890	7,070	22,953
Arizona	767,670	47,324	48,769	17,524	190,636	33,697	12,910	49,867	151,943	18,839	25,485	37,885	132,791
Arkansas	338,415	13,092	25,311	10,598	63,281	15,913	7,575	16,992	98,596	7,772	11,539	22,696	45,050
California	5,914,961	211,769	362,487	223,024	1,378,764	230,441	92,927	572,945	1,046,898	195,896	325,335	249,314	1,025,161
Colorado	810,509	43,936	52,135	16,472	201,297	30,963	12,455	64,742	145,773	24,928	33,029	35,721	152,058
Connecticut	670,881	12,159	37,323	13,269	132,745	18,187	7,947	47,209	176,989	23,376	57,646	41,524	102,507
Delaware	126,924	2,771	6,956	2,909	29,897	4,087	1,934	8,132	30,516	4,512	6,014	9,152	20,044
Dist. Of Col.	308,704	16,555	6,183	7,749	48,103	3,606	495	6,659	40,306	34,374	34,997	15,706	93,971
Florida	2,678,127	157,315	150,310	77,264	644,928	95,076	43,303	202,974	629,204	81,596	87,481	119,865	388,811
Georgia	1,183,780	47,539	73,374	38,585	309,600	47,965	17,736	64,588	252,400	35,638	65,181	46,629	184,545
Hawaii	229,008	41,160	14,779	2,741	36,048	8,677	3,245	19,713	40,549	6,793	14,321	11,312	29,670
Idaho	177,676	9,594	12,909	3,909	29,818	8,920	4,541	12,336	36,991	4,363	8,564	10,407	35,324
Illinois	*2,125,978*	*58,915*	*122,300*	*38,420*	*478,419*	*75,985*	*33,506*	*128,419*	*483,112*	*75,761*	*124,931*	*116,228*	*389,982*
Indiana	881,337	25,073	66,303	18,510	168,252	38,055	16,138	52,253	237,931	21,081	59,019	47,386	131,336
Percent U.S.	1.90	1.30	2.36	1.49	1.73	2.26	2.21	1.70	2.21	1.44	2.20	1.87	1.71
Rank	18	26	14	21	21	13	14	21	14	22	13	18	22
Iowa	485,868	15,168	32,848	11,547	91,951	19,503	10,380	35,696	121,901	11,045	31,497	33,752	70,580
Kansas	425,538	11,376	31,095	9,622	83,870	16,301	10,273	22,508	111,112	10,109	18,836	24,405	76,031
Kentucky	*538,052*	*17,524*	*37,989*	*16,522*	*100,493*	*23,623*	*9,741*	*29,576*	*158,283*	*16,354*	*26,413*	*25,573*	*75,961*
Louisiana	654,195	25,909	41,201	27,926	110,189	23,073	13,681	51,232	178,385	27,447	34,969	31,127	89,056
Maine	216,839	12,331	12,733	5,685	31,783	8,463	4,104	12,906	58,948	5,293	13,649	18,680	32,264
Maryland	954,660	26,359	52,552	26,569	210,453	29,297	12,238	52,415	219,884	28,708	54,882	54,467	186,836
Massachusetts	1,443,816	36,658	69,214	18,727	278,643	36,810	14,987	69,710	374,171	47,614	167,657	83,895	245,730
Michigan	*1,530,673*	*42,256*	*97,489*	*30,290*	*334,109*	*58,160*	*24,085*	*90,339*	*402,993*	*39,375*	*60,658*	*93,029*	*257,890*
Minnesota	920,451	33,152	54,120	13,651	190,688	31,853	13,365	71,913	213,835	25,365	50,575	67,967	153,967
Mississippi	335,965	22,070	22,262	17,148	49,729	13,459	8,130	35,073	82,526	10,211	16,155	14,124	45,078
Missouri	943,538	35,169	61,434	19,295	177,092	38,503	15,312	63,478	244,819	26,440	68,121	49,442	144,433
Montana	156,989	11,285	10,455	3,660	22,254	7,290	3,482	13,023	37,269	3,923	6,763	10,465	27,120
Nebraska	312,864	8,416	21,771	7,078	78,983	12,410	5,994	17,432	70,818	7,313	18,708	14,292	49,649
Nevada	439,494	195,392	20,476	4,486	57,207	11,818	4,103	38,158	45,709	7,174	4,364	7,915	42,692
New Hampshire	223,512	10,523	13,864	3,394	41,906	8,387	3,747	15,111	53,960	5,543	18,914	15,045	33,118
New Jersey	1,419,443	80,337	74,307	25,651	324,373	41,541	16,766	72,747	354,757	52,611	71,277	63,983	241,093
New Mexico	268,494	16,517	16,324	7,876	45,052	11,004	4,881	16,226	54,835	7,026	10,609	15,037	63,107
New York	3,466,159	84,207	167,691	112,613	613,996	82,669	35,227	232,851	860,626	162,828	323,396	304,992	485,063
North Carolina	1,092,581	39,004	77,297	29,719	259,405	44,784	20,767	60,368	246,068	24,625	48,352	66,971	175,221
North Dakota	121,300	5,941	8,390	2,343	17,373	4,580	2,253	7,728	36,539	2,251	4,851	9,831	19,220
Ohio	*1,838,391*	*40,767*	*119,315*	*32,138*	*377,879*	*67,590*	*27,702*	*105,266*	*511,121*	*52,150*	*100,168*	*103,224*	*301,071*
Oklahoma	509,699	12,742	39,255	15,456	106,760	26,476	9,708	25,456	126,767	14,295	19,027	27,627	86,130
Oregon	564,113	24,894	35,728	12,977	121,609	23,478	10,672	40,084	117,747	15,729	28,004	38,759	94,432
Pennsylvania	2,112,097	58,309	115,612	34,985	344,046	73,257	28,443	107,063	611,138	68,227	197,250	142,571	331,196
Rhode Island	189,451	4,216	10,178	2,444	35,471	5,243	2,268	9,250	55,921	5,814	18,393	13,756	26,497
South Carolina	504,835	27,662	37,809	19,891	116,209	21,580	12,103	31,696	89,616	15,129	22,115	29,035	81,990
South Dakota	133,172	8,588	8,832	2,875	16,703	5,168	2,972	11,456	37,135	2,633	7,114	8,763	20,933
Tennessee	879,019	40,981	59,944	22,387	189,174	33,072	15,192	55,214	218,909	19,970	41,842	33,004	149,330
Texas	3,069,567	99,622	202,201	124,141	711,027	128,434	56,291	167,799	718,084	99,888	118,313	119,712	524,055
Utah	360,785	17,013	23,991	4,916	83,518	14,553	5,952	26,663	69,588	7,206	27,917	13,164	66,304
Vermont	121,277	12,031	6,352	2,970	17,089	4,139	2,181	7,684	29,962	2,767	12,718	5,871	17,513
Virginia	1,175,451	50,171	72,154	37,305	280,473	37,795	16,175	62,421	227,097	30,259	54,650	52,626	254,325
Washington	926,536	33,174	57,397	20,602	183,019	36,198	17,298	70,128	202,890	28,160	43,756	57,295	176,619
West Virginia	236,140	10,330	16,506	6,835	33,375	8,840	5,393	11,278	*72,613*	*8,101*	*10,457*	*18,073*	34,339
Wisconsin	845,334	34,673	53,091	14,450	150,652	30,531	13,385	55,441	230,414	19,719	45,524	65,956	131,498
Wyoming	76,829	10,474	6,201	1,900	11,135	3,663	2,088	6,035	12,053	2,013	2,300	5,661	13,306

Percent Change in Service Industry Employment
1990 to 1996

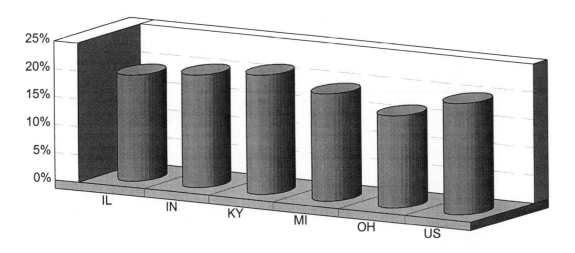

Source: U.S. Bureau of Economic Analysis
EDIN table(s): EMSE

1.42 Employment by Industry: Mining and Government 1996

	Mining					Government			
	Total	Coal Mining	Oil & Gas Extraction	Metal Mining	Nonmetallic Minerals Exc. Fuels		Total	Federal Civilian	Military	State And Local
United States	880,300	100,900	604,500	60,500	114,400		21,693,000	2,878,000	2,245,000	16,570,000
Alabama	12,311	6,659	NA	NA	2,796		380,781	53,191	45,784	281,806
Alaska	11,189	NA	8,871	1,854	NA		93,995	17,050	24,348	52,597
Arizona	17,064	887	2,633	12,126	1,418		334,652	42,386	34,206	258,060
Arkansas	6,774	NA	NA	NA	1,571		196,607	20,837	20,004	155,766
California	45,502	84	35,586	3,858	5,974		2,390,523	289,827	259,770	1,840,926
Colorado	24,805	2,263	18,188	2,737	1,617		354,375	54,173	44,191	256,011
Connecticut	1,957	2	1,159	9	787		229,307	23,307	19,281	186,719
Delaware	119	NA	29	NA	NA		63,178	5,712	9,647	47,819
Dist. Of Col.	378	NA	360	NA	NA		260,387	190,226	25,223	44,938
Florida	13,751	26	6,930	216	6,579		1,032,043	118,260	116,221	797,562
Georgia	9,442	8	1,494	23	7,917		661,788	95,650	94,693	471,445
Hawaii	488	0	NA	4	NA		166,879	30,828	57,943	78,108
Idaho	3,897	7	444	2,138	1,308		104,575	12,706	9,526	82,343
Illinois	*23,760*	*6,241*	*13,216*	*112*	*4,191*		*868,013*	*99,611*	*60,200*	*708,202*
Indiana	**9,614**	**2,885**	**3,442**	**17**	**3,270**		**412,878**	**40,549**	**23,330**	**348,999**
Percent U.S.	*1.09*	*2.86*	*0.57*	*0.03*	*2.86*		*1.90*	*1.41*	*1.04*	*2.11*
Rank	*21*	*10*	*19*	*30*	*12*		*17*	*23*	*30*	*15*
Iowa	2,872	NA	NA	4	2,165		243,350	20,553	14,075	208,722
Kansas	23,157	93	21,731	9	1,324		271,429	28,714	30,375	212,340
Kentucky	*26,760*	*19,878*	*4,146*	*15*	*2,721*		*322,941*	*38,619*	*48,573*	*235,749*
Louisiana	59,219	NA	57,034	NA	1,907		399,654	35,439	44,495	319,720
Maine	330	NA	NA	15	146		101,942	12,606	11,230	78,106
Maryland	2,672	552	1,452	4	664		502,671	151,717	56,167	294,787
Massachusetts	2,386	10	NA	NA	1,301		432,404	54,695	27,164	350,545
Michigan	*14,152*	*3*	*9,100*	*2,251*	*2,798*		*650,984*	*56,552*	*24,568*	*569,864*
Minnesota	9,287	11	1,282	5,987	2,007		376,598	33,637	20,508	322,453
Mississippi	8,943	2	8,118	4	819		251,534	26,379	36,536	188,619
Missouri	7,374	NA	2,364	NA	3,441		438,511	62,298	41,674	334,539
Montana	6,980	957	2,811	2,362	850		83,623	12,679	9,098	61,846
Nebraska	2,393	3	NA	NA	959		162,175	15,484	16,949	129,742
Nevada	16,254	NA	NA	13,647	1,493		112,046	13,299	12,047	86,700
New Hampshire	737	0	170	11	556		79,486	8,005	4,475	67,006
New Jersey	3,659	10	1,703	16	1,930		580,879	68,975	31,532	480,372
New Mexico	19,663	1,719	13,679	2,185	2,080		187,701	30,062	21,641	135,998
New York	9,362	12	4,920	417	4,013		1,405,512	142,728	61,778	1,201,006
North Carolina	5,316	16	1,320	80	3,900		691,000	60,970	125,307	504,723
North Dakota	4,742	1,028	3,098	8	608		72,612	8,854	15,194	48,564
Ohio	*23,675*	*4,024*	*14,353*	*113*	*5,185*		*797,835*	*86,091*	*39,328*	*672,416*
Oklahoma	62,245	405	59,860	85	1,895		310,643	43,092	45,265	222,286
Oregon	3,052	6	721	440	1,885		250,698	29,645	13,413	207,640
Pennsylvania	26,524	12,096	8,200	48	6,180		767,516	120,998	48,371	598,147
Rhode Island	309	2	NA	NA	170		73,733	10,393	9,957	53,383
South Carolina	2,448	2	578	213	1,655		353,613	27,659	58,887	267,067
South Dakota	2,894	6	588	1,461	839		68,941	10,787	8,683	49,471
Tennessee	7,124	879	2,268	973	3,004		405,203	53,306	30,216	321,681
Texas	263,419	2,956	254,199	705	5,559		1,612,910	184,262	173,403	1,255,245
Utah	9,184	2,180	2,900	3,045	1,059		181,321	30,498	16,842	133,981
Vermont	739	NA	NA	6	633		48,892	5,409	4,879	38,604
Virginia	13,194	7,271	2,565	31	3,327		787,993	175,603	182,370	430,020
Washington	5,410	632	1,519	780	2,479		520,658	67,518	79,450	373,690
West Virginia	31,110	21,463	8,579	77	991		147,666	19,489	9,821	118,356
Wisconsin	3,574	9	926	104	2,535		386,605	29,501	19,853	337,251
Wyoming	18,090	4,788	9,410	661	3,231		61,740	7,171	6,509	48,060

Percent Change in Mining and Government Employment
1990 to 1996

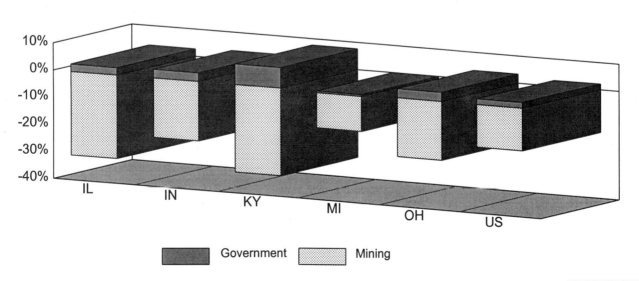

Government   Mining

Source: U.S. Bureau of Economic Analysis
EDIN table(s): EMMI, EMGV

1.43 Projected Employment by Industry 2005 *(Thousands of Jobs)*

	Total Employment	Farm	Non-farm	Private	Ag., Forest., and Fish.	Mining	Construction	Manufacturing	Trans- port., Public Utilities	Wholesale Trade	Retail Trade	Finance, Insurance & Real Estate	Services	Govt.
United States	167,817.0	2,962.2	164,854.8	140,842.4	2,116.8	796.0	8,372.9	18,886.8	7,766.3	7,821.9	28,019.6	12,178.8	54,883.3	24,012.4
Alabama	2,467.9	58.1	2,409.8	1,998.1	28.6	10.1	132.2	421.7	114.9	108.3	406.0	125.8	650.4	411.7
Alaska	425.6	0.7	424.9	320.6	14.4	12.0	21.5	21.6	31.5	11.5	66.4	24.4	117.3	104.3
Arizona	2,685.9	24.0	2,661.9	2,270.4	46.7	16.5	159.1	207.9	116.5	118.5	478.2	222.3	904.6	391.5
Arkansas	1,512.0	63.1	1,448.9	1,240.9	23.3	5.8	78.8	272.4	82.2	58.6	252.4	73.2	394.1	208.0
California	20,203.5	278.5	19,925.0	17,153.9	393.3	43.0	945.8	1,937.5	841.5	953.9	3,276.8	1,650.5	7,111.8	2,771.1
Colorado	2,828.6	39.8	2,788.8	2,373.8	35.0	22.9	150.8	213.6	150.0	127.4	485.2	220.3	968.6	415.0
Connecticut	2,217.6	10.3	2,207.3	1,951.8	21.1	2.0	96.0	274.9	87.3	97.7	350.4	245.3	777.1	255.5
Delaware	509.1	3.8	505.2	437.5	5.3	0.3	29.4	66.6	19.9	16.3	86.7	58.2	154.8	67.7
Dist. Of Col.	843.1	0.0	843.1	545.3	11.7	0.5	10.2	14.6	24.0	6.5	50.7	44.1	383.1	297.8
Florida	9,233.7	118.0	9,115.6	7,903.0	181.0	11.0	522.3	533.6	417.8	427.0	1,703.9	709.9	3,396.4	1,212.6
Georgia	4,751.7	61.7	4,690.0	3,952.7	47.9	9.7	242.3	603.6	276.3	285.3	807.5	297.2	1,382.8	737.3
Hawaii	891.8	16.5	875.3	687.6	11.2	0.6	48.9	20.8	55.5	32.6	155.3	73.9	288.9	187.7
Idaho	748.5	34.9	713.6	598.7	21.6	2.7	47.0	85.5	31.5	34.0	131.2	45.5	199.6	114.9
Illinois	*7,549.5*	*102.8*	*7,446.7*	*6,533.2*	*70.4*	*21.9*	*334.3*	*956.4*	*398.0*	*403.1*	*1,213.8*	*640.7*	*2,494.4*	*913.5*
Indiana	**3,718.2**	**78.3**	**3,639.9**	**3,181.7**	**34.0**	**7.9**	**195.7**	**673.3**	**187.3**	**166.2**	**668.5**	**216.3**	**1,032.4**	**458.2**
Percent U.S.	*2.22*	*2.64*	*2.21*	*2.26*	*1.61*	*0.99*	*2.34*	*3.56*	*2.41*	*2.12*	*2.39*	*1.78*	*1.88*	*1.91*
Rank	*14*	*13*	*15*	*14*	*21*	*25*	*14*	*9*	*14*	*17*	*13*	*22*	*19*	*16*
Iowa	1,887.1	116.2	1,770.9	1,522.5	31.2	2.9	90.0	247.9	78.7	94.3	325.2	125.6	526.9	248.4
Kansas	1,808.4	77.7	1,730.7	1,421.0	25.4	22.0	82.9	200.0	84.5	87.1	301.9	108.5	508.7	309.7
Kentucky	*2,295.0*	*114.9*	*2,180.1*	*1,834.7*	*27.0*	*23.4*	*125.2*	*317.3*	*114.7*	*88.9*	*402.2*	*111.0*	*624.9*	*345.4*
Louisiana	2,414.1	38.5	2,375.6	1,948.3	29.2	49.0	148.0	200.7	130.4	107.6	403.7	133.1	746.7	427.3
Maine	798.3	12.1	786.2	670.2	13.8	0.3	44.8	97.8	31.0	31.1	156.2	47.1	247.9	116.0
Maryland	3,200.1	20.6	3,179.4	2,635.8	35.8	2.6	190.2	178.0	132.0	128.3	542.8	257.3	1,168.9	543.6
Massachusetts	4,072.0	12.8	4,059.2	3,581.4	34.5	2.2	165.5	418.0	153.5	191.9	651.2	316.5	1,648.2	477.8
Michigan	*5,444.3*	*70.5*	*5,373.8*	*4,679.1*	*52.5*	*13.3*	*238.1*	*909.4*	*190.8*	*245.5*	*971.5*	*356.6*	*1,701.6*	*694.7*
Minnesota	3,307.5	106.0	3,201.5	2,794.6	30.8	9.3	144.8	445.3	146.1	163.9	555.9	236.5	1,062.0	406.9
Mississippi	1,473.1	50.3	1,422.8	1,161.7	18.0	7.7	72.3	282.7	64.2	53.0	237.9	67.7	358.1	261.1
Missouri	3,548.7	117.2	3,431.5	2,978.8	37.7	6.3	179.9	430.0	205.0	169.1	600.0	239.7	1,111.3	452.7
Montana	570.0	33.0	537.0	443.5	10.0	7.0	28.7	29.6	28.3	23.4	108.5	31.3	176.7	93.5
Nebraska	1,193.7	69.1	1,124.6	945.8	18.1	2.3	54.9	112.0	63.1	65.1	201.4	85.4	343.6	178.8
Nevada	1,125.0	5.1	1,119.8	990.5	9.9	15.4	81.5	40.5	50.4	38.9	172.9	73.5	507.7	129.3
New Hampshire	765.2	4.2	760.9	671.3	8.0	0.7	38.9	99.0	25.7	34.0	157.4	53.7	254.0	89.6
New Jersey	4,911.0	15.2	4,895.8	4,241.1	37.4	3.3	203.5	476.4	292.3	328.1	739.6	432.3	1,728.4	654.7
New Mexico	1,039.0	20.8	1,018.2	806.7	15.0	19.4	62.7	53.6	40.4	38.5	189.1	57.8	330.2	211.5
New York	10,423.5	66.2	10,357.3	8,818.7	69.9	9.2	382.1	874.6	481.2	493.5	1,454.8	1,077.5	3,976.0	1,538.6
North Carolina	4,924.9	71.4	4,853.5	4,095.1	55.8	5.0	286.1	891.5	211.1	223.8	816.5	272.2	1,333.2	758.4
North Dakota	450.2	39.9	410.3	333.2	6.0	3.8	21.1	23.0	24.2	22.4	77.0	25.2	130.4	77.1
Ohio	*6,833.8*	*93.9*	*6,739.9*	*5,877.7*	*61.4*	*20.8*	*332.0*	*1,060.3*	*279.5*	*318.9*	*1,222.0*	*443.8*	*2,139.1*	*862.2*
Oklahoma	2,007.2	83.9	1,923.3	1,591.3	29.1	60.5	96.5	186.1	99.6	78.7	332.8	113.8	594.2	332.0
Oregon	2,069.9	54.3	2,015.6	1,734.8	41.8	2.8	102.5	238.8	94.3	107.9	366.9	141.2	638.8	280.8
Pennsylvania	7,110.3	74.0	7,036.3	6,215.3	63.4	22.2	343.1	900.5	337.9	319.8	1,199.8	518.0	2,510.6	821.0
Rhode Island	609.4	1.6	607.9	526.2	5.7	0.3	24.5	84.0	18.0	23.1	101.6	44.8	224.2	81.7
South Carolina	2,328.7	29.3	2,299.5	1,886.7	23.1	2.5	142.6	397.4	89.8	77.9	412.6	127.7	613.1	412.8
South Dakota	528.3	40.6	487.7	407.9	7.5	3.2	25.8	50.2	22.3	24.2	93.7	32.3	148.8	79.8
Tennessee	3,508.4	100.7	3,407.7	2,959.3	30.5	6.8	184.9	564.1	183.1	169.3	591.4	188.9	1,040.4	448.4
Texas	11,992.3	248.2	11,744.1	9,971.5	162.4	234.4	658.2	1,092.2	604.5	594.6	2,027.8	843.7	3,753.8	1,772.6
Utah	1,397.5	17.4	1,380.1	1,165.3	11.7	8.6	80.3	142.1	68.3	62.3	244.5	97.0	450.6	214.8
Vermont	411.0	10.0	401.0	347.0	5.8	0.8	25.5	48.4	15.1	17.4	71.9	24.1	137.9	54.0
Virginia	4,410.4	51.6	4,358.7	3,493.8	44.0	12.5	259.2	421.5	195.2	167.8	712.1	299.1	1,382.3	864.9
Washington	3,712.2	66.5	3,645.7	3,064.3	70.6	4.9	209.5	370.6	159.1	186.7	629.1	268.6	1,165.1	581.4
West Virginia	891.3	21.7	869.6	719.4	7.4	22.0	52.3	84.5	49.2	35.1	161.0	41.6	266.3	150.2
Wisconsin	3,430.1	103.2	3,327.0	2,901.8	34.8	3.2	159.8	602.2	150.3	153.5	590.0	218.9	989.1	425.2
Wyoming	338.6	13.4	325.2	256.2	6.0	18.3	20.9	12.4	18.6	9.3	64.0	19.5	87.3	69.0

Projected Employment Index 2005 to 2045
2005 = 100

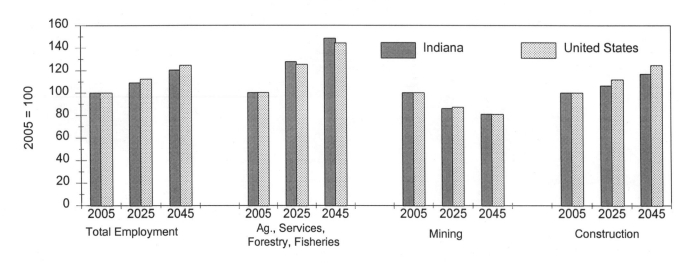

Source: U.S. Bureau of Economic Analysis, B.E.A. Regional Projections
EDIN table(s): PPE1, PPE2

1.44 Projected Employment by Industry 2025 *(Thousands of Jobs)*

	Total Employment	Farm	Non-farm	Private	Ag., Forest., and Fish.	Mining	Construction	Manufacturing	Trans-port., Public Utilities	Wholesale Trade	Retail Trade	Finance, Insurance, & Real Estate	Services	Govt.
United States	188,329.0	2,554.6	185,774.4	160,109.1	2,647.2	694.6	9,370.8	18,316.7	8,525.9	8,437.1	31,360.6	13,560.4	67,195.9	25,665.3
Alabama	2,734.6	49.7	2,684.9	2,254.1	36.5	8.7	144.1	424.3	127.3	117.4	451.8	140.0	804.0	430.8
Alaska	490.2	0.6	489.6	380.3	16.8	12.0	24.6	22.9	35.5	13.0	79.6	28.1	147.9	109.3
Arizona	3,246.9	21.8	3,225.1	2,779.0	60.8	17.0	192.1	217.3	140.3	140.8	564.9	262.4	1,183.3	446.1
Arkansas	1,649.0	53.4	1,595.6	1,377.5	29.6	5.1	84.7	279.4	90.8	61.6	275.1	79.5	471.7	218.1
California	23,696.7	247.3	23,449.4	20,339.6	483.6	38.1	1,150.1	1,901.9	961.3	1,066.9	3,887.0	1,917.3	8,933.4	3,109.8
Colorado	3,349.0	35.1	3,313.9	2,846.1	44.9	19.4	171.8	219.9	178.1	148.6	567.6	247.5	1,248.3	467.8
Connecticut	2,479.7	8.9	2,470.8	2,191.3	26.2	1.8	108.2	243.9	95.6	107.0	390.1	270.7	947.8	279.5
Delaware	575.3	3.1	572.2	499.7	6.7	0.3	32.8	65.1	21.8	17.9	97.2	66.1	191.9	72.5
Dist. Of Col.	888.4	0.0	888.4	608.4	0.4	0.4	10.2	14.1	23.6	5.8	50.8	44.4	444.5	280.0
Florida	10,999.0	107.3	10,891.7	9,516.8	222.6	10.1	607.6	531.6	475.9	490.7	1,995.4	811.8	4,371.0	1,374.9
Georgia	5,577.8	51.2	5,526.6	4,714.1	60.3	9.8	279.9	605.0	319.4	317.9	949.4	350.1	1,822.5	812.5
Hawaii	1,010.0	14.6	995.4	798.2	14.2	0.6	54.4	19.6	62.0	36.2	174.8	83.2	353.3	197.2
Idaho	843.0	29.8	813.2	689.9	28.1	2.5	49.3	90.6	35.0	37.4	148.3	51.9	246.7	123.3
Illinois	*8,281.3*	*86.3*	*8,195.0*	*7,242.2*	*91.6*	*17.9*	*361.0*	*913.0*	*428.1*	*416.2*	*1,328.9*	*708.2*	*2,977.3*	*952.8*
Indiana	**4,056.5**	**66.8**	**3,989.6**	**3,506.4**	**43.4**	**6.8**	**208.6**	**659.0**	**206.2**	**178.6**	**727.4**	**236.5**	**1,240.0**	**483.2**
Percent U.S.	*2.15*	*2.61*	*2.15*	*2.19*	*1.64*	*0.98*	*2.23*	*3.60*	*2.42*	*2.12*	*2.32*	*1.74*	*1.85*	*1.88*
Rank	*15*	*14*	*15*	*15*	*20*	*26*	*14*	*9*	*14*	*16*	*14*	*22*	*20*	*16*
Iowa	1,973.1	97.8	1,875.2	1,626.6	39.5	2.8	94.2	242.5	81.9	94.4	336.0	135.4	599.9	248.6
Kansas	1,977.0	67.0	1,910.0	1,580.3	33.4	18.6	89.9	199.9	88.8	91.4	330.6	117.5	610.1	329.7
Kentucky	*2,490.0*	*99.3*	*2,390.7*	*2,027.9*	*34.5*	*18.3*	*133.5*	*316.2*	*125.4*	*93.3*	*440.2*	*118.7*	*747.8*	*362.8*
Louisiana	2,640.3	31.9	2,608.4	2,161.5	35.3	41.4	158.3	199.5	135.1	113.8	439.0	146.5	892.6	446.9
Maine	887.1	10.6	876.5	753.7	15.5	0.3	48.5	92.2	33.6	33.5	174.4	53.2	302.4	122.8
Maryland	3,602.5	17.5	3,585.1	3,019.1	45.0	2.2	207.3	164.4	143.3	137.7	602.1	286.1	1,431.0	566.0
Massachusetts	4,518.6	11.1	4,507.4	3,998.8	40.9	2.1	187.2	365.5	161.6	202.6	713.8	346.2	1,979.0	508.6
Michigan	*5,825.7*	*59.5*	*5,766.2*	*5,053.5*	*66.3*	*12.1*	*256.3*	*864.9*	*196.6*	*253.8*	*1,037.2*	*382.9*	*1,983.4*	*712.7*
Minnesota	3,617.3	89.7	3,527.6	3,101.0	38.0	8.8	156.8	451.5	156.0	169.5	601.5	256.3	1,262.8	426.6
Mississippi	1,591.2	41.6	1,549.6	1,281.9	22.4	6.6	78.7	287.3	70.2	55.4	258.4	73.6	429.3	267.7
Missouri	3,883.4	100.5	3,782.9	3,308.1	47.7	5.6	193.6	417.7	220.0	175.4	656.3	262.6	1,329.2	474.8
Montana	629.7	30.1	599.6	501.7	12.6	6.9	31.2	29.8	29.8	25.1	119.8	33.2	213.3	97.9
Nebraska	1,286.7	59.6	1,227.1	1,042.2	22.7	2.1	59.5	112.5	67.2	67.7	217.0	92.9	400.6	184.9
Nevada	1,410.5	4.6	1,405.9	1,251.5	13.5	15.9	99.2	46.7	61.4	49.0	217.1	92.8	656.0	154.4
New Hampshire	867.8	3.6	864.2	766.2	10.3	0.7	43.1	92.8	28.7	38.2	178.9	61.4	312.0	98.0
New Jersey	5,399.6	13.3	5,386.2	4,694.7	44.6	3.0	226.8	415.0	311.9	351.2	802.2	468.8	2,071.1	691.5
New Mexico	1,216.3	18.7	1,197.7	966.3	19.5	17.8	73.4	56.3	45.1	44.4	222.0	66.3	421.5	231.4
New York	10,879.1	57.2	10,821.9	9,290.5	81.3	8.0	390.0	732.4	479.3	490.1	1,501.2	1,097.2	4,510.9	1,531.4
North Carolina	5,615.0	54.5	5,560.5	4,734.2	70.5	5.0	322.9	873.4	236.2	249.4	930.6	317.9	1,728.4	826.3
North Dakota	475.3	34.5	440.8	363.4	7.6	3.4	22.5	24.1	25.7	22.0	79.9	26.7	151.5	77.4
Ohio	*7,338.3*	*79.6*	*7,258.7*	*6,365.7*	*77.2*	*17.8*	*357.6*	*1,006.3*	*290.2*	*329.2*	*1,306.8*	*475.9*	*2,504.7*	*893.0*
Oklahoma	2,185.8	75.0	2,110.8	1,769.3	37.8	50.8	107.2	185.7	107.9	83.0	362.3	123.5	711.0	341.5
Oregon	2,342.1	47.8	2,294.4	1,991.7	52.0	2.8	115.4	237.0	105.6	117.4	414.3	159.4	787.7	302.7
Pennsylvania	7,614.8	63.8	7,551.0	6,711.4	78.4	18.1	358.3	804.2	352.0	325.6	1,269.9	561.0	2,943.8	839.6
Rhode Island	668.9	1.4	667.6	581.3	6.6	0.3	26.9	75.2	19.1	24.7	111.1	49.2	268.0	86.3
South Carolina	2,649.2	22.9	2,626.3	2,174.3	28.9	2.5	162.5	391.9	102.1	86.7	467.1	148.0	784.7	452.0
South Dakota	579.4	35.2	544.2	460.9	9.5	3.2	28.2	55.8	24.2	25.5	101.5	35.4	177.5	83.3
Tennessee	3,926.8	87.2	3,839.6	3,357.5	39.5	6.3	204.3	555.7	209.8	182.1	661.5	208.8	1,289.5	482.1
Texas	13,662.8	219.8	13,443.0	11,515.6	207.3	200.7	738.9	1,103.1	681.1	648.1	2,295.3	957.5	4,683.5	1,927.4
Utah	1,734.5	15.1	1,719.4	1,473.1	15.7	8.0	99.9	157.6	82.7	74.9	303.5	120.3	610.5	246.3
Vermont	461.3	8.7	452.6	394.7	7.3	0.8	27.9	46.6	16.6	19.7	80.8	27.0	167.9	57.9
Virginia	5,035.7	41.9	4,993.7	4,077.5	55.6	10.4	296.5	416.3	217.2	185.2	811.8	347.4	1,737.2	916.2
Washington	4,385.5	60.3	4,325.2	3,683.1	88.9	4.9	242.9	392.6	183.5	213.1	745.4	307.0	1,504.9	642.1
West Virginia	945.2	18.5	926.6	774.4	9.8	16.3	54.1	80.0	50.7	35.6	170.6	44.2	313.1	152.2
Wisconsin	3,762.5	86.6	3,676.0	3,224.0	44.1	3.1	175.1	603.6	164.8	162.5	640.0	240.4	1,190.3	452.0
Wyoming	372.4	12.0	360.4	288.0	7.6	16.4	22.8	13.0	19.7	9.8	72.2	21.5	105.0	72.4

Projected Employment Index 2005 to 2045
2005 = 100

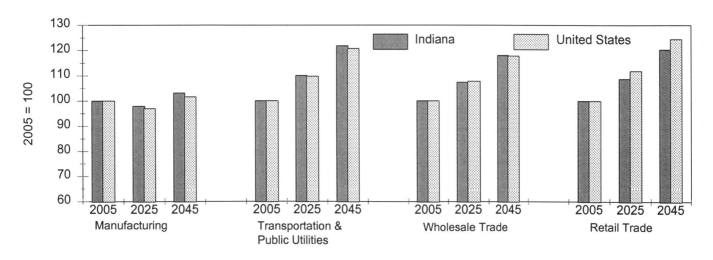

Source: U.S. Bureau of Economic Analysis, B.E.A. Regional Projections
EDIN table(s): PPE1, PPE2

1.45 Projected Employment by Industry 2045 *(Thousands of Jobs)*

	Total Employment	Farm	Non-farm	Private	Ag., Forest., and Fish.	Mining	Construction	Manufacturing	Trans-Port., Public Utilities	Wholesale Trade	Retail Trade	Finance, Insurance, & Real Estate	Services	Govt.
United States	208,789.0	2,415.2	206,373.8	178,644.1	3,053.1	644.5	10,425.2	19,190.6	9,375.9	9,215.3	34,873.5	14,982.2	76,883.9	27,729.7
Alabama	3,058.8	46.9	3,011.9	2,545.4	42.5	8.1	160.6	451.5	141.8	130.5	509.7	157.3	943.5	466.5
Alaska	544.1	0.6	543.5	428.0	18.7	11.8	27.3	24.9	39.2	14.4	90.3	31.2	170.2	115.5
Arizona	3,710.4	21.1	3,689.3	3,194.5	71.6	17.9	220.8	235.4	161.3	160.4	640.6	296.3	1,390.2	494.8
Arkansas	1,814.3	49.8	1,764.5	1,529.8	34.5	4.7	93.1	300.4	100.8	67.0	303.9	87.5	537.9	234.7
California	26,735.9	237.1	26,498.8	23,067.3	552.0	35.8	1,314.7	2,001.8	1,074.0	1,180.3	4,431.5	2,157.0	10,320.1	3,431.5
Colorado	3,807.5	33.8	3,773.7	3,254.8	52.5	17.5	193.9	237.8	203.5	168.7	644.2	273.6	1,463.2	518.9
Connecticut	2,752.8	8.4	2,744.3	2,437.9	30.2	1.8	121.3	244.6	105.3	118.2	434.0	297.7	1,084.9	306.4
Delaware	633.0	2.8	630.2	552.9	7.7	0.3	36.0	68.5	23.6	19.5	105.2	73.6	218.5	77.3
Dist. Of Col.	960.4	0.0	960.4	672.3	16.9	0.4	10.7	14.5	24.6	5.8	54.5	47.0	497.9	288.1
Florida	12,402.7	103.0	12,299.7	10,787.6	254.2	10.0	683.4	560.8	525.9	546.8	2,235.8	900.6	5,070.2	1,512.1
Georgia	6,377.2	47.6	6,329.6	5,432.2	69.7	10.2	319.0	643.1	361.2	351.7	1,091.2	401.6	2,184.6	897.4
Hawaii	1,112.2	14.0	1,098.3	890.1	16.4	0.6	59.8	20.2	68.3	39.6	192.7	91.9	400.5	208.2
Idaho	940.6	28.0	912.7	778.6	33.1	2.4	54.2	98.8	39.0	41.4	166.3	58.4	284.9	134.1
Illinois	*9,092.8*	*80.5*	*9,012.3*	*7,993.3*	*107.9*	*16.0*	*395.4*	*950.0*	*466.4*	*445.8*	*1,464.2*	*780.6*	*3,367.0*	*1,019.0*
Indiana	4,473.3	62.9	4,410.4	3,887.5	50.5	6.4	228.8	694.2	228.1	196.2	804.7	261.0	1,417.6	522.9
Percent U.S.	2.14	2.60	2.14	2.18	1.65	0.99	2.19	3.62	2.43	2.13	2.31	1.74	1.84	1.89
Rank	15	14	15	15	19	26	14	9	14	16	14	22	20	17
Iowa	2,117.3	91.4	2,026.0	1,765.2	45.9	2.9	101.8	255.2	87.9	99.7	360.4	147.2	664.1	260.8
Kansas	2,144.2	63.3	2,081.0	1,729.5	39.4	16.7	97.7	211.7	94.9	97.7	360.2	127.0	684.2	351.5
Kentucky	*2,731.4*	*93.9*	*2,637.5*	*2,247.4*	*40.2*	*15.8*	*146.0*	*335.0*	*139.1*	*101.6*	*488.1*	*129.2*	*852.5*	*390.1*
Louisiana	2,868.8	29.6	2,839.2	2,366.0	39.8	36.9	170.7	210.9	144.1	122.2	477.7	160.2	1,003.3	473.2
Maine	980.4	10.1	970.4	838.1	17.0	0.3	53.3	95.1	36.9	36.6	193.6	59.2	346.1	132.3
Maryland	3,998.9	16.4	3,982.6	3,376.7	51.9	2.1	227.5	168.2	157.0	150.1	666.7	316.1	1,637.0	605.9
Massachusetts	4,994.3	10.6	4,983.7	4,433.3	46.0	2.2	210.1	365.9	174.4	219.8	787.9	380.1	2,247.0	550.4
Michigan	*6,377.1*	*55.5*	*6,321.5*	*5,558.4*	*76.9*	*11.8*	*283.5*	*903.3*	*212.1*	*274.7*	*1,139.0*	*419.3*	*2,237.9*	*763.1*
Minnesota	3,964.2	83.8	3,880.4	3,423.2	43.5	8.9	171.9	483.5	169.4	181.7	658.2	279.6	1,426.3	457.2
Mississippi	1,732.8	38.7	1,694.1	1,411.6	25.8	6.0	86.3	306.1	77.3	59.7	283.4	80.5	486.5	282.5
Missouri	4,262.0	94.7	4,167.2	3,657.3	55.4	5.4	211.9	437.7	239.4	188.3	723.2	288.8	1,507.2	509.9
Montana	684.4	29.3	655.1	551.5	14.5	7.0	33.9	31.3	31.7	27.0	130.7	35.3	240.1	103.6
Nebraska	1,391.4	56.3	1,335.1	1,139.7	26.2	2.0	65.0	119.8	72.6	72.2	235.6	101.2	445.1	195.4
Nevada	1,641.4	4.4	1,636.9	1,461.4	16.3	17.0	114.3	53.0	70.6	57.4	254.0	108.9	769.9	175.5
New Hampshire	969.7	3.4	966.3	858.8	12.0	0.7	48.0	95.9	31.9	42.7	200.2	68.9	358.5	107.5
New Jersey	5,903.7	12.7	5,891.0	5,150.1	50.2	3.0	251.2	410.0	337.3	382.6	875.9	509.9	2,330.1	740.9
New Mexico	1,366.1	18.2	1,347.9	1,097.3	23.1	16.8	83.0	61.1	49.8	49.8	250.6	73.8	489.3	250.6
New York	11,627.4	54.1	11,573.3	9,975.5	90.1	7.7	414.4	713.1	500.4	513.0	1,603.6	1,156.7	4,976.5	1,598.0
North Carolina	6,290.9	49.1	6,241.7	5,342.2	81.6	5.2	362.2	920.5	262.6	277.0	1,047.0	358.9	2,027.2	899.5
North Dakota	506.6	32.7	473.9	393.9	8.8	3.1	24.3	26.1	27.6	22.7	84.9	28.4	167.8	80.0
Ohio	*8,012.4*	*74.5*	*7,937.9*	*6,981.3*	*89.4*	*16.4*	*392.6*	*1,044.4*	*313.0*	*354.3*	*1,430.2*	*519.8*	*2,821.3*	*956.6*
Oklahoma	2,373.3	72.2	2,301.1	1,940.7	44.4	45.2	118.2	197.0	117.6	89.1	395.1	133.8	800.3	360.4
Oregon	2,623.0	45.6	2,577.4	2,244.7	59.9	2.9	129.7	251.1	117.9	129.6	465.7	178.6	909.3	332.7
Pennsylvania	8,261.6	60.3	8,201.3	7,311.3	89.9	16.6	385.3	808.4	377.7	346.2	1,376.0	611.5	3,299.6	890.0
Rhode Island	735.6	1.3	734.3	641.4	7.4	0.3	29.8	76.1	20.8	26.9	122.4	54.1	303.5	92.9
South Carolina	2,938.4	20.9	2,917.4	2,428.5	33.4	2.5	181.3	411.7	113.3	95.4	519.3	165.0	906.7	488.9
South Dakota	633.8	33.4	600.4	511.7	11.0	3.4	31.0	62.2	26.6	27.5	111.0	38.7	200.2	88.7
Tennessee	4,364.8	82.5	4,282.3	3,757.9	46.3	6.3	227.3	585.4	235.3	199.4	738.5	230.9	1,488.4	524.4
Texas	15,168.3	210.4	14,958.0	12,870.3	241.9	180.1	820.3	1,178.3	755.9	707.5	2,550.5	1,061.9	5,373.9	2,087.7
Utah	2,018.3	14.3	2,004.0	1,727.8	18.8	7.9	117.0	174.1	95.3	86.2	354.8	140.4	733.4	276.2
Vermont	512.4	8.2	504.2	441.5	8.5	0.8	30.8	48.6	18.3	22.0	90.2	30.1	192.2	62.7
Virginia	5,641.1	38.5	5,602.6	4,618.1	64.4	9.5	334.4	439.8	241.1	205.0	912.6	392.6	2,018.6	984.5
Washington	4,961.1	59.0	4,902.1	4,200.6	103.0	5.0	274.3	422.7	205.8	237.8	847.6	343.9	1,760.5	701.5
West Virginia	1,022.9	17.4	1,005.5	844.7	11.7	13.8	58.0	82.8	54.2	37.9	185.4	48.0	353.0	160.8
Wisconsin	4,148.5	80.6	4,067.9	3,578.2	51.3	3.2	194.1	643.8	181.9	177.0	704.7	265.2	1,357.0	489.7
Wyoming	404.4	11.6	392.8	316.1	8.9	15.4	24.7	14.1	21.3	10.5	79.8	23.4	118.0	76.7

Projected Employment Index 2005 to 2045
2005 = 100

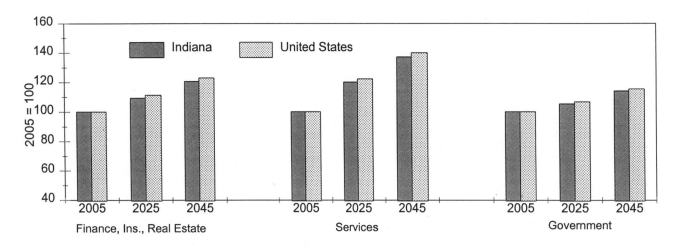

Source: U.S. Bureau of Economic Analysis, B.E.A. Regional Projections
EDIN Table(s): PPE1, PPE2

1.46 Percent Change in Projected Employment by Industry 2005 to 2045

	Total Employment	Farm	Non-farm	Private	Ag., Forest., and Fish.	Mining	Construction	Manufacturing	Transport., Public Utilities	Wholesale Trade	Retail Trade	Finance, Insurance, & Real Estate	Services	Govt.
United States	24.4	-18.5	25.2	26.8	44.2	-19.0	24.5	1.6	20.7	17.8	24.5	23.0	40.1	15.5
Alabama	23.9	-19.3	25.0	27.4	48.6	-19.8	21.5	7.1	23.4	20.5	25.5	25.0	45.1	13.3
Alaska	27.8	-14.3	27.9	33.5	29.9	-1.7	27.0	15.3	24.4	25.2	36.0	27.9	45.1	10.7
Arizona	38.1	-12.1	38.6	40.7	53.3	8.5	38.8	13.2	38.5	35.4	34.0	33.3	53.7	26.4
Arkansas	20.0	-21.1	21.8	23.3	48.1	-19.0	18.1	10.3	22.6	14.3	20.4	19.5	36.5	12.8
California	32.3	-14.9	33.0	34.5	40.4	-16.7	39.0	3.3	27.6	23.7	35.2	30.7	45.1	23.8
Colorado	34.6	-15.1	35.3	37.1	50.0	-23.6	28.6	11.3	35.7	32.4	32.8	24.2	51.1	25.0
Connecticut	24.1	-18.4	24.3	24.9	43.1	-10.0	26.4	-11.0	20.6	21.0	23.9	21.4	39.6	19.9
Delaware	24.3	-26.3	24.7	26.4	45.3	0.0	22.4	2.9	18.6	19.6	21.3	26.5	41.1	14.2
Dist. Of Col.	13.9	0.0	13.9	23.3	44.4	-20.0	4.9	-0.7	2.5	-10.8	7.5	6.6	30.0	-3.3
Florida	34.3	-12.7	34.9	36.5	40.4	-9.1	30.8	5.1	25.9	28.1	31.2	26.9	49.3	24.7
Georgia	34.2	-22.9	35.0	37.4	45.5	5.2	31.7	6.5	30.7	23.3	35.1	35.1	58.0	21.7
Hawaii	24.7	-15.2	25.5	29.5	46.4	0.0	22.3	-2.9	23.1	21.5	24.1	24.4	38.6	16.7
Idaho	25.7	-19.8	27.9	30.0	53.2	-11.1	15.3	15.6	23.8	21.8	26.8	28.4	42.7	16.7
Illinois	*20.4*	*-21.7*	*21.0*	*22.3*	*53.3*	*-26.9*	*18.3*	*-0.7*	*17.2*	*10.6*	*20.6*	*21.8*	*35.0*	*11.5*
Indiana	**20.3**	**-19.7**	**21.2**	**22.2**	**48.5**	**-19.0**	**16.9**	**3.1**	**21.8**	**18.1**	**20.4**	**20.7**	**37.3**	**14.1**
Rank	*30*	*34*	*32*	*37*	*16*	*35*	*42*	*32*	*22*	*23*	*33*	*29*	*26*	*22*
Iowa	12.2	-21.3	14.4	15.9	47.1	0.0	13.1	2.9	11.7	5.7	10.8	17.2	26.0	5.0
Kansas	18.6	-18.5	20.2	21.7	55.1	-24.1	17.9	5.8	12.3	12.2	19.3	17.1	34.5	13.5
Kentucky	*19.0*	*-18.3*	*21.0*	*22.5*	*48.9*	*-32.5*	*16.6*	*5.6*	*21.3*	*14.3*	*21.4*	*16.4*	*36.4*	*12.9*
Louisiana	18.8	-23.1	19.5	21.4	36.3	-24.7	15.3	5.1	10.5	13.6	18.3	20.4	34.4	10.7
Maine	22.8	-16.5	23.4	25.1	23.2	0.0	19.0	-2.8	19.0	17.7	23.9	25.7	39.6	14.1
Maryland	25.0	-20.4	25.3	28.1	45.0	-19.2	19.6	-5.5	18.9	17.0	22.8	22.9	40.0	11.5
Massachusetts	22.6	-17.2	22.8	23.8	33.3	0.0	26.9	-12.5	13.6	14.5	21.0	20.1	36.3	15.2
Michigan	*17.1*	*-21.3*	*17.6*	*18.8*	*46.5*	*-11.3*	*19.1*	*-0.7*	*11.2*	*11.9*	*17.2*	*17.6*	*31.5*	*9.8*
Minnesota	19.9	-20.9	21.2	22.5	41.2	-4.3	18.7	8.6	15.9	10.9	18.4	18.2	34.3	12.4
Mississippi	17.6	-23.1	19.1	21.5	43.3	-22.1	19.4	8.3	20.4	12.6	19.1	18.9	35.9	4.2
Missouri	20.1	-19.2	21.4	22.8	46.9	-14.3	17.8	1.8	16.8	11.4	20.5	20.5	35.6	12.6
Montana	20.1	-11.2	22.0	24.4	45.0	0.0	18.1	5.7	12.0	15.4	20.5	12.8	35.9	10.8
Nebraska	16.6	-18.5	18.7	20.5	44.8	-13.0	18.4	7.0	15.1	10.9	17.0	18.5	29.5	9.3
Nevada	45.9	-13.7	46.2	47.5	64.6	10.4	40.2	30.9	40.1	47.6	46.9	48.2	51.6	35.7
New Hampshire	26.7	-19.0	27.0	27.9	50.0	0.0	23.4	-3.1	24.1	25.6	27.2	28.3	41.1	20.0
New Jersey	20.2	-16.4	20.3	21.4	34.2	-9.1	23.4	-13.9	15.4	16.6	18.4	18.0	34.8	13.2
New Mexico	31.5	-12.5	32.4	36.0	54.0	-13.4	32.4	14.0	23.3	29.4	32.5	27.7	48.2	18.5
New York	11.5	-18.3	11.7	13.1	28.9	-16.3	8.5	-18.5	4.0	4.0	10.2	7.4	25.2	3.9
North Carolina	27.7	-31.2	28.6	30.5	46.2	4.0	26.6	3.3	24.4	23.8	28.2	31.9	52.1	18.6
North Dakota	12.5	-18.0	15.5	18.2	46.7	-18.4	15.2	13.5	14.0	1.3	10.3	12.7	28.7	3.8
Ohio	*17.2*	*-20.7*	*17.8*	*18.8*	*45.6*	*-21.2*	*18.3*	*-1.5*	*12.0*	*11.1*	*17.0*	*17.1*	*31.9*	*10.9*
Oklahoma	18.2	-13.9	19.6	22.0	52.6	-25.3	22.5	5.9	18.1	13.2	18.7	17.6	34.7	14.2
Oregon	26.7	-16.0	27.9	29.4	43.3	3.6	26.5	5.2	25.0	20.1	26.9	26.5	42.3	18.5
Pennsylvania	16.2	-18.5	16.6	17.6	41.8	-25.2	12.3	-10.2	11.8	8.3	14.7	18.1	31.4	8.4
Rhode Island	20.7	-18.8	20.8	21.9	29.8	0.0	21.6	-9.4	15.6	16.5	20.5	20.8	35.4	13.7
South Carolina	26.2	-28.7	26.9	28.7	44.6	0.0	27.1	3.6	26.2	22.5	25.9	29.2	47.9	18.4
South Dakota	20.0	-17.7	23.1	25.4	46.7	6.2	20.2	23.9	19.3	13.6	18.5	19.8	34.5	11.2
Tennessee	24.4	-18.1	25.7	27.0	51.8	-7.4	22.9	3.8	28.5	17.8	24.9	22.2	43.1	16.9
Texas	26.5	-15.2	27.4	29.1	49.0	-23.2	24.6	7.9	25.0	19.0	25.8	25.9	43.2	17.8
Utah	44.4	-17.8	45.2	48.3	60.7	-8.1	45.7	22.5	39.5	38.4	45.1	44.7	62.8	28.6
Vermont	24.7	-18.0	25.7	27.2	46.6	0.0	20.8	0.4	21.2	26.4	25.5	24.9	39.4	16.1
Virginia	27.9	-25.4	28.5	32.2	46.4	-24.0	29.0	4.3	23.5	22.2	28.2	31.3	46.0	13.8
Washington	33.6	-11.3	34.5	37.1	45.9	2.0	30.9	14.1	29.4	27.4	34.7	28.0	51.1	20.7
West Virginia	14.8	-19.8	15.6	17.4	58.1	-37.3	10.9	-2.0	10.2	8.0	15.2	15.4	32.6	7.1
Wisconsin	20.9	-21.9	22.3	23.3	47.4	0.0	21.5	6.9	21.0	15.3	19.4	21.2	37.2	15.2
Wyoming	19.4	-13.4	20.8	23.4	48.3	-15.8	18.2	13.7	14.5	12.9	24.7	20.0	35.2	11.2

Percent Change in Projected Employment 2005 to 2045
Indiana's Top 5 Most Volatile Industries

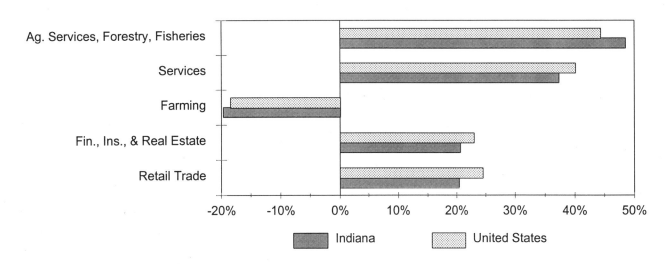

Source: U.S. Bureau of Economic Analysis, B.E.A. Regional Projections to 2045
EDIN Table(s): PPE1, PPE2

Earnings
1.47 Earnings by Industry 1996 *($MIL)*

	Total Earnings	Farm	Manufacturing	Mining	Contract Construction	Wholesale and Retail	Finance, Insurance, & Real Estate	Transportation, Communication, and Public Utilities	Services	Ag. Serv., Forestry, Fisheries	Government
United States	4,548,138	46,649	820,893	39,044	254,790	699,860	375,626	308,977	1,280,038	29,770	692,491
Alabama	59,680	886	13,209	631	3,662	9,053	3,314	4,050	13,531	378	10,966
Alaska	11,585	9	605	891	886	1,468	454	1,146	2,428	228	3,470
Arizona	65,124	687	8,924	811	4,751	11,232	5,587	3,868	18,503	611	10,149
Arkansas	33,277	1,847	7,575	162	1,933	5,226	1,559	2,763	6,933	259	5,019
California	570,328	7,419	88,845	2,064	28,043	86,772	45,560	35,211	185,394	6,072	84,950
Colorado	71,865	644	8,630	1,302	5,175	11,351	5,596	6,912	20,686	467	11,103
Connecticut	74,876	186	15,501	91	3,463	10,796	9,360	3,937	22,442	405	8,695
Delaware	15,446	119	4,375	7	1,071	1,854	1,937	695	3,404	62	1,923
Dist. Of Col.	34,297	0	963	14	379	1,175	1,865	1,337	14,268	337	13,959
Florida	207,974	1,774	18,897	399	12,656	38,386	18,603	13,952	68,762	2,190	32,355
Georgia	126,017	1,952	21,100	350	7,161	22,573	8,916	12,018	32,206	704	19,036
Hawaii	21,242	184	793	19	1,459	3,411	1,757	1,745	6,415	142	5,317
Idaho	16,713	767	2,990	170	1,451	2,679	853	1,089	3,775	224	2,716
Illinois	*227,762*	*1,704*	*45,138*	*775*	*12,327*	*34,837*	*21,842*	*16,614*	*64,746*	*1,052*	*28,728*
Indiana	**94,928**	**896**	**30,533**	**354**	**6,003**	**14,115**	**5,325**	**5,801**	**19,924**	**411**	**11,565**
Percent U.S.	*2.09*	*1.92*	*3.72*	*0.91*	*2.36*	*2.02*	*1.42*	*1.88*	*1.56*	*1.38*	*1.67*
Rank	*15*	*17*	*8*	*23*	*14*	*18*	*22*	*18*	*21*	*22*	*19*
Iowa	44,805	3,046	9,419	79	2,717	7,070	3,125	2,691	9,672	356	6,630
Kansas	40,976	1,118	7,718	396	2,459	7,010	2,425	3,197	9,355	266	7,034
Kentucky	*53,736*	*1,085*	*12,016*	*1,348*	*3,109*	*8,250*	*2,673*	*3,935*	*12,009*	*366*	*8,945*
Louisiana	58,224	642	8,204	2,721	4,194	8,694	3,080	4,517	15,894	320	9,960
Maine	17,012	109	3,213	5	1,108	2,931	1,057	988	4,562	192	2,847
Maryland	85,910	318	7,970	72	5,734	13,104	6,733	5,045	27,835	508	18,591
Massachusetts	130,453	153	22,625	66	5,919	20,026	13,230	6,909	45,744	670	15,111
Michigan	*170,929*	*457*	*56,591*	*403*	*8,517*	*24,711*	*9,111*	*8,321*	*40,575*	*752*	*21,491*
Minnesota	88,848	1,795	18,968	454	5,012	14,988	7,263	5,587	22,794	401	11,586
Mississippi	32,084	842	7,136	245	1,885	4,708	1,453	2,193	7,259	226	6,136
Missouri	87,682	811	17,437	240	5,605	14,288	6,294	7,390	23,074	441	12,102
Montana	10,831	246	834	290	809	1,927	601	912	2,931	102	2,180
Nebraska	27,911	2,157	3,912	59	1,635	4,276	1,990	2,389	6,683	293	4,516
Nevada	30,802	53	1,464	826	3,498	4,277	2,151	1,789	12,593	182	3,970
New Hampshire	19,780	45	4,531	20	1,161	3,629	1,289	1,155	5,547	113	2,291
New Jersey	162,871	263	25,948	214	7,218	27,224	14,212	14,360	49,326	721	23,385
New Mexico	22,057	352	1,721	759	1,570	3,359	1,119	1,307	6,133	152	5,585
New York	375,518	541	47,006	319	13,318	46,807	70,376	22,883	118,131	1,292	54,846
North Carolina	119,692	2,970	29,457	180	7,596	18,523	7,360	7,543	26,003	699	19,360
North Dakota	9,351	764	697	186	617	1,663	489	812	2,275	73	1,776
Ohio	*185,451*	*948*	*51,493*	*825*	*10,134*	*29,465*	*11,525*	*10,509*	*45,475*	*835*	*24,242*
Oklahoma	43,300	360	7,001	2,062	2,144	6,590	2,294	3,586	10,571	247	8,446
Oregon	52,780	742	10,083	80	3,969	9,510	3,402	3,333	13,378	599	7,684
Pennsylvania	199,478	906	41,734	1,488	11,096	29,707	15,225	13,608	58,923	984	25,808
Rhode Island	15,242	30	2,978	8	712	2,187	1,081	760	4,929	106	2,453
South Carolina	51,786	425	13,050	77	3,604	8,168	2,736	2,936	11,080	319	9,393
South Dakota	10,829	1,052	1,418	118	636	1,783	677	710	2,606	139	1,693
Tennessee	85,928	311	19,341	275	5,252	14,556	5,141	6,271	22,817	414	11,549
Texas	319,149	1,973	53,041	13,220	19,821	50,701	21,755	27,836	82,349	1,868	46,585
Utah	30,300	181	4,581	418	2,383	4,978	2,150	2,260	8,151	120	5,078
Vermont	8,916	130	1,823	21	607	1,402	498	511	2,513	63	1,348
Virginia	115,007	479	15,470	635	6,953	16,371	7,805	7,639	32,995	618	26,042
Washington	97,384	1,734	16,298	194	6,272	15,413	5,988	6,640	26,704	1,169	16,972
West Virginia	20,947	-14	3,375	1,561	1,321	3,014	844	1,693	5,130	76	3,946
Wisconsin	84,118	491	23,874	119	5,249	12,666	5,629	4,966	19,289	488	11,348
Wyoming	6,911	61	391	1,022	536	953	314	659	1,311	54	1,610

Real Percent Change in Earnings
By Industry 1990 to 1996

	Illinois	Indiana	Kentucky	Michigan	Ohio	United States
Ag. Services, For., Fish.	12.6%	24.8%	22.2%	32.0%	20.5%	13.5%
Mining	-31.5%	-24.6%	-32.2%	-11.3%	1.4%	-5.4%
Construction	0.5%	19.0%	18.6%	13.6%	10.5%	4.8%
Manufacturing	6.5%	15.9%	12.5%	17.7%	3.9%	3.9%
Trans., & Pub. Utils.	12.9%	7.2%	17.7%	9.7%	7.8%	13.9%
Wholesale Trade	-1.0%	14.3%	18.1%	17.6%	13.3%	8.2%
Retail Trade	5.7%	15.9%	17.9%	8.5%	13.3%	8.8%
Fin., Ins., & Real Est.	40.5%	32.3%	29.1%	30.3%	27.8%	32.5%
Services	22.8%	23.5%	27.2%	22.8%	17.3%	21.2%
Government	11.1%	6.5%	13.2%	4.3%	9.2%	6.5%

Source: Bureau of Economic Analysis
EDIN Table(s): PITE

1.48 Percent Distribution of Earnings by Industry 1996

	Total Earnings ($Mil)	Farm	Manufacturing	Mining	Contract Construction	Wholesale and Retail	Finance, Insurance, & Real Estate	Transportation, Communication, and Public Utilities	Services	Ag. Serv,. Forestry, Fisheries	Government
United States	4,548,138	1.0	18.0	0.9	5.6	15.4	8.3	6.8	28.1	0.7	15.2
Alabama	59,680	1.5	22.1	1.1	6.1	15.2	5.6	6.8	22.7	0.6	18.4
Alaska	11,585	0.1	5.2	7.7	7.6	12.7	3.9	9.9	21.0	2.0	30.0
Arizona	65,124	1.1	13.7	1.2	7.3	17.2	8.6	5.9	28.4	0.9	15.6
Arkansas	33,277	5.6	22.8	0.5	5.8	15.7	4.7	8.3	20.8	0.8	15.1
California	570,328	1.3	15.6	0.4	4.9	15.2	8.0	6.2	32.5	1.1	14.9
Colorado	71,865	0.9	12.0	1.8	7.2	15.8	7.8	9.6	28.8	0.6	15.4
Connecticut	74,876	0.2	20.7	0.1	4.6	14.4	12.5	5.3	30.0	0.5	11.6
Delaware	15,446	0.8	28.3	0.0	6.9	12.0	12.5	4.5	22.0	0.4	12.4
Dist. Of Col.	34,297	0.0	2.8	0.0	1.1	3.4	5.4	3.9	41.6	1.0	40.7
Florida	207,974	0.9	9.1	0.2	6.1	18.5	8.9	6.7	33.1	1.1	15.6
Georgia	126,017	1.5	16.7	0.3	5.7	17.9	7.1	9.5	25.6	0.6	15.1
Hawaii	21,242	0.9	3.7	0.1	6.9	16.1	8.3	8.2	30.2	0.7	25.0
Idaho	16,713	4.6	17.9	1.0	8.7	16.0	5.1	6.5	22.6	1.3	16.3
Illinois	*227,762*	*0.7*	*19.8*	*0.3*	*5.4*	*15.3*	*9.6*	*7.3*	*28.4*	*0.5*	*12.6*
Indiana	**94,928**	**0.9**	**32.2**	**0.4**	**6.3**	**14.9**	**5.6**	**6.1**	**21.0**	**0.4**	**12.2**
Percent U.S.	2.09	—	—	—	—	—	—	—	—	—	—
Rank	15	22	2	24	21	37	34	33	48	45	48
Iowa	44,805	6.8	21.0	0.2	6.1	15.8	7.0	6.0	21.6	0.8	14.8
Kansas	40,976	2.7	18.8	1.0	6.0	17.1	5.9	7.8	22.8	0.6	17.2
Kentucky	*53,736*	*2.0*	*22.4*	*2.5*	*5.8*	*15.4*	*5.0*	*7.3*	*22.3*	*0.7*	*16.6*
Louisiana	58,224	1.1	14.1	4.7	7.2	14.9	5.3	7.8	27.3	0.5	17.1
Maine	17,012	0.6	18.9	0.0	6.5	17.2	6.2	5.8	26.8	1.1	16.7
Maryland	85,910	0.4	9.3	0.1	6.7	15.3	7.8	5.9	32.4	0.6	21.6
Massachusetts	130,453	0.1	17.3	0.1	4.5	15.4	10.1	5.3	35.1	0.5	11.6
Michigan	*170,929*	*0.3*	*33.1*	*0.2*	*5.0*	*14.5*	*5.3*	*4.9*	*23.7*	*0.4*	*12.6*
Minnesota	88,848	2.0	21.3	0.5	5.6	16.9	8.2	6.3	25.7	0.5	13.0
Mississippi	32,084	2.6	22.2	0.8	5.9	14.7	4.5	6.8	22.6	0.7	19.1
Missouri	87,682	0.9	19.9	0.3	6.4	16.3	7.2	8.4	26.3	0.5	13.8
Montana	10,831	2.3	7.7	2.7	7.5	17.8	5.5	8.4	27.1	0.9	20.1
Nebraska	27,911	7.7	14.0	0.2	5.9	15.3	7.1	8.6	23.9	1.0	16.2
Nevada	30,802	0.2	4.8	2.7	11.4	13.9	7.0	5.8	40.9	0.6	12.9
New Hampshire	19,780	0.2	22.9	0.1	5.9	18.3	6.5	5.8	28.0	0.6	11.6
New Jersey	162,871	0.2	15.9	0.1	4.4	16.7	8.7	8.8	30.3	0.4	14.4
New Mexico	22,057	1.6	7.8	3.4	7.1	15.2	5.1	5.9	27.8	0.7	25.3
New York	375,518	0.1	12.5	0.1	3.5	12.5	18.7	6.1	31.5	0.3	14.6
North Carolina	119,692	2.5	24.6	0.2	6.3	15.5	6.1	6.3	21.7	0.6	16.2
North Dakota	9,351	8.2	7.5	2.0	6.6	17.8	5.2	8.7	24.3	0.8	19.0
Ohio	*185,451*	*0.5*	*27.8*	*0.4*	*5.5*	*15.9*	*6.2*	*5.7*	*24.5*	*0.5*	*13.1*
Oklahoma	43,300	0.8	16.2	4.8	5.0	15.2	5.3	8.3	24.4	0.6	19.5
Oregon	52,780	1.4	19.1	0.2	7.5	18.0	6.4	6.3	25.3	1.1	14.6
Pennsylvania	199,478	0.5	20.9	0.7	5.6	14.9	7.6	6.8	29.5	0.5	12.9
Rhode Island	15,242	0.2	19.5	0.1	4.7	14.3	7.1	5.0	32.3	0.7	16.1
South Carolina	51,786	0.8	25.2	0.1	7.0	15.8	5.3	5.7	21.4	0.6	18.1
South Dakota	10,829	9.7	13.1	1.1	5.9	16.5	6.3	6.6	24.1	1.3	15.6
Tennessee	85,928	0.4	22.5	0.3	6.1	16.9	6.0	7.3	26.6	0.5	13.4
Texas	319,149	0.6	16.6	4.1	6.2	15.9	6.8	8.7	25.8	0.6	14.6
Utah	30,300	0.6	15.1	1.4	7.9	16.4	7.1	7.5	26.9	0.4	16.8
Vermont	8,916	1.5	20.4	0.2	6.8	15.7	5.6	5.7	28.2	0.7	15.1
Virginia	115,007	0.4	13.5	0.6	6.0	14.2	6.8	6.6	28.7	0.5	22.6
Washington	97,384	1.8	16.7	0.2	6.4	15.8	6.1	6.8	27.4	1.2	17.4
West Virginia	20,947	-0.1	16.1	7.5	6.3	14.4	4.0	8.1	24.5	0.4	18.8
Wisconsin	84,118	0.6	28.4	0.1	6.2	15.1	6.7	5.9	22.9	0.6	13.5
Wyoming	6,911	0.9	5.7	14.8	7.8	13.8	4.5	9.5	19.0	0.8	23.3

Percent Distribution of Earnings
1996

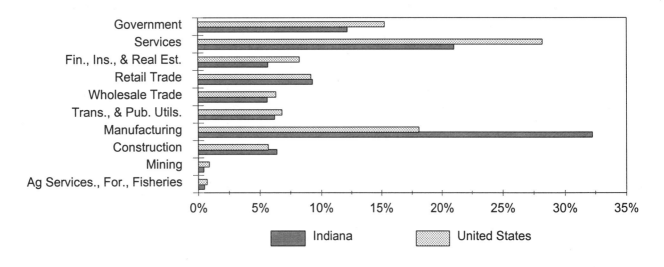

1.49 Earnings by Industry: Agriculture and Construction 1996 *($000)*

	Ag. Services, Forestry, Fisheries, & Other	Ag. Services	Forestry, Fisheries, and Other	Forestry	Fisheries	Other	Construction	General Building Contractors	Heavy Construct. Contractors	Special Trade Contractors
United States	29,770,000	26,845,000	2,925,000	711,000	1,544,000	670,000	254,790,000	59,255,000	32,802,000	162,733,000
Alabama	378,404	324,396	54,008	41,981	12,027	0	3,661,658	1,015,013	474,513	2,172,132
Alaska	228,282	27,638	200,644	5,052	195,592	0	886,242	229,055	217,476	439,711
Arizona	611,081	604,263	6,818	5,963	855	0	4,750,924	1,028,462	519,036	3,203,426
Arkansas	259,435	240,004	19,431	17,690	1,741	0	1,933,430	445,410	268,055	1,219,965
California	6,071,758	5,870,527	201,231	52,267	126,970	21,994	28,042,868	6,990,372	3,052,310	18,000,186
Colorado	466,630	462,956	3,674	1,420	2,254	0	5,175,004	1,197,411	616,757	3,360,836
Connecticut	404,597	396,394	8,203	855	7,348	0	3,463,210	682,090	363,021	2,418,099
Delaware	61,798	59,770	2,028	55	1,973	0	1,070,636	208,737	128,411	733,488
Dist. Of Col.	336,649	9,797	326,852	1	34	326,817	379,444	151,995	69,052	158,397
Florida	2,190,450	2,068,583	121,867	37,176	81,621	3,070	12,655,819	2,933,273	1,546,470	8,176,076
Georgia	704,383	629,912	74,471	59,919	14,552	0	7,161,167	1,797,923	769,117	4,594,127
Hawaii	142,160	125,674	16,486	NA	NA	0	1,459,424	459,425	188,031	811,968
Idaho	224,399	209,420	14,979	11,334	3,645	0	1,450,793	348,980	232,899	868,914
Illinois	*1,051,724*	*1,034,137*	*17,587*	*3,369*	*3,480*	*10,738*	*12,326,508*	*2,665,129*	*1,119,524*	*8,541,855*
Indiana	411,025	407,541	3,484	1,371	2,113	0	6,003,487	1,559,228	737,055	3,707,204
Percent U.S.	*1.38*	*1.52*	*0.12*	*0.19*	*0.14*	*0.00*	*2.36*	*2.63*	*2.25*	*2.28*
Rank	*22*	*21*	*41*	*33*	*34*	*—*	*14*	*13*	*14*	*15*
Iowa	356,344	353,973	2,371	NA	NA	0	2,717,072	584,904	355,405	1,776,763
Kansas	266,137	264,730	1,407	NA	NA	0	2,458,648	539,058	379,284	1,540,306
Kentucky	*365,946*	*361,424*	*4,522*	*1,049*	*3,473*	*0*	*3,108,547*	*668,331*	*450,517*	*1,989,699*
Louisiana	319,765	228,230	91,535	23,856	60,521	7,158	4,194,370	685,237	1,492,676	2,016,457
Maine	192,089	97,901	94,188	16,296	77,892	0	1,108,483	227,229	172,785	708,469
Maryland	508,084	483,996	24,088	3,378	20,710	0	5,734,344	1,426,931	550,444	3,756,969
Massachusetts	669,922	547,241	122,681	1,243	121,438	0	5,918,577	1,317,672	674,976	3,925,929
Michigan	*752,108*	*734,507*	*17,601*	*11,373*	*6,228*	*0*	*8,516,831*	*1,957,596*	*662,614*	*5,896,621*
Minnesota	401,306	393,480	7,826	4,197	3,629	0	5,012,471	1,007,720	588,392	3,416,359
Mississippi	226,243	185,675	40,568	24,487	16,081	0	1,885,451	515,344	311,940	1,058,167
Missouri	441,424	438,621	2,803	1,997	806	0	5,605,275	1,345,105	574,198	3,685,972
Montana	102,285	90,389	11,896	7,734	4,162	0	808,651	196,228	166,827	445,596
Nebraska	293,475	292,344	1,131	620	511	0	1,634,539	342,283	317,157	975,099
Nevada	181,704	175,127	6,577	NA	NA	0	3,497,647	767,227	469,932	2,260,488
New Hampshire	113,135	103,991	9,144	4,178	4,966	0	1,160,775	258,397	106,145	796,233
New Jersey	720,899	697,006	23,893	921	22,972	0	7,218,105	1,536,793	834,701	4,846,611
New Mexico	152,468	150,546	1,922	1,116	806	0	1,569,695	457,495	244,793	867,407
New York	1,292,470	980,481	311,989	7,679	14,315	289,995	13,318,396	2,693,241	1,418,071	9,207,084
North Carolina	699,124	636,310	62,814	29,768	33,046	0	7,596,201	2,005,419	896,213	4,694,569
North Dakota	72,864	72,063	801	NA	NA	0	616,986	122,364	140,179	354,443
Ohio	*834,878*	*828,518*	*6,360*	*3,133*	*3,227*	*0*	*10,134,321*	*2,225,729*	*1,090,838*	*6,817,754*
Oklahoma	246,692	242,557	4,135	2,741	1,394	0	2,143,522	423,721	289,995	1,429,806
Oregon	599,184	407,975	191,209	122,833	68,376	0	3,969,131	965,440	461,901	2,541,790
Pennsylvania	984,142	967,176	16,966	11,170	2,726	3,070	11,096,172	2,571,566	1,143,208	7,381,398
Rhode Island	105,930	69,130	36,800	133	36,667	0	712,114	192,063	57,849	462,202
South Carolina	319,101	260,292	58,809	49,449	9,360	0	3,603,639	1,185,865	363,380	2,054,394
South Dakota	139,045	137,213	1,832	1,261	571	0	635,569	156,555	96,546	382,468
Tennessee	414,318	405,020	9,298	6,824	2,474	0	5,251,536	1,432,820	516,465	3,302,251
Texas	1,868,467	1,764,650	103,817	24,990	71,669	7,158	19,821,426	3,906,156	4,523,412	11,391,858
Utah	120,182	109,207	10,975	133	10,842	0	2,383,069	557,036	248,761	1,577,272
Vermont	63,072	61,489	1,583	1,261	322	0	606,565	157,653	51,193	397,719
Virginia	617,750	580,028	37,722	13,143	24,579	0	6,953,362	1,657,593	963,924	4,331,845
Washington	1,168,803	657,315	511,488	77,024	434,464	0	6,272,366	1,787,851	872,500	3,612,015
West Virginia	75,744	74,223	1,521	1,322	199	0	1,320,969	318,008	321,899	681,062
Wisconsin	487,694	472,234	15,460	10,333	5,127	0	5,248,766	1,240,153	540,965	3,467,648
Wyoming	54,431	48,926	5,505	4,460	1,045	0	535,795	109,714	150,188	275,893

Agriculture and Construction
Percent Change in Real Earnings
1990 to 1996

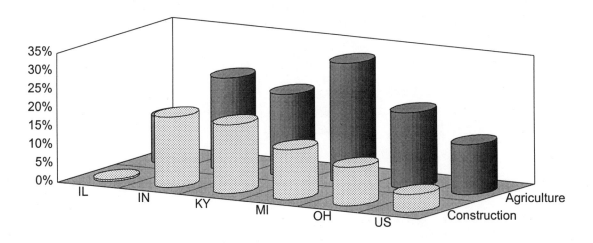

Source: U.S Bureau of Economic Analysis
EDIN Table(s): PIAG, PICO

1.50 Earnings by Industry: Manufacturing - Nondurable Goods 1996 *($000)*

	Total Manufacturing	Non-Durable Goods	Food and Kindred	Textile Mill	Apparel and Other Textile	Paper and Allied	Printing and Publishing	Chemical and Allied	Petroleum and Coal Products	Tobacco Manufacturers	Rubber and Misc. Plastics	Leather and Leather Goods
United States	820,893,000	317,115,000	57,853,000	17,713,000	19,824,000	31,576,000	63,527,000	76,440,000	10,546,000	2,868,000	34,195,000	2,573,000
Alabama	13,209,020	5,830,922	875,680	1,018,357	807,717	1,147,942	491,674	723,337	90,799	17,362	655,980	2,074
Alaska	605,320	424,335	277,930	NA	1,267	NA	50,778	NA	NA	13	1,348	142
Arizona	8,923,848	1,775,237	348,314	30,625	64,522	89,673	706,042	297,021	6,209	115	223,163	9,553
Arkansas	7,574,601	3,345,171	1,330,975	99,755	148,553	627,685	311,791	280,114	46,705	57	437,602	61,934
California	88,844,924	27,592,356	6,487,468	571,614	3,592,682	1,774,556	6,905,193	3,804,044	1,822,282	1,774	2,477,212	155,491
Colorado	8,630,253	2,794,661	933,638	9,780	100,741	118,767	998,580	211,311	52,291	113	309,672	59,768
Connecticut	15,501,020	4,550,801	385,170	69,117	158,251	520,476	1,139,022	1,627,606	92,198	68,741	443,958	46,262
Delaware	4,374,738	3,517,098	248,296	NA	32,319	116,776	86,742	2,795,219	NA	13	NA	NA
Dist. Of Col.	18,896,724	6,948,272	1,486,367	120,543	539,561	648,823	2,260,212	1,009,422	89,666	60,493	663,477	69,708
Florida	962,769	823,434	13,557	1,478	524	5,334	749,231	46,505	6,645	NA	NA	9
Georgia	21,099,547	11,442,740	2,311,334	3,130,508	741,022	1,572,630	1,615,943	997,420	43,001	234,056	776,955	19,871
Hawaii	792,867	587,186	186,262	NA	55,582	NA	250,405	NA	57,194	51	6,403	NA
Idaho	2,990,155	911,168	513,264	920	7,844	116,958	131,244	107,780	1,692	54	27,876	3,536
Illinois	*45,137,752*	*17,849,775*	*4,026,345*	*93,015*	*338,446*	*1,452,109*	*4,411,519*	*4,456,685*	*605,843*	*19,241*	*2,342,802*	*103,770*
Indiana	30,532,977	8,529,818	1,146,124	38,126	200,641	582,231	1,371,518	3,158,313	235,831	1,269	1,755,519	40,246
Percent U.S.	3.72	2.69	1.98	0.22	1.01	1.84	2.16	4.13	2.24	0.04	5.13	1.56
Rank	8	12	20	27	20	23	16	8	11	15	5	20
Iowa	9,418,591	3,631,625	1,683,991	13,591	104,064	227,255	695,963	332,801	10,835	53	534,601	28,471
Kansas	7,717,727	2,797,764	992,078	4,380	84,621	165,671	703,798	299,611	133,319	52	409,394	4,840
Kentucky	*12,016,319*	*4,720,234*	*822,453*	*190,310*	*534,103*	*460,330*	*704,362*	*843,626*	*244,663*	*274,095*	*616,235*	*30,057*
Louisiana	8,203,838	4,932,987	559,803	103,756	145,073	603,339	288,845	2,278,964	792,865	437	158,485	1,420
Maine	3,212,899	1,669,279	161,992	133,317	48,409	772,048	180,612	72,084	14,265	39	102,771	183,742
Maryland	7,969,697	3,629,034	746,921	NA	183,635	299,819	1,185,978	754,399	NA	36	341,202	31,406
Massachusetts	22,624,720	7,291,356	830,780	570,991	370,897	879,291	2,254,994	1,101,475	118,036	255	1,044,565	120,072
Michigan	*56,590,731*	*10,946,186*	*1,700,414*	*19,882*	*837,938*	*1,003,820*	*1,888,860*	*2,954,866*	*122,713*	*313*	*2,290,396*	*126,984*
Minnesota	18,967,549	7,945,098	2,148,425	50,932	102,372	2,044,086	2,073,442	588,713	166,558	118	696,799	73,653
Mississippi	7,135,996	2,726,025	635,977	111,333	423,243	456,657	216,323	358,483	143,707	57	373,977	6,268
Missouri	17,437,019	7,489,473	1,893,115	19,666	394,136	532,487	1,685,400	2,135,067	100,720	548	599,988	128,346
Montana	833,533	303,820	73,299	198	11,968	42,102	75,823	23,100	66,950	39	8,551	1,790
Nebraska	3,911,724	1,978,911	1,162,996	6,965	32,801	72,922	300,888	156,547	6,312	26	225,196	14,258
Nevada	1,464,062	504,629	107,168	1,182	21,074	14,875	189,471	57,454	5,441	NA	105,739	NA
New Hampshire	4,531,126	1,285,001	98,567	131,345	50,613	195,342	300,759	63,284	9,396	26	358,889	76,780
New Jersey	25,948,499	16,497,527	2,007,158	410,764	750,383	961,723	2,856,447	7,709,518	588,073	NA	1,097,528	NA
New Mexico	1,721,076	496,074	119,161	15,020	41,042	12,878	190,789	31,643	44,531	26	37,642	3,342
New York	47,005,633	21,955,460	2,726,212	561,912	2,763,023	1,440,574	8,432,760	3,976,079	354,460	306,221	1,175,766	218,453
North Carolina	29,456,678	15,225,253	1,506,086	4,963,472	1,148,712	1,067,408	1,077,394	2,892,695	39,036	1,046,973	1,424,531	58,926
North Dakota	696,866	272,399	149,173	NA	4,306	NA	65,842	11,789	17,579	14	20,030	580
Ohio	*51,492,877*	*15,719,848*	*2,328,870*	*153,523*	*313,935*	*1,612,206*	*2,842,777*	*4,446,135*	*504,648*	*277*	*3,420,099*	*97,378*
Oklahoma	7,000,934	2,469,796	478,706	26,507	126,722	181,578	333,447	435,248	366,729	19	509,172	11,668
Oregon	10,082,984	2,277,709	714,823	43,510	63,761	462,520	568,743	154,361	NA	NA	229,156	11,442
Pennsylvania	41,734,086	17,273,997	3,112,766	643,319	946,061	1,631,261	3,117,207	5,252,078	732,171	36,460	1,654,321	148,353
Rhode Island	2,977,578	1,089,693	85,349	235,844	21,575	81,671	262,018	134,518	1,256	14	238,569	28,879
South Carolina	13,050,118	7,668,999	442,677	2,325,958	549,682	873,605	434,997	2,084,374	24,381	645	931,340	1,340
South Dakota	1,418,364	427,694	244,711	NA	28,783	NA	77,843	5,837	930	31	45,163	764
Tennessee	19,341,225	8,269,130	1,249,435	525,585	844,911	932,005	1,252,267	2,085,529	59,992	65,761	1,166,891	86,754
Texas	53,041,124	24,366,331	3,054,624	98,240	1,268,317	1,216,370	2,732,193	11,970,788	2,163,192	4,589	1,681,270	176,748
Utah	4,580,756	1,299,393	349,392	10,226	74,456	83,106	340,436	232,817	71,356	40	133,753	3,811
Vermont	1,823,360	506,864	133,858	14,558	23,791	81,930	163,114	25,373	6,051	39	57,790	360
Virginia	15,470,185	7,540,756	1,145,581	901,148	341,444	839,411	1,616,930	1,154,691	30,449	717,961	774,822	18,319
Washington	16,297,938	4,246,625	1,376,805	38,120	179,531	898,763	882,270	406,702	175,854	178	277,151	11,251
West Virginia	3,375,192	1,474,040	119,404	23,567	31,206	40,947	142,206	1,004,421	29,703	7,188	64,142	11,256
Wisconsin	23,874,415	9,031,138	2,291,576	96,002	165,118	2,552,123	1,871,016	731,406	26,396	56	1,133,620	163,825
Wyoming	391,066	231,938	27,930	313	2,622	423	40,892	102,847	48,332	23	7,112	1,444

Manufacturing
Percent Change in Real Earnings
1990 to 1996

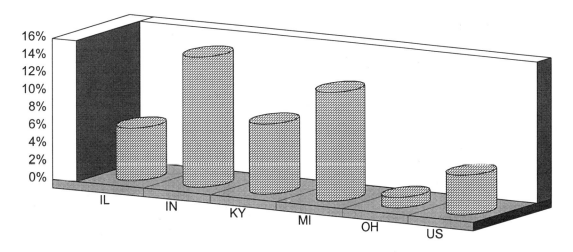

Source: U.S. Bureau of Economic Analysis
EDIN Table(s): PIMA

1.51 Earnings by Industry: Manufacturing - Durable Goods 1996 *($000)*

	Total Manufacturing¹	Durable Goods	Lumber and Wood	Furniture and Fixtures	Primary Metal Industries	Fabricated Metal	Machinery Except Electrical	Electric and Electronic Equip.	Transport. Eq. Except Motor Vehicles	Motor Vehicles and Equip.	Stone, Clay and Glass	Instruments and Related
United States	820,893,000	503,778,000	26,591,000	15,346,000	36,498,000	58,318,000	101,874,000	77,076,000	44,997,000	62,731,000	22,422,000	44,797,000
Alabama	13,209,020	7,378,098	1,143,472	298,500	1,238,611	792,664	1,108,518	876,054	634,837	670,896	353,715	117,255
Alaska	605,320	180,985	122,817	1,885	1,163	12,187	9,906	1,852	10,834	493	15,338	2,421
Arizona	8,923,848	7,148,611	247,752	112,301	314,368	438,080	581,493	2,502,355	1,587,849	273,559	325,747	625,814
Arkansas	7,574,601	4,229,430	674,690	250,028	460,790	706,759	574,770	618,649	197,899	320,430	176,233	160,873
California	88,844,924	61,252,608	1,868,008	1,528,726	1,619,264	5,101,878	12,995,242	13,741,522	8,085,045	1,735,841	2,000,051	10,957,693
Colorado	8,630,253	5,835,592	167,903	158,442	189,862	491,253	1,631,717	855,965	675,859	104,865	427,143	994,455
Connecticut	15,501,020	10,950,219	102,221	100,559	456,931	1,580,139	1,898,088	1,836,411	2,911,726	163,416	238,978	1,360,196
Delaware	4,374,738	857,640	14,865	15,077	74,502	73,567	61,353	NA	NA	327,611	31,507	212,489
Dist. Of Col.	962,769	139,335	1,285	4,063	3,902	1,568	9,276	NA	NA	6,948	5,136	2,625
Florida	18,896,724	11,948,452	660,013	376,869	249,635	1,081,363	1,591,548	2,809,386	2,169,620	312,515	842,367	1,555,265
Georgia	21,099,547	9,656,807	1,500,234	316,734	681,113	828,947	1,318,700	1,375,009	1,347,140	891,323	743,150	439,186
Hawaii	792,867	205,681	15,086	12,219	340	17,952	10,098	4,985	21,332	2,022	104,790	1,130
Idaho	2,990,155	2,078,987	750,454	31,911	8,740	99,453	521,301	498,849	44,791	37,435	47,261	17,439
Illinois	*45,137,752*	*27,287,977*	*439,244*	*514,143*	*2,288,821*	*4,564,500*	*8,193,389*	*5,254,991*	*571,214*	*2,053,241*	*976,078*	*1,569,204*
Indiana	30,532,977	22,003,159	911,128	749,551	3,880,048	2,346,001	3,223,746	2,597,995	1,047,728	5,367,286	721,551	794,197
Percent U.S.	3.72	4.37	3.43	4.88	10.63	4.02	3.16	3.37	2.33	8.56	3.22	1.77
Rank	8	8	10	5	3	8	12	9	14	3	12	16
Iowa	9,418,591	5,786,966	323,181	209,742	412,939	658,762	2,030,653	1,057,739	NA	491,644	242,486	NA
Kansas	7,717,727	4,919,963	123,589	45,330	126,617	339,548	886,190	315,130	2,160,803	493,433	234,541	149,434
Kentucky	*12,016,319*	*7,296,085*	*378,927*	*138,381*	*850,067*	*787,102*	*1,362,397*	*1,052,551*	*173,677*	*1,891,978*	*394,338*	*130,718*
Louisiana	8,203,838	3,270,851	522,042	18,636	110,485	487,129	598,420	231,522	752,897	225,232	205,089	60,909
Maine	3,212,899	1,543,620	347,900	39,481	19,803	109,697	169,194	279,464	469,836	15,385	43,585	28,058
Maryland	7,969,697	4,340,663	123,072	107,429	501,410	331,967	794,226	665,304	313,947	310,937	264,467	865,679
Massachusetts	22,624,720	15,333,364	158,708	159,638	478,208	1,886,037	3,863,317	3,452,206	1,078,560	77,762	378,645	3,185,118
Michigan	*56,590,731*	*45,644,545*	*656,058*	*1,762,502*	*2,001,328*	*5,920,129*	*6,745,314*	*1,526,401*	*540,941*	*24,353,858*	*995,649*	*819,341*
Minnesota	18,967,549	11,022,451	847,773	229,718	332,327	1,515,229	3,566,875	1,343,900	274,383	339,298	368,703	1,934,120
Mississippi	7,135,996	4,409,971	831,011	661,268	154,011	433,840	584,327	682,146	555,635	190,653	181,178	50,156
Missouri	17,437,019	9,947,546	356,718	434,613	532,546	1,334,742	1,410,851	1,130,574	1,645,653	2,054,583	411,218	424,312
Montana	833,533	529,713	281,865	13,242	47,040	24,558	53,916	6,828	9,656	7,367	35,515	11,186
Nebraska	3,911,724	1,932,813	NA	103,469	82,112	276,287	497,535	378,847	NA	140,843	93,432	176,994
Nevada	1,464,062	959,433	48,385	25,071	54,260	138,278	108,447	105,055	22,790	12,196	152,144	95,722
New Hampshire	4,531,126	3,246,125	162,750	33,038	195,402	319,523	952,240	789,529	47,411	24,150	80,137	581,010
New Jersey	25,948,499	9,450,972	137,509	232,675	640,105	1,355,559	1,760,467	1,583,612	163,542	447,261	723,782	1,889,801
New Mexico	1,721,076	1,225,002	53,728	17,513	65,296	53,156	75,222	514,369	95,882	47,112	94,589	128,716
New York	47,005,633	25,050,173	448,386	473,238	1,022,238	2,192,066	5,438,980	4,199,524	576,627	2,230,529	1,303,014	5,811,797
North Carolina	29,456,678	14,231,445	1,248,170	1,982,904	705,757	1,151,891	3,451,288	2,520,649	204,053	1,291,937	827,910	620,339
North Dakota	696,866	424,467	NA	NA	NA	39,473	181,270	39,344	20,529	54,559	22,960	NA
Ohio	*51,492,877*	*35,773,029*	*908,245*	*534,631*	*5,588,885*	*5,662,534*	*7,639,772*	*3,178,900*	*1,522,712*	*7,180,663*	*1,874,859*	*1,156,427*
Oklahoma	7,000,934	4,531,138	120,351	74,376	192,219	756,287	1,249,032	343,575	548,995	652,068	323,688	168,299
Oregon	10,082,984	7,805,275	2,278,808	113,977	549,597	520,105	1,016,987	1,701,454	320,704	414,528	188,260	563,450
Pennsylvania	41,734,086	24,460,089	1,126,541	580,337	4,411,837	3,534,086	4,759,170	3,102,165	1,877,443	923,060	1,760,409	1,589,555
Rhode Island	2,977,578	1,887,885	22,054	57,586	212,502	242,284	171,521	196,606	106,677	29,791	53,101	221,538
South Carolina	13,050,118	5,381,119	468,301	126,323	401,091	631,426	1,463,744	854,105	146,447	648,465	361,349	168,947
South Dakota	1,418,364	990,670	88,263	NA	NA	56,865	458,356	102,747	6,322	54,842	40,875	74,634
Tennessee	19,341,225	11,072,095	667,178	834,368	735,666	1,592,041	1,597,647	1,438,025	411,712	2,362,592	667,247	410,802
Texas	53,041,124	28,674,793	1,312,025	512,957	1,355,925	3,565,149	7,393,990	6,520,487	3,018,633	780,183	1,427,942	2,066,057
Utah	4,580,756	3,281,363	122,086	109,799	362,927	296,841	522,984	278,272	535,327	304,762	176,396	342,018
Vermont	1,823,360	1,316,496	132,478	60,828	35,726	106,221	161,789	513,670	89,756	23,847	84,369	61,694
Virginia	15,470,185	7,929,429	772,874	495,227	500,433	728,182	1,013,021	1,503,744	1,299,678	646,382	402,644	458,539
Washington	16,297,938	12,051,313	1,542,083	132,838	603,018	511,748	1,075,387	632,202	5,935,266	277,853	348,980	729,637
West Virginia	3,375,192	1,901,152	267,147	16,427	709,963	229,112	187,992	72,963	111,550	26,885	196,925	62,102
Wisconsin	23,874,415	14,843,277	957,005	503,486	997,758	2,376,736	4,863,806	1,689,574	378,201	1,434,064	425,934	872,857
Wyoming	391,066	159,128	39,123	2,800	12,592	17,099	38,528	6,184	5,782	2,417	26,595	3,534

Durable Manufacturing
Percent Change in Real Earnings
1990 to 1996

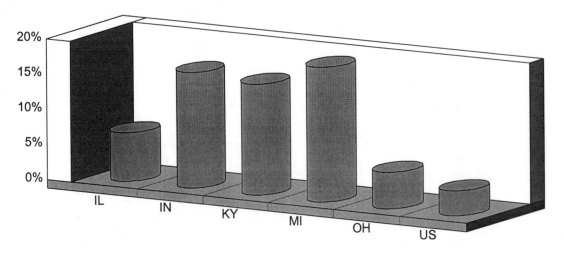

Footnote: ¹Includes categories not shown separately.
Source: U.S. Bureau of Economic Analysis
EDIN Table(s): PIMA

1.52 Earnings by Industry: Transportation and Public Utilities 1996 *($000)*

	Total	Railroad Transportation	Trucking and Warehousing	Water Transportation	Other Transportation	Local & Inter-urban Passenger	Air Transportation	Pipelines Except Natural Gas	Transportation Services	Communication	Electric, Gas and Sanitary
United States	308,977,000	12,889,000	67,322,000	7,321,000	73,564,000	10,933,000	44,138,000	946,000	17,547,000	85,767,000	62,114,000
Alabama	4,049,949	204,296	1,245,158	NA	NA	NA	212,846	3,879	85,810	1,061,269	1,075,149
Alaska	1,145,773	0	138,485	90,175	549,710	44,265	335,591	121,025	48,829	191,509	175,894
Arizona	3,868,134	139,868	758,971	4,939	1,221,696	136,143	895,596	10,326	179,631	949,817	792,843
Arkansas	2,763,157	218,887	1,180,681	15,765	278,929	36,732	174,985	11,612	55,600	524,030	544,865
California	35,210,503	789,461	6,533,000	1,248,397	9,466,016	1,172,759	5,454,984	99,730	2,738,543	10,339,444	6,834,185
Colorado	6,911,638	279,272	917,101	1,802	1,282,218	137,555	869,334	7,942	267,387	3,388,154	1,043,091
Connecticut	3,936,928	NA	566,682	100,961	NA	326,707	313,061	NA	332,025	1,255,786	1,001,433
Delaware	695,059	NA	176,458	16,838	NA	33,100	49,492	NA	21,288	117,399	220,666
Dist. Of Col.	1,337,123	NA	28,563	6,023	NA	39,918	44,403	NA	61,438	802,106	239,669
Florida	13,952,009	456,926	2,475,507	708,004	4,014,054	463,495	2,468,149	5,379	1,077,031	4,250,810	2,046,708
Georgia	12,018,433	389,019	2,101,433	90,753	3,296,284	151,630	2,545,012	31,424	568,218	4,693,102	1,447,842
Hawaii	1,745,382	0	142,588	165,013	846,347	132,740	511,232	0	202,375	350,404	241,030
Idaho	1,088,893	109,315	351,904	3,926	142,121	20,106	81,963	1,411	38,641	143,740	337,887
Illinois	*16,614,201*	*996,584*	*3,709,259*	*145,722*	*4,603,386*	*561,930*	*2,756,089*	*32,814*	*1,252,553*	*4,077,953*	*3,081,297*
Indiana	**5,801,047**	**354,295**	**2,366,989**	**94,891**	**895,973**	**127,541**	**591,801**	**15,891**	**160,740**	**854,369**	**1,234,530**
Percent U.S.	*1.88*	*2.75*	*3.52*	*1.30*	*1.22*	*1.17*	*1.34*	*1.68*	*0.92*	*1.00*	*1.99*
Rank	*18*	*13*	*9*	*16*	*20*	*25*	*22*	*12*	*26*	*25*	*15*
Iowa	2,691,157	211,931	1,093,876	19,262	275,867	34,640	167,821	7,406	66,000	513,445	576,776
Kansas	3,196,592	405,445	824,241	913	406,770	51,668	195,664	35,417	124,021	912,631	646,592
Kentucky	*3,934,875*	*249,426*	*1,014,783*	*101,044*	*1,262,313*	*73,486*	*1,077,003*	*4,690*	*107,134*	*526,836*	*780,473*
Louisiana	4,516,544	202,957	860,996	877,241	684,136	174,961	295,399	50,079	163,697	860,027	1,031,187
Maine	987,550	NA	303,319	NA	NA	32,924	63,112	NA	26,249	213,716	283,992
Maryland	5,044,542	NA	981,466	142,798	NA	239,268	517,062	NA	241,618	1,702,323	1,081,604
Massachusetts	6,909,445	147,525	994,686	NA	NA	508,452	826,938	NA	443,530	1,814,160	2,067,639
Michigan	*8,321,194*	*331,423*	*2,101,648*	*63,400*	*2,010,736*	*184,813*	*1,194,330*	*15,188*	*616,405*	*1,652,220*	*2,161,767*
Minnesota	5,587,177	337,415	1,292,090	39,129	1,921,439	246,962	1,327,793	18,958	327,726	987,455	1,009,649
Mississippi	2,193,336	105,571	736,315	85,429	263,374	39,242	171,202	10,650	42,280	489,041	513,606
Missouri	7,389,761	442,304	2,047,828	61,481	1,441,491	178,116	930,423	10,182	322,770	2,162,007	1,234,650
Montana	912,137	166,042	247,580	441	135,824	23,732	74,274	5,402	32,416	122,512	239,738
Nebraska	2,389,232	624,237	851,315	989	237,889	35,248	144,422	4,264	53,955	401,925	272,877
Nevada	1,788,995	55,568	286,535	NA	NA	274,083	260,268	NA	76,224	377,842	451,371
New Hampshire	1,154,678	21,163	189,812	NA	NA	53,003	93,290	NA	32,771	219,063	538,826
New Jersey	14,359,956	122,789	2,691,213	533,779	3,161,624	866,774	1,447,192	8,073	839,585	5,675,352	2,175,199
New Mexico	1,306,825	106,070	298,174	834	239,232	54,647	143,278	9,818	31,489	262,043	400,472
New York	22,882,529	428,473	2,562,236	423,462	6,251,438	1,804,531	3,121,552	6,068	1,319,087	9,019,595	4,197,325
North Carolina	7,543,196	144,907	2,259,413	32,962	1,773,863	103,434	1,261,407	6,163	402,859	1,590,915	1,741,136
North Dakota	812,281	111,134	228,007	107	95,920	19,415	41,315	5,078	30,112	101,161	275,952
Ohio	*10,508,901*	*506,451*	*3,331,883*	*140,782*	*1,902,624*	*235,567*	*1,144,711*	*30,992*	*491,354*	*2,513,463*	*2,113,698*
Oklahoma	3,586,451	96,406	863,430	5,933	928,096	30,644	738,401	57,125	101,926	759,344	933,242
Oregon	3,333,193	165,339	1,103,107	NA	NA	98,085	384,136	NA	186,797	619,299	664,786
Pennsylvania	13,607,830	739,058	3,103,580	196,157	3,098,003	645,134	1,861,498	40,294	551,077	3,176,642	3,294,390
Rhode Island	759,611	11,603	140,455	19,042	131,715	45,911	53,243	0	32,561	229,316	227,480
South Carolina	2,936,231	111,079	919,317	73,837	406,707	NA	231,182	NA	125,207	588,047	837,244
South Dakota	709,707	39,721	306,643	428	90,146	19,892	52,847	2,357	15,050	115,712	157,057
Tennessee	6,270,988	265,096	2,239,951	NA	NA	155,986	1,668,036	NA	208,824	1,239,115	414,916
Texas	27,836,048	959,559	4,619,655	588,778	7,483,434	465,823	4,434,427	228,596	2,354,588	7,078,983	7,105,639
Utah	2,259,873	133,348	685,925	928	543,197	26,353	442,732	3,445	70,667	405,890	490,585
Vermont	510,589	11,477	142,821	5,790	86,173	25,594	41,173	0	19,406	132,661	131,667
Virginia	7,638,671	411,832	1,423,976	213,243	1,653,510	216,150	1,073,313	4,868	359,179	2,674,265	1,261,845
Washington	6,640,058	280,260	1,251,228	512,906	1,435,172	133,098	882,320	6,131	413,623	2,453,165	707,327
West Virginia	1,693,472	191,023	418,422	37,896	116,048	26,578	67,520	1,163	20,787	312,394	617,689
Wisconsin	4,966,051	233,346	2,080,479	27,238	867,528	297,004	371,466	6,328	192,730	799,027	958,433
Wyoming	659,095	192,284	132,816	159	68,238	10,874	32,712	11,465	13,187	65,516	200,082

Transportation and Public Utilities
Percent Change in Real Earnings
1990 to 1996

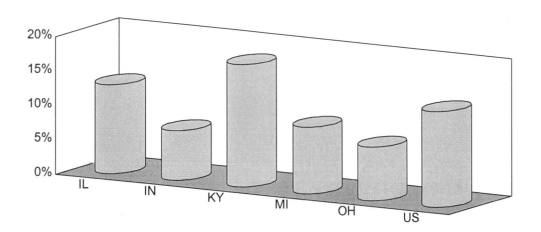

Source: U.S. Bureau of Economic Analysis
EDIN Table(s): PITR

1.53 Earnings by Industry: Wholesale and Retail 1996 ($000)

	Wholesale	Retail	Building Materials & Farm Equipment	General Merchandise Stores	Food Stores	Auto Dealers & Service Stations	Apparel and Accessory Stores	Furniture and Home Furnishings	Eating and Drinking Places	Misc. Retail
United States	284,507,000	415,353,000	23,369,000	44,842,000	64,393,000	71,286,000	19,219,000	25,005,000	98,164,000	69,075,000
Alabama	3,384,018	5,668,810	344,138	683,113	867,965	1,138,858	281,743	301,823	1,243,972	807,198
Alaska	345,211	1,123,060	63,868	156,779	183,687	173,032	25,547	39,965	282,224	197,958
Arizona	4,032,490	7,199,747	357,772	622,593	1,220,200	1,497,969	206,801	523,504	1,683,169	1,087,739
Arkansas	1,670,497	3,555,902	220,487	869,595	487,438	617,675	95,850	151,535	670,047	443,275
California	35,216,143	51,555,524	2,320,705	4,525,772	8,725,163	8,131,458	2,830,691	3,619,856	12,509,179	8,892,700
Colorado	4,279,674	7,070,792	429,798	622,687	1,113,264	1,225,253	237,205	425,730	1,933,118	1,083,737
Connecticut	4,796,152	5,999,721	334,806	561,665	1,015,514	974,652	337,045	375,475	1,145,899	1,254,665
Delaware	590,780	1,263,353	69,901	120,968	181,859	217,511	46,887	82,803	332,146	211,278
Dist. Of Col.	298,358	877,265	13,785	41,925	114,980	32,063	56,171	22,966	452,227	143,148
Florida	13,921,306	24,465,240	1,234,029	2,493,699	3,928,415	4,338,352	1,097,492	1,587,046	6,202,692	3,583,515
Georgia	10,694,991	11,878,475	814,595	1,334,160	1,643,040	2,118,034	533,941	739,778	3,096,310	1,598,617
Hawaii	790,945	2,620,268	60,626	234,643	308,546	271,094	191,726	86,649	786,510	680,474
Idaho	909,808	1,768,521	146,682	170,464	354,819	355,461	43,356	101,594	365,523	230,622
Illinois	*16,315,790*	*18,521,158*	*1,061,606*	*2,265,086*	*2,483,939*	*2,954,403*	*845,621*	*1,182,381*	*4,625,542*	*3,102,580*
Indiana	5,303,457	8,811,991	607,552	1,074,464	1,139,982	1,618,137	280,352	457,398	2,155,996	1,478,110
Percent U.S.	*1.86*	*2.12*	*2.60*	*2.40*	*1.77*	*2.27*	*1.46*	*1.83*	*2.20*	*2.14*
Rank	*18*	*16*	*11*	*15*	*18*	*15*	*21*	*18*	*16*	*13*
Iowa	2,925,849	4,143,840	317,093	469,448	644,943	845,022	147,710	227,641	857,980	634,003
Kansas	3,002,000	4,007,812	251,894	482,637	559,233	719,209	204,544	232,409	970,073	587,813
Kentucky	*2,835,925*	*5,414,447*	*347,269*	*664,367*	*834,540*	*963,127*	*178,583*	*304,417*	*1,344,395*	*777,749*
Louisiana	3,231,663	5,462,367	308,099	630,085	922,609	1,025,141	192,804	266,330	1,381,096	736,203
Maine	916,486	2,015,401	124,284	177,342	323,580	327,306	81,776	71,348	440,820	468,945
Maryland	4,847,143	8,257,405	430,642	723,662	1,532,592	1,426,376	333,328	595,691	1,849,101	1,366,013
Massachusetts	8,741,404	11,284,966	531,101	901,562	1,828,315	1,440,597	780,802	617,009	2,749,436	2,436,144
Michigan	*10,485,860*	*14,225,117*	*910,142*	*2,126,986*	*1,795,921*	*2,804,356*	*511,439*	*797,373*	*3,262,699*	*2,016,201*
Minnesota	7,014,170	7,974,041	459,406	1,116,631	992,716	1,381,290	287,804	557,342	1,729,499	1,449,353
Mississippi	1,491,608	3,215,929	220,810	445,912	549,310	665,424	103,387	152,267	618,603	460,216
Missouri	6,004,391	8,284,493	555,698	1,150,124	1,048,738	1,674,909	317,078	416,531	1,974,971	1,146,444
Montana	573,288	1,354,324	114,410	129,428	190,024	267,666	32,068	75,443	348,113	197,172
Nebraska	1,750,234	2,526,484	165,397	279,196	352,543	488,470	83,147	152,331	563,290	442,110
Nevada	1,302,141	2,974,907	144,602	289,249	461,479	561,337	126,314	164,134	712,948	514,844
New Hampshire	1,325,635	2,302,853	149,706	236,504	338,164	423,763	87,866	137,160	475,160	454,530
New Jersey	14,173,551	13,050,197	585,270	1,145,701	2,491,554	2,010,121	908,401	868,932	2,502,860	2,537,358
New Mexico	899,192	2,459,675	155,781	226,243	349,550	467,968	73,105	137,855	639,763	409,410
New York	21,645,614	25,160,935	1,157,447	2,291,435	4,094,254	2,935,490	1,923,912	1,394,679	5,889,688	5,474,030
North Carolina	7,132,382	11,391,110	871,728	1,175,084	1,726,788	2,128,027	437,454	788,389	2,743,461	1,520,179
North Dakota	743,501	919,086	61,957	98,086	117,315	216,969	26,282	45,504	202,782	150,191
Ohio	*12,041,874*	*17,423,370*	*956,837*	*1,964,284*	*2,664,104*	*2,980,258*	*772,194*	*1,013,117*	*4,124,883*	*2,947,693*
Oklahoma	2,213,201	4,377,056	246,422	488,687	605,689	870,891	148,924	256,515	1,090,480	669,448
Oregon	3,818,224	5,691,769	342,677	744,026	876,190	1,091,317	245,831	283,712	1,347,920	760,096
Pennsylvania	11,328,990	18,377,169	1,288,383	1,976,141	3,115,895	2,923,976	833,268	915,479	3,766,721	3,557,756
Rhode Island	778,652	1,408,126	57,102	106,795	228,415	203,118	53,298	52,352	354,693	352,353
South Carolina	2,517,739	5,649,974	389,715	556,113	891,893	996,026	237,973	368,001	1,414,641	795,612
South Dakota	645,920	1,136,645	86,278	107,467	142,854	253,109	29,385	58,776	249,121	209,655
Tennessee	5,500,288	9,055,854	564,851	1,050,551	1,213,039	1,821,628	393,831	442,180	2,195,122	1,374,652
Texas	21,189,657	29,510,551	1,418,988	3,625,299	4,478,211	5,468,755	1,201,703	1,747,784	7,192,145	4,377,666
Utah	1,750,124	3,228,365	198,056	305,162	492,975	647,293	113,838	250,787	644,740	575,514
Vermont	459,287	942,876	63,745	49,200	167,677	163,060	33,238	38,558	208,836	218,562
Virginia	6,284,122	10,086,953	510,661	1,143,996	1,527,795	1,952,617	377,960	818,147	2,301,220	1,454,557
Washington	6,093,147	9,319,522	595,105	939,869	1,627,025	1,527,160	515,742	549,836	2,169,871	1,394,914
West Virginia	1,003,406	2,011,499	127,172	248,631	356,989	398,391	54,910	97,329	446,367	281,710
Wisconsin	5,053,754	7,611,987	535,704	933,080	988,363	1,381,106	232,704	381,984	1,737,240	1,421,806
Wyoming	236,958	715,618	44,218	65,404	92,907	170,775	25,969	29,155	178,708	108,482

Wholesale and Retail Trade
Percent Change in Real Earnings
1990 to 1996

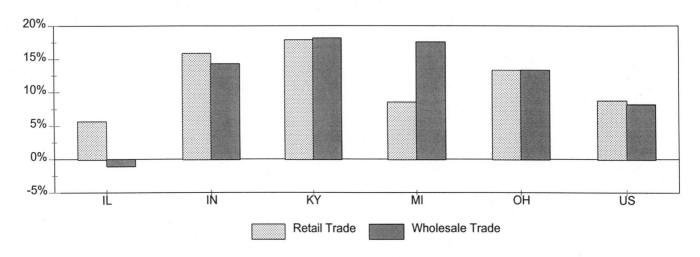

Legend: Retail Trade, Wholesale Trade

Source: U.S. Bureau of Economic Analysis
EDIN Table(s): PIRT

1.54 Earnings by Industry: Finance, Insurance, and Real Estate 1996 *($000)*

	Finance, Insurance & Real Estate	Banking and Credit Agencies	Other Finance, Insurance, Real Estate	Security & Commodity Brokers & Services	Insurance Carriers	Insurance Agents, Brokers & Services	Real Estate	Holding & Other Investment Companies
United States	375,626,000	102,128,000	273,498,000	71,501,000	71,366,000	42,143,000	68,152,000	20,336,000
Alabama	3,314,143	1,125,998	2,188,145	196,875	670,384	434,475	725,452	160,959
Alaska	454,487	152,361	302,126	23,699	48,738	58,846	95,468	75,375
Arizona	5,587,076	1,827,471	3,759,605	371,159	795,856	696,029	1,725,241	171,320
Arkansas	1,559,441	501,747	1,057,694	170,953	244,656	260,063	306,766	75,256
California	45,559,844	12,242,271	33,317,573	6,505,527	6,860,354	5,281,064	12,355,056	2,315,572
Colorado	5,596,444	1,375,603	4,220,841	684,240	1,086,018	606,466	1,389,654	454,463
Connecticut	9,360,132	1,648,678	7,711,454	1,535,593	3,849,362	746,275	956,117	624,107
Delaware	1,937,102	1,222,340	714,762	155,447	231,890	90,796	179,712	56,917
Dist. Of Col.	1,864,983	564,340	1,300,643	307,088	230,532	59,850	509,656	193,517
Florida	18,603,202	5,037,976	13,565,226	2,297,625	3,190,386	2,330,652	4,925,354	821,209
Georgia	8,916,168	2,621,568	6,294,600	842,681	1,818,876	1,256,676	1,814,683	561,684
Hawaii	1,757,155	490,026	1,267,129	60,723	194,648	174,065	733,518	104,175
Idaho	853,172	306,746	546,426	52,748	128,196	143,962	201,156	20,364
Illinois	*21,841,613*	*5,863,941*	*15,977,672*	*4,056,542*	*5,207,776*	*2,149,719*	*3,319,012*	*1,244,623*
Indiana	5,325,132	1,696,185	3,628,947	335,131	1,445,284	742,826	998,238	107,468
Percent U.S.	*1.42*	*1.66*	*1.33*	*0.47*	*2.03*	*1.76*	*1.46*	*0.53*
Rank	*22*	*20*	*22*	*23*	*15*	*18*	*19*	*31*
Iowa	3,125,040	948,712	2,176,328	166,756	1,092,805	512,623	305,903	98,241
Kansas	2,424,947	711,351	1,713,596	156,410	557,883	470,418	391,234	137,651
Kentucky	*2,673,166*	*960,293*	*1,712,873*	*250,788*	*424,530*	*440,418*	*420,891*	*176,246*
Louisiana	3,080,035	1,073,218	2,006,817	190,489	561,516	616,567	437,065	201,180
Maine	1,057,133	317,033	740,100	67,079	360,662	159,947	137,064	15,348
Maryland	6,732,522	1,778,462	4,954,060	945,545	1,367,566	740,245	1,767,274	133,430
Massachusetts	13,230,152	3,110,387	10,119,765	3,934,012	2,617,967	1,210,692	1,821,821	535,273
Michigan	*9,111,449*	*2,998,059*	*6,113,390*	*683,030*	*1,995,582*	*1,266,376*	*1,573,741*	*594,661*
Minnesota	7,262,971	1,817,962	5,445,009	1,241,563	1,978,022	894,667	928,498	402,259
Mississippi	1,453,136	604,356	848,780	71,715	259,956	288,197	188,483	40,429
Missouri	6,293,588	1,939,335	4,354,253	971,557	1,320,878	834,942	927,101	299,775
Montana	601,220	195,559	405,661	56,271	76,712	107,885	130,873	33,920
Nebraska	1,989,888	564,283	1,425,605	144,246	687,982	325,474	203,718	64,185
Nevada	2,151,028	508,159	1,642,869	100,686	219,910	199,372	1,051,532	71,369
New Hampshire	1,289,380	276,435	1,012,945	98,206	432,662	180,725	237,768	63,584
New Jersey	14,212,462	3,102,981	11,109,481	3,179,324	3,681,427	1,669,337	1,955,441	623,952
New Mexico	1,119,283	377,252	742,031	73,518	152,697	164,883	322,130	28,803
New York	70,375,711	15,445,215	54,930,496	32,919,145	6,825,559	4,262,600	6,533,628	4,389,564
North Carolina	7,360,442	2,758,611	4,601,831	665,112	1,345,341	978,167	1,311,813	301,398
North Dakota	489,181	195,122	294,059	33,406	102,588	94,579	57,683	5,803
Ohio	*11,524,570*	*3,589,975*	*7,934,595*	*970,920*	*2,940,032*	*1,355,816*	*1,953,699*	*714,128*
Oklahoma	2,293,775	770,576	1,523,199	136,998	432,222	400,571	402,999	150,409
Oregon	3,401,837	1,055,285	2,346,552	288,746	672,300	449,938	789,117	146,451
Pennsylvania	15,224,776	4,173,287	11,051,489	1,653,120	4,322,175	1,949,702	2,269,938	856,554
Rhode Island	1,080,512	324,262	756,250	85,019	306,972	136,767	166,661	60,831
South Carolina	2,736,149	902,273	1,833,876	150,673	533,368	420,251	670,505	59,079
South Dakota	676,645	330,122	346,523	38,864	84,635	132,398	81,771	8,855
Tennessee	5,141,369	1,701,029	3,440,340	533,533	998,389	721,886	976,196	210,336
Texas	21,754,821	5,731,283	16,023,538	2,007,713	4,044,702	3,240,258	4,923,883	1,806,982
Utah	2,150,234	755,310	1,394,924	131,292	320,814	292,117	492,376	158,325
Vermont	498,283	170,204	328,079	33,034	114,232	80,055	80,409	20,349
Virginia	7,804,932	2,715,612	5,089,320	678,524	1,326,704	728,635	2,044,597	310,860
Washington	5,988,337	1,707,953	4,280,384	595,452	1,209,584	792,619	1,448,640	234,089
West Virginia	843,856	307,916	535,940	49,245	139,649	172,910	133,822	40,314
Wisconsin	5,628,985	1,433,871	4,195,114	571,962	1,809,211	770,257	709,087	334,597
Wyoming	314,091	99,006	215,085	31,016	45,810	48,942	69,556	19,761

Finance, Insurance & Real Estate
Percent Change in Real Earnings
1990 to 1996

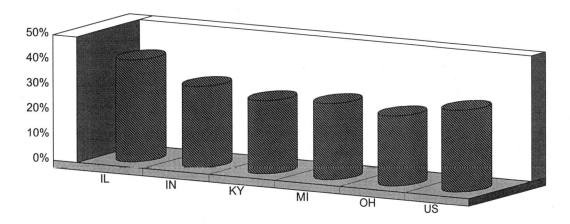

Source: U.S. Bureau of Economic Analysis
EDIN Table(s): PIFI

1.55 Earnings by Industry: Services 1996 *($000)*

	Total [1]	Hotels and Other Lodging	Personal Services	Private Households	Business Services	Auto Repair and Garages	Amusement and Recreation Services	Health Services	Legal Services	Education Services	Social Services
United States	1,280,038	39,675	39,163	11,212	262,237	37,362	42,608	388,834	91,945	53,200	45,092
Alabama	13,531	215	514	160	2,123	473	226	5,160	1,047	336	371
Alaska	2,428	144	75	17	347	92	85	633	125	48	150
Arizona	18,503	911	664	145	4,047	729	711	5,501	1,048	426	655
Arkansas	6,933	149	304	69	1,123	284	125	3,068	326	151	307
California	185,394	4,474	5,436	2,208	43,815	5,737	7,705	43,015	13,311	5,786	4,854
Colorado	20,686	759	648	143	5,358	680	1,100	5,103	1,145	476	601
Connecticut	22,442	267	664	163	5,189	500	830	7,130	1,361	1,420	867
Delaware	3,404	47	108	29	628	101	100	1,218	292	117	158
Dist. Of Col.	14,268	586	119	91	1,377	74	104	1,752	3,665	1,176	456
Florida	68,762	3,091	2,041	744	13,355	1,995	3,843	22,958	4,787	1,751	2,090
Georgia	32,206	1,040	1,000	323	8,157	1,058	880	9,551	2,040	1,223	739
Hawaii	6,415	1,285	208	31	848	191	272	1,727	406	310	212
Idaho	3,775	121	139	29	503	164	113	1,228	183	98	147
Illinois	*64,746*	*1,278*	*1,825*	*341*	*15,135*	*1,861*	*1,941*	*16,850*	*5,632*	*2,849*	*2,210*
Indiana	**19,924**	**366**	**834**	**140**	**3,315**	**782**	**632**	**8,077**	**1,015**	**855**	**784**
Percent U.S.	*1.56*	*0.92*	*2.13*	*1.25*	*1.26*	*2.09*	*1.48*	*2.08*	*1.10*	*1.61*	*1.74*
Rank	*21*	*29*	*16*	*23*	*22*	*16*	*24*	*14*	*25*	*19*	*18*
Iowa	9,672	193	402	83	1,663	371	391	3,672	475	482	500
Kansas	9,355	162	394	69	1,788	328	161	3,451	400	270	361
Kentucky	*12,009*	*250*	*491*	*117*	*1,854*	*446*	*281*	*5,267*	*736*	*359*	*385*
Louisiana	15,894	438	503	200	2,275	413	912	5,746	1,482	632	404
Maine	4,562	164	135	46	536	167	97	1,828	271	239	311
Maryland	27,835	842	746	265	6,079	726	726	7,972	1,772	1,198	1,056
Massachusetts	45,744	915	1,015	203	9,652	948	947	13,377	3,208	4,177	1,681
Michigan	*40,575*	*587*	*1,311*	*238*	*8,635*	*1,293*	*1,088*	*14,156*	*2,241*	*1,029*	*1,612*
Minnesota	22,794	484	792	113	5,083	734	864	7,380	1,421	828	1,173
Mississippi	7,259	411	271	120	801	248	611	2,781	475	239	206
Missouri	23,074	573	860	154	3,832	868	1,028	8,072	1,447	1,367	753
Montana	2,931	131	109	24	347	130	114	1,129	152	70	151
Nebraska	6,683	92	252	48	1,710	245	169	2,176	337	279	232
Nevada	12,593	5,438	324	41	1,387	283	877	1,964	435	59	121
New Hampshire	5,547	156	197	32	1,142	212	150	1,848	296	404	249
New Jersey	49,326	2,890	1,188	289	11,570	1,159	1,111	14,594	3,126	1,554	1,241
New Mexico	6,133	231	195	56	899	204	153	1,749	324	143	244
New York	118,131	2,322	2,439	1,397	21,680	1,870	4,288	33,504	13,157	7,207	6,411
North Carolina	26,003	580	1,029	235	5,517	865	643	8,925	1,296	1,085	1,019
North Dakota	2,275	64	102	17	276	88	59	1,067	84	56	120
Ohio	*45,475*	*688*	*1,680*	*259*	*8,219*	*1,470*	*1,327*	*16,974*	*2,773*	*1,738*	*1,797*
Oklahoma	10,571	152	430	111	2,002	505	204	3,789	710	294	399
Oregon	13,378	380	488	94	2,899	551	392	4,344	742	404	627
Pennsylvania	58,923	995	1,733	299	9,255	1,680	1,456	21,588	4,144	4,920	2,751
Rhode Island	4,929	75	138	22	856	116	91	1,934	310	460	247
South Carolina	11,080	433	470	139	1,984	415	385	3,352	784	329	409
South Dakota	2,606	103	102	17	295	95	113	1,146	108	101	142
Tennessee	22,817	764	869	172	3,989	666	703	8,596	984	862	509
Texas	82,349	1,841	2,792	985	19,380	2,639	2,010	24,598	6,728	2,075	1,826
Utah	8,151	243	255	36	1,896	305	250	2,233	360	407	200
Vermont	2,513	190	71	24	340	82	62	875	144	236	103
Virginia	32,995	859	1,005	336	8,313	835	621	7,942	1,614	1,018	902
Washington	26,704	617	821	168	6,967	849	867	7,426	1,495	676	940
West Virginia	5,130	148	189	43	556	138	92	2,366	419	141	258
Wisconsin	19,289	408	728	113	3,070	632	637	7,668	1,037	818	1,071
Wyoming	1,311	122	60	13	170	63	62	377	78	22	80

Services
Percent Change in Real Earnings
1990 to 1996

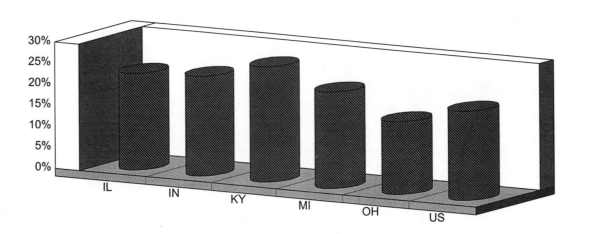

Footnote: [1]Includes categories not shown separately.
Source: U.S. Bureau of Economic Analysis
EDIN Table(s): PISE

1.56 Earnings by Industry: Mining and Government 1996 *($000)*

	Mining					Government			
	Total	Coal Mining	Oil and Gas Extraction	Metal Mining	Nonmetallic Minerals Exc. Fuels	Total	Federal Civilian	Military	State and Local
United States	39,044,000	7,053,000	23,830,000	3,257,000	4,904,000	692,491,000	132,171,000	48,833,000	511,487,000
Alabama	631,331	432,444	NA	NA	117,037	10,965,820	2,574,308	874,055	7,517,457
Alaska	891,477	NA	788,855	72,393	NA	3,469,754	765,866	645,657	2,058,231
Arizona	811,181	60,815	16,391	693,010	40,965	10,149,113	1,866,290	796,193	7,486,630
Arkansas	161,601	NA	NA	NA	46,731	5,019,036	889,086	283,384	3,846,566
California	2,063,547	59,247	1,496,316	156,542	351,442	84,949,757	12,967,945	6,157,575	65,824,237
Colorado	1,302,447	194,498	865,006	180,585	62,358	11,102,893	2,467,723	1,114,080	7,521,090
Connecticut	91,144	1,771	39,071	68	50,234	8,695,119	1,124,200	381,366	7,189,553
Delaware	6,687	NA	2,043	NA	NA	1,923,118	242,886	171,789	1,508,443
Dist. Of Col.	14,291	NA	10,231	NA	NA	13,958,754	11,286,320	748,363	1,924,071
Florida	398,564	18,152	91,722	8,807	279,883	32,355,125	5,351,029	2,967,852	24,036,244
Georgia	350,033	2,850	5,069	83	342,031	19,036,360	4,009,867	2,211,312	12,815,181
Hawaii	18,716	0	NA	29	NA	5,317,041	1,220,840	1,583,920	2,512,281
Idaho	170,337	5,363	4,540	85,705	74,729	2,715,541	518,188	164,548	2,032,805
Illinois	*775,297*	*439,883*	*136,822*	*1,255*	*197,337*	*28,727,863*	*4,671,313*	*1,195,927*	*22,860,623*
Indiana	**354,146**	**205,702**	**22,894**	**36**	**125,514**	**11,565,394**	**1,767,126**	**227,210**	**9,571,058**
Percent U.S.	*0.91*	*2.92*	*0.10*	*0.00*	*2.56*	*1.67*	*1.34*	*0.47*	*1.87*
Rank	*23*	*10*	*24*	*37*	*14*	*19*	*23*	*37*	*18*
Iowa	79,449	NA	NA	71	73,987	6,630,314	852,196	124,594	5,653,524
Kansas	395,845	10,061	344,138	0	41,646	7,033,899	1,207,334	688,122	5,138,443
Kentucky	*1,348,202*	*1,179,738*	*61,392*	*89*	*106,983*	*8,945,274*	*1,564,442*	*1,122,960*	*6,257,872*
Louisiana	2,720,726	NA	2,570,944	NA	109,245	9,959,595	1,523,801	800,044	7,635,750
Maine	4,520	NA	NA	390	2,218	2,846,764	576,917	201,111	2,068,736
Maryland	72,143	26,586	5,021	31	40,505	18,591,185	7,425,849	1,366,486	9,798,850
Massachusetts	65,912	10,406	NA	NA	49,334	15,111,413	2,621,590	368,699	12,121,124
Michigan	*402,763*	*9,265*	*153,704*	*125,441*	*114,353*	*21,490,936*	*2,446,997*	*258,672*	*18,785,267*
Minnesota	453,527	7,970	19,951	344,237	81,369	11,586,161	1,538,158	194,400	9,853,603
Mississippi	244,984	1,843	222,320	71	20,750	6,136,298	1,091,487	672,736	4,372,075
Missouri	239,796	NA	9,127	NA	118,296	12,102,134	2,690,943	637,007	8,774,184
Montana	289,637	60,311	76,324	119,275	33,727	2,179,793	526,949	163,060	1,489,784
Nebraska	59,408	9,510	NA	NA	33,325	4,515,811	623,544	395,501	3,496,766
Nevada	826,020	NA	NA	747,487	63,419	3,969,845	630,708	289,965	3,049,172
New Hampshire	20,131	0	892	95	19,144	2,290,875	369,634	43,196	1,878,045
New Jersey	214,493	6,831	18,545	364	188,753	23,384,666	3,308,453	514,188	19,562,025
New Mexico	758,843	114,410	439,615	111,240	93,578	5,584,987	1,328,669	547,633	3,708,685
New York	319,230	8,746	111,658	30,978	167,848	54,845,639	6,602,548	924,766	47,318,325
North Carolina	179,696	13,120	6,017	607	159,952	19,360,166	2,586,190	3,079,985	13,693,991
North Dakota	186,112	67,139	99,105	3	19,865	1,776,447	338,563	345,989	1,091,895
Ohio	*824,619*	*274,284*	*269,867*	*70,046*	*210,422*	*24,242,348*	*3,918,997*	*643,038*	*19,680,313*
Oklahoma	2,061,843	35,962	1,966,322	2,606	56,953	8,446,176	1,948,818	987,696	5,509,662
Oregon	79,878	5,743	2,576	1,685	69,874	7,684,273	1,333,940	143,305	6,207,028
Pennsylvania	1,487,761	1,062,697	194,057	291	230,716	25,807,987	5,460,525	551,200	19,796,262
Rhode Island	8,326	1,782	NA	NA	5,792	2,453,493	438,306	220,532	1,794,655
South Carolina	76,736	2,162	3,169	10,695	60,710	9,392,542	1,166,076	1,186,028	7,040,438
South Dakota	118,091	2,228	9,311	76,316	30,236	1,692,723	424,178	152,051	1,116,494
Tennessee	275,427	94,543	15,920	39,330	125,634	11,549,355	2,596,408	384,407	8,568,540
Texas	13,219,572	219,417	12,728,204	30,420	241,531	46,585,329	8,090,909	4,099,587	34,394,833
Utah	417,582	129,562	84,826	166,182	37,012	5,077,579	1,286,799	260,550	3,530,230
Vermont	21,326	NA	NA	25	20,022	1,347,680	228,775	41,589	1,077,316
Virginia	634,923	447,712	45,847	982	140,382	26,041,949	8,250,258	5,561,612	12,230,079
Washington	194,174	47,803	11,012	36,552	98,807	16,972,487	3,056,057	1,925,884	11,990,546
West Virginia	1,560,899	1,369,969	152,333	2,490	36,107	3,946,023	851,331	93,552	3,001,140
Wisconsin	118,690	7,634	8,351	4,504	98,201	11,347,889	1,251,671	183,420	9,912,798
Wyoming	1,021,917	307,847	503,246	29,731	181,093	1,610,277	289,993	136,204	1,184,080

Government and Mining
Percent Change in Real Earnings
1990 to 1996

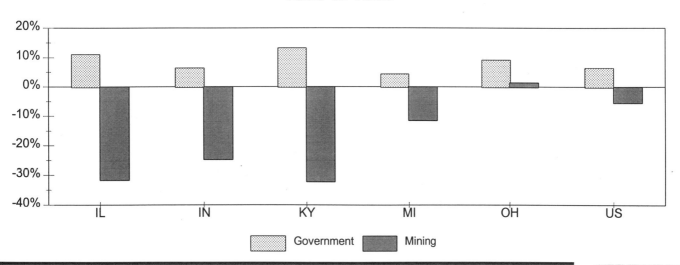

Source: U.S Bureau of Economic Analysis
EDIN Table(s): PIMI, PIGV

1.57 Projected Earnings by Industry by Place of Work 2005 *(Millions of 1987 Dollars)*

	Total Earnings	Farm	Non-farm	Private	Ag. Services, Forestry, Fisheries	Mining	Construc-tion	Manu-facturing	Transport. and Public Utilities	Wholesale Trade	Retail Trade	Finance, & Insurance & Real Estate	Services	Govt., & Govt. Enterprises
United States	3,878,404	44,495	3,833,909	3,236,903	29,548	27,100	196,458	606,963	245,174	235,817	348,287	323,129	1,224,426	597,006
Alabama	50,551	1,022	49,529	40,512	395	447	2,497	10,823	3,330	2,800	4,575	2,666	12,979	9,018
Alaska	11,429	7	11,422	8,218	377	821	764	610	1,155	324	1,068	432	2,667	3,204
Arizona	55,321	677	54,644	45,461	536	577	3,295	6,683	3,183	3,166	5,895	4,475	17,651	9,183
Arkansas	27,488	1,118	26,369	22,218	294	101	1,325	6,158	2,167	1,444	2,903	1,431	6,394	4,151
California	523,966	6,387	517,579	439,163	5,514	1,778	27,401	68,480	28,978	30,144	47,762	42,127	186,979	78,416
Colorado	62,102	861	61,240	51,209	445	947	3,488	6,813	5,190	3,613	5,837	4,886	19,990	10,032
Connecticut	63,613	236	63,377	55,618	353	61	2,735	11,070	3,112	3,918	5,186	8,713	20,471	7,759
Delaware	12,108	96	12,012	10,404	57	15	696	2,877	605	484	1,033	1,492	3,147	1,607
Dist. Of Col.	29,311	0	29,311	18,166	360	6	277	636	1,005	265	714	1,499	13,403	11,146
Florida	193,381	2,452	190,929	160,944	2,321	250	10,644	15,073	11,719	12,058	21,123	16,868	70,889	29,985
Georgia	107,295	1,295	106,000	89,462	650	283	4,971	16,183	9,616	9,175	9,572	8,047	30,967	16,538
Hawaii	21,425	194	21,231	16,466	178	18	1,729	724	1,699	827	2,615	1,724	6,952	4,765
Idaho	14,966	1,032	13,934	11,637	258	166	1,034	2,827	804	755	1,502	716	3,576	2,297
Illinois	*188,059*	*948*	*187,111*	*163,844*	*1,117*	*539*	*9,575*	*33,139*	*13,302*	*13,407*	*15,309*	*18,877*	*58,581*	*23,267*
Indiana	77,975	791	77,183	67,007	463	252	4,326	21,931	4,904	4,492	7,061	4,859	18,721	10,177
Percent U.S.	*2.01*	*1.78*	*2.01*	*2.07*	*1.57*	*0.93*	*2.20*	*3.61*	*2.00*	*1.90*	*2.03*	*1.50*	*1.53*	*1.70*
Rank	*15*	*23*	*15*	*15*	*20*	*23*	*15*	*9*	*18*	*18*	*17*	*21*	*21*	*17*
Iowa	34,754	1,358	33,396	28,185	441	62	1,824	7,049	2,016	2,306	3,317	2,683	8,487	5,212
Kansas	35,109	1,261	33,848	27,618	353	251	1,629	5,803	2,619	2,328	3,362	2,214	9,059	6,230
Kentucky	*44,523*	*1,132*	*43,391*	*35,918*	*326*	*873*	*2,371*	*9,138*	*3,058*	*2,198*	*4,440*	*2,353*	*11,162*	*7,473*
Louisiana	48,730	420	48,310	39,713	325	1,754	3,126	6,493	3,552	2,697	4,409	2,704	14,653	8,597
Maine	15,530	180	15,351	12,791	178	6	885	2,683	764	759	1,859	1,007	4,649	2,560
Maryland	75,829	311	75,518	60,501	507	48	4,546	5,986	4,175	4,047	7,064	6,347	27,781	15,017
Massachusetts	106,145	220	105,925	93,186	576	49	4,293	15,225	5,031	6,777	8,774	10,402	42,060	12,739
Michigan	*131,769*	*791*	*130,978*	*112,911*	*704*	*329*	*5,740*	*37,497*	*6,188*	*7,965*	*11,078*	*7,603*	*35,808*	*18,067*
Minnesota	71,855	1,166	70,689	61,197	443	328	3,528	14,470	4,398	5,235	6,347	6,079	20,370	9,492
Mississippi	26,139	496	25,643	20,807	240	138	1,342	6,120	1,623	1,248	2,581	1,326	6,190	4,837
Missouri	72,384	596	71,788	62,156	487	199	3,675	12,884	6,219	5,043	6,801	5,611	21,239	9,632
Montana	9,907	514	9,393	7,480	121	257	571	699	816	506	1,189	506	2,816	1,912
Nebraska	23,078	1,684	21,394	17,534	267	143	1,104	2,808	1,925	1,560	2,027	1,768	5,933	3,859
Nevada	27,634	87	27,547	24,019	143	626	2,298	1,083	1,567	1,097	2,414	1,461	13,330	3,528
New Hampshire	16,694	60	16,635	14,560	111	13	856	3,192	806	1,060	1,999	1,222	5,301	2,074
New Jersey	139,632	269	139,363	119,274	610	104	6,030	18,722	10,561	12,118	11,117	12,331	47,681	20,089
New Mexico	19,813	479	19,334	14,503	144	539	1,160	1,321	1,144	842	2,149	955	6,250	4,830
New York	304,082	615	303,467	257,930	1,206	225	10,083	31,515	16,447	17,400	19,868	55,401	105,785	45,538
North Carolina	101,868	2,222	99,646	82,879	669	116	5,501	23,425	6,096	6,164	9,546	6,156	25,207	16,767
North Dakota	7,505	598	6,907	5,463	84	131	411	521	674	540	727	425	1,949	1,444
Ohio	*150,956*	*1,027*	*149,929*	*129,683*	*829*	*426*	*7,527*	*37,778*	*7,721*	*9,382*	*13,667*	*10,002*	*42,352*	*20,246*
Oklahoma	36,989	1,090	35,900	28,811	311	1,467	1,623	5,135	3,039	1,862	3,602	2,073	9,699	7,089
Oregon	44,230	843	43,387	36,564	585	90	2,585	7,261	2,791	3,043	4,736	2,838	12,635	6,823
Pennsylvania	166,197	923	165,273	144,211	971	696	8,607	29,326	10,762	9,609	15,061	12,916	56,264	21,062
Rhode Island	13,468	38	13,430	11,300	98	7	575	2,341	523	660	1,262	1,042	4,793	2,130
South Carolina	46,279	290	45,988	37,227	296	59	2,914	11,315	2,379	1,996	4,837	2,411	11,020	8,761
South Dakota	9,312	984	8,328	6,793	134	98	473	1,079	519	545	974	553	2,418	1,535
Tennessee	73,335	511	72,824	62,948	373	164	3,775	15,725	5,028	4,573	7,265	4,261	21,784	9,876
Texas	272,134	3,450	268,684	227,784	1,989	8,865	14,277	36,550	22,553	17,875	25,121	18,868	81,686	40,900
Utah	26,775	268	26,507	22,003	100	324	1,561	3,713	2,033	1,529	2,546	1,799	8,398	4,505
Vermont	7,971	118	7,854	6,661	71	21	515	1,399	395	438	845	463	2,514	1,193
Virginia	98,435	364	98,071	75,859	578	412	5,542	11,706	6,117	5,103	8,395	6,993	31,014	22,212
Washington	86,424	1,546	84,878	70,022	1,255	147	5,357	12,541	4,964	5,294	8,235	5,573	26,656	14,856
West Virginia	17,205	117	17,088	13,860	90	904	987	2,399	1,426	817	1,633	741	4,863	3,228
Wisconsin	70,315	1,104	69,211	59,498	543	86	3,985	17,724	3,907	4,125	6,250	4,941	17,937	9,713
Wyoming	6,413	250	6,163	4,725	77	884	427	313	572	206	638	292	1,316	1,438

Projected Earnings Index 2005 to 2045
2005 = 100

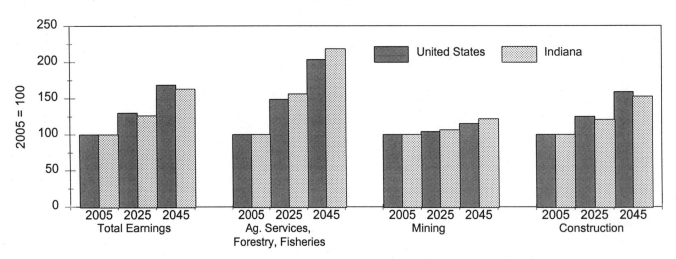

Source: U.S. Bureau of Economic Analysis, B.E.A. Regional Projections
EDIN table(s): PPI1, PPI2

1.58 Projected Earnings by Industry by Place of Work 2025 *(Millions of 1987 Dollars)*

	Total Earnings	Farm	Non-farm	Private	Ag. Services, Forestry, Fisheries	Mining	Construction	Manufacturing	Transport. and Public Utilities	Wholesale Trade	Retail Trade	Finance, Insurance & Real Estate	Services	Govt., & Govt. Enterprises
United States	5,039,010	47,382	4,991,628	4,253,734	43,907	28,234	245,214	687,989	304,876	291,174	425,900	455,658	1,770,784	737,895
Alabama	65,488	1,072	64,416	53,505	598	513	3,062	13,049	4,226	3,498	5,579	3,783	19,196	10,911
Alaska	14,924	8	14,916	11,042	534	954	982	738	1,465	410	1,379	627	3,954	3,874
Arizona	77,435	705	76,730	64,562	831	703	4,475	8,207	4,294	4,329	7,693	6,828	27,201	12,168
Arkansas	34,969	1,136	33,833	28,775	457	102	1,600	7,550	2,702	1,787	3,497	2,051	9,029	5,058
California	710,085	6,510	703,576	602,576	8,030	1,834	36,766	77,890	37,295	38,469	60,915	63,108	278,269	101,000
Colorado	85,913	900	85,013	71,816	691	955	4,475	8,216	7,003	4,847	7,576	7,199	30,853	13,197
Connecticut	81,751	241	81,510	71,665	516	68	3,354	11,507	3,863	4,914	6,273	12,138	29,032	9,845
Delaware	15,814	89	15,726	13,724	84	16	858	3,295	753	605	1,267	2,229	4,619	2,001
Dist. Of Col.	35,320	0	35,320	23,705	521	7	302	696	1,113	267	778	1,907	18,115	11,615
Florida	269,037	2,618	266,419	226,837	3,496	274	13,902	17,649	15,118	16,027	26,945	25,136	108,290	39,582
Georgia	147,200	1,234	145,966	124,622	988	337	6,512	19,378	12,706	11,598	12,258	12,141	48,704	21,344
Hawaii	28,273	217	28,056	22,265	267	23	2,096	803	2,162	1,053	3,213	2,488	10,160	5,791
Idaho	19,828	1,114	18,713	15,818	404	189	1,238	3,652	1,022	960	1,882	1,081	5,390	2,896
Illinois	*237,682*	*891*	*236,791*	*208,886*	*1,712*	*499*	*11,507*	*36,569*	*16,016*	*15,792*	*18,162*	*26,405*	*82,224*	*27,905*
Indiana	**98,504**	**907**	**97,597**	**85,086**	**723**	**268**	**5,219**	**25,122**	**6,095**	**5,604**	**8,483**	**6,967**	**26,608**	**12,510**
Percent U.S.	*1.95*	*1.92*	*1.96*	*2.00*	*1.65*	*0.95*	*2.13*	*3.65*	*2.00*	*1.92*	*1.99*	*1.53*	*1.50*	*1.70*
Rank	*15*	*21*	*15*	*15*	*20*	*24*	*16*	*9*	*17*	*18*	*16*	*21*	*22*	*17*
Iowa	42,473	1,586	40,887	34,873	654	70	2,159	8,025	2,361	2,653	3,757	3,722	11,472	6,014
Kansas	44,499	1,293	43,206	35,554	551	241	1,962	6,820	3,142	2,823	4,042	3,068	12,904	7,652
Kentucky	*56,580*	*1,274*	*55,306*	*46,139*	*502*	*807*	*2,861*	*10,954*	*3,778*	*2,664*	*5,377*	*3,233*	*15,963*	*9,167*
Louisiana	61,763	456	61,307	50,751	475	1,727	3,826	7,535	4,144	3,309	5,255	3,763	20,716	10,556
Maine	19,976	195	19,781	16,625	239	8	1,084	2,980	932	941	2,266	1,426	6,749	3,156
Maryland	97,747	325	97,422	79,692	757	52	5,366	6,386	5,123	4,965	8,439	8,954	39,650	17,730
Massachusetts	135,091	234	134,857	119,160	788	56	5,245	15,451	5,979	8,181	10,398	14,413	58,648	15,698
Michigan	*161,632*	*878*	*160,755*	*139,391*	*1,078*	*361*	*6,881*	*41,539*	*7,259*	*9,452*	*12,886*	*10,505*	*49,430*	*21,363*
Minnesota	91,454	1,319	90,135	78,643	656	374	4,250	17,186	5,304	6,195	7,491	8,408	28,779	11,492
Mississippi	33,215	539	32,676	26,898	364	137	1,675	7,310	2,013	1,502	3,076	1,885	8,936	5,778
Missouri	91,670	634	91,036	79,421	733	211	4,396	14,660	7,558	6,003	8,141	7,854	29,867	11,615
Montana	12,837	598	12,238	9,888	187	314	728	808	989	619	1,457	703	4,083	2,351
Nebraska	29,014	1,725	27,288	22,635	403	137	1,363	3,310	2,386	1,849	2,408	2,455	8,323	4,654
Nevada	40,329	94	40,235	35,364	229	753	3,092	1,441	2,175	1,589	3,321	2,453	20,310	4,871
New Hampshire	21,941	64	21,877	19,218	170	15	1,075	3,543	1,011	1,365	2,488	1,795	7,754	2,659
New Jersey	175,989	279	175,710	151,277	846	119	7,240	19,156	12,705	14,813	13,111	16,965	66,323	24,433
New Mexico	27,112	509	26,603	20,440	225	578	1,552	1,632	1,437	1,126	2,794	1,437	9,658	6,163
New York	364,474	643	363,830	311,582	1,616	237	11,126	30,541	18,418	19,542	22,268	69,653	138,183	52,248
North Carolina	135,659	2,174	133,485	112,022	1,034	133	7,097	27,709	7,805	7,911	12,017	9,291	39,025	21,463
North Dakota	9,195	641	8,554	6,879	126	137	507	638	822	601	818	577	2,652	1,675
Ohio	*187,304*	*1,096*	*186,209*	*161,881*	*1,252*	*413*	*9,072*	*42,053*	*9,048*	*11,154*	*16,060*	*13,839*	*58,990*	*24,328*
Oklahoma	46,525	1,242	45,282	36,804	505	1,494	2,026	6,062	3,775	2,259	4,302	2,868	13,514	8,478
Oregon	58,464	924	57,540	48,887	859	110	3,266	8,473	3,574	3,837	5,869	4,136	18,762	8,653
Pennsylvania	205,166	1,003	204,162	179,503	1,400	665	9,823	30,469	12,592	11,239	17,347	17,721	78,248	24,659
Rhode Island	17,162	37	17,125	14,516	132	8	699	2,483	631	814	1,510	1,444	6,794	2,609
South Carolina	62,007	296	61,711	50,444	439	69	3,803	13,799	3,023	2,571	6,052	3,631	17,056	11,267
South Dakota	11,889	1,030	10,859	9,002	196	122	578	1,412	628	672	1,158	776	3,462	1,858
Tennessee	96,356	559	95,797	83,455	571	183	4,738	18,627	6,583	5,660	8,879	6,110	32,104	12,342
Texas	361,841	3,868	357,974	305,955	3,055	9,157	18,030	43,576	29,090	22,361	31,189	27,769	121,728	52,019
Utah	38,935	287	38,647	32,625	165	355	2,191	4,870	2,808	2,128	3,494	2,933	13,683	6,022
Vermont	10,393	128	10,264	8,770	108	24	637	1,569	487	572	1,040	651	3,684	1,494
Virginia	130,953	338	130,616	103,575	880	394	7,108	13,529	7,745	6,491	10,459	10,454	46,517	27,041
Washington	118,148	1,758	116,391	97,326	1,765	175	6,824	15,491	6,501	6,970	10,627	8,217	40,754	19,065
West Virginia	21,068	153	20,915	17,056	146	805	1,150	2,551	1,690	948	1,911	996	6,859	3,859
Wisconsin	89,737	1,276	88,460	76,470	831	98	4,901	20,689	4,829	4,979	7,485	7,039	25,619	11,991
Wyoming	8,192	283	7,909	6,133	121	952	538	393	696	258	808	424	1,943	1,776

Projected Earnings Index 2005 to 2045
2005 = 100

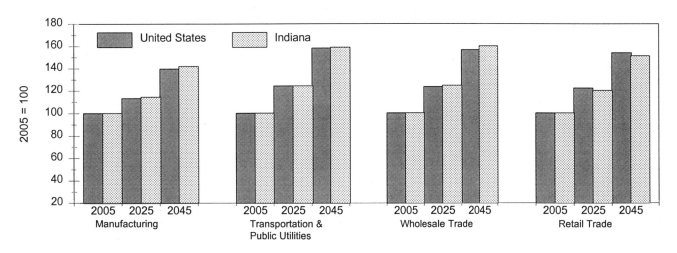

Source: U.S. Bureau of Economic Analysis, B.E.A. Regional Projections
EDIN table(s): PPI1, PPI2

1.59 Projected Earnings by Industry by Place of Work 2045 *(Millions of 1987 Dollars)*

	Total Earnings	Farm	Non-farm	Private	Ag. Services, Forestry, Fisheries	Mining	Construction	Manufacturing	Transport. and Public Utilities	Wholesale Trade	Retail Trade	Finance, Insurance & Real Estate	Services	Govt., & Govt. Enterprises
United States	6,538,618	54,180	6,484,438	5,550,378	60,121	31,240	312,074	848,599	387,987	369,578	536,553	615,958	2,388,268	934,060
Alabama	86,079	1,220	84,859	70,988	827	605	3,924	16,543	5,479	4,539	7,142	5,215	26,713	13,871
Alaska	19,166	10	19,156	14,358	715	1,103	1,254	937	1,869	519	1,761	849	5,351	4,798
Arizona	103,562	797	102,765	86,920	1,162	881	5,913	10,491	5,676	5,747	9,943	9,532	37,577	15,845
Arkansas	45,188	1,268	43,920	37,523	642	112	2,017	9,663	3,465	2,287	4,404	2,813	12,121	6,398
California	936,254	7,248	929,005	799,110	10,864	2,030	47,875	96,098	48,066	49,345	78,015	87,655	379,163	129,896
Colorado	114,873	1,026	113,847	96,612	967	1,031	5,806	10,475	9,279	6,410	9,822	9,917	42,906	17,235
Connecticut	105,886	271	105,614	92,951	703	80	4,242	13,577	4,926	6,309	7,890	16,308	38,917	12,663
Delaware	20,449	95	20,354	17,843	115	18	1,075	4,084	948	766	1,555	3,080	6,204	2,511
Dist. Of Col.	44,388	0	44,388	30,728	709	7	361	832	1,343	309	941	2,467	23,759	13,660
Florida	356,195	2,962	353,233	302,155	4,817	323	17,966	21,998	19,331	20,822	34,154	34,430	148,314	51,078
Georgia	197,716	1,338	196,378	168,598	1,366	421	8,568	24,527	16,689	14,821	15,952	17,144	69,110	27,780
Hawaii	36,532	254	36,278	29,107	367	28	2,600	976	2,758	1,341	4,011	3,383	13,643	7,170
Idaho	26,110	1,283	24,826	21,107	569	229	1,572	4,786	1,322	1,243	2,410	1,520	7,456	3,719
Illinois	*305,263*	*955*	*304,308*	*269,402*	*2,382*	*521*	*14,397*	*44,575*	*20,093*	*19,635*	*22,607*	*35,665*	*109,528*	*34,906*
Indiana	127,154	1,074	126,080	110,159	1,011	307	6,598	31,166	7,791	7,193	10,687	9,527	35,880	15,921
Percent U.S.	1.94	1.98	1.94	1.98	1.68	0.98	2.11	3.67	2.01	1.95	1.99	1.55	1.50	1.70
Rank	15	21	15	15	19	24	16	9	17	18	16	22	22	17
Iowa	53,559	1,834	51,726	44,346	896	85	2,686	9,924	2,929	3,261	4,573	4,989	15,004	7,380
Kansas	56,559	1,458	55,102	45,565	773	253	2,437	8,512	3,901	3,522	5,003	4,071	17,093	9,536
Kentucky	*73,018*	*1,499*	*71,519*	*59,911*	*701*	*830*	*3,604*	*13,851*	*4,846*	*3,383*	*6,794*	*4,335*	*21,568*	*11,608*
Louisiana	78,549	528	78,021	64,811	644	1,821	4,772	9,356	5,106	4,154	6,487	5,023	27,448	13,210
Maine	25,832	225	25,608	21,608	311	10	1,369	3,625	1,181	1,199	2,850	1,934	9,131	3,999
Maryland	126,376	368	126,009	103,949	1,039	57	6,642	7,649	6,488	6,285	10,514	12,109	53,167	22,059
Massachusetts	174,061	267	173,794	153,874	1,036	68	6,617	18,147	7,454	10,307	12,943	19,356	77,946	19,919
Michigan	*206,400*	*1,023*	*205,377*	*178,616*	*1,494*	*419*	*8,694*	*51,022*	*9,077*	*11,902*	*16,017*	*14,186*	*65,805*	*26,762*
Minnesota	117,672	1,526	116,147	101,715	894	456	5,333	21,681	6,662	7,716	9,288	11,270	38,414	14,432
Mississippi	42,725	628	42,096	34,911	505	146	2,129	9,206	2,563	1,887	3,837	2,573	12,065	7,185
Missouri	117,758	727	117,031	102,454	1,010	243	5,500	18,093	9,515	7,501	10,174	10,609	39,809	14,577
Montana	16,426	717	15,709	12,771	262	382	927	993	1,228	773	1,815	932	5,460	2,938
Nebraska	36,872	1,931	34,941	29,163	556	152	1,721	4,157	3,029	2,289	2,975	3,284	11,001	5,778
Nevada	54,980	109	54,871	48,397	324	944	4,056	1,916	2,908	2,173	4,410	3,600	28,067	6,474
New Hampshire	28,723	74	28,648	25,212	237	19	1,378	4,328	1,299	1,773	3,156	2,477	10,546	3,436
New Jersey	224,077	315	223,762	193,152	1,118	142	9,000	22,319	15,852	18,730	16,181	22,580	87,232	30,610
New Mexico	35,807	588	35,219	27,360	319	643	2,033	2,095	1,833	1,476	3,600	1,989	13,371	7,859
New York	454,095	732	453,363	389,600	2,088	271	13,335	34,834	22,171	23,632	26,887	88,623	177,766	63,758
North Carolina	178,692	2,427	176,265	148,676	1,445	162	9,227	34,921	10,104	10,243	15,422	12,952	54,200	27,589
North Dakota	11,474	738	10,736	8,709	174	150	635	815	1,032	720	981	758	3,443	2,028
Ohio	*239,226*	*1,251*	*237,975*	*207,393*	*1,726*	*451*	*11,425*	*51,421*	*11,283*	*13,995*	*19,951*	*18,603*	*78,538*	*30,582*
Oklahoma	59,007	1,475	57,532	47,037	721	1,596	2,569	7,614	4,786	2,823	5,326	3,814	17,787	10,495
Oregon	77,017	1,076	75,941	64,699	1,169	136	4,217	10,587	4,639	4,956	7,492	5,724	25,778	11,242
Pennsylvania	259,992	1,162	258,830	228,349	1,885	726	11,949	35,939	15,553	13,903	21,250	23,634	103,511	30,481
Rhode Island	22,114	42	22,072	18,781	172	10	880	2,973	794	1,036	1,888	1,941	9,088	3,292
South Carolina	81,108	337	80,771	66,380	601	84	4,922	17,467	3,865	3,301	7,662	4,994	23,486	14,391
South Dakota	15,264	1,180	14,084	11,763	266	154	727	1,858	790	851	1,438	1,044	4,636	2,321
Tennessee	126,135	646	125,489	109,720	793	220	6,092	23,379	8,584	7,227	11,237	8,384	43,804	15,769
Texas	471,925	4,545	467,380	401,011	4,259	9,833	23,017	55,029	37,578	28,400	39,371	38,082	165,442	66,369
Utah	53,343	331	53,012	45,051	238	412	2,954	6,360	3,755	2,864	4,657	4,266	19,545	7,961
Vermont	13,534	149	13,385	11,478	149	30	808	1,920	619	745	1,316	882	5,008	1,907
Virginia	172,170	371	171,798	137,861	1,219	423	9,188	16,825	9,965	8,377	13,322	14,558	63,985	33,938
Washington	156,225	2,107	154,118	129,675	2,352	215	8,738	19,566	8,449	9,106	13,668	11,373	56,210	24,443
West Virginia	26,633	194	26,439	21,626	208	822	1,415	3,064	2,096	1,171	2,366	1,323	9,160	4,813
Wisconsin	116,050	1,467	114,583	99,339	1,154	120	6,234	25,918	6,148	6,289	9,381	9,610	34,486	15,244
Wyoming	10,409	335	10,075	7,851	172	1,062	681	506	873	327	1,026	575	2,629	2,224

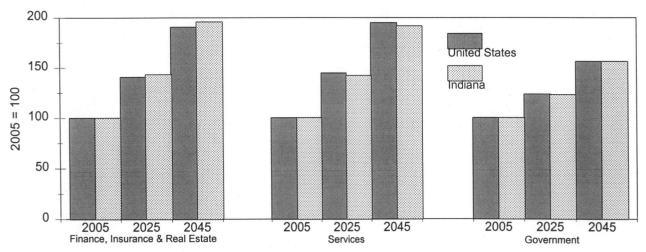

Projected Earning Index 2005 to 2045
2005 = 100

(Bar chart comparing United States and Indiana for Finance, Insurance & Real Estate; Services; and Government, at 2005, 2025, and 2045, with 2005 = 100)

Source: U.S. Bureau of Economic Analysis, B.E.A. Regional Projections
EDIN table(s): PPI1, PPI2

1.60 Percent Change in Projected Earnings by Industry by Place of Work 2005 to 2045 (*Millions of 1987 Dollars*)

	Total Earnings	Farm	Non-farm	Private	Ag. Services, Forestry, Fisheries	Mining	Construction	Manufacturing	Transport. & Public Utilities	Wholesale Trade	Retail Trade	Finance, Insurance & Real Estate	Services	Govt., & Government Enterprises
United States	68.6	21.8	69.1	71.5	103.5	15.3	58.9	39.8	58.2	56.7	54.1	90.6	95.1	56.5
Alabama	70.3	19.4	71.3	75.2	109.4	35.5	57.1	52.9	64.5	62.1	56.1	95.6	105.8	53.8
Alaska	67.7	30.1	67.7	74.7	89.8	34.3	64.2	53.6	61.8	60.4	64.9	96.4	100.6	49.8
Arizona	87.2	17.8	88.1	91.2	116.9	52.6	79.4	57.0	78.3	81.5	68.7	113.0	112.9	72.5
Arkansas	64.4	13.4	66.6	68.9	118.4	10.8	52.2	56.9	59.9	58.3	51.7	96.6	89.6	54.1
California	78.7	13.5	79.5	82.0	97.0	14.1	74.7	40.3	65.9	63.7	63.3	108.1	102.8	65.7
Colorado	85.0	19.2	85.9	88.7	117.1	8.9	66.5	53.7	78.8	77.4	68.3	103.0	114.6	71.8
Connecticut	66.5	15.0	66.6	67.1	99.3	30.5	55.1	22.7	58.3	61.0	52.2	87.2	90.1	63.2
Delaware	68.9	-0.9	69.5	71.5	102.7	15.1	54.6	42.0	56.6	58.4	50.5	106.4	97.1	56.2
Dist. Of Col.	51.4	0.0	51.4	69.2	97.0	14.5	30.1	30.8	33.6	16.6	31.8	64.6	77.3	22.6
Florida	84.2	20.8	85.0	87.7	107.5	29.2	68.8	45.9	65.0	72.7	61.7	104.1	109.2	70.3
Georgia	84.3	3.3	85.3	88.5	110.3	49.1	72.3	51.6	73.5	61.5	66.7	113.1	123.2	68.0
Hawaii	70.5	30.6	70.9	76.8	106.5	53.3	50.4	34.8	62.3	62.2	53.4	96.3	96.2	50.5
Idaho	74.5	24.4	78.2	81.4	120.6	38.1	52.1	69.3	64.5	64.7	60.4	112.3	108.5	61.9
Illinois	*62.3*	*0.7*	*62.6*	*64.4*	*113.2*	*-3.3*	*50.4*	*34.5*	*51.1*	*46.5*	*47.7*	*88.9*	*87.0*	*50.0*
Indiana	**63.1**	**35.8**	**63.4**	**64.4**	**118.5**	**21.8**	**52.5**	**42.1**	**58.9**	**60.1**	**51.4**	**96.1**	**91.7**	**56.4**
Rank	**35**	**4**	**36**	**40**	**9**	**29**	**34**	**30**	**22**	**21**	**28**	**23**	**29**	**20**
Iowa	54.1	35.0	54.9	57.3	103.2	36.6	47.3	40.8	45.3	41.4	37.9	85.9	76.8	41.6
Kansas	61.1	15.6	62.8	65.0	118.8	1.1	49.6	46.7	49.0	51.3	48.8	83.9	88.7	53.1
Kentucky	*64.0*	*32.4*	*64.8*	*66.8*	*115.1*	*-4.9*	*52.0*	*51.6*	*58.5*	*53.9*	*53.0*	*84.3*	*93.2*	*55.3*
Louisiana	61.2	25.6	61.5	63.2	98.1	3.8	52.7	44.1	43.7	54.0	47.1	85.7	87.3	53.7
Maine	66.3	24.9	66.8	68.9	75.3	50.8	54.6	35.1	54.6	57.8	53.3	92.0	96.4	56.2
Maryland	66.7	18.3	66.9	71.8	104.9	18.2	46.1	27.8	55.4	55.3	48.8	90.8	91.4	46.9
Massachusetts	64.0	21.6	64.1	65.1	79.8	38.4	54.1	19.2	48.2	52.1	47.5	86.1	85.3	56.4
Michigan	*56.6*	*29.3*	*56.8*	*58.2*	*112.2*	*27.4*	*51.5*	*36.1*	*46.7*	*49.4*	*44.6*	*86.6*	*83.8*	*48.1*
Minnesota	63.8	30.9	64.3	66.2	102.0	39.1	51.2	49.8	51.5	47.4	46.3	85.4	88.6	52.0
Mississippi	63.4	26.7	64.2	67.8	110.6	5.9	58.6	50.4	58.0	51.2	48.7	94.1	94.9	48.6
Missouri	62.7	22.0	63.0	64.8	107.2	22.1	49.7	40.4	53.0	48.8	49.6	89.1	87.4	51.3
Montana	65.8	39.4	67.3	70.7	116.6	48.6	62.3	42.1	50.6	52.9	52.6	84.2	93.9	53.7
Nebraska	59.8	14.7	63.3	66.3	108.2	6.9	55.8	48.1	57.4	46.7	46.7	85.8	85.4	49.7
Nevada	99.0	25.8	99.2	101.5	126.2	50.7	76.5	77.0	85.6	98.0	82.7	146.4	110.6	83.5
New Hampshire	72.0	24.5	72.2	73.2	113.1	40.9	60.8	35.6	61.2	67.3	57.9	102.7	99.0	65.7
New Jersey	60.5	17.1	60.6	61.9	83.4	35.8	49.3	19.2	50.1	54.6	45.6	83.1	82.9	52.4
New Mexico	80.7	22.7	82.2	88.6	121.7	19.4	75.2	58.6	60.3	75.3	67.5	108.4	113.9	62.7
New York	49.3	19.0	49.4	51.1	73.1	20.3	32.3	10.5	34.8	35.8	35.3	60.0	68.0	40.0
North Carolina	75.4	9.2	76.9	79.4	115.8	39.9	67.7	49.1	65.8	66.2	61.6	110.4	115.0	64.5
North Dakota	52.9	23.4	55.4	59.4	107.6	14.3	54.3	56.5	53.1	33.3	35.0	78.4	76.6	40.4
Ohio	*58.5*	*21.8*	*58.7*	*59.9*	*108.3*	*5.9*	*51.8*	*36.1*	*46.1*	*49.2*	*46.0*	*86.0*	*85.4*	*51.1*
Oklahoma	59.5	35.4	60.3	63.3	131.7	8.8	58.3	48.3	57.5	51.6	47.9	84.0	83.4	48.1
Oregon	74.1	27.6	75.0	76.9	100.0	50.9	63.2	45.8	66.2	62.9	58.2	101.7	104.0	64.8
Pennsylvania	56.4	25.8	56.6	58.3	94.2	4.3	38.8	22.6	44.5	44.7	41.1	83.0	84.0	44.7
Rhode Island	64.2	10.7	64.3	66.2	76.0	44.1	53.0	27.0	51.8	56.9	49.6	86.2	89.6	54.5
South Carolina	75.3	16.2	75.6	78.3	102.9	43.3	68.9	54.4	62.5	65.3	58.4	107.1	113.1	64.3
South Dakota	63.9	20.0	69.1	73.2	97.7	56.5	53.5	72.2	52.1	56.1	47.7	89.0	91.7	51.2
Tennessee	72.0	26.5	72.3	74.3	112.7	34.0	61.4	48.7	70.7	58.0	54.7	96.7	101.1	59.7
Texas	73.4	31.7	74.0	76.0	114.2	10.9	61.2	50.6	66.6	58.9	56.7	101.8	102.5	62.3
Utah	99.2	23.8	100.0	104.8	138.6	27.1	89.3	71.3	84.7	87.3	82.9	137.2	132.7	76.7
Vermont	69.8	26.8	70.4	72.3	108.0	47.6	57.0	37.3	56.5	70.1	55.9	90.6	99.2	59.8
Virginia	74.9	1.9	75.2	81.7	111.0	2.6	65.8	43.7	62.9	64.1	58.7	108.2	106.3	52.8
Washington	80.8	36.3	81.6	85.2	87.4	45.6	63.1	56.0	70.2	72.0	66.0	104.1	110.9	64.5
West Virginia	54.8	65.6	54.7	56.0	131.7	-9.0	43.4	27.7	47.0	43.4	44.9	78.5	88.3	49.1
Wisconsin	65.0	32.9	65.6	67.0	112.3	39.4	56.4	46.2	57.4	52.4	50.1	94.5	92.3	56.9
Wyoming	62.3	33.9	63.5	66.2	122.9	20.2	59.4	62.0	52.7	58.7	60.8	97.1	99.7	54.6

Percent Change in Projected Earnings 2005 to 2045
Indiana's Top 5 Most Volatile Industries

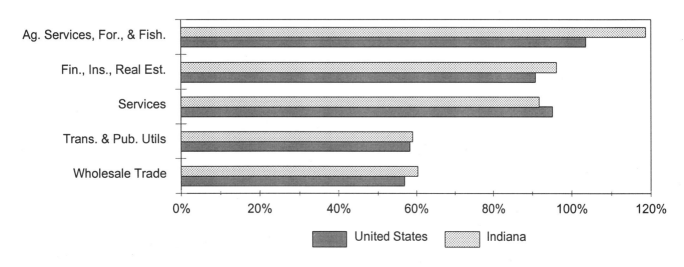

Social Welfare
1.61 Social Security: Beneficiaries and Benefits ($000) 1995

	Total		Retirement Benefits		Survivor Benefits		Disability Benefits		Beneficiaries Aged 65 & Older	
	Beneficiaries	Benefits ($000)	Beneficiaries	Benefits ($000)	Beneficiaries	Benefits ($000)	Beneficiaries	Benefits ($000)	Beneficiaries	Benefits ($000)
United States	43,386,897	28,147,981	30,141,246	20,462,198	7,388,084	4,530,860	5,857,567	3,154,922	31,452,810	21,789,778
Alabama	778,021	457,993	481,689	301,247	158,173	86,987	138,159	69,758	515,562	326,856
Alaska	44,335	27,209	27,886	18,462	8,741	4,727	7,708	4,020	26,689	18,256
Arizona	706,954	468,490	512,439	352,876	102,418	63,856	92,097	51,758	516,461	363,677
Arkansas	509,462	294,953	322,298	197,474	92,022	49,909	95,142	47,570	341,228	211,813
California	3,979,717	2,640,961	2,862,894	1,972,466	619,698	388,889	497,125	279,607	2,939,886	2,078,930
Colorado	495,117	313,916	338,236	222,710	79,307	49,333	77,574	41,874	348,836	235,341
Connecticut	565,539	412,723	425,963	323,618	80,263	54,991	59,313	34,113	440,891	340,658
Delaware	119,746	82,193	85,838	61,489	19,165	12,377	14,743	8,326	86,997	63,530
Dist. Of Col.	77,163	43,437	53,433	31,203	14,723	7,329	9,007	4,904	57,699	34,253
Florida	2,985,768	1,977,286	2,247,977	1,534,927	423,976	268,539	313,815	173,820	2,294,903	1,603,201
Georgia	1,009,272	608,769	636,096	409,254	191,748	105,725	181,428	93,790	663,644	432,047
Hawaii	166,089	107,660	130,103	86,914	22,159	13,178	13,827	7,567	127,698	87,455
Idaho	177,910	112,539	126,756	83,264	27,935	17,190	23,219	12,086	128,683	86,767
Illinois	*1,830,425*	*1,268,042*	*1,293,218*	*934,877*	*318,981*	*209,860*	*218,226*	*123,305*	*1,367,841*	*1,010,718*
Indiana	970,250	661,684	673,683	481,110	165,973	108,884	130,594	71,690	703,848	511,968
Percent U.S.	*2.24*	*2.35*	*2.24*	*2.35*	*2.25*	*2.40*	*2.23*	*2.27*	*2.24*	*2.35*
Rank	*14*	*12*	*12*	*12*	*15*	*11*	*18*	*17*	*12*	*12*
Iowa	540,171	354,601	393,685	266,024	91,178	59,162	55,308	29,415	418,988	288,909
Kansas	434,369	291,020	313,544	218,406	72,370	47,065	48,455	25,548	331,468	235,619
Kentucky	*708,941*	*415,888*	*419,712*	*260,068*	*138,784*	*78,068*	*150,445*	*77,753*	*456,439*	*286,875*
Louisiana	701,733	405,894	409,499	251,881	163,317	90,852	128,917	63,162	452,656	286,076
Maine	236,551	142,366	162,705	102,228	36,034	21,561	37,812	18,579	168,540	108,250
Maryland	675,738	448,195	481,458	330,798	121,809	75,447	72,471	41,949	502,850	352,123
Massachusetts	1,045,899	696,171	747,728	517,963	151,869	98,777	146,302	79,432	786,637	556,132
Michigan	*1,594,430*	*1,106,033*	*1,098,597*	*795,678*	*278,603*	*184,962*	*217,230*	*125,392*	*1,145,508*	*845,831*
Minnesota	715,782	462,868	523,484	348,372	115,478	73,143	76,820	41,353	546,898	370,516
Mississippi	492,717	271,361	287,967	171,600	98,298	49,792	106,452	49,969	306,311	184,919
Missouri	975,979	623,934	671,031	448,359	167,585	102,447	137,363	73,129	702,197	478,182
Montana	150,831	94,835	104,074	67,803	25,174	15,507	21,583	11,526	108,006	72,294
Nebraska	281,528	182,128	205,604	137,145	46,754	29,944	29,170	15,038	217,667	148,661
Nevada	230,204	154,795	169,465	117,347	30,619	19,421	30,120	18,025	165,384	117,475
New Hampshire	185,015	123,809	134,253	93,827	25,100	16,388	25,662	13,593	135,367	96,461
New Jersey	1,313,653	956,414	966,771	734,955	204,246	137,300	142,636	84,158	1,007,920	778,802
New Mexico	255,133	150,344	168,838	105,339	45,286	24,934	41,009	20,071	171,600	110,046
New York	2,971,608	2,076,669	2,111,060	1,547,180	464,167	300,185	396,381	229,304	2,182,590	1,631,002
North Carolina	1,233,066	758,479	822,480	536,537	205,264	113,321	205,322	108,621	849,047	556,166
North Dakota	115,577	70,337	82,526	51,254	21,868	13,312	11,183	5,772	89,539	57,066
Ohio	*1,902,055*	*1,263,491*	*1,301,336*	*895,771*	*353,966*	*230,890*	*246,753*	*136,831*	*1,399,125*	*985,196*
Oklahoma	576,236	356,726	393,559	253,481	106,889	63,140	75,788	40,106	414,532	272,499
Oregon	538,917	361,823	399,214	276,362	79,028	51,409	60,675	34,053	407,565	288,185
Pennsylvania	2,330,182	1,590,539	1,693,439	1,192,171	404,854	268,232	231,889	130,134	1,801,735	1,292,406
Rhode Island	189,851	126,675	139,959	97,341	25,127	16,123	24,765	13,213	145,043	102,671
South Carolina	624,446	379,999	401,819	261,070	110,822	59,884	111,805	59,046	411,422	269,381
South Dakota	134,936	79,994	96,014	58,809	23,886	13,899	15,036	7,286	102,525	64,374
Tennessee	928,980	559,771	590,252	378,364	171,917	96,749	166,811	84,657	623,905	404,715
Texas	2,470,558	1,526,199	1,649,494	1,067,468	496,499	292,366	324,565	166,365	1,734,405	1,154,692
Utah	222,751	143,713	158,271	107,297	35,813	22,145	28,667	14,272	158,730	110,965
Vermont	98,316	62,801	68,447	45,986	15,426	9,453	14,443	7,362	70,607	48,319
Virginia	947,405	590,169	639,890	416,942	166,813	97,796	140,702	75,431	669,420	442,384
Washington	793,298	541,392	577,033	408,136	117,621	77,441	98,644	55,815	588,886	424,683
West Virginia	387,373	241,421	232,397	152,047	82,094	49,540	72,882	39,834	258,822	172,430
Wisconsin	881,830	594,410	641,824	448,055	138,670	90,988	101,336	55,368	665,058	472,823
Wyoming	71,000	46,376	49,677	33,860	11,762	7,432	9,561	5,084	50,476	35,214

Percent of Population Receiving Social Security Benefits 1995

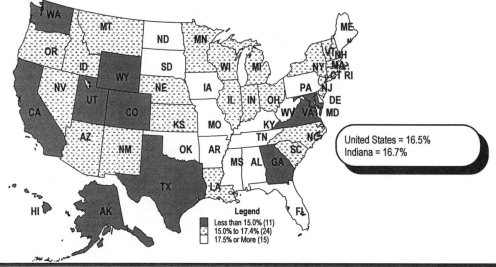

United States = 16.5%
Indiana = 16.7%

Legend
Less than 15.0% (11)
15.0% to 17.4% (24)
17.5% or More (15)

Source: U.S. Department of Health and Human Services
EDIN table(s): SSBB

1.62 Medicare: Hospital Insurance for Enrollees, Number of Hospitals and Number of Beds 1995

	Enrollees (000)				Hospitals				Number of Beds			
	Aged	Percent Change 1994-95	Disabled	Percent Change 1994-95	Total	Percent Change 1994-95	Short-Stay	Long-Stay	Total	Percent Change 1994-95	Short-Stay	Long-Stay
United States	32,093	1.0	4,266	6.3	6,314	-0.6	5,194	1,120	1,045,229	-1.7	915,532	129,697
Alabama	535	1.1	101	6.3	129	0.0	111	18	21,180	-0.4	19,584	1,596
Alaska	28	3.7	5	0.0	25	0.0	22	3	1,586	-1.6	1,378	208
Arizona	531	2.7	66	8.2	87	0.0	68	19	11,795	-0.2	10,423	1,372
Arkansas	356	0.9	67	8.1	94	-3.1	78	16	12,071	-3.9	10,642	1,429
California	3,106	1.5	392	5.4	527	-1.5	438	89	92,687	-1.9	84,801	7,886
Colorado	362	2.0	54	8.0	85	-2.3	64	21	11,874	-3.5	9,502	2,372
Connecticut	454	0.9	47	9.3	51	0.0	35	16	13,949	0.1	11,089	2,860
Delaware	90	2.3	11	10.0	12	0.0	7	5	2,572	0.0	2,174	398
Dist. Of Col.	66	-1.5	8	0.0	15	7.1	11	4	4,955	0.5	3,969	986
Florida	2,385	1.1	232	7.9	277	-1.4	210	67	58,450	-0.4	53,171	5,279
Georgia	694	1.5	134	7.2	196	0.0	160	36	29,020	-0.2	24,957	4,063
Hawaii	137	3.0	11	0.0	26	0.0	22	4	2,768	-0.6	2,335	433
Idaho	133	1.5	16	6.7	49	2.1	42	7	2,996	-1.6	2,721	275
Illinois	*1,429*	*0.2*	*172*	*5.5*	*227*	*0.0*	*199*	*28*	*53,242*	*0.3*	*49,984*	*3,258*
Indiana	724	0.8	99	4.2	157	-1.3	116	41	25,780	-7.0	23,371	2,409
Percent U.S.	2.26	—	2.32	—	2.49	—	2.23	3.66	2.47	—	2.55	1.86
Rank	13	31	18	42	11	40	19	8	14	50	14	18
Iowa	431	0.2	43	4.9	122	-0.8	118	4	12,904	-3.4	12,477	427
Kansas	346	0.3	35	6.1	146	-2.0	130	16	12,882	-6.5	11,287	1,595
Kentucky	*475*	*0.9*	*105*	*8.3*	*122*	*-0.8*	*104*	*18*	*18,401*	*-0.4*	*16,103*	*2,298*
Louisiana	481	1.1	93	4.5	193	-0.5	131	62	18,238	-26.7	13,633	4,605
Maine	173	0.6	27	8.0	44	0.0	39	5	4,858	-0.5	4,227	631
Maryland	537	1.3	60	7.1	73	-1.4	50	23	17,329	0.1	13,188	4,141
Massachusetts	822	0.2	108	8.0	137	0.0	90	47	24,862	-1.8	18,000	6,862
Michigan	*1,169*	*1.0*	*170*	*5.6*	*193*	*0.0*	*170*	*23*	*36,028*	*-0.9*	*31,875*	*4,153*
Minnesota	569	0.7	60	5.3	153	-0.7	143	10	18,677	-0.8	16,711	1,966
Mississippi	324	0.6	72	7.5	109	0.0	102	7	12,857	3.3	12,386	471
Missouri	727	0.4	100	5.3	149	-0.7	124	25	27,287	-1.1	25,039	2,248
Montana	114	1.8	16	6.7	55	0.0	53	2	3,089	-0.4	3,035	54
Nebraska	227	0.4	22	10.0	99	-1.0	91	8	7,948	-2.6	7,122	826
Nevada	171	4.9	22	10.0	33	0.0	25	8	3,879	-0.8	3,337	542
New Hampshire	138	1.5	17	6.3	31	0.0	26	5	3,834	8.1	3,251	583
New Jersey	1,044	0.6	110	4.8	114	1.8	88	26	34,150	0.6	29,818	4,332
New Mexico	179	2.3	28	3.7	57	-1.7	43	14	5,343	-3.5	4,645	698
New York	2,248	0.0	302	6.3	273	-0.4	225	48	85,447	-0.2	69,065	16,382
North Carolina	876	1.7	149	8.0	145	0.0	127	18	27,360	-0.2	24,198	3,162
North Dakota	93	0.0	9	0.0	51	-1.9	49	2	4,120	-0.6	3,724	396
Ohio	*1,457*	*0.8*	*196*	*4.8*	*217*	*-0.9*	*185*	*32*	*54,112*	*-0.2*	*49,287*	*4,825*
Oklahoma	430	0.7	56	7.7	150	0.7	123	27	16,066	-0.1	14,177	1,889
Oregon	418	0.7	47	6.8	67	0.0	63	4	8,470	-0.5	8,108	362
Pennsylvania	1,876	0.4	190	4.4	264	-1.5	206	58	48,244	-2.7	39,358	8,886
Rhode Island	148	0.0	19	5.6	18	0.0	12	6	4,611	-0.4	3,290	1,321
South Carolina	422	1.7	81	8.0	77	1.3	64	13	13,349	-0.9	12,066	1,283
South Dakota	105	0.0	11	0.0	60	0.0	58	2	3,635	0.5	3,490	145
Tennessee	650	1.3	119	7.2	154	0.0	128	26	28,073	-0.8	25,604	2,469
Texas	1,834	2.0	236	7.3	517	-0.6	394	123	65,530	-1.4	56,984	8,546
Utah	166	1.8	20	11.1	52	0.0	42	10	5,576	0.6	4,611	965
Vermont	72	1.4	10	0.0	16	-5.9	14	2	1,994	-5.2	1,830	164
Virginia	703	1.7	105	7.1	125	-0.8	98	27	24,178	1.4	21,455	2,723
Washington	608	1.5	74	7.3	99	0.0	90	9	14,546	-2.3	12,530	2,016
West Virginia	274	0.4	55	3.8	68	0.0	57	11	10,210	1.1	9,400	810
Wisconsin	682	0.9	79	4.0	145	-1.4	124	21	20,537	-5.8	18,538	1,999
Wyoming	53	1.9	7	16.7	29	0.0	25	4	1,680	-0.7	1,582	98

Beds Per 1,000 Persons
1995

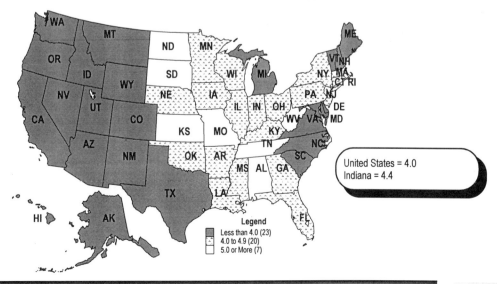

United States = 4.0
Indiana = 4.4

Legend
Less than 4.0 (23)
4.0 to 4.9 (20)
5.0 or More (7)

Source: U.S. Department of Health and Human Services, Social Security Bulletin, Annual Statistical Supplement
EDIN table(s): SSHI

1.63 Public Welfare: Aid to Families with Dependent Children 1994

	Monthly Average Number			Total Payments ($000)	Monthly Average Per		Emergency Assistance		
	Families	Total Recipients	Children		Family ($)	Recipient ($)	Avg. Monthly # of Families	Total Payments to Families ($000)	Avg. Monthly Payment per Family ($)
United States	5,035,385	14,164,286	9,569,985	22,827,399	377.78	134.30	60,450	802,258	1,105.95
Alabama	49,578	129,222	94,110	90,249	151.70	58.20	NA	8,283	NA
Alaska	12,722	37,798	23,963	112,186	734.88	247.34	NA	NA	NA
Arizona	71,895	199,682	135,600	267,046	309.53	111.45	160	8,700	4,531.19
Arkansas	25,733	68,203	48,726	56,545	183.12	69.09	NA	3,288	NA
California	916,019	2,661,010	1,818,293	6,159,537	560.35	192.89	7,234	281,321	3,240.72
Colorado	40,984	116,887	79,022	155,700	316.59	111.00	NA	32,079	NA
Connecticut	59,862	167,601	112,456	399,055	555.52	198.42	NA	19,076	NA
Delaware	11,390	27,138	18,314	39,210	286.87	120.40	150	1,470	816.59
Dist. Of Col.	27,222	74,142	51,192	127,577	390.55	143.39	730	158	NA
Florida	243,685	658,238	455,841	816,761	279.31	103.40	1,968	12,292	520.51
Georgia	141,236	391,561	273,747	427,949	252.50	91.08	1,138	15,453	1,131.61
Hawaii	20,836	63,284	41,905	166,599	666.33	219.38	1,108	NA	NA
Idaho	8,762	23,315	15,734	30,634	291.35	109.50	NA	6,980	NA
Illinois	*241,339*	*715,003*	*488,437*	*935,601*	*323.06*	*109.04*	*1,973*	*17,524*	*740.17*
Indiana	72,598	212,065	143,005	238,554	273.83	93.74	NA	55,898	NA
Percent U.S.	*1.44*	*1.50*	*1.49*	*1.05*	—	—	—	—	—
Rank	*21*	*19*	*18*	*21*	*39*	*39*	*NA*	*3*	*NA*
Iowa	39,512	110,214	71,534	167,644	353.58	126.76	412	2,933	593.20
Kansas	29,819	85,525	58,072	122,391	342.03	119.25	193	17,839	7,702.54
Kentucky	*79,128*	*204,264*	*134,876*	*195,851*	*206.26*	*79.90*	*NA*	*650*	*NA*
Louisiana	85,601	245,464	177,124	165,529	161.14	56.20	NA	NA	NA
Maine	22,661	63,357	39,537	105,623	388.42	138.93	345	750	181.20
Maryland	80,547	224,162	152,272	315,596	326.51	117.32	2,149	12,527	485.76
Massachusetts	109,961	301,271	193,743	715,717	542.40	197.97	2,061	47,058	1,902.73
Michigan	*219,986*	*652,427*	*431,223*	*1,103,954*	*418.19*	*141.01*	*1,230*	*18,337*	*1,242.31*
Minnesota	61,619	182,187	121,105	374,799	506.88	171.43	1,909	15,498	676.54
Mississippi	55,652	154,927	113,172	80,232	120.14	43.16	NA	NA	NA
Missouri	92,124	262,888	177,947	286,217	258.91	90.73	438	14,336	2,727.64
Montana	11,858	34,633	22,602	48,898	343.65	117.66	28	563	1,675.35
Nebraska	15,665	44,356	30,429	60,758	323.21	114.15	142	3,141	1,843.45
Nevada	14,557	38,876	27,218	48,937	280.15	104.90	435	1,223	234.20
New Hampshire	11,467	30,204	19,309	61,562	447.38	169.85	380	1,617	354.50
New Jersey	122,100	331,998	224,720	521,729	356.08	130.96	7,445	42,897	480.16
New Mexico	34,119	103,506	67,092	149,531	365.22	120.39	NA	7	NA
New York	459,157	1,264,063	817,592	2,997,670	544.05	197.62	14,024	206,229	1,225.45
North Carolina	130,611	329,809	220,993	354,198	225.99	89.50	3,433	8,832	214.40
North Dakota	5,688	15,852	10,465	24,784	363.11	130.29	678	4,383	538.69
Ohio	*246,478*	*670,376*	*446,853*	*925,506*	*312.91*	*115.05*	*3,527*	*4,557*	*107.68*
Oklahoma	46,794	130,510	89,784	163,419	291.03	104.35	52	101	161.15
Oregon	41,602	111,954	74,841	193,665	387.93	144.15	1,613	10,942	565.33
Pennsylvania	210,756	620,118	417,368	931,189	368.19	125.14	921	24,443	2,211.62
Rhode Island	22,694	62,905	41,483	137,097	503.43	181.62	NA	2,983	NA
South Carolina	51,412	137,496	100,889	114,008	184.80	69.10	NA	2,388	NA
South Dakota	6,793	18,689	13,391	24,322	298.36	108.45	222	1,794	673.28
Tennessee	109,738	294,733	200,178	212,140	161.10	59.98	NA	2,129	NA
Texas	284,682	788,687	550,260	545,325	159.63	57.62	2,152	8,650	334.98
Utah	17,622	49,115	32,673	74,256	351.15	125.99	120	336	233.22
Vermont	9,868	27,772	17,171	64,337	543.32	193.05	248	873	293.51
Virginia	74,760	193,612	133,562	252,368	281.31	108.62	39	72	153.85
Washington	103,138	291,598	186,872	612,880	495.19	175.15	596	6,273	877.07
West Virginia	40,385	112,548	70,951	125,324	258.60	92.79	1,109	2,534	190.44
Wisconsin	76,217	222,434	141,575	416,622	455.52	156.08	454	3,059	561.54
Wyoming	5,650	16,053	10,924	20,775	306.41	107.85	235	3,493	1,238.51

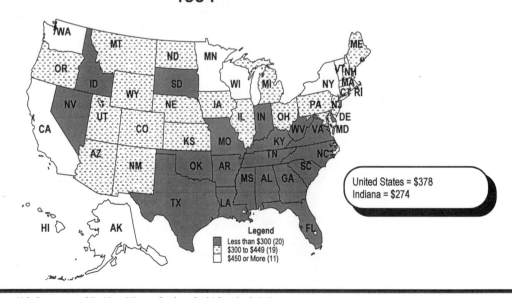

Average Monthly Payment Per Family
1994

United States = $378
Indiana = $274

Legend
Less than $300 (20)
$300 to $449 (19)
$450 or More (11)

Source: U.S. Department of Health and Human Services, Social Security Bulletin
EDIN table(s): WELA

1.64 Federal Funds or Obligations *(Fiscal Year)* 1996 *($MIL)*

	←Direct Fed. Expend. Or Obligation→			Grant Awards	Salaries & Wages		Direct Payments For Individuals			Procurement Contract Awards		Other Federal Expenditure Or Obligation	Other Federal Assistance
	Total	Defense	All Other Agencies		Total	Defense	Total	Retirement Disability	All Other	Total	Defense		
United States	1,398,228	232,050	1,166,178	241,474	169,731	72,955	760,958	468,439	292,519	200,543	128,629	25,522	548,838
Alabama	23,548	4,081	19,467	3,671	2,898	1,484	13,752	8,699	5,053	2,937	1,839	291	4,332
Alaska	4,378	1,462	2,916	1,140	1,327	794	1,054	641	413	804	565	53	775
Arizona	21,951	4,836	17,116	3,396	2,523	1,092	12,384	8,163	4,221	3,485	2,921	163	5,019
Arkansas	12,164	995	11,169	2,203	1,037	368	8,109	5,237	2,872	453	249	361	2,354
California	157,631	33,086	124,545	28,965	18,038	9,189	81,136	45,601	35,535	27,724	19,972	1,768	51,083
Colorado	20,011	5,109	14,902	2,709	3,235	1,318	9,021	6,058	2,963	4,656	3,010	391	6,607
Connecticut	18,142	3,345	14,798	3,472	1,418	473	9,904	5,825	4,079	3,123	2,685	225	4,787
Delaware	3,408	442	2,966	700	411	234	2,116	1,330	785	154	102	27	1,811
Dist. Of Col.	22,678	2,492	20,187	3,408	11,304	1,194	2,728	1,649	1,080	4,580	1,197	657	740
Florida	79,614	12,664	66,951	9,055	7,660	3,685	53,695	33,198	20,497	8,126	5,880	1,078	176,552
Georgia	34,857	8,397	26,459	5,501	5,904	3,322	18,276	11,480	6,797	4,741	3,982	435	10,818
Hawaii	7,990	3,258	4,732	1,105	2,409	2,085	3,348	2,139	1,210	1,027	907	101	5,643
Idaho	5,489	481	5,008	897	630	201	2,919	1,938	981	945	132	98	1,286
Illinois	*51,586*	*3,279*	*48,307*	*9,610*	*5,440*	*1,590*	*32,487*	*19,361*	*13,126*	*3,165*	*1,185*	*884*	*11,891*
Indiana	24,250	2,563	21,687	3,747	1,970	690	15,283	9,969	5,315	2,090	1,574	1,160	9,985
Percent U.S.	1.73	1.10	1.86	1.55	1.16	0.95	2.01	2.13	1.82	1.04	1.22	4.55	1.82
Rank	18	24	18	21	27	29	16	15	17	26	20	5	12
Iowa	13,415	635	12,780	2,099	944	124	7,818	5,263	2,555	778	372	1,776	5,658
Kansas	12,359	1,856	10,503	1,737	1,700	787	7,157	4,766	2,391	1,110	780	655	2,792
Kentucky	*19,742*	*2,539*	*17,203*	*3,445*	*2,442*	*1,356*	*11,468*	*7,404*	*4,064*	*2,005*	*859*	*383*	*2,716*
Louisiana	22,048	2,418	19,630	4,728	2,084	911	12,767	7,167	5,600	2,086	1,077	384	29,858
Maine	6,819	1,326	5,492	1,348	722	369	3,782	2,458	1,323	907	792	59	1,112
Maryland	37,110	7,461	29,649	4,283	7,324	2,565	14,744	9,531	5,213	8,522	4,090	2,237	8,558
Massachusetts	36,136	5,684	30,452	7,415	2,857	585	19,416	10,752	8,664	6,081	4,696	367	6,892
Michigan	*39,633*	*2,176*	*37,457*	*7,846*	*2,778*	*523*	*26,464*	*16,252*	*10,212*	*2,189*	*1,250*	*356*	*6,129*
Minnesota	18,994	1,433	17,560	3,923	1,655	222	10,886	7,042	3,844	1,535	964	995	7,383
Mississippi	15,184	3,293	11,891	2,726	1,571	955	8,335	5,026	3,308	2,326	1,963	226	4,556
Missouri	35,321	10,819	24,502	4,440	3,185	1,127	15,966	10,079	5,887	10,594	9,218	1,137	4,729
Montana	4,972	392	4,580	1,003	632	195	2,447	1,681	766	263	90	628	1,295
Nebraska	7,591	1,082	6,509	1,235	1,031	518	4,296	2,980	1,316	585	367	444	4,529
Nevada	7,514	1,062	6,452	934	850	392	4,277	2,843	1,434	1,407	290	47	2,707
New Hampshire	5,049	836	4,213	934	448	97	2,936	2,028	908	672	567	60	965
New Jersey	38,467	4,153	34,315	6,529	3,556	1,220	24,355	14,091	10,264	3,750	2,577	276	21,153
New Mexico	12,141	1,878	10,263	2,126	1,686	849	4,508	3,030	1,479	3,676	680	143	1,488
New York	95,798	5,341	90,456	26,118	7,157	1,277	55,294	31,229	24,065	6,320	3,559	910	18,045
North Carolina	33,370	5,909	27,461	6,300	4,898	3,185	19,620	12,877	6,742	2,293	1,655	258	11,329
North Dakota	3,605	552	3,054	811	644	391	1,696	1,110	586	210	106	244	2,143
Ohio	*50,601*	*5,166*	*45,434*	*9,394*	*4,612*	*1,845*	*31,541*	*19,830*	*11,711*	*4,583*	*2,736*	*471*	*5,990*
Oklahoma	16,843	2,948	13,895	2,584	2,721	1,697	10,021	6,542	3,479	1,205	777	313	2,815
Oregon	14,246	722	13,524	3,058	1,410	192	8,908	5,843	3,064	610	201	260	3,188
Pennsylvania	64,610	6,274	58,336	11,017	5,625	1,797	41,535	24,879	16,655	5,531	3,773	902	9,846
Rhode Island	5,719	773	4,945	1,172	634	340	3,428	1,985	1,443	423	329	62	1,769
South Carolina	18,354	3,290	15,064	3,007	2,203	1,485	10,497	6,987	3,510	2,505	1,016	142	13,894
South Dakota	3,867	369	3,497	864	534	183	2,017	1,330	688	249	110	202	1,648
Tennessee	27,520	2,259	25,261	4,527	2,702	494	15,705	9,740	5,964	4,317	1,132	269	4,088
Texas	86,783	17,533	69,250	13,937	11,249	5,680	46,390	27,582	18,807	13,840	9,074	1,367	38,855
Utah	8,153	1,341	6,812	1,508	1,478	761	3,984	2,807	1,177	1,072	393	110	2,192
Vermont	2,784	323	2,461	665	270	47	1,534	985	549	295	225	20	444
Virginia	50,688	21,795	28,893	3,992	12,322	9,158	18,790	13,460	5,330	14,529	10,346	1,055	11,614
Washington	29,563	6,245	23,318	4,998	4,574	2,773	14,964	9,814	5,151	4,603	2,381	424	5,645
West Virginia	10,066	462	9,603	2,146	815	117	6,492	4,252	2,240	514	203	99	1,239
Wisconsin	20,095	1,000	19,095	4,024	1,377	209	13,123	8,719	4,403	1,162	556	409	3,693
Wyoming	2,504	326	2,177	706	395	171	1,215	828	387	153	92	35	446

Defense as a Percent of
Total Direct Federal Expenditures 1996

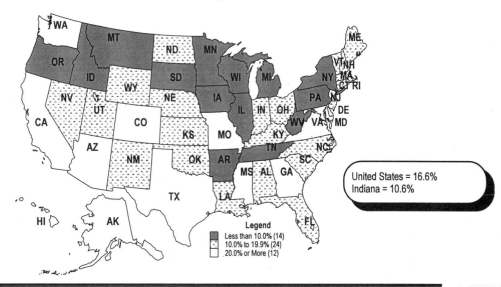

United States = 16.6%
Indiana = 10.6%

Legend
Less than 10.0% (14)
10.0% to 19.9% (24)
20.0% or More (12)

Source: U.S. Bureau of the Census
EDIN table(s): CFFR

1.65 State Government Tax Collections 1996 *($000)*

	Total Taxes	Percent Change 1995-96	Total Property Taxes	Percent Change 1995-96	Total Sales and Gross Receipts Taxes	Percent Change 1995-96	Total General Sales Taxes	Total Selective Sales Taxes	Total License Taxes	Total Other Taxes
United States	418,576,126	4.9	9,943,863	4.5	205,577,827	4.4	139,302,749	66,275,078	26,942,023	176,112,413
Alabama	5,257,771	3.5	134,252	13.6	2,773,974	4.9	1,439,145	1,334,829	422,841	1,926,704
Alaska	1,519,082	-21.0	56,168	-2.0	99,124	-1.9	0	99,124	78,896	1,284,894
Arizona	6,409,395	3.0	363,315	9.7	3,658,165	1.6	2,720,378	937,787	391,385	1,996,530
Arkansas	3,708,744	9.3	7,363	15.1	1,939,666	2.7	1,375,906	563,760	216,315	1,545,400
California	57,746,664	8.4	3,375,264	6.2	24,092,750	6.5	18,980,224	5,112,526	3,034,776	27,243,874
Colorado	4,820,163	6.4	0	-100.0	2,037,377	6.5	1,321,500	715,877	255,753	2,527,033
Connecticut	7,830,181	4.8	38	216.7	3,932,300	6.0	2,444,896	1,487,404	330,986	3,566,857
Delaware	1,688,349	6.3	0	NA	252,744	4.4	0	252,744	533,401	902,204
Dist. Of Col.	NA	NA	NA	NA	NA	NA	NA	NA	NA	NA
Florida	19,699,256	6.0	754,482	6.9	15,240,514	6.4	11,428,999	3,811,515	1,315,384	2,388,876
Georgia	10,292,371	8.5	35,651	8.4	4,785,987	7.3	3,823,895	962,092	420,202	5,050,531
Hawaii	3,069,300	6.8	0	NA	1,894,579	5.5	1,431,802	462,777	85,456	1,089,265
Idaho	1,857,006	7.1	0	-100.0	911,552	12.0	600,112	311,440	96,233	849,221
Illinois	*17,277,319*	*4.1*	*212,144*	*3.5*	*8,485,929*	*0.7*	*5,057,457*	*3,428,472*	*951,871*	*7,627,375*
Indiana	8,437,031	4.9	2,876	-9.4	3,761,281	5.2	2,867,644	893,637	201,776	4,471,098
Percent U.S.	2.02	—	0.03	—	1.83	—	2.06	1.35	0.75	2.54
Rank	17	23	32	42	18	21	15	25	35	14
Iowa	4,440,540	0.8	0	NA	2,147,520	3.9	1,456,221	691,299	414,215	1,878,805
Kansas	3,978,761	5.7	40,362	6.1	1,930,900	1.9	1,401,023	529,877	203,098	1,804,401
Kentucky	*6,489,256*	*3.3*	*411,635*	*3.3*	*3,065,661*	*4.7*	*1,784,031*	*1,281,630*	*381,299*	*2,630,661*
Louisiana	4,906,283	4.9	20,304	-44.7	2,558,812	6.3	1,621,872	936,940	418,327	1,908,840
Maine	1,896,564	4.6	43,467	3.3	935,796	1.2	657,955	277,841	114,473	802,828
Maryland	8,166,692	1.3	226,767	-5.5	3,554,952	1.6	2,000,298	1,554,654	357,725	4,027,248
Massachusetts	12,453,370	7.3	102	-41.0	3,887,937	4.0	2,610,094	1,277,843	395,522	8,169,809
Michigan	*19,128,687*	*7.9*	*1,640,411*	*10.2*	*8,324,240*	*8.6*	*6,586,563*	*1,737,677*	*982,069*	*8,181,967*
Minnesota	10,055,523	7.8	8,288	-4.0	4,407,349	5.7	2,900,125	1,507,224	638,071	5,001,815
Mississippi	3,862,541	7.3	23,733	3.2	2,602,402	7.4	1,831,963	770,439	249,480	986,926
Missouri	7,300,119	8.1	14,626	4.2	3,353,325	2.3	2,453,924	899,401	597,734	3,334,434
Montana	1,256,416	3.5	229,692	0.1	269,478	8.2	0	269,478	147,824	609,422
Nebraska	2,369,462	6.7	4,114	18.5	1,224,525	3.1	814,748	409,777	158,146	982,677
Nevada	2,889,254	7.1	55,094	-4.7	2,434,901	7.7	1,571,703	863,198	312,972	86,287
New Hampshire	837,092	-8.7	424	226.2	428,740	-20.7	0	428,740	108,038	299,890
New Jersey	14,384,897	5.7	2,770	-50.6	7,363,746	5.6	4,318,373	3,045,373	752,861	6,265,520
New Mexico	3,060,637	7.6	36,560	33.3	1,735,760	7.4	1,283,843	451,917	164,818	1,123,499
New York	34,150,039	-0.4	0	NA	11,913,517	1.2	6,963,058	4,950,459	973,607	21,262,915
North Carolina	11,882,318	4.0	11,448	-91.1	5,143,859	5.8	2,970,566	2,173,293	732,907	5,994,104
North Dakota	985,327	2.8	2,079	4.4	559,751	2.1	282,131	277,620	77,715	345,782
Ohio	*15,649,492*	*3.1*	*17,227*	*27.5*	*7,604,288*	*1.6*	*4,991,363*	*2,612,925*	*1,218,717*	*6,809,260*
Oklahoma	4,617,778	4.6	0	NA	1,870,060	1.0	1,210,391	659,669	658,576	2,089,142
Oregon	4,415,725	3.0	91	-52.8	591,357	8.2	0	591,357	580,688	3,243,589
Pennsylvania	18,725,016	2.5	220,796	-3.6	8,815,643	1.9	5,740,703	3,074,940	1,819,745	7,868,832
Rhode Island	1,549,195	3.9	9,125	11.0	778,189	1.2	465,133	313,056	80,448	681,433
South Carolina	5,113,034	7.3	11,892	-16.8	2,603,702	5.4	1,919,340	684,362	389,432	2,108,008
South Dakota	730,251	5.2	0	NA	572,364	6.4	383,423	188,941	90,336	67,551
Tennessee	6,184,562	4.7	0	NA	4,744,381	3.9	3,537,315	1,207,066	609,567	830,614
Texas	21,259,072	4.8	0	NA	17,223,664	4.8	10,811,287	6,412,377	3,047,806	987,602
Utah	2,913,960	8.9	0	NA	1,470,506	8.2	1,170,120	300,386	98,909	1,344,545
Vermont	841,029	4.9	10,562	9.6	403,847	2.4	182,528	221,319	71,538	355,082
Virginia	8,900,413	1.3	18,808	-4.4	3,588,976	4.2	1,995,787	1,593,189	418,817	4,873,812
Washington	10,586,463	3.8	1,800,457	6.8	7,867,511	3.0	6,182,443	1,685,068	492,932	425,563
West Virginia	2,770,888	1.4	2,416	3.4	1,452,499	-0.5	797,289	655,210	155,827	1,160,146
Wisconsin	9,616,833	6.5	84,437	37.2	4,010,185	4.2	2,708,052	1,302,133	664,401	4,857,810
Wyoming	625,966	-6.1	83,611	-3.2	274,217	0.8	210,952	63,265	74,243	193,895

Percent Change in Total State Government Tax Collections 1992 to 1996

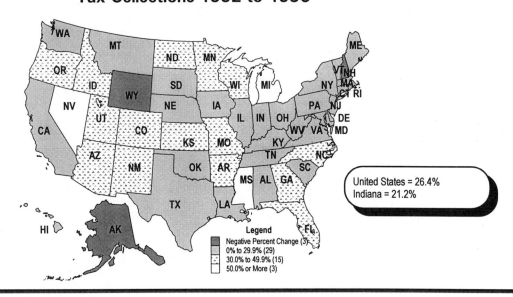

United States = 26.4%
Indiana = 21.2%

Legend
- Negative Percent Change (3)
- 0% to 29.9% (29)
- 30.0% to 49.9% (15)
- 50.0% or More (3)

Source: U.S. Bureau of the Census
EDIN table(s): GOVT

1.66 Per Capita State Government Finances 1995 *($)*

	Total Revenue	General Revenue	Utility Revenue	Liquor Store Revenue	Insurance Trust Revenue	Total Expenditures	Intergovernmental Expenditure	Direct Expenditure	Exhibit: Salaries & Wages
United States	3,447	2,819	15	12	602	3,192	919	2,273	478
Alabama	2,887	2,488	0	31	368	2,714	616	2,098	574
Alaska	13,722	12,183	39	0	1,500	9,270	1,814	7,456	1,479
Arizona	2,986	2,492	5	0	489	2,646	947	1,700	396
Arkansas	2,966	2,603	0	0	363	2,663	638	2,025	543
California	3,745	2,984	4	0	757	3,458	1,421	2,037	416
Colorado	3,084	2,453	0	0	631	2,616	721	1,895	473
Connecticut	4,189	3,682	7	0	500	4,145	736	3,410	748
Delaware	4,799	4,343	8	0	448	4,156	711	3,446	977
Dist. Of Col.	NA	NA	NA	NA	NA	NA	NA	NA	NA
Florida	2,637	2,189	0	0	448	2,453	773	1,680	420
Georgia	2,817	2,378	0	0	439	2,660	674	1,986	415
Hawaii	4,867	4,296	0	0	572	5,067	121	4,946	1,428
Idaho	3,306	2,709	0	39	558	2,889	811	2,078	479
Illinois	*2,932*	*2,457*	*0*	*0*	*476*	*2,789*	*675*	*2,113*	*346*
Indiana	**2,802**	**2,559**	**0**	**0**	**243**	**2,634**	**881**	**1,752**	**412**
Rank	*46*	*34*	*—*	*—*	*50*	*42*	*16*	*47*	*44*
Iowa	3,261	2,846	0	29	386	3,021	910	2,111	593
Kansas	2,875	2,532	0	0	343	2,774	860	1,914	533
Kentucky	*3,328*	*2,872*	*0*	*0*	*456*	*2,952*	*723*	*2,229*	*550*
Louisiana	3,214	2,779	0	0	435	3,331	687	2,644	666
Maine	3,391	2,960	0	55	376	3,368	604	2,763	492
Maryland	3,259	2,716	18	0	525	2,989	610	2,379	506
Massachusetts	3,968	3,547	11	0	410	3,998	780	3,217	502
Michigan	*3,700*	*3,164*	*0*	*48*	*487*	*3,631*	*1,423*	*2,207*	*513*
Minnesota	3,976	3,299	0	0	677	3,553	1,221	2,332	556
Mississippi	3,078	2,616	0	49	413	2,749	845	1,904	426
Missouri	2,928	2,351	0	0	577	2,344	650	1,694	398
Montana	3,785	3,040	0	43	702	3,434	787	2,647	538
Nebraska	2,819	2,563	0	0	256	2,596	699	1,898	568
Nevada	3,580	2,546	53	0	981	2,994	931	2,063	469
New Hampshire	2,848	2,329	0	184	335	2,697	326	2,371	473
New Jersey	4,113	3,190	54	0	869	4,104	994	3,109	608
New Mexico	3,937	3,359	0	0	578	3,776	1,167	2,609	714
New York	5,017	3,853	116	0	1,048	4,487	1,389	3,098	539
North Carolina	3,070	2,664	0	0	406	2,840	926	1,914	443
North Dakota	3,820	3,343	0	0	477	3,452	682	2,770	637
Ohio	*3,704*	*2,535*	*0*	*33*	*1,136*	*3,138*	*855*	*2,283*	*398*
Oklahoma	2,794	2,356	76	0	362	2,742	747	1,995	498
Oregon	4,134	3,005	0	56	1,074	3,512	949	2,563	521
Pennsylvania	3,315	2,715	0	56	544	3,263	748	2,515	396
Rhode Island	4,198	3,420	8	0	770	4,308	509	3,800	720
South Carolina	3,286	2,616	165	0	504	3,164	644	2,520	644
South Dakota	2,867	2,422	0	0	444	2,578	462	2,117	500
Tennessee	2,454	2,192	0	0	262	2,556	621	1,935	428
Texas	2,639	2,155	0	0	484	2,384	630	1,754	327
Utah	3,242	2,718	0	41	482	2,963	741	2,221	634
Vermont	3,545	3,196	0	48	301	3,442	528	2,914	659
Virginia	2,870	2,456	0	37	377	2,575	649	1,926	533
Washington	4,341	3,087	0	47	1,208	3,904	983	2,920	616
West Virginia	3,626	3,079	0	25	523	3,425	686	2,739	451
Wisconsin	3,284	2,994	0	0	291	3,182	1,117	2,065	464
Wyoming	4,666	4,066	0	68	532	4,261	1,409	2,852	630

Education Expenditures as a Percent of Total Expenditures 1995

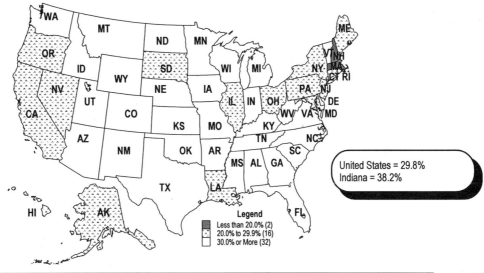

United States = 29.8%
Indiana = 38.2%

Legend
Less than 20.0% (2)
20.0% to 29.9% (16)
30.0% or More (32)

1.67 State Government Finances 1995 ($): Per Capita General Expenditure by Function

	Education	Public Welfare	Hospitals	Health	Highways	Police Protection	Correction	Natural Resources	Parks and Recreation	Govt. Administration	Interest On General Debt
United States	952.21	743.15	111.13	117.71	218.82	24.60	99.42	47.80	12.98	99.46	93.38
Alabama	1,034.78	538.74	190.79	115.60	217.36	19.63	54.40	43.71	2.50	70.35	45.56
Alaska	2,082.76	1,064.03	52.60	238.71	958.68	91.54	242.76	399.97	24.27	589.91	456.34
Arizona	853.73	585.14	13.09	116.05	219.38	26.03	103.55	37.72	6.16	78.84	42.69
Arkansas	946.95	611.39	136.34	96.75	246.79	20.38	64.77	54.08	14.67	69.68	47.18
California	950.55	902.62	79.95	166.42	152.61	28.46	116.36	56.68	8.16	101.11	84.41
Colorado	984.92	569.87	39.08	59.96	208.13	13.09	85.32	42.55	10.23	77.47	62.11
Connecticut	859.42	888.41	287.42	105.56	228.93	32.24	146.95	21.49	17.50	175.69	258.26
Delaware	1,282.50	577.30	79.01	201.03	343.79	66.00	153.52	51.00	58.28	288.53	305.98
Dist. Of Col.	NA	NA	NA	NA	NA	NA	NA	NA	NA	NA	NA
Florida	765.60	497.42	35.82	137.17	211.45	19.83	112.89	77.08	7.50	86.43	61.60
Georgia	1,019.40	637.42	88.59	83.75	184.07	18.99	106.17	49.83	25.65	55.12	43.07
Hawaii	1,386.24	752.75	183.28	256.42	237.78	16.73	92.87	79.79	106.61	236.04	251.72
Idaho	1,075.48	418.33	38.80	73.39	314.52	24.75	65.35	98.52	19.01	83.37	80.22
Illinois	*718.95*	*745.91*	*66.39*	*103.91*	*224.06*	*22.96*	*68.96*	*26.31*	*18.98*	*64.51*	*116.74*
Indiana	**1,006.42**	**552.66**	**84.28**	**65.66**	**240.99**	**20.44**	**60.47**	**26.58**	**6.22**	**57.37**	**49.19**
Rank	22	37	32	48	24	32	38	45	44	49	39
Iowa	1,114.42	580.63	184.61	66.43	344.35	18.94	62.16	71.47	6.77	101.31	40.94
Kansas	1,121.09	472.66	128.18	72.33	322.98	16.15	74.63	58.11	3.49	90.72	27.60
Kentucky	*1,052.37*	*719.28*	*87.38*	*65.88*	*238.83*	*29.35*	*57.28*	*65.39*	*21.62*	*104.14*	*92.66*
Louisiana	977.68	892.75	273.41	89.65	183.81	32.10	81.41	71.61	21.79	74.20	138.15
Maine	842.81	1,013.22	50.88	124.71	247.75	22.99	50.89	68.76	11.60	113.48	140.70
Maryland	757.32	586.24	60.89	146.31	233.10	45.36	148.09	62.11	14.35	129.48	99.73
Massachusetts	675.32	1,017.15	123.64	206.98	280.38	40.65	108.70	29.97	16.37	177.60	258.91
Michigan	*1,454.48*	*647.06*	*153.30*	*197.13*	*191.86*	*23.02*	*124.05*	*32.21*	*6.32*	*76.90*	*74.93*
Minnesota	1,205.56	850.99	126.79	95.72	224.81	24.91	53.42	72.26	16.87	107.46	59.67
Mississippi	925.04	604.78	129.42	71.57	216.83	18.46	51.72	60.90	33.34	66.79	42.88
Missouri	804.85	542.36	82.89	91.65	217.82	23.69	49.82	44.67	5.06	75.07	65.73
Montana	1,127.14	532.62	43.62	133.88	342.96	32.64	57.05	146.74	5.87	137.51	135.48
Nebraska	879.40	559.36	153.99	117.53	332.63	24.77	51.92	78.17	11.90	72.81	50.99
Nevada	883.39	400.07	37.89	45.49	271.48	21.40	88.88	31.42	9.34	101.98	64.60
New Hampshire	485.21	821.37	36.72	102.64	178.82	23.24	51.07	32.32	11.65	117.00	325.21
New Jersey	932.16	852.54	130.80	82.26	266.71	37.24	103.89	34.32	41.77	112.11	147.04
New Mexico	1,402.32	521.53	179.37	158.63	413.99	29.32	95.56	51.57	17.63	135.72	57.92
New York	964.63	1,421.75	199.58	132.56	168.00	19.16	125.32	17.77	15.52	154.33	187.11
North Carolina	1,078.68	558.77	102.52	117.61	252.68	26.89	113.92	54.62	8.24	83.53	35.85
North Dakota	1,150.31	683.13	84.44	76.13	421.69	10.35	28.24	135.34	11.52	101.49	84.22
Ohio	*887.00*	*680.93*	*107.21*	*101.07*	*205.21*	*16.99*	*94.32*	*23.55*	*6.88*	*85.04*	*73.21*
Oklahoma	1,028.36	505.23	87.56	88.67	221.41	14.57	75.32	39.06	14.69	95.18	49.30
Oregon	982.39	660.92	147.12	119.31	312.77	36.51	89.45	80.01	8.67	215.57	116.94
Pennsylvania	801.60	920.37	136.23	105.30	207.75	29.23	79.08	36.17	7.93	91.48	102.26
Rhode Island	894.02	911.40	94.35	243.66	268.77	28.96	115.53	34.90	29.02	183.42	307.26
South Carolina	962.99	666.28	158.51	169.74	161.77	33.09	94.76	42.61	11.19	71.46	49.02
South Dakota	705.91	513.75	66.95	79.67	354.31	21.57	55.80	107.13	21.32	114.08	145.66
Tennessee	818.62	723.91	95.04	106.65	232.13	16.26	80.75	32.08	17.48	75.46	35.35
Texas	869.79	568.00	99.25	66.65	162.23	12.82	138.35	32.79	3.19	69.12	40.14
Utah	1,272.59	473.46	144.36	71.81	181.44	18.73	73.98	57.81	20.63	128.95	61.11
Vermont	1,043.88	873.14	16.15	82.17	268.38	46.29	70.36	92.83	15.10	190.77	171.38
Virginia	903.49	423.74	157.44	82.27	299.67	43.69	117.63	20.84	9.75	111.25	77.16
Washington	1,339.18	686.73	94.62	157.33	282.98	28.83	88.89	94.32	18.44	80.10	90.68
West Virginia	1,090.60	862.17	45.79	71.82	362.47	20.33	42.25	82.81	20.23	129.66	80.47
Wisconsin	981.81	616.82	84.47	98.71	217.61	10.93	99.46	78.20	11.83	80.07	96.07
Wyoming	1,304.83	525.38	69.91	154.14	598.48	25.54	61.60	186.72	29.00	155.30	100.57

State Government Per Capita Expenditures 1995

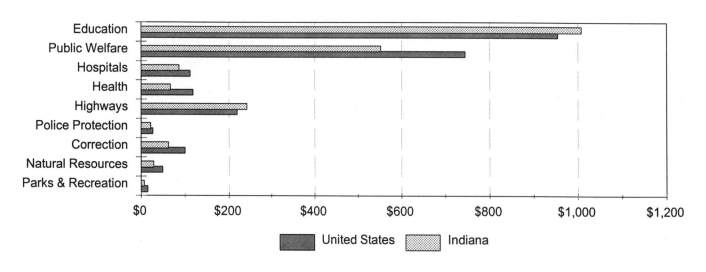

Education, Public Welfare, Hospitals, Health, Highways, Police Protection, Correction, Natural Resources, Parks & Recreation

$0 $200 $400 $600 $800 $1,000 $1,200

United States   Indiana

Source: U.S. Bureau of the Census
EDIN table(s): GOVF

1.68 Income and Apportionment of State-Administered Lottery Funds ($000) 1994

	Income -- Ticket Sales Excluding Commissions	Percent Change 1993-94	Prizes	Percent Change 1993-94	Administration	Percent Change 1993-94	Proceeds Available From Ticket Sales	Percent Change 1993-94
United States	31,713,277	6.4	18,692,622	7.6	1,767,188	4.6	11,253,467	4.8
Alabama	0	NA	0	NA	0	NA	0	NA
Alaska	0	NA	0	NA	0	NA	0	NA
Arizona	243,285	-9.5	135,319	-10.2	24,200	-11.8	83,766	-7.6
Arkansas	0	NA	0	NA	0	NA	0	NA
California	2,144,503	5.9	1,132,429	4.7	203,913	12.0	808,161	6.0
Colorado	310,343	-5.9	191,987	-4.4	26,811	-4.2	91,545	-9.2
Connecticut	669,936	5.3	401,787	4.1	27,605	4.8	240,544	7.5
Delaware	126,773	16.6	58,198	3.3	4,291	-49.7	64,284	46.4
Dist. Of Col.	0	NA	0	NA	0	NA	0	NA
Florida	1,962,014	-7.7	1,023,808	-9.3	117,145	-4.0	821,061	-6.3
Georgia	1,434,785	11.1	789,174	13.7	106,577	9.8	539,034	7.8
Hawaii	0	NA	0	NA	0	NA	0	NA
Idaho	91,162	3.6	55,250	4.4	15,902	-1.4	20,010	5.7
Illinois	*1,473,813*	*0.4*	*838,968*	*-2.3*	*56,835*	*-4.3*	*578,010*	*5.2*
Indiana	**572,925**	**1.8**	**349,844**	**0.0**	**31,666**	**6.2**	**191,415**	**4.5**
Rank	*16*	*25*	*16*	*24*	*19*	*12*	*15*	*17*
Iowa	169,998	-8.7	102,820	-8.7	24,774	0.6	42,404	-13.3
Kansas	167,506	2.9	96,088	4.4	20,039	3.5	51,379	0.0
Kentucky	*509,175*	*6.1*	*321,640*	*6.1*	*30,940*	*4.0*	*156,595*	*6.6*
Louisiana	265,852	-4.9	144,590	-4.9	17,821	-6.1	103,441	-4.6
Maine	148,690	-2.9	83,639	-5.6	15,767	-5.9	49,284	3.1
Maryland	1,052,673	7.0	609,373	11.8	48,898	17.1	394,402	-0.8
Massachusetts	2,850,344	8.4	2,139,703	10.4	69,721	-3.1	640,920	3.5
Michigan	*1,329,265*	*4.5*	*736,073*	*5.3*	*51,578*	*4.1*	*541,614*	*3.5*
Minnesota	355,632	12.0	230,848	17.7	60,366	2.5	64,418	3.0
Mississippi	0	NA	0	NA	0	NA	0	NA
Missouri	396,371	2.4	229,520	3.5	37,588	8.6	129,263	-1.2
Montana	29,997	-3.1	15,914	-1.5	6,447	1.5	7,636	-9.6
Nebraska	81,830	3.6	42,618	8.4	16,564	3.6	22,648	-4.4
Nevada	0	NA	0	NA	0	NA	0	NA
New Hampshire	153,097	15.6	97,940	15.4	6,707	19.2	48,450	15.4
New Jersey	1,501,768	0.8	795,667	-0.4	43,379	-7.7	662,722	2.7
New Mexico	0	NA	0	NA	0	NA	0	NA
New York	3,295,255	18.8	1,826,657	24.2	82,797	21.4	1,385,801	12.2
North Carolina	0	NA	0	NA	0	NA	0	NA
North Dakota	0	NA	0	NA	0	NA	0	NA
Ohio	*2,234,615*	*9.1*	*1,363,071*	*10.2*	*83,276*	*-2.9*	*788,268*	*8.5*
Oklahoma	0	NA	0	NA	0	NA	0	NA
Oregon	944,940	6.7	599,013	6.9	200,710	5.4	145,217	7.7
Pennsylvania	1,585,279	6.5	890,675	9.6	60,728	9.8	633,876	2.3
Rhode Island	395,992	38.2	303,402	46.3	4,854	5.5	87,736	17.7
South Carolina	0	NA	0	NA	0	NA	0	NA
South Dakota	118,858	41.7	16,444	-15.0	7,580	-13.1	94,834	69.8
Tennessee	0	NA	0	NA	0	NA	0	NA
Texas	3,101,735	13.1	1,951,060	15.1	63,294	20.2	1,087,381	9.2
Utah	0	NA	0	NA	0	NA	0	NA
Vermont	74,741	4.2	44,288	6.6	5,605	6.5	24,848	-0.1
Virginia	901,212	2.4	480,404	-1.4	85,929	9.3	334,879	6.7
Washington	389,881	-2.8	223,756	7.8	56,143	3.0	109,982	-20.8
West Virginia	171,709	10.5	93,689	10.2	18,695	15.6	59,325	9.5
Wisconsin	457,323	-7.1	276,966	-7.3	32,043	0.5	148,314	-8.2
Wyoming	0	NA	0	NA	0	NA	0	NA

Percent Distribution of State Administered Lottery Funds
1996

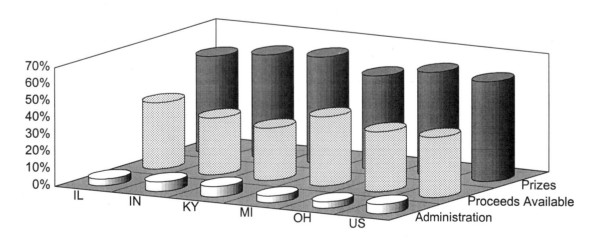

Source: U.S. Bureau of the Census
EDIN table(s): GOVL

Agriculture
1.69 Selected Farm Statistics 1995

	Number of Farms (000)	Percent Change 1990-95	Land in Farms (Mil of Acres)	Percent Change 1990-95	Value Land Per Acre	Per Acre ($)	Per Farm ($)	Total ($Mil)	Building Value ($ Mil)
						Land and Building Value			
United States	2,068.0	-3.14	970.0	-1.5	644	832	390,241	807,017	182,595
Alabama	47.0	0.00	10.2	1.0	874	1,262	273,926	12,874	3,956
Alaska	NA	NA	NA	NA	NA	NA	NA	NA	NA
Arizona	7.4	-5.13	35.4	-1.7	311	347	1,659,790	12,282	1,266
Arkansas	44.0	-6.38	15.0	-3.2	745	983	335,170	14,747	3,570
California	80.0	-5.88	30.0	-2.6	1,787	2,215	830,705	66,456	12,861
Colorado	25.0	-5.66	32.7	-1.2	414	520	680,790	17,019	3,495
Connecticut	3.8	-2.56	0.4	0.0	4,801	6,567	656,676	2,495	671
Delaware	2.5	-13.79	0.6	0.0	1,871	2,689	613,163	1,532	466
Dist. Of Col.	NA	NA	NA	NA	NA	NA	NA	NA	NA
Florida	39.0	-4.88	10.3	-5.5	1,897	2,219	586,166	22,860	3,323
Georgia	45.0	-6.25	12.0	-4.0	879	1,256	335,011	15,075	4,529
Hawaii	NA	NA	NA	NA	NA	NA	NA	NA	NA
Idaho	21.5	-1.38	13.5	-1.5	650	836	524,927	11,285	2,511
Illinois	*77.0*	*-7.23*	*28.1*	*-1.4*	*1,586*	*1,863*	*679,824*	*52,346*	*7,776*
Indiana	**63.0**	**-7.35**	**15.9**	**-2.5**	**1,233**	**1,654**	**417,486**	**26,301**	**6,700**
Percent U.S.	*3.05*	—	*1.64*	—	—	—	—	*3.26*	*3.67*
Rank	*13*	*39*	*19*	*31*	*15*	*15*	*23*	*8*	*9*
Iowa	100.0	-3.85	33.2	-0.9	1,103	1,349	447,862	44,786	8,181
Kansas	66.0	-4.35	47.8	-0.2	447	535	387,469	25,572	4,211
Kentucky	*89.0*	*-4.30*	*14.0*	*-0.7*	*874*	*1,250*	*196,607*	*17,498*	*5,263*
Louisiana	27.0	-15.63	8.5	-4.5	858	1,082	340,694	9,198	1,908
Maine	7.6	5.56	1.4	-6.7	911	1,245	221,195	1,681	451
Maryland	14.3	-5.92	2.2	-4.4	2,643	3,707	570,305	8,155	2,341
Massachusetts	5.8	-15.94	0.6	-14.3	3,945	5,398	530,449	3,077	828
Michigan	*54.0*	*0.00*	*10.7*	*-0.9*	*894*	*1,329*	*263,309*	*14,218*	*4,654*
Minnesota	87.0	-2.25	29.8	-0.7	685	936	320,772	27,907	7,480
Mississippi	40.0	0.00	12.9	-0.8	659	886	285,804	11,432	2,928
Missouri	106.0	-1.85	30.0	-1.3	650	880	249,160	26,204	37,633
Montana	22.0	-10.93	59.7	-1.3	226	277	751,336	16,529	3,012
Nebraska	56.0	-1.75	47.1	0.0	503	596	501,325	28,074	4,404
Nevada	2.5	0.00	8.8	-1.1	203	289	1,017,399	2,543	752
New Hampshire	2.3	-20.69	0.4	-20.0	1,818	2,486	475,600	1,094	294
New Jersey	9.0	11.11	0.9	0.0	6,221	8,052	760,423	6,843	1,555
New Mexico	13.5	0.00	44.0	-1.1	197	225	732,042	9,882	1,234
New York	36.0	-6.49	7.7	-8.3	855	1,380	295,209	10,627	4,042
North Carolina	58.0	-6.45	9.2	-5.2	1,305	1,749	277,456	16,092	4,088
North Dakota	32.0	-5.88	40.3	-0.5	320	373	470,020	15,040	2,145
Ohio	*74.0*	*-11.90*	*15.2*	*-3.2*	*1,270*	*1,800*	*369,717*	*27,359*	*8,049*
Oklahoma	71.0	1.43	34.0	3.0	420	547	262,099	18,609	4,335
Oregon	38.5	5.48	17.5	-1.7	598	844	383,790	14,775	4,304
Pennsylvania	50.0	-5.66	7.7	-4.9	1,506	2,339	360,259	18,012	6,414
Rhode Island	0.7	0.00	0.1	0.0	5,079	6,947	625,225	438	118
South Carolina	22.0	-12.00	5.1	-1.9	961	1,337	306,795	6,749	1,897
South Dakota	33.0	-5.71	44.0	-0.7	244	302	403,219	13,306	2,550
Tennessee	82.0	-7.87	12.0	-3.2	969	1,336	195,546	16,034	4,411
Texas	202.0	8.60	129.0	-2.3	454	550	351,329	70,968	12,379
Utah	13.4	1.52	11.1	-1.8	473	606	502,341	6,731	1,477
Vermont	6.0	-14.29	1.4	-6.7	1,082	1,479	337,675	2,026	544
Virginia	47.0	2.17	8.6	-3.4	1,274	1,771	324,075	15,231	4,275
Washington	36.0	-2.70	15.8	-1.3	799	1,065	467,364	16,825	4,205
West Virginia	20.0	-2.44	3.7	0.0	636	910	168,394	3,367	1,015
Wisconsin	80.0	0.00	16.9	-4.0	618	1,065	225,049	18,003	7,554
Wyoming	9.2	3.37	34.6	-0.6	156	192	721,025	6,633	1,231

Average Size of Farms in Acres
1995

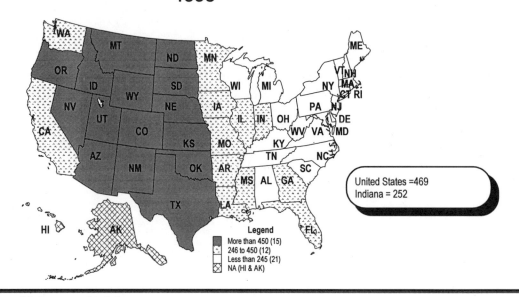

United States = 469
Indiana = 252

Legend
More than 450 (15)
246 to 450 (12)
Less than 245 (21)
NA (HI & AK)

Source: U.S. Department of Agriculture
EDIN table(s): FARM

1.70 Farm Income 1996 ($000)

	Marketing Cash Receipts						Other Income	
	Total	Percent Change 1991-96	Livestock and Products	Percent Change 1991-96	Crops	Percent Change 1991-96	Total	Government Payments
United States	210,124,831	17.6	101,242,988	5.7	108,881,843	31.4	24,099,618	7,285,541
Alabama	3,219,649	8.0	2,431,463	8.8	788,186	5.5	648,520	75,550
Alaska	29,394	10.3	6,108	-5.3	23,286	15.3	5,064	1,258
Arizona	2,161,432	18.5	838,827	4.2	1,322,605	29.9	190,087	57,993
Arkansas	6,030,256	37.4	3,458,229	20.8	2,572,027	68.7	784,264	361,818
California	23,790,583	30.9	6,552,170	15.0	17,238,413	38.1	1,374,957	295,460
Colorado	4,462,760	15.9	3,001,081	8.4	1,461,679	35.1	518,210	176,101
Connecticut	492,312	14.1	239,899	12.2	252,413	15.9	39,620	1,791
Delaware	762,323	20.5	580,166	28.7	182,157	0.2	84,583	4,888
Dist. Of Col.	NA	NA	NA	NA	NA	NA	NA	NA
Florida	6,179,967	-0.9	1,238,137	-2.2	4,941,830	-0.6	248,569	22,872
Georgia	5,791,660	42.4	3,402,874	46.7	2,388,786	36.7	763,290	114,524
Hawaii	486,945	-12.5	70,351	-26.9	416,594	-9.5	28,088	580
Idaho	3,725,786	23.2	1,654,423	15.3	2,071,363	30.3	321,648	116,009
Illinois	*9,187,488*	*16.0*	*2,259,326*	*-11.9*	*6,928,162*	*29.4*	*837,988*	*386,767*
Indiana	5,716,526	21.8	2,070,654	-1.2	3,645,872	40.4	544,137	213,703
Percent U.S.	*2.72*	—	*2.05*	—	*3.35*	—	*2.26*	*2.93*
Rank	*14*	*15*	*19*	*31*	*9*	*12*	*21*	*14*
Iowa	13,255,688	20.3	5,971,251	-2.8	7,284,437	49.4	1,063,573	501,694
Kansas	8,747,484	8.6	5,470,035	-4.6	3,277,449	41.1	1,109,839	555,139
Kentucky	*3,557,304*	*9.4*	*1,725,204*	*-2.1*	*1,832,100*	*22.9*	*573,632*	*74,542*
Louisiana	2,329,662	43.8	708,024	8.3	1,621,638	67.9	337,905	176,471
Maine	492,592	8.0	269,063	2.8	223,529	15.0	40,988	4,638
Maryland	1,557,991	12.0	927,861	8.8	630,130	17.2	219,963	17,647
Massachusetts	481,128	5.4	112,497	-13.1	368,631	12.7	44,255	1,548
Michigan	*3,769,903*	*10.4*	*1,565,877*	*9.0*	*2,204,026*	*11.4*	*397,750*	*109,585*
Minnesota	8,980,895	16.9	4,414,243	15.2	4,566,652	18.7	887,130	348,804
Mississippi	3,512,846	49.1	1,980,213	46.8	1,532,633	52.3	547,905	184,925
Missouri	5,234,082	21.7	2,775,566	4.7	2,458,516	48.9	730,254	289,279
Montana	2,118,431	25.4	904,885	-4.6	1,213,546	63.9	448,862	240,874
Nebraska	9,588,566	1.0	5,517,287	-10.3	4,071,279	21.8	935,146	388,819
Nevada	300,334	0.9	167,768	-22.2	132,566	61.5	43,828	2,605
New Hampshire	161,933	17.2	73,328	10.8	88,605	23.0	19,904	1,093
New Jersey	801,955	21.8	197,379	-0.4	604,576	31.4	98,432	3,258
New Mexico	1,702,766	17.0	1,197,489	16.2	505,277	18.9	161,105	59,000
New York	3,104,741	6.2	2,103,980	10.8	1,000,761	-2.5	217,910	43,289
North Carolina	8,240,677	51.3	4,842,059	72.0	3,398,618	29.0	1,364,807	75,702
North Dakota	3,491,678	33.0	596,769	-16.5	2,894,909	51.5	593,649	351,520
Ohio	*5,373,969*	*22.3*	*2,188,366*	*14.2*	*3,185,603*	*28.6*	*753,194*	*163,120*
Oklahoma	3,975,457	-7.6	2,851,094	-11.9	1,124,363	5.5	588,932	236,707
Oregon	3,072,605	12.5	755,157	-22.3	2,317,448	31.7	769,344	74,262
Pennsylvania	4,307,856	16.2	3,032,734	13.1	1,275,122	24.0	359,641	37,111
Rhode Island	83,660	18.2	12,087	-11.2	71,573	25.2	6,888	156
South Carolina	1,624,833	31.8	760,621	34.2	864,212	29.6	189,145	42,868
South Dakota	3,949,844	9.7	1,953,959	-15.4	1,995,885	54.7	499,537	229,605
Tennessee	2,381,107	25.5	1,038,719	-2.5	1,342,388	61.5	422,278	79,917
Texas	14,696,454	3.6	9,393,878	-4.8	5,302,576	22.8	2,175,920	764,778
Utah	916,875	19.0	690,109	16.0	226,766	29.2	136,831	21,006
Vermont	543,420	20.8	445,811	18.5	97,609	32.6	40,202	4,035
Virginia	2,486,857	9.6	1,589,937	5.2	896,920	18.3	306,841	30,423
Washington	5,853,208	30.1	1,860,587	16.3	3,992,621	37.7	801,152	156,039
West Virginia	403,062	14.1	323,300	14.9	79,762	10.7	83,027	4,538
Wisconsin	6,290,982	9.3	4,508,836	2.2	1,782,146	32.8	607,255	156,849
Wyoming	696,905	-23.1	513,307	-28.6	183,598	-2.1	133,569	24,381

Crops as a Percent of Total Cash Receipts
1996

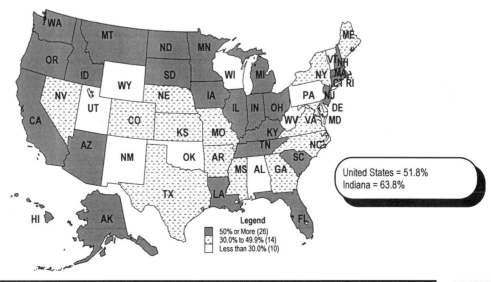

United States = 51.8%
Indiana = 63.8%

Legend
- 50% or More (26)
- 30.0% to 49.9% (14)
- Less than 30.0% (10)

Source: U.S. Bureau of Economic Analysis
EDIN table(s): FMIN

1.71 Average Price ($) Received for Livestock (Per 100 Pounds) 1995

	Cows	Percent Change 1990-95	Steers And Heifers	Percent Change 1990-95	Beef Cattle	Percent Change 1990-95	Calves	Percent Change 1990-95	Hogs	Percent Change 1990-95	Sheep	Percent Change 1990-95	Lambs	Percent Change 1990-95
United States	35.70	-30.68	65.10	-17.39	61.80	-17.16	73.10	-23.54	40.50	-24.58	28.00	20.69	78.20	40.90
Alabama	35.90	-29.61	57.80	-27.02	51.40	-26.15	59.70	-33.74	35.80	-27.82	25.00	NA	65.00	NA
Alaska	56.00	7.69	80.00	14.29	66.10	6.61	84.00	10.53	55.00	-29.49	50.00	66.67	85.00	30.77
Arizona	33.80	-34.11	63.70	-16.73	60.40	-15.76	74.20	-19.26	40.60	-25.64	29.00	20.83	79.00	27.21
Arkansas	37.20	-27.49	61.60	-25.42	49.20	-25.57	58.40	-38.27	40.00	-18.20	NA	NA	NA	NA
California	33.50	-33.79	57.00	-25.39	47.00	-27.69	69.40	-22.37	39.70	-32.02	24.80	31.22	79.20	31.78
Colorado	36.90	-30.51	66.60	-16.75	64.70	-17.58	75.20	-24.65	42.00	-24.73	27.30	13.28	79.60	46.32
Connecticut	40.00	-23.08	50.00	-20.63	48.00	-21.31	50.00	-35.06	37.00	-24.49	37.00	8.82	115.00	15.00
Delaware	38.60	-28.39	49.80	-31.02	45.40	-31.00	66.80	-37.57	38.00	-25.34	NA	NA	NA	NA
Dist. Of Col.	NA	NA	NA	NA	NA	NA	NA	NA	NA	NA	NA	NA	NA	NA
Florida	35.40	-32.44	57.20	-27.41	44.30	-25.55	70.00	-28.43	34.20	-30.63	NA	NA	NA	NA
Georgia	35.40	-31.66	56.50	-26.05	42.30	-30.77	66.30	-25.51	39.70	-25.09	NA	NA	NA	NA
Hawaii	29.80	-12.87	49.30	-4.27	38.10	-21.28	47.40	-15.21	80.20	1.01	NA	NA	NA	NA
Idaho	34.70	-29.33	62.10	-15.74	55.30	-18.68	66.00	-29.11	38.30	-25.34	26.10	50.87	74.80	52.97
Illinois	*35.70*	*-29.72*	*64.60*	*-15.67*	*63.80*	*-15.72*	*101.70*	*-14.54*	*38.90*	*-27.83*	*26.20*	*50.57*	*65.70*	*23.73*
Indiana	**37.90**	**-25.98**	**65.00**	**-11.32**	**56.20**	**-15.99**	**65.90**	**-20.70**	**39.10**	**-25.67**	**25.60**	**26.11**	**77.00**	**50.10**
Rank	9	8	11	5	19	9	33	7	22	35	30	22	26	9
Iowa	36.30	-30.99	65.50	-16.13	61.10	-19.50	69.90	-26.88	41.40	-24.31	26.70	31.53	77.60	45.59
Kansas	39.10	-27.19	65.80	-16.81	65.00	-16.67	75.90	-21.27	38.90	-22.97	27.30	18.70	80.20	44.50
Kentucky	*35.40*	*-28.63*	*58.90*	*-25.91*	*53.30*	*-24.82*	*63.70*	*-28.91*	*39.40*	*-26.63*	*26.00*	*52.94*	*72.00*	*44.00*
Louisiana	34.40	-30.51	55.60	-29.80	41.40	-30.77	62.50	-33.58	35.50	-22.83	31.00	16.98	77.00	37.50
Maine	45.00	-15.09	60.00	-6.25	57.00	-8.06	50.00	-35.06	37.00	-24.49	45.00	32.35	100.00	0.00
Maryland	38.60	-28.39	49.80	-31.02	45.40	-31.00	66.80	-37.57	38.00	-25.34	32.50	43.81	82.80	44.50
Massachusetts	35.00	-30.00	50.00	-20.63	47.00	-21.67	50.00	-35.06	37.00	-24.49	41.00	20.59	115.00	9.52
Michigan	*37.00*	*-27.88*	*58.50*	*-17.37*	*52.00*	*-17.72*	*69.30*	*-30.00*	*39.70*	*-24.09*	*22.60*	*41.25*	*79.50*	*44.55*
Minnesota	36.40	-28.21	58.60	-21.76	56.60	-19.49	72.90	-27.10	41.90	-24.09	23.50	18.69	75.30	40.22
Mississippi	36.00	-28.85	56.00	-29.47	46.00	-23.71	61.20	-35.10	40.10	-23.18	NA	NA	NA	NA
Missouri	35.00	-32.82	62.20	-26.48	55.90	-29.15	68.20	-27.29	39.10	-27.32	21.70	10.15	71.50	40.75
Montana	37.90	-25.69	66.70	-19.93	59.80	-15.30	69.50	-27.07	39.10	-21.80	26.80	52.27	81.40	68.53
Nebraska	36.50	-29.81	66.80	-16.50	66.00	-13.84	76.20	-23.80	42.00	-23.36	26.80	22.37	80.10	48.33
Nevada	34.90	-26.83	60.80	-20.31	54.20	-21.56	69.10	-23.56	38.20	-13.18	20.50	20.59	77.00	61.43
New Hampshire	40.00	-21.57	50.00	-21.88	48.00	-21.31	40.00	-47.37	37.00	-24.49	33.00	-2.94	105.00	5.00
New Jersey	39.30	-22.02	58.80	-9.82	42.70	-20.34	74.20	-30.65	34.10	-29.98	34.90	1.45	83.20	37.07
New Mexico	37.80	-27.45	62.10	-19.66	52.40	-22.94	68.80	-28.93	40.90	-19.33	28.00	6.06	77.20	53.78
New York	35.30	-27.52	52.50	-21.05	37.20	-27.20	68.30	-34.33	36.90	-25.30	31.40	46.05	89.60	52.12
North Carolina	35.80	-33.21	65.80	-11.32	50.10	-21.10	63.90	-26.13	41.80	-19.31	28.40	35.24	68.30	36.60
North Dakota	36.10	-28.94	63.30	-24.46	55.70	-26.71	69.20	-28.44	35.30	-29.96	23.90	14.90	75.90	48.24
Ohio	*33.30*	*-33.67*	*62.50*	*-17.33*	*59.70*	*-16.74*	*70.40*	*-19.91*	*40.30*	*-23.09*	*28.70*	*42.08*	*77.90*	*42.94*
Oklahoma	35.30	-30.51	65.60	-22.18	62.50	-14.50	70.50	-25.55	38.60	-24.90	34.00	57.41	75.00	47.35
Oregon	34.80	-29.12	59.50	-24.78	52.10	-25.04	66.40	-25.23	44.40	-18.83	23.30	33.14	72.30	39.58
Pennsylvania	37.00	-27.17	63.30	-13.76	56.60	-13.72	91.80	-18.04	38.00	-30.02	31.50	48.58	77.50	32.25
Rhode Island	35.00	-32.69	50.00	-20.63	47.00	-22.95	50.00	-35.06	37.00	-24.49	NA	NA	NA	NA
South Carolina	37.00	-28.85	53.40	-29.83	48.70	-16.03	65.50	-29.72	38.30	-26.20	NA	NA	NA	NA
South Dakota	36.20	-30.38	66.10	-19.00	61.60	-19.58	68.70	-31.98	41.70	-22.92	27.60	18.45	80.20	47.97
Tennessee	33.80	-33.33	58.00	-25.06	50.20	-23.36	59.60	-32.35	38.10	-24.40	28.70	24.78	81.50	45.80
Texas	33.70	-36.53	64.70	-18.00	62.20	-19.01	71.80	-23.86	35.50	-26.35	33.40	12.08	78.50	33.28
Utah	37.50	-26.33	63.10	-17.84	61.40	-16.80	71.10	-24.28	33.80	-29.88	21.00	12.30	77.00	58.76
Vermont	35.00	-31.37	50.00	-21.88	47.00	-22.95	50.00	-34.21	37.00	-24.49	36.00	5.88	95.00	-3.06
Virginia	34.20	-30.91	58.80	-24.32	50.90	-27.60	62.90	-25.47	41.20	-22.99	26.80	57.65	80.80	52.45
Washington	34.80	-29.41	63.90	-17.23	59.60	-18.69	66.90	-24.49	40.80	-19.53	23.40	37.65	70.80	33.33
West Virginia	31.80	-31.61	57.60	-25.68	46.50	-36.21	60.10	-28.88	33.60	-36.12	22.70	41.88	76.20	49.41
Wisconsin	36.60	-28.38	60.50	-16.90	46.70	-24.07	108.00	-22.86	38.30	-27.46	23.50	95.83	76.10	40.41
Wyoming	37.90	-33.86	67.10	-22.25	62.40	-18.22	70.20	-30.50	40.40	-24.06	25.90	45.51	80.20	60.40

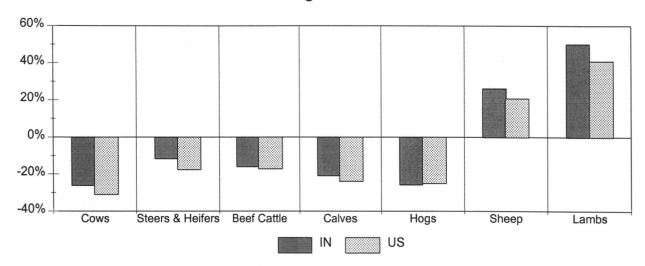

Average Price Received for Livestock
Percent Change 1990 to 1995

Legend: IN, US

Source: U.S. Department of Agriculture
EDIN table(s): FMLV

1.72 Crops - Season Average Price *($)* and Value of Production *($000)* 1995

	Average Price per Bushel					Value of Production				
	Wheat	Corn	Oats	Soy-beans	Hay (Tons)	Wheat	Corn	Oats	Soy-beans	Hay (Tons)
United States	4.55	3.24	1.67	6.72	82.20	9,787,213	24,117,503	280,547	14,616,758	11,041,844
Alabama	3.90	3.50	1.85	7.10	50.00	11,232	57,750	1,489	38,340	75,600
Alaska	NA	NA	NA	NA	NA	NA	NA	NA	NA	NA
Arizona	4.64	3.70	NA	NA	78.50	47,038	13,838	NA	NA	109,496
Arkansas	3.61	3.10	1.75	6.85	61.50	169,670	30,303	2,678	605,540	115,359
California	4.33	3.95	2.09	NA	98.50	141,249	94,800	5,330	NA	780,299
Colorado	4.64	3.33	2.17	NA	88.50	488,528	306,793	4,440	NA	348,840
Connecticut	NA	NA	NA	NA	120.00	NA	NA	NA	NA	17,066
Delaware	4.10	3.75	NA	6.95	106.00	17,843	54,731	NA	32,387	3,268
Dist. Of Col.	NA	NA	NA	NA	NA	NA	NA	NA	NA	NA
Florida	3.15	3.20	NA	6.50	83.00	1,210	17,280	NA	4,732	47,725
Georgia	3.39	3.55	1.70	6.71	65.00	38,646	111,825	2,975	56,163	97,500
Hawaii	NA	NA	NA	NA	NA	NA	NA	NA	NA	NA
Idaho	4.45	4.50	1.95	NA	87.00	460,048	22,050	3,120	NA	434,785
Illinois	*3.89*	*3.30*	*1.74*	*6.88*	*82.00*	*264,948*	*3,729,000*	*9,326*	*2,602,704*	*287,190*
Indiana	**3.96**	**3.38**	**1.59**	**6.73**	**76.00**	**156,816**	**2,024,282**	**3,244**	**1,323,858**	**178,160**
Percent U.S.	—	—	—	—	—	1.60	8.39	1.16	9.06	1.61
Rank	27	21	28	14	25	17	5	19	4	25
Iowa	4.05	3.20	1.76	6.65	81.00	4,961	4,487,040	25,740	2,709,476	457,763
Kansas	4.59	3.24	1.71	6.69	75.00	1,312,740	791,467	6,430	342,863	436,573
Kentucky	*3.84*	*3.27*	*NA*	*7.01*	*69.00*	*93,619*	*402,602*	*NA*	*290,214*	*398,790*
Louisiana	3.70	2.95	NA	6.63	46.00	10,656	68,455	NA	172,380	34,224
Maine	NA	NA	1.34	NA	84.00	NA	NA	2,171	NA	35,138
Maryland	4.15	3.65	1.90	6.95	106.00	59,760	153,300	695	81,524	58,593
Massachusetts	4.10	3.20	NA	NA	116.00	152,520	798,560	NA	NA	22,320
Michigan	*NA*	*NA*	*1.90*	*6.52*	*66.00*	*NA*	*NA*	*9,747*	*388,592*	*331,995*
Minnesota	4.71	3.14	1.59	6.59	72.50	338,652	2,298,009	28,620	1,547,991	494,497
Mississippi	4.40	3.00	NA	6.76	51.00	27,588	78,375	NA	255,528	85,068
Missouri	3.84	3.48	2.00	6.84	67.00	184,205	521,791	2,726	908,010	460,999
Montana	4.63	3.00	1.75	NA	66.00	904,112	5,760	8,260	NA	346,840
Nebraska	4.56	3.22	1.83	6.56	59.00	392,616	2,752,134	8,235	662,429	407,700
Nevada	4.43	NA	NA	NA	96.00	3,760	NA	NA	NA	141,735
New Hampshire	NA	NA	NA	NA	110.00	NA	NA	NA	NA	15,060
New Jersey	3.80	3.75	NA	6.70	119.00	6,931	27,203	NA	20,341	33,855
New Mexico	4.50	2.95	NA	NA	114.00	14,850	34,456	NA	NA	171,275
New York	4.20	3.85	1.65	NA	85.50	28,875	246,593	8,762	NA	285,436
North Carolina	3.65	3.54	1.50	6.95	72.00	102,784	265,146	2,925	185,913	92,810
North Dakota	5.05	3.16	1.52	6.49	43.00	1,495,226	127,316	32,832	120,454	209,240
Ohio	*3.96*	*3.32*	*1.68*	*6.70*	*78.00*	*292,288*	*1,245,332*	*11,592*	*1,026,038*	*330,940*
Oklahoma	4.41	3.70	1.80	6.65	73.50	481,572	60,125	1,404	36,575	277,064
Oregon	4.79	4.11	1.89	NA	99.50	289,119	13,810	6,417	NA	303,615
Pennsylvania	4.25	3.86	1.91	6.81	94.50	43,244	363,149	18,030	64,355	431,085
Rhode Island	NA	NA	NA	NA	129.00	NA	NA	NA	NA	1,800
South Carolina	3.60	3.40	1.65	6.93	64.00	32,256	81,991	2,599	88,150	46,080
South Dakota	4.68	3.23	1.88	6.28	57.50	420,038	625,167	21,620	471,000	507,300
Tennessee	3.90	3.50	NA	6.88	44.00	62,322	223,020	NA	237,773	172,560
Texas	4.19	3.19	2.19	6.52	72.00	316,764	690,954	11,038	39,120	517,212
Utah	4.74	3.88	2.05	NA	66.00	42,415	7,760	1,292	NA	169,554
Vermont	NA	NA	NA	NA	85.00	NA	NA	NA	NA	47,443
Virginia	3.70	3.35	NA	6.85	86.50	65,120	102,259	NA	77,268	221,850
Washington	4.83	3.45	1.75	NA	97.00	742,500	66,861	1,960	NA	328,878
West Virginia	4.00	3.85	2.20	NA	64.50	2,496	15,400	462	NA	67,488
Wisconsin	3.65	3.11	1.63	6.60	61.50	29,456	1,081,347	30,481	227,040	414,020
Wyoming	4.60	3.90	1.85	NA	71.50	36,540	19,469	3,907	NA	189,756

Value of Production (Billions of Dollars)
Corn and Soybeans 1995

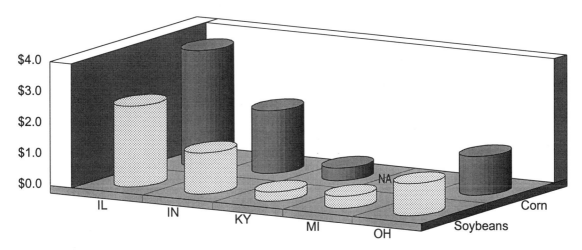

Source: U.S. Department of Agriculture
EDIN table(s): FMPR

1.73 Production and Yield for Selected Crops 1995

	Production (000)					Yield per Acre				
	Corn for Grain (Bushels)	Soy- beans (Bushels)	Wheat (Bushels)	Oats (Bushels)	Hay (Tons)	Corn for Grain (Bushels)	Soy- beans (Bushels)	Wheat (Bushels)	Oats (Bushels)	Hay (Tons)
United States	7,373,876	2,176,814	2,182,591	162,027	69,651	113.5	35.3	35.8	54.7	2.0
Alabama	16,500	5,400	2,880	805	1,512	75.0	24.0	36.0	35.0	2.1
Alaska	NA	NA	NA	NA	NA	NA	NA	NA	NA	NA
Arizona	3,740	NA	10,354	1,530	105	170.0	26.0	84.9	85.0	3.5
Arkansas	9,775	88,400	47,000	NA	1,948	115.0	NA	47.0	NA	1.9
California	24,000	NA	32,725	2,550	1,855	160.0	NA	66.4	85.0	3.5
Colorado	92,130	NA	105,260	2,046	918	111.0	NA	38.4	62.0	1.8
Connecticut	NA	NA	NA	NA	110	NA	NA	NA	NA	1.9
Delaware	14,595	4,660	4,352	NA	16	105.0	20.0	64.0	NA	2.3
Dist. Of Col.	NA	NA	NA	NA	NA	NA	NA	NA	NA	NA
Florida	5,400	728	384	NA	575	90.0	26.0	32.0	NA	2.5
Georgia	31,500	8,370	11,400	1,750	1,500	90.0	27.0	38.0	50.0	2.5
Hawaii	NA	NA	NA	NA	NA	NA	NA	NA	NA	NA
Idaho	4,900	NA	103,320	1,600	570	140.0	NA	77.7	80.0	1.9
Illinois	*1,130,000*	*378,300*	*68,110*	*5,360*	*1,118*	*113.0*	*39.0*	*49.0*	*67.0*	*2.6*
Indiana	598,900	196,710	39,600	2,040	1,120	113.0	39.5	60.0	68.0	2.8
Percent U.S.	*8.12*	*9.04*	*1.81*	*1.26*	*1.61*	—	—	—	—	—
Rank	*5*	*4*	*17*	*19*	*23*	*18*	*5*	*10*	*8*	*3*
Iowa	1,402,200	407,440	1,225	14,625	805	123.0	44.0	35.0	65.0	2.3
Kansas	244,280	51,250	286,000	3,760	3,325	124.0	25.0	26.0	47.0	1.9
Kentucky	*123,120*	*41,400*	*24,380*	*NA*	*4,620*	*108.0*	*36.0*	*53.0*	*NA*	*2.2*
Louisiana	23,205	26,000	2,880	NA	744	105.0	25.0	36.0	NA	2.4
Maine	NA	NA	NA	1,620	389	NA	NA	NA	60.0	1.9
Maryland	42,000	11,730	14,400	366	315	105.0	23.0	64.0	61.0	2.1
Massachusetts	NA	NA	NA	NA	144	NA	NA	NA	NA	1.8
Michigan	*249,550*	*59,600*	*37,200*	*5,130*	*720*	*115.0*	*40.0*	*60.0*	*57.0*	*2.4*
Minnesota	731,850	234,900	71,849	18,000	1,955	119.0	40.5	32.0	48.0	2.3
Mississippi	26,125	37,800	6,270	NA	1,668	95.0	21.0	38.0	NA	2.3
Missouri	149,940	132,750	47,970	1,363	5,558	102.0	29.5	39.0	47.0	2.0
Montana	1,920	NA	195,750	4,720	1,360	120.0	NA	36.0	59.0	1.7
Nebraska	854,700	100,980	86,100	4,500	2,340	111.0	33.0	41.0	50.0	1.3
Nevada	NA	NA	850	NA	425	NA	NA	85.0	NA	1.7
New Hampshire	NA	NA	NA	NA	110	NA	NA	NA	NA	2.0
New Jersey	7,254	3,036	1,824	NA	180	93.0	22.0	57.0	NA	1.8
New Mexico	11,680	NA	3,300	NA	190	160.0	NA	22.0	NA	1.9
New York	64,050	NA	6,875	5,310	1,758	105.0	NA	55.0	59.0	1.9
North Carolina	74,900	26,750	28,160	1,950	1,224	107.0	25.0	44.0	65.0	2.4
North Dakota	40,290	18,560	300,300	21,600	2,015	79.0	29.0	27.0	48.0	1.6
Ohio	*375,100*	*153,140*	*73,810*	*6,900*	*1,375*	*121.0*	*38.0*	*61.0*	*69.0*	*2.5*
Oklahoma	16,250	5,500	109,200	780	2,730	125.0	20.0	21.0	39.0	1.5
Oregon	3,360	NA	60,438	3,395	1,365	160.0	NA	66.9	97.0	2.1
Pennsylvania	94,080	9,450	10,175	9,440	2,147	96.0	30.0	55.0	59.0	1.9
Rhode Island	NA	NA	NA	NA	10	NA	NA	NA	NA	2.0
South Carolina	24,115	12,720	8,960	1,575	720	91.0	24.0	32.0	45.0	2.4
South Dakota	193,550	75,000	90,736	11,500	2,550	79.0	30.0	33.0	46.0	1.5
Tennessee	63,720	34,560	15,980	NA	3,740	118.0	32.0	47.0	NA	2.2
Texas	216,600	6,000	75,600	5,040	7,560	114.0	25.0	27.0	42.0	2.1
Utah	2,000	NA	8,950	630	300	100.0	NA	53.9	70.0	2.0
Vermont	NA	NA	NA	NA	359	NA	NA	NA	NA	1.8
Virginia	30,525	11,280	17,600	NA	2,109	111.0	24.0	64.0	NA	1.9
Washington	19,380	NA	153,770	1,120	728	190.0	NA	59.3	80.0	2.8
West Virginia	4,000	NA	624	210	936	100.0	NA	52.0	42.0	1.8
Wisconsin	347,700	34,400	8,070	18,700	840	114.0	43.0	56.4	55.0	2.1
Wyoming	4,992	NA	7,960	2,112	990	104.0	NA	36.2	64.0	1.5

Yield Per Acre
Corn and Soybeans 1995

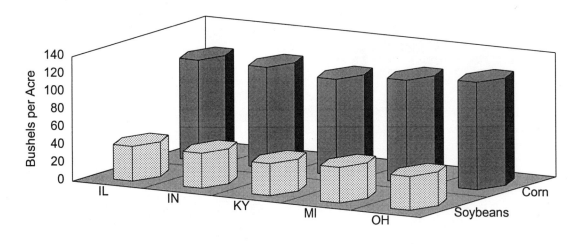

Source: U.S. Department of Agriculture
EDIN table(s): FMCH

1.74 Farm Income and Expenses 1996 *($000)*

	Production Expenses	Percent Change 1991-1996	Inventory Change Value	Cash Receipts & Other Income	Realized Net Income	Percent Change 1991-1996	Net Income Including Corporate Farms	Percent Change 1991-1996	Net Farm Proprietor's Income	Percent Change 1991-1996	Farm Labor & Proprietor's Income	Percent Change 1991-1996
United States	198,982,050	17.11	3,064,842	234,224,449	35,242,399	14.76	38,307,241	29.12	31,536,000	18.09	46,649,000	19.59
Alabama	3,026,637	20.15	17,040	3,868,169	841,532	-13.14	858,572	-19.40	759,273	-24.49	886,452	-21.21
Alaska	28,314	4.99	264	34,458	6,144	18.04	6,408	23.21	4,653	3.31	8,649	4.22
Arizona	1,710,493	22.09	-27,855	2,351,519	641,026	15.95	613,171	-5.02	449,160	-19.12	687,398	-5.22
Arkansas	5,053,087	10.97	64,013	6,814,520	1,761,433	219.87	1,825,446	130.83	1,626,943	117.75	1,847,400	86.27
California	20,399,045	26.54	-103,710	25,165,540	4,766,495	46.52	4,662,785	31.18	3,493,443	12.40	7,419,447	25.96
Colorado	4,468,910	15.19	69,508	4,980,970	512,060	8.89	581,568	4.02	382,573	-17.67	643,599	0.06
Connecticut	398,827	12.98	2,981	531,932	133,105	11.42	136,086	34.62	91,384	7.94	186,386	13.99
Delaware	746,978	25.75	10,786	846,906	99,928	-7.09	110,714	-5.10	91,034	-14.29	118,886	-8.33
Dist. Of Col.	NA	NA	NA	NA	NA	NA	NA	NA	NA	NA	NA	NA
Florida	4,908,007	21.60	13,352	6,428,536	1,520,529	-37.47	1,533,881	-37.83	903,027	-53.90	1,773,580	-34.90
Georgia	4,608,902	35.06	43,093	6,554,950	1,946,048	57.86	1,989,141	42.59	1,729,279	32.45	1,951,619	29.16
Hawaii	559,132	1.89	-3,013	515,033	-44,099	-212.07	-47,112	-245.30	1,584	-93.36	183,675	-11.40
Idaho	3,503,048	32.74	71,117	4,047,434	544,386	-22.38	615,503	-10.31	466,680	-22.70	767,341	-4.31
Illinois	*9,100,616*	*14.07*	*586,062*	*10,025,476*	*924,860*	*11.97*	*1,510,922*	*486.35*	*1,392,766*	*462.00*	*1,704,281*	*206.60*
Indiana	**5,597,244**	**11.39**	**132,358**	**6,260,663**	**663,419**	**236.18**	**795,777**	**-738.18**	**687,316**	**-926.31**	**895,796**	**623.70**
Percent U.S.	*2.81*	—	*4.32*	*2.67*	*1.88*	—	*2.08*	—	*2.18*	—	*1.92*	—
Rank	*11*	*38*	*10*	*14*	*18*	*1*	*16*	*50*	*17*	*50*	*17*	*1*
Iowa	11,589,878	10.22	372,258	14,319,261	2,729,383	60.84	3,101,641	149.80	2,775,142	135.72	3,045,672	109.91
Kansas	8,960,771	12.29	364,934	9,857,323	896,552	-28.57	1,261,486	38.32	870,136	12.77	1,117,925	15.45
Kentucky	*3,273,819*	*14.71*	*83,105*	*4,130,936*	*857,117*	*6.17*	*940,222*	*13.53*	*889,376*	*10.51*	*1,085,193*	*10.45*
Louisiana	2,142,931	7.13	33,884	2,667,567	524,636	-1,470.81	558,520	107.37	493,758	94.32	641,548	52.65
Maine	506,991	12.94	16,638	533,580	26,589	-50.14	43,227	-5.14	35,107	-14.72	108,622	4.10
Maryland	1,569,099	16.50	36,299	1,777,954	208,855	-8.59	245,154	14.88	205,895	4.69	317,836	9.88
Massachusetts	423,250	9.82	-12,861	525,383	102,133	-17.67	89,272	-21.53	58,839	-37.85	152,909	-11.67
Michigan	*3,927,482*	*8.80*	*-253,304*	*4,167,653*	*240,171*	*17.90*	*-13,133*	*-107.20*	*-9,536*	*-105.60*	*457,150*	*-17.46*
Minnesota	8,367,657	15.74	60,613	9,868,025	1,500,368	8.72	1,560,981	95.89	1,411,581	85.83	1,795,325	64.83
Mississippi	3,385,128	18.43	76,784	4,060,751	675,623	-2,123.37	752,407	157.87	675,872	144.10	842,281	83.21
Missouri	5,667,511	18.56	384,247	5,964,336	296,825	65.28	681,072	121.01	619,451	110.30	810,974	69.08
Montana	2,342,972	22.91	-86,412	2,567,293	224,321	-14.06	137,909	-71.92	108,144	-75.33	245,551	-53.80
Nebraska	8,751,416	8.89	711,316	10,523,712	1,772,296	-27.39	2,483,612	24.95	1,894,239	7.75	2,157,130	9.48
Nevada	340,682	23.31	15,439	344,162	3,480	-93.81	18,919	-64.59	14,101	-69.64	52,734	-28.70
New Hampshire	151,726	11.32	-5,304	181,837	30,111	21.33	24,807	7.02	18,759	-7.65	45,230	7.38
New Jersey	732,634	18.47	6,375	900,387	167,753	38.08	174,128	41.42	123,725	17.39	262,817	21.08
New Mexico	1,594,657	24.88	-5,441	1,863,871	269,214	-17.03	263,773	-25.71	210,614	-33.67	352,047	-14.77
New York	3,184,968	11.91	20,521	3,322,651	137,683	-53.72	158,204	-44.19	135,042	-48.66	541,281	-8.92
North Carolina	6,665,225	55.82	150,743	9,605,484	2,940,259	47.88	3,091,002	38.31	2,595,436	25.95	2,969,956	23.92
North Dakota	3,794,400	24.31	387,601	4,085,327	290,927	5.51	678,528	109.00	660,755	106.23	763,889	90.00
Ohio	*5,094,394*	*12.37*	*-255,531*	*6,127,163*	*1,032,769*	*100.18*	*777,238*	*151.60*	*689,778*	*136.50*	*948,379*	*74.64*
Oklahoma	4,343,298	4.29	38,900	4,564,389	221,091	-70.25	259,991	-53.17	211,364	-58.10	359,553	-44.01
Oregon	3,521,105	27.35	25,721	3,841,949	320,844	-30.80	346,565	-6.26	258,137	-20.09	741,861	12.74
Pennsylvania	4,179,390	13.74	49,569	4,667,497	488,107	32.18	537,676	103.12	473,936	89.97	906,278	49.54
Rhode Island	59,934	31.60	-349	90,548	30,614	-3.65	30,265	-4.09	19,033	-25.85	29,644	-14.93
South Carolina	1,449,435	25.36	19,409	1,813,978	364,543	51.04	383,952	29.13	326,393	18.61	424,783	16.05
South Dakota	3,756,036	14.81	352,453	4,449,381	693,345	-13.83	1,045,798	28.73	952,289	22.80	1,051,532	22.99
Tennessee	2,569,231	18.49	-45,915	2,803,385	234,154	140.77	188,239	-34.60	177,368	-36.58	311,187	-22.80
Texas	14,768,041	6.72	-537,427	16,872,374	2,104,333	-7.19	1,566,906	-30.19	1,226,314	-38.58	1,973,461	-26.66
Utah	961,178	37.47	21,863	1,053,706	92,528	-48.99	114,391	-36.80	91,719	-43.96	181,242	-18.52
Vermont	487,821	13.01	-5,775	583,622	95,801	56.48	90,026	62.00	83,432	55.71	130,432	41.94
Virginia	2,485,331	18.50	41,971	2,793,698	308,367	-31.33	350,338	-22.10	297,091	-28.62	479,103	-17.54
Washington	5,567,525	31.65	216,474	6,654,360	1,086,835	18.38	1,303,309	81.25	960,197	53.74	1,733,628	50.45
West Virginia	519,598	25.17	-19,509	486,089	-33,509	-780.52	-53,018	2,655.61	-40,253	2,855.43	-14,184	-162.26
Wisconsin	6,835,459	14.18	-123,676	6,898,237	62,778	-82.26	-60,898	-122.36	-46,789	-118.22	490,535	-30.90
Wyoming	901,837	-0.31	53,233	830,474	-71,363	-169.65	-18,130	-109.69	-9,560	-105.80	60,987	-71.35

Realized Net Income as a Percent of Cash Receipts
1996

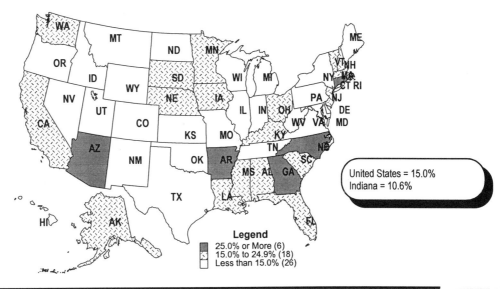

United States = 15.0%
Indiana = 10.6%

Legend
25.0% or More (6)
15.0% to 24.9% (18)
Less than 15.0% (26)

Source: U.S. Bureau of Economic Analysis
EDIN table(s): FMIN

Energy and Transportation

1.75 Electric Utility Industry: Sales *(Kilowatt hours in Millions)* and Revenues 1996 *($000)*

	Sales				Revenues			
	Total [1]	Residential	Commercial	Industrial	Total [1]	Residential	Commercial	Industrial
United States	3,090,846	1,071,232	883,230	1,041,068	211,849,407	89,765,126	67,478,564	48,007,679
Alabama	71,707	24,478	13,189	33,551	3,827,168	1,629,471	855,510	1,301,104
Alaska	4,720	1,737	2,240	582	472,218	192,834	208,023	48,459
Arizona	51,364	18,837	17,173	12,940	3,768,543	1,670,154	1,335,024	646,579
Arkansas	36,289	12,977	7,430	15,243	2,232,019	1,011,295	501,718	672,881
California	217,293	70,701	88,095	54,418	20,685,063	8,021,944	8,543,977	3,777,162
Colorado	35,425	11,503	13,956	9,161	2,139,889	853,362	820,746	397,878
Connecticut	28,569	11,027	11,117	6,045	2,943,884	1,295,828	1,126,482	468,200
Delaware	9,728	3,296	2,954	3,418	674,146	297,082	207,787	162,193
Dist. Of Col.	10,137	1,614	7,905	252	744,568	125,402	584,746	10,966
Florida	173,533	89,178	62,649	16,344	12,450,217	7,131,298	4,104,406	852,899
Georgia	101,265	37,888	29,208	32,921	6,601,334	2,985,105	2,101,711	1,409,682
Hawaii	9,379	2,670	2,768	3,884	1,137,030	381,005	359,091	389,506
Idaho	21,051	6,429	5,809	8,579	830,714	336,506	247,934	233,149
Illinois	*125,496*	*37,451*	*37,391*	*42,125*	*9,662,309*	*3,878,159*	*2,982,816*	*2,217,180*
Indiana	84,360	26,946	18,267	38,565	4,570,538	1,825,231	1,089,644	1,603,082
Percent U.S.	*2.73*	*2.52*	*2.07*	*3.70*	*2.16*	*2.03*	*1.61*	*3.34*
Rank	*13*	*14*	*16*	*8*	*14*	*15*	*19*	*9*
Iowa	34,805	11,487	7,414	14,589	2,075,691	946,350	481,813	568,055
Kansas	33,142	11,241	11,148	10,374	2,185,014	897,681	756,515	499,422
Kentucky	*80,999*	*21,378*	*10,778*	*45,768*	*3,030,250*	*1,175,320*	*555,950*	*1,155,441*
Louisiana	74,996	24,192	15,885	32,475	4,502,025	1,799,838	1,116,182	1,399,064
Maine	11,870	3,672	2,866	5,198	1,117,929	462,512	297,911	336,241
Maryland	56,810	22,893	16,042	17,100	3,959,134	1,893,633	1,104,057	894,157
Massachusetts	47,074	16,156	20,265	10,053	4,723,836	1,772,028	2,019,675	846,073
Michigan	*95,821*	*28,823*	*31,731*	*34,412*	*6,821,534*	*2,432,007*	*2,521,469*	*1,773,985*
Minnesota	55,135	17,312	9,985	27,119	3,059,611	1,237,322	614,731	1,155,525
Mississippi	38,892	14,498	7,843	15,837	2,344,773	1,025,390	552,029	705,196
Missouri	65,986	26,701	23,158	15,184	4,146,348	1,896,855	1,411,958	785,187
Montana	13,845	3,826	3,274	6,566	666,761	239,173	180,828	233,333
Nebraska	22,041	7,865	6,173	6,304	1,169,907	506,035	341,338	233,263
Nevada	22,697	7,471	5,134	9,300	1,332,187	517,419	337,796	440,096
New Hampshire	9,188	3,462	2,949	2,586	1,032,481	452,231	330,311	230,214
New Jersey	67,048	22,655	29,854	13,938	7,028,297	2,708,780	3,078,346	1,135,778
New Mexico	17,190	4,284	5,271	5,992	1,155,093	383,797	416,747	262,979
New York	131,208	40,167	52,209	26,498	14,520,528	5,614,305	6,348,403	1,483,244
North Carolina	108,126	41,279	30,626	34,259	7,069,062	3,331,652	1,953,026	1,633,377
North Dakota	8,086	3,525	2,055	2,063	461,847	218,687	128,236	94,194
Ohio	*162,671*	*45,797*	*37,013*	*75,263*	*10,275,380*	*3,954,960*	*2,856,055*	*3,174,432*
Oklahoma	42,688	16,941	11,292	12,184	2,379,061	1,141,167	662,085	461,395
Oregon	47,236	16,811	13,308	16,523	2,267,193	953,701	691,526	588,091
Pennsylvania	127,346	43,638	35,298	46,991	10,147,478	4,246,571	2,952,705	2,790,962
Rhode Island	6,608	2,472	2,588	1,371	692,083	290,997	263,455	118,274
South Carolina	66,899	22,456	14,311	29,265	3,843,570	1,722,084	924,945	1,143,312
South Dakota	7,612	3,314	2,148	1,826	476,201	237,345	142,685	81,282
Tennessee	81,923	29,662	5,209	45,893	4,259,930	1,762,686	347,788	2,064,306
Texas	275,184	97,973	70,608	94,449	16,836,744	7,565,446	4,718,205	3,773,358
Utah	19,576	5,383	6,019	7,336	1,036,777	373,863	358,857	266,378
Vermont	5,105	1,985	1,649	1,421	506,082	218,993	167,506	112,514
Virginia	87,249	34,167	24,680	19,052	5,328,693	2,618,959	1,457,128	762,825
Washington	89,050	30,749	20,538	34,354	3,696,603	1,520,341	990,214	1,061,738
West Virginia	26,073	9,229	5,923	10,826	1,358,843	588,130	337,939	422,744
Wisconsin	58,349	18,691	15,233	23,727	3,077,887	1,282,263	865,859	879,957
Wyoming	12,004	2,341	2,605	6,944	524,933	141,930	124,677	250,368

Residential Sales and Revenues as a Percent of Total Sales and Revenues
1996

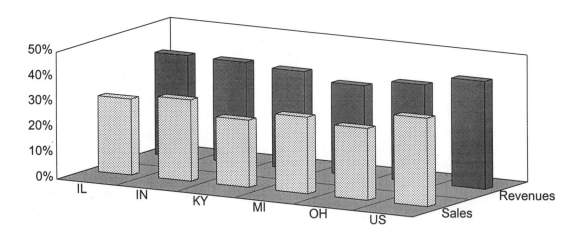

Footnote: [1] Total includes category not shown separately.
Source: Edison Electric Institute, The Statistical Yearbook of the Electric Utility Industry
EDIN table(s): ELSA, ELRE

1.76 Electric Utility Industry: Number of Customers and Revenue and Use Per Total Ultimate Customer 1996

| | Number of Customers | | | | Average Annual | | Average Revenue Per KWH. Sold (¢) | Percent Change 1995-96 |
	Total	Residential	Commercial	Industrial	Other	Revenue Per Customer ($)	KWH Use per Customer		
United States	119,998,835	105,339,532	13,203,067	578,254	877,982	1,765.43	25,757.00	6.85	-0.72
Alabama	2,079,626	1,791,479	270,659	13,284	4,204	1,840.32	34,480.00	5.34	-2.38
Alaska	246,740	204,664	35,634	1,417	5,025	1,913.83	19,128.00	10.01	-0.50
Arizona	1,790,413	1,584,317	175,657	5,039	25,400	2,104.85	28,689.00	7.34	-3.67
Arkansas	1,291,601	1,124,285	128,124	24,454	14,738	1,728.10	28,097.00	6.15	-1.91
California	12,712,192	11,060,258	1,581,199	31,933	38,802	1,627.18	17,093.00	9.52	-3.94
Colorado	1,839,707	1,537,879	210,222	1,805	89,801	1,163.17	19,256.00	6.04	-1.15
Connecticut	1,452,821	1,337,928	104,442	6,064	4,387	2,026.32	19,664.00	10.30	-2.00
Dist. Of Col.	350,492	314,079	35,014	583	816	1,923.43	27,754.00	6.93	0.29
Delaware	218,979	192,017	26,930	1	31	3,400.18	46,291.00	7.35	3.23
Florida	7,564,029	6,677,852	811,654	22,004	52,519	1,645.98	22,942.00	7.17	2.28
Georgia	3,474,016	3,087,650	342,065	14,273	30,028	1,900.20	29,149.00	6.52	-1.36
Hawaii	411,691	354,416	52,428	692	4,155	2,761.85	22,782.00	12.12	7.35
Idaho	548,131	462,364	80,738	2,136	2,893	1,515.54	38,404.00	3.95	-3.42
Illinois	*5,098,313*	*4,606,467*	*465,747*	*4,972*	*21,127*	*1,895.20*	*24,615.00*	*7.70*	*0.13*
Indiana	2,701,164	2,407,913	266,253	17,795	9,203	1,692.06	31,231.00	5.42	0.18
Percent U.S.	*2.25*	*2.29*	*2.02*	*3.08*	*1.05*	*95.84*	*121.25*	*79.12*	*—*
Rank	*14*	*14*	*17*	*8*	*33*	*28*	*13*	*39*	*21*
Iowa	1,383,714	1,196,236	167,880	3,903	15,695	1,500.09	25,154.00	5.96	-1.16
Kansas	1,278,834	1,085,175	169,135	15,177	9,347	1,708.60	25,916.00	6.59	0.46
Kentucky	*1,920,163*	*1,676,045*	*211,594*	*13,169*	*19,355*	*1,578.12*	*42,184.00*	*3.74*	*-8.33*
Louisiana	1,984,930	1,745,316	201,783	14,525	23,306	2,268.10	37,783.00	6.00	4.17
Maine	698,539	604,964	71,883	3,430	18,262	1,600.38	16,993.00	9.42	-0.63
Maryland	2,095,347	1,882,887	200,054	11,124	1,282	1,889.49	27,112.00	6.97	-1.27
Massachusetts	2,728,192	2,414,603	287,770	14,080	11,739	1,731.49	17,255.00	10.03	-0.89
Michigan	*4,342,613*	*3,892,621*	*418,820*	*13,382*	*17,790*	*1,570.84*	*22,065.00*	*7.12*	*0.71*
Minnesota	2,164,129	1,927,642	201,224	10,381	24,882	1,413.78	25,477.00	5.55	-0.54
Mississippi	1,274,872	1,092,333	163,544	8,722	10,273	1,839.22	30,507.00	6.03	0.84
Missouri	2,692,417	2,369,678	298,433	10,811	13,495	1,540.01	24,508.00	6.28	0.32
Montana	456,210	380,813	64,936	4,126	6,335	1,461.52	30,349.00	4.82	3.66
Nebraska	875,537	709,546	116,716	6,661	42,614	1,336.22	25,175.00	5.31	-1.67
Nevada	741,303	646,716	92,078	1,167	1,342	1,797.09	30,618.00	5.87	-3.77
New Hampshire	594,042	503,535	76,405	2,561	11,541	1,738.06	15,467.00	11.24	-4.10
New Jersey	3,422,423	3,021,193	377,597	13,554	10,079	2,053.60	19,591.00	10.48	0.38
New Mexico	774,804	661,751	96,862	6,057	10,134	1,490.82	22,186.00	6.72	-1.18
New York	7,360,269	6,485,210	832,543	10,650	31,866	1,972.83	17,826.00	11.07	0.09
North Carolina	3,711,980	3,218,694	453,460	13,200	26,626	1,904.39	29,129.00	6.54	-0.61
North Dakota	335,195	283,609	44,294	2,508	4,784	1,377.85	24,124.00	5.71	0.00
Ohio	*5,184,123*	*4,620,237*	*513,464*	*31,556*	*18,866*	*1,982.09*	*31,379.00*	*6.32*	*1.12*
Oklahoma	1,667,639	1,441,610	192,686	16,212	17,131	1,426.60	25,598.00	5.57	0.00
Oregon	1,507,907	1,308,433	185,101	5,462	8,911	1,503.54	31,326.00	4.80	2.78
Pennsylvania	5,438,258	4,833,642	566,703	29,112	8,801	1,865.94	23,417.00	7.97	0.50
Rhode Island	450,847	403,407	43,891	2,639	910	1,535.07	14,656.00	10.47	0.87
South Carolina	1,879,383	1,627,280	233,542	4,683	13,878	2,045.12	35,596.00	5.75	1.05
South Dakota	366,299	309,041	46,003	2,013	9,242	1,300.03	20,781.00	6.26	0.97
Tennessee	2,403,912	2,058,651	295,855	37,763	11,643	1,772.08	34,079.00	5.20	-0.19
Texas	8,404,289	7,296,264	946,305	72,482	89,238	2,003.35	32,743.00	6.12	0.16
Utah	732,653	646,575	69,247	11,867	4,964	1,415.10	26,719.00	5.30	-0.19
Vermont	314,334	271,672	38,088	1,139	3,435	1,610.01	16,242.00	9.91	3.88
Virginia	2,884,102	2,557,651	281,759	5,284	39,408	1,847.61	30,252.00	6.11	-2.40
Washington	2,501,062	2,217,593	248,961	12,308	22,200	1,478.01	35,605.00	4.15	1.97
West Virginia	912,004	791,687	106,906	11,205	2,206	1,489.95	28,589.00	5.21	-2.43
Wisconsin	2,443,865	2,172,308	256,149	5,657	9,751	1,259.43	23,876.00	5.27	-1.68
Wyoming	292,730	241,346	44,630	3,232	3,522	1,793.23	41,008.00	4.37	1.16

Average Revenue Per Kilowatt Hour Sold
1996

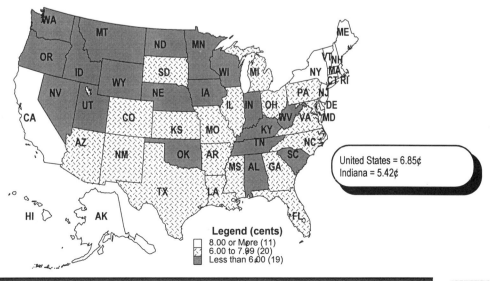

United States = 6.85¢
Indiana = 5.42¢

Legend (cents)
☐ 8.00 or More (11)
▨ 6.00 to 7.99 (20)
▩ Less than 6.00 (19)

Source: Edison Electric Institute, The Statistical Yearbook of the Electric Utility Industry
EDIN table(s): ELUC, ELRU

1.77 Motor Vehicle Registrations 1995

	Motor Vehicle		Automobiles		Buses		Trucks		Motorcycles	
	Private and Commercial	Publicly Owned	Private and Commercial	Publicly Owned	Private and Commercial	Publicly Owned	Private and Commercial	Publicly Owned	Private and Commercial	Publicly Owned
United States	197,941,202	3,588,819	134,803,214	1,262,831	287,873	397,631	62,850,115	1,928,357	3,727,738	39,291
Alabama	3,506,241	46,594	1,827,309	14,785	2,141	6,310	1,676,791	25,499	37,445	481
Alaska	531,948	10,238	302,517	2,026	1,845	163	227,586	8,049	12,909	8
Arizona	2,836,517	36,808	1,864,959	16,113	1,298	3,131	970,260	17,564	68,379	791
Arkansas	1,588,484	24,715	797,844	9,389	1,236	4,425	789,404	10,901	17,195	22
California	22,003,184	428,565	14,677,140	172,667	27,142	15,757	7,298,902	240,141	518,927	13,126
Colorado	2,773,372	38,418	1,695,078	9,726	1,544	4,065	1,076,750	24,627	88,058	62
Connecticut	2,585,404	36,852	2,068,111	11,176	7,949	800	509,344	24,876	48,690	275
Delaware	582,068	9,840	397,933	6,838	1,552	582	182,583	2,420	9,141	27
Dist. Of Col.	231,829	10,866	201,811	4,300	2,337	380	27,681	6,186	1,193	430
Florida	10,108,556	260,839	7,503,240	91,638	4,938	35,326	2,600,378	133,875	184,526	5,586
Georgia	6,030,523	89,674	4,203,418	22,162	3,529	12,022	1,823,576	55,490	71,392	926
Hawaii	788,644	13,482	527,269	5,858	3,446	937	257,929	6,687	12,901	308
Idaho	1,015,488	27,586	581,050	5,516	1,264	2,097	433,174	19,973	33,362	127
Illinois	*8,895,577*	*77,432*	*6,553,045*	*58,623*	*15,132*	*1,296*	*2,327,400*	*17,513*	*184,101*	*115*
Indiana	**4,998,778**	**73,184**	**3,349,440**	**20,857**	**9,101**	**15,189**	**1,640,237**	**37,138**	**95,936**	**458**
Percent U.S.	*2.53*	*2.04*	*2.48*	*1.65*	*3.16*	*3.82*	*2.61*	*1.93*	*2.57*	*1.17*
Rank	*14*	*14*	*15*	*17*	*12*	*7*	*12*	*15*	*12*	*17*
Iowa	2,768,041	45,977	1,817,008	11,728	1,413	7,989	949,620	26,260	111,342	161
Kansas	2,057,510	26,998	1,078,381	7,268	1,534	2,245	977,595	17,485	42,825	295
Kentucky	*2,593,760*	*37,636*	*1,608,650*	*21,130*	*1,876*	*9,751*	*983,234*	*6,755*	*32,992*	*4*
Louisiana	3,228,587	56,994	1,927,080	31,234	15,119	5,226	1,286,388	20,534	36,318	458
Maine	948,251	18,594	618,357	5,714	646	2,130	329,248	10,750	25,886	86
Maryland	3,614,865	39,334	2,692,109	12,971	6,559	4,666	916,197	21,697	38,698	135
Massachusetts	4,452,695	49,274	3,491,479	15,546	10,447	479	950,769	33,249	74,237	6
Michigan	*7,541,832*	*132,258*	*5,269,744*	*45,071*	*9,658*	*14,591*	*2,262,430*	*72,596*	*126,590*	*1,312*
Minnesota	3,835,771	46,058	2,540,595	11,409	6,669	8,983	1,288,507	25,666	117,592	299
Mississippi	2,109,720	33,833	1,397,995	10,227	3,368	6,316	708,357	17,280	29,636	NA
Missouri	4,223,510	31,513	2,739,026	7,581	4,597	7,659	1,479,887	16,273	54,900	39
Montana	943,263	25,205	531,726	6,724	1,144	1,850	410,393	16,631	20,824	106
Nebraska	1,436,197	30,438	838,592	10,165	1,141	4,654	596,464	15,619	18,732	219
Nevada	1,023,471	23,755	583,499	9,655	1,482	262	438,490	13,838	21,215	457
New Hampshire	1,108,103	13,925	727,841	3,622	1,467	296	378,795	10,007	49,445	NA
New Jersey	5,757,742	148,574	4,637,039	52,065	16,557	3,057	1,104,146	93,452	87,918	716
New Mexico	1,449,742	33,985	819,250	12,825	2,480	955	628,012	20,205	30,946	234
New York	10,078,418	195,618	7,846,764	70,568	20,524	25,252	2,211,130	99,798	168,248	1,431
North Carolina	5,567,054	115,201	3,652,169	32,992	9,105	26,218	1,905,780	55,991	66,748	459
North Dakota	680,309	14,366	367,761	3,897	613	1,563	311,935	8,906	16,864	30
Ohio	*9,685,675*	*124,595*	*7,155,205*	*37,998*	*11,695*	*21,120*	*2,518,775*	*65,477*	*217,917*	*585*
Oklahoma	2,790,946	65,133	1,618,877	10,614	2,032	12,754	1,170,037	41,765	55,146	334
Oregon	2,727,140	57,832	1,606,254	22,820	3,610	7,932	1,117,276	27,080	60,489	747
Pennsylvania	8,373,355	107,171	5,971,808	41,841	26,770	7,104	2,374,777	58,226	170,322	1,013
Rhode Island	690,502	8,708	542,032	3,181	1,679	12	146,791	5,515	16,893	86
South Carolina	2,790,279	43,052	1,855,653	9,612	4,556	10,432	930,070	23,008	34,355	215
South Dakota	690,186	18,427	375,187	4,401	713	1,850	314,286	12,176	25,155	29
Tennessee	5,310,413	89,880	3,913,546	21,851	3,410	13,696	1,393,457	54,333	69,840	218
Texas	13,217,925	463,810	8,427,262	177,696	15,718	56,058	4,774,945	230,056	125,890	4,227
Utah	1,422,680	24,186	790,387	9,492	422	784	631,871	13,910	22,000	171
Vermont	481,568	10,691	314,123	3,111	633	1,256	166,812	6,324	18,113	NA
Virginia	5,530,144	82,989	3,941,693	33,898	2,447	14,788	1,586,004	34,303	57,832	367
Washington	4,443,371	59,407	2,942,316	17,487	2,956	4,726	1,498,099	37,194	95,047	748
West Virginia	1,372,017	53,192	839,379	17,202	951	2,541	531,687	33,449	17,831	663
Wisconsin	3,935,087	58,241	2,410,607	13,158	8,518	4,398	1,515,962	40,685	168,287	650
Wyoming	584,460	16,876	363,656	4,393	910	1,558	219,894	10,925	16,510	49

Private and Public Autos Per 1,000 Persons 1995

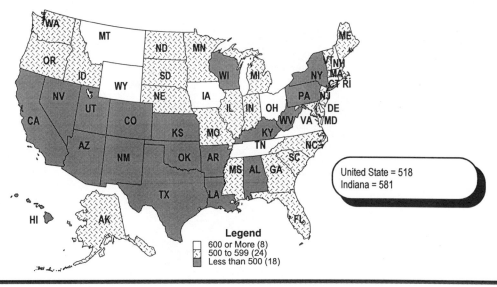

United State = 518
Indiana = 581

Legend
☐ 600 or More (8)
▨ 500 to 599 (24)
▦ Less than 500 (18)

Source: U.S. Department of Transportation
EDIN table(s): REGT

1.78 Existing Road and Street Mileage 1995

	Total Mileage	Rural — Total	Rural — Under State Control	Rural — Under Local Control	Rural — Under Federal Control	Urban — Total	Urban — Under State Control	Urban — Under Local Control	Urban — Under Federal Control
United States	3,912,226	3,092,520	690,952	2,231,110	170,458	819,706	111,781	706,416	1,509
Alabama	93,313	73,227	9,083	63,207	937	20,086	1,890	18,188	8
Alaska	13,486	11,705	5,421	4,405	1,879	1,781	485	1,295	1
Arizona	54,561	38,239	5,484	18,733	14,022	16,322	655	15,622	45
Arkansas	77,222	69,565	15,027	52,912	1,626	7,657	1,227	6,430	NA
California	170,389	87,869	14,371	55,828	17,670	82,520	3,880	78,633	7
Colorado	84,499	71,014	8,221	54,467	8,326	13,485	1,029	12,456	NA
Connecticut	20,500	8,873	2,140	6,729	4	11,627	1,837	9,790	NA
Delaware	5,631	3,711	3,463	241	7	1,920	1,500	420	NA
Dist. Of Col.	1,421	NA	NA	NA	NA	1,421	1,354	NA	67
Florida	113,778	65,440	6,976	57,155	1,309	48,338	4,945	43,393	NA
Georgia	111,273	84,871	14,930	68,876	1,065	26,402	2,983	23,382	37
Hawaii	4,133	2,293	845	1,376	72	1,840	357	1,443	40
Idaho	59,733	56,187	4,850	27,541	23,796	3,546	272	3,262	12
Illinois	*137,413*	*101,846*	*12,417*	*89,188*	*241*	*35,567*	*4,773*	*30,769*	*25*
Indiana	92,780	73,313	9,569	63,744	NA	19,467	1,742	17,725	NA
Percent U.S.	*2.37*	*2.37*	*1.38*	*2.86*	*—*	*2.37*	*1.56*	*2.51*	*—*
Rank	*18*	*19*	*26*	*15*	*—*	*14*	*20*	*13*	*—*
Iowa	112,702	103,365	9,146	94,103	116	9,337	999	8,333	5
Kansas	133,323	123,632	10,009	113,623	NA	9,691	672	9,019	NA
Kentucky	*72,998*	*62,700*	*25,053*	*37,410*	*237*	*10,298*	*2,430*	*7,704*	*164*
Louisiana	60,119	46,200	14,661	30,924	615	13,919	1,997	11,922	NA
Maine	22,577	19,957	7,734	12,055	168	2,620	812	1,804	4
Maryland	29,680	15,781	3,746	11,996	39	13,899	1,664	11,840	395
Massachusetts	30,751	10,904	1,644	9,171	89	19,847	1,989	17,836	22
Michigan	*117,611*	*89,528*	*7,642*	*81,864*	*22*	*28,083*	*2,000*	*26,083*	*NA*
Minnesota	130,391	115,225	12,124	101,475	1,626	15,166	1,180	13,986	NA
Mississippi	73,102	65,183	9,760	54,611	812	7,919	852	7,045	22
Missouri	122,616	106,306	30,652	74,690	964	16,310	1,718	14,592	NA
Montana	69,537	67,138	7,985	44,891	14,262	2,399	169	2,230	NA
Nebraska	92,755	87,650	9,934	77,565	151	5,105	339	4,766	NA
Nevada	44,936	40,483	4,744	23,176	12,563	4,453	530	3,919	4
New Hampshire	15,086	12,173	3,614	8,423	136	2,913	406	2,507	NA
New Jersey	35,646	11,241	1,479	9,740	22	24,405	1,805	22,582	18
New Mexico	61,289	55,187	10,879	34,912	9,396	6,102	610	5,492	NA
New York	112,193	71,873	11,619	60,227	27	40,320	4,695	35,586	39
North Carolina	96,809	74,660	69,068	3,932	1,660	22,149	9,267	12,633	249
North Dakota	86,830	85,010	7,195	76,989	826	1,820	205	1,615	NA
Ohio	*114,563*	*81,424*	*16,420*	*64,975*	*29*	*33,139*	*4,083*	*29,053*	*3*
Oklahoma	112,517	99,561	12,111	87,431	19	12,956	1,004	11,950	2
Oregon	83,944	73,789	10,296	33,389	30,104	10,155	819	9,302	34
Pennsylvania	118,648	85,376	36,136	48,273	967	33,272	8,093	25,179	NA
Rhode Island	5,893	1,321	324	988	9	4,572	810	3,762	NA
South Carolina	64,293	53,750	34,782	18,366	602	10,543	6,910	3,633	NA
South Dakota	83,360	81,422	7,683	71,777	1,962	1,938	189	1,748	1
Tennessee	85,599	68,403	11,642	56,394	367	17,196	2,395	14,801	NA
Texas	296,186	213,985	68,028	145,032	925	82,201	10,451	71,722	28
Utah	41,044	34,817	5,030	22,808	6,979	6,227	762	5,450	15
Vermont	14,184	12,850	2,662	10,117	71	1,334	176	1,149	9
Virginia	69,142	50,767	48,548	565	1,654	18,375	8,439	9,684	252
Washington	79,710	62,098	17,762	37,548	6,788	17,612	1,168	16,444	NA
West Virginia	35,110	31,952	30,661	658	633	3,158	1,353	1,805	NA
Wisconsin	111,489	95,507	10,966	83,550	991	15,982	1,467	14,515	NA
Wyoming	35,461	33,149	6,416	23,060	3,673	2,312	394	1,917	1

Percent of Total Road Mileage Under Local Control 1995

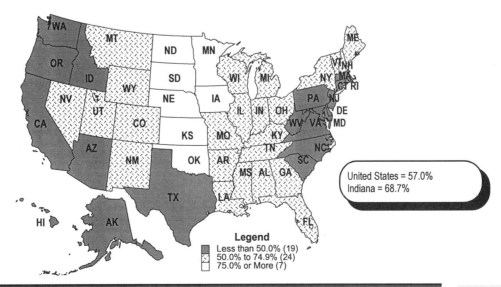

United States = 57.0%
Indiana = 68.7%

Legend
Less than 50.0% (19)
50.0% to 74.9% (24)
75.0% or More (7)

Source: U.S. Department of Transportation
EDIN table(s): TRRM

1.79 Highway Revenues 1995 *($000)*

	Total Receipts	State Highway User Tax Revenues	Road and Crossing Tolls	Other State Imposts, General Fund	Misc. Income	Federal Funds	Transfers From Local Govt.	Bond Proceeds
United States	68,175,518	35,825,806	3,489,143	3,423,701	1,910,482	18,050,359	1,159,196	4,316,831
Alabama	1,030,837	659,670	NA	18,523	3,625	337,699	690	10,630
Alaska	438,198	42,836	16,030	123,838	23,826	231,668	NA	NA
Arizona	1,191,475	649,348	NA	123,718	41,262	212,855	164,292	NA
Arkansas	713,855	422,421	NA	20,551	29,576	241,307	NA	NA
California	5,805,441	3,548,650	134,756	NA	125,486	1,599,031	397,518	NA
Colorado	932,046	573,061	NA	106,175	2,126	246,304	4,380	NA
Connecticut	1,222,053	445,994	239	14,244	74,105	361,142	3,017	323,312
Delaware	429,296	141,992	100,817	25,567	16,826	74,030	NA	70,064
Dist. Of Col.	139,758	44,596	NA	NA	NA	56,429	NA	38,733
Florida	3,210,104	1,500,310	347,243	99,909	110,587	832,098	103,532	216,425
Georgia	1,372,068	380,590	14,459	137,613	38,426	554,728	15,995	230,257
Hawaii	424,847	123,669	NA	1,672	12,321	181,689	NA	105,496
Idaho	357,133	230,695	NA	NA	NA	121,193	5,245	NA
Illinois	*3,114,184*	*1,629,456*	*297,554*	*75,343*	*59,610*	*825,338*	*23,972*	*202,911*
Indiana	**1,363,069**	**824,294**	**69,294**	**6,279**	**39,540**	**384,582**	**28,917**	**10,163**
Percent U.S.	*2.00*	*2.30*	*1.99*	*0.18*	*2.07*	*2.13*	*2.49*	*0.24*
Rank	*17*	*15*	*14*	*34*	*19*	*16*	*8*	*21*
Iowa	1,073,287	627,258	NA	131,027	14,735	296,892	3,375	NA
Kansas	907,779	388,891	52,313	183,325	57,329	199,870	26,051	NA
Kentucky	*1,454,469*	*843,455*	*10,799*	*103,439*	*59,768*	*247,827*	*118*	*189,063*
Louisiana	1,236,606	626,784	34,180	280,811	31,864	227,057	NA	35,910
Maine	379,619	183,545	40,741	1,440	7,529	136,364	NA	10,000
Maryland	1,376,063	676,571	128,167	97,271	48,184	339,730	12,176	73,964
Massachusetts	2,478,230	756,701	163,747	183,903	62,810	943,789	63	367,217
Michigan	*1,820,995*	*1,086,291*	*19,304*	*122,301*	*102,019*	*462,492*	*28,588*	*NA*
Minnesota	1,284,864	934,916	NA	4,284	55,971	262,133	21,830	5,730
Mississippi	711,099	424,123	NA	45,079	37,995	201,024	2,878	NA
Missouri	1,308,605	732,941	NA	157,816	15,441	393,447	8,960	NA
Montana	345,642	183,072	NA	5,101	9,893	146,874	702	NA
Nebraska	567,461	282,928	NA	115,556	4,415	151,287	13,275	NA
Nevada	438,032	286,865	NA	1,372	14,756	131,596	3,443	NA
New Hampshire	325,148	169,571	48,110	NA	26,097	74,708	5,568	1,094
New Jersey	1,776,002	558,584	545,944	NA	160,679	509,867	928	NA
New Mexico	512,915	333,811	NA	7,309	13,667	157,358	770	NA
New York	5,066,150	1,774,826	654,003	303,959	138,679	625,239	NA	1,569,444
North Carolina	1,962,649	1,190,646	1,519	184,149	58,357	513,087	14,891	NA
North Dakota	266,826	122,840	NA	4,266	3,897	123,663	12,160	NA
Ohio	*2,707,031*	*1,757,589*	*105,084*	*36,709*	*36,224*	*753,798*	*17,627*	*NA*
Oklahoma	811,647	426,227	105,345	26,596	17,076	219,418	16,985	NA
Oregon	898,252	582,954	NA	26,383	26,545	241,283	21,087	NA
Pennsylvania	3,446,430	1,926,588	334,757	NA	86,757	730,954	15,657	351,717
Rhode Island	292,454	75,632	9,693	NA	554	176,420	NA	30,155
South Carolina	682,535	401,292	NA	NA	5,555	253,198	2,467	20,023
South Dakota	293,532	115,158	NA	36,949	2,782	133,261	5,382	NA
Tennessee	1,244,488	824,790	80	71,296	7,241	328,622	12,459	NA
Texas	3,765,214	2,568,743	47,661	20,724	50,165	1,009,189	42,115	26,617
Utah	486,161	247,958	330	71,113	1,310	162,999	2,451	NA
Vermont	200,559	115,197	NA	122	6,470	77,733	1,037	NA
Virginia	2,178,313	1,049,223	83,973	419,483	60,113	391,995	31,059	142,467
Washington	1,806,004	1,029,594	76,972	NA	29,356	447,243	42,786	180,053
West Virginia	786,341	448,091	46,029	12,951	19,609	259,561	100	NA
Wisconsin	1,256,047	774,100	NA	566	49,605	283,022	43,368	105,386
Wyoming	283,705	80,469	NA	14,969	9,719	177,266	1,282	NA

Federal Funds as a Percent of Total Receipts
1995

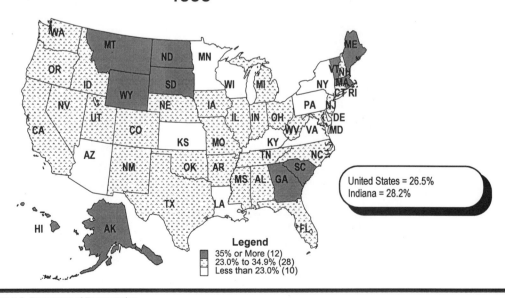

United States = 26.5%
Indiana = 28.2%

Legend
35% or More (12)
23.0% to 34.9% (28)
Less than 23.0% (10)

Source: U.S. Department of Transportation
EDIN table(s): TRRD

1.80 Disbursements for Highways 1995 *($000)*

	Total Disbursements	Capital Outlay	Percent Total	Maintenance and Traffic Services	Admin. and Highway Police	Bond Interest	Grants-in-Aid to Local Governments	Bond Retirement
United States	67,260,818	32,500,624	48.3	10,405,045	9,223,383	2,254,985	10,279,304	2,597,477
Alabama	1,001,737	436,663	43.6	221,082	126,088	3,480	197,899	16,525
Alaska	438,198	254,068	58.0	123,161	49,669	773	5,832	4,695
Arizona	1,199,273	454,795	37.9	76,205	105,776	88,230	380,007	94,260
Arkansas	665,735	370,697	55.7	116,415	58,476	NA	120,147	NA
California	5,966,475	2,348,070	39.4	564,006	1,297,384	2,716	1,748,554	5,745
Colorado	922,112	378,603	41.1	171,212	112,615	NA	259,682	NA
Connecticut	1,153,096	596,585	51.7	67,855	103,733	164,922	20,911	199,090
Delaware	441,222	240,412	54.5	60,087	67,664	41,976	3,000	28,083
Dist. Of Col.	139,758	78,060	55.9	19,508	17,991	11,356	NA	12,843
Florida	3,401,753	2,103,664	61.8	425,667	325,136	169,933	317,358	59,995
Georgia	1,436,829	881,477	61.3	259,122	173,432	61,143	2,602	59,053
Hawaii	307,206	214,054	69.7	17,591	32,199	11,098	8,488	23,776
Idaho	349,964	165,509	47.3	57,632	39,049	NA	87,774	NA
Illinois	*2,984,784*	*1,575,878*	*52.8*	*347,388*	*356,869*	*144,383*	*451,479*	*108,787*
Indiana	**1,367,729**	**650,052**	**47.5**	**208,483**	**118,357**	**47,015**	**327,342**	**16,480**
Percent U.S.	*2.03*	*2.00*	*—*	*2.00*	*1.28*	*2.08*	*3.18*	*0.63*
Rank	*15*	*17*	*29*	*15*	*25*	*14*	*9*	*25*
Iowa	1,077,704	459,382	42.6	116,465	125,109	NA	376,748	NA
Kansas	1,019,160	635,892	62.4	106,755	88,059	57,147	127,247	4,060
Kentucky	*1,342,126*	*666,794*	*49.7*	*204,855*	*110,529*	*91,649*	*118,215*	*150,084*
Louisiana	1,194,645	552,283	46.2	135,863	173,623	71,277	43,838	217,761
Maine	379,282	161,258	42.5	116,521	51,257	13,331	19,380	17,535
Maryland	1,289,354	544,898	42.3	153,552	261,589	26,469	291,548	11,298
Massachusetts	2,500,788	1,480,228	59.2	123,484	325,782	165,466	120,388	285,440
Michigan	*1,973,894*	*739,443*	*37.5*	*201,078*	*265,825*	*35,896*	*723,097*	*8,555*
Minnesota	1,210,014	510,421	42.2	150,436	136,530	3,553	409,074	NA
Mississippi	661,610	402,619	60.9	65,727	84,958	7,426	76,693	24,187
Missouri	1,313,107	665,559	50.7	251,071	196,910	NA	199,567	NA
Montana	388,416	183,346	47.2	66,800	51,204	8,680	28,671	49,715
Nebraska	578,157	285,384	49.4	58,682	47,012	NA	187,079	NA
Nevada	484,112	292,805	60.5	57,283	52,533	5,529	45,542	30,420
New Hampshire	328,027	138,938	42.4	80,184	54,383	21,322	19,963	13,237
New Jersey	2,101,667	811,965	38.6	335,496	380,930	295,155	84,904	193,217
New Mexico	534,803	336,610	62.9	71,731	91,226	1,880	28,976	4,380
New York	4,514,566	2,132,192	47.2	848,487	582,900	298,449	231,417	421,121
North Carolina	1,871,498	1,010,399	54.0	447,896	285,804	1,791	99,768	25,840
North Dakota	270,095	154,641	57.3	37,647	29,924	NA	47,883	NA
Ohio	*2,636,791*	*1,029,082*	*39.0*	*419,478*	*297,557*	*30,306*	*769,968*	*90,400*
Oklahoma	828,008	375,426	45.3	113,093	114,220	40,459	173,855	10,955
Oregon	887,786	315,752	35.6	124,043	126,229	2,550	308,217	10,995
Pennsylvania	3,153,335	1,443,354	45.8	789,490	388,842	140,214	172,518	218,917
Rhode Island	290,143	200,683	69.2	43,309	18,063	14,772	NA	13,316
South Carolina	668,381	380,460	56.9	131,337	122,584	20	33,980	NA
South Dakota	285,683	187,358	65.6	39,955	31,375	NA	26,995	NA
Tennessee	1,229,518	609,410	49.6	219,049	149,703	1,310	245,856	4,190
Texas	3,592,957	1,803,125	50.2	768,466	671,529	25,488	317,519	6,830
Utah	431,264	232,600	53.9	72,000	58,651	NA	68,013	NA
Vermont	194,205	83,084	42.8	38,565	43,517	1,762	24,623	2,654
Virginia	2,107,426	908,891	43.1	688,408	263,151	46,746	177,359	22,871
Washington	1,841,555	768,337	41.7	198,404	318,726	47,737	444,811	63,540
West Virginia	780,879	457,244	58.6	190,589	75,477	18,324	NA	39,245
Wisconsin	1,251,993	631,874	50.5	135,591	131,095	33,252	292,799	27,382
Wyoming	271,998	160,300	58.9	67,841	32,139	NA	11,718	NA

Capital Outlay as a Percent of Total Disbursements
1995

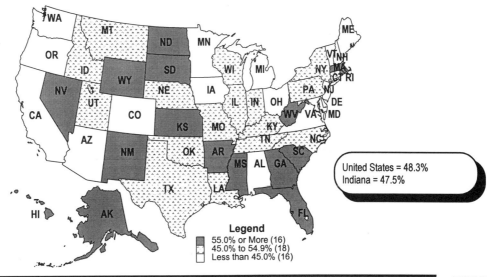

United States = 48.3%
Indiana = 47.5%

Legend
- 55.0% or More (16)
- 45.0% to 54.9% (18)
- Less than 45.0% (16)

Source: U.S. Department of Transportation
EDIN table(s): TRRD

Business
1.81 Total Industries: Establishments, Employees, and Payroll 1995 *($Mil)*

	Number of Establishments	Number of Employees	Annual Payroll	Average Employee Per Establishment	Payroll Per Employee ($)	Percent Change 1993-95 Establishments	Employees	Annual Payroll[1]
United States	6,613,218	100,334,745	2,666,412	15	26,575	3.3	5.9	7.3
Alabama	96,053	1,553,309	34,477	16	22,196	4.3	7.3	6.8
Alaska	17,264	181,975	5,960	11	32,752	4.9	5.5	3.4
Arizona	99,583	1,507,132	36,517	15	24,229	6.9	13.7	16.9
Arkansas	60,231	891,175	18,223	15	20,448	4.9	9.0	10.5
California	740,583	10,959,318	321,816	15	29,365	0.5	2.2	3.7
Colorado	118,192	1,558,141	40,433	13	25,950	8.7	9.6	12.1
Connecticut	91,189	1,415,400	47,127	16	33,296	0.8	0.6	4.2
Delaware	20,991	324,498	9,363	15	28,854	5.5	6.4	4.1
Dist. Of Col.	19,451	413,757	14,643	21	35,390	0.7	-0.5	2.6
Florida	398,232	5,208,285	119,273	13	22,901	3.5	8.4	9.0
Georgia	179,006	2,920,361	73,622	16	25,210	6.5	10.2	11.1
Hawaii	29,942	423,822	10,696	14	25,237	-0.7	-2.8	-3.5
Idaho	32,972	379,161	8,440	11	22,260	8.6	10.1	12.7
Illinois	*293,694*	*4,950,462*	*143,854*	*17*	*29,059*	*3.3*	*5.4*	*7.6*
Indiana	**141,253**	**2,403,189**	**59,554**	**17**	**24,781**	**4.0**	**6.4**	**7.5**
Percent U.S.	*2.14*	*2.40*	*2.23*	—	*93.25*	—	—	—
Rank	*15*	*14*	*14*	*3*	*24*	*23*	*26*	*30*
Iowa	78,464	1,138,402	25,120	15	22,066	2.0	6.2	9.1
Kansas	70,894	982,066	22,826	14	23,243	2.8	5.8	8.1
Kentucky	*85,123*	*1,347,087*	*30,097*	*16*	*22,342*	*2.9*	*6.9*	*7.5*
Louisiana	96,063	1,452,355	33,644	15	23,165	2.8	5.5	7.7
Maine	36,298	432,290	9,800	12	22,670	3.1	4.9	4.9
Maryland	122,350	1,820,731	49,135	15	26,986	2.9	5.4	6.3
Massachusetts	160,350	2,735,963	83,414	17	30,488	2.6	3.9	6.5
Michigan	*226,973*	*3,704,315*	*107,301*	*16*	*28,966*	*3.7*	*7.3*	*10.4*
Minnesota	125,927	2,072,503	54,783	16	26,433	4.5	6.6	9.0
Mississippi	57,095	871,814	17,382	15	19,938	2.9	9.4	8.8
Missouri	139,980	2,169,026	53,346	15	24,594	2.8	6.3	8.6
Montana	29,109	260,973	5,053	9	19,362	6.0	6.2	6.4
Nebraska	47,128	674,779	14,513	14	21,508	2.3	6.4	9.8
Nevada	37,219	672,260	16,527	18	24,584	10.5	15.7	17.0
New Hampshire	34,647	464,122	11,778	13	25,377	4.2	8.7	8.5
New Jersey	220,991	3,184,458	102,819	14	32,288	3.0	2.7	4.5
New Mexico	40,631	506,634	11,050	12	21,811	4.5	8.0	8.7
New York	467,262	6,782,174	225,157	15	33,198	1.5	2.2	5.0
North Carolina	181,972	2,992,175	70,232	16	23,472	5.7	8.4	10.2
North Dakota	20,269	230,090	4,466	11	19,410	2.6	6.5	7.4
Ohio	*263,739*	*4,550,590*	*117,902*	*17*	*25,909*	*2.8*	*6.7*	*7.8*
Oklahoma	81,395	1,055,227	23,037	13	21,831	2.7	5.2	2.9
Oregon	93,468	1,185,415	29,798	13	25,137	6.2	10.4	14.1
Pennsylvania	283,998	4,702,892	123,512	17	26,263	1.2	3.1	5.0
Rhode Island	27,766	379,595	9,480	14	24,974	1.5	2.0	3.8
South Carolina	87,990	1,395,070	31,292	16	22,430	4.6	6.7	7.9
South Dakota	22,708	268,483	5,134	12	19,122	3.8	8.3	12.7
Tennessee	124,814	2,153,264	51,089	17	23,726	4.7	9.3	10.7
Texas	438,262	6,786,893	174,888	15	25,768	4.2	8.0	9.4
Utah	45,882	744,430	17,040	16	22,890	10.3	12.7	14.6
Vermont	20,542	224,327	5,041	11	22,472	1.9	4.0	5.6
Virginia	162,378	2,481,306	63,266	15	25,497	4.3	6.5	7.7
Washington	151,925	1,948,923	53,451	13	27,426	4.3	4.8	8.0
West Virginia	40,599	530,596	11,928	13	22,480	3.1	6.1	5.5
Wisconsin	133,238	2,186,060	53,654	16	24,544	2.9	6.2	7.9
Wyoming	17,133	157,472	3,459	9	21,966	5.3	8.4	6.9

Percent Change in Annual Payroll for All Industries
1993 to 1995

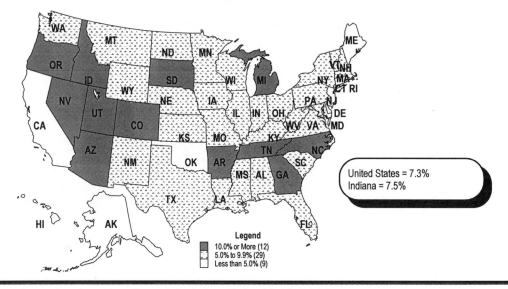

United States = 7.3%
Indiana = 7.5%

Legend
10.0% or More (12)
5.0% to 9.9% (29)
Less than 5.0% (9)

[1]Footnote: Percent change in annual payroll was calculated using real (adjusted for inflation) dollars.
Source: U.S. Bureau of the Census, County Business Patterns
EDIN table(s): EMIE, EMIP

1.82 Agriculture Services, Forestry, and Fisheries: Establishments, Employees, and Payroll 1995 ($Mil)

	Number of Establishments	Number of Employees	Annual Payroll	Average Employee Per Establishment	Payroll Per Employee ($)	Percent Change 1993-95 Establishments	Percent Change 1993-95 Employees	Percent Change 1993-95 Annual Payroll[1]
United States	108,353	630,157	12,099	6	19,200	8.0	7.1	12.3
Alabama	1,528	10,023	179	7	17,859	16.9	28.3	33.1
Alaska	396	1,803	55	5	30,505	9.7	NA	NA
Arizona	1,970	15,122	244	8	16,135	5.3	13.8	19.7
Arkansas	992	6,796	110	7	16,186	10.3	14.4	17.6
California	12,130	100,249	1,912	8	19,073	3.1	5.3	9.9
Colorado	1,998	10,449	206	5	19,715	10.4	19.5	19.5
Connecticut	2,028	7,356	184	4	25,014	8.2	-12.6	9.4
Delaware	347	1,721	32	5	18,594	5.2	4.5	1.5
Dist. Of Col.	40	189	6	5	31,746	-2.4	NA	NA
Florida	8,363	53,767	851	6	15,828	6.2	5.4	6.8
Georgia	2,952	19,524	347	7	17,773	15.5	25.0	26.5
Hawaii	359	2,717	59	8	21,715	2.0	-2.0	-4.8
Idaho	705	4,567	69	6	15,108	19.7	17.6	21.6
Illinois	*4,064*	*22,551*	*545*	*6*	*24,167*	*7.2*	*-0.9*	*9.2*
Indiana	**2,136**	**12,404**	**225**	**6**	**18,139**	**8.1**	**11.5**	**15.7**
Percent U.S.	1.97	1.97	1.86	—	94.47	—	—	—
Rank	17	17	19	13	27	30	18	16
Iowa	1,258	6,581	132	5	20,058	9.9	5.9	11.2
Kansas	1,205	5,842	100	5	17,117	6.3	15.2	18.9
Kentucky	*1,247*	*7,323*	*127*	*6*	*17,343*	*11.7*	*6.3*	*14.0*
Louisiana	1,316	7,184	117	5	16,286	12.5	10.0	8.1
Maine	670	2,637	57	4	21,615	15.5	-2.0	15.4
Maryland	2,187	15,108	302	7	19,989	5.5	14.5	14.5
Massachusetts	2,970	10,822	272	4	25,134	6.6	-11.6	12.5
Michigan	*3,623*	*17,336*	*385*	*5*	*22,208*	*7.0*	*4.9*	*14.8*
Minnesota	1,768	8,215	173	5	21,059	10.8	7.6	14.3
Mississippi	845	4,510	71	5	15,743	12.1	6.2	0.8
Missouri	2,167	10,572	178	5	16,837	10.7	6.3	8.6
Montana	504	1,606	27	3	16,812	12.5	-2.5	-4.8
Nebraska	982	3,875	68	4	17,548	8.9	-4.3	4.4
Nevada	660	4,617	84	7	18,194	12.1	44.6	42.7
New Hampshire	610	2,247	48	4	21,362	10.3	-0.8	14.2
New Jersey	4,165	15,250	365	4	23,934	5.3	-4.3	10.6
New Mexico	513	2,933	45	6	15,343	7.3	9.0	9.8
New York	5,702	23,749	576	4	24,254	5.3	-3.6	8.5
North Carolina	3,144	17,473	299	6	17,112	11.4	13.1	15.7
North Dakota	321	1,022	17	3	16,634	3.2	NA	NA
Ohio	*4,454*	*23,124*	*448*	*5*	*19,374*	*10.0*	*5.0*	*14.0*
Oklahoma	1,191	6,467	93	5	14,381	8.5	10.7	9.3
Oregon	1,975	14,653	276	7	18,836	8.9	26.6	33.3
Pennsylvania	4,172	21,049	435	5	20,666	6.2	-8.3	-1.4
Rhode Island	581	1,663	38	3	22,850	13.3	-24.6	9.6
South Carolina	1,550	9,064	161	6	17,763	8.1	13.2	16.1
South Dakota	351	1,371	23	4	16,776	4.2	-0.8	15.2
Tennessee	1,686	9,859	156	6	15,823	17.8	20.1	23.7
Texas	6,467	44,413	752	7	16,932	6.8	14.6	16.2
Utah	675	3,220	53	5	16,460	15.2	31.0	32.7
Vermont	382	1,506	31	4	20,584	3.5	2.9	9.3
Virginia	2,787	19,168	348	7	18,155	10.8	20.1	16.6
Washington	3,537	22,274	524	6	23,525	10.5	1.7	8.2
West Virginia	395	2,721	44	7	16,171	6.5	15.7	23.1
Wisconsin	2,005	10,439	233	5	22,320	10.7	1.4	5.6
Wyoming	280	1,026	17	4	16,569	8.5	11.4	15.5

Agriculture Services, Forestry, and Fisheries
Payroll Per Employee 1995

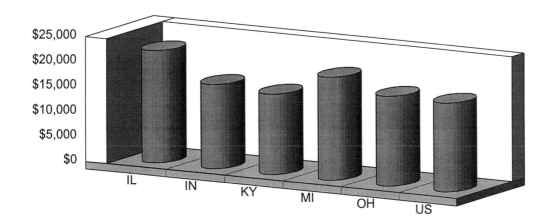

[1]Footnote: Percent change in annual payroll was calculated using real (adjusted for inflation) dollars.
Source: U.S. Bureau of the Census, County Business Patterns
EDIN table(s): EMIE, EMIP

1.83 Mining: Establishments, Employees, and Payroll 1995 ($Mil)

	Number of Establishments	Number of Employees	Annual Payroll	Average Employee Per Establishment	Payroll Per Employee ($)	Percent Change 1993-95 Establishment	Employees	Annual Payroll[1]
United States	27,356	627,483	25,697	23	40,953	-4.1	3.2	-0.7
Alabama	308	10,127	445	33	43,942	-2.8	-3.0	-0.1
Alaska	151	10,463	783	69	74,835	-10.1	5.6	-0.1
Arizona	210	13,296	540	63	40,614	-5.4	-10.2	-10.6
Arkansas	295	3,518	100	12	28,425	-3.9	0.5	4.6
California	1,057	32,480	1,596	31	49,138	-5.5	0.2	-0.5
Colorado	1,053	17,016	802	16	47,132	-2.1	1.3	-1.3
Connecticut	99	1,294	58	13	44,822	3.1	-3.2	-30.1
Delaware	20	131	3	7	22,901	17.6	-16.6	-59.2
Dist. Of Col.	14	107	9	8	84,112	-6.7	16.3	22.3
Florida	283	7,617	299	27	39,254	-5.0	4.8	13.8
Georgia	230	7,514	280	33	37,264	1.3	5.2	13.9
Hawaii	7	217	10	31	46,083	-41.7	-13.5	-13.5
Idaho	127	2,621	105	21	40,061	-3.8	-3.8	0.9
Illinois	*755*	*14,370*	*607*	*19*	*42,241*	*-6.7*	*-10.9*	*-6.7*
Indiana	**381**	**6,351**	**246**	**17**	**38,734**	**1.9**	**-5.7**	**-1.2**
Percent U.S.	*1.39*	*1.01*	*0.96*	*—*	*94.58*	*—*	*—*	*—*
Rank	*17*	*24*	*25*	*28*	*28*	*12*	*34*	*28*
Iowa	199	1,930	60	10	31,088	2.1	-1.8	-6.4
Kansas	1,051	9,813	313	9	31,896	-4.5	-6.4	-9.5
Kentucky	*886*	*26,215*	*950*	*30*	*36,239*	*-11.2*	*-11.5*	*-12.3*
Louisiana	1,534	46,176	1,929	30	41,775	-1.4	3.5	-1.1
Maine	36	67	2	2	29,851	33.3	-28.0	-4.8
Maryland	102	2,115	85	21	40,189	-1.0	4.7	7.8
Massachusetts	103	1,275	59	12	46,275	9.6	10.9	14.6
Michigan	*484*	*8,376*	*316*	*17*	*37,727*	*-4.3*	*-1.9*	*-2.4*
Minnesota	169	7,121	323	42	45,359	1.8	0.0	11.4
Mississippi	377	5,067	141	13	27,827	-5.5	1.6	-0.6
Missouri	337	5,001	185	15	36,993	2.4	6.7	-2.7
Montana	282	5,094	213	18	41,814	-4.4	-3.9	3.9
Nebraska	146	1,169	34	8	29,085	-7.0	-12.4	-7.6
Nevada	236	11,422	547	48	47,890	2.2	6.8	13.9
New Hampshire	45	365	15	8	41,096	12.5	19.7	18.9
New Jersey	132	3,575	207	27	57,902	-4.3	0.8	-3.4
New Mexico	614	15,632	572	25	36,592	-4.5	-3.7	-7.3
New York	413	5,735	299	14	52,136	-2.6	-15.1	-16.3
North Carolina	225	4,179	152	19	36,372	3.2	12.9	11.3
North Dakota	227	4,078	177	18	43,404	-0.4	-2.6	2.1
Ohio	*931*	*14,447*	*529*	*16*	*36,617*	*-3.4*	*-14.5*	*-16.7*
Oklahoma	2,411	35,086	1,342	15	38,249	-6.4	-10.4	-14.5
Oregon	155	1,734	57	11	32,872	4.0	9.7	10.7
Pennsylvania	1,060	20,120	762	19	37,873	-5.7	-6.0	-2.4
Rhode Island	19	110	3	6	27,273	-17.4	-6.0	-28.6
South Carolina	102	1,654	54	16	32,648	5.2	-1.4	0.8
South Dakota	63	2,047	78	32	38,105	1.6	-6.3	-1.0
Tennessee	248	4,531	144	18	31,781	-6.8	-0.1	4.6
Texas	6,955	183,762	7,222	26	39,301	-4.1	24.7	6.5
Utah	323	8,897	362	28	40,688	-6.9	-1.0	-9.4
Vermont	58	685	25	12	36,496	-1.7	-3.1	-4.8
Virginia	519	14,505	509	28	35,091	1.4	-7.0	-10.8
Washington	197	3,192	138	16	43,233	-2.0	-7.9	1.8
West Virginia	937	27,470	1,204	29	43,830	-10.5	-4.6	6.2
Wisconsin	170	2,453	99	14	40,359	-0.6	-16.3	0.2
Wyoming	620	15,263	704	25	46,125	-3.1	-3.2	1.5

Mining
Payroll Per Employee 1995

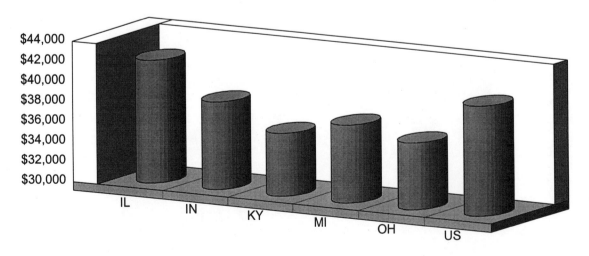

[1]Footnote: Percent change in annual payroll was calculated using real (adjusted for inflation) dollars.
Source: U.S. Bureau of the Census, County Business Patterns
EDIN table(s): EMIE, EMIP

1.84 Contract Construction: Establishments, Employees, and Payroll 1995 *($Mil)*

	Number of Establishments	Number of Employees	Annual Payroll	Average Employee Per Establishment	Payroll Per Employee ($)	Percent Change 1993-95 Establishment	Employees	Annual Payroll[1]
United States	634,030	5,038,839	147,275	8	29,228	6.0	11.4	11.7
Alabama	9,121	92,845	2,099	10	22,608	10.0	8.6	10.8
Alaska	2,001	11,211	569	6	50,754	10.6	-4.0	6.4
Arizona	10,063	121,286	3,018	12	24,883	12.9	34.2	33.9
Arkansas	5,508	41,502	881	8	21,228	10.8	17.6	14.8
California	60,360	495,037	15,412	8	31,133	-2.2	4.1	7.1
Colorado	13,209	104,428	3,023	8	28,948	19.3	22.5	18.6
Connecticut	8,985	52,048	2,035	6	39,099	1.7	2.7	8.8
Delaware	2,236	17,170	516	8	30,052	4.0	0.7	5.6
Dist. Of Col.	308	5,009	182	16	36,335	-7.8	-12.6	-13.4
Florida	36,078	310,556	7,280	9	23,442	0.4	7.6	9.1
Georgia	16,751	147,220	3,789	9	25,737	12.9	18.4	20.5
Hawaii	2,443	25,943	999	11	38,507	-7.5	-19.0	-19.5
Idaho	4,936	34,542	998	7	28,892	16.4	53.5	63.7
Illinois	*27,371*	*209,515*	*7,824*	*8*	*37,343*	*6.3*	*11.8*	*9.7*
Indiana	**15,286**	**129,903**	**3,791**	**8**	**29,183**	**8.6**	**14.4**	**14.3**
Percent U.S.	*2.41*	*2.58*	*2.57*	*—*	*99.85*	*—*	*—*	*—*
Rank	*14*	*13*	*14*	*15*	*22*	*21*	*18*	*21*
Iowa	7,688	51,070	1,471	7	28,804	7.4	13.8	17.7
Kansas	6,813	51,976	1,422	8	27,359	6.7	13.8	15.7
Kentucky	*8,395*	*71,112*	*1,698*	*8*	*23,878*	*7.2*	*12.9*	*9.2*
Louisiana	7,444	104,257	2,748	14	26,358	9.6	10.3	16.5
Maine	4,181	19,384	539	5	27,806	3.2	0.9	3.4
Maryland	14,356	138,594	4,032	10	29,092	2.1	11.4	7.6
Massachusetts	14,320	89,493	3,241	6	36,215	3.9	9.5	9.5
Michigan	*22,941*	*145,235*	*4,951*	*6*	*34,090*	*7.9*	*12.9*	*18.0*
Minnesota	12,072	81,676	3,064	7	37,514	7.3	5.0	13.3
Mississippi	4,600	41,395	911	9	22,007	9.3	12.8	15.4
Missouri	14,711	115,160	3,477	8	30,193	6.8	21.6	28.5
Montana	3,227	15,137	405	5	26,756	10.5	19.2	12.0
Nebraska	4,877	36,259	939	7	25,897	7.6	27.9	25.3
Nevada	3,901	56,366	1,731	14	30,710	13.6	28.7	19.5
New Hampshire	3,592	18,055	536	5	29,687	6.6	14.6	14.1
New Jersey	21,622	128,121	4,562	6	35,607	5.8	6.8	2.6
New Mexico	4,788	41,853	936	9	22,364	9.7	25.7	27.1
New York	36,810	232,937	8,443	6	36,246	1.1	2.5	2.2
North Carolina	21,757	173,506	4,086	8	23,550	11.6	17.7	19.3
North Dakota	1,950	12,406	342	6	27,567	9.7	12.0	15.0
Ohio	*26,048*	*200,139*	*6,102*	*8*	*30,489*	*6.9*	*11.1*	*8.2*
Oklahoma	6,630	49,284	1,130	7	22,928	7.4	9.4	7.7
Oregon	11,339	68,028	2,116	6	31,105	16.0	29.6	35.0
Pennsylvania	26,955	202,946	6,265	8	30,870	2.9	3.5	3.5
Rhode Island	2,998	13,233	435	4	32,872	2.7	9.7	9.5
South Carolina	9,534	96,581	2,255	10	23,348	8.2	7.7	11.2
South Dakota	2,333	13,371	311	6	23,259	7.6	15.4	12.1
Tennessee	11,014	104,583	2,738	9	26,180	11.7	19.7	22.7
Texas	34,447	388,558	10,314	11	26,544	8.7	13.2	15.2
Utah	6,319	48,560	1,254	8	25,824	26.6	36.3	33.9
Vermont	2,465	11,772	315	5	26,758	-1.9	11.7	12.3
Virginia	18,859	158,172	4,035	8	25,510	5.7	12.2	11.4
Washington	19,468	125,167	3,832	6	30,615	4.4	5.8	5.3
West Virginia	4,366	29,410	692	7	23,529	11.3	21.9	5.4
Wisconsin	14,512	94,917	3,225	7	33,977	6.3	5.6	7.6
Wyoming	2,042	11,911	308	6	25,858	9.7	13.1	10.2

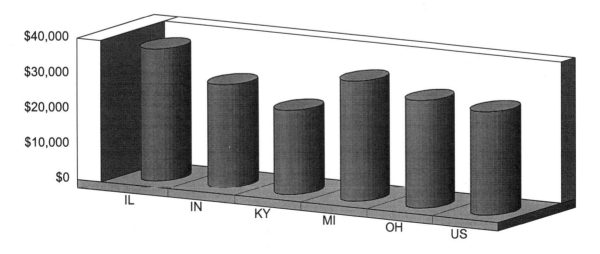

Contract Construction
Payroll Per Employee 1995

[1]Footnote: Percent change in annual payroll was calculated using real (adjusted for inflation) dollars.
Source: U.S. Bureau of the Census, County Business Patterns
EDIN table(s): EMIE, EMIP

1.85 Manufacturing: Establishments, Employees, and Payroll 1995 *($Mil)*

	Number of Establishments	Number of Employees	Annual Payroll	Average Employee Per Establishment	Payroll Per Employee ($)	Percent Change 1993-95 Establishments	Employees	Annual Payroll[1]
United States	389,925	18,612,597	631,000	48	33,902	0.9	2.4	4.3
Alabama	6,672	393,859	10,333	59	26,235	0.9	2.7	3.4
Alaska	574	13,503	431	24	31,919	7.7	-5.1	-5.7
Arizona	5,035	199,783	7,112	40	35,599	3.1	11.3	17.7
Arkansas	4,190	250,755	5,850	60	23,330	3.1	6.5	8.5
California	50,232	1,842,438	68,845	37	37,366	-0.4	-1.9	0.0
Colorado	5,732	189,247	6,529	33	34,500	3.9	-0.1	2.0
Connecticut	6,138	288,198	12,504	47	43,387	-1.6	-8.0	-1.4
Delaware	758	65,631	2,908	87	44,308	3.0	1.7	-3.6
Dist. Of Col.	447	12,361	629	28	50,886	-2.6	-10.6	-1.7
Florida	16,680	482,473	14,126	29	29,278	-0.7	1.0	3.2
Georgia	10,236	598,223	17,194	58	28,742	2.5	5.5	7.0
Hawaii	956	17,067	496	18	29,062	-5.6	-13.5	-11.3
Idaho	2,057	72,066	2,201	35	30,541	5.4	6.1	8.9
Illinois	*19,015*	*1,011,741*	*36,296*	*53*	*35,875*	*0.3*	*3.4*	*3.5*
Indiana	9,591	672,734	23,035	70	34,241	1.6	5.7	5.9
Percent U.S.	*2.46*	*3.61*	*3.65*	—	*101.00*	—	—	—
Rank	*14*	*9*	*9*	*4*	*16*	*29*	*16*	*21*
Iowa	4,046	248,812	7,588	61	30,497	2.0	7.5	7.1
Kansas	3,579	195,294	6,095	55	31,209	2.1	3.3	6.2
Kentucky	*4,532*	*305,321*	*9,089*	*67*	*29,769*	*1.9*	*7.4*	*10.3*
Louisiana	4,097	178,627	6,026	44	33,735	-0.8	-1.3	4.0
Maine	2,283	90,548	2,678	40	29,575	2.2	2.3	3.3
Maryland	4,288	187,771	6,771	44	36,060	-0.2	-3.5	-0.4
Massachusetts	10,136	457,310	17,982	45	39,321	-0.7	-3.8	1.3
Michigan	*16,781*	*960,243*	*40,626*	*57*	*42,308*	*2.3*	*5.9*	*9.7*
Minnesota	8,505	414,087	14,731	49	35,575	4.9	5.4	8.2
Mississippi	3,896	249,760	5,624	64	22,518	0.9	2.9	1.4
Missouri	8,111	422,933	13,404	52	31,693	0.9	2.9	4.8
Montana	1,452	22,454	572	15	25,474	4.6	-1.1	-4.3
Nebraska	2,071	112,951	3,121	55	27,631	0.8	9.3	10.6
Nevada	1,553	35,526	1,043	23	29,359	13.9	22.1	16.8
New Hampshire	2,481	99,834	3,300	40	33,055	4.0	6.6	6.6
New Jersey	12,741	546,357	22,469	43	41,125	-3.6	-0.1	3.0
New Mexico	1,657	43,895	1,293	26	29,457	0.5	2.9	2.1
New York	25,859	963,231	36,297	37	37,683	-2.9	-3.7	-1.2
North Carolina	12,217	870,344	23,384	71	26,868	1.6	2.6	4.2
North Dakota	739	22,188	560	30	25,239	6.0	15.4	17.4
Ohio	*18,647*	*1,093,560*	*39,986*	*59*	*36,565*	*1.4*	*4.5*	*6.1*
Oklahoma	4,246	166,744	4,695	39	28,157	0.7	3.1	0.2
Oregon	7,124	227,601	7,673	32	33,713	1.4	7.9	15.1
Pennsylvania	17,932	935,945	31,893	52	34,076	-0.3	0.1	3.0
Rhode Island	2,640	84,782	2,558	32	30,171	-2.3	-5.6	-4.7
South Carolina	5,024	375,427	10,646	75	28,357	2.0	1.5	2.6
South Dakota	979	45,222	1,133	46	25,054	4.7	18.9	28.7
Tennessee	8,045	537,213	14,990	67	27,903	2.9	4.6	5.6
Texas	22,880	1,012,788	34,413	44	33,978	3.0	4.6	6.2
Utah	2,811	121,960	3,449	43	28,280	4.5	10.1	8.4
Vermont	1,410	45,298	1,395	32	30,796	3.6	1.7	2.1
Virginia	6,813	404,233	12,414	59	30,710	2.7	0.0	2.8
Washington	8,994	335,543	12,435	37	37,059	2.9	2.2	4.9
West Virginia	1,899	82,159	2,629	43	31,999	4.7	2.0	4.1
Wisconsin	10,540	596,622	19,279	57	32,314	2.2	8.7	9.2
Wyoming	604	9,935	272	16	27,378	4.5	6.0	7.0

Manufacturing
Payroll Per Employee 1995

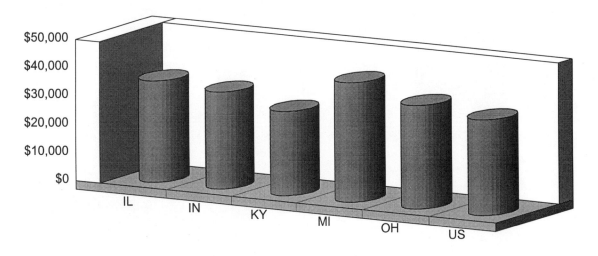

[1]Footnote: Percent change in annual payroll was calculated using real (adjusted for inflation) dollars.
Source: U.S. Bureau of the Census, County Business Patterns
EDIN table(s): EMIE, EMIP

1.86 Transportation and Public Utilities: Establishments, Employees, and Payroll 1995 *($Mil)*

	Number of Establishments	Number of Employees	Annual Payroll	Average Employee Per Establishment	Payroll Per Employee ($)	Prcent Change 1993-95 Establishments	Employees	Annual Payroll[1]
United States	284,986	5,924,252	200,880	21	33,908	6.9	5.4	5.0
Alabama	4,571	85,160	2,718	19	31,916	8.7	4.8	1.9
Alaska	1,472	22,697	928	15	40,886	4.8	10.6	10.1
Arizona	3,827	94,628	2,937	25	31,037	11.9	8.5	11.0
Arkansas	3,538	58,811	1,726	17	29,348	8.7	10.2	12.4
California	27,180	645,494	22,338	24	34,606	2.5	3.8	0.7
Colorado	4,649	110,665	4,057	24	36,660	11.3	12.0	16.1
Connecticut	3,146	71,262	2,752	23	38,618	3.6	-1.1	6.6
Delaware	860	14,209	467	17	32,866	5.4	3.8	5.8
Dist. Of Col.	737	18,549	871	25	46,957	-2.4	-5.8	2.4
Florida	16,245	315,115	9,589	19	30,430	10.6	7.5	4.4
Georgia	7,828	211,325	7,556	27	35,755	11.9	6.9	4.4
Hawaii	1,566	41,693	1,325	27	31,780	1.6	0.7	-0.9
Idaho	1,756	18,217	507	10	27,831	8.3	4.2	7.0
Illinois	*13,269*	*302,838*	*10,940*	*23*	*36,125*	*7.0*	*3.3*	*4.0*
Indiana	**6,374**	**129,403**	**3,954**	**20**	**30,556**	**9.0**	**6.3**	**4.5**
Percent U.S.	*2.24*	*2.18*	*1.97*	—	*90.11*	—	—	—
Rank	*16*	*15*	*18*	*22*	*36*	*11*	*20*	*28*
Iowa	4,472	63,424	1,783	14	28,112	7.9	15.5	16.1
Kansas	3,579	62,310	1,926	17	30,910	9.0	13.0	10.5
Kentucky	*4,368*	*83,039*	*2,550*	*19*	*30,708*	*3.8*	*10.2*	*6.5*
Louisiana	5,377	99,125	3,122	18	31,496	6.3	2.4	4.0
Maine	1,879	19,767	564	11	28,532	4.0	-1.2	2.6
Maryland	4,865	102,159	3,474	21	34,006	6.0	9.8	8.7
Massachusetts	5,857	126,764	4,501	22	35,507	2.3	3.9	2.1
Michigan	*7,793*	*160,095*	*5,974*	*21*	*37,315*	*5.8*	*6.0*	*8.5*
Minnesota	5,706	112,963	3,625	20	32,090	7.0	6.4	2.9
Mississippi	3,591	47,042	1,359	13	28,889	12.4	9.0	6.3
Missouri	7,288	146,603	4,674	20	31,882	8.0	4.6	5.2
Montana	1,571	17,252	500	11	28,982	-0.9	-1.4	1.4
Nebraska	2,630	38,920	1,113	15	28,597	7.1	12.3	12.5
Nevada	1,541	36,985	1,128	24	30,499	12.2	19.0	14.1
New Hampshire	1,261	22,066	667	17	30,227	5.3	11.1	-3.1
New Jersey	10,457	252,839	9,923	24	39,246	5.4	2.0	4.7
New Mexico	1,734	29,286	846	17	28,888	7.5	1.8	-3.6
New York	18,413	408,813	15,935	22	38,979	3.8	1.6	1.9
North Carolina	7,325	156,650	5,192	21	33,144	12.0	3.2	5.8
North Dakota	1,435	15,428	426	11	27,612	7.9	6.1	6.4
Ohio	*10,092*	*222,686*	*7,294*	*22*	*32,755*	*7.5*	*7.5*	*5.0*
Oklahoma	3,651	67,766	2,263	19	33,394	6.9	2.9	0.8
Oregon	4,131	65,339	2,121	16	32,461	7.3	1.3	2.6
Pennsylvania	10,679	262,314	8,847	25	33,727	1.2	2.1	1.5
Rhode Island	904	12,873	439	14	34,102	7.4	-8.2	1.1
South Carolina	3,396	64,604	2,019	19	31,252	9.9	5.6	5.8
South Dakota	1,484	14,012	346	9	24,693	4.5	-3.2	-1.7
Tennessee	5,713	130,729	4,055	23	31,018	8.9	4.9	9.6
Texas	20,771	453,865	15,489	22	34,127	10.3	10.3	10.7
Utah	1,824	49,710	1,548	27	31,141	11.5	7.4	5.0
Vermont	872	10,081	300	12	29,759	3.6	1.1	4.2
Virginia	6,827	141,942	4,945	21	34,838	8.2	5.2	3.3
Washington	6,379	128,066	4,563	20	35,630	6.3	6.8	9.9
West Virginia	2,256	33,220	1,023	15	30,795	8.1	5.4	4.9
Wisconsin	6,925	115,078	3,358	17	29,180	7.3	5.3	5.6
Wyoming	922	10,371	327	11	31,530	7.7	-0.4	-2.2

Transportation
Payroll Per Employee 1995

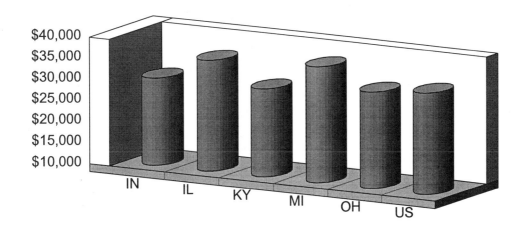

[1]Footnote: Percent change in annual payroll was calculated using real (adjusted for inflation) dollars.
Source: U.S. Bureau of the Census, County Business Patterns
EDIN table(s): EMIE, EMIP

1.87 Wholesale Trade: Establishments, Employees, and, Payroll 1995 *($Mil)*

	Number of Establishments	Number of Employees	Annual Payroll	Average Employee Per Establishment	Payroll Per Employee ($)	Percent Change 1993-95 Establishments	Employees	Annual Payroll[1]
United States	517,737	6,606,186	226,993	13	34,361	1.7	5.6	7.6
Alabama	7,380	91,060	2,536	12	27,850	1.9	8.5	11.3
Alaska	977	8,862	319	9	35,996	1.0	-1.7	-6.9
Arizona	7,376	88,673	2,745	12	30,956	7.5	15.6	18.8
Arkansas	4,447	49,857	1,275	11	25,573	1.1	8.0	9.8
California	61,649	821,002	30,568	13	37,233	3.3	4.0	6.2
Colorado	8,358	101,742	3,390	12	33,320	4.1	9.0	10.3
Connecticut	6,355	91,574	4,027	14	43,975	-0.1	5.4	6.1
Delaware	1,169	16,214	626	14	38,609	3.8	-10.0	-18.7
Dist. Of Col.	468	6,640	269	14	40,512	-3.3	-1.9	-7.3
Florida	32,907	321,405	9,851	10	30,650	3.4	8.3	11.0
Georgia	15,885	217,390	7,700	14	35,420	3.8	8.3	14.4
Hawaii	2,213	22,304	676	10	30,308	-0.8	-4.5	-3.3
Idaho	2,420	26,793	730	11	27,246	2.4	1.9	21.0
Illinois	*25,254*	*382,112*	*14,732*	*15*	*38,554*	*0.7*	*7.8*	*12.7*
Indiana	**10,636**	**132,665**	**4,024**	**12**	**30,332**	**1.1**	**7.0**	**11.6**
Percent U.S.	*2.05*	*2.01*	*1.77*	—	*88.27*	—	—	—
Rank	*16*	*16*	*19*	*23*	*30*	*24*	*18*	*14*
Iowa	6,874	77,981	2,146	11	27,520	-2.7	6.4	13.1
Kansas	6,010	71,149	2,124	12	29,853	0.1	6.4	9.0
Kentucky	*6,147*	*80,457*	*2,198*	*13*	*27,319*	*0.8*	*2.8*	*2.6*
Louisiana	7,507	86,269	2,352	11	27,264	-0.8	2.7	4.0
Maine	2,075	25,020	682	12	27,258	0.0	3.0	6.2
Maryland	7,505	109,709	3,879	15	35,357	0.9	1.4	-0.4
Massachusetts	11,318	166,532	6,846	15	41,109	0.1	4.9	6.5
Michigan	*15,737*	*215,440*	*8,044*	*14*	*37,338*	*1.4*	*7.8*	*11.6*
Minnesota	10,804	150,077	5,298	14	35,302	1.7	11.0	12.8
Mississippi	3,970	45,330	1,141	11	25,171	0.8	3.1	5.3
Missouri	11,518	147,146	4,674	13	31,764	0.0	5.7	8.9
Montana	1,860	17,596	424	9	24,096	-3.1	2.6	4.8
Nebraska	3,994	51,466	1,346	13	26,153	-2.1	-0.3	3.5
Nevada	2,427	27,183	855	11	31,453	9.6	14.0	15.7
New Hampshire	2,346	25,450	873	11	34,303	3.9	11.9	12.9
New Jersey	19,576	304,347	12,683	16	41,673	2.5	2.2	3.0
New Mexico	2,655	26,678	683	10	25,602	2.5	12.4	14.0
New York	42,331	462,249	18,195	11	39,362	0.9	1.8	1.2
North Carolina	14,067	173,976	5,557	12	31,941	3.1	8.4	11.2
North Dakota	2,030	20,630	519	10	25,158	-4.2	3.4	7.8
Ohio	*19,982*	*298,491*	*10,004*	*15*	*33,515*	*1.5*	*5.8*	*10.8*
Oklahoma	6,114	68,689	1,946	11	28,331	0.7	6.9	6.5
Oregon	6,861	89,284	2,934	13	32,861	2.1	9.3	13.4
Pennsylvania	20,328	276,222	9,448	14	34,204	-0.5	2.9	6.8
Rhode Island	1,856	21,200	652	11	30,755	0.3	7.0	7.3
South Carolina	5,840	68,968	2,001	12	29,013	3.6	14.2	16.8
South Dakota	1,812	18,912	446	10	23,583	-0.9	6.0	12.6
Tennessee	9,589	131,645	4,016	14	30,506	0.3	7.9	9.2
Texas	38,134	476,759	16,140	13	33,854	1.5	6.8	10.7
Utah	3,602	49,915	1,451	14	29,069	5.9	17.5	23.8
Vermont	1,179	13,021	367	11	28,185	3.5	6.5	7.1
Virginia	9,621	129,199	4,188	13	32,415	0.7	1.2	1.4
Washington	11,449	134,026	4,420	12	32,979	2.9	-0.6	-10.6
West Virginia	2,450	27,621	751	11	27,189	-1.7	4.4	6.0
Wisconsin	9,690	131,916	4,049	14	30,694	1.7	5.4	7.3
Wyoming	985	7,340	192	7	26,158	-0.4	1.3	3.8

Wholesale Trade
Payroll Per Employee 1995

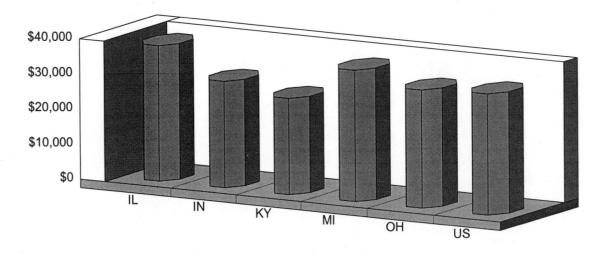

[1]Footnote: Percent change in annual payroll was calculated using real (adjusted for inflation) dollars.
Source: U.S. Bureau of the Census, County Business Patterns
EDIN table(s): EMIE, EMIP

1.88 Retail Trade: Establishments, Employees, and Payroll 1995 *($Mil)*

	Number of Establishments	Number of Employees	Annual Payroll	Average Employee Per Establishment	Payroll Per Employee ($)	Percent Change 1993-95 Establishments	Percent Change 1993-95 Employees	Percent Change 1993-95 Annual Payroll[1]
United States	1,567,884	21,084,574	300,040	13	14,230	1.1	6.6	7.6
Alabama	25,323	335,404	3,964	13	11,819	2.5	13.8	7.9
Alaska	3,943	44,699	854	11	19,106	2.8	10.9	10.9
Arizona	22,875	349,628	4,984	15	14,255	3.1	9.9	13.8
Arkansas	15,924	189,863	2,499	12	13,162	4.1	10.4	13.0
California	160,075	2,195,189	35,392	14	16,123	-1.3	1.5	3.3
Colorado	25,367	348,983	5,045	14	14,456	6.1	11.6	14.8
Connecticut	21,043	265,490	4,449	13	16,758	-0.5	3.7	4.4
Delaware	4,948	67,097	930	14	13,861	2.4	8.6	7.5
Dist. Of Col.	3,736	52,101	951	14	18,253	0.0	6.3	18.1
Florida	90,869	1,260,237	17,589	14	13,957	0.9	5.6	5.4
Georgia	43,433	640,340	8,578	15	13,396	2.5	13.9	13.8
Hawaii	8,034	110,914	1,790	14	16,139	1.4	-0.4	-0.2
Idaho	7,837	92,515	1,233	12	13,328	6.9	10.4	12.8
Illinois	*66,428*	*948,331*	*13,833*	*14*	*14,587*	*1.0*	*4.5*	*5.9*
Indiana	34,845	516,374	6,475	15	12,539	2.1	9.2	11.2
Percent U.S.	*2.22*	*2.45*	*2.16*	*—*	*88.12*	*—*	*—*	*—*
Rank	*14*	*14*	*15*	*2*	*38*	*19*	*15*	*11*
Iowa	19,784	249,528	2,958	13	11,854	-1.1	3.9	5.4
Kansas	16,845	217,049	2,817	13	12,979	0.1	5.8	9.6
Kentucky	*22,468*	*309,598*	*3,796*	*14*	*12,261*	*-0.3*	*8.7*	*9.1*
Louisiana	23,366	324,669	4,017	14	12,373	0.3	6.6	8.8
Maine	9,626	103,469	1,464	11	14,149	1.5	5.2	4.9
Maryland	28,262	410,357	6,309	15	15,374	0.0	7.6	7.1
Massachusetts	39,369	532,729	8,377	14	15,725	1.9	6.0	8.0
Michigan	*55,122*	*797,021*	*11,071*	*14*	*13,890*	*0.5*	*6.0*	*9.2*
Minnesota	28,495	433,092	5,945	15	13,727	0.9	5.9	8.7
Mississippi	15,664	179,165	2,169	11	12,106	1.0	9.6	10.5
Missouri	33,075	447,052	6,092	14	13,627	0.8	7.0	9.0
Montana	7,458	74,859	898	10	11,996	4.9	8.3	7.6
Nebraska	11,500	146,895	1,712	13	11,655	-0.3	4.8	9.6
Nevada	8,364	123,067	1,974	15	16,040	7.2	14.6	16.5
New Hampshire	8,737	110,927	1,618	13	14,586	0.7	9.8	9.7
New Jersey	50,123	593,263	10,201	12	17,195	1.2	4.9	4.1
New Mexico	10,042	130,785	1,731	13	13,235	3.4	7.6	10.9
New York	110,862	1,181,842	18,789	11	15,898	-0.3	4.3	3.6
North Carolina	45,936	606,963	8,187	13	13,488	1.9	9.0	12.0
North Dakota	4,912	57,724	647	12	11,209	0.3	6.5	9.5
Ohio	*64,551*	*988,550*	*13,230*	*15*	*13,383*	*0.7*	*9.9*	*10.7*
Oklahoma	20,006	242,130	3,005	12	12,411	0.6	6.9	7.1
Oregon	20,699	268,148	3,976	13	14,828	3.3	7.4	8.8
Pennsylvania	71,686	953,719	13,082	13	13,717	-0.3	4.9	6.5
Rhode Island	6,645	76,747	1,077	12	14,033	1.4	6.9	6.4
South Carolina	23,891	305,591	3,835	13	12,549	2.2	8.9	8.8
South Dakota	5,773	66,077	750	11	11,350	1.3	7.7	7.6
Tennessee	32,108	455,184	6,151	14	13,513	2.5	13.3	12.2
Texas	103,250	1,466,975	20,778	14	14,164	2.2	7.2	9.5
Utah	10,326	160,846	2,162	16	13,441	7.7	10.4	18.2
Vermont	5,319	51,538	688	10	13,349	1.3	4.8	3.9
Virginia	38,662	549,803	7,662	14	13,936	1.6	7.6	8.0
Washington	33,238	432,370	6,692	13	15,477	2.6	4.0	5.2
West Virginia	10,787	126,618	1,511	12	11,934	0.9	10.5	7.5
Wisconsin	32,277	450,941	5,583	14	12,381	0.2	5.7	7.4
Wyoming	3,976	42,118	520	11	12,346	2.6	7.1	7.3

Retail Trade
Payroll Per Employee 1995

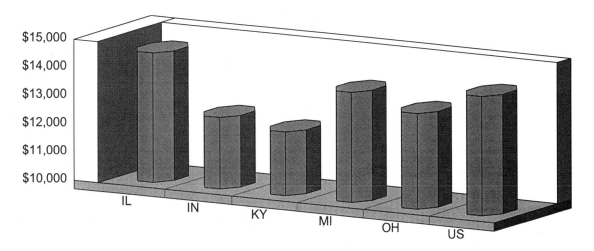

[1]Footnote: Percent change in annual payroll was calculated using real (adjusted for inflation) dollars.
Source: U.S. Bureau of the Census, County Business Patterns
EDIN table(s): EMIE, EMIP

1.89 Finance, Insurance, and Real Estate: Establishments, Employees, And Payroll 1995 *($Mil)*

	Number of Establishments	Number of Employees	Annual Payroll	Average Employee Per Establishment	Payroll Per Employee ($)	Percent Change 1993-95 Establishments	Employees	Annual Payroll[1]
United States	628,499	6,998,156	256,162	11	36,604	3.3	1.3	4.9
Alabama	7,968	77,948	2,239	10	28,724	1.8	1.0	7.0
Alaska	1,151	9,695	311	8	32,078	0.9	4.2	-1.4
Arizona	10,223	104,917	3,254	10	31,015	10.2	12.3	14.7
Arkansas	4,964	39,092	1,027	8	26,271	6.0	3.9	1.4
California	73,484	792,727	29,741	11	37,517	-2.5	-4.7	-1.9
Colorado	12,848	116,929	3,678	9	31,455	12.7	5.5	6.3
Connecticut	8,420	144,114	6,901	17	47,886	0.2	-3.4	3.7
Delaware	3,405	42,809	1,515	13	35,390	13.7	21.5	30.2
Dist. Of Col.	2,203	30,373	1,408	14	46,357	-4.3	-19.5	-5.5
Florida	42,659	395,150	11,939	9	30,214	5.1	5.1	7.4
Georgia	16,578	181,778	6,041	11	33,233	6.8	1.8	3.7
Hawaii	3,845	38,917	1,192	10	30,629	-4.7	-3.6	-5.6
Idaho	2,801	20,449	511	7	24,989	10.8	9.0	8.8
Illinois	*29,524*	*404,604*	*16,232*	*14*	*40,118*	*3.6*	*1.3*	*6.7*
Indiana	12,597	128,762	3,709	10	28,805	5.9	1.0	1.6
Percent U.S.	2.00	1.84	1.45	—	78.69	—	—	—
Rank	17	19	20	22	33	13	31	33
Iowa	7,286	80,838	2,292	11	28,353	3.7	4.2	4.7
Kansas	6,803	61,252	1,739	9	28,391	1.5	0.2	1.4
Kentucky	*7,215*	*65,840*	*1,785*	*9*	*27,111*	*5.0*	*0.1*	*0.0*
Louisiana	9,325	79,825	2,179	9	27,297	2.5	-0.1	5.1
Maine	2,666	25,568	752	10	29,412	1.6	1.4	-2.4
Maryland	11,687	143,694	4,984	12	34,685	3.0	-1.4	-1.2
Massachusetts	13,219	231,300	9,993	17	43,204	0.3	2.7	7.0
Michigan	*18,193*	*200,997*	*6,421*	*11*	*31,946*	*5.0*	*-1.0*	*4.2*
Minnesota	11,888	142,981	5,149	12	36,012	6.3	7.0	8.1
Mississippi	5,090	37,925	955	7	25,181	-4.2	-1.8	0.9
Missouri	12,771	143,687	4,391	11	30,559	2.0	2.8	3.6
Montana	2,458	14,840	357	6	24,057	8.7	1.7	-0.1
Nebraska	4,566	53,709	1,554	12	28,934	3.3	-1.8	1.8
Nevada	4,479	37,577	1,037	8	27,597	19.3	25.7	18.5
New Hampshire	2,734	28,108	883	10	31,415	2.3	-2.1	1.2
New Jersey	19,143	241,289	10,245	13	42,459	2.5	-1.9	5.4
New Mexico	3,784	29,031	721	8	24,836	9.4	3.7	6.9
New York	55,394	758,802	46,480	14	61,254	2.1	2.3	9.2
North Carolina	15,366	156,581	4,918	10	31,409	5.7	10.3	15.1
North Dakota	1,976	13,929	335	7	24,051	2.5	5.3	6.3
Ohio	*23,339*	*270,106*	*8,108*	*12*	*30,018*	*3.8*	*2.6*	*6.6*
Oklahoma	7,648	61,190	1,608	8	26,279	1.8	-4.2	-3.0
Oregon	8,691	79,553	2,316	9	29,113	11.1	9.2	8.6
Pennsylvania	23,695	328,988	10,650	14	32,372	0.7	-2.2	1.5
Rhode Island	1,983	25,405	806	13	31,726	-1.6	-4.3	-4.6
South Carolina	7,864	68,741	1,864	9	27,116	5.8	2.3	8.9
South Dakota	2,183	18,418	430	8	23,347	4.0	4.2	9.1
Tennessee	10,882	109,083	3,345	10	30,665	4.1	3.5	6.3
Texas	41,528	440,607	14,240	11	32,319	4.6	3.3	4.6
Utah	4,532	44,958	1,228	10	27,314	13.0	15.9	18.6
Vermont	1,516	12,894	391	9	30,324	-0.2	4.4	11.7
Virginia	15,202	165,377	5,362	11	32,423	3.4	4.0	2.8
Washington	14,405	123,342	3,847	9	31,190	4.8	-1.6	-2.9
West Virginia	3,224	24,571	574	8	23,361	1.7	-2.8	-2.8
Wisconsin	11,776	141,858	4,356	12	30,707	2.2	1.2	3.6
Wyoming	1,318	7,028	168	5	23,904	5.6	-3.1	-9.7

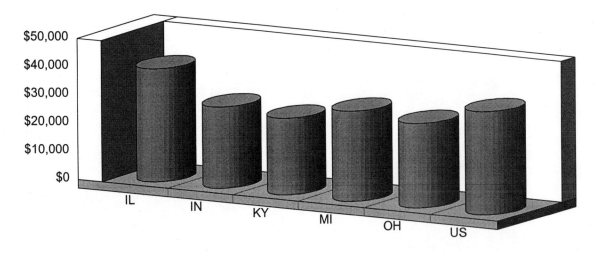

Finance, Insurance and Real Estate
Payroll Per Employee 1995

[1]Footnote: Percent change in annual payroll was calculated using real (adjusted for inflation) dollars.
Source: U.S. Bureau of the Census, County Business Patterns
EDIN table(s): EMIE, EMIP

1.90 Services: Establishments, Employees, and Payroll 1995 *($Mil)*

	Number of Establishments	Number of Employees	Annual Payroll	Average Employee Per Establishment	Payroll Per Employee ($)	Percent Change 1993-95 Establishments	Percent Change 1993-95 Employees	Percent Change 1993-95 Annual Payroll[1]
United States	2,385,532	34,707,165	864,352	15	24,904	4.2	7.6	10.3
Alabama	32,164	455,428	9,946	14	21,839	5.3	7.9	9.5
Alaska	6,380	58,836	1,705	9	28,979	5.8	5.5	2.7
Arizona	37,104	518,668	11,666	14	22,492	6.9	14.8	17.4
Arkansas	19,886	250,252	4,743	13	18,953	4.7	9.8	12.5
California	286,617	4,020,703	115,735	14	28,785	1.7	4.9	7.2
Colorado	43,812	556,824	13,622	13	24,464	7.9	10.3	16.3
Connecticut	34,383	493,299	14,203	14	28,792	2.1	5.4	8.2
Delaware	6,939	98,989	2,357	14	23,811	4.2	6.8	6.9
Dist. Of Col.	11,244	288,083	10,311	26	35,792	2.8	2.0	3.5
Florida	148,955	2,055,425	47,635	14	23,175	4.8	13.1	13.3
Georgia	63,170	892,581	22,064	14	24,719	7.7	12.2	15.1
Hawaii	10,353	163,866	4,145	16	25,295	1.7	-0.3	0.6
Idaho	10,039	106,856	2,080	11	19,465	7.4	5.9	1.0
Illinois	*105,928*	*1,651,684*	*42,735*	*16*	*25,874*	*5.2*	*7.5*	*11.1*
Indiana	48,162	672,660	14,072	14	20,920	3.9	4.5	8.3
Percent U.S.	2.02	1.94	1.63	—	84.00	—	—	—
Rank	16	17	20	19	37	33	46	37
Iowa	26,044	357,401	6,683	14	18,699	2.6	4.8	9.9
Kansas	24,261	306,628	6,281	13	20,484	4.4	6.2	9.6
Kentucky	*29,173*	*397,088*	*7,883*	*14*	*19,852*	*4.3*	*7.0*	*9.6*
Louisiana	35,055	524,549	11,133	15	21,224	3.8	8.6	11.6
Maine	12,456	145,448	3,053	12	20,990	4.6	9.0	8.4
Maryland	47,779	709,497	19,270	15	27,160	5.0	7.0	11.5
Massachusetts	61,916	1,117,921	32,109	18	28,722	4.4	6.2	9.3
Michigan	*79,733*	*1,183,964*	*29,218*	*15*	*24,678*	*3.9*	*9.9*	*11.5*
Minnesota	45,123	720,520	16,452	16	22,834	5.7	7.0	9.6
Mississippi	18,277	260,329	4,992	14	19,176	3.5	19.4	20.3
Missouri	48,728	729,257	16,255	15	22,290	3.0	6.9	10.6
Montana	10,070	91,885	1,654	9	18,001	8.0	8.2	12.7
Nebraska	15,803	228,883	4,620	14	20,185	3.0	6.3	11.1
Nevada	13,626	338,878	8,116	25	23,950	8.3	12.4	16.9
New Hampshire	12,577	156,799	3,832	12	24,439	6.3	10.2	12.0
New Jersey	81,509	1,097,636	32,125	13	29,267	4.7	4.0	6.4
New Mexico	14,413	185,934	4,217	13	22,680	4.1	8.4	11.4
New York	168,217	2,740,020	80,030	16	29,208	2.8	3.8	8.0
North Carolina	60,073	830,091	18,419	14	22,189	7.1	13.5	15.5
North Dakota	6,422	82,296	1,441	13	17,510	3.1	4.9	2.8
Ohio	*93,469*	*1,436,027*	*32,158*	*15*	*22,394*	*3.0*	*6.9*	*9.1*
Oklahoma	28,658	355,989	6,937	12	19,487	4.3	8.0	7.6
Oregon	31,672	370,089	8,315	12	22,468	6.3	12.8	15.9
Pennsylvania	105,108	1,698,011	42,065	16	24,773	2.3	5.3	8.0
Rhode Island	9,967	143,376	3,434	14	23,951	2.1	5.8	10.5
South Carolina	29,802	403,114	8,441	14	20,939	5.4	9.5	12.2
South Dakota	7,481	88,848	1,613	12	18,155	6.0	6.8	10.6
Tennessee	44,274	668,472	15,466	15	23,136	5.3	11.1	15.0
Texas	158,992	2,313,642	55,458	15	23,970	4.9	8.6	11.2
Utah	15,030	255,698	5,526	17	21,611	7.4	11.6	15.1
Vermont	7,104	77,302	1,526	11	19,741	3.4	3.7	7.0
Virginia	61,294	896,580	23,772	15	26,514	6.0	9.5	13.5
Washington	52,559	642,944	16,956	12	26,372	5.0	8.8	21.8
West Virginia	14,009	176,497	3,498	13	19,819	3.6	6.3	6.9
Wisconsin	43,972	639,997	13,450	15	21,016	3.5	5.9	8.6
Wyoming	5,750	51,401	937	9	18,229	5.6	17.1	17.8

Services
Payroll Per Employee 1995

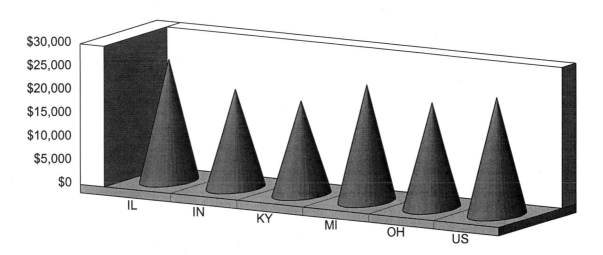

[1]Footnote: Percent change in annual payroll was calculated using real (adjusted for inflation) dollars.
Source: U.S. Bureau of the Census, County Business Patterns
EDIN table(s): EMIE, EMIP

SECTION 1

INDIANA FACTBOOK
Page 91

1.91 Building Permits: New Privately Owned Housing - Units and Valuation 1996 *($000)*

	Total Units	Value	1 Unit Number	1 Unit Value	2 Units Number	2 Units Value	3 & 4 Units Number	3 & 4 Units Value	5 Units or More Number	5 Units or More Value
United States	1,425,616	134,175,811	1,069,472	116,535,045	33,608	2,069,137	32,230	1,861,424	290,306	13,710,205
Alabama	19,868	1,508,738	14,566	1,301,462	216	10,131	285	10,333	4,801	186,812
Alaska	2,640	316,425	1,810	249,435	212	21,770	101	10,540	517	34,680
Arizona	53,715	5,448,566	41,311	4,759,903	426	30,839	418	29,026	11,560	628,798
Arkansas	11,144	777,153	7,671	673,828	564	22,974	432	12,679	2,477	67,672
California	92,060	12,472,294	73,532	11,130,529	1,138	110,365	2,457	200,184	14,933	1,031,216
Colorado	41,135	4,274,869	30,361	3,621,681	862	81,568	1,128	85,941	8,784	485,679
Connecticut	8,537	987,222	7,590	941,093	86	6,786	129	7,541	732	31,802
Delaware	4,370	351,730	4,218	342,781	26	1,448	4	271	122	7,230
Dist. Of Col.	0	0	0	0	0	0	0	0	0	0
Florida	125,020	11,471,660	91,040	9,361,145	1,488	99,500	2,411	186,202	30,081	1,824,813
Georgia	74,874	6,075,222	59,397	5,429,227	990	36,723	539	20,291	13,948	588,981
Hawaii	3,927	486,062	2,698	373,848	58	7,105	51	7,508	1,120	97,601
Idaho	10,755	1,058,954	9,180	983,104	294	22,387	559	25,428	722	28,035
Illinois	*49,592*	*5,198,763*	*35,912*	*4,423,251*	*1,628*	*109,291*	*2,796*	*166,745*	*9,256*	*499,476*
Indiana	**37,219**	**3,719,252**	**29,863**	**3,428,866**	**1,288**	**80,660**	**576**	**32,859**	**5,492**	**176,867**
Percent U.S.	*2.61*	*2.77*	*2.79*	*2.94*	*3.83*	*3.90*	*1.79*	*1.77*	*1.89*	*1.29*
Rank	*16*	*13*	*13*	*12*	*9*	*11*	*20*	*18*	*19*	*23*
Iowa	12,027	1,050,537	7,923	862,899	442	30,113	441	24,158	3,221	133,367
Kansas	14,676	1,322,385	10,121	1,124,060	872	52,382	422	16,639	3,261	129,304
Kentucky	*18,778*	*1,484,079*	*14,056*	*1,314,348*	*748*	*32,251*	*652*	*23,328*	*3,322*	*114,152*
Louisiana	17,998	1,436,403	14,422	1,308,078	426	14,246	272	7,778	2,878	106,301
Maine	4,685	436,422	4,463	425,650	46	1,879	41	2,116	135	6,777
Maryland	25,108	2,284,010	22,594	2,170,591	68	3,687	66	4,889	2,380	104,843
Massachusetts	17,261	2,055,225	15,077	1,927,960	466	32,361	144	11,063	1,574	83,841
Michigan	*52,355*	*5,179,181*	*43,421*	*4,733,581*	*758*	*52,184*	*889*	*53,696*	*7,287*	*339,720*
Minnesota	27,043	2,902,560	22,085	2,581,526	376	34,575	774	57,676	3,808	228,783
Mississippi	10,367	709,629	8,061	633,815	158	5,720	233	5,748	1,915	64,346
Missouri	26,298	2,275,667	20,107	2,008,419	2,004	101,620	1,458	55,071	2,729	110,557
Montana	2,678	209,026	1,494	149,625	214	16,066	259	13,664	711	29,671
Nebraska	10,091	681,359	5,717	540,899	342	19,531	90	4,443	3,942	116,486
Nevada	37,242	2,854,151	23,810	2,258,801	220	14,052	716	41,463	12,496	539,835
New Hampshire	4,926	516,839	4,233	473,734	88	5,430	36	4,257	569	33,418
New Jersey	24,173	2,134,126	20,853	1,985,727	880	47,616	211	14,716	2,229	86,067
New Mexico	10,180	1,083,501	8,842	1,029,456	26	1,114	83	3,473	1,229	49,458
New York	34,895	3,110,079	20,215	2,380,716	3,166	177,108	1,094	76,539	10,420	475,716
North Carolina	66,997	6,042,572	51,796	5,418,435	990	51,955	773	41,310	13,438	530,872
North Dakota	2,324	181,018	1,479	147,765	36	2,496	50	3,578	759	27,179
Ohio	*49,280*	*5,000,781*	*35,719*	*4,430,635*	*1,736*	*112,136*	*2,392*	*109,762*	*9,433*	*348,248*
Oklahoma	10,640	980,991	8,757	906,920	370	15,041	73	2,659	1,440	56,371
Oregon	27,814	2,759,925	17,232	2,225,636	1,156	86,248	918	54,988	8,508	393,053
Pennsylvania	37,895	3,549,886	32,439	3,299,216	544	27,673	796	39,251	4,116	183,746
Rhode Island	2,462	219,557	2,077	202,375	106	5,837	23	839	256	10,506
South Carolina	29,403	2,464,112	22,511	2,145,657	402	14,902	375	17,460	6,115	286,093
South Dakota	3,648	278,738	2,418	220,148	120	7,690	133	6,654	977	44,246
Tennessee	40,522	3,334,418	28,217	2,739,338	824	32,769	775	28,440	10,706	533,871
Texas	118,823	9,934,738	83,103	8,480,809	1,570	69,613	1,629	53,131	32,521	1,331,185
Utah	23,481	2,111,224	16,663	1,748,741	624	45,128	904	56,997	5,290	260,358
Vermont	2,070	201,383	1,872	190,788	68	3,740	7	362	123	6,493
Virginia	45,919	3,947,353	35,163	3,534,235	640	35,528	470	27,614	9,646	349,976
Washington	39,597	3,772,982	27,015	3,019,875	1,564	113,722	1,588	111,299	9,430	528,086
West Virginia	3,616	276,125	2,908	246,997	58	2,955	84	4,676	566	21,497
Wisconsin	33,296	3,047,212	21,811	2,472,467	2,140	153,535	1,334	77,446	8,011	343,764
Wyoming	2,192	200,707	1,649	174,970	84	4,687	139	8,693	320	12,357

One Unit Structures as a Percent of Total Units
1996

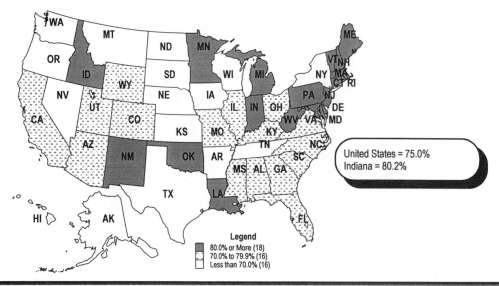

United States = 75.0%
Indiana = 80.2%

Legend
- 80.0% or More (18)
- 70.0% to 79.9% (16)
- Less than 70.0% (16)

Source: U.S. Bureau of the Census
EDIN table(s): BPHR, BPVR

Gross State Product

1.92 Gross State Product in Constant 1992 Dollars *(Millions)* 1984 to 1994 - Part I

	Total				Farms				Construction			
	1984	1989	1994	% Chg 1984 to 1994	1984	1989	1994	% Chg 1984 to 1994	1984	1989	1994	% Chg 1984 to 1994
United States	4,975,332	5,927,883	6,509,565	30.8	56,590	64,855	83,119	46.9	209,048	250,951	252,698	20.9
Alabama	64,037	74,533	84,612	32.1	815	1,115	1,529	87.6	2,194	2,788	3,282	49.6
Alaska	23,189	24,714	22,180	-4.4	13	14	18	38.5	2,101	747	974	-53.6
Arizona	59,065	72,159	89,557	51.6	645	836	819	27.0	4,367	3,712	4,802	10.0
Arkansas	36,334	39,872	48,358	33.1	1,209	1,363	2,058	70.2	1,406	1,301	1,732	23.2
California	641,150	822,183	835,391	30.3	6,558	8,581	11,296	72.2	26,996	36,753	27,427	1.6
Colorado	73,396	77,047	95,446	30.0	912	1,052	1,193	30.8	4,316	2,938	4,913	13.8
Connecticut	81,425	104,935	104,480	28.3	169	205	284	68.0	3,383	5,111	3,422	1.2
Delaware	15,487	22,189	25,173	62.5	130	232	223	71.5	744	776	835	12.2
Dist. Of Col.	38,418	44,208	44,747	16.5	0	0	0	NA	503	617	402	-20.1
Florida	211,649	269,420	301,960	42.7	2,377	3,348	3,437	44.6	12,365	14,256	13,696	10.8
Georgia	117,416	147,638	175,188	49.2	1,417	1,665	2,519	77.8	5,474	6,329	6,295	15.0
Hawaii	25,446	32,382	34,723	36.5	264	293	285	8.0	987	1,803	2,018	104.5
Idaho	16,199	18,027	23,044	42.3	882	1,171	1,274	44.4	710	760	1,442	103.1
Illinois	*253,418*	*288,101*	*317,414*	*25.3*	*2,513*	*2,818*	*3,555*	*41.5*	*9,680*	*12,512*	*13,221*	*36.6*
Indiana	**99,813**	**115,002**	**131,802**	**32.0**	**1,674**	**1,632**	**1,860**	**11.1**	**3,612**	**4,949**	**6,094**	**68.7**
Percent U.S.	*2.01*	*1.94*	*2.02*	*—*	*2.96*	*2.52*	*2.24*	*—*	*1.73*	*1.97*	*2.41*	*—*
Rank	*15*	*16*	*15*	*23*	*10*	*13*	*16*	*47*	*20*	*17*	*15*	*6*
Iowa	52,545	56,763	65,462	24.6	3,089	3,185	4,285	38.7	1,689	1,741	2,534	50.0
Kansas	48,966	53,267	59,058	20.6	1,562	1,534	2,558	63.8	2,024	1,817	2,255	11.4
Kentucky	*64,277*	*71,510*	*83,417*	*29.8*	*1,613*	*1,535*	*1,888*	*17.0*	*2,252*	*2,663*	*3,218*	*42.9*
Louisiana	96,054	92,574	97,016	1.0	696	623	892	28.2	5,137	3,273	4,201	-18.2
Maine	19,811	25,266	24,637	24.4	181	206	224	23.8	856	1,505	1,072	25.2
Maryland	94,477	121,370	125,676	33.0	444	558	608	36.9	4,845	7,880	6,134	26.6
Massachusetts	138,821	176,724	177,710	28.0	227	249	300	32.2	5,045	7,198	5,578	10.6
Michigan	*185,000*	*206,095*	*227,493*	*23.0*	*1,289*	*1,494*	*1,503*	*16.6*	*4,974*	*7,563*	*8,056*	*62.0*
Minnesota	90,701	104,770	118,923	31.1	2,681	2,873	2,854	6.5	3,520	4,424	4,992	41.8
Mississippi	36,584	40,357	48,180	31.7	906	790	1,270	40.2	1,305	1,314	1,741	33.4
Missouri	100,505	113,182	121,845	21.2	1,392	1,538	1,771	27.2	4,075	4,536	5,465	34.1
Montana	14,207	13,813	16,058	13.0	442	691	844	91.0	745	464	712	-4.4
Nebraska	31,070	33,719	39,644	27.6	2,011	2,484	3,195	58.9	1,049	1,053	1,608	53.3
Nevada	22,819	30,821	41,529	82.0	99	129	144	45.5	1,147	2,137	2,900	152.8
New Hampshire	19,493	26,609	28,140	44.4	51	81	95	86.3	1,101	1,512	968	-12.1
New Jersey	179,943	229,130	242,255	34.6	292	358	485	66.1	7,483	10,927	8,692	16.2
New Mexico	26,577	27,381	36,570	37.6	293	479	570	94.5	1,365	1,087	1,671	22.4
New York	460,338	531,816	545,091	18.4	1,116	1,306	1,414	26.7	14,255	19,812	15,637	9.7
North Carolina	125,484	156,211	177,549	41.5	1,750	1,978	3,458	97.6	4,384	5,966	6,643	51.5
North Dakota	12,708	11,434	12,971	2.1	1,049	790	1,300	23.9	677	404	552	-18.5
Ohio	*213,785*	*239,630*	*262,205*	*22.6*	*1,657*	*1,770*	*2,145*	*29.5*	*7,073*	*9,036*	*9,933*	*40.4*
Oklahoma	61,928	59,163	63,534	2.6	984	1,312	1,609	63.5	2,565	1,557	1,942	-24.3
Oregon	50,684	58,566	70,398	38.9	869	1,116	1,498	72.4	1,523	2,226	3,235	112.4
Pennsylvania	227,173	260,160	280,163	23.3	1,397	1,648	1,825	30.6	8,754	11,887	11,124	27.1
Rhode Island	18,517	23,363	22,711	22.6	36	45	56	55.6	604	1,044	771	27.6
South Carolina	54,644	67,834	76,793	40.5	493	524	732	48.5	2,210	3,401	3,260	47.5
South Dakota	12,201	13,202	16,526	35.4	1,163	1,043	1,661	42.8	404	432	616	52.5
Tennessee	84,332	101,584	120,686	43.1	980	877	1,256	28.2	3,248	3,912	4,390	35.2
Texas	363,168	393,323	461,857	27.2	3,165	3,292	5,442	71.9	19,997	14,212	18,794	-6.0
Utah	28,885	31,317	39,677	37.4	231	322	422	82.7	1,581	1,162	2,019	27.7
Vermont	9,273	12,297	12,652	36.4	160	207	237	48.1	466	704	538	15.5
Virginia	127,750	159,687	170,825	33.7	748	1,039	1,160	55.1	5,053	8,329	6,986	38.3
Washington	94,897	115,275	136,405	43.7	1,417	1,569	2,236	57.8	4,223	5,035	6,699	58.6
West Virginia	27,479	29,314	33,546	22.1	137	163	202	47.4	976	1,075	1,572	61.1
Wisconsin	91,329	103,477	119,984	31.4	2,226	2,503	2,328	4.6	2,911	3,893	5,077	74.4
Wyoming	13,124	12,683	15,560	18.6	166	220	300	80.7	695	417	555	-20.1

Gross State Product
Percent Change 1984 to 1994

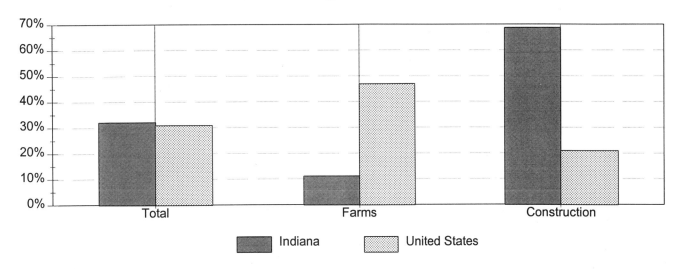

Legend: Indiana, United States

Source: U.S. Bureau of Economic Analysis
EDIN table(s): GSPR

1.93 Gross State Product in Constant 1992 Dollars *(Millions)* 1984 to 1994 - Part II

	Manufacturing				Manufacturing - Durable Goods				Manufacturing - Nondurable Goods			
	1984	1989	1994	% Chg 1984 to 1994	1984	1989	1994	% Chg 1984 to 1994	1984	1989	1994	% Chg to 1984 to 1994
United States	952,257	1,099,291	1,173,159	23.2	525,792	607,934	664,053	26.3	425,145	491,357	509,106	19.7
Alabama	14,301	17,186	18,784	31.3	6,808	7,982	9,100	33.7	7,493	9,204	9,684	29.2
Alaska	712	1,246	1,034	45.2	148	493	255	72.3	565	753	779	37.9
Arizona	6,998	9,019	13,764	96.7	5,368	6,694	11,084	106.5	1,629	2,325	2,680	64.5
Arkansas	8,446	10,073	12,127	43.6	4,398	5,109	6,477	47.3	4,048	4,964	5,650	39.6
California	99,168	122,986	120,475	21.5	62,659	80,048	77,465	23.6	36,509	42,938	43,009	17.8
Colorado	8,636	9,626	12,201	41.3	5,144	5,440	7,366	43.2	3,492	4,186	4,834	38.4
Connecticut	18,645	19,724	18,470	-0.9	13,241	13,543	12,366	-6.6	5,404	6,181	6,105	13.0
Delaware	4,670	5,214	5,120	9.6	1,233	1,260	1,388	12.6	3,437	3,955	3,732	8.6
Dist. Of Col.	1,439	1,740	1,175	-18.3	98	231	155	58.2	1,341	1,509	1,020	-23.9
Florida	21,913	25,790	26,034	18.8	12,122	14,652	15,017	23.9	9,791	11,138	11,016	12.5
Georgia	23,274	27,316	32,223	38.5	9,241	10,887	12,739	37.9	14,033	16,429	19,484	38.8
Hawaii	1,166	1,459	1,058	-9.3	142	272	280	97.2	1,024	1,187	778	-24.0
Idaho	2,546	3,476	4,406	73.1	1,213	2,039	2,895	138.7	1,333	1,437	1,511	13.4
Illinois	*48,606*	*55,276*	*61,511*	*26.6*	*25,698*	*30,639*	*35,637*	*38.7*	*22,907*	*24,638*	*25,873*	*12.9*
Indiana	30,212	34,801	40,595	34.4	21,378	23,366	28,403	32.9	8,835	11,435	12,193	38.0
Percent U.S.	3.17	3.17	3.46	148.28	4.07	3.84	4.28	125.10	2.08	2.33	2.39	192.89
Rank	10	10	9	20	8	8	8	30	18	15	16	13
Iowa	11,056	13,904	16,564	49.8	6,154	7,885	9,938	61.5	4,902	6,019	6,626	35.2
Kansas	8,568	9,706	10,331	20.6	4,471	5,031	5,518	23.4	4,097	4,675	4,812	17.5
Kentucky	*18,719*	*20,099*	*22,775*	*21.7*	*7,635*	*9,781*	*12,007*	*57.3*	*11,084*	*10,318*	*10,768*	*-2.9*
Louisiana	12,274	17,799	16,409	33.7	3,446	3,716	4,064	17.9	8,829	14,083	12,345	39.8
Maine	4,346	4,811	4,441	2.2	1,871	2,169	2,038	8.9	2,475	2,642	2,403	-2.9
Maryland	10,158	11,791	11,184	10.1	5,120	6,117	5,692	11.2	5,039	5,674	5,492	9.0
Massachusetts	28,995	32,468	30,490	5.2	19,442	22,765	20,749	6.7	9,552	9,703	9,741	2.0
Michigan	*60,388*	*59,025*	*67,426*	*11.7*	*48,784*	*44,554*	*51,076*	*4.7*	*11,604*	*14,470*	*16,350*	*40.9*
Minnesota	18,683	22,930	24,459	30.9	10,262	13,311	14,456	40.9	8,421	9,619	10,003	18.8
Mississippi	7,773	9,572	11,362	46.2	4,645	5,477	6,651	43.2	3,128	4,094	4,711	50.6
Missouri	22,422	25,975	25,934	15.7	13,819	14,608	13,971	1.1	8,603	11,367	11,963	39.1
Montana	1,166	1,247	1,163	-0.3	659	814	647	-1.8	507	433	517	2.0
Nebraska	4,173	4,869	5,928	42.1	2,174	2,384	3,114	43.2	1,999	2,485	2,814	40.8
Nevada	977	1,242	1,929	97.4	580	742	1,234	112.8	397	500	695	75.1
New Hampshire	4,563	5,690	6,128	34.3	3,074	4,033	4,445	44.6	1,489	1,657	1,683	13.0
New Jersey	35,151	38,828	35,627	1.4	15,077	14,377	12,235	-18.8	20,074	24,451	23,393	16.5
New Mexico	1,564	1,703	5,187	231.6	806	1,087	4,531	462.2	758	616	656	-13.5
New York	70,470	72,216	69,319	-1.6	35,011	37,072	35,998	2.8	35,459	35,144	33,321	-6.0
North Carolina	42,791	52,834	55,987	30.8	13,166	17,501	19,427	47.6	29,625	35,333	36,560	23.4
North Dakota	683	795	958	40.3	265	420	537	102.6	417	375	421	1.0
Ohio	*62,378*	*67,227*	*71,776*	*15.1*	*41,647*	*44,976*	*47,529*	*14.1*	*20,731*	*22,251*	*24,247*	*17.0*
Oklahoma	8,564	10,195	10,797	26.1	4,826	6,487	6,562	36.0	3,738	3,708	4,235	13.3
Oregon	10,351	12,553	13,970	35.0	7,649	9,283	10,532	37.7	2,701	3,270	3,438	27.3
Pennsylvania	49,328	51,670	56,528	14.6	26,085	28,602	29,900	14.6	23,242	23,068	26,629	14.6
Rhode Island	4,185	4,615	4,111	-1.8	2,894	3,402	2,755	-4.8	1,291	1,213	1,356	5.0
South Carolina	13,746	17,552	21,623	57.3	4,723	6,380	8,320	76.2	9,023	11,172	13,302	47.4
South Dakota	1,126	1,278	1,953	73.4	647	821	1,440	122.6	479	457	512	6.9
Tennessee	20,395	24,970	29,680	45.5	9,773	12,107	15,492	58.5	10,622	12,863	14,188	33.6
Texas	52,651	66,769	74,029	40.6	24,349	29,678	39,922	64.0	28,302	37,091	34,106	20.5
Utah	3,876	4,529	5,681	46.6	2,591	3,046	3,713	43.3	1,285	1,484	1,967	53.1
Vermont	1,900	2,497	2,261	19.0	1,305	1,848	1,594	22.1	595	649	667	12.1
Virginia	25,158	26,669	28,045	11.5	7,880	10,055	10,656	35.2	17,278	16,615	17,389	0.6
Washington	14,908	20,896	19,268	29.2	9,855	14,363	13,070	32.6	5,053	6,533	6,198	22.7
West Virginia	4,599	5,471	5,577	21.3	2,117	2,487	2,403	13.5	2,482	2,983	3,174	27.9
Wisconsin	24,851	29,407	34,659	39.5	14,468	17,741	21,008	45.2	10,382	11,666	13,650	31.5
Wyoming	536	552	623	16.2	155	154	199	28.4	380	398	424	11.6

Gross State Product
Percent Change 1984 to 1994

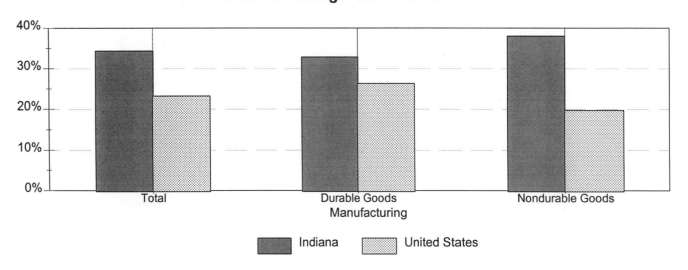

Manufacturing

Indiana   United States

Source: U.S. Bureau of Economic Analysis
EDIN table(s): GSPR

1.94 Gross State Product in Constant 1992 Dollars *(Millions)* 1984 to 1994 - Part III

	Transport., Comm., and Public Utilities				Wholesale Trade				Retail Trade			
	1984	1989	1994	% Chg 1984 to 1994	1984	1989	1994	% Chg 1984 to 1994	1984	1989	1994	% Chg 1984 to 1994
United States	421,147	477,669	584,152	38.7	290,190	367,439	451,425	55.6	465,555	552,731	595,075	27.8
Alabama	6,327	7,143	8,512	34.5	3,354	4,089	5,390	60.7	6,342	7,397	8,708	37.3
Alaska	3,805	3,788	3,849	1.2	566	502	657	16.1	1,491	1,265	1,501	0.7
Arizona	4,614	5,774	8,041	74.3	2,758	3,912	5,549	101.2	6,527	8,037	9,790	50.0
Arkansas	3,640	4,330	5,978	64.2	1,814	2,189	3,008	65.8	3,794	4,013	5,066	33.5
California	45,096	54,560	60,636	34.5	36,836	49,930	58,508	58.8	62,728	76,644	77,724	23.9
Colorado	6,364	7,420	10,629	67.0	3,953	4,406	6,197	56.8	7,769	7,878	9,794	26.1
Connecticut	5,304	6,272	7,403	39.6	4,504	6,699	7,163	59.0	7,234	9,677	8,599	18.9
Delaware	994	1,271	1,303	31.1	615	818	1,023	66.3	1,069	1,384	1,476	38.1
Dist. Of Col.	1,983	2,282	2,496	25.9	555	590	564	1.6	1,488	1,636	1,334	-10.3
Florida	17,982	21,522	28,804	60.2	11,983	17,108	22,132	84.7	23,581	31,778	34,913	48.1
Georgia	11,467	14,671	21,069	83.7	9,325	12,865	15,986	71.4	11,307	14,275	16,307	44.2
Hawaii	2,107	2,833	3,346	58.8	823	1,135	1,382	67.9	2,549	3,679	3,964	55.5
Idaho	1,459	1,460	2,113	44.8	831	962	1,423	71.2	1,683	1,880	2,442	45.1
Illinois	*23,154*	*25,321*	*30,750*	*32.8*	*17,528*	*22,208*	*26,037*	*48.5*	*22,974*	*26,459*	*26,879*	*17.0*
Indiana	8,744	10,077	10,988	25.7	4,791	6,253	8,193	71.0	9,592	11,143	12,425	29.5
Percent U.S.	2.08	2.11	1.88	—	1.65	1.70	1.81	—	2.06	2.02	2.09	—
Rank	15	15	16	35	20	20	18	14	15	16	16	23
Iowa	4,434	4,596	5,188	17.0	3,258	3,656	4,611	41.5	4,760	4,976	5,821	22.3
Kansas	5,474	6,435	7,250	32.4	3,082	3,504	4,442	44.1	4,468	5,058	5,811	30.1
Kentucky	*4,982*	*5,663*	*8,015*	*60.9*	*2,827*	*3,503*	*4,662*	*64.9*	*5,818*	*6,449*	*7,465*	*28.3*
Louisiana	9,850	8,961	10,731	8.9	4,807	4,670	5,653	17.6	8,622	7,856	8,505	-1.4
Maine	1,494	1,678	1,790	19.8	943	1,375	1,476	56.5	2,131	2,975	3,082	44.6
Maryland	6,759	8,903	10,706	58.4	5,301	7,114	8,013	51.2	9,263	12,129	11,501	24.2
Massachusetts	8,737	10,159	12,352	41.4	8,080	11,435	12,937	60.1	12,043	15,913	14,424	19.8
Michigan	*12,742*	*14,764*	*15,498*	*21.6*	*9,176*	*12,418*	*16,003*	*74.4*	*15,646*	*18,426*	*19,472*	*24.5*
Minnesota	7,467	8,151	9,226	23.6	6,118	7,433	9,833	60.7	8,512	9,728	10,863	27.6
Mississippi	3,688	4,579	6,004	62.8	1,780	2,132	2,776	56.0	4,106	4,144	4,887	19.0
Missouri	10,362	11,797	13,001	25.5	6,096	7,604	9,194	50.8	9,919	11,031	12,189	22.9
Montana	1,753	1,770	2,101	19.9	786	769	1,025	30.4	1,403	1,336	1,672	19.2
Nebraska	3,114	3,218	4,523	45.2	2,061	2,434	3,076	49.2	2,826	2,946	3,403	20.4
Nevada	2,001	2,577	3,252	62.5	777	1,228	1,945	150.3	2,248	3,027	3,985	77.3
New Hampshire	1,358	1,188	2,231	64.3	899	1,370	1,703	89.4	1,928	2,857	2,842	47.4
New Jersey	16,660	19,514	24,720	48.4	12,792	17,907	22,846	78.6	14,754	19,243	18,631	26.3
New Mexico	2,674	2,704	3,555	32.9	1,029	1,162	1,608	56.3	2,497	2,726	3,465	38.8
New York	37,514	37,834	44,771	19.3	30,486	33,159	34,877	14.4	32,807	40,295	39,032	19.0
North Carolina	9,493	11,518	13,748	44.8	6,100	8,675	11,428	87.3	11,194	14,148	15,940	42.4
North Dakota	1,279	1,159	1,458	14.0	930	968	1,226	31.8	1,150	1,112	1,260	9.6
Ohio	*18,190*	*19,019*	*21,743*	*19.5*	*11,408*	*14,196*	*18,116*	*58.8*	*19,849*	*22,757*	*25,292*	*27.4*
Oklahoma	5,707	5,403	7,023	23.1	3,293	3,304	3,960	20.3	6,381	5,955	6,501	1.9
Oregon	4,589	4,625	5,688	23.9	3,202	4,213	5,755	79.7	4,656	5,367	6,609	41.9
Pennsylvania	19,826	22,348	26,257	32.4	12,240	15,222	17,607	43.8	20,644	24,932	25,878	25.4
Rhode Island	968	1,204	1,666	72.1	907	1,231	1,245	37.3	1,762	2,286	2,150	22.0
South Carolina	4,465	5,500	6,158	37.9	2,695	3,489	4,269	58.4	5,319	6,854	7,847	47.5
South Dakota	1,087	1,051	1,325	21.9	700	800	1,052	50.3	1,265	1,296	1,612	27.4
Tennessee	6,158	7,140	10,273	66.8	5,221	6,815	9,024	72.8	9,235	11,057	13,543	46.6
Texas	34,630	38,216	51,285	48.1	22,571	25,829	34,569	53.2	34,630	35,783	41,593	20.1
Utah	3,084	3,068	3,870	25.5	1,554	1,850	2,474	59.2	2,713	3,087	4,164	53.5
Vermont	749	898	1,179	57.4	439	676	852	94.1	943	1,264	1,291	36.9
Virginia	9,729	12,008	14,901	53.2	5,627	7,944	9,475	68.4	10,669	13,981	14,460	35.5
Washington	6,949	8,384	11,178	60.9	6,206	7,923	10,636	71.4	9,452	11,531	14,116	49.3
West Virginia	3,363	3,543	4,428	31.7	1,374	1,456	1,794	30.6	2,669	2,751	2,983	11.8
Wisconsin	6,912	7,436	8,512	23.1	4,706	5,912	7,570	60.9	8,163	9,473	10,850	32.9
Wyoming	1,942	1,933	2,628	35.3	481	397	480	-0.2	978	835	1,015	3.8

Gross State Product
Percent Change 1984 to 1994

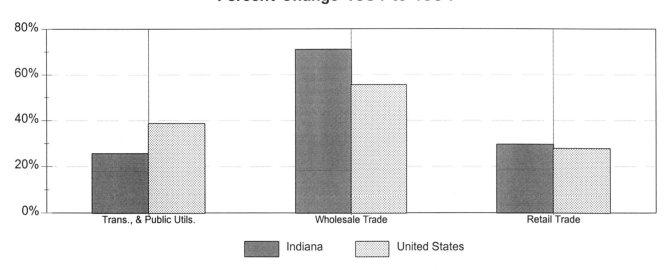

Source: U.S. Bureau of Economic Analysis
EDIN table(s): GSPR

	Finance, Insurance, and Real Estate				Services				Government			
	1984	1989	1994	% Chg 1984 to 1994	1984	1989	1994	% Chg 1984 to 1994	1984	1989	1994	% Chg 1984 to 1994
United States	941,118	1,101,764	1,193,505	26.8	914,419	1,145,691	1,249,534	36.6	704,049	780,447	815,970	15.9
Alabama	8,790	9,103	10,112	15.0	9,108	11,426	13,017	42.9	11,678	13,082	13,556	16.1
Alaska	2,701	2,185	2,355	-12.8	2,567	2,289	2,473	-3.7	4,632	4,524	4,491	-3.0
Arizona	11,590	13,270	15,938	37.5	11,012	14,783	16,874	53.2	9,814	11,717	12,321	25.5
Arkansas	5,270	4,858	5,304	0.6	5,183	5,904	6,712	29.5	4,996	5,254	5,686	13.8
California	135,136	188,112	186,955	38.3	134,110	174,781	180,501	34.6	85,730	100,160	100,711	17.5
Colorado	14,802	13,530	15,780	6.6	13,450	15,995	19,273	43.3	11,764	12,390	13,230	12.5
Connecticut	18,292	26,406	27,526	50.5	14,832	20,563	21,316	43.7	8,790	9,834	9,804	11.5
Delaware	3,309	7,308	9,719	193.7	2,074	3,021	3,169	52.8	1,842	2,109	2,234	21.3
Dist. Of Col.	4,957	6,813	6,482	30.8	10,920	13,800	14,655	34.2	16,563	16,713	17,621	6.4
Florida	46,043	57,497	63,897	38.8	44,293	59,353	67,469	52.3	28,808	36,203	38,401	33.3
Georgia	18,231	23,532	26,674	46.3	17,397	24,415	29,780	71.2	18,629	21,386	22,885	22.8
Hawaii	5,596	7,499	7,970	42.4	5,037	6,400	7,055	40.1	6,842	7,155	7,439	8.7
Idaho	2,542	2,378	2,898	14.0	2,615	2,917	3,506	34.1	2,583	2,693	3,130	21.2
Illinois	*49,776*	*53,650*	*58,559*	*17.6*	*48,466*	*57,274*	*62,353*	*28.7*	*28,872*	*30,374*	*31,947*	*10.7*
Indiana	**14,444**	**15,009**	**17,052**	**18.1**	**14,639**	**17,627**	**19,728**	**34.8**	**11,391**	**12,567**	**13,557**	**19.0**
Percent U.S.	*1.53*	*1.36*	*1.43*	—	*1.60*	*1.54*	*1.58*	—	*1.62*	*1.61*	*1.66*	—
Rank	*22*	*20*	*20*	*30*	*21*	*20*	*20*	*27*	*21*	*20*	*18*	*17*
Iowa	8,801	8,119	8,802	0.0	8,232	8,822	9,330	13.3	6,830	7,365	7,671	12.3
Kansas	7,601	7,268	7,292	-4.1	7,763	8,714	9,281	19.6	7,370	7,976	8,657	17.5
Kentucky	*8,337*	*8,339*	*8,925*	*7.1*	*8,666*	*10,421*	*11,509*	*32.8*	*8,990*	*10,180*	*11,203*	*24.6*
Louisiana	17,021	12,170	12,423	-27.0	14,102	14,200	15,494	9.9	11,491	10,720	11,712	1.9
Maine	3,199	4,282	4,375	36.8	3,282	4,425	4,447	35.5	3,254	3,763	3,478	6.9
Maryland	18,566	24,953	27,385	47.5	18,898	25,940	27,561	45.8	19,892	21,529	21,913	10.2
Massachusetts	28,419	38,822	40,230	41.6	31,968	42,508	44,026	37.7	14,842	17,178	16,558	11.6
Michigan	*27,852*	*30,834*	*34,065*	*22.3*	*29,967*	*36,447*	*39,322*	*31.2*	*21,734*	*23,513*	*24,412*	*12.3*
Minnesota	16,006	17,119	20,391	27.4	15,835	19,324	22,204	40.2	11,023	12,107	13,154	19.3
Mississippi	4,947	4,855	5,293	7.0	4,771	5,170	7,013	47.0	6,390	6,894	7,198	12.6
Missouri	15,233	15,945	17,487	14.8	18,210	20,902	22,399	23.0	12,228	13,150	13,538	10.7
Montana	2,310	1,875	2,124	-8.1	2,321	2,418	2,829	21.9	2,516	2,415	2,576	2.4
Nebraska	5,244	5,095	5,448	3.9	4,924	5,661	6,250	26.9	5,443	5,686	5,835	7.2
Nevada	3,757	5,281	7,565	101.4	8,348	10,669	13,971	67.4	3,032	3,624	4,366	44.0
New Hampshire	3,930	5,905	6,040	53.7	3,476	5,195	5,310	52.8	2,113	2,686	2,670	26.4
New Jersey	35,601	50,507	53,568	50.5	35,179	46,926	50,531	43.6	21,543	24,176	26,225	21.7
New Mexico	4,352	3,917	4,815	10.6	4,494	5,227	6,166	37.2	5,776	5,945	6,488	12.3
New York	123,311	143,860	156,596	27.0	96,250	120,012	120,633	25.3	53,060	61,880	61,277	15.5
North Carolina	16,194	19,069	21,926	35.4	15,201	20,396	24,474	61.0	17,643	20,735	23,000	30.4
North Dakota	1,843	1,524	1,556	-15.6	2,018	1,974	2,121	5.1	2,179	2,058	2,081	-4.5
Ohio	*31,559*	*35,103*	*38,656*	*22.5*	*35,610*	*42,147*	*44,408*	*24.7*	*24,313*	*26,391*	*27,842*	*14.5*
Oklahoma	9,707	7,065	7,660	-21.1	9,306	9,718	9,993	7.4	10,572	10,151	10,266	-2.9
Oregon	9,163	9,383	11,659	27.2	8,600	10,498	12,305	43.1	7,343	8,022	8,920	21.5
Pennsylvania	40,457	45,803	50,403	24.6	45,120	55,573	57,802	28.1	27,500	28,618	29,796	8.3
Rhode Island	3,729	5,206	5,095	36.6	3,610	4,768	4,771	32.2	2,637	2,821	2,699	2.4
South Carolina	7,781	8,758	9,594	23.3	6,866	9,213	10,806	57.4	10,778	12,130	12,021	11.5
South Dakota	2,426	2,967	3,282	35.3	1,880	2,053	2,494	32.7	1,966	2,051	2,201	12.0
Tennessee	12,525	13,618	15,223	21.5	14,671	18,642	21,961	49.7	11,361	13,885	14,553	28.1
Texas	66,444	57,980	64,276	-3.3	58,499	68,501	79,562	36.0	46,314	50,693	55,384	19.6
Utah	4,715	4,309	5,500	16.6	4,852	6,016	7,670	58.1	5,498	5,766	6,239	13.5
Vermont	1,638	2,202	2,147	31.1	1,730	2,304	2,502	44.6	1,177	1,444	1,538	30.7
Virginia	20,433	27,616	28,904	41.5	19,930	28,181	31,484	58.0	29,438	32,541	33,544	13.9
Washington	17,390	20,343	24,223	39.3	15,844	19,619	25,827	63.0	17,829	18,500	20,481	14.9
West Virginia	4,000	3,492	3,595	-10.1	4,289	4,492	5,048	17.7	3,987	3,969	4,382	9.9
Wisconsin	15,317	15,641	18,204	18.8	14,805	16,876	18,795	27.0	11,013	11,822	13,154	19.4
Wyoming	1,943	1,389	1,556	-19.9	1,273	1,190	1,358	6.7	2,044	1,900	1,920	-6.1

Gross State Product
Percent Change 1984 to 1994

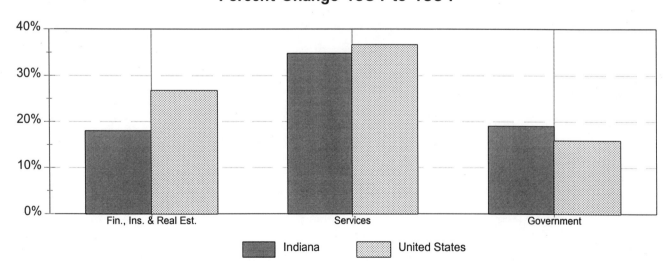

Source: U.S. Bureau of Economic Analysis
EDIN table(s): GSPR

SECTION 2

Counties in Perspective:
Indiana and 92 Counties

**Population Density
Persons Per Square Mile
1997**

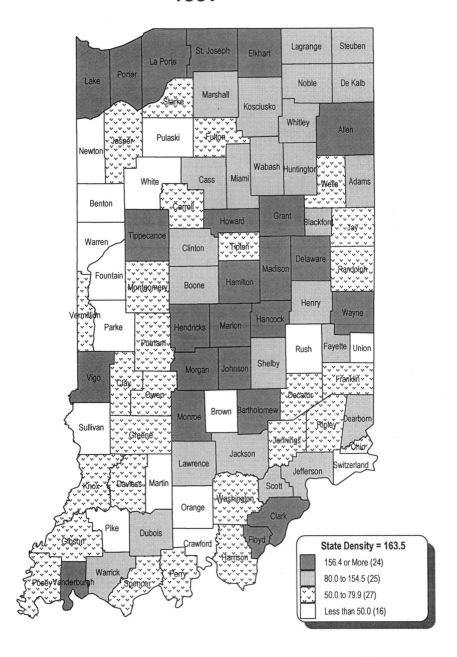

State Density = 163.5

156.4 or More (24)
80.0 to 154.5 (25)
50.0 to 79.9 (27)
Less than 50.0 (16)

Population Density: EDIN Table(s) POPD, POPE.

Percent Change in Population
1990 to 1997

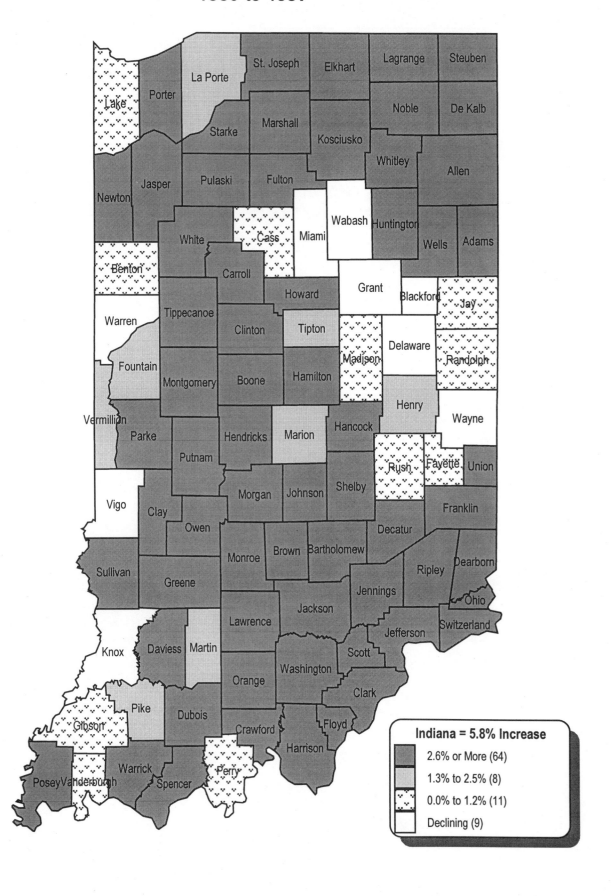

Indiana = 5.8% Increase

2.6% or More (64)

1.3% to 2.5% (8)

0.0% to 1.2% (11)

Declining (9)

Percent Change in Population: EDIN table(s): POPU, POPE

Population
2.1 Counts and Estimates 1980 TO 1997

	Census Counts				Estimates					
	1980	Percent of State	1990	Percent of State	1992	1993	1994	1995	1996	1997
Indiana	5,490,210	100.00	5,544,159	100.00	5,647,853	5,700,243	5,741,540	5,787,839	5,828,090	5,864,108
Adams	29,619	0.54	31,095	0.56	31,467	31,645	32,058	32,387	32,653	32,837
Allen	294,335	5.36	300,836	5.43	304,322	305,856	306,880	308,021	310,073	312,091
Bartholomew	65,088	1.19	63,657	1.15	65,234	66,032	66,847	67,883	68,372	68,734
Benton	10,218	0.19	9,441	0.17	9,647	9,623	9,592	9,698	9,594	9,557
Blackford	15,570	0.28	14,067	0.25	14,030	13,961	13,911	14,045	14,112	14,020
Boone	36,446	0.66	38,147	0.69	39,479	40,192	40,887	41,678	42,366	42,985
Brown	12,377	0.23	14,080	0.25	14,663	14,940	14,913	15,097	15,329	15,591
Carroll	19,722	0.36	18,809	0.34	19,276	19,313	19,534	19,551	19,606	19,989
Cass	40,936	0.75	38,413	0.69	38,538	38,602	38,461	38,449	38,644	38,573
Clark	88,838	1.62	87,777	1.58	89,309	89,996	90,654	91,379	92,326	93,212
Clay	24,862	0.45	24,705	0.45	25,112	25,664	25,756	26,247	26,487	26,531
Clinton	31,545	0.57	30,974	0.56	31,741	32,019	32,250	32,455	32,920	33,232
Crawford	9,820	0.18	9,914	0.18	10,022	10,176	10,348	10,351	10,536	10,499
Daviess	27,836	0.51	27,533	0.50	27,864	28,048	28,163	28,509	28,651	28,851
Dearborn	34,291	0.62	38,835	0.70	41,178	42,127	43,266	44,392	45,298	46,576
Decatur	23,841	0.43	23,645	0.43	24,282	24,422	24,660	24,906	25,077	25,362
Dekalb	33,606	0.61	35,324	0.64	36,634	36,988	37,423	37,763	38,131	38,722
Delaware	128,587	2.34	119,659	2.16	119,463	119,690	118,924	118,745	118,274	117,625
Dubois	34,238	0.62	36,616	0.66	37,498	37,859	38,179	38,776	39,019	39,139
Elkhart	137,330	2.50	156,198	2.82	159,182	161,699	163,825	166,594	168,811	170,725
Fayette	28,272	0.51	26,015	0.47	26,140	26,207	26,205	26,223	26,214	26,133
Floyd	61,205	1.11	64,404	1.16	67,088	68,118	68,990	69,847	70,636	71,465
Fountain	19,033	0.35	17,808	0.32	17,901	17,938	17,974	18,033	18,194	18,235
Franklin	19,612	0.36	19,580	0.35	19,860	19,982	20,216	20,967	21,326	21,582
Fulton	19,335	0.35	18,840	0.34	19,119	19,449	19,654	19,848	20,159	20,351
Gibson	33,156	0.60	31,913	0.58	31,796	32,017	31,953	31,941	31,964	31,948
Grant	80,934	1.47	74,169	1.34	74,135	73,797	73,634	73,620	73,271	72,818
Greene	30,416	0.55	30,410	0.55	31,366	31,983	32,281	32,642	32,898	33,074
Hamilton	82,027	1.49	108,936	1.96	120,934	127,337	134,124	140,771	147,710	154,785
Hancock	43,939	0.80	45,527	0.82	47,420	48,128	49,410	50,895	51,980	53,071
Harrison	27,276	0.50	29,890	0.54	30,646	31,273	31,869	32,531	33,226	33,999
Hendricks	69,804	1.27	75,717	1.37	79,503	81,952	84,086	86,529	89,230	92,291
Henry	53,336	0.97	48,139	0.87	48,601	48,650	48,849	49,070	48,957	48,867
Howard	86,896	1.58	80,827	1.46	82,242	82,852	83,047	83,246	83,837	83,586
Huntington	35,596	0.65	35,427	0.64	35,762	36,144	36,365	36,757	36,938	37,144
Jackson	36,523	0.67	37,730	0.68	38,625	39,113	39,346	40,230	40,446	40,884
Jasper	26,138	0.48	24,960	0.45	25,935	26,532	27,284	27,793	28,282	28,697
Jay	23,239	0.42	21,512	0.39	21,744	21,714	21,694	21,719	21,708	21,692
Jefferson	30,419	0.55	29,797	0.54	30,308	30,469	30,669	30,800	30,978	31,292
Jennings	22,854	0.42	23,661	0.43	24,325	24,940	25,482	26,068	26,682	27,217
Johnson	77,240	1.41	88,109	1.59	93,553	96,525	98,837	101,525	104,296	106,888
Knox	41,838	0.76	39,884	0.72	39,978	39,976	40,001	39,690	39,602	39,686
Kosciusko	59,555	1.08	65,294	1.18	65,900	66,723	67,878	68,984	69,745	70,363
Lagrange	25,550	0.47	29,477	0.53	30,214	30,551	31,026	31,761	32,132	32,719
Lake	522,917	9.52	475,594	8.58	479,168	479,491	479,827	479,755	479,016	479,339
Laporte	108,632	1.98	107,066	1.93	108,917	109,417	109,482	109,416	109,260	109,080
Lawrence	42,472	0.77	42,836	0.77	43,334	43,874	44,402	44,986	45,278	45,539
Madison	139,336	2.54	130,669	2.36	131,425	131,818	132,454	132,420	132,370	131,840
Marion	765,233	13.94	797,159	14.38	810,568	813,122	815,293	815,011	814,854	813,670
Marshall	39,155	0.71	42,182	0.76	43,125	43,530	44,103	44,648	45,169	45,337
Martin	11,001	0.20	10,369	0.19	10,431	10,437	10,554	10,492	10,585	10,510
Miami	39,820	0.73	36,897	0.67	36,935	36,233	34,287	32,398	32,465	33,199
Monroe	98,783	1.80	108,978	1.97	110,526	112,625	113,581	115,238	115,917	116,653
Montgomery	35,501	0.65	34,436	0.62	35,080	35,486	35,795	36,075	36,213	36,285
Morgan	51,999	0.95	55,920	1.01	58,492	59,371	60,815	61,904	63,215	64,787
Newton	14,844	0.27	13,551	0.24	13,871	13,978	14,068	14,383	14,550	14,683
Noble	35,443	0.65	37,877	0.68	38,637	39,410	40,002	40,802	41,478	41,918
Ohio	5,114	0.09	5,315	0.10	5,316	5,459	5,467	5,430	5,451	5,458
Orange	18,677	0.34	18,409	0.33	18,552	18,696	18,807	18,967	19,204	19,378
Owen	15,841	0.29	17,281	0.31	18,255	18,792	19,215	19,601	20,095	20,257
Parke	16,372	0.30	15,410	0.28	15,686	15,898	15,926	16,114	16,352	16,446
Perry	19,346	0.35	19,107	0.34	18,933	19,011	19,015	19,119	19,156	19,306
Pike	13,465	0.25	12,509	0.23	12,416	12,503	12,554	12,506	12,558	12,758
Porter	119,816	2.18	128,932	2.33	134,102	135,789	137,561	140,044	142,116	144,084
Posey	26,414	0.48	25,968	0.47	26,055	26,141	26,218	26,331	26,443	26,640
Pulaski	13,258	0.24	12,643	0.23	12,899	12,937	13,002	13,115	13,091	13,212
Putnam	29,163	0.53	30,315	0.55	31,346	31,823	32,510	32,915	33,412	33,706
Randolph	29,997	0.55	27,148	0.49	27,035	27,159	27,156	27,382	27,493	27,480
Ripley	24,398	0.44	24,616	0.44	25,423	25,932	26,339	26,666	26,933	27,177
Rush	19,604	0.36	18,129	0.33	18,236	18,360	18,419	18,293	18,198	18,236
St. Joseph	241,617	4.40	247,052	4.46	250,212	253,218	254,873	256,479	257,338	258,056
Scott	20,422	0.37	20,991	0.38	21,504	21,948	22,109	22,402	22,635	22,818
Shelby	39,887	0.73	40,307	0.73	41,183	41,827	42,196	42,735	42,816	43,151
Spencer	19,361	0.35	19,490	0.35	19,700	19,849	20,097	20,315	20,506	20,690
Starke	21,997	0.40	22,747	0.41	22,500	22,241	22,218	22,568	23,352	23,759
Steuben	24,694	0.45	27,446	0.50	28,287	28,748	29,222	30,113	30,786	31,102
Sullivan	21,107	0.38	18,993	0.34	18,989	19,284	20,044	20,323	20,116	20,280
Switzerland	7,153	0.13	7,738	0.14	7,987	8,096	8,124	8,257	8,393	8,636
Tippecanoe	121,702	2.22	130,598	2.36	133,048	135,077	135,890	137,304	138,164	138,307
Tipton	16,819	0.31	16,119	0.29	16,126	16,327	16,340	16,418	16,413	16,395
Union	6,860	0.12	6,976	0.13	7,134	7,271	7,303	7,337	7,325	7,272
Vanderburgh	167,515	3.05	165,058	2.98	166,718	167,377	167,353	167,114	167,150	166,837
Vermillion	18,229	0.33	16,773	0.30	16,628	16,807	16,746	16,812	16,834	16,997
Vigo	112,385	2.05	106,107	1.91	107,077	107,336	106,725	106,347	106,043	104,940
Wabash	36,640	0.67	35,069	0.63	34,766	34,657	34,609	34,738	34,609	34,525
Warren	8,976	0.16	8,176	0.15	8,168	8,180	8,101	8,222	8,141	8,170
Warrick	41,474	0.76	44,920	0.81	46,489	47,417	48,446	49,214	49,983	50,831
Washington	21,932	0.40	23,717	0.43	24,411	24,909	25,333	26,039	26,641	27,143
Wayne	76,058	1.39	71,951	1.30	71,912	72,262	72,156	72,215	71,879	71,800
Wells	25,401	0.46	25,948	0.47	26,052	26,121	26,206	26,462	26,565	26,773
White	23,867	0.43	23,265	0.42	23,758	24,017	24,175	24,578	25,043	25,041
Whitley	26,215	0.48	27,651	0.50	28,405	28,760	29,017	29,420	29,796	29,969

Footnote: 1980 and 1990 are Census figures. 1992-1997 data are estimates.
Source: U.S. Bureau of the Census
EDIN table(s): POPU, POPE

2.2 Ten Year Changes in Population 1960 to 2000

| | Census Counts | | | | | | | | | Projections | | |
| | 1960-1970 | | | 1970-1980 | | | 1980-1990 | | | 1990-2000 | | |
	Number	Percent	Rank	Number	Percent	Rank	Number	Percent	Rank	Number	Percent	Rank
Indiana	532,894	11.4	—	294,818	5.7	—	53,949	1.0	—	158,841	2.9	—
Adams	2,228	9.0	37	2,748	10.2	44	1,476	5.0	25	2,505	8.1	5
Allen	48,259	20.8	10	13,880	4.9	59	6,501	2.2	35	14,364	4.8	23
Bartholomew	8,824	18.3	17	8,066	14.1	27	-1,431	-2.2	58	1,143	1.8	43
Benton	-650	-5.5	90	-1,044	-9.3	92	-777	-7.6	82	59	0.6	54
Blackford	1,096	7.4	47	-318	-2.0	86	-1,503	-9.7	90	-467	-3.3	85
Boone	3,327	12.1	28	5,576	18.1	19	1,701	4.7	26	1,753	4.6	24
Brown	2,033	28.9	8	3,320	36.7	4	1,703	13.8	4	820	5.8	13
Carroll	800	4.7	58	1,988	11.2	42	-913	-4.6	66	91	0.5	57
Cass	-475	-1.2	83	480	1.2	76	-2,523	-6.2	73	-413	-1.1	73
Clark	13,081	20.8	10	12,962	17.1	22	-1,061	-1.2	50	-577	-0.7	66
Clay	-274	-1.1	82	929	3.9	66	-157	-0.6	47	-205	-0.8	71
Clinton	-218	-0.7	81	998	3.3	68	-571	-1.8	56	326	1.1	49
Crawford	-346	-4.1	88	1,787	22.2	15	94	1.0	40	286	2.9	37
Daviess	-34	-0.1	78	1,234	4.6	61	-303	-1.1	49	467	1.7	45
Dearborn	756	2.6	65	4,861	16.5	23	4,544	13.3	6	2,865	7.4	8
Decatur	2,719	13.6	22	1,103	4.9	59	-196	-0.8	48	355	1.5	46
Dekalb	2,566	9.1	36	2,769	9.0	49	1,718	5.1	24	1,776	5.0	20
Delaware	18,281	16.5	20	-632	-0.5	81	-8,928	-6.9	76	1,841	1.5	46
Dubois	3,471	12.6	25	3,304	10.7	43	2,378	6.9	20	1,584	4.3	25
Elkhart	19,739	18.5	16	10,801	8.5	52	18,868	13.7	5	13,402	8.6	4
Fayette	1,762	7.2	48	2,056	7.8	54	-2,257	-8.0	83	-415	-1.6	75
Floyd	4,225	8.2	41	5,583	10.0	47	3,199	5.2	23	2,496	3.9	28
Fountain	-449	-2.4	85	776	4.3	64	-1,225	-6.4	75	-608	-3.4	88
Franklin	-72	-0.4	80	2,669	15.8	25	-32	-0.2	45	820	4.2	27
Fulton	27	0.2	76	2,351	13.8	29	-495	-2.6	60	160	0.8	52
Gibson	495	1.7	72	2,712	8.9	50	-1,243	-3.7	62	-613	-1.9	76
Grant	8,214	10.8	32	-3,021	-3.6	87	-6,765	-8.4	85	-2,469	-3.3	85
Greene	567	2.2	68	3,522	13.1	33	-6	0.0	44	-10	0.0	59
Hamilton	14,400	35.9	4	27,495	50.4	1	26,909	32.8	1	18,864	17.3	1
Hancock	8,431	31.6	6	8,843	25.2	11	1,588	3.6	30	1,973	4.3	25
Harrison	1,216	6.3	54	6,853	33.6	5	2,614	9.6	9	1,610	5.4	16
Hendricks	13,078	32.0	5	15,830	29.3	7	5,913	8.5	12	4,383	5.8	13
Henry	3,704	7.6	45	733	1.4	74	-5,197	-9.7	90	-1,639	-3.4	88
Howard	13,689	19.7	13	3,698	4.4	63	-6,069	-7.0	77	-327	-0.4	61
Huntington	1,156	3.4	61	626	1.8	72	-169	-0.5	46	673	1.9	42
Jackson	2,631	8.6	39	3,336	10.1	45	1,207	3.3	33	870	2.3	40
Jasper	1,587	8.4	40	5,709	27.9	8	-1,178	-4.5	65	740	3.0	35
Jay	1,003	4.4	59	-336	-1.4	84	-1,727	-7.4	80	-112	-0.5	63
Jefferson	2,945	12.2	27	3,413	12.6	36	-622	-2.0	57	-297	-1.0	72
Jennings	2,187	12.7	24	3,400	17.5	21	807	3.5	31	639	2.7	39
Johnson	17,434	39.9	3	16,102	26.3	10	10,869	14.1	3	5,991	6.8	10
Knox	-15	0.0	77	292	0.7	78	-1,954	-4.7	68	-884	-2.2	80
Kosciusko	7,754	19.2	14	11,428	23.7	12	5,739	9.6	9	5,006	7.7	6
Lagrange	3,510	20.2	12	4,660	22.3	14	3,927	15.4	2	4,323	14.7	2
Lake	32,984	6.4	53	-23,336	-4.3	91	-47,323	-9.0	88	-5,194	-1.1	73
Laporte	10,231	10.8	32	3,290	3.1	69	-1,566	-1.4	52	1,134	1.1	49
Lawrence	1,474	4.0	60	4,434	11.7	40	364	0.9	41	-36	-0.1	60
Madison	12,703	10.1	35	814	0.6	79	-8,667	-6.2	73	-2,469	-1.9	76
Marion	96,202	13.8	21	-28,536	-3.6	87	31,926	4.2	27	44,141	5.5	15
Marshall	2,543	7.8	44	4,169	11.9	38	3,027	7.7	16	2,118	5.0	20
Martin	361	3.4	61	32	0.3	80	-632	-5.7	71	-69	-0.7	66
Miami	1,246	3.3	63	574	1.5	73	-2,923	-7.3	79	-4,497	-12.2	92
Monroe	25,996	43.9	2	13,562	15.9	24	10,195	10.3	8	9,922	9.1	3
Montgomery	1,841	5.7	55	1,571	4.6	61	-1,065	-3.0	61	264	0.8	52
Morgan	10,301	30.4	7	7,823	17.7	20	3,921	7.5	18	3,480	6.2	11
Newton	104	0.9	74	3,238	27.9	8	-1,293	-8.7	86	-51	-0.4	61
Noble	3,220	11.4	30	4,061	12.9	35	2,434	6.9	20	2,323	6.1	12
Ohio	124	3.0	64	825	19.2	17	201	3.9	29	285	5.4	16
Orange	91	0.5	75	1,709	10.1	45	-268	-1.4	52	-109	-0.6	64
Owen	763	6.7	50	3,678	30.2	6	1,440	9.1	11	1,219	7.1	9
Parke	-176	-1.2	83	1,744	11.9	38	-962	-5.9	72	-310	-2.0	78
Perry	1,843	10.7	34	271	1.4	74	-239	-1.2	50	-107	-0.6	64
Pike	-516	-4.0	87	1,184	9.6	48	-956	-7.1	78	-409	-3.3	85
Porter	26,835	44.5	1	32,702	37.5	3	9,116	7.6	17	4,068	3.2	34
Posey	2,526	13.1	23	4,674	21.5	16	-446	-1.7	55	232	0.9	51
Pulaski	-303	-2.4	85	724	5.8	57	-615	-4.6	66	57	0.5	57
Putnam	2,005	8.0	43	2,231	8.3	53	1,152	4.0	28	1,085	3.6	30
Randolph	481	1.7	72	1,082	3.7	67	-2,849	-9.5	89	-848	-3.1	84
Ripley	497	2.4	67	3,260	15.4	26	218	0.9	41	884	3.6	30
Rush	-41	-0.2	79	-748	-3.7	89	-1,475	-7.5	81	-129	-0.7	66
St. Joseph	6,213	2.6	65	-3,210	-1.3	83	5,435	2.2	35	7,448	3.0	35
Scott	2,501	17.1	19	3,278	19.1	18	569	2.8	34	709	3.4	32
Shelby	3,704	10.9	31	2,090	5.5	58	420	1.1	39	493	1.2	48
Spencer	1,060	6.6	51	2,227	13.0	34	129	0.7	43	110	0.6	54
Starke	1,369	7.6	45	2,717	14.1	27	750	3.4	32	653	2.9	37
Steuben	2,975	17.3	18	4,535	22.5	13	2,752	11.1	7	1,454	5.3	18
Sullivan	-1,832	-8.4	91	1,218	6.1	56	-2,114	-10.0	92	-393	-2.1	79
Switzerland	-786	-11.1	92	847	13.4	32	585	8.2	14	162	2.1	41
Tippecanoe	20,256	22.7	9	12,324	11.3	41	8,896	7.3	19	9,802	7.5	7
Tipton	794	5.0	57	169	1.0	77	-700	-4.2	63	-119	-0.7	66
Union	125	1.9	69	278	4.2	65	116	1.7	38	124	1.8	43
Vanderburgh	2,978	1.8	71	-1,257	-0.7	82	-2,457	-1.5	54	-1,158	-0.7	66
Vermillion	-890	-5.0	89	1,436	8.6	51	-1,456	-8.0	83	-973	-5.8	91
Vigo	6,070	5.6	56	-2,143	-1.9	85	-6,278	-5.6	70	-2,307	-2.2	80
Wabash	2,948	9.0	37	1,087	3.1	69	-1,571	-4.3	64	-969	-2.8	83
Warren	160	1.9	69	271	3.1	69	-800	-8.9	87	-376	-4.6	90
Warrick	4,395	18.6	15	13,502	48.3	2	3,446	8.3	13	2,280	5.1	19
Washington	1,459	8.2	41	2,654	13.8	29	1,785	8.1	15	883	3.7	29
Wayne	5,070	6.8	49	-3,051	-3.9	90	-4,107	-5.4	69	-1,751	-2.4	82
Wells	2,601	12.3	26	1,580	6.6	55	547	2.2	35	852	3.3	33
White	1,286	6.5	52	2,872	13.7	31	-602	-2.5	59	135	0.6	54
Whitley	2,441	11.6	29	2,820	12.1	37	1,436	5.5	22	1,349	4.9	22

Footnote: 1980 and 1990 are Census data, 1995 forward are from 1993 projection edition.
Source: IU Kelley School of Business (IBRC), U.S. Bureau of the Census
EDIN table(s): POPU, PPAT

2.3 Components of Population Change 1990 To 1997

	Population 1990	Births	Deaths	Natural Increase	Rank	Net Migration	Rank
Indiana	5,544,159	609,996	376,758	233,238	–	86,714	–
Adams	31,095	4,335	1,929	2,406	21	-664	79
Allen	300,836	36,894	18,037	18,857	3	-7,602	90
Bartholomew	63,657	7,109	3,981	3,128	16	1,949	22
Benton	9,441	934	702	232	79	-116	68
Blackford	14,067	1,345	1,147	198	81	-245	72
Boone	38,147	4,143	2,683	1,460	35	3,378	12
Brown	14,080	1,136	777	359	71	1,152	38
Carroll	18,809	1,895	1,229	666	56	514	51
Cass	38,413	3,650	3,037	613	57	-453	75
Clark	87,777	8,844	6,510	2,334	22	3,104	13
Clay	24,705	2,471	2,217	254	76	1,572	27
Clinton	30,974	3,425	2,575	850	52	1,408	31
Crawford	9,914	910	853	57	87	528	50
Daviess	27,533	3,318	2,248	1,070	44	248	56
Dearborn	38,835	4,134	2,513	1,621	32	6,120	5
Decatur	23,645	2,581	1,706	875	51	842	44
Dekalb	35,324	3,990	2,256	1,734	30	1,664	26
Delaware	119,659	10,689	8,140	2,549	20	-4,583	88
Dubois	36,616	4,248	2,299	1,949	27	574	49
Elkhart	156,198	19,578	9,217	10,361	5	4,166	9
Fayette	26,015	2,492	1,960	532	65	-414	74
Floyd	64,404	6,788	4,512	2,276	24	4,785	8
Fountain	17,808	1,705	1,420	285	75	142	58
Franklin	19,580	2,120	1,104	1,016	48	986	41
Fulton	18,840	1,904	1,489	415	69	1,096	39
Gibson	31,913	2,999	2,500	499	66	-464	76
Grant	74,169	7,382	5,618	1,764	29	-3,115	86
Greene	30,410	2,884	2,506	378	70	2,286	21
Hamilton	108,936	15,234	5,115	10,119	6	35,730	1
Hancock	45,527	4,551	2,734	1,817	28	5,727	7
Harrison	29,890	2,922	1,839	1,083	43	3,026	14
Hendricks	75,717	7,555	4,112	3,443	13	13,131	3
Henry	48,139	4,519	3,700	819	53	-91	66
Howard	80,827	8,781	5,208	3,573	12	-814	80
Huntington	35,427	3,793	2,561	1,232	37	485	53
Jackson	37,730	4,067	2,785	1,282	36	1,872	24
Jasper	24,960	2,643	1,664	979	49	2,758	16
Jay	21,512	2,411	1,633	778	55	-598	78
Jefferson	29,797	2,930	2,382	548	64	947	42
Jennings	23,661	2,725	1,519	1,206	39	2,350	19
Johnson	88,109	9,999	5,643	4,356	9	14,423	2
Knox	39,884	3,463	3,436	27	89	-225	71
Kosciusko	65,294	7,788	3,942	3,846	11	1,223	35
Lagrange	29,477	4,709	1,526	3,183	15	59	61
Lake	475,594	54,119	33,703	20,416	2	-16,671	91
Laporte	107,066	10,438	7,312	3,126	17	-1,112	82
Lawrence	42,836	4,258	3,454	804	54	1,899	23
Madison	130,669	12,551	9,786	2,765	18	-1,594	85
Marion	797,159	104,617	53,804	50,813	1	-34,302	92
Marshall	42,182	4,492	2,847	1,645	31	1,510	30
Martin	10,369	1,039	794	245	78	-104	67
Miami	36,897	3,801	2,181	1,620	33	-5,318	89
Monroe	108,978	8,536	4,604	3,932	10	3,743	11
Montgomery	34,436	3,750	2,666	1,084	42	765	46
Morgan	55,920	6,257	3,509	2,748	19	6,119	6
Newton	13,551	1,224	1,023	201	80	931	43
Noble	37,877	4,703	2,412	2,291	23	1,750	25
Ohio	5,315	456	350	106	85	37	63
Orange	18,409	1,756	1,508	248	77	721	48
Owen	17,281	1,787	1,199	588	61	2,388	18
Parke	15,410	1,344	1,331	13	90	1,023	40
Perry	19,107	1,546	1,391	155	83	44	62
Pike	12,509	1,113	1,006	107	84	142	58
Porter	128,932	12,119	6,983	5,136	8	10,016	4
Posey	25,968	2,558	1,537	1,021	47	-349	73
Pulaski	12,643	1,414	1,078	336	73	233	57
Putnam	30,315	3,090	2,037	1,053	45	2,338	20
Randolph	27,148	2,582	2,119	463	68	-131	69
Ripley	24,616	2,903	1,864	1,039	46	1,522	29
Rush	18,129	1,878	1,302	576	62	-469	77
St. Joseph	247,052	27,577	17,067	10,510	4	494	52
Scott	20,991	2,206	1,605	601	58	1,226	34
Shelby	40,307	4,195	2,719	1,476	34	1,368	32
Spencer	19,490	1,876	1,412	464	67	736	47
Starke	22,747	2,399	1,823	576	62	436	54
Steuben	27,446	3,042	1,818	1,224	38	2,432	17
Sullivan	18,993	1,780	1,851	-71	91	1,358	33
Switzerland	7,738	742	643	99	86	799	45
Tippecanoe	130,598	13,170	7,022	6,148	7	1,561	28
Tipton	16,119	1,456	1,167	289	74	-13	64
Union	6,976	688	492	196	82	100	60
Vanderburgh	165,058	16,710	13,421	3,289	14	-1,510	84
Vermillion	16,773	1,555	1,643	-88	92	312	55
Vigo	106,107	10,584	8,439	2,145	25	-3,312	87
Wabash	35,069	3,131	2,791	340	72	-884	81
Warren	8,176	664	615	49	88	-55	65
Warrick	44,920	4,532	2,545	1,987	26	3,924	10
Washington	23,717	2,367	1,772	595	59	2,831	15
Wayne	71,951	6,894	5,712	1,182	40	-1,333	83
Wells	25,948	2,712	1,756	956	50	-131	69
White	23,265	2,414	1,821	593	60	1,183	37
Whitley	27,651	2,978	1,860	1,118	41	1,200	36

Footnote: Components of change do not equal total change due to rounding.
Source: U.S. Bureau of the Census
EDIN table(s): POPU, POCH

Percent of Population Under Age 20
1996

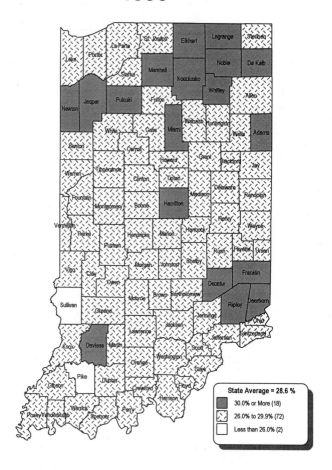

State Average = 28.6 %

- 30.0% or More (18)
- 26.0% to 29.9% (72)
- Less than 26.0% (2)

Percent of Population 65 Years & Older
1996

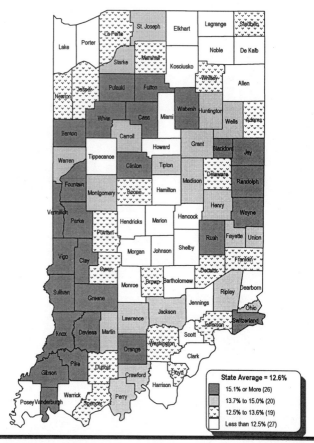

State Average = 12.6%

- 15.1% or More (26)
- 13.7% to 15.0% (20)
- 12.5% to 13.6% (19)
- Less than 12.5% (27)

Percent of Population Under Age 20: EDIN Table PAGE
Percent of Population 65 Years and Older: EDIN Table PAGE.

2.4 Population by Age Groups 1996

	Total	Under 5 Years	5 - 14 Years	15 - 24 Years	25 - 34 Years	35 - 44 Years	45 - 54 Years	55 - 64 Years	65 Years and Over	Percent 0 - 14	Percent 65 and Over
Indiana	5,840,528	409,635	825,734	835,837	870,642	952,351	723,278	488,237	734,814	21.2	12.6
Adams	32,686	2,778	5,661	4,555	4,457	4,817	3,604	2,358	4,456	25.8	13.6
Allen	310,803	23,989	46,269	42,095	49,162	53,348	36,414	24,111	35,415	22.6	11.4
Bartholomew	68,441	4,726	9,209	8,953	9,866	11,820	10,019	6,003	7,845	20.4	11.5
Benton	9,669	681	1,505	1,106	1,276	1,411	1,167	879	1,644	22.6	17.0
Blackford	14,134	949	1,842	1,783	1,878	2,202	1,941	1,365	2,174	19.7	15.4
Boone	42,453	3,058	6,216	4,726	6,165	7,510	5,902	3,416	5,460	21.8	12.9
Brown	15,485	928	2,051	1,801	2,053	2,793	2,375	1,538	1,946	19.2	12.6
Carroll	19,643	1,321	2,787	2,372	2,684	3,122	2,625	1,797	2,935	20.9	14.9
Cass	38,829	2,552	5,545	4,702	5,303	6,177	5,011	3,549	5,990	20.9	15.4
Clark	92,530	5,873	12,927	12,207	14,057	16,030	12,112	8,089	11,235	20.3	12.1
Clay	26,491	1,746	3,777	3,186	3,600	3,942	3,254	2,467	4,519	20.8	17.1
Clinton	32,876	2,373	4,931	4,016	4,565	5,052	3,971	2,841	5,127	22.2	15.6
Crawford	10,559	705	1,555	1,429	1,409	1,639	1,348	949	1,525	21.4	14.4
Daviess	28,760	2,209	4,482	3,546	3,780	4,301	3,284	2,490	4,668	23.3	16.2
Dearborn	45,236	3,288	7,160	5,672	6,345	7,752	5,829	3,784	5,406	23.1	12.0
Decatur	25,105	1,776	3,995	3,328	3,595	3,834	3,099	2,078	3,400	23.0	13.5
Dekalb	38,272	2,884	6,046	5,020	5,904	6,194	4,576	3,010	4,638	23.3	12.1
Delaware	118,600	6,989	13,839	25,396	14,901	17,061	15,068	10,140	15,206	17.6	12.8
Dubois	39,088	3,072	5,898	4,980	6,279	6,182	4,623	3,134	4,920	22.9	12.6
Elkhart	168,941	13,965	25,310	23,138	25,382	28,265	20,771	13,074	19,036	23.2	11.3
Fayette	26,237	1,573	3,749	3,593	3,277	4,352	3,443	2,420	3,830	20.3	14.6
Floyd	70,746	4,745	10,173	8,998	10,198	12,477	9,126	5,979	9,050	21.1	12.8
Fountain	18,207	1,192	2,527	2,201	2,347	2,637	2,516	1,731	3,056	20.4	16.8
Franklin	21,530	1,557	3,473	2,872	2,958	3,458	2,664	1,851	2,697	23.4	12.5
Fulton	20,223	1,365	2,956	2,240	2,782	3,014	2,615	1,971	3,280	21.4	16.2
Gibson	32,058	2,041	4,544	3,879	4,449	4,985	4,018	3,008	5,134	20.5	16.0
Grant	73,469	4,572	9,607	11,374	9,280	11,346	10,111	7,112	10,067	19.3	13.7
Greene	32,942	2,048	4,555	4,003	4,344	5,082	4,381	3,073	5,456	20.0	16.6
Hamilton	147,719	11,664	22,975	16,543	23,287	29,758	20,806	10,670	12,016	23.4	8.1
Hancock	52,000	3,294	7,906	6,616	6,992	9,650	7,839	4,321	5,382	21.5	10.4
Harrison	33,349	2,208	5,289	4,215	4,801	5,871	4,330	2,808	3,827	22.5	11.5
Hendricks	89,343	5,997	13,350	11,565	13,334	16,562	12,893	7,035	8,607	21.7	9.6
Henry	49,135	2,889	6,405	6,272	6,547	8,019	6,928	4,775	7,300	18.9	14.9
Howard	84,126	5,790	11,895	10,916	11,765	13,917	12,216	7,750	9,877	21.0	11.7
Huntington	37,024	2,694	5,640	4,915	5,386	5,682	4,376	2,997	5,334	22.5	14.4
Jackson	40,467	2,737	5,930	5,291	5,877	6,331	5,231	3,506	5,564	21.4	13.7
Jasper	28,368	1,985	4,540	4,131	3,767	4,492	3,667	2,230	3,556	23.0	12.5
Jay	21,733	1,438	3,091	2,801	2,816	3,265	2,963	1,985	3,374	20.8	15.5
Jefferson	31,039	1,940	4,228	4,649	4,315	4,924	4,108	2,668	4,207	19.9	13.6
Jennings	26,747	1,872	3,823	3,697	3,869	4,336	3,716	2,308	3,126	21.3	11.7
Johnson	104,280	7,143	15,128	14,720	15,645	18,764	14,015	7,946	10,919	21.4	10.5
Knox	39,667	2,374	5,009	6,977	5,022	5,587	4,648	3,567	6,483	18.6	16.3
Kosciusko	69,932	5,588	10,895	9,152	10,341	11,238	8,697	5,699	8,322	23.6	11.9
Lagrange	32,103	3,125	5,920	4,751	4,299	4,672	3,615	2,359	3,362	28.2	10.5
Lake	479,940	33,873	73,726	65,782	69,431	77,414	59,108	42,038	58,568	22.4	12.2
Laporte	109,604	7,121	15,057	14,213	16,441	18,865	13,853	9,634	14,420	20.2	13.2
Lawrence	45,361	2,867	6,188	5,841	6,053	7,336	6,262	4,217	6,597	20.0	14.5
Madison	132,782	8,257	17,519	18,519	18,193	21,653	17,750	12,188	18,703	19.4	14.1
Marion	817,525	63,108	108,658	112,313	147,801	132,277	91,720	65,637	96,011	21.0	11.7
Marshall	45,173	3,438	7,026	5,565	6,397	7,218	5,492	3,957	6,080	23.2	13.5
Martin	10,581	701	1,567	1,355	1,441	1,677	1,388	981	1,471	21.4	13.9
Miami	32,686	2,548	5,061	4,345	4,974	5,240	3,916	2,677	3,925	23.3	12.0
Monroe	116,176	6,316	11,457	34,668	18,344	16,549	11,286	7,375	10,181	15.3	8.8
Montgomery	36,349	2,464	4,900	5,000	5,209	5,497	4,755	3,286	5,238	20.3	14.4
Morgan	63,244	4,339	9,525	8,520	9,147	10,801	9,036	5,329	6,547	21.9	10.4
Newton	14,611	1,005	2,372	1,760	1,987	2,331	1,954	1,230	1,972	23.1	13.5
Noble	41,449	3,286	6,530	5,635	6,045	6,655	4,980	3,298	5,020	23.7	12.1
Ohio	5,490	354	810	654	817	841	732	506	776	21.2	14.1
Orange	19,221	1,306	2,759	2,413	2,628	2,993	2,389	1,761	2,972	21.1	15.5
Owen	20,158	1,366	2,926	2,491	2,687	3,236	2,737	1,991	2,724	21.3	13.5
Parke	16,339	1,034	2,121	1,976	2,189	2,542	2,237	1,642	2,598	19.3	15.9
Perry	19,210	1,166	2,749	2,592	2,957	2,973	2,252	1,682	2,839	20.4	14.8
Pike	12,569	760	1,650	1,496	1,714	1,958	1,741	1,243	2,007	19.2	16.0
Porter	142,363	9,500	21,948	19,900	20,221	26,473	19,263	11,029	14,029	22.1	9.9
Posey	26,505	1,949	4,047	3,157	3,968	4,581	3,366	2,216	3,221	22.6	12.2
Pulaski	13,103	979	2,013	1,638	1,761	1,906	1,533	1,201	2,072	22.8	15.8
Putnam	33,451	2,022	4,308	5,832	4,639	5,041	4,175	3,053	4,381	18.9	13.1
Randolph	27,530	1,750	3,777	3,551	3,562	4,252	3,635	2,725	4,278	20.1	15.5
Ripley	26,932	1,914	4,163	3,554	3,742	4,130	3,278	2,289	3,862	22.6	14.3
Rush	18,285	1,213	2,745	2,467	2,471	2,777	2,230	1,629	2,753	21.6	15.1
St. Joseph	257,740	18,324	34,900	39,963	36,986	41,132	28,197	21,657	36,581	20.7	14.2
Scott	22,652	1,584	3,345	3,199	3,227	3,599	3,121	1,863	2,714	21.8	12.0
Shelby	42,951	3,068	6,277	5,567	6,456	7,026	5,555	3,704	5,298	21.8	12.3
Spencer	20,540	1,383	3,098	2,508	3,032	3,297	2,696	1,793	2,733	21.8	13.3
Starke	23,399	1,680	3,519	3,106	3,286	3,325	2,903	2,157	3,423	22.2	14.6
Steuben	30,831	2,185	4,279	4,378	4,288	4,906	3,963	2,744	4,088	21.0	13.3
Sullivan	20,115	1,161	2,689	2,503	2,518	3,378	2,593	1,781	3,492	19.1	17.4
Switzerland	8,380	544	1,256	986	1,078	1,267	1,158	802	1,289	21.5	15.4
Tippecanoe	138,324	8,795	15,615	36,552	21,437	19,836	13,864	8,822	13,403	17.6	9.7
Tipton	16,453	999	2,339	2,057	2,171	2,724	2,299	1,403	2,461	20.3	15.0
Union	7,345	485	1,098	990	974	1,213	949	600	1,036	21.6	14.1
Vanderburgh	167,716	11,211	21,370	22,310	25,321	26,064	19,751	15,127	26,562	19.4	15.8
Vermillion	16,791	975	2,302	2,051	2,120	2,670	2,243	1,486	2,944	19.5	17.5
Vigo	106,389	6,512	13,336	18,415	14,832	16,171	11,925	8,831	16,367	18.7	15.4
Wabash	34,661	2,259	4,926	4,942	4,619	5,283	4,329	3,048	5,255	20.7	15.2
Warren	8,188	562	1,128	969	1,029	1,310	1,174	791	1,225	20.6	15.0
Warrick	50,070	3,359	7,788	6,343	7,172	9,541	7,027	3,722	5,118	22.3	10.2
Washington	26,689	1,757	4,053	3,532	3,832	4,196	3,419	2,261	3,639	21.8	13.6
Wayne	72,017	4,619	9,728	9,918	9,505	11,014	9,347	6,876	11,010	19.9	15.3
Wells	26,651	2,007	4,194	3,160	3,972	4,202	3,298	2,175	3,643	23.3	13.7
White	25,081	1,641	3,736	2,953	3,341	4,052	2,997	2,375	3,986	21.4	15.9
Whitley	29,863	2,196	4,543	3,816	4,268	5,058	3,487	2,564	3,931	22.6	13.2

Source: U.S. Bureau of the Census
EDIN table(s): PAGE

2.5 Female Population by Age Groups 1996

	Total	Under 5 Years	5 - 14 Years	15 - 24 Years	25 - 34 Years	35 - 44 Years	45 - 54 Years	55 - 64 Years	65 Years and Over	0 - 14	65 and Over
Indiana	2,994,337	200,062	401,500	409,842	440,207	479,705	368,053	255,429	439,539	20.1	14.7
Adams	16,576	1,362	2,727	2,194	2,211	2,369	1,822	1,230	2,661	24.7	16.1
Allen	159,539	11,713	22,612	20,771	24,877	26,948	18,600	12,621	21,397	21.5	13.4
Bartholomew	35,023	2,314	4,500	4,443	5,052	5,957	5,053	3,062	4,642	19.5	13.3
Benton	4,924	310	717	565	626	687	589	471	959	20.9	19.5
Blackford	7,249	449	865	853	950	1,109	986	718	1,319	18.1	18.2
Boone	21,894	1,489	2,990	2,343	3,171	3,830	3,003	1,706	3,362	20.5	15.4
Brown	7,691	463	939	847	1,066	1,393	1,152	765	1,066	18.2	13.9
Carroll	9,972	660	1,343	1,146	1,339	1,536	1,322	923	1,703	20.1	17.1
Cass	20,110	1,269	2,685	2,293	2,667	3,144	2,558	1,847	3,647	19.7	18.1
Clark	48,121	2,856	6,293	6,082	7,234	8,258	6,269	4,321	6,808	19.0	14.1
Clay	13,754	884	1,801	1,512	1,832	1,961	1,703	1,313	2,748	19.5	20.0
Clinton	16,907	1,174	2,359	1,921	2,313	2,551	2,026	1,478	3,085	20.9	18.2
Crawford	5,291	346	751	683	699	795	670	503	844	20.7	16.0
Daviess	14,800	1,108	2,120	1,724	1,892	2,162	1,691	1,338	2,765	21.8	18.7
Dearborn	22,936	1,645	3,457	2,724	3,312	3,792	2,886	1,922	3,198	22.2	13.9
Decatur	12,655	828	1,948	1,569	1,802	1,907	1,587	1,070	1,944	21.9	15.4
Dekalb	19,446	1,414	3,007	2,380	2,967	3,014	2,353	1,537	2,774	22.7	14.3
Delaware	61,942	3,534	6,728	12,955	7,518	8,862	7,693	5,311	9,341	16.6	15.1
Dubois	19,813	1,551	2,879	2,460	3,028	3,047	2,322	1,612	2,914	22.4	14.7
Elkhart	85,893	6,768	12,318	11,387	12,621	14,147	10,428	6,811	11,413	22.2	13.3
Fayette	13,485	776	1,814	1,682	1,719	2,196	1,727	1,267	2,304	19.2	17.1
Floyd	36,835	2,350	4,974	4,466	5,334	6,391	4,663	3,161	5,496	19.9	14.9
Fountain	9,389	587	1,226	1,054	1,170	1,360	1,251	886	1,855	19.3	19.8
Franklin	10,810	769	1,679	1,354	1,467	1,675	1,327	941	1,598	22.6	14.8
Fulton	10,373	658	1,438	1,122	1,376	1,519	1,331	1,035	1,894	20.2	18.3
Gibson	16,594	1,027	2,229	1,900	2,213	2,489	2,041	1,615	3,080	19.6	18.6
Grant	37,891	2,245	4,673	5,730	4,816	5,745	5,124	3,628	5,930	18.3	15.7
Greene	16,886	986	2,220	1,933	2,164	2,522	2,244	1,601	3,216	19.0	19.0
Hamilton	75,029	5,665	11,385	8,224	12,137	15,048	10,327	5,300	6,943	22.7	9.3
Hancock	26,297	1,569	3,849	3,165	3,555	4,962	3,880	2,147	3,170	20.6	12.1
Harrison	16,739	1,079	2,519	2,052	2,417	2,893	2,120	1,443	2,216	21.5	13.2
Hendricks	44,061	2,935	6,502	5,002	6,454	8,301	6,362	3,465	5,040	21.4	11.4
Henry	25,409	1,456	3,116	3,051	3,352	4,033	3,520	2,507	4,374	18.0	17.2
Howard	43,740	2,849	5,769	5,466	6,082	7,233	6,221	4,042	6,078	19.7	13.9
Huntington	18,986	1,320	2,742	2,384	2,665	2,842	2,225	1,558	3,250	21.4	17.1
Jackson	20,779	1,363	2,893	2,615	2,961	3,170	2,638	1,832	3,307	20.5	15.9
Jasper	14,264	960	2,180	1,960	1,895	2,276	1,777	1,140	2,076	22.0	14.6
Jay	11,130	664	1,488	1,353	1,432	1,640	1,509	1,050	1,994	19.3	17.9
Jefferson	15,784	966	2,001	2,316	2,133	2,452	2,097	1,392	2,427	18.8	15.4
Jennings	13,453	888	1,870	1,796	1,936	2,195	1,798	1,178	1,792	20.5	13.3
Johnson	53,368	3,486	7,400	7,163	7,956	9,529	7,031	4,122	6,681	20.4	12.5
Knox	20,326	1,182	2,437	3,003	2,494	2,813	2,418	1,933	4,046	17.8	19.9
Kosciusko	35,466	2,730	5,314	4,563	5,204	5,608	4,348	2,918	4,781	22.7	13.5
Lagrange	16,066	1,550	2,864	2,303	2,152	2,289	1,843	1,182	1,883	27.5	11.7
Lake	248,641	16,489	36,083	32,921	36,437	39,879	30,664	22,150	34,018	21.1	13.7
Laporte	53,579	3,446	7,311	6,531	7,372	8,716	6,783	5,026	8,394	20.1	15.7
Lawrence	23,258	1,383	3,002	2,787	3,105	3,693	3,168	2,218	3,902	18.9	16.8
Madison	67,543	3,982	8,487	8,882	8,832	10,766	8,848	6,365	11,381	18.5	16.9
Marion	428,174	30,831	52,972	57,580	75,856	68,452	48,189	35,362	58,932	19.6	13.8
Marshall	22,881	1,682	3,346	2,679	3,179	3,541	2,829	2,038	3,587	22.0	15.7
Martin	5,349	354	741	659	715	841	708	492	839	20.5	15.7
Miami	16,678	1,219	2,475	2,140	2,537	2,602	1,991	1,384	2,330	22.1	14.0
Monroe	59,687	3,105	5,468	18,084	8,958	8,290	5,779	3,885	6,118	14.4	10.3
Montgomery	18,240	1,163	2,368	2,132	2,561	2,773	2,386	1,706	3,151	19.4	17.3
Morgan	32,033	2,125	4,611	4,175	4,643	5,442	4,539	2,697	3,801	21.0	11.9
Newton	7,395	485	1,154	847	1,019	1,143	976	615	1,156	22.2	15.6
Noble	20,928	1,607	3,146	2,729	3,004	3,242	2,543	1,683	2,974	22.7	14.2
Ohio	2,806	189	381	313	420	389	379	253	482	20.3	17.2
Orange	9,814	637	1,351	1,163	1,310	1,511	1,207	909	1,726	20.3	17.6
Owen	10,161	662	1,431	1,253	1,341	1,621	1,352	977	1,524	20.6	15.0
Parke	8,479	488	1,043	938	1,195	1,330	1,117	857	1,511	18.1	17.8
Perry	9,409	590	1,348	1,124	1,292	1,358	1,112	912	1,673	20.6	17.8
Pike	6,336	347	760	723	855	944	904	640	1,163	17.5	18.4
Porter	72,247	4,704	10,723	9,812	10,596	13,173	9,412	5,567	8,260	21.4	11.4
Posey	13,325	935	1,929	1,565	2,022	2,256	1,650	1,138	1,830	21.5	13.7
Pulaski	6,612	508	956	788	855	920	756	621	1,208	22.1	18.3
Putnam	16,300	1,031	2,121	2,685	1,962	2,345	2,089	1,490	2,577	19.3	15.8
Randolph	14,120	854	1,803	1,723	1,814	2,152	1,836	1,426	2,512	18.8	17.8
Ripley	13,669	934	2,031	1,742	1,863	2,021	1,636	1,212	2,230	21.7	16.3
Rush	9,378	601	1,326	1,216	1,212	1,405	1,151	847	1,620	20.5	17.3
St. Joseph	132,954	8,881	16,982	19,540	18,711	20,677	14,575	11,588	22,000	19.5	16.5
Scott	11,593	806	1,642	1,551	1,628	1,849	1,557	932	1,628	21.1	14.0
Shelby	21,951	1,503	3,111	2,774	3,266	3,442	2,766	1,914	3,175	21.0	14.5
Spencer	10,234	707	1,530	1,170	1,475	1,571	1,332	920	1,529	21.9	14.9
Starke	11,825	786	1,696	1,478	1,651	1,662	1,503	1,106	1,943	21.0	16.4
Steuben	15,382	1,062	2,102	1,977	2,148	2,418	1,962	1,394	2,319	20.6	15.1
Sullivan	9,989	541	1,307	1,118	1,212	1,511	1,224	952	2,124	18.5	21.3
Switzerland	4,251	294	602	471	541	627	576	412	728	21.1	17.1
Tippecanoe	68,068	4,304	7,429	16,387	10,378	9,872	7,044	4,593	8,061	17.2	11.8
Tipton	8,417	469	1,119	993	1,117	1,357	1,153	741	1,468	18.9	17.4
Union	3,757	230	530	486	504	613	464	321	609	20.2	16.2
Vanderburgh	88,369	5,451	10,546	11,419	12,822	13,093	10,285	8,210	16,543	18.1	18.7
Vermillion	8,772	472	1,151	993	1,086	1,347	1,080	818	1,825	18.5	20.8
Vigo	54,312	3,153	6,555	8,410	7,259	7,848	6,113	4,725	10,249	17.9	18.9
Wabash	17,829	1,099	2,333	2,430	2,326	2,637	2,191	1,596	3,217	19.2	18.0
Warren	4,126	242	545	484	523	649	593	401	689	19.1	16.7
Warrick	25,304	1,610	3,777	3,041	3,720	4,834	3,503	1,880	2,939	21.3	11.6
Washington	13,327	873	1,885	1,638	1,912	2,072	1,680	1,195	2,072	20.7	15.5
Wayne	37,483	2,166	4,662	4,965	4,821	5,676	4,876	3,634	6,683	18.2	17.8
Wells	13,651	948	1,991	1,552	2,030	2,076	1,712	1,143	2,199	21.5	16.1
White	12,870	837	1,833	1,416	1,706	1,986	1,539	1,230	2,323	20.7	18.0
Whitley	15,135	1,080	2,184	1,849	2,155	2,433	1,786	1,352	2,296	21.6	15.2

2.6 Male Population by Age Groups 1996

	Total	Under 5 Years	5 - 14 Years	15 - 24 Years	25 - 34 Years	35 - 44 Years	45 - 54 Years	55 - 64 Years	65 Years and Over	Percent 0 - 14	Percent 65 and Over
Indiana	2,846,191	209,573	424,234	425,995	430,435	472,646	355,225	232,808	295,275	22.3	10.4
Adams	16,110	1,416	2,934	2,361	2,246	2,448	1,782	1,128	1,795	27.0	11.1
Allen	151,264	12,276	23,657	21,324	24,285	26,400	17,814	11,490	14,018	23.8	9.3
Bartholomew	33,418	2,412	4,709	4,510	4,814	5,863	4,966	2,941	3,203	21.3	9.6
Benton	4,745	371	788	541	650	724	578	408	685	24.4	14.4
Blackford	6,885	500	977	930	928	1,093	955	647	855	21.5	12.4
Boone	20,559	1,569	3,226	2,383	2,994	3,680	2,899	1,710	2,098	23.3	10.2
Brown	7,794	465	1,112	954	987	1,400	1,223	773	880	20.2	11.3
Carroll	9,671	661	1,444	1,226	1,345	1,586	1,303	874	1,232	21.8	12.7
Cass	18,719	1,283	2,860	2,409	2,636	3,033	2,453	1,702	2,343	22.1	12.5
Clark	44,409	3,017	6,634	6,125	6,823	7,772	5,843	3,768	4,427	21.7	10.0
Clay	12,737	862	1,976	1,674	1,768	1,981	1,551	1,154	1,771	22.3	13.9
Clinton	15,969	1,199	2,572	2,095	2,252	2,501	1,945	1,363	2,042	23.6	12.8
Crawford	5,268	359	804	746	710	844	678	446	681	22.1	12.9
Daviess	13,960	1,101	2,362	1,822	1,888	2,139	1,593	1,152	1,903	24.8	13.6
Dearborn	22,300	1,643	3,703	2,948	3,033	3,960	2,943	1,862	2,208	24.0	9.9
Decatur	12,450	948	2,047	1,759	1,793	1,927	1,512	1,008	1,456	24.1	11.7
Dekalb	18,826	1,470	3,039	2,640	2,937	3,180	2,223	1,473	1,864	24.0	9.9
Delaware	56,658	3,455	7,111	12,441	7,383	8,199	7,375	4,829	5,865	18.6	10.4
Dubois	19,275	1,521	3,019	2,520	3,251	3,135	2,301	1,522	2,006	23.6	10.4
Elkhart	83,048	7,197	12,992	11,751	12,761	14,118	10,343	6,263	7,623	24.3	9.2
Fayette	12,752	797	1,935	1,911	1,558	2,156	1,716	1,153	1,526	21.4	12.0
Floyd	33,911	2,395	5,199	4,532	4,864	6,086	4,463	2,818	3,554	22.4	10.5
Fountain	8,818	605	1,301	1,147	1,177	1,277	1,265	845	1,201	21.6	13.6
Franklin	10,720	788	1,794	1,518	1,491	1,783	1,337	910	1,099	24.1	10.3
Fulton	9,850	707	1,518	1,118	1,406	1,495	1,284	936	1,386	22.6	14.1
Gibson	15,464	1,014	2,315	1,979	2,236	2,496	1,977	1,393	2,054	21.5	13.3
Grant	35,578	2,327	4,934	5,644	4,464	5,601	4,987	3,484	4,137	20.4	11.6
Greene	16,056	1,062	2,335	2,070	2,180	2,560	2,137	1,472	2,240	21.2	14.0
Hamilton	72,690	5,999	11,590	8,319	11,150	14,710	10,479	5,370	5,073	24.2	7.0
Hancock	25,703	1,725	4,057	3,451	3,437	4,688	3,959	2,174	2,212	22.5	8.6
Harrison	16,610	1,129	2,770	2,163	2,384	2,978	2,210	1,365	1,611	23.5	9.7
Hendricks	45,282	3,062	6,848	6,563	6,880	8,261	6,531	3,570	3,567	21.9	7.9
Henry	23,726	1,433	3,289	3,221	3,195	3,986	3,408	2,268	2,926	19.9	12.3
Howard	40,386	2,941	6,126	5,450	5,683	6,684	5,995	3,708	3,799	22.5	9.4
Huntington	18,038	1,374	2,898	2,531	2,721	2,840	2,151	1,439	2,084	23.7	11.6
Jackson	19,688	1,374	3,037	2,676	2,916	3,161	2,593	1,674	2,257	22.4	11.5
Jasper	14,104	1,025	2,360	2,171	1,872	2,216	1,890	1,090	1,480	24.0	10.5
Jay	10,603	774	1,603	1,448	1,384	1,625	1,454	935	1,380	22.4	13.0
Jefferson	15,255	974	2,227	2,333	2,182	2,472	2,011	1,276	1,780	21.0	11.7
Jennings	13,294	984	1,953	1,901	1,933	2,141	1,918	1,130	1,334	22.1	10.0
Johnson	50,912	3,657	7,728	7,557	7,689	9,235	6,984	3,824	4,238	22.4	8.3
Knox	19,341	1,192	2,572	3,974	2,528	2,774	2,230	1,634	2,437	19.5	12.6
Kosciusko	34,466	2,858	5,581	4,589	5,137	5,630	4,349	2,781	3,541	24.5	10.3
Lagrange	16,037	1,575	3,056	2,448	2,147	2,383	1,772	1,177	1,479	28.9	9.2
Lake	231,299	17,384	37,643	32,861	32,994	37,535	28,444	19,888	24,550	23.8	10.6
Laporte	56,025	3,675	7,746	7,682	9,069	10,149	7,070	4,608	6,026	20.4	10.8
Lawrence	22,103	1,484	3,186	3,054	2,948	3,643	3,094	1,999	2,695	21.1	12.2
Madison	65,239	4,275	9,032	9,637	9,361	10,887	8,902	5,823	7,322	20.4	11.2
Marion	389,351	32,277	55,686	54,733	71,945	63,825	43,531	30,275	37,079	22.6	9.5
Marshall	22,292	1,756	3,680	2,886	3,218	3,677	2,663	1,919	2,493	24.4	11.2
Martin	5,232	347	826	696	726	836	680	489	632	22.4	12.1
Miami	16,008	1,329	2,586	2,205	2,437	2,638	1,925	1,293	1,595	24.5	10.0
Monroe	56,489	3,211	5,989	16,584	9,386	8,259	5,507	3,490	4,063	16.3	7.2
Montgomery	18,109	1,301	2,532	2,868	2,648	2,724	2,369	1,580	2,087	21.2	11.5
Morgan	31,211	2,214	4,914	4,345	4,504	5,359	4,497	2,632	2,746	22.8	8.8
Newton	7,216	520	1,218	913	968	1,188	978	615	816	24.1	11.3
Noble	20,521	1,679	3,384	2,906	3,041	3,413	2,437	1,615	2,046	24.7	10.0
Ohio	2,684	165	429	341	397	452	353	253	294	22.1	11.0
Orange	9,407	669	1,408	1,250	1,318	1,482	1,182	852	1,246	22.1	13.2
Owen	9,997	704	1,495	1,238	1,346	1,615	1,385	1,014	1,200	22.0	12.0
Parke	7,860	546	1,078	1,038	994	1,212	1,120	785	1,087	20.7	13.8
Perry	9,801	576	1,401	1,468	1,665	1,615	1,140	770	1,166	20.2	11.9
Pike	6,233	413	890	773	859	1,014	837	603	844	20.9	13.5
Porter	70,116	4,796	11,225	10,088	9,625	13,300	9,851	5,462	5,769	22.8	8.2
Posey	13,180	1,014	2,118	1,592	1,946	2,325	1,716	1,078	1,391	23.8	10.6
Pulaski	6,491	471	1,057	850	906	986	777	580	864	23.5	13.3
Putnam	17,151	991	2,187	3,147	2,677	2,696	2,086	1,563	1,804	18.5	10.5
Randolph	13,410	896	1,974	1,828	1,748	2,100	1,799	1,299	1,766	21.4	13.2
Ripley	13,263	980	2,132	1,812	1,879	2,109	1,642	1,077	1,632	23.5	12.3
Rush	8,907	612	1,419	1,251	1,259	1,372	1,079	782	1,133	22.8	12.7
St. Joseph	124,786	9,443	17,918	20,423	18,275	20,455	13,622	10,069	14,581	21.9	11.7
Scott	11,059	778	1,703	1,648	1,599	1,750	1,564	931	1,086	22.4	9.8
Shelby	21,000	1,565	3,166	2,793	3,190	3,584	2,789	1,790	2,123	22.5	10.1
Spencer	10,306	676	1,568	1,338	1,557	1,726	1,364	873	1,204	21.8	11.7
Starke	11,574	894	1,823	1,628	1,635	1,663	1,400	1,051	1,480	23.5	12.8
Steuben	15,449	1,123	2,177	2,401	2,140	2,488	2,001	1,350	1,769	21.4	11.5
Sullivan	10,126	620	1,382	1,385	1,306	1,867	1,369	829	1,368	19.8	13.5
Switzerland	4,129	250	654	515	537	640	582	390	561	21.9	13.6
Tippecanoe	70,256	4,491	8,186	20,165	11,059	9,964	6,820	4,229	5,342	18.0	7.6
Tipton	8,036	530	1,220	1,064	1,054	1,367	1,146	662	993	21.8	12.4
Union	3,588	255	568	504	470	600	485	279	427	22.9	11.9
Vanderburgh	79,347	5,760	10,824	10,891	12,499	12,971	9,466	6,917	10,019	20.9	12.6
Vermillion	8,019	503	1,151	1,058	1,034	1,323	1,163	668	1,119	20.6	14.0
Vigo	52,077	3,359	6,781	10,005	7,573	8,323	5,812	4,106	6,118	19.5	11.7
Wabash	16,832	1,160	2,593	2,512	2,293	2,646	2,138	1,452	2,038	22.3	12.1
Warren	4,062	320	583	485	506	661	581	390	536	22.2	13.2
Warrick	24,766	1,749	4,011	3,302	3,452	4,707	3,524	1,842	2,179	23.3	8.8
Washington	13,362	884	2,168	1,894	1,920	2,124	1,739	1,066	1,567	22.8	11.7
Wayne	34,534	2,453	5,066	4,953	4,684	5,338	4,471	3,242	4,327	21.8	12.5
Wells	13,000	1,059	2,203	1,608	1,942	2,126	1,586	1,032	1,444	25.1	11.1
White	12,211	804	1,903	1,537	1,635	2,066	1,458	1,145	1,663	22.2	13.6
Whitley	14,728	1,116	2,359	1,967	2,113	2,625	1,701	1,212	1,635	23.6	11.1

Source: U.S. Bureau of the Census
EDIN table(s): PAMF

2.7 Population Projections by Age Groups 2005

	Total Population	Rank	0 - 17	18 - 24	25 - 39	40 - 59	60 - 74	75 and Over	Median Age	0 - 17	Rank	75 and Over	Rank
					Age Groups						Percent		
Indiana	5,776,200	—	1,408,010	623,900	1,192,420	1,578,830	641,870	331,190	35.3	24.4	—	5.7	—
Adams	35,100	41	10,540	3,910	6,890	8,290	3,360	2,120	31.0	30.0	2	6.0	53
Allen	321,500	3	83,720	32,650	62,220	93,340	33,020	16,610	35.5	26.0	10	5.2	79
Bartholomew	65,200	23	15,380	6,200	12,290	19,030	8,660	3,640	38.3	23.6	47	5.6	69
Benton	9,600	88	2,570	1,040	1,700	2,410	1,120	730	34.2	26.8	7	7.6	7
Blackford	13,400	83	3,180	1,320	2,510	3,690	1,780	970	38.0	23.7	45	7.2	19
Boone	40,500	33	9,800	4,220	6,900	12,330	4,930	2,320	38.0	24.2	35	5.7	65
Brown	15,000	80	2,950	1,370	2,630	4,550	2,410	1,100	43.1	19.7	92	7.3	14
Carroll	19,100	71	4,590	1,880	3,550	5,220	2,400	1,440	37.4	24.0	39	7.5	9
Cass	38,100	37	9,230	3,700	7,180	10,460	4,600	2,910	37.1	24.2	35	7.6	7
Clark	87,000	16	19,450	8,350	17,500	26,350	10,510	4,790	38.2	22.4	78	5.5	73
Clay	24,600	61	5,980	2,520	4,720	6,640	2,970	1,800	36.5	24.3	32	7.3	14
Clinton	31,600	47	8,020	3,270	5,960	8,580	3,620	2,150	35.5	25.4	17	6.8	31
Crawford	10,400	86	2,690	1,020	2,060	2,800	1,210	630	34.9	25.9	12	6.1	52
Daviess	28,400	53	7,740	3,120	5,360	7,180	2,970	2,040	33.4	27.3	5	7.2	19
Dearborn	42,700	29	10,250	4,670	8,190	12,390	4,870	2,360	36.0	24.0	39	5.5	73
Decatur	24,400	63	6,030	2,560	4,940	6,600	2,830	1,430	35.0	24.7	29	5.9	58
Dekalb	38,100	37	9,600	4,040	7,470	10,920	3,980	2,040	35.0	25.2	18	5.4	76
Delaware	123,100	11	29,520	19,350	24,270	28,870	14,040	7,010	32.7	24.0	39	5.7	65
Dubois	39,000	34	9,470	4,200	7,330	11,390	4,280	2,300	36.6	24.3	32	5.9	58
Elkhart	174,300	5	44,910	18,040	34,320	49,130	18,790	9,150	35.6	25.8	14	5.2	79
Fayette	25,600	59	5,920	2,330	5,270	6,870	3,270	1,910	37.4	23.1	57	7.5	9
Floyd	67,700	22	16,030	6,830	12,960	20,120	7,730	4,000	37.3	23.7	45	5.9	58
Fountain	17,100	77	3,910	1,730	3,260	4,430	2,320	1,400	37.9	22.9	64	8.2	2
Franklin	20,900	68	5,200	2,180	4,130	5,540	2,410	1,410	34.7	24.9	26	6.7	40
Fulton	19,200	70	4,830	2,010	3,300	5,050	2,470	1,520	36.6	25.2	18	7.9	3
Gibson	31,300	48	7,220	3,200	5,960	8,790	3,980	2,200	37.9	23.1	57	7.0	26
Grant	70,700	20	16,540	6,940	13,920	18,710	9,780	4,780	37.7	23.4	50	6.8	31
Greene	30,500	49	6,910	2,990	5,850	8,400	3,930	2,380	38.5	22.7	69	7.8	4
Hamilton	132,900	9	29,960	14,820	21,910	46,400	14,820	4,940	39.8	22.5	74	3.7	92
Hancock	48,300	25	10,760	4,980	9,180	14,600	6,370	2,380	38.2	22.3	80	4.9	84
Harrison	32,000	45	7,390	3,400	6,180	9,470	3,760	1,840	37.0	23.1	57	5.8	64
Hendricks	81,500	17	18,180	8,710	15,130	25,720	10,140	3,620	38.4	22.3	80	4.4	89
Henry	46,000	27	10,200	4,160	8,840	13,010	6,410	3,400	39.6	22.2	83	7.4	12
Howard	80,900	18	19,440	7,870	15,240	22,610	10,870	4,870	37.6	24.0	39	6.0	53
Huntington	36,700	39	9,190	3,900	7,290	10,080	4,010	2,210	35.3	25.0	22	6.0	53
Jackson	39,000	34	9,100	3,860	7,830	10,970	4,740	2,450	37.1	23.3	52	6.3	50
Jasper	26,100	57	6,580	2,830	5,590	6,740	2,960	1,440	34.5	25.2	18	5.5	73
Jay	21,500	67	5,600	2,080	4,070	5,530	2,700	1,540	35.7	26.0	10	7.2	19
Jefferson	29,300	51	6,590	3,060	6,260	8,010	3,640	1,750	37.0	22.5	74	6.0	53
Jennings	24,600	61	5,580	2,450	4,940	7,010	3,190	1,380	37.5	22.7	69	5.6	69
Johnson	95,700	15	21,840	9,820	19,260	29,060	10,950	4,800	37.4	22.8	65	5.0	83
Knox	38,700	36	8,760	4,680	8,720	9,500	4,460	2,600	34.9	22.6	72	6.7	40
Kosciusko	72,500	19	19,500	7,630	13,750	19,500	8,110	4,060	34.5	26.9	6	5.6	69
Lagrange	36,000	40	11,810	4,030	7,340	7,940	3,310	1,630	28.9	32.8	1	4.5	88
Lake	474,000	2	122,950	48,260	94,160	127,340	53,250	28,090	34.7	25.9	12	5.9	58
Laporte	108,900	13	25,330	10,340	24,920	28,980	12,430	6,940	36.0	23.3	52	6.4	47
Lawrence	42,700	29	9,480	4,110	8,430	12,180	5,560	2,950	38.6	22.2	83	6.9	29
Madison	127,500	10	28,990	12,480	26,630	34,130	16,570	8,700	37.4	22.7	69	6.8	31
Marion	855,200	1	220,760	76,930	217,210	222,280	77,900	40,080	34.0	25.8	14	4.7	87
Marshall	45,300	28	11,250	4,850	8,500	12,680	5,230	2,830	35.8	24.8	27	6.2	51
Martin	10,400	86	2,430	1,050	1,990	2,840	1,340	710	37.4	23.4	50	6.8	31
Miami	33,200	44	9,100	3,640	6,580	8,650	3,360	1,890	33.7	27.4	4	5.7	65
Monroe	123,000	12	26,840	26,990	27,790	25,960	10,320	5,120	28.7	21.8	87	4.2	90
Montgomery	34,900	42	8,510	3,480	6,830	9,470	4,360	2,260	37.0	24.4	31	6.5	43
Morgan	60,700	24	14,570	6,190	11,910	17,560	7,540	2,960	36.5	24.0	39	4.9	84
Newton	13,700	82	3,450	1,440	2,550	3,630	1,730	880	34.8	25.2	18	6.4	47
Noble	41,300	31	11,010	4,440	8,060	11,200	4,390	2,210	34.1	26.7	8	5.4	76
Ohio	5,700	92	1,340	550	1,070	1,600	700	410	37.8	23.5	48	7.2	19
Orange	18,400	75	4,290	1,850	3,640	5,070	2,280	1,260	36.9	23.3	52	6.8	31
Owen	19,000	72	4,580	1,880	3,560	5,180	2,540	1,230	37.1	24.1	37	6.5	43
Parke	15,000	80	3,450	1,540	2,770	3,940	2,090	1,250	38.5	23.0	61	8.3	1
Perry	19,000	72	4,120	2,160	4,080	5,170	2,120	1,350	36.0	21.7	88	7.1	24
Pike	12,000	85	2,700	1,180	2,230	3,390	1,670	870	39.3	22.5	74	7.3	14
Porter	134,400	8	28,560	15,190	27,570	40,010	16,300	6,800	37.4	21.3	90	5.1	81
Posey	26,500	55	6,100	2,820	4,900	7,950	3,130	1,570	37.8	23.0	61	5.9	58
Pulaski	12,900	84	3,580	1,340	2,380	3,280	1,460	880	33.8	27.8	3	6.8	31
Putnam	31,700	46	6,870	4,170	8,040	7,310	3,570	1,710	33.8	21.7	88	5.4	76
Randolph	26,200	56	6,090	2,450	5,210	6,960	3,480	1,970	37.5	23.2	55	7.5	9
Ripley	26,000	58	6,860	2,710	5,060	6,940	2,930	1,530	34.4	26.4	9	5.9	58
Rush	18,200	76	4,490	1,830	3,740	4,760	2,030	1,300	34.8	24.7	29	7.1	24
St. Joseph	256,700	4	62,490	28,470	52,680	69,800	26,590	16,720	35.6	24.3	32	6.5	43
Scott	22,000	66	5,490	2,160	4,580	6,010	2,620	1,130	35.4	25.0	22	5.1	81
Shelby	41,100	32	9,360	4,290	8,050	12,270	4,800	2,320	37.5	22.8	65	5.6	69
Spencer	19,800	69	4,750	2,010	3,810	5,740	2,400	1,120	36.8	24.0	39	5.7	65
Starke	23,700	64	6,060	2,460	4,710	6,060	2,790	1,650	34.6	25.6	16	7.0	26
Steuben	29,200	52	6,860	3,290	5,480	8,010	3,630	1,950	36.9	23.5	48	6.7	40
Sullivan	18,500	74	4,260	1,850	3,860	5,010	2,130	1,350	36.3	23.0	61	7.3	14
Switzerland	8,000	89	1,780	810	1,570	2,200	1,080	560	37.8	22.3	80	7.0	26
Tippecanoe	145,200	7	34,990	30,040	31,270	31,600	11,820	5,510	28.3	24.1	37	3.8	91
Tipton	16,000	78	3,600	1,570	3,130	4,500	2,090	1,110	38.1	22.5	74	6.9	29
Union	7,200	91	1,640	720	1,470	2,010	900	470	36.9	22.8	65	6.5	43
Vanderburgh	163,200	6	37,770	15,510	32,170	47,070	18,830	11,890	38.3	23.1	57	7.3	14
Vermillion	15,600	79	3,420	1,570	3,120	4,440	2,030	1,060	38.2	21.9	85	6.8	31
Vigo	103,300	14	23,350	13,310	22,030	26,500	11,170	6,980	34.8	22.6	72	6.8	31
Wabash	33,900	43	7,720	4,100	6,320	9,130	4,230	2,440	36.7	22.8	65	7.2	19
Warren	7,700	90	1,630	790	1,480	2,120	1,120	590	39.5	21.2	91	7.7	5
Warrick	48,100	26	10,790	4,960	9,280	15,020	5,690	2,320	37.8	22.4	78	4.8	86
Washington	24,900	60	5,460	2,510	5,100	7,170	3,050	1,590	37.7	21.9	85	6.4	47
Wayne	69,900	21	16,230	7,300	13,340	18,920	8,960	5,180	37.6	23.2	55	7.4	12
Wells	27,300	54	6,770	2,970	5,020	7,640	3,090	1,850	36.0	24.8	27	6.8	31
White	23,600	65	5,890	2,340	4,350	6,460	2,750	1,810	36.3	25.0	22	7.7	5
Whitley	29,600	50	7,390	3,080	5,610	8,500	3,210	1,780	35.6	25.0	22	6.0	53

Footnote: Projections are the 1993 edition. Numbers may not sum to total due to rounding.
Source: IU Kelley School of Business (IBRC)
EDIN table(s): PPTA, PPAT

2.8 Population Under Age 18 1990 to 2000

	1990			2000			Change 1990 to 2000			
	Number	Percent of State	Percent of County	Number	Percent of State	Percent of County	Number	Rank	Percent	Rank
Indiana	1,455,964	100.00	—	1,441,970	100.00	—	-13,994	—	-1.0	—
Adams	9,860	0.68	31.70	10,310	0.71	30.70	450	10	4.6	6
Allen	83,504	5.74	27.80	85,850	5.95	27.20	2,346	5	2.8	10
Bartholomew	16,475	1.13	25.90	16,020	1.11	24.70	-455	50	-2.8	28
Benton	2,658	0.18	28.20	2,590	0.18	27.30	-68	21	-2.6	27
Blackford	3,572	0.25	25.40	3,330	0.23	24.50	-242	30	-6.8	53
Boone	10,437	0.72	27.40	10,200	0.71	25.60	-237	29	-2.3	24
Brown	3,468	0.24	24.60	3,120	0.22	20.90	-348	42	-10.0	73
Carroll	4,976	0.34	26.50	4,700	0.33	24.90	-276	37	-5.5	44
Cass	10,157	0.70	26.40	9,380	0.65	24.70	-777	72	-7.6	56
Clark	22,549	1.55	25.70	20,470	1.42	23.50	-2,079	89	-9.2	67
Clay	6,452	0.44	26.10	6,090	0.42	24.90	-362	45	-5.6	45
Clinton	8,552	0.59	27.60	8,240	0.57	26.30	-312	39	-3.6	33
Crawford	2,728	0.19	27.50	2,650	0.18	26.00	-78	23	-2.9	29
Daviess	7,955	0.55	28.90	7,860	0.55	28.10	-95	25	-1.2	20
Dearborn	11,106	0.76	28.60	10,630	0.74	25.50	-476	51	-4.3	39
Decatur	6,822	0.47	28.90	6,170	0.43	25.70	-652	67	-9.6	70
Dekalb	10,225	0.70	28.90	9,790	0.68	26.40	-435	49	-4.3	39
Delaware	26,415	1.81	22.10	29,300	2.03	24.10	2,885	4	10.9	3
Dubois	10,294	0.71	28.10	9,960	0.69	26.10	-334	41	-3.2	31
Elkhart	44,477	3.05	28.50	46,200	3.20	27.20	1,723	7	3.9	8
Fayette	6,903	0.47	26.50	5,990	0.42	23.40	-913	76	-13.2	88
Floyd	17,042	1.17	26.50	16,620	1.15	24.80	-422	48	-2.5	25
Fountain	4,612	0.32	25.90	4,120	0.29	24.00	-492	56	-10.7	79
Franklin	5,786	0.40	29.60	5,290	0.37	25.90	-496	58	-8.6	62
Fulton	5,016	0.34	26.60	4,890	0.34	25.70	-126	27	-2.5	25
Gibson	8,199	0.56	25.70	7,510	0.52	24.00	-689	68	-8.4	60
Grant	18,370	1.26	24.80	17,300	1.20	24.10	-1,070	80	-5.8	47
Greene	7,729	0.53	25.40	7,110	0.49	23.40	-619	65	-8.0	59
Hamilton	31,623	2.17	29.00	32,000	2.22	25.00	377	11	1.2	12
Hancock	12,545	0.86	27.60	11,200	0.78	23.60	-1,345	85	-10.7	79
Harrison	8,450	0.58	28.30	7,680	0.53	24.40	-770	71	-9.1	65
Hendricks	21,112	1.45	27.90	19,260	1.34	24.00	-1,852	88	-8.8	63
Henry	11,837	0.81	24.60	10,620	0.74	22.80	-1,217	84	-10.3	75
Howard	21,542	1.48	26.70	20,150	1.40	25.00	-1,392	86	-6.5	48
Huntington	9,804	0.67	27.70	9,440	0.65	26.10	-364	46	-3.7	35
Jackson	10,180	0.70	27.00	9,380	0.65	24.30	-800	74	-7.9	58
Jasper	7,173	0.49	28.70	6,670	0.46	26.00	-503	60	-7.0	54
Jay	5,700	0.39	26.50	5,620	0.39	26.30	-80	24	-1.4	21
Jefferson	7,455	0.51	25.00	6,960	0.48	23.60	-495	57	-6.6	51
Jennings	6,386	0.44	27.00	5,850	0.41	24.10	-536	62	-8.4	60
Johnson	23,817	1.64	27.00	22,960	1.59	24.40	-857	75	-3.6	33
Knox	9,235	0.63	23.20	9,190	0.64	23.60	-45	20	-0.5	18
Kosciusko	18,774	1.29	28.80	19,620	1.36	27.90	846	8	4.5	7
Lagrange	10,342	0.71	35.10	11,170	0.77	33.00	828	9	8.0	5
Lake	133,167	9.15	28.00	124,500	8.63	26.50	-8,667	92	-6.5	48
Laporte	27,113	1.86	25.30	25,920	1.80	24.00	-1,193	82	-4.4	42
Lawrence	10,934	0.75	25.50	9,940	0.69	23.20	-994	78	-9.1	65
Madison	32,375	2.22	24.80	30,260	2.10	23.60	-2,115	90	-6.5	48
Marion	203,185	13.96	25.50	220,080	15.26	26.20	16,895	1	8.3	4
Marshall	12,028	0.83	28.50	11,550	0.80	26.10	-478	52	-4.0	36
Martin	2,802	0.19	27.00	2,540	0.18	24.70	-262	34	-9.4	68
Miami	10,484	0.72	28.40	9,350	0.65	28.90	-1,134	81	-10.8	81
Monroe	20,067	1.38	18.40	26,350	1.83	22.20	6,283	3	31.3	1
Montgomery	8,680	0.60	25.20	8,750	0.61	25.20	70	14	0.8	13
Morgan	15,569	1.07	27.80	14,920	1.03	25.10	-649	66	-4.2	37
Newton	3,924	0.27	29.00	3,510	0.24	26.00	-414	47	-10.6	78
Noble	11,113	0.76	29.30	11,170	0.77	27.80	57	15	0.5	14
Ohio	1,392	0.10	26.20	1,350	0.09	24.10	-42	19	-3.0	30
Orange	4,922	0.34	26.70	4,440	0.31	24.30	-482	54	-9.8	72
Owen	4,625	0.32	26.80	4,600	0.32	24.90	-25	18	-0.5	18
Parke	3,869	0.27	25.10	3,590	0.25	23.80	-279	38	-7.2	55
Perry	4,950	0.34	25.90	4,350	0.30	22.90	-600	64	-12.1	87
Pike	3,064	0.21	24.50	2,830	0.20	23.40	-234	28	-7.6	56
Porter	35,523	2.44	27.60	30,850	2.14	23.20	-4,673	91	-13.2	88
Posey	7,284	0.50	28.00	6,550	0.45	25.00	-734	69	-10.1	74
Pulaski	3,619	0.25	28.60	3,550	0.25	28.00	-69	22	-1.9	23
Putnam	7,006	0.48	23.10	7,120	0.49	22.70	114	13	1.6	11
Randolph	7,026	0.48	25.90	6,240	0.43	23.70	-786	73	-11.2	83
Ripley	7,019	0.48	28.50	6,910	0.48	27.10	-109	26	-1.6	22
Rush	5,060	0.35	27.90	4,570	0.32	25.40	-490	55	-9.7	71
St. Joseph	62,463	4.29	25.30	64,700	4.49	25.40	2,237	6	3.6	9
Scott	5,832	0.40	27.80	5,580	0.39	25.70	-252	31	-4.3	39
Shelby	11,005	0.76	27.30	9,970	0.69	24.40	-1,035	79	-9.4	68
Spencer	5,320	0.37	27.30	4,840	0.34	24.70	-480	53	-9.0	64
Starke	6,380	0.44	28.00	6,110	0.42	26.10	-270	35	-4.2	37
Steuben	7,176	0.49	26.10	7,170	0.50	24.80	-6	17	-0.1	17
Sullivan	4,836	0.33	25.50	4,340	0.30	23.30	-496	58	-10.3	75
Switzerland	2,092	0.14	27.00	1,840	0.13	23.30	-252	31	-12.0	85
Tippecanoe	27,384	1.88	21.00	34,570	2.40	24.60	7,186	2	26.2	2
Tipton	4,215	0.29	26.10	3,710	0.26	23.20	-505	61	-12.0	85
Union	1,950	0.13	28.00	1,690	0.12	23.80	-260	33	-13.3	90
Vanderburgh	39,410	2.71	23.90	39,540	2.74	24.10	130	12	0.3	15
Vermillion	4,170	0.29	24.90	3,590	0.25	22.70	-580	63	-13.9	91
Vigo	24,379	1.67	23.00	24,380	1.69	23.50	1	16	0.0	16
Wabash	9,217	0.63	26.30	8,250	0.57	24.20	-967	77	-10.5	77
Warren	2,141	0.15	26.20	1,780	0.12	22.80	-361	44	-16.9	92
Warrick	12,723	0.87	28.30	11,310	0.78	24.00	-1,413	87	-11.1	82
Washington	6,493	0.45	27.40	5,740	0.40	23.30	-753	70	-11.6	84
Wayne	18,143	1.25	25.20	16,940	1.17	24.10	-1,203	83	-6.6	51
Wells	7,378	0.51	28.40	7,050	0.49	26.30	-328	40	-4.4	42
White	6,288	0.43	27.00	5,930	0.41	25.30	-358	43	-5.7	46
Whitley	7,855	0.54	28.40	7,580	0.53	26.10	-275	36	-3.5	32

Footnote: Projections are the 1993 edition.
Source: IU Kelley School of Business (IBRC)
EDIN table(s): PPTA

2.9 Population Over Age 18 1990 to 2000

| | 1990 | | | 2000 | | | Change 1990 to 2000 | |
	Number	Percent of State	Percent of County	Number	Percent of State	Percent of County	Number	Rank
Indiana	4,088,195	100.00	—	4,261,070	100.00	—	172,875	—
Adams	21,235	0.52	68.30	23,300	0.55	69.30	2,065	24
Allen	217,332	5.32	72.20	229,350	5.38	72.80	12,018	3
Bartholomew	47,182	1.15	74.10	48,720	1.14	75.20	1,538	30
Benton	6,783	0.17	71.80	6,850	0.16	72.10	67	74
Blackford	10,495	0.26	74.60	10,240	0.24	75.30	-255	82
Boone	27,710	0.68	72.60	29,650	0.70	74.30	1,940	26
Brown	10,612	0.26	75.40	11,810	0.28	79.30	1,198	38
Carroll	13,833	0.34	73.50	14,240	0.33	75.30	407	57
Cass	28,256	0.69	73.60	28,620	0.67	75.30	364	63
Clark	65,228	1.60	74.30	66,690	1.57	76.50	1,462	32
Clay	18,253	0.45	73.90	18,430	0.43	75.20	177	70
Clinton	22,422	0.55	72.40	23,050	0.54	73.60	628	50
Crawford	7,186	0.18	72.50	7,570	0.18	74.20	384	61
Daviess	19,578	0.48	71.10	20,100	0.47	71.80	522	52
Dearborn	27,729	0.68	71.40	31,100	0.73	74.60	3,371	15
Decatur	16,823	0.41	71.10	17,840	0.42	74.30	1,017	41
Dekalb	25,099	0.61	71.10	27,330	0.64	73.70	2,231	23
Delaware	93,244	2.28	77.90	92,210	2.16	75.90	-1,034	88
Dubois	26,322	0.64	71.90	28,270	0.66	74.00	1,948	25
Elkhart	111,721	2.73	71.50	123,400	2.90	72.80	11,679	4
Fayette	19,112	0.47	73.50	19,570	0.46	76.40	458	55
Floyd	47,362	1.16	73.50	50,290	1.18	75.20	2,928	17
Fountain	13,196	0.32	74.10	13,060	0.31	75.90	-136	81
Franklin	13,794	0.34	70.40	15,110	0.35	74.10	1,316	34
Fulton	13,824	0.34	73.40	14,110	0.33	74.30	286	66
Gibson	23,714	0.58	74.30	23,800	0.56	76.00	86	73
Grant	55,799	1.36	75.20	54,360	1.28	75.80	-1,439	90
Greene	22,681	0.55	74.60	23,320	0.55	76.70	639	49
Hamilton	77,313	1.89	71.00	95,820	2.25	75.00	18,507	2
Hancock	32,982	0.81	72.40	36,280	0.85	76.40	3,298	16
Harrison	21,440	0.52	71.70	23,790	0.56	75.50	2,350	20
Hendricks	54,605	1.34	72.10	60,800	1.43	75.90	6,195	7
Henry	36,302	0.89	75.40	35,890	0.84	77.20	-412	85
Howard	59,285	1.45	73.30	60,400	1.42	75.00	1,115	40
Huntington	25,623	0.63	72.30	26,620	0.62	73.70	997	44
Jackson	27,550	0.67	73.00	29,180	0.68	75.60	1,630	29
Jasper	17,787	0.44	71.30	18,990	0.45	73.90	1,203	37
Jay	15,812	0.39	73.50	15,780	0.37	73.70	-32	78
Jefferson	22,342	0.55	75.00	22,520	0.53	76.30	178	69
Jennings	17,275	0.42	73.00	18,480	0.43	76.00	1,205	36
Johnson	64,292	1.57	73.00	71,150	1.67	75.60	6,858	6
Knox	30,649	0.75	76.80	29,760	0.70	76.30	-889	87
Kosciusko	46,520	1.14	71.20	50,740	1.19	72.20	4,220	9
Lagrange	19,135	0.47	64.90	22,610	0.53	66.90	3,475	14
Lake	342,427	8.38	72.00	345,910	8.12	73.50	3,483	13
Laporte	79,953	1.96	74.70	82,240	1.93	76.00	2,287	21
Lawrence	31,902	0.78	74.50	32,880	0.77	76.80	978	47
Madison	98,294	2.40	75.20	97,890	2.30	76.40	-404	84
Marion	593,974	14.53	74.50	621,190	14.58	73.80	27,216	1
Marshall	30,154	0.74	71.50	32,750	0.77	73.90	2,596	19
Martin	7,567	0.19	73.00	7,750	0.18	75.20	183	68
Miami	26,413	0.65	71.60	23,100	0.54	71.30	-3,313	92
Monroe	88,911	2.17	81.60	92,590	2.17	77.90	3,679	12
Montgomery	25,756	0.63	74.80	25,960	0.61	74.80	204	67
Morgan	40,351	0.99	72.20	44,520	1.04	74.90	4,169	10
Newton	9,627	0.24	71.00	10,000	0.23	74.10	373	62
Noble	26,764	0.65	70.70	29,020	0.68	72.20	2,256	22
Ohio	3,923	0.10	73.80	4,210	0.10	75.20	287	65
Orange	13,487	0.33	73.30	13,880	0.33	75.80	393	59
Owen	12,656	0.31	73.20	13,930	0.33	75.30	1,274	35
Parke	11,541	0.28	74.90	11,540	0.27	76.40	-1	76
Perry	14,157	0.35	74.10	14,620	0.34	76.90	463	54
Pike	9,445	0.23	75.50	9,320	0.22	77.00	-125	80
Porter	93,409	2.28	72.40	102,150	2.40	76.80	8,741	5
Posey	18,684	0.46	72.00	19,690	0.46	75.20	1,006	42
Pulaski	9,024	0.22	71.40	9,180	0.22	72.30	156	71
Putnam	23,309	0.57	76.90	24,300	0.57	77.40	991	46
Randolph	20,122	0.49	74.10	20,040	0.47	76.20	-82	79
Ripley	17,597	0.43	71.50	18,590	0.44	72.90	993	45
Rush	13,069	0.32	72.10	13,460	0.32	74.80	391	60
St. Joseph	184,589	4.52	74.70	189,830	4.45	74.60	5,241	8
Scott	15,159	0.37	72.20	16,160	0.38	74.50	1,001	43
Shelby	29,302	0.72	72.70	30,830	0.72	75.60	1,528	31
Spencer	14,170	0.35	72.70	14,770	0.35	75.40	600	51
Starke	16,367	0.40	72.00	17,300	0.41	73.90	933	48
Steuben	20,270	0.50	73.90	21,730	0.51	75.20	1,460	33
Sullivan	14,157	0.35	74.50	14,290	0.34	76.80	133	72
Switzerland	5,646	0.14	73.00	6,100	0.14	77.20	454	56
Tippecanoe	103,214	2.52	79.00	105,820	2.48	75.40	2,606	18
Tipton	11,904	0.29	73.90	12,240	0.29	76.50	336	64
Union	5,026	0.12	72.00	5,420	0.13	76.30	394	58
Vanderburgh	125,648	3.07	76.10	124,340	2.92	75.90	-1,308	89
Vermillion	12,603	0.31	75.10	12,240	0.29	77.50	-363	83
Vigo	81,728	2.00	77.00	79,440	1.86	76.50	-2,288	91
Wabash	25,852	0.63	73.70	25,840	0.61	75.80	-12	77
Warren	6,035	0.15	73.80	6,060	0.14	77.70	25	75
Warrick	32,197	0.79	71.70	35,900	0.84	76.10	3,703	11
Washington	17,224	0.42	72.60	18,860	0.44	76.70	1,636	28
Wayne	53,808	1.32	74.80	53,300	1.25	75.90	-508	86
Wells	18,570	0.45	71.60	19,760	0.46	73.70	1,190	39
White	16,977	0.42	73.00	17,480	0.41	74.70	503	53
Whitley	19,796	0.48	71.60	21,440	0.50	73.90	1,644	27

Footnote: Projections are the 1993 edition.
Source: IU Kelley School of Business (IBRC)
EDIN table(s): PPTA

2.10 Population by Race and Hispanic Origin 1990

	Total	White	African-American	Native American	Asian American	Other Races	Hispanic Origin (Of Any Race)
			Percent of Total				
Indiana	**5,544,159**	**90.56**	**7.79**	**0.23**	**0.68**	**0.74**	**1.78**
Adams	31,095	98.18	0.12	0.14	0.19	1.37	2.60
Allen	300,836	87.78	10.08	0.30	0.88	0.96	1.93
Bartholomew	63,657	97.04	1.58	0.15	0.96	0.27	0.68
Benton	9,441	99.45	0.06	0.17	0.01	0.31	1.14
Blackford	14,067	99.37	0.05	0.31	0.11	0.16	0.64
Boone	38,147	99.13	0.22	0.24	0.25	0.17	0.66
Brown	14,080	99.20	0.09	0.33	0.13	0.24	0.67
Carroll	18,809	99.53	0.10	0.12	0.02	0.24	0.64
Cass	38,413	98.31	0.86	0.36	0.30	0.17	0.60
Clark	87,777	93.75	5.36	0.22	0.41	0.27	0.64
Clay	24,705	99.26	0.46	0.17	0.06	0.06	0.27
Clinton	30,974	98.98	0.12	0.16	0.20	0.55	1.46
Crawford	9,914	99.54	0.09	0.26	0.11	0.00	0.16
Daviess	27,533	99.42	0.36	0.09	0.07	0.06	0.31
Dearborn	38,835	98.98	0.65	0.14	0.19	0.04	0.32
Decatur	23,645	99.15	0.16	0.08	0.55	0.06	0.39
Dekalb	35,324	99.11	0.10	0.26	0.25	0.28	0.91
Delaware	119,659	92.96	5.99	0.23	0.54	0.29	0.71
Dubois	36,616	99.59	0.09	0.08	0.15	0.09	0.67
Elkhart	156,198	93.79	4.55	0.29	0.64	0.73	1.88
Fayette	26,015	97.87	1.67	0.14	0.27	0.05	0.32
Floyd	64,404	95.36	4.10	0.14	0.27	0.12	0.39
Fountain	17,808	99.54	0.02	0.14	0.15	0.15	0.49
Franklin	19,580	99.57	0.05	0.17	0.14	0.07	0.27
Fulton	18,840	98.49	0.80	0.25	0.19	0.27	0.72
Gibson	31,913	97.60	1.87	0.12	0.33	0.09	0.42
Grant	74,169	91.44	6.80	0.40	0.50	0.85	2.04
Greene	30,410	99.47	0.03	0.15	0.21	0.13	0.48
Hamilton	108,936	98.01	0.62	0.15	1.09	0.13	0.67
Hancock	45,527	99.22	0.10	0.13	0.39	0.16	0.73
Harrison	29,890	99.17	0.41	0.19	0.12	0.10	0.42
Hendricks	75,717	98.42	0.90	0.21	0.36	0.11	0.47
Henry	48,139	98.56	0.98	0.16	0.16	0.13	0.44
Howard	80,827	93.31	5.44	0.28	0.57	0.40	1.31
Huntington	35,427	98.83	0.15	0.43	0.38	0.21	0.79
Jackson	37,730	98.83	0.37	0.17	0.50	0.13	0.32
Jasper	24,960	98.79	0.44	0.24	0.16	0.36	1.27
Jay	21,512	99.07	0.14	0.15	0.31	0.33	0.70
Jefferson	29,797	97.93	1.22	0.19	0.41	0.24	0.41
Jennings	23,661	98.67	0.88	0.13	0.22	0.10	0.38
Johnson	88,109	98.12	0.96	0.16	0.61	0.15	0.71
Knox	39,884	98.05	1.22	0.17	0.45	0.11	0.51
Kosciusko	65,294	98.11	0.47	0.18	0.49	0.75	1.93
Lagrange	29,477	98.91	0.15	0.20	0.31	0.43	1.23
Lake	475,594	70.27	24.54	0.18	0.58	4.43	9.36
Laporte	107,066	89.93	8.95	0.24	0.40	0.48	1.47
Lawrence	42,836	99.30	0.25	0.21	0.18	0.06	0.34
Madison	130,669	91.63	7.55	0.23	0.32	0.27	0.68
Marion	797,159	77.15	21.28	0.21	0.95	0.40	1.06
Marshall	42,182	98.40	0.18	0.17	0.36	0.89	1.97
Martin	10,369	99.54	0.12	0.14	0.14	0.08	0.14
Miami	36,897	94.27	3.02	1.55	0.61	0.55	1.47
Monroe	108,978	94.29	2.60	0.20	2.49	0.42	1.25
Montgomery	34,436	98.65	0.58	0.20	0.40	0.17	0.46
Morgan	55,920	99.49	0.02	0.24	0.16	0.09	0.41
Newton	13,551	99.15	0.07	0.29	0.18	0.32	1.31
Noble	37,877	98.89	0.15	0.22	0.26	0.48	1.65
Ohio	5,315	98.87	0.77	0.15	0.17	0.04	0.13
Orange	18,409	98.94	0.69	0.22	0.11	0.04	0.32
Owen	17,281	99.34	0.25	0.27	0.10	0.03	0.32
Parke	15,410	98.78	0.77	0.27	0.10	0.08	0.62
Perry	19,107	98.49	1.10	0.17	0.17	0.07	0.35
Pike	12,509	99.68	0.02	0.13	0.15	0.02	0.32
Porter	128,932	97.98	0.35	0.19	0.73	0.75	2.99
Posey	25,968	98.54	1.09	0.15	0.13	0.10	0.40
Pulaski	12,643	98.94	0.51	0.17	0.16	0.22	0.84
Putnam	30,315	96.31	2.72	0.25	0.51	0.20	0.60
Randolph	27,148	99.26	0.21	0.18	0.14	0.22	0.71
Ripley	24,616	99.53	0.06	0.18	0.15	0.07	0.25
Rush	18,129	98.74	0.78	0.08	0.33	0.06	0.34
St. Joseph	247,052	87.83	9.79	0.34	1.01	1.02	2.11
Scott	20,991	99.33	0.08	0.12	0.24	0.24	0.71
Shelby	40,307	98.60	0.82	0.17	0.35	0.06	0.29
Spencer	19,490	99.00	0.57	0.19	0.17	0.07	0.46
Starke	22,747	98.68	0.32	0.38	0.21	0.41	1.61
Steuben	27,446	98.91	0.19	0.23	0.48	0.19	0.70
Sullivan	18,993	99.54	0.08	0.21	0.08	0.10	0.31
Switzerland	7,738	99.44	0.19	0.21	0.13	0.03	0.28
Tippecanoe	130,598	93.43	2.04	0.25	3.69	0.60	1.59
Tipton	16,119	99.20	0.06	0.12	0.32	0.30	0.75
Union	6,976	99.13	0.29	0.22	0.30	0.07	0.36
Vanderburgh	165,058	91.61	7.52	0.17	0.56	0.14	0.53
Vermillion	16,773	99.51	0.09	0.19	0.17	0.05	0.36
Vigo	106,107	92.75	5.58	0.28	1.09	0.30	0.94
Wabash	35,069	98.27	0.39	0.74	0.35	0.25	0.92
Warren	8,176	99.56	0.01	0.21	0.18	0.04	0.28
Warrick	44,920	98.56	0.83	0.18	0.35	0.08	0.37
Washington	23,717	99.61	0.10	0.12	0.08	0.10	0.46
Wayne	71,951	93.86	5.27	0.21	0.41	0.24	0.52
Wells	25,948	99.27	0.04	0.15	0.16	0.38	1.01
White	23,265	99.41	0.01	0.21	0.18	0.19	0.75
Whitley	27,651	99.36	0.10	0.26	0.13	0.14	0.46

Source: U.S. Bureau of the Census
EDIN table(s): RACE

2.11 Changes in Population by Race and Hispanic Origin 1980 to 1990

	Change 1980 to 1990						Percent Change 1980 to 1990					
	White	African-American	Native American	Asian American	Other Races	Hispanic Origin (Of Any Race)	White	African-American	Native American	Asian American	Other Races	Hispanic Origin (Of Any Race)
Indiana	11,883	17,603	3,029	13,262	8,158	12,270	0.2	4.2	31.3	54.5	24.8	14.2
Adams	1,430	33	-17	3	27	-11	4.9	1,100.0	-28.8	5.3	6.8	-1.3
Allen	245	4,317	287	760	892	1,125	0.1	16.6	47.4	40.3	44.4	24.0
Bartholomew	-1,722	-20	40	341	-70	-34	-2.7	-2.0	70.2	126.8	-29.0	-7.2
Benton	-787	2	7	1	0	31	-7.7	50.0	77.8	NA	0.0	40.3
Blackford	-1,560	5	22	8	22	37	-10.0	250.0	100.0	100.0	NA	69.8
Boone	1,621	40	40	-17	17	49	4.5	93.0	80.0	-15.3	34.7	24.4
Brown	1,641	-18	47	-1	34	56	13.3	-58.1	NA	-5.3	NA	147.4
Carroll	-919	2	-8	-3	15	20	-4.7	11.8	-26.7	-50.0	50.0	19.8
Cass	-2,675	-15	82	40	45	59	-6.6	-4.3	146.4	54.1	214.3	34.5
Clark	-1,686	414	43	72	96	247	-2.0	9.7	28.9	25.4	68.1	78.9
Clay	-185	-20	36	-2	14	4	-0.7	-15.0	720.0	-11.8	NA	6.5
Clinton	-680	12	-13	-2	112	-30	-2.2	50.0	-20.3	-3.2	196.5	-6.2
Crawford	110	-8	-12	4	0	-31	1.1	-47.1	-31.6	57.1	NA	-66.0
Daviess	-342	58	-24	-11	16	-55	-1.2	141.5	-48.0	-35.5	NA	-39.0
Dearborn	4,567	42	-9	-60	4	-8	13.5	20.0	-14.5	-44.4	36.4	-6.0
Decatur	-345	39	8	90	12	18	-1.5	NA	72.7	230.8	600.0	24.3
Dekalb	1,675	-17	40	-1	21	43	5.0	-31.5	78.4	-1.1	26.9	15.5
Delaware	-8,657	-542	47	94	130	3	-7.2	-7.0	20.7	17.2	60.5	0.4
Dubois	2,341	11	5	22	-1	130	6.9	50.0	20.0	66.7	-3.0	114.0
Elkhart	16,379	1,474	51	444	520	1,196	12.6	26.2	12.7	80.3	84.3	68.9
Fayette	-2,163	-38	-40	-10	-6	9	-7.8	-8.0	-51.9	-12.7	-33.3	12.2
Floyd	2,743	354	65	46	27	-8	4.7	15.5	240.7	35.7	50.9	-3.1
Fountain	-1,244	4	15	-15	15	53	-6.6	NA	150.0	-35.7	136.4	151.4
Franklin	-47	8	26	-32	13	-70	-0.2	400.0	325.0	-54.2	NA	-57.4
Fulton	-510	27	-24	-31	43	24	-2.7	21.8	-33.8	-46.3	537.5	21.6
Gibson	-1,290	24	8	1	14	-21	-4.0	4.2	26.7	1.0	93.3	-13.6
Grant	-6,807	-181	35	161	27	116	-9.1	-3.5	13.3	75.9	4.4	8.3
Greene	-67	-1	21	7	34	81	-0.2	-9.1	80.8	12.1	566.7	124.6
Hamilton	25,574	382	112	791	50	195	31.5	129.9	219.6	198.2	53.8	36.8
Hancock	1,540	11	20	-17	34	94	3.5	33.3	51.3	-8.8	82.9	39.3
Harrison	2,596	-33	39	-7	19	16	9.6	-21.0	205.3	-16.3	158.3	14.5
Hendricks	5,302	332	121	136	22	62	7.7	94.1	336.1	97.8	37.3	21.3
Henry	-5,174	-56	15	7	11	-60	-9.8	-10.6	23.8	9.9	21.2	-21.9
Howard	-6,287	141	-11	135	-47	74	-7.7	3.3	-4.6	41.9	-12.6	7.5
Huntington	-251	-12	33	17	44	149	-0.7	-18.8	27.3	14.7	137.5	112.9
Jackson	1,063	2	41	73	28	-8	2.9	1.5	164.0	62.9	140.0	-6.2
Jasper	-1,220	55	50	-47	-16	57	-4.7	98.2	500.0	-54.0	-15.1	21.9
Jay	-1,803	-27	16	56	31	34	-7.8	-47.4	100.0	509.1	79.5	29.1
Jefferson	-607	-107	8	30	54	3	-2.0	-22.8	16.0	32.6	284.2	2.5
Jennings	708	99	-11	-12	23	-29	3.1	90.0	-26.2	-19.0	NA	-24.4
Johnson	10,518	-23	25	339	10	161	13.9	-2.6	21.9	173.8	7.9	34.5
Knox	-2,221	165	17	98	-13	17	-5.4	51.4	32.7	122.5	-22.8	9.0
Kosciusko	5,408	84	0	31	216	356	9.2	37.3	0.0	10.7	79.7	39.5
Lagrange	3,682	28	40	72	105	238	14.5	175.0	210.5	360.0	500.0	191.9
Lake	-40,207	-9,378	56	430	1,728	732	-10.7	-7.4	6.9	18.4	8.9	1.7
Laporte	-2,566	924	42	45	-11	271	-2.6	10.7	19.4	11.7	-2.1	20.8
Lawrence	304	68	44	-63	11	-19	0.7	165.9	100.0	-45.0	73.3	-11.6
Madison	-9,118	200	78	-75	248	97	-7.1	2.1	35.3	-15.3	240.8	12.3
Marion	13,849	14,199	212	2,512	1,154	1,372	2.3	9.1	14.3	49.6	56.7	19.4
Marshall	2,764	23	33	95	112	199	7.1	43.4	84.6	169.6	42.6	31.5
Martin	-573	12	-6	-71	6	-40	-5.3	NA	-30.0	-83.5	300.0	-74.1
Miami	-3,302	117	242	-66	86	110	-8.7	11.7	73.6	-22.8	73.5	25.3
Monroe	8,677	194	106	1,179	37	275	9.2	7.3	96.4	76.9	8.7	25.2
Montgomery	-1,358	148	19	96	30	83	-3.8	279.2	38.8	228.6	107.1	109.2
Morgan	3,835	-4	96	-40	34	125	7.4	-30.8	234.1	-30.5	242.9	121.4
Newton	-1,306	-1	2	-3	15	40	-8.9	-10.0	5.4	-11.1	53.6	29.2
Noble	2,285	28	34	75	12	192	6.5	93.3	69.4	326.1	7.1	44.3
Ohio	217	-13	3	-8	2	2	4.3	-24.1	60.0	-47.1	NA	40.0
Orange	-202	-87	15	9	-3	-23	-1.1	-40.7	60.0	75.0	-27.3	-28.0
Owen	1,463	6	-3	-30	4	-5	9.3	15.8	-6.1	-62.5	200.0	-8.3
Parke	-1,044	75	-5	9	3	21	-6.4	174.4	-10.6	128.6	33.3	28.4
Perry	-421	195	-19	-7	13	46	-2.2	1,300.0	-37.3	-17.9	1,300.0	230.0
Pike	-862	-31	-37	-26	0	-44	-6.5	-91.2	-69.8	-57.8	0.0	-52.4
Porter	8,201	159	21	458	277	1,203	6.9	53.9	9.5	94.2	40.4	45.3
Posey	-400	17	-68	-11	16	-17	-1.5	6.4	-64.2	-24.4	177.8	-14.0
Pulaski	-656	25	16	-12	12	-8	-5.0	62.5	320.0	-37.5	75.0	-7.0
Putnam	633	334	42	94	49	67	2.2	67.9	120.0	156.7	376.9	58.3
Randolph	-2,877	14	6	-28	36	4	-9.6	33.3	14.0	-43.1	156.5	2.1
Ripley	189	10	20	-18	17	-20	0.8	166.7	83.3	-32.1	NA	-24.4
Rush	-1,548	34	-11	58	-8	-15	-8.0	31.5	-42.3	2,900.0	-42.1	-19.7
St. Joseph	725	2,302	375	1,136	897	1,694	0.3	10.5	79.6	82.9	55.1	48.3
Scott	567	8	17	-33	10	-62	2.8	100.0	212.5	-39.8	25.0	-29.5
Shelby	311	51	17	75	-34	2	0.8	18.3	34.0	111.9	-57.6	1.7
Spencer	152	-24	0	-11	12	37	0.8	-17.8	0.0	-25.0	600.0	71.2
Starke	634	17	17	21	61	261	2.9	30.4	24.6	77.8	184.8	246.2
Steuben	2,757	-30	14	66	-55	92	11.3	-37.0	28.0	100.0	-50.9	91.1
Sullivan	-2,146	5	0	8	19	4	-10.2	50.0	0.0	114.3	NA	7.3
Switzerland	587	8	1	-13	2	-35	3.9	114.3	6.7	-56.5	NA	-61.4
Tippecanoe	4,574	739	169	3,067	347	727	3.9	38.5	111.9	174.9	79.4	53.8
Tipton	-713	10	-3	20	-14	-5	-4.3	NA	-13.0	64.5	-22.6	-4.0
Union	99	12	-1	1	5	6	1.5	150.0	-6.3	5.0	NA	31.6
Vanderburgh	-3,229	321	15	301	135	142	-2.1	2.7	5.6	48.9	140.6	19.2
Vermillion	-1,470	4	17	-5	-2	-8	-8.1	36.4	113.3	-15.2	-20.0	-11.6
Vigo	-6,545	-131	-1	388	11	31	-6.2	-2.2	-0.3	50.2	3.5	3.2
Wabash	-1,687	-19	134	-49	50	120	-4.7	-12.1	107.2	-28.5	135.1	59.7
Warren	-812	-1	8	2	3	-19	-9.1	-50.0	88.9	15.4	NA	-45.2
Warrick	3,399	78	-20	-36	25	58	8.3	26.6	-19.4	-18.7	250.0	52.7
Washington	1,745	14	0	5	21	-23	8.0	155.6	0.0	38.5	1,050.0	-17.6
Wayne	-4,186	-101	2	122	56	37	-5.8	-2.6	1.3	70.1	47.1	11.0
Wells	480	10	22	7	28	51	1.9	NA	122.2	20.6	39.4	24.2
White	-652	2	42	-34	40	56	-2.7	NA	525.0	-45.3	800.0	47.1
Whitley	1,422	13	-27	11	17	64	5.5	81.3	-27.0	42.3	77.3	103.2

Source: U.S. Bureau of the Census
EDIN table(s): RACE

2.12 Urban and Rural Population 1990

	Total Population	Land Area (Square Miles)	Population Per Square Mile	Urban	Rural Total	Rural Farm	Rural Non-farm	Percent Change 1980-90 Urban	Percent Change 1980-90 Rural Total	Percent Change 1980-90 Rural Farm	Percent Change 1980-90 Rural Non-farm
Indiana	5,544,156	35,870.1	154.6	3,596,017	1,948,142	188,133	1,760,009	2.0	-0.9	-44.0	8.0
Adams	31,095	339.4	91.6	12,203	18,892	4,322	14,570	2.1	6.9	-33.6	30.6
Allen	300,836	657.3	457.7	248,686	52,150	4,946	47,204	5.1	-9.7	-47.1	-2.4
Bartholomew	63,657	406.9	156.5	32,171	31,486	2,450	29,036	3.5	-7.4	-32.1	-4.4
Benton	9,441	406.3	23.2	0	9,441	1,141	8,300	NA	-7.6	-50.2	4.7
Blackford	14,067	165.1	85.2	7,112	6,955	1,149	5,806	-8.5	-10.8	-41.6	-0.4
Boone	38,147	422.7	90.2	17,588	20,559	2,258	18,301	14.2	-2.3	-45.3	8.2
Brown	14,080	312.3	45.1	0	14,080	349	13,731	NA	13.8	-66.0	21.0
Carroll	18,809	372.3	50.5	2,531	16,278	2,006	14,272	-16.8	-2.4	-51.0	13.4
Cass	38,413	412.9	93.0	16,812	21,601	2,227	19,374	-6.1	-6.2	-49.9	4.2
Clark	87,774	375.2	234.0	65,102	22,675	1,310	21,365	1.5	-8.2	-60.8	0.0
Clay	24,705	357.6	69.1	7,640	17,065	1,811	15,254	-2.7	0.3	-44.4	10.9
Clinton	30,974	405.1	76.5	14,754	16,220	2,019	14,201	-2.7	-1.0	-45.3	11.9
Crawford	9,914	305.7	32.4	0	9,914	522	9,392	NA	1.0	-62.7	11.5
Daviess	27,533	430.7	63.9	10,838	16,695	3,639	13,056	-4.3	1.1	-35.5	20.1
Dearborn	38,835	305.2	127.2	16,067	22,768	1,662	21,106	33.7	2.2	-39.8	8.2
Decatur	23,645	372.6	63.5	9,286	14,359	2,499	11,860	0.3	-1.6	-39.8	13.7
Dekalb	35,324	362.9	97.3	17,329	17,995	2,508	15,487	11.8	-0.6	-51.0	19.3
Delaware	119,659	393.3	304.2	89,712	29,947	2,246	27,701	-5.3	-11.5	-49.0	-5.9
Dubois	36,616	430.1	85.1	15,272	21,344	2,149	19,195	5.5	8.0	-44.8	21.0
Elkhart	156,198	463.8	336.8	104,890	51,308	5,856	45,452	18.7	4.9	-25.2	10.6
Fayette	26,015	215.0	121.0	15,550	10,465	1,338	9,127	-8.7	-7.0	-34.7	-0.8
Floyd	64,404	148.0	435.1	40,930	23,474	670	22,804	4.3	7.0	-58.1	12.1
Fountain	17,808	395.7	45.0	6,204	11,604	1,707	9,897	-7.7	-5.7	-43.3	6.4
Franklin	19,580	386.0	50.7	3,397	16,183	2,546	13,637	-4.2	0.7	-28.5	9.1
Fulton	18,840	368.5	51.1	5,969	12,871	2,396	10,475	18.2	-9.9	-39.1	1.2
Gibson	31,913	488.5	65.3	10,909	21,004	2,247	18,757	-26.2	14.3	-35.7	26.1
Grant	74,169	414.0	179.1	45,332	28,837	2,613	26,224	-7.2	-10.1	-39.6	-5.6
Greene	30,410	542.1	56.1	8,406	22,004	1,937	20,067	-6.8	2.8	-49.8	14.4
Hamilton	108,936	398.0	273.7	75,350	33,586	2,350	31,236	68.4	-9.9	-50.0	-4.2
Hancock	45,527	306.2	148.7	17,517	28,010	2,266	25,744	8.6	0.7	-44.2	8.4
Harrison	29,890	485.3	61.6	2,827	27,063	2,189	24,874	3.8	10.2	-60.9	31.3
Hendricks	75,717	408.4	185.4	27,408	48,309	2,700	45,609	15.1	5.0	-40.8	10.1
Henry	48,139	393.0	122.5	17,753	30,386	2,687	27,699	-22.9	0.3	-44.5	8.8
Howard	80,827	293.1	275.8	56,803	24,024	2,089	21,935	-7.1	-6.8	-38.2	-2.1
Huntington	35,427	382.6	92.6	16,389	19,038	2,349	16,689	1.2	-1.8	-46.2	11.1
Jackson	37,730	509.3	74.1	18,448	19,282	2,009	17,273	3.9	2.7	-50.1	17.2
Jasper	24,960	559.9	44.6	5,045	19,915	2,394	17,521	-32.8	6.9	-38.9	19.1
Jay	21,512	383.7	56.1	9,070	12,442	2,930	9,512	-10.1	-5.4	-34.6	9.7
Jefferson	29,797	361.4	82.5	15,616	14,181	2,176	12,005	-5.5	2.1	-41.7	18.2
Jennings	23,661	377.3	62.7	5,311	18,350	1,979	16,371	-7.9	7.4	-37.8	17.7
Johnson	88,109	320.2	275.2	66,178	21,931	1,907	20,024	23.2	-6.8	-41.9	-1.2
Knox	39,884	515.9	77.3	23,216	16,668	1,920	14,748	-9.2	2.5	-48.4	17.6
Kosciusko	65,294	537.5	121.5	17,681	47,613	3,875	43,738	10.1	9.5	-36.7	17.0
Lagrange	29,477	379.6	77.7	0	29,477	5,639	23,838	NA	15.4	-25.6	32.6
Lake	475,594	497.0	956.9	453,887	21,707	1,135	20,572	-8.7	-16.0	-54.9	-11.8
Laporte	107,066	598.3	179.0	60,593	46,473	2,527	43,946	-5.4	4.3	-38.8	8.6
Lawrence	42,836	448.9	95.4	18,486	24,350	1,328	23,022	-3.0	4.0	-53.1	11.8
Madison	130,669	452.2	289.0	87,438	43,231	2,597	40,634	-7.0	-4.5	-50.6	1.6
Marion	797,159	396.4	2,011.0	797,159	0	0	0	4.2	NA	NA	NA
Marshall	42,182	444.3	94.9	13,028	29,154	3,211	25,943	15.7	4.5	-42.6	16.3
Martin	10,369	336.2	30.8	2,890	7,479	695	6,784	-5.7	-5.8	-52.4	4.8
Miami	36,897	375.8	98.2	17,114	19,783	2,407	17,376	-7.2	-7.5	-42.8	1.2
Monroe	108,978	394.4	276.3	74,306	34,672	1,224	33,448	10.9	9.1	-38.8	12.4
Montgomery	34,436	504.6	68.2	13,584	20,852	2,269	18,583	1.9	-6.0	-46.6	3.6
Morgan	55,920	406.5	137.6	17,218	38,702	1,916	36,786	3.3	9.5	-42.9	15.0
Newton	13,551	401.9	33.7	0	13,551	1,061	12,490	NA	-8.7	-53.3	-0.7
Noble	37,877	411.1	92.1	11,216	26,661	3,298	23,363	7.5	6.6	-39.7	19.6
Ohio	5,315	86.7	61.3	0	5,315	668	4,647	NA	3.9	-27.5	10.8
Orange	18,409	399.6	46.1	3,542	14,867	1,236	13,631	-2.6	-1.2	-47.0	7.2
Owen	17,281	385.2	44.9	2,536	14,745	1,018	13,727	-7.2	12.5	-64.8	34.3
Parke	15,410	444.8	34.6	2,706	12,704	1,165	11,539	-2.8	-6.5	-59.9	8.0
Perry	19,107	381.4	50.1	8,088	11,019	887	10,132	-7.1	3.5	-54.9	16.8
Pike	12,509	336.2	37.2	0	12,509	913	11,596	-100.0	19.4	-45.5	31.7
Porter	128,932	418.2	308.3	86,403	42,529	1,386	41,143	11.6	0.4	-54.7	4.7
Posey	25,968	408.5	63.6	7,217	18,751	1,352	17,399	-5.7	0.0	-56.2	11.0
Pulaski	12,643	433.7	29.2	0	12,643	1,462	11,181	NA	-4.6	-61.3	17.9
Putnam	30,315	480.3	63.1	8,984	21,331	2,072	19,259	6.9	2.8	-49.8	15.8
Randolph	27,148	452.9	59.9	8,707	18,441	3,618	14,823	-11.4	-8.6	-31.7	-0.4
Ripley	24,616	446.4	55.1	3,869	20,747	2,762	17,985	11.5	-0.9	-40.0	10.2
Rush	18,129	408.3	44.4	5,533	12,596	2,797	9,799	-9.5	-6.6	-34.9	6.6
St. Joseph	247,052	457.3	540.2	214,194	32,858	2,691	30,167	5.7	-15.9	-45.7	-11.5
Scott	20,991	190.4	110.2	9,644	11,347	980	10,367	-2.8	8.1	-44.9	18.9
Shelby	40,307	412.7	97.7	15,336	24,971	2,433	22,538	2.3	0.3	-44.0	9.7
Spencer	19,490	398.7	48.9	0	19,490	2,254	17,236	-100.0	16.2	-36.1	30.1
Starke	22,747	309.3	73.5	3,711	19,036	1,508	17,528	1.0	3.9	-45.4	12.6
Steuben	27,446	308.7	88.9	5,824	21,622	1,596	20,026	6.2	12.6	-48.1	24.1
Sullivan	18,993	447.2	42.5	4,663	14,330	1,353	12,977	-2.3	-12.3	-56.2	-2.0
Switzerland	7,738	221.2	35.0	0	7,738	1,700	6,038	NA	8.2	-34.0	31.9
Tippecanoe	130,598	499.8	261.3	99,840	30,758	2,218	28,540	9.4	1.1	-43.7	7.8
Tipton	16,119	260.4	61.9	4,751	11,368	1,483	9,885	-9.7	-1.6	-33.3	5.9
Union	6,976	161.6	43.2	0	6,976	1,014	5,962	NA	1.7	-28.3	9.5
Vanderburgh	165,058	234.6	703.6	141,028	24,030	1,003	23,027	-1.7	-0.2	-38.7	2.6
Vermillion	16,773	256.9	65.3	5,040	11,733	748	10,985	-4.3	-9.5	-56.8	-2.2
Vigo	106,107	403.3	263.1	76,943	29,164	1,436	27,728	2.8	-22.4	-61.2	-18.1
Wabash	35,069	413.2	84.9	18,510	16,559	2,610	13,949	-2.5	-6.2	-40.3	5.0
Warren	8,176	364.9	22.4	0	8,176	1,360	6,816	NA	-8.9	-39.3	1.2
Warrick	44,920	384.1	117.0	25,197	19,723	1,150	18,573	17.5	-1.6	-41.9	2.9
Washington	23,717	514.5	46.1	5,619	18,098	2,119	15,979	6.2	8.7	-50.9	29.6
Wayne	71,951	403.6	178.3	38,649	33,302	2,337	30,965	-6.5	-4.1	-43.9	1.3
Wells	25,948	370.0	70.1	9,020	16,928	2,913	14,015	3.6	1.4	-39.4	17.9
White	23,265	505.3	46.0	5,237	18,028	1,940	16,088	1.5	-3.6	-46.5	6.7
Whitley	27,651	335.5	82.4	9,005	18,646	2,301	16,345	76.9	-11.7	-54.1	1.4

Footnote: Urban - places of 2,500 or more persons. Rural - all persons living on farms.
Source: U.S. Bureau of the Census
EDIN table(s): POPD, PURB

2.13 Population 15 Years and Older by Sex and Marital Status 1990

	Total Male	Total Female	Never Married Male	Never Married Female	Married Male	Married Female	Separated Male	Separated Female	Widowed Male	Widowed Female	Divorced Male	Divorced Female
Indiana	2,064,662	2,263,865	569,459	481,644	1,244,234	1,239,148	24,707	33,317	50,574	274,357	175,688	235,399
Adams	10,946	11,833	2,832	2,335	7,198	7,182	82	107	255	1,444	579	765
Allen	109,800	120,644	31,257	27,279	65,851	65,735	1,318	1,927	2,418	12,919	8,956	12,784
Bartholomew	23,998	26,133	5,436	4,473	15,728	15,666	230	274	513	2,865	2,091	2,855
Benton	3,425	3,784	755	599	2,299	2,296	25	37	104	568	242	284
Blackford	5,291	5,870	1,141	875	3,513	3,510	45	56	156	869	436	560
Boone	13,848	15,549	2,740	2,387	9,780	9,762	130	127	293	1,936	905	1,337
Brown	5,534	5,704	1,102	833	3,752	3,737	52	62	131	561	497	511
Carroll	7,120	7,582	1,510	1,122	4,904	4,911	52	45	169	948	485	556
Cass	14,186	15,883	3,391	2,658	9,010	9,006	171	206	397	2,305	1,217	1,708
Clark	32,369	36,848	8,050	6,972	19,975	19,935	442	628	780	4,672	3,122	4,641
Clay	9,081	10,255	1,965	1,535	6,067	6,048	82	102	283	1,698	684	872
Clinton	11,247	12,588	2,382	1,925	7,585	7,594	109	161	325	1,837	846	1,071
Crawford	3,766	3,933	869	618	2,405	2,404	34	26	115	556	343	329
Daviess	9,878	10,985	2,270	1,798	6,484	6,485	68	93	299	1,676	757	933
Dearborn	14,246	15,242	3,441	2,614	9,317	9,317	134	186	319	1,779	1,035	1,346
Decatur	8,716	9,281	2,110	1,591	5,669	5,644	75	90	227	1,120	635	836
Dekalb	12,968	13,792	3,100	2,324	8,420	8,404	137	160	291	1,633	1,020	1,271
Delaware	45,765	52,095	15,444	14,818	25,042	25,017	463	662	1,008	6,238	3,808	5,360
Dubois	13,540	14,349	3,491	2,786	8,837	8,818	79	89	320	1,748	813	908
Elkhart	56,986	61,542	14,203	12,118	36,081	35,886	762	954	1,086	6,408	4,854	6,176
Fayette	9,744	10,758	2,337	1,705	6,103	6,131	121	137	242	1,519	941	1,266
Floyd	23,494	26,733	5,775	4,992	14,745	14,753	256	458	630	3,402	2,088	3,128
Fountain	6,652	7,360	1,404	1,059	4,471	4,459	65	58	204	1,209	508	575
Franklin	7,262	7,567	1,823	1,466	4,757	4,760	65	58	157	808	460	475
Fulton	6,994	7,649	1,394	1,104	4,682	4,694	70	84	225	1,064	623	703
Gibson	11,864	13,209	2,632	2,055	7,889	7,902	94	123	359	1,993	890	1,136
Grant	28,048	31,101	7,416	6,454	16,959	16,786	250	354	652	3,876	2,771	3,631
Greene	11,455	12,554	2,404	1,672	7,619	7,609	92	123	354	1,986	986	1,164
Hamilton	39,708	42,532	8,507	7,327	27,879	27,891	289	388	604	3,183	2,429	3,743
Hancock	17,092	18,157	3,812	3,001	11,682	11,675	134	163	366	1,844	1,098	1,474
Harrison	11,159	11,708	2,514	1,881	7,435	7,419	99	106	218	1,344	893	958
Hendricks	29,309	29,206	7,067	4,580	19,443	19,178	282	295	520	2,776	1,997	2,377
Henry	18,290	20,319	4,060	3,223	11,988	11,998	198	260	490	2,785	1,554	2,053
Howard	29,521	33,543	6,996	6,074	18,767	18,768	301	491	647	3,991	2,810	4,219
Huntington	12,927	14,214	3,070	2,574	8,491	8,470	122	145	314	1,827	930	1,198
Jackson	13,995	15,328	3,132	2,464	9,263	9,256	122	151	338	2,007	1,140	1,450
Jasper	9,278	9,755	2,407	1,868	6,048	6,037	77	82	191	1,121	555	647
Jay	7,967	8,840	1,774	1,433	5,265	5,255	72	81	208	1,208	648	863
Jefferson	11,309	12,321	2,980	2,488	6,814	6,771	122	175	307	1,515	1,086	1,372
Jennings	9,038	9,436	2,337	1,808	5,626	5,610	96	90	194	1,092	785	836
Johnson	32,733	35,795	7,841	6,637	21,349	21,295	338	429	670	3,911	2,535	3,523
Knox	15,454	16,680	4,996	3,429	8,726	8,683	139	195	470	2,682	1,123	1,691
Kosciusko	23,792	25,521	5,243	4,425	16,023	16,017	210	263	541	2,677	1,775	2,139
Lagrange	10,290	10,563	2,659	2,222	6,777	6,753	74	72	205	942	575	574
Lake	171,701	193,410	52,924	48,006	96,135	95,897	2,951	4,613	5,305	24,939	14,386	19,955
Laporte	42,904	41,647	12,533	8,004	24,137	23,154	587	597	1,133	5,390	4,514	4,502
Lawrence	16,134	17,758	3,497	2,699	10,706	10,723	125	178	463	2,465	1,343	1,693
Madison	50,265	53,887	13,254	10,141	29,822	29,399	589	682	1,264	7,077	5,336	6,588
Marion	290,049	334,169	88,850	84,540	157,060	156,722	5,479	8,009	7,240	38,855	31,420	46,043
Marshall	15,454	16,614	3,542	2,810	10,248	10,233	142	160	393	2,029	1,129	1,382
Martin	3,907	4,141	955	698	2,511	2,518	26	24	95	548	320	353
Miami	13,685	14,420	3,181	2,294	9,022	8,969	143	147	290	1,648	1,049	1,362
Monroe	43,839	48,109	20,546	20,339	19,451	19,412	319	427	582	3,626	2,941	4,305
Montgomery	13,319	13,867	3,348	2,061	8,446	8,441	111	130	346	1,897	1,068	1,338
Morgan	20,911	22,258	4,574	3,572	14,131	14,128	210	255	400	2,305	1,596	1,998
Newton	4,999	5,290	1,151	862	3,293	3,296	43	63	151	684	361	385
Noble	13,881	14,719	3,299	2,504	9,079	9,065	108	125	330	1,716	1,065	1,309
Ohio	1,983	2,150	420	315	1,334	1,332	19	24	55	323	155	156
Orange	6,902	7,464	1,552	1,152	4,470	4,454	52	61	174	1,024	654	773
Owen	6,559	6,877	1,366	1,010	4,412	4,397	57	60	171	817	553	593
Parke	5,858	6,412	1,372	959	3,793	3,835	47	85	178	952	468	581
Perry	7,583	7,427	2,009	1,191	4,560	4,422	109	84	199	1,100	706	630
Pike	4,808	5,192	982	731	3,218	3,215	44	31	133	795	431	420
Porter	47,980	51,428	12,743	10,753	30,385	30,338	380	528	965	5,152	3,507	4,657
Posey	9,635	10,196	2,092	1,642	6,580	6,568	57	84	214	1,110	692	792
Pulaski	4,685	4,933	1,044	716	3,140	3,124	27	31	128	727	346	335
Putnam	12,625	11,871	3,905	2,687	7,079	6,790	149	117	289	1,394	1,203	883
Randolph	10,204	11,271	2,242	1,735	6,814	6,832	109	155	260	1,504	779	1,045
Ripley	9,093	9,755	2,242	1,768	5,879	5,852	63	92	274	1,345	635	698
Rush	6,688	7,358	1,559	1,243	4,388	4,391	67	91	195	1,012	479	621
St. Joseph	91,924	102,326	28,879	25,170	52,055	51,956	1,244	1,743	2,444	13,265	7,302	10,192
Scott	7,797	8,442	1,803	1,316	4,988	4,979	69	100	203	1,119	734	928
Shelby	14,997	16,208	3,377	2,801	9,744	9,744	146	166	344	1,931	1,386	1,566
Spencer	7,520	7,528	1,919	1,158	4,849	4,827	43	42	195	972	514	529
Starke	8,460	9,051	2,029	1,524	5,360	5,352	90	112	294	1,294	687	769
Steuben	10,645	10,825	2,802	1,843	6,678	6,664	78	110	252	1,242	835	966
Sullivan	7,026	7,983	1,461	1,166	4,718	4,703	50	70	265	1,378	532	666
Switzerland	2,926	3,072	682	433	1,885	1,867	31	42	80	454	248	276
Tippecanoe	54,099	53,253	24,285	18,469	25,313	24,911	408	522	879	4,802	3,214	4,549
Tipton	6,031	6,634	1,317	1,099	4,015	4,008	50	64	163	872	486	591
Union	2,568	2,834	569	470	1,708	1,708	28	36	70	369	193	251
Vanderburgh	60,684	70,887	15,979	14,502	36,167	36,153	567	793	1,794	10,404	6,177	9,035
Vermillion	6,213	7,117	1,406	1,124	4,001	3,994	57	72	206	1,222	543	705
Vigo	41,570	44,135	13,499	10,357	22,481	21,879	712	544	1,121	6,453	3,757	4,902
Wabash	13,029	14,480	3,232	2,724	8,406	8,392	87	119	330	1,985	974	1,260
Warren	3,090	3,311	629	501	2,179	2,169	21	31	78	402	183	208
Warrick	16,667	17,783	3,646	2,872	11,476	11,482	104	159	339	1,755	1,102	1,515
Washington	8,974	9,376	2,053	1,428	5,741	5,715	97	99	246	1,220	837	914
Wayne	26,576	30,507	6,617	5,849	16,489	16,449	392	575	761	4,259	2,317	3,375
Wells	9,301	10,382	1,941	1,681	6,486	6,498	81	93	199	1,281	594	829
White	8,608	9,432	1,764	1,375	5,802	5,782	74	80	233	1,353	735	842
Whitley	10,221	10,935	2,319	1,749	6,882	6,882	87	119	256	1,349	677	836

Source: U.S. Bureau of the Census
EDIN table(s): PMAR

Percent Change in the Number of Non-family Households
1980 to 1990

Indiana = 25.3% Increase

- 30.0% or More (22)
- 21.0% to 29.9% (27)
- 15.5% to 20.9% (22)
- Less than 15.5% (21)

Percent Change in the Number of Family Households
1980 to 1990

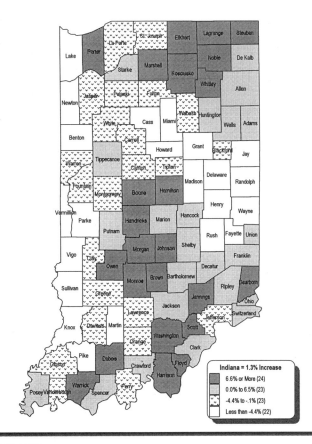

Indiana = 1.3% Increase

- 6.6% or More (24)
- 0.0% to 6.5% (23)
- -4.4% to -.1% (23)
- Less than -4.4% (22)

Percent Change in the Number of Nonfamily Households: EDIN Table HHTC.
Percent Change in the Number of Family Households: EDIN Table HHTC.

2.14 Persons in Family Households by Relationship 1990

	Total	In Family Household	Persons Percent Change 1980-1990	House-holder	Spouse	Total	Children of Householder Natural Born or Adopted	Stepchild	Grandchild	Other Relatives	Non-relatives
Indiana	5,544,159	4,677,147	-2.7	1,480,351	1,202,020	1,740,331	1,628,874	111,457	80,599	103,376	70,470
Adams	31,095	27,941	2.2	8,075	6,994	12,024	11,529	495	206	416	226
Allen	300,836	255,502	-0.8	79,624	64,009	99,104	93,857	5,247	3,826	5,120	3,819
Bartholomew	63,657	55,821	-5.4	18,141	15,273	19,728	18,379	1,349	823	1,029	827
Benton	9,441	8,280	-9.6	2,598	2,246	3,114	2,915	199	101	125	96
Blackford	14,067	12,370	-11.3	4,043	3,435	4,344	3,998	346	163	190	195
Boone	38,147	33,838	3.1	10,816	9,553	12,228	11,366	862	397	501	343
Brown	14,080	12,455	11.4	4,076	3,615	4,115	3,778	337	227	240	182
Carroll	18,809	16,701	-7.0	5,389	4,785	5,909	5,445	464	200	228	190
Cass	38,413	32,684	-8.9	10,609	8,794	11,864	10,909	955	414	555	448
Clark	87,777	75,969	-5.6	24,355	19,253	27,927	25,947	1,980	1,450	1,840	1,144
Clay	24,705	21,663	-2.9	6,932	5,895	7,863	7,247	616	361	369	243
Clinton	30,974	27,081	-3.6	8,610	7,359	9,910	9,160	750	417	446	339
Crawford	9,914	8,813	-2.6	2,754	2,324	3,238	2,969	269	141	190	166
Daviess	27,533	24,144	-3.3	7,404	6,314	9,514	9,032	482	267	372	273
Dearborn	38,835	34,945	10.7	10,692	9,046	13,495	12,511	984	538	764	410
Decatur	23,645	21,045	-3.3	6,455	5,492	8,184	7,668	516	264	396	254
Dekalb	35,324	31,296	1.7	9,617	8,186	12,082	11,192	890	420	540	451
Delaware	119,659	91,246	-13.1	30,186	24,240	32,060	29,887	2,173	1,541	1,773	1,446
Dubois	36,616	32,174	3.7	9,847	8,633	12,718	12,157	561	200	473	303
Elkhart	156,198	134,883	10.4	41,751	34,802	50,947	47,609	3,338	2,039	2,781	2,563
Fayette	26,015	22,683	-11.4	7,313	5,922	8,259	7,610	649	407	443	339
Floyd	64,404	56,423	2.3	18,058	14,286	21,003	19,687	1,316	950	1,320	806
Fountain	17,808	15,559	-8.9	5,044	4,349	5,497	5,055	442	209	266	194
Franklin	19,580	17,735	-2.6	5,303	4,634	7,030	6,673	357	247	341	180
Fulton	18,840	16,361	-5.5	5,351	4,584	5,739	5,258	481	219	255	213
Gibson	31,913	27,747	-6.3	9,003	7,724	9,961	9,338	623	352	429	278
Grant	74,169	61,982	-11.9	20,196	16,269	21,855	20,235	1,620	1,317	1,248	1,097
Greene	30,410	26,445	-2.0	8,692	7,403	9,242	8,518	724	376	452	280
Hamilton	108,936	98,345	29.3	30,854	27,398	37,138	35,138	2,000	747	1,390	818
Hancock	45,527	41,401	0.7	12,886	11,395	15,410	14,392	1,018	651	637	422
Harrison	29,890	27,084	6.1	8,437	7,234	10,108	9,412	696	394	560	351
Hendricks	75,717	67,715	5.3	21,220	18,762	25,170	23,480	1,690	798	1,104	661
Henry	48,139	42,236	-12.2	13,976	11,682	14,621	13,553	1,068	672	706	579
Howard	80,827	69,941	-10.9	22,729	18,281	25,772	23,882	1,890	1,167	1,162	830
Huntington	35,427	30,664	-2.2	9,643	8,257	11,501	10,691	810	397	486	380
Jackson	37,730	33,508	0.8	10,701	9,011	12,221	11,334	887	525	608	442
Jasper	24,960	21,871	-6.8	6,726	5,879	8,389	7,966	423	271	390	216
Jay	21,512	18,889	-10.1	6,035	5,135	6,898	6,431	467	252	302	267
Jefferson	29,797	24,654	-5.5	8,023	6,556	8,736	8,134	602	410	531	398
Jennings	23,661	20,654	1.6	6,430	5,451	7,654	7,026	628	372	449	298
Johnson	88,109	76,620	9.8	24,260	20,701	28,310	26,360	1,950	1,016	1,400	933
Knox	39,884	31,246	-11.1	10,248	8,444	11,212	10,483	729	384	573	385
Kosciusko	65,294	57,589	7.5	17,924	15,576	21,662	20,228	1,434	709	969	749
Lagrange	29,477	26,856	12.4	7,402	6,608	11,944	11,411	533	231	422	249
Lake	475,594	418,783	-11.8	125,761	91,980	168,153	160,352	7,801	11,999	14,110	6,780
Laporte	107,066	88,561	-7.2	27,906	22,487	32,998	30,794	2,204	1,634	2,031	1,505
Lawrence	42,836	37,535	-2.5	12,171	10,409	13,300	12,180	1,120	613	629	413
Madison	130,669	109,346	-10.8	35,804	28,617	39,023	35,793	3,230	2,081	2,110	1,711
Marion	797,159	644,041	-0.8	205,652	150,965	237,402	222,455	14,947	15,905	19,980	14,137
Marshall	42,182	37,275	5.1	11,508	9,945	14,240	13,380	860	426	654	502
Martin	10,369	9,010	-9.0	2,840	2,430	3,381	3,182	199	110	144	105
Miami	36,897	32,422	-9.5	10,284	8,763	12,178	11,198	980	351	449	397
Monroe	108,978	68,578	4.4	22,953	18,753	23,345	21,846	1,499	807	1,477	1,243
Montgomery	34,436	29,016	-6.0	9,578	8,209	10,136	9,256	880	303	475	315
Morgan	55,920	50,953	5.1	15,885	13,673	18,728	17,209	1,519	859	1,079	729
Newton	13,551	12,050	-11.0	3,710	3,208	4,600	4,292	308	178	208	146
Noble	37,877	33,557	4.8	10,308	8,804	12,856	11,965	891	410	632	547
Ohio	5,315	4,704	0.7	1,497	1,293	1,682	1,563	119	71	101	60
Orange	18,409	16,114	-3.3	5,169	4,341	5,848	5,408	440	217	310	229
Owen	17,281	15,396	7.3	4,936	4,264	5,392	4,915	477	254	332	218
Parke	15,410	13,226	-10.1	4,343	3,695	4,599	4,209	390	210	237	142
Perry	19,107	16,312	-7.8	5,137	4,313	6,152	5,718	434	198	338	174
Pike	12,509	10,975	-9.0	3,658	3,140	3,721	3,469	252	140	183	133
Porter	128,932	112,615	5.0	34,634	29,509	43,407	40,699	2,708	1,449	2,260	1,356
Posey	25,968	23,257	-4.3	7,331	6,432	8,753	8,207	546	233	307	201
Pulaski	12,643	11,123	-7.6	3,485	3,061	4,143	3,841	302	132	190	112
Putnam	30,315	23,377	-1.8	7,549	6,600	8,211	7,495	716	338	427	252
Randolph	27,148	23,842	-12.8	7,789	6,673	8,438	7,817	621	294	368	280
Ripley	24,616	21,860	-2.1	6,646	5,686	8,504	8,079	425	313	470	241
Rush	18,129	15,908	-9.3	4,985	4,265	5,922	5,521	401	278	281	177
St. Joseph	247,052	200,500	-2.1	63,629	50,364	74,959	71,016	3,943	3,478	4,735	3,335
Scott	20,991	18,761	-0.8	5,881	4,806	6,983	6,437	546	367	421	303
Shelby	40,307	35,524	-2.1	11,169	9,454	13,031	12,002	1,029	589	723	558
Spencer	19,490	17,201	-1.5	5,388	4,739	6,531	6,161	370	152	256	135
Starke	22,747	20,145	0.6	6,186	5,154	7,566	7,034	532	396	509	334
Steuben	27,446	23,348	9.1	7,446	6,468	8,418	7,797	621	264	413	339
Sullivan	18,993	16,509	-12.5	5,338	4,598	5,867	5,473	394	243	299	164
Switzerland	7,738	6,764	3.6	2,099	1,813	2,463	2,327	136	125	157	107
Tippecanoe	130,598	88,444	1.8	28,742	24,096	31,620	29,797	1,823	986	1,749	1,251
Tipton	16,119	14,243	-7.1	4,554	3,916	5,204	4,863	341	196	215	158
Union	6,976	6,147	-3.2	1,958	1,653	2,245	2,047	198	97	126	68
Vanderburgh	165,058	134,071	-5.6	44,311	34,952	47,516	44,532	2,984	2,257	3,034	2,001
Vermillion	16,773	14,264	-11.7	4,650	3,888	5,110	4,720	390	219	253	144
Vigo	106,107	81,679	-9.7	26,608	21,191	29,284	27,126	2,158	1,328	1,972	1,296
Wabash	35,069	29,474	-6.3	9,450	8,136	10,676	9,936	740	371	450	391
Warren	8,176	7,375	-10.2	2,378	2,120	2,603	2,433	170	76	124	74
Warrick	44,920	40,750	5.6	12,761	11,191	15,217	14,192	1,025	523	633	425
Washington	23,717	21,014	4.7	6,597	5,550	7,786	7,153	633	323	443	315
Wayne	71,951	60,219	-9.7	19,766	15,903	21,256	19,699	1,557	1,023	1,346	925
Wells	25,948	23,011	-0.6	7,249	6,323	8,675	8,139	536	231	318	215
White	23,265	20,340	-5.1	6,567	5,666	7,295	6,737	558	222	307	283
Whitley	27,651	24,469	2.4	7,677	6,735	9,214	8,560	654	262	320	261

Source: U.S. Bureau of the Census
EDIN table(s): PHTR

2.15 Persons in Non-family Households by Relationship 1990

	Number of Persons in Non-family Households	Percent of Total Persons	Householder Living Alone	Householder Not Living Alone	Non-relatives	In Group Quarters Institutionalized Persons	In Group Quarters Other Persons
Indiana	705,020	12.7	496,841	88,163	120,016	81,686	80,306
Adams	2,680	8.6	2,185	210	285	463	11
Allen	40,663	13.5	28,239	5,470	6,954	3,126	1,545
Bartholomew	7,066	11.1	5,246	805	1,015	673	97
Benton	1,043	11.0	842	84	117	118	0
Blackford	1,570	11.2	1,259	134	177	127	0
Boone	3,581	9.4	2,744	362	475	728	0
Brown	1,544	11.0	1,095	199	250	81	0
Carroll	1,890	10.0	1,511	167	212	215	3
Cass	4,706	12.3	3,589	461	656	1,004	19
Clark	10,422	11.9	7,760	1,177	1,485	1,152	234
Clay	2,714	11.0	2,254	196	264	320	8
Clinton	3,245	10.5	2,528	312	405	647	1
Crawford	1,017	10.3	819	87	111	84	0
Daviess	2,851	10.4	2,419	189	243	538	0
Dearborn	3,425	8.8	2,621	329	475	436	29
Decatur	2,268	9.6	1,760	212	296	332	0
Dekalb	3,656	10.3	2,713	395	548	330	42
Delaware	20,374	17.0	11,704	3,287	5,383	1,155	6,884
Dubois	3,606	9.8	2,847	329	430	480	356
Elkhart	18,620	11.9	12,268	2,694	3,658	1,797	898
Fayette	2,958	11.4	2,394	238	326	364	10.
Floyd	6,978	10.8	5,277	750	951	950	53
Fountain	2,050	11.5	1,632	182	236	196	3
Franklin	1,525	7.8	1,209	124	192	125	195
Fulton	2,305	12.2	1,776	218	311	174	0
Gibson	3,682	11.5	3,013	283	386	377	107
Grant	8,853	11.9	6,554	951	1,348	1,622	1,712
Greene	3,565	11.7	2,957	261	347	383	17
Hamilton	9,677	8.9	6,616	1,364	1,697	726	188
Hancock	3,565	7.8	2,718	355	492	519	42
Harrison	2,554	8.5	1,929	252	373	217	35
Hendricks	5,640	7.4	4,289	600	751	2,354	8
Henry	5,220	10.8	4,245	421	554	675	8
Howard	9,977	12.3	7,873	921	1,183	782	127
Huntington	3,702	10.4	2,809	378	515	665	396
Jackson	3,809	10.1	2,973	358	478	411	2
Jasper	2,027	8.1	1,630	171	226	369	693
Jay	2,371	11.0	1,932	194	245	238	14
Jefferson	3,313	11.1	2,545	329	439	841	989
Jennings	2,277	9.6	1,670	251	356	723	7
Johnson	8,440	9.6	6,050	1,044	1,346	1,725	1,324
Knox	5,851	14.7	4,230	667	954	660	2,127
Kosciusko	6,580	10.1	4,708	817	1,055	630	495
Lagrange	2,192	7.4	1,533	274	385	424	5
Lake	51,969	10.9	39,592	5,395	6,982	3,215	1,627
Laporte	12,476	11.7	9,085	1,497	1,894	5,984	45
Lawrence	4,620	10.8	3,654	410	556	617	64
Madison	16,140	12.4	12,385	1,615	2,140	4,048	1,135
Marion	138,789	17.4	93,696	20,123	24,970	9,725	4,604
Marshall	4,255	10.1	3,185	453	617	494	158
Martin	1,103	10.6	916	80	107	81	175
Miami	3,648	9.9	2,863	337	448	256	571
Monroe	25,288	23.2	11,216	5,182	8,890	778	14,334
Montgomery	4,215	12.2	3,234	423	558	519	686
Morgan	4,480	8.0	3,179	536	765	472	15
Newton	1,344	9.9	988	141	215	156	1
Noble	3,693	9.7	2,657	453	583	516	111
Ohio	553	10.4	428	55	70	58	0
Orange	2,039	11.1	1,583	198	258	239	17
Owen	1,739	10.1	1,251	207	281	144	2
Parke	1,664	10.8	1,377	125	162	520	0
Perry	1,885	9.9	1,574	134	177	902	8
Pike	1,426	11.4	1,157	110	159	108	0
Porter	12,650	9.8	8,873	1,652	2,125	1,129	2,538
Posey	2,471	9.5	1,942	235	294	226	14
Pulaski	1,401	11.1	1,124	113	164	113	6
Putnam	2,827	9.3	2,169	278	380	2,010	2,101
Randolph	3,036	11.2	2,390	272	374	261	9
Ripley	2,402	9.8	1,953	179	270	328	26
Rush	1,730	9.5	1,373	146	211	478	13
St. Joseph	34,391	13.9	24,427	4,309	5,655	3,079	9,082
Scott	1,978	9.4	1,527	185	266	246	6
Shelby	4,281	10.6	3,095	497	689	359	143
Spencer	1,742	8.9	1,451	123	168	199	348
Starke	2,261	9.9	1,719	236	306	341	0
Steuben	3,323	12.1	2,324	424	575	194	581
Sullivan	2,210	11.6	1,885	141	184	274	0
Switzerland	870	11.2	654	86	130	104	0
Tippecanoe	25,694	19.7	11,603	5,273	8,818	1,701	14,759
Tipton	1,677	10.4	1,316	156	205	148	51
Union	731	10.5	546	72	113	82	16
Vanderburgh	26,486	16.0	19,516	2,953	4,017	3,060	1,441
Vermillion	2,260	13.5	1,808	180	272	249	0
Vigo	15,738	14.8	11,284	1,912	2,542	3,555	5,135
Wabash	3,650	10.4	2,832	348	470	1,164	781
Warren	704	8.6	577	60	67	96	1
Warrick	3,563	7.9	2,650	406	507	607	0
Washington	2,413	10.2	1,836	231	346	258	32
Wayne	9,225	12.8	6,881	940	1,404	1,558	949
Wells	2,487	9.6	1,973	216	298	440	10
White	2,709	11.6	2,099	260	350	216	0
Whitley	2,732	9.9	2,029	304	399	423	27

Source: U.S. Bureau of the Census
EDIN table(s): PHTR

2.16 Households by Type and Presence of Own Children 1990

	Households		Married Couple			Male Householder, No Wife Present			Female Householder, No Husband Present		
	Total	Family	Total	With Related Children	No Related Children	Total	With Related Children	No Related Children	Total	With Related Children	No Related Children
Indiana	2,065,355	1,480,351	1,202,020	586,033	615,987	60,703	33,658	27,045	217,628	146,179	71,449
Adams	10,470	8,075	6,994	3,672	3,322	282	154	128	799	513	286
Allen	113,333	79,624	64,009	32,199	31,810	3,268	1,844	1,424	12,347	8,672	3,675
Bartholomew	24,192	18,141	15,273	7,364	7,909	649	379	270	2,219	1,477	742
Benton	3,524	2,598	2,246	1,062	1,184	94	52	42	258	172	86
Blackford	5,436	4,043	3,435	1,558	1,877	141	90	51	467	290	177
Boone	13,922	10,816	9,553	4,819	4,734	307	184	123	956	622	334
Brown	5,370	4,076	3,615	1,576	2,039	155	95	60	306	186	120
Carroll	7,067	5,389	4,785	2,206	2,579	173	96	77	431	274	157
Cass	14,659	10,609	8,794	4,132	4,662	394	241	153	1,421	960	461
Clark	33,292	24,355	19,253	9,458	9,795	1,025	575	450	4,077	2,711	1,366
Clay	9,382	6,932	5,895	2,825	3,070	226	141	85	811	480	331
Clinton	11,450	8,610	7,359	3,616	3,743	285	180	105	966	635	331
Crawford	3,660	2,754	2,324	1,196	1,128	133	69	64	297	192	105
Daviess	10,012	7,404	6,314	3,125	3,189	254	148	106	836	522	314
Dearborn	13,642	10,692	9,046	4,796	4,250	402	212	190	1,244	785	459
Decatur	8,427	6,455	5,492	2,832	2,660	237	134	103	726	485	241
Dekalb	12,725	9,617	8,186	4,345	3,841	379	223	156	1,052	689	363
Delaware	45,177	30,186	24,240	10,687	13,553	1,146	604	542	4,800	3,264	1,536
Dubois	13,023	9,847	8,633	4,568	4,065	344	156	188	870	553	317
Elkhart	56,713	41,751	34,802	17,695	17,107	1,777	1,090	687	5,172	3,618	1,554
Fayette	9,945	7,313	5,922	2,854	3,068	298	181	117	1,093	770	323
Floyd	24,085	18,058	14,286	7,039	7,247	735	363	372	3,037	2,014	1,023
Fountain	6,858	5,044	4,349	1,960	2,389	193	107	86	502	320	182
Franklin	6,636	5,303	4,634	2,553	2,081	221	107	114	448	261	187
Fulton	7,345	5,351	4,584	2,093	2,491	212	118	94	555	381	174
Gibson	12,299	9,003	7,724	3,680	4,044	304	171	133	975	623	352
Grant	27,701	20,196	16,269	7,255	9,014	771	480	291	3,156	2,205	951
Greene	11,910	8,692	7,403	3,505	3,898	316	174	142	973	621	352
Hamilton	38,834	30,854	27,398	14,671	12,727	758	413	345	2,698	1,843	855
Hancock	15,959	12,886	11,395	5,800	5,595	408	237	171	1,083	680	403
Harrison	10,618	8,437	7,234	3,771	3,463	319	185	134	884	549	335
Hendricks	26,109	21,220	18,762	9,785	8,977	614	345	269	1,844	1,154	690
Henry	18,642	13,976	11,682	5,215	6,467	559	322	237	1,735	1,126	609
Howard	31,523	22,729	18,281	8,686	9,595	877	524	353	3,571	2,558	1,013
Huntington	12,830	9,643	8,257	4,114	4,143	350	212	138	1,036	692	344
Jackson	14,032	10,701	9,011	4,505	4,506	411	216	195	1,279	822	457
Jasper	8,527	6,726	5,879	3,051	2,828	211	125	86	636	416	220
Jay	8,161	6,035	5,135	2,349	2,786	218	132	86	682	463	219
Jefferson	10,897	8,023	6,556	3,199	3,357	328	188	140	1,139	756	383
Jennings	8,351	6,430	5,451	2,720	2,731	252	135	117	727	459	268
Johnson	31,354	24,260	20,701	10,694	10,007	849	500	349	2,710	1,821	889
Knox	15,145	10,248	8,444	3,859	4,585	362	180	182	1,442	923	519
Kosciusko	23,449	17,924	15,576	7,804	7,772	655	401	254	1,693	1,157	536
Lagrange	9,209	7,402	6,608	3,611	2,997	268	147	121	526	324	202
Lake	170,748	125,761	91,980	45,455	46,525	6,679	3,189	3,490	27,102	18,275	8,827
Laporte	38,488	27,906	22,487	10,708	11,779	1,231	687	544	4,188	2,762	1,426
Lawrence	16,235	12,171	10,409	4,954	5,455	407	234	173	1,355	845	510
Madison	49,804	35,804	28,617	12,958	15,659	1,499	839	660	5,688	3,933	1,755
Marion	319,471	205,652	150,965	71,797	79,168	10,455	5,810	4,645	44,232	30,355	13,877
Marshall	15,146	11,508	9,945	4,974	4,971	426	235	191	1,137	766	371
Martin	3,836	2,840	2,430	1,192	1,238	107	55	52	303	177	126
Miami	13,484	10,284	8,763	4,566	4,197	368	227	141	1,153	773	380
Monroe	39,351	22,953	18,753	8,590	10,163	930	521	409	3,270	2,181	1,089
Montgomery	13,235	9,578	8,209	3,793	4,416	338	188	150	1,031	683	348
Morgan	19,600	15,885	13,673	6,989	6,684	562	351	211	1,650	1,097	553
Newton	4,839	3,710	3,208	1,650	1,558	141	86	55	361	224	137
Noble	13,418	10,308	8,804	4,530	4,274	415	255	160	1,089	738	351
Ohio	1,980	1,497	1,293	636	657	54	29	25	150	84	66
Orange	6,950	5,169	4,341	2,107	2,234	213	123	90	615	392	223
Owen	6,394	4,936	4,264	1,979	2,285	192	122	70	480	310	170
Parke	5,845	4,343	3,695	1,648	2,047	163	82	81	485	317	168
Perry	6,845	5,137	4,313	2,123	2,190	201	93	108	623	394	229
Pike	4,925	3,658	3,140	1,414	1,726	150	86	64	368	222	146
Porter	45,159	34,634	29,509	15,536	13,973	1,343	733	610	3,782	2,473	1,309
Posey	9,508	7,331	6,432	3,332	3,100	219	118	101	680	452	228
Pulaski	4,722	3,485	3,061	1,525	1,536	124	78	46	300	195	105
Putnam	9,996	7,549	6,600	3,144	3,456	258	137	121	691	436	255
Randolph	10,451	7,789	6,673	3,029	3,644	234	135	99	882	591	291
Ripley	8,778	6,646	5,686	3,054	2,632	293	160	133	667	405	262
Rush	6,504	4,985	4,265	2,102	2,163	188	110	78	532	348	184
St. Joseph	92,365	63,629	50,364	23,528	26,836	2,695	1,443	1,252	10,570	7,064	3,506
Scott	7,593	5,881	4,806	2,496	2,310	227	144	83	848	557	291
Shelby	14,761	11,169	9,454	4,741	4,713	500	291	209	1,215	765	450
Spencer	6,962	5,388	4,739	2,398	2,341	186	91	95	463	297	166
Starke	8,141	6,186	5,154	2,605	2,549	286	162	124	746	483	263
Steuben	10,194	7,446	6,468	3,014	3,454	279	165	114	699	456	243
Sullivan	7,364	5,338	4,598	2,169	2,429	189	108	81	551	315	236
Switzerland	2,839	2,099	1,813	877	936	87	51	36	199	135	64
Tippecanoe	45,618	28,742	24,096	11,729	12,367	1,050	563	487	3,596	2,397	1,199
Tipton	6,026	4,554	3,916	1,875	2,041	175	103	72	463	286	177
Union	2,576	1,958	1,653	825	828	80	45	35	225	156	69
Vanderburgh	66,780	44,311	34,952	15,729	19,223	1,734	924	810	7,625	5,082	2,543
Vermillion	6,638	4,650	3,888	1,805	2,083	178	101	77	584	368	216
Vigo	39,804	26,608	21,191	9,800	11,391	1,154	670	484	4,263	2,754	1,509
Wabash	12,630	9,450	8,136	3,868	4,268	356	203	153	958	611	347
Warren	3,015	2,378	2,120	990	1,130	77	41	36	181	105	76
Warrick	15,817	12,761	11,191	6,004	5,187	356	211	145	1,214	824	390
Washington	8,664	6,597	5,550	2,778	2,772	267	149	118	780	521	259
Wayne	27,587	19,766	15,903	7,236	8,667	734	425	309	3,129	2,193	936
Wells	9,438	7,249	6,323	3,249	3,074	216	129	87	710	456	254
White	8,926	6,567	5,666	2,632	3,034	265	165	100	636	441	195
Whitley	10,010	7,677	6,735	3,396	3,339	262	161	101	680	447	233

Footnote: Own children are related by birth, marriage or adoption.
Source: U.S. Bureau of the Census
EDIN table(s): HHTC

2.17 Household Type and Relationship of Persons Under 18 Years 1990

	Total Persons in Households	Total	In Married Couple Family	Own Child — Male Householder, No Wife Present	Female Householder, No Husband Present	Other Relatives	Non-relatives	In Group Quarters — Total	Institutionalized Persons	Other Persons
Indiana	1,450,304	1,339,888	1,069,169	45,666	225,053	83,040	25,751	5,660	3,753	1,907
Adams	9,860	9,529	8,480	232	817	224	98	0	0	0
Allen	83,258	77,668	61,317	2,472	13,879	4,126	1,389	246	186	60
Bartholomew	16,417	15,235	12,656	510	2,069	850	316	58	35	23
Benton	2,658	2,508	2,148	77	283	100	49	0	0	0
Blackford	3,572	3,337	2,789	142	406	165	65	0	0	0
Boone	10,366	9,801	8,649	255	897	411	148	71	71	0
Brown	3,468	3,159	2,769	128	262	232	72	0	0	0
Carroll	4,975	4,695	4,136	140	419	204	74	1	0	1
Cass	10,102	9,458	7,654	313	1,491	416	223	55	50	5
Clark	22,436	20,647	16,018	719	3,910	1,415	347	113	60	53
Clay	6,452	6,016	5,111	190	715	330	98	0	0	0
Clinton	8,552	7,930	6,669	260	1,001	434	181	0	0	0
Crawford	2,728	2,525	2,159	96	270	143	55	0	0	0
Daviess	7,954	7,559	6,529	216	814	270	114	1	1	0
Dearborn	11,095	10,346	8,877	276	1,193	562	175	11	1	10
Decatur	6,792	6,363	5,368	196	799	312	109	30	30	0
Dekalb	10,225	9,570	8,211	298	1,061	437	208	0	0	0
Delaware	26,279	24,232	18,511	808	4,913	1,481	538	136	79	57
Dubois	10,163	9,835	8,747	214	874	221	99	131	1	130
Elkhart	44,322	41,015	34,027	1,462	5,526	2,173	1,076	155	87	68
Fayette	6,901	6,378	4,966	230	1,182	396	119	2	1	1
Floyd	16,956	15,727	12,140	442	3,145	967	240	86	77	9
Fountain	4,610	4,309	3,646	150	513	206	82	2	1	1
Franklin	5,786	5,434	4,862	151	421	261	86	0	0	0
Fulton	5,016	4,675	3,919	173	583	220	114	0	0	0
Gibson	8,199	7,729	6,592	244	893	343	110	0	0	0
Grant	18,339	16,550	12,515	656	3,379	1,365	408	31	18	13
Greene	7,719	7,225	6,045	243	937	368	114	10	0	10
Hamilton	31,566	30,471	27,213	568	2,690	776	304	57	0	57
Hancock	12,518	11,729	10,439	320	970	638	140	27	3	24
Harrison	8,442	7,858	6,776	248	834	412	165	8	0	8
Hendricks	20,703	19,614	17,484	447	1,683	834	236	409	408	1
Henry	11,828	11,000	8,978	444	1,578	639	176	9	7	2
Howard	21,491	19,933	15,365	694	3,874	1,196	338	51	29	22
Huntington	9,802	9,202	7,810	314	1,078	433	153	2	1	1
Jackson	10,172	9,452	7,911	295	1,246	524	176	8	8	0
Jasper	7,145	6,765	5,921	175	669	285	86	28	27	1
Jay	5,692	5,337	4,471	182	684	243	104	8	0	8
Jefferson	7,435	6,850	5,506	235	1,109	414	159	20	12	8
Jennings	6,370	5,841	4,945	195	701	394	128	16	9	7
Johnson	23,555	22,107	18,873	666	2,568	1,054	377	262	32	230
Knox	9,218	8,653	7,007	246	1,400	386	165	17	2	15
Kosciusko	18,757	17,708	15,374	544	1,790	745	284	17	0	17
Lagrange	10,142	9,735	9,030	225	480	263	135	200	198	2
Lake	132,813	118,166	83,766	4,150	30,250	12,313	2,188	354	244	110
Laporte	27,103	24,886	19,677	944	4,265	1,662	520	10	9	1
Lawrence	10,904	10,120	8,632	323	1,165	588	181	30	9	21
Madison	32,287	29,502	22,430	1,106	5,966	2,113	631	88	78	10
Marion	202,436	181,049	126,860	7,738	46,451	16,644	4,513	749	610	139
Marshall	12,005	11,324	9,745	355	1,224	452	219	23	15	8
Martin	2,709	2,560	2,189	84	287	107	39	93	0	93
Miami	10,483	9,977	8,415	322	1,240	350	149	1	0	1
Monroe	19,956	18,661	14,762	707	3,192	822	445	111	0	111
Montgomery	8,623	8,150	6,844	269	1,037	317	146	57	54	3
Morgan	15,562	14,342	12,313	461	1,568	882	317	7	2	5
Newton	3,924	3,638	3,157	133	348	185	99	0	0	0
Noble	11,063	10,389	8,910	376	1,103	455	206	50	0	50
Ohio	1,392	1,315	1,159	49	107	63	14	0	0	0
Orange	4,922	4,597	3,781	181	635	222	93	0	0	0
Owen	4,624	4,225	3,582	160	483	281	107	1	1	0
Parke	3,785	3,525	2,931	112	482	206	52	84	84	0
Perry	4,947	4,659	3,934	130	595	213	67	3	3	0
Pike	3,064	2,867	2,447	110	310	135	55	0	0	0
Porter	35,400	33,402	28,711	1,001	3,690	1,504	467	123	92	31
Posey	7,280	6,967	6,088	168	711	226	85	4	0	4
Pulaski	3,619	3,407	2,982	109	316	140	67	0	0	0
Putnam	6,991	6,540	5,717	194	629	337	108	15	14	1
Randolph	7,024	6,583	5,475	192	916	292	141	2	2	0
Ripley	7,014	6,574	5,731	213	630	350	86	5	0	5
Rush	4,862	4,514	3,854	158	502	275	67	198	198	0
St. Joseph	62,102	57,362	43,911	2,026	11,425	3,552	1,100	361	205	156
Scott	5,831	5,308	4,272	191	845	392	118	1	1	0
Shelby	10,944	10,056	8,582	386	1,088	617	261	61	0	61
Spencer	5,312	5,098	4,495	116	487	145	66	8	0	8
Starke	6,343	5,795	4,877	235	683	415	129	37	37	0
Steuben	7,169	6,732	5,773	234	725	280	148	7	0	7
Sullivan	4,836	4,505	3,887	146	472	251	69	0	0	0
Switzerland	2,091	1,910	1,623	73	214	130	51	1	1	0
Tippecanoe	27,244	25,775	21,363	814	3,598	1,061	383	140	60	80
Tipton	4,215	3,963	3,450	132	381	192	57	0	0	0
Union	1,942	1,798	1,497	64	237	105	39	8	1	7
Vanderburgh	39,252	36,252	27,402	1,253	7,597	2,248	699	158	113	45
Vermillion	4,170	3,881	3,187	154	540	191	94	0	0	0
Vigo	24,206	22,385	17,341	916	4,128	1,329	448	173	142	31
Wabash	8,990	8,435	7,189	309	937	377	171	227	227	0
Warren	2,141	2,040	1,825	55	160	77	22	0	0	0
Warrick	12,711	11,993	10,503	286	1,204	539	170	12	12	0
Washington	6,492	6,027	5,047	212	768	325	132	1	0	1
Wayne	17,998	16,574	12,604	592	3,378	1,041	348	145	71	74
Wells	7,376	7,015	6,149	169	697	252	102	2	2	0
White	6,286	5,930	5,004	234	692	231	120	2	2	0
Whitley	7,825	7,405	6,483	233	689	288	129	30	30	0

Source: U.S. Bureau of the Census
EDIN table(s): PH18

2.18 Household Type and Relationship of Persons 65 Years and Over 1990

| | In Family Households | | | | | In Non-family Households | | | | | | |
| | Total | Householder | Spouse | Other Relatives | Non-relatives | Total | Male Householder | | | Female Householder | | |
							Total	Living Alone	Not Living Alone	Total	Living Alone	Not Living Alone
Indiana	429,236	237,682	156,501	32,920	2,133	219,190	43,540	40,753	2,787	171,111	167,684	3,427
Adams	2,600	1,413	1,040	143	4	1,184	210	205	5	960	952	8
Allen	21,106	11,604	7,908	1,509	85	10,776	2,040	1,924	116	8,510	8,313	197
Bartholomew	4,635	2,603	1,697	315	20	2,196	425	402	23	1,737	1,706	31
Benton	976	549	372	49	6	492	100	97	3	389	387	2
Blackford	1,288	730	481	71	6	738	122	114	8	601	596	5
Boone	2,907	1,570	1,141	193	3	1,455	242	223	19	1,189	1,166	23
Brown	1,213	682	454	74	3	513	130	125	5	372	357	15
Carroll	1,789	1,004	719	63	3	818	162	151	11	641	637	4
Cass	3,528	1,956	1,353	205	14	1,943	341	324	17	1,557	1,525	32
Clark	6,387	3,576	2,211	567	33	3,338	621	583	38	2,651	2,608	43
Clay	2,491	1,393	938	147	13	1,417	263	250	13	1,137	1,122	15
Clinton	2,796	1,561	1,087	137	11	1,435	258	235	23	1,154	1,141	13
Crawford	858	484	294	64	16	485	130	122	8	346	343	3
Daviess	2,595	1,451	1,019	122	3	1,405	268	254	14	1,115	1,101	14
Dearborn	2,920	1,614	1,025	261	20	1,327	288	278	10	1,013	996	17
Decatur	1,974	1,106	737	122	9	932	215	201	14	705	692	13
Dekalb	2,637	1,463	1,010	157	7	1,319	233	219	14	1,061	1,052	9
Delaware	9,008	5,045	3,381	532	50	5,206	937	880	57	4,152	4,064	88
Dubois	2,607	1,496	951	155	5	1,401	258	243	15	1,121	1,107	14
Elkhart	11,077	6,006	4,268	751	52	5,246	956	883	73	4,179	4,097	82
Fayette	2,230	1,259	814	148	9	1,273	242	232	10	1,014	997	17
Floyd	5,005	2,766	1,746	463	30	2,482	465	437	28	1,965	1,921	44
Fountain	1,802	1,010	681	104	7	1,000	174	158	16	811	795	16
Franklin	1,479	842	500	123	14	694	148	135	13	528	519	9
Fulton	1,903	1,062	763	75	3	971	203	190	13	756	747	9
Gibson	2,923	1,641	1,133	146	3	1,764	343	325	18	1,386	1,367	19
Grant	6,112	3,388	2,304	371	49	3,128	570	534	36	2,506	2,467	39
Greene	2,988	1,684	1,142	151	11	1,658	347	330	17	1,288	1,277	11
Hamilton	6,037	3,250	2,223	542	22	2,347	440	411	29	1,861	1,827	34
Hancock	2,972	1,629	1,101	221	21	1,366	267	247	20	1,075	1,063	12
Harrison	2,230	1,234	787	203	6	983	211	203	8	756	742	14
Hendricks	4,861	2,613	1,778	442	28	2,018	376	357	19	1,604	1,580	24
Henry	4,465	2,517	1,708	221	19	2,290	408	388	20	1,851	1,830	21
Howard	5,714	3,212	2,122	368	12	3,207	560	530	30	2,597	2,557	40
Huntington	2,964	1,657	1,171	129	7	1,424	253	246	7	1,156	1,141	15
Jackson	3,171	1,796	1,168	190	17	1,586	301	287	14	1,271	1,251	20
Jasper	2,039	1,110	790	129	10	874	156	145	11	705	697	8
Jay	2,076	1,172	797	101	6	1,049	186	178	8	850	842	8
Jefferson	2,428	1,353	882	170	23	1,231	291	275	16	914	893	21
Jennings	1,742	985	614	135	8	860	191	179	12	651	638	13
Johnson	5,398	2,959	1,937	482	20	2,515	459	423	36	2,012	1,980	32
Knox	3,507	1,968	1,326	200	13	2,303	417	398	19	1,841	1,810	31
Kosciusko	5,054	2,789	1,942	302	21	2,139	445	406	39	1,642	1,599	43
Lagrange	2,036	1,127	801	105	3	813	187	176	11	603	583	20
Lake	39,545	22,059	12,518	4,653	315	16,942	4,056	3,765	291	12,418	12,087	331
Laporte	9,007	4,986	3,243	735	43	4,339	940	878	62	3,291	3,208	83
Lawrence	3,744	2,106	1,392	224	22	1,977	384	366	18	1,565	1,547	18
Madison	11,311	6,293	4,278	685	55	6,096	1,109	1,045	64	4,875	4,798	77
Marion	55,709	30,814	19,284	5,267	344	31,467	6,394	5,901	493	24,236	23,529	707
Marshall	3,530	1,923	1,356	239	12	1,633	343	328	15	1,260	1,237	23
Martin	874	515	298	58	3	490	113	105	8	367	364	3
Miami	2,679	1,512	1,016	135	16	1,410	251	228	23	1,131	1,114	17
Monroe	5,766	3,141	2,145	446	34	2,984	553	517	36	2,372	2,305	67
Montgomery	2,897	1,597	1,128	162	10	1,669	325	308	17	1,309	1,284	25
Morgan	3,774	2,082	1,329	339	24	1,622	328	309	19	1,264	1,241	23
Newton	1,079	618	396	62	3	589	132	124	8	445	438	7
Noble	2,865	1,564	1,105	186	10	1,351	262	246	16	1,061	1,046	15
Ohio	444	245	168	30	1	246	53	49	4	192	191	1
Orange	1,747	989	644	109	5	873	194	177	17	659	646	13
Owen	1,529	850	567	104	8	678	166	153	13	499	490	9
Parke	1,480	827	560	84	9	818	169	163	6	633	625	8
Perry	1,749	976	626	140	7	908	180	172	8	717	712	5
Pike	1,186	687	433	65	1	681	152	143	9	520	519	1
Porter	8,297	4,433	2,899	920	45	3,625	726	672	54	2,818	2,761	57
Posey	1,947	1,097	734	104	12	993	222	211	11	754	742	12
Pulaski	1,226	684	476	63	3	674	138	130	8	523	512	11
Putnam	2,356	1,312	890	144	10	1,176	233	220	13	918	907	11
Randolph	2,630	1,454	1,030	136	10	1,315	258	245	13	1,037	1,019	18
Ripley	2,098	1,175	742	169	12	1,095	252	243	9	830	821	9
Rush	1,634	936	604	88	6	816	158	151	7	648	640	8
St. Joseph	21,463	11,725	7,966	1,662	110	11,130	2,260	2,108	152	8,663	8,463	170
Scott	1,511	869	510	119	13	780	162	150	12	601	589	12
Shelby	3,077	1,701	1,147	221	8	1,545	282	268	14	1,232	1,208	24
Spencer	1,544	869	569	101	5	791	185	177	8	596	590	6
Starke	2,060	1,136	754	160	10	985	257	241	16	715	707	8
Steuben	2,345	1,277	932	131	5	1,105	235	217	18	835	815	20
Sullivan	1,936	1,080	741	110	5	1,237	264	251	13	954	945	9
Switzerland	695	399	254	39	3	385	89	83	6	283	272	11
Tippecanoe	7,171	3,953	2,715	480	23	3,831	712	658	54	3,043	2,966	77
Tipton	1,448	798	567	82	1	778	153	145	8	616	604	12
Union	606	338	226	36	6	292	60	57	3	226	224	2
Vanderburgh	14,974	8,259	5,543	1,108	64	8,928	1,627	1,532	95	7,118	6,983	135
Vermillion	1,582	882	606	91	3	1,105	211	200	11	877	859	18
Vigo	9,242	5,102	3,370	725	45	5,550	1,040	980	60	4,428	4,349	79
Wabash	3,081	1,690	1,218	166	7	1,406	246	223	23	1,137	1,120	17
Warren	810	461	308	41	0	334	70	65	5	257	253	4
Warrick	2,935	1,583	1,087	252	13	1,213	272	255	17	918	900	18
Washington	1,989	1,112	724	134	19	1,003	223	211	12	749	733	16
Wayne	6,487	3,577	2,454	429	27	3,465	667	630	37	2,716	2,671	45
Wells	2,171	1,187	862	115	7	994	155	147	8	826	815	11
White	2,271	1,252	903	109	7	1,217	234	214	20	958	948	10
Whitley	2,207	1,228	868	104	7	1,048	206	189	17	818	802	16

Source: U.S. Bureau of the Census
EDIN table(s): PH65

Birth Rates Per 1,000 Population
1995

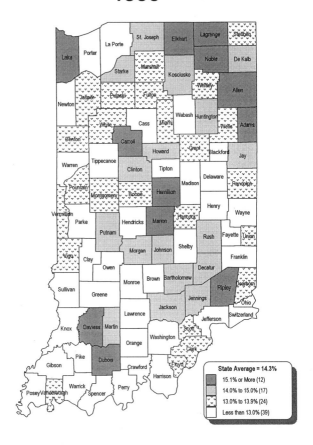

State Average = 14.3%
- 15.1% or More (12)
- 14.0% to 15.0% (17)
- 13.0% to 13.9% (24)
- Less than 13.0% (39)

Deaths by Major Cause
Indiana - 1995

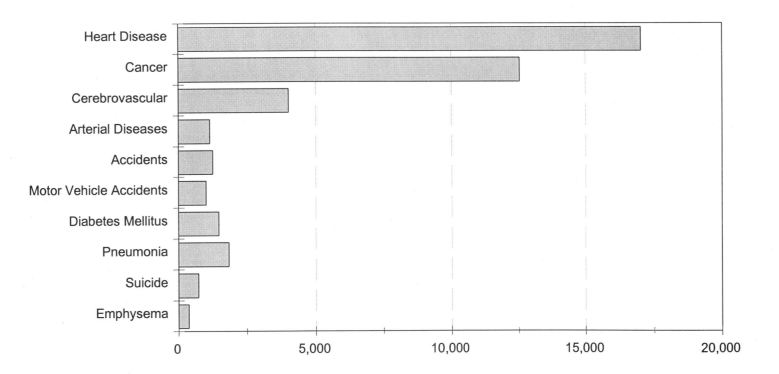

Birth Rates Per 1,000 Population: EDIN Table VITB.
Deaths by Major Cause: EDIN Table VITD.

SECTION 2
INDIANA FACTBOOK
Page 119

Vital Statistics

2.19 Vital Statistics and Fertility Rates 1995

| | Births | | Deaths | | Fertility Rates | | | | | | |
	Number	Rate per 1,000 Persons	Number	Rate per 1,000 Persons	General	Age 15 to 19	Age 20 to 24	Age 25 to 29	Age 30 to 34	Age 35 to 39	Age 40 to 44
Indiana	**82,944**	**14.3**	**53,053**	**9.2**	**62.30**	**57.70**	**113.30**	**111.70**	**71.30**	**25.20**	**4.20**
Adams	623	19.3	297	9.2	92.20	40.70	175.20	186.90	109.30	47.70	12.30
Allen	4,933	16.0	2,425	7.9	67.90	60.30	122.40	124.50	78.30	29.60	5.60
Bartholomew	1,024	15.0	585	8.6	66.10	64.50	126.70	128.50	78.40	26.40	2.70
Benton	132	13.6	97	10.0	69.70	67.10	150.60	144.80	63.40	21.70	0.00
Blackford	171	12.1	146	10.4	58.30	64.00	167.90	82.10	57.60	9.70	3.40
Boone	544	13.0	376	9.0	58.60	39.20	92.80	110.40	93.40	37.10	2.20
Brown	129	8.5	123	8.1	39.60	25.30	113.60	66.80	45.90	25.10	1.40
Carroll	295	15.1	161	8.2	73.50	40.80	193.10	151.60	77.30	19.80	8.00
Cass	490	12.7	436	11.3	60.40	66.90	161.90	106.50	52.80	16.00	2.60
Clark	1,199	13.1	919	10.0	55.50	55.20	134.80	91.30	60.10	16.50	1.50
Clay	335	12.7	329	12.5	63.10	75.60	177.10	99.90	44.60	17.00	1.10
Clinton	462	14.2	368	11.3	68.10	56.70	168.30	117.40	66.70	24.80	6.50
Crawford	110	10.5	115	11.1	50.50	86.70	133.10	51.50	39.80	12.20	0.00
Daviess	444	15.5	333	11.7	76.80	57.50	179.30	141.90	88.70	17.40	9.60
Dearborn	590	13.3	363	8.2	60.60	35.40	102.60	129.70	82.90	27.50	6.40
Decatur	360	14.4	224	9.0	67.90	64.30	134.30	137.90	71.80	18.50	2.20
Dekalb	544	14.3	331	8.7	65.00	63.70	158.70	106.40	60.60	21.40	2.90
Delaware	1,408	11.9	1,173	9.9	47.40	35.40	67.40	108.80	60.50	13.80	2.00
Dubois	597	15.4	328	8.5	69.90	31.80	107.90	136.90	100.80	37.50	4.30
Elkhart	2,737	16.4	1,314	7.9	71.90	76.80	140.30	127.60	75.90	23.20	4.60
Fayette	335	12.7	309	11.8	59.10	90.10	153.00	94.10	44.90	11.10	1.00
Floyd	933	13.3	580	8.3	57.80	65.80	117.20	103.70	68.50	19.20	2.60
Fountain	243	13.5	186	10.3	67.70	65.90	169.10	121.10	59.50	21.80	6.10
Franklin	247	11.8	174	8.3	56.00	50.70	112.50	119.20	59.20	21.80	3.80
Fulton	277	13.9	223	11.2	69.60	70.00	197.80	114.00	65.00	18.30	2.80
Gibson	411	12.8	337	10.5	61.60	57.40	140.40	120.20	55.80	22.40	1.70
Grant	984	13.3	825	11.2	60.40	71.00	134.10	104.40	51.60	12.80	2.40
Greene	414	12.7	324	9.9	62.50	65.50	158.10	104.70	50.90	19.60	4.10
Hamilton	2,316	16.5	729	5.2	68.20	19.20	79.80	138.30	127.50	47.60	6.60
Hancock	687	13.5	391	7.7	59.80	37.80	129.90	136.30	83.00	26.10	3.30
Harrison	390	12.0	271	8.3	53.80	45.10	131.10	100.50	54.90	22.50	2.20
Hendricks	1,067	12.3	604	7.0	55.10	32.20	92.00	129.90	87.30	23.70	3.00
Henry	611	12.4	527	10.7	57.90	59.10	138.90	115.40	53.80	11.70	4.10
Howard	1,207	14.4	699	8.4	64.10	76.40	141.80	106.40	71.50	18.90	3.00
Huntington	523	14.2	363	9.9	66.30	68.40	146.20	117.10	64.20	17.00	3.00
Jackson	576	14.3	390	9.7	65.40	71.10	142.10	124.10	60.00	16.70	1.30
Jasper	365	13.1	240	8.6	59.70	45.60	125.60	127.10	63.60	19.00	4.50
Jay	310	14.2	234	10.8	69.00	63.40	160.30	126.30	73.80	18.60	1.20
Jefferson	398	12.9	310	10.0	57.40	55.90	107.00	107.30	61.70	20.90	1.60
Jennings	374	14.3	210	8.0	63.70	66.70	167.70	107.70	54.60	16.20	0.90
Johnson	1,456	14.3	825	8.1	60.10	42.50	103.60	120.70	85.30	28.20	2.80
Knox	483	12.0	516	13.0	56.80	44.60	122.80	103.80	56.30	21.40	5.10
Kosciusko	1,040	15.0	560	8.1	67.70	64.10	153.30	114.10	65.50	23.00	5.60
Lagrange	662	20.9	220	6.9	99.20	45.70	240.70	165.10	105.50	45.20	14.30
Lake	7,339	15.2	4,784	10.0	66.40	72.50	129.10	110.50	67.70	30.70	5.30
Laporte	1,325	12.0	994	9.1	57.80	61.90	126.20	98.30	64.90	18.20	4.40
Lawrence	562	12.5	503	11.2	58.40	71.70	150.30	94.20	50.30	15.60	1.70
Madison	1,660	12.5	1,385	10.4	58.00	63.20	122.20	113.90	53.50	15.50	2.40
Marion	13,920	17.0	7,582	9.3	68.50	80.20	110.50	99.60	79.40	30.90	5.40
Marshall	606	13.5	418	9.3	64.20	58.50	119.80	121.40	71.20	25.90	7.80
Martin	149	14.1	108	10.3	67.20	53.90	219.60	90.90	56.50	26.20	0.00
Miami	424	13.0	292	9.0	58.20	66.20	132.50	83.70	53.20	18.40	6.40
Monroe	1,162	10.1	662	5.7	32.70	13.80	27.10	74.80	66.10	25.90	5.90
Montgomery	494	13.7	368	10.2	66.20	61.70	147.90	111.80	73.70	22.50	3.70
Morgan	909	14.6	520	8.4	64.30	55.50	144.10	134.80	61.00	19.90	4.90
Newton	151	10.5	147	10.2	50.70	38.60	169.80	93.90	46.60	9.90	0.00
Noble	692	16.9	304	7.4	77.50	71.60	193.60	126.30	68.50	23.80	5.30
Ohio	57	10.6	53	9.7	50.90	54.20	132.50	51.50	61.90	20.50	0.00
Orange	236	12.4	199	10.5	59.30	71.40	158.70	95.20	49.20	16.10	1.30
Owen	238	12.1	177	9.0	57.30	68.90	155.10	100.00	42.00	11.30	3.80
Parke	187	11.6	180	11.2	56.40	55.20	142.90	95.50	66.70	11.10	3.10
Perry	206	10.8	192	10.0	54.10	66.00	127.90	89.30	45.60	13.80	1.60
Pike	125	9.9	149	11.9	49.00	44.20	112.80	81.40	62.50	16.20	0.00
Porter	1,724	12.3	1,064	7.6	51.20	33.60	86.70	109.90	74.10	23.20	3.50
Posey	327	12.3	181	6.9	55.40	36.00	131.40	106.70	61.90	22.80	3.80
Pulaski	174	13.4	153	11.7	68.30	55.70	154.30	158.00	49.00	13.70	5.10
Putnam	461	14.0	286	8.7	65.10	49.80	108.00	156.00	52.00	33.30	5.40
Randolph	369	13.5	275	10.0	64.60	61.70	186.20	123.70	41.20	17.90	2.80
Ripley	420	15.7	260	9.7	74.40	64.30	146.40	150.30	71.60	31.90	4.00
Rush	264	14.3	190	10.4	67.60	58.30	161.30	139.90	61.10	13.80	1.50
St. Joseph	3,762	14.6	2,350	9.1	63.40	55.50	93.20	119.80	82.10	28.10	5.00
Scott	301	13.3	245	10.9	59.50	81.50	141.70	91.10	45.40	12.10	2.20
Shelby	550	12.8	410	9.6	57.70	56.80	127.40	105.10	57.50	15.30	3.00
Spencer	257	12.6	195	9.6	61.00	51.40	144.80	106.50	64.70	28.60	2.60
Starke	340	15.0	254	11.3	72.90	88.50	179.40	107.00	54.20	22.00	7.70
Steuben	415	13.8	236	7.8	64.40	54.20	133.90	121.90	70.80	23.10	3.40
Sullivan	247	12.4	256	12.6	62.00	59.50	193.80	127.20	36.80	10.20	2.60
Switzerland	101	12.3	117	14.2	62.50	59.10	172.10	132.30	28.20	16.70	6.50
Tippecanoe	1,740	12.9	980	7.1	47.50	23.70	47.10	106.10	76.10	31.30	6.30
Tipton	187	11.4	172	10.4	53.50	33.50	128.10	117.30	59.60	17.90	3.00
Union	96	13.2	86	11.7	59.80	63.80	146.30	113.80	52.80	19.40	0.00
Vanderburgh	2,203	13.1	1,822	10.9	58.90	71.60	100.30	101.40	61.90	22.00	1.60
Vermillion	221	13.1	199	11.8	63.80	58.60	167.00	148.00	52.50	9.10	1.50
Vigo	1,413	13.3	1,181	11.1	59.60	57.10	109.90	101.00	58.20	23.10	3.80
Wabash	445	12.8	393	11.3	59.10	48.20	143.40	106.00	49.50	15.90	4.60
Warren	85	10.1	87	10.6	49.60	49.30	108.10	102.00	59.60	8.70	3.20
Warrick	621	12.6	357	7.2	53.90	41.40	113.40	117.40	73.90	20.70	1.70
Washington	335	12.8	246	9.4	60.30	69.40	129.20	94.00	55.90	32.00	3.80
Wayne	903	12.4	772	10.7	57.20	59.60	120.10	110.80	48.70	17.00	3.20
Wells	360	13.6	245	9.3	63.30	65.70	126.80	129.90	61.10	17.50	2.10
White	336	13.7	252	10.2	66.80	70.80	165.60	123.90	66.50	19.60	2.20
Whitley	409	13.9	282	9.6	63.90	46.40	137.80	141.50	61.40	28.80	3.50

Source: Indiana State Department of Health, IU Kelley School of Business (IBRC)
EDIN table(s): VITB, VITD, FERR

Natural Increase in the Population
1993 to 1995

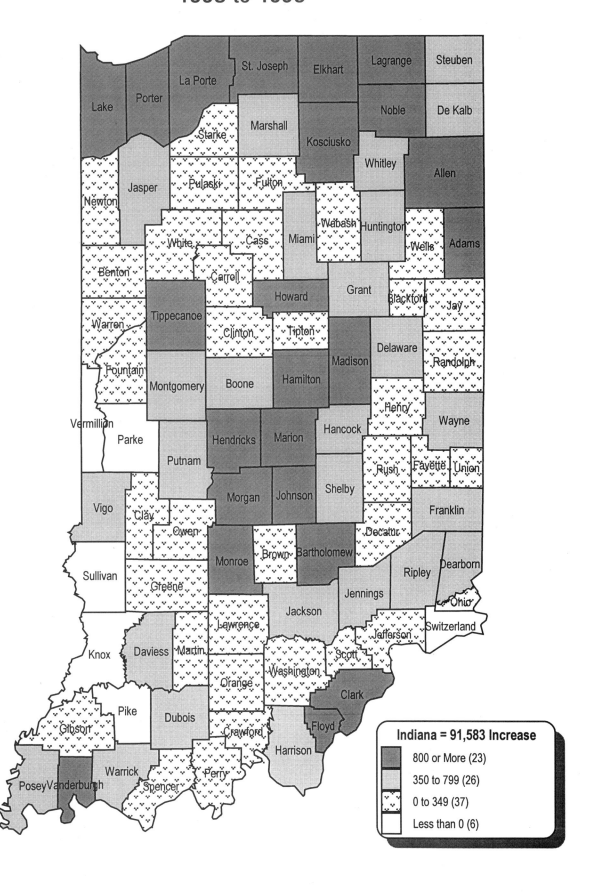

Indiana = 91,583 Increase

- 800 or More (23)
- 350 to 799 (26)
- 0 to 349 (37)
- Less than 0 (6)

Natural Increase in the Population: EDIN Table VITB and VITD.

SECTION 2

INDIANA FACTBOOK
Page 121

2.20 Number of Deaths by Major Cause 1995

	All Causes	Heart Disease	Cancer	Cerebrovascular	Arterial Diseases	Accidents	Motor Vehicle Accidents	Diabetes Mellitus	Pneumonia	Suicide	Emphysema
Indiana	53,053	17,000	12,523	3,986	1,116	1,209	983	1,440	1,810	691	362
Adams	297	93	76	28	5	5	10	10	10	4	0
Allen	2,425	806	594	178	42	64	33	65	65	34	13
Bartholomew	585	196	139	40	6	11	14	14	22	6	2
Benton	97	21	21	15	6	4	1	2	7	2	0
Blackford	146	47	32	9	2	1	3	8	9	2	0
Boone	376	125	91	30	3	9	3	2	6	4	5
Brown	123	28	39	11	2	3	4	5	3	3	0
Carroll	161	47	42	13	2	-5	3	3	6	4	0
Cass	436	139	93	33	16	12	9	12	17	10	2
Clark	919	321	216	84	26	15	14	21	27	10	3
Clay	329	123	68	40	5	4	8	13	1	7	0
Clinton	368	136	78	32	7	10	9	7	14	2	1
Crawford	115	42	20	0	2	-2	2	2	8	2	2
Daviess	333	92	76	30	7	10	7	18	11	3	2
Dearborn	363	119	83	26	7	10	10	6	17	4	2
Decatur	224	86	48	17	1	8	9	9	4	1	0
Dekalb	331	102	78	38	5	6	7	13	3	7	1
Delaware	1,173	390	277	89	28	25	23	31	26	14	9
Dubois	328	119	77	23	11	5	6	4	9	4	1
Elkhart	1,314	453	296	94	17	30	39	44	30	17	16
Fayette	309	106	74	21	6	5	4	7	6	5	0
Floyd	580	191	152	47	13	10	4	16	32	6	5
Fountain	186	59	59	13	1	3	6	5	6	2	0
Franklin	174	59	40	12	5	12	4	9	6	2	0
Fulton	223	80	53	21	6	2	2	8	4	4	0
Gibson	337	102	85	25	6	9	14	12	5	5	4
Grant	825	286	204	44	14	19	14	31	20	7	1
Greene	324	122	71	16	9	5	7	14	8	3	3
Hamilton	729	194	176	54	15	12	19	22	31	24	10
Hancock	391	121	93	23	8	13	7	11	18	7	1
Harrison	271	81	60	13	11	6	16	2	11	7	3
Hendricks	604	167	174	41	10	14	5	15	20	9	5
Henry	527	176	122	44	2	10	17	14	15	9	3
Howard	699	203	177	62	13	14	14	15	29	12	4
Huntington	363	144	65	32	11	8	9	11	13	4	0
Jackson	390	132	91	38	5	17	8	15	5	4	1
Jasper	240	85	61	13	8	9	3	5	7	0	1
Jay	234	72	58	24	4	2	6	9	6	2	2
Jefferson	310	118	60	24	5	8	7	4	17	6	1
Jennings	210	60	56	18	3	5	7	3	13	3	2
Johnson	825	262	166	67	18	21	13	18	45	8	15
Knox	516	164	124	64	13	7	9	8	23	2	2
Kosciusko	560	180	144	35	12	19	14	20	27	3	3
Lagrange	220	70	49	18	4	13	5	8	9	2	0
Lake	4,784	1,607	1,122	300	74	96	72	186	117	44	30
Laporte	994	323	255	49	18	28	15	33	39	17	10
Lawrence	503	164	95	49	11	14	18	14	22	6	7
Madison	1,385	440	352	94	24	40	21	35	39	21	8
Marion	7,582	2,190	1,742	494	196	162	93	192	271	98	63
Marshall	418	117	99	39	3	5	14	19	18	4	5
Martin	108	36	23	13	0	2	2	3	4	0	1
Miami	292	102	75	15	14	10	9	3	6	2	0
Monroe	662	178	187	57	20	16	7	12	33	12	3
Montgomery	368	123	76	35	5	10	7	5	23	4	3
Morgan	520	173	129	44	13	8	17	13	21	5	5
Newton	147	49	37	5	6	3	4	4	6	3	0
Noble	304	102	75	34	4	9	10	5	9	6	1
Ohio	53	20	14	9	0	0	1	1	2	0	0
Orange	199	57	47	9	9	8	4	3	18	3	0
Owen	177	65	37	16	7	5	1	4	10	1	1
Parke	180	83	30	11	3	8	7	4	4	4	0
Perry	192	75	29	14	11	3	4	5	13	5	0
Pike	149	64	35	16	5	1	2	3	3	2	3
Porter	1,064	321	269	63	29	28	30	29	21	21	12
Posey	181	53	52	15	2	5	2	2	6	5	1
Pulaski	153	51	33	17	0	5	8	6	2	4	2
Putnam	286	112	73	14	3	8	3	3	10	3	2
Randolph	275	108	59	12	5	8	3	6	8	4	1
Ripley	260	72	58	29	4	6	7	3	14	6	2
Rush	190	52	45	9	6	2	5	13	6	1	4
St. Joseph	2,350	768	531	203	57	39	33	64	67	22	11
Scott	245	75	61	13	3	2	3	4	18	1	1
Shelby	410	125	106	32	18	16	4	4	18	2	2
Spencer	195	67	44	18	2	4	6	7	6	0	0
Starke	254	85	48	29	5	3	9	3	13	3	5
Steuben	236	70	59	11	3	6	5	5	11	3	1
Sullivan	256	71	52	29	6	8	6	4	9	3	1
Switzerland	117	36	27	9	2	6	3	4	9	2	0
Tippecanoe	980	317	242	77	19	15	16	18	38	11	1
Tipton	172	42	48	16	3	5	5	3	8	3	0
Union	86	36	19	7	1	0	1	0	5	1	0
Vanderburgh	1,822	567	429	148	35	48	30	45	73	28	20
Vermillion	199	75	39	14	4	4	3	4	9	4	1
Vigo	1,181	382	268	100	35	22	11	26	39	13	6
Wabash	393	121	88	39	6	10	14	14	7	4	3
Warren	87	23	28	3	2	2	0	1	3	1	0
Warrick	357	116	98	20	7	8	3	12	13	3	3
Washington	246	84	69	18	3	2	6	5	17	4	1
Wayne	772	268	180	52	12	21	10	24	23	11	10
Wells	245	64	54	34	6	6	4	6	11	5	0
White	252	72	58	19	9	6	5	8	6	3	4
Whitley	282	80	69	25	4	8	12	2	11	7	3

Source: Indiana State Department of Health
EDIN table(s): VITD

2.21 Number of Highway Deaths 1986 to 1996

	1986	1987	1988	1989	1990	1991	1992	1993	1994	1995	1996
Indiana	1,038	1,056	1,104	973	1,044	1,022	903	893	977	959	982
Adams	1	5	10	5	4	6	3	6	4	7	4
Allen	43	47	60	52	44	38	37	35	50	35	36
Bartholomew	17	12	20	8	19	10	12	12	9	15	15
Benton	3	3	2	3	1	0	1	3	2	0	2
Blackford	0	0	3	1	4	1	2	6	0	2	3
Boone	11	4	14	12	11	8	9	4	14	8	10
Brown	0	5	8	2	4	5	4	5	4	1	6
Carroll	6	3	5	1	2	2	2	6	9	4	5
Cass	10	9	10	14	10	14	5	13	7	9	3
Clark	15	14	15	13	12	20	14	17	10	16	6
Clay	8	6	5	5	4	3	6	0	8	8	7
Clinton	5	6	9	9	12	15	6	5	15	8	6
Crawford	0	3	2	3	6	3	2	2	3	2	2
Daviess	8	13	6	4	6	10	8	6	4	5	8
Dearborn	6	14	10	9	4	9	10	3	7	10	9
Decatur	8	6	7	4	6	5	5	4	10	3	9
Dekalb	11	11	10	5	8	15	13	11	10	8	12
Delaware	20	17	16	23	19	26	16	23	17	20	19
Dubois	3	3	11	7	10	2	6	4	4	6	3
Elkhart	43	49	32	31	36	25	26	34	32	39	42
Fayette	1	2	3	5	2	5	5	0	5	2	3
Floyd	10	5	5	13	5	11	9	9	10	7	9
Fountain	1	6	5	0	2	6	4	3	3	4	6
Franklin	2	6	2	9	7	3	3	8	3	3	7
Fulton	12	4	8	6	7	3	8	6	6	2	9
Gibson	6	8	6	6	5	5	7	7	4	15	6
Grant	22	8	23	11	14	5	9	11	9	10	15
Greene	6	6	17	8	7	5	10	8	7	4	3
Hamilton	18	16	22	12	15	13	13	12	9	15	11
Hancock	9	6	12	7	11	3	4	10	9	9	5
Harrison	10	13	8	6	6	11	5	4	12	14	8
Hendricks	19	18	9	10	17	12	13	6	10	8	19
Henry	3	10	12	7	21	19	16	12	9	10	12
Howard	22	7	15	17	5	17	16	5	15	9	5
Huntington	3	11	14	4	9	13	5	12	14	12	9
Jackson	11	5	11	5	10	11	6	8	9	8	9
Jasper	8	6	6	6	14	9	9	4	10	6	7
Jay	4	6	2	7	8	4	6	5	3	6	5
Jefferson	7	6	5	3	4	4	6	4	9	7	7
Jennings	5	5	8	5	4	32	5	5	9	5	5
Johnson	15	10	7	17	12	8	10	5	11	11	10
Knox	7	3	7	2	10	12	11	5	13	7	5
Kosciusko	24	9	27	21	21	15	11	19	24	14	21
Lagrange	14	5	5	7	13	9	7	8	8	9	19
Lake	56	75	74	77	74	65	66	56	80	61	65
Laporte	25	31	17	31	37	35	26	31	28	17	27
Lawrence	18	9	4	9	6	5	11	12	9	15	9
Madison	22	15	22	24	27	24	11	13	27	18	13
Marion	120	113	100	88	94	74	83	80	77	91	105
Marshall	15	15	18	12	9	12	10	11	7	12	13
Martin	3	1	3	2	3	1	3	2	3	3	3
Miami	7	5	6	4	7	12	9	10	6	7	8
Monroe	20	21	14	13	12	17	10	14	15	11	9
Montgomery	5	6	14	12	7	6	7	6	9	7	11
Morgan	13	14	10	10	9	10	10	15	4	13	8
Newton	3	3	9	7	8	6	4	11	5	5	3
Noble	4	19	10	11	8	11	15	9	11	18	11
Ohio	1	0	1	1	1	0	2	1	0	2	0
Orange	2	2	6	2	3	3	3	1	4	5	6
Owen	5	6	6	3	4	6	5	3	5	1	3
Parke	6	9	8	3	8	6	7	2	5	4	2
Perry	3	0	2	6	4	2	0	7	3	5	3
Pike	1	3	0	4	5	5	5	1	1	2	8
Porter	21	36	38	20	38	28	26	29	20	26	28
Posey	3	4	14	2	5	5	1	8	4	5	3
Pulaski	5	3	3	3	4	5	4	0	4	6	3
Putnam	5	6	6	11	8	10	8	4	11	6	4
Randolph	7	11	5	8	4	7	3	10	12	7	9
Ripley	3	8	0	4	4	10	6	2	5	8	5
Rush	6	3	3	7	3	4	3	2	4	13	4
St. Joseph	34	41	40	40	40	41	21	24	25	35	39
Scott	3	4	2	4	7	4	10	10	4	6	5
Shelby	8	12	5	5	7	9	3	13	5	6	6
Spencer	2	4	8	5	6	5	8	5	5	5	5
Starke	6	11	17	6	10	9	6	7	9	13	7
Steuben	5	10	16	7	9	14	12	6	9	5	8
Sullivan	3	8	8	1	2	7	3	2	5	2	5
Switzerland	1	4	1	6	1	4	2	1	1	2	3
Tippecanoe	16	17	14	19	23	16	20	23	14	20	19
Tipton	2	2	0	10	5	5	4	4	1	2	7
Union	2	2	2	2	2	2	3	1	0	1	2
Vanderburgh	20	19	21	19	17	19	17	11	17	21	12
Vermillion	5	4	6	3	2	2	6	3	7	5	11
Vigo	24	28	16	15	13	17	8	12	24	14	17
Wabash	7	13	5	6	14	8	14	10	10	15	12
Warren	3	2	2	2	2	13	3	4	2	2	2
Warrick	11	7	5	11	7	7	11	7	9	4	3
Washington	7	7	5	1	9	11	3	5	5	4	5
Wayne	11	9	13	17	8	9	9	9	6	9	15
Wells	3	5	8	4	4	6	6	7	7	4	5
White	15	7	11	4	6	13	6	6	6	6	2
Whitley	12	11	12	7	7	4	5	8	7	7	5

Source: Indiana State Police
EDIN table(s): RDTH

Percent Change in the Number of Health Professionals
Indiana - 1990 to 1997

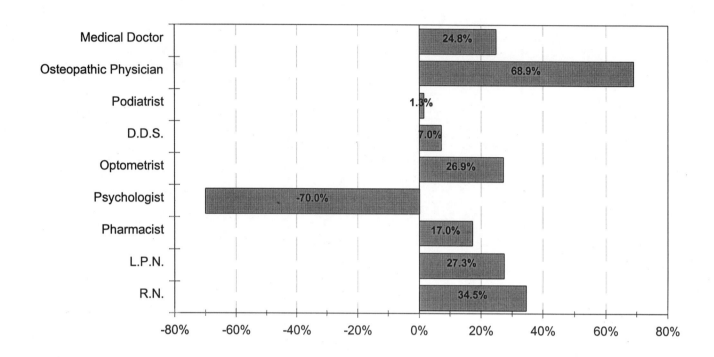

Highway Deaths
Indiana - 1986 to 1996

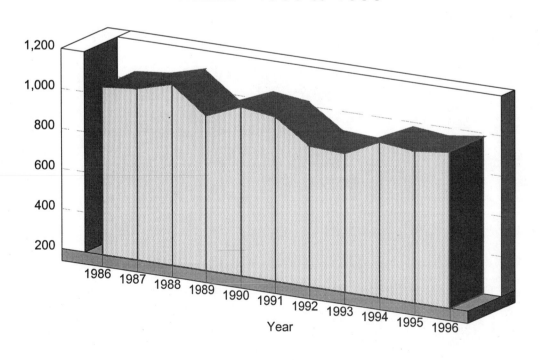

Percent Change in the Number of Health Professionals: EDIN Table HLHP.
Highway Deaths: EDIN Table RDTH.

2.22 Number of Health Professionals *(Either Live or Work in County)* 1997

	Total [1]	Medical Doctor	Osteopathic Physician	Podiatrist	D.D.S.	Optometrist	Psychologist	Pharmacist	L.P.N.	R.N.
Indiana	138,349	10,952	554	228	3,010	958	1,026	5,457	21,247	61,331
Adams	608	16	0	1	11	4	1	12	128	319
Allen	9,060	731	33	14	176	53	63	319	1,299	4,173
Bartholomew	1,704	158	4	6	37	16	14	54	372	646
Benton	163	6	0	0	2	0	1	7	34	76
Blackford	221	8	1	0	3	4	1	5	64	102
Boone	1,425	152	6	1	28	8	11	83	186	640
Brown	179	4	1	0	2	1	1	6	49	66
Carroll	349	7	0	0	7	2	0	14	68	170
Cass	748	44	5	1	11	6	5	21	152	324
Clark	1,922	157	0	2	31	16	3	54	495	811
Clay	585	14	1	0	6	4	4	15	177	277
Clinton	573	16	0	1	10	4	1	22	121	276
Crawford	133	1	0	0	1	1	0	1	57	49
Daviess	544	18	8	1	6	5	0	24	96	261
Dearborn	711	48	3	2	8	6	3	37	157	313
Decatur	444	19	0	0	7	6	1	22	99	188
Dekalb	713	29	6	1	15	2	2	17	126	363
Delaware	2,825	284	3	4	56	16	61	87	563	1,055
Dubois	799	58	8	2	19	10	2	23	120	368
Elkhart	3,007	206	22	6	65	20	13	109	370	1,473
Fayette	433	23	1	0	6	6	0	18	120	174
Floyd	1,563	125	0	5	38	14	6	66	261	710
Fountain	344	9	0	0	5	1	1	14	95	146
Franklin	199	4	0	0	4	1	0	5	49	92
Fulton	335	16	3	1	7	3	0	15	62	155
Gibson	774	22	9	1	14	4	2	30	127	400
Grant	1,839	111	12	3	35	9	7	46	409	841
Greene	632	16	0	1	15	5	3	20	205	264
Hamilton	5,557	576	16	5	124	39	39	415	344	2,589
Hancock	1,375	76	0	2	16	8	2	97	178	680
Harrison	611	20	1	0	12	4	1	20	165	267
Hendricks	2,399	117	8	3	56	15	6	119	302	1,194
Henry	983	44	1	1	20	10	3	27	220	443
Howard	1,876	124	2	7	49	16	10	59	292	886
Huntington	761	28	3	0	13	5	1	25	146	388
Jackson	717	36	0	1	12	8	3	32	171	292
Jasper	647	12	3	0	8	6	2	28	118	332
Jay	332	12	4	0	7	3	0	10	97	132
Jefferson	758	41	2	1	17	7	7	26	189	273
Jennings	390	11	1	0	7	3	2	7	133	132
Johnson	2,832	134	3	5	70	31	11	147	416	1,339
Knox	1,342	73	16	2	16	11	10	41	165	674
Kosciusko	1,051	63	11	1	25	10	6	52	160	461
Lagrange	336	10	1	0	8	1	0	11	71	160
Lake	10,198	828	83	35	255	58	41	389	1,003	5,154
Laporte	2,345	178	11	5	60	13	7	65	291	1,144
Lawrence	869	56	1	1	20	9	3	34	205	335
Madison	2,881	165	0	7	57	18	11	83	626	1,255
Marion	25,144	3,206	76	41	682	135	235	1,021	2,894	9,896
Marshall	749	45	10	0	20	8	1	34	91	357
Martin	224	2	0	0	3	2	0	6	45	114
Miami	580	22	0	1	9	3	1	13	148	266
Monroe	2,579	256	5	4	64	49	78	86	400	909
Montgomery	605	39	1	0	20	5	4	23	122	233
Morgan	1,181	54	8	1	25	11	5	47	250	512
Newton	156	3	2	0	3	2	1	10	32	76
Noble	591	23	1	1	12	5	1	15	143	256
Ohio	82	0	0	0	2	0	0	0	21	51
Orange	299	13	1	0	6	4	1	11	84	100
Owen	248	5	0	0	4	1	1	10	105	87
Parke	288	11	0	0	4	0	1	16	84	126
Perry	267	11	0	0	8	2	2	10	80	106
Pike	267	5	1	0	4	1	0	7	69	136
Porter	3,735	199	26	6	81	21	42	143	343	2,011
Posey	488	9	1	0	8	3	0	24	97	242
Pulaski	255	6	2	0	4	3	1	8	47	125
Putnam	538	18	3	1	13	4	5	17	129	247
Randolph	522	16	1	0	9	4	2	16	167	210
Ripley	598	32	0	1	13	3	1	30	121	268
Rush	292	11	0	0	5	2	0	12	65	138
St. Joseph	6,286	551	74	14	144	47	89	279	694	2,728
Scott	363	15	0	0	6	1	0	12	126	123
Shelby	736	26	0	1	14	6	1	24	198	316
Spencer	341	3	1	0	4	1	1	8	69	189
Starke	310	8	1	0	3	0	0	5	55	193
Steuben	482	21	1	0	12	7	3	19	87	231
Sullivan	570	15	0	1	7	2	0	17	183	261
Switzerland	112	4	0	0	1	1	0	2	37	48
Tippecanoe	3,698	306	1	6	56	23	58	227	370	1,400
Tipton	328	14	2	0	5	2	0	6	41	167
Union	132	2	0	0	2	0	0	0	38	57
Vanderburgh	4,983	526	7	10	106	42	42	158	612	2,147
Vermillion	313	9	1	0	3	2	0	7	95	141
Vigo	2,773	236	13	4	61	13	54	82	536	1,230
Wabash	689	32	2	1	13	9	2	25	163	255
Warren	115	4	0	0	1	1	0	4	26	61
Warrick	1,558	75	6	0	21	6	9	64	215	760
Washington	416	11	0	0	7	1	0	13	149	162
Wayne	1,610	121	8	3	42	9	11	51	356	653
Wells	639	46	2	2	7	9	1	17	115	304
White	457	18	0	0	9	3	1	22	76	221
Whitley	657	17	4	0	10	3	1	20	116	356

Footnote: [1] Includes categories not shown separately.
Source: Health Professionals Bureau
EDIN table(s): HLHP

Students Enrolled in Indiana Higher Education as a Percent of the Population in the Students' Home Counties 1995

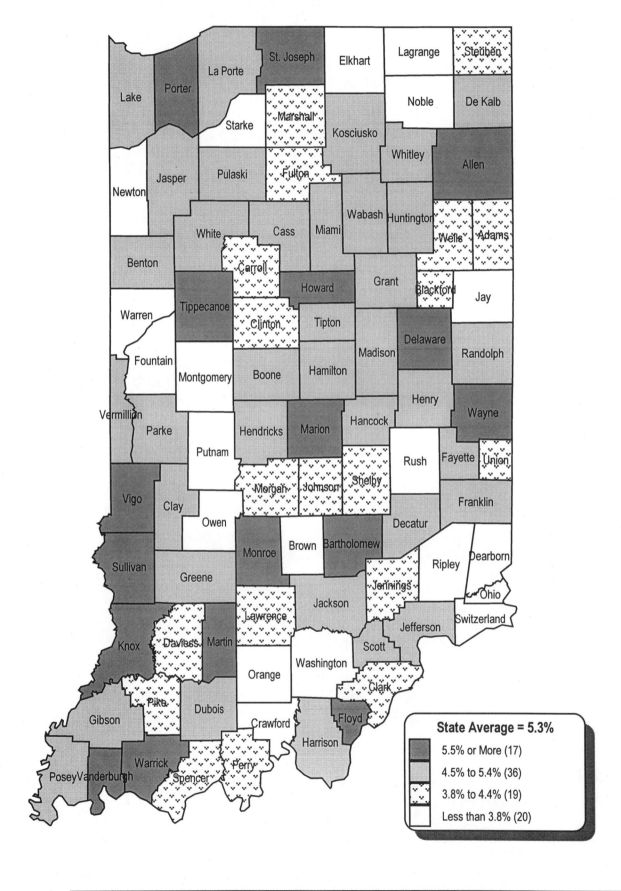

State Average = 5.3%

- 5.5% or More (17)
- 4.5% to 5.4% (36)
- 3.8% to 4.4% (19)
- Less than 3.8% (20)

Students Enrolled in Indiana Higher Education: EDIN Table EDHI.

Education

2.23 Higher Education by Reported County of Residence 1995

	Students Counted 1995	Percent Change 1994-95	Male		African-American		Other Minority		Attending Full-time		Over Age 25		On Campus	
			Number	Percent	Number	Percent	Number	Percent	Number	Percent	Number	Percent	Number	Percent
Indiana	308,451	-1.8	134,176	43.5	21,592	7.0	10,796	3.5	112,585	36.5	132,017	42.8	41,641	13.5
Adams	1,249	-5.7	582	46.6	2	0.2	36	2.9	580	46.4	390	31.2	231	18.5
Allen	19,152	-4.6	8,408	43.9	1,551	8.1	689	3.6	6,588	34.4	8,216	42.9	1,954	10.2
Bartholomew	4,314	3.1	1,993	46.2	78	1.8	104	2.4	1,277	29.6	2,045	47.4	526	12.2
Benton	516	-3.7	208	40.3	0	0.0	3	0.6	268	51.9	181	35.1	114	22.0
Blackford	579	-9.0	254	43.9	0	0.0	8	1.4	301	52.0	219	37.9	116	20.0
Boone	2,164	0.7	935	43.2	11	0.5	28	1.3	896	41.4	829	38.3	426	19.7
Brown	419	1.5	185	44.2	1	0.2	7	1.7	136	32.5	206	49.2	49	11.6
Carroll	748	-0.7	307	41.0	4	0.6	11	1.5	314	42.0	277	37.0	122	16.3
Cass	2,084	-12.8	802	38.5	10	0.5	27	1.3	765	36.7	973	46.7	319	15.3
Clark	3,825	-7.0	1,614	42.2	176	4.6	65	1.7	1,170	30.6	1,622	42.4	383	10.0
Clay	1,264	-1.6	562	44.5	10	0.8	9	0.7	506	40.0	546	43.2	99	7.8
Clinton	1,418	-1.8	588	41.5	1	0.1	31	2.2	552	38.9	614	43.3	230	16.2
Crawford	385	2.4	156	40.6	0	0.0	3	0.8	152	39.5	146	37.8	62	16.0
Daviess	1,121	-9.6	480	42.8	8	0.7	7	0.6	535	47.7	365	32.6	193	17.2
Dearborn	1,039	0.1	448	43.1	9	0.9	9	0.9	365	35.1	450	43.3	232	22.3
Decatur	1,233	4.9	580	47.0	1	0.1	31	2.5	451	36.6	492	39.9	261	21.2
Dekalb	1,820	-0.3	815	44.8	2	0.1	29	1.6	653	35.9	752	41.3	244	13.4
Delaware	8,180	-3.5	3,779	46.2	515	6.3	180	2.2	3,763	46.0	3,182	38.9	753	9.2
Dubois	1,993	3.1	787	39.5	2	0.1	12	0.6	759	38.1	512	25.7	387	19.4
Elkhart	5,318	7.9	2,452	46.1	85	1.6	160	3.0	1,835	34.5	2,361	44.4	963	18.1
Fayette	1,185	0.9	469	39.6	19	1.6	13	1.1	425	35.9	461	38.9	213	18.0
Floyd	3,960	-3.6	1,727	43.6	91	2.3	63	1.6	1,216	30.7	1,659	41.9	404	10.2
Fountain	629	-10.8	257	40.9	0	0.0	8	1.3	326	51.8	195	31.0	164	26.0
Franklin	1,098	-1.3	502	45.7	0	0.0	9	0.8	473	43.1	345	31.4	296	27.0
Fulton	789	6.5	315	39.9	0	0.0	11	1.4	294	37.3	342	43.4	154	19.5
Gibson	1,685	-2.4	687	40.8	30	1.8	25	1.5	714	42.4	716	42.5	278	16.5
Grant	3,458	-5.5	1,542	44.6	173	5.0	138	4.0	1,428	41.3	1,383	40.0	692	20.0
Greene	1,511	-3.7	616	40.8	2	0.1	18	1.2	632	41.8	607	40.2	187	12.4
Hamilton	6,460	-2.0	2,849	44.1	58	0.9	174	2.7	2,623	40.6	2,649	41.0	1,208	18.7
Hancock	2,659	-3.7	1,197	45.0	3	0.1	51	1.9	1,058	39.8	973	36.6	553	20.8
Harrison	1,646	-3.1	726	44.1	3	0.2	20	1.2	543	33.0	644	39.1	221	13.4
Hendricks	4,354	-1.4	1,977	45.4	30	0.7	57	1.3	1,755	40.3	1,707	39.2	823	18.9
Henry	2,303	-0.9	972	42.2	30	1.3	28	1.2	970	42.1	896	38.9	403	17.5
Howard	5,727	-9.3	2,617	45.7	286	5.0	200	3.5	1,632	28.5	2,640	46.1	613	10.7
Huntington	1,839	-3.0	862	46.9	4	0.2	46	2.5	660	35.9	791	43.0	294	16.0
Jackson	1,938	0.4	895	46.2	2	0.1	33	1.7	653	33.7	849	43.8	302	15.6
Jasper	1,260	1.1	533	42.3	8	0.6	29	2.3	587	46.6	440	34.9	236	18.7
Jay	778	-3.8	307	39.4	0	0.0	7	0.9	390	50.1	269	34.6	168	21.6
Jefferson	1,646	-8.5	662	40.2	20	1.2	18	1.1	487	29.6	838	50.9	240	14.6
Jennings	999	1.7	420	42.0	8	0.8	16	1.6	308	30.8	463	46.3	161	16.1
Johnson	4,025	0.4	1,783	44.3	28	0.7	72	1.8	1,525	37.9	1,610	40.0	648	16.1
Knox	2,385	-2.9	1,037	43.5	33	1.4	29	1.2	1,061	44.5	887	37.2	167	7.0
Kosciusko	3,405	17.2	1,468	43.1	27	0.8	99	2.9	984	28.9	1,645	48.3	497	14.6
Lagrange	622	3.5	283	45.5	0	0.0	14	2.3	296	47.6	193	31.1	149	23.9
Lake	25,839	-1.2	10,413	40.3	5,685	22.0	3,101	12.0	9,560	37.0	9,870	38.2	2,997	11.6
Laporte	5,405	-3.3	2,448	45.3	303	5.6	200	3.7	1,859	34.4	2,394	44.3	724	13.4
Lawrence	1,734	-8.7	782	45.1	2	0.1	36	2.1	687	39.6	697	40.2	239	13.8
Madison	6,732	1.6	3,151	46.8	505	7.5	101	1.5	2,794	41.5	2,841	42.2	1,077	16.0
Marion	46,715	-3.4	19,714	42.2	7,895	16.9	1,635	3.5	15,696	33.6	22,049	47.2	5,699	12.2
Marshall	1,891	9.8	908	48.0	8	0.4	62	3.3	709	37.5	817	43.2	363	19.2
Martin	576	2.7	235	40.8	0	0.0	7	1.2	230	39.9	219	38.0	73	12.7
Miami	1,594	-5.6	695	43.6	35	2.2	46	2.9	575	36.1	697	43.7	285	17.9
Monroe	10,608	-6.2	5,028	47.4	414	3.9	488	4.6	4,668	44.0	5,251	49.5	934	8.8
Montgomery	1,348	-5.3	604	44.8	7	0.5	40	3.0	574	42.6	519	38.5	307	22.8
Morgan	2,445	-4.1	1,002	41.0	2	0.1	39	1.6	885	36.2	1,020	41.7	362	14.8
Newton	377	-7.8	162	43.0	2	0.5	9	2.4	194	51.5	124	32.9	91	24.2
Noble	1,421	2.1	624	43.9	3	0.2	31	2.2	551	38.8	539	37.9	246	17.3
Ohio	131	5.6	43	32.8	0	0.0	0	0.0	48	36.6	48	36.4	43	33.1
Orange	616	-5.5	249	40.5	5	0.8	4	0.7	261	42.4	206	33.4	125	20.3
Owen	617	-4.8	241	39.1	1	0.2	6	1.0	222	36.0	291	47.1	72	11.6
Parke	752	4.0	280	37.2	20	2.6	9	1.2	296	39.4	322	42.8	73	9.7
Perry	842	-2.8	367	43.6	22	2.6	11	1.3	333	39.5	329	39.1	178	21.1
Pike	533	1.7	214	40.2	0	0.0	4	0.8	217	40.7	194	36.4	69	13.0
Porter	8,222	0.8	3,577	43.5	41	0.5	444	5.4	3,165	38.5	3,248	39.5	1,126	13.7
Posey	1,406	-1.1	627	44.6	14	1.0	14	1.0	457	32.5	636	45.2	149	10.6
Pulaski	594	12.5	260	43.7	4	0.7	7	1.2	275	46.3	190	32.0	151	25.4
Putnam	1,218	3.7	542	44.5	35	2.9	23	1.9	512	42.0	474	38.9	200	16.4
Randolph	1,342	-1.3	574	42.8	1	0.1	19	1.4	558	41.6	527	39.3	197	14.7
Ripley	828	3.0	290	35.0	0	0.0	4	0.5	309	37.3	301	36.4	170	20.5
Rush	664	9.8	262	39.5	7	1.1	5	0.8	288	43.4	238	35.8	172	25.9
St. Joseph	17,213	2.5	7,763	45.1	1,601	9.3	568	3.3	5,043	29.3	8,211	47.7	2,393	13.9
Scott	1,047	-6.3	414	39.5	2	0.2	16	1.5	310	29.6	480	45.8	136	13.0
Shelby	1,830	-4.7	780	42.6	7	0.4	18	1.0	675	36.9	781	42.7	335	18.3
Spencer	812	8.3	337	41.5	3	0.4	3	0.4	331	40.8	292	36.0	188	23.2
Starke	709	8.6	316	44.6	1	0.1	18	2.5	281	39.6	278	39.2	131	18.5
Steuben	1,202	0.5	549	45.7	8	0.7	28	2.3	508	42.3	457	38.0	224	18.6
Sullivan	1,112	3.3	507	45.6	7	0.6	14	1.3	431	38.8	427	38.4	116	10.4
Switzerland	184	-10.7	71	38.6	0	0.0	0	0.0	75	40.8	88	47.8	42	23.0
Tippecanoe	8,975	0.7	4,102	45.7	224	2.5	521	5.8	3,419	38.1	4,380	48.8	915	10.2
Tipton	809	-6.1	365	45.1	1	0.1	13	1.6	296	36.6	277	34.2	144	17.8
Union	305	0.3	109	35.7	3	1.0	7	2.4	120	39.3	109	35.6	59	19.2
Vanderburgh	11,253	-1.3	4,726	42.0	596	5.3	214	1.9	3,815	33.9	4,929	43.8	1,362	12.1
Vermillion	816	-3.2	341	41.8	1	0.1	8	1.0	313	38.4	288	35.3	69	8.5
Vigo	7,444	-5.8	3,365	45.2	462	6.2	216	2.9	2,948	39.6	3,149	42.3	588	7.9
Wabash	1,705	3.6	789	46.3	3	0.2	41	2.4	617	36.2	631	37.0	278	16.3
Warren	228	-2.1	94	41.4	0	0.0	7	3.1	109	47.8	88	38.8	42	18.5
Warrick	3,135	0.6	1,379	44.0	22	0.7	47	1.5	1,125	35.9	1,329	42.4	423	13.5
Washington	922	-8.3	372	40.3	0	0.0	9	1.0	334	36.2	346	37.5	123	13.3
Wayne	4,272	0.4	1,722	40.3	235	5.5	68	1.6	1,273	29.8	1,918	44.9	568	13.3
Wells	995	0.2	480	48.2	0	0.0	14	1.4	436	43.8	352	35.4	161	16.2
White	1,256	-3.5	549	43.7	1	0.1	24	1.9	530	42.2	487	38.8	208	16.6
Whitley	1,423	-3.9	663	46.6	4	0.3	13	0.9	511	35.9	542	38.1	218	15.3

Source: Indiana Commission for Higher Education
EDIN table(s): EDHI

Value of Owner Occupied Housing
Indiana - 1990

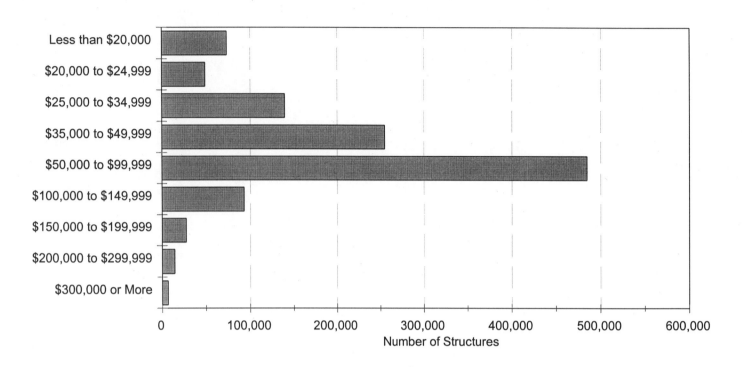

Contract Rent
Indiana - 1990

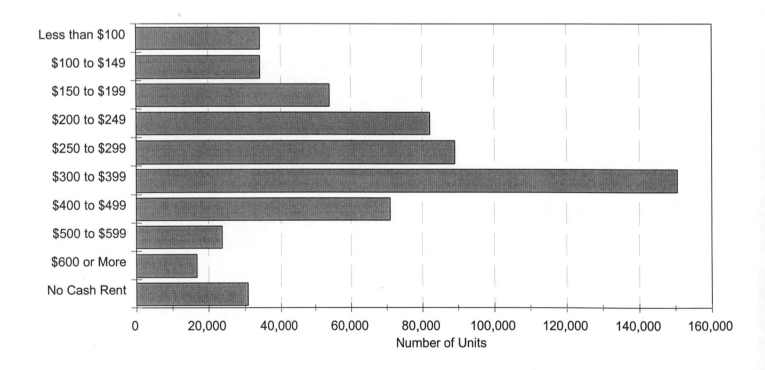

Value of Owner Occupied Housing: EDIN Table HSVL.
Contract Rent: EDIN Table HSCR.

Housing
2.24 Tenure by Race and Vacancy Status 1990

	Total Housing Units	Total Occupied Units	Owner Occupied				Renter Occupied				Total Vacant Units	Vacancy Rate
			Total	Percent Change 1980-90	White	African-American	Total	Percent Change 1980-90	White	African-American		
Indiana	2,246,046	2,065,355	1,450,898	5.0	1,369,211	68,482	614,457	12.7	520,642	80,573	180,691	8.0
Adams	10,931	10,470	8,206	5.0	8,107	3	2,264	24.9	2,198	2	461	4.2
Allen	122,923	113,333	79,567	6.9	73,750	4,738	33,766	12.8	27,678	5,330	9,590	7.8
Bartholomew	25,432	24,192	17,703	3.5	17,397	177	6,489	13.9	6,178	189	1,240	4.9
Benton	3,833	3,524	2,569	-4.0	2,557	1	955	-2.4	952	1	309	8.1
Blackford	5,856	5,436	4,202	-6.1	4,185	0	1,234	11.9	1,227	0	420	7.2
Boone	14,516	13,922	10,607	11.7	10,550	14	3,315	5.3	3,280	11	594	4.1
Brown	6,997	5,370	4,436	22.9	4,410	5	934	13.6	927	0	1,627	23.3
Carroll	8,431	7,067	5,515	1.5	5,496	4	1,552	-0.2	1,549	1	1,364	16.2
Cass	15,633	14,659	10,899	-3.2	10,799	47	3,760	8.9	3,689	41	974	6.2
Clark	35,313	33,292	22,760	4.9	21,978	666	10,532	12.9	9,508	923	2,021	5.7
Clay	10,606	9,382	7,440	-0.8	7,381	41	1,942	12.3	1,930	8	1,224	11.5
Clinton	12,100	11,450	8,244	0.1	8,204	2	3,206	3.7	3,170	7	650	5.4
Crawford	4,374	3,660	3,118	5.2	3,112	0	542	8.6	537	1	714	16.3
Daviess	10,985	10,012	7,810	1.4	7,764	33	2,202	1.3	2,187	7	973	8.9
Dearborn	14,532	13,642	10,683	17.3	10,603	54	2,959	24.2	2,916	34	890	6.1
Decatur	9,098	8,427	6,372	3.0	6,347	0	2,055	9.3	2,033	0	671	7.4
Dekalb	13,601	12,725	10,333	9.3	10,271	7	2,392	20.4	2,369	1	876	6.4
Delaware	48,793	45,177	30,193	-3.3	28,876	1,159	14,984	11.4	13,305	1,477	3,616	7.4
Dubois	13,964	13,023	10,248	14.1	10,227	3	2,775	24.8	2,754	9	941	6.7
Elkhart	60,182	56,713	40,745	14.7	39,374	1,011	15,968	26.5	14,337	1,296	3,469	5.8
Fayette	10,525	9,945	6,950	-3.5	6,822	104	2,995	8.7	2,903	78	580	5.5
Floyd	25,238	24,085	17,283	9.7	16,837	384	6,802	19.2	6,248	517	1,153	4.6
Fountain	7,344	6,858	5,259	-1.2	5,236	1	1,599	-3.1	1,592	0	486	6.6
Franklin	7,176	6,636	5,275	8.2	5,259	3	1,361	7.9	1,355	1	540	7.5
Fulton	8,656	7,345	5,681	-1.6	5,604	40	1,664	16.4	1,639	13	1,311	15.1
Gibson	13,454	12,299	9,672	0.4	9,480	155	2,627	3.1	2,533	69	1,155	8.6
Grant	29,904	27,701	19,758	-2.7	18,605	930	7,943	4.1	6,942	840	2,203	7.4
Greene	13,337	11,910	9,578	0.6	9,545	2	2,332	17.0	2,316	1	1,427	10.7
Hamilton	41,074	38,834	29,849	40.6	29,402	156	8,985	48.9	8,756	97	2,240	5.5
Hancock	16,495	15,959	12,766	11.5	12,691	7	3,193	5.8	3,170	4	536	3.2
Harrison	11,456	10,618	9,060	17.0	8,999	30	1,558	16.2	1,540	13	838	7.3
Hendricks	26,962	26,109	21,525	13.9	21,414	28	4,584	21.3	4,543	9	853	3.2
Henry	19,835	18,642	14,024	-2.9	13,893	90	4,618	6.0	4,507	82	1,193	6.0
Howard	33,820	31,523	22,716	-1.1	21,688	867	8,807	9.0	7,879	772	2,297	6.8
Huntington	13,629	12,830	9,840	2.6	9,763	8	2,990	8.0	2,956	4	799	5.9
Jackson	14,820	14,032	10,815	3.9	10,741	36	3,217	26.5	3,138	21	788	5.3
Jasper	8,984	8,527	6,428	2.0	6,400	3	2,099	5.6	2,074	5	457	5.1
Jay	8,905	8,161	6,330	-5.3	6,298	10	1,831	9.4	1,798	4	744	8.4
Jefferson	11,921	10,897	7,979	2.8	7,874	82	2,918	15.3	2,834	46	1,024	8.6
Jennings	9,129	8,351	6,681	10.9	6,600	61	1,670	29.6	1,640	22	778	8.5
Johnson	33,289	31,354	23,206	20.2	23,000	58	8,148	35.0	8,010	43	1,935	5.8
Knox	16,730	15,145	10,687	-5.7	10,620	39	4,458	7.6	4,320	90	1,585	9.5
Kosciusko	30,516	23,449	18,529	13.3	18,304	60	4,920	9.1	4,807	36	7,067	23.2
Lagrange	12,218	9,209	7,496	16.9	7,455	2	1,713	26.1	1,691	0	3,009	24.6
Lake	183,014	170,748	115,720	-2.3	91,585	20,426	55,028	-2.9	31,950	19,760	12,266	6.7
Laporte	42,268	38,488	28,132	1.4	26,772	1,166	10,356	7.1	9,003	1,229	3,780	8.9
Lawrence	17,587	16,235	12,943	2.2	12,872	25	3,292	14.9	3,265	15	1,352	7.7
Madison	53,353	49,804	36,395	-2.8	34,799	1,446	13,409	7.1	11,698	1,591	3,549	6.7
Marion	349,403	319,471	182,039	8.0	154,279	25,932	137,432	17.9	99,944	35,356	29,932	8.6
Marshall	16,820	15,146	11,619	7.7	11,510	15	3,527	23.7	3,470	6	1,674	10.0
Martin	4,116	3,836	3,133	3.4	3,124	1	703	-7.7	696	3	280	6.8
Miami	14,639	13,484	9,516	-0.9	9,257	106	3,968	-2.8	3,607	253	1,155	7.9
Monroe	41,948	39,351	21,558	12.7	21,169	193	17,793	20.0	16,217	677	2,597	6.2
Montgomery	13,957	13,235	9,555	-0.6	9,494	26	3,680	9.9	3,608	39	722	5.2
Morgan	20,500	19,600	15,455	14.0	15,409	1	4,145	14.9	4,117	1	900	4.4
Newton	5,276	4,839	3,723	-3.7	3,695	2	1,116	-6.3	1,105	0	437	8.3
Noble	15,516	13,418	10,485	9.5	10,434	1	2,933	18.0	2,896	5	2,098	13.5
Ohio	2,161	1,980	1,557	9.4	1,542	12	423	6.8	419	3	181	8.4
Orange	7,732	6,950	5,635	2.7	5,596	22	1,315	7.1	1,281	24	782	10.1
Owen	8,011	6,394	5,307	13.0	5,280	10	1,087	16.3	1,079	3	1,617	20.2
Parke	7,189	5,845	4,617	-4.3	4,606	4	1,228	8.8	1,221	3	1,344	18.7
Perry	7,404	6,845	5,461	-2.3	5,446	1	1,384	18.0	1,376	1	559	7.6
Pike	5,487	4,925	4,070	-2.8	4,065	0	855	-0.7	850	1	562	10.2
Porter	47,240	45,159	33,963	13.7	33,499	56	11,196	20.8	10,940	70	2,081	4.4
Posey	10,401	9,508	7,633	8.0	7,573	49	1,875	-6.7	1,816	50	893	8.6
Pulaski	5,541	4,722	3,661	-1.7	3,631	16	1,061	10.2	1,047	6	819	14.8
Putnam	10,981	9,996	7,584	2.3	7,522	47	2,412	21.0	2,360	30	985	9.0
Randolph	11,327	10,451	7,900	-4.8	7,857	15	2,551	5.7	2,531	5	876	7.7
Ripley	9,587	8,778	6,660	1.8	6,634	2	2,118	27.4	2,107	0	809	8.4
Rush	7,014	6,504	4,678	-3.2	4,635	34	1,826	1.1	1,804	16	510	7.3
St. Joseph	97,956	92,365	66,492	4.4	61,758	3,975	25,873	15.0	20,971	4,184	5,591	5.7
Scott	8,078	7,593	5,864	7.5	5,835	0	1,729	35.7	1,720	1	485	6.0
Shelby	15,654	14,761	10,847	2.5	10,741	64	3,914	20.6	3,831	57	893	5.7
Spencer	7,636	6,962	5,661	9.2	5,619	24	1,301	5.3	1,270	18	674	8.8
Starke	9,888	8,141	6,344	6.0	6,282	15	1,797	21.7	1,772	4	1,747	17.7
Steuben	15,768	10,194	8,053	14.4	8,009	14	2,141	24.8	2,095	11	5,574	35.4
Sullivan	8,487	7,364	5,892	-9.3	5,878	5	1,472	1.3	1,467	1	1,123	13.2
Switzerland	3,732	2,839	2,245	9.6	2,231	4	594	19.0	591	2	893	23.9
Tippecanoe	48,134	45,618	26,059	7.1	25,498	205	19,559	19.6	17,379	583	2,516	5.2
Tipton	6,427	6,026	4,632	-0.9	4,605	0	1,394	5.6	1,385	3	401	6.2
Union	2,813	2,576	1,863	6.0	1,851	7	713	9.2	708	1	237	8.4
Vanderburgh	72,637	66,780	43,287	2.6	41,272	1,802	23,493	7.6	20,506	2,762	5,857	8.1
Vermillion	7,288	6,638	5,322	-5.8	5,300	3	1,316	3.1	1,307	2	650	8.9
Vigo	44,203	39,804	27,568	-4.1	26,510	955	12,236	6.0	10,930	940	4,399	10.0
Wabash	13,394	12,630	9,380	-0.5	9,273	16	3,250	3.0	3,183	10	764	5.7
Warren	3,275	3,015	2,371	1.0	2,362	1	644	-13.3	642	0	260	7.9
Warrick	16,926	15,817	12,917	14.6	12,773	87	2,900	17.8	2,851	28	1,109	6.6
Washington	9,520	8,664	6,933	10.9	6,915	1	1,731	32.7	1,722	1	856	9.0
Wayne	29,586	27,587	18,650	-2.2	17,903	656	8,937	6.9	8,143	706	1,999	6.8
Wells	9,928	9,438	7,443	4.9	7,406	3	1,995	14.0	1,974	1	490	4.9
White	11,875	8,926	6,780	-1.0	6,755	0	2,146	10.2	2,131	0	2,949	24.8
Whitley	10,852	10,010	8,259	8.6	8,226	3	1,751	19.9	1,734	0	842	7.8

2.25 Tenure by Age of Householder: Owner, Renter Occupied 1990

| | ←Total Occupied Units→ | | ←15 to 24 Years→ | | ←25 to 44 Years→ | | ←45 to 64 Years→ | | ←65 to 74 Years→ | | ←75 Years and Older→ | |
	Owner	Renter	Owner	Renter	Owner	Renter	Owner	Renter	Owner	Renter	Owner	Renter
Indiana	1,450,898	614,457	26,669	91,714	568,343	320,753	501,250	104,293	213,772	46,334	140,864	51,363
Adams	8,206	2,264	243	337	3,366	1,077	2,531	333	1,193	224	873	293
Allen	79,567	33,766	1,589	5,172	35,104	17,968	26,177	5,169	10,297	2,406	6,400	3,051
Bartholomew	17,703	6,489	407	857	6,852	3,556	6,581	1,174	2,330	470	1,533	432
Benton	2,569	955	35	98	793	531	834	195	509	70	398	61
Blackford	4,202	1,234	97	139	1,441	611	1,477	218	690	105	497	161
Boone	10,607	3,315	153	325	4,451	1,697	3,748	547	1,331	289	924	457
Brown	4,436	934	83	99	1,659	495	1,679	171	635	82	380	87
Carroll	5,515	1,552	95	189	2,009	814	1,899	254	921	122	591	173
Cass	10,899	3,760	162	474	3,843	1,920	3,726	680	1,882	329	1,286	357
Clark	22,760	10,532	333	1,171	9,095	5,584	8,239	2,022	3,256	837	1,837	918
Clay	7,440	1,942	185	202	2,604	859	2,409	330	1,230	245	1,012	306
Clinton	8,244	3,206	159	393	2,945	1,712	2,735	533	1,396	255	1,009	313
Crawford	3,118	542	112	78	1,179	221	1,013	97	432	60	382	86
Daviess	7,810	2,202	195	259	2,889	989	2,394	452	1,331	225	1,001	277
Dearborn	10,683	2,959	162	338	4,489	1,451	3,699	588	1,431	280	902	302
Decatur	6,372	2,055	140	267	2,454	1,062	2,117	361	972	158	689	207
Dekalb	10,333	2,392	310	331	4,466	1,270	3,229	362	1,307	186	1,021	243
Delaware	30,193	14,984	612	4,031	10,145	6,754	11,225	2,276	4,846	914	3,365	1,009
Dubois	10,248	2,775	235	368	4,509	1,435	3,160	441	1,333	234	1,011	297
Elkhart	40,745	15,968	1,084	2,566	17,273	8,311	13,692	2,646	5,276	984	3,420	1,461
Fayette	6,950	2,995	143	356	2,382	1,476	2,503	570	1,142	303	780	290
Floyd	17,283	6,802	249	876	7,086	3,464	5,909	1,305	2,420	595	1,619	562
Fountain	5,259	1,599	111	216	1,636	783	1,825	292	962	141	725	167
Franklin	5,275	1,361	94	168	2,111	684	1,845	216	720	122	505	171
Fulton	5,681	1,664	115	181	1,913	897	1,924	294	951	140	778	152
Gibson	9,672	2,627	209	299	3,533	1,241	3,169	478	1,538	268	1,223	341
Grant	19,758	7,943	354	1,064	6,772	3,937	7,603	1,507	3,074	695	1,955	740
Greene	9,578	2,332	242	304	3,352	1,104	3,158	431	1,592	214	1,234	279
Hamilton	29,849	8,985	322	1,016	14,816	5,214	10,384	1,531	2,848	570	1,479	654
Hancock	12,766	3,193	143	361	5,296	1,734	4,855	599	1,555	239	917	260
Harrison	9,060	1,558	248	213	3,858	816	3,015	267	1,112	118	827	144
Hendricks	21,525	4,584	319	479	9,599	2,488	7,823	808	2,445	382	1,339	427
Henry	14,024	4,618	231	549	4,785	2,362	5,071	868	2,262	412	1,675	427
Howard	22,716	8,807	385	1,209	8,541	4,704	8,684	1,631	3,155	638	1,951	625
Huntington	9,840	2,990	203	475	3,912	1,583	3,119	472	1,500	212	1,106	248
Jackson	10,815	3,217	289	427	4,088	1,705	3,570	585	1,584	220	1,284	280
Jasper	6,428	2,099	93	305	2,419	1,093	2,259	387	923	175	734	139
Jay	6,330	1,831	141	239	2,135	904	2,179	355	1,066	150	809	183
Jefferson	7,979	2,918	167	393	3,019	1,445	2,730	585	1,236	242	827	253
Jennings	6,681	1,670	219	203	2,540	872	2,362	328	911	131	649	136
Johnson	23,206	8,148	444	1,096	10,608	4,235	8,149	1,392	2,650	635	1,355	790
Knox	10,687	4,458	187	838	3,590	1,952	3,579	773	1,818	383	1,513	512
Kosciusko	18,529	4,920	513	745	7,679	2,777	6,106	753	2,546	301	1,685	344
Lagrange	7,496	1,713	262	286	3,178	897	2,417	252	995	127	644	151
Lake	115,720	55,028	1,371	5,170	41,440	29,646	43,387	11,201	19,137	4,910	10,385	4,101
Laporte	28,132	10,356	454	1,293	10,298	5,463	9,856	1,907	4,567	890	2,957	803
Lawrence	12,943	3,292	301	419	4,789	1,543	4,518	610	1,900	336	1,435	384
Madison	36,395	13,409	618	1,937	12,417	6,839	13,357	2,359	5,934	1,116	4,069	1,158
Marion	182,039	137,432	2,745	19,266	75,311	75,837	61,653	23,215	26,658	9,318	15,672	9,796
Marshall	11,619	3,527	222	454	4,500	1,959	3,923	562	1,704	224	1,270	328
Martin	3,133	703	81	81	1,181	311	1,062	125	516	95	293	91
Miami	9,516	3,968	187	682	3,595	2,311	3,260	555	1,413	212	1,061	208
Monroe	21,558	17,793	498	5,954	8,868	8,671	7,579	1,715	2,793	639	1,820	814
Montgomery	9,555	3,680	186	517	3,578	1,799	3,316	608	1,415	347	1,060	409
Morgan	15,455	4,145	337	480	6,445	2,204	5,706	754	1,839	357	1,128	350
Newton	3,723	1,116	52	111	1,372	603	1,273	233	563	76	463	93
Noble	10,485	2,933	310	445	4,408	1,484	3,419	465	1,413	235	935	304
Ohio	1,557	423	23	56	612	190	540	69	229	43	153	65
Orange	5,635	1,315	162	136	2,067	657	1,847	239	915	136	644	147
Owen	5,307	1,087	156	130	1,985	552	1,867	189	758	83	541	133
Parke	4,617	1,228	81	136	1,531	599	1,640	229	758	114	607	150
Perry	5,461	1,384	129	150	2,061	638	1,757	237	898	148	616	211
Pike	4,070	855	107	89	1,443	406	1,356	165	630	86	534	109
Porter	33,963	11,196	452	1,548	14,775	6,118	12,341	1,948	4,100	822	2,295	760
Posey	7,633	1,875	160	201	3,305	973	2,441	355	993	151	734	195
Pulaski	3,661	1,061	73	146	1,259	567	1,180	152	644	96	505	100
Putnam	7,584	2,412	138	343	2,704	1,194	2,757	397	1,155	199	830	279
Randolph	7,900	2,551	156	324	2,649	1,333	2,766	474	1,284	205	1,045	215
Ripley	6,660	2,118	120	231	2,546	1,033	2,226	365	1,014	189	754	300
Rush	4,678	1,826	73	185	1,555	1,012	1,593	344	845	132	612	153
St. Joseph	66,492	25,873	1,210	3,892	25,895	13,263	21,379	4,108	10,715	1,988	7,293	2,622
Scott	5,864	1,729	139	270	2,244	880	2,091	337	770	144	620	98
Shelby	10,847	3,914	187	501	4,274	2,087	3,775	722	1,497	285	1,114	319
Spencer	5,661	1,301	142	139	2,266	634	1,920	211	769	120	564	197
Starke	6,344	1,797	133	234	2,181	941	2,189	355	1,054	140	787	127
Steuben	8,053	2,141	215	359	3,116	1,067	2,761	329	1,184	150	777	236
Sullivan	5,892	1,472	118	146	2,022	629	1,876	275	1,042	190	834	232
Switzerland	2,245	594	46	42	760	293	803	124	365	55	271	80
Tippecanoe	26,059	19,559	487	6,195	10,754	9,470	8,903	2,101	3,591	825	2,324	968
Tipton	4,632	1,394	75	135	1,645	728	1,619	257	721	121	572	153
Union	1,863	713	46	94	675	364	645	128	276	53	221	74
Vanderburgh	43,287	23,493	557	3,529	15,828	11,433	14,256	4,173	7,435	2,156	5,211	2,202
Vermillion	5,322	1,316	89	155	1,827	605	1,742	250	885	144	779	162
Vigo	27,568	12,236	530	2,422	9,736	5,822	8,951	1,773	4,924	1,052	3,427	1,167
Wabash	9,380	3,250	167	462	3,454	1,636	3,255	583	1,490	236	1,014	333
Warren	2,371	644	36	73	798	350	853	117	408	45	276	59
Warrick	12,917	2,900	216	390	5,919	1,576	4,435	508	1,476	202	871	224
Washington	6,933	1,731	213	218	2,661	870	2,300	318	1,013	141	746	184
Wayne	18,650	8,937	287	1,246	6,190	4,376	6,816	1,712	3,155	765	2,202	838
Wells	7,443	1,995	197	266	3,058	1,020	2,418	311	1,023	163	747	235
White	6,780	2,146	84	227	2,438	1,143	2,238	352	1,200	181	820	243
Whitley	8,259	1,751	229	243	3,494	940	2,603	249	1,101	131	832	188

Source: U.S. Bureau of the Census
EDIN table(s): HSTR

2.26 Number of Persons Per Housing Unit 1990

	1 Person			2 Persons			3 Persons			4 or More Persons		
	Total	Owner	Renter	Total	Owner	Renter	Total	Owner	Renter	Total	Owner	Renter
Indiana	496,841	265,757	231,084	668,710	503,842	164,868	366,268	269,016	97,252	533,536	412,283	121,253
Adams	2,185	1,328	857	3,205	2,642	563	1,718	1,355	363	3,362	2,881	481
Allen	28,239	13,981	14,258	35,818	26,606	9,212	19,480	14,740	4,740	29,796	24,240	5,556
Bartholomew	5,246	3,014	2,232	8,155	6,406	1,749	4,715	3,565	1,150	6,076	4,718	1,358
Benton	842	597	245	1,198	942	256	528	371	157	956	659	297
Blackford	1,259	833	426	1,875	1,581	294	990	773	217	1,312	1,015	297
Boone	2,744	1,549	1,195	4,602	3,774	828	2,639	2,097	542	3,937	3,187	750
Brown	1,095	795	300	2,029	1,753	276	930	782	148	1,316	1,106	210
Carroll	1,511	994	517	2,529	2,159	370	1,166	907	259	1,861	1,455	406
Cass	3,589	2,215	1,374	4,983	4,068	915	2,459	1,807	652	3,628	2,809	819
Clark	7,760	3,974	3,786	10,585	7,826	2,759	6,484	4,618	1,866	8,463	6,342	2,121
Clay	2,254	1,510	744	3,038	2,592	446	1,654	1,328	326	2,436	2,010	426
Clinton	2,528	1,555	973	3,826	2,995	831	1,961	1,432	529	3,135	2,262	873
Crawford	819	626	193	1,147	1,020	127	690	595	95	1,004	877	127
Daviess	2,419	1,585	834	3,227	2,672	555	1,607	1,236	371	2,759	2,317	442
Dearborn	2,621	1,599	1,022	4,127	3,389	738	2,597	2,083	514	4,297	3,612	685
Decatur	1,760	1,135	625	2,612	2,124	488	1,492	1,128	364	2,563	1,985	578
Dekalb	2,713	1,829	884	3,832	3,267	565	2,322	1,925	397	3,858	3,312	546
Delaware	11,704	6,420	5,284	15,428	11,224	4,204	8,063	5,404	2,659	9,982	7,145	2,837
Dubois	2,847	1,655	1,192	3,869	3,138	731	2,350	1,945	405	3,957	3,510	447
Elkhart	12,268	6,645	5,623	18,522	14,153	4,369	9,995	7,505	2,490	15,928	12,442	3,486
Fayette	2,394	1,353	1,041	3,267	2,524	743	1,766	1,250	516	2,518	1,823	695
Floyd	5,277	2,950	2,327	7,765	5,785	1,980	4,781	3,512	1,269	6,262	5,036	1,226
Fountain	1,632	1,122	510	2,365	1,966	399	1,159	872	287	1,702	1,299	403
Franklin	1,209	785	424	1,916	1,622	294	1,288	1,039	249	2,223	1,829	394
Fulton	1,776	1,233	543	2,619	2,207	412	1,175	903	272	1,775	1,338	437
Gibson	3,013	1,999	1,014	4,034	3,354	680	2,156	1,722	434	3,096	2,597	499
Grant	6,554	3,680	2,874	9,456	7,371	2,085	4,972	3,697	1,275	6,719	5,010	1,709
Greene	2,957	2,104	853	4,004	3,460	544	2,105	1,702	403	2,844	2,312	532
Hamilton	6,616	3,555	3,061	12,762	9,919	2,843	7,534	6,052	1,482	11,922	10,323	1,599
Hancock	2,718	1,685	1,033	5,061	4,237	824	3,154	2,598	556	5,026	4,246	780
Harrison	1,929	1,435	494	3,346	2,940	406	2,139	1,875	264	3,204	2,810	394
Hendricks	4,289	2,776	1,513	8,356	7,157	1,199	5,366	4,532	834	8,098	7,060	1,038
Henry	4,245	2,714	1,531	6,522	5,321	1,201	3,461	2,594	867	4,414	3,395	1,019
Howard	7,873	4,556	3,317	10,370	8,050	2,320	5,739	4,278	1,461	7,541	5,832	1,709
Huntington	2,809	1,818	991	4,149	3,414	735	2,248	1,755	493	3,624	2,853	771
Jackson	2,973	1,977	996	4,577	3,742	835	2,626	2,045	581	3,856	3,051	805
Jasper	1,630	1,051	579	2,757	2,214	543	1,441	1,050	391	2,699	2,113	586
Jay	1,932	1,304	628	2,770	2,307	463	1,415	1,111	304	2,044	1,608	436
Jefferson	2,545	1,486	1,059	3,619	2,868	751	2,139	1,585	554	2,594	2,040	554
Jennings	1,670	1,157	513	2,714	2,303	411	1,511	1,242	269	2,456	1,979	477
Johnson	6,050	3,060	2,990	10,090	7,768	2,322	6,192	4,839	1,353	9,022	7,539	1,483
Knox	4,230	2,458	1,772	5,055	3,828	1,227	2,427	1,747	680	3,433	2,654	779
Kosciusko	4,708	3,170	1,538	7,963	6,665	1,298	4,086	3,256	830	6,692	5,438	1,254
Lagrange	1,533	1,058	475	2,957	2,500	457	1,495	1,208	287	3,224	2,730	494
Lake	39,592	19,811	19,781	49,915	36,026	13,889	31,159	22,064	9,095	50,082	37,819	12,263
Laporte	9,085	5,382	3,703	12,617	9,875	2,742	6,771	5,088	1,683	10,015	7,787	2,228
Lawrence	3,654	2,400	1,254	5,417	4,608	809	3,048	2,504	544	4,116	3,431	685
Madison	12,385	7,514	4,871	16,868	13,413	3,455	8,885	6,561	2,324	11,666	8,907	2,759
Marion	93,696	36,831	56,865	102,522	64,221	38,301	53,112	33,589	19,523	70,141	47,398	22,743
Marshall	3,185	2,037	1,148	4,915	4,059	856	2,600	1,970	630	4,446	3,553	893
Martin	916	630	286	1,181	1,046	135	716	598	118	1,023	859	164
Miami	2,863	1,875	988	4,373	3,454	919	2,487	1,693	794	3,761	2,494	1,267
Monroe	11,216	4,125	7,091	13,368	7,981	5,387	6,800	4,157	2,643	7,967	5,295	2,672
Montgomery	3,234	1,803	1,431	4,634	3,688	946	2,286	1,681	605	3,081	2,383	698
Morgan	3,179	2,066	1,113	6,362	5,268	1,094	3,981	3,113	868	6,078	5,008	1,070
Newton	988	702	286	1,510	1,242	268	855	647	208	1,486	1,132	354
Noble	2,657	1,674	983	4,421	3,668	753	2,324	1,857	467	4,016	3,286	730
Ohio	428	271	157	661	549	112	340	277	63	551	460	91
Orange	1,583	1,116	467	2,306	1,992	314	1,278	1,066	212	1,783	1,461	322
Owen	1,251	939	312	2,277	1,998	279	1,149	949	200	1,717	1,421	296
Parke	1,377	961	416	2,053	1,765	288	1,019	810	209	1,396	1,081	315
Perry	1,574	1,003	571	2,156	1,820	336	1,239	1,047	192	1,876	1,591	285
Pike	1,157	843	314	1,702	1,488	214	921	786	135	1,145	953	192
Porter	8,873	4,968	3,905	13,952	10,688	3,264	8,540	6,805	1,735	13,794	11,502	2,292
Posey	1,942	1,329	613	3,029	2,553	476	1,772	1,420	352	2,765	2,331	434
Pulaski	1,124	774	350	1,522	1,307	215	781	602	179	1,295	978	317
Putnam	2,169	1,322	847	3,469	2,879	590	1,770	1,352	418	2,588	2,031	557
Randolph	2,390	1,590	800	3,643	3,018	625	1,834	1,356	478	2,584	1,936	648
Ripley	1,953	1,138	815	2,602	2,123	479	1,545	1,200	345	2,678	2,199	479
Rush	1,373	881	492	2,109	1,684	425	1,155	831	324	1,867	1,282	585
St. Joseph	24,427	13,390	11,037	29,925	23,161	6,764	15,512	11,850	3,662	22,501	18,091	4,410
Scott	1,527	1,091	436	2,332	1,889	443	1,617	1,258	359	2,117	1,626	491
Shelby	3,095	1,865	1,230	4,756	3,763	993	2,736	2,082	654	4,174	3,137	1,037
Spencer	1,451	991	460	2,192	1,860	332	1,296	1,084	212	2,023	1,726	297
Starke	1,719	1,258	461	2,576	2,139	437	1,445	1,080	365	2,401	1,867	534
Steuben	2,324	1,492	832	3,570	3,025	545	1,687	1,375	312	2,613	2,161	452
Sullivan	1,885	1,309	576	2,406	2,069	337	1,216	1,001	215	1,857	1,513	344
Switzerland	654	456	198	918	787	131	482	391	91	785	611	174
Tippecanoe	11,603	4,741	6,862	15,429	9,313	6,116	7,888	4,781	3,107	10,698	7,224	3,474
Tipton	1,316	902	414	2,004	1,642	362	1,087	839	248	1,619	1,249	370
Union	546	346	200	861	659	202	479	333	146	690	525	165
Vanderburgh	19,516	9,211	10,305	21,968	15,649	6,319	11,227	7,892	3,335	14,069	10,535	3,534
Vermillion	1,808	1,279	529	2,117	1,816	301	1,144	939	205	1,569	1,288	281
Vigo	11,284	6,182	5,102	12,942	9,703	3,239	6,072	4,054	1,818	8,906	6,829	2,077
Wabash	2,832	1,685	1,147	4,319	3,503	816	2,158	1,634	524	3,321	2,558	763
Warren	577	416	161	1,067	929	138	558	431	127	813	595	218
Warrick	2,650	1,765	885	4,996	4,181	815	3,283	2,720	563	4,888	4,251	637
Washington	1,836	1,324	512	2,775	2,304	471	1,630	1,324	306	2,423	1,981	442
Wayne	6,881	3,734	3,147	9,354	7,081	2,273	4,869	3,305	1,564	6,483	4,530	1,953
Wells	1,973	1,215	758	3,041	2,600	441	1,641	1,312	329	2,783	2,316	467
White	2,099	1,404	695	3,121	2,574	547	1,393	1,054	339	2,313	1,748	565
Whitley	2,029	1,391	638	3,356	2,929	427	1,666	1,394	272	2,959	2,545	414

Source: U.S. Bureau of the Census
EDIN table(s): HSTP

2.27 Number of Rooms and Number of Units in Structure 1990

	Total Units	Rooms in Unit						Units in Structure				Mobile Home Or Trailer
		1 Room	2 Rooms	3 Rooms	4 Rooms	5 Rooms	6 or More Rooms	1 Unit	2 Units	3 to 4 Units	5 or More Units	
Indiana	2,246,046	16,897	51,873	174,660	409,164	552,864	1,040,588	1,631,605	81,406	89,395	267,554	156,821
Adams	10,931	17	106	555	1,578	2,295	6,380	8,782	313	251	749	761
Allen	122,923	846	3,095	10,485	18,024	24,680	65,793	87,610	5,096	5,122	18,481	5,759
Bartholomew	25,432	171	459	1,531	4,302	6,675	12,294	19,532	594	875	2,286	2,004
Benton	3,833	7	25	142	449	807	2,403	3,377	81	26	111	196
Blackford	5,856	18	57	300	1,031	1,466	2,984	4,665	182	199	175	582
Boone	14,516	83	167	968	1,644	3,139	8,515	11,751	490	417	900	777
Brown	6,997	67	176	474	1,350	1,866	3,064	5,755	60	49	82	965
Carroll	8,431	37	144	547	1,302	1,889	4,512	6,975	216	167	132	876
Cass	15,633	69	199	925	2,073	3,838	8,529	12,332	873	513	661	1,149
Clark	35,313	97	690	3,256	7,152	9,399	14,719	24,306	947	1,586	5,119	3,086
Clay	10,606	64	215	670	2,279	2,927	4,451	8,299	257	163	355	1,379
Clinton	12,100	70	209	781	1,773	2,933	6,334	9,746	481	448	652	672
Crawford	4,374	37	69	323	1,120	1,130	1,695	3,014	17	12	79	1,208
Daviess	10,985	26	169	653	2,161	3,209	4,767	8,817	273	173	514	1,084
Dearborn	14,532	82	260	931	2,187	3,579	7,493	11,187	707	392	830	1,249
Decatur	9,098	27	100	477	1,590	2,283	4,621	7,490	276	114	285	846
Dekalb	13,601	39	162	705	1,852	2,796	8,047	10,434	451	423	483	1,655
Delaware	48,793	284	1,156	4,240	10,027	12,952	20,134	35,647	2,609	2,285	5,024	2,868
Dubois	13,964	81	262	954	2,368	3,402	6,897	10,495	644	470	808	1,368
Elkhart	60,182	450	1,334	4,744	10,263	12,862	30,529	43,146	2,550	3,146	6,179	4,751
Fayette	10,525	63	182	686	2,110	2,911	4,573	8,001	572	403	750	707
Floyd	25,238	80	481	1,760	4,389	6,744	11,784	19,264	1,037	1,047	2,906	760
Fountain	7,344	20	91	421	1,331	1,845	3,636	5,837	153	251	133	915
Franklin	7,176	39	82	342	1,170	1,892	3,651	5,453	159	83	205	1,157
Fulton	8,656	46	164	630	1,607	1,938	4,271	6,779	185	193	280	1,155
Gibson	13,454	72	223	859	3,167	3,760	5,373	10,193	222	229	672	1,963
Grant	29,904	154	665	2,461	4,770	7,399	14,455	22,577	1,559	1,147	2,064	2,291
Greene	13,337	59	300	804	3,276	3,693	5,205	9,848	212	137	435	2,549
Hamilton	41,074	133	425	1,881	4,960	6,912	26,763	31,833	796	1,311	4,799	2,116
Hancock	16,495	44	146	756	1,977	3,343	10,229	13,914	651	458	727	662
Harrison	11,456	58	131	532	2,089	2,968	5,678	8,792	162	128	199	2,018
Hendricks	26,962	90	310	1,071	3,284	5,902	16,305	22,366	705	521	1,353	1,881
Henry	19,835	80	262	1,173	3,459	4,937	9,924	15,991	707	626	1,119	1,246
Howard	33,820	137	733	2,489	5,347	8,654	16,460	25,914	1,076	1,352	3,372	1,849
Huntington	13,629	30	128	755	1,851	2,964	7,901	10,775	699	378	573	1,084
Jackson	14,820	80	173	771	3,090	4,455	6,251	11,377	259	343	826	1,902
Jasper	8,984	25	103	426	1,356	2,148	4,926	7,278	262	204	292	845
Jay	8,905	23	84	548	1,478	2,155	4,617	7,280	290	216	258	779
Jefferson	11,921	108	297	850	2,254	3,010	5,402	8,753	391	410	855	1,370
Jennings	9,129	82	127	455	1,995	2,647	3,823	6,468	151	156	217	2,050
Johnson	33,289	346	643	2,194	5,205	7,821	17,080	24,566	872	1,109	4,126	2,293
Knox	16,730	69	491	1,389	3,762	4,565	6,454	12,783	691	700	1,207	1,226
Kosciusko	30,516	167	567	1,995	6,347	6,900	14,540	22,408	898	772	1,032	5,082
Lagrange	12,218	70	277	950	2,489	2,550	5,882	9,239	193	160	349	2,155
Lake	183,014	1,459	3,944	14,026	36,314	50,985	76,286	131,299	11,798	10,405	24,677	3,287
Laporte	42,268	247	712	2,925	7,543	11,004	19,837	31,527	2,895	1,542	3,316	2,626
Lawrence	17,587	138	351	1,151	3,865	5,048	7,034	13,415	318	420	852	2,399
Madison	53,353	228	848	3,923	10,051	14,290	24,013	41,425	2,682	2,114	3,180	3,500
Marion	349,403	4,721	10,855	36,683	67,418	88,839	140,887	219,471	9,318	19,673	90,763	7,160
Marshall	16,820	114	248	940	2,757	3,758	9,003	13,321	466	506	802	1,556
Martin	4,116	25	44	258	1,024	1,101	1,664	2,892	96	56	64	961
Miami	14,639	39	155	785	2,480	3,685	7,495	11,035	603	392	518	1,975
Monroe	41,948	976	2,609	4,928	9,322	8,754	15,359	23,139	1,344	2,151	11,114	3,821
Montgomery	13,957	42	221	1,090	2,273	3,158	7,173	10,685	627	625	797	1,133
Morgan	20,500	90	287	1,095	3,655	5,279	10,094	16,115	741	468	925	2,105
Newton	5,276	19	40	238	735	1,240	3,004	4,504	147	61	102	401
Noble	15,516	70	213	1,029	2,765	3,553	7,886	11,617	564	356	705	2,119
Ohio	2,161	6	39	164	419	584	949	1,510	74	32	104	427
Orange	7,732	59	152	560	1,855	2,083	3,023	5,471	95	132	282	1,662
Owen	8,011	93	143	527	1,972	2,304	2,972	5,341	82	82	124	2,246
Parke	7,189	38	148	463	1,433	1,867	3,240	5,445	78	142	162	1,251
Perry	7,404	30	187	470	1,558	2,040	3,119	5,614	163	91	466	979
Pike	5,487	36	78	329	1,390	1,560	2,094	4,181	59	55	90	1,057
Porter	47,240	229	660	2,500	8,063	11,029	24,759	35,238	1,656	2,001	4,158	3,845
Posey	10,401	53	206	707	2,057	2,694	4,684	8,097	188	183	460	1,411
Pulaski	5,541	43	80	306	1,037	1,332	2,743	4,354	51	58	147	896
Putnam	10,981	48	189	683	1,931	2,918	5,212	8,153	246	383	550	1,566
Randolph	11,327	34	117	541	1,692	2,787	6,156	9,105	447	209	390	1,084
Ripley	9,587	68	174	617	1,658	2,261	4,809	7,195	278	208	613	1,198
Rush	7,014	21	65	324	974	1,507	4,123	5,882	194	205	265	413
St. Joseph	97,956	536	2,279	7,466	17,847	22,874	46,954	75,802	3,020	3,633	12,393	2,247
Scott	8,078	25	110	487	1,828	2,552	3,076	5,989	130	135	344	1,384
Shelby	15,654	96	247	1,126	2,409	4,038	7,738	12,815	604	474	813	786
Spencer	7,636	61	137	484	1,511	1,907	3,536	5,954	146	139	188	1,138
Starke	9,888	34	163	560	1,960	2,721	4,450	8,199	133	71	240	1,149
Steuben	15,768	86	318	1,076	3,298	3,647	7,343	11,155	390	183	714	3,207
Sullivan	8,487	23	126	532	1,756	2,436	3,614	6,666	118	83	293	1,155
Switzerland	3,732	45	93	261	867	933	1,533	2,490	39	44	112	990
Tippecanoe	48,134	829	2,702	5,547	8,433	10,166	20,457	28,768	2,081	2,630	11,632	2,750
Tipton	6,427	15	51	273	863	1,453	3,772	5,157	218	164	171	675
Union	2,813	4	15	183	466	628	1,517	2,142	68	38	151	392
Vanderburgh	72,637	613	3,415	8,388	15,708	18,307	26,206	50,348	3,426	3,778	12,867	1,607
Vermillion	7,288	27	107	512	1,747	2,030	2,865	5,837	68	105	280	943
Vigo	44,203	383	1,529	4,166	9,015	11,906	17,204	32,176	1,753	2,890	3,827	3,144
Wabash	13,394	40	215	918	2,038	2,868	7,315	10,237	584	553	627	1,290
Warren	3,275	7	19	127	455	813	1,854	2,754	27	35	59	379
Warrick	16,926	46	226	880	3,086	4,099	8,589	13,395	356	519	834	1,708
Washington	9,520	53	133	522	2,065	2,571	4,176	7,029	189	137	208	1,823
Wayne	29,586	249	630	2,117	4,844	7,537	14,209	21,828	1,956	1,473	2,376	1,672
Wells	9,928	34	102	538	1,298	2,128	5,828	7,890	296	188	512	973
White	11,875	76	219	705	2,463	2,995	5,417	9,229	316	183	236	1,819
Whitley	10,852	42	133	671	1,678	2,355	5,973	8,665	259	225	397	1,222

Source: U.S. Bureau of the Census
EDIN table(s): HSRU

2.28 Value of Structure 1990

	Total Units	Less Than $20,000	$20,000 to $24,999	$25,000 to $34,999	$35,000 to $49,999	$50,000 to $99,999	$100,000 to $149,999	$150,000 to $199,999	$200,000 to $299,999	$300,000 or More	Median Value
Indiana	1,137,766	72,896	48,329	138,196	254,864	484,025	92,829	26,991	13,675	5,961	53,900
Adams	5,679	240	188	720	1,599	2,566	303	46	14	3	51,100
Allen	67,581	3,360	2,125	6,321	12,462	33,435	6,602	1,854	1,006	416	59,900
Bartholomew	13,942	428	380	1,325	3,308	6,491	1,279	456	213	62	57,200
Benton	1,985	336	167	370	506	541	52	8	2	3	38,100
Blackford	3,015	636	370	685	677	609	32	3	2	1	32,300
Boone	8,227	198	144	554	1,397	3,580	1,225	535	424	170	71,100
Brown	2,568	104	58	159	441	1,431	294	63	17	1	64,900
Carroll	3,832	321	235	616	1,024	1,447	148	27	12	2	45,400
Cass	8,157	943	665	1,610	2,139	2,438	265	61	29	7	40,300
Clark	17,747	532	439	1,897	5,998	7,758	863	176	65	19	50,000
Clay	5,088	988	491	1,023	1,123	1,348	96	18	1	0	35,500
Clinton	6,417	732	490	1,255	1,705	1,975	208	36	12	4	40,900
Crawford	1,299	320	143	285	282	253	15	1	0	0	31,800
Daviess	5,172	721	399	975	1,268	1,596	162	32	14	5	40,600
Dearborn	7,537	374	215	627	1,481	4,049	622	126	39	4	59,900
Decatur	4,503	324	248	741	1,320	1,620	188	50	9	3	44,900
Dekalb	7,192	330	306	1,026	1,976	2,956	462	92	37	7	49,700
Delaware	24,707	2,997	1,815	4,378	6,118	7,823	1,105	296	135	40	42,300
Dubois	7,478	312	220	712	1,610	3,893	543	111	57	20	58,000
Elkhart	32,211	717	573	2,253	6,705	17,932	2,660	771	422	178	62,300
Fayette	5,361	416	348	1,140	1,738	1,556	127	26	9	1	41,100
Floyd	14,578	600	457	1,368	3,309	7,124	1,337	232	109	42	57,600
Fountain	3,538	546	299	776	959	869	68	13	5	3	37,000
Franklin	2,909	149	93	360	723	1,330	205	38	10	1	53,300
Fulton	3,699	353	260	726	974	1,232	117	29	7	1	42,200
Gibson	6,749	827	442	1,090	1,569	2,489	266	42	23	1	44,400
Grant	15,413	1,810	1,170	2,973	4,109	4,668	497	126	42	18	40,400
Greene	5,612	1,023	495	1,097	1,401	1,499	88	6	2	1	36,800
Hamilton	25,265	172	174	466	1,466	9,322	7,212	3,247	2,041	1,165	106,500
Hancock	10,372	196	160	566	1,489	5,762	1,719	374	95	11	72,000
Harrison	4,966	256	172	580	1,354	2,298	257	42	5	2	51,800
Hendricks	17,199	163	107	511	1,673	11,094	2,747	664	195	45	75,700
Henry	10,874	1,857	1,101	2,165	2,463	3,007	235	31	9	6	36,800
Howard	19,097	936	762	2,680	4,779	8,253	1,263	280	125	19	51,700
Huntington	7,348	526	414	1,345	2,094	2,629	261	57	20	2	44,200
Jackson	7,375	668	433	1,213	2,124	2,555	274	67	36	5	43,900
Jasper	4,554	173	150	469	1,136	2,310	255	48	10	3	55,100
Jay	4,361	1,032	460	962	1,035	791	64	14	3	0	32,400
Jefferson	5,424	382	295	841	1,616	1,938	258	69	17	8	44,900
Jennings	3,761	335	208	613	1,280	1,231	72	13	7	2	43,700
Johnson	18,918	185	177	745	2,968	10,279	3,064	951	454	95	72,200
Knox	8,233	1,220	677	1,509	1,947	2,406	324	78	54	18	39,800
Kosciusko	12,806	386	332	1,085	2,777	6,187	1,250	396	240	153	60,600
Lagrange	4,414	151	158	479	1,066	2,191	301	54	12	2	55,100
Lake	100,099	5,633	3,978	11,653	22,577	43,686	8,880	2,408	935	349	54,800
Laporte	22,276	788	773	2,925	5,847	9,448	1,573	474	311	137	52,700
Lawrence	8,765	983	578	1,655	2,462	2,789	236	48	9	5	42,000
Madison	29,882	2,857	2,020	5,458	7,629	10,481	1,066	268	84	19	43,700
Marion	161,643	7,912	5,212	16,387	31,952	74,447	16,397	4,938	2,764	1,634	61,400
Marshall	8,323	346	331	1,163	2,383	3,530	410	79	50	31	49,600
Martin	1,730	290	137	322	468	472	34	3	2	2	38,700
Miami	6,529	799	530	1,317	1,651	2,028	178	17	6	3	40,300
Monroe	15,748	300	213	858	2,845	8,470	1,981	661	331	89	66,600
Montgomery	7,147	460	354	1,094	1,899	2,869	352	74	40	5	48,100
Morgan	11,097	329	223	841	2,497	5,811	1,024	250	103	19	59,700
Newton	2,809	303	188	483	706	1,033	82	9	4	1	43,300
Noble	7,076	341	313	943	2,074	2,958	351	73	17	6	49,100
Ohio	822	59	41	125	256	305	30	4	2	0	45,400
Orange	3,105	537	263	593	889	756	59	4	3	1	37,400
Owen	2,435	288	136	441	650	830	76	12	2	0	43,000
Parke	2,807	506	244	520	673	764	78	12	7	3	37,900
Perry	3,568	374	229	637	1,015	1,202	89	14	7	1	42,600
Pike	2,570	522	227	504	603	664	38	5	4	3	35,700
Porter	27,644	212	229	976	5,003	15,096	3,762	1,302	727	337	69,600
Posey	5,523	301	195	506	1,051	2,991	378	76	19	6	58,800
Pulaski	2,188	249	179	405	619	642	76	11	6	1	40,300
Putnam	4,702	287	188	605	1,166	2,152	255	35	11	3	51,600
Randolph	5,361	794	530	1,301	1,436	1,197	77	15	7	4	35,500
Ripley	3,915	255	182	581	1,002	1,548	252	57	30	8	49,000
Rush	3,227	372	249	615	841	1,035	89	17	7	2	41,200
St. Joseph	58,123	3,322	2,817	8,374	14,035	23,031	4,276	1,313	705	250	50,800
Scott	3,766	426	306	865	1,163	911	77	11	7	0	38,000
Shelby	8,459	410	361	1,152	2,175	3,652	578	80	43	8	51,300
Spencer	3,480	350	201	496	847	1,387	145	35	16	3	47,000
Starke	4,248	434	299	825	1,265	1,295	104	19	5	2	40,900
Steuben	5,181	185	152	499	1,089	2,394	509	196	112	45	59,800
Sullivan	3,941	986	421	765	829	851	66	13	8	2	32,300
Switzerland	947	125	95	194	257	251	18	4	1	2	37,700
Tippecanoe	21,221	395	320	1,313	4,517	10,308	2,910	951	410	97	66,000
Tipton	3,316	171	150	451	845	1,463	185	33	11	7	50,900
Union	1,185	100	87	234	343	388	26	6	1	0	41,800
Vanderburgh	37,618	2,229	1,453	4,604	9,422	15,757	2,788	790	390	185	52,100
Vermillion	3,854	857	425	867	846	770	76	7	4	2	32,300
Vigo	22,080	3,699	1,772	3,821	4,847	6,501	1,003	266	115	56	40,000
Wabash	6,667	515	424	1,330	1,805	2,287	241	45	17	3	43,400
Warren	1,453	244	116	241	380	411	48	10	1	2	39,700
Warrick	9,979	289	240	798	1,818	5,370	980	307	152	25	64,800
Washington	3,664	440	271	740	1,017	1,081	87	21	5	2	40,000
Wayne	14,856	1,615	1,076	2,639	3,898	4,813	530	176	81	28	42,400
Wells	5,068	257	181	584	1,310	2,310	332	70	20	4	53,000
White	5,115	328	262	716	1,491	1,952	261	66	28	11	46,900
Whitley	5,391	147	143	489	1,283	2,877	381	47	15	9	57,300

Footnote: Specified owner occupied housing units
Source: U.S. Bureau of the Census
EDIN table(s): HSVL

2.29 Contract Rent 1990

	Total Units	With Cash Rent — Less Than $100	$100 to $149	$150 to $199	$200 to $249	$250 to $299	$300 to $399	$400 to $499	$500 to $599	$600 to $699	$700 to $999	$1,000 or More	No Cash Rent	Median Contract Rent ($)
Indiana	585,269	34,205	34,226	53,949	82,034	88,936	150,284	70,851	23,628	7,971	6,283	2,311	30,591	291
Adams	2,036	218	182	312	403	390	323	44	11	2	1	2	148	229
Allen	33,069	1,345	1,209	1,795	3,942	5,549	10,076	5,541	1,754	421	330	160	947	320
Bartholomew	6,125	347	315	470	790	883	2,117	683	182	49	20	8	261	305
Benton	730	70	89	161	171	73	40	7	1	0	0	0	118	196
Blackford	1,122	127	195	303	254	90	46	4	1	1	0	2	99	181
Boone	2,950	187	144	183	388	515	816	249	132	54	63	39	180	297
Brown	746	30	43	48	119	115	154	71	21	9	0	0	136	278
Carroll	1,276	88	125	299	277	187	125	23	6	4	0	1	141	210
Cass	3,430	265	341	668	775	623	412	51	2	3	0	2	288	219
Clark	10,167	786	741	719	1,231	1,905	3,190	689	132	55	102	71	546	285
Clay	1,758	154	284	350	330	251	149	11	3	2	1	0	223	197
Clinton	2,857	164	229	379	676	625	518	47	5	1	0	3	210	241
Crawford	437	113	65	84	51	16	6	0	0	0	0	0	102	142
Daviess	1,970	246	261	485	395	194	106	50	2	2	1	1	227	188
Dearborn	2,729	189	212	335	543	445	607	126	28	13	5	2	224	248
Decatur	1,687	121	145	293	379	258	252	49	14	1	7	2	166	227
Dekalb	2,171	99	106	245	463	496	519	64	13	2	2	1	161	259
Delaware	14,536	978	994	1,933	2,819	2,270	2,995	853	389	295	227	73	710	254
Dubois	2,584	200	215	359	520	486	529	40	12	5	5	7	206	240
Elkhart	15,409	679	715	695	1,324	1,795	5,998	2,530	550	337	67	14	705	335
Fayette	2,760	267	238	439	702	579	320	35	9	3	0	1	167	225
Floyd	6,578	737	533	603	887	1,039	1,520	702	163	53	3	6	332	267
Fountain	1,388	141	247	344	303	138	48	5	1	1	0	0	160	183
Franklin	1,040	79	114	256	236	120	74	16	3	2	1	1	138	200
Fulton	1,450	92	149	277	276	308	194	14	5	0	0	0	135	225
Gibson	2,427	291	302	567	529	285	140	21	5	0	0	1	286	192
Grant	7,506	523	774	1,228	1,583	1,416	1,227	163	72	19	14	4	483	231
Greene	2,079	237	258	484	446	220	113	11	1	0	0	3	306	190
Hamilton	8,510	216	173	241	420	692	2,014	2,153	1,068	519	404	222	388	412
Hancock	2,932	88	117	238	398	544	1,039	246	49	15	12	2	184	299
Harrison	1,253	114	147	183	248	164	171	33	7	3	3	0	180	219
Hendricks	4,193	144	143	252	497	625	1,177	642	263	87	79	38	246	327
Henry	4,273	356	480	963	886	594	521	81	14	5	35	5	333	210
Howard	8,477	593	478	593	1,367	1,638	2,571	537	179	17	6	5	493	279
Huntington	2,698	144	177	289	498	496	770	132	14	3	2	2	171	266
Jackson	2,939	257	222	390	643	449	555	121	23	12	10	6	251	237
Jasper	1,721	86	118	293	487	345	171	35	5	0	1	1	179	228
Jay	1,580	166	290	417	316	170	59	9	1	1	0	0	151	181
Jefferson	2,661	304	257	473	608	386	365	26	8	5	2	0	227	215
Jennings	1,442	99	133	252	354	223	170	30	9	1	0	1	170	221
Johnson	7,769	322	271	374	691	912	2,561	1,273	615	131	187	60	372	339
Knox	4,153	469	396	616	821	673	596	161	35	7	31	8	340	226
Kosciusko	4,520	182	229	368	769	947	1,300	340	60	22	12	5	286	280
Lagrange	1,365	96	101	176	276	242	275	60	5	2	0	0	132	244
Lake	53,934	3,794	3,412	5,190	7,434	7,911	12,374	7,581	2,828	417	361	190	2,442	287
Laporte	9,897	572	597	998	1,861	1,974	2,307	806	148	48	26	7	553	266
Lawrence	3,062	302	283	502	620	501	436	72	9	3	0	1	333	222
Madison	12,871	820	861	1,814	2,516	2,326	2,872	587	138	19	18	3	897	250
Marion	135,791	5,869	4,446	5,833	11,458	17,869	44,668	27,239	9,249	3,193	1,833	725	3,409	345
Marshall	3,111	109	176	347	641	653	766	148	28	2	2	1	238	263
Martin	626	76	112	173	98	32	18	10	3	2	1	0	101	172
Miami	3,625	227	245	555	577	430	641	194	46	19	6	0	685	238
Monroe	17,452	585	576	825	1,734	2,679	5,072	2,889	1,140	586	685	183	498	339
Montgomery	3,324	215	215	454	625	659	740	164	27	5	3	1	216	253
Morgan	3,786	262	243	252	483	673	1,151	330	58	19	7	6	302	287
Newton	859	71	107	160	221	100	67	7	1	0	2	0	123	207
Noble	2,660	218	160	287	538	522	570	148	11	2	1	3	200	253
Ohio	367	27	62	89	85	37	24	5	0	1	0	0	37	193
Orange	1,138	149	164	242	260	75	79	16	2	1	1	0	149	188
Owen	909	87	87	184	172	128	82	12	4	0	0	0	153	206
Parke	984	113	146	169	172	130	70	11	0	0	0	0	173	193
Perry	1,270	186	190	252	299	151	68	3	2	0	0	1	118	190
Pike	750	82	131	170	113	48	43	3	0	0	0	0	160	174
Porter	10,810	267	229	425	970	1,580	4,200	1,879	552	169	84	28	427	340
Posey	1,673	174	217	281	299	241	211	52	11	7	1	1	178	213
Pulaski	854	42	102	236	228	97	29	4	2	0	0	0	114	198
Putnam	2,094	180	139	303	392	381	383	89	18	4	6	6	193	242
Randolph	2,153	235	328	594	456	196	139	6	1	0	0	2	196	185
Ripley	1,807	187	204	315	362	219	246	73	13	3	0	1	184	215
Rush	1,420	141	176	316	331	163	102	14	5	0	1	2	169	199
St. Joseph	25,217	1,261	1,155	1,558	2,651	3,615	7,304	4,171	1,454	491	347	167	1,043	325
Scott	1,591	155	146	278	338	248	230	39	1	2	0	1	153	221
Shelby	3,497	166	183	310	653	763	921	192	55	11	11	8	224	271
Spencer	1,109	124	151	247	219	132	64	17	4	0	1	0	150	191
Starke	1,534	99	192	360	355	242	95	4	6	1	0	2	178	204
Steuben	1,969	155	143	164	286	338	504	162	19	4	5	2	187	271
Sullivan	1,292	185	277	282	206	82	36	9	1	0	0	0	214	164
Switzerland	423	57	79	78	80	35	15	2	1	0	0	0	75	174
Tippecanoe	19,075	675	580	974	2,198	2,762	5,629	3,023	949	607	1,063	112	505	335
Tipton	1,183	69	82	184	241	172	246	34	4	4	1	0	146	238
Union	538	67	77	119	132	47	24	2	1	0	0	0	69	188
Vanderburgh	23,097	1,482	1,430	2,330	4,513	4,424	5,486	1,668	585	97	109	69	904	265
Vermillion	1,195	121	197	267	199	149	73	7	4	0	2	1	175	186
Vigo	11,860	729	1,045	1,988	2,462	2,093	1,903	589	193	43	38	8	769	236
Wabash	2,872	177	212	463	702	597	407	41	12	7	3	2	249	233
Warren	455	46	92	100	95	25	23	1	0	0	0	0	73	176
Warrick	2,740	152	196	283	463	500	636	153	76	21	18	6	236	266
Washington	1,409	126	177	297	292	189	112	8	1	1	1	1	204	200
Wayne	8,354	609	783	1,410	1,832	1,504	1,416	249	64	15	5	8	459	231
Wells	1,750	107	164	298	348	322	331	60	5	1	2	2	110	236
White	1,845	141	193	349	435	290	204	33	13	2	3	1	181	217
Whitley	1,534	103	107	212	300	261	338	67	12	0	3	0	131	247

Source: U.S. Bureau of the Census
EDIN table(s): HSCR

2.30 Persons by Type of Group Quarters 1990

	Total Persons In Group Quarters	Institutionalized						Non-Institutionalized
		Total	Correctional	Nursing Homes	Mental Hospitals	Juvenile Institutions	Other	
Indiana	**161,992**	**81,686**	**21,726**	**50,845**	**3,015**	**2,823**	**3,277**	**86,337**
Adams	474	463	51	396	5	0	11	22
Allen	4,671	3,126	356	2,415	68	183	104	2,281
Bartholomew	770	673	81	534	0	33	25	167
Benton	118	118	6	112	0	0	0	0
Blackford	127	127	4	123	0	0	0	0
Boone	728	728	38	551	0	90	49	0
Brown	81	81	18	63	0	0	0	0
Carroll	218	215	20	195	0	0	0	6
Cass	1,023	1,004	54	367	472	29	82	32
Clark	1,386	1,152	116	927	97	0	12	346
Clay	328	320	34	284	0	0	2	16
Clinton	648	647	24	623	0	0	0	1
Crawford	84	84	7	77	0	0	0	0
Daviess	538	538	40	498	0	0	0	0
Dearborn	465	436	26	396	14	0	0	46
Decatur	332	332	25	267	0	31	9	0
Dekalb	372	330	36	294	0	0	0	84
Delaware	8,039	1,155	64	1,012	0	79	0	7,171
Dubois	836	480	4	476	0	0	0	537
Elkhart	2,695	1,797	372	1,295	63	44	23	947
Fayette	374	364	65	299	0	0	0	14
Floyd	1,003	950	70	787	0	0	93	90
Fountain	199	196	20	176	0	0	0	3
Franklin	320	125	13	112	0	0	0	390
Fulton	174	174	28	146	0	0	0	0
Gibson	484	377	21	356	0	0	0	107
Grant	3,334	1,622	163	1,411	34	14	0	1,755
Greene	400	383	23	360	0	0	0	34
Hamilton	914	726	0	726	0	0	0	317
Hancock	561	519	58	435	0	0	26	84
Harrison	252	217	24	176	0	0	17	35
Hendricks	2,362	2,354	1,442	508	0	401	3	16
Henry	683	675	44	409	0	0	222	8
Howard	909	782	109	568	43	18	44	181
Huntington	1,061	665	44	616	0	0	5	494
Jackson	413	411	23	380	0	8	0	4
Jasper	1,062	369	164	177	0	28	0	693
Jay	252	238	29	209	0	0	0	26
Jefferson	1,830	841	107	343	301	0	90	989
Jennings	730	723	18	110	0	0	595	7
Johnson	3,049	1,725	156	1,510	51	0	8	2,051
Knox	2,787	660	47	597	16	0	0	2,127
Kosciusko	1,125	630	48	582	0	0	0	524
Lagrange	429	424	27	161	7	229	0	10
Lake	4,842	3,215	389	2,422	34	213	157	1,957
Laporte	6,029	5,984	5,228	716	0	0	40	62
Lawrence	681	617	51	566	0	0	0	128
Madison	5,183	4,048	2,918	971	99	59	1	1,187
Marion	14,329	9,725	1,893	6,172	640	257	763	5,043
Marshall	652	494	42	170	0	0	282	299
Martin	256	81	7	74	0	0	0	337
Miami	827	256	36	220	0	0	0	582
Monroe	15,112	778	180	586	12	0	0	14,518
Montgomery	1,205	519	37	426	0	56	0	700
Morgan	487	472	62	410	0	0	0	21
Newton	157	156	8	148	0	0	0	1
Noble	627	516	146	370	0	0	0	187
Ohio	58	58	0	58	0	0	0	0
Orange	256	239	31	208	0	0	0	34
Owen	146	144	31	113	0	0	0	4
Parke	520	520	174	152	104	90	0	0
Perry	910	902	748	154	0	0	0	8
Pike	108	108	0	108	0	0	0	0
Porter	3,667	1,129	122	874	18	105	10	2,655
Posey	240	226	46	180	0	0	0	28
Pulaski	119	113	30	83	0	0	0	12
Putnam	4,111	2,010	1,674	320	0	10	6	2,101
Randolph	270	261	24	237	0	0	0	18
Ripley	354	328	12	314	0	0	2	52
Rush	491	478	24	233	0	218	3	26
St. Joseph	12,161	3,079	308	2,525	61	141	44	9,451
Scott	252	246	25	220	0	0	1	12
Shelby	502	359	37	322	0	0	0	260
Spencer	547	199	9	190	0	0	0	488
Starke	341	341	78	263	0	0	0	0
Steuben	775	194	21	136	0	0	37	592
Sullivan	274	274	26	248	0	0	0	0
Switzerland	104	104	8	96	0	0	0	0
Tippecanoe	16,460	1,701	81	1,455	100	10	55	14,864
Tipton	199	148	25	123	0	0	0	102
Union	98	82	9	73	0	0	0	32
Vanderburgh	4,501	3,060	396	2,126	411	41	86	1,684
Vermillion	249	249	22	227	0	0	0	0
Vigo	8,690	3,555	2,113	1,244	31	148	19	5,241
Wabash	1,945	1,164	70	769	0	190	135	781
Warren	97	96	15	81	0	0	0	2
Warrick	607	607	73	525	0	9	0	0
Washington	290	258	39	215	0	0	4	60
Wayne	2,507	1,558	196	783	319	53	207	1,119
Wells	450	440	68	352	15	0	5	20
White	216	216	17	199	0	0	0	0
Whitley	450	423	58	329	0	36	0	54

Source: U.S. Bureau of the Census
EDIN table(s): PTGQ

Per Capita Personal Income ($)
1995

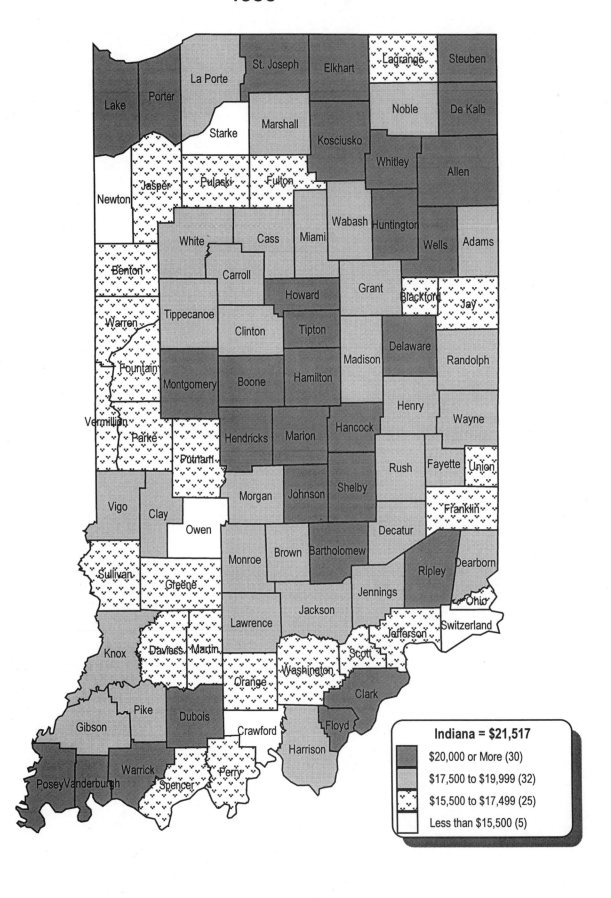

Indiana = $21,517

$20,000 or More (30)

$17,500 to $19,999 (32)

$15,500 to $17,499 (25)

Less than $15,500 (5)

Per Capita Personal Income ($): EDIN Table PIRE.

Income

2.31 Personal Income 1995 *($000)*

	Total Earnings by Place of Work	Net Earnings by Place of Work	Plus Residence Adjustment	Net Earnings by Place of Residence	Plus Dividends, Interest, Rent	Plus Transfer Payments	Personal Income by Place of Residence	Per Capita Income ($)	Rank
Indiana	90,885,424	84,742,049	2,253,042	86,995,091	19,257,888	18,477,338	124,730,317	21,517	—
Adams	401,384	374,371	65,205	439,576	107,121	84,778	631,475	19,479	41
Allen	6,412,192	5,976,361	-664,904	5,311,457	1,261,398	935,917	7,508,772	24,339	4
Bartholomew	1,540,769	1,438,703	-258,300	1,180,403	262,243	191,691	1,634,337	24,047	5
Benton	57,408	52,064	52,382	104,446	32,525	32,115	169,086	17,408	63
Blackford	119,670	111,089	45,400	156,489	30,089	49,129	235,707	16,764	75
Boone	392,906	365,264	447,514	812,778	206,828	106,766	1,126,372	26,963	2
Brown	70,267	65,366	144,220	209,586	43,382	30,801	283,769	18,707	51
Carroll	151,894	141,251	119,377	260,628	62,384	50,933	373,945	19,114	44
Cass	435,607	406,374	74,119	480,493	109,674	141,503	731,670	18,991	49
Clark	1,204,825	1,122,291	159,754	1,282,045	234,646	320,549	1,837,240	20,069	28
Clay	243,521	226,334	78,793	305,127	64,012	98,162	467,301	17,771	61
Clinton	333,397	309,573	109,939	419,512	101,956	104,778	626,246	19,279	43
Crawford	42,209	38,753	54,707	93,460	15,723	37,712	146,895	14,154	92
Daviess	257,569	239,398	43,622	283,020	86,097	108,194	477,311	16,708	76
Dearborn	352,818	327,992	289,030	617,022	104,912	122,272	844,206	18,996	48
Decatur	345,975	321,186	21,448	342,634	73,137	70,605	486,376	19,514	40
Dekalb	615,127	574,107	-1,866	572,241	119,056	97,570	788,867	20,846	24
Delaware	1,809,669	1,690,745	-65,090	1,625,655	359,258	398,681	2,383,594	20,044	29
Dubois	772,821	720,051	-126,166	593,885	188,106	107,643	889,634	22,932	12
Elkhart	3,745,833	3,493,140	-753,892	2,739,248	603,515	437,626	3,780,389	22,660	13
Fayette	390,821	363,248	-52,418	310,830	70,046	99,235	480,111	18,296	56
Floyd	759,547	707,666	380,495	1,088,161	225,933	230,834	1,544,928	22,083	16
Fountain	129,893	119,636	66,090	185,726	50,118	60,621	296,465	16,411	80
Franklin	95,868	88,274	141,295	229,569	61,534	52,389	343,492	16,333	82
Fulton	208,875	193,732	32,825	226,557	55,154	63,483	345,194	17,349	65
Gibson	274,987	254,423	108,750	363,173	108,043	115,580	586,796	18,345	55
Grant	1,069,399	996,253	-57,723	938,530	202,657	287,993	1,429,180	19,388	42
Greene	219,128	202,574	121,068	323,642	87,552	121,427	532,621	16,303	83
Hamilton	2,446,233	2,278,907	1,306,331	3,585,238	797,608	290,507	4,673,353	33,163	1
Hancock	470,738	438,952	461,283	900,235	150,415	137,097	1,187,747	23,325	9
Harrison	223,715	207,756	225,228	432,984	83,343	93,158	609,485	18,692	52
Hendricks	750,152	699,479	878,785	1,578,264	287,676	197,749	2,063,689	23,819	7
Henry	487,126	453,672	201,679	655,351	121,995	191,168	968,514	19,704	35
Howard	2,207,375	2,069,860	-581,856	1,488,004	234,276	280,110	2,002,390	24,013	6
Huntington	464,938	432,392	89,330	521,722	113,702	109,138	744,562	20,244	27
Jackson	561,068	522,385	7,462	529,847	111,868	124,369	766,084	19,021	47
Jasper	276,117	256,632	48,418	305,050	81,762	76,203	463,015	16,619	78
Jay	211,989	196,971	30,706	227,677	47,138	74,719	349,534	16,058	85
Jefferson	379,940	354,068	-20,370	333,698	85,274	109,300	528,272	17,126	72
Jennings	205,905	191,961	120,385	312,346	45,404	109,013	466,763	17,875	59
Johnson	999,343	930,140	814,382	1,744,522	327,100	259,945	2,331,567	22,934	11
Knox	493,393	461,953	-129	461,824	121,401	163,087	746,312	18,778	50
Kosciusko	1,115,072	1,038,147	30,685	1,068,832	265,278	179,153	1,513,263	21,893	17
Lagrange	416,252	388,633	19,055	407,688	77,738	66,239	551,665	17,370	64
Lake	6,885,307	6,409,717	507,353	6,917,070	1,389,352	1,748,039	10,054,461	20,923	23
Laporte	1,395,071	1,300,155	165,480	1,465,635	337,566	353,588	2,156,789	19,673	36
Lawrence	528,741	491,986	80,399	572,385	102,135	164,619	839,139	18,607	53
Madison	1,772,605	1,647,953	176,813	1,824,766	347,722	470,522	2,643,010	19,928	31
Marion	20,976,027	19,595,942	-5,417,474	14,178,468	3,190,320	2,902,899	20,271,687	24,826	3
Marshall	567,169	527,841	94,232	622,073	136,465	115,406	873,944	19,536	39
Martin	279,725	266,966	-153,115	113,851	26,270	39,845	179,966	17,117	73
Miami	274,136	255,215	119,585	374,800	81,281	115,915	571,996	17,637	62
Monroe	1,698,795	1,598,043	-89,267	1,508,776	369,971	268,227	2,146,974	18,603	54
Montgomery	571,016	531,446	-46,103	485,343	122,871	115,136	723,350	20,011	30
Morgan	390,485	362,503	564,966	927,469	135,358	164,419	1,227,246	19,792	33
Newton	93,277	85,651	58,206	143,857	37,734	40,041	221,632	15,394	88
Noble	574,810	536,462	73,148	609,610	90,779	104,613	805,002	19,710	34
Ohio	15,682	14,304	52,644	66,948	10,653	15,356	92,957	17,085	74
Orange	180,592	167,407	24,564	191,971	39,636	65,738	297,345	15,651	87
Owen	100,086	92,448	108,402	200,850	44,860	54,878	300,588	15,306	89
Parke	83,601	77,289	103,861	181,150	43,393	52,548	277,091	17,188	69
Perry	150,060	139,328	50,550	189,878	52,643	61,347	303,868	15,874	86
Pike	101,595	93,942	47,644	141,586	34,612	48,388	224,586	17,921	58
Porter	1,915,775	1,787,484	718,769	2,506,253	454,205	353,836	3,314,294	23,627	8
Posey	369,641	344,125	54,528	398,653	88,754	77,061	564,468	21,402	20
Pulaski	132,072	122,944	17,393	140,337	45,449	40,001	225,787	17,217	68
Putnam	316,751	295,419	97,132	392,551	88,341	88,742	569,634	17,295	66
Randolph	255,094	236,870	88,089	324,959	68,372	94,761	488,092	17,788	60
Ripley	385,796	358,354	23,185	381,539	96,857	82,932	561,328	21,019	22
Rush	148,814	137,968	79,596	217,564	51,624	60,386	329,574	17,971	57
St. Joseph	4,210,145	3,914,134	42,580	3,956,714	930,224	853,767	5,740,705	22,350	14
Scott	173,261	160,670	98,290	258,960	39,003	76,053	374,016	16,691	77
Shelby	495,144	461,312	183,934	645,246	109,896	122,572	877,714	20,492	26
Spencer	205,672	191,132	48,857	239,989	53,754	58,284	352,027	17,291	67
Starke	123,805	114,789	98,552	213,341	41,165	71,208	325,714	14,427	90
Steuben	474,165	441,630	-3,168	438,462	88,569	92,787	619,818	20,536	25
Sullivan	147,291	136,750	75,937	212,687	52,094	83,426	348,207	17,145	70
Switzerland	40,669	37,327	39,465	76,792	13,007	27,167	116,966	14,164	91
Tippecanoe	2,361,634	2,219,496	-283,403	1,936,093	461,079	329,587	2,726,759	19,842	32
Tipton	119,442	111,426	153,071	264,497	50,786	50,507	365,790	22,208	15
Union	36,491	33,685	49,260	82,945	16,844	22,041	121,830	16,555	79
Vanderburgh	3,254,278	3,024,685	-630,195	2,394,490	805,078	654,166	3,853,734	23,008	10
Vermillion	173,733	161,031	30,133	191,164	40,372	56,644	288,180	17,134	71
Vigo	1,600,977	1,491,111	-211,610	1,279,501	359,893	393,926	2,033,320	19,093	45
Wabash	426,741	396,830	29,581	426,411	118,783	117,283	662,477	19,045	46
Warren	54,933	51,110	35,909	87,019	22,408	23,536	132,963	16,132	84
Warrick	461,263	428,971	335,989	764,960	159,403	131,541	1,055,904	21,428	19
Washington	172,294	159,900	137,829	297,729	50,391	79,123	427,243	16,385	81
Wayne	1,055,552	981,101	-56,108	924,993	224,655	267,172	1,416,820	19,593	38
Wells	314,932	293,206	112,912	406,118	91,205	75,609	572,932	21,633	18
White	302,026	281,356	35,367	316,723	79,492	87,554	483,769	19,655	37
Whitley	354,518	330,508	122,232	452,740	83,487	84,200	620,427	21,059	21

Footnote: Please see the "Glossary" preceding the Table of Contents for an explanation of the difference between per capita money income from the Census Bureau and per capita personal income from the Bureau of Economic Analysis.

Source: U.S. Bureau of Economic Analysis
EDIN table(s): PIRE

Net Income Flows Caused by Commuting
1995

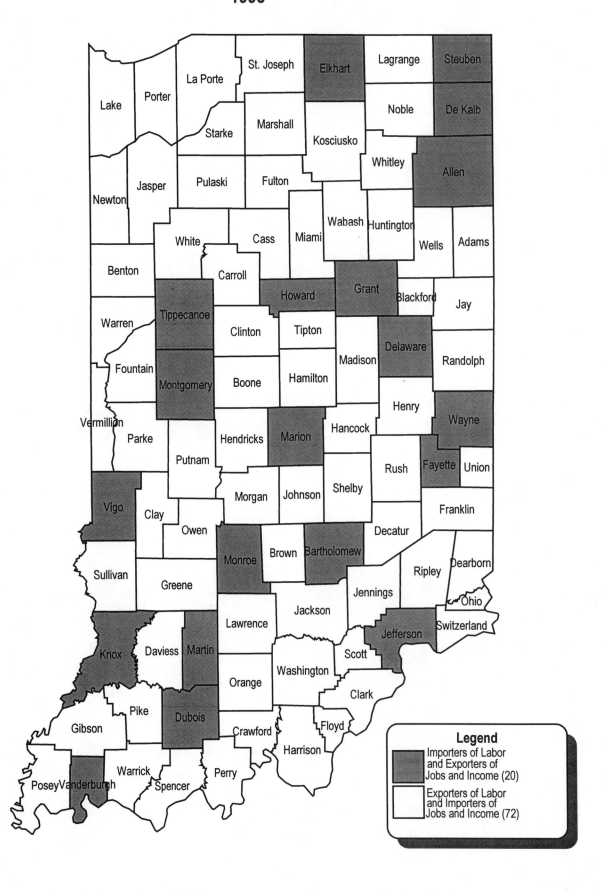

Legend

Importers of Labor and Exporters of Jobs and Income (20)

Exporters of Labor and Importers of Jobs and Income (72)

Net Income Flows Caused by Commuting: EDIN Table PIRE.

2.32 History of Personal Income 1975 to 1995

	Personal Income			Percent of State			Real Percent Change Adjusted for Inflation			Rank
	1975	1985	1995	1975	1985	1995	1975-85	1985-95	1975-95	
Indiana	30,924,251	70,147,689	124,730,317	100.0	100.0	100.0	19.7	25.0	49.6	—
Adams	149,915	360,119	631,475	0.5	0.5	0.5	26.8	23.3	56.3	33
Allen	1,754,616	4,041,578	7,508,772	5.7	5.8	6.0	21.6	30.6	58.8	29
Bartholomew	377,221	926,752	1,634,337	1.2	1.3	1.3	29.6	24.0	60.7	28
Benton	80,222	127,055	169,086	0.3	0.2	0.1	-16.4	-6.4	-21.8	92
Blackford	85,925	170,865	235,707	0.3	0.2	0.2	4.9	-3.0	1.8	87
Boone	220,428	569,386	1,126,372	0.7	0.8	0.9	36.3	39.1	89.6	14
Brown	50,050	141,493	283,769	0.2	0.2	0.2	49.2	41.0	110.3	3
Carroll	134,248	236,045	373,945	0.4	0.3	0.3	-7.2	11.4	3.3	86
Cass	242,845	482,461	731,670	0.8	0.7	0.6	4.8	6.6	11.8	80
Clark	434,420	1,050,097	1,837,240	1.4	1.5	1.5	27.6	23.0	56.9	32
Clay	121,062	278,535	467,301	0.4	0.4	0.4	21.4	17.9	43.2	47
Clinton	201,253	373,407	626,246	0.7	0.5	0.5	-2.1	17.9	15.4	77
Crawford	36,209	87,735	146,895	0.1	0.1	0.1	27.9	17.7	50.5	37
Daviess	139,862	295,890	477,311	0.5	0.4	0.4	11.6	13.4	26.6	64
Dearborn	162,845	448,994	844,206	0.5	0.6	0.7	45.5	32.2	92.3	11
Decatur	128,632	278,682	486,376	0.4	0.4	0.4	14.3	22.7	40.3	53
Dekalb	179,876	411,658	788,867	0.6	0.6	0.6	20.8	34.7	62.7	26
Delaware	672,172	1,452,319	2,383,594	2.2	2.1	1.9	14.0	15.4	31.6	56
Dubois	175,162	496,178	889,634	0.6	0.7	0.7	49.5	26.0	88.4	15
Elkhart	776,536	1,966,456	3,780,389	2.5	2.8	3.0	33.6	35.1	80.6	20
Fayette	145,794	308,636	480,111	0.5	0.4	0.4	11.7	9.4	22.2	69
Floyd	311,906	799,270	1,544,928	1.0	1.1	1.2	35.2	35.9	83.7	16
Fountain	108,399	202,327	296,465	0.4	0.3	0.2	-1.5	3.0	1.5	88
Franklin	86,264	206,059	343,492	0.3	0.3	0.3	26.1	17.2	47.7	41
Fulton	100,436	215,812	345,194	0.3	0.3	0.3	13.4	12.4	27.5	58
Gibson	187,136	414,480	586,796	0.6	0.6	0.5	16.9	-0.5	16.3	75
Grant	446,383	951,908	1,429,180	1.4	1.4	1.2	12.5	5.5	18.8	74
Greene	137,006	325,051	532,621	0.4	0.5	0.4	25.2	15.2	44.2	45
Hamilton	495,501	1,697,002	4,673,353	1.6	2.4	3.8	80.7	93.6	249.9	1
Hancock	230,793	597,712	1,187,747	0.8	0.9	1.0	36.7	39.7	90.9	13
Harrison	110,940	315,081	609,485	0.4	0.5	0.5	49.9	36.0	103.8	6
Hendricks	367,004	990,206	2,063,689	1.2	1.4	1.7	42.4	46.5	108.6	5
Henry	291,803	580,221	968,514	0.9	0.8	0.8	4.9	17.3	23.1	67
Howard	526,793	1,194,158	2,002,390	1.7	1.7	1.6	19.6	17.9	41.0	50
Huntington	202,586	419,332	744,562	0.7	0.6	0.6	9.2	24.8	36.3	54
Jackson	179,930	423,538	766,084	0.6	0.6	0.6	24.2	27.2	57.9	31
Jasper	142,252	300,527	463,015	0.5	0.4	0.4	11.5	8.3	20.7	71
Jay	123,235	232,495	349,534	0.4	0.3	0.3	-0.4	5.7	5.2	85
Jefferson	133,561	303,181	528,272	0.4	0.4	0.4	19.8	22.5	46.7	44
Jennings	87,580	227,656	466,763	0.3	0.3	0.4	37.2	44.1	97.7	7
Johnson	398,788	1,137,484	2,331,567	1.3	1.6	1.9	50.5	44.1	116.9	2
Knox	217,614	480,936	746,312	0.7	0.7	0.6	16.6	9.1	27.2	60
Kosciusko	307,385	798,600	1,513,263	1.0	1.1	1.2	37.1	33.2	82.6	18
Lagrange	103,900	277,397	551,665	0.3	0.4	0.4	40.9	39.8	97.0	8
Lake	3,268,579	6,161,048	10,054,461	10.6	8.8	8.1	-0.5	14.7	14.1	78
Laporte	629,309	1,307,201	2,156,789	2.0	1.9	1.7	9.6	16.0	27.1	62
Lawrence	203,801	478,788	839,139	0.7	0.7	0.7	24.0	23.2	52.7	35
Madison	804,059	1,698,133	2,643,010	2.6	2.4	2.1	11.4	9.4	21.9	70
Marion	5,000,596	11,176,347	20,271,687	16.2	15.9	16.3	17.9	27.5	50.4	38
Marshall	220,250	478,135	873,944	0.7	0.7	0.7	14.6	28.5	47.2	42
Martin	47,409	108,462	179,966	0.2	0.2	0.1	20.7	16.6	40.8	51
Miami	218,999	435,020	571,996	0.7	0.6	0.5	4.8	-7.6	-3.1	90
Monroe	414,021	1,107,986	2,146,974	1.3	1.6	1.7	41.2	36.2	92.4	10
Montgomery	210,673	432,055	723,350	0.7	0.6	0.6	8.2	17.7	27.4	59
Morgan	251,812	637,622	1,227,246	0.8	0.9	1.0	33.6	35.3	80.8	19
Newton	77,354	163,346	221,632	0.3	0.2	0.2	11.4	-4.6	6.3	84
Noble	171,044	411,565	805,002	0.6	0.6	0.7	27.0	37.5	74.6	22
Ohio	21,753	55,539	92,957	0.1	0.1	0.1	34.7	17.7	58.5	30
Orange	78,456	190,803	297,345	0.3	0.3	0.2	28.3	9.6	40.6	52
Owen	53,150	153,672	300,588	0.2	0.2	0.2	52.6	37.5	109.8	4
Parke	83,748	170,320	277,091	0.3	0.2	0.2	7.3	14.4	22.7	68
Perry	86,896	205,703	303,868	0.3	0.3	0.2	24.9	3.8	29.7	57
Pike	83,079	164,391	224,586	0.3	0.2	0.2	4.4	-4.0	0.3	89
Porter	670,196	1,641,297	3,314,294	2.2	2.3	2.7	29.2	42.0	83.5	17
Posey	138,896	357,311	564,468	0.5	0.5	0.5	35.8	11.1	50.8	36
Pulaski	78,634	149,462	225,787	0.3	0.2	0.2	0.3	6.2	6.5	83
Putnam	149,813	339,949	569,634	0.5	0.5	0.5	19.7	17.8	41.1	49
Randolph	159,005	333,400	488,092	0.5	0.5	0.4	10.6	2.9	13.9	79
Ripley	115,421	285,728	561,328	0.4	0.4	0.5	30.6	38.1	80.4	21
Rush	112,804	214,999	329,574	0.4	0.3	0.3	0.6	7.8	8.4	82
St. Joseph	1,416,662	3,239,042	5,740,705	4.6	4.6	4.6	20.7	24.6	50.3	39
Scott	84,576	206,509	374,016	0.3	0.3	0.3	28.8	27.3	64.1	24
Shelby	217,663	495,834	877,714	0.7	0.7	0.7	20.2	24.4	49.6	40
Spencer	88,718	220,290	352,027	0.3	0.3	0.3	31.0	12.3	47.2	42
Starke	100,897	197,294	325,714	0.3	0.3	0.3	3.2	16.1	19.8	72
Steuben	117,537	318,220	619,818	0.4	0.5	0.5	42.9	36.9	95.6	9
Sullivan	108,500	225,466	348,207	0.4	0.3	0.3	9.7	8.6	19.1	73
Switzerland	27,778	66,179	116,966	0.1	0.1	0.1	25.7	24.2	56.2	34
Tippecanoe	621,288	1,479,518	2,726,759	2.0	2.1	2.2	25.7	29.6	62.8	25
Tipton	102,228	229,445	365,790	0.3	0.3	0.3	18.4	12.1	32.7	55
Union	40,468	75,940	121,830	0.1	0.1	0.1	-1.0	12.8	11.7	81
Vanderburgh	991,712	2,378,403	3,853,734	3.2	3.4	3.1	26.6	13.9	44.2	45
Vermillion	92,562	196,542	288,180	0.3	0.3	0.2	12.1	3.1	15.5	76
Vigo	600,228	1,252,515	2,033,320	1.9	1.8	1.6	10.1	14.1	25.7	65
Wabash	193,156	417,913	662,477	0.6	0.6	0.5	14.2	11.4	27.2	60
Warren	55,044	94,791	132,963	0.2	0.1	0.1	-9.1	-1.4	-10.4	91
Warrick	203,818	601,749	1,055,904	0.7	0.9	0.9	55.8	23.4	92.2	12
Washington	98,214	227,344	427,243	0.3	0.3	0.3	22.2	32.1	61.4	27
Wayne	414,076	860,610	1,416,820	1.3	1.2	1.1	9.7	15.7	26.9	63
Wells	150,199	319,315	572,932	0.5	0.5	0.5	12.2	26.1	41.5	48
White	144,883	274,985	483,769	0.5	0.4	0.4	0.2	23.7	23.9	66
Whitley	137,799	316,720	620,427	0.5	0.5	0.5	21.3	37.7	67.0	23

Footnote: Deflator: 1995 = 107.8, 1985 = 75.8, 1975 = 40
Source: U.S. Bureau of Economic Analysis
EDIN table(s): PIRE

Total Personal Income Real Percent Change
(Adjusted for Inflation)
1985 to 1995

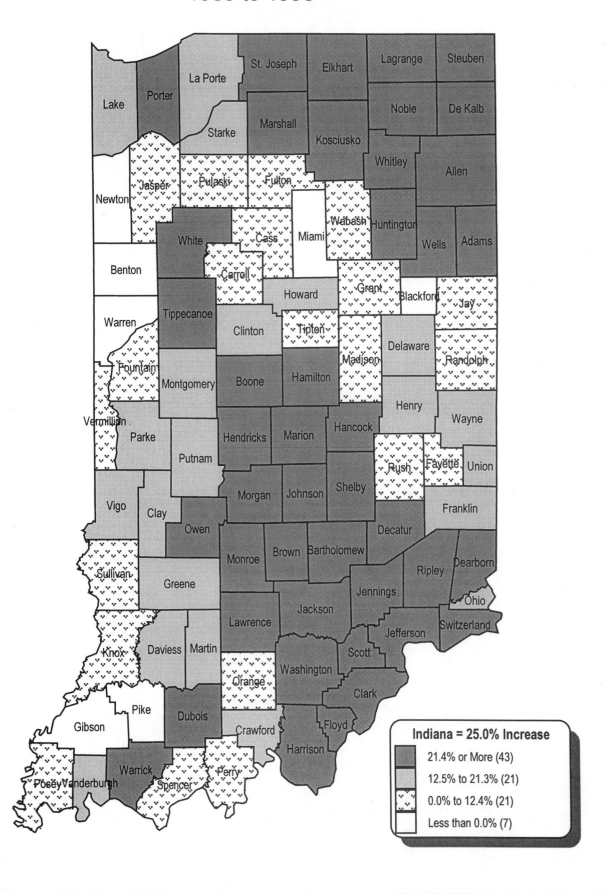

Indiana = 25.0% Increase

21.4% or More (43)
12.5% to 21.3% (21)
0.0% to 12.4% (21)
Less than 0.0% (7)

Total Personal Income Real Percent Change: EDIN Table PIRE.

2.33 History of Per Capita Personal Income 1975 to 1995

	Per Capita Income			Percent of State			Real Percent Change Adjusted for Inflation			Rank
	1975	1985	1995	1975	1985	1995	1975-85	1985-95	1975-95	
Indiana	5,779	12,849	21,517	100.00	100.00	100.00	17.3	17.7	38.1	—
Adams	5,311	11,893	19,479	91.90	92.56	90.53	18.2	15.1	36.1	39
Allen	6,072	13,963	24,339	105.07	108.67	113.12	21.3	22.5	48.7	11
Bartholomew	6,200	14,618	24,047	107.28	113.77	111.76	24.4	15.6	43.9	21
Benton	7,426	12,993	17,408	128.50	101.12	80.90	-7.7	-5.8	-13.0	92
Blackford	5,403	11,476	16,764	93.49	89.31	77.91	12.1	2.7	15.1	80
Boone	6,746	15,331	26,963	116.73	119.32	125.31	19.9	23.6	48.3	13
Brown	4,719	10,984	18,707	81.66	85.49	86.94	22.8	19.7	47.1	17
Carroll	7,112	12,566	19,114	123.07	97.80	88.83	-6.8	6.9	-0.3	88
Cass	5,949	12,110	18,991	102.94	94.25	88.26	7.4	10.2	18.4	75
Clark	5,212	11,841	20,069	90.19	92.16	93.27	19.9	19.1	42.8	24
Clay	4,983	11,304	17,771	86.23	87.98	82.59	19.7	10.5	32.3	48
Clinton	6,384	12,130	19,279	110.47	94.40	89.60	0.3	11.7	12.0	81
Crawford	4,019	8,784	14,154	69.54	68.36	65.78	15.3	13.3	30.6	54
Daviess	5,193	10,481	16,708	89.86	81.57	77.65	6.5	12.1	19.4	71
Dearborn	5,251	12,629	18,996	90.86	98.29	88.28	26.9	5.7	34.2	45
Decatur	5,419	11,907	19,514	93.77	92.67	90.69	16.0	15.2	33.6	47
Dekalb	5,505	12,208	20,846	95.26	95.01	96.88	17.0	20.0	40.5	31
Delaware	5,158	11,900	20,044	89.25	92.61	93.15	21.7	18.4	44.2	19
Dubois	5,405	14,031	22,932	93.53	109.20	106.58	37.0	14.9	57.4	4
Elkhart	5,906	13,351	22,660	102.20	103.91	105.31	19.3	19.3	42.3	26
Fayette	5,189	11,376	18,296	89.79	88.54	85.03	15.7	13.1	30.8	53
Floyd	5,470	12,883	22,083	94.65	100.26	102.63	24.3	20.5	49.8	8
Fountain	5,623	10,867	16,411	97.30	84.57	76.27	2.0	6.2	8.3	84
Franklin	4,821	10,380	16,333	83.42	80.78	75.91	13.6	10.6	25.7	64
Fulton	5,485	11,455	17,349	94.91	89.15	80.63	10.2	6.5	17.3	77
Gibson	5,890	12,570	18,345	101.92	97.83	85.26	12.6	2.6	15.5	79
Grant	5,361	12,406	19,388	92.77	96.55	90.11	22.1	9.9	34.2	45
Greene	4,673	10,777	16,303	80.86	83.87	75.77	21.7	6.3	29.4	56
Hamilton	7,336	19,009	33,163	126.94	147.94	154.12	36.7	22.6	67.7	1
Hancock	5,753	13,677	23,325	99.55	106.44	108.40	25.5	19.9	50.4	7
Harrison	4,669	11,011	18,692	80.79	85.70	86.87	24.4	19.3	48.5	12
Hendricks	5,982	13,837	23,819	103.51	107.69	110.70	22.1	21.0	47.7	15
Henry	5,434	11,685	19,704	94.03	90.94	91.57	13.5	18.5	34.5	43
Howard	6,062	14,139	24,013	104.90	110.04	111.60	23.1	19.4	47.0	18
Huntington	5,724	12,051	20,244	99.05	93.79	94.08	11.1	18.1	31.2	50
Jackson	5,206	11,404	19,021	90.08	88.75	88.40	15.6	17.3	35.5	41
Jasper	6,219	11,780	16,619	107.61	91.68	77.24	0.0	-0.8	-0.9	89
Jay	5,058	10,584	16,058	87.52	82.37	74.63	10.4	6.7	17.8	76
Jefferson	4,646	10,401	17,126	80.39	80.95	79.59	18.1	15.8	36.7	36
Jennings	4,012	9,786	17,875	69.42	76.16	83.07	28.7	28.4	65.3	2
Johnson	5,776	13,922	22,934	99.95	108.35	106.59	27.2	15.8	47.3	16
Knox	5,303	11,440	18,778	91.76	89.03	87.27	13.8	15.4	31.4	49
Kosciusko	5,713	12,758	21,893	98.86	99.29	101.75	17.8	20.6	42.2	27
Lagrange	4,351	10,026	17,370	75.29	78.03	80.73	21.6	21.8	48.1	14
Lake	6,046	12,630	20,923	104.62	98.30	97.24	10.2	16.5	28.4	61
Laporte	5,862	12,253	19,673	101.44	95.36	91.43	10.3	12.9	24.5	66
Lawrence	4,960	11,415	18,607	85.83	88.84	86.48	21.4	14.6	39.2	33
Madison	5,762	12,802	19,928	99.71	99.63	92.62	17.2	9.4	28.3	62
Marion	6,389	14,412	24,826	110.56	112.16	115.38	19.0	21.1	44.1	20
Marshall	5,826	11,610	19,536	100.81	90.36	90.79	5.2	18.3	24.4	67
Martin	4,215	10,054	17,117	72.94	78.25	79.55	25.9	19.7	50.7	6
Miami	5,373	11,417	17,637	92.97	88.86	81.97	12.1	8.6	21.8	69
Monroe	4,609	10,850	18,603	79.75	84.44	86.46	24.2	20.5	49.7	9
Montgomery	5,950	12,333	20,011	102.96	95.98	93.00	9.4	14.1	24.8	65
Morgan	5,231	11,839	19,792	90.52	92.14	91.98	19.4	17.5	40.4	32
Newton	5,842	11,693	15,394	101.09	91.00	71.54	5.6	-7.5	-2.2	90
Noble	5,104	11,247	19,710	88.32	87.53	91.60	16.3	23.2	43.3	22
Ohio	4,443	10,440	17,085	76.88	81.25	79.40	24.0	15.0	42.7	25
Orange	4,437	10,147	15,651	76.78	78.97	72.74	20.7	8.4	30.9	52
Owen	3,761	9,591	15,306	65.08	74.64	71.13	34.6	12.2	51.0	5
Parke	5,361	10,782	17,188	92.77	83.91	79.88	6.1	12.1	18.9	72
Perry	4,563	10,592	15,874	78.96	82.43	73.77	22.5	5.4	29.1	59
Pike	6,647	12,560	17,921	115.02	97.75	83.29	-0.3	0.3	0.0	87
Porter	6,776	13,420	23,627	117.25	104.44	109.81	4.5	23.8	29.4	56
Posey	5,904	13,501	21,402	102.16	105.07	99.47	20.7	11.4	34.5	43
Pulaski	6,010	11,394	17,217	104.00	88.68	80.02	0.0	6.2	6.3	85
Putnam	5,501	11,649	17,295	95.19	90.66	80.38	11.7	4.4	16.6	78
Randolph	5,341	11,703	17,788	92.42	91.08	82.67	15.6	6.9	23.6	68
Ripley	4,907	11,704	21,019	84.91	91.09	97.69	25.9	26.2	58.9	3
Rush	5,545	11,506	17,971	95.95	89.55	83.52	9.5	9.8	20.2	70
St. Joseph	5,882	13,472	22,350	101.78	104.85	103.87	20.9	16.6	41.0	30
Scott	4,360	10,031	16,691	75.45	78.07	77.57	21.4	17.0	42.0	28
Shelby	5,506	12,467	20,492	95.28	97.03	95.24	19.5	15.6	38.1	34
Spencer	4,923	11,112	17,291	85.19	86.48	80.36	19.1	9.4	30.3	55
Starke	4,797	9,170	14,427	83.01	71.37	67.05	0.9	10.6	11.6	82
Steuben	5,110	12,571	20,536	88.42	97.84	95.44	29.8	14.8	49.1	10
Sullivan	5,353	11,292	17,145	92.63	87.88	79.68	11.3	6.7	18.8	73
Switzerland	4,083	9,025	14,164	70.65	70.24	65.83	16.6	10.3	28.7	60
Tippecanoe	5,386	11,774	19,842	93.20	91.63	92.22	15.4	18.5	36.7	36
Tipton	6,057	14,128	22,208	104.81	109.95	103.21	23.1	10.5	36.0	40
Union	5,984	10,697	16,555	103.55	83.25	76.94	-5.7	8.8	2.6	86
Vanderburgh	6,009	14,230	23,000	103.98	110.75	106.93	25.0	13.7	42.0	28
Vermillion	5,358	11,132	17,134	92.72	86.64	79.63	9.6	8.2	18.6	74
Vigo	5,402	11,414	19,093	93.48	88.83	88.73	11.5	17.6	31.1	51
Wabash	5,461	11,939	19,045	94.50	92.92	88.51	15.4	12.1	29.4	56
Warren	6,347	11,379	16,132	109.83	88.56	74.97	-5.4	-0.3	-5.7	91
Warrick	5,806	13,703	21,428	100.47	106.65	99.59	24.5	9.9	36.9	35
Washington	4,806	9,973	16,385	83.16	77.62	76.15	9.5	15.5	26.5	63
Wayne	5,325	11,765	19,593	92.14	91.56	91.06	16.6	17.1	36.5	38
Wells	5,927	12,779	21,633	102.56	99.46	100.54	13.8	19.0	35.4	42
White	6,561	11,845	19,655	113.53	92.19	91.35	-4.7	16.7	11.1	83
Whitley	5,455	11,913	21,059	94.39	92.72	97.87	15.2	24.3	43.2	23

Footnote: Deflator: 1995 = 107.8, 1985 = 75.8, 1975 = 40
Source: U.S. Bureau of Economic Analysis
EDIN table(s): PIRE

2.34 Selected Calculations of Personal Income 1995

	Personal Income Received From									Per Capita Personal Income	
	Earnings			Dividends, Interest, Rent			Transfer Payments				
	Number	% Chg. 1985-95	Rank	Number	% Chg. 1985-95	Rank	Number	% Chg. 1985-96	Rank	Number	Rank
Indiana	86,995,091	81.1	—	19,257,888	53.3	—	18,477,338	93.4	—	21,517	—
Adams	439,576	86.0	34	107,121	34.1	49	84,778	93.4	39	19,479	41
Allen	5,311,457	88.3	32	1,261,398	66.1	16	935,917	102.5	18	24,339	4
Bartholomew	1,180,403	81.5	36	262,243	46.5	30	191,691	96.6	29	24,047	5
Benton	104,446	38.7	88	32,525	0.0	91	32,115	67.1	89	17,408	63
Blackford	156,489	33.3	90	30,089	14.1	84	49,129	81.3	71	16,764	75
Boone	812,778	103.9	11	206,828	79.9	4	106,766	91.1	44	26,963	2
Brown	209,586	106.9	9	43,382	73.0	7	30,801	103.5	16	18,707	51
Carroll	260,628	68.4	55	62,384	20.0	70	50,933	73.6	84	19,114	44
Cass	480,493	52.7	80	109,674	19.2	73	141,503	86.5	59	18,991	49
Clark	1,282,045	74.4	45	234,646	49.8	27	320,549	102.5	18	20,069	28
Clay	305,127	79.0	41	64,012	14.5	82	98,162	88.0	57	17,771	61
Clinton	419,512	75.1	43	101,956	35.7	45	104,778	78.6	77	19,279	43
Crawford	93,460	68.2	56	15,723	16.9	79	37,712	101.4	22	14,154	92
Daviess	283,020	63.2	66	86,097	32.6	53	108,194	88.0	57	16,708	76
Dearborn	617,022	96.9	19	104,912	41.7	33	122,272	98.7	25	18,996	48
Decatur	342,634	90.2	30	73,137	26.4	59	70,605	73.8	83	19,514	40
Dekalb	572,241	101.8	13	119,056	53.3	22	97,570	93.2	40	20,846	24
Delaware	1,625,655	66.7	57	359,258	36.7	42	398,681	85.8	62	20,044	29
Dubois	593,885	79.7	40	188,106	67.2	13	107,643	102.0	22	22,932	12
Elkhart	2,739,248	95.3	21	603,515	71.8	9	437,626	105.9	12	22,660	13
Fayette	310,830	59.0	73	70,046	14.1	84	99,235	92.0	42	8,296	56
Floyd	1,088,161	98.0	18	225,933	66.9	14	230,834	101.8	21	22,083	16
Fountain	185,726	51.4	82	50,118	16.3	80	60,621	65.8	90	16,411	80
Franklin	229,569	65.4	62	61,534	47.4	29	52,389	105.6	14	16,333	82
Fulton	226,557	65.6	61	55,154	20.8	68	63,483	90.5	46	17,349	65
Gibson	363,173	40.0	86	108,043	17.2	76	115,580	84.0	67	18,345	55
Grant	938,530	42.4	85	202,657	37.9	39	287,993	97.4	27	19,388	42
Greene	323,642	66.2	59	87,552	34.8	46	121,427	85.7	63	16,303	83
Hamilton	3,585,238	180.4	1	797,608	162.6	1	290,507	153.1	2	33,163	1
Hancock	900,235	102.7	12	150,415	68.0	12	137,097	113.9	7	23,325	9
Harrison	432,984	100.1	16	83,343	50.6	26	93,158	114.7	5	18,692	52
Hendricks	1,578,264	110.2	3	287,676	94.4	2	197,749	116.8	3	23,819	7
Henry	655,351	71.7	49	121,995	17.7	75	191,168	101.3	23	19,704	35
Howard	1,488,004	69.7	53	234,276	33.3	51	280,110	98.0	26	24,013	6
Huntington	521,722	91.1	27	113,702	36.9	41	109,138	72.4	87	20,244	27
Jackson	529,847	93.7	23	111,868	32.8	52	124,369	89.0	53	19,021	47
Jasper	305,050	54.5	79	81,762	30.6	54	76,203	88.1	56	16,619	78
Jay	227,677	58.4	76	47,138	0.3	90	74,719	78.8	76	16,058	85
Jefferson	333,698	74.6	44	85,274	51.8	25	109,300	95.5	33	17,126	72
Jennings	312,346	98.9	17	45,404	37.8	40	109,013	189.5	1	17,875	59
Johnson	1,744,522	109.3	6	327,100	79.2	5	259,945	114.2	6	22,934	11
Knox	461,824	59.9	70	121,401	19.8	72	163,087	79.5	73	18,778	50
Kosciusko	1,068,832	93.1	24	265,278	68.1	11	179,153	105.7	13	21,893	17
Lagrange	407,688	109.7	5	77,738	56.4	19	66,239	99.3	24	17,370	64
Lake	6,917,070	64.8	63	1,389,352	40.6	36	1,748,039	79.1	75	20,923	23
Laporte	1,465,635	64.1	64	337,566	48.0	28	353,588	90.3	47	19,673	36
Lawrence	572,385	81.3	37	102,135	30.1	56	164,619	94.6	37	18,607	53
Madison	1,824,766	57.4	77	347,722	21.7	64	470,522	86.1	60	19,928	31
Marion	14,178,468	80.7	38	3,190,320	73.4	6	2,902,899	95.0	35	24,826	3
Marshall	622,073	94.6	22	136,465	39.6	37	115,406	89.9	48	19,536	39
Martin	113,851	66.5	58	26,270	40.7	35	39,845	86.0	61	17,117	73
Miami	374,800	24.8	92	81,281	20.4	69	115,915	72.6	86	17,637	62
Monroe	1,508,776	92.9	25	369,971	85.0	3	268,227	112.7	9	18,603	54
Montgomery	485,343	70.5	51	122,871	41.2	34	115,136	90.6	45	20,011	30
Morgan	927,469	96.8	20	135,358	58.4	17	164,419	103.2	17	19,792	33
Newton	143,857	32.6	91	37,734	15.2	81	40,041	81.2	72	15,394	88
Noble	609,610	110.0	4	90,779	33.4	50	104,613	96.6	29	19,710	34
Ohio	66,948	78.1	42	10,653	17.1	78	15,356	73.4	85	17,085	74
Orange	191,971	56.8	78	39,636	24.8	60	65,738	79.5	73	15,651	87
Owen	200,850	104.1	10	44,860	57.0	18	54,878	105.6	14	15,306	89
Parke	181,150	73.2	47	43,393	27.8	58	52,548	65.2	91	17,188	69
Perry	189,878	48.3	84	52,643	23.7	61	61,347	74.7	81	15,874	86
Pike	141,586	34.0	89	34,612	10.0	87	48,388	77.3	80	17,921	58
Porter	2,506,253	107.2	8	454,205	73.0	7	353,836	109.1	11	23,627	8
Posey	398,653	63.5	65	88,754	21.8	62	77,061	89.9	48	21,402	20
Pulaski	140,337	58.7	74	45,449	17.9	74	40,001	78.1	79	17,217	68
Putnam	392,551	69.8	52	88,341	42.3	32	88,742	89.9	48	17,295	66
Randolph	324,959	51.4	82	68,372	2.1	89	94,761	82.8	69	17,788	60
Ripley	381,539	107.9	7	96,857	66.7	15	82,932	88.2	55	21,019	22
Rush	217,564	59.3	71	51,624	14.5	82	60,386	81.4	70	17,971	57
St. Joseph	3,956,714	80.1	39	930,224	54.2	21	853,767	94.3	38	22,350	14
Scott	258,960	89.8	31	39,003	30.4	55	76,053	89.4	52	16,691	77
Shelby	645,246	85.8	35	109,896	29.5	57	122,572	92.7	41	20,492	26
Spencer	239,989	61.4	69	53,754	34.5	48	58,284	84.3	65	17,291	67
Starke	213,341	74.4	45	41,165	13.5	86	71,208	84.0	67	14,427	90
Steuben	438,462	101.8	13	88,569	52.5	24	92,787	116.3	4	20,536	25
Sullivan	212,687	62.0	68	52,094	6.6	88	83,426	84.2	66	17,145	70
Switzerland	76,792	86.8	33	13,007	21.1	65	27,167	89.6	51	14,164	91
Tippecanoe	1,936,093	90.9	28	461,079	55.4	20	329,587	95.5	33	19,842	32
Tipton	264,497	69.3	54	50,786	17.2	76	50,507	69.2	88	22,208	15
Union	82,945	73.1	48	16,844	0.0	91	22,041	97.3	28	16,555	79
Vanderburgh	2,394,490	59.1	72	805,078	53.0	23	654,166	88.6	54	23,008	10
Vermillion	191,164	51.6	81	40,372	21.8	62	56,644	51.9	92	17,134	71
Vigo	1,279,501	63.0	67	359,893	45.7	31	393,926	78.5	78	19,093	45
Wabash	426,411	58.6	75	118,783	38.7	38	117,283	84.7	64	19,045	46
Warren	87,019	39.0	87	22,408	19.9	71	23,536	74.2	82	16,132	84
Warrick	764,960	71.7	49	159,403	69.9	10	131,541	111.2	10	21,428	19
Washington	297,729	100.2	15	50,391	21.0	67	79,123	113.9	7	16,385	81
Wayne	924,993	66.2	59	224,645	36.5	43	267,172	91.4	43	19,593	38
Wells	406,118	90.7	29	91,205	34.6	47	75,609	96.0	32	21,633	18
White	316,723	92.6	26	79,492	21.1	65	87,554	94.9	36	19,655	37
Whitley	452,740	113.2	2	83,487	35.9	44	84,200	96.3	31	21,059	21

Source: U.S. Bureau of Economic Analysis
EDIN table(s): PIRE

2.35 Transfer Payments Part I 1995 ($000)

	Total Payments [1]	Total Govt. Payments to Individuals [1]	Retirement & Disability Insurance	Old Age, Survivors, Disability	Railroad Retirement & Disability	Federal Civilian Employee and Military Retirement	State & Local Govt. Employee Retirement	Worker's Comp. (Fed. & State)	Other	Medical Payments
Indiana	18,477,338	17,570,304	9,678,436	7,893,191	224,785	773,482	724,510	24,481	37,987	5,808,073
Adams	84,778	79,727	46,667	40,767	537	2,051	3,194	56	62	26,578
Allen	935,917	887,686	500,756	412,588	13,182	28,210	44,704	901	1,171	289,269
Bartholomew	191,691	181,049	105,569	91,544	662	3,956	8,921	183	303	57,434
Benton	32,115	30,597	19,276	17,063	271	878	1,010	NA	NA	8,978
Blackford	49,129	46,915	27,459	24,386	162	1,441	1,401	NA	NA	14,729
Boone	106,766	100,228	59,627	47,137	967	4,771	6,467	170	115	33,661
Brown	30,801	28,440	16,587	11,756	187	2,947	1,638	NA	NA	8,086
Carroll	50,933	47,884	31,044	26,176	563	2,130	2,095	NA	NA	13,055
Cass	141,503	135,470	76,063	58,313	7,693	5,706	4,148	123	80	47,481
Clark	320,549	306,192	165,810	127,585	4,672	21,429	10,882	645	597	104,196
Clay	98,162	94,049	54,788	45,802	1,452	4,069	2,339	116	1,010	30,107
Clinton	104,778	99,683	60,327	48,625	5,009	3,065	3,488	70	70	30,836
Crawford	37,712	36,079	17,875	14,572	367	2,103	780	NA	NA	12,364
Daviess	108,194	103,722	56,168	35,963	4,171	12,949	2,394	372	319	36,573
Dearborn	122,272	115,335	66,234	55,813	1,128	3,971	4,960	130	232	37,256
Decatur	70,605	66,696	38,476	32,087	850	2,823	2,587	NA	97	21,556
Dekalb	97,570	91,636	54,217	42,887	4,093	2,558	4,397	73	209	30,730
Delaware	398,681	380,142	194,562	167,746	2,180	9,341	14,296	311	688	124,422
Dubois	107,643	101,587	58,874	49,335	722	3,903	4,683	80	151	35,479
Elkhart	437,626	411,517	242,238	204,546	7,509	9,104	20,154	189	736	124,484
Fayette	99,235	95,103	47,453	42,240	227	2,072	2,716	NA	150	35,843
Floyd	230,834	219,881	119,028	91,123	4,342	14,093	8,842	343	285	72,314
Fountain	60,621	57,797	34,755	29,135	995	2,830	1,684	70	NA	17,959
Franklin	52,389	49,111	27,427	23,319	295	1,613	2,035	NA	123	15,295
Fulton	63,483	60,369	37,429	31,987	959	2,548	1,845	NA	50	18,188
Gibson	115,580	110,550	64,492	53,205	2,478	4,151	3,454	66	1,138	34,983
Grant	287,993	276,468	150,621	125,802	755	14,610	8,523	521	410	91,144
Greene	121,427	116,314	70,545	47,407	1,256	16,755	2,997	636	1,494	33,307
Hamilton	290,507	268,517	164,332	114,154	1,116	22,422	25,270	844	526	88,071
Hancock	137,097	129,159	79,492	58,446	1,044	11,890	7,339	537	236	40,594
Harrison	93,158	88,063	51,650	40,545	1,126	6,241	3,445	154	139	26,501
Hendricks	197,749	184,206	114,491	81,774	4,343	14,810	12,730	510	324	57,558
Henry	191,168	183,463	95,584	84,480	630	4,560	5,457	159	298	70,452
Howard	280,110	267,014	150,196	126,536	904	10,723	11,407	288	338	87,284
Huntington	109,138	103,383	64,115	53,355	3,137	3,016	4,308	84	215	30,702
Jackson	124,369	118,052	69,928	60,611	772	4,200	4,027	70	248	36,026
Jasper	76,203	71,841	41,015	35,546	1,065	1,646	2,592	NA	118	22,645
Jay	74,719	71,294	40,225	36,147	428	1,555	1,908	NA	142	24,469
Jefferson	109,300	104,483	52,812	39,640	500	9,378	2,975	116	203	39,490
Jennings	109,013	104,921	41,610	33,979	1,777	3,385	2,212	64	193	55,222
Johnson	259,945	244,044	149,121	114,078	3,948	15,907	14,264	582	342	75,029
Knox	163,087	156,803	77,709	62,849	1,678	7,732	3,690	170	1,590	58,300
Kosciusko	179,153	168,334	102,360	85,770	1,550	5,845	8,490	85	620	51,203
Lagrange	66,239	61,291	36,854	30,892	741	2,426	2,605	NA	154	18,408
Lake	1,748,039	1,672,575	834,059	719,945	25,399	23,914	61,727	1,308	1,766	578,729
Laporte	353,588	336,333	190,350	163,243	6,138	7,404	12,995	217	353	110,384
Lawrence	164,619	157,568	88,939	66,732	1,327	15,625	4,641	458	156	52,755
Madison	470,522	449,759	245,998	214,134	2,226	13,166	15,264	432	776	152,937
Marion	2,902,899	2,775,335	1,444,188	1,099,236	28,297	181,801	124,069	6,966	3,819	929,635
Marshall	115,406	108,389	65,387	55,668	1,047	3,369	5,002	80	221	33,417
Martin	39,845	38,220	22,539	13,372	313	7,894	871	70	NA	11,272
Miami	115,915	110,828	65,183	42,194	7,827	10,917	3,927	258	60	32,805
Monroe	268,227	250,215	139,537	106,933	1,406	17,565	12,486	788	359	73,182
Montgomery	115,136	109,494	60,416	51,388	577	4,089	4,203	85	74	39,647
Morgan	164,419	154,709	90,078	72,371	1,701	7,445	7,948	276	337	49,379
Newton	40,041	37,787	20,998	17,905	408	1,190	1,449	NA	NA	12,601
Noble	104,613	98,222	58,494	49,258	1,446	2,795	4,443	73	479	31,651
Ohio	15,356	14,513	8,090	6,721	53	732	560	NA	NA	4,935
Orange	65,738	62,766	31,135	24,654	283	4,461	1,524	72	141	22,959
Owen	54,878	51,804	29,959	24,267	643	3,153	1,676	70	150	15,304
Parke	52,548	50,033	28,209	23,226	672	2,373	1,573	56	309	16,319
Perry	61,347	58,357	32,968	28,942	79	2,201	1,663	NA	NA	18,726
Pike	48,388	46,417	25,487	20,006	1,746	1,730	1,318	NA	654	15,835
Porter	353,836	331,871	193,401	157,850	6,579	7,070	21,092	367	443	108,395
Posey	77,061	72,919	40,449	34,242	594	2,157	3,254	63	139	24,355
Pulaski	40,001	37,974	22,152	19,259	608	1,033	1,200	NA	NA	12,001
Putnam	88,742	83,592	49,457	40,644	1,085	4,313	3,216	137	62	25,976
Randolph	94,761	90,481	52,109	46,114	731	2,449	2,574	61	180	29,065
Ripley	82,932	78,737	43,345	36,159	370	3,735	2,842	68	171	27,178
Rush	60,386	57,499	32,705	28,019	166	2,583	1,860	NA	NA	19,290
St. Joseph	853,767	813,427	458,307	399,341	3,974	21,575	31,956	654	807	265,134
Scott	76,053	72,524	35,181	29,244	322	2,743	2,089	NA	737	26,680
Shelby	122,572	115,878	61,610	48,061	981	6,803	5,501	179	85	43,525
Spencer	58,284	55,099	30,580	25,383	219	2,785	2,031	60	102	18,558
Starke	71,208	67,671	37,563	31,953	2,108	1,462	1,814	NA	191	21,826
Steuben	92,787	88,087	53,741	46,760	882	2,654	3,319	57	69	27,086
Sullivan	83,426	80,318	42,544	34,608	578	3,906	1,800	93	1,559	29,414
Switzerland	27,167	25,882	13,259	11,137	78	1,349	668	NA	NA	8,821
Tippecanoe	329,587	308,442	177,896	142,517	3,715	14,823	16,080	452	309	81,805
Tipton	50,507	47,932	28,273	23,702	691	1,716	2,084	NA	NA	15,624
Union	22,041	20,900	11,778	10,070	92	918	646	NA	NA	6,758
Vanderburgh	654,166	627,888	334,558	284,520	8,977	18,287	20,890	379	1,505	213,795
Vermillion	56,644	54,013	30,627	23,628	1,280	2,684	1,786	51	1,198	17,482
Vigo	393,926	377,259	196,079	155,127	8,181	18,083	11,212	532	2,944	127,550
Wabash	117,283	111,827	62,799	54,677	694	3,096	3,671	86	575	39,644
Warren	23,536	22,223	13,086	11,083	204	999	742	NA	NA	6,991
Warrick	131,541	123,820	72,537	59,778	767	4,823	6,452	109	608	40,112
Washington	79,123	75,044	40,189	34,049	476	3,002	2,326	63	273	24,793
Wayne	267,172	255,790	140,236	121,808	2,966	7,283	7,489	116	574	81,886
Wells	75,609	71,465	44,513	38,078	561	2,446	3,271	90	67	22,735
White	87,554	83,723	52,041	45,196	1,446	2,809	2,489	NA	64	25,884
Whitley	84,200	79,600	49,546	42,278	1,429	2,259	3,464	51	65	24,977

Footnote: [1] Includes items not shown separately.
Source: U.S. Bureau of Economic Analysis
EDIN table(s): PITP

	Income Maintenance Benefits [1]	Supplemental Security Income (SSI)	Aid to Families with Dependent Children (AFDC)	Food Stamps	Other	Total Unemployment Insurance Compensation [1]	Total Veterans Benefits [1]	Federal Ed. & Training Assistance	Total Payments to Nonprofit Institutions	Business Payments to Individuals
Indiana	1,317,225	351,605	198,573	364,190	402,857	238,520	327,972	20,489	555,443	351,591
Adams	4,255	984	444	1,095	1,732	901	1,021	80	3,093	1,958
Allen	66,141	16,270	10,939	20,241	18,691	9,249	14,943	1,097	29,535	18,696
Bartholomew	12,631	3,949	1,357	2,581	4,744	1,188	3,587	246	6,517	4,125
Benton	1,447	313	174	349	611	346	459	NA	930	588
Blackford	3,068	627	404	894	1,143	626	899	NA	1,356	858
Boone	3,826	912	278	758	1,878	851	1,836	141	4,004	2,534
Brown	2,220	327	273	639	981	539	864	58	1,446	915
Carroll	1,969	408	190	387	984	680	953	62	1,867	1,182
Cass	7,850	2,144	956	2,225	2,525	1,294	2,416	153	3,695	2,338
Clark	22,018	6,722	3,134	5,285	6,877	5,978	7,326	387	8,792	5,565
Clay	5,774	1,993	566	1,111	2,104	1,125	2,007	80	2,519	1,594
Clinton	5,595	1,479	603	1,309	2,204	1,019	1,599	101	3,120	1,975
Crawford	3,638	1,104	396	752	1,386	1,087	1,017	NA	1,000	633
Daviess	7,025	1,667	782	1,455	3,121	1,478	2,208	82	2,739	1,733
Dearborn	6,906	1,756	931	1,865	2,354	2,059	2,461	167	4,248	2,689
Decatur	4,473	1,174	392	1,008	1,899	683	1,273	81	2,394	1,515
Dekalb	3,930	1,158	306	874	1,592	929	1,470	131	3,634	2,300
Delaware	36,718	10,995	4,874	9,658	11,191	5,279	7,438	405	11,353	7,186
Dubois	3,130	877	235	525	1,493	1,520	2,217	111	3,709	2,347
Elkhart	27,145	7,808	3,860	7,152	8,325	8,258	6,234	532	15,988	10,121
Fayette	7,612	2,357	1,069	1,815	2,371	2,255	1,689	84	2,530	1,602
Floyd	16,908	5,023	2,737	4,311	4,837	4,328	4,896	247	6,707	4,246
Fountain	3,120	972	300	685	1,163	638	1,154	62	1,729	1,095
Franklin	3,491	978	406	832	1,275	1,302	1,399	66	2,008	1,270
Fulton	2,810	606	347	635	1,222	569	1,186	74	1,907	1,207
Gibson	5,849	1,435	687	1,390	2,337	1,408	2,237	120	3,081	1,949
Grant	21,433	5,991	3,102	6,015	6,325	3,994	6,433	298	7,057	4,468
Greene	6,991	2,102	749	1,459	2,681	2,742	2,421	127	3,131	1,982
Hamilton	7,815	1,892	867	1,890	3,166	2,168	4,796	407	13,466	8,524
Hancock	4,717	1,013	450	1,106	2,148	1,398	2,478	182	4,861	3,077
Harrison	5,745	1,455	776	1,706	1,808	1,738	2,122	122	3,120	1,975
Hendricks	5,562	1,192	517	1,442	2,411	1,828	3,952	317	8,293	5,250
Henry	11,956	3,195	1,449	2,948	4,364	1,847	3,159	183	4,719	2,986
Howard	20,607	6,672	2,933	5,060	5,942	2,390	4,905	357	8,020	5,076
Huntington	4,304	1,152	428	1,010	1,714	1,379	1,783	127	3,524	2,231
Jackson	7,805	2,524	739	1,589	2,953	1,258	2,653	128	3,868	2,449
Jasper	4,190	914	544	1,273	1,459	1,954	1,030	89	2,671	1,691
Jay	4,438	1,205	404	1,019	1,810	864	1,092	71	2,098	1,327
Jefferson	7,555	2,173	941	1,687	2,754	1,882	1,872	109	2,950	1,867
Jennings	5,677	1,702	613	1,297	2,065	534	1,631	86	2,506	1,586
Johnson	11,194	2,789	1,271	3,163	3,971	2,402	4,740	333	9,738	6,163
Knox	11,982	3,389	1,664	2,764	4,165	1,929	3,370	149	3,848	2,436
Kosciusko	7,404	1,669	649	1,531	3,555	3,211	2,620	230	6,625	4,194
Lagrange	3,406	610	165	409	2,222	1,438	886	72	3,030	1,918
Lake	197,117	47,004	39,221	60,554	50,338	26,927	22,199	1,727	46,212	29,252
Laporte	22,957	5,787	3,574	6,854	6,742	5,188	4,881	465	10,567	6,688
Lawrence	9,146	3,195	814	1,977	3,160	2,859	3,443	156	4,318	2,733
Madison	35,409	10,579	5,286	9,033	10,511	4,971	7,513	514	12,715	8,048
Marion	260,822	68,359	44,750	80,780	66,933	30,759	53,284	3,027	78,112	49,452
Marshall	5,299	1,009	500	1,262	2,528	1,442	2,119	156	4,297	2,720
Martin	2,667	849	282	607	929	568	1,076	NA	995	630
Miami	8,081	2,118	1,071	2,149	2,743	1,766	2,684	162	3,115	1,972
Monroe	17,449	4,982	1,990	4,352	6,125	3,939	5,473	330	11,030	6,982
Montgomery	5,747	1,835	678	1,445	1,789	1,166	1,447	123	3,455	2,187
Morgan	9,729	2,233	1,011	2,830	3,655	1,764	3,174	232	5,946	3,764
Newton	2,492	463	369	696	964	806	752	50	1,381	873
Noble	4,726	1,277	375	861	2,213	1,312	1,653	134	3,913	2,478
Ohio	836	176	80	154	426	190	411	NA	516	327
Orange	5,225	1,637	468	1,182	1,938	1,637	1,631	69	1,820	1,152
Owen	4,023	806	564	1,205	1,448	1,088	1,245	66	1,882	1,192
Parke	3,584	1,049	379	769	1,387	659	1,110	59	1,540	975
Perry	3,736	1,104	372	761	1,499	1,350	1,397	74	1,831	1,159
Pike	3,177	889	416	859	1,013	690	1,108	NA	1,207	764
Porter	14,475	3,753	1,883	4,048	4,791	7,269	5,245	532	13,451	8,514
Posey	5,124	1,281	726	1,258	1,859	1,049	1,693	102	2,536	1,606
Pulaski	2,536	592	282	640	1,022	413	749	NA	1,242	785
Putnam	4,357	1,289	384	987	1,697	1,056	1,694	119	3,154	1,996
Randolph	6,750	1,425	975	1,946	2,404	1,066	1,232	98	2,621	1,659
Ripley	4,783	1,310	508	1,093	1,872	1,433	1,746	89	2,569	1,626
Rush	3,367	897	340	637	1,493	1,047	915	59	1,768	1,119
St. Joseph	61,936	15,545	11,227	18,248	16,916	8,624	12,257	873	24,703	15,637
Scott	8,036	2,777	1,085	1,937	2,237	954	1,461	65	2,161	1,368
Shelby	6,293	1,520	784	1,611	2,378	1,824	2,222	148	4,100	2,594
Spencer	3,351	806	390	803	1,352	1,066	1,195	74	1,950	1,235
Starke	5,832	1,710	629	1,487	2,006	1,125	1,112	79	2,166	1,371
Steuben	4,007	954	383	1,108	1,562	940	1,433	100	2,878	1,822
Sullivan	4,965	1,395	607	1,382	1,581	1,596	1,612	66	1,903	1,205
Switzerland	2,070	528	234	505	803	701	953	NA	787	498
Tippecanoe	18,687	4,827	2,440	5,281	6,139	2,759	9,757	409	12,949	8,196
Tipton	2,062	511	218	558	775	736	1,081	61	1,577	998
Union	1,443	348	166	327	602	327	526	NA	699	442
Vanderburgh	49,899	14,516	7,859	14,198	13,326	8,729	12,807	593	16,092	10,186
Vermillion	3,605	956	437	803	1,409	939	1,201	64	1,611	1,020
Vigo	28,085	9,649	3,455	6,704	8,277	5,114	7,802	408	10,206	6,461
Wabash	5,347	1,526	585	1,132	2,104	661	1,999	112	3,341	2,115
Warren	1,365	362	113	249	641	248	454	NA	804	509
Warrick	6,108	1,597	633	1,537	2,341	1,871	2,727	173	4,728	2,993
Washington	6,414	1,989	731	1,470	2,224	1,558	1,844	87	2,498	1,581
Wayne	23,548	6,654	3,481	6,509	6,904	3,281	5,324	261	6,970	4,412
Wells	2,411	562	277	602	970	547	1,010	84	2,538	1,606
White	3,483	813	405	1,020	1,245	766	1,318	81	2,346	1,485
Whitley	2,334	485	235	581	1,033	1,195	1,271	108	2,817	1,783

Footnote: [1] Includes items not shown separately.
Source: U.S. Bureau of Economic Analysis
EDIN table(s): PITP

Non-Farm Wage and Salary Employment by Industry
Indiana - 1995

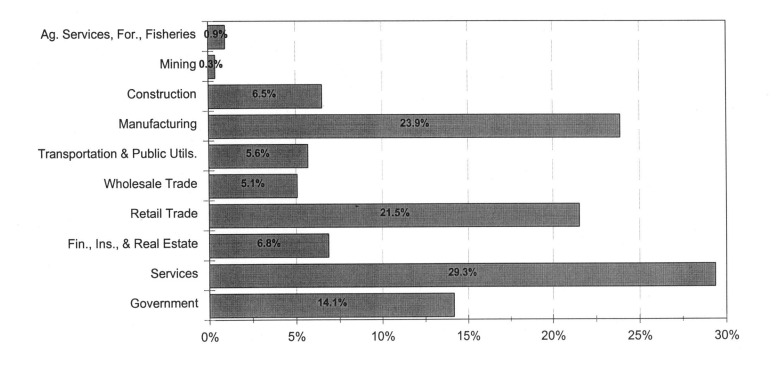

Percent Change in Non-Farm Wage and Salary Employment by Industry
Indiana - 1985 to 1995

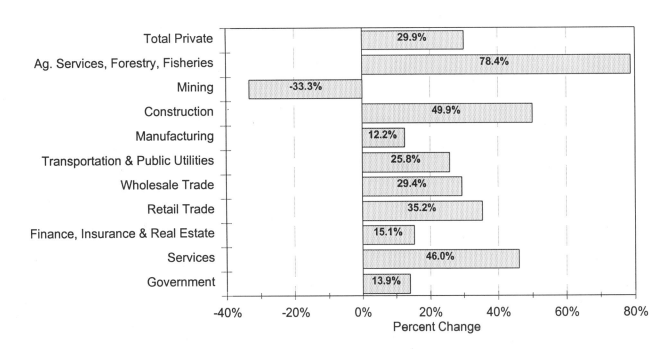

Non-Farm Wage and Salary Employment by Industry: EDIN Table EMPT.
Percent Change in Non-Farm Wage and Salary Employment by Industry: EDIN Table EMPT.

Employment and Earnings
2.37 Non-farm Wage and Salary Employment by Industry 1995

	Total Private	Ag. Services, Forestry, Fisheries	Mining	Construction	Manufacturing	Transport. & Public Utilities	Wholesale Trade	Retail Trade	Services	Finance, Insurance & Real Estate	Government
Indiana	**2,916,516**	**27,692**	**10,184**	**188,740**	**696,635**	**164,362**	**147,336**	**626,545**	**855,753**	**199,269**	**411,955**
Adams	16,328	203	NA	1,283	6,884	411	NA	3,412	2,855	705	1,897
Allen	201,567	1,716	244	12,468	41,259	12,837	13,873	39,628	62,164	17,378	17,999
Bartholomew	43,313	224	56	2,589	17,547	1,742	1,191	7,896	9,319	2,749	5,333
Benton	3,028	63	0	168	616	186	NA	584	NA	245	615
Blackford	4,584	54	11	204	1,887	156	136	896	1,010	230	826
Boone	15,788	NA	NA	2,021	1,977	638	1,001	3,616	4,806	1,232	2,080
Brown	3,836	70	NA	481	139	131	43	1,291	1,465	213	768
Carroll	6,280	NA	NA	535	2,086	209	368	1,075	1,416	420	859
Cass	15,347	NA	NA	938	4,918	608	819	3,597	3,363	732	3,527
Clark	43,440	320	129	3,682	7,640	4,473	1,904	11,961	11,416	1,915	6,759
Clay	8,920	96	NA	NA	2,652	739	204	2,102	1,985	423	1,325
Clinton	12,853	183	NA	818	5,118	368	417	2,475	2,892	555	1,891
Crawford	2,026	33	NA	208	187	188	13	570	NA	120	507
Daviess	11,131	158	441	1,224	2,073	828	651	2,386	2,867	503	1,614
Dearborn	12,709	162	NA	1,470	2,321	1,034	420	3,059	3,372	868	2,157
Decatur	12,960	NA	NA	544	5,298	562	433	2,409	2,893	535	1,321
Dekalb	21,270	203	61	1,039	10,438	612	456	3,281	4,222	958	1,833
Delaware	59,448	NA	NA	3,505	11,384	6,412	1,811	14,056	18,625	2,980	10,698
Dubois	29,023	206	190	1,422	12,777	1,112	1,627	4,944	5,491	1,254	2,016
Elkhart	126,139	771	91	5,913	60,503	4,749	6,435	18,809	24,106	4,762	7,144
Fayette	11,919	75	NA	412	5,101	254	281	2,321	3,025	441	1,560
Floyd	27,995	411	21	2,542	7,452	675	1,352	5,632	7,852	2,058	5,134
Fountain	5,598	122	NA	294	1,786	216	211	1,361	1,266	339	952
Franklin	4,320	72	11	507	442	367	160	1,130	1,389	242	826
Fulton	8,783	209	12	569	3,254	369	241	1,877	1,849	403	1,249
Gibson	11,940	182	291	539	2,480	1,067	413	3,111	3,257	600	1,340
Grant	33,915	NA	NA	1,342	10,407	1,229	842	7,586	10,446	1,717	4,734
Greene	9,302	120	681	910	1,553	460	287	2,318	2,475	498	1,903
Hamilton	76,117	1,493	414	6,106	9,509	3,394	5,951	15,661	21,188	12,401	6,757
Hancock	16,486	NA	NA	2,015	3,167	615	716	3,992	4,509	1,138	2,890
Harrison	9,785	207	78	774	2,226	584	361	2,616	2,488	451	1,651
Hendricks	27,306	NA	NA	3,164	1,381	3,116	955	7,334	8,986	1,882	5,457
Henry	15,266	232	16	1,051	3,653	573	439	4,272	4,126	904	3,568
Howard	50,355	377	103	2,014	20,286	1,418	1,084	11,030	11,843	2,200	5,928
Huntington	18,810	153	67	931	7,761	503	624	3,607	4,407	757	2,101
Jackson	20,880	NA	NA	1,216	6,577	928	1,245	5,751	3,956	1,013	2,446
Jasper	10,811	198	23	1,105	1,406	1,731	376	2,819	2,533	620	1,716
Jay	8,614	NA	NA	393	3,538	259	202	1,569	2,211	309	1,192
Jefferson	13,853	135	NA	NA	4,274	NA	245	3,272	3,901	585	2,484
Jennings	7,759	NA	NA	835	2,134	278	196	1,945	1,916	337	2,275
Johnson	41,193	NA	NA	3,909	6,348	1,188	1,138	13,504	11,844	2,773	5,135
Knox	17,044	278	451	835	2,319	1,258	1,082	4,552	5,034	1,235	5,254
Kosciusko	37,859	NA	NA	1,764	16,142	1,323	1,092	6,563	8,930	1,647	2,839
Lagrange	15,139	230	NA	840	7,145	406	608	2,534	2,885	484	1,339
Lake	205,705	1,527	149	15,392	40,925	13,663	9,287	45,922	66,513	12,327	27,747
Laporte	48,722	657	82	2,847	12,701	2,462	2,330	11,282	13,873	2,488	7,904
Lawrence	18,190	135	120	1,121	5,858	641	533	4,471	4,508	803	2,624
Madison	54,461	541	82	2,938	14,255	1,827	1,497	13,161	17,630	2,530	7,180
Marion	574,729	3,252	775	33,314	83,700	41,037	43,106	115,354	197,113	57,078	83,618
Marshall	22,650	200	NA	1,041	9,082	980	733	4,071	5,478	1,057	2,218
Martin	3,446	54	NA	NA	743	550	100	724	780	164	4,815
Miami	10,141	NA	NA	741	2,940	550	373	2,376	2,401	580	2,754
Monroe	53,550	586	255	3,820	10,060	2,048	1,641	14,692	16,568	3,880	18,457
Montgomery	20,682	279	NA	767	8,340	726	477	4,101	5,147	836	2,077
Morgan	16,477	313	110	1,959	2,609	874	435	4,524	4,677	976	2,773
Newton	4,274	78	33	370	1,453	165	272	712	926	265	757
Noble	20,919	204	27	1,065	11,231	565	493	2,916	3,742	676	2,605
Ohio	669	33	0	86	14	23	11	198	280	24	258
Orange	7,817	179	NA	734	2,880	NA	116	1,190	1,986	309	1,062
Owen	4,492	104	11	463	1,071	373	98	999	1,055	318	891
Parke	3,432	69	NA	230	597	250	97	816	1,101	269	1,111
Perry	5,783	NA	NA	409	1,669	231	119	1,546	1,338	355	1,522
Pike	3,112	29	392	134	230	772	85	481	815	174	698
Porter	57,816	671	34	5,161	12,257	3,855	2,723	12,572	17,355	3,188	8,490
Posey	9,931	140	268	1,151	3,118	800	426	1,394	2,258	376	1,286
Pulaski	4,684	86	38	220	1,466	235	380	936	1,056	267	1,013
Putnam	12,853	144	51	767	2,780	509	246	3,693	4,004	659	2,603
Randolph	9,095	122	18	504	3,562	452	369	1,787	1,907	374	1,532
Ripley	12,894	NA	NA	748	5,045	752	320	2,231	2,929	659	1,393
Rush	6,107	NA	NA	468	1,634	333	302	1,287	1,675	318	1,222
St. Joseph	140,314	1,069	71	8,520	23,904	6,394	8,783	29,859	52,037	9,677	14,182
Scott	7,068	NA	NA	401	2,435	224	118	1,903	1,617	287	1,285
Shelby	17,863	181	133	1,509	6,484	544	888	3,075	4,180	869	2,268
Spencer	8,126	93	281	321	1,511	1,572	444	1,132	2,503	269	956
Starke	4,992	95	NA	282	1,295	279	183	1,348	1,282	225	1,302
Steuben	18,931	127	NA	837	8,047	940	573	4,095	3,705	603	1,589
Sullivan	5,614	74	273	312	644	669	248	1,416	1,601	377	1,841
Switzerland	1,882	25	NA	151	708	NA	39	210	512	94	446
Tippecanoe	69,064	NA	NA	4,246	16,947	2,302	1,849	16,225	21,502	5,042	20,027
Tipton	4,358	168	NA	363	813	208	281	1,145	1,099	278	1,139
Union	1,557	49	NA	94	102	125	48	478	469	189	435
Vanderburgh	113,901	619	886	7,931	19,376	5,788	7,210	25,335	38,754	8,002	9,867
Vermillion	5,243	43	23	383	1,413	441	91	1,332	1,326	191	1,012
Vigo	56,749	347	128	4,006	8,931	2,796	2,363	16,962	18,372	2,844	9,325
Wabash	16,970	204	76	994	5,947	608	615	3,266	4,383	877	2,139
Warren	2,026	NA	NA	129	600	87	159	345	557	86	397
Warrick	15,476	206	729	1,403	3,368	813	628	2,985	4,431	913	1,824
Washington	7,307	93	17	483	2,780	347	148	1,450	1,638	351	1,390
Wayne	38,450	227	80	1,950	9,323	2,500	1,842	8,419	12,249	1,860	5,067
Wells	11,650	NA	NA	601	3,503	469	450	2,747	3,179	511	1,604
White	12,200	172	14	555	4,860	700	639	2,410	2,410	440	1,516
Whitley	13,129	148	NA	767	5,379	478	395	2,568	2,868	523	1,835

2.38 Percent Change in Non-farm Wage and Salary Employment by Industry 1985 to 1995

	Total Private	Ag. Services, Forestry, Fisheries	Mining	Construction	Manufacturing	Transport. & Public Utilities	Wholesale Trade	Retail Trade	Services	Finance, Insurance & Real Estate	Government
Indiana	**29.9**	**78.4**	**-33.3**	**49.9**	**12.2**	**25.8**	**29.4**	**35.2**	**46.0**	**15.1**	**13.9**
Adams	27.8	47.1	NA	69.7	15.0	2.8	NA	51.2	34.0	25.9	38.1
Allen	29.3	100.9	-29.3	43.8	14.0	11.8	29.1	31.1	49.9	9.4	13.8
Bartholomew	34.4	79.2	9.8	72.5	21.8	20.9	27.2	34.8	55.1	43.7	23.7
Benton	21.9	16.7	NA	-8.7	100.7	-16.6	NA	27.2	NA	-8.2	0.0
Blackford	-11.0	58.8	NA	63.2	-23.3	19.1	-32.0	-2.6	1.5	-18.4	5.2
Boone	31.8	NA	NA	95.5	7.3	-2.1	68.5	36.9	33.2	-3.2	28.1
Brown	33.3	112.1	NA	70.0	-13.7	24.8	34.4	41.9	28.7	2.4	44.4
Carroll	32.8	NA	NA	50.3	80.8	-8.7	-38.6	25.4	31.7	16.7	9.8
Cass	9.3	NA	NA	51.0	-0.8	-22.0	2.8	19.3	20.0	-16.4	15.6
Clark	40.4	201.9	4.0	109.8	-2.4	69.0	69.7	43.3	58.2	6.8	-0.4
Clay	44.6	84.6	NA	NA	102.9	118.0	9.7	29.7	31.2	2.9	11.8
Clinton	33.5	144.0	NA	13.3	59.6	-6.1	-1.9	20.1	40.1	-15.7	20.3
Crawford	10.9	65.0	NA	36.8	-15.8	40.3	-23.5	18.8	NA	-16.7	27.4
Daviess	35.0	41.1	-26.1	91.3	75.1	12.3	42.5	30.7	29.8	3.5	15.3
Dearborn	30.4	102.5	NA	85.6	-17.1	19.3	58.5	55.4	54.7	11.1	25.9
Decatur	66.8	NA	NA	68.9	85.1	7.7	24.4	61.1	90.3	3.5	10.1
Dekalb	43.2	118.3	190.5	91.7	43.8	20.2	-37.8	48.2	50.1	41.9	19.7
Delaware	29.8	NA	NA	59.0	1.3	147.3	-3.4	25.0	40.0	2.4	8.8
Dubois	40.4	40.1	-14.8	20.1	39.6	42.2	62.9	48.3	49.6	6.3	28.0
Elkhart	33.8	69.5	56.9	72.7	26.0	23.6	29.1	41.2	49.1	20.2	23.3
Fayette	8.3	102.7	NA	12.3	-4.1	-8.6	5.2	34.7	25.2	-24.5	24.8
Floyd	49.0	129.6	5.0	70.3	62.6	-6.4	107.0	29.6	57.9	13.0	27.9
Fountain	18.5	16.2	NA	40.7	22.7	-8.1	13.4	23.2	20.6	-7.1	6.0
Franklin	45.3	105.7	-15.4	106.9	-32.3	69.9	24.0	65.9	87.2	-6.9	19.5
Fulton	24.8	95.3	-33.3	53.4	11.8	23.4	7.6	51.6	30.8	-12.0	28.1
Gibson	8.9	64.0	-42.0	15.9	-9.9	-8.3	18.0	33.7	22.9	-6.4	5.3
Grant	7.5	NA	NA	21.3	-16.0	-2.6	13.6	22.2	33.1	3.6	1.7
Greene	26.7	103.4	35.4	60.2	30.5	-29.6	-1.0	34.8	34.6	-4.2	24.1
Hamilton	117.0	210.4	81.6	97.3	73.4	27.6	124.5	127.5	125.1	196.2	74.7
Hancock	53.6	NA	NA	102.5	46.6	5.3	97.2	66.4	49.5	7.0	26.6
Harrison	52.0	35.3	-13.3	78.3	77.7	29.8	-3.0	90.8	38.2	-12.4	30.2
Hendricks	61.5	NA	NA	130.1	8.1	NA	64.9	76.8	NA	23.2	49.6
Henry	17.1	47.8	-11.1	44.8	-4.1	5.5	20.9	34.2	25.7	-4.5	4.0
Howard	19.2	76.2	77.6	28.9	-0.2	-8.5	27.1	32.7	60.4	11.4	25.5
Huntington	40.3	84.3	-21.2	69.0	40.3	6.6	52.9	35.5	54.4	-0.4	19.9
Jackson	54.4	NA	NA	72.5	45.7	22.8	38.6	85.3	49.2	28.1	25.1
Jasper	28.6	115.2	-8.0	11.5	20.3	38.6	-8.7	56.0	24.1	-0.2	31.2
Jay	23.0	NA	NA	45.0	17.2	-1.1	-2.9	14.9	61.3	-10.4	-1.2
Jefferson	40.9	175.5	NA	NA	45.0	NA	-1.2	53.8	NA	-3.0	-4.2
Jennings	63.3	NA	NA	NA	58.7	-2.1	237.9	88.1	51.2	0.3	11.2
Johnson	55.8	NA	NA	113.5	34.7	44.5	78.6	69.1	55.1	12.3	33.3
Knox	15.6	104.4	-54.5	23.2	17.7	38.2	-9.6	24.5	26.5	0.7	24.2
Kosciusko	38.3	NA	NA	38.6	39.1	2.3	48.8	42.1	51.9	-2.0	24.6
Lagrange	71.7	96.6	NA	88.3	96.9	0.5	-16.5	73.4	84.2	8.8	6.2
Lake	14.5	87.1	140.3	23.2	-17.0	11.5	37.8	19.3	37.2	11.2	6.3
Laporte	23.4	73.4	51.9	47.3	0.5	9.2	90.7	37.0	34.3	2.2	20.5
Lawrence	42.8	32.4	-14.3	46.0	38.4	-3.0	72.5	68.7	44.6	5.7	20.5
Madison	6.1	40.5	34.4	41.4	-26.3	-0.9	17.5	23.4	36.8	-10.3	15.2
Marion	29.0	59.8	-44.9	38.7	-5.0	45.1	29.2	28.9	51.4	17.6	6.6
Marshall	41.6	47.1	NA	37.7	43.5	4.1	40.4	41.2	61.5	4.3	25.5
Martin	26.0	NA	NA	NA	11.4	48.6	7.5	19.1	41.3	-5.2	-11.0
Miami	9.3	NA	NA	47.3	5.8	-16.5	3.6	13.7	16.6	-18.3	-51.0
Monroe	36.5	85.4	-26.1	61.9	27.4	7.4	18.1	36.7	47.0	28.8	17.4
Montgomery	40.1	244.4	NA	29.3	51.3	2.1	-36.1	48.0	47.9	-0.2	23.0
Morgan	40.6	108.7	23.6	109.5	15.0	39.4	69.3	48.5	38.9	-0.3	23.6
Newton	9.2	NA	NA	50.4	35.8	1.9	8.8	1.1	-15.8	-5.4	-2.6
Noble	47.6	119.4	170.0	49.0	57.1	32.6	-17.7	34.7	65.2	-9.7	48.9
Ohio	-13.9	3.1	NA	-3.4	-54.8	-58.2	-64.5	-3.4	2.2	-60.0	25.9
Orange	16.5	193.4	NA	51.0	17.4	NA	-14.7	14.8	13.6	-8.6	11.8
Owen	61.5	65.1	-81.0	97.0	153.2	48.6	127.9	50.5	30.4	35.3	38.8
Parke	10.5	-11.5	NA	-5.3	27.8	-9.1	-25.4	14.0	14.9	15.9	35.3
Perry	3.9	NA	NA	33.2	-19.1	7.4	50.6	30.7	17.3	-9.7	30.5
Pike	-22.2	31.8	-67.1	NA	62.0	NA	23.2	-9.4	10.7	-7.9	20.3
Porter	42.0	161.1	-49.3	116.3	5.9	70.2	130.6	44.2	52.0	12.2	26.6
Posey	9.7	122.2	-26.4	-19.2	15.6	49.3	-2.7	4.9	33.3	-25.4	15.5
Pulaski	26.5	30.3	15.2	49.7	35.6	9.8	1.6	36.8	32.2	-12.5	17.7
Putnam	44.4	8.3	-42.0	56.2	162.0	-3.4	-82.0	117.2	37.1	7.0	31.1
Randolph	-12.0	-3.2	-61.7	8.2	-25.8	-13.4	-8.4	12.8	1.0	-24.3	9.1
Ripley	39.2	NA	NA	91.8	35.9	24.1	38.5	43.8	35.4	38.7	33.0
Rush	30.7	NA	NA	58.1	25.9	22.9	-4.7	48.3	46.4	-16.5	4.3
St. Joseph	25.9	68.6	-20.2	49.7	-4.2	23.9	28.3	28.2	42.7	16.0	18.3
Scott	40.7	NA	NA	NA	54.4	-10.0	-19.7	69.2	36.9	-16.8	18.8
Shelby	31.9	54.7	77.3	73.6	30.7	-1.6	57.2	24.3	37.2	-1.3	21.5
Spencer	29.8	190.6	-44.5	8.4	35.6	100.3	66.3	12.5	29.6	-17.0	20.7
Starke	22.3	111.1	NA	32.4	67.7	3.3	12.3	16.3	12.0	-27.4	17.4
Steuben	69.9	69.3	NA	69.1	99.7	2.8	113.8	75.1	62.6	-13.9	37.7
Sullivan	10.5	32.1	-33.9	-33.8	7.3	-13.3	7.8	43.3	44.0	-14.1	74.5
Switzerland	40.9	38.9	NA	86.4	21.4	NA	95.0	19.3	102.4	-1.1	37.2
Tippecanoe	38.3	NA	NA	74.1	46.4	13.9	9.9	32.4	44.0	11.6	16.4
Tipton	16.9	63.1	NA	41.8	31.8	12.4	4.1	22.7	6.4	-15.2	8.4
Union	18.8	40.0	NA	-2.1	18.6	28.9	9.1	27.5	13.3	21.2	14.2
Vanderburgh	22.3	68.7	-46.8	27.4	-1.9	14.0	27.1	26.3	37.7	29.1	20.7
Vermillion	7.7	-48.8	-94.2	64.4	-10.9	21.2	-21.6	51.0	38.0	-23.3	13.5
Vigo	26.8	129.8	-04.0	76.2	-5.4	8.1	3.9	42.6	38.8	12.5	0.9
Wabash	18.2	75.9	111.1	49.9	0.8	7.8	13.5	32.6	31.6	17.9	15.1
Warren	7.3	NA	NA	33.0	21.0	-13.9	65.6	-0.6	0.2	-30.1	2.1
Warrick	7.4	68.9	-52.3	30.9	-19.5	3.2	45.7	32.5	43.1	-2.2	25.3
Washington	29.4	63.2	-58.5	32.3	37.6	16.4	32.1	22.2	39.8	-10.9	22.4
Wayne	24.5	55.5	-2.4	53.1	-6.9	124.0	57.0	20.4	55.7	-15.8	9.6
Wells	29.5	NA	NA	37.8	35.7	40.4	-39.4	61.4	25.7	-4.7	26.9
White	47.3	97.7	-6.7	30.0	101.1	-3.0	61.8	37.2	36.4	-36.7	18.1
Whitley	42.0	124.2	NA	35.0	39.6	41.4	80.4	35.7	75.1	-20.9	36.1

Source: U.S. Bureau of Economic Analysis
EDIN table(s): EMPT

2.39 Annual Average Employment and Unemployment 1994 to 1996

	Labor Force			Persons Employed			Persons Unemployed			Unemployment Rate	
	1994	1996	Percent Change	1994	1996	Percent Change	1994	1996	Percent Change	1994	1996
Indiana	3,048,900	3,072,000	0.8	2,898,400	2,945,300	1.6	150,500	126,700	-15.8	4.9	4.1
Adams	16,010	16,400	2.4	15,390	15,740	2.3	620	660	6.5	3.9	4.0
Allen	171,840	173,660	1.1	164,290	167,520	2.0	7,550	6,140	-18.7	4.4	3.5
Bartholomew	38,750	39,530	2.0	37,410	38,410	2.7	1,340	1,120	-16.4	3.5	2.8
Benton	5,280	5,375	1.8	4,970	5,145	3.5	310	230	-25.8	5.8	4.2
Blackford	6,385	6,350	-0.5	5,930	5,995	1.1	455	355	-22.0	7.1	5.6
Boone	22,700	23,320	2.7	21,990	22,780	3.6	710	540	-23.9	3.1	2.3
Brown	8,325	8,475	1.8	8,090	8,290	2.5	235	185	-21.3	2.8	2.2
Carroll	11,640	12,000	3.1	11,150	11,670	4.7	490	330	-32.7	4.2	2.8
Cass	18,820	19,600	4.1	17,120	18,500	8.1	1,700	1,100	-35.3	9.0	5.6
Clark	49,810	50,410	1.2	47,170	48,290	2.4	2,640	2,120	-19.7	5.3	4.2
Clay	12,640	12,800	1.3	11,890	12,020	1.1	750	780	4.0	6.0	6.1
Clinton	15,540	15,960	2.7	14,950	15,430	3.2	590	530	-10.2	3.8	3.3
Crawford	4,790	4,620	-3.5	4,275	4,165	-2.6	515	455	-11.7	10.8	9.9
Daviess	13,260	13,500	1.8	12,670	12,980	2.4	590	520	-11.9	4.4	3.9
Dearborn	21,440	22,170	3.4	20,070	21,010	4.7	1,370	1,160	-15.3	6.4	5.2
Decatur	15,140	14,930	-1.4	14,550	14,480	-0.5	590	450	-23.7	3.9	3.0
Dekalb	20,870	21,200	1.6	19,910	20,450	2.7	960	750	-21.9	4.6	3.5
Delaware	65,220	62,790	-3.7	61,520	59,880	-2.7	3,700	2,910	-21.4	5.7	4.6
Dubois	21,890	22,350	2.1	21,190	21,710	2.5	700	640	-8.6	3.2	2.8
Elkhart	93,280	94,340	1.1	90,340	90,640	0.3	2,940	3,700	25.9	3.2	3.9
Fayette	12,830	11,890	-7.3	11,600	11,110	-4.2	1,230	780	-36.6	9.6	6.6
Floyd	36,440	37,240	2.2	34,860	35,840	2.8	1,580	1,400	-11.4	4.3	3.7
Fountain	8,800	8,505	-3.4	8,195	8,070	-1.5	605	435	-28.1	6.9	5.1
Franklin	10,460	10,800	3.3	9,760	10,300	5.5	700	500	-28.6	6.7	4.7
Fulton	10,100	10,240	1.4	9,610	9,810	2.1	490	430	-12.2	4.9	4.2
Gibson	16,350	15,730	-3.8	15,120	14,920	-1.3	1,230	810	-34.1	7.5	5.2
Grant	36,940	35,680	-3.4	34,070	33,620	-1.3	2,870	2,060	-28.2	7.8	5.8
Greene	15,570	15,270	-1.9	14,100	14,060	-0.3	1,470	1,210	-17.7	9.4	7.9
Hamilton	76,540	80,940	5.7	74,830	79,570	6.3	1,710	1,370	-19.9	2.2	1.7
Hancock	27,140	28,190	3.9	26,240	27,390	4.4	900	800	-11.1	3.3	2.8
Harrison	16,700	17,260	3.4	15,970	16,520	3.4	730	740	1.4	4.4	4.3
Hendricks	46,220	48,040	3.9	45,050	47,060	4.5	1,170	980	-16.2	2.5	2.0
Henry	25,220	25,150	-0.3	23,490	23,860	1.6	1,730	1,290	-25.4	6.9	5.1
Howard	42,890	43,320	1.0	40,450	41,730	3.2	2,440	1,590	-34.8	5.7	3.7
Huntington	20,210	20,430	1.1	19,150	19,640	2.6	1,060	790	-25.5	5.3	3.9
Jackson	20,830	20,980	0.7	19,930	20,130	1.0	900	850	-5.6	4.3	4.0
Jasper	13,920	14,380	3.3	13,130	13,560	3.3	790	820	3.8	5.6	5.7
Jay	11,460	12,040	5.1	10,790	11,450	6.1	670	590	-11.9	5.9	4.9
Jefferson	14,920	14,820	-0.7	14,190	14,030	-1.1	730	790	8.2	4.9	5.3
Jennings	13,580	14,050	3.5	13,130	13,590	3.5	450	460	2.2	3.3	3.3
Johnson	55,350	57,300	3.5	53,550	55,890	4.4	1,800	1,410	-21.7	3.3	2.5
Knox	20,350	21,260	4.5	19,410	20,260	4.4	940	1,000	6.4	4.6	4.7
Kosciusko	36,420	39,130	7.4	35,240	37,840	7.4	1,180	1,290	9.3	3.2	3.3
Lagrange	16,440	16,950	3.1	15,830	16,260	2.7	610	690	13.1	3.7	4.1
Lake	228,660	227,180	-0.6	212,420	214,370	0.9	16,240	12,810	-21.1	7.1	5.6
Laporte	54,490	54,030	-0.8	51,730	51,290	-0.9	2,760	2,740	-0.7	5.1	5.1
Lawrence	23,840	24,310	2.0	22,070	22,590	2.4	1,770	1,720	-2.8	7.4	7.1
Madison	66,280	66,740	0.7	62,810	63,780	1.5	3,470	2,960	-14.7	5.2	4.4
Marion	451,190	453,630	0.5	430,330	437,270	1.6	20,860	16,360	-21.6	4.6	3.6
Marshall	26,040	26,170	0.5	25,160	25,220	0.2	880	950	8.0	3.4	3.6
Martin	5,190	5,260	1.3	4,905	4,955	1.0	285	305	7.0	5.5	5.8
Miami	16,550	14,930	-9.8	15,510	14,030	-9.5	1,040	900	-13.5	6.3	6.1
Monroe	60,570	60,880	0.5	58,200	59,210	1.7	2,370	1,670	-29.5	3.9	2.7
Montgomery	20,520	19,670	-4.1	19,950	19,080	-4.4	570	590	3.5	2.8	3.0
Morgan	32,710	33,480	2.4	31,300	32,360	3.4	1,410	1,120	-20.6	4.3	3.4
Newton	6,760	6,420	-5.0	6,380	6,060	-5.0	380	360	-5.3	5.6	5.6
Noble	23,800	24,810	4.2	22,950	23,880	4.1	850	930	9.4	3.6	3.8
Ohio	2,665	2,665	0.0	2,495	2,525	1.2	170	140	-17.6	6.4	5.3
Orange	9,595	9,005	-6.1	8,720	8,140	-6.7	875	865	-1.1	9.1	9.6
Owen	9,860	10,420	5.7	9,245	9,930	7.4	615	490	-20.3	6.2	4.7
Parke	7,895	7,700	-2.5	7,420	7,300	-1.6	475	400	-15.8	6.0	5.2
Perry	9,600	9,135	-4.8	8,735	8,445	-3.3	865	690	-20.2	9.0	7.6
Pike	6,200	6,210	0.2	5,815	5,880	1.1	385	330	-14.3	6.2	5.3
Porter	71,420	72,520	1.5	67,990	69,760	2.6	3,430	2,760	-19.5	4.8	3.8
Posey	13,830	13,850	0.1	13,250	13,340	0.7	580	510	-12.1	4.2	3.7
Pulaski	6,195	6,175	-0.3	5,825	5,825	0.0	370	350	-5.4	6.0	5.6
Putnam	16,930	16,670	-1.5	16,360	16,060	-1.8	570	610	7.0	3.4	3.7
Randolph	12,270	12,700	3.5	11,140	11,670	4.8	1,130	1,030	-8.8	9.2	8.1
Ripley	13,360	13,670	2.3	12,640	13,060	3.3	720	610	-15.3	5.4	4.4
Rush	9,765	10,240	4.9	9,300	9,850	5.9	465	390	-16.1	4.8	3.8
St. Joseph	134,240	135,840	1.2	128,330	130,440	1.6	5,910	5,400	-8.6	4.4	4.0
Scott	10,330	10,650	3.1	9,820	10,110	3.0	510	540	5.9	4.9	5.1
Shelby	22,770	23,230	2.0	21,730	22,370	2.9	1,040	860	-17.3	4.6	3.7
Spencer	10,860	11,000	1.8	10,170	10,520	3.4	690	540	-21.7	6.4	4.9
Starke	11,210	11,260	0.4	10,560	10,580	0.2	650	680	4.6	5.8	6.0
Steuben	16,810	17,050	1.4	16,160	16,420	1.6	650	630	-3.1	3.8	3.7
Sullivan	10,260	10,050	-2.0	9,330	9,220	-1.2	930	830	-10.8	9.1	8.2
Switzerland	4,185	3,965	-5.3	3,950	3,685	-6.7	235	280	19.1	5.6	7.1
Tippecanoe	70,040	71,910	2.7	67,660	69,930	3.4	2,380	1,980	-16.8	3.4	2.7
Tipton	8,740	8,940	2.3	8,345	8,635	3.5	395	305	-22.8	4.5	3.4
Union	3,935	3,920	-0.4	3,700	3,735	0.9	235	185	-21.3	5.9	4.7
Vanderburgh	91,240	90,380	-0.9	86,560	86,670	0.1	4,680	3,710	-20.7	5.1	4.1
Vermillion	8,265	8,115	-1.8	7,555	7,505	-0.7	710	610	-14.1	8.6	7.5
Vigo	54,020	53,330	-1.3	50,450	49,920	-1.1	3,570	3,410	-4.5	6.6	6.4
Wabash	18,490	17,660	-4.5	17,680	16,920	-4.3	810	740	-8.6	4.4	4.2
Warren	3,970	3,930	-1.0	3,780	3,790	0.3	190	140	-26.3	4.8	3.5
Warrick	27,130	27,250	0.4	25,760	26,220	1.8	1,370	1,030	-24.8	5.0	3.8
Washington	11,430	11,720	2.5	10,720	10,910	1.8	710	810	14.1	6.2	6.9
Wayne	39,270	38,710	-1.4	36,670	36,930	0.7	2,600	1,780	-31.5	6.6	4.6
Wells	14,390	14,670	1.9	13,830	14,180	2.5	560	490	-12.5	3.9	3.3
White	16,080	14,490	-9.9	15,220	13,540	-11.0	860	950	10.5	5.3	6.5
Whitley	15,820	16,140	2.0	15,220	15,650	2.8	600	490	-18.3	3.8	3.0

Source: Indiana Department of Workforce Development
EDIN table(s): LFAA

Manufacturing as a Percent of Total Earnings
1995

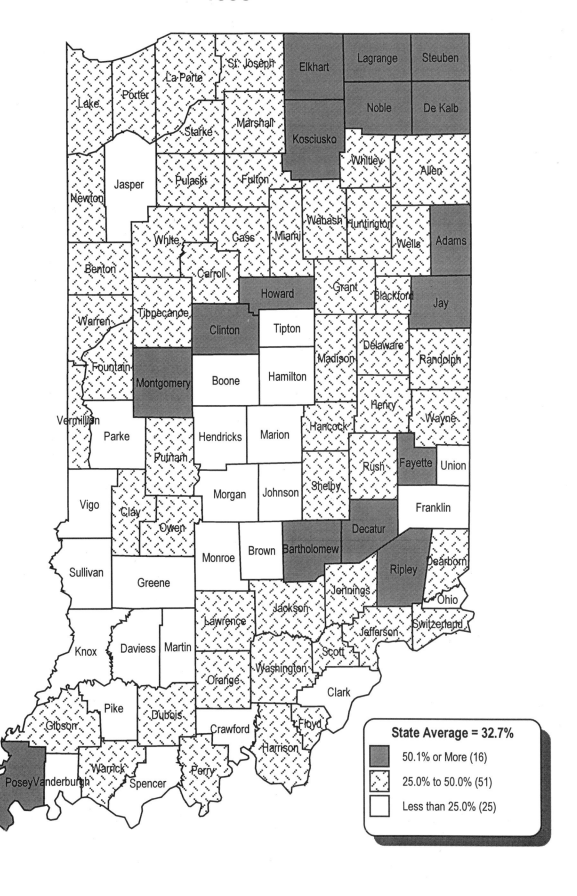

State Average = 32.7%

▨	50.1% or More (16)
⬚	25.0% to 50.0% (51)
☐	Less than 25.0% (25)

Manufacturing as a Percent of Total Earnings: EDIN Table PITE.

SECTION 2
INDIANA FACTBOOK
Page 149

2.40 Earnings by Industry 1995 *($000)*

	Total Earnings	Farm	Manufacturing	Mining	Contract Construction	Wholesale & Retail	Finance, Insurance & Real Estate	Transportation, Communication, Public Utilities	Services	Ag. Serv., Forestry, Fisheries	Government
Indiana	90,885,424	87,204	29,695,708	343,054	5,654,537	13,648,609	4,721,068	5,699,848	19,340,517	407,984	11,286,895
Adams	401,384	8,200	212,850	NA	24,430	NA	7,862	10,716	36,978	4,319	40,418
Allen	6,412,192	10,834	2,016,250	5,789	388,924	1,005,041	501,562	545,737	1,406,068	26,557	505,430
Bartholomew	1,540,769	2,012	844,149	2,537	65,568	146,734	79,810	58,332	199,960	2,502	139,165
Benton	57,408	-13,575	17,671	0	2,508	NA	3,585	5,818	NA	663	13,553
Blackford	119,670	2,226	57,215	382	4,474	13,089	3,568	4,015	14,842	503	19,356
Boone	392,906	3,161	58,566	NA	60,121	76,092	21,870	17,586	95,858	NA	51,975
Brown	70,267	150	3,885	142	8,932	15,031	2,798	3,127	19,603	580	16,019
Carroll	151,894	5,782	63,809	NA	9,999	22,302	4,307	5,273	19,304	NA	18,807
Cass	435,607	6,466	153,704	NA	27,721	66,628	12,670	16,363	59,769	NA	85,354
Clark	1,204,825	-1,148	258,068	4,897	119,337	218,279	32,795	159,332	233,930	3,608	175,727
Clay	243,521	4,780	90,795	NA	NA	32,965	6,372	25,868	29,222	921	31,063
Clinton	333,397	-2,028	168,547	NA	17,950	39,474	8,024	10,535	40,961	2,472	47,415
Crawford	42,209	-369	4,236	NA	3,556	6,673	1,908	3,307	NA	393	10,931
Daviess	257,569	7,988	48,240	17,928	25,785	46,519	8,206	21,462	41,209	1,615	38,617
Dearborn	352,818	-1,811	94,631	55	40,343	51,656	12,875	37,870	59,260	2,977	54,962
Decatur	345,975	3,567	182,962	NA	11,099	41,525	7,445	18,021	43,392	NA	31,146
Dekalb	615,127	4,134	385,275	2,437	23,755	51,198	10,510	20,929	69,113	2,520	45,256
Delaware	1,809,669	4,033	563,707	NA	98,932	227,269	53,938	150,174	419,068	NA	281,581
Dubois	772,821	5,870	382,073	5,205	44,293	117,645	18,846	34,130	110,064	2,660	52,035
Elkhart	3,745,833	6,396	2,181,490	1,351	182,987	462,179	88,220	136,041	479,778	15,526	191,865
Fayette	390,821	-3,794	241,364	455	7,303	35,624	6,772	8,572	54,568	930	39,027
Floyd	759,547	NA	213,227	805	68,900	108,213	36,950	23,093	168,254	9,504	130,639
Fountain	129,893	-6,158	55,434	65	5,864	21,542	5,366	6,949	18,343	1,608	20,880
Franklin	95,868	-4,339	14,166	274	11,528	15,971	4,622	11,762	23,073	695	18,116
Fulton	208,875	-5,013	91,767	369	18,164	27,388	5,902	10,034	27,395	4,193	28,676
Gibson	274,987	2,045	73,702	3,458	12,556	45,204	7,354	46,809	47,915	2,437	33,507
Grant	1,069,399	4,872	486,353	NA	35,756	118,805	33,327	37,330	208,770	NA	137,418
Greene	219,128	-4,160	28,075	36,337	18,439	39,829	6,985	11,666	36,373	1,407	44,177
Hamilton	2,446,233	-2,069	381,050	10,126	228,796	541,192	348,146	133,139	593,640	27,238	184,975
Hancock	470,738	2,132	142,111	NA	62,054	74,449	15,999	18,392	78,185	NA	73,333
Harrison	223,715	196	66,963	2,139	14,950	37,697	7,305	17,150	34,273	3,673	39,369
Hendricks	750,152	4,343	39,814	NA	88,088	129,906	27,918	155,287	156,149	NA	142,678
Henry	487,126	-1,105	216,505	686	23,414	66,331	14,009	13,598	68,631	2,630	82,427
Howard	2,207,375	8,466	1,475,395	2,179	51,916	176,285	44,607	49,361	242,899	4,755	151,512
Huntington	464,938	381	226,917	2,862	22,870	60,742	12,210	17,079	66,299	1,629	53,949
Jackson	561,068	4,307	232,198	NA	29,216	116,169	15,606	37,445	64,874	NA	58,830
Jasper	276,117	-3,356	42,028	665	30,300	48,183	8,396	68,476	39,839	1,598	39,988
Jay	211,989	3,163	107,323	NA	5,938	23,200	4,809	6,929	28,918	NA	29,085
Jefferson	379,940	307	142,497	86	NA	46,292	7,740	NA	79,197	1,433	58,692
Jennings	205,905	-2,126	56,723	NA	21,657	30,250	4,350	5,798	34,946	NA	52,151
Johnson	999,343	3,715	218,631	NA	104,709	207,160	45,378	35,576	246,244	NA	131,608
Knox	493,393	12,343	66,601	17,845	19,547	83,174	25,588	38,322	99,213	3,025	127,735
Kosciusko	1,115,072	805	659,903	NA	44,349	116,053	25,900	44,546	150,550	NA	68,421
Lagrange	416,252	11,884	247,246	221	16,644	39,968	7,000	10,762	44,944	4,964	32,619
Lake	6,885,307	-231	2,170,457	2,897	560,802	957,586	238,970	518,303	1,669,819	24,044	742,660
Laporte	1,395,071	11,682	451,870	1,437	81,571	218,031	38,961	101,620	283,971	9,485	196,443
Lawrence	528,741	-4,169	257,735	3,767	24,214	65,570	10,806	19,103	86,653	1,535	63,527
Madison	1,772,605	1,910	839,696	2,554	69,954	206,983	48,841	45,574	359,233	8,200	189,660
Marion	20,976,027	311	4,644,284	16,147	1,101,738	3,577,509	1,787,905	1,461,284	5,549,155	56,786	2,780,908
Marshall	567,169	5,046	270,355	189	22,506	71,722	22,456	30,827	88,338	2,704	53,026
Martin	279,725	2,917	21,946	NA	NA	10,574	2,490	15,934	11,975	1,931	203,701
Miami	274,136	-3,470	84,794	NA	15,308	38,850	7,789	17,982	33,549	NA	76,463
Monroe	1,698,795	-794	349,086	8,532	120,557	225,891	73,189	68,335	357,351	7,721	488,927
Montgomery	571,016	5,605	300,736	396	18,193	70,345	12,625	20,078	92,382	2,553	48,103
Morgan	390,485	-417	77,629	3,466	44,454	66,530	14,011	29,744	82,735	3,325	69,008
Newton	93,277	-13,678	40,195	1,302	7,846	16,987	3,613	5,263	13,909	697	17,143
Noble	574,810	841	351,750	736	25,475	49,827	7,426	15,105	58,761	1,874	63,015
Ohio	15,682	-1,452	2,353	0	1,472	2,459	151	647	4,307	124	5,621
Orange	180,592	-2,139	68,227	NA	20,978	18,322	5,182	NA	28,446	3,359	25,414
Owen	100,086	-2,108	31,722	372	7,338	13,026	3,478	10,974	15,548	1,413	18,323
Parke	83,601	360	14,992	85	3,488	11,556	4,190	7,072	17,963	692	23,203
Perry	150,060	-2,852	45,501	NA	10,119	20,362	8,196	7,044	22,288	NA	36,234
Pike	101,595	-2,267	7,933	20,009	2,247	9,178	3,079	35,155	11,575	326	14,360
Porter	1,915,775	2,999	687,768	208	177,877	264,910	50,332	137,518	366,219	9,486	218,458
Posey	369,641	-647	195,779	2,595	36,969	27,356	5,244	27,355	41,135	1,271	32,584
Pulaski	132,072	968	51,389	1,572	5,162	21,175	4,566	6,179	16,250	898	23,913
Putnam	316,751	977	84,003	1,821	15,493	55,878	9,124	20,250	65,269	1,220	62,716
Randolph	255,094	2,723	118,273	572	10,782	38,624	5,999	13,568	26,316	3,046	35,191
Ripley	385,796	-1,289	198,542	NA	17,954	33,858	15,939	20,768	61,806	NA	33,557
Rush	148,814	-2,959	51,215	NA	8,759	24,004	4,040	8,236	26,302	NA	27,927
St. Joseph	4,210,145	1,711	1,153,203	1,180	264,204	707,725	218,581	213,051	1,280,915	15,758	353,817
Scott	173,261	-822	69,036	NA	8,401	25,967	4,894	8,630	24,588	NA	30,326
Shelby	495,144	4,746	230,981	4,565	34,289	65,398	9,841	15,492	70,905	2,287	56,640
Spencer	205,672	756	44,465	8,723	6,279	25,374	3,678	56,672	35,507	1,648	22,570
Starke	123,805	2,888	33,949	55	6,127	19,974	2,562	7,070	20,648	905	29,627
Steuben	474,165	-991	245,252	NA	20,379	65,231	9,986	33,622	63,200	1,397	36,048
Sullivan	147,291	-1,653	15,038	9,397	4,246	20,169	6,192	25,664	26,353	725	41,160
Switzerland	40,669	-4,287	16,816	NA	2,888	3,900	1,398	NA	6,144	120	9,541
Tippecanoe	2,361,634	-6,494	750,829	NA	130,504	261,100	118,274	73,746	464,044	NA	556,022
Tipton	119,442	6,437	28,555	93	6,938	22,996	3,662	4,686	18,079	1,524	26,472
Union	36,491	-1,260	4,924	55	1,849	7,805	2,686	3,968	6,413	1,285	8,766
Vanderburgh	3,254,278	1,592	718,128	38,523	308,305	569,154	194,995	198,143	940,340	7,195	277,903
Vermillion	173,733	-4,903	77,094	815	11,289	19,605	3,165	15,811	23,410	2,072	25,375
Vigo	1,600,977	-1,396	338,808	1,726	132,853	313,116	55,993	90,656	413,288	4,189	251,746
Wabash	426,741	933	196,315	226	23,636	53,286	12,121	16,072	68,043	2,894	53,215
Warren	54,933	2,745	18,689	NA	2,326	8,588	860	3,480	8,141	NA	9,060
Warrick	461,263	-4,005	174,500	35,963	33,772	51,590	13,535	28,044	75,419	3,512	48,933
Washington	172,294	-752	72,606	692	10,529	21,503	4,369	9,500	21,892	1,036	30,919
Wayne	1,055,552	-4,074	337,675	1,369	56,547	211,039	33,680	66,195	228,683	1,899	122,539
Wells	314,932	2,967	125,260	NA	13,733	53,055	6,444	13,362	60,143	NA	38,054
White	302,026	5,873	138,696	546	11,466	46,221	8,166	22,145	33,435	1,816	33,662
Whitley	354,518	5,857	172,543	90	18,041	38,788	7,974	14,585	49,865	2,645	44,130

Source: U.S. Bureau of Economic Analysis
EDIN table(s): PITE

2.41 Percent Distribution of Earnings by Industry 1995

	Total Earnings ($000)	Farm	Manufacturing	Mining	Contract Construction	Wholesale & Retail	Finance, Insurance & Real Estate	Transport, Communication Public Utilities	Services	Ag. Serv., Forestry, Fisheries	Government
Indiana	**90,885,424**	**0.1**	**32.7**	**0.4**	**6.2**	**15.0**	**5.2**	**6.3**	**21.3**	**0.4**	**12.4**
Adams	401,384	2.0	53.0	NA	6.1	9.9	2.0	2.7	9.2	1.1	10.1
Allen	6,412,192	0.2	31.4	0.1	6.1	15.7	7.8	8.5	21.9	0.4	7.9
Bartholomew	1,540,769	0.1	54.8	0.2	4.3	9.5	5.2	3.8	13.0	0.2	9.0
Benton	57,408	-23.6	30.8	0.0	4.4	10.5	6.2	10.1	NA	1.2	23.6
Blackford	119,670	1.9	47.8	0.3	3.7	10.9	3.0	3.4	12.4	0.4	16.2
Boone	392,906	0.8	14.9	NA	15.3	19.4	5.6	4.5	24.4	NA	13.2
Brown	70,267	0.2	5.5	0.2	12.7	21.4	4.0	4.5	27.9	0.8	22.8
Carroll	151,894	3.8	42.0	NA	6.6	14.7	2.8	3.5	12.7	NA	12.4
Cass	435,607	1.5	35.3	NA	6.4	15.3	2.9	3.8	13.7	NA	19.6
Clark	1,204,825	-0.1	21.4	0.4	9.9	18.1	2.7	13.2	19.4	0.3	14.6
Clay	243,521	2.0	37.3	NA	NA	13.5	2.6	10.6	12.0	0.4	12.8
Clinton	333,397	-0.6	50.6	NA	5.4	11.8	2.4	3.2	12.3	0.7	14.2
Crawford	42,209	-0.9	10.0	NA	8.4	15.8	4.5	7.8	NA	0.9	25.9
Daviess	257,569	3.1	18.7	7.0	10.0	18.1	3.2	8.3	16.0	0.6	15.0
Dearborn	352,818	-0.5	26.8	0.0	11.4	14.6	3.6	10.7	16.8	0.8	15.6
Decatur	345,975	1.0	52.9	NA	3.2	12.0	2.2	5.2	12.5	NA	9.0
Dekalb	615,127	0.7	62.6	0.4	3.9	8.3	1.7	3.4	11.2	0.4	7.4
Delaware	1,809,669	0.2	31.1	NA	5.5	12.6	3.0	8.3	23.2	NA	15.6
Dubois	772,821	0.8	49.4	0.7	5.7	15.2	2.4	4.4	14.2	0.3	6.7
Elkhart	3,745,833	0.2	58.2	0.0	4.9	12.3	2.4	3.6	12.8	0.4	5.1
Fayette	390,821	-1.0	61.8	0.1	1.9	9.1	1.7	2.2	14.0	0.2	10.0
Floyd	759,547	NA	28.1	0.1	9.1	14.2	4.9	3.0	22.2	1.3	17.2
Fountain	129,893	-4.7	42.7	0.1	4.5	16.6	4.1	5.3	14.1	1.2	16.1
Franklin	95,868	-4.5	14.8	0.3	12.0	16.7	4.8	12.3	24.1	0.7	18.9
Fulton	208,875	-2.4	43.9	0.2	8.7	13.1	2.8	4.8	13.1	2.0	13.7
Gibson	274,987	0.7	26.8	1.3	4.6	16.4	2.7	17.0	17.4	0.9	12.2
Grant	1,069,399	0.5	45.5	NA	3.3	11.1	3.1	3.5	19.5	NA	12.9
Greene	219,128	-1.9	12.8	16.6	8.4	18.2	3.2	5.3	16.6	0.6	20.2
Hamilton	2,446,233	-0.1	15.6	0.4	9.4	22.1	14.2	5.4	24.3	1.1	7.6
Hancock	470,738	0.5	30.2	NA	13.2	15.8	3.4	3.9	16.6	NA	15.6
Harrison	223,715	0.1	29.9	1.0	6.7	16.9	3.3	7.7	15.3	1.6	17.6
Hendricks	750,152	0.6	5.3	NA	11.7	17.3	3.7	20.7	20.8	NA	19.0
Henry	487,126	-0.2	44.4	0.1	4.8	13.6	2.9	2.8	14.1	0.5	16.9
Howard	2,207,375	0.4	66.8	0.1	2.4	8.0	2.0	2.2	11.0	0.2	6.9
Huntington	464,938	0.1	48.8	0.6	4.9	13.1	2.6	3.7	14.3	0.4	11.6
Jackson	561,068	0.8	41.4	NA	5.2	20.7	2.8	6.7	11.6	NA	10.5
Jasper	276,117	-1.2	15.2	0.2	11.0	17.5	3.0	24.8	14.4	0.6	14.5
Jay	211,989	1.5	50.6	NA	2.8	10.9	2.3	3.3	13.6	NA	13.7
Jefferson	379,940	0.1	37.5	0.0	NA	12.2	2.0	NA	20.8	0.4	15.4
Jennings	205,905	-1.0	27.5	NA	10.5	14.7	2.1	2.8	17.0	NA	25.3
Johnson	999,343	0.4	21.9	NA	10.5	20.7	4.5	3.6	24.6	NA	13.2
Knox	493,393	2.5	13.5	3.6	4.0	16.9	5.2	7.8	20.1	0.6	25.9
Kosciusko	1,115,072	0.1	59.2	NA	4.0	10.4	2.3	4.0	13.5	NA	6.1
Lagrange	416,252	2.9	59.4	0.1	4.0	9.6	1.7	2.6	10.8	1.2	7.8
Lake	6,885,307	0.0	31.5	0.0	8.1	13.9	3.5	7.5	24.3	0.3	10.8
Laporte	1,395,051	0.8	32.4	0.1	5.8	15.6	2.8	7.3	20.4	0.7	14.1
Lawrence	528,741	-0.8	48.7	0.7	4.6	12.4	2.0	3.6	16.4	0.3	12.0
Madison	1,772,605	0.1	47.4	0.1	3.9	11.7	2.8	2.6	20.3	0.5	10.7
Marion	20,976,027	0.0	22.1	0.1	5.3	17.1	8.5	7.0	26.5	0.3	13.3
Marshall	567,169	0.9	47.7	0.0	4.0	12.6	4.0	5.4	15.6	0.5	9.3
Martin	279,725	1.0	7.8	NA	NA	3.8	0.9	5.7	4.3	0.7	72.8
Miami	274,136	-1.3	30.9	NA	5.6	14.2	2.8	6.6	12.2	NA	27.9
Monroe	1,698,795	0.0	20.5	0.5	7.1	13.3	4.3	4.0	21.0	0.5	28.8
Montgomery	571,016	1.0	52.7	0.1	3.2	12.3	2.2	3.5	16.2	0.4	8.4
Morgan	390,485	-0.1	19.9	0.9	11.4	17.0	3.6	7.6	21.2	0.9	17.7
Newton	93,277	-14.7	43.1	1.4	8.4	18.2	3.9	5.6	14.9	0.7	18.4
Noble	574,810	0.1	61.2	0.1	4.4	8.7	1.3	2.6	10.2	0.3	11.0
Ohio	15,682	-9.3	15.0	0.0	9.4	15.7	1.0	4.1	27.5	0.8	35.8
Orange	180,592	-1.2	37.8	NA	11.6	10.1	2.9	NA	15.8	1.9	14.1
Owen	100,086	-2.1	31.7	0.4	7.3	13.0	3.5	11.0	15.5	1.4	18.3
Parke	83,601	0.4	17.9	0.1	4.2	13.8	5.0	8.5	21.5	0.8	27.8
Perry	150,060	-1.9	30.3	NA	6.7	13.6	5.5	4.7	14.9	NA	24.1
Pike	101,595	-2.2	7.8	19.7	2.2	9.0	3.0	34.6	11.4	0.3	14.1
Porter	1,915,775	0.2	35.9	0.0	9.3	13.8	2.6	7.2	19.1	0.5	11.4
Posey	369,641	-0.2	53.0	0.7	10.0	7.4	1.4	7.4	11.1	0.3	8.8
Pulaski	132,072	0.7	38.9	1.2	3.9	16.0	3.5	4.7	12.3	0.7	18.1
Putnam	316,751	0.3	26.5	0.6	4.9	17.6	2.9	6.4	20.6	0.4	19.8
Randolph	255,094	1.1	46.4	0.2	4.2	15.1	2.4	5.3	10.3	1.2	13.8
Ripley	385,796	-0.3	51.5	NA	4.7	8.8	4.1	5.4	16.0	NA	8.7
Rush	148,814	-2.0	34.4	NA	5.9	16.1	2.7	5.5	17.7	NA	18.8
St. Joseph	4,210,145	0.0	27.4	0.0	6.3	16.8	5.2	5.1	30.4	0.4	8.4
Scott	173,261	-0.5	39.8	NA	4.8	15.0	2.8	5.0	14.2	NA	17.5
Shelby	495,144	1.0	46.6	0.9	6.9	13.2	2.0	3.1	14.3	0.5	11.4
Spencer	205,672	0.4	21.6	4.2	3.1	12.3	1.8	27.6	17.3	0.8	11.0
Starke	123,805	2.3	27.4	0.0	4.9	16.1	2.1	5.7	16.7	0.7	23.9
Steuben	474,165	-0.2	51.7	NA	4.3	13.8	2.1	7.1	13.3	0.3	7.6
Sullivan	147,291	-1.1	10.2	6.4	2.9	13.7	4.2	17.4	17.9	0.5	27.9
Switzerland	40,669	-10.5	41.3	NA	7.1	9.6	3.4	NA	15.1	0.3	23.5
Tippecanoe	2,361,634	-0.3	31.8	NA	5.5	11.1	5.0	3.1	19.6	NA	23.5
Tipton	119,442	5.4	23.9	0.1	5.8	19.3	3.1	3.9	15.1	1.3	22.2
Union	36,491	-3.5	13.5	0.2	5.1	21.4	7.4	10.9	17.6	3.5	24.0
Vanderburgh	3,254,278	0.0	22.1	1.2	9.5	17.5	6.0	6.1	28.9	0.2	8.5
Vermillion	173,733	-2.8	44.4	0.5	6.5	11.3	1.8	9.1	13.5	1.2	14.6
Vigo	1,600,977	-0.1	21.2	0.1	8.3	19.0	3.5	5.7	25.0	0.3	15.7
Wabash	426,741	0.2	46.0	0.1	5.5	12.5	2.8	3.8	15.9	0.7	12.5
Warren	54,933	5.0	34.0	NA	4.2	15.6	1.6	6.3	14.8	NA	16.5
Warrick	461,263	-0.9	37.8	7.8	7.3	11.2	2.9	6.1	16.4	0.8	10.6
Washington	172,294	-0.4	42.1	0.4	6.1	12.5	2.5	5.5	12.7	0.6	17.9
Wayne	1,055,552	-0.4	32.0	0.1	5.4	20.0	3.2	6.3	21.7	0.2	11.6
Wells	314,932	0.9	39.8	NA	4.4	16.8	2.0	4.2	19.1	NA	12.1
White	302,026	1.9	45.9	0.2	3.8	15.3	2.7	7.3	11.1	0.6	11.1
Whitley	354,518	1.7	48.7	0.0	5.1	10.9	2.2	4.1	14.1	0.7	12.4

Source: U.S. Bureau of Economic Analysis
EDIN table(s): PITE

Retail Trade as a Percent of Total Earnings 1995

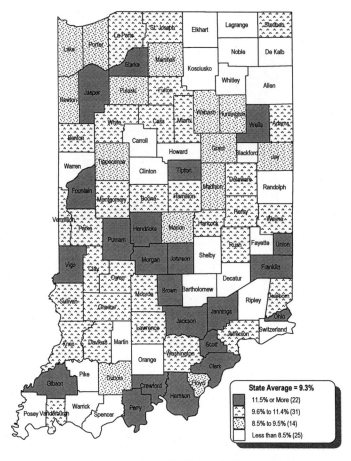

State Average = 9.3%
- 11.5% or More (22)
- 9.6% to 11.4% (31)
- 8.5% to 9.5% (14)
- Less than 8.5% (25)

Services as a Percent of Total Earnings 1995

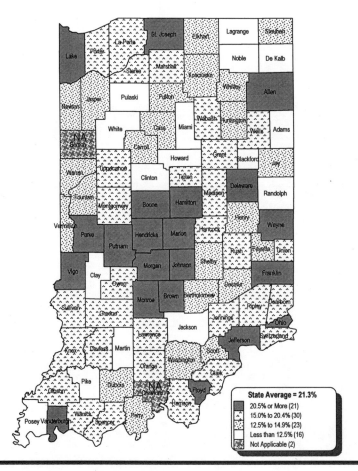

State Average = 21.3%
- 20.5% or More (21)
- 15.0% to 20.4% (30)
- 12.5% to 14.9% (23)
- Less than 12.5% (16)
- Not Applicable (2)

Retail Trade as a Percent of Total Earnings: EDIN Table PITE.
Services as a Percent of Total Earnings: EDIN Table PITE.

2.42 Wages and Salaries 1989 to 1995

	Disbursements ($000)			Employment by Place of Work			Average Wage per Job ($)		
	1989	1992	1995	1989	1992	1995	1989	1992	1995
Indiana	52,852,700	61,498,240	72,681,087	2,592,024	2,678,795	2,906,624	20,391	22,957	25,005
Adams	247,819	247,316	307,464	13,851	13,112	15,303	17,892	18,862	20,092
Allen	3,935,561	4,427,230	5,138,133	181,093	183,915	193,982	21,732	24,072	26,488
Bartholomew	809,273	976,497	1,257,638	35,545	38,564	44,098	22,768	25,321	28,519
Benton	36,662	42,805	51,887	2,525	2,669	2,921	14,520	16,038	17,763
Blackford	84,905	82,263	94,381	4,986	4,312	4,624	17,029	19,078	20,411
Boone	198,812	238,765	282,145	12,032	12,505	13,329	16,524	19,094	21,168
Brown	29,117	36,784	44,372	2,523	2,808	3,012	11,541	13,100	14,732
Carroll	69,435	90,865	115,122	4,514	5,217	5,749	15,382	17,417	20,025
Cass	283,546	319,022	351,651	16,581	16,482	16,476	17,101	19,356	21,343
Clark	658,167	816,997	959,522	36,896	40,680	43,973	17,838	20,084	21,821
Clay	112,011	132,496	170,353	6,523	7,150	8,366	17,172	18,531	20,363
Clinton	181,483	220,462	275,937	10,711	11,373	12,685	16,944	19,385	21,753
Crawford	21,413	23,618	29,619	1,719	1,708	1,847	12,457	13,828	16,036
Daviess	139,209	167,863	186,530	9,270	9,964	10,377	15,017	16,847	17,975
Dearborn	201,105	223,606	263,968	10,656	10,576	11,770	18,872	21,143	22,427
Decatur	166,856	209,055	270,726	9,352	10,654	12,563	17,842	19,622	21,549
Dekalb	330,566	387,857	494,628	16,640	17,288	19,974	19,866	22,435	24,764
Delaware	1,043,004	1,237,343	1,453,097	54,331	58,049	62,380	19,197	21,315	23,294
Dubois	425,840	506,978	626,429	23,064	24,764	27,939	18,463	20,472	22,421
Elkhart	2,169,047	2,403,783	2,984,094	107,227	104,277	119,219	20,229	23,052	25,030
Fayette	274,151	290,062	322,908	12,083	11,671	11,824	22,689	24,853	27,310
Floyd	365,813	463,706	587,135	21,443	23,434	27,594	17,060	19,788	21,278
Fountain	74,710	77,400	100,416	4,850	4,640	5,358	15,404	16,681	18,741
Franklin	50,526	54,970	68,196	3,288	3,503	3,948	15,367	15,692	17,274
Fulton	114,384	138,104	164,970	6,978	7,258	8,243	16,392	19,028	20,013
Gibson	185,819	213,679	218,090	10,682	11,268	10,979	17,396	18,963	19,864
Grant	739,996	786,333	868,189	33,375	33,518	34,441	22,172	23,460	25,208
Greene	121,081	147,159	163,094	7,866	8,407	8,787	15,393	17,504	18,561
Hamilton	870,709	1,286,020	1,796,518	40,700	51,206	64,345	21,393	25,115	27,920
Hancock	221,273	273,548	335,795	11,924	13,031	14,452	18,557	20,992	23,235
Harrison	103,826	131,055	169,561	7,124	7,589	8,941	14,574	17,269	18,964
Hendricks	366,126	435,953	555,783	19,560	21,094	24,327	18,718	20,667	22,846
Henry	264,028	294,503	380,032	14,259	14,200	15,449	18,517	20,740	24,599
Howard	1,211,830	1,312,233	1,703,790	44,525	45,878	50,147	27,217	28,603	33,976
Huntington	252,280	298,368	378,743	15,363	15,687	18,365	16,421	19,020	20,623
Jackson	276,264	348,703	442,582	15,829	17,758	20,144	17,453	19,636	21,971
Jasper	153,292	171,803	220,771	8,853	9,002	10,621	17,315	19,085	20,786
Jay	118,363	136,465	165,125	7,240	7,591	8,409	16,348	17,977	19,637
Jefferson	229,146	268,369	304,045	12,882	13,649	14,326	17,788	19,662	21,223
Jennings	103,722	113,494	157,934	6,657	6,381	8,385	15,581	17,786	18,835
Johnson	457,271	583,891	763,722	29,523	31,529	37,456	15,489	18,519	20,390
Knox	258,757	317,614	381,946	16,619	17,693	19,543	15,570	17,951	19,544
Kosciusko	622,212	723,620	882,375	30,142	30,608	34,660	20,643	23,642	25,458
Lagrange	164,690	194,146	308,309	10,037	10,537	13,944	16,408	18,425	22,111
Lake	4,604,299	5,059,366	5,614,021	205,566	205,157	208,705	22,398	24,661	26,899
Laporte	862,323	992,691	1,119,763	46,429	46,842	49,776	18,573	21,192	22,496
Lawrence	278,980	314,941	408,098	14,675	14,776	17,319	19,011	21,314	23,564
Madison	1,259,137	1,262,884	1,465,529	52,532	51,632	52,812	23,969	24,459	27,750
Marion	12,627,964	15,017,530	17,263,721	549,212	563,526	599,120	22,993	26,649	28,815
Marshall	284,917	347,703	445,520	16,766	18,108	21,287	16,994	19,202	20,929
Martin	205,820	253,056	235,880	7,883	8,137	7,571	26,109	31,099	31,156
Miami	240,552	263,793	221,439	13,465	12,947	10,570	17,865	20,375	20,950
Monroe	956,294	1,168,172	1,350,293	55,843	58,913	63,610	17,125	19,829	21,228
Montgomery	325,449	409,812	466,546	16,771	18,626	19,965	19,405	22,002	23,368
Morgan	210,142	250,404	300,005	13,298	13,959	15,176	15,803	17,939	19,768
Newton	62,497	74,204	81,588	4,054	4,190	4,228	15,416	17,710	19,297
Noble	283,234	333,830	462,690	16,518	17,562	20,803	17,147	19,009	22,242
Ohio	7,527	8,917	10,315	641	671	689	11,743	13,289	14,971
Orange	105,106	115,033	140,393	7,049	6,892	7,575	14,911	16,691	18,534
Owen	40,862	55,822	69,753	3,134	3,497	3,943	13,038	15,963	17,690
Parke	47,174	54,751	60,605	3,405	3,513	3,669	13,854	15,585	16,518
Perry	90,187	102,752	117,016	5,619	5,875	6,140	16,050	17,490	19,058
Pike	77,954	85,748	80,855	3,370	3,219	3,117	23,132	26,638	25,940
Porter	1,011,308	1,227,205	1,522,979	46,468	51,594	56,400	21,764	23,786	27,003
Posey	196,967	230,323	275,066	8,653	8,778	9,418	22,763	26,239	29,206
Pulaski	78,854	89,744	102,178	4,387	4,572	4,858	17,974	19,629	21,033
Putnam	152,928	198,021	252,041	10,164	11,880	13,307	15,046	16,668	18,940
Randolph	175,818	153,041	186,177	9,813	8,183	8,973	17,917	18,702	20,749
Ripley	215,551	257,210	303,276	10,703	11,199	12,542	20,139	22,967	24,181
Rush	78,831	95,711	116,601	5,136	5,468	6,150	15,349	17,504	18,960
St. Joseph	2,422,628	2,772,538	3,334,273	122,888	124,758	136,858	19,714	22,223	24,363
Scott	80,769	108,290	135,236	5,541	6,520	7,181	14,577	16,609	18,832
Shelby	251,208	319,623	395,902	14,843	15,387	16,877	16,924	20,772	23,458
Spencer	128,563	128,778	163,966	6,955	6,618	7,725	18,485	19,459	21,225
Starke	67,037	76,554	91,120	4,893	4,844	5,116	13,701	15,804	17,811
Steuben	253,585	292,739	374,706	14,614	15,408	18,058	17,352	18,999	20,750
Sullivan	81,298	99,594	114,175	4,898	5,286	6,034	16,598	18,841	18,922
Switzerland	21,129	26,064	33,061	1,662	1,779	2,024	12,713	14,651	16,334
Tippecanoe	1,333,867	1,620,890	1,937,302	68,813	73,017	79,462	19,384	22,199	24,380
Tipton	67,312	79,606	90,672	4,088	4,191	4,387	16,466	18,995	20,668
Union	17,120	20,205	24,186	1,311	1,437	1,534	13,059	14,061	15,767
Vanderburgh	1,927,887	2,291,630	2,626,144	98,526	103,300	111,696	19,567	22,184	23,512
Vermillion	121,580	151,923	143,022	5,313	5,775	5,341	22,883	26,307	26,778
Vigo	941,586	1,146,782	1,300,339	52,114	55,951	59,491	18,068	20,496	21,858
Wabash	265,806	291,403	336,567	15,096	14,930	15,510	17,608	19,518	21,700
Warren	31,728	37,308	39,932	1,925	1,902	1,939	16,482	19,615	20,594
Warrick	334,233	354,467	349,869	13,238	13,666	13,285	25,248	25,938	26,336
Washington	99,867	106,269	131,839	6,666	6,259	7,104	14,982	16,979	18,558
Wayne	627,458	678,837	832,634	34,249	33,705	38,206	18,320	20,141	21,793
Wells	172,746	200,384	244,516	9,966	9,970	11,065	17,334	20,099	22,098
White	160,598	181,687	234,730	9,551	9,948	11,989	16,815	18,264	19,579
Whitley	219,920	237,202	276,823	11,479	11,229	12,744	19,158	21,124	21,722

Footnote: Employment estimates used to compute the average are a job not person count. People holding more than one job are counted in the estimate for each job they hold.
Source: U.S. Bureau of Economic Analysis
EDIN table(s): WAGE

Supplemental Security Income Payments ($000)
1995

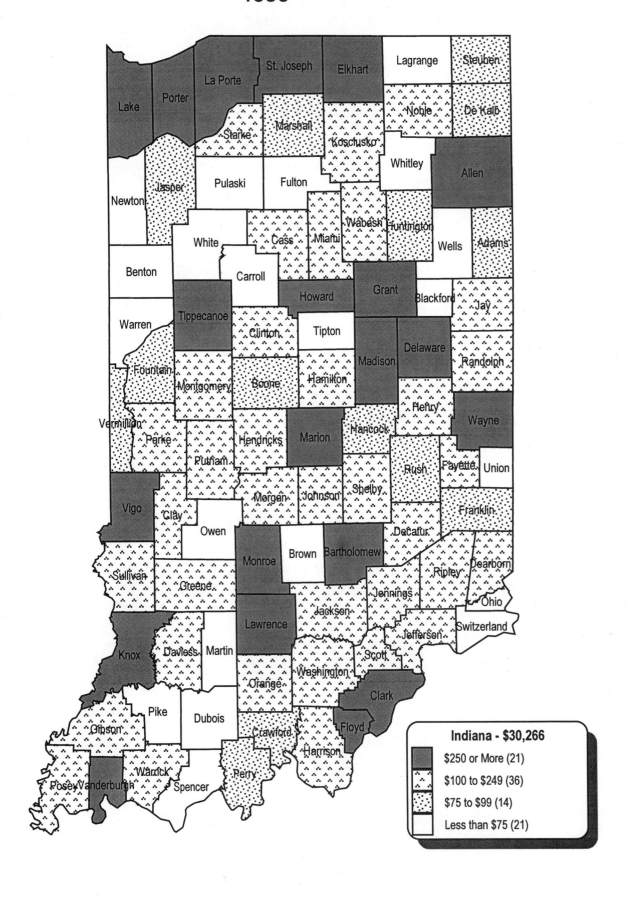

Indiana - $30,266

■	$250 or More (21)
⋰	$100 to $249 (36)
∴	$75 to $99 (14)
□	Less than $75 (21)

Supplemental Security Income Payments ($000): EDIN Table SSRP.

Social Welfare
2.43 Supplemental Security Income 1995

	Total Persons	Aged	Adults Blind	Adults Disabled	Children Blind	Children Disabled	Age 65 Plus [1]	Payments ($000)
Indiana	88,756	9,440	934	58,615	150	19,617	15,288	30,266
Adams	218	21	0	148	0	49	37	93
Allen	4,191	365	33	2,706	13	1,074	592	1,430
Bartholomew	1,006	113	6	695	1	191	184	339
Benton	87	13	2	45	0	27	20	27
Blackford	173	18	1	119	1	34	31	52
Boone	261	35	4	161	1	60	50	88
Brown	96	21	0	58	0	17	28	27
Carroll	103	15	0	52	0	36	22	31
Cass	623	56	4	419	3	141	82	177
Clark	1,657	141	17	1,183	1	315	274	596
Clay	503	67	5	348	1	82	104	180
Clinton	386	40	3	266	1	76	66	122
Crawford	299	46	1	206	0	46	70	94
Daviess	460	63	1	307	1	88	102	142
Dearborn	443	41	3	326	0	73	78	143
Decatur	293	55	1	185	0	52	77	106
Dekalb	325	28	5	228	1	63	46	93
Delaware	2,752	217	24	1,989	4	518	371	965
Dubois	259	48	1	167	0	43	71	69
Elkhart	1,966	178	24	1,152	6	606	268	682
Fayette	563	60	8	410	0	85	93	214
Floyd	1,241	137	18	842	4	240	236	412
Fountain	282	37	2	184	1	58	62	89
Franklin	248	43	3	158	1	43	59	83
Fulton	163	17	2	108	0	36	29	58
Gibson	392	57	6	258	0	71	90	118
Grant	1,574	138	18	1,098	1	319	237	490
Greene	538	73	8	358	1	98	108	185
Hamilton	584	68	6	378	2	130	117	153
Hancock	292	44	3	194	0	51	69	77
Harrison	411	57	7	276	0	71	95	142
Hendricks	345	51	7	228	1	58	74	107
Henry	823	81	9	587	2	144	135	244
Howard	1,551	110	13	1,010	4	414	181	557
Huntington	312	36	5	196	1	74	51	96
Jackson	666	66	6	469	1	124	104	229
Jasper	232	26	3	136	1	66	41	78
Jay	316	41	4	190	0	81	58	100
Jefferson	648	95	9	445	4	95	148	214
Jennings	531	38	11	402	1	79	77	141
Johnson	709	85	9	456	1	158	132	231
Knox	941	118	15	647	0	161	185	287
Kosciusko	462	56	5	303	0	98	77	157
Lagrange	149	13	1	105	0	30	25	45
Lake	10,702	994	114	7,138	17	2,439	1,749	4,041
Laporte	1,400	116	16	932	2	334	196	475
Lawrence	824	91	7	613	3	110	151	287
Madison	2,552	218	20	1,745	3	566	373	880
Marion	16,862	1,908	207	10,612	21	4,114	3,057	5,917
Marshall	275	36	1	173	1	64	49	96
Martin	234	32	1	160	1	40	63	71
Miami	564	67	5	348	0	144	92	185
Monroe	1,224	106	17	910	3	188	189	425
Montgomery	493	67	3	295	2	126	93	148
Morgan	598	81	4	416	0	97	130	174
Newton	134	26	3	75	1	29	31	42
Noble	354	47	2	237	0	68	67	108
Ohio	61	8	2	45	0	6	18	15
Orange	420	49	14	296	1	60	81	134
Owen	231	41	1	147	0	42	59	74
Parke	292	35	0	217	0	40	62	100
Perry	296	47	0	194	3	52	78	94
Pike	255	33	1	187	0	34	54	72
Porter	996	100	11	688	0	197	148	333
Posey	345	48	4	235	0	58	65	111
Pulaski	160	24	1	106	1	28	33	47
Putnam	336	57	2	194	1	82	77	104
Randolph	359	46	1	212	0	100	70	115
Ripley	338	41	1	245	0	51	68	114
Rush	223	35	6	148	0	34	47	80
St. Joseph	3,898	428	32	2,331	5	1,102	636	1,364
Scott	693	55	6	512	2	118	108	232
Shelby	482	58	3	310	0	111	87	128
Spencer	227	43	3	151	0	30	61	65
Starke	384	35	6	289	0	54	59	137
Steuben	281	40	2	178	0	61	57	86
Sullivan	372	41	3	239	1	88	66	115
Switzerland	161	36	0	97	0	28	57	43
Tippecanoe	1,250	116	11	793	4	326	170	419
Tipton	140	20	2	96	1	21	38	36
Union	96	21	0	51	0	24	24	29
Vanderburgh	3,718	381	45	2,516	8	768	654	1,223
Vermillion	252	30	3	176	0	43	53	81
Vigo	2,418	228	26	1,656	5	503	389	849
Wabash	453	37	7	283	2	124	57	128
Warren	96	14	2	51	0	29	22	31
Warrick	434	56	3	265	0	110	79	132
Washington	520	58	4	371	1	86	100	192
Wayne	1,609	169	10	1,062	0	368	281	559
Wells	155	19	2	98	0	36	36	58
White	226	33	5	128	0	60	43	64
Whitley	154	29	1	102	0	22	36	43

Footnote: [1] Includes blind and disabled over age 65.
Source: U.S. Department of Health and Human Services
EDIN table(s): SSRP

Percent of Vote Cast for Winning Party
Governor
1996

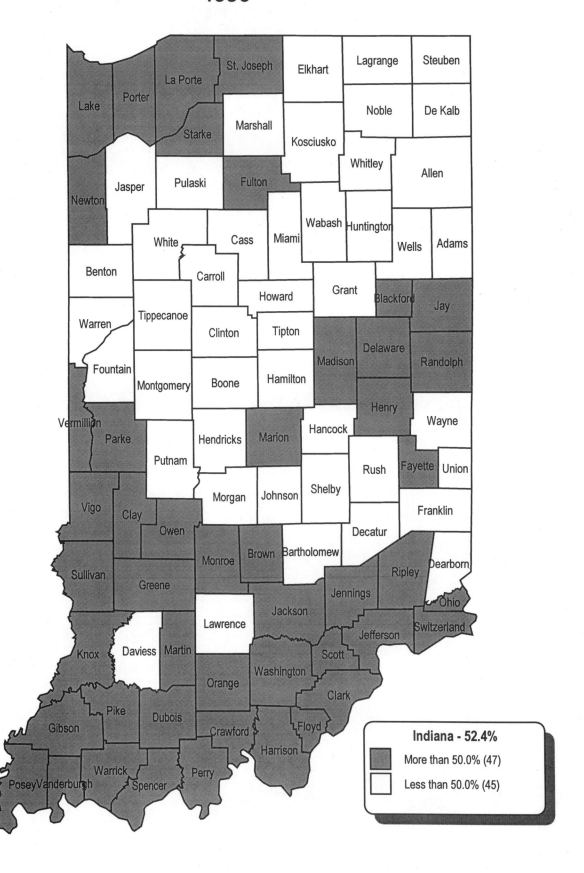

Indiana - 52.4%

More than 50.0% (47)

Less than 50.0% (45)

Percent of Vote Cast for Winning Party, Governor: EDIN Table VOTE.

Government

2.44 Percent of Vote Cast for Winning Party 1976 to 1996

Year Winning Party	President						Governor					
	1976 Dem	1980 Rep	1984 Rep	1988 Rep	1992 Dem	1996 Dem	1976 Rep	1980 Rep	1984 Rep	1988 Dem	1992 Dem	1996 Dem
Indiana	45.7	56.0	61.7	60.2	36.8	46.9	56.8	57.7	52.2	53.0	62.0	52.4
Adams	43.4	53.2	66.6	67.8	29.2	37.9	54.3	54.2	53.4	55.4	62.7	47.4
Allen	38.0	57.6	65.7	64.9	32.6	41.2	62.7	61.6	59.1	48.1	59.9	45.6
Bartholomew	42.8	58.7	69.4	66.0	30.2	41.4	59.1	62.4	57.9	46.9	61.0	44.7
Benton	39.6	64.3	70.4	66.3	28.2	40.2	64.7	64.5	52.8	49.2	57.4	45.5
Blackford	51.9	53.1	60.8	59.5	36.1	53.0	53.3	59.9	46.7	57.4	66.7	54.5
Boone	37.9	66.1	74.4	73.4	22.9	29.0	64.0	68.6	61.6	38.9	50.4	38.2
Brown	48.6	54.5	56.7	60.9	32.1	44.7	54.9	56.1	50.2	52.6	64.6	52.0
Carroll	42.5	60.5	66.1	62.5	29.9	40.3	63.5	59.9	49.6	51.1	58.3	44.7
Cass	41.7	62.9	68.7	65.1	29.3	40.3	62.0	58.6	55.5	53.0	56.9	48.0
Clark	56.1	49.7	57.5	53.0	47.6	55.3	49.1	52.6	53.1	62.4	71.5	64.5
Clay	48.2	59.1	64.9	60.8	32.5	42.6	55.5	52.8	47.1	63.1	66.9	57.3
Clinton	44.5	58.4	67.1	65.8	28.6	39.1	58.7	62.4	53.6	48.0	44.1	43.1
Crawford	55.0	52.5	53.6	55.1	45.3	56.9	48.3	53.3	47.7	58.9	62.8	65.4
Daviess	41.8	60.9	68.3	65.7	30.4	36.9	59.6	56.6	56.4	51.0	56.1	48.1
Dearborn	50.4	56.4	64.7	61.6	32.9	43.0	48.5	47.0	56.8	53.0	54.7	48.5
Decatur	43.7	58.5	70.0	67.4	27.0	40.0	57.1	54.0	52.9	51.6	62.0	46.6
Dekalb	43.2	56.5	64.8	65.7	31.0	41.4	56.7	58.5	56.2	41.6	54.1	45.5
Delaware	48.3	53.8	60.0	56.8	38.6	52.9	52.5	60.0	50.1	56.1	66.1	51.6
Dubois	53.2	47.5	62.8	62.3	36.8	48.7	47.7	45.2	50.5	61.0	65.6	61.0
Elkhart	38.7	61.5	72.0	70.1	28.1	36.6	69.1	66.1	59.5	46.0	54.8	42.2
Fayette	48.9	55.9	62.9	58.9	37.1	48.3	50.8	55.2	53.1	54.5	62.1	50.9
Floyd	52.5	48.9	58.9	56.3	44.4	52.6	50.1	51.8	54.8	58.6	68.0	62.2
Fountain	45.2	62.2	64.9	60.6	33.6	36.9	59.5	61.7	54.1	52.3	59.8	39.7
Franklin	47.2	59.1	69.6	65.7	30.1	40.3	49.9	37.0	55.4	56.9	59.3	49.4
Fulton	40.1	62.5	70.1	65.0	29.9	42.9	66.6	53.0	52.4	28.8	57.8	50.1
Gibson	54.0	50.3	54.6	51.8	46.7	54.6	48.1	45.5	44.8	65.3	69.5	61.7
Grant	44.1	61.7	66.8	62.8	32.1	42.2	57.6	63.9	54.1	50.0	59.4	46.9
Greene	52.5	52.9	60.7	55.9	39.9	47.9	52.8	49.1	49.1	61.3	65.7	58.5
Hamilton	26.2	74.2	82.3	80.4	18.4	24.9	75.0	78.4	69.1	29.7	50.8	31.2
Hancock	37.7	66.7	73.6	71.2	23.0	32.2	63.2	68.4	57.4	44.8	56.1	43.6
Harrison	53.1	54.2	60.6	57.5	42.2	49.3	49.2	54.5	56.0	65.3	70.8	69.0
Hendricks	34.7	68.9	75.7	74.1	21.3	29.6	66.9	70.3	61.6	37.6	50.9	40.7
Henry	46.4	60.0	62.6	59.0	34.0	47.3	56.3	60.5	29.6	55.8	62.2	52.5
Howard	42.8	59.2	67.7	63.2	30.0	41.7	59.9	59.0	53.4	50.0	60.1	46.0
Huntington	41.0	59.6	69.8	74.9	24.1	34.1	62.0	60.6	58.4	46.8	55.1	43.0
Jackson	49.6	55.8	64.8	62.8	35.0	46.7	53.0	53.8	54.3	56.8	61.0	51.4
Jasper	37.0	68.1	69.1	64.7	30.7	40.7	67.2	69.3	63.0	49.4	48.8	45.9
Jay	46.8	58.1	64.9	62.2	36.3	48.4	55.0	64.3	54.4	54.4	62.2	58.0
Jefferson	51.7	52.2	59.2	56.6	41.8	53.0	49.8	54.8	49.4	57.6	60.8	59.7
Jennings	49.2	56.0	65.5	60.3	33.7	48.6	51.0	49.7	51.4	58.6	55.3	53.2
Johnson	37.7	66.3	74.9	73.0	23.3	32.2	64.2	68.9	59.3	42.5	55.6	43.0
Knox	51.0	53.6	62.3	58.1	38.9	52.3	52.0	50.1	50.6	60.8	62.0	62.6
Kosciusko	33.1	68.8	77.9	76.7	21.5	29.0	70.6	69.3	64.6	41.7	50.1	37.1
Lagrange	41.9	62.5	71.3	68.7	28.1	40.1	63.1	62.8	56.4	52.1	54.4	47.1
Lake	56.7	46.0	44.3	43.0	55.2	67.7	42.8	43.8	39.3	67.9	68.7	67.8
Laporte	44.8	55.3	59.0	53.6	41.7	58.5	57.5	60.1	46.0	63.0	65.5	60.7
Lawrence	45.3	62.7	66.7	64.7	33.1	41.3	55.6	60.5	58.1	53.2	58.1	48.4
Madison	47.5	57.3	61.9	56.9	37.7	50.7	53.1	60.4	51.4	54.3	65.2	51.2
Marion	44.6	53.7	58.3	58.6	37.8	48.3	55.8	58.5	52.5	48.1	61.5	53.5
Marshall	39.2	62.2	68.8	65.4	29.6	40.2	70.6	63.2	55.1	48.8	56.6	48.2
Martin	50.8	53.3	63.1	58.7	37.1	44.8	49.1	48.7	47.6	61.5	63.4	57.0
Miami	42.7	60.6	68.8	64.5	28.5	38.8	60.6	56.9	55.1	49.7	57.1	44.8
Monroe	35.2	49.4	59.1	56.0	45.2	52.5	62.1	58.9	51.6	51.8	67.3	55.2
Montgomery	35.5	66.6	75.0	74.6	23.1	33.2	67.1	69.0	60.0	41.0	54.7	38.7
Morgan	39.0	68.5	75.9	72.4	22.2	31.1	63.5	67.7	60.6	41.6	50.3	44.5
Newton	40.8	66.8	68.5	65.0	32.9	47.8	60.1	64.3	58.6	51.2	52.6	50.9
Noble	45.1	56.3	65.7	65.3	32.2	42.9	56.3	56.6	54.2	55.5	57.8	47.5
Ohio	55.6	52.2	58.3	55.8	38.6	49.7	48.7	47.1	53.1	56.1	59.0	58.9
Orange	47.6	59.3	69.4	65.4	36.8	47.3	53.9	59.2	63.6	51.7	54.3	56.5
Owen	51.2	56.1	66.5	60.3	33.7	42.3	53.4	57.1	50.7	55.8	62.2	52.7
Parke	44.2	62.8	69.3	63.2	34.2	43.8	59.7	61.4	52.0	56.3	63.0	54.9
Perry	57.7	45.9	49.9	49.3	51.5	63.4	44.0	43.6	41.0	66.2	69.0	72.1
Pike	55.5	48.1	53.0	51.7	46.5	56.1	47.7	43.2	43.0	64.4	67.5	62.6
Porter	38.6	64.2	64.1	60.4	36.8	51.2	62.9	66.3	55.4	56.1	59.5	55.5
Posey	50.5	53.7	59.1	57.1	40.4	51.7	62.9	52.4	48.8	61.3	69.0	61.7
Pulaski	42.5	62.1	66.9	62.1	33.0	42.7	61.7	58.2	52.4	52.9	59.3	49.5
Putnam	45.3	60.4	69.4	64.6	28.9	39.9	60.5	62.9	52.3	51.8	58.6	49.9
Randolph	43.3	62.6	66.8	62.9	32.8	46.5	60.4	66.3	56.4	52.0	58.7	50.2
Ripley	47.2	56.4	68.0	63.8	31.8	43.6	53.9	39.4	57.2	52.7	56.7	51.6
Rush	39.0	64.3	69.9	67.4	27.1	40.2	64.4	63.1	52.3	50.9	59.8	47.4
St. Joseph	49.0	49.1	54.2	50.6	44.2	54.4	63.8	53.6	47.9	58.9	70.3	58.7
Scott	60.7	46.8	66.9	50.4	52.0	60.2	42.5	47.3	54.1	61.1	69.9	65.5
Shelby	44.0	61.2	59.1	65.1	28.1	40.9	59.1	60.8	54.2	50.0	59.1	48.0
Spencer	53.3	54.4	57.4	54.8	44.9	51.8	47.4	53.5	43.6	55.0	61.5	58.1
Starke	51.4	55.3	72.0	51.8	42.2	55.4	55.7	51.3	60.6	62.5	64.7	58.2
Steuben	38.8	62.9	53.1	68.6	31.7	42.8	62.8	64.3	44.7	50.0	56.6	47.0
Sullivan	57.7	49.0	54.1	49.4	45.9	56.0	47.8	43.1	38.4	70.5	74.6	67.0
Switzerland	61.6	47.1	55.5	51.4	45.3	54.2	40.0	43.2	46.4	61.0	64.2	60.6
Tippecanoe	37.5	56.9	64.8	62.9	34.5	43.3	66.5	64.2	50.1	44.5	60.3	47.0
Tipton	41.2	63.8	70.5	67.2	27.0	38.4	61.1	63.5	57.2	46.9	57.9	45.8
Union	41.4	63.5	70.4	65.5	30.3	43.3	60.3	61.4	64.2	45.8	51.4	47.5
Vanderburgh	47.7	51.1	56.7	55.3	44.0	52.3	55.5	55.6	51.1	56.0	71.0	58.5
Vermillion	56.1	49.9	54.3	47.3	46.6	58.2	48.4	48.6	41.3	71.9	76.0	66.6
Vigo	50.8	51.9	58.4	53.1	42.8	53.3	51.7	48.8	43.4	67.0	74.6	61.7
Wabash	39.8	60.8	70.3	68.4	29.9	39.6	65.3	62.8	59.4	48.1	57.0	45.1
Warren	44.2	64.1	65.4	59.0	34.1	45.4	59.4	61.5	55.4	54.2	60.7	48.1
Warrick	51.7	52.4	61.3	56.6	41.8	50.2	51.5	50.7	50.3	57.7	68.2	58.1
Washington	53.0	56.3	62.6	59.4	40.7	48.4	50.1	56.2	57.3	56.1	60.7	60.4
Wayne	42.2	60.5	64.8	61.4	36.4	47.2	60.2	63.8	58.1	50.4	57.1	49.3
Wells	42.8	56.1	69.4	68.9	27.3	37.2	61.5	59.5	60.6	49.7	56.0	42.7
White	38.2	64.5	69.3	65.4	29.2	42.2	68.8	66.7	50.3	52.1	59.1	46.7
Whitley	43.8	55.7	67.2	67.4	29.6	41.2	57.0	58.3	55.6	53.1	57.5	47.4

Source: Indiana Secretary of State
EDIN table(s): VOTE

Percent of Vote Cast for Winning Party
President
1996

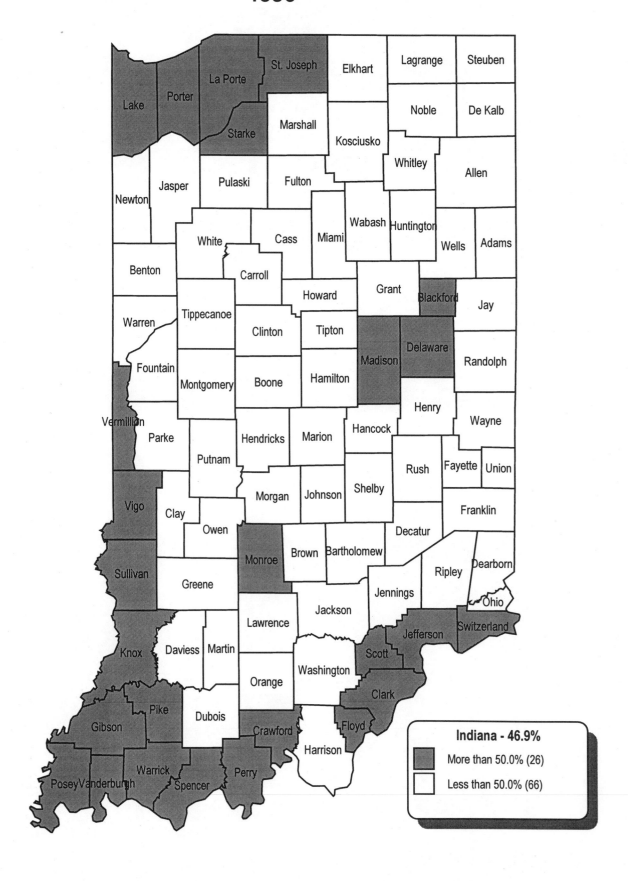

Indiana - 46.9%

More than 50.0% (26)

Less than 50.0% (66)

Percent of Vote Cast for Winning Party, President: EDIN Table VOTE.

2.45 Number of Motor Vehicle Registrations 1996

	Total	Passenger Cars	Trucks	Trailers	Tractors	Semi Trailers	House Cars	Re-declared Weight	Motor-cycles	School Buses	Farm Tractors	Other
Indiana	5,347,748	3,500,863	1,228,442	374,091	9,405	52,337	59,410	1,404	96,052	3,308	153	22,283
Adams	29,243	17,388	7,687	2,560	46	395	347	7	623	1	4	185
Allen	283,265	203,854	51,313	18,031	443	2,104	2,082	66	4,769	59	10	534
Bartholomew	68,801	43,583	17,565	4,924	113	386	834	23	1,261	10	1	101
Benton	10,476	5,476	3,270	875	70	97	173	0	145	0	0	370
Blackford	14,356	8,517	3,829	1,152	30	195	256	2	298	0	0	77
Boone	43,459	27,141	10,396	3,633	142	382	540	14	861	20	2	328
Brown	16,297	9,274	4,972	1,375	16	28	234	8	331	36	0	23
Carroll	22,309	11,466	6,768	2,296	196	441	341	5	466	0	1	329
Cass	37,861	22,762	10,059	3,098	142	265	550	10	758	1	0	216
Clark	86,021	55,621	19,981	5,632	39	2,478	925	18	1,154	79	0	94
Clay	26,434	14,791	8,227	1,874	77	226	406	15	531	1	0	286
Clinton	32,184	18,870	8,797	2,428	128	340	438	11	657	0	1	514
Crawford	11,179	5,823	3,869	1,028	26	91	162	7	121	34	0	18
Daviess	26,532	13,966	8,459	2,206	121	402	412	10	457	69	1	429
Dearborn	43,121	27,278	11,129	3,054	23	260	493	12	744	108	0	20
Decatur	25,079	13,563	8,060	2,015	87	125	320	5	424	49	0	431
Dekalb	40,312	23,846	10,078	4,163	72	392	635	12	826	0	0	288
Delaware	102,569	67,927	22,764	7,467	181	579	1,328	25	1,523	167	1	607
Dubois	40,091	21,334	13,467	3,176	122	659	425	9	546	56	1	296
Elkhart	158,225	103,455	32,933	14,156	163	1,827	1,988	62	3,314	31	2	294
Fayette	25,174	15,318	7,050	1,698	29	66	309	6	514	1	6	177
Floyd	61,363	41,599	13,338	4,249	14	475	766	6	823	13	0	80
Fountain	17,720	9,899	5,642	1,395	36	154	203	4	287	9	0	91
Franklin	21,443	12,085	6,920	1,633	19	143	184	9	322	71	0	57
Fulton	21,253	11,747	6,151	2,113	75	146	341	6	470	2	5	197
Gibson	32,322	18,230	9,754	2,473	115	394	505	3	479	61	0	308
Grant	68,508	44,790	15,252	5,018	128	621	981	15	1,449	3	3	248
Greene	32,569	17,802	10,516	2,614	86	89	491	18	634	62	1	256
Hamilton	134,564	100,362	21,297	8,941	113	522	1,020	33	2,144	8	6	118
Hancock	54,850	33,754	13,717	4,662	111	775	739	15	977	3	0	97
Harrison	36,562	20,313	11,582	3,272	42	231	517	6	458	79	0	62
Hendricks	91,256	57,013	22,260	7,762	174	600	1,178	37	1,853	52	0	327
Henry	51,091	30,849	13,657	4,207	90	320	767	20	911	29	3	238
Howard	79,325	52,662	16,891	6,188	128	313	1,062	23	1,855	44	15	144
Huntington	36,033	21,680	9,153	3,246	119	325	540	6	720	0	0	244
Jackson	41,310	22,938	12,864	3,461	109	525	585	20	686	7	0	115
Jasper	31,250	17,128	8,464	2,489	116	1,559	407	12	565	12	0	498
Jay	21,304	12,433	6,148	1,686	47	80	295	4	503	0	0	108
Jefferson	28,176	16,846	8,161	2,163	40	131	282	7	470	21	0	55
Jennings	26,396	13,844	9,092	2,243	45	186	387	14	463	74	0	48
Johnson	96,393	64,319	21,898	6,638	115	312	967	20	1,822	3	5	294
Knox	36,922	21,145	10,664	2,662	241	533	431	12	533	80	0	621
Kosciusko	71,227	43,350	16,774	7,905	126	400	1,048	21	1,438	1	3	161
Lagrange	26,166	13,904	7,193	3,724	22	326	356	8	516	0	0	117
Lake	356,457	271,978	55,735	16,305	258	2,753	2,528	54	6,001	258	1	586
Laporte	100,992	67,945	21,083	6,860	159	1,206	1,167	15	2,177	3	0	377
Lawrence	44,645	25,133	14,088	3,619	55	93	721	13	758	87	0	78
Madison	124,464	80,309	27,933	10,070	222	844	2,036	28	2,260	170	22	570
Marion	699,785	524,715	120,405	28,237	1,086	9,298	3,803	142	10,659	410	5	1,025
Marshall	44,236	25,548	11,677	4,085	131	407	734	11	1,038	15	3	587
Martin	10,737	5,671	3,576	840	32	215	124	2	183	26	0	68
Miami	34,635	20,175	9,095	3,039	94	244	616	17	974	1	1	379
Monroe	87,382	58,707	19,560	5,784	109	417	909	31	1,662	79	0	124
Montgomery	35,793	20,553	10,420	2,748	97	283	464	9	688	40	2	489
Morgan	65,079	37,377	18,764	5,876	101	439	1,018	18	1,317	45	0	124
Newton	15,368	8,804	4,319	1,355	34	99	259	0	334	0	2	154
Noble	41,414	23,957	11,411	4,119	61	424	523	8	811	0	1	99
Ohio	5,626	3,225	1,721	495	3	21	55	3	86	0	0	17
Orange	19,303	9,937	6,564	1,626	81	332	263	8	374	43	0	75
Owen	20,588	10,872	6,954	1,846	37	70	330	10	373	39	1	56
Parke	16,068	8,598	5,066	1,577	68	174	237	5	238	35	2	68
Perry	18,687	10,067	6,264	1,671	13	177	200	6	246	19	0	24
Pike	13,535	7,066	4,662	1,168	44	55	206	3	182	21	0	128
Porter	125,044	86,220	24,246	8,630	151	724	1,467	20	3,310	23	0	253
Posey	27,935	14,685	8,797	2,407	102	674	461	9	464	22	0	314
Pulaski	15,015	7,616	4,682	1,415	122	216	217	11	258	0	0	478
Putnam	31,790	17,814	9,691	3,066	47	99	460	18	476	10	7	102
Randolph	28,085	16,163	8,016	2,300	64	353	449	17	529	4	0	190
Ripley	28,001	15,842	8,624	2,141	69	272	360	14	401	44	0	234
Rush	18,789	10,185	5,853	1,558	61	278	209	2	322	20	1	300
St. Joseph	221,807	161,664	37,307	11,922	219	4,018	2,094	25	4,144	115	0	299
Scott	22,099	13,162	6,584	1,580	21	61	259	6	367	38	0	21
Shelby	43,051	25,185	12,197	3,489	121	299	514	27	897	59	0	263
Spencer	21,226	11,182	7,145	1,833	85	211	314	7	223	25	0	201
Starke	22,984	13,566	6,364	1,993	73	157	325	9	402	0	1	94
Steuben	32,742	19,377	8,031	3,920	27	222	482	6	590	0	0	87
Sullivan	20,567	10,768	6,721	1,635	74	292	336	3	361	35	2	340
Switzerland	8,018	4,244	2,828	690	12	38	80	4	106	11	0	5
Tippecanoe	106,810	74,753	22,410	5,563	189	352	1,104	15	2,106	1	3	314
Tipton	18,605	10,277	5,256	1,899	75	159	322	9	343	32	17	216
Union	7,839	4,198	2,478	693	13	57	100	0	159	11	2	128
Vanderburgh	150,555	102,325	33,515	8,383	112	2,170	1,431	42	2,181	72	0	324
Vermillion	17,573	9,932	5,272	1,329	35	209	267	3	341	26	0	159
Vigo	90,440	59,279	21,812	5,402	146	688	1,172	35	1,659	6	0	241
Wabash	35,741	20,260	9,428	3,364	77	660	522	9	786	0	3	632
Warren	9,667	4,924	3,148	924	20	99	100	6	124	0	0	322
Warrick	49,517	30,023	13,329	3,904	55	258	634	7	936	77	0	294
Washington	26,159	14,246	8,808	1,983	57	161	290	4	532	25	0	53
Wayne	64,783	42,965	14,950	4,097	56	483	713	25	1,310	0	5	179
Wells	28,223	16,224	7,422	2,809	61	225	465	14	585	1	1	416
White	27,513	15,362	7,782	2,625	142	177	357	16	438	4	0	610
Whitley	31,385	17,840	8,388	3,632	57	276	463	4	640	0	0	85

Source: Indiana Bureau of Motor Vehicles
EDIN table(s): REGT

Percent Change in Passenger Cars
1986 to 1996

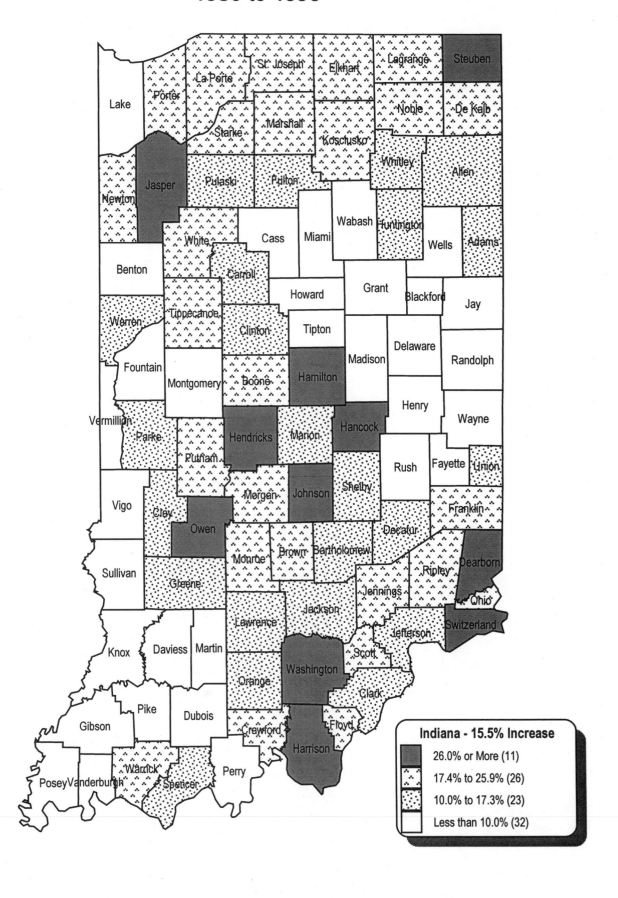

Indiana - 15.5% Increase

- 26.0% or More (11)
- 17.4% to 25.9% (26)
- 10.0% to 17.3% (23)
- Less than 10.0% (32)

Percent Change in Passenger Cars: EDIN Table REGT.

2.46 History of Motor Vehicle Registrations 1986 to 1996

	Total				Passenger Cars				Trucks			
	1986	1996	Change 1986-96	Percent Change 1986-96	1986	1996	Change 1986-96	Percent Change 1986-96	1986	1996	Change 1986-96	Percent Change 1986-96
Indiana	4,533,362	5,347,748	814,386	18.0	3,031,756	3,500,863	469,107	15.5	900,697	1,228,442	327,745	36.4
Adams	25,851	29,243	3,392	13.1	15,805	17,388	1,583	10.0	5,821	7,687	1,866	32.1
Allen	259,773	283,265	23,492	9.0	180,317	203,854	23,537	13.1	37,368	51,313	13,945	37.3
Bartholomew	58,631	68,801	10,170	17.3	38,352	43,583	5,231	13.6	12,276	17,565	5,289	43.1
Benton	9,771	10,476	705	7.2	5,285	5,476	191	3.6	2,738	3,270	532	19.4
Blackford	13,506	14,356	850	6.3	8,105	8,517	412	5.1	3,049	3,829	780	25.6
Boone	34,109	43,459	9,350	27.4	21,653	27,141	5,488	25.3	7,394	10,396	3,002	40.6
Brown	12,352	16,297	3,945	31.9	7,403	9,274	1,871	25.3	3,386	4,972	1,586	46.8
Carroll	19,135	22,309	3,174	16.6	10,138	11,466	1,328	13.1	5,446	6,768	1,322	24.3
Cass	34,999	37,861	2,862	8.2	21,920	22,762	842	3.8	7,966	10,059	2,093	26.3
Clark	75,009	86,021	11,012	14.7	50,164	55,621	5,457	10.9	14,584	19,981	5,397	37.0
Clay	22,438	26,434	3,996	17.8	12,807	14,791	1,984	15.5	6,380	8,227	1,847	28.9
Clinton	27,005	32,184	5,179	19.2	16,391	18,870	2,479	15.1	6,577	8,797	2,220	33.8
Crawford	8,780	11,179	2,399	27.3	4,791	5,823	1,032	21.5	2,863	3,869	1,006	35.1
Daviess	23,694	26,532	2,838	12.0	13,103	13,966	863	6.6	6,650	8,459	1,809	27.2
Dearborn	31,463	43,121	11,658	37.1	20,246	27,278	7,032	34.7	7,130	11,129	3,999	56.1
Decatur	20,767	25,079	4,312	20.8	11,861	13,563	1,702	14.3	5,628	8,060	2,432	43.2
Dekalb	32,310	40,312	8,002	24.8	20,054	23,846	3,792	18.9	6,831	10,078	3,247	47.5
Delaware	95,617	102,569	6,952	7.3	64,328	67,927	3,599	5.6	17,917	22,764	4,847	27.1
Dubois	33,610	40,091	6,481	19.3	19,627	21,334	1,707	8.7	9,452	13,467	4,015	42.5
Elkhart	129,484	158,225	28,741	22.2	84,827	103,455	18,628	22.0	24,371	32,933	8,562	35.1
Fayette	21,810	25,174	3,364	15.4	14,067	15,318	1,251	8.9	4,906	7,050	2,144	43.7
Floyd	50,717	61,363	10,646	21.0	35,298	41,599	6,301	17.9	9,735	13,338	3,603	37.0
Fountain	15,775	17,720	1,945	12.3	9,188	9,899	711	7.7	4,448	5,642	1,194	26.8
Franklin	16,714	21,443	4,729	28.3	9,876	12,085	2,209	22.4	4,692	6,920	2,228	47.5
Fulton	18,278	21,253	2,975	16.3	10,335	11,747	1,412	13.7	4,773	6,151	1,378	28.9
Gibson	29,940	32,322	2,382	8.0	17,552	18,230	678	3.9	8,302	9,754	1,452	17.5
Grant	63,199	68,508	5,309	8.4	42,444	44,790	2,346	5.5	11,851	15,252	3,401	28.7
Greene	27,237	32,569	5,332	19.6	15,275	17,802	2,527	16.5	8,132	10,516	2,384	29.3
Hamilton	85,832	134,564	48,732	56.8	60,553	100,362	39,809	65.7	13,042	21,297	8,255	63.3
Hancock	41,747	54,850	13,103	31.4	26,728	33,754	7,026	26.3	9,052	13,717	4,665	51.5
Harrison	26,823	36,562	9,739	36.3	15,391	20,313	4,922	32.0	7,810	11,582	3,772	48.3
Hendricks	69,689	91,256	21,567	30.9	44,349	57,013	12,664	28.6	15,224	22,260	7,036	46.2
Henry	44,133	51,091	6,958	15.8	28,584	30,849	2,265	7.9	9,711	13,657	3,946	40.6
Howard	72,763	79,325	6,562	9.0	50,533	52,662	2,129	4.2	12,665	16,891	4,226	33.4
Huntington	30,712	36,033	5,321	17.3	19,445	21,680	2,235	11.5	6,481	9,153	2,672	41.2
Jackson	34,276	41,310	7,034	20.5	19,746	22,938	3,192	16.2	9,201	12,864	3,663	39.8
Jasper	22,826	31,250	8,424	36.9	13,049	17,128	4,079	31.3	5,864	8,464	2,600	44.3
Jay	20,014	21,304	1,290	6.4	12,079	12,433	354	2.9	4,781	6,148	1,367	28.6
Jefferson	22,877	28,176	5,299	23.2	14,372	16,846	2,474	17.2	5,750	8,161	2,411	41.9
Jennings	19,224	26,396	7,172	37.3	11,204	13,844	2,640	23.6	5,491	9,092	3,601	65.6
Johnson	70,496	96,393	25,897	36.7	48,640	64,319	15,679	32.2	13,834	21,898	8,064	58.3
Knox	35,125	36,922	1,797	5.1	20,617	21,145	528	2.6	8,859	10,664	1,805	20.4
Kosciusko	57,485	71,227	13,742	23.9	35,143	43,350	8,207	23.4	12,334	16,774	4,440	36.0
Lagrange	20,122	26,166	6,044	30.0	11,372	13,904	2,532	22.3	4,903	7,193	2,290	46.7
Lake	330,626	356,457	25,831	7.8	256,028	271,978	15,950	6.2	42,553	55,735	13,182	31.0
Laporte	83,318	100,992	17,674	21.2	57,412	67,945	10,533	18.3	14,982	21,083	6,101	40.7
Lawrence	37,116	44,645	7,529	20.3	22,156	25,133	2,977	13.4	9,892	14,088	4,196	42.4
Madison	112,929	124,464	11,535	10.2	76,257	80,309	4,052	5.3	20,810	27,933	7,123	34.2
Marion	599,047	699,785	100,738	16.8	457,229	524,715	67,486	14.8	87,352	120,405	33,053	37.8
Marshall	36,651	44,236	7,585	20.7	21,605	25,548	3,943	18.3	8,606	11,677	3,071	35.7
Martin	10,035	10,737	702	7.0	5,499	5,671	172	3.1	2,863	3,576	713	24.9
Miami	33,357	34,635	1,278	3.8	20,587	20,175	-412	-2.0	7,582	9,095	1,513	20.0
Monroe	69,683	87,382	17,699	25.4	47,066	58,707	11,641	24.7	14,081	19,560	5,479	38.9
Montgomery	31,495	35,793	4,298	13.6	18,847	20,553	1,706	9.1	7,867	10,420	2,553	32.5
Morgan	48,565	65,079	16,514	34.0	30,137	37,377	7,240	24.0	12,047	18,764	6,717	55.8
Newton	12,686	15,368	2,682	21.1	7,263	8,804	1,541	21.2	3,255	4,319	1,064	32.7
Noble	32,966	41,414	8,448	25.6	19,541	23,957	4,416	22.6	7,971	11,411	3,440	43.2
Ohio	4,439	5,626	1,187	26.7	2,663	3,225	562	21.1	1,206	1,721	515	42.7
Orange	16,121	19,303	3,182	19.7	8,901	9,937	1,036	11.6	4,818	6,564	1,746	36.2
Owen	14,412	20,588	6,176	42.9	7,912	10,872	2,960	37.4	4,385	6,954	2,569	58.6
Parke	14,155	16,068	1,913	13.5	7,789	8,598	809	10.4	4,250	5,066	816	19.2
Perry	16,787	18,687	1,900	11.3	9,609	10,067	458	4.8	4,611	6,264	1,653	35.8
Pike	12,809	13,535	726	5.7	6,954	7,066	112	1.6	4,015	4,662	647	16.1
Porter	98,875	125,044	26,169	26.5	69,633	86,220	16,587	23.8	16,099	24,246	8,147	50.6
Posey	24,599	27,935	3,336	13.6	13,740	14,685	945	6.9	7,294	8,797	1,503	20.6
Pulaski	12,956	15,015	2,059	15.9	6,883	7,616	733	10.6	3,657	4,682	1,025	28.0
Putnam	24,550	31,790	7,240	29.5	14,193	17,814	3,621	25.5	6,867	9,691	2,824	41.1
Randolph	25,930	28,085	2,155	8.3	15,383	16,163	780	5.1	6,439	8,016	1,577	24.5
Ripley	22,005	28,001	5,996	27.2	12,870	15,842	2,972	23.1	5,953	8,624	2,671	44.9
Rush	16,163	18,789	2,626	16.2	9,363	10,185	822	8.8	4,399	5,853	1,454	33.1
St. Joseph	188,621	221,807	33,186	17.6	136,791	161,664	24,873	18.2	28,207	37,307	9,100	32.3
Scott	16,892	22,099	5,207	30.8	10,503	13,162	2,659	25.3	4,401	6,584	2,183	49.6
Shelby	35,641	43,051	7,410	20.8	22,065	25,185	3,120	14.1	8,861	12,197	3,336	37.6
Spencer	18,256	21,226	2,970	16.3	9,876	11,182	1,306	13.2	5,927	7,145	1,218	20.6
Starke	18,433	22,984	4,551	24.7	11,230	13,566	2,336	20.8	4,546	6,364	1,818	40.0
Steuben	24,195	32,742	8,547	35.3	14,659	19,377	4,718	32.2	5,339	8,031	2,692	50.4
Sullivan	18,332	20,567	2,235	12.2	10,151	10,768	617	6.1	5,342	6,721	1,379	25.8
Switzerland	5,890	8,018	2,128	36.1	3,341	4,244	903	27.0	1,864	2,828	964	51.7
Tippecanoe	87,962	106,810	18,848	21.4	61,047	74,753	13,706	22.5	16,379	22,410	6,031	36.8
Tipton	16,618	18,605	1,987	12.0	9,604	10,277	673	7.0	4,109	5,256	1,147	27.9
Union	6,666	7,839	1,173	17.6	3,668	4,198	530	14.4	1,811	2,478	667	36.8
Vanderburgh	138,480	150,555	12,075	8.7	95,072	102,325	7,253	7.6	27,435	33,515	6,080	22.2
Vermillion	15,787	17,573	1,786	11.3	9,086	9,932	846	9.3	4,413	5,272	859	19.5
Vigo	82,997	90,440	7,443	9.0	54,994	59,279	4,285	7.8	17,999	21,812	3,813	21.2
Wabash	31,456	35,741	4,285	13.6	18,769	20,260	1,491	7.9	7,232	9,428	2,196	30.4
Warren	8,355	9,667	1,312	15.7	4,439	4,924	485	10.9	2,564	3,148	584	22.8
Warrick	39,598	49,517	9,919	25.0	24,358	30,023	5,665	23.3	10,216	13,329	3,113	30.5
Washington	19,526	26,159	6,633	34.0	11,127	14,246	3,119	28.0	5,951	8,808	2,857	48.0
Wayne	57,560	64,783	7,223	12.5	39,641	42,965	3,324	8.4	11,191	14,950	3,759	33.6
Wells	24,822	28,223	3,401	13.7	14,777	16,224	1,447	9.8	5,331	7,422	2,091	39.2
White	22,667	27,513	4,846	21.4	12,666	15,362	2,696	21.3	5,791	7,782	1,991	34.4
Whitley	26,215	31,385	5,170	19.7	15,355	17,840	2,485	16.2	6,266	8,388	2,122	33.9

Source: Indiana Bureau of Motor Vehicles
EDIN table(s): REGT

2.47 Veteran Population Estimates And Selected Expenditures 1996

	Total Veterans	Percent of State	Number of War Veterans — Total	Persian Gulf	Vietnam	Korean Conflict	World War II	World War I	Peacetime Veterans	Expenditures ($) — Total	Percent of State
Indiana	587,400	100.00	448,900	40,700	180,700	95,000	152,400	200	141,695	604,532,638	100.00
Adams	2,290	0.39	1,770	100	710	410	630	0	510	1,082,989	0.18
Allen	30,900	5.26	23,360	2,280	9,650	4,940	7,520	10	7,541	38,799,502	6.42
Bartholomew	7,370	1.25	5,560	490	2,250	1,240	1,820	0	1,811	3,693,371	0.61
Benton	930	0.16	720	60	270	180	260	0	216	449,591	0.07
Blackford	1,570	0.27	1,240	70	390	280	550	0	337	940,405	0.16
Boone	4,180	0.71	3,170	230	1,330	670	1,090	0	1,007	1,811,553	0.30
Brown	1,880	0.32	1,440	120	560	330	500	0	436	931,873	0.15
Carroll	1,770	0.30	1,340	100	560	310	430	0	439	991,630	0.16
Cass	4,260	0.73	3,230	270	1,410	720	980	0	1,025	2,572,284	0.43
Clark	11,200	1.91	8,550	780	3,560	1,680	2,920	0	2,650	7,836,952	1.30
Clay	2,680	0.46	2,110	140	740	470	860	0	574	2,114,176	0.35
Clinton	3,020	0.51	2,370	180	820	530	950	0	658	1,580,723	0.26
Crawford	1,200	0.20	940	50	350	190	400	0	266	1,122,542	0.19
Daviess	2,780	0.47	2,220	110	860	460	890	0	562	2,287,213	0.38
Dearborn	4,590	0.78	3,500	290	1,470	720	1,170	0	1,082	2,479,506	0.41
Decatur	2,430	0.41	1,880	200	730	380	660	0	735	1,299,059	0.21
Dekalb	3,520	0.60	2,610	310	1,060	590	770	0	904	1,462,437	0.24
Delaware	11,990	2.04	9,180	900	3,310	2,180	3,210	10	2,811	7,430,420	1.23
Dubois	3,350	0.57	2,530	210	900	620	930	0	825	2,224,097	0.37
Elkhart	14,310	2.44	10,800	1,080	4,690	2,160	3,320	10	3,512	6,406,765	1.06
Fayette	2,890	0.49	2,320	160	780	490	990	0	573	1,803,524	0.30
Floyd	7,210	1.23	5,570	440	2,300	1,100	1,980	0	1,647	5,144,113	0.85
Fountain	2,140	0.36	1,700	110	580	330	770	0	444	1,199,962	0.20
Franklin	1,820	0.31	1,400	110	610	340	400	0	429	1,429,438	0.24
Fulton	2,260	0.38	1,730	130	650	410	610	0	528	1,185,765	0.20
Gibson	3,560	0.61	2,790	160	1,060	590	1,110	0	769	2,358,227	0.39
Grant	9,050	1.54	7,060	490	2,790	1,500	2,590	10	1,991	80,187,559	13.26
Greene	4,140	0.70	3,230	250	1,120	690	1,330	0	902	2,510,218	0.42
Hamilton	12,620	2.15	9,540	730	4,730	1,890	2,590	10	3,074	4,908,339	0.81
Hancock	5,350	0.91	4,090	280	1,860	880	1,250	0	1,257	2,566,387	0.42
Harrison	3,370	0.57	2,480	220	1,060	560	750	0	888	2,144,925	0.35
Hendricks	8,960	1.53	6,790	550	3,320	1,360	1,850	0	2,168	3,987,541	0.66
Henry	5,560	0.95	4,350	330	1,730	990	1,490	0	1,212	3,295,740	0.55
Howard	9,480	1.61	7,160	730	3,000	1,500	2,240	0	2,325	5,068,645	0.84
Huntington	3,350	0.57	2,510	230	1,070	470	850	0	841	1,808,136	0.30
Jackson	4,040	0.69	3,090	280	1,050	740	1,160	0	958	2,712,162	0.45
Jasper	2,430	0.41	1,850	150	730	400	650	0	573	942,319	0.16
Jay	2,110	0.36	1,700	150	610	340	680	0	412	1,112,013	0.18
Jefferson	3,620	0.62	2,830	190	990	600	1,180	0	797	1,973,830	0.33
Jennings	2,580	0.44	1,960	140	790	410	700	0	622	1,699,223	0.28
Johnson	9,760	1.66	7,370	670	3,120	1,590	2,320	10	2,396	4,950,572	0.82
Knox	4,220	0.72	3,250	280	1,300	730	1,070	0	969	3,498,492	0.58
Kosciusko	6,580	1.12	5,060	410	2,110	1,120	1,650	0	1,521	2,591,685	0.43
Lagrange	1,860	0.32	1,400	120	630	330	370	0	464	916,325	0.15
Lake	48,360	8.23	37,350	3,090	15,000	7,950	13,000	10	11,016	22,102,722	3.66
Laporte	13,220	2.25	10,070	920	4,310	2,090	3,200	0	3,145	4,966,962	0.82
Lawrence	5,090	0.87	3,910	310	1,450	930	1,390	0	1,193	3,706,572	0.61
Madison	14,570	2.48	11,170	1,070	4,390	2,420	3,790	10	3,391	7,442,461	1.23
Marion	82,150	13.99	61,490	7,100	24,390	12,300	20,320	30	20,656	226,378,325	37.45
Marshall	4,330	0.74	3,350	310	1,450	700	1,040	0	975	2,098,277	0.35
Martin	1,210	0.21	920	80	330	190	350	0	291	1,067,321	0.18
Miami	3,780	0.64	2,790	360	1,240	590	710	0	991	2,809,594	0.46
Monroe	9,260	1.58	6,980	860	2,570	1,450	2,400	0	2,286	5,638,983	0.93
Montgomery	3,750	0.64	2,930	240	1,060	630	1,120	0	820	1,432,288	0.24
Morgan	6,310	1.07	4,590	530	1,990	970	1,290	0	1,723	3,266,046	0.54
Newton	1,380	0.23	1,080	80	420	230	400	0	307	731,328	0.12
Noble	3,640	0.62	2,800	260	1,220	580	870	0	840	1,630,082	0.27
Ohio	630	0.11	480	50	200	80	180	0	140	425,469	0.07
Orange	1,990	0.34	1,520	140	530	360	560	0	469	1,714,299	0.28
Owen	2,100	0.36	1,590	130	580	340	620	0	509	1,601,407	0.26
Parke	1,970	0.34	1,540	90	540	360	620	0	418	1,114,529	0.18
Perry	2,300	0.39	1,770	160	650	360	680	0	525	1,496,619	0.25
Pike	1,400	0.24	1,110	70	430	230	430	0	287	1,146,627	0.19
Porter	14,670	2.50	11,210	920	5,330	2,230	3,200	10	3,457	5,206,391	0.86
Posey	2,810	0.48	2,180	130	1,060	430	660	0	641	1,779,034	0.29
Pulaski	1,280	0.22	970	90	340	240	340	0	318	826,086	0.14
Putnam	3,610	0.61	2,660	290	930	620	940	0	960	1,737,378	0.29
Randolph	2,760	0.47	2,160	180	820	520	740	0	606	1,101,974	0.18
Ripley	2,570	0.44	1,980	140	840	410	680	0	583	1,659,502	0.27
Rush	1,760	0.30	1,340	150	450	310	490	0	425	895,309	0.15
St. Joseph	25,730	4.38	20,100	1,680	7,570	4,180	7,590	10	5,623	12,125,878	2.01
Scott	2,060	0.35	1,560	130	560	380	580	0	494	1,472,894	0.24
Shelby	4,270	0.73	3,270	280	1,340	660	1,130	0	1,004	2,294,365	0.38
Spencer	2,160	0.37	1,650	150	730	380	460	0	509	1,249,227	0.21
Starke	2,410	0.41	1,900	150	670	410	750	0	505	1,114,950	0.18
Steuben	3,190	0.54	2,470	190	1,050	560	770	0	731	1,456,177	0.24
Sullivan	2,160	0.37	1,720	100	640	370	690	0	440	1,707,024	0.28
Switzerland	850	0.14	640	50	290	140	190	0	199	1,026,112	0.17
Tippecanoe	11,360	1.93	8,670	1,090	3,300	1,860	2,800	10	2,688	10,100,417	1.67
Tipton	1,760	0.30	1,400	100	550	260	540	0	370	1,057,646	0.17
Union	580	0.10	410	40	190	80	110	0	170	467,647	0.08
Vanderburgh	17,960	3.06	14,030	1,040	5,310	3,000	5,330	10	3,926	13,526,813	2.24
Vermillion	1,890	0.32	1,460	100	660	330	440	0	433	1,245,901	0.21
Vigo	11,710	1.99	9,070	880	3,490	1,820	3,280	0	2,641	7,884,528	1.30
Wabash	3,130	0.53	2,320	210	930	580	700	0	809	1,967,175	0.33
Warren	900	0.15	730	50	290	170	250	0	174	487,798	0.08
Warrick	4,600	0.78	3,470	270	1,610	740	1,000	0	1,131	2,808,730	0.46
Washington	2,540	0.43	1,920	180	690	450	690	0	613	1,953,779	0.32
Wayne	8,040	1.37	6,270	550	2,170	1,370	2,470	0	1,770	5,383,400	0.89
Wells	2,440	0.42	1,900	130	760	390	700	0	538	1,058,519	0.18
White	2,520	0.43	1,980	140	740	450	750	0	534	1,391,275	0.23
Whitley	3,120	0.53	2,380	200	1,080	480	720	0	740	1,264,570	0.21

Items do not sum to total due to rounding.
Source: U.S. Veterans Administration
EDIN table(s): VETP, VAEX

Adjusted Gross Personal Income:
Percent of Returns over $50,000
1994

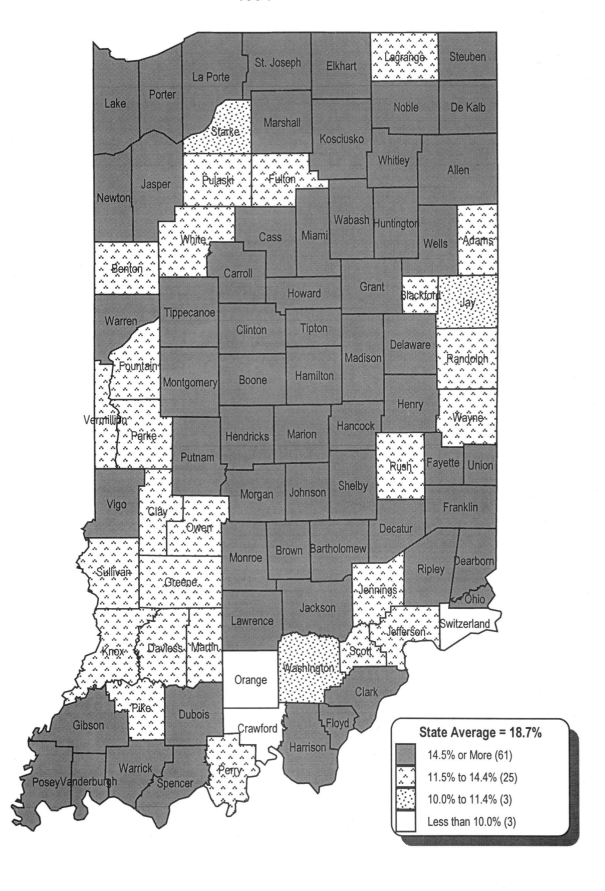

State Average = 18.7%

- 14.5% or More (61)
- 11.5% to 14.4% (25)
- 10.0% to 11.4% (3)
- Less than 10.0% (3)

2.48 Adjusted Gross Personal Income: Number of Returns 1994

	Total Number	Total Amount ($000)	Mean Amount ($000)	Less Than Zero	Zero to $9,999	$10,000 to $19,999	$20,000 to $29,999	$30,000 to $39,999	$40,000 to $49,999	$50,000 to $74,999	Over $75,000	Percent Over $50,000
Indiana	2,621,909	81,326,689	31.0	10,081	742,258	525,040	363,705	267,834	222,336	312,699	177,956	18.7
Adams	14,233	382,022	26.8	85	4,202	2,980	2,119	1,662	1,282	1,457	546	14.1
Allen	142,726	4,794,173	33.6	347	38,153	28,111	19,616	14,629	12,435	18,536	11,001	20.7
Bartholomew	31,191	1,103,779	35.4	78	7,969	5,818	4,228	3,220	2,976	4,201	2,701	22.1
Benton	4,319	110,005	25.5	32	1,231	889	674	497	436	396	164	13.0
Blackford	6,302	157,245	25.0	25	1,898	1,332	972	712	533	623	207	13.2
Boone	18,577	795,096	42.8	96	4,738	3,052	2,304	1,824	1,889	2,589	2,305	26.3
Brown	6,339	183,347	28.9	25	1,732	1,268	868	701	601	765	379	18.0
Carroll	8,800	244,399	27.8	45	2,443	1,651	1,274	1,028	873	1,050	436	16.9
Cass	17,854	487,515	27.3	73	5,403	3,858	2,520	1,851	1,533	1,796	820	14.7
Clark	40,641	1,082,411	26.6	85	10,890	9,340	6,157	4,401	3,395	4,411	1,962	15.7
Clay	10,944	278,383	25.4	52	3,249	2,225	1,715	1,311	979	1,039	374	12.9
Clinton	14,614	402,851	27.6	49	4,097	2,819	2,126	1,608	1,406	1,825	684	17.2
Crawford	4,099	87,089	21.2	21	1,304	865	738	442	276	273	80	8.6
Daviess	12,153	289,301	23.8	98	3,926	2,808	1,735	1,197	919	1,036	436	12.1
Dearborn	17,557	527,634	30.1	63	4,608	3,178	2,379	1,972	1,763	2,576	1,018	20.5
Decatur	11,305	303,094	26.8	50	3,256	2,067	1,824	1,377	1,042	1,243	446	14.9
Dekalb	17,300	621,814	35.9	58	4,511	3,265	2,579	2,017	1,780	2,251	839	17.9
Delaware	48,583	1,485,890	30.6	116	15,669	10,127	6,282	4,668	3,865	5,850	3,216	18.7
Dubois	17,970	583,545	32.5	58	4,746	3,187	2,831	1,987	1,910	2,207	1,064	18.2
Elkhart	73,660	2,425,803	32.9	217	18,891	15,041	11,667	8,412	6,634	8,250	4,548	17.4
Fayette	11,700	317,820	27.2	61	3,685	2,200	1,688	1,192	1,008	1,275	691	16.8
Floyd	30,040	874,758	29.1	77	8,134	6,138	3,938	2,911	2,523	3,945	2,374	21.0
Fountain	7,940	208,168	26.2	40	2,342	1,600	1,237	961	723	796	251	13.2
Franklin	8,738	247,386	28.3	57	2,638	1,607	1,255	986	780	953	462	16.2
Fulton	8,775	223,774	25.5	47	2,619	1,860	1,328	1,009	773	834	305	13.0
Gibson	14,364	380,143	26.5	51	4,267	2,863	2,023	1,563	1,259	1,817	621	17.0
Grant	32,138	824,087	25.6	101	9,545	6,492	4,586	3,174	2,478	3,840	1,922	17.9
Greene	13,599	337,793	24.8	60	4,270	2,838	1,958	1,515	1,100	1,344	514	13.7
Hamilton	58,463	3,347,063	57.3	220	13,234	7,362	5,947	4,814	4,658	9,786	12,442	38.0
Hancock	22,447	828,116	36.9	78	5,450	3,754	2,688	2,082	2,031	3,822	2,531	28.3
Harrison	13,636	363,091	26.6	66	3,833	2,848	1,992	1,585	1,213	1,505	614	15.5
Hendricks	36,459	1,408,809	38.6	121	8,497	5,538	4,192	3,471	3,509	6,837	4,284	30.5
Henry	22,221	818,475	36.8	71	6,470	4,776	3,127	2,178	1,694	2,516	1,389	17.6
Howard	38,594	1,321,403	34.2	84	10,612	6,932	4,054	3,114	3,397	6,158	4,243	26.9
Huntington	16,851	470,176	27.9	43	4,573	3,493	2,508	1,912	1,521	2,057	744	16.6
Jackson	17,662	484,063	27.4	80	5,061	3,793	2,634	1,896	1,615	1,879	704	14.6
Jasper	11,676	341,601	29.3	58	3,302	2,148	1,585	1,371	1,172	1,458	582	17.5
Jay	8,683	228,562	26.3	56	2,925	2,237	1,523	1,149	799	756	238	11.4
Jefferson	13,097	344,465	26.3	53	3,755	2,905	2,013	1,409	1,094	1,329	539	14.3
Jennings	10,482	260,131	24.8	38	2,917	2,469	1,689	1,172	903	991	303	12.3
Johnson	43,453	1,595,502	36.7	108	10,605	7,376	5,581	4,488	4,139	6,638	4,518	25.7
Knox	16,856	434,263	25.8	72	5,853	3,486	2,326	1,735	1,312	1,480	792	13.5
Kosciusko	31,774	1,040,698	32.8	140	8,058	6,018	4,802	3,788	3,047	3,954	1,967	18.6
Lagrange	13,259	377,104	28.4	91	3,645	2,649	2,291	1,808	1,183	1,178	414	12.0
Lake	196,967	6,048,116	30.7	391	55,328	37,501	25,045	20,159	18,906	27,029	12,608	20.1
Laporte	47,165	1,401,386	29.7	162	13,845	8,156	6,580	4,900	4,209	5,701	2,612	17.6
Lawrence	19,260	530,889	27.6	62	5,402	4,074	2,706	2,087	1,617	2,256	1,056	17.2
Madison	59,961	1,822,071	30.4	110	16,880	12,938	7,890	5,326	4,456	7,469	4,892	20.6
Marion	370,659	12,223,533	33.0	805	80,640	80,115	57,637	38,705	30,344	44,023	28,390	19.5
Marshall	19,433	567,718	29.2	93	5,480	3,876	2,927	2,381	1,783	2,031	882	15.0
Martin	4,643	116,894	25.2	11	1,280	1,081	732	535	396	448	160	13.1
Miami	14,821	386,178	26.1	49	4,282	3,155	2,037	1,621	1,260	1,677	740	16.3
Monroe	44,978	1,348,817	30.0	107	14,109	9,210	5,733	4,237	3,428	4,770	3,384	18.1
Montgomery	16,473	482,678	29.3	55	4,302	3,034	2,520	1,871	1,604	2,134	853	18.1
Morgan	25,667	828,134	32.3	86	6,452	4,744	3,342	2,879	2,583	3,739	1,842	21.7
Newton	5,915	155,186	26.2	33	1,709	1,095	870	731	589	683	205	15.0
Noble	18,633	539,139	28.9	60	4,737	3,666	3,195	2,141	1,880	2,237	717	15.9
Ohio	1,990	53,239	26.8	7	536	399	299	228	211	234	76	15.6
Orange	7,913	108,802	13.7	35	2,376	2,032	1,337	844	551	514	225	9.3
Owen	7,814	187,574	24.0	46	2,241	1,633	1,243	947	659	803	242	13.4
Parke	6,550	163,256	24.9	44	1,952	1,435	988	715	562	616	240	13.1
Perry	8,248	206,863	25.1	24	2,607	1,763	1,337	860	684	778	215	12.0
Pike	5,429	131,845	24.3	19	1,651	1,175	854	557	496	518	159	12.5
Porter	59,666	2,220,169	37.2	151	15,364	9,307	6,488	5,625	6,020	10,818	5,893	28.0
Posey	11,548	371,695	32.2	40	3,052	1,972	1,477	1,147	1,051	1,944	865	24.3
Pulaski	5,843	152,458	26.1	49	1,744	1,180	946	684	516	510	214	12.4
Putnam	13,136	367,705	28.0	52	3,635	2,554	1,931	1,577	1,220	1,573	594	16.5
Randolph	12,007	297,388	24.8	51	3,588	2,713	1,892	1,350	982	1,079	352	11.9
Ripley	11,294	314,866	27.9	58	3,310	2,176	1,762	1,219	1,014	1,261	494	15.5
Rush	8,309	211,524	25.5	60	2,422	1,645	1,333	992	704	800	353	13.9
St. Joseph	112,270	3,624,896	32.3	273	32,293	23,407	15,852	11,528	9,115	12,253	7,549	17.6
Scott	8,108	215,079	26.5	30	2,666	2,113	1,560	1,032	695	771	241	12.5
Shelby	18,537	554,494	29.9	58	4,767	3,634	2,628	2,192	1,763	2,329	1,166	18.9
Spencer	8,560	233,516	27.3	55	2,502	1,624	1,210	1,021	859	971	318	15.1
Starke	9,351	216,207	23.1	53	2,955	2,117	1,468	1,011	729	777	241	10.9
Steuben	13,757	395,820	28.8	73	3,726	2,715	2,241	1,583	1,232	1,551	636	15.9
Sullivan	8,886	204,907	23.1	35	2,865	1,926	1,225	889	645	803	298	12.4
Switzerland	2,984	68,495	23.0	22	837	759	471	350	259	223	63	9.6
Tippecanoe	56,042	1,751,649	31.3	137	16,294	11,270	7,182	5,326	4,637	6,830	4,366	20.0
Tipton	7,690	238,616	31.0	24	2,186	1,423	939	738	630	1,068	672	22.6
Union	2,972	74,768	25.2	21	862	627	399	367	262	335	101	14.7
Vanderburgh	76,003	2,358,078	31.0	202	22,302	16,519	10,239	7,825	5,983	8,130	4,803	17.0
Vermillion	7,380	185,631	25.2	20	2,268	1,559	1,087	790	599	759	278	14.1
Vigo	46,630	1,263,867	27.1	141	14,895	9,623	6,211	4,542	3,542	4,384	2,492	14.7
Wabash	15,721	428,837	27.3	75	4,498	3,165	2,323	1,881	1,498	1,611	670	14.5
Warren	3,532	94,442	26.7	30	946	707	570	421	318	378	162	15.3
Warrick	21,575	743,446	34.5	59	5,797	3,698	2,622	2,267	2,102	3,222	1,808	23.3
Washington	9,977	233,283	23.4	80	2,823	2,334	1,722	1,142	809	810	257	10.7
Wayne	31,344	820,947	26.2	115	9,860	6,884	4,456	3,287	2,294	2,902	1,446	13.9
Wells	12,038	361,901	30.1	51	3,294	2,132	1,828	1,377	1,176	1,531	650	18.1
White	11,731	305,289	26.0	58	3,570	2,435	1,787	1,304	992	1,093	492	13.5
Whitley	13,376	403,005	30.1	50	3,454	2,493	1,920	1,454	1,403	1,898	704	19.5

Footnote: Items do not sum to total because Indiana figures include nonresident tax payments.
Source: Indiana Department of Revenue
EDIN table(s): TAXN

Average Net Property Tax Rate Payable in 1995

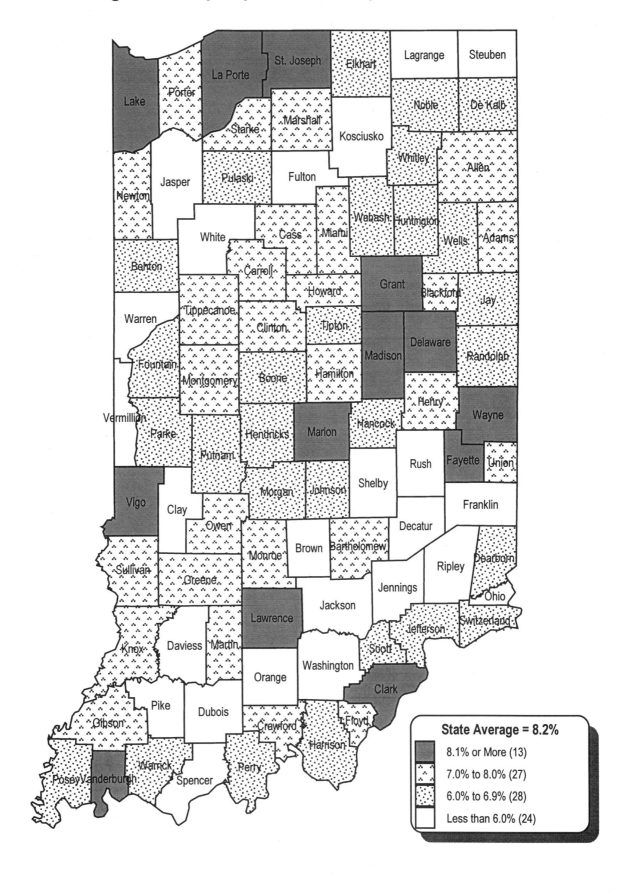

State Average = 8.2%

- 8.1% or More (13)
- 7.0% to 8.0% (27)
- 6.0% to 6.9% (28)
- Less than 6.0% (24)

Adjusted Gross Personal Income: EDIN Table TAXR.

2.49 Average County Property Tax Rates Payable in 1995 ($000)

	Assessed Valuation	Rank	Assessed Value Per Capita	Levy	Gross Rate	State Property Tax Replacement Credit	Net Levy	Average Net Rate	Rank	Percent of State
Indiana	48,634,955	—	8.39	4,683,924	9.631	690,366	3,993,558	8.211	—	100.00
Adams	263,191	48	8.12	22,096	8.395	3,345	18,751	7.125	37	86.77
Allen	2,835,784	3	9.19	264,498	9.327	38,364	226,134	7.974	15	97.11
Bartholomew	707,222	19	10.41	63,424	8.968	9,900	53,523	7.568	24	92.17
Benton	114,454	81	11.78	8,601	7.515	1,514	7,087	6.192	64	75.41
Blackford	87,893	87	6.25	8,131	9.251	1,309	6,822	7.762	19	94.53
Boone	395,869	30	9.48	30,809	7.783	3,655	27,154	6.859	43	83.53
Brown	112,742	82	7.43	7,389	6.554	1,153	6,235	5.531	80	67.36
Carroll	183,005	64	9.35	15,082	8.241	1,996	13,086	7.151	33	87.09
Cass	288,844	43	7.50	24,731	8.562	3,906	20,825	7.210	30	87.81
Clark	630,500	20	6.89	66,094	10.483	10,245	55,849	8.858	7	107.88
Clay	171,557	67	6.52	11,671	6.803	2,241	9,430	5.497	82	66.95
Clinton	253,327	50	7.80	23,028	9.090	3,837	19,192	7.576	23	92.27
Crawford	51,588	90	4.97	4,895	9.489	781	4,114	7.975	14	97.13
Daviess	213,754	56	7.48	13,777	6.445	2,082	11,695	5.471	84	66.63
Dearborn	332,026	36	7.47	26,183	7.886	3,658	22,525	6.784	46	82.62
Decatur	233,589	53	9.37	13,876	5.940	2,351	11,525	4.934	90	60.09
Dekalb	331,401	37	8.76	24,823	7.490	3,906	20,917	6.312	62	76.87
Delaware	746,036	16	6.27	91,148	12.218	12,918	78,229	10.486	3	127.71
Dubois	414,519	27	10.68	27,416	6.614	3,865	23,551	5.682	76	69.20
Elkhart	1,759,621	5	10.55	142,372	8.091	22,090	120,283	6.836	44	83.25
Fayette	196,387	62	7.48	19,060	9.706	3,007	16,053	8.174	13	99.55
Floyd	495,063	24	7.08	43,839	8.855	7,238	36,602	7.393	25	90.04
Fountain	135,004	77	7.47	9,663	7.158	1,515	8,148	6.036	67	73.51
Franklin	139,237	76	6.62	9,138	6.563	1,467	7,672	5.510	81	67.11
Fulton	178,032	66	8.95	12,124	6.810	1,949	10,175	5.715	74	69.60
Gibson	296,517	40	9.27	25,384	8.561	4,020	21,365	7.205	31	87.75
Grant	510,803	22	6.93	52,036	10.187	7,752	44,284	8.670	9	105.59
Greene	181,429	65	5.55	15,245	8.403	2,026	13,219	7.286	26	88.73
Hamilton	1,873,091	4	13.29	149,796	7.997	15,862	133,934	7.150	34	87.08
Hancock	407,457	28	8.00	31,957	7.843	4,624	27,334	6.708	48	81.70
Harrison	205,083	59	6.29	15,227	7.425	2,160	13,066	6.371	58	77.59
Hendricks	716,587	18	8.27	54,888	7.660	6,827	48,061	6.707	49	81.68
Henry	293,883	42	5.98	27,177	9.248	4,314	22,862	7.779	18	94.74
Howard	915,460	10	10.98	79,425	8.676	12,744	66,681	7.284	27	88.71
Huntington	280,000	44	7.61	23,483	8.387	4,030	19,454	6.948	41	84.62
Jackson	373,498	33	9.27	20,652	5.529	3,872	16,780	4.493	92	54.72
Jasper	353,960	35	12.70	23,896	6.751	3,933	19,962	5.640	77	68.69
Jay	159,082	72	7.31	12,503	7.859	2,397	10,105	6.352	60	77.36
Jefferson	248,428	51	8.05	19,470	7.838	2,974	16,497	6.641	50	80.88
Jennings	159,816	71	6.12	9,593	6.003	1,719	7,874	4.927	91	60.00
Johnson	864,613	11	8.50	65,277	7.550	8,783	56,494	6.534	57	79.58
Knox	268,171	45	6.75	24,333	9.074	3,596	20,737	7.733	21	94.18
Kosciusko	730,507	17	10.57	48,853	6.688	6,367	42,486	5.816	71	70.83
Lagrange	264,257	47	8.32	17,281	6.539	2,791	14,489	5.483	83	66.78
Lake	3,073,868	2	6.40	597,733	19.446	87,976	509,757	16.584	1	201.97
Laporte	826,227	12	7.54	83,046	10.051	14,624	68,422	8.281	12	100.85
Lawrence	232,696	54	5.16	23,016	9.891	3,607	19,409	8.341	11	101.58
Madison	807,113	13	6.09	84,382	10.455	12,540	71,842	8.901	5	108.40
Marion	8,007,858	1	9.81	831,728	10.386	120,879	710,849	8.877	6	108.11
Marshall	390,296	31	8.72	33,616	8.613	5,277	28,339	7.261	28	88.43
Martin	61,742	88	5.87	5,130	8.308	708	4,422	7.162	32	87.22
Miami	203,164	60	6.26	18,201	8.959	2,592	15,609	7.683	22	93.57
Monroe	782,777	14	6.78	70,450	9.000	9,294	61,156	7.813	17	95.15
Montgomery	396,576	29	10.97	32,167	8.111	3,897	28,270	7.129	35	86.82
Morgan	417,390	26	6.73	29,704	7.117	4,356	25,348	6.073	66	73.96
Newton	133,037	78	9.24	11,281	8.480	1,801	9,480	7.126	36	86.79
Noble	316,599	38	7.75	25,020	7.903	4,118	20,902	6.602	54	80.40
Ohio	25,181	92	4.63	1,569	6.231	313	1,256	4.988	89	60.75
Orange	131,056	79	6.90	8,116	6.193	1,370	6,746	5.147	88	62.68
Owen	98,551	85	5.02	8,173	8.293	1,051	7,121	7.226	29	88.00
Parke	105,334	84	6.53	8,083	7.673	1,380	6,703	6.364	59	77.51
Perry	110,044	83	5.75	8,143	7.400	1,271	6,872	6.245	63	76.06
Pike	162,114	69	12.94	11,286	6.962	1,773	9,514	5.869	70	71.48
Porter	1,421,160	7	10.13	127,692	8.985	17,736	109,956	7.737	20	94.23
Posey	430,110	25	16.31	33,577	7.807	5,043	28,534	6.634	51	80.79
Pulaski	139,451	75	10.63	10,025	7.189	1,631	8,394	6.019	68	73.30
Putnam	261,660	49	7.94	18,459	7.055	2,307	16,152	6.173	65	75.18
Randolph	208,935	58	7.61	16,969	8.122	2,750	14,219	6.805	45	82.88
Ripley	197,077	61	7.38	13,171	6.683	1,943	11,228	5.697	75	69.38
Rush	163,502	68	8.92	11,582	7.084	2,131	9,451	5.780	72	70.39
St. Joseph	1,620,265	6	6.31	217,636	13.432	30,591	187,045	11.544	2	140.59
Scott	129,901	80	5.80	9,895	7.618	1,396	8,500	6.543	56	79.69
Shelby	377,013	32	8.80	24,371	6.464	3,789	20,582	5.459	85	66.48
Spencer	294,256	41	14.45	18,573	6.312	2,799	15,773	5.360	87	65.28
Starke	145,022	73	6.42	11,896	8.203	1,625	10,271	7.083	39	86.26
Steuben	362,216	34	12.00	24,800	6.847	3,533	21,267	5.871	69	71.50
Sullivan	195,085	63	9.61	18,367	9.415	2,861	15,506	7.948	16	96.80
Switzerland	46,641	91	5.65	3,669	7.867	617	3,052	6.544	55	79.70
Tippecanoe	1,241,429	8	9.03	100,888	8.127	13,756	87,132	7.019	40	85.48
Tipton	142,277	74	8.64	11,393	8.008	1,959	9,434	6.631	52	80.76
Union	54,253	89	7.37	4,469	8.238	618	3,851	7.099	38	86.46
Vanderburgh	1,232,424	9	7.36	135,322	10.980	21,764	113,558	9.214	4	112.22
Vermillion	218,545	55	12.99	13,736	6.285	1,893	11,843	5.419	86	66.00
Vigo	760,853	15	7.14	78,784	10.355	12,409	66,376	8.724	8	106.25
Wabash	267,163	46	7.68	22,099	8.272	3,564	18,535	6.938	42	84.50
Warren	88,260	86	10.71	6,216	7.043	1,153	5,063	5.737	73	69.87
Warrick	566,088	21	11.49	41,230	7.283	5,468	35,762	6.317	61	76.93
Washington	160,919	70	6.17	10,798	6.710	1,889	8,908	5.536	78	67.42
Wayne	496,819	23	6.87	51,401	10.346	8,780	42,621	8.579	10	104.48
Wells	212,562	57	8.03	16,423	7.726	2,366	14,057	6.613	53	80.54
White	301,909	39	12.27	19,602	6.493	2,889	16,713	5.536	78	67.42
Whitley	244,251	52	8.29	19,690	8.062	3,192	16,498	6.755	47	82.27

Source: Indiana State Board of Tax Commissioners, U.S. Bureau of the Census.
EDIN table(s): TAXR, POPE

2.50 Assessed Value of Real Estate by Type of Property ($000) 1994

	Total Gross Value	Exemptions and Deductions		Total Net Value	Percent Distribution by Sector				
		Total	Tax Exempt		Agriculture	Commercial	Industrial	Residential	Utility
Indiana	**38,751,882**	**6,973,463**	**2,839,034**	**31,778,419**	**14.0**	**22.7**	**9.0**	**53.1**	**1.2**
Adams	205,861	35,573	11,595	170,288	31.0	14.8	18.4	35.3	0.5
Allen	2,322,375	387,972	157,587	1,934,403	5.7	23.0	8.9	61.6	0.7
Bartholomew	527,500	78,318	16,841	449,182	12.1	20.4	10.5	56.6	0.4
Benton	94,804	8,409	2,102	86,395	68.7	5.8	0.6	24.6	0.3
Blackford	73,681	13,719	2,417	59,962	33.9	13.7	12.9	39.2	0.3
Boone	341,697	56,708	30,154	284,989	25.3	12.8	3.0	58.4	0.4
Brown	97,110	9,983	470	87,127	46.1	13.5	0.1	40.3	0.1
Carroll	153,691	26,397	10,321	127,294	43.1	11.7	5.6	38.9	0.7
Cass	231,704	36,256	9,478	195,448	29.5	15.6	8.0	46.5	0.4
Clark	481,810	89,610	19,586	392,200	9.2	30.5	5.5	54.4	0.5
Clay	134,451	22,051	4,788	112,400	44.5	15.2	5.3	34.7	0.3
Clinton	197,798	34,749	11,506	163,049	38.4	14.5	7.5	39.4	0.2
Crawford	42,379	8,504	2,081	33,875	68.8	14.6	0.3	15.9	0.5
Daviess	166,636	26,556	7,831	140,079	41.2	26.0	0.0	32.3	0.5
Dearborn	234,360	35,433	6,755	198,927	22.5	7.8	2.5	63.2	4.1
Decatur	168,374	35,920	15,940	132,454	38.3	18.6	6.0	36.5	0.6
Dekalb	238,695	44,391	9,857	194,304	27.3	14.5	13.7	44.0	0.5
Delaware	571,505	107,775	33,738	463,730	11.4	36.0	6.5	45.1	1.0
Dubois	355,787	57,358	28,224	298,429	17.2	15.1	16.7	50.5	0.4
Elkhart	1,289,175	172,175	73,154	1,117,001	6.5	19.7	27.7	45.7	0.5
Fayette	143,935	24,759	8,572	119,176	22.9	13.9	11.1	51.4	0.8
Floyd	435,850	83,198	30,472	352,652	7.6	21.0	4.3	65.9	1.3
Fountain	113,457	15,910	4,288	97,547	55.2	4.5	0.5	39.5	0.3
Franklin	119,365	18,059	5,499	101,306	53.2	2.7	0.2	43.7	0.1
Fulton	137,459	26,914	12,223	110,544	31.3	5.5	0.7	62.2	0.3
Gibson	203,635	44,043	21,182	159,592	32.8	8.9	6.8	43.8	7.7
Grant	431,183	115,693	66,866	315,490	15.6	18.1	11.5	54.5	0.2
Greene	142,696	26,165	6,453	116,531	41.1	16.4	4.2	37.6	0.7
Hamilton	1,469,016	222,449	114,470	1,246,567	6.8	20.4	2.1	70.0	0.7
Hancock	340,362	44,931	8,964	295,431	18.0	10.0	5.0	66.6	0.4
Harrison	177,144	34,009	12,581	143,135	34.2	16.7	3.3	45.3	0.5
Hendricks	595,624	77,302	20,056	518,323	4.6	12.2	1.4	80.4	1.4
Henry	236,238	43,903	9,767	192,335	27.3	13.6	4.0	54.4	0.6
Howard	671,193	165,261	94,979	505,932	12.6	16.2	10.5	60.0	0.8
Huntington	228,816	50,890	23,009	177,927	30.8	14.4	10.9	43.3	0.6
Jackson	258,290	45,326	11,136	212,964	20.8	21.1	3.8	52.6	1.8
Jasper	221,650	21,561	5,152	200,089	35.9	9.0	5.3	35.9	13.9
Jay	131,497	21,719	5,008	109,778	46.8	10.9	0.0	41.4	0.9
Jefferson	182,922	39,137	16,681	143,785	20.3	21.6	2.8	47.2	8.1
Jennings	126,815	23,062	4,040	103,753	29.7	12.2	4.5	53.4	0.2
Johnson	718,672	100,158	34,457	618,514	9.0	20.2	4.2	66.2	0.3
Knox	203,970	62,224	37,755	141,746	31.2	11.3	1.8	54.4	1.3
Kosciusko	573,519	102,747	58,503	470,772	18.6	14.1	8.9	57.8	0.6
Lagrange	223,087	40,036	20,148	183,051	33.9	12.4	9.5	43.8	0.4
Lake	2,270,834	502,839	160,280	1,767,996	1.4	27.6	17.8	51.0	2.1
Laporte	651,599	119,567	43,765	532,032	11.9	9.2	1.9	74.9	2.1
Lawrence	186,728	44,401	13,527	142,327	22.2	19.4	6.0	52.0	0.5
Madison	690,228	153,846	54,914	536,382	13.6	18.4	8.1	59.7	0.3
Marion	6,634,329	1,022,042	432,481	5,612,287	0.4	41.6	5.4	51.5	1.0
Marshall	314,294	52,687	22,753	261,608	24.9	13.0	9.5	51.9	0.7
Martin	50,617	9,451	2,243	41,166	39.3	14.1	1.9	44.4	0.4
Miami	195,362	53,893	29,793	141,469	41.0	14.1	8.2	36.0	0.7
Monroe	689,448	125,229	61,503	564,219	8.8	25.9	5.6	59.0	0.7
Montgomery	269,687	49,396	11,059	220,291	30.8	14.9	15.4	38.5	0.5
Morgan	337,498	46,006	10,553	291,492	22.0	13.7	2.5	60.8	1.1
Newton	105,625	11,022	2,049	94,602	50.7	8.8	5.9	34.3	0.3
Noble	252,489	47,484	15,003	205,006	22.3	15.2	12.7	49.3	0.5
Ohio	22,971	4,941	1,016	18,030	54.1	5.8	0.0	39.9	0.2
Orange	111,050	21,190	8,713	89,860	29.7	21.0	11.6	36.9	0.8
Owen	84,335	14,811	4,060	69,524	47.1	11.8	1.6	39.2	0.2
Parke	93,598	14,062	4,199	79,536	51.3	11.4	0.9	35.7	0.8
Perry	96,422	19,642	5,138	76,780	32.1	2.8	0.7	63.8	0.6
Pike	87,490	12,502	4,350	74,988	34.5	6.5	9.0	33.3	16.8
Porter	1,068,477	165,301	56,497	903,176	4.6	8.2	28.7	57.2	1.4
Posey	252,619	24,148	5,848	228,471	22.8	8.4	23.4	38.6	6.8
Pulaski	106,238	12,894	2,968	93,344	47.1	3.5	4.7	44.3	0.3
Putnam	215,299	50,650	22,424	164,649	37.0	11.9	5.4	45.2	0.5
Randolph	188,186	41,103	22,381	147,083	27.5	15.5	5.7	50.8	0.4
Ripley	152,516	22,326	4,798	130,190	37.7	12.5	8.1	41.3	0.5
Rush	132,749	16,159	3,955	116,590	47.9	16.0	3.6	32.1	0.4
St. Joseph	1,692,888	428,339	229,110	1,264,549	3.9	23.8	16.3	55.1	0.9
Scott	109,763	22,153	4,211	87,609	25.9	17.4	5.4	51.1	0.2
Shelby	284,987	45,357	8,411	239,629	27.6	15.1	11.6	44.8	0.9
Spencer	150,070	23,378	11,841	126,692	38.7	0.3	0.3	47.1	13.6
Starke	118,547	21,678	5,806	96,870	36.1	17.7	4.7	41.1	0.4
Steuben	266,123	32,506	9,683	233,617	16.4	13.8	9.2	60.3	0.3
Sullivan	112,008	14,202	210	97,806	30.1	8.8	-0.3	48.0	13.4
Switzerland	38,114	5,677	1,133	32,437	65.6	4.1	0.0	18.2	12.1
Tippecanoe	949,626	172,080	84,687	777,546	12.7	25.9	7.5	53.4	0.6
Tipton	126,846	31,195	18,487	95,650	44.9	11.9	5.2	37.7	0.3
Union	44,108	5,697	1,463	38,412	58.9	8.0	0.0	32.6	0.5
Vanderburgh	1,024,599	204,949	83,852	819,651	3.1	32.0	6.1	58.1	0.6
Vermillion	93,355	16,494	2,673	76,861	28.5	15.1	16.8	34.6	4.9
Vigo	679,594	220,886	145,483	458,708	14.8	34.6	9.9	38.4	2.2
Wabash	212,036	47,402	23,402	164,634	26.5	11.8	7.1	54.1	0.5
Warren	74,710	8,212	2,097	66,498	82.1	1.5	2.6	13.6	0.2
Warrick	338,415	43,504	7,362	294,911	20.1	13.2	11.5	53.4	1.8
Washington	125,498	19,441	3,323	106,057	47.6	12.9	5.0	34.4	0.2
Wayne	438,412	117,634	61,614	320,778	17.2	27.5	9.0	45.5	0.8
Wells	198,652	50,105	30,874	148,547	32.6	10.3	8.2	48.7	0.2
White	204,714	20,875	4,486	183,839	36.3	9.9	6.3	46.1	1.4
Whitley	192,338	26,797	5,870	165,541	34.8	8.7	16.1	40.1	0.3

Source: Indiana State Board of Tax Commissioners
EDIN table(s): TAXA, TAXB

2.51 Assessed Valuation of Personal Property ($000) 1994

	Total Gross Value	Total Exemptions	Total Net Value	Railroads and Utilities	Vehicles	Boats and Motors	Farm Implements	Livestock, Poultry, Grain	Inventory	Depreciable Assets
							Percent Distribution of Personal Property by Sector			
Indiana	**13,559,487**	**1,527,039**	**12,032,448**	**2,194,359**	**1.2**	**0.0**	**3.1**	**1.5**	**32.9**	**61.3**
Adams	75,464	1,650	73,814	7,904	1.1	0.0	8.0	5.3	44.3	41.3
Allen	717,156	77,233	639,924	93,775	0.8	0.0	1.0	0.4	34.8	63.0
Bartholomew	214,117	22,971	191,146	18,301	0.9	0.0	2.0	0.8	27.7	68.6
Benton	19,231	215	19,015	3,457	1.6	0.0	28.7	12.5	32.6	24.5
Blackford	27,297	3,874	23,422	3,539	1.7	0.0	5.4	2.3	29.2	61.4
Boone	50,188	896	49,293	10,719	3.9	0.0	15.3	5.6	29.9	45.2
Brown	9,484	57	9,426	4,294	11.7	0.6	6.3	2.2	37.5	41.7
Carroll	33,768	1,737	32,031	5,897	2.7	0.0	19.3	12.6	27.7	37.7
Cass	70,489	2,315	68,174	8,882	1.7	0.0	7.7	4.0	38.8	47.7
Clark	150,197	4,973	145,224	23,788	1.2	0.0	1.2	0.6	40.5	56.6
Clay	36,392	152	36,240	6,532	1.6	0.0	7.7	3.2	37.4	50.1
Clinton	69,388	8,494	60,894	8,097	1.6	0.0	9.0	5.2	29.9	54.3
Crawford	12,888	26	12,861	7,440	11.5	0.8	7.8	8.6	20.2	51.2
Daviess	52,923	484	52,440	8,263	2.0	0.0	13.6	9.7	28.8	45.8
Dearborn	71,870	875	70,995	33,183	2.0	0.0	3.7	1.6	38.3	54.3
Decatur	72,076	5,474	66,601	8,092	1.1	0.0	8.5	5.7	35.2	49.4
Dekalb	100,348	10,499	89,849	12,810	1.1	0.0	3.2	1.7	31.3	62.6
Delaware	224,329	44,440	179,889	30,558	1.1	0.0	1.6	0.4	41.4	55.5
Dubois	108,965	3,783	105,183	12,946	0.6	0.0	6.6	5.1	45.1	42.6
Elkhart	489,220	16,032	473,189	45,162	0.9	0.0	1.3	1.1	54.8	41.9
Fayette	74,090	10,620	63,470	6,199	0.9	0.0	3.9	2.0	23.8	69.5
Floyd	78,990	2,359	76,631	24,108	1.6	0.0	0.5	0.2	39.7	57.8
Fountain	24,016	2,132	21,884	5,288	2.7	0.1	16.0	7.1	31.8	42.3
Franklin	19,633	53	19,580	5,609	8.1	0.0	21.4	13.2	23.5	33.9
Fulton	42,191	1,360	40,831	7,435	2.5	0.0	15.3	6.3	33.1	42.7
Gibson	104,590	2,003	102,587	51,824	2.6	0.0	15.1	3.5	27.8	51.1
Grant	173,454	28,866	144,588	15,476	1.0	0.0	2.7	1.0	26.7	68.6
Greene	48,248	489	47,759	13,096	2.8	0.0	7.9	5.2	25.0	59.2
Hamilton	217,890	711	217,179	46,479	1.7	0.0	2.2	1.0	39.1	56.0
Hancock	76,352	9,925	66,427	13,983	3.3	0.0	6.9	2.3	21.1	66.4
Harrison	41,804	3,077	38,727	10,089	2.4	0.0	7.8	4.7	30.3	54.8
Hendricks	88,220	762	87,458	28,320	5.0	0.0	6.8	2.3	37.8	48.1
Henry	71,963	2,412	69,551	15,546	2.8	0.0	6.0	2.8	34.1	54.3
Howard	332,280	27,557	304,723	22,224	0.7	0.0	1.2	0.8	20.0	77.3
Huntington	80,621	5,923	74,699	11,352	1.6	0.0	6.9	3.3	35.6	52.6
Jackson	115,666	15,022	100,644	13,592	0.7	0.0	6.1	3.5	48.7	41.0
Jasper	130,486	778	129,708	86,732	3.8	0.0	15.0	8.2	31.9	41.1
Jay	42,538	5,196	37,342	7,794	1.8	0.0	10.4	5.5	29.9	52.5
Jefferson	70,606	6,645	63,961	25,864	1.3	0.0	4.1	1.7	37.5	55.4
Jennings	27,060	339	26,721	6,800	3.8	0.0	13.3	6.4	26.8	49.7
Johnson	139,425	9,461	129,964	29,591	1.6	0.0	3.0	1.0	42.1	52.4
Knox	70,815	3,329	67,486	19,016	1.1	0.0	11.6	3.2	36.6	47.5
Kosciusko	187,719	12,358	175,360	27,144	2.7	0.1	5.9	3.2	35.0	53.1
Lagrange	58,828	1,816	57,013	11,671	3.4	0.2	12.1	9.8	35.5	39.0
Lake	1,275,540	256,411	1,019,130	116,734	0.2	0.0	0.1	0.0	20.4	79.2
Laporte	217,867	33,066	184,801	49,670	1.7	0.1	3.2	1.2	39.7	54.2
Lawrence	71,234	16,978	54,256	13,084	1.8	0.0	2.4	2.1	30.9	62.8
Madison	217,418	25,641	191,777	23,327	2.1	0.0	2.3	0.6	28.1	66.9
Marion	2,217,982	251,979	1,966,003	275,258	0.5	0.0	0.0	0.0	37.2	62.2
Marshall	111,982	6,716	105,266	17,853	2.7	0.0	5.7	2.6	34.9	53.9
Martin	14,042	740	13,302	3,890	1.7	0.0	8.6	9.2	21.3	59.1
Miami	43,241	696	42,545	6,680	4.0	0.0	10.9	6.1	39.9	39.0
Monroe	166,591	22,155	144,437	30,175	2.0	0.0	0.7	0.3	37.4	59.6
Montgomery	152,005	30,476	121,528	10,963	0.6	0.0	3.8	2.1	39.6	53.8
Morgan	64,027	903	63,124	24,303	5.2	0.0	4.5	2.4	40.4	47.3
Newton	24,337	131	24,205	4,630	2.2	0.0	19.4	9.5	24.9	43.9
Noble	103,576	11,498	92,078	15,833	1.2	0.0	4.4	2.3	31.1	60.9
Ohio	3,471	31	3,441	2,043	7.0	0.1	59.1	12.6	19.9	1.3
Orange	27,406	802	26,604	7,070	4.1	0.0	6.0	4.8	44.4	40.8
Owen	18,769	59	18,710	7,198	4.3	0.2	10.5	5.4	37.8	41.8
Parke	16,246	22	16,224	6,763	5.8	0.0	26.8	10.3	21.7	35.4
Perry	21,639	716	20,923	3,606	2.3	0.0	6.3	3.9	37.8	49.6
Pike	86,847	132	86,715	59,365	2.2	0.0	9.5	3.5	13.3	71.3
Porter	487,915	73,122	414,793	62,312	1.0	0.0	0.7	0.2	23.3	74.8
Posey	190,827	2,061	188,765	33,021	0.6	0.0	3.6	0.6	25.5	69.7
Pulaski	33,863	467	33,396	5,084	2.2	0.0	19.3	11.7	31.6	35.1
Putnam	55,285	3,639	51,646	11,867	2.4	0.0	7.0	3.6	25.6	61.3
Randolph	45,778	524	45,254	11,626	2.5	0.0	14.0	6.4	36.6	40.5
Ripley	45,556	949	44,607	7,708	2.8	0.0	7.7	3.3	29.5	56.7
Rush	36,039	2,155	33,884	5,944	1.2	0.0	20.0	10.9	26.5	41.5
St. Joseph	582,142	155,348	426,794	68,934	0.8	0.0	0.6	0.2	28.2	70.2
Scott	35,239	6,264	28,976	5,102	1.2	0.0	3.7	1.5	23.7	70.0
Shelby	101,018	15,223	85,795	15,275	1.1	0.0	6.4	2.7	23.8	66.0
Spencer	152,423	1,771	150,651	115,023	1.6	0.0	14.6	5.6	33.3	44.9
Starke	26,276	610	25,666	8,022	3.0	0.0	13.8	1.9	44.0	37.2
Steuben	83,191	6,531	76,660	10,220	2.8	0.1	2.6	1.3	33.8	59.5
Sullivan	86,119	13	86,106	53,202	2.1	0.0	16.0	3.2	36.9	41.8
Switzerland	10,405	50	10,356	5,481	0.8	0.2	20.3	10.9	21.9	46.0
Tippecanoe	391,368	48,287	343,081	33,142	0.8	0.0	1.4	0.5	31.4	65.9
Tipton	28,939	1,043	27,897	5,523	2.6	0.0	17.7	8.3	31.7	39.7
Union	10,423	6	10,417	3,116	18.4	0.0	27.4	18.3	19.7	16.3
Vanderburgh	357,735	64,186	293,549	29,471	0.9	0.0	0.7	0.1	40.3	57.9
Vermillion	127,185	27,803	99,382	22,434	0.4	0.0	1.4	0.5	30.1	67.7
Vigo	260,261	46,882	213,379	50,698	0.8	0.0	1.0	0.2	26.9	71.1
Wabash	68,250	6,118	62,132	9,340	2.2	0.0	8.2	5.5	36.6	47.4
Warren	13,672	19	13,653	3,370	1.9	0.0	28.6	13.9	28.5	27.1
Warrick	190,566	4,247	186,319	19,842	0.4	0.0	0.9	0.3	13.7	84.6
Washington	35,280	1,818	33,462	11,142	1.2	0.0	10.8	8.9	35.7	43.4
Wayne	141,330	31,551	109,779	16,899	1.1	0.0	2.8	1.5	37.3	57.4
Wells	55,037	5,492	49,544	7,143	1.4	0.0	8.8	3.6	33.6	52.6
White	70,497	1,383	69,114	14,383	1.5	0.0	11.7	6.3	34.6	45.8
Whitley	59,368	946	58,422	11,720	2.3	0.1	8.7	5.0	36.4	47.6

Source: Indiana State Board of Tax Commissioners
EDIN table(s): TAXA, TAXC

Average Acres Per Farm
1992

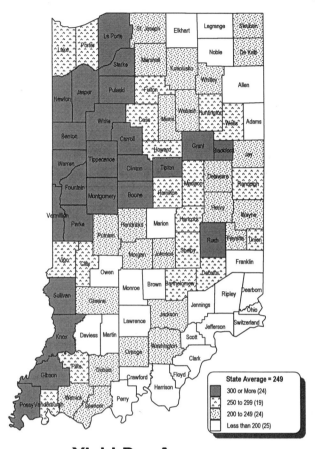

State Average = 249

- 300 or More (24)
- 250 to 299 (19)
- 200 to 249 (24)
- Less than 200 (25)

Yield Per Acre
Indiana - 1995 and 1996

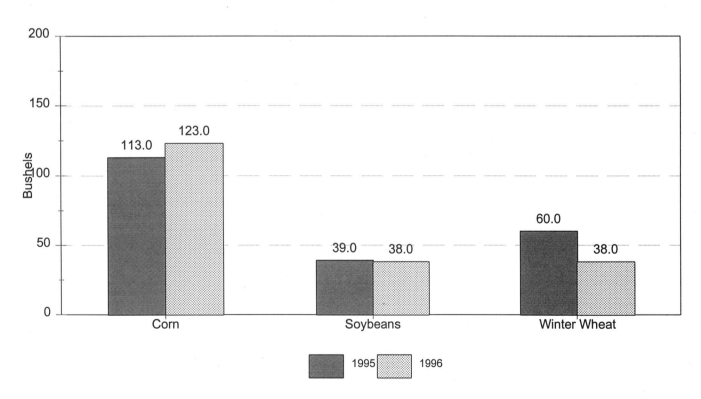

Average Acres Per Farm: EDIN Table FMSC.
Yield Per Acre: EDIN Tabe FMPD.

SECTION 2
INDIANA FACTBOOK
Page 169

	Total Number of Farms	Percent Change 1987-92	Farms with Sales of $10,000 or More			Number of Farms by Size			Principal Occupation of Operator		Tenure of Operator		
			Number	% Chg. 1987-92	% of All Farms	Less Than 50 Acres	50 to 500 Acres	500 or More Acres	Farming	Other	Full Owners	Part Owners	Tenants
Indiana	62,778	-11.0	36,688	-9.4	58.4	19,375	34,196	9,207	31,547	31,231	35,868	20,504	6,406
Adams	1,102	-7.8	767	-11.2	69.6	430	574	98	561	541	650	373	79
Allen	1,463	-11.3	892	-9.1	61.0	515	798	150	641	822	812	489	162
Bartholomew	645	-13.8	396	-7.5	61.4	218	315	112	321	324	337	241	67
Benton	500	-18.6	451	-16.0	90.2	51	241	208	383	117	143	224	133
Blackford	273	-25.0	165	-23.6	60.4	71	149	53	126	147	137	113	23
Boone	711	-13.5	463	-16.9	65.1	250	307	154	372	339	370	255	86
Brown	168	-16.0	53	10.4	31.5	42	123	3	63	105	120	45	3
Carroll	659	-14.4	470	-17.5	71.3	213	303	143	356	303	327	247	85
Cass	804	-12.6	530	-12.8	65.9	261	397	146	391	413	417	301	86
Clark	641	-7.2	259	0.8	40.4	227	369	45	288	353	438	155	48
Clay	568	-12.1	346	-4.4	60.9	167	292	109	300	268	291	246	31
Clinton	675	-15.7	514	-14.0	76.1	189	312	174	410	265	284	272	119
Crawford	382	-8.6	88	-4.3	23.0	86	278	18	129	253	313	59	10
Daviess	1,181	-6.0	772	-6.9	65.4	476	584	121	595	586	745	339	97
Dearborn	738	-7.3	193	11.6	26.2	173	555	10	262	476	549	147	42
Decatur	731	-10.4	523	-10.1	71.5	186	422	123	447	284	387	236	108
Dekalb	671	-18.6	367	-18.6	54.7	177	415	79	305	366	400	231	40
Delaware	688	-17.5	381	-16.8	55.4	263	331	94	332	356	375	242	71
Dubois	923	-6.0	596	-2.5	64.6	230	603	90	475	448	588	269	66
Elkhart	1,447	-7.0	932	-4.0	64.4	630	739	78	703	744	848	455	144
Fayette	456	-11.3	295	-4.5	64.7	123	262	71	252	204	281	116	59
Floyd	336	-14.7	82	12.3	24.4	149	180	7	112	224	238	85	13
Fountain	633	-8.7	401	-13.8	63.3	162	305	166	374	259	324	217	92
Franklin	849	-7.8	435	-5.2	51.2	194	600	55	403	446	521	214	114
Fulton	690	-10.7	450	-13.0	65.2	189	389	112	361	329	385	250	55
Gibson	720	-14.9	467	-14.2	64.9	210	353	157	414	306	336	299	85
Grant	630	-15.3	406	-15.1	64.4	194	306	130	358	272	291	262	77
Greene	958	-2.9	390	4.0	40.7	250	608	100	397	561	628	264	66
Hamilton	648	-16.1	373	-18.7	57.6	254	294	100	331	317	346	220	82
Hancock	625	-10.5	364	-12.3	58.2	262	272	91	291	334	338	221	66
Harrison	1,167	-10.0	375	-3.6	32.1	392	724	51	474	693	856	265	46
Hendricks	792	-14.5	430	-12.8	54.3	315	368	109	360	432	447	257	88
Henry	848	-9.6	509	-9.4	60.0	312	414	122	393	455	473	284	91
Howard	566	-16.4	412	-11.0	72.8	174	298	94	334	232	260	225	81
Huntington	704	-13.9	468	-12.0	66.5	187	386	131	370	334	372	266	66
Jackson	851	-11.6	482	-10.9	56.6	256	473	122	427	424	463	331	57
Jasper	716	-8.2	546	-10.8	76.3	184	306	226	481	235	304	271	141
Jay	852	-7.6	512	-11.9	60.1	256	499	97	397	455	536	260	56
Jefferson	914	-5.0	416	20.2	45.5	309	562	43	358	556	667	191	56
Jennings	658	-1.9	283	-2.1	43.0	222	377	59	267	391	435	174	49
Johnson	586	-9.8	328	-9.9	56.0	239	243	104	298	288	319	196	71
Knox	688	-17.4	537	-12.8	78.1	167	335	186	447	241	281	312	95
Kosciusko	1,123	-15.4	685	-13.7	61.0	376	610	137	553	570	703	344	76
Lagrange	1,391	-3.2	1,001	1.4	72.0	517	802	72	795	596	957	344	90
Lake	482	-12.5	298	-11.3	61.8	144	246	92	271	211	228	160	94
Laporte	826	-9.6	545	-4.9	66.0	237	409	180	448	378	403	314	109
Lawrence	849	-1.8	297	-3.3	35.0	220	559	70	306	543	620	187	42
Madison	848	-11.3	486	-11.6	57.3	338	366	144	426	422	449	296	103
Marion	276	-23.5	121	-19.9	43.8	175	76	25	125	151	162	72	42
Marshall	956	-12.3	567	-13.2	59.3	292	538	126	500	456	538	320	98
Martin	375	3.9	177	8.6	47.2	108	230	37	155	220	276	84	15
Miami	771	-5.7	503	-6.5	65.2	234	413	124	415	356	431	258	82
Monroe	508	-12.9	136	-8.1	26.8	167	331	10	185	323	371	117	20
Montgomery	762	-19.1	556	-15.0	73.0	200	372	190	460	302	353	312	97
Morgan	647	-9.3	285	-9.2	44.0	241	329	77	298	349	402	176	69
Newton	390	-18.8	320	-18.2	82.1	70	162	158	278	112	142	144	104
Noble	993	-6.1	519	-12.5	52.3	315	579	99	423	570	657	273	63
Ohio	267	-5.7	93	36.8	34.8	74	186	7	103	164	190	62	15
Orange	524	-7.4	213	-3.6	40.6	100	366	58	224	300	373	132	19
Owen	622	-6.5	205	-9.3	33.0	171	402	49	247	375	439	150	33
Parke	491	-16.4	299	-15.1	60.9	100	280	111	271	220	262	178	51
Perry	486	-7.6	154	-5.5	31.7	107	352	27	177	309	345	115	26
Pike	309	-19.1	187	-16.9	60.5	85	177	47	153	156	147	123	39
Porter	496	-16.9	297	-17.0	59.9	162	241	93	264	232	215	201	80
Posey	491	-10.9	366	-9.4	74.5	118	229	144	294	197	183	226	82
Pulaski	630	-12.3	449	-17.2	71.3	154	305	171	390	240	310	269	51
Putnam	826	-7.3	413	-3.5	50.0	253	462	111	378	448	490	281	55
Randolph	936	-12.8	606	-13.1	64.7	281	504	151	494	442	510	345	81
Ripley	963	-10.1	475	-5.9	49.3	284	608	71	425	538	588	297	78
Rush	761	-8.8	615	-10.1	80.8	179	420	162	517	244	365	281	115
St. Joseph	768	-14.4	423	-9.0	55.1	303	373	92	377	391	403	276	89
Scott	357	-8.5	137	-1.4	38.4	124	199	34	145	212	250	95	12
Shelby	749	-14.5	496	-10.8	66.2	250	357	142	425	324	352	287	110
Spencer	730	-9.7	411	0.7	56.3	205	446	79	320	410	441	232	57
Starke	387	-13.8	211	-18.5	54.5	114	182	91	201	186	188	141	58
Steuben	500	-12.7	263	-15.2	52.6	133	298	69	248	252	285	174	41
Sullivan	544	-9.2	351	-6.1	64.5	162	266	116	291	253	291	191	62
Switzerland	654	-0.9	235	32.0	35.9	208	430	16	264	390	464	124	66
Tippecanoe	790	-10.3	493	-9.7	62.4	259	364	167	390	400	405	258	127
Tipton	449	-18.5	340	-16.0	75.7	115	222	112	259	190	156	210	83
Union	268	-10.7	202	-12.6	75.4	42	169	57	170	98	119	108	41
Vanderburgh	305	-19.3	199	-7.9	65.2	117	143	45	174	131	150	116	39
Vermillion	307	-21.9	183	-14.9	59.6	68	163	76	187	120	166	108	33
Vigo	536	-14.0	272	-9.3	50.7	195	250	91	246	290	284	198	54
Wabash	810	-6.4	537	-6.3	66.3	237	469	104	434	376	457	255	98
Warren	435	-10.5	307	-10.0	70.6	97	196	142	271	164	199	173	63
Warrick	392	-9.3	213	7.0	54.3	122	212	58	182	210	191	152	49
Washington	937	-9.4	429	1.4	45.8	249	598	90	443	494	720	186	31
Wayne	828	-6.8	468	-12.7	56.5	241	471	116	408	420	505	217	106
Wells	722	-17.5	540	-10.6	74.8	179	412	131	392	330	332	312	78
White	695	-11.6	557	-10.2	80.1	161	315	219	465	230	307	281	107
Whitley	759	-13.8	434	-7.5	57.2	237	446	76	321	438	462	230	67

Source: U.S. Bureau of the Census
EDIN table(s): FMSZ

2.53 Selected Farm Characteristics 1992

	Total Number of Farms	Percent of State	Acres Per Farm	Crop Sales ($000)	Percent of State	Poultry & Products	Percent of State	Dairy Products	Percent of State	Value $000	Average Per Farm	Rank
						←——Livestock Sales ($000)——→				←——Machinery and Equipment——→		
Indiana	62,778	100.00	249	2,698,335	100.00	429,369	100.00	258,282	100.00	3,474,495	55,440	—
Adams	1,102	1.76	179	30,525	1.13	13,629	3.17	11,522	4.46	58,666	53,381	52
Allen	1,463	2.33	195	50,395	1.87	259	0.06	5,430	2.10	84,201	57,870	42
Bartholomew	645	1.03	256	33,774	1.25	3	0.00	1,332	0.52	33,023	51,278	57
Benton	500	0.80	541	58,318	2.16	NA	NA	230	0.09	52,779	105,981	3
Blackford	273	0.43	320	14,765	0.55	NA	NA	235	0.09	14,873	54,681	50
Boone	711	1.13	314	49,053	1.82	NA	NA	1,513	0.59	45,438	63,998	36
Brown	168	0.27	134	1,274	0.05	3	0.00	NA	NA	3,045	18,234	91
Carroll	659	1.05	334	47,572	1.76	7,297	1.70	499	0.19	59,331	90,443	4
Cass	804	1.28	283	45,755	1.70	NA	NA	2,977	1.15	57,259	71,843	18
Clark	641	1.02	165	12,282	0.46	NA	NA	1,685	0.65	22,647	35,221	76
Clay	568	0.90	286	29,581	1.10	NA	NA	1,703	0.66	35,270	62,204	38
Clinton	675	1.08	350	50,545	1.87	2,327	0.54	58	0.02	53,737	79,492	11
Crawford	382	0.61	156	1,189	0.04	NA	NA	585	0.23	9,526	24,937	87
Daviess	1,181	1.88	188	38,375	1.42	26,243	6.11	4,171	1.61	55,494	46,870	63
Dearborn	738	1.18	117	4,845	0.18	15	0.00	1,076	0.42	16,765	22,686	88
Decatur	731	1.16	277	36,621	1.36	2	0.00	2,776	1.07	48,087	65,692	30
Dekalb	671	1.07	228	18,736	0.69	NA	NA	6,018	2.33	32,866	49,054	58
Delaware	688	1.10	246	33,799	1.25	5	0.00	1,212	0.47	36,262	52,706	54
Dubois	923	1.47	210	21,459	0.80	77,003	17.93	6,273	2.43	50,020	54,134	51
Elkhart	1,447	2.30	133	27,726	1.03	10,773	2.51	33,542	12.99	57,873	40,050	71
Fayette	456	0.73	245	14,264	0.53	NA	NA	1,040	0.40	20,401	45,035	65
Floyd	336	0.54	89	2,550	0.09	NA	NA	211	0.08	5,766	17,212	92
Fountain	633	1.01	362	40,512	1.50	NA	NA	200	0.08	39,061	61,805	40
Franklin	849	1.35	175	13,764	0.51	2	0.00	4,094	1.59	26,948	31,667	78
Fulton	690	1.10	282	31,594	1.17	NA	NA	4,461	1.73	44,297	64,105	35
Gibson	720	1.15	335	52,414	1.94	992	0.23	1,946	0.75	61,551	85,606	7
Grant	630	1.00	312	42,562	1.58	1,147	0.27	1,869	0.72	49,356	78,344	12
Greene	958	1.53	217	22,023	0.82	6,336	1.48	2,267	0.88	34,385	35,930	75
Hamilton	648	1.03	251	40,024	1.48	13	0.00	966	0.37	37,737	60,477	41
Hancock	625	1.00	261	34,338	1.27	NA	NA	125	0.05	41,360	65,966	27
Harrison	1,167	1.86	139	12,590	0.47	NA	NA	3,866	1.50	36,054	31,135	81
Hendricks	792	1.26	236	37,998	1.41	67	0.02	1,039	0.40	36,216	45,843	64
Henry	848	1.35	225	37,256	1.38	8	0.00	1,368	0.53	39,961	47,068	62
Howard	566	0.90	263	34,631	1.28	32	0.01	1,431	0.55	40,499	71,680	19
Huntington	704	1.12	267	33,697	1.25	NA	NA	2,247	0.87	51,766	73,846	16
Jackson	851	1.36	238	28,953	1.07	NA	NA	4,138	1.60	47,175	55,566	45
Jasper	716	1.14	422	58,781	2.18	4,991	1.16	415	0.16	61,549	85,485	8
Jay	852	1.36	215	26,119	0.97	20,170	4.70	4,739	1.83	41,137	48,798	59
Jefferson	914	1.46	143	16,736	0.62	6	0.00	1,780	0.69	27,284	29,851	83
Jennings	658	1.05	190	14,740	0.55	NA	NA	813	0.31	25,404	38,608	73
Johnson	586	0.93	238	32,872	1.22	NA	NA	2,219	0.86	32,967	56,161	43
Knox	688	1.10	444	68,349	2.53	12,967	3.02	1,143	0.44	56,991	82,715	9
Kosciusko	1,123	1.79	224	37,800	1.40	41,946	9.77	8,804	3.41	72,973	64,922	32
Lagrange	1,391	2.22	135	34,579	1.28	9,749	2.27	16,442	6.37	53,600	38,953	72
Lake	482	0.77	299	28,554	1.06	129	0.03	2,086	0.81	32,019	66,429	26
Laporte	826	1.32	324	51,521	1.91	14	0.00	10,042	3.89	58,963	71,211	22
Lawrence	849	1.35	187	7,231	0.27	NA	NA	1,070	0.41	26,612	31,272	80
Madison	848	1.35	263	53,215	1.97	NA	NA	968	0.37	54,938	64,862	33
Marion	276	0.44	141	14,104	0.52	19	0.00	NA	NA	14,387	52,507	55
Marshall	956	1.52	230	34,072	1.26	1,586	0.37	11,499	4.45	53,224	55,557	46
Martin	375	0.60	191	5,101	0.19	11,849	2.76	232	0.09	15,141	40,484	70
Miami	771	1.23	245	32,396	1.20	NA	NA	5,427	2.10	48,887	63,407	37
Monroe	508	0.81	117	2,902	0.11	5	0.00	614	0.24	9,736	19,165	90
Montgomery	762	1.21	371	57,710	2.14	NA	NA	335	0.13	58,690	76,921	13
Morgan	647	1.03	216	22,460	0.83	4	0.00	502	0.19	28,555	44,135	67
Newton	390	0.62	530	43,794	1.62	NA	NA	NA	NA	42,191	107,630	2
Noble	993	1.58	185	24,066	0.89	3,667	0.85	7,948	3.08	43,266	43,484	68
Ohio	267	0.43	121	2,661	0.10	NA	NA	NA	NA	5,726	21,447	89
Orange	524	0.83	222	7,054	0.26	NA	NA	1,235	0.48	16,977	32,462	77
Owen	622	0.99	182	8,985	0.33	NA	NA	732	0.28	16,215	26,026	86
Parke	491	0.78	370	27,650	1.02	NA	NA	858	0.33	32,302	65,789	29
Perry	486	0.77	165	3,325	0.12	NA	NA	814	0.32	14,951	30,827	82
Pike	309	0.49	276	13,074	0.48	3,248	0.76	NA	NA	13,813	44,414	66
Porter	496	0.79	287	27,361	1.01	4	0.00	1,264	0.49	32,321	65,163	31
Posey	491	0.78	450	48,615	1.80	NA	NA	2,255	0.87	53,386	109,173	1
Pulaski	630	1.00	385	43,549	1.61	NA	NA	2,623	1.02	50,961	80,890	10
Putnam	826	1.32	247	28,991	1.07	NA	NA	1,723	0.67	34,371	41,662	69
Randolph	936	1.49	253	40,201	1.49	5,865	1.37	2,177	0.84	51,981	55,476	47
Ripley	963	1.53	170	20,551	0.76	NA	NA	2,950	1.14	35,183	36,573	74
Rush	761	1.21	306	43,050	1.60	7	0.00	3,461	1.34	54,502	71,618	20
St. Joseph	768	1.22	224	33,639	1.25	NA	NA	5,056	1.96	42,992	56,052	44
Scott	357	0.57	177	7,763	0.29	6	0.00	509	0.20	9,179	26,225	85
Shelby	749	1.19	290	50,625	1.88	6	0.00	2,184	0.85	54,502	72,961	17
Spencer	730	1.16	240	26,262	0.97	4,267	0.99	2,243	0.87	40,093	55,149	49
Starke	387	0.62	349	24,456	0.91	NA	NA	331	0.13	23,841	61,925	39
Steuben	500	0.80	243	12,661	0.47	NA	NA	6,148	2.38	23,979	48,540	60
Sullivan	544	0.87	333	36,072	1.34	NA	NA	260	0.10	41,160	75,662	15
Switzerland	654	1.04	121	7,745	0.29	0	0.00	2,143	0.83	19,299	29,554	84
Tippecanoe	790	1.26	326	51,747	1.92	NA	NA	764	0.30	52,048	65,800	28
Tipton	449	0.72	358	40,445	1.50	NA	NA	NA	NA	39,394	87,738	5
Union	268	0.43	299	13,024	0.48	NA	NA	1,024	0.40	17,749	66,476	25
Vanderburgh	305	0.49	265	19,417	0.72	NA	NA	951	0.37	20,739	68,219	23
Vermillion	307	0.49	389	21,544	0.80	NA	NA	62	0.02	20,839	67,659	24
Vigo	536	0.85	270	26,212	0.97	3	0.00	627	0.24	28,255	52,715	53
Wabash	810	1.29	244	30,789	1.14	13,715	3.19	3,752	1.45	57,870	71,444	21
Warren	435	0.69	464	39,510	1.46	NA	NA	97	0.04	33,144	76,194	14
Warrick	392	0.62	245	15,513	0.57	NA	NA	749	0.29	20,393	52,157	56
Washington	937	1.49	202	12,986	0.48	10,630	2.48	6,064	2.35	29,389	31,399	79
Wayne	828	1.32	229	37,497	1.39	NA	NA	3,926	1.52	39,531	47,743	61
Wells	722	1.15	275	37,838	1.40	908	0.21	3,216	1.25	46,824	64,853	34
White	695	1.11	410	61,958	2.30	NA	NA	951	0.37	60,927	87,539	6
Whitley	759	1.21	214	22,708	0.84	1,644	0.38	4,407	1.71	41,450	55,192	48

Footnote: Data are for all farms.
Source: U.S. Bureau of the Census
EDIN table(s): FMSC

Components of Farm Income
Indiana - 1990 to 1995

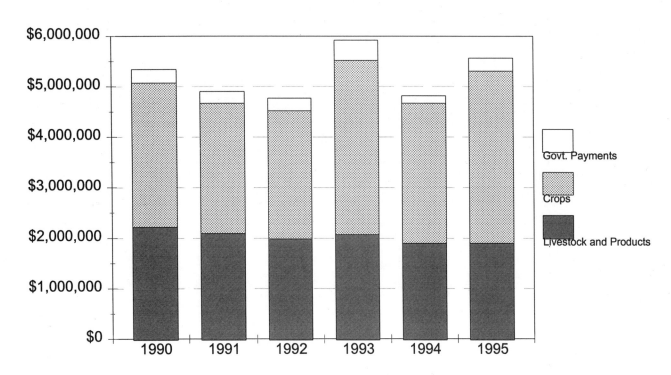

Production Expenses as a Percent of Cash Receipts
Indiana - 1995

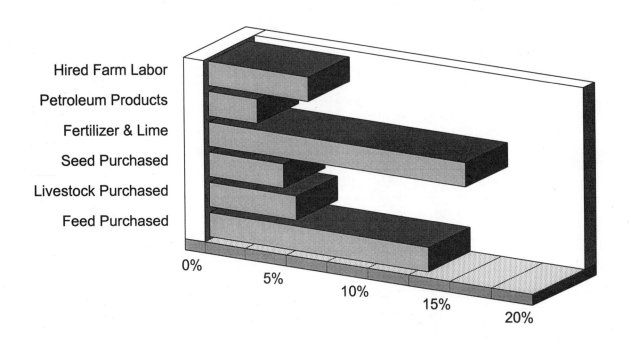

Components of Farm Income: EDIN Table FMIN.
Production Expenses as a Percent of Cash Receipts: EDIN Table FMIN.

2.54 Farm Income and Expenses Part I 1995 ($000)

	Marketing Cash Receipts	Livestock and Products	Crops	Other Income Total[1]	Govt. Payments	Production Expenses Total[1]	Feed Purchased	Livestock Purchased	Seed Purchased	Fertilizer & Lime	Petroleum Products	Hired Farm Labor
Indiana	5,316,374	1,906,905	3,409,469	597,313	246,066	5,426,203	711,966	283,293	242,428	835,107	157,982	323,868
Adams	97,001	51,722	45,279	7,343	2,535	90,774	19,424	7,126	3,314	10,775	2,479	5,011
Allen	102,753	28,640	74,113	10,123	2,717	95,733	6,764	5,775	5,063	14,908	2,980	4,613
Bartholomew	55,245	11,770	43,475	6,646	2,979	52,751	4,259	1,474	2,827	10,471	1,661	1,942
Benton	68,071	4,022	64,049	12,569	5,879	86,615	1,114	536	4,576	15,684	2,372	3,385
Blackford	27,523	8,606	18,917	2,730	1,538	25,646	2,966	1,319	1,274	4,652	859	1,431
Boone	81,056	22,560	58,496	9,540	3,681	80,090	10,168	1,899	3,793	12,683	2,500	5,305
Brown	2,360	962	1,398	580	222	2,663	329	NA	81	226	83	153
Carroll	113,677	56,150	57,527	8,698	3,595	107,603	21,175	8,105	4,237	15,016	2,679	6,528
Cass	84,659	26,250	58,409	8,484	3,388	78,606	7,838	4,118	4,146	13,199	2,606	5,280
Clark	21,144	5,121	16,023	2,920	903	24,931	1,349	722	1,315	4,153	728	1,807
Clay	45,315	7,453	37,862	7,594	2,063	41,916	2,983	1,424	2,469	8,945	1,443	1,923
Clinton	94,105	34,641	59,464	9,626	3,609	99,157	13,357	2,825	4,142	14,867	3,069	6,456
Crawford	14,193	13,159	1,034	1,540	488	16,164	7,649	1,427	101	549	250	810
Daviess	117,637	69,765	47,872	11,051	3,580	114,332	36,920	8,405	3,396	14,287	2,500	5,432
Dearborn	9,637	4,359	5,278	2,047	261	13,255	900	599	512	1,177	421	393
Decatur	88,470	37,850	50,620	9,565	4,318	85,002	10,878	8,064	3,225	12,637	2,410	4,607
Dekalb	41,284	15,138	26,146	7,761	4,268	41,820	4,238	1,486	2,146	6,348	1,323	2,612
Delaware	55,246	8,134	47,112	6,783	2,522	51,987	2,894	1,865	2,866	9,641	1,659	3,617
Dubois	146,405	122,395	24,010	8,371	2,876	147,508	64,811	14,741	2,667	11,174	2,557	8,164
Elkhart	107,010	70,365	36,645	8,123	2,061	106,478	22,971	8,498	3,517	11,266	2,859	5,869
Fayette	27,175	11,828	15,347	4,000	1,747	31,980	2,935	1,635	1,421	4,518	1,041	1,271
Floyd	4,257	1,420	2,837	1,181	134	5,440	215	75	194	523	114	227
Fountain	58,227	7,711	50,516	8,403	4,467	64,175	2,558	1,402	3,723	10,725	1,757	2,356
Franklin	34,940	20,202	14,738	4,157	1,519	40,410	5,401	2,129	1,480	5,155	1,157	1,195
Fulton	53,816	16,928	36,888	7,078	3,689	58,957	5,434	2,299	3,020	11,161	1,953	2,813
Gibson	79,882	13,773	66,109	9,329	4,040	77,459	5,302	1,306	4,774	17,544	2,364	2,946
Grant	70,249	12,631	57,618	6,520	2,543	65,219	4,718	2,541	3,322	12,024	2,255	3,271
Greene	46,371	18,402	27,969	5,489	1,694	52,254	8,121	2,579	2,054	8,659	1,711	2,954
Hamilton	53,765	8,822	44,943	6,642	2,015	61,750	3,851	1,895	3,421	10,245	1,742	5,834
Hancock	54,494	10,587	43,907	6,989	2,345	53,198	4,090	1,938	2,685	8,735	1,832	2,367
Harrison	43,098	31,241	11,857	5,218	1,265	51,579	9,957	4,986	1,294	4,761	1,136	5,334
Hendricks	59,351	9,673	49,678	7,197	2,230	56,960	3,711	1,203	3,154	10,588	1,621	3,534
Henry	59,770	14,274	45,496	8,032	2,894	63,696	3,735	3,339	3,516	11,722	2,077	4,291
Howard	71,343	23,303	48,040	6,375	2,550	60,923	7,509	2,907	2,588	8,905	1,871	3,387
Huntington	61,053	18,939	42,114	6,869	2,581	62,050	6,682	2,736	3,182	10,066	1,925	2,927
Jackson	80,694	43,506	37,188	7,427	2,957	80,707	16,686	8,531	3,132	9,971	2,035	6,161
Jasper	109,723	40,779	68,944	12,741	6,534	115,888	13,694	9,565	5,160	17,540	3,166	5,764
Jay	72,400	37,650	34,750	7,558	3,728	71,961	17,332	5,774	2,540	8,513	1,763	3,209
Jefferson	23,303	5,361	17,942	3,702	761	26,987	1,340	593	1,140	4,208	789	1,991
Jennings	39,321	21,706	17,615	4,033	1,512	42,472	9,877	2,957	1,362	4,981	903	1,605
Johnson	49,937	9,418	40,519	5,573	2,179	47,815	2,959	1,853	2,367	7,636	1,436	4,246
Knox	123,330	28,914	94,416	10,525	5,301	109,314	8,554	6,843	5,972	21,065	3,123	7,055
Kosciusko	137,818	90,032	47,786	8,973	4,042	144,779	37,940	13,974	4,442	14,135	3,366	10,723
Lagrange	101,265	60,910	40,355	9,114	2,385	100,812	22,541	9,840	2,488	9,781	2,490	10,892
Lake	44,146	4,623	39,523	6,289	3,027	46,180	943	423	2,813	6,890	1,528	3,234
Laporte	105,403	24,763	80,640	10,173	5,218	95,159	7,281	3,782	4,630	15,840	3,374	7,741
Lawrence	16,094	8,328	7,766	3,697	1,668	23,017	2,406	856	755	2,865	640	1,186
Madison	79,573	12,283	67,290	8,487	3,108	79,782	2,723	4,042	4,576	13,727	2,228	5,259
Marion	18,309	5,281	13,028	2,476	390	22,251	1,223	773	1,900	2,480	661	3,225
Marshall	72,024	23,341	48,683	7,754	3,157	67,106	6,368	2,697	3,388	11,098	2,519	3,503
Martin	30,646	24,191	6,455	2,878	885	29,227	11,523	3,143	529	2,089	568	1,094
Miami	68,752	27,168	41,584	7,035	2,526	74,568	8,503	5,253	4,007	12,134	2,234	3,646
Monroe	9,741	6,626	3,115	1,684	458	12,207	800	682	276	1,029	358	660
Montgomery	105,412	35,248	70,164	10,793	4,618	100,606	14,023	3,214	4,874	17,207	2,677	6,381
Morgan	38,388	7,683	30,705	5,715	2,038	40,897	2,644	1,282	2,128	7,467	1,253	2,576
Newton	74,970	24,307	50,663	10,199	6,244	91,642	11,244	3,157	3,469	11,920	1,946	4,077
Noble	56,618	24,547	32,071	6,245	2,983	59,264	5,680	3,706	2,527	8,796	1,734	3,951
Ohio	3,094	1,815	1,279	639	97	5,668	465	335	153	497	227	503
Orange	19,872	11,953	7,919	3,608	1,685	25,088	5,070	1,551	863	3,180	602	2,165
Owen	15,501	4,507	10,994	4,097	1,326	19,791	1,345	529	1,028	4,150	666	727
Parke	41,503	7,160	34,343	7,126	3,258	42,362	2,109	995	2,452	8,638	1,677	2,196
Perry	11,160	7,347	3,813	3,560	559	16,655	3,175	692	443	1,583	426	373
Pike	21,939	7,098	14,841	2,537	1,277	24,359	3,469	892	1,322	5,341	738	1,059
Porter	49,108	6,588	42,520	5,683	2,831	45,306	2,341	689	2,700	7,853	1,625	2,222
Posey	74,150	13,314	60,836	7,438	3,126	75,825	5,267	1,272	3,969	15,983	2,273	3,420
Pulaski	85,327	31,559	53,768	8,336	4,629	84,797	13,863	3,704	3,729	13,989	2,634	4,838
Putnam	54,738	14,162	40,576	7,289	3,346	55,167	5,320	2,772	2,481	9,717	1,679	3,106
Randolph	79,836	26,585	53,251	6,359	2,647	77,128	10,271	2,898	3,982	14,066	2,169	4,392
Ripley	43,992	18,675	25,317	6,301	2,000	47,546	6,190	2,406	2,059	7,681	1,704	2,599
Rush	85,001	31,219	53,782	11,896	4,447	90,279	9,040	4,782	4,167	15,483	2,650	3,913
St. Joseph	64,342	14,663	49,679	6,746	2,810	65,316	6,433	1,545	3,052	9,662	2,467	4,788
Scott	11,218	2,018	9,200	2,007	806	13,228	754	91	582	2,532	422	949
Shelby	75,206	13,124	62,082	8,735	3,804	70,628	3,656	2,099	4,080	13,426	2,524	4,065
Spencer	50,539	19,409	31,130	5,003	1,796	51,527	7,368	1,983	2,550	8,940	1,590	3,175
Starke	47,051	3,720	43,331	6,355	3,475	44,616	1,399	1,325	2,068	8,958	1,512	3,028
Steuben	29,308	11,962	17,346	5,399	3,333	33,626	3,998	1,473	1,681	5,491	1,099	1,828
Sullivan	47,332	7,142	40,190	5,930	2,908	49,264	1,979	1,570	2,751	10,305	1,684	2,265
Switzerland	10,902	5,493	5,409	1,503	244	18,676	2,220	393	591	1,857	556	1,247
Tippecanoe	78,962	20,275	58,687	10,154	4,459	88,955	8,002	2,954	4,067	14,410	2,642	5,758
Tipton	69,870	17,933	51,937	7,552	2,152	66,142	5,908	3,135	2,792	10,805	1,790	6,400
Union	26,630	11,074	15,556	3,977	1,712	28,208	2,497	1,380	1,623	4,699	1,037	1,218
Vanderburgh	26,679	3,040	23,639	3,415	1,594	25,609	859	444	1,549	5,023	760	1,720
Vermillion	30,081	4,702	25,379	4,481	1,802	36,465	1,181	890	1,698	5,085	904	2,075
Vigo	36,837	3,974	32,863	3,677	1,641	39,730	1,353	739	2,253	6,706	1,363	3,225
Wabash	102,456	60,967	41,489	8,592	3,110	109,137	22,139	13,386	3,367	11,542	2,599	7,693
Warren	47,189	3,697	43,492	8,031	4,556	46,196	923	505	3,044	9,478	1,656	2,490
Warrick	21,596	3,777	17,819	3,393	1,692	26,886	1,680	284	1,263	6,149	868	1,448
Washington	45,281	30,334	14,947	6,570	2,806	51,167	13,116	3,262	1,610	6,397	1,242	2,694
Wayne	59,059	18,380	40,679	7,107	3,554	69,611	6,372	2,806	2,520	9,041	2,629	6,937
Wells	67,461	17,179	50,282	6,701	2,517	64,306	5,372	3,285	3,180	11,403	2,020	2,236
White	118,478	43,356	75,122	11,693	5,820	112,994	17,232	5,603	4,478	17,990	3,135	6,619
Whitley	56,227	23,243	32,984	6,779	3,332	52,223	6,233	4,265	2,311	7,686	1,628	2,273

Footnote: [1] Includes items not shown separately.
Source: U.S. Bureau of Economic Analysis
EDIN table(s): FMIN

2.55 Farm Income and Expenses Part II 1995 *($000)*

	Inventory Change Value			Cash Receipts, Other Income	Less Production Expenses	Realized Net Income	Net Income Including Corporate Farms	Net Farm Proprietor's Income	Farm Labor & Proprietor's Income
	Total	Livestock	Crops						
Indiana	-633,685	-48,272	-585,413	5,913,687	5,426,203	487,484	-146,201	-135,726	87,204
Adams	-7,918	-987	-6,931	104,344	90,774	13,570	5,652	5,007	8,200
Allen	-8,691	-834	-7,857	112,876	95,733	17,143	8,452	7,885	10,834
Bartholomew	-8,202	-425	-7,777	61,891	52,751	9,140	938	808	2,012
Benton	-11,007	-201	-10,806	80,640	86,615	-5,975	-16,982	-15,422	-13,575
Blackford	-3,133	-215	-2,918	30,253	25,646	4,607	1,474	1,261	2,226
Boone	-11,119	-496	-10,623	90,596	80,090	10,506	-613	-528	3,161
Brown	-244	-65	-179	2,940	2,663	277	NA	NA	150
Carroll	-13,142	-1,341	-11,801	122,375	107,603	14,772	1,630	1,242	5,782
Cass	-10,740	-778	-9,962	93,143	78,606	14,537	3,797	3,401	6,466
Clark	-1,760	-334	-1,426	24,064	24,931	-867	-2,627	-2,532	-1,148
Clay	-7,040	-278	-6,762	52,909	41,916	10,993	3,953	3,506	4,780
Clinton	-11,977	-992	-10,985	103,731	99,157	4,574	-7,403	-6,291	-2,028
Crawford	-310	-223	-87	15,733	16,164	-431	-741	-727	-369
Daviess	-9,752	-1,366	-8,386	128,688	114,332	14,356	4,604	3,969	7,988
Dearborn	-581	-287	-294	11,684	13,255	-1,571	-2,152	-2,026	-1,811
Decatur	-11,894	-1,151	-10,743	98,035	85,002	13,033	1,139	838	3,567
Dekalb	-4,514	-377	-4,137	49,045	41,820	7,225	2,711	2,358	4,134
Delaware	-8,026	-301	-7,725	62,029	51,987	10,042	2,016	1,824	4,033
Dubois	-7,150	-1,486	-5,664	154,776	147,508	7,268	118	75	5,870
Elkhart	-6,199	-1,282	-4,917	115,133	106,478	8,655	2,456	2,326	6,396
Fayette	-4,494	-485	-4,009	31,175	31,980	-805	-5,299	-4,583	-3,794
Floyd	-170	-104	-66	5,438	5,440	NA	-172	-166	NA
Fountain	-10,193	-330	-9,863	66,630	64,175	2,455	-7,738	-7,198	-6,158
Franklin	-4,050	-756	-3,294	39,097	40,410	-1,313	-5,363	-5,092	-4,339
Fulton	-8,906	-519	-8,387	60,894	58,957	1,937	-6,969	-6,585	-5,013
Gibson	-11,602	-384	-11,218	89,211	77,459	11,752	150	134	2,045
Grant	-8,459	-362	-8,097	76,769	65,219	11,550	3,091	2,694	4,872
Greene	-5,943	-613	-5,330	51,860	52,254	-394	-6,337	-5,999	-4,160
Hamilton	-6,512	-328	-6,184	60,407	61,750	-1,343	-7,855	-6,187	-2,069
Hancock	-7,870	-434	-7,436	61,483	53,198	8,285	415	356	2,132
Harrison	-1,730	-658	-1,072	48,316	51,579	-3,263	-4,993	-4,335	196
Hendricks	-7,669	-396	-7,273	66,548	56,960	9,588	1,919	1,768	4,343
Henry	-8,198	-521	-7,677	67,802	63,696	4,106	-4,092	-3,682	-1,105
Howard	-8,920	-661	-8,259	77,718	60,923	16,795	7,875	6,475	8,466
Huntington	-7,338	-521	-6,817	67,922	62,050	5,872	-1,466	-1,364	381
Jackson	-8,101	-758	-7,343	88,121	80,707	7,414	-687	-634	4,307
Jasper	-14,676	-897	-13,779	122,464	115,888	6,576	-8,100	-6,946	-3,356
Jay	-6,822	-558	-6,264	79,958	71,961	7,997	1,175	1,058	3,163
Jefferson	-1,302	-313	-989	27,005	26,987	NA	-1,284	-1,208	307
Jennings	-4,344	-336	-4,008	43,354	42,472	882	-3,462	-3,290	-2,126
Johnson	-7,061	-337	-6,724	55,510	47,815	7,695	634	595	3,715
Knox	-14,084	-529	-13,555	133,855	109,314	24,541	10,457	7,306	12,343
Kosciusko	-10,649	-1,402	-9,247	146,791	144,779	2,012	-8,637	-7,461	805
Lagrange	-6,056	-1,335	-4,721	110,379	100,812	9,567	3,511	3,140	11,884
Lake	-7,095	-135	-6,960	50,435	46,180	4,255	-2,840	-2,447	-231
Laporte	-13,971	-598	-13,373	115,576	95,159	20,417	6,446	5,800	11,682
Lawrence	-2,114	-653	-1,461	19,791	23,017	-3,226	-5,340	-4,999	-4,169
Madison	-10,545	-421	-10,124	88,060	79,782	8,278	-2,267	-1,890	1,910
Marion	-1,310	-113	-1,197	20,785	22,251	-1,466	-2,776	-2,369	311
Marshall	-9,663	-625	-9,038	79,778	67,106	12,672	3,009	2,855	5,046
Martin	-2,065	-422	-1,643	33,524	29,227	4,297	2,232	2,116	2,917
Miami	-7,760	-726	-7,034	75,787	74,568	1,219	-6,541	-5,688	-3,470
Monroe	-571	-243	-328	11,425	12,207	-782	-1,353	-1,327	-794
Montgomery	-13,902	-1,149	-12,753	116,205	100,606	15,599	1,697	1,493	5,605
Morgan	-5,799	-338	-5,461	44,103	40,897	3,206	-2,593	-2,239	-417
Newton	-11,410	-357	-11,053	85,169	91,642	-6,473	-17,883	-16,179	-13,678
Noble	-5,591	-581	-5,010	62,863	59,264	3,599	-1,992	-1,802	841
Ohio	148	-121	269	3,733	5,668	-1,935	-1,787	-1,769	-1,452
Orange	-2,183	-411	-1,772	23,480	25,088	-1,608	-3,791	-3,383	-2,139
Owen	-2,400	-345	-2,055	19,598	19,791	-193	-2,593	-2,471	-2,108
Parke	-7,698	-322	-7,376	48,629	42,362	6,267	-1,431	-1,269	360
Perry	-1,149	-335	-814	14,720	16,655	-1,935	-3,084	-3,041	-2,852
Pike	-3,314	-157	-3,157	24,476	24,359	117	-3,197	-3,019	-2,267
Porter	-7,807	-202	-7,605	54,791	45,306	9,485	1,678	1,480	2,999
Posey	-9,497	-247	-9,250	81,588	75,825	5,763	-3,734	-3,202	-647
Pulaski	-11,171	-536	-10,635	93,663	84,797	8,866	-2,305	-2,077	968
Putnam	-8,102	-621	-7,481	62,027	55,167	6,860	-1,242	-1,188	977
Randolph	-8,598	-660	-7,938	86,195	77,128	9,067	469	429	2,723
Ripley	-6,109	-619	-5,490	50,293	47,546	2,747	-3,362	-3,197	-1,289
Rush	-12,693	-947	-11,746	96,897	90,279	6,618	-6,075	-5,505	-2,959
St. Joseph	-8,104	-320	-7,784	71,088	65,316	5,772	-2,332	-2,085	1,711
Scott	-1,636	-134	-1,502	13,225	13,228	NA	-1,639	-1,377	-822
Shelby	-11,320	-452	-10,868	83,941	70,628	13,313	1,993	1,692	4,746
Spencer	-5,751	-584	-5,167	55,542	51,527	4,015	-1,736	-1,586	756
Starke	-6,682	-150	-6,532	53,406	44,616	8,790	2,108	1,319	2,888
Steuben	-3,448	-313	-3,135	34,707	33,626	1,081	-2,367	-2,260	-991
Sullivan	-7,451	-250	-7,201	53,262	49,264	3,998	-3,453	-3,236	-1,653
Switzerland	796	-240	1,036	12,405	18,676	-6,271	-5,475	-5,233	-4,287
Tippecanoe	-11,780	-661	-11,119	89,116	88,955	161	-11,619	-10,594	-6,494
Tipton	-8,415	-373	-8,042	77,422	66,142	11,280	2,865	2,176	6,437
Union	-4,504	-370	-4,134	30,607	28,208	2,399	-2,105	-1,894	-1,260
Vanderburgh	-4,176	-90	-4,086	30,094	25,609	4,485	309	273	1,592
Vermillion	-4,794	-183	-4,611	34,562	36,465	-1,903	-6,697	-6,125	-4,903
Vigo	-6,023	-150	-5,873	40,514	39,730	784	-5,239	-4,128	-1,396
Wabash	-8,234	-1,316	-6,918	111,048	109,137	1,911	-6,323	-4,800	933
Warren	-7,941	-188	-7,753	55,220	46,196	9,024	1,083	976	2,745
Warrick	-3,521	-176	-3,345	24,989	26,886	-1,897	-5,418	-4,918	-4,005
Washington	-3,528	-857	-2,671	51,851	51,167	684	-2,844	-2,582	-752
Wayne	-6,630	-680	-5,950	66,166	69,611	-3,445	-10,075	-9,375	-4,074
Wells	-8,111	-459	-7,652	74,162	64,306	9,856	1,745	1,522	2,967
White	-15,650	-832	-14,818	130,171	112,994	17,177	1,527	1,262	5,873
Whitley	-5,865	-654	-5,211	63,006	52,223	10,783	4,918	4,333	5,857

Source: U.S. Bureau of Economic Analysis
EDIN table(s): FMIN

2.56 Production and Yield for Selected Crops 1996

| | Production (000) | | | | Yield per Acre (Bushels) | | | | | | | |
| | Corn For Grain (Bushels) | Soybeans (Bushels) | Winter Wheat (Bushels) | Hay (Tons) | – Corn for Grain – | | – Soybeans – | | – Winter Wheat – | | – Hay (Tons) – | |
					1995	1996	1995	1996	1995	1996	1995	1996
Indiana	670,350.0	203,680.0	27,360.0	2,020.0	113.0	123.0	39.0	38.0	60.0	38.0	3.3	2.8
Adams	4,471.5	2,729.4	723.2	34.3	126.0	120.0	37.0	34.0	65.0	38.0	4.1	3.6
Allen	6,500.0	4,169.3	1,719.5	33.5	130.0	124.0	41.0	37.0	70.0	46.0	4.3	3.5
Bartholomew	9,122.3	2,948.1	448.2	15.0	117.0	117.0	39.0	40.0	63.0	43.0	3.1	2.6
Benton	17,877.1	4,823.9	69.4	7.0	87.0	138.0	40.0	42.0	71.0	35.0	3.9	4.4
Blackford	2,644.1	1,859.9	147.5	4.7	108.0	118.0	36.0	37.0	67.0	34.0	3.3	2.9
Boone	11,442.6	3,867.0	231.3	13.0	106.0	113.0	40.0	38.0	77.0	39.0	4.3	3.0
Brown	241.8	51.1	NA	9.1	106.0	97.0	41.0	39.0	NA	NA	2.6	2.7
Carroll	16,447.0	3,050.0	362.9	10.4	120.0	149.0	42.0	46.0	68.0	44.0	4.1	3.3
Cass	14,251.1	3,121.6	316.7	19.4	115.0	141.0	42.0	44.0	59.0	37.0	4.0	3.4
Clark	1,911.2	939.8	348.9	33.5	104.0	127.0	37.0	34.0	45.0	35.0	3.4	2.4
Clay	5,365.7	1,904.6	203.3	13.6	123.0	108.0	39.0	35.0	53.0	30.0	2.9	2.7
Clinton	15,607.8	4,360.7	286.1	9.3	102.0	133.0	41.0	41.0	74.0	33.0	4.2	3.4
Crawford	266.8	73.1	NA	24.5	98.0	103.0	36.0	39.0	NA	NA	2.6	2.5
Daviess	10,576.3	2,142.8	321.4	33.6	120.0	122.0	39.0	40.0	53.0	35.0	2.7	2.8
Dearborn	550.5	278.6	53.7	32.0	112.0	92.0	33.0	33.0	47.0	28.0	2.8	2.2
Decatur	10,158.2	2,595.3	395.0	21.4	132.0	121.0	46.0	42.0	66.0	38.0	3.2	3.6
Dekalb	2,583.6	1,565.0	732.1	20.6	108.0	98.0	38.0	28.0	57.0	46.0	4.1	2.8
Delaware	5,210.4	3,134.4	266.6	10.1	121.0	106.0	38.0	37.0	67.0	33.0	3.1	3.5
Dubois	8,482.8	1,677.6	396.4	51.8	102.0	124.0	38.0	44.0	47.0	32.0	3.0	2.7
Elkhart	4,991.7	1,713.3	219.4	65.0	115.0	110.0	39.0	34.0	60.0	39.0	3.9	3.6
Fayette	3,829.4	1,103.6	224.5	18.1	116.0	115.0	38.0	39.0	NA	36.0	3.7	3.3
Floyd	173.9	89.9	37.6	15.0	105.0	102.0	36.0	36.0	NA	38.0	2.4	2.5
Fountain	12,926.1	3,628.8	171.4	22.6	112.0	130.0	39.0	42.0	66.0	35.0	3.3	3.4
Franklin	3,830.3	876.5	157.2	29.9	115.0	113.0	41.0	36.0	59.0	31.0	3.4	2.5
Fulton	11,086.9	2,167.7	214.2	24.3	109.0	127.0	35.0	35.0	NA	36.0	3.2	3.6
Gibson	15,100.1	4,291.5	1,484.8	13.7	114.0	136.0	37.0	44.0	60.0	45.0	3.1	2.9
Grant	7,310.6	3,566.7	271.5	16.3	116.0	118.0	40.0	39.0	66.0	41.0	3.1	3.5
Greene	5,421.4	1,344.7	90.2	48.8	122.0	107.0	39.0	36.0	45.0	36.0	2.4	2.4
Hamilton	7,028.3	2,851.6	233.0	12.2	104.0	118.0	39.0	38.0	76.0	39.0	3.5	2.9
Hancock	7,940.3	3,290.1	206.0	7.1	113.0	125.0	39.0	40.0	76.0	37.0	3.1	2.5
Harrison	2,385.9	707.8	298.5	65.6	101.0	107.0	35.0	36.0	48.0	41.0	3.6	2.7
Hendricks	7,815.7	2,499.5	253.5	15.2	120.0	122.0	43.0	39.0	69.0	40.0	3.4	2.5
Henry	7,367.3	3,341.4	153.8	19.5	111.0	117.0	36.0	39.0	67.0	28.0	4.2	2.9
Howard	10,253.6	2,838.2	244.5	9.4	123.0	143.0	42.0	42.0	74.0	41.0	4.0	3.4
Huntington	5,047.1	3,488.5	526.3	15.7	112.0	119.0	37.0	34.0	63.0	41.0	3.4	2.9
Jackson	9,377.7	2,948.1	486.1	26.5	114.0	129.0	39.0	40.0	55.0	39.0	2.6	2.5
Jasper	19,244.8	3,865.8	70.9	10.8	99.0	125.0	34.0	39.0	NA	30.0	3.1	3.7
Jay	4,224.1	2,710.2	412.8	23.6	109.0	93.0	34.0	31.0	60.0	31.0	3.3	2.7
Jefferson	1,434.4	987.2	NA	35.5	112.0	101.0	38.0	35.0	NA	NA	3.0	2.5
Jennings	3,872.3	1,707.9	182.8	20.5	117.0	115.0	38.0	35.0	61.0	36.0	2.7	2.7
Johnson	5,951.8	2,149.5	281.0	16.6	121.0	109.0	44.0	36.0	63.0	40.0	4.2	3.0
Knox	15,275.5	4,379.9	886.7	16.7	123.0	131.0	35.0	38.0	52.0	36.0	2.5	2.2
Kosciusko	10,685.9	2,584.1	411.7	31.9	111.0	119.0	38.0	35.0	56.0	41.0	3.1	3.1
Lagrange	5,195.7	1,175.1	273.7	56.0	115.0	104.0	40.0	41.0	55.0	43.0	3.9	3.0
Lake	6,837.9	1,757.2	NA	8.6	113.0	113.0	40.0	28.0	65.0	NA	3.0	2.1
Laporte	15,419.3	2,204.0	235.1	38.5	129.0	127.0	40.0	30.0	59.0	39.0	4.5	3.2
Lawrence	1,849.1	492.4	NA	58.7	98.0	90.0	33.0	31.0	40.0	NA	3.1	2.3
Madison	11,563.3	4,264.1	244.3	11.4	119.0	130.0	43.0	42.0	70.0	35.0	3.6	2.9
Marion	1,129.2	644.2	84.5	3.0	107.0	121.0	39.0	38.0	67.0	40.0	3.8	2.3
Marshall	9,449.4	2,465.8	291.3	37.1	113.0	108.0	39.0	30.0	61.0	35.0	4.2	3.0
Martin	1,953.2	552.7	57.2	12.2	114.0	119.0	41.0	43.0	45.0	30.0	2.5	2.3
Miami	9,253.9	2,868.8	376.2	21.1	111.0	132.0	40.0	41.0	65.0	43.0	3.8	3.5
Monroe	568.2	137.6	NA	40.3	95.0	103.0	34.0	31.0	NA	NA	3.7	2.8
Montgomery	14,720.0	4,503.9	305.6	24.6	115.0	124.0	41.0	41.0	71.0	38.0	4.5	3.6
Morgan	6,057.0	1,929.6	113.1	19.0	122.0	127.0	42.0	40.0	68.0	22.0	3.6	2.5
Newton	15,718.6	3,040.9	NA	4.2	99.0	128.0	38.0	41.0	68.0	NA	3.1	2.6
Noble	4,935.5	1,712.5	312.0	30.7	110.0	113.0	39.0	37.0	57.0	42.0	3.4	3.0
Ohio	NA	NA	NA	16.4	NA	NA	NA	NA	NA	NA	2.4	2.5
Orange	1,946.1	640.6	171.9	40.0	97.0	116.0	39.0	43.0	50.0	45.0	2.7	2.4
Owen	1,523.3	573.4	103.8	28.6	110.0	93.0	37.0	29.0	47.0	28.0	2.8	2.4
Parke	7,019.8	2,216.2	248.8	13.6	117.0	111.0	41.0	35.0	NA	33.0	4.2	2.6
Perry	1,126.5	201.0	34.4	33.0	105.0	115.0	40.0	31.0	41.0	29.0	3.0	2.2
Pike	4,253.2	1,349.4	198.7	6.7	99.0	126.0	36.0	40.0	56.0	32.0	2.4	2.3
Porter	8,018.3	1,796.5	188.9	16.0	128.0	136.0	41.0	34.0	64.0	38.0	3.4	3.7
Posey	10,721.5	3,953.2	1,435.2	8.8	120.0	140.0	38.0	42.0	53.0	43.0	3.1	3.0
Pulaski	13,087.5	2,489.0	191.1	13.2	103.0	110.0	33.0	34.0	58.0	34.0	2.8	3.4
Putnam	9,075.0	2,484.1	185.3	27.7	117.0	126.0	44.0	40.0	72.0	35.0	3.2	2.6
Randolph	7,280.6	3,495.8	483.6	17.4	119.0	110.0	37.0	36.0	66.0	35.0	3.5	2.9
Ripley	4,677.7	2,126.8	175.0	26.8	121.0	103.0	39.0	39.0	59.0	31.0	3.2	2.4
Rush	12,884.2	3,587.2	268.9	21.4	120.0	127.0	42.0	41.0	72.0	32.0	4.3	3.7
St. Joseph	7,877.2	1,572.8	226.5	15.2	121.0	107.0	42.0	30.0	NA	40.0	4.0	2.9
Scott	1,859.1	886.0	125.4	15.6	109.0	128.0	38.0	40.0	NA	38.0	3.1	3.0
Shelby	11,320.4	3,858.6	381.2	17.2	115.0	122.0	40.0	40.0	65.0	38.0	3.5	3.4
Spencer	7,148.8	1,957.3	577.3	27.9	101.0	124.0	33.0	36.0	51.0	37.0	2.9	2.1
Starke	6,607.5	562.1	NA	5.7	114.0	103.0	33.0	27.0	NA	NA	3.7	2.9
Steuben	3,138.7	883.6	240.3	34.2	105.0	106.0	39.0	35.0	50.0	39.0	3.8	3.1
Sullivan	7,240.3	2,345.6	464.7	14.2	111.0	112.0	36.0	36.0	44.0	41.0	3.8	2.7
Switzerland	NA	NA	NA	30.8	NA	NA	NA	NA	68.0	NA	2.5	2.3
Tippecanoe	15,311.1	3,722.8	364.0	21.3	108.0	132.0	41.0	41.0	68.0	38.0	3.7	3.7
Tipton	10,169.7	3,463.6	157.9	4.5	112.0	131.0	44.0	44.0	75.0	40.0	3.3	3.0
Union	4,421.8	1,187.0	156.9	5.4	128.0	120.0	44.0	43.0	NA	30.0	3.9	2.2
Vanderburgh	5,173.9	1,480.0	370.7	4.8	110.0	136.0	40.0	40.0	57.0	37.0	3.9	3.0
Vermillion	5,007.1	1,661.7	115.9	9.8	112.0	126.0	40.0	40.0	NA	39.0	3.4	3.9
Vigo	4,584.3	1,515.7	255.7	7.2	111.0	97.0	34.0	28.0	59.0	43.0	2.9	2.6
Wabash	7,464.9	2,620.9	488.1	19.6	113.0	124.0	40.0	37.0	58.0	40.0	3.9	3.1
Warren	13,689.6	3,369.8	161.2	13.0	92.0	140.0	40.0	43.0	66.0	38.0	4.1	3.6
Warrick	4,918.0	1,145.3	252.7	14.8	96.0	123.0	34.0	37.0	46.0	32.0	2.4	2.5
Washington	4,303.0	969.4	198.4	75.3	100.0	121.0	36.0	39.0	48.0	31.0	2.9	2.5
Wayne	5,772.3	2,393.7	250.3	22.2	107.0	107.0	36.0	36.0	68.0	31.0	4.0	2.3
Wells	6,400.0	3,838.9	557.7	10.6	114.0	123.0	36.0	38.0	68.0	39.0	4.3	3.3
White	21,404.0	4,704.6	224.4	12.0	117.0	148.0	40.0	43.0	65.0	35.0	3.6	2.7
Whitley	3,337.9	2,198.7	726.2	26.4	120.0	109.0	41.0	34.0	68.0	42.0	3.5	3.2

Source: U.S. Department of Agriculture and Purdue University
EDIN table(s): FMPD

Number of Establishments by Industry: Percent Change
Indiana - 1990 to 1995

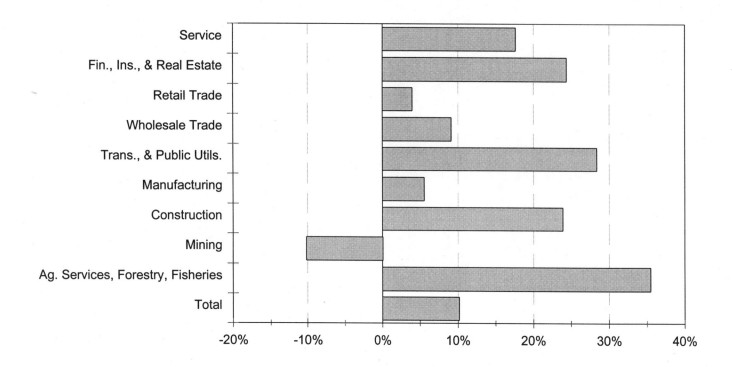

Payroll Per Employee by Industry: Real Percent Change
Indiana - 1990 to 1995

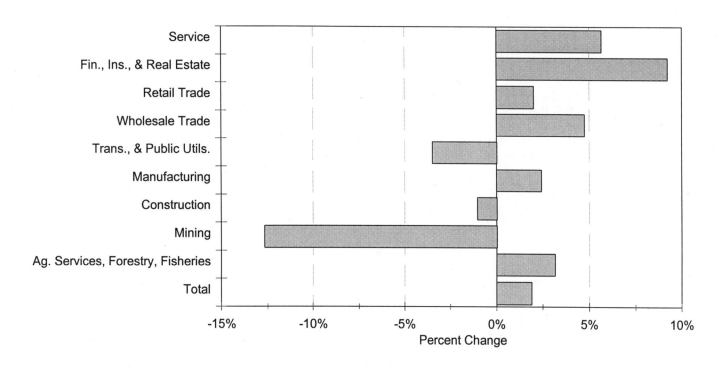

Number of Establishments by Industry: Percent Change: EDIN Table EMIE.
Payroll Per employee by Industry: Percent Change: EDIN Table EMIP.

Business

2.57 Total Industries: Establishments, Employees, and Payroll 1995

	Number of Establishments	Number of Employees	Annual Payroll ($000)	Average Employee Per Establishment	Payroll Per Employee ($)	Rank	Percent Change 1990 to 1995				Rank
							Establishments	Employees	Annual Payroll	Payroll Per Employee	
Indiana	141,253	2,403,189	59,553,716	17	24,781	—	10.1	11.8	13.8	1.9	—
Adams	724	13,045	263,642	18	20,210	58	4.2	16.9	14.4	-2.1	74
Allen	8,557	166,194	4,215,336	19	25,364	13	5.9	-0.8	-2.2	-1.4	70
Bartholomew	1,925	36,088	914,546	19	25,342	14	12.8	11.3	0.6	-9.6	87
Benton	273	2,010	33,987	7	16,909	85	16.2	0.1	-15.4	-15.6	90
Blackford	284	4,002	77,963	14	19,481	63	0.0	6.5	-0.8	-6.9	85
Boone	1,136	11,078	219,565	10	19,820	60	16.6	23.0	24.9	1.5	52
Brown	365	1,952	26,809	5	13,734	91	17.4	3.9	19.7	15.2	3
Carroll	385	4,658	92,750	12	19,912	59	7.8	36.4	42.6	4.6	35
Cass	869	14,786	310,102	17	20,973	47	-3.2	5.6	11.8	5.9	28
Clark	2,314	35,410	754,530	15	21,308	41	17.1	18.6	18.1	-0.4	62
Clay	548	6,535	126,579	12	19,369	65	21.2	41.6	39.7	-1.4	70
Clinton	727	10,617	238,316	15	22,447	32	4.8	27.5	42.3	11.6	9
Crawford	152	1,141	16,548	8	14,503	90	13.4	19.2	24.7	4.6	35
Daviess	731	8,086	138,870	11	17,174	82	10.6	10.3	2.5	-7.1	86
Dearborn	952	10,581	224,096	11	21,179	44	33.5	22.4	10.4	-9.8	88
Decatur	591	9,670	212,374	16	21,962	35	10.3	26.9	30.6	2.9	43
Dekalb	882	17,384	431,224	20	24,806	17	12.8	26.7	42.3	12.3	6
Delaware	2,753	49,968	1,179,784	18	23,611	23	6.0	13.0	16.2	2.9	43
Dubois	1,163	25,321	579,985	22	22,905	27	9.8	20.3	23.7	2.9	43
Elkhart	4,993	110,515	2,675,544	22	24,210	21	7.7	17.1	18.1	0.9	55
Fayette	541	10,197	276,876	19	27,153	8	9.1	-1.8	-0.6	1.2	53
Floyd	1,605	22,233	453,960	14	20,418	56	21.0	33.4	39.9	4.9	33
Fountain	385	4,369	85,856	11	19,651	62	2.4	8.3	12.7	4.0	38
Franklin	320	3,158	58,590	10	18,553	72	14.3	36.3	51.6	11.2	10
Fulton	489	6,982	144,752	14	20,732	51	2.9	16.1	14.7	-1.2	69
Gibson	732	8,868	150,836	12	17,009	84	0.8	4.4	-20.6	-24.0	92
Grant	1,562	30,836	740,615	20	24,018	22	-0.3	-0.2	-0.2	-0.1	60
Greene	701	6,304	95,241	9	15,108	89	19.4	17.4	11.8	-4.7	82
Hamilton	4,275	56,343	1,581,219	13	28,064	6	35.5	43.0	51.8	6.2	27
Hancock	1,103	11,533	264,179	10	22,906	26	18.3	25.2	25.9	0.5	57
Harrison	617	7,062	125,824	11	17,817	78	15.1	36.6	35.9	-0.5	63
Hendricks	1,732	17,517	383,667	10	21,903	36	34.2	42.1	46.5	3.1	42
Henry	950	11,764	288,174	12	24,496	20	3.0	10.0	23.2	12.0	8
Howard	1,944	42,992	1,530,179	22	35,592	1	5.9	13.8	27.7	12.2	7
Huntington	898	18,286	486,344	20	26,597	10	17.2	34.8	88.7	40.0	1
Jackson	1,002	18,167	387,367	18	21,323	40	15.4	21.0	37.7	13.8	4
Jasper	742	8,470	173,805	11	20,520	53	23.5	38.8	32.5	-4.6	79
Jay	460	6,900	129,841	15	18,818	68	10.0	8.3	6.6	-1.5	72
Jefferson	699	11,573	246,457	17	21,296	42	7.4	9.4	18.9	8.7	17
Jennings	400	7,603	144,978	19	19,069	66	14.9	51.8	64.0	8.0	19
Johnson	2,524	32,446	638,689	13	19,685	61	22.2	25.8	34.6	7.0	24
Knox	1,039	14,453	263,220	14	18,212	75	1.3	27.8	34.9	5.6	31
Kosciusko	1,781	29,564	778,527	17	26,334	11	9.7	10.1	16.4	5.7	30
Lagrange	650	10,445	228,766	16	21,902	37	21.5	31.2	40.5	7.2	23
Lake	9,958	167,675	4,553,952	17	27,159	7	8.2	0.3	1.0	0.7	56
Laporte	2,621	39,137	880,008	15	22,485	30	13.4	7.2	7.0	-0.2	61
Lawrence	886	13,960	315,000	16	22,564	29	14.2	25.8	20.0	-4.6	79
Madison	2,712	42,875	1,101,332	16	25,687	12	5.2	-2.0	-5.0	-3.0	77
Marion	23,910	500,953	14,373,627	21	28,693	3	7.5	7.1	12.2	4.7	34
Marshall	1,101	18,193	384,009	17	21,108	46	10.1	38.9	44.9	4.3	37
Martin	227	2,307	42,617	10	18,473	73	9.1	-1.7	0.1	1.9	50
Miami	652	7,433	138,687	11	18,658	69	8.5	17.3	21.3	3.4	40
Monroe	2,815	41,990	852,257	15	20,297	57	10.4	8.9	11.0	1.9	50
Montgomery	901	16,314	400,312	18	24,538	19	5.4	13.9	20.0	5.4	32
Morgan	1,197	12,080	227,462	10	18,830	67	20.3	11.7	23.9	10.9	12
Newton	267	2,913	54,124	11	18,580	70	7.2	15.9	9.4	-5.6	83
Noble	904	18,757	408,134	21	21,759	38	4.0	28.7	31.9	2.5	47
Ohio	61	487	5,446	8	11,183	92	-9.0	39.1	36.7	-1.8	73
Orange	394	6,787	120,300	17	17,725	80	12.9	15.3	27.5	10.6	13
Owen	289	2,732	50,199	9	18,374	74	18.9	21.4	30.5	7.4	21
Parke	294	2,272	36,215	8	15,940	87	5.4	8.9	6.5	-2.1	74
Perry	392	4,685	84,470	12	18,030	76	9.5	14.1	17.1	2.6	46
Pike	194	2,086	51,615	11	24,744	18	-4.9	21.7	29.7	6.6	26
Porter	2,964	47,796	1,346,531	16	28,172	5	20.9	22.0	29.1	5.8	29
Posey	520	7,405	218,251	14	29,473	2	7.9	17.8	26.5	7.4	21
Pulaski	321	3,692	79,659	12	21,576	39	13.0	18.6	14.0	-3.9	78
Putnam	651	10,191	181,136	16	17,774	79	15.6	32.3	43.4	8.4	18
Randolph	587	7,347	153,927	13	20,951	48	3.0	-2.3	-0.3	2.0	49
Ripley	678	10,242	277,369	15	27,082	9	17.1	12.4	16.1	3.2	41
Rush	395	4,323	84,180	11	19,473	64	11.3	30.0	42.2	9.4	16
St. Joseph	6,611	117,353	2,756,584	18	23,490	24	4.8	12.5	12.8	0.3	58
Scott	434	5,757	103,759	13	18,023	77	25.1	46.7	52.4	3.8	39
Shelby	909	14,709	328,250	16	22,316	34	11.7	21.0	30.1	7.6	20
Spencer	396	5,584	127,212	14	22,782	28	5.0	15.2	14.4	-0.7	65
Starke	331	3,791	65,476	11	17,271	81	0.3	22.6	39.0	13.3	5
Steuben	920	15,562	321,193	17	20,640	52	16.5	24.9	23.5	-1.1	67
Sullivan	410	4,230	87,814	10	20,760	50	15.5	20.4	14.9	-4.6	79
Switzerland	112	1,273	20,670	11	16,237	86	20.4	11.9	22.5	9.5	14
Tippecanoe	2,992	55,580	1,402,484	19	25,234	15	9.5	14.4	25.3	9.5	14
Tipton	324	3,384	71,948	10	21,261	43	4.9	29.9	44.5	11.2	10
Union	139	855	13,271	6	15,522	88	-1.4	24.6	26.1	1.2	53
Vanderburgh	5,196	102,461	2,404,682	20	23,469	25	3.5	10.5	9.4	-1.0	66
Vermillion	283	4,099	116,287	14	28,370	4	2.9	33.1	62.5	22.1	2
Vigo	2,682	46,777	978,201	17	20,912	40	8.5	10.3	3.6	-6.1	84
Wabash	874	13,203	295,414	15	22,375	33	11.6	3.8	4.0	0.2	59
Warren	109	986	16,909	9	17,149	83	11.2	26.6	25.2	-1.1	67
Warrick	969	10,796	268,400	11	24,861	16	12.0	1.0	-16.8	-17.7	91
Washington	429	5,490	101,943	13	18,569	71	18.8	11.8	11.1	-0.6	64
Wayne	1,775	30,046	634,999	17	21,134	45	8.9	8.4	10.6	2.1	48
Wells	628	9,257	207,995	15	22,469	31	9.4	16.0	23.9	6.8	25
White	689	9,526	195,026	14	20,473	54	15.4	44.1	29.4	-10.2	89
Whitley	655	10,195	208,645	16	20,465	55	15.3	40.1	37.2	-2.1	74

Footnote: Percent change in annual payroll and payroll per employee were calculated using real (adjusted for inflation) dollars.
Source: U.S. Bureau of the Census, County Business Patterns
EDIN table(s): EMIE, EMIP

2.58 Ag. Services, Forestry, and Fisheries: Establishments, Employees, and Payroll 1995

	Number of Establishments	Number of Employees	Annual Payroll ($000)	Average Employee Per Establishment	Payroll Per Employee ($)	Rank	Percent Change 1990 to 1995 Establishments	Employees	Annual Payroll	Payroll Per Employee	Rank
Indiana	2,136	12,404	224,652	6	18,111	—	35.4	34.6	38.8	3.1	—
Adams	13	55	1,696	4	30,836	1	44.4	189.5	306.9	40.6	3
Allen	142	958	17,338	7	18,098	22	24.6	34.7	30.0	-3.5	34
Bartholomew	26	110	1,692	4	15,382	39	44.4	35.8	53.2	12.8	19
Benton	4	8	92	2	11,500	58	-20.0	NA	NA	NA	50
Blackford	2	NA	NA	NA	NA	62	0.0	NA	NA	NA	50
Boone	36	184	3,999	5	21,734	7	28.6	4.0	0.2	-3.6	35
Brown	3	4	77	1	19,250	13	200.0	NA	NA	NA	50
Carroll	10	NA	NA	NA	NA	62	25.0	NA	NA	NA	50
Cass	18	NA	NA	NA	NA	62	20.0	NA	NA	NA	50
Clark	37	140	2,015	4	14,393	46	42.3	91.8	125.1	17.4	9
Clay	12	NA	NA	NA	NA	62	50.0	NA	NA	NA	50
Clinton	13	25	694	2	27,760	3	-13.3	47.1	119.8	49.4	2
Crawford	0	0	0	NA	NA	62	NA	NA	NA	NA	50
Daviess	14	32	487	2	15,219	40	40.0	-30.4	-10.4	28.8	4
Dearborn	15	44	606	3	13,773	50	66.7	37.5	45.0	5.5	24
Decatur	9	86	2,133	10	24,802	5	0.0	115.0	76.2	-18.1	45
Dekalb	15	47	704	3	14,979	41	36.4	74.1	10.7	-36.4	49
Delaware	44	1,206	20,305	27	16,837	29	18.9	25.8	9.8	-12.7	42
Dubois	11	43	610	4	14,186	48	22.2	7.5	26.6	17.8	8
Elkhart	66	296	5,556	4	18,770	18	34.7	26.5	26.2	-0.2	31
Fayette	7	14	199	2	14,214	47	16.7	NA	NA	NA	50
Floyd	21	172	2,720	8	15,814	37	75.0	129.3	135.7	2.8	29
Fountain	7	NA	NA	NA	NA	62	40.0	NA	NA	NA	50
Franklin	2	NA	NA	NA	NA	62	-60.0	NA	NA	NA	50
Fulton	6	23	415	4	18,043	23	20.0	9.5	13.1	3.3	27
Gibson	13	NA	NA	NA	NA	62	62.5	NA	NA	NA	50
Grant	13	72	1,190	6	16,528	31	8.3	35.8	54.1	13.5	16
Greene	8	NA	NA	NA	NA	62	166.7	NA	NA	NA	50
Hamilton	114	810	18,303	7	22,596	6	58.3	80.0	110.7	17.0	11
Hancock	27	100	1,784	4	17,840	25	50.0	33.3	116.7	62.6	1
Harrison	13	51	620	4	12,157	56	18.2	-46.9	-49.4	-4.8	38
Hendricks	32	141	2,262	4	16,043	34	3.2	54.9	49.4	-3.6	35
Henry	18	75	1,417	4	18,893	16	28.6	11.9	15.3	3.0	28
Howard	23	83	1,747	4	21,048	9	9.5	-29.1	-16.9	17.2	10
Huntington	18	67	1,329	4	19,836	11	80.0	NA	NA	NA	50
Jackson	12	35	642	3	18,343	21	20.0	NA	NA	NA	50
Jasper	20	111	1,841	6	16,586	30	66.7	79.0	50.3	-16.0	44
Jay	5	NA	NA	NA	NA	62	25.0	NA	NA	NA	50
Jefferson	14	52	488	4	9,385	60	27.3	0.0	13.3	13.3	17
Jennings	5	15	446	3	29,733	2	25.0	NA	NA	NA	50
Johnson	44	186	3,438	4	18,484	19	29.4	50.0	79.6	19.7	6
Knox	10	99	1,338	10	13,515	51	-9.1	57.1	65.6	5.4	25
Kosciusko	28	96	1,828	3	19,042	15	40.0	57.4	81.0	15.0	14
Lagrange	11	61	994	6	16,295	32	22.2	24.5	26.3	1.4	30
Lake	116	801	14,702	7	18,355	20	30.3	55.2	65.1	6.3	23
Laporte	47	203	5,349	4	26,350	4	51.6	-0.5	16.1	16.7	12
Lawrence	10	41	505	4	12,317	55	66.7	46.4	84.3	25.9	5
Madison	40	176	2,866	4	16,284	33	33.3	11.4	17.3	5.3	26
Marion	293	2,026	38,923	7	19,212	14	38.2	30.1	46.8	12.8	19
Marshall	21	65	1,033	3	15,892	36	90.9	NA	NA	NA	50
Martin	2	NA	NA	NA	NA	62	-33.3	NA	NA	NA	50
Miami	6	NA	NA	NA	NA	62	200.0	NA	NA	NA	50
Monroe	44	268	4,205	6	15,690	38	37.5	NA	NA	NA	50
Montgomery	17	57	1,101	3	19,316	12	54.5	14.0	31.0	14.9	15
Morgan	26	91	1,719	4	18,890	17	73.3	139.5	101.5	-15.9	43
Newton	2	NA	NA	NA	NA	62	-33.3	NA	NA	NA	50
Noble	20	NA	NA	NA	NA	62	53.8	NA	NA	NA	50
Ohio	2	NA	NA	NA	NA	62	0.0	NA	NA	NA	50
Orange	5	NA	NA	NA	NA	62	25.0	NA	NA	NA	50
Owen	7	19	282	3	14,842	42	133.3	NA	NA	NA	50
Parke	5	NA	NA	NA	NA	62	150.0	NA	NA	NA	50
Perry	6	11	95	2	8,636	61	50.0	83.3	38.7	-24.3	47
Pike	2	NA	NA	NA	NA	62	100.0	NA	NA	NA	50
Porter	54	222	3,984	4	17,946	24	86.2	98.2	131.1	16.6	13
Posey	7	12	253	2	21,083	8	16.7	-36.8	-32.5	6.8	22
Pulaski	6	NA	NA	NA	NA	62	20.0	NA	NA	NA	50
Putnam	10	31	356	3	11,484	59	0.0	-11.4	5.0	18.6	7
Randolph	10	NA	NA	NA	NA	62	-9.1	NA	NA	NA	50
Ripley	19	61	723	3	11,852	57	137.5	NA	NA	NA	50
Rush	4	NA	NA	NA	NA	62	-33.3	NA	NA	NA	50
St. Joseph	94	538	9,239	6	17,173	28	36.2	25.1	22.8	-1.8	33
Scott	5	NA	NA	NA	NA	62	0.0	NA	NA	NA	50
Shelby	16	44	875	3	19,886	10	77.8	-12.0	-15.5	-4.0	37
Spencer	3	NA	NA	NA	NA	62	-40.0	NA	NA	NA	50
Starke	3	35	457	12	13,057	53	200.0	NA	NA	NA	50
Steuben	13	NA	NA	NA	NA	62	85.7	NA	NA	NA	50
Sullivan	3	NA	NA	NA	NA	62	50.0	NA	NA	NA	50
Switzerland	2	NA	NA	NA	NA	62	NA	NA	NA	NA	50
Tippecanoe	49	318	5,539	6	17,418	27	19.5	39.5	57.7	13.0	18
Tipton	6	15	262	3	17,467	26	0.0	36.4	11.2	-18.5	46
Union	4	NA	NA	NA	NA	62	33.3	NA	NA	NA	50
Vanderburgh	58	389	5,633	7	14,481	45	28.9	55.6	38.5	-11.0	40
Vermillion	2	NA	NA	NA	NA	62	0.0	NA	NA	NA	50
Vigo	33	156	2,092	5	13,410	52	37.5	13.9	13.5	-0.3	32
Wabash	14	51	815	4	15,980	35	40.0	24.4	9.2	-12.2	41
Warren	2	NA	NA	NA	NA	62	-33.3	NA	NA	NA	50
Warrick	21	67	936	3	13,970	49	40.0	NA	NA	NA	50
Washington	8	NA	NA	NA	NA	62	166.7	NA	NA	NA	50
Wayne	17	48	606	3	12,625	54	41.7	-15.8	-21.2	-6.4	39
Wells	10	56	830	6	14,821	43	-9.1	30.2	-14.7	-34.5	48
White	16	NA	NA	NA	NA	62	14.3	NA	NA	NA	50
Whitley	12	38	551	3	14,500	44	71.4	35.7	52.1	12.1	21

Footnote: Percent change in annual payroll and payroll per employee were calculated using real (adjusted for inflation) dollars.
Source: U.S. Bureau of the Census, County Business Patterns
EDIN table(s): EMIE, EMIP

2.59 Mining: Establishments, Employees, and Payroll 1995

	Number of Establishments	Number of Employees	Annual Payroll ($000)	Average Employee Per Establishment	Payroll Per Employee ($)	Rank	Percent Change 1990 to 1995 Establishments	Employees	Annual Payroll	Payroll Per Employee	Rank
Indiana	381	6,351	246,113	17	38,752	—	-10.1	-17.3	-27.8	-12.7	—
Adams	3	NA	NA	NA	NA	30	50.0	NA	NA	NA	20
Allen	8	117	4,053	15	34,641	18	-38.5	-3.3	-8.9	-5.8	12
Bartholomew	3	NA	NA	NA	NA	30	50.0	NA	NA	NA	20
Benton	0	0	0	NA	NA	30	NA	NA	NA	NA	20
Blackford	2	NA	NA	NA	NA	30	0.0	NA	NA	NA	20
Boone	1	NA	NA	NA	NA	30	0.0	NA	NA	NA	20
Brown	0	0	NA	NA	NA	30	NA	NA	NA	NA	20
Carroll	1	NA	NA	NA	NA	30	-50.0	NA	NA	NA	20
Cass	1	NA	NA	NA	NA	30	0.0	NA	NA	NA	20
Clark	7	135	4,443	19	32,911	20	16.7	36.4	48.0	8.6	9
Clay	2	NA	NA	NA	NA	30	-75.0	NA	NA	NA	20
Clinton	0	0	0	NA	NA	30	NA	NA	NA	NA	20
Crawford	4	NA	NA	NA	NA	30	-33.3	NA	NA	NA	20
Daviess	12	340	13,428	28	39,494	11	20.0	-46.1	-57.2	-20.6	15
Dearborn	1	NA	NA	NA	NA	30	NA	NA	NA	NA	20
Decatur	2	NA	NA	NA	NA	30	-33.3	NA	NA	NA	20
Dekalb	4	36	1,414	9	39,278	12	-42.9	-42.9	-22.3	35.9	4
Delaware	2	NA	NA	NA	NA	30	0.0	NA	NA	NA	20
Dubois	5	135	5,381	27	39,859	10	0.0	-36.0	-11.5	38.4	3
Elkhart	3	NA	NA	NA	NA	30	50.0	NA	NA	NA	20
Fayette	3	11	386	4	35,091	17	0.0	NA	NA	NA	20
Floyd	0	0	0	NA	NA	30	NA	NA	NA	NA	20
Fountain	1	NA	NA	NA	NA	30	0.0	NA	NA	NA	20
Franklin	2	NA	NA	NA	NA	30	-50.0	NA	NA	NA	20
Fulton	0	0	0	NA	NA	30	NA	NA	NA	NA	20
Gibson	12	NA	NA	NA	NA	30	-42.9	NA	NA	NA	20
Grant	3	NA	NA	NA	NA	30	0.0	NA	NA	NA	20
Greene	3	NA	NA	NA	NA	30	-66.7	NA	NA	NA	20
Hamilton	9	110	4,710	12	42,818	5	28.6	31.0	18.3	-9.7	13
Hancock	2	NA	NA	NA	NA	30	0.0	NA	NA	NA	20
Harrison	6	89	2,563	15	28,798	24	50.0	45.9	89.7	30.0	6
Hendricks	2	NA	NA	NA	NA	30	0.0	NA	NA	NA	20
Henry	0	0	0	NA	NA	30	-100.0	NA	NA	NA	20
Howard	4	NA	NA	NA	NA	30	0.0	NA	NA	NA	20
Huntington	2	NA	NA	NA	NA	30	100.0	NA	NA	NA	20
Jackson	2	NA	NA	NA	NA	30	100.0	NA	NA	NA	20
Jasper	2	NA	NA	NA	NA	30	-66.7	NA	NA	NA	20
Jay	2	NA	NA	NA	NA	30	-60.0	NA	NA	NA	20
Jefferson	0	0	0	NA	NA	30	NA	NA	NA	NA	20
Jennings	3	NA	NA	NA	NA	30	0.0	NA	NA	NA	20
Johnson	4	16	737	4	46,063	3	NA	NA	NA	NA	20
Knox	10	264	12,169	26	46,095	2	25.0	340.0	481.0	32.1	5
Kosciusko	2	NA	NA	NA	NA	30	100.0	NA	NA	NA	20
Lagrange	1	NA	NA	NA	NA	30	NA	NA	NA	NA	20
Lake	8	40	1,086	5	27,150	26	700.0	NA	NA	NA	20
Laporte	3	18	552	6	30,667	23	NA	NA	NA	NA	20
Lawrence	4	63	2,619	16	41,571	9	0.0	NA	NA	NA	20
Madison	4	NA	NA	NA	NA	30	0.0	NA	NA	NA	20
Marion	22	405	17,225	18	42,531	6	-8.3	-15.6	-39.3	-28.1	18
Marshall	2	NA	NA	NA	NA	30	100.0	NA	NA	NA	20
Martin	0	0	0	NA	NA	30	NA	NA	NA	NA	20
Miami	2	NA	NA	NA	NA	30	-33.3	NA	NA	NA	20
Monroe	9	178	7,701	20	43,264	4	28.6	13.4	37.3	21.1	8
Montgomery	1	NA	NA	NA	NA	30	-66.7	NA	NA	NA	20
Morgan	6	96	3,386	16	35,271	16	100.0	68.4	147.0	46.6	2
Newton	1	NA	NA	NA	NA	30	0.0	NA	NA	NA	20
Noble	3	NA	NA	NA	NA	30	200.0	NA	NA	NA	20
Ohio	0	0	0	NA	NA	30	NA	NA	NA	NA	20
Orange	3	NA	NA	NA	NA	30	200.0	NA	NA	NA	20
Owen	0	0	0	NA	NA	30	-100.0	NA	NA	NA	20
Parke	1	NA	NA	NA	NA	30	0.0	NA	NA	NA	20
Perry	0	0	0	NA	NA	30	-100.0	NA	NA	NA	20
Pike	10	179	6,650	18	37,151	15	-9.1	NA	NA	NA	20
Porter	1	NA	NA	NA	NA	30	-80.0	NA	NA	NA	20
Posey	14	43	966	3	22,465	28	-22.2	-65.3	-74.1	-25.2	17
Pulaski	3	40	1,508	13	37,700	14	200.0	NA	NA	NA	20
Putnam	6	74	2,375	12	32,095	21	-14.3	-2.6	-7.9	-5.4	11
Randolph	1	NA	NA	NA	NA	30	NA	NA	NA	NA	20
Ripley	4	NA	NA	NA	NA	30	0.0	NA	NA	NA	20
Rush	1	NA	NA	NA	NA	30	-50.0	NA	NA	NA	20
St. Joseph	4	24	802	6	33,417	19	-33.3	-25.0	-23.8	1.6	10
Scott	1	NA	NA	NA	NA	30	0.0	NA	NA	NA	20
Shelby	5	98	2,358	20	24,061	27	400.0	NA	NA	NA	20
Spencer	13	128	3,635	10	28,398	25	0.0	-12.3	-32.0	-22.4	16
Starke	0	0	0	NA	NA	30	-100.0	NA	NA	NA	20
Steuben	2	NA	NA	NA	NA	30	0.0	NA	NA	NA	20
Sullivan	10	472	19,868	47	42,093	8	150.0	NA	NA	NA	20
Switzerland	1	NA	NA	NA	NA	30	0.0	NA	NA	NA	20
Tippecanoe	7	59	1,829	8	31,000	22	16.7	NA	NA	NA	20
Tipton	0	0	0	NA	NA	30	NA	NA	NA	NA	20
Union	0	0	0	NA	NA	30	NA	NA	NA	NA	20
Vanderburgh	48	659	27,970	14	42,443	7	-22.6	46.4	115.0	46.8	1
Vermillion	3	NA	NA	NA	NA	30	0.0	NA	NA	NA	20
Vigo	13	130	2,434	10	18,723	29	-23.5	18.2	-19.6	-31.9	19
Wabash	0	0	0	NA	NA	30	NA	NA	NA	NA	20
Warren	1	NA	NA	NA	NA	30	0.0	NA	NA	NA	20
Warrick	10	603	28,286	60	46,909	1	-23.1	-8.2	-20.4	-13.3	14
Washington	2	NA	NA	NA	NA	30	0.0	NA	NA	NA	20
Wayne	4	44	1,691	11	38,432	13	0.0	29.4	67.0	29.1	7
Wells	2	NA	NA	NA	NA	30	-60.0	NA	NA	NA	20
White	1	NA	NA	NA	NA	30	0.0	NA	NA	NA	20
Whitley	0	0	0	NA	NA	30	NA	NA	NA	NA	20

Footnote: Percent change in annual payroll and payroll per employee were calculated using real (adjusted for inflation) dollars.
Source: U.S. Bureau of the Census, County Business Patterns
EDIN table(s): EMIE, EMIP

2.60 Contract Construction: Establishments, Employees, and Payroll 1995

	Number of Establishments	Number of Employees	Annual Payroll ($000)	Average Employee Per Establishment	Payroll Per Employee ($)	Rank	Percent Change 1990 to 1995 Establishments	Employees	Annual Payroll	Payroll Per Employee	Rank
Indiana	15,286	129,903	3,791,435	8	29,187	—	23.9	15.0	13.9	-1.0	—
Adams	76	433	10,795	6	24,931	40	7.0	7.4	11.9	4.1	35
Allen	895	8,808	272,632	10	30,953	10	14.2	11.1	7.3	-3.4	54
Bartholomew	214	2,397	70,903	11	29,580	15	29.7	63.8	49.5	-8.8	67
Benton	23	79	1,456	3	18,430	71	27.8	NA	NA	NA	86
Blackford	16	52	1,236	3	23,769	45	77.8	-45.3	-8.3	67.5	2
Boone	175	1,376	37,278	8	27,092	26	27.7	34.9	26.7	-6.1	64
Brown	47	146	2,434	3	16,671	80	30.6	-30.8	19.8	73.1	1
Carroll	59	217	3,127	4	14,410	87	7.3	14.8	-17.0	-27.7	84
Cass	76	488	17,094	6	35,029	3	-9.5	12.4	49.7	33.1	5
Clark	276	2,063	56,534	7	27,404	25	38.0	-5.7	7.6	14.1	16
Clay	56	169	2,543	3	15,047	86	69.7	83.7	104.5	11.3	21
Clinton	97	667	16,088	7	24,120	42	27.6	46.9	68.7	14.8	14
Crawford	19	113	1,586	6	14,035	89	90.0	NA	NA	NA	86
Daviess	104	583	10,535	6	18,070	75	30.0	58.0	48.8	-5.8	63
Dearborn	151	990	17,436	7	17,612	77	42.5	-24.9	-44.6	-26.3	83
Decatur	70	250	3,975	4	15,900	83	22.8	43.7	47.1	2.4	40
Dekalb	98	504	12,829	5	25,454	32	46.3	38.8	64.7	18.6	9
Delaware	277	3,165	91,196	11	28,814	17	26.5	13.7	18.7	4.4	34
Dubois	130	945	27,122	7	28,701	18	12.1	12.2	7.3	-4.4	60
Elkhart	479	3,924	116,228	8	29,620	13	13.0	17.9	15.2	-2.3	52
Fayette	39	177	3,260	5	18,418	72	-13.3	7.9	-1.2	-8.5	66
Floyd	250	1,841	46,407	7	25,207	37	34.4	28.7	50.6	17.0	10
Fountain	41	137	3,068	3	22,394	51	20.6	17.1	67.4	42.9	4
Franklin	50	235	3,662	5	15,583	85	47.1	55.6	34.2	-13.8	75
Fulton	44	315	12,223	7	38,803	1	-2.2	-20.3	-19.3	1.2	44
Gibson	76	304	5,981	4	19,674	66	7.0	18.8	5.4	-11.3	69
Grant	134	1,000	32,109	7	32,109	8	12.6	18.6	14.4	-3.5	56
Greene	105	481	10,265	5	21,341	58	61.5	36.6	20.6	-11.7	70
Hamilton	550	5,602	154,550	10	27,588	23	26.4	39.1	41.9	2.0	42
Hancock	221	1,241	27,771	6	22,378	52	50.3	43.3	54.8	8.0	27
Harrison	95	375	7,207	4	19,219	69	43.9	30.7	46.3	12.0	20
Hendricks	326	1,869	49,127	6	26,285	30	63.8	56.7	70.4	8.7	25
Henry	94	609	13,231	6	21,726	55	3.3	-11.5	-25.4	-15.7	77
Howard	170	1,179	33,450	7	28,372	21	13.3	23.7	26.4	2.2	41
Huntington	96	401	11,456	4	28,569	20	28.0	10.2	24.0	12.5	18
Jackson	112	626	14,206	6	22,693	50	33.3	8.3	18.4	9.3	24
Jasper	118	720	17,958	6	24,942	39	43.9	59.3	75.8	10.4	22
Jay	41	127	2,002	3	15,764	84	17.1	22.1	27.1	4.1	35
Jefferson	69	399	8,292	6	20,782	60	23.2	69.1	62.3	-4.0	58
Jennings	55	460	11,709	8	25,454	32	52.8	69.1	49.3	-11.7	70
Johnson	366	2,276	54,664	6	24,018	43	50.6	34.8	26.6	-6.1	64
Knox	84	438	8,439	5	19,267	68	10.5	-16.7	-28.2	-13.8	75
Kosciusko	202	907	23,537	4	25,950	31	19.5	4.9	10.9	5.8	31
Lagrange	70	533	13,461	8	25,255	36	89.2	89.7	102.3	6.7	30
Lake	1,061	11,736	425,137	11	36,225	2	28.3	11.5	11.7	0.2	45
Laporte	271	2,041	69,329	8	33,968	4	24.9	7.3	23.8	15.4	13
Lawrence	90	486	11,872	5	24,428	41	57.9	32.1	29.8	-1.7	49
Madison	261	1,458	36,831	6	25,261	35	22.0	-2.8	-8.0	-5.3	61
Marion	1,956	26,868	839,040	14	31,228	9	8.8	1.1	-2.1	-3.2	53
Marshall	122	489	9,440	4	19,305	67	34.1	11.6	-11.3	-20.5	80
Martin	28	128	2,805	5	21,914	54	47.4	91.0	48.0	-22.6	81
Miami	86	416	8,292	5	19,933	65	62.3	63.8	57.0	-4.2	59
Monroe	313	2,532	67,818	8	26,784	28	16.8	14.1	11.7	-2.0	51
Montgomery	94	391	6,510	4	16,650	81	13.3	19.9	19.7	-0.2	46
Morgan	216	1,097	22,122	5	20,166	63	54.3	66.2	68.9	1.6	43
Newton	37	161	4,310	4	26,770	29	42.3	28.8	-9.0	-29.3	85
Noble	96	496	12,494	5	25,190	38	11.6	7.1	18.1	10.2	23
Ohio	15	55	1,281	4	23,291	46	15.4	NA	NA	NA	86
Orange	48	793	22,449	17	28,309	22	45.5	27.9	43.9	12.5	18
Owen	38	200	4,773	5	23,865	44	35.7	60.0	39.6	-12.8	73
Parke	24	60	994	3	16,567	82	-4.0	-39.4	-55.0	-25.8	82
Perry	45	268	5,939	6	22,160	53	40.6	67.5	81.3	8.2	26
Pike	10	25	321	3	12,840	90	-9.1	NA	NA	NA	86
Porter	431	3,538	108,709	8	30,726	12	41.8	34.3	29.0	-3.9	57
Posey	88	780	21,132	9	27,092	26	6.0	54.5	59.9	3.5	37
Pulaski	31	92	1,582	3	17,196	79	47.6	37.3	19.3	-13.1	74
Putnam	81	370	8,009	5	21,646	57	52.8	4.8	8.0	3.0	38
Randolph	62	208	3,965	3	19,063	70	6.9	-51.5	-25.4	53.8	3
Ripley	87	396	8,222	5	20,763	61	20.8	3.9	9.1	4.9	33
Rush	45	200	3,626	4	18,130	74	9.8	23.5	22.5	-0.8	48
St. Joseph	644	6,349	195,297	10	30,760	11	10.3	14.6	13.8	-0.7	47
Scott	47	158	2,908	3	18,405	73	42.4	21.5	2.5	-15.7	77
Shelby	125	747	17,175	6	22,992	48	8.7	-9.8	-3.6	6.8	29
Spencer	46	158	2,820	3	17,848	76	35.3	11.3	-2.9	-12.7	72
Starke	32	84	1,466	3	17,452	78	39.1	6.3	23.9	16.5	11
Steuben	102	458	10,485	4	22,893	49	27.5	35.5	43.4	5.8	31
Sullivan	35	111	1,574	3	14,180	88	40.0	9.9	-12.1	-20.0	79
Switzerland	11	39	780	4	20,000	64	57.1	NA	NA	NA	86
Tippecanoe	327	2,717	80,416	8	29,597	14	33.5	31.4	50.1	14.2	15
Tipton	32	164	3,442	5	20,988	59	3.2	47.7	85.4	25.5	6
Union	12	NA	NA	NA	NA	91	-7.7	NA	NA	NA	86
Vanderburgh	514	7,468	241,954	15	32,399	6	18.2	19.9	17.7	-1.8	50
Vermillion	31	173	5,560	6	32,139	7	34.8	32.1	18.7	-10.1	68
Vigo	259	2,832	91,770	11	32,405	5	46.3	19.7	13.0	-5.6	62
Wabash	66	370	10,164	6	27,470	24	37.5	16.4	25.2	7.6	28
Warren	12	NA	NA	NA	NA	91	50.0	NA	NA	NA	86
Warrick	175	884	17,846	5	20,188	62	25.0	20.8	24.0	2.7	39
Washington	39	165	4,718	4	28,594	19	21.9	24.1	44.5	16.5	11
Wayne	159	1,003	29,097	6	29,010	16	19.5	16.1	40.7	21.2	7
Wells	82	379	9,577	5	25,269	34	46.4	44.7	64.1	13.4	17
White	64	267	6,212	4	23,266	47	33.3	23.0	18.9	-3.4	54
Whitley	87	381	8,275	4	21,719	56	29.9	46.0	73.3	18.7	8

Footnote: Percent change in annual payroll and payroll per employee were calculated using real (adjusted for inflation) dollars.
Source: U.S. Bureau of the Census, County Business Patterns
EDIN table(s): EMIE, EMIP

2.61 Manufacturing: Establishments, Employees, and Payroll 1995

	Number of Establishments	Number of Employees	Annual Payroll ($000)	Average Employee Per Establishment	Payroll Per Employee ($)	Rank	Percent Change 1990 to 1995				Rank
							Establishments	Employees	Annual Payroll	Payroll Per Employee	
Indiana	9,591	672,734	23,034,890	70	34,241	—	5.5	6.8	9.4	2.4	—
Adams	78	7,020	170,727	90	24,320	61	-1.3	7.8	7.9	0.1	49
Allen	588	37,609	1,317,389	64	35,029	16	1.9	-8.0	-8.8	-0.9	54
Bartholomew	142	14,026	430,880	99	30,720	29	9.2	-5.7	-24.6	-20.0	85
Benton	18	520	10,529	29	20,248	82	28.6	NA	NA	NA	88
Blackford	33	2,159	51,876	65	24,028	66	-10.8	4.8	-5.1	-9.4	78
Boone	64	1,807	43,589	28	24,122	64	-4.5	1.9	-0.3	-2.1	63
Brown	21	107	1,724	5	16,112	88	16.7	1.9	-23.3	-24.7	86
Carroll	31	2,180	54,628	70	25,059	53	29.2	94.1	85.9	-4.2	68
Cass	60	5,592	138,872	93	24,834	55	-4.8	-6.2	-7.1	-0.9	54
Clark	140	6,856	213,949	49	31,206	26	27.3	3.8	2.8	-1.0	56
Clay	33	2,504	65,435	76	26,132	49	0.0	76.7	75.6	-0.6	53
Clinton	45	4,766	146,784	106	30,798	28	4.7	34.2	55.5	15.9	10
Crawford	20	120	1,497	6	12,475	90	25.0	10.1	-4.3	-13.0	81
Daviess	44	2,106	37,831	48	17,963	85	-6.4	8.2	9.3	1.0	46
Dearborn	50	2,342	81,888	47	34,965	17	28.2	-8.0	-10.7	-2.9	65
Decatur	49	4,368	126,996	89	29,074	35	16.7	15.6	20.3	4.1	35
Dekalb	115	9,667	307,627	84	31,822	24	13.9	36.1	51.3	11.2	18
Delaware	180	11,565	453,073	64	39,176	10	2.9	0.7	8.4	7.7	25
Dubois	123	12,831	327,342	104	25,512	51	0.0	21.1	25.0	3.2	39
Elkhart	945	60,695	1,683,067	64	27,730	39	2.1	19.3	17.3	-1.7	60
Fayette	30	5,259	201,314	175	38,280	12	-14.3	-6.4	-4.9	1.6	42
Floyd	123	7,076	166,759	58	23,567	69	9.8	33.6	33.8	0.1	49
Fountain	27	2,010	52,866	74	26,301	48	8.0	25.9	18.1	-6.2	72
Franklin	13	928	22,730	71	24,494	59	0.0	30.2	61.8	24.3	6
Fulton	55	3,340	76,260	61	22,832	73	0.0	3.9	2.6	-1.3	58
Gibson	41	2,434	60,161	59	24,717	57	5.1	-8.8	-18.5	-10.6	79
Grant	94	10,073	385,596	107	38,280	11	5.6	-8.0	-11.6	-3.9	67
Greene	29	1,522	21,779	52	14,309	89	3.6	1.8	-17.0	-18.5	84
Hamilton	182	7,502	229,718	41	30,621	30	15.2	31.0	44.2	10.0	20
Hancock	71	2,936	104,772	41	35,685	15	20.3	11.0	5.9	-4.6	69
Harrison	38	2,282	52,317	60	22,926	71	18.8	50.4	33.7	-11.1	80
Hendricks	66	1,422	41,519	22	29,198	33	24.5	41.4	73.8	22.9	7
Henry	54	3,374	149,632	62	44,349	7	1.9	6.6	30.3	22.2	8
Howard	75	19,496	1,093,127	260	56,069	1	11.9	8.3	28.8	18.9	9
Huntington	89	10,265	353,799	115	34,467	19	17.1	50.3	115.4	43.3	2
Jackson	90	6,793	184,399	75	27,145	43	3.4	15.7	48.2	28.1	4
Jasper	30	1,494	33,660	50	22,530	75	11.1	13.3	14.9	1.5	45
Jay	36	3,477	79,301	97	22,807	74	5.9	0.7	3.1	2.4	40
Jefferson	47	4,084	112,215	87	27,477	41	-2.1	5.9	14.8	8.5	23
Jennings	43	2,567	55,610	60	21,663	79	16.2	55.5	54.8	-0.4	51
Johnson	136	5,616	167,684	41	29,858	31	16.2	10.2	17.7	6.8	27
Knox	43	2,105	50,315	49	23,903	68	-6.5	29.4	19.2	-7.8	76
Kosciusko	182	15,130	525,765	83	34,750	18	5.8	13.8	21.7	6.9	26
Lagrange	81	5,464	151,375	67	27,704	40	5.2	26.2	42.6	13.0	14
Lake	422	39,585	1,747,371	94	44,142	8	3.4	-12.6	-8.7	4.5	34
Laporte	203	12,795	362,982	63	28,369	38	1.5	3.0	2.6	-0.4	51
Lawrence	76	5,620	180,312	74	32,084	23	8.6	19.6	9.8	-8.2	77
Madison	133	11,810	556,958	89	47,160	3	7.3	-29.2	-21.2	11.4	17
Marion	1,318	83,556	3,809,183	63	45,588	4	1.5	-1.8	10.2	12.2	16
Marshall	128	8,973	222,300	70	24,774	56	2.4	64.4	62.7	-1.0	56
Martin	16	714	18,106	45	25,359	52	-11.1	-23.7	-12.5	14.7	12
Miami	43	2,612	63,488	61	24,306	63	16.2	18.0	20.5	2.2	41
Monroe	131	9,587	280,991	73	29,310	32	1.6	2.1	5.6	3.4	37
Montgomery	61	8,264	269,724	135	32,638	21	24.5	14.3	21.8	6.6	28
Morgan	77	2,361	62,231	31	26,358	47	30.5	-14.3	9.1	27.2	5
Newton	24	1,513	30,976	63	20,473	80	33.3	39.8	33.4	-4.6	69
Noble	144	10,885	280,171	76	25,739	50	-5.9	20.6	26.4	4.8	33
Ohio	1	NA	NA	NA	NA	91	-50.0	NA	NA	NA	88
Orange	32	2,919	54,583	91	18,699	84	10.3	17.0	21.0	3.4	37
Owen	25	1,019	24,770	41	24,308	62	13.6	25.5	42.4	13.4	13
Parke	16	616	13,814	39	22,425	76	-11.1	21.7	28.7	5.7	30
Perry	31	1,594	35,165	51	22,061	77	3.3	-8.5	-3.5	5.5	31
Pike	10	190	4,546	19	23,926	67	-16.7	2.7	41.0	37.2	3
Porter	147	12,254	607,032	83	49,537	2	24.6	6.1	19.7	12.9	15
Posey	32	2,936	130,898	92	44,584	6	10.3	12.7	24.6	10.5	19
Pulaski	22	1,418	38,181	64	26,926	44	4.8	4.9	-2.5	-7.0	73
Putnam	30	2,544	62,296	85	24,487	60	11.1	42.0	38.9	-2.2	64
Randolph	65	3,571	97,209	55	27,222	42	27.5	-6.3	-7.6	-1.4	59
Ripley	47	4,546	165,141	97	36,327	14	42.4	11.3	17.3	5.4	32
Rush	30	1,248	33,262	42	26,652	46	7.1	31.5	33.7	1.6	42
St. Joseph	498	23,779	766,049	48	32,215	22	1.4	9.6	10.5	0.8	47
Scott	37	2,496	57,261	67	22,941	70	15.6	53.8	50.7	-2.0	62
Shelby	80	6,740	194,803	84	28,903	37	2.6	28.0	32.8	3.8	36
Spencer	19	1,945	44,472	102	22,865	72	-29.6	2.0	-1.7	-3.7	66
Starke	23	1,315	28,964	57	22,026	78	15.0	52.4	75.4	15.1	11
Steuben	107	7,487	180,549	70	24,115	65	13.8	40.7	29.9	-7.7	75
Sullivan	28	614	12,227	22	19,914	83	7.7	NA	NA	NA	88
Switzerland	8	688	12,077	86	17,554	86	0.0	12.4	23.5	9.8	21
Tippecanoe	129	16,197	613,620	126	37,885	13	15.2	25.7	26.3	0.4	48
Tipton	20	935	25,175	47	26,925	45	42.9	66.1	37.9	-17.0	82
Union	6	NA	NA	NA	NA	91	100.0	NA	NA	NA	88
Vanderburgh	266	19,511	642,724	73	32,942	20	-4.0	2.0	0.1	-1.9	61
Vermillion	12	1,557	69,881	130	44,882	5	0.0	122.4	273.5	67.9	1
Vigo	142	8,436	266,406	59	31,580	25	0.0	-19.4	-23.8	-5.6	71
Wabash	77	6,017	174,667	78	29,029	36	-3.8	-9.1	-3.9	5.8	29
Warren	10	300	5,030	30	16,767	87	0.0	96.1	45.2	-25.9	87
Warrick	49	3,292	135,463	67	41,149	9	22.5	NA	NA	NA	88
Washington	46	2,935	60,050	64	20,460	81	12.2	7.8	-0.4	-7.6	74
Wayne	142	7,678	237,899	54	30,985	27	5.2	3.4	12.4	8.8	22
Wells	48	3,531	103,021	74	29,176	34	14.3	18.7	28.6	8.4	24
White	58	4,613	113,326	80	24,567	58	41.5	72.0	42.0	-17.5	83
Whitley	68	3,979	99,690	59	25,054	54	23.6	48.2	50.6	1.6	42

Footnote: Percent change in annual payroll and payroll per employee were calculated using real (adjusted for inflation) dollars.
Source: U.S. Bureau of the Census, County Business Patterns
EDIN table(s): EMIE, EMIP

2.62 Transportation And Public Utilities: Establishments, Employees, And Payroll 1995

	Number of Establishments	Number of Employees	Annual Payroll ($000)	Average Employee Per Establishment	Payroll Per Employee ($)	Rank	Percent Change 1990 to 1995				Rank
							Establishments	Employees	Annual Payroll	Payroll Per Employee	
Indiana	6,374	129,403	3,953,635	20	30,553	—	28.2	6.8	3.1	-3.5	—
Adams	25	230	6,491	9	28,222	35	19.0	19.2	7.0	-10.2	67
Allen	318	12,152	405,639	38	33,380	12	20.9	-25.3	-22.9	3.3	22
Bartholomew	105	1,622	43,661	15	26,918	43	15.4	5.3	33.3	26.6	4
Benton	20	129	2,785	6	21,589	76	66.7	-47.8	-63.8	-30.7	87
Blackford	9	69	1,833	8	26,565	47	-25.0	-43.9	-44.0	-0.1	33
Boone	43	498	13,305	12	26,717	44	19.4	29.4	65.9	28.2	3
Brown	18	61	1,508	3	24,721	62	260.0	NA	NA	NA	88
Carroll	21	131	2,772	6	21,160	79	40.0	7.4	7.5	0.1	31
Cass	41	485	10,123	12	20,872	80	10.8	35.5	12.1	-17.3	79
Clark	164	3,580	111,794	22	31,227	21	23.3	4.8	5.0	0.2	30
Clay	40	429	8,676	11	20,224	83	66.7	37.1	8.5	-20.9	82
Clinton	37	211	5,468	6	25,915	52	37.0	-9.1	-20.4	-12.5	72
Crawford	7	NA	NA	NA	NA	89	16.7	NA	NA	NA	88
Daviess	53	499	11,739	9	23,525	68	29.3	32.4	39.1	5.1	18
Dearborn	63	818	29,425	13	35,972	6	61.5	31.9	29.1	-2.1	40
Decatur	37	421	11,636	11	27,639	38	32.1	19.3	34.3	12.6	14
Dekalb	37	364	10,381	10	28,519	34	37.0	109.2	144.2	16.7	11
Delaware	91	5,575	115,848	61	20,780	81	18.2	114.7	109.9	-2.2	42
Dubois	73	616	17,579	8	28,537	33	40.4	15.4	15.0	-0.3	35
Elkhart	157	2,749	69,244	18	25,189	56	36.5	5.5	-4.6	-9.6	65
Fayette	22	229	6,088	10	26,585	45	83.3	44.0	27.0	-11.8	71
Floyd	46	615	20,101	13	32,685	17	58.6	36.7	25.3	-8.3	62
Fountain	30	112	3,064	4	27,357	40	36.4	-17.0	-16.8	0.3	29
Franklin	26	121	3,161	5	26,124	49	36.8	49.4	55.2	3.9	21
Fulton	27	250	5,819	9	23,276	72	3.8	-12.0	-19.3	-8.4	63
Gibson	52	284	7,286	5	25,655	54	40.5	-12.6	-16.3	-4.2	49
Grant	66	815	20,451	12	25,093	57	40.4	12.6	9.7	-2.5	43
Greene	43	228	5,555	5	24,364	64	38.7	-8.8	1.1	10.9	15
Hamilton	140	2,832	96,415	20	34,045	9	34.6	-21.8	-27.5	-7.3	58
Hancock	55	520	12,990	9	24,981	60	34.1	31.3	27.4	-3.0	44
Harrison	37	307	7,696	8	25,068	58	-5.1	0.3	0.4	0.1	31
Hendricks	90	2,444	95,468	27	39,062	3	23.3	14.3	5.5	-7.7	59
Henry	52	439	10,712	8	24,401	63	44.4	30.7	23.2	-5.7	52
Howard	59	1,058	32,595	18	30,808	23	-7.8	-11.8	-12.1	-0.3	35
Huntington	39	503	12,578	13	25,006	59	95.0	78.4	67.3	-6.2	54
Jackson	53	670	26,392	13	39,391	2	55.9	2.1	22.6	20.0	9
Jasper	70	1,007	39,212	14	38,939	4	84.2	34.3	16.1	-13.5	74
Jay	20	147	4,009	7	27,272	41	66.7	14.0	9.9	-3.6	46
Jefferson	24	604	22,065	25	36,531	5	-11.1	-1.9	0.5	2.5	26
Jennings	26	117	1,932	5	16,513	88	23.8	-5.6	-3.0	2.8	25
Johnson	86	848	25,310	10	29,847	28	53.6	-15.2	-17.8	-3.1	45
Knox	85	1,012	24,508	12	24,217	65	26.9	15.7	19.0	2.9	24
Kosciusko	69	633	18,738	9	29,602	30	25.5	-31.0	-27.6	4.9	20
Lagrange	35	159	5,241	5	32,962	15	84.2	-7.6	-13.5	-6.4	56
Lake	451	8,593	293,155	19	34,116	8	17.8	-11.3	-8.6	3.1	23
Laporte	111	1,528	53,103	14	34,753	7	26.1	-9.7	-5.2	5.0	19
Lawrence	44	329	8,936	7	27,161	42	29.4	14.6	5.2	-8.2	60
Madison	99	1,204	27,404	12	22,761	73	22.2	22.2	30.1	6.4	17
Marion	872	38,974	1,246,582	45	31,985	19	26.2	14.9	10.6	-3.7	47
Marshall	64	686	20,349	11	29,663	29	42.2	12.8	8.3	-4.1	48
Martin	19	230	4,367	12	18,987	85	46.2	69.1	18.9	-29.7	86
Miami	35	358	8,604	10	24,034	66	20.7	-3.2	-5.3	-2.1	40
Monroe	100	1,680	49,629	17	29,541	31	42.9	-5.2	-14.4	-9.7	66
Montgomery	60	365	9,044	6	24,778	61	33.3	-3.2	-13.0	-10.2	67
Morgan	61	621	18,875	10	30,395	24	45.2	24.9	45.1	16.1	13
Newton	24	NA	NA	NA	NA	89	50.0	NA	NA	NA	88
Noble	35	268	7,563	8	28,220	36	25.0	-19.0	-2.3	20.6	7
Ohio	1	NA	NA	NA	NA	89	-66.7	NA	NA	NA	88
Orange	25	176	4,817	7	27,369	39	4.2	0.0	-8.2	-8.2	60
Owen	41	201	4,117	5	20,483	82	127.8	24.8	45.9	16.9	10
Parke	24	166	3,895	7	23,464	70	33.3	78.5	36.2	-23.7	84
Perry	31	163	4,312	5	26,454	48	40.9	-33.5	-11.9	32.4	2
Pike	23	631	26,210	27	41,537	1	109.1	250.6	442.2	54.7	1
Porter	156	3,314	102,310	21	30,872	22	44.4	49.1	40.6	-5.7	52
Posey	39	709	16,631	18	23,457	71	34.5	93.7	91.7	-1.1	38
Pulaski	20	88	2,535	4	28,807	32	25.0	27.5	16.2	-8.9	64
Putnam	33	374	12,508	11	33,444	11	6.5	21.0	46.0	20.6	7
Randolph	40	472	11,088	12	23,492	69	42.9	83.7	42.4	-22.5	83
Ripley	41	307	6,603	7	21,508	77	41.4	-20.1	-30.9	-13.6	75
Rush	27	292	5,757	11	19,716	84	35.0	30.4	7.6	-17.5	80
St. Joseph	231	5,249	158,694	23	30,233	26	24.9	7.7	-4.2	-11.0	70
Scott	23	119	2,546	5	21,395	78	109.1	112.5	99.2	-6.3	55
Shelby	50	412	11,452	8	27,796	37	42.9	24.8	23.8	-0.9	37
Spencer	44	1,300	43,730	30	33,638	10	29.4	49.9	53.0	2.1	28
Starke	21	76	1,958	4	25,763	53	10.5	-14.6	5.2	23.2	6
Steuben	39	675	22,362	17	33,129	13	18.2	-21.0	-30.8	-12.5	72
Sullivan	37	677	21,368	18	31,563	20	12.1	92.3	97.2	2.5	26
Switzerland	12	40	883	3	22,075	75	50.0	42.9	79.0	25.3	5
Tippecanoe	134	1,949	50,839	15	26,085	50	35.4	26.1	7.5	-14.8	77
Tipton	22	77	1,375	4	17,857	87	100.0	-8.3	-25.9	-19.1	81
Union	9	39	1,289	4	33,051	14	-18.2	-25.0	-12.7	16.4	12
Vanderburgh	209	4,982	151,227	24	30,355	25	8.9	7.3	7.1	-0.2	34
Vermillion	28	346	11,212	12	32,405	18	47.4	16.9	8.9	-6.8	57
Vigo	98	1,591	47,928	16	30,124	27	-3.9	-15.8	-16.7	-1.1	38
Wabash	50	392	10,421	8	26,584	46	6.4	-3.9	-13.9	-10.4	69
Warren	11	NA	NA	NA	NA	89	10.0	NA	NA	NA	88
Warrick	55	418	9,360	8	22,392	74	22.2	-12.6	-24.5	-13.7	76
Washington	39	193	3,622	5	18,767	86	129.4	75.5	68.0	-4.2	49
Wayne	81	993	25,055	12	25,232	55	30.6	9.4	-9.2	-17.0	78
Wells	26	268	6,349	10	23,690	67	-13.3	-16.0	-8.2	9.3	16
White	48	614	15,972	13	26,013	51	50.0	40.5	3.3	-26.5	85
Whitley	20	517	16,934	26	32,754	16	33.3	57.1	49.1	-5.1	51

Footnote: Percent change in annual payroll and payroll per employee were calculated using real (adjusted for inflation) dollars.
Source: U.S. Bureau of the Census, County Business Patterns
EDIN table(s): EMIE, EMIP

SECTION 2

INDIANA FACTBOOK

2.63 Wholesale: Establishments, Employees, and Payroll 1995

	Number of Establishments	Number of Employees	Annual Payroll ($000)	Average Employee Per Establishment	Payroll Per Employee ($)	Rank	Percent Change 1990 to 1995				Rank
							Establishments	Employees	Annual Payroll	Payroll Per Employee	
Indiana	10,636	132,665	4,024,186	12	30,333	—	9.1	6.4	11.4	4.7	—
Adams	51	419	10,517	8	25,100	36	6.3	12.0	13.2	1.1	52
Allen	765	12,596	357,669	16	28,395	21	-2.9	-0.3	-0.3	0.0	55
Bartholomew	123	1,124	32,382	9	28,810	19	2.5	-12.2	-6.6	6.3	40
Benton	33	377	6,967	11	18,480	86	-15.4	16.0	-6.5	-19.4	83
Blackford	20	166	3,146	8	18,952	84	17.6	18.6	-0.1	-15.8	81
Boone	91	580	17,082	6	29,452	16	-1.1	-4.3	2.6	7.2	35
Brown	14	63	1,218	5	19,333	83	40.0	NA	NA	NA	85
Carroll	36	289	8,977	8	31,062	10	-25.0	-15.5	2.4	21.2	13
Cass	65	770	19,467	12	25,282	34	-20.7	5.8	19.4	12.9	24
Clark	145	1,723	39,354	12	22,840	58	14.2	16.3	12.8	-2.9	62
Clay	29	196	4,345	7	22,168	63	26.1	NA	NA	NA	85
Clinton	65	577	12,589	9	21,818	67	1.6	10.5	9.2	-1.2	58
Crawford	7	NA	NA	NA	NA	90	75.0	NA	NA	NA	85
Daviess	38	491	12,082	13	24,607	41	0.0	16.9	21.6	4.0	46
Dearborn	49	343	7,845	7	22,872	57	32.4	53.8	60.1	4.1	45
Decatur	46	445	10,428	10	23,434	52	-9.8	7.0	14.6	7.2	35
Dekalb	52	517	15,042	10	29,095	17	23.8	3.6	48.9	43.7	5
Delaware	180	2,017	53,065	11	26,309	29	11.8	3.2	9.4	6.0	42
Dubois	99	1,734	55,050	18	31,747	8	5.3	6.6	13.5	6.5	39
Elkhart	480	6,283	190,822	13	30,371	13	18.5	11.5	25.7	12.8	25
Fayette	24	312	6,840	13	21,923	64	33.3	-25.4	-14.3	14.8	17
Floyd	109	1,074	26,195	10	24,390	43	17.2	25.5	26.5	0.8	53
Fountain	31	165	3,670	5	22,242	62	-3.1	2.5	4.9	2.3	49
Franklin	14	99	2,379	7	24,030	48	-26.3	-31.7	-22.6	13.3	21
Fulton	40	244	8,531	6	34,963	6	-7.0	-6.5	62.1	73.4	1
Gibson	44	343	7,198	8	20,985	74	7.3	29.9	28.1	-1.4	59
Grant	88	862	19,369	10	22,470	61	2.3	4.6	1.1	-3.4	63
Greene	39	285	6,219	7	21,821	66	0.0	13.1	59.9	41.3	7
Hamilton	521	4,867	191,985	9	39,446	2	41.2	25.9	42.5	13.2	22
Hancock	72	699	21,236	10	30,381	12	1.4	42.9	38.9	-2.8	61
Harrison	39	333	7,184	9	21,574	71	-2.5	-17.0	-14.4	3.1	47
Hendricks	94	590	16,540	6	28,034	22	28.8	30.5	87.4	43.6	6
Henry	54	385	8,234	7	21,387	72	-8.5	-0.3	-9.0	-8.7	72
Howard	124	894	27,663	7	30,943	11	12.7	-4.5	21.5	27.2	11
Huntington	72	690	14,896	10	21,588	70	14.3	47.4	37.6	-6.6	68
Jackson	46	973	21,141	21	21,728	68	-2.1	12.6	0.3	-10.9	76
Jasper	58	458	11,731	8	25,614	31	13.7	14.8	9.7	-4.4	66
Jay	26	259	5,878	10	22,695	59	-13.3	-2.3	3.7	6.1	41
Jefferson	34	279	5,503	8	19,724	81	-2.9	32.9	47.3	10.9	27
Jennings	20	259	6,259	13	24,166	47	0.0	87.7	123.0	18.8	16
Johnson	138	894	23,273	6	26,032	30	22.1	3.2	10.9	7.4	33
Knox	85	1,005	22,730	12	22,617	60	-4.5	-4.6	-2.5	2.3	49
Kosciusko	136	1,021	27,350	8	26,787	28	9.7	-9.7	-1.5	9.1	29
Lagrange	47	629	9,221	13	14,660	89	34.3	48.0	9.7	-25.9	84
Lake	624	8,083	253,221	13	31,328	9	15.6	4.9	13.8	8.5	31
Laporte	174	2,358	63,715	14	27,021	27	25.2	-0.1	-4.4	-4.3	64
Lawrence	40	504	10,262	13	20,361	79	11.1	100.8	77.2	-11.7	77
Madison	116	1,545	38,194	13	24,721	40	4.5	3.5	18.8	14.8	17
Marion	2,309	38,192	1,383,764	17	36,232	4	10.8	7.4	14.6	6.7	38
Marshall	95	853	23,812	9	27,916	23	31.9	59.1	63.6	2.8	48
Martin	9	62	1,510	7	24,355	44	-30.8	-38.6	-7.7	50.4	4
Miami	47	338	7,819	7	23,133	54	23.7	46.3	53.1	4.7	44
Monroe	138	1,408	33,058	10	23,479	51	21.1	-7.6	-16.6	-9.8	75
Montgomery	60	414	10,484	7	25,324	33	5.3	-49.4	-33.3	31.7	9
Morgan	67	377	8,993	6	23,854	50	17.5	27.8	56.2	22.2	12
Newton	29	194	4,874	7	25,124	35	26.1	50.4	61.6	7.5	32
Noble	56	493	13,639	9	27,665	26	-20.0	-41.5	-30.1	19.5	15
Ohio	2	NA	NA	NA	NA	90	0.0	NA	NA	NA	85
Orange	22	136	2,645	6	19,449	82	0.0	-16.6	10.9	32.9	8
Owen	16	65	1,340	4	20,615	75	14.3	NA	NA	NA	85
Parke	13	91	1,696	7	18,637	85	-35.0	-21.6	-32.4	-13.9	79
Perry	21	252	8,599	12	34,123	7	10.5	36.2	73.5	27.3	10
Pike	16	84	3,132	5	37,286	3	14.3	-34.4	-0.6	51.4	3
Porter	184	1,786	51,906	10	29,063	18	18.7	10.5	21.9	10.3	28
Posey	32	364	10,832	11	29,758	14	-17.9	3.7	18.8	14.5	19
Pulaski	33	478	11,828	14	24,745	39	-2.9	7.4	15.2	7.3	34
Putnam	33	181	3,812	5	21,061	73	0.0	23.1	21.9	-1.0	57
Randolph	46	311	6,306	7	20,277	80	-6.1	9.5	7.2	-2.1	60
Ripley	45	639	29,263	14	45,795	1	28.6	NA	NA	NA	85
Rush	40	284	7,037	7	24,778	38	17.6	26.2	42.9	13.2	22
St. Joseph	575	7,709	227,785	13	29,548	15	15.9	11.8	13.8	1.7	51
Scott	21	149	2,584	7	17,342	88	-8.7	-2.6	-10.7	-8.3	70
Shelby	60	622	17,767	10	28,564	20	-6.3	16.9	11.9	-4.3	64
Spencer	37	362	8,637	10	23,859	49	19.4	7.1	-2.5	-8.9	73
Starke	33	186	3,811	6	20,489	76	17.9	10.1	25.3	13.9	20
Steuben	59	398	9,267	7	23,284	53	22.9	1.3	21.5	20.0	14
Sullivan	28	166	3,589	6	21,620	69	27.3	-18.2	-12.7	6.8	37
Switzerland	8	NA	NA	NA	NA	90	166.7	NA	NA	NA	85
Tippecanoe	136	1,486	36,348	11	24,460	42	-9.3	-7.5	-15.4	-8.5	71
Tipton	24	374	13,281	16	35,511	5	14.3	57.1	163.9	67.9	2
Union	11	66	1,351	6	20,470	77	0.0	4.8	-1.1	-5.6	67
Vanderburgh	434	6,105	169,352	14	27,740	25	-2.0	-5.0	-13.6	-9.0	74
Vermillion	12	61	1,082	5	17,738	87	-20.0	-21.8	-33.1	-14.5	80
Vigo	172	2,093	53,158	12	25,398	32	-3.4	9.3	9.0	-0.3	56
Wabash	63	505	11,612	8	22,994	56	-1.6	7.9	-5.0	-12.0	78
Warren	13	130	3,158	10	24,292	45	-13.3	41.3	16.9	-17.3	82
Warrick	46	258	6,459	6	25,035	37	-6.1	NA	NA	NA	85
Washington	25	169	3,452	7	20,426	78	31.6	52.3	69.6	11.4	26
Wayne	115	1,912	53,096	17	27,770	24	8.5	-11.3	-18.0	-7.5	69
Wells	48	980	21,456	20	21,894	65	23.1	29.8	36.4	5.0	43
White	60	487	11,255	8	23,111	55	20.0	9.4	19.0	8.7	30
Whitley	42	506	12,246	12	24,202	46	2.4	50.1	51.2	0.7	54

Footnote: Percent change in annual payroll and payroll per employee were calculated using real (adjusted for inflation) dollars.
Source: U.S. Bureau of the Census, County Business Patterns
EDIN table(s): EMIE, EMIP

2.64 Retail: Establishments, Employees, And Payroll 1995

	Number of Establishments	Number of Employees	Annual Payroll ($000)	Average Employee Per Establishment	Payroll Per Employee ($)	Rank	Percent Change 1990 to 1995				Rank
							Establishments	Employees	Annual Payroll	Payroll Per Employee	
Indiana	34,845	516,374	6,474,879	15	12,539	—	3.8	10.8	13.0	2.0	—
Adams	203	2,604	28,522	13	10,953	59	4.6	23.6	17.4	-5.0	81
Allen	1,960	35,560	450,550	18	12,670	11	1.4	7.5	9.0	1.5	50
Bartholomew	449	6,530	79,844	15	12,227	23	9.8	17.0	22.9	5.1	33
Benton	73	379	3,733	5	9,850	85	19.7	14.8	18.5	3.2	41
Blackford	84	697	7,032	8	10,089	78	-5.6	-6.6	-5.3	1.3	52
Boone	255	2,850	32,605	11	11,440	42	10.9	15.2	15.4	0.2	60
Brown	146	714	8,159	5	11,427	44	9.0	-7.3	2.1	10.1	9
Carroll	79	842	8,279	11	9,833	86	-7.1	-0.2	-12.2	-12.0	87
Cass	257	3,139	35,428	12	11,286	48	-1.5	12.5	15.3	2.4	45
Clark	638	10,296	133,342	16	12,951	9	8.5	21.9	21.6	-0.2	63
Clay	139	1,537	16,211	11	10,547	69	16.8	26.1	26.4	0.3	59
Clinton	174	1,852	20,506	11	11,072	58	-5.9	0.5	4.0	3.5	40
Crawford	46	432	4,231	9	9,794	87	0.0	16.4	26.8	8.9	14
Daviess	187	1,910	19,888	10	10,413	73	3.3	1.7	-1.0	-2.7	72
Dearborn	229	2,810	33,355	12	11,870	34	23.8	32.4	39.5	5.3	31
Decatur	156	2,144	25,909	14	12,084	28	10.6	35.2	52.2	12.6	6
Dekalb	218	2,641	29,401	12	11,133	55	3.8	17.9	17.6	-0.3	64
Delaware	745	11,677	135,131	16	11,572	37	1.9	2.9	-3.8	-6.5	85
Dubois	302	4,147	57,505	14	13,867	5	2.7	14.5	26.0	10.0	10
Elkhart	1,034	15,354	190,433	15	12,403	19	2.9	15.8	17.9	1.8	49
Fayette	147	1,893	21,036	13	11,113	57	6.5	5.6	13.2	7.3	20
Floyd	322	3,841	43,914	12	11,433	43	2.2	4.3	0.1	-4.0	77
Fountain	113	1,096	11,740	10	10,712	65	-10.3	-7.2	-0.5	7.2	21
Franklin	94	719	6,979	8	9,707	89	17.5	33.1	25.0	-6.1	84
Fulton	131	1,432	14,168	11	9,894	84	5.6	28.8	27.6	-0.9	66
Gibson	186	2,528	25,931	14	10,258	76	-12.3	35.7	29.8	-4.3	78
Grant	454	6,363	70,899	14	11,142	54	-4.0	10.8	8.7	-1.9	69
Greene	180	1,777	18,252	10	10,271	75	3.4	10.6	21.6	9.9	11
Hamilton	739	12,039	176,690	16	14,676	2	21.9	38.3	37.8	-0.4	65
Hancock	215	2,834	32,579	13	11,496	39	4.9	11.1	15.4	3.9	38
Harrison	161	1,973	20,845	12	10,565	68	10.3	48.8	56.8	5.4	30
Hendricks	382	5,270	68,274	14	12,955	8	26.5	40.1	51.1	7.9	19
Henry	267	3,094	38,828	12	12,549	15	-3.6	5.0	11.7	6.3	24
Howard	576	9,214	115,001	16	12,481	18	-2.9	13.3	18.9	5.0	34
Huntington	229	2,503	31,610	11	12,629	14	7.0	0.4	20.2	19.7	4
Jackson	305	4,816	72,389	16	15,031	1	25.5	39.5	35.0	-3.2	74
Jasper	189	2,324	24,341	12	10,474	72	15.2	58.7	30.6	-17.7	92
Jay	124	1,143	12,821	9	11,217	53	-1.6	-3.2	-2.6	0.6	55
Jefferson	228	2,716	30,593	12	11,264	49	16.3	33.3	39.3	4.5	37
Jennings	106	1,438	20,989	14	14,596	3	6.0	58.5	112.7	34.2	2
Johnson	689	11,736	142,882	17	12,175	24	14.5	28.1	35.6	5.8	29
Knox	303	3,920	39,856	13	10,167	77	0.7	13.3	14.0	0.6	55
Kosciusko	437	5,205	63,096	12	12,122	26	4.0	13.3	10.7	-2.3	71
Lagrange	192	1,868	20,392	10	10,916	60	18.5	27.9	24.3	-2.8	73
Lake	2,627	38,879	486,183	15	12,505	17	0.7	1.1	4.9	3.7	39
Laporte	727	8,987	108,918	12	12,120	27	14.1	12.2	15.6	3.0	42
Lawrence	262	3,419	37,294	13	10,908	61	3.1	22.4	28.9	5.3	31
Madison	740	10,634	134,313	14	12,631	13	-1.3	6.3	12.6	5.9	28
Marion	5,453	96,851	1,400,718	18	14,463	4	2.9	4.9	6.9	2.0	48
Marshall	283	3,174	33,393	11	10,521	71	8.4	25.4	26.4	0.8	54
Martin	59	546	5,428	9	9,941	83	5.4	15.2	25.1	8.6	15
Miami	170	1,724	20,528	10	11,907	32	-3.4	-0.2	4.7	4.9	35
Monroe	730	12,412	133,928	17	10,790	64	1.0	13.7	20.7	6.1	27
Montgomery	228	2,772	32,065	12	11,567	38	-3.4	13.8	14.5	0.6	55
Morgan	265	3,798	43,243	14	11,386	45	-4.3	6.2	4.7	-1.4	68
Newton	71	524	5,275	7	10,067	79	-11.3	-14.8	-28.6	-16.2	91
Noble	205	2,360	26,721	12	11,322	47	1.0	19.5	20.6	0.9	53
Ohio	14	124	1,131	9	9,121	92	0.0	14.8	17.4	2.2	47
Orange	111	856	8,561	8	10,001	82	1.8	-1.0	14.2	15.4	5
Owen	64	680	7,160	11	10,529	70	16.4	15.4	17.1	1.4	51
Parke	87	615	5,912	7	9,613	90	3.6	17.4	1.4	-13.6	90
Perry	118	1,279	12,866	11	10,059	80	7.3	43.4	32.8	-7.4	86
Pike	39	282	2,751	7	9,755	88	-32.8	-15.3	-19.6	-5.1	82
Porter	658	9,851	122,169	15	12,402	20	8.6	12.0	22.9	9.7	12
Posey	115	1,012	12,449	9	12,301	22	3.6	1.5	1.7	0.2	60
Pulaski	76	599	7,265	8	12,129	25	10.1	1.0	6.0	4.9	35
Putnam	173	2,924	39,339	17	13,454	6	15.3	67.1	112.7	27.3	3
Randolph	145	1,314	13,934	9	10,604	67	-4.6	-5.5	0.4	6.3	24
Ripley	160	1,614	18,145	10	11,242	51	-10.1	-4.7	1.3	6.3	24
Rush	94	1,065	11,509	11	10,807	63	8.0	8.8	12.0	3.0	42
St. Joseph	1,570	25,455	307,442	16	12,078	29	-1.3	6.4	8.9	2.3	46
Scott	125	1,530	17,162	12	11,217	52	14.7	28.0	38.9	8.5	17
Shelby	205	2,658	30,497	13	11,474	40	15.2	18.6	31.1	10.6	8
Spencer	91	794	9,513	9	11,981	31	-9.0	31.2	30.0	-0.9	66
Starke	104	1,079	11,101	10	10,288	74	-6.3	2.8	-10.7	-13.1	88
Steuben	280	3,203	39,561	11	12,351	21	14.8	22.1	32.2	8.3	18
Sullivan	98	929	9,936	9	10,695	66	-3.9	4.1	7.2	2.9	44
Switzerland	26	156	1,701	6	10,904	62	-18.8	-0.6	6.3	7.0	22
Tippecanoe	787	14,032	164,428	18	11,718	36	3.6	8.8	18.7	9.1	13
Tipton	78	759	8,899	10	11,725	35	-8.2	-8.2	-20.4	-13.3	89
Union	41	362	4,527	9	12,506	16	0.0	28.4	28.9	0.4	58
Vanderburgh	1,250	22,742	274,140	18	12,054	30	-1.3	3.2	-1.8	-4.9	80
Vermillion	93	1,076	13,901	12	12,919	10	8.1	16.6	14.2	-2.0	70
Vigo	741	15,120	197,511	20	13,063	7	7.9	23.1	23.2	0.1	62
Wabash	226	2,454	28,085	11	11,445	41	6.1	13.2	7.3	-5.3	83
Warren	18	69	658	4	9,536	91	20.0	-17.9	15.7	40.8	1
Warrick	218	2,372	23,758	11	10,016	81	13.5	19.9	14.1	-4.8	79
Washington	111	939	11,868	8	12,639	12	7.8	-4.3	6.8	11.5	7
Wayne	466	6,859	81,469	15	11,878	33	0.6	4.2	0.6	-3.4	75
Wells	153	1,616	17,981	11	11,127	56	1.3	-4.0	2.7	7.0	22
White	186	1,783	20,221	10	11,341	46	16.3	16.7	12.5	-3.6	76
Whitley	161	2,235	25,153	14	11,254	50	10.3	25.2	35.9	8.6	15

Footnote: Percent change in annual payroll and payroll per employee were calculated using real (adjusted for inflation) dollars.
Source: U.S. Bureau of the Census, County Business Patterns
EDIN table(s): EMIE, EMIP

2.65 Finance, Insurance, and Real Estate: Establishments, Employees, and Payroll 1995

	Number of Establishments	Number of Employees	Annual Payroll ($000)	Average Employee Per Establishment	Payroll Per Employee ($)	Rank	Percent Change 1990 to 1995				Rank
							Establishments	Employees	Annual Payroll	Payroll Per Employee	
Indiana	12,597	128,762	3,709,445	10	28,809	—	24.3	3.8	13.4	9.2	—
Adams	58	326	6,525	6	20,015	65	26.1	17.3	17.5	0.2	63
Allen	827	11,917	407,844	14	34,224	3	15.8	-9.4	-0.4	10.0	29
Bartholomew	184	2,318	89,713	13	38,703	1	34.3	-1.4	44.1	46.2	4
Benton	21	138	2,698	7	19,551	70	16.7	-1.4	-12.1	-10.8	85
Blackford	20	161	2,811	8	17,460	85	5.3	8.8	-1.4	-9.4	83
Boone	91	566	11,522	6	20,357	60	51.7	5.0	-6.5	-11.0	87
Brown	23	82	1,396	4	17,024	89	43.8	5.1	-3.6	-8.3	82
Carroll	32	202	3,642	6	18,030	83	33.3	-12.6	-3.0	10.9	28
Cass	60	382	8,706	6	22,791	29	5.3	-21.9	-12.5	12.0	24
Clark	169	1,052	21,654	6	20,584	56	56.5	24.2	27.2	2.4	51
Clay	39	228	4,582	6	20,096	63	30.0	1.3	-3.5	-4.8	76
Clinton	58	326	6,678	6	20,485	58	18.4	-12.8	-6.5	7.2	39
Crawford	15	74	1,577	5	21,311	46	50.0	27.6	31.5	3.1	49
Daviess	55	274	5,818	5	21,234	48	48.6	-6.5	-6.0	0.5	61
Dearborn	87	539	11,173	6	20,729	52	40.3	21.1	21.5	0.3	62
Decatur	42	249	5,852	6	23,502	26	5.0	6.4	24.6	17.1	20
Dekalb	54	307	6,927	6	22,564	32	20.0	-9.4	30.1	43.7	5
Delaware	243	1,872	41,834	8	22,347	35	19.1	15.9	16.2	0.2	63
Dubois	93	684	15,471	7	22,618	30	24.0	23.0	22.5	-0.4	67
Elkhart	370	2,776	68,891	8	24,817	17	24.2	-5.1	-5.3	-0.3	66
Fayette	53	256	4,712	5	18,406	80	43.2	-0.4	0.4	0.8	59
Floyd	151	974	22,946	6	23,559	25	39.8	23.4	25.6	1.7	55
Fountain	27	148	2,397	5	16,196	91	-3.6	-18.2	-16.8	1.7	55
Franklin	23	148	3,801	6	25,682	12	53.3	-17.8	9.4	33.0	8
Fulton	38	207	5,547	5	26,797	10	46.2	1.0	16.5	15.4	21
Gibson	56	284	5,639	5	19,856	67	0.0	-7.8	-7.7	0.1	65
Grant	147	1,099	26,686	7	24,282	19	5.0	-11.4	7.8	21.8	15
Greene	57	309	5,292	5	17,126	88	46.2	10.4	-3.7	-12.7	88
Hamilton	483	7,613	286,683	16	37,657	2	56.8	70.8	86.2	9.0	33
Hancock	76	397	7,912	5	19,929	66	18.8	7.3	0.7	-6.2	79
Harrison	42	244	5,969	6	24,463	18	27.3	15.1	49.0	29.4	9
Hendricks	161	683	16,970	4	24,846	15	71.3	16.4	23.6	6.2	42
Henry	77	530	12,158	7	22,940	27	51.0	7.1	10.0	2.7	50
Howard	186	1,350	34,252	7	25,372	13	39.8	1.0	24.6	23.4	12
Huntington	79	411	9,057	5	22,036	40	17.9	10.2	12.6	2.1	52
Jackson	86	499	11,044	6	22,132	39	43.3	-33.6	-19.6	21.1	17
Jasper	62	326	7,845	5	24,064	21	31.9	-0.3	43.0	43.4	6
Jay	40	208	4,676	5	22,481	33	53.8	9.5	35.1	23.4	12
Jefferson	55	264	5,863	5	22,208	38	27.9	8.6	6.4	-2.1	71
Jennings	36	198	3,310	6	16,717	90	89.5	92.2	93.4	0.6	60
Johnson	238	1,544	39,120	6	25,337	14	42.5	39.7	65.0	18.1	18
Knox	82	607	13,029	7	21,465	44	15.5	-4.6	1.9	6.8	41
Kosciusko	131	803	18,383	6	22,893	28	36.5	11.5	20.3	7.8	38
Lagrange	36	263	5,451	7	20,726	53	28.6	2.7	-0.4	-3.1	72
Lake	851	6,730	167,074	8	24,825	16	16.6	-4.2	6.4	11.1	26
Laporte	192	1,067	24,111	6	22,597	31	16.4	-9.9	-17.0	-7.9	81
Lawrence	71	408	7,780	6	19,069	75	34.0	3.0	-2.5	-5.3	77
Madison	251	1,334	29,827	5	22,359	34	15.7	-12.9	-11.1	2.1	52
Marion	2,544	43,742	1,392,812	17	31,842	5	18.2	0.0	9.0	8.9	34
Marshall	79	438	11,554	6	26,379	11	31.7	-30.1	-5.6	35.1	7
Martin	16	105	2,038	7	19,410	71	23.1	23.5	15.6	-6.4	80
Miami	57	274	5,531	5	20,186	62	18.8	-35.2	-31.2	6.1	44
Monroe	274	2,163	46,069	8	21,299	47	28.0	-6.8	1.4	8.8	35
Montgomery	74	366	8,131	5	22,216	37	17.5	-4.4	-3.3	1.2	58
Morgan	95	485	9,915	5	20,443	59	43.9	16.9	23.1	5.3	45
Newton	19	103	2,468	5	23,961	22	18.8	9.6	17.1	6.9	40
Noble	62	253	5,340	4	21,107	51	14.8	-26.9	-25.5	1.9	54
Ohio	5	21	237	4	11,286	92	25.0	NA	NA	NA	NA
Orange	28	204	3,846	7	18,853	76	55.6	-11.3	-20.1	-9.9	84
Owen	17	124	2,366	7	19,081	74	-5.6	11.7	5.0	-6.0	78
Parke	25	124	2,209	5	17,815	84	56.3	21.6	16.1	-4.5	74
Perry	28	274	5,410	10	19,745	68	-3.4	14.2	1.8	-10.9	86
Pike	16	120	2,475	8	20,625	55	14.3	-16.7	1.5	21.8	15
Porter	242	1,581	37,318	7	23,604	24	29.4	6.7	18.8	11.4	25
Posey	31	209	4,326	7	20,699	54	40.9	-3.7	-7.8	-4.3	73
Pulaski	31	176	3,174	6	18,034	82	14.8	-25.1	-11.6	18.0	19
Putnam	47	294	6,400	6	21,769	41	23.7	-3.3	6.3	9.9	30
Randolph	40	233	4,665	6	20,021	64	8.1	-14.0	-6.2	9.1	32
Ripley	53	594	19,714	11	33,189	4	60.6	157.1	357.5	77.9	1
Rush	35	174	3,213	5	18,466	79	34.6	17.6	23.0	4.6	47
St. Joseph	578	6,251	173,049	11	27,683	7	31.4	13.4	15.2	1.6	57
Scott	30	146	3,261	5	22,336	36	25.0	15.0	19.2	3.7	48
Shelby	81	293	6,362	4	21,713	42	22.7	-6.1	8.2	15.3	22
Spencer	31	182	3,144	6	17,275	87	19.2	11.7	11.2	-0.4	67
Starke	21	83	1,685	4	20,301	61	0.0	-55.9	-45.2	24.1	11
Steuben	52	270	7,399	5	27,404	9	20.9	-10.0	32.0	46.6	3
Sullivan	40	226	4,374	6	19,354	73	29.0	11.9	36.6	22.1	14
Switzerland	9	51	884	6	17,333	86	80.0	15.9	10.7	-4.5	74
Tippecanoe	305	4,125	124,059	14	30,075	6	19.6	16.8	24.1	6.2	42
Tipton	26	156	3,022	6	19,372	72	8.3	-25.4	-6.0	26.0	10
Union	12	96	1,969	8	20,510	57	33.3	57.4	74.7	11.0	27
Vanderburgh	485	6,548	180,907	14	27,628	8	13.1	34.5	33.2	-1.0	69
Vermillion	22	132	2,387	6	18,083	81	10.0	NA	NA	NA	NA
Vigo	207	1,706	40,877	8	23,961	23	6.7	-1.8	3.3	5.2	46
Wabash	117	448	8,351	4	18,641	77	98.3	10.1	-5.6	-14.2	89
Warren	14	119	2,214	9	18,605	78	75.0	-1.7	66.0	68.8	2
Warrick	77	376	7,941	5	21,120	50	26.2	-0.3	12.9	13.2	23
Washington	35	164	3,234	5	19,720	69	12.9	-23.7	-35.9	-16.0	90
Wayne	157	1,149	24,267	7	21,120	49	21.7	-0.4	-1.4	-1.0	69
Wells	51	240	5,119	5	21,329	45	27.5	10.6	21.0	9.4	31
White	52	263	6,343	5	24,118	20	2.0	-26.9	-21.2	7.9	37
Whitley	49	304	6,538	6	21,507	43	25.6	3.8	12.8	8.7	36

Footnote: Percent change in annual payroll and payroll per employee were calculated using real (adjusted for inflation) dollars.
Source: U.S. Bureau of the Census, County Business Patterns
EDIN table(s): EMIE, EMIP

2.66 Services: Establishments, Employees, and Payroll 1995

	Number of Establishments	Number of Employees	Annual Payroll ($000)	Average Employee Per Establishment	Payroll Per Employee ($)	Rank	Percent Change 1990 to 1995				Rank
							Establishments	Employees	Annual Payroll	Payroll Per Employee	
Indiana	**48,162**	**672,660**	**14,071,972**	**14**	**20,920**	**—**	**17.6**	**22.9**	**29.8**	**5.6**	**—**
Adams	212	1,923	27,305	9	14,199	70	11.0	57.4	72.1	9.4	58
Allen	2,987	46,359	981,041	16	21,162	6	14.8	9.5	11.5	1.8	75
Bartholomew	661	7,893	163,663	12	20,735	9	20.0	55.4	78.6	14.9	40
Benton	74	374	5,697	5	15,233	57	29.8	12.7	25.7	11.6	50
Blackford	96	677	9,689	7	14,312	69	10.3	56.4	72.0	10.0	54
Boone	365	3,194	59,870	9	18,745	23	27.2	59.7	81.1	13.4	44
Brown	89	767	10,182	9	13,275	79	17.1	22.5	46.7	19.7	23
Carroll	104	706	9,646	7	13,663	74	26.8	40.1	69.4	20.9	20
Cass	283	3,776	75,095	13	19,887	12	8.4	23.0	64.3	33.7	6
Clark	718	9,548	171,195	13	17,930	32	20.7	44.9	62.6	12.2	48
Clay	191	1,275	16,675	7	13,078	81	24.0	45.1	73.1	19.3	24
Clinton	226	2,180	29,406	10	13,489	76	16.5	69.8	70.7	0.5	78
Crawford	30	220	2,785	7	12,659	84	15.4	11.7	36.1	21.8	18
Daviess	220	1,850	27,045	8	14,619	63	14.0	38.2	60.0	15.8	38
Dearborn	295	2,673	41,986	9	15,707	51	52.8	101.6	134.3	16.2	36
Decatur	169	1,678	24,514	10	14,609	64	19.0	68.3	95.1	15.9	37
Dekalb	281	3,298	46,823	12	14,197	71	16.6	14.3	5.6	-7.6	86
Delaware	961	12,811	268,082	13	20,926	7	11.9	13.9	24.9	9.6	57
Dubois	318	4,157	73,792	13	17,751	33	20.0	37.5	39.6	1.6	76
Elkhart	1,424	18,356	349,417	13	19,036	18	15.5	20.2	33.8	11.3	52
Fayette	211	2,045	33,012	10	16,143	47	15.3	6.2	23.5	16.3	34
Floyd	566	6,627	124,742	12	18,823	21	35.1	65.0	86.1	12.8	46
Fountain	104	659	8,329	6	12,639	85	22.4	6.1	18.3	11.5	51
Franklin	95	876	15,260	9	17,420	37	30.1	93.0	124.8	16.5	33
Fulton	145	1,169	21,777	8	18,629	25	18.9	134.7	181.2	19.8	22
Gibson	244	2,321	27,763	10	11,962	88	11.4	21.2	24.5	2.7	71
Grant	546	10,496	182,533	19	17,391	39	3.2	0.7	25.2	24.3	12
Greene	230	1,610	23,834	7	14,804	61	36.9	80.3	105.6	14.0	42
Hamilton	1,493	14,930	421,554	10	28,235	1	57.5	80.4	104.1	13.2	45
Hancock	357	2,776	54,546	8	19,649	14	24.4	66.3	98.3	19.2	25
Harrison	180	1,397	21,350	8	15,283	56	33.3	49.3	75.8	17.8	27
Hendricks	557	5,029	92,402	9	18,374	26	39.6	68.5	95.0	15.7	39
Henry	323	3,252	53,890	10	16,571	46	11.0	28.0	53.6	20.0	21
Howard	708	9,668	190,735	14	19,728	13	14.0	37.9	41.4	2.5	73
Huntington	265	3,388	49,725	13	14,677	62	26.2	27.1	70.9	34.5	5
Jackson	287	3,740	56,334	13	15,063	60	7.5	36.8	68.0	22.8	17
Jasper	187	2,009	36,683	11	18,259	28	30.8	61.0	89.4	17.7	28
Jay	158	1,484	19,942	9	13,438	78	21.5	68.1	82.3	8.5	60
Jefferson	220	3,163	61,285	14	19,376	17	10.0	-2.6	23.5	26.8	10
Jennings	103	2,511	43,556	24	17,346	40	12.0	43.7	63.4	13.7	43
Johnson	803	9,305	181,286	12	19,483	16	28.5	40.3	74.4	24.3	12
Knox	333	4,998	90,731	15	18,153	29	6.4	69.3	98.6	17.3	31
Kosciusko	578	5,744	99,274	10	17,283	41	19.4	11.7	15.1	3.0	69
Lagrange	169	1,461	22,447	9	15,364	55	15.0	54.8	82.1	17.6	29
Lake	3,722	53,114	1,164,626	14	21,927	4	13.7	11.8	12.4	0.6	77
Laporte	861	10,109	191,511	12	18,945	19	15.9	17.3	19.5	1.9	74
Lawrence	279	3,071	55,314	11	18,012	31	24.6	43.2	57.5	10.0	54
Madison	1,039	14,630	272,669	14	18,638	24	12.6	30.1	35.7	4.3	67
Marion	8,982	169,807	4,238,278	19	24,959	2	14.6	15.3	21.2	5.2	63
Marshall	301	3,506	61,836	12	17,637	34	4.2	26.0	40.2	11.3	52
Martin	76	522	8,336	7	15,969	50	31.0	-3.7	-0.7	3.1	68
Miami	201	1,654	22,838	8	13,808	73	9.2	63.3	83.8	12.6	47
Monroe	1,040	11,700	228,077	11	19,494	15	20.9	18.0	29.6	9.8	56
Montgomery	296	3,669	62,849	12	17,130	43	11.3	38.7	47.9	6.6	62
Morgan	372	3,139	56,751	8	18,079	30	27.8	29.7	36.4	5.2	63
Newton	57	292	3,171	5	10,860	89	5.6	-18.7	-51.8	-40.7	91
Noble	280	3,911	60,207	14	15,394	54	23.9	157.1	211.8	21.3	19
Ohio	20	250	2,372	13	9,488	91	5.3	174.7	127.8	-17.1	88
Orange	116	1,654	21,870	14	13,222	80	31.8	28.3	74.0	35.6	3
Owen	75	420	5,341	6	12,717	83	17.2	34.6	28.4	-4.6	81
Parke	98	582	7,428	6	12,763	82	18.1	-7.8	-3.5	4.7	66
Perry	109	842	12,073	8	14,338	68	17.2	37.4	71.5	24.8	11
Pike	66	572	5,476	9	9,573	90	10.0	78.8	57.2	-12.1	87
Porter	1,065	15,213	312,725	14	20,556	10	29.9	44.6	57.6	9.0	59
Posey	157	1,336	20,734	9	15,519	53	19.8	21.7	35.9	11.7	49
Pulaski	97	774	13,238	8	17,103	44	24.4	142.6	126.8	-6.5	84
Putnam	232	3,391	45,979	15	13,559	75	20.2	16.1	33.1	14.7	41
Randolph	171	1,201	16,190	7	13,480	77	5.6	16.3	53.4	31.9	7
Ripley	215	2,046	28,465	10	13,913	72	36.9	11.6	-12.6	-21.6	89
Rush	115	1,011	19,145	9	18,937	20	17.3	92.2	174.7	42.9	2
St. Joseph	2,363	41,835	917,279	18	21,926	5	8.8	19.6	20.1	0.4	79
Scott	141	1,126	16,169	8	14,360	67	45.4	89.6	123.9	18.1	26
Shelby	281	3,092	46,897	11	15,167	59	23.2	21.6	49.9	23.3	16
Spencer	110	693	10,805	6	15,592	52	22.2	11.1	13.9	2.6	72
Starke	89	929	16,011	10	17,235	42	12.7	55.1	91.8	23.7	15
Steuben	252	3,017	50,596	12	16,770	45	27.3	18.4	38.1	16.7	32
Sullivan	128	1,017	14,619	8	14,375	66	34.7	52.9	96.9	28.7	8
Switzerland	32	190	2,390	6	12,579	87	45.5	-8.2	7.9	17.5	30
Tippecanoe	1,094	14,670	325,130	13	22,163	3	16.0	8.3	34.1	23.9	14
Tipton	109	898	16,454	8	18,323	27	14.7	64.2	108.8	27.2	9
Union	42	NA	NA	NA	NA	92	5.0	NA	NA	NA	92
Vanderburgh	1,901	34,031	710,287	18	20,872	8	12.8	19.4	23.0	2.9	70
Vermillion	77	721	11,531	9	15,993	49	0.0	34.5	94.2	44.4	1
Vigo	992	14,680	275,642	15	18,777	22	17.5	29.5	38.2	6.7	61
Wabash	252	2,947	51,259	12	17,394	38	9.6	30.6	51.9	16.3	34
Warren	26	256	3,225	10	12,598	86	13.0	6.2	-0.7	-6.5	84
Warrick	309	2,518	38,257	8	15,193	58	19.8	34.8	32.2	-1.9	80
Washington	123	898	14,383	7	16,017	48	29.5	50.4	103.4	35.2	4
Wayne	623	10,342	181,697	17	17,569	35	16.4	22.1	28.5	5.2	63
Wells	202	2,177	43,326	11	19,902	11	26.3	31.9	25.8	-4.6	81
White	198	1,425	20,488	7	14,378	65	13.1	66.1	55.8	-6.2	83
Whitley	209	2,230	39,156	11	17,559	36	21.5	45.3	6.4	-26.8	90

Footnote: Percent change in annual payroll and payroll per employee were calculated using real (adjusted for inflation) dollars.
Source: U.S. Bureau of the Census, County Business Patterns
EDIN table(s): EMIE, EMIP

Economic Census
2.67 Share of Area's Retail Sales 1992

	Building Materials	General Merchandise	Food Stores	Automotive Dealers	Gasoline Stations	Apparel and Accessory	Furniture and Furnishings	Eating and Drinking	Drug and Proprietary	Misc. Retail
Indiana	5.77	13.97	17.27	20.86	8.69	3.77	4.21	10.29	4.68	10.48
Adams	5.07	NA	16.88	38.70	7.31	1.11	3.30	8.16	3.33	NA
Allen	6.68	16.09	15.62	22.26	5.77	4.55	5.42	11.11	4.66	7.85
Bartholomew	6.16	17.49	19.53	13.39	9.79	8.25	3.76	11.36	4.13	6.12
Benton	4.85	NA	26.27	NA	19.23	0.00	NA	8.44	NA	NA
Blackford	1.75	5.48	30.68	24.93	10.43	0.53	2.76	10.67	7.98	4.79
Boone	6.36	NA	20.11	14.39	21.90	2.54	4.57	11.68	NA	NA
Brown	NA	NA	21.16	0.00	9.81	4.28	5.23	18.47	NA	30.57
Carroll	7.68	NA	20.08	36.20	7.99	0.61	1.39	12.11	5.30	NA
Cass	6.48	17.57	17.33	20.88	8.84	4.78	3.12	9.24	6.45	5.31
Clark	8.76	18.80	15.92	23.57	7.05	NA	3.53	8.91	3.51	NA
Clay	5.85	NA	10.82	41.41	16.07	0.00	1.77	5.39	NA	NA
Clinton	NA	NA	24.89	20.23	9.85	1.17	2.02	10.54	NA	7.53
Crawford	5.43	NA	43.96	3.69	30.32	NA	0.00	7.44	NA	NA
Daviess	24.52	16.88	16.47	12.18	7.48	2.57	2.37	7.21	3.82	6.49
Dearborn	NA	NA	NA	NA	8.49	NA	2.82	7.22	NA	NA
Decatur	4.54	NA	14.67	28.02	13.74	1.86	2.50	9.85	NA	6.10
Dekalb	3.32	NA	24.08	25.07	12.42	1.08	1.78	10.17	'4.13	NA
Delaware	5.16	16.20	18.80	21.56	8.30	2.78	4.63	10.66	4.31	7.59
Dubois	3.60	12.24	14.34	34.19	4.95	3.57	2.77	6.70	2.54	15.10
Elkhart	8.91	14.69	17.72	26.74	7.66	2.18	2.73	10.58	4.07	4.72
Fayette	2.81	15.41	20.96	19.32	9.76	3.30	1.40	10.82	8.59	7.62
Floyd	5.33	NA	26.83	7.78	11.22	NA	6.47	12.85	7.72	NA
Fountain	6.58	2.75	24.46	31.19	6.91	0.87	2.41	13.40	NA	NA
Franklin	4.09	NA	34.84	20.47	9.20	NA	NA	9.96	7.88	6.14
Fulton	4.82	NA	24.59	20.59	7.39	1.19	1.81	10.30	6.79	NA
Gibson	3.95	13.01	23.42	19.68	16.38	2.47	1.74	8.87	4.75	5.75
Grant	5.30	16.44	19.42	24.10	8.28	2.89	3.47	9.62	3.61	6.84
Greene	8.99	NA	26.56	17.74	10.19	0.79	1.69	10.14	5.46	NA
Hamilton	7.01	NA	13.18	17.72	8.83	1.72	6.21	10.64	4.23	NA
Hancock	3.17	NA	18.46	24.48	19.55	0.49	2.39	9.72	7.98	NA
Harrison	5.58	NA	23.27	20.02	10.33	0.00	1.84	10.99	4.87	NA
Hendricks	6.36	NA	19.60	21.40	12.90	1.38	2.46	9.11	4.25	NA
Henry	5.48	8.13	17.56	25.62	16.06	2.37	2.89	9.05	5.23	7.62
Howard	6.15	NA	17.41	NA	7.37	NA	4.24	11.06	NA	5.91
Huntington	6.12	NA	23.24	17.52	10.50	2.86	3.08	14.73	NA	NA
Jackson	7.98	12.25	18.42	20.96	14.54	4.45	4.15	8.99	3.60	4.66
Jasper	13.11	2.44	15.53	15.29	30.36	2.12	2.56	7.61	6.26	4.71
Jay	3.12	NA	26.66	19.70	11.56	0.68	5.46	12.94	NA	NA
Jefferson	5.62	17.41	22.51	19.04	7.59	3.53	4.51	9.30	4.39	6.09
Jennings	8.24	NA	19.76	24.90	13.36	NA	0.28	6.87	NA	8.60
Johnson	5.07	NA	13.41	16.15	7.77	6.07	6.01	9.69	NA	NA
Knox	6.53	14.34	18.53	21.62	9.22	6.64	2.76	8.97	5.40	6.00
Kosciusko	7.95	13.05	17.09	23.18	7.85	3.39	4.42	10.72	4.28	8.07
Lagrange	11.29	NA	17.27	18.65	18.10	0.49	5.61	11.17	3.49	NA
Lake	4.87	13.19	18.35	18.31	12.58	5.23	4.60	9.45	5.91	7.50
Laporte	6.37	12.46	17.28	18.48	11.49	10.09	4.07	8.80	5.18	5.79
Lawrence	5.29	17.04	23.30	20.51	8.99	4.08	2.79	9.11	4.63	4.25
Madison	6.38	NA	19.14	24.93	8.39	2.28	3.61	9.64	6.93	NA
Marion	4.78	12.81	14.45	19.95	6.10	4.61	5.32	11.56	4.25	16.18
Marshall	9.84	7.25	15.40	30.02	13.62	3.21	1.25	9.31	5.34	4.76
Martin	NA	3.08	26.05	34.99	13.01	NA	NA	9.19	NA	3.57
Miami	6.76	5.27	18.69	30.61	12.49	2.46	3.36	9.04	6.89	4.44
Monroe	5.34	15.17	19.22	17.50	6.42	4.74	5.03	13.80	3.85	8.94
Montgomery	5.13	16.77	20.50	22.47	11.30	1.22	2.48	9.82	5.16	5.15
Morgan	5.97	NA	20.74	26.18	11.10	1.91	2.24	11.43	4.46	NA
Newton	6.14	NA	29.03	14.10	22.30	NA	1.25	9.08	12.14	NA
Noble	3.34	12.79	22.38	21.67	9.93	1.52	2.42	9.42	4.78	11.75
Ohio	NA	0.00	NA	NA	0.00	NA	0.00	10.87	NA	NA
Orange	4.39	6.65	34.22	13.44	20.73	0.76	NA	7.44	7.33	NA
Owen	1.99	NA	17.62	NA	12.15	NA	0.47	7.32	NA	2.64
Parke	8.41	NA	28.93	13.47	15.58	NA	NA	11.41	7.65	NA
Perry	1.72	19.72	24.12	25.13	7.55	1.46	3.50	8.81	5.46	2.54
Pike	2.65	NA	29.95	NA	24.06	NA	3.25	5.44	NA	3.42
Porter	6.18	9.63	21.07	23.38	14.03	1.88	2.97	10.19	5.04	5.63
Posey	2.82	NA	17.56	32.54	12.49	1.01	2.42	6.97	6.29	NA
Pulaski	8.10	NA	16.26	32.24	NA	NA	1.59	6.41	7.60	3.13
Putnam	7.37	NA	23.91	16.93	11.93	2.00	1.98	11.29	5.84	NA
Randolph	3.30	14.13	24.88	19.95	11.86	0.82	4.68	8.62	6.60	5.17
Ripley	6.27	4.95	26.80	27.44	7.77	0.93	3.08	10.04	6.76	5.96
Rush	3.81	NA	20.36	25.23	10.19	0.46	3.42	8.80	6.20	NA
St. Joseph	5.05	15.99	17.75	21.48	5.32	4.20	5.03	10.53	5.43	9.23
Scott	5.58	NA	21.42	21.95	14.56	NA	1.49	11.09	4.62	NA
Shelby	4.33	NA	21.36	28.39	11.50	3.38	2.29	9.51	NA	NA
Spencer	7.06	NA	25.69	27.03	16.31	NA	3.88	8.06	4.31	5.83
Starke	11.36	11.70	23.53	12.07	14.28	NA	3.12	9.54	NA	NA
Steuben	6.10	NA	17.44	15.52	19.29	7.10	3.54	9.76	2.56	NA
Sullivan	3.51	NA	20.91	NA	20.88	0.99	2.97	10.54	NA	5.20
Switzerland	NA	NA	35.80	NA	NA	NA	NA	12.00	NA	10.08
Tippecanoe	NA	NA	14.54	22.00	5.99	3.56	4.37	11.40	NA	8.16
Tipton	2.75	NA	17.08	NA	6.99	NA	1.43	7.87	NA	3.78
Union	NA	0.00	NA	19.22	8.31	1.50	NA	8.86	NA	13.15
Vanderburgh	6.47	NA	14.91	19.83	5.44	6.23	6.18	10.82	3.71	NA
Vermillion	4.88	NA	18.83	34.42	7.72	NA	0.60	10.18	NA	NA
Vigo	3.23	NA	9.50	8.96	4.91	NA	2.66	6.95	NA	NA
Wabash	9.20	12.48	20.68	18.93	7.58	3.90	3.18	9.29	7.18	7.59
Warren	NA	0.00	NA	NA	NA	0.00	NA	12.38	0.00	NA
Warrick	4.50	NA	28.76	19.28	11.53	0.26	2.73	9.24	5.65	NA
Washington	9.32	5.92	25.28	25.38	9.48	NA	1.63	8.85	6.81	NA
Wayne	6.56	16.84	17.76	23.05	7.48	2.10	3.80	10.36	3.86	8.19
Wells	3.63	5.96	29.92	24.62	9.48	1.29	5.06	10.93	NA	NA
White	6.98	NA	25.66	22.24	9.21	2.37	1.09	11.09	4.01	NA
Whitley	5.16	NA	25.52	17.79	12.65	0.35	1.84	9.03	5.88	NA

Footnote: Data are for establishments with payroll.
Source: U.S. Bureau of the Census
EDIN table(s): SALE

2.68 Selected Manufacturing Characteristics 1992 *(Part I)*

	Establishments				Employees		Payroll		Production Workers			
	Total	Percent Change 1987-92	20 or More Employees	Percent of State	Total (000)	Percent Change 1987-92	($MIL)	Percent Change 1987-92	Number (000)	Percent Change 1987-92	Hours (MIL)	Wages ($MIL)
Indiana	**9,278**	**7.37**	**3,876**	**100.00**	**620.3**	**3.04**	**19,129.5**	**21.41**	**434.3**	**1.78**	**885.7**	**11,660.1**
Adams	74	-2.63	38	0.98	5.6	-12.50	135.3	-0.73	4.4	-16.98	8.6	93.2
Allen	576	8.27	229	5.91	35.9	-1.91	1,169.4	18.01	23.1	1.76	47.2	623.9
Bartholomew	139	26.36	61	1.57	16.6	10.67	527.9	17.91	9.7	12.79	19.6	240.5
Benton	12	-14.29	6	0.15	0.4	0.00	7.0	40.00	0.4	33.33	0.6	5.7
Blackford	33	-2.94	19	0.49	1.7	-15.00	43.5	12.69	1.3	-13.33	2.6	29.3
Boone	59	-6.35	18	0.46	1.5	0.00	33.5	16.32	1.1	10.00	2.1	19.0
Brown	19	5.56	0	0.00	0.1	0.00	1.2	-7.69	NA	NA	0.1	0.7
Carroll	30	15.38	7	0.18	1.7	41.67	37.9	66.96	1.4	40.00	2.8	29.3
Cass	55	-6.78	33	0.85	5.4	-1.82	121.9	8.16	4.3	-2.27	8.1	80.6
Clark	130	16.07	49	1.26	6.9	-2.82	188.7	5.89	5.3	0.00	10.4	124.9
Clay	33	6.45	7	0.18	NA	NA	NA	NA	NA	NA	NA	NA
Clinton	42	-6.67	23	0.59	4.0	11.11	101.1	50.90	3.2	10.34	6.4	70.5
Crawford	19	11.76	1	0.03	0.1	0.00	1.8	28.57	0.1	0.00	0.2	1.5
Daviess	44	4.76	15	0.39	2.0	33.33	30.1	46.83	1.6	23.08	2.9	21.0
Dearborn	46	31.43	12	0.31	NA	NA	NA	NA	NA	NA	NA	NA
Decatur	44	15.79	16	0.41	4.0	42.86	109.8	60.53	3.3	37.50	7.0	88.4
Dekalb	103	11.96	56	1.44	8.6	26.47	234.1	54.73	6.4	23.08	13.1	154.2
Delaware	182	-3.19	75	1.93	10.6	-5.36	383.5	17.17	7.2	-8.86	15.4	219.6
Dubois	123	17.14	71	1.83	11.2	15.46	255.8	36.43	8.9	14.10	18.3	175.3
Elkhart	931	8.89	482	12.44	52.3	4.60	1,343.5	22.05	38.0	5.26	74.6	784.2
Fayette	32	-3.03	13	0.34	5.1	-7.27	185.0	13.08	4.1	-6.82	8.6	138.7
Floyd	117	14.71	57	1.47	5.3	NA	129.5	NA	4.0	NA	8.4	81.9
Fountain	26	-3.70	9	0.23	1.7	-5.56	40.5	3.85	1.3	0.00	2.4	28.3
Franklin	14	16.67	6	0.15	0.5	-28.57	10.1	-21.09	0.4	-33.33	0.8	7.8
Fulton	55	10.00	27	0.70	2.5	-10.71	55.2	8.02	2.0	-9.09	4.0	37.5
Gibson	44	22.22	16	0.41	2.6	23.81	64.0	48.15	1.9	11.76	4.0	38.5
Grant	86	-5.49	38	0.98	9.9	-8.33	365.4	12.85	7.8	-9.30	17.3	280.9
Greene	29	11.54	11	0.28	1.4	55.56	22.8	79.53	1.2	71.43	2.4	17.9
Hamilton	166	20.29	61	1.57	5.8	16.00	155.5	45.06	3.5	9.37	7.5	73.4
Hancock	59	-6.35	18	0.46	2.6	-25.71	82.0	-17.00	1.5	7.14	3.0	31.4
Harrison	38	35.71	13	0.34	1.8	NA	39.8	NA	1.4	NA	3.0	30.0
Hendricks	60	13.21	15	0.39	1.1	-15.38	24.7	38.76	0.8	-11.11	1.5	13.9
Henry	54	0.00	22	0.57	3.2	-5.88	109.4	24.89	2.5	-3.85	5.1	79.9
Howard	77	2.67	29	0.75	17.9	-1.10	784.9	17.68	11.1	-17.16	25.3	428.8
Huntington	86	16.22	41	1.06	8.9	12.66	266.5	28.19	6.7	8.06	13.9	187.2
Jackson	86	13.16	35	0.90	4.6	6.98	114.9	52.79	3.6	5.88	7.8	71.7
Jasper	25	8.70	11	0.28	1.2	-7.69	24.9	6.87	0.9	-18.18	1.9	17.6
Jay	34	6.25	23	0.59	3.2	6.67	64.5	21.47	2.7	22.73	4.7	47.2
Jefferson	47	14.63	21	0.54	3.3	0.00	82.7	20.20	2.6	-7.14	4.9	54.6
Jennings	43	53.57	15	0.39	1.5	7.14	33.0	28.40	1.2	0.00	2.4	22.6
Johnson	130	19.27	40	1.03	5.5	25.00	139.4	47.05	4.1	20.59	7.7	84.1
Knox	45	0.00	17	0.44	1.8	5.88	43.6	24.93	1.4	7.69	2.6	29.4
Kosciusko	186	6.90	87	2.24	13.9	14.88	438.4	55.79	9.7	12.79	18.9	260.3
Lagrange	75	8.70	29	0.75	4.0	-2.44	96.3	26.88	3.0	-3.23	5.9	61.1
Lake	418	10.29	158	4.08	41.7	-0.95	1,636.2	21.73	29.9	-3.55	61.7	1,110.5
Laporte	193	2.66	90	2.32	12.1	2.54	311.4	17.29	8.1	0.00	16.3	183.2
Lawrence	70	9.38	26	0.67	4.9	11.36	143.2	16.61	4.2	16.67	7.4	114.2
Madison	132	0.00	49	1.26	15.5	-7.74	619.7	3.46	11.4	-8.80	23.4	452.6
Marion	1,314	4.78	483	12.46	83.4	0.85	2,970.1	16.74	47.9	-5.34	101.0	1,562.8
Marshall	131	7.38	68	1.75	6.5	14.04	152.9	38.87	5.2	10.64	10.9	102.7
Martin	17	30.77	5	0.13	0.7	0.00	16.1	14.18	0.6	20.00	1.3	12.9
Miami	41	-12.77	21	0.54	2.1	-19.23	48.5	-1.22	1.6	-11.11	3.3	32.4
Monroe	123	13.89	39	1.01	8.7	6.10	240.9	30.36	6.8	-1.45	12.6	169.9
Montgomery	55	34.15	23	0.59	8.0	45.45	232.3	81.91	6.2	47.62	12.0	158.1
Morgan	63	8.62	20	0.52	2.4	-17.24	55.6	14.64	1.7	-26.09	3.4	32.9
Newton	18	38.46	8	0.21	1.2	NA	23.7	NA	1.0	NA	2.2	18.6
Noble	143	0.00	82	2.12	8.4	10.53	191.2	36.47	6.7	8.06	13.5	130.3
Ohio	2	0.00	0	0.00	NA	NA	NA	NA	NA	NA	NA	NA
Orange	35	6.06	16	0.41	2.4	-7.69	46.6	13.94	2.1	-4.55	4.3	34.9
Owen	23	21.05	8	0.21	0.8	60.00	16.9	79.79	0.6	50.00	1.2	10.6
Parke	19	-13.64	7	0.18	0.5	0.00	10.6	43.24	0.4	0.00	0.9	8.5
Perry	34	6.25	13	0.34	1.7	6.25	34.5	10.58	1.4	0.00	2.8	26.5
Pike	11	0.00	3	0.08	0.2	100.00	3.4	61.90	0.1	0.00	0.3	2.4
Porter	132	26.92	46	1.19	11.9	11.21	477.5	35.50	8.6	11.69	17.9	342.7
Posey	31	3.33	13	0.34	NA	NA	NA	NA	NA	NA	NA	NA
Pulaski	27	58.82	10	0.26	1.6	33.33	35.9	33.46	1.2	33.33	1.9	23.8
Putnam	27	12.50	11	0.28	2.1	133.33	45.3	155.93	1.6	128.57	3.6	30.7
Randolph	54	-3.57	26	0.67	2.8	-39.13	76.8	-25.44	2.1	-43.24	4.4	48.3
Ripley	40	14.29	18	0.46	5.0	35.14	181.1	98.79	2.6	13.04	5.5	57.7
Rush	30	11.11	10	0.26	1.1	10.00	25.7	37.43	0.8	0.00	1.5	16.5
St. Joseph	486	-0.61	188	4.85	20.0	-13.79	622.0	3.75	12.6	-14.86	24.7	308.5
Scott	32	10.34	12	0.31	2.2	46.67	46.1	55.22	1.8	63.64	4.0	33.4
Shelby	75	0.00	32	0.83	5.2	18.18	136.8	46.15	3.7	15.63	8.0	81.5
Spencer	19	-20.83	11	0.28	1.4	7.69	33.1	44.54	1.1	10.00	2.3	21.4
Starke	25	25.00	10	0.26	1.0	11.11	19.2	38.13	0.8	14.29	1.5	12.5
Steuben	101	21.69	58	1.50	5.8	23.40	138.9	38.62	4.3	19.44	8.9	93.7
Sullivan	28	3.70	7	0.18	0.6	20.00	10.9	60.29	0.4	0.00	0.9	7.4
Switzerland	9	12.50	4	0.10	0.6	20.00	8.8	41.94	0.5	0.00	0.9	6.3
Tippecanoe	118	11.32	48	1.24	14.3	22.22	483.5	47.01	9.9	22.22	19.8	298.1
Tipton	17	70.00	7	0.18	0.7	75.00	20.9	106.93	0.5	66.67	0.9	11.1
Union	5	0.00	0	0.00	NA	NA	0.9	NA	NA	NA	NA	0.4
Vanderburgh	268	-1.47	101	2.61	19.3	-8.53	573.4	-3.68	12.8	-1.54	26.6	313.2
Vermillion	15	0.00	7	0.18	NA	NA	NA	NA	NA	NA	NA	NA
Vigo	138	6.15	61	1.57	9.0	-7.22	256.4	-3.21	5.9	-3.28	12.1	155.9
Wabash	70	-11.39	37	0.95	5.7	-1.72	140.9	15.59	4.5	2.27	9.3	97.6
Warren	9	50.00	2	0.05	0.1	0.00	2.6	136.36	0.1	0.00	0.2	1.9
Warrick	42	-4.55	12	0.31	NA	NA	NA	NA	NA	NA	NA	NA
Washington	43	34.38	15	0.39	2.4	4.35	47.3	15.09	2.1	5.00	4.1	36.8
Wayne	138	6.15	67	1.73	6.9	-21.59	193.1	-4.07	4.8	-28.36	9.8	117.1
Wells	44	2.33	24	0.62	2.9	-6.45	76.5	28.57	2.1	-12.50	4.3	43.7
White	47	20.51	22	0.57	3.3	37.50	74.9	90.59	2.6	36.84	5.1	56.6
Whitley	58	16.00	26	0.67	3.3	43.48	82.4	82.71	2.7	50.00	5.3	62.9

Source: U.S. Bureau of the Census, Census of Manufactures
EDIN table(s): MANF

2.69 Selected Manufacturing Characteristics 1992 (Part II)

	Value Added by Manufacture ($MIL)	Percent Change 1987-92	Value Added Per Production Worker	Value Added Per Dollar of Wages	Rank	Cost of Materials ($MIL)	Percent of State	Value of Shipments ($MIL)	New Capital Expenditures Total ($MIL)	New Capital Expenditures Per Production Worker
Indiana	49,801.8	26.79	114,671.4	4.3	—	55,423.2	100.00	104,971.1	4,125.3	9,499
Adams	335.7	4.03	76,295.5	3.6	50	657.6	1.19	982.6	20.7	4,705
Allen	2,491.2	29.83	107,844.2	4.0	33	2,277.9	4.11	4,789.7	121.9	5,277
Bartholomew	1,129.7	2.57	116,463.9	4.7	19	1,551.3	2.80	2,676.7	109.7	11,309
Benton	17.1	17.12	42,750.0	3.0	75	19.3	0.03	36.2	NA	NA
Blackford	168.6	55.54	129,692.3	5.8	9	145.2	0.26	311.9	5.0	3,846
Boone	60.9	16.67	55,363.6	3.2	65	54.3	0.10	115.6	2.3	2,091
Brown	2.5	13.64	NA	3.6	50	2.3	0.00	4.7	NA	NA
Carroll	96.8	74.10	69,142.9	3.3	64	210.3	0.38	305.0	6.4	4,571
Cass	253.1	-9.12	58,860.5	3.1	70	405.0	0.73	654.0	23.5	5,465
Clark	894.8	11.14	168,830.2	7.2	4	572.4	1.03	1,404.9	45.5	8,585
Clay	NA	NA	NA	NA	85	NA	NA	NA	NA	NA
Clinton	400.2	28.85	125,062.5	5.7	10	626.1	1.13	1,023.4	45.3	14,156
Crawford	3.3	-37.74	33,000.0	2.2	84	5.5	0.01	8.7	NA	NA
Daviess	106.0	101.90	66,250.0	5.0	14	168.8	0.30	279.8	3.3	2,063
Dearborn	NA	NA	NA	NA	85	NA	NA	NA	NA	NA
Decatur	364.4	44.55	110,424.2	4.1	30	288.0	0.52	656.7	24.6	7,455
Dekalb	500.2	42.39	78,156.3	3.2	65	633.1	1.14	1,135.8	33.3	5,203
Delaware	737.1	20.58	102,375.0	3.4	58	671.8	1.21	1,427.7	39.3	5,458
Dubois	560.7	48.18	63,000.0	3.2	65	625.3	1.13	1,182.0	28.9	3,247
Elkhart	2,989.0	13.19	78,657.9	3.8	41	3,902.2	7.04	6,943.1	125.8	3,311
Fayette	467.1	17.87	113,926.8	3.4	58	468.9	0.85	939.7	26.6	6,488
Floyd	340.2	NA	85,050.0	4.2	29	339.7	0.61	685.7	19.5	4,875
Fountain	99.8	49.85	76,769.2	3.5	52	68.4	0.12	162.0	5.5	4,231
Franklin	30.1	-4.75	75,250.0	3.9	36	55.4	0.10	87.0	NA	NA
Fulton	168.3	8.09	84,150.0	4.5	22	153.2	0.28	320.8	7.7	3,850
Gibson	97.8	-12.29	51,473.7	2.5	81	297.2	0.54	399.1	9.8	5,158
Grant	688.9	51.04	88,320.5	2.5	81	831.3	1.50	1,519.1	48.5	6,218
Greene	39.8	85.12	33,166.7	2.2	84	156.6	0.28	196.7	2.9	2,417
Hamilton	451.7	78.75	129,057.1	6.2	7	282.7	0.51	736.2	20.1	5,743
Hancock	121.4	71.71	80,933.3	3.9	36	208.2	0.38	329.5	20.8	13,867
Harrison	110.1	NA	78,642.9	3.7	46	107.1	0.19	214.5	9.4	6,714
Hendricks	47.0	39.88	58,750.0	3.4	58	48.7	0.09	94.9	1.6	2,000
Henry	205.7	12.84	82,280.0	2.6	79	252.2	0.46	452.5	14.1	5,640
Howard	1,364.2	19.49	122,900.9	3.2	65	1,407.8	2.54	2,727.3	NA	NA
Huntington	1,805.6	253.21	269,492.5	9.6	1	2,027.0	3.66	3,831.6	29.2	4,358
Jackson	275.8	45.31	76,611.1	3.8	41	338.2	0.61	612.8	27.8	7,722
Jasper	61.2	15.47	68,000.0	3.5	52	73.1	0.13	137.0	5.5	6,111
Jay	147.8	6.87	54,740.7	3.1	70	147.3	0.27	297.5	7.1	2,630
Jefferson	191.1	-7.55	73,500.0	3.5	52	183.2	0.33	366.1	9.6	3,692
Jennings	87.9	61.58	73,250.0	3.9	36	61.6	0.11	150.4	2.5	2,083
Johnson	296.9	28.97	72,414.6	3.5	52	476.5	0.86	769.3	27.5	6,707
Knox	101.6	16.11	72,571.4	3.5	52	146.3	0.26	250.3	23.3	16,643
Kosciusko	1,478.7	77.84	152,443.3	5.7	10	805.1	1.45	2,274.7	95.2	9,814
Lagrange	266.5	55.12	88,833.3	4.4	26	254.9	0.46	517.1	8.0	2,667
Lake	4,598.1	22.26	153,782.6	4.1	30	7,163.3	12.92	11,753.6	437.2	14,622
Laporte	789.3	20.58	97,444.4	4.3	28	763.6	1.38	1,558.4	36.9	4,556
Lawrence	305.7	25.03	72,785.7	2.7	78	410.1	0.74	711.6	8.0	1,905
Madison	1,009.2	3.68	88,526.3	2.2	84	1,209.8	2.18	2,240.4	46.8	4,105
Marion	7,926.8	36.35	165,486.4	5.1	13	6,070.2	10.95	13,902.8	714.2	14,910
Marshall	481.1	73.43	92,519.2	4.7	19	583.2	1.05	1,062.6	43.4	8,346
Martin	60.7	8.01	101,166.7	4.7	19	57.6	0.10	118.4	2.2	3,667
Miami	130.1	7.34	81,312.5	4.0	33	118.6	0.21	248.4	8.0	5,000
Monroe	527.2	-30.95	77,529.4	3.1	70	1,391.0	2.51	1,943.2	64.3	9,456
Montgomery	583.2	85.73	94,064.5	3.7	46	648.2	1.17	1,230.9	95.4	15,387
Morgan	147.0	21.89	86,470.6	4.5	22	109.4	0.20	257.5	5.7	3,353
Newton	84.4	NA	84,400.0	4.5	22	47.6	0.09	132.1	4.3	4,300
Noble	506.7	53.08	75,626.9	3.9	36	517.7	0.93	1,020.9	25.2	3,761
Ohio	NA	NA	NA	NA	85	NA	NA	NA	NA	NA
Orange	87.1	5.96	41,476.2	2.5	81	168.4	0.30	249.7	2.8	1,333
Owen	55.4	86.53	92,333.3	5.2	12	28.3	0.05	83.1	2.0	3,333
Parke	32.5	70.16	81,250.0	3.8	41	33.8	0.06	66.1	NA	NA
Perry	69.1	-0.86	49,357.1	2.6	79	59.8	0.11	130.5	3.1	2,214
Pike	15.6	NA	156,000.0	6.5	6	10.5	0.02	24.1	NA	NA
Porter	1,528.2	6.25	177,697.7	4.5	22	2,007.5	3.62	3,517.9	299.5	34,826
Posey	NA	NA	NA	NA	85	NA	NA	NA	NA	NA
Pulaski	88.5	36.79	73,750.0	3.7	46	107.7	0.19	203.9	4.6	3,833
Putnam	121.1	139.33	75,687.5	3.9	36	155.1	0.28	276.8	21.2	13,250
Randolph	165.2	-19.65	78,666.7	3.4	58	137.2	0.25	305.3	6.3	3,000
Ripley	468.6	81.21	180,230.8	8.1	2	181.6	0.33	651.9	23.1	8,885
Rush	117.5	78.57	146,875.0	7.1	5	61.7	0.11	180.9	6.2	7,750
St. Joseph	1,493.9	25.55	118,563.5	4.8	17	1,531.9	2.76	2,961.0	99.6	7,905
Scott	136.8	40.89	76,000.0	4.1	30	222.3	0.40	355.2	12.7	7,056
Shelby	309.6	33.16	83,675.7	3.8	41	287.7	0.52	596.3	29.5	7,973
Spencer	79.5	59.96	72,272.7	3.7	46	60.2	0.11	138.7	NA	NA
Starke	39.1	19.21	48,875.0	3.1	70	42.7	0.08	80.8	2.0	2,500
Steuben	370.9	34.63	86,255.8	4.0	33	323.7	0.58	699.0	27.4	6,372
Sullivan	25.5	60.38	63,750.0	3.4	58	25.7	0.05	50.8	1.6	4,000
Switzerland	48.3	49.54	96,600.0	7.7	3	35.9	0.06	74.4	1.7	3,400
Tippecanoe	1,433.7	52.29	144,818.2	4.8	17	2,487.2	4.49	3,935.0	154.1	15,566
Tipton	35.6	30.40	71,200.0	3.2	65	39.0	0.07	74.0	NA	NA
Union	2.0	NA	NA	5.0	14	4.3	0.01	6.2	NA	NA
Vanderburgh	1,528.0	-23.84	119,375.0	4.9	16	1,417.9	2.56	2,901.7	133.2	10,406
Vermillion	NA	NA	NA	NA	85	NA	NA	NA	NA	NA
Vigo	969.3	2.83	164,288.1	6.2	7	723.0	1.30	1,694.0	NA	NA
Wabash	336.2	11.21	74,711.1	3.4	58	391.8	0.71	722.4	17.2	3,822
Warren	5.9	25.53	59,000.0	3.1	70	8.0	0.01	13.9	NA	NA
Warrick	NA	NA	NA	NA	85	NA	NA	NA	NA	NA
Washington	112.1	14.86	53,381.0	3.0	75	92.7	0.17	208.1	6.5	3,095
Wayne	440.1	15.36	91,687.5	3.8	41	433.4	0.78	876.3	26.2	5,458
Wells	191.4	11.41	91,142.9	4.4	26	180.9	0.33	372.0	17.7	8,429
White	196.6	121.65	75,615.4	3.5	52	280.0	0.51	475.7	9.3	3,577
Whitley	185.5	102.07	68,703.7	2.9	77	272.4	0.49	457.7	8.0	2,963

Source: U.S. Bureau of the Census, Census of Manufactures
EDIN table(s): MANF

2.70 New Residential Buildings: Permit Authorized Construction, Reported and Imputed - Units and Cost ($000) 1996

	Total				1 Family		2 Family		3 & 4 Family		5 or More Family	
	Units	Percent State	Cost	Percent State	Units	Cost	Units	Cost	Units	Cost	Units	Cost
Indiana	37,417	100.00	3,737,072	100.00	30,061	3,446,686	1,288	80,660	576	32,859	5,492	176,867
Adams	138	0.37	11,536	0.31	118	11,036	NA	NA	NA	NA	20	500
Allen	1,900	5.08	253,478	6.78	1,743	247,804	32	2,082	10	484	115	3,108
Bartholomew	366	0.98	44,207	1.18	360	43,847	6	360	NA	NA	NA	NA
Benton	27	0.07	1,457	0.04	23	1,217	4	240	NA	NA	NA	NA
Blackford	65	0.17	5,226	0.14	61	4,926	4	300	NA	NA	NA	NA
Boone	471	1.26	61,355	1.64	343	57,899	NA	NA	NA	NA	128	3,456
Brown	189	0.51	15,369	0.41	173	14,630	10	527	NA	NA	6	212
Carroll	84	0.22	5,930	0.16	84	5,930	NA	NA	NA	NA	NA	NA
Cass	79	0.21	6,224	0.17	75	6,099	4	125	NA	NA	NA	NA
Clark	798	2.13	74,648	2.00	664	67,330	74	4,667	28	1,452	32	1,200
Clay	49	0.13	3,134	0.08	47	3,071	2	63	NA	NA	NA	NA
Clinton	192	0.51	15,210	0.41	124	12,420	NA	NA	4	340	64	2,450
Crawford	1	0.00	125	0.00	1	125	NA	NA	NA	NA	NA	NA
Daviess	33	0.09	3,957	0.11	29	3,692	4	265	NA	NA	NA	NA
Dearborn	501	1.34	47,537	1.27	393	43,095	36	1,483	15	828	57	2,130
Decatur	118	0.32	9,316	0.25	86	8,316	NA	NA	NA	NA	32	1,000
Dekalb	279	0.75	27,067	0.72	224	25,442	14	408	NA	NA	41	1,217
Delaware	273	0.73	31,448	0.84	255	30,299	10	689	8	460	NA	NA
Dubois	218	0.58	23,227	0.62	176	21,357	34	1,629	NA	NA	8	241
Elkhart	1,177	3.15	105,753	2.83	994	96,059	40	3,943	42	3,314	101	2,438
Fayette	89	0.24	5,425	0.15	89	5,425	NA	NA	NA	NA	NA	NA
Floyd	558	1.49	57,530	1.54	406	51,270	28	1,328	NA	NA	124	4,932
Fountain	13	0.03	1,087	0.03	13	1,087	NA	NA	NA	NA	NA	NA
Franklin	115	0.31	12,348	0.33	112	12,179	NA	NA	3	169	NA	NA
Fulton	45	0.12	4,436	0.12	35	4,086	NA	NA	NA	NA	10	350
Gibson	47	0.13	2,987	0.08	29	2,465	18	522	NA	NA	NA	NA
Grant	195	0.52	14,519	0.39	176	14,302	6	72	3	45	10	100
Greene	0	0.00	0	0.00	NA	NA	NA	NA	NA	NA	NA	NA
Hamilton	3,064	8.19	422,202	11.30	2,846	412,885	26	1,591	4	160	188	7,566
Hancock	634	1.69	73,007	1.95	534	69,077	32	2,001	3	140	65	1,789
Harrison	262	0.70	28,000	0.75	262	28,000	NA	NA	NA	NA	NA	NA
Hendricks	1,524	4.07	159,570	4.27	1,220	147,863	28	2,176	4	222	272	9,309
Henry	198	0.53	16,296	0.44	160	15,428	10	468	NA	NA	28	400
Howard	659	1.76	56,587	1.51	335	42,863	84	6,725	NA	NA	240	7,000
Huntington	180	0.48	18,330	0.49	178	18,261	2	69	NA	NA	NA	NA
Jackson	399	1.07	23,873	0.64	209	18,126	6	254	4	140	180	5,353
Jasper	238	0.64	19,776	0.53	206	18,221	24	1,356	NA	NA	8	200
Jay	50	0.13	4,115	0.11	50	4,115	NA	NA	NA	NA	NA	NA
Jefferson	214	0.57	14,105	0.38	206	13,848	8	257	NA	NA	NA	NA
Jennings	201	0.54	13,247	0.35	117	10,130	20	967	NA	NA	64	2,150
Johnson	2,201	5.88	199,277	5.33	1,296	172,275	46	4,379	3	223	856	22,400
Knox	105	0.28	7,184	0.19	73	5,903	16	602	16	679	NA	NA
Kosciusko	521	1.39	49,463	1.32	505	48,081	12	1,132	4	250	NA	NA
Lagrange	225	0.60	15,160	0.41	223	15,060	2	100	NA	NA	NA	NA
Lake	1,935	5.17	217,289	5.81	1,573	190,682	124	11,062	42	2,793	196	12,751
Laporte	537	1.44	47,722	1.28	518	46,919	6	323	7	280	6	200
Lawrence	58	0.16	3,519	0.09	34	2,619	20	790	4	110	NA	NA
Madison	774	2.07	52,750	1.41	351	41,474	28	1,130	3	275	392	9,872
Marion	4,185	11.18	445,870	11.93	3,272	406,049	18	947	183	11,175	712	27,699
Marshall	316	0.84	22,870	0.61	255	20,973	26	897	NA	NA	35	1,000
Martin	2	0.01	95	0.00	2	95	NA	NA	NA	NA	NA	NA
Miami	99	0.26	7,745	0.21	97	7,585	2	160	NA	NA	NA	NA
Monroe	879	2.35	74,088	1.98	639	66,261	44	2,162	15	1,118	181	4,547
Montgomery	175	0.47	12,545	0.34	167	12,253	8	292	NA	NA	NA	NA
Morgan	678	1.81	66,121	1.77	646	64,913	20	858	NA	NA	12	350
Newton	108	0.29	9,176	0.25	108	9,176	NA	NA	NA	NA	NA	NA
Noble	409	1.09	31,055	0.83	299	27,824	4	281	NA	NA	106	2,950
Ohio	69	0.18	3,936	0.11	37	2,886	NA	NA	NA	NA	32	1,050
Orange	3	0.01	65	0.00	3	65	NA	NA	NA	NA	NA	NA
Owen	30	0.08	1,950	0.05	10	1,500	20	450	NA	NA	NA	NA
Parke	36	0.10	3,074	0.08	36	3,074	NA	NA	NA	NA	NA	NA
Perry	88	0.24	5,460	0.15	62	4,850	2	50	NA	NA	24	560
Pike	66	0.18	3,684	0.10	54	3,234	NA	NA	NA	NA	12	450
Porter	1,256	3.36	145,156	3.88	1,010	132,131	56	4,920	43	3,136	147	4,969
Posey	69	0.18	7,865	0.21	67	7,744	2	121	NA	NA	NA	NA
Pulaski	8	0.02	1,010	0.03	8	1,010	NA	NA	NA	NA	NA	NA
Putnam	305	0.82	25,381	0.68	285	24,576	4	355	16	450	NA	NA
Randolph	82	0.22	6,473	0.17	74	6,176	4	217	4	80	NA	NA
Ripley	190	0.51	17,003	0.45	176	16,476	4	185	NA	NA	10	342
Rush	61	0.16	4,296	0.11	45	3,596	NA	NA	16	700	NA	NA
St. Joseph	1,303	3.48	135,935	3.64	1,019	125,874	10	397	NA	NA	274	9,664
Scott	161	0.43	7,931	0.21	104	5,846	6	135	NA	NA	51	1,950
Shelby	206	0.55	21,095	0.56	196	20,363	6	332	4	400	NA	NA
Spencer	106	0.28	5,591	0.15	104	5,503	2	88	NA	NA	NA	NA
Starke	125	0.33	6,643	0.18	125	6,643	NA	NA	NA	NA	NA	NA
Steuben	316	0.84	29,367	0.79	286	27,811	30	1,556	NA	NA	NA	NA
Sullivan	43	0.11	2,871	0.08	27	2,305	NA	NA	NA	NA	16	566
Switzerland	30	0.08	1,800	0.05	30	1,800	NA	NA	NA	NA	NA	NA
Tippecanoe	1,257	3.36	108,972	2.92	744	88,280	110	6,620	40	2,133	363	11,940
Tipton	82	0.22	8,157	0.22	78	8,029	4	128	NA	NA	NA	NA
Union	37	0.10	2,853	0.08	37	2,853	NA	NA	NA	NA	NA	NA
Vanderburgh	662	1.77	48,658	1.30	532	46,273	NA	NA	4	200	126	2,185
Vermillion	45	0.12	3,736	0.10	45	3,736	NA	NA	NA	NA	NA	NA
Vigo	418	1.12	31,069	0.83	272	26,268	34	1,878	36	923	76	2,000
Wabash	147	0.39	11,286	0.30	123	10,566	NA	NA	NA	NA	24	720
Warren	57	0.15	3,568	0.10	57	3,568	NA	NA	NA	NA	NA	NA
Warrick	401	1.07	46,485	1.24	383	44,761	14	1,544	4	180	NA	NA
Washington	30	0.08	2,537	0.07	30	2,537	NA	NA	NA	NA	NA	NA
Wayne	379	1.01	30,549	0.82	369	30,273	6	277	4	NA	NA	NA
Wells	123	0.33	14,292	0.38	117	13,908	6	385	NA	NA	NA	NA
White	180	0.48	12,170	0.33	112	9,749	20	821	NA	NA	48	1,600
Whitley	196	0.52	20,573	0.55	190	20,053	6	520	NA	NA	NA	NA

Source: U.S. Bureau of the Census
EDIN table(s): BPAS

2.71 New Residential Buildings: 1986 to 1996

	1986 to 1996	Percent of State	1986	1987	1988	1989	1990	1991	1992	1993	1994	1995	1996
Indiana	325,766	100.00	29,686	27,286	25,173	26,474	24,846	24,114	29,010	31,279	34,597	35,884	37,417
Adams	1,472	0.45	128	85	119	191	120	124	173	81	182	131	138
Allen	21,274	6.53	3,321	2,477	1,646	1,953	1,469	1,422	1,595	1,798	1,804	1,889	1,900
Bartholomew	3,730	1.14	251	327	314	235	208	227	379	586	350	487	366
Benton	201	0.06	9	6	4	34	21	2	24	29	21	24	27
Blackford	402	0.12	13	22	12	27	57	31	31	21	60	63	65
Boone	3,102	0.95	174	177	339	220	186	265	276	274	390	330	471
Brown	1,429	0.44	130	108	98	116	115	117	141	121	147	147	189
Carroll	677	0.21	30	31	39	65	59	56	68	74	84	87	84
Cass	755	0.23	45	102	46	70	55	71	59	101	52	75	79
Clark	5,526	1.70	315	277	407	399	384	542	500	554	699	651	798
Clay	332	0.10	21	3	9	6	17	49	28	59	55	36	49
Clinton	1,012	0.31	26	14	61	84	96	67	86	104	139	143	192
Crawford	38	0.01	1	1	0	0	0	0	1	1	32	1	1
Daviess	359	0.11	26	52	23	23	47	30	25	23	46	31	33
Dearborn	4,209	1.29	362	308	326	313	303	397	356	397	455	491	501
Decatur	1,314	0.40	69	71	73	69	152	73	105	91	237	256	118
Dekalb	2,084	0.64	191	132	167	186	196	188	147	177	176	245	279
Delaware	3,528	1.08	295	290	288	286	258	401	420	343	329	345	273
Dubois	2,649	0.81	284	287	278	173	227	210	225	240	229	278	218
Elkhart	11,617	3.57	1,655	1,128	1,286	1,043	744	629	892	1,032	988	1,043	1,177
Fayette	811	0.25	75	32	43	51	96	71	78	77	132	67	89
Floyd	5,091	1.56	450	390	387	578	485	459	484	442	451	407	558
Fountain	131	0.04	3	30	5	5	10	15	17	6	17	10	13
Franklin	927	0.28	35	100	77	72	85	65	75	83	110	110	115
Fulton	335	0.10	32	22	12	17	20	23	31	50	46	37	45
Gibson	172	0.05	6	20	14	15	8	8	13	11	14	16	47
Grant	1,888	0.58	119	168	174	161	115	213	141	167	231	204	195
Greene	0	0.00	0	0	0	0	0	0	0	0	0	0	0
Hamilton	24,195	7.43	1,692	1,822	1,942	1,732	1,778	1,691	2,087	2,682	2,885	2,820	3,064
Hancock	4,837	1.48	244	299	444	394	300	405	476	525	568	548	634
Harrison	2,346	0.72	178	190	175	199	162	158	228	280	271	243	262
Hendricks	10,408	3.19	600	795	720	695	660	720	1,118	960	1,123	1,493	1,524
Henry	1,571	0.48	57	68	165	81	162	150	142	173	192	183	198
Howard	3,633	1.12	340	173	162	201	200	182	255	383	488	590	659
Huntington	1,568	0.48	70	93	104	161	96	118	150	149	281	166	180
Jackson	1,748	0.54	66	92	38	85	180	152	141	170	190	235	399
Jasper	1,851	0.57	25	19	42	82	101	137	214	278	333	382	238
Jay	297	0.09	10	6	9	12	16	14	22	59	50	49	50
Jefferson	1,232	0.38	66	41	67	72	78	75	168	123	134	194	214
Jennings	1,124	0.35	59	71	70	54	85	60	113	125	136	150	201
Johnson	11,435	3.51	816	889	710	610	644	916	935	1,142	1,117	1,455	2,201
Knox	1,046	0.32	92	52	64	136	92	68	84	127	104	122	105
Kosciusko	4,608	1.41	336	359	491	448	356	329	500	389	406	473	521
Lagrange	2,146	0.66	130	156	221	200	183	178	193	194	227	239	225
Lake	17,309	5.31	861	1,058	1,336	1,364	1,385	2,152	1,646	1,753	1,989	1,830	1,935
Laporte	4,611	1.42	247	276	329	452	344	397	407	464	563	595	537
Lawrence	638	0.20	47	42	52	46	47	42	55	63	109	77	58
Madison	3,702	1.14	149	347	209	244	221	244	345	332	432	405	774
Marion	51,964	15.95	7,575	5,914	4,378	4,674	4,328	2,870	4,127	3,786	4,524	5,603	4,185
Marshall	2,401	0.74	178	165	182	193	191	170	150	214	308	334	316
Martin	NA	NA	NA	NA	NA	NA	NA	NA	NA	1	37	4	2
Miami	707	0.22	114	76	55	37	50	51	35	46	72	72	99
Monroe	9,426	2.89	956	630	534	790	541	753	1,107	1,045	1,212	979	879
Montgomery	1,890	0.58	83	105	167	182	205	135	178	249	207	204	175
Morgan	5,269	1.62	306	316	304	369	349	445	580	609	604	709	678
Newton	566	0.17	9	10	22	27	39	37	74	59	92	89	108
Noble	2,796	0.86	173	196	251	310	214	177	176	260	288	342	409
Ohio	579	0.18	48	48	61	64	72	39	45	48	37	48	69
Orange	103	0.03	25	10	6	22	11	3	5	0	2	16	3
Owen	144	0.04	0	5	32	9	34	7	4	0	8	15	30
Parke	644	0.20	26	28	26	28	33	95	77	89	89	117	36
Perry	621	0.19	48	50	37	49	56	68	50	46	40	89	88
Pike	300	0.09	8	1	2	0	0	57	36	35	34	61	66
Porter	11,044	3.39	375	534	640	1,274	908	1,060	1,274	1,025	1,501	1,197	1,256
Posey	944	0.29	111	90	93	101	74	68	108	88	79	63	69
Pulaski	89	0.03	7	7	6	6	5	9	3	13	15	10	8
Putnam	1,381	0.42	24	15	21	135	58	67	72	157	267	260	305
Randolph	511	0.16	66	82	27	29	23	18	39	47	41	57	82
Ripley	1,651	0.51	132	148	161	109	114	107	157	161	185	187	190
Rush	585	0.18	28	54	77	27	40	50	43	65	76	64	61
St. Joseph	14,343	4.40	1,163	1,504	1,275	1,390	1,489	843	1,311	1,527	1,388	1,150	1,303
Scott	1,040	0.32	40	52	57	60	66	57	107	144	136	160	161
Shelby	2,145	0.66	93	300	128	144	233	148	175	209	266	243	206
Spencer	773	0.24	64	62	57	46	57	43	107	70	78	83	106
Starke	908	0.28	50	47	63	83	59	64	81	86	124	126	125
Steuben	2,671	0.82	355	200	203	181	199	176	263	272	260	246	316
Sullivan	245	0.08	5	5	11	7	53	16	21	23	34	27	43
Switzerland	290	0.09	14	22	42	21	36	20	24	24	28	29	30
Tippecanoe	9,528	2.92	632	956	675	644	752	930	885	948	1,018	831	1,257
Tipton	523	0.16	18	37	39	44	36	24	37	58	72	76	82
Union	291	0.09	11	18	19	18	14	29	38	38	46	23	37
Vanderburgh	6,903	2.12	1,133	623	560	397	600	439	618	685	590	596	662
Vermillion	322	0.10	19	15	16	20	31	34	42	36	22	42	45
Vigo	3,892	1.19	407	341	393	190	354	183	370	568	370	298	418
Wabash	1,025	0.31	44	73	57	75	63	80	133	106	100	147	147
Warren	317	0.10	24	28	30	31	21	23	37	4	6	56	57
Warrick	4,113	1.26	464	449	291	273	322	267	311	436	367	532	401
Washington	355	0.11	59	27	22	49	50	18	13	23	49	15	30
Wayne	2,566	0.79	180	180	181	228	135	139	104	289	372	379	379
Wells	1,363	0.42	218	138	90	114	97	100	94	110	142	137	123
White	973	0.30	71	43	44	51	62	67	85	106	137	127	180
Whitley	2,121	0.65	149	174	241	313	149	185	165	161	200	188	196

Source: U.S. Bureau of the Census
EDIN table(s): BPAS

2.72 Retail Sales Tax ($000) 1994 to 1996

	1994			1995			1996		
	Total Sales	Taxable Sales	Sales Tax Remitted	Total Sales	Taxable Sales	Sales Tax Remitted	Total Sales	Taxable Sales	Sales Tax Remitted
Indiana	207,876,484	48,959,325	2,627,359	223,453,478	50,700,083	2,788,459	231,232,682	54,219,134	2,952,252
Adams	1,310,706	136,189	6,930	1,280,857	144,014	7,260	1,392,499	154,884	7,422
Allen	9,024,577	2,105,598	117,667	10,259,003	2,295,859	121,779	10,339,289	2,380,863	128,212
Bartholomew	3,383,294	399,639	25,110	4,201,526	394,905	26,444	4,146,044	422,092	27,127
Benton	107,134	25,880	1,398	118,384	28,811	1,473	124,215	31,956	1,630
Blackford	181,053	39,567	2,014	217,336	37,698	2,017	206,034	42,396	2,158
Boone	464,187	165,334	8,656	637,821	180,277	9,177	509,677	185,831	9,835
Brown	73,233	53,995	2,667	72,803	54,567	2,850	76,515	56,370	2,803
Carroll	513,516	62,955	3,227	681,556	62,522	3,191	614,169	62,861	3,223
Cass	496,980	150,384	8,058	499,857	144,893	8,219	512,613	161,830	8,783
Clark	2,247,689	492,234	26,371	2,380,743	526,999	28,317	2,588,450	578,394	30,224
Clay	673,373	87,192	4,498	700,227	77,147	4,245	624,999	83,751	4,302
Clinton	395,873	96,949	4,911	383,087	99,282	5,049	325,648	99,842	5,100
Crawford	31,341	18,017	939	30,516	18,448	831	30,589	18,531	979
Daviess	394,168	122,901	6,741	410,819	138,676	6,929	426,280	141,027	7,284
Dearborn	452,810	128,246	6,716	446,315	134,226	6,961	468,779	144,394	7,453
Decatur	929,201	91,483	5,266	834,188	91,626	5,290	766,167	106,659	6,048
Dekalb	1,158,697	163,635	8,658	1,170,912	182,038	10,005	1,463,912	186,267	10,661
Delaware	1,481,985	484,352	25,360	1,615,629	554,537	26,109	1,796,337	505,919	27,167
Dubois	2,738,598	407,393	20,721	2,766,444	408,813	21,284	3,121,322	428,775	22,932
Elkhart	10,055,063	912,466	48,348	9,861,365	825,447	61,159	10,179,313	982,666	54,541
Fayette	346,622	85,517	4,686	313,649	83,838	4,638	345,814	81,768	4,603
Floyd	1,068,231	188,915	9,898	1,220,586	205,059	10,525	1,296,510	217,835	11,375
Fountain	199,847	61,611	3,158	224,718	83,501	3,255	243,049	67,787	3,491
Franklin	116,698	47,199	2,401	116,232	48,746	2,482	126,918	56,216	2,830
Fulton	309,892	73,737	3,911	313,409	75,785	3,997	304,180	81,635	4,337
Gibson	435,759	97,383	5,012	375,352	96,962	4,980	423,790	111,495	5,789
Grant	800,206	269,382	14,563	888,855	285,854	14,970	1,041,611	293,315	15,466
Greene	264,059	111,424	5,710	271,424	107,599	6,481	313,986	104,615	5,723
Hamilton	2,737,430	1,031,065	54,852	2,991,478	1,115,177	59,590	3,454,813	1,256,474	67,799
Hancock	944,699	172,774	10,919	1,029,006	223,641	11,199	1,111,808	241,399	12,432
Harrison	367,427	114,058	5,761	384,223	115,610	5,868	381,155	123,326	6,284
Hendricks	1,663,996	837,389	47,038	1,823,416	922,048	49,888	1,984,746	1,003,523	53,336
Henry	621,450	223,155	11,666	715,149	231,296	11,973	702,268	236,029	12,887
Howard	5,020,336	408,274	26,783	5,246,028	434,845	27,666	6,619,918	451,006	27,222
Huntington	599,992	141,548	7,132	630,308	142,147	7,161	536,504	147,074	7,446
Jackson	1,372,052	321,745	16,905	1,530,294	323,352	18,838	1,938,139	306,307	17,626
Jasper	446,566	137,314	7,392	437,901	144,715	7,808	411,144	138,459	8,213
Jay	363,974	66,097	3,386	369,436	73,211	3,645	350,334	78,365	4,381
Jefferson	581,613	102,368	5,289	644,681	102,671	5,337	666,501	107,442	5,511
Jennings	234,087	69,365	3,470	253,784	69,691	3,544	269,884	74,993	3,811
Johnson	1,494,418	415,035	21,735	1,628,024	454,489	23,999	1,429,773	522,452	27,357
Knox	792,491	164,138	8,939	823,846	170,190	9,142	820,901	173,293	9,491
Kosciusko	1,551,852	402,898	20,986	1,422,162	420,442	22,292	1,229,092	335,178	18,283
Lagrange	616,427	129,628	6,788	736,881	136,659	7,155	904,841	142,433	7,498
Lake	10,364,548	4,234,985	153,565	8,980,969	2,840,129	153,533	9,102,723	2,921,738	160,924
Laporte	2,407,652	424,394	22,881	2,435,158	413,052	23,394	2,579,291	443,842	24,731
Lawrence	402,764	147,207	7,876	422,373	163,145	8,442	447,110	155,420	8,315
Madison	2,491,232	591,319	34,524	2,732,992	611,189	33,434	2,606,685	581,131	31,221
Marion	39,035,660	9,233,109	511,261	40,401,770	9,438,286	528,128	41,138,149	10,028,614	554,831
Marshall	925,377	162,668	8,499	904,772	177,181	8,877	889,117	184,358	9,317
Martin	77,839	32,915	1,656	81,340	31,704	1,598	87,671	31,217	1,606
Miami	262,379	95,349	5,119	290,322	106,993	5,344	324,107	111,517	5,785
Monroe	1,638,811	563,632	29,698	1,641,897	588,797	30,714	1,734,453	595,873	31,753
Montgomery	1,160,392	164,972	9,452	1,159,740	168,430	9,515	1,192,185	171,007	9,751
Morgan	406,525	202,877	10,631	440,216	223,313	11,482	463,760	231,897	12,785
Newton	131,988	30,971	1,484	139,369	31,930	1,495	132,113	30,264	1,564
Noble	817,199	125,592	6,457	856,482	133,947	8,903	1,001,567	138,690	7,147
Ohio	14,930	7,431	375	14,645	7,525	369	17,756	10,100	1,228
Orange	303,410	62,638	3,510	319,193	65,368	3,683	332,239	67,812	3,830
Owen	91,458	34,963	1,850	95,966	40,333	2,004	226,036	150,647	2,117
Parke	85,410	46,676	2,494	91,515	49,568	2,502	94,335	52,718	2,614
Perry	253,984	78,560	4,143	280,708	81,879	4,342	293,349	89,339	5,199
Pike	84,578	17,791	856	86,015	19,015	944	108,112	20,744	1,056
Porter	2,874,861	527,952	28,684	2,826,828	543,076	28,787	2,925,075	587,997	31,084
Posey	491,980	61,212	3,605	496,841	64,739	3,764	657,532	77,389	4,134
Pulaski	265,540	61,241	3,143	278,124	71,230	3,642	275,525	70,333	3,674
Putnam	332,362	97,342	4,993	359,469	104,888	5,227	399,984	110,922	5,581
Randolph	391,127	81,961	4,154	421,862	82,052	4,212	445,155	88,762	4,472
Ripley	360,514	135,698	7,227	353,289	136,589	7,452	361,076	140,029	7,775
Rush	288,868	67,802	3,459	278,274	71,844	3,624	310,485	76,193	4,040
St. Joseph	5,575,406	1,134,557	62,773	5,896,230	1,172,201	64,208	5,949,747	1,267,357	69,509
Scott	374,720	76,094	3,881	377,811	79,406	4,010	392,256	80,063	4,091
Shelby	789,853	183,327	9,463	814,139	183,490	9,587	786,131	176,625	9,302
Spencer	222,855	52,841	2,678	233,394	68,187	2,870	250,775	59,612	3,019
Starke	189,249	68,309	3,424	187,677	87,529	3,371	212,698	68,654	3,469
Steuben	723,009	167,792	8,412	671,874	184,858	8,177	796,786	200,942	10,399
Sullivan	215,733	57,627	3,019	251,854	60,837	3,051	190,589	53,718	2,901
Switzerland	36,664	13,441	667	40,170	14,267	721	40,950	14,641	744
Tippecanoe	4,750,598	631,136	32,840	5,376,122	671,181	34,521	5,768,873	672,553	34,840
Tipton	269,864	63,896	3,215	269,815	62,711	3,324	318,748	63,455	3,351
Union	52,607	17,051	897	50,969	16,429	854	49,248	16,610	868
Vanderburgh	6,189,541	1,294,685	72,904	5,494,680	1,305,328	72,138	5,940,383	1,409,325	77,203
Vermillion	357,734	62,613	3,357	278,282	63,337	3,524	316,476	72,301	3,789
Vigo	1,972,300	495,206	26,534	2,181,841	512,599	27,823	1,922,074	500,948	27,467
Wabash	521,538	140,910	7,964	486,590	140,337	8,587	539,720	141,697	8,715
Warren	91,238	16,739	940	89,250	18,771	1,007	93,168	21,410	1,091
Warrick	414,606	102,487	5,233	402,394	104,708	5,345	427,345	108,283	5,582
Washington	301,554	75,075	3,808	305,895	79,190	4,007	322,716	80,099	4,109
Wayne	1,649,661	474,245	23,698	1,799,203	504,754	24,851	1,681,762	503,579	25,415
Wells	559,279	84,941	4,343	585,538	90,845	4,620	594,371	90,078	4,696
White	646,578	119,405	6,057	822,213	122,786	6,233	683,481	134,642	6,939
Whitley	709,062	115,555	6,360	597,652	119,984	8,466	622,554	125,902	6,950

Footnote: County figures do not sum to state totals because state figures include sales and tax remitted from out-of-state corporations doing business in Indiana. Sales tax remitted includes prior years and penalties.
Source: Indiana Department of Revenue
EDIN table(s): RSTX

SECTION 3

Indiana Counties in Profile

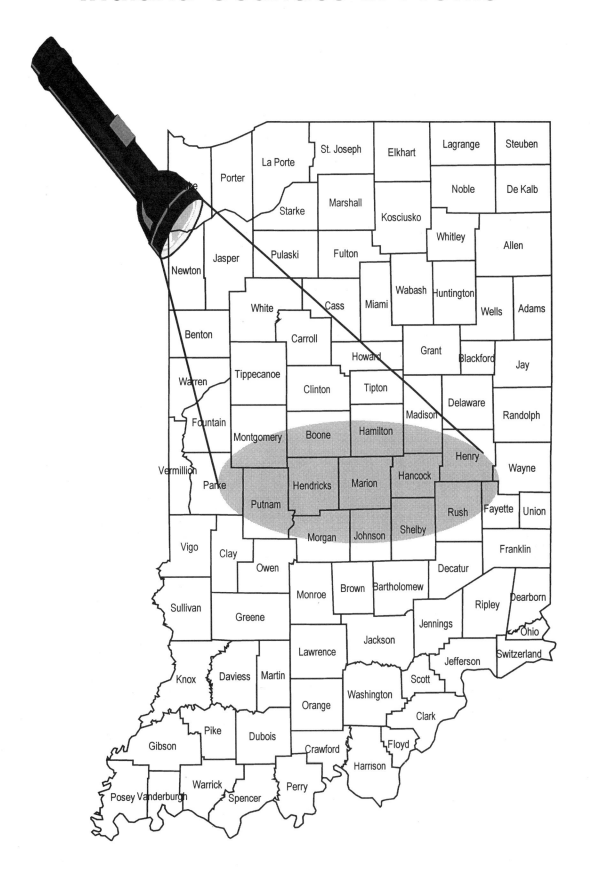

INdiANA

Population 1997 (Est.)	5,864,108	# Households 1995 (Projection)	2,102,500	Personal Income 1995 ($000)	$90,885,424
Land Area (Sq. Mi.)	35,870.1	% Family	71.9%	Avg. Wage Per Job 1995	$25,005
Population Density 1997	163.5	% Non-Family	28.1%	Employed in 1996	2,945,300
% Under 20 1996	28.6%	% Living Alone	23.9%	Unemployed in 1996	126,700
% 65 & Over 1996	12.6%	Births 1995	82,944	Unemployment Rate 1996	4.1%
% White 1996	90.7%	Births to Teens 1995	12,193	Avg. Covered Payroll 1996 ($000)	$17,816,712
% African-Amer. 1996	8.2%	Deaths 1995	53,053	Average Weekly Earnings in Manufacturing 1996	$698.75
% Hispanic* 1996	2.2%	Marriages 1995	50,628	Registered Vehicles 1996	5,347,748

*May be of any race.

Percent of Total Population By Sex and Age

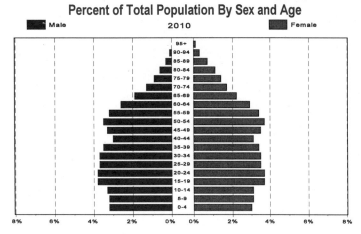

Male — 2010 — Female

Population Projections

Age Groups	2000	2010	% Change
0-17	1,441,970	1,370,840	-4.9%
18-24	634,730	611,820	-3.6%
25-39	1,198,450	1,236,790	3.2%
40-59	1,498,250	1,549,600	3.4%
60-74	607,630	743,290	22.3%
75 +	322,010	325,260	1.0%
Total	5,703,000	5,837,600	2.4%

Personal Income
Real 1995 Dollars ($000)

	1990	1995	% Chg.
Total Earnings by Place of Work	79,713,016	90,885,424	14.0%
Less Personal Contributions for Social Insurance	5,167,727	6,143,375	18.9%
Net Income by Place of Work	74,545,288	84,742,049	13.7%
Plus Residence Adjustment	1,727,477	2,253,042	30.4%
Net Income by Place of Residence	76,272,765	86,995,091	14.1%
Plus Dividends, Rent and Interest	19,212,631	19,257,888	0.2%
Plus Transfer Payments	15,316,834	18,477,338	20.6%
Personal Income by Place of Residence	110,802,230	124,730,317	12.6%
Per Capita Income ($)	19,947	21,517	7.9%
Rank	NA	NA	NA

Educational Attainment 1990

Graduate or Prof. Degree
Bachelor's Degree
Associate Degree
Some College No Degree
High School Graduate
9th-12th No Diploma
Less than 9th Grade

0   500,000   1,000,000   1,500,000

High School Grad or Higher
Percent: 76%

Population Change by Decade
(1990-2000 projected)

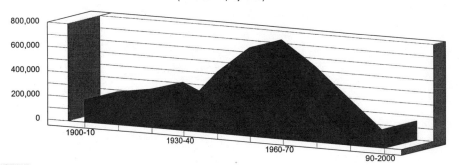

800,000
600,000
400,000
200,000
0

1900-10   1930-40   1960-70   90-2000

For EDIN tables, sources and footnotes, see page 380.

Occupation of Employed Persons Age 16 & Over

	1990	% Chg. 80-90
Managerial & Professional	586,305	30.9
Technical, Sales & Admin. Support	778,109	18.7
Service Occupations	348,349	13.3
Farming, Forestry and Fishing	59,132	-10.5
Precision Production, Craft & Repair	338,548	2.6
Operators, Fabricators	518,252	-7.4

Top 5 Counties Commuting in 1990

From Indiana Into:		Into Indiana From:	
Illinois	52,424	Illinois	21,895
Kentucky	39,608	Michigan	21,467
Ohio	17,805	Kentucky	18,720
Michigan	6,244	Ohio	14,328

2,462,256 persons lived and worked in this county.
124,926 lived in the county but worked elsewhere.

Number of Establishments
(% Change 1990-1995)

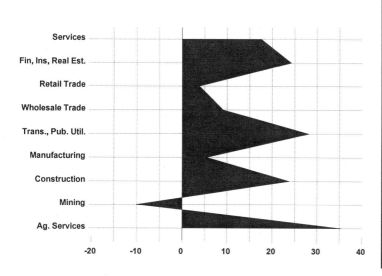

Establishments by Sector 1995

Industry	Number of Establishments	% with fewer than 10 employees
Ag. Services	2,136	85.5%
Mining	381	58.5%
Construction	15,286	80.7%
Manufacturing	9,591	40.8%
Transportation, Public Utilities	6,374	67.8%
Wholesale Trade	10,636	67.8%
Retail Trade	34,845	64.1%
Finance, Insurance, Real Estate	12,597	81.4%
Services	48,162	77.7%

Private Industry	Employment		Real Earnings ($000)		Average Earnings Per Job	
	1995	% Chg. 90-95	1995	Real % Chg. 90-95	1995	Real % Chg. 90-95
Ag. Services	27,692	26.7%	407,984	25.2%	14,733	-1.2%
Mining	10,184	-17.3%	343,054	-24.6%	33,686	-8.8%
Construction	188,740	14.2%	5,654,537	14.8%	29,959	0.6%
Manufacturing	696,635	7.9%	29,695,708	15.5%	42,627	7.0%
Transportation, Public Utilities	164,362	7.6%	5,699,848	8.0%	34,679	0.4%
Wholesale Trade	147,336	9.9%	5,177,525	14.3%	35,141	4.0%
Retail Trade	626,545	14.2%	8,471,084	14.4%	13,520	0.2%
Finance, Insurance, Real Estate	199,269	5.1%	4,721,068	22.3%	23,692	16.3%
Services	855,753	16.8%	19,340,517	23.2%	22,601	5.5%

For EDIN tables, sources and footnotes, see page 380.

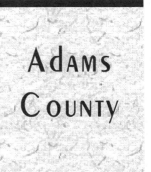

Adams County

Population 1997 (Est.)	32,837	# Households 1995 (Projection)	10,800	Personal Income 1995 ($000)	$401,384
Land Area (Sq. Mi.)	339.4	% Family	77.5%	Avg. Wage Per Job 1995	$20,092
Population Density 1997	96.8	% Non-Family	22.7%	Employed in 1996	15,740
% Under 20 1996	33.7%	% Living Alone	20.7%	Unemployed in 1996	660
% 65 & Over 1996	13.6%	Births 1995	623	Unemployment Rate 1996	4.0%
% White 1996	99.4%	Births to Teens 1995	50	Avg. Covered Payroll 1996 ($000)	$74,673
% African-Amer. 1996	0.1%	Deaths 1995	297	Average Weekly Earnings in Manufacturing 1996	$529.00
% Hispanic* 1996	3.4%	Marriages 1995	269	Registered Vehicles 1996	29,243

*May be of any race.

Percent of Total Population By Sex and Age

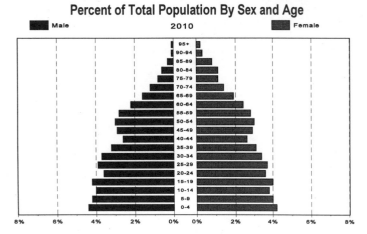

Male   2010   Female

Population Projections

Age Groups	2000	2010	% Change
0-17	10,310	10,890	5.6%
18-24	3,830	3,830	0.0%
25-39	6,500	7,740	19.1%
40-59	7,720	8,330	7.9%
60-74	3,100	3,970	28.1%
75 +	2,150	1,990	-7.4%
Total	33,600	36,700	9.2%

Personal Income
Real 1995 Dollars ($000)

	1990	1995	% Chg.
Total Earnings by Place of Work	364,910	401,384	10.0%
Less Personal Contributions for Social Insurance	22,763	27,013	18.7%
Net Income by Place of Work	342,147	374,371	9.4%
Plus Residence Adjustment	31,488	65,205	107.1%
Net Income by Place of Residence	373,635	439,576	17.6%
Plus Dividends, Rent and Interest	114,412	107,121	-6.4%
Plus Transfer Payments	70,464	84,778	20.3%
Personal Income by Place of Residence	558,511	631,475	13.1%
Per Capita Income ($)	17,930	19,479	8.6%
Rank	47	41	32

Educational Attainment 1990

Graduate or Prof. Degree
Bachelor's Degree
Associate Degree
Some College No Degree
High School Graduate
9th-12th No Diploma
Less than 9th Grade

0   2,000   4,000   6,000   8,000   10,000

High School Grad or Higher
Percent: 74%
Rank in State: 40

Population Change by Decade
(1990-2000 projected)

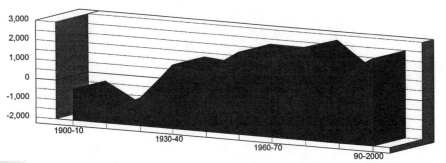

1900-10   1930-40   1960-70   90-2000

For EDIN tables, sources and footnotes, see page 380.

Occupation of Employed Persons Age 16 & Over

	1990	% Chg. 80-90
Managerial & Professional	2,369	37.3
Technical, Sales & Admin. Support	3,333	32.8
Service Occupations	1,764	22.7
Farming, Forestry and Fishing	707	-23.9
Precision Production, Craft & Repair	2,169	10.7
Operators, Fabricators	3,779	0.9

Top 5 Counties Commuting in 1990

From Adams Into:		Into Adams From:	
Allen	2,180	Jay	1,298
Wells	599	Outside Indiana	1,071
Outside Indiana	315	Allen	623
Jay	182	Wells	434
Huntington	33	Blackford	198

10,329 persons lived and worked in this county.
3,450 lived in the county but worked elsewhere.

Number of Establishments
(% Change 1990-1995)

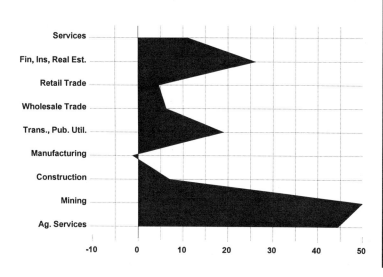

Establishments by Sector 1995

Industry	Number of Establishments	% with fewer than 10 employees
Ag. Services	13	92.3%
Mining	3	33.3%
Construction	76	78.9%
Manufacturing	78	30.8%
Transportation, Public Utilities	25	64.0%
Wholesale Trade	51	78.4%
Retail Trade	203	68.5%
Finance, Insurance, Real Estate	58	84.5%
Services	212	89.2%

Private Industry	Employment		Real Earnings ($000)		Average Earnings Per Job	
	1995	% Chg. 90-95	1995	Real % Chg. 90-95	1995	Real % Chg. 90-95
Ag. Services	203	62.4%	4,319	78.6%	21,276	10.0%
Mining	NA	NA	NA	NA	NA	NA
Construction	1,283	NA	24,430	NA	19,041	NA
Manufacturing	6,884	14.6%	212,850	16.9%	30,920	2.1%
Transportation, Public Utilities	411	7.0%	10,716	6.8%	26,073	-0.2%
Wholesale Trade	NA	NA	NA	NA	NA	NA
Retail Trade	3,412	25.9%	39,751	26.1%	11,650	0.2%
Finance, Insurance, Real Estate	705	13.2%	7,862	22.2%	11,152	8.0%
Services	2,855	16.6%	36,978	8.5%	12,952	-6.9%

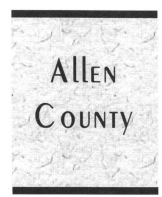

Allen County

Population 1997 (Est.)	312,091	# Households 1995 (Projection)	116,300	Personal Income 1995 ($000)	$6,412,192
Land Area (Sq. Mi.)	657.3	% Family	70.8%	Avg. Wage Per Job 1995	$26,488
Population Density 1997	474.8	% Non-Family	29.3%	Employed in 1996	167,520
% Under 20 1996	29.7%	% Living Alone	24.6%	Unemployed in 1996	6,140
% 65 & Over 1996	11.4%	Births 1995	4,933	Unemployment Rate 1996	3.5%
% White 1996	87.5%	Births to Teens 1995	651	Avg. Covered Payroll 1996 ($000)	$1,234,727
% African-Amer. 1996	11.0%	Deaths 1995	2,425	Average Weekly Earnings in Manufacturing 1996	$762.25
% Hispanic* 1996	2.5%	Marriages 1995	2,723	Registered Vehicles 1996	283,265

*May be of any race.

Percent of Total Population By Sex and Age

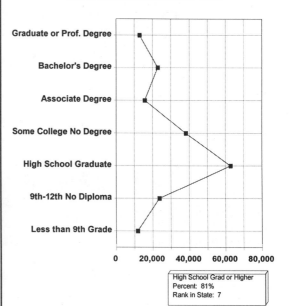

Population Projections

Age Groups	2000	2010	% Change
0-17	85,850	80,640	-6.1%
18-24	31,620	33,370	5.5%
25-39	65,750	65,200	-0.8%
40-59	85,480	91,400	6.9%
60-74	30,580	40,270	31.7%
75 +	15,920	16,470	3.5%
Total	315,200	327,400	3.9%

Personal Income
Real 1995 Dollars ($000)

	1990	1995	% Chg.
Total Earnings by Place of Work	5,736,276	6,412,192	11.8%
Less Personal Contributions for Social Insurance	380,589	435,831	14.5%
Net Income by Place of Work	5,355,687	5,976,361	11.6%
Plus Residence Adjustment	-576,519	-664,904	15.3%
Net Income by Place of Residence	4,779,169	5,311,457	11.1%
Plus Dividends, Rent and Interest	1,304,287	1,261,398	-3.3%
Plus Transfer Payments	750,353	935,917	24.7%
Personal Income by Place of Residence	6,833,809	7,508,772	9.9%
Per Capita Income ($)	22,678	24,339	7.3%
Rank	4	4	50

Educational Attainment 1990

High School Grad or Higher
Percent: 81%
Rank in State: 7

Population Change by Decade
(1990-2000 projected)

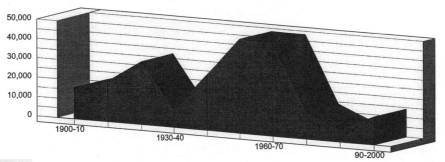

For EDIN tables, sources and footnotes, see page 380.

Occupation of Employed Persons Age 16 & Over

	1990	% Chg. 80-90
Managerial & Professional	39,889	34.8
Technical, Sales & Admin. Support	49,952	15.9
Service Occupations	18,626	5.8
Farming, Forestry and Fishing	1,275	-17.5
Precision Production, Craft & Repair	17,369	1.2
Operators, Fabricators	25,193	-1.4

Top 5 Counties Commuting in 1990

From Allen Into:		Into Allen From:	
Huntington	2,047	Outside Indiana	5,243
Outside Indiana	1,925	Whitley	3,970
Whitley	1,691	Wells	3,218
Dekalb	1,339	Dekalb	2,917
Noble	784	Huntington	2,485

139,681 persons lived and worked in this county.
10,619 lived in the county but worked elsewhere.

Number of Establishments
(% Change 1990-1995)

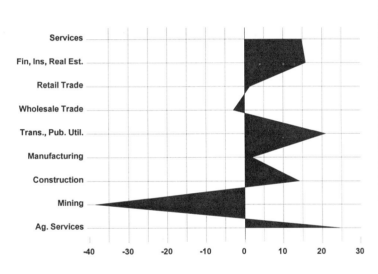

Establishments by Sector 1995

Industry	Number of Establishments	% with fewer than 10 employees
Ag. Services	142	83.1%
Mining	8	62.5%
Construction	895	75.5%
Manufacturing	588	39.5%
Transportation, Public Utilities	318	57.9%
Wholesale Trade	765	62.5%
Retail Trade	1,960	58.3%
Finance, Insurance, Real Estate	827	79.6%
Services	2,987	72.0%

Private Industry	Employment		Real Earnings ($000)		Average Earnings Per Job	
	1995	% Chg. 90-95	1995	Real % Chg. 90-95	1995	Real % Chg. 90-95
Ag. Services	1,716	18.8%	26,557	19.5%	15,476	0.6%
Mining	244	-13.8%	5,789	-3.8%	23,725	11.6%
Construction	12,468	8.9%	388,924	12.0%	31,194	2.9%
Manufacturing	41,259	9.9%	2,016,250	16.2%	48,868	5.8%
Transportation, Public Utilities	12,837	-5.8%	545,737	15.2%	42,513	22.4%
Wholesale Trade	13,873	4.0%	469,829	5.9%	33,866	1.8%
Retail Trade	39,628	3.9%	535,212	1.5%	13,506	-2.4%
Finance, Insurance, Real Estate	17,378	-4.0%	501,562	6.3%	28,862	10.7%
Services	62,164	20.5%	1,406,068	14.6%	22,619	-4.8%

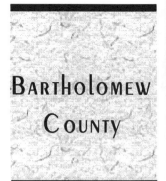

BARTHOLOMEW COUNTY

Population 1997 (Est.)	68,734	# Households 1995 (Projection)	24,600	Personal Income 1995 ($000)	$1,540,769
Land Area (Sq. Mi.)	406.9	% Family	75.0%	Avg. Wage Per Job 1995	$28,519
Population Density 1997	168.9	% Non-Family	24.9%	Employed in 1996	38,410
% Under 20 1996	27.5%	% Living Alone	21.7%	Unemployed in 1996	1,120
% 65 & Over 1996	11.5%	Births 1995	1,024	Unemployment Rate 1996	2.8%
% White 1996	96.8%	Births to Teens 1995	155	Avg. Covered Payroll 1996 ($000)	$307,865
% African-Amer. 1996	1.8%	Deaths 1995	585	Average Weekly Earnings in Manufacturing 1996	$765.75
% Hispanic* 1996	0.9%	Marriages 1995	729	Registered Vehicles 1996	68,801

*May be of any race.

Percent of Total Population By Sex and Age

Male 2010 Female

8% 6% 4% 2% 0% 0% 2% 4% 6% 8%

95+ 90-94 85-89 80-84 75-79 70-74 65-69 60-64 55-59 50-54 45-49 40-44 35-39 30-34 25-29 20-24 15-19 10-14 5-9 0-4

Population Projections

Age Groups	2000	2010	% Change
0-17	16,020	14,520	-9.4%
18-24	6,100	6,400	4.9%
25-39	12,750	12,810	0.5%
40-59	18,800	17,930	-4.6%
60-74	7,630	9,980	30.8%
75 +	3,440	3,830	11.3%
Total	64,800	65,500	1.1%

Personal Income
Real 1995 Dollars ($000)

	1990	1995	% Chg.
Total Earnings by Place of Work	1,198,485	1,540,769	28.6%
Less Personal Contributions for Social Insurance	77,788	102,066	31.2%
Net Income by Place of Work	1,120,696	1,438,703	28.4%
Plus Residence Adjustment	-163,709	-258,300	57.8%
Net Income by Place of Residence	956,987	1,180,403	23.3%
Plus Dividends, Rent and Interest	247,387	262,243	6.0%
Plus Transfer Payments	155,119	191,691	23.6%
Personal Income by Place of Residence	1,359,494	1,634,337	20.2%
Per Capita Income ($)	21,298	24,047	12.9%
Rank	11	5	6

Educational Attainment 1990

Graduate or Prof. Degree
Bachelor's Degree
Associate Degree
Some College No Degree
High School Graduate
9th-12th No Diploma
Less than 9th Grade

0 4,000 8,000 12,000 16,000

High School Grad or Higher
Percent: 77%
Rank in State: 22

Population Change by Decade
(1990-2000 projected)

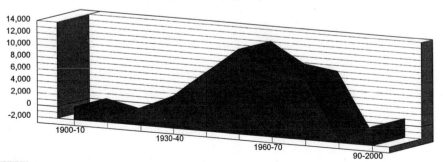

14,000 12,000 10,000 8,000 6,000 4,000 2,000 0 -2,000

1900-10 1930-40 1960-70 90-2000

Occupation of Employed Persons Age 16 & Over

	1990	% Chg. 80-90
Managerial & Professional	7,957	25.0
Technical, Sales & Admin. Support	8,861	14.4
Service Occupations	4,006	16.4
Farming, Forestry and Fishing	614	-16.9
Precision Production, Craft & Repair	4,138	6.8
Operators, Fabricators	5,888	-9.1

Top 5 Counties Commuting in 1990

From Bartholomew Into:		Into Bartholomew From:	
Johnson	1,402	Jennings	2,193
Marion	890	Jackson	1,950
Jackson	577	Brown	962
Jennings	240	Johnson	898
Outside Indiana	236	Decatur	893

26,455   persons lived and worked in this county.

4,310   lived in the county but worked elsewhere.

Number of Establishments
(% Change 1990-1995)

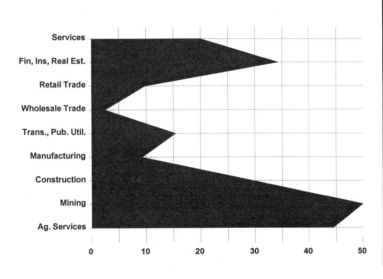

Establishments by Sector 1995

Industry	Number of Establishments	% with fewer than 10 employees
Ag. Services	26	88.5%
Mining	3	66.7%
Construction	214	83.6%
Manufacturing	142	33.1%
Transportation, Public Utilities	105	60.0%
Wholesale Trade	123	67.5%
Retail Trade	449	66.4%
Finance, Insurance, Real Estate	184	81.0%
Services	661	77.9%

Private Industry	Employment		Real Earnings ($000)		Average Earnings Per Job	
	1995	% Chg. 90-95	1995	Real % Chg. 90-95	1995	Real % Chg. 90-95
Ag. Services	224	16.7%	2,502	0.4%	11,170	-14.0%
Mining	56	-37.1%	2,537	-44.7%	45,304	-12.1%
Construction	2,589	27.5%	65,568	22.4%	25,326	-4.0%
Manufacturing	17,547	24.9%	844,149	37.4%	48,108	10.1%
Transportation, Public Utilities	1,742	-13.3%	58,332	-2.7%	33,486	12.3%
Wholesale Trade	1,191	12.7%	38,040	30.9%	31,940	16.2%
Retail Trade	7,896	12.5%	108,694	22.2%	13,766	8.6%
Finance, Insurance, Real Estate	2,749	11.8%	79,810	19.3%	29,032	6.6%
Services	9,319	16.9%	199,960	32.4%	21,457	13.2%

BENTON COUNTY

Population 1997 (Est.)	9,557	# Households 1995 (Projection)	3,400	Personal Income 1995 ($000)	$57,408
Land Area (Sq. Mi.)	406.3	% Family	74.4%	Avg. Wage Per Job 1995	$17,763
Population Density 1997	23.5	% Non-Family	26.5%	Employed in 1996	5,145
% Under 20 1996	29.2%	% Living Alone	24.1%	Unemployed in 1996	230
% 65 & Over 1996	17.0%	Births 1995	132	Unemployment Rate 1996	4.2%
% White 1996	99.7%	Births to Teens 1995	21	Avg. Covered Payroll 1996 ($000)	$12,672
% African-Amer. 1996	0.1%	Deaths 1995	97	Average Weekly Earnings in Manufacturing 1996	$389.25
% Hispanic* 1996	1.4%	Marriages 1995	82	Registered Vehicles 1996	10,476

*May be of any race.

Percent of Total Population By Sex and Age

■ Male   2010   ■ Female

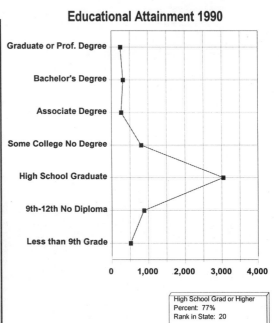

Population Projections

Age Groups	2000	2010	% Change
0-17	2,590	2,570	-0.8%
18-24	1,050	980	-6.7%
25-39	1,600	2,010	25.6%
40-59	2,360	2,300	-2.5%
60-74	1,090	1,190	9.2%
75 +	750	690	-8.0%
Total	9,500	9,700	2.1%

Personal Income
Real 1995 Dollars ($000)

	1990	1995	% Chg.
Total Earnings by Place of Work	67,229	57,408	-14.6%
Less Personal Contributions for Social Insurance	4,110	5,344	30.0%
Net Income by Place of Work	63,120	52,064	-17.5%
Plus Residence Adjustment	43,034	52,382	21.7%
Net Income by Place of Residence	106,153	104,446	-1.6%
Plus Dividends, Rent and Interest	40,613	32,525	-19.9%
Plus Transfer Payments	26,914	32,115	19.3%
Personal Income by Place of Residence	173,680	169,086	-2.6%
Per Capita Income ($)	18,368	17,408	-5.2%
Rank	37	63	90

Educational Attainment 1990

(Chart: values for Graduate or Prof. Degree, Bachelor's Degree, Associate Degree, Some College No Degree, High School Graduate, 9th-12th No Diploma, Less than 9th Grade; x-axis 0 to 4,000)

High School Grad or Higher
Percent: 77%
Rank in State: 20

Population Change by Decade
(1990-2000 projected)

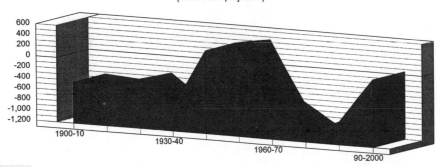

(y-axis: 600, 400, 200, 0, -200, -400, -600, -800, -1,000, -1,200; x-axis: 1900-10, 1930-40, 1960-70, 90-2000)

For EDIN tables, sources and footnotes, see page 380.

Occupation of Employed Persons Age 16 & Over

	1990	% Chg. 80-90
Managerial & Professional	719	41.5
Technical, Sales & Admin. Support	1,040	2.6
Service Occupations	622	16.3
Farming, Forestry and Fishing	540	-17.1
Precision Production, Craft & Repair	574	-5.9
Operators, Fabricators	934	-14.7

Top 5 Counties Commuting in 1990

From Benton Into:		Into Benton From:	
Tippecanoe	1,284	Tippecanoe	230
Newton	309	Warren	153
Outside Indiana	139	Outside Indiana	48
Jasper	88	Newton	48
White	38	Fountain	28

2,353 persons lived and worked in this county.

1,983 lived in the county but worked elsewhere.

Number of Establishments
(% Change 1990-1995)

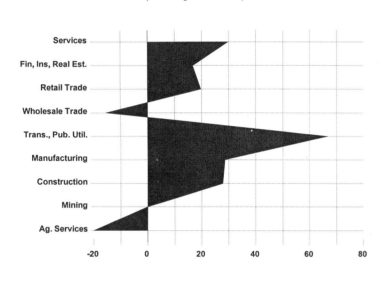

Establishments by Sector 1995

Industry	Number of Establishments	% with fewer than 10 employees
Ag. Services	4	100.0%
Mining	0	NA
Construction	23	91.3%
Manufacturing	18	38.9%
Transportation, Public Utilities	20	80.0%
Wholesale Trade	33	69.7%
Retail Trade	73	83.6%
Finance, Insurance, Real Estate	21	85.7%
Services	74	87.8%

Private Industry	Employment		Real Earnings ($000)		Average Earnings Per Job	
	1995	% Chg. 90-95	1995	Real % Chg. 90-95	1995	Real % Chg. 90-95
Ag. Services	63	23.5%	663	-12.5%	10,524	-29.2%
Mining	0	NA	0	NA	NA	NA
Construction	168	58.5%	2,508	2.8%	14,929	-35.1%
Manufacturing	616	35.4%	17,671	70.2%	28,687	25.7%
Transportation, Public Utilities	186	39.8%	5,818	70.7%	31,280	22.1%
Wholesale Trade	NA	NA	NA	NA	NA	NA
Retail Trade	584	16.6%	6,055	14.1%	10,368	-2.1%
Finance, Insurance, Real Estate	245	13.4%	3,585	11.8%	14,633	-1.4%
Services	NA	NA	NA	NA	NA	NA

For EDIN tables, sources and footnotes, see page 380.

Blackford County

Population 1997 (Est.)	14,020	# Households 1995 (Projection)	5,300	Personal Income 1995 ($000)	$119,670
Land Area (Sq. Mi.)	165.1	% Family	74.2%	Avg. Wage Per Job 1995	$20,411
Population Density 1997	84.9	% Non-Family	25.7%	Employed in 1996	5,995
% Under 20 1996	27.0%	% Living Alone	23.4%	Unemployed in 1996	355
% 65 & Over 1996	15.4%	Births 1995	171	Unemployment Rate 1996	5.6%
% White 1996	99.5%	Births to Teens 1995	30	Avg. Covered Payroll 1996 ($000)	$23,522
% African-Amer. 1996	0.1%	Deaths 1995	146	Average Weekly Earnings in Manufacturing 1996	$506.75
% Hispanic* 1996	0.7%	Marriages 1995	134	Registered Vehicles 1996	14,356

*May be of any race.

Percent of Total Population By Sex and Age

Male — 2010 — Female

(Population pyramid chart with age groups from 0-4 to 95+, scale 8% to 8%)

Population Projections

Age Groups	2000	2010	% Change
0-17	3,330	3,040	-8.7%
18-24	1,280	1,320	3.1%
25-39	2,630	2,690	2.3%
40-59	3,590	3,410	-5.0%
60-74	1,780	2,000	12.4%
75 +	960	900	-6.2%
Total	13,600	13,400	-1.5%

Personal Income
Real 1995 Dollars ($000)

	1990	1995	% Chg.
Total Earnings by Place of Work	125,006	119,670	-4.3%
Less Personal Contributions for Social Insurance	8,157	8,581	5.2%
Net Income by Place of Work	116,849	111,089	-4.9%
Plus Residence Adjustment	37,280	45,400	21.8%
Net Income by Place of Residence	154,129	156,489	1.5%
Plus Dividends, Rent and Interest	33,656	30,089	-10.6%
Plus Transfer Payments	42,216	49,129	16.4%
Personal Income by Place of Residence	230,002	235,707	2.5%
Per Capita Income ($)	16,341	16,764	2.6%
Rank	70	75	81

Educational Attainment 1990

(Chart showing educational attainment levels: Graduate or Prof. Degree, Bachelor's Degree, Associate Degree, Some College No Degree, High School Graduate, 9th-12th No Diploma, Less than 9th Grade; scale 0 to 5,000)

High School Grad or Higher
Percent: 73%
Rank in State: 52

Population Change by Decade
(1990-2000 projected)

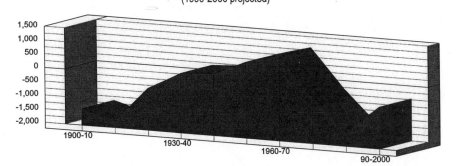

(3D area chart, scale -2,000 to 1,500, decades from 1900-10 to 90-2000)

For EDIN tables, sources and footnotes, see page 380.

Occupation of Employed Persons Age 16 & Over			Top 5 Counties Commuting in 1990				
	1990	% Chg. 80-90	From Blackford Into:		Into Blackford From:		
Managerial & Professional	1,037	16.4	Delaware	641	Delaware	317	
Technical, Sales & Admin. Support	1,425	4.3	Grant	614	Grant	257	
Service Occupations	783	6.4	Wells	392	Jay	210	
Farming, Forestry and Fishing	244	-3.9	Jay	234	Wells	138	
Precision Production, Craft & Repair	786	-19.5	Adams	198	Allen	30	
Operators, Fabricators	2,156	5.7					

3,875 persons lived and worked in this county.

2,367 lived in the county but worked elsewhere.

Number of Establishments
(% Change 1990-1995)

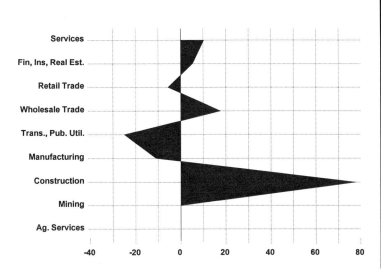

Establishments by Sector 1995		
Industry	Number of Establishments	% with fewer than 10 employees
Ag. Services	2	100.0%
Mining	2	100.0%
Construction	16	87.5%
Manufacturing	33	30.3%
Transportation, Public Utilities	9	88.9%
Wholesale Trade	20	80.0%
Retail Trade	84	72.6%
Finance, Insurance, Real Estate	20	75.0%
Services	96	87.5%

Private Industry	Employment		Real Earnings ($000)		Average Earnings Per Job	
	1995	% Chg. 90-95	1995	Real % Chg. 90-95	1995	Real % Chg. 90-95
Ag. Services	54	5.9%	503	26.3%	9,315	19.3%
Mining	11	NA	382	110.9%	34,727	NA
Construction	204	19.3%	4,474	57.1%	21,931	31.7%
Manufacturing	1,887	-10.9%	57,215	-11.0%	30,321	-0.1%
Transportation, Public Utilities	156	13.0%	4,015	25.5%	25,737	11.0%
Wholesale Trade	136	-9.9%	3,142	0.6%	23,103	11.7%
Retail Trade	896	-8.8%	9,947	-6.8%	11,102	2.2%
Finance, Insurance, Real Estate	230	-9.1%	3,568	0.3%	15,513	10.3%
Services	1,010	3.4%	14,842	13.9%	14,695	10.1%

For EDIN tables, sources and footnotes, see page 380.

Boone County

Population 1997 (Est.)	42,985	# Households 1995 (Projection)	14,100	Personal Income 1995 ($000)	$392,906
Land Area (Sq. Mi.)	422.7	% Family	78.2%	Avg. Wage Per Job 1995	$21,168
Population Density 1997	101.7	% Non-Family	22.0%	Employed in 1996	22,780
% Under 20 1996	28.4%	% Living Alone	19.4%	Unemployed in 1996	540
% 65 & Over 1996	12.9%	Births 1995	544	Unemployment Rate 1996	2.3%
% White 1996	99.2%	Births to Teens 1995	53	Avg. Covered Payroll 1996 ($000)	$68,112
% African-Amer. 1996	0.2%	Deaths 1995	376	Average Weekly Earnings in Manufacturing 1996	$535.25
% Hispanic* 1996	0.9%	Marriages 1995	317	Registered Vehicles 1996	43,459

*May be of any race.

Percent of Total Population By Sex and Age

2010 — Male / Female

(Age groups from 0-4 to 95+; horizontal axis 8% to 8%)

Population Projections

Age Groups	2000	2010	% Change
0-17	10,200	9,530	-6.6%
18-24	4,180	4,060	-2.9%
25-39	6,800	8,180	20.3%
40-59	12,070	10,970	-9.1%
60-74	4,310	6,080	41.1%
75 +	2,290	2,310	0.9%
Total	39,900	41,100	3.0%

Personal Income
Real 1995 Dollars ($000)

	1990	1995	% Chg.
Total Earnings by Place of Work	346,217	392,906	13.5%
Less Personal Contributions for Social Insurance	21,982	27,642	25.7%
Net Income by Place of Work	324,235	365,264	12.7%
Plus Residence Adjustment	333,815	447,514	34.1%
Net Income by Place of Residence	658,050	812,778	23.5%
Plus Dividends, Rent and Interest	171,596	206,828	20.5%
Plus Transfer Payments	86,017	106,766	24.1%
Personal Income by Place of Residence	915,663	1,126,372	23.0%
Per Capita Income ($)	23,914	26,963	12.8%
Rank	2	2	8

Educational Attainment 1990

(Chart categories: Graduate or Prof. Degree, Bachelor's Degree, Associate Degree, Some College No Degree, High School Graduate, 9th-12th No Diploma, Less than 9th Grade; horizontal axis 0 to 10,000)

High School Grad or Higher
Percent: 83%
Rank in State: 4

Population Change by Decade
(1990-2000 projected)

(Chart, vertical axis -2,000 to 6,000; horizontal axis decades 1900-10, 1930-40, 1960-70, 90-2000)

For EDIN tables, sources and footnotes, see page 380.

Occupation of Employed Persons Age 16 & Over

	1990	% Chg. 80-90
Managerial & Professional	5,068	38.0
Technical, Sales & Admin. Support	6,222	24.5
Service Occupations	2,346	17.4
Farming, Forestry and Fishing	779	-6.6
Precision Production, Craft & Repair	2,419	3.3
Operators, Fabricators	2,716	-3.4

Top 5 Counties Commuting in 1990

From Boone Into:		Into Boone From:	
Marion	7,521	Marion	1,159
Hamilton	1,297	Hamilton	481
Clinton	360	Clinton	410
Hendricks	313	Hendricks	301
Montgomery	291	Montgomery	243

8,770 persons lived and worked in this county.
10,458 lived in the county but worked elsewhere.

Number of Establishments
(% Change 1990-1995)

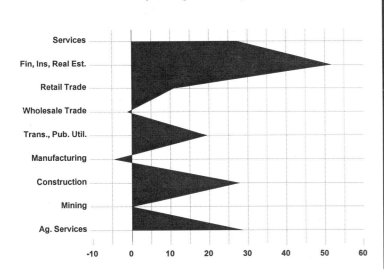

Establishments by Sector 1995

Industry	Number of Establishments	% with fewer than 10 employees
Ag. Services	36	83.3%
Mining	1	100.0%
Construction	175	83.4%
Manufacturing	64	56.2%
Transportation, Public Utilities	43	62.8%
Wholesale Trade	91	79.1%
Retail Trade	255	67.1%
Finance, Insurance, Real Estate	91	86.8%
Services	365	81.6%

Private Industry	Employment		Real Earnings ($000)		Average Earnings Per Job	
	1995	% Chg. 90-95	1995	Real % Chg. 90-95	1995	Real % Chg. 90-95
Ag. Services	NA	NA	NA	NA	NA	NA
Mining	NA	NA	NA	NA	NA	NA
Construction	2,021	29.6%	60,121	41.0%	29,748	8.8%
Manufacturing	1,977	-0.4%	58,566	-3.0%	29,624	-2.6%
Transportation, Public Utilities	638	17.7%	17,586	30.0%	27,564	10.4%
Wholesale Trade	1,001	19.0%	31,879	24.6%	31,847	4.7%
Retail Trade	3,616	14.1%	44,213	12.9%	12,227	-1.1%
Finance, Insurance, Real Estate	1,232	-2.5%	21,870	40.3%	17,752	43.9%
Services	4,806	8.5%	95,858	26.4%	19,945	16.5%

BROWN COUNTY

Population 1997 (Est.)	15,591	# Households 1995 (Projection)	5,700	Personal Income 1995 ($000)	$70,267
Land Area (Sq. Mi.)	312.3	% Family	76.0%	Avg. Wage Per Job 1995	$14,732
Population Density 1997	49.9	% Non-Family	24.6%	Employed in 1996	8,290
% Under 20 1996	26.0%	% Living Alone	21.1%	Unemployed in 1996	185
% 65 & Over 1996	12.6%	Births 1995	129	Unemployment Rate 1996	2.2%
% White 1996	99.3%	Births to Teens 1995	12	Avg. Covered Payroll 1996 ($000)	$10,577
% African-Amer. 1996	0.2%	Deaths 1995	123	Average Weekly Earnings in Manufacturing 1996	$310.75
% Hispanic* 1996	0.9%	Marriages 1995	302	Registered Vehicles 1996	16,297

*May be of any race.

Percent of Total Population By Sex and Age

■ Male   2010   ■ Female

(Population pyramid chart showing age groups from 0-4 to 95+, with scale from 8% to 0% to 8% for Male and Female)

Population Projections

Age Groups	2000	2010	% Change
0-17	3,120	2,800	-10.3%
18-24	1,460	1,230	-15.8%
25-39	2,530	2,940	16.2%
40-59	4,660	3,990	-14.4%
60-74	2,200	2,740	24.5%
75 +	960	1,220	27.1%
Total	14,900	14,900	0.0%

Personal Income
Real 1995 Dollars ($000)

	1990	1995	% Chg.
Total Earnings by Place of Work	64,911	70,267	8.3%
Less Personal Contributions for Social Insurance	4,174	4,901	17.4%
Net Income by Place of Work	60,737	65,366	7.6%
Plus Residence Adjustment	111,231	144,220	29.7%
Net Income by Place of Residence	171,969	209,586	21.9%
Plus Dividends, Rent and Interest	40,091	43,382	8.2%
Plus Transfer Payments	23,371	30,801	31.8%
Personal Income by Place of Residence	235,431	283,769	20.5%
Per Capita Income ($)	16,625	18,707	12.5%
Rank	66	51	10

Educational Attainment 1990

(Line chart showing educational attainment categories: Graduate or Prof. Degree, Bachelor's Degree, Associate Degree, Some College No Degree, High School Graduate, 9th-12th No Diploma, Less than 9th Grade; x-axis from 0 to 4,000)

High School Grad or Higher
Percent: 76%
Rank in State: 25

Population Change by Decade
(1990-2000 projected)

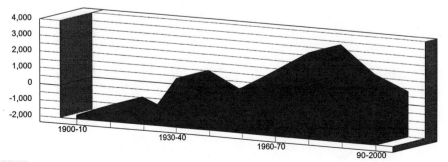

(Area chart showing population change by decade from 1900-10 to 90-2000, y-axis from -2,000 to 4,000)

Occupation of Employed Persons Age 16 & Over

	1990	% Chg. 80-90
Managerial & Professional	1,416	32.7
Technical, Sales & Admin. Support	1,836	37.9
Service Occupations	920	30.7
Farming, Forestry and Fishing	184	130.0
Precision Production, Craft & Repair	1,182	33.3
Operators, Fabricators	1,235	12.7

Top 5 Counties Commuting in 1990

From Brown Into:		Into Brown From:	
Marion	1,477	Bartholomew	168
Bartholomew	962	Monroe	124
Monroe	642	Morgan	60
Johnson	619	Johnson	52
Morgan	189	Marion	50

2,562 persons lived and worked in this county.
4,115 lived in the county but worked elsewhere.

Number of Establishments
(% Change 1990-1995)

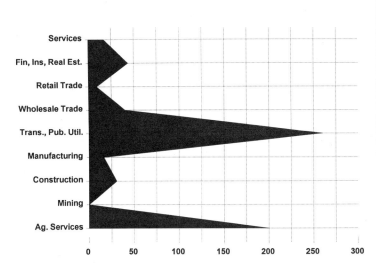

Establishments by Sector 1995

Industry	Number of Establishments	% with fewer than 10 employees
Ag. Services	3	100.0%
Mining	0	NA
Construction	47	97.9%
Manufacturing	21	85.7%
Transportation, Public Utilities	18	88.9%
Wholesale Trade	14	92.9%
Retail Trade	146	87.0%
Finance, Insurance, Real Estate	23	87.0%
Services	89	82.0%

Private Industry	Employment		Real Earnings ($000)		Average Earnings Per Job	
	1995	% Chg. 90-95	1995	Real % Chg. 90-95	1995	Real % Chg. 90-95
Ag. Services	70	55.6%	580	41.5%	8,286	-9.0%
Mining	NA	NA	142	-64.2%	NA	NA
Construction	481	5.3%	8,932	2.1%	18,570	-3.0%
Manufacturing	139	33.7%	3,885	0.4%	27,950	-24.9%
Transportation, Public Utilities	131	13.9%	3,127	61.8%	23,870	42.0%
Wholesale Trade	43	10.3%	790	-49.3%	18,372	-54.0%
Retail Trade	1,291	4.4%	14,241	9.0%	11,031	4.5%
Finance, Insurance, Real Estate	213	-7.0%	2,798	98.8%	13,136	113.8%
Services	1,465	0.5%	19,603	3.9%	13,381	3.4%

For EDIN tables, sources and footnotes, see page 380.

Carroll County

Population 1997 (Est.)	19,989	# Households 1995 (Projection)	7,100	Personal Income 1995 ($000)	$151,894
Land Area (Sq. Mi.)	372.3	% Family	75.6%	Avg. Wage Per Job 1995	$20,025
Population Density 1997	53.7	% Non-Family	23.9%	Employed in 1996	11,670
% Under 20 1996	28.0%	% Living Alone	21.7%	Unemployed in 1996	330
% 65 & Over 1996	14.9%	Births 1995	295	Unemployment Rate 1996	2.8%
% White 1996	99.8%	Births to Teens 1995	28	Avg. Covered Payroll 1996 ($000)	$26,962
% African-Amer. 1996	0.1%	Deaths 1995	161	Average Weekly Earnings in Manufacturing 1996	$479.00
% Hispanic* 1996	0.8%	Marriages 1995	177	Registered Vehicles 1996	22,309

*May be of any race.

Percent of Total Population By Sex and Age

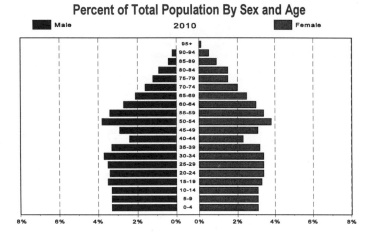

Male   2010   Female

Population Projections

Age Groups	2000	2010	% Change
0-17	4,700	4,500	-4.3%
18-24	1,960	1,840	-6.1%
25-39	3,400	3,940	15.9%
40-59	5,180	4,860	-6.2%
60-74	2,330	2,700	15.9%
75 +	1,370	1,360	-0.7%
Total	18,900	19,200	1.6%

Personal Income
Real 1995 Dollars ($000)

	1990	1995	% Chg.
Total Earnings by Place of Work	151,221	151,894	0.4%
Less Personal Contributions for Social Insurance	7,761	10,643	37.1%
Net Income by Place of Work	143,460	141,251	-1.5%
Plus Residence Adjustment	100,363	119,377	18.9%
Net Income by Place of Residence	243,823	260,628	6.9%
Plus Dividends, Rent and Interest	70,466	62,384	-11.5%
Plus Transfer Payments	45,280	50,933	12.5%
Personal Income by Place of Residence	359,570	373,945	4.0%
Per Capita Income ($)	19,107	19,114	0.0%
Rank	24	44	87

Educational Attainment 1990

Graduate or Prof. Degree
Bachelor's Degree
Associate Degree
Some College No Degree
High School Graduate
9th-12th No Diploma
Less than 9th Grade

High School Grad or Higher
Percent: 76%
Rank in State: 28

Population Change by Decade
(1990-2000 projected)

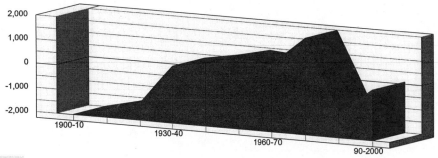

1900-10   1930-40   1960-70   90-2000

For EDIN tables, sources and footnotes, see page 380.

Occupation of Employed Persons Age 16 & Over		
	1990	% Chg. 80-90
Managerial & Professional	1,534	27.0
Technical, Sales & Admin. Support	2,062	11.1
Service Occupations	1,137	4.1
Farming, Forestry and Fishing	645	-33.8
Precision Production, Craft & Repair	1,321	5.8
Operators, Fabricators	2,313	-5.8

Top 5 Counties Commuting in 1990			
From Carroll Into:		Into Carroll From:	
Tippecanoe	1,969	Tippecanoe	317
White	829	White	247
Howard	659	Cass	98
Cass	477	Howard	94
Clinton	190	Clinton	85

4,440 persons lived and worked in this county.
4,453 lived in the county but worked elsewhere.

Number of Establishments
(% Change 1990-1995)

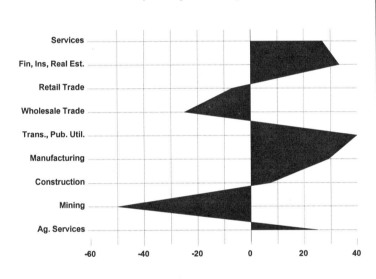

Establishments by Sector 1995		
Industry	Number of Establishments	% with fewer than 10 employees
Ag. Services	10	100.0%
Mining	1	0.0%
Construction	59	94.9%
Manufacturing	31	48.4%
Transportation, Public Utilities	21	81.0%
Wholesale Trade	36	75.0%
Retail Trade	79	68.4%
Finance, Insurance, Real Estate	32	84.4%
Services	104	87.5%

Private Industry	Employment		Real Earnings ($000)		Average Earnings Per Job	
	1995	% Chg. 90-95	1995	Real % Chg. 90-95	1995	Real % Chg. 90-95
Ag. Services	NA	NA	NA	NA	NA	NA
Mining	NA	NA	NA	NA	NA	NA
Construction	535	13.6%	9,999	7.8%	18,690	-5.1%
Manufacturing	2,086	86.6%	63,809	93.5%	30,589	3.7%
Transportation, Public Utilities	209	14.2%	5,273	22.4%	25,230	7.2%
Wholesale Trade	368	-21.7%	11,804	-6.0%	32,076	20.0%
Retail Trade	1,075	9.5%	10,498	-11.0%	9,766	-18.7%
Finance, Insurance, Real Estate	420	6.6%	4,307	6.2%	10,255	-0.4%
Services	1,416	9.3%	19,304	16.2%	13,633	6.3%

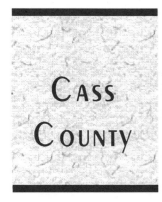

CASS COUNTY

Population 1997 (Est.)	38,573	# Households 1995 (Projection)	14,500	Personal Income 1995 ($000)	$435,607
Land Area (Sq. Mi.)	412.9	% Family	72.0%	Avg. Wage Per Job 1995	$21,343
Population Density 1997	93.4	% Non-Family	27.9%	Employed in 1996	18,500
% Under 20 1996	28.0%	% Living Alone	24.8%	Unemployed in 1996	1,100
% 65 & Over 1996	15.4%	Births 1995	490	Unemployment Rate 1996	5.6%
% White 1996	98.4%	Births to Teens 1995	88	Avg. Covered Payroll 1996 ($000)	$88,175
% African-Amer. 1996	0.9%	Deaths 1995	436	Average Weekly Earnings in Manufacturing 1996	$489.00
% Hispanic* 1996	0.8%	Marriages 1995	419	Registered Vehicles 1996	37,861

*May be of any race.

Percent of Total Population By Sex and Age

■ Male   2010   ■ Female

(population pyramid chart with age groups 0-4 through 95+, axis from 8% to 8%)

Population Projections

Age Groups	2000	2010	% Change
0-17	9,380	9,070	-3.3%
18-24	4,000	3,580	-10.5%
25-39	7,000	7,930	13.3%
40-59	10,180	9,670	-5.0%
60-74	4,520	5,130	13.5%
75 +	2,920	2,760	-5.5%
Total	38,000	38,100	0.3%

Personal Income
Real 1995 Dollars ($000)

	1990	1995	% Chg.
Total Earnings by Place of Work	419,227	435,607	3.9%
Less Personal Contributions for Social Insurance	26,167	29,233	11.7%
Net Income by Place of Work	393,060	406,374	3.4%
Plus Residence Adjustment	49,241	74,119	50.5%
Net Income by Place of Residence	442,301	480,493	8.6%
Plus Dividends, Rent and Interest	124,308	109,674	-11.8%
Plus Transfer Payments	119,515	141,503	18.4%
Personal Income by Place of Residence	686,125	731,670	6.6%
Per Capita Income ($)	17,863	18,991	6.3%
Rank	48	49	58

Educational Attainment 1990

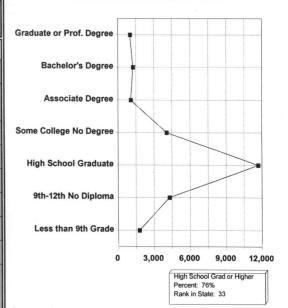

High School Grad or Higher
Percent: 76%
Rank in State: 33

Population Change by Decade
(1990-2000 projected)

(3D area chart showing population change from 1900-10 to 90-2000, y-axis from -4,000 to 3,000)

For EDIN tables, sources and footnotes, see page 380.

Occupation of Employed Persons Age 16 & Over

	1990	% Chg. 80-90
Managerial & Professional	2,989	8.6
Technical, Sales & Admin. Support	4,067	-3.1
Service Occupations	2,802	7.2
Farming, Forestry and Fishing	757	-11.0
Precision Production, Craft & Repair	2,783	6.1
Operators, Fabricators	3,962	-20.6

Top 5 Counties Commuting in 1990

From Cass Into:		Into Cass From:	
Howard	1,651	Carroll	477
Miami	450	Miami	452
White	289	White	383
Fulton	194	Howard	312
Tippecanoe	134	Pulaski	238

13,480 persons lived and worked in this county.

3,559 lived in the county but worked elsewhere.

Number of Establishments
(% Change 1990-1995)

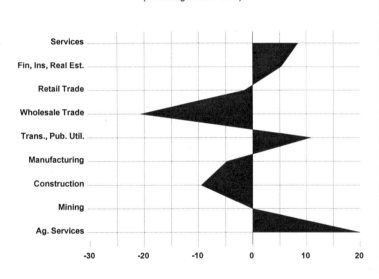

Establishments by Sector 1995

Industry	Number of Establishments	% with fewer than 10 employees
Ag. Services	18	66.7%
Mining	1	0.0%
Construction	76	84.2%
Manufacturing	60	28.3%
Transportation, Public Utilities	41	58.5%
Wholesale Trade	65	67.7%
Retail Trade	257	66.5%
Finance, Insurance, Real Estate	60	83.3%
Services	283	83.7%

Private Industry	Employment		Real Earnings ($000)		Average Earnings Per Job	
	1995	% Chg. 90-95	1995	Real % Chg. 90-95	1995	Real % Chg. 90-95
Ag. Services	NA	NA	NA	NA	NA	NA
Mining	NA	NA	NA	NA	NA	NA
Construction	938	24.7%	27,721	44.9%	29,553	16.2%
Manufacturing	4,918	-9.5%	153,704	-2.7%	31,253	7.5%
Transportation, Public Utilities	608	6.1%	16,363	8.6%	26,913	2.3%
Wholesale Trade	819	7.1%	22,725	8.5%	27,747	1.3%
Retail Trade	3,597	2.9%	43,903	8.4%	12,205	5.3%
Finance, Insurance, Real Estate	732	-16.4%	12,670	1.2%	17,309	21.1%
Services	3,363	4.2%	59,769	16.6%	17,773	11.9%

CLARK COUNTY

Population 1997 (Est.)	93,212	# Households 1995 (Projection)	33,400	Personal Income 1995 ($000)	$1,204,825
Land Area (Sq. Mi.)	375.2	% Family	73.3%	Avg. Wage Per Job 1995	$21,821
Population Density 1997	248.4	% Non-Family	26.7%	Employed in 1996	48,290
% Under 20 1996	27.6%	% Living Alone	23.3%	Unemployed in 1996	2,120
% 65 & Over 1996	12.1%	Births 1995	1,199	Unemployment Rate 1996	4.2%
% White 1996	93.3%	Births to Teens 1995	180	Avg. Covered Payroll 1996 ($000)	$231,835
% African-Amer. 1996	5.9%	Deaths 1995	919	Average Weekly Earnings in Manufacturing 1996	$578.75
% Hispanic* 1996	0.8%	Marriages 1995	808	Registered Vehicles 1996	86,021

*May be of any race.

Percent of Total Population By Sex and Age

Male | 2010 | Female

(Age groups from 0-4 to 95+)

8% 6% 4% 2% 0% 0% 2% 4% 6% 8%

Population Projections

Age Groups	2000	2010	% Change
0-17	20,470	18,450	-9.9%
18-24	8,830	7,970	-9.7%
25-39	18,320	18,200	-0.7%
40-59	25,020	25,040	0.1%
60-74	9,920	12,160	22.6%
75 +	4,600	4,700	2.2%
Total	87,200	86,600	-0.7%

Personal Income
Real 1995 Dollars ($000)

	1990	1995	% Chg.
Total Earnings by Place of Work	1,053,935	1,204,825	14.3%
Less Personal Contributions for Social Insurance	68,199	82,534	21.0%
Net Income by Place of Work	985,736	1,122,291	13.9%
Plus Residence Adjustment	146,764	159,754	8.9%
Net Income by Place of Residence	1,132,500	1,282,045	13.2%
Plus Dividends, Rent and Interest	229,923	234,646	2.1%
Plus Transfer Payments	264,995	320,549	21.0%
Personal Income by Place of Residence	1,627,417	1,837,240	12.9%
Per Capita Income ($)	18,557	20,069	8.1%
Rank	29	28	38

Educational Attainment 1990

(chart categories: Graduate or Prof. Degree, Bachelor's Degree, Associate Degree, Some College No Degree, High School Graduate, 9th-12th No Diploma, Less than 9th Grade)

0 6,000 12,000 18,000 24,000

High School Grad or Higher
Percent: 73%
Rank in State: 54

Population Change by Decade
(1990-2000 projected)

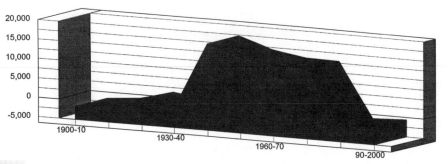

20,000 | 15,000 | 10,000 | 5,000 | 0 | -5,000

1900-10 1930-40 1960-70 90-2000

For EDIN tables, sources and footnotes, see page 380.

Occupation of Employed Persons Age 16 & Over

	1990	% Chg. 80-90
Managerial & Professional	8,119	20.4
Technical, Sales & Admin. Support	14,062	18.0
Service Occupations	6,283	32.1
Farming, Forestry and Fishing	634	5.8
Precision Production, Craft & Repair	5,109	-7.8
Operators, Fabricators	8,240	-11.6

Top 5 Counties Commuting in 1990

From Clark Into:		Into Clark From:	
Outside Indiana	15,793	Outside Indiana	6,943
Floyd	3,283	Floyd	4,615
Scott	189	Harrison	1,069
Washington	181	Washington	993
Harrison	163	Scott	654

21,557 persons lived and worked in this county.

20,089 lived in the county but worked elsewhere.

Number of Establishments
(% Change 1990-1995)

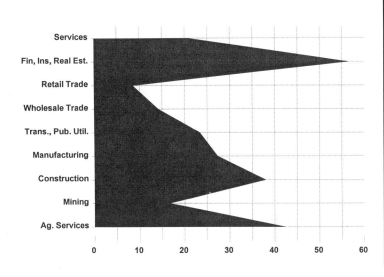

Establishments by Sector 1995

Industry	Number of Establishments	% with fewer than 10 employees
Ag. Services	37	89.2%
Mining	7	42.9%
Construction	276	79.7%
Manufacturing	140	42.1%
Transportation, Public Utilities	164	62.2%
Wholesale Trade	145	66.2%
Retail Trade	638	62.7%
Finance, Insurance, Real Estate	169	82.8%
Services	718	76.9%

Private Industry	Employment		Real Earnings ($000)		Average Earnings Per Job	
	1995	% Chg. 90-95	1995	Real % Chg. 90-95	1995	Real % Chg. 90-95
Ag. Services	320	47.5%	3,608	0.7%	11,275	-31.7%
Mining	129	4.0%	4,897	64.6%	37,961	58.2%
Construction	3,682	44.4%	119,337	31.3%	32,411	-9.1%
Manufacturing	7,640	6.6%	258,068	3.3%	33,779	-3.1%
Transportation, Public Utilities	4,473	18.7%	159,332	27.4%	35,621	7.3%
Wholesale Trade	1,904	23.3%	48,997	23.1%	25,734	-0.2%
Retail Trade	11,961	21.6%	169,282	24.7%	14,153	2.6%
Finance, Insurance, Real Estate	1,915	5.8%	32,795	42.4%	17,125	34.6%
Services	11,416	17.6%	233,930	23.1%	20,491	4.7%

For EDIN tables, sources and footnotes, see page 380.

Clay County

Population 1997 (Est.)	26,531	# Households 1995 (Projection)	9,300	Personal Income 1995 ($000)	$243,521
Land Area (Sq. Mi.)	357.6	% Family	74.0%	Avg. Wage Per Job 1995	$20,363
Population Density 1997	74.2	% Non-Family	25.6%	Employed in 1996	12,020
% Under 20 1996	27.7%	% Living Alone	23.5%	Unemployed in 1996	780
% 65 & Over 1996	17.1%	Births 1995	335	Unemployment Rate 1996	6.1%
% White 1996	99.3%	Births to Teens 1995	63	Avg. Covered Payroll 1996 ($000)	$37,411
% African-Amer. 1996	0.5%	Deaths 1995	329	Average Weekly Earnings in Manufacturing 1996	$520.25
% Hispanic* 1996	0.3%	Marriages 1995	268	Registered Vehicles 1996	26,434

*May be of any race.

Percent of Total Population By Sex and Age

■ Male 2010 ▨ Female

95+ / 90-94 / 85-89 / 80-84 / 75-79 / 70-74 / 65-69 / 60-64 / 55-59 / 50-54 / 45-49 / 40-44 / 35-39 / 30-34 / 25-29 / 20-24 / 15-19 / 10-14 / 5-9 / 0-4

8% 6% 4% 2% 0% 0% 2% 4% 6% 8%

Population Projections

Age Groups	2000	2010	% Change
0-17	6,090	5,960	-2.1%
18-24	2,570	2,360	-8.2%
25-39	4,610	5,210	13.0%
40-59	6,380	6,330	-0.8%
60-74	2,990	3,250	8.7%
75 +	1,880	1,660	-11.7%
Total	24,500	24,800	1.2%

Personal Income
Real 1995 Dollars ($000)

	1990	1995	% Chg.
Total Earnings by Place of Work	186,348	243,521	30.7%
Less Personal Contributions for Social Insurance	12,341	17,187	39.3%
Net Income by Place of Work	174,007	226,334	30.1%
Plus Residence Adjustment	75,706	78,793	4.1%
Net Income by Place of Residence	249,713	305,127	22.2%
Plus Dividends, Rent and Interest	69,276	64,012	-7.6%
Plus Transfer Payments	79,610	98,162	23.3%
Personal Income by Place of Residence	398,599	467,301	17.2%
Per Capita Income ($)	16,110	17,771	10.3%
Rank	74	61	18

Educational Attainment 1990

Graduate or Prof. Degree / Bachelor's Degree / Associate Degree / Some College No Degree / High School Graduate / 9th-12th No Diploma / Less than 9th Grade

0 2,000 4,000 6,000 8,000

High School Grad or Higher
Percent: 76%
Rank in State: 33

Population Change by Decade
(1990-2000 projected)

1,000 / 0 / -1,000 / -2,000 / -3,000 / -4,000

1900-10   1930-40   1960-70   90-2000

For EDIN tables, sources and footnotes, see page 380.

Occupation of Employed Persons Age 16 & Over			Top 5 Counties Commuting in 1990				
	1990	% Chg. 80-90	From Clay Into:			Into Clay From:	
Managerial & Professional	1,820	22.7	Vigo	2,652		Vigo	632
Technical, Sales & Admin. Support	2,771	6.8	Putnam	560		Parke	230
Service Occupations	1,737	29.6	Marion	456		Putnam	193
Farming, Forestry and Fishing	441	-18.3	Greene	276		Greene	113
Precision Production, Craft & Repair	1,447	3.4	Hendricks	114		Owen	92
Operators, Fabricators	2,279	-12.6	5,745	persons lived and worked in this county.			
			4,499	lived in the county but worked elsewhere.			

Number of Establishments
(% Change 1990-1995)

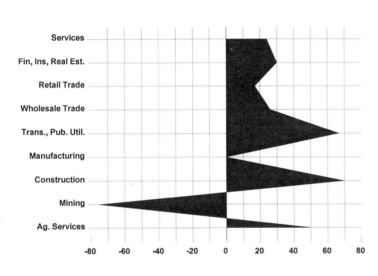

Establishments by Sector 1995

Industry	Number of Establishments	% with fewer than 10 employees
Ag. Services	12	91.7%
Mining	2	50.0%
Construction	56	92.9%
Manufacturing	33	48.5%
Transportation, Public Utilities	40	62.5%
Wholesale Trade	29	75.9%
Retail Trade	139	67.6%
Finance, Insurance, Real Estate	39	89.7%
Services	191	88.0%

Private Industry	Employment		Real Earnings ($000)		Average Earnings Per Job	
	1995	% Chg. 90-95	1995	Real % Chg. 90-95	1995	Real % Chg. 90-95
Ag. Services	96	88.2%	921	151.8%	9,594	33.8%
Mining	NA	NA	NA	NA	NA	NA
Construction	NA	NA	NA	NA	NA	NA
Manufacturing	2,652	86.0%	90,795	103.0%	34,236	9.1%
Transportation, Public Utilities	739	28.5%	25,868	56.3%	35,004	21.6%
Wholesale Trade	204	2.0%	6,163	0.2%	30,211	-1.7%
Retail Trade	2,102	19.7%	26,802	15.5%	12,751	-3.5%
Finance, Insurance, Real Estate	423	-2.3%	6,372	6.3%	15,064	8.8%
Services	1,985	18.7%	29,222	36.8%	14,721	15.3%

Clinton County

Population 1997 (Est.)	33,232	# Households 1995 (Projection)	11,300	Personal Income 1995 ($000)	$333,397
Land Area (Sq. Mi.)	405.1	% Family	75.9%	Avg. Wage Per Job 1995	$21,753
Population Density 1997	82.0	% Non-Family	24.5%	Employed in 1996	15,430
% Under 20 1996	29.2%	% Living Alone	21.8%	Unemployed in 1996	530
% 65 & Over 1996	15.6%	Births 1995	462	Unemployment Rate 1996	3.3%
% White 1996	99.4%	Births to Teens 1995	59	Avg. Covered Payroll 1996 ($000)	$68,030
% African-Amer. 1996	0.2%	Deaths 1995	368	Average Weekly Earnings in Manufacturing 1996	$546.00
% Hispanic* 1996	1.9%	Marriages 1995	330	Registered Vehicles 1996	32,184

*May be of any race.

Percent of Total Population By Sex and Age

■ Male   2010   ▨ Female

(Population pyramid chart showing age groups from 0-4 to 95+, with horizontal scale from 8% to 0% on left (Male) and 0% to 8% on right (Female))

Population Projections

Age Groups	2000	2010	% Change
0-17	8,240	7,820	-5.1%
18-24	3,340	3,190	-4.5%
25-39	5,900	6,630	12.4%
40-59	8,050	8,200	1.9%
60-74	3,530	4,050	14.7%
75 +	2,230	2,060	-7.6%
Total	31,300	31,900	1.9%

Personal Income
Real 1995 Dollars ($000)

	1990	1995	% Chg.
Total Earnings by Place of Work	304,313	333,397	9.6%
Less Personal Contributions for Social Insurance	18,837	23,824	26.5%
Net Income by Place of Work	285,476	309,573	8.4%
Plus Residence Adjustment	88,079	109,939	24.8%
Net Income by Place of Residence	373,556	419,512	12.3%
Plus Dividends, Rent and Interest	104,464	101,956	-2.4%
Plus Transfer Payments	87,752	104,778	19.4%
Personal Income by Place of Residence	565,772	626,246	10.7%
Per Capita Income ($)	18,225	19,279	5.8%
Rank	41	43	63

Educational Attainment 1990

(Line chart showing educational attainment categories from "Less than 9th Grade" to "Graduate or Prof. Degree" on vertical axis, with horizontal scale from 0 to 10,000)

High School Grad or Higher
Percent: 76%
Rank in State: 28

Population Change by Decade
(1990-2000 projected)

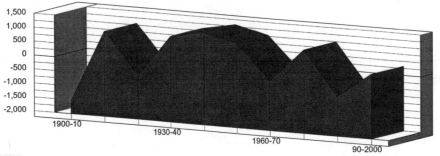

(3D area chart with vertical scale from -2,000 to 1,500, horizontal axis labeled 1900-10, 1930-40, 1960-70, 90-2000)

For EDIN tables, sources and footnotes, see page 380.

Occupation of Employed Persons Age 16 & Over

	1990	% Chg. 80-90
Managerial & Professional	2,417	18.0
Technical, Sales & Admin. Support	3,450	13.0
Service Occupations	1,752	-2.6
Farming, Forestry and Fishing	767	-10.6
Precision Production, Craft & Repair	2,168	7.8
Operators, Fabricators	3,362	-9.7

Top 5 Counties Commuting in 1990

From Clinton Into:		Into Clinton From:	
Tippecanoe	2,156	Tippecanoe	424
Howard	715	Boone	360
Marion	688	Carroll	190
Boone	410	Howard	149
Hamilton	165	Marion	77

9,051 persons lived and worked in this county.

4,653 lived in the county but worked elsewhere.

Number of Establishments
(% Change 1990-1995)

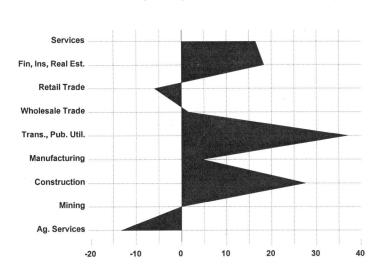

Establishments by Sector 1995

Industry	Number of Establishments	% with fewer than 10 employees
Ag. Services	13	100.0%
Mining	0	NA
Construction	97	87.6%
Manufacturing	45	33.3%
Transportation, Public Utilities	37	81.1%
Wholesale Trade	65	81.5%
Retail Trade	174	70.7%
Finance, Insurance, Real Estate	58	93.1%
Services	226	88.1%

Private Industry	Employment		Real Earnings ($000)		Average Earnings Per Job	
	1995	% Chg. 90-95	1995	Real % Chg. 90-95	1995	Real % Chg. 90-95
Ag. Services	183	38.6%	2,472	59.3%	13,508	14.9%
Mining	NA	NA	NA	NA	NA	NA
Construction	818	-12.7%	17,950	-23.7%	21,944	-12.6%
Manufacturing	5,118	31.4%	168,547	37.6%	32,932	4.7%
Transportation, Public Utilities	368	38.9%	10,535	32.9%	28,628	-4.3%
Wholesale Trade	417	-17.1%	12,259	-9.8%	29,398	8.8%
Retail Trade	2,475	5.8%	27,215	7.0%	10,996	1.1%
Finance, Insurance, Real Estate	555	-10.0%	8,024	-6.4%	14,458	4.1%
Services	2,892	18.0%	40,961	29.8%	14,164	10.0%

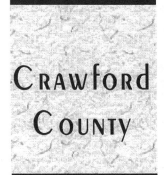

CRAWFORD COUNTY

Population 1997 (Est.)	10,499	# Households 1995 (Projection)	3,700	Personal Income 1995 ($000)	$42,209
Land Area (Sq. Mi.)	305.7	% Family	75.4%	Avg. Wage Per Job 1995	$16,036
Population Density 1997	34.3	% Non-Family	24.3%	Employed in 1996	4,165
% Under 20 1996	29.1%	% Living Alone	21.9%	Unemployed in 1996	455
% 65 & Over 1996	14.4%	Births 1995	110	Unemployment Rate 1996	9.9%
% White 1996	99.5%	Births to Teens 1995	34	Avg. Covered Payroll 1996 ($000)	$6,831
% African-Amer. 1996	0.1%	Deaths 1995	115	Average Weekly Earnings in Manufacturing 1996	$263.75
% Hispanic* 1996	0.2%	Marriages 1995	92	Registered Vehicles 1996	11,179

*May be of any race.

Percent of Total Population By Sex and Age

■ Male   2010   ■ Female

(Population pyramid chart with age groups from 0-4 to 95+, x-axis from 8% to 0% to 8%)

Population Projections

Age Groups	2000	2010	% Change
0-17	2,650	2,680	1.1%
18-24	1,090	990	-9.2%
25-39	1,960	2,240	14.3%
40-59	2,700	2,680	-0.7%
60-74	1,200	1,360	13.3%
75 +	620	600	-3.2%
Total	10,200	10,600	3.9%

Personal Income
Real 1995 Dollars ($000)

	1990	1995	% Chg.
Total Earnings by Place of Work	40,405	42,209	4.5%
Less Personal Contributions for Social Insurance	2,842	3,456	21.6%
Net Income by Place of Work	37,563	38,753	3.2%
Plus Residence Adjustment	45,650	54,707	19.8%
Net Income by Place of Residence	83,214	93,460	12.3%
Plus Dividends, Rent and Interest	15,964	15,723	-1.5%
Plus Transfer Payments	29,600	37,712	27.4%
Personal Income by Place of Residence	128,778	146,895	14.1%
Per Capita Income ($)	12,977	14,154	9.1%
Rank	92	92	27

Educational Attainment 1990

(Line chart with categories: Graduate or Prof. Degree, Bachelor's Degree, Associate Degree, Some College No Degree, High School Graduate, 9th-12th No Diploma, Less than 9th Grade; x-axis from 0 to 2,500)

High School Grad or Higher
Percent: 60%
Rank in State: 91

Population Change by Decade
(1990-2000 projected)

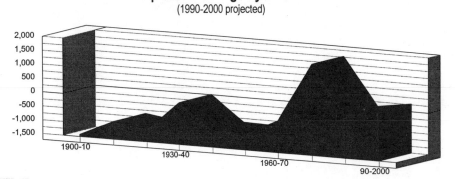

(Area chart, y-axis from -1,500 to 2,000, x-axis decades: 1900-10, 1930-40, 1960-70, 90-2000)

For EDIN tables, sources and footnotes, see page 380.

Occupation of Employed Persons Age 16 & Over

	1990	% Chg. 80-90
Managerial & Professional	512	24.6
Technical, Sales & Admin. Support	678	17.5
Service Occupations	670	85.1
Farming, Forestry and Fishing	183	-12.0
Precision Production, Craft & Repair	678	16.9
Operators, Fabricators	1,184	-1.1

Top 5 Counties Commuting in 1990

From Crawford Into:		Into Crawford From:	
Outside Indiana	518	Harrison	141
Dubois	448	Perry	64
Harrison	424	Orange	57
Orange	228	Outside Indiana	35
Clark	199	Dubois	13

1,639 persons lived and worked in this county.

2,215 lived in the county but worked elsewhere.

Number of Establishments
(% Change 1990-1995)

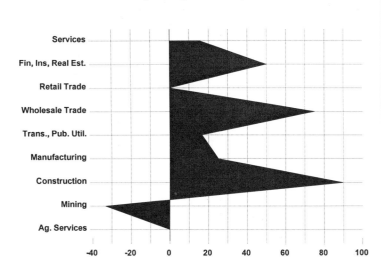

Establishments by Sector 1995

Industry	Number of Establishments	% with fewer than 10 employees
Ag. Services	0	NA
Mining	4	25.0%
Construction	19	89.5%
Manufacturing	20	70.0%
Transportation, Public Utilities	7	100.0%
Wholesale Trade	7	100.0%
Retail Trade	46	73.9%
Finance, Insurance, Real Estate	15	80.0%
Services	30	90.0%

Private Industry	Employment		Real Earnings ($000)		Average Earnings Per Job	
	1995	% Chg. 90-95	1995	Real % Chg. 90-95	1995	Real % Chg. 90-95
Ag. Services	33	17.9%	393	41.6%	11,909	20.2%
Mining	NA	NA	NA	NA	NA	NA
Construction	208	42.5%	3,556	77.4%	17,096	24.5%
Manufacturing	187	-5.1%	4,236	-32.5%	22,652	-28.9%
Transportation, Public Utilities	188	22.9%	3,307	28.3%	17,590	4.4%
Wholesale Trade	13	-66.7%	281	-51.7%	21,615	44.9%
Retail Trade	570	8.0%	6,392	12.0%	11,214	3.7%
Finance, Insurance, Real Estate	120	-16.7%	1,908	9.6%	15,900	31.5%
Services	NA	NA	NA	NA	NA	NA

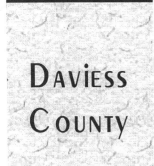

DAVIESS COUNTY

Population 1997 (Est.)	28,851	# Households 1995 (Projection)	9,900	Personal Income 1995 ($000)	$257,569
Land Area (Sq. Mi.)	430.7	% Family	73.7%	Avg. Wage Per Job 1995	$17,975
Population Density 1997	67.0	% Non-Family	26.1%	Employed in 1996	12,980
% Under 20 1996	30.4%	% Living Alone	24.1%	Unemployed in 1996	520
% 65 & Over 1996	16.2%	Births 1995	444	Unemployment Rate 1996	3.9%
% White 1996	99.4%	Births to Teens 1995	56	Avg. Covered Payroll 1996 ($000)	$43,727
% African-Amer. 1996	0.4%	Deaths 1995	333	Average Weekly Earnings in Manufacturing 1996	$356.50
% Hispanic* 1996	0.4%	Marriages 1995	201	Registered Vehicles 1996	26,532

*May be of any race.

Percent of Total Population By Sex and Age

Male   2010   Female

Age groups (top to bottom): 95+, 90-94, 85-89, 80-84, 75-79, 70-74, 65-69, 60-64, 55-59, 50-54, 45-49, 40-44, 35-39, 30-34, 25-29, 20-24, 15-19, 10-14, 5-9, 0-4

Axis: 8% 6% 4% 2% 0% 0% 2% 4% 6% 8%

Population Projections

Age Groups	2000	2010	% Change
0-17	7,860	7,720	-1.8%
18-24	3,030	3,030	0.0%
25-39	5,220	6,150	17.8%
40-59	6,760	6,800	0.6%
60-74	2,980	3,370	13.1%
75 +	2,110	1,870	-11.4%
Total	28,000	28,900	3.2%

Personal Income
Real 1995 Dollars ($000)

	1990	1995	% Chg.
Total Earnings by Place of Work	244,816	257,569	5.2%
Less Personal Contributions for Social Insurance	15,599	18,171	16.5%
Net Income by Place of Work	229,217	239,398	4.4%
Plus Residence Adjustment	41,124	43,622	6.1%
Net Income by Place of Residence	270,341	283,020	4.7%
Plus Dividends, Rent and Interest	87,697	86,097	-1.8%
Plus Transfer Payments	90,507	108,194	19.5%
Personal Income by Place of Residence	448,545	477,311	6.4%
Per Capita Income ($)	16,273	16,708	2.7%
Rank	73	76	80

Educational Attainment 1990

Categories (top to bottom): Graduate or Prof. Degree, Bachelor's Degree, Associate Degree, Some College No Degree, High School Graduate, 9th-12th No Diploma, Less than 9th Grade

Axis: 0 2,000 4,000 6,000 8,000

High School Grad or Higher
Percent: 66%
Rank in State: 79

Population Change by Decade
(1990-2000 projected)

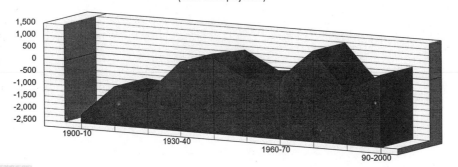

Axis: 1,500 1,000 500 0 -500 -1,000 -1,500 -2,000 -2,500

1900-10   1930-40   1960-70   90-2000

Occupation of Employed Persons Age 16 & Over		
	1990	% Chg. 80-90
Managerial & Professional	1,844	13.3
Technical, Sales & Admin. Support	2,889	16.4
Service Occupations	1,806	29.1
Farming, Forestry and Fishing	815	-21.1
Precision Production, Craft & Repair	1,757	6.9
Operators, Fabricators	2,623	8.0

Top 5 Counties Commuting in 1990			
From Daviess Into:		Into Daviess From:	
Martin	1,114	Knox	504
Dubois	551	Martin	307
Knox	307	Pike	248
Pike	227	Greene	164
Greene	151	Outside Indiana	105

8,676 persons lived and worked in this county.
2,963 lived in the county but worked elsewhere.

Number of Establishments
(% Change 1990-1995)

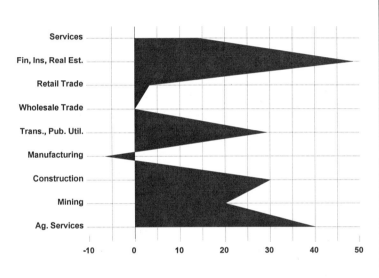

Establishments by Sector 1995		
Industry	Number of Establishments	% with fewer than 10 employees
Ag. Services	14	100.0%
Mining	12	58.3%
Construction	104	85.6%
Manufacturing	44	40.9%
Transportation, Public Utilities	53	69.8%
Wholesale Trade	38	63.2%
Retail Trade	187	71.1%
Finance, Insurance, Real Estate	55	87.3%
Services	220	87.3%

Private Industry	Employment		Real Earnings ($000)		Average Earnings Per Job	
	1995	% Chg. 90-95	1995	Real % Chg. 90-95	1995	Real % Chg. 90-95
Ag. Services	158	27.4%	1,615	10.8%	10,222	-13.1%
Mining	441	-37.8%	17,928	-39.8%	40,653	-3.2%
Construction	1,224	38.6%	25,785	46.6%	21,066	5.8%
Manufacturing	2,073	3.8%	48,240	10.9%	23,271	6.8%
Transportation, Public Utilities	828	11.4%	21,462	17.8%	25,920	5.7%
Wholesale Trade	651	28.9%	18,901	38.3%	29,034	7.3%
Retail Trade	2,386	2.7%	27,618	6.4%	11,575	3.7%
Finance, Insurance, Real Estate	503	-4.7%	8,206	6.0%	16,314	11.3%
Services	2,867	8.4%	41,209	23.3%	14,374	13.8%

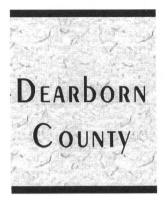

DEARBORN COUNTY

Population 1997 (Est.)	46,576	# Households 1995 (Projection)	14,300	Personal Income 1995 ($000)	$352,818
Land Area (Sq. Mi.)	305.2	% Family	78.6%	Avg. Wage Per Job 1995	$22,427
Population Density 1997	152.6	% Non-Family	21.6%	Employed in 1996	21,010
% Under 20 1996	30.3%	% Living Alone	19.2%	Unemployed in 1996	1,160
% 65 & Over 1996	12.0%	Births 1995	590	Unemployment Rate 1996	5.2%
% White 1996	98.8%	Births to Teens 1995	52	Avg. Covered Payroll 1996 ($000)	$65,126
% African-Amer. 1996	0.7%	Deaths 1995	363	Average Weekly Earnings in Manufacturing 1996	$693.75
% Hispanic* 1996	0.4%	Marriages 1995	313	Registered Vehicles 1996	43,121

*May be of any race.

Percent of Total Population By Sex and Age

Male 2010 Female

95+
90-94
85-89
80-84
75-79
70-74
65-69
60-64
55-59
50-54
45-49
40-44
35-39
30-34
25-29
20-24
15-19
10-14
5-9
0-4

8% 6% 4% 2% 0% 0% 2% 4% 6% 8%

Population Projections

Age Groups	2000	2010	% Change
0-17	10,630	10,240	-3.7%
18-24	4,780	4,210	-11.9%
25-39	7,690	9,380	22.0%
40-59	11,910	11,680	-1.9%
60-74	4,490	5,720	27.4%
75 +	2,230	2,360	5.8%
Total	41,700	43,600	4.6%

Personal Income
Real 1995 Dollars ($000)

	1990	1995	% Chg.
Total Earnings by Place of Work	308,482	352,818	14.4%
Less Personal Contributions for Social Insurance	20,692	24,826	20.0%
Net Income by Place of Work	287,790	327,992	14.0%
Plus Residence Adjustment	227,261	289,030	27.2%
Net Income by Place of Residence	515,051	617,022	19.8%
Plus Dividends, Rent and Interest	100,425	104,912	4.5%
Plus Transfer Payments	101,212	122,272	20.8%
Personal Income by Place of Residence	716,688	844,206	17.8%
Per Capita Income ($)	18,361	18,996	3.5%
Rank	38	48	76

Educational Attainment 1990

Graduate or Prof. Degree
Bachelor's Degree
Associate Degree
Some College No Degree
High School Graduate
9th-12th No Diploma
Less than 9th Grade

0   3,000   6,000   9,000   12,000

High School Grad or Higher
Percent: 74%
Rank in State: 48

Population Change by Decade
(1990-2000 projected)

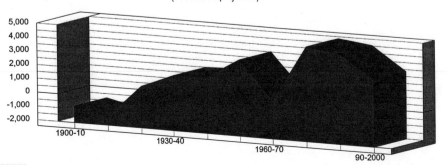

5,000
4,000
3,000
2,000
1,000
0
-1,000
-2,000

1900-10   1930-40   1960-70   90-2000

For EDIN tables, sources and footnotes, see page 380.

Occupation of Employed Persons Age 16 & Over		
	1990	% Chg. 80-90
Managerial & Professional	3,570	58.5
Technical, Sales & Admin. Support	4,815	52.7
Service Occupations	2,125	28.5
Farming, Forestry and Fishing	326	0.6
Precision Production, Craft & Repair	2,859	16.8
Operators, Fabricators	3,954	2.1

Top 5 Counties Commuting in 1990			
From Dearborn Into:		Into Dearborn From:	
Outside Indiana	8,446	Outside Indiana	1,162
Ripley	1,109	Ohio	809
Franklin	90	Ripley	614
Marion	42	Switzerland	347
Decatur	40	Franklin	178

7,336 persons lived and worked in this county.
9,972 lived in the county but worked elsewhere.

Number of Establishments
(% Change 1990-1995)

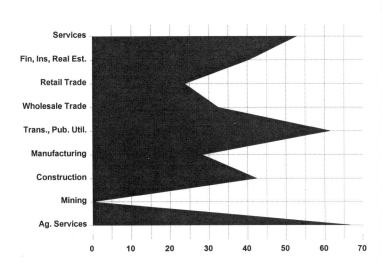

Establishments by Sector 1995		
Industry	Number of Establishments	% with fewer than 10 employees
Ag. Services	15	93.3%
Mining	1	100.0%
Construction	151	85.4%
Manufacturing	50	54.0%
Transportation, Public Utilities	63	71.4%
Wholesale Trade	49	75.5%
Retail Trade	229	69.4%
Finance, Insurance, Real Estate	87	85.1%
Services	295	84.7%

Private Industry	Employment		Real Earnings ($000)		Average Earnings Per Job	
	1995	% Chg. 90-95	1995	Real % Chg. 90-95	1995	Real % Chg. 90-95
Ag. Services	162	31.7%	2,977	23.4%	18,377	-6.3%
Mining	NA	NA	55	-82.6%	NA	NA
Construction	1,470	37.5%	40,343	38.7%	27,444	0.9%
Manufacturing	2,321	0.0%	94,631	-0.5%	40,772	-0.5%
Transportation, Public Utilities	1,034	1.5%	37,870	6.5%	36,625	5.0%
Wholesale Trade	420	35.5%	11,849	31.6%	28,212	-2.8%
Retail Trade	3,059	12.8%	39,807	14.4%	13,013	1.4%
Finance, Insurance, Real Estate	868	6.2%	12,875	13.4%	14,833	6.7%
Services	3,372	22.1%	59,260	42.4%	17,574	16.6%

Decatur County

Population 1997 (Est.)	25,362	# Households 1995 (Projection)	8,500	Personal Income 1995 ($000)	$345,975
Land Area (Sq. Mi.)	372.6	% Family	77.1%	Avg. Wage Per Job 1995	$21,549
Population Density 1997	68.1	% Non-Family	23.3%	Employed in 1996	14,480
% Under 20 1996	30.6%	% Living Alone	20.7%	Unemployed in 1996	450
% 65 & Over 1996	13.5%	Births 1995	360	Unemployment Rate 1996	3.0%
% White 1996	99.1%	Births to Teens 1995	57	Avg. Covered Payroll 1996 ($000)	$69,514
% African-Amer. 1996	0.1%	Deaths 1995	224	Average Weekly Earnings in Manufacturing 1996	$575.25
% Hispanic* 1996	0.5%	Marriages 1995	235	Registered Vehicles 1996	25,079

*May be of any race.

Percent of Total Population By Sex and Age

Male   2010   Female

(population pyramid chart, age groups 0-4 through 95+, scale 8% 6% 4% 2% 0% 0% 2% 4% 6% 8%)

Population Projections

Age Groups	2000	2010	% Change
0-17	6,170	5,980	-3.1%
18-24	2,760	2,370	-14.1%
25-39	4,750	5,410	13.9%
40-59	6,200	6,360	2.6%
60-74	2,710	3,230	19.2%
75 +	1,420	1,420	0.0%
Total	24,000	24,800	3.3%

Personal Income
Real 1995 Dollars ($000)

	1990	1995	% Chg.
Total Earnings by Place of Work	267,016	345,975	29.6%
Less Personal Contributions for Social Insurance	17,411	24,789	42.4%
Net Income by Place of Work	249,605	321,186	28.7%
Plus Residence Adjustment	20,909	21,448	2.6%
Net Income by Place of Residence	270,514	342,634	26.7%
Plus Dividends, Rent and Interest	77,125	73,137	-5.2%
Plus Transfer Payments	62,264	70,605	13.4%
Personal Income by Place of Residence	409,903	486,376	18.7%
Per Capita Income ($)	17,323	19,514	12.6%
Rank	52	40	9

Educational Attainment 1990

(chart plotting values for each category from 0 to 8,000)

- Graduate or Prof. Degree
- Bachelor's Degree
- Associate Degree
- Some College No Degree
- High School Graduate
- 9th-12th No Diploma
- Less than 9th Grade

0   2,000   4,000   6,000   8,000

High School Grad or Higher
Percent: 72%
Rank in State: 58

Population Change by Decade
(1990-2000 projected)

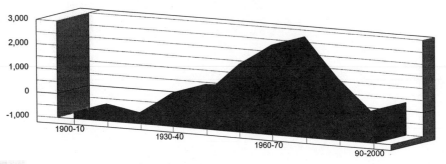

3,000 / 2,000 / 1,000 / 0 / -1,000

1900-10   1930-40   1960-70   90-2000

For EDIN tables, sources and footnotes, see page 380.

Occupation of Employed Persons Age 16 & Over

	1990	% Chg. 80-90
Managerial & Professional	1,723	28.0
Technical, Sales & Admin. Support	2,626	26.2
Service Occupations	1,436	25.6
Farming, Forestry and Fishing	658	-28.9
Precision Production, Craft & Repair	1,644	18.1
Operators, Fabricators	3,127	14.0

Top 5 Counties Commuting in 1990

From Decatur Into:		Into Decatur From:	
Bartholomew	893	Ripley	657
Ripley	465	Franklin	289
Shelby	440	Shelby	231
Marion	400	Bartholomew	216
Outside Indiana	117	Jennings	171

8,129 persons lived and worked in this county.

2,854 lived in the county but worked elsewhere.

Number of Establishments
(% Change 1990-1995)

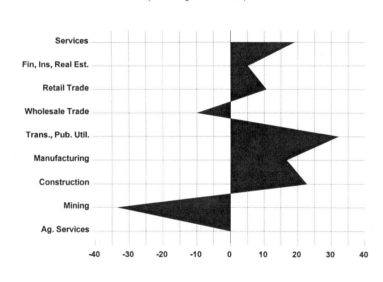

Establishments by Sector 1995

Industry	Number of Establishments	% with fewer than 10 employees
Ag. Services	9	77.8%
Mining	2	50.0%
Construction	70	95.7%
Manufacturing	49	42.9%
Transportation, Public Utilities	37	64.9%
Wholesale Trade	46	63.0%
Retail Trade	156	66.7%
Finance, Insurance, Real Estate	42	88.1%
Services	169	79.3%

Private Industry	Employment		Real Earnings ($000)		Average Earnings Per Job	
	1995	% Chg. 90-95	1995	Real % Chg. 90-95	1995	Real % Chg. 90-95
Ag. Services	NA	NA	NA	NA	NA	NA
Mining	NA	NA	NA	NA	NA	NA
Construction	544	18.0%	11,099	23.4%	20,403	4.6%
Manufacturing	5,298	29.3%	182,962	36.8%	34,534	5.8%
Transportation, Public Utilities	562	7.0%	18,021	33.4%	32,066	24.6%
Wholesale Trade	433	-3.8%	13,624	-5.6%	31,464	-1.9%
Retail Trade	2,409	24.4%	27,901	23.8%	11,582	-0.5%
Finance, Insurance, Real Estate	535	15.1%	7,445	37.3%	13,916	19.4%
Services	2,893	50.6%	43,392	60.5%	14,999	6.6%

DeKalb County

Population 1997 (Est.)	38,722	# Households 1995 (Projection)	13,200	Personal Income 1995 ($000)	$615,127
Land Area (Sq. Mi.)	362.9	% Family	76.0%	Avg. Wage Per Job 1995	$24,764
Population Density 1997	106.7	% Non-Family	23.8%	Employed in 1996	20,450
% Under 20 1996	30.7%	% Living Alone	20.8%	Unemployed in 1996	750
% 65 & Over 1996	12.1%	Births 1995	544	Unemployment Rate 1996	3.5%
% White 1996	99.3%	Births to Teens 1995	82	Avg. Covered Payroll 1996 ($000)	$125,511
% African-Amer. 1996	0.1%	Deaths 1995	331	Average Weekly Earnings in Manufacturing 1996	$624.25
% Hispanic* 1996	1.2%	Marriages 1995	394	Registered Vehicles 1996	40,312

*May be of any race.

Percent of Total Population By Sex and Age

Male — 2010 — Female

8% 6% 4% 2% 0% 0% 2% 4% 6% 8%

95+, 90-94, 85-89, 80-84, 75-79, 70-74, 65-69, 60-64, 55-59, 50-54, 45-49, 40-44, 35-39, 30-34, 25-29, 20-24, 15-19, 10-14, 5-9, 0-4

Population Projections

Age Groups	2000	2010	% Change
0-17	9,790	9,580	-2.1%
18-24	4,120	3,830	-7.0%
25-39	7,560	8,230	8.9%
40-59	9,950	10,680	7.3%
60-74	3,740	4,640	24.1%
75 +	1,960	2,020	3.1%
Total	37,100	39,000	5.1%

Personal Income
Real 1995 Dollars ($000)

	1990	1995	% Chg.
Total Earnings by Place of Work	487,908	615,127	26.1%
Less Personal Contributions for Social Insurance	31,856	41,020	28.8%
Net Income by Place of Work	456,052	574,107	25.9%
Plus Residence Adjustment	14,455	-1,866	-112.9%
Net Income by Place of Residence	470,507	572,241	21.6%
Plus Dividends, Rent and Interest	105,402	119,056	13.0%
Plus Transfer Payments	79,075	97,570	23.4%
Personal Income by Place of Residence	654,984	788,867	20.4%
Per Capita Income ($)	18,473	20,846	12.8%
Rank	32	24	7

Educational Attainment 1990

Graduate or Prof. Degree
Bachelor's Degree
Associate Degree
Some College No Degree
High School Graduate
9th-12th No Diploma
Less than 9th Grade

0   3,000   6,000   9,000   12,000

High School Grad or Higher
Percent: 78%
Rank in State: 18

Population Change by Decade
(1990-2000 projected)

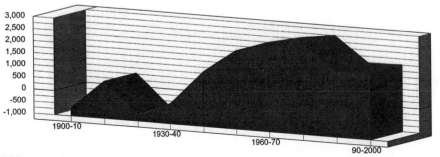

3,000 / 2,500 / 2,000 / 1,500 / 1,000 / 500 / 0 / -500 / -1,000

1900-10   1930-40   1960-70   90-2000

For EDIN tables, sources and footnotes, see page 380.

Occupation of Employed Persons Age 16 & Over

	1990	% Chg. 80-90
Managerial & Professional	2,791	34.8
Technical, Sales & Admin. Support	3,920	27.4
Service Occupations	1,831	18.2
Farming, Forestry and Fishing	569	-2.4
Precision Production, Craft & Repair	2,692	32.9
Operators, Fabricators	5,944	20.2

Top 5 Counties Commuting in 1990

From Dekalb Into:		Into Dekalb From:	
Allen	2,917	Allen	1,339
Noble	1,326	Steuben	1,065
Steuben	827	Outside Indiana	954
Outside Indiana	265	Noble	711
Whitley	119	Lagrange	124

11,851 persons lived and worked in this county.
5,625 lived in the county but worked elsewhere.

Number of Establishments
(% Change 1990-1995)

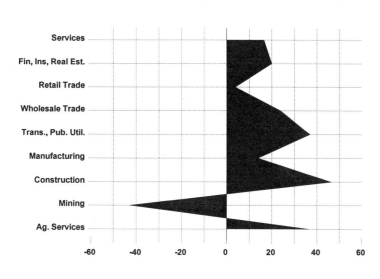

Establishments by Sector 1995

Industry	Number of Establishments	% with fewer than 10 employees
Ag. Services	15	100.0%
Mining	4	50.0%
Construction	98	85.7%
Manufacturing	115	34.8%
Transportation, Public Utilities	37	75.7%
Wholesale Trade	52	75.0%
Retail Trade	218	65.6%
Finance, Insurance, Real Estate	54	83.3%
Services	281	76.5%

Private Industry	Employment		Real Earnings ($000)		Average Earnings Per Job	
	1995	% Chg. 90-95	1995	Real % Chg. 90-95	1995	Real % Chg. 90-95
Ag. Services	203	16.0%	2,520	5.4%	12,414	-9.2%
Mining	61	69.4%	2,437	116.6%	39,951	27.8%
Construction	1,039	51.2%	23,755	52.7%	22,863	1.0%
Manufacturing	10,438	21.9%	385,275	31.6%	36,911	8.0%
Transportation, Public Utilities	612	-6.0%	20,929	-2.1%	34,198	4.1%
Wholesale Trade	456	9.1%	12,949	26.2%	28,397	15.7%
Retail Trade	3,281	18.8%	38,249	20.0%	11,658	1.0%
Finance, Insurance, Real Estate	958	4.9%	10,510	47.5%	10,971	40.6%
Services	4,222	19.8%	69,113	30.8%	16,370	9.1%

For EDIN tables, sources and footnotes, see page 380.

Delaware County

Population 1997 (Est.)	117,625	# Households 1995 (Projection)	45,400	Personal Income 1995 ($000)	$1,809,669
Land Area (Sq. Mi.)	393.3	% Family	67.0%	Avg. Wage Per Job 1995	$23,294
Population Density 1997	299.1	% Non-Family	33.1%	Employed in 1996	59,880
% Under 20 1996	27.7%	% Living Alone	25.9%	Unemployed in 1996	2,910
% 65 & Over 1996	12.8%	Births 1995	1,408	Unemployment Rate 1996	4.6%
% White 1996	92.4%	Births to Teens 1995	222	Avg. Covered Payroll 1996 ($000)	$339,269
% African-Amer. 1996	6.6%	Deaths 1995	1,173	Average Weekly Earnings in Manufacturing 1996	$791.50
% Hispanic* 1996	0.9%	Marriages 1995	1,043	Registered Vehicles 1996	102,569

*May be of any race.

Percent of Total Population By Sex and Age

Male — 2010 — Female

(Population pyramid chart showing age groups from 0-4 to 95+, male on left, female on right, scale 8% to 0% to 8%)

Population Projections

Age Groups	2000	2010	% Change
0-17	29,300	29,570	0.9%
18-24	19,980	19,670	-1.6%
25-39	23,840	24,130	1.2%
40-59	28,300	29,250	3.4%
60-74	13,200	15,580	18.0%
75 +	6,890	6,810	-1.2%
Total	121,500	125,000	2.9%

Personal Income
Real 1995 Dollars ($000)

	1990	1995	% Chg.
Total Earnings by Place of Work	1,577,398	1,809,669	14.7%
Less Personal Contributions for Social Insurance	99,784	118,924	19.2%
Net Income by Place of Work	1,477,614	1,690,745	14.4%
Plus Residence Adjustment	22,810	-65,090	-385.4%
Net Income by Place of Residence	1,500,424	1,625,655	8.3%
Plus Dividends, Rent and Interest	377,399	359,258	-4.8%
Plus Transfer Payments	341,509	398,681	16.7%
Personal Income by Place of Residence	2,219,332	2,383,594	7.4%
Per Capita Income ($)	18,544	20,044	8.1%
Rank	30	29	40

Educational Attainment 1990

(Line chart with categories: Graduate or Prof. Degree, Bachelor's Degree, Associate Degree, Some College No Degree, High School Graduate, 9th-12th No Diploma, Less than 9th Grade; scale 0 to 30,000)

High School Grad or Higher
Percent: 75%
Rank in State: 38

Population Change by Decade
(1990-2000 projected)

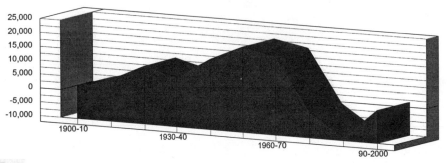

(Area chart with scale -10,000 to 25,000; x-axis labels 1900-10, 1930-40, 1960-70, 90-2000)

For EDIN tables, sources and footnotes, see page 380.

Occupation of Employed Persons Age 16 & Over

	1990	% Chg. 80-90
Managerial & Professional	12,185	7.0
Technical, Sales & Admin. Support	16,717	8.4
Service Occupations	8,850	11.2
Farming, Forestry and Fishing	873	-0.3
Precision Production, Craft & Repair	6,599	4.7
Operators, Fabricators	9,873	-17.4

Top 5 Counties Commuting in 1990

From Delaware Into:		Into Delaware From:	
Madison	2,238	Madison	1,855
Marion	1,121	Henry	1,682
Jay	586	Randolph	1,572
Grant	480	Blackford	641
Randolph	471	Jay	565

46,695 persons lived and worked in this county.

7,312 lived in the county but worked elsewhere.

Number of Establishments
(% Change 1990-1995)

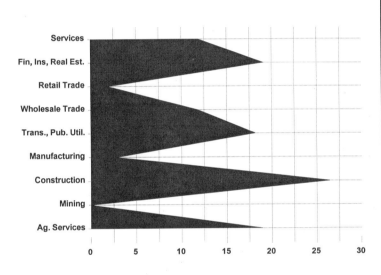

Establishments by Sector 1995

Industry	Number of Establishments	% with fewer than 10 employees
Ag. Services	44	86.4%
Mining	2	50.0%
Construction	277	78.3%
Manufacturing	180	31.1%
Transportation, Public Utilities	91	63.7%
Wholesale Trade	180	65.0%
Retail Trade	745	61.7%
Finance, Insurance, Real Estate	243	81.1%
Services	961	74.8%

Private Industry	Employment		Real Earnings ($000)		Average Earnings Per Job	
	1995	% Chg. 90-95	1995	Real % Chg. 90-95	1995	Real % Chg. 90-95
Ag. Services	NA	NA	NA	NA	NA	NA
Mining	NA	NA	NA	NA	NA	NA
Construction	3,505	16.1%	98,932	19.8%	28,226	3.1%
Manufacturing	11,384	-0.6%	563,707	12.1%	49,517	12.8%
Transportation, Public Utilities	6,412	111.6%	150,174	79.4%	23,421	-15.2%
Wholesale Trade	1,811	-15.1%	53,364	-9.3%	29,467	6.9%
Retail Trade	14,056	14.1%	173,905	1.7%	12,372	-10.9%
Finance, Insurance, Real Estate	2,980	1.5%	53,938	20.4%	18,100	18.6%
Services	18,625	12.6%	419,068	23.0%	22,500	9.2%

For EDIN tables, sources and footnotes, see page 380.

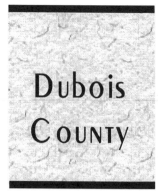

Dubois County

Population 1997 (Est.)	39,139	# Households 1995 (Projection)	13,500	Personal Income 1995 ($000)	$772,821
Land Area (Sq. Mi.)	430.1	% Family	76.1%	Avg. Wage Per Job 1995	$22,421
Population Density 1997	91.0	% Non-Family	24.0%	Employed in 1996	21,710
% Under 20 1996	29.6%	% Living Alone	21.6%	Unemployed in 1996	640
% 65 & Over 1996	12.6%	Births 1995	597	Unemployment Rate 1996	2.8%
% White 1996	99.6%	Births to Teens 1995	41	Avg. Covered Payroll 1996 ($000)	$156,815
% African-Amer. 1996	0.1%	Deaths 1995	328	Average Weekly Earnings in Manufacturing 1996	$506.25
% Hispanic* 1996	0.9%	Marriages 1995	309	Registered Vehicles 1996	40,091

*May be of any race.

Percent of Total Population By Sex and Age

■ Male   2010   ■ Female

8%	6%	4%	2%	0%	0%	2%	4%	6%	8%

(Age groups: 95+, 90-94, 85-89, 80-84, 75-79, 70-74, 65-69, 60-64, 55-59, 50-54, 45-49, 40-44, 35-39, 30-34, 25-29, 20-24, 15-19, 10-14, 5-9, 0-4)

Population Projections

Age Groups	2000	2010	% Change
0-17	9,960	9,220	-7.4%
18-24	3,970	4,030	1.5%
25-39	7,820	8,030	2.7%
40-59	10,230	11,190	9.4%
60-74	4,050	4,970	22.7%
75 +	2,200	2,310	5.0%
Total	38,200	39,800	4.2%

Personal Income
Real 1995 Dollars ($000)

	1990	1995	% Chg.
Total Earnings by Place of Work	653,732	772,821	18.2%
Less Personal Contributions for Social Insurance	42,101	52,770	25.3%
Net Income by Place of Work	611,631	720,051	17.7%
Plus Residence Adjustment	-92,999	-126,166	35.7%
Net Income by Place of Residence	518,632	593,885	14.5%
Plus Dividends, Rent and Interest	181,226	188,106	3.8%
Plus Transfer Payments	86,139	107,643	25.0%
Personal Income by Place of Residence	785,997	889,634	13.2%
Per Capita Income ($)	21,430	22,932	7.0%
Rank	10	12	54

Educational Attainment 1990

(Categories: Graduate or Prof. Degree, Bachelor's Degree, Associate Degree, Some College No Degree, High School Graduate, 9th-12th No Diploma, Less than 9th Grade)

0	3,000	6,000	9,000	12,000

High School Grad or Higher
Percent: 72%
Rank in State: 59

Population Change by Decade
(1990-2000 projected)

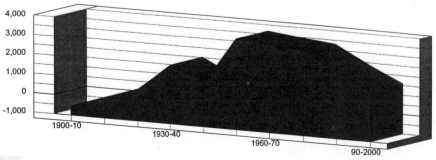

(Y-axis: -1,000 to 4,000; X-axis decades: 1900-10, 1930-40, 1960-70, 90-2000)

For EDIN tables, sources and footnotes, see page 380.

Occupation of Employed Persons Age 16 & Over

	1990	% Chg. 80-90
Managerial & Professional	3,207	30.8
Technical, Sales & Admin. Support	4,607	37.0
Service Occupations	2,014	9.5
Farming, Forestry and Fishing	916	-15.7
Precision Production, Craft & Repair	2,798	18.3
Operators, Fabricators	5,738	16.9

Top 5 Counties Commuting in 1990

From Dubois Into:		Into Dubois From:	
Spencer	475	Pike	1,346
Orange	164	Spencer	1,245
Pike	149	Perry	840
Martin	132	Martin	717
Warrick	100	Daviess	551

17,535 persons lived and worked in this county.

1,548 lived in the county but worked elsewhere.

Number of Establishments
(% Change 1990-1995)

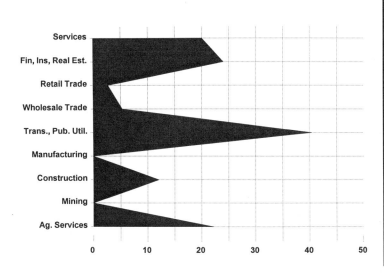

Establishments by Sector 1995

Industry	Number of Establishments	% with fewer than 10 employees
Ag. Services	11	90.9%
Mining	5	60.0%
Construction	130	80.8%
Manufacturing	123	26.8%
Transportation, Public Utilities	73	75.3%
Wholesale Trade	99	64.6%
Retail Trade	302	67.2%
Finance, Insurance, Real Estate	93	86.0%
Services	318	75.5%

Private Industry	Employment		Real Earnings ($000)		Average Earnings Per Job	
	1995	% Chg. 90-95	1995	Real % Chg. 90-95	1995	Real % Chg. 90-95
Ag. Services	206	12.6%	2,660	23.2%	12,913	9.4%
Mining	190	-9.1%	5,205	9.1%	27,395	20.0%
Construction	1,422	9.3%	44,293	16.1%	31,148	6.2%
Manufacturing	12,777	18.1%	382,073	23.4%	29,903	4.4%
Transportation, Public Utilities	1,112	20.3%	34,130	19.3%	30,692	-0.9%
Wholesale Trade	1,627	7.8%	48,181	9.4%	29,613	1.5%
Retail Trade	4,944	25.8%	69,464	20.6%	14,050	-4.1%
Finance, Insurance, Real Estate	1,254	-5.1%	18,846	15.3%	15,029	21.5%
Services	5,491	27.0%	110,064	40.1%	20,044	10.3%

ELKHART COUNTY

Population 1997 (Est.)	170,725	# Households 1995 (Projection)	60,300	Personal Income 1995 ($000)	$3,745,833
Land Area (Sq. Mi.)	463.8	% Family	74.0%	Avg. Wage Per Job 1995	$25,030
Population Density 1997	368.1	% Non-Family	26.0%	Employed in 1996	90,640
% Under 20 1996	30.2%	% Living Alone	21.4%	Unemployed in 1996	3,700
% 65 & Over 1996	11.3%	Births 1995	2,737	Unemployment Rate 1996	3.9%
% White 1996	93.9%	Births to Teens 1995	445	Avg. Covered Payroll 1996 ($000)	$734,585
% African-Amer. 1996	5.0%	Deaths 1995	1,314	Average Weekly Earnings in Manufacturing 1996	$591.75
% Hispanic* 1996	2.4%	Marriages 1995	1,597	Registered Vehicles 1996	158,225

*May be of any race.

Percent of Total Population By Sex and Age

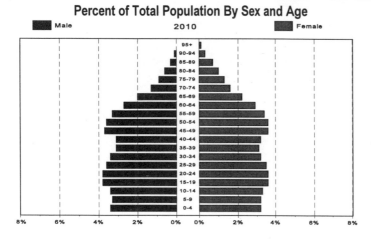

Male 2010 Female

Population Projections

Age Groups	2000	2010	% Change
0-17	46,200	43,240	-6.4%
18-24	17,010	18,590	9.3%
25-39	35,830	35,510	-0.9%
40-59	45,060	49,130	9.0%
60-74	16,810	22,590	34.4%
75 +	8,690	9,350	7.6%
Total	169,600	178,400	5.2%

Personal Income
Real 1995 Dollars ($000)

	1990	1995	% Chg.
Total Earnings by Place of Work	3,079,759	3,745,833	21.6%
Less Personal Contributions for Social Insurance	205,206	252,693	23.1%
Net Income by Place of Work	2,874,554	3,493,140	21.5%
Plus Residence Adjustment	-625,578	-753,892	20.5%
Net Income by Place of Residence	2,248,976	2,739,248	21.8%
Plus Dividends, Rent and Interest	611,698	603,515	-1.3%
Plus Transfer Payments	353,457	437,626	23.8%
Personal Income by Place of Residence	3,214,131	3,780,389	17.6%
Per Capita Income ($)	20,554	22,660	10.2%
Rank	14	13	19

Educational Attainment 1990

Graduate or Prof. Degree
Bachelor's Degree
Associate Degree
Some College No Degree
High School Graduate
9th-12th No Diploma
Less than 9th Grade

0   10,000   20,000   30,000   40,000

High School Grad or Higher
Percent: 73%
Rank in State: 54

Population Change by Decade
(1990-2000 projected)

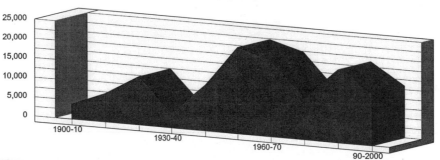

25,000
20,000
15,000
10,000
5,000
0

1900-10   1930-40   1960-70   90-2000

For EDIN tables, sources and footnotes, see page 380.

Occupation of Employed Persons Age 16 & Over

	1990	% Chg. 80-90
Managerial & Professional	16,351	35.3
Technical, Sales & Admin. Support	21,820	32.6
Service Occupations	8,189	23.3
Farming, Forestry and Fishing	1,570	1.0
Precision Production, Craft & Repair	11,091	23.9
Operators, Fabricators	21,567	26.4

Top 5 Counties Commuting in 1990

From Elkhart Into:		Into Elkhart From:	
St. Joseph	3,601	St. Joseph	10,742
Outside Indiana	965	Outside Indiana	8,087
Lagrange	856	Kosciusko	3,437
Kosciusko	808	Lagrange	2,182
Marshall	310	Marshall	1,692

72,405 persons lived and worked in this county.
7,091 lived in the county but worked elsewhere.

Number of Establishments
(% Change 1990-1995)

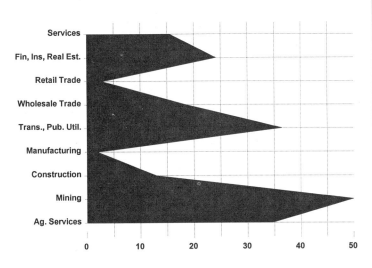

Establishments by Sector 1995

Industry	Number of Establishments	% with fewer than 10 employees
Ag. Services	66	84.8%
Mining	3	33.3%
Construction	479	79.1%
Manufacturing	945	31.9%
Transportation, Public Utilities	157	66.2%
Wholesale Trade	480	61.7%
Retail Trade	1,034	62.0%
Finance, Insurance, Real Estate	370	84.1%
Services	1,424	76.7%

Private Industry	Employment		Real Earnings ($000)		Average Earnings Per Job	
	1995	% Chg. 90-95	1995	Real % Chg. 90-95	1995	Real % Chg. 90-95
Ag. Services	771	21.0%	15,526	41.4%	20,137	16.8%
Mining	91	-1.1%	1,351	46.4%	14,846	48.0%
Construction	5,913	24.3%	182,987	30.8%	30,947	5.2%
Manufacturing	60,503	16.4%	2,181,490	25.2%	36,056	7.6%
Transportation, Public Utilities	4,749	3.0%	136,041	-3.0%	28,646	-5.8%
Wholesale Trade	6,435	13.1%	214,697	15.6%	33,364	2.2%
Retail Trade	18,809	19.8%	247,482	20.6%	13,158	0.7%
Finance, Insurance, Real Estate	4,762	-6.4%	88,220	1.0%	18,526	7.8%
Services	24,106	14.5%	479,778	27.5%	19,903	11.4%

FAYETTE COUNTY

Population 1997 (Est.)	26,133	# Households 1995 (Projection)	9,900	Personal Income 1995 ($000)	$390,821
Land Area (Sq. Mi.)	215.0	% Family	73.5%	Avg. Wage Per Job 1995	$27,310
Population Density 1997	121.5	% Non-Family	26.9%	Employed in 1996	11,110
% Under 20 1996	28.3%	% Living Alone	24.5%	Unemployed in 1996	780
% 65 & Over 1996	14.6%	Births 1995	335	Unemployment Rate 1996	6.6%
% White 1996	97.7%	Births to Teens 1995	91	Avg. Covered Payroll 1996 ($000)	$80,020
% African-Amer. 1996	1.8%	Deaths 1995	309	Average Weekly Earnings in Manufacturing 1996	$807.25
% Hispanic* 1996	0.4%	Marriages 1995	272	Registered Vehicles 1996	25,174

*May be of any race.

Percent of Total Population By Sex and Age

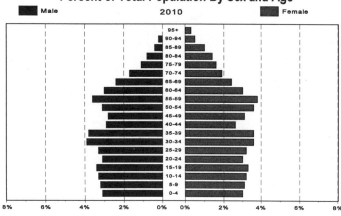

Population Projections

Age Groups	2000	2010	% Change
0-17	5,990	5,820	-2.8%
18-24	2,710	2,230	-17.7%
25-39	4,950	5,490	10.9%
40-59	6,890	6,500	-5.7%
60-74	3,170	3,680	16.1%
75 +	1,850	1,840	-0.5%
Total	25,600	25,600	0.0%

Personal Income
Real 1995 Dollars ($000)

	1990	1995	% Chg.
Total Earnings by Place of Work	381,522	390,821	2.4%
Less Personal Contributions for Social Insurance	25,465	27,573	8.3%
Net Income by Place of Work	356,058	363,248	2.0%
Plus Residence Adjustment	-55,606	-52,418	-5.7%
Net Income by Place of Residence	300,452	310,830	3.5%
Plus Dividends, Rent and Interest	74,358	70,046	-5.8%
Plus Transfer Payments	79,576	99,235	24.7%
Personal Income by Place of Residence	454,386	480,111	5.7%
Per Capita Income ($)	17,473	18,296	4.7%
Rank	51	56	68

Educational Attainment 1990

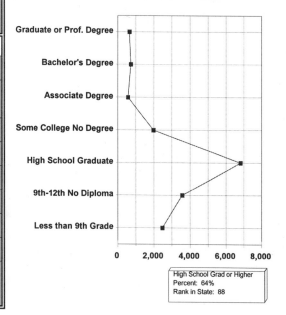

High School Grad or Higher
Percent: 64%
Rank in State: 88

Population Change by Decade
(1990-2000 projected)

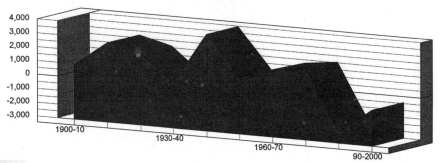

For EDIN tables, sources and footnotes, see page 380.

Occupation of Employed Persons Age 16 & Over

	1990	% Chg. 80-90
Managerial & Professional	1,843	13.8
Technical, Sales & Admin. Support	2,467	5.2
Service Occupations	1,607	16.8
Farming, Forestry and Fishing	369	-19.6
Precision Production, Craft & Repair	1,615	11.5
Operators, Fabricators	3,414	-3.3

Top 5 Counties Commuting in 1990

From Fayette Into:		Into Fayette From:	
Wayne	622	Wayne	890
Rush	310	Franklin	764
Marion	263	Union	429
Outside Indiana	172	Rush	301
Franklin	110	Henry	173

9,168 persons lived and worked in this county.

1,888 lived in the county but worked elsewhere.

Number of Establishments
(% Change 1990-1995)

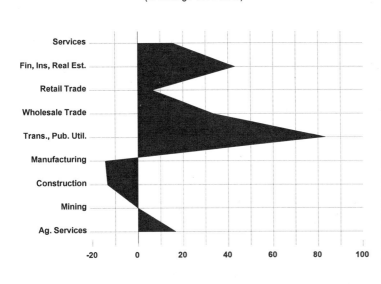

Establishments by Sector 1995

Industry	Number of Establishments	% with fewer than 10 employees
Ag. Services	7	100.0%
Mining	3	100.0%
Construction	39	92.3%
Manufacturing	30	36.7%
Transportation, Public Utilities	22	68.2%
Wholesale Trade	24	62.5%
Retail Trade	147	62.6%
Finance, Insurance, Real Estate	53	88.7%
Services	211	81.5%

Private Industry	Employment		Real Earnings ($000)		Average Earnings Per Job	
	1995	% Chg. 90-95	1995	Real % Chg. 90-95	1995	Real % Chg. 90-95
Ag. Services	75	31.6%	930	69.7%	12,400	29.0%
Mining	NA	NA	455	-0.5%	NA	NA
Construction	412	9.6%	7,303	9.2%	17,726	-0.3%
Manufacturing	5,101	-14.8%	241,364	-1.5%	47,317	15.5%
Transportation, Public Utilities	254	-17.5%	8,572	-4.1%	33,748	16.3%
Wholesale Trade	281	-1.7%	7,578	26.1%	26,968	28.3%
Retail Trade	2,321	17.9%	28,046	24.4%	12,084	5.6%
Finance, Insurance, Real Estate	441	3.8%	6,772	10.9%	15,356	6.8%
Services	3,025	9.8%	54,568	21.7%	18,039	10.9%

Floyd County

Population 1997 (Est.)	71,465	# Households 1995 (Projection)	24,700	Personal Income 1995 ($000)	$759,547
Land Area (Sq. Mi.)	148.0	% Family	74.9%	Avg. Wage Per Job 1995	$21,278
Population Density 1997	482.9	% Non-Family	24.9%	Employed in 1996	35,840
% Under 20 1996	28.1%	% Living Alone	21.9%	Unemployed in 1996	1,400
% 65 & Over 1996	12.8%	Births 1995	933	Unemployment Rate 1996	3.7%
% White 1996	95.0%	Births to Teens 1995	158	Avg. Covered Payroll 1996 ($000)	$141,636
% African-Amer. 1996	4.5%	Deaths 1995	580	Average Weekly Earnings in Manufacturing 1996	$513.00
% Hispanic* 1996	0.5%	Marriages 1995	643	Registered Vehicles 1996	61,363

*May be of any race.

Percent of Total Population By Sex and Age

Male   2010   Female

(Age groups from 0-4 to 95+, scale 8% to 8%)

Population Projections

Age Groups	2000	2010	% Change
0-17	16,620	15,430	-7.2%
18-24	6,960	6,470	-7.0%
25-39	12,920	14,140	9.4%
40-59	19,310	18,740	-3.0%
60-74	7,260	9,450	30.2%
75 +	3,840	3,880	1.0%
Total	66,900	68,100	1.8%

Personal Income
Real 1995 Dollars ($000)

	1990	1995	% Chg.
Total Earnings by Place of Work	599,716	759,547	26.7%
Less Personal Contributions for Social Insurance	38,716	51,881	34.0%
Net Income by Place of Work	561,000	707,666	26.1%
Plus Residence Adjustment	342,607	380,495	11.1%
Net Income by Place of Residence	903,607	1,088,161	20.4%
Plus Dividends, Rent and Interest	217,131	225,933	4.1%
Plus Transfer Payments	193,221	230,834	19.5%
Personal Income by Place of Residence	1,313,959	1,544,928	17.6%
Per Capita Income ($)	20,273	22,083	8.9%
Rank	16	16	29

Educational Attainment 1990

(Chart with categories: Graduate or Prof. Degree, Bachelor's Degree, Associate Degree, Some College No Degree, High School Graduate, 9th-12th No Diploma, Less than 9th Grade; scale 0 to 16,000)

High School Grad or Higher
Percent: 73%
Rank in State: 51

Population Change by Decade
(1990-2000 projected)

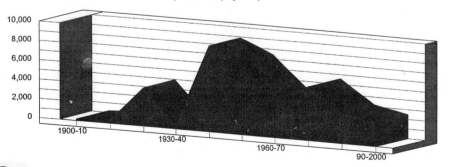

(scale 0 to 10,000; periods 1900-10, 1930-40, 1960-70, 90-2000)

For EDIN tables, sources and footnotes, see page 380.

Occupation of Employed Persons Age 16 & Over		
	1990	% Chg. 80-90
Managerial & Professional	7,316	46.6
Technical, Sales & Admin. Support	9,345	17.0
Service Occupations	3,606	10.6
Farming, Forestry and Fishing	308	16.2
Precision Production, Craft & Repair	3,923	2.9
Operators, Fabricators	5,808	-6.1

Top 5 Counties Commuting in 1990			
From Floyd Into:		Into Floyd From:	
Outside Indiana	11,377	Clark	3,283
Clark	4,615	Outside Indiana	2,755
Harrison	436	Harrison	1,765
Washington	62	Washington	492
Scott	49	Crawford	178

12,917 persons lived and worked in this county.
16,825 lived in the county but worked elsewhere.

Number of Establishments
(% Change 1990-1995)

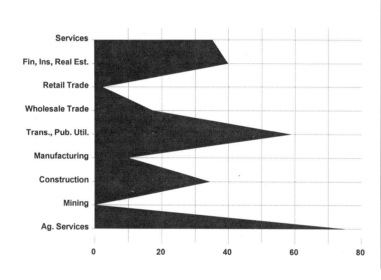

Establishments by Sector 1995		
Industry	Number of Establishments	% with fewer than 10 employees
Ag. Services	21	81.0%
Mining	0	NA
Construction	250	78.4%
Manufacturing	123	35.8%
Transportation, Public Utilities	46	71.7%
Wholesale Trade	109	68.8%
Retail Trade	322	65.8%
Finance, Insurance, Real Estate	151	83.4%
Services	566	79.0%

Private Industry	Employment		Real Earnings ($000)		Average Earnings Per Job	
	1995	% Chg. 90-95	1995	Real % Chg. 90-95	1995	Real % Chg. 90-95
Ag. Services	411	44.2%	9,504	64.1%	23,124	13.8%
Mining	21	-30.0%	805	158.7%	38,333	269.6%
Construction	2,542	28.4%	68,900	40.8%	27,105	9.7%
Manufacturing	7,452	39.3%	213,227	37.1%	28,613	-1.6%
Transportation, Public Utilities	675	-10.1%	23,093	-10.6%	34,212	-0.6%
Wholesale Trade	1,352	31.0%	37,955	22.4%	28,073	-6.5%
Retail Trade	5,632	19.2%	70,258	16.7%	12,475	-2.1%
Finance, Insurance, Real Estate	2,058	2.6%	36,950	15.6%	17,954	12.6%
Services	7,852	27.9%	168,254	38.8%	21,428	8.5%

For EDIN tables, sources and footnotes, see page 380.

FOUNTAIN COUNTY

Population 1997 (Est.)	18,235	# Households 1995 (Projection)	6,700	Personal Income 1995 ($000)	$129,893
Land Area (Sq. Mi.)	395.7	% Family	73.6%	Avg. Wage Per Job 1995	$18,741
Population Density 1997	46.1	% Non-Family	26.9%	Employed in 1996	8,070
% Under 20 1996	27.3%	% Living Alone	24.2%	Unemployed in 1996	435
% 65 & Over 1996	16.8%	Births 1995	243	Unemployment Rate 1996	5.1%
% White 1996	99.7%	Births to Teens 1995	40	Avg. Covered Payroll 1996 ($000)	$25,797
% African-Amer. 1996	0.0%	Deaths 1995	186	Average Weekly Earnings in Manufacturing 1996	$548.25
% Hispanic* 1996	0.6%	Marriages 1995	162	Registered Vehicles 1996	17,720

*May be of any race.

Percent of Total Population By Sex and Age

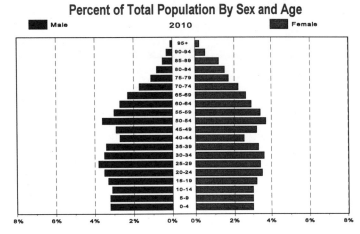

■ Male   2010   ■ Female

Population Projections

Age Groups	2000	2010	% Change
0-17	4,120	3,800	-7.8%
18-24	1,760	1,620	-8.0%
25-39	3,140	3,570	13.7%
40-59	4,470	4,210	-5.8%
60-74	2,250	2,450	8.9%
75 +	1,440	1,320	-8.3%
Total	17,200	17,000	-1.2%

Personal Income
Real 1995 Dollars ($000)

	1990	1995	% Chg.
Total Earnings by Place of Work	120,640	129,893	7.7%
Less Personal Contributions for Social Insurance	8,223	10,257	24.7%
Net Income by Place of Work	112,417	119,636	6.4%
Plus Residence Adjustment	65,774	66,090	0.5%
Net Income by Place of Residence	178,190	185,726	4.2%
Plus Dividends, Rent and Interest	55,544	50,118	-9.8%
Plus Transfer Payments	50,736	60,621	19.5%
Personal Income by Place of Residence	284,470	296,465	4.2%
Per Capita Income ($)	15,975	16,411	2.7%
Rank	76	80	79

Educational Attainment 1990

Graduate or Prof. Degree
Bachelor's Degree
Associate Degree
Some College No Degree
High School Graduate
9th-12th No Diploma
Less than 9th Grade

0   2,000   4,000   6,000

High School Grad or Higher
Percent: 73%
Rank in State: 52

Population Change by Decade
(1990-2000 projected)

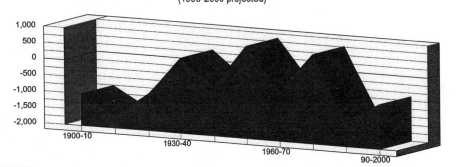

1,000
500
0
-500
-1,000
-1,500
-2,000

1900-10   1930-40   1960-70   90-2000

For EDIN tables, sources and footnotes, see page 380.

Occupation of Employed Persons Age 16 & Over

	1990	% Chg. 80-90
Managerial & Professional	1,244	15.5
Technical, Sales & Admin. Support	1,604	4.6
Service Occupations	1,284	17.3
Farming, Forestry and Fishing	444	-17.5
Precision Production, Craft & Repair	1,216	-11.9
Operators, Fabricators	2,089	-9.1

Top 5 Counties Commuting in 1990

From Fountain Into:		Into Fountain From:	
Outside Indiana	1,189	Warren	691
Tippecanoe	792	Outside Indiana	180
Montgomery	780	Vermillion	175
Warren	192	Tippecanoe	83
Vermillion	135	Parke	69

4,445 persons lived and worked in this county.

3,324 lived in the county but worked elsewhere.

Number of Establishments
(% Change 1990-1995)

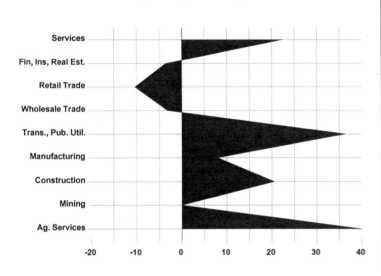

Establishments by Sector 1995

Industry	Number of Establishments	% with fewer than 10 employees
Ag. Services	7	100.0%
Mining	1	100.0%
Construction	41	92.7%
Manufacturing	27	59.3%
Transportation, Public Utilities	30	90.0%
Wholesale Trade	31	90.3%
Retail Trade	113	73.5%
Finance, Insurance, Real Estate	27	85.2%
Services	104	94.2%

Private Industry	Employment		Real Earnings ($000)		Average Earnings Per Job	
	1995	% Chg. 90-95	1995	Real % Chg. 90-95	1995	Real % Chg. 90-95
Ag. Services	122	-1.6%	1,608	-17.6%	13,180	-16.2%
Mining	NA	NA	65	-87.3%	NA	NA
Construction	294	-1.7%	5,864	10.6%	19,946	12.5%
Manufacturing	1,786	21.9%	55,434	22.7%	31,038	0.6%
Transportation, Public Utilities	216	0.0%	6,949	18.7%	32,171	18.7%
Wholesale Trade	211	8.2%	6,480	31.4%	30,711	21.4%
Retail Trade	1,361	5.0%	15,062	4.5%	11,067	-0.5%
Finance, Insurance, Real Estate	339	2.1%	5,366	52.8%	15,829	49.6%
Services	1,266	5.5%	18,343	25.0%	14,489	18.5%

FRANKLIN COUNTY

Population 1997 (Est.)	21,582	# Households 1995 (Projection)	6,800	Personal Income 1995 ($000)	$95,868
Land Area (Sq. Mi.)	386.0	% Family	80.0%	Avg. Wage Per Job 1995	$17,274
Population Density 1997	55.9	% Non-Family	20.7%	Employed in 1996	10,300
% Under 20 1996	31.3%	% Living Alone	18.8%	Unemployed in 1996	500
% 65 & Over 1996	12.5%	Births 1995	247	Unemployment Rate 1996	4.7%
% White 1996	99.6%	Births to Teens 1995	39	Avg. Covered Payroll 1996 ($000)	$16,653
% African-Amer. 1996	0.1%	Deaths 1995	174	Average Weekly Earnings in Manufacturing 1996	$501.75
% Hispanic* 1996	0.4%	Marriages 1995	154	Registered Vehicles 1996	21,443

*May be of any race.

Percent of Total Population By Sex and Age

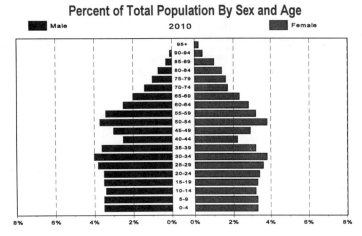

2010 — Male / Female

Population Projections

Age Groups	2000	2010	% Change
0-17	5,290	5,170	-2.3%
18-24	2,380	2,050	-13.9%
25-39	3,740	4,660	24.6%
40-59	5,420	5,230	-3.5%
60-74	2,290	2,700	17.9%
75 +	1,280	1,450	13.3%
Total	20,400	21,300	4.4%

Personal Income
Real 1995 Dollars ($000)

	1990	1995	% Chg.
Total Earnings by Place of Work	90,550	95,868	5.9%
Less Personal Contributions for Social Insurance	5,936	7,594	27.9%
Net Income by Place of Work	84,614	88,274	4.3%
Plus Residence Adjustment	128,446	141,295	10.0%
Net Income by Place of Residence	213,060	229,569	7.7%
Plus Dividends, Rent and Interest	59,884	61,534	2.8%
Plus Transfer Payments	42,056	52,389	24.6%
Personal Income by Place of Residence	315,000	343,492	9.0%
Per Capita Income ($)	16,062	16,333	1.7%
Rank	75	82	83

Educational Attainment 1990

```
Graduate or Prof. Degree
Bachelor's Degree
Associate Degree
Some College No Degree
High School Graduate
9th-12th No Diploma
Less than 9th Grade

0    2,000    4,000    6,000
```

High School Grad or Higher
Percent: 65%
Rank in State: 84

Population Change by Decade
(1990-2000 projected)

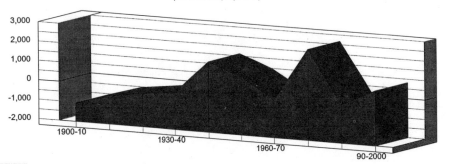

```
3,000
2,000
1,000
0
-1,000
-2,000

1900-10    1930-40    1960-70    90-2000
```

For EDIN tables, sources and footnotes, see page 380.

Occupation of Employed Persons Age 16 & Over

	1990	% Chg. 80-90
Managerial & Professional	1,280	25.7
Technical, Sales & Admin. Support	1,833	36.9
Service Occupations	1,243	51.0
Farming, Forestry and Fishing	497	-25.5
Precision Production, Craft & Repair	1,378	19.6
Operators, Fabricators	2,626	8.5

Top 5 Counties Commuting in 1990

From Franklin Into:		Into Franklin From:	
Outside Indiana	2,169	Outside Indiana	303
Ripley	1,469	Ripley	238
Fayette	764	Fayette	110
Decatur	289	Union	109
Dearborn	178	Dearborn	90

3,205 persons lived and worked in this county.

5,472 lived in the county but worked elsewhere.

Number of Establishments
(% Change 1990-1995)

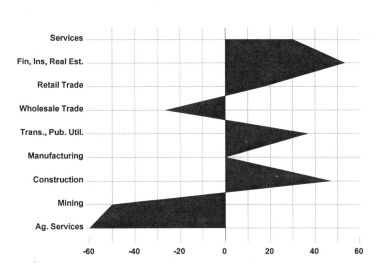

Establishments by Sector 1995

Industry	Number of Establishments	% with fewer than 10 employees
Ag. Services	2	100.0%
Mining	2	0.0%
Construction	50	86.0%
Manufacturing	13	15.4%
Transportation, Public Utilities	26	92.3%
Wholesale Trade	14	78.6%
Retail Trade	94	77.7%
Finance, Insurance, Real Estate	23	87.0%
Services	95	88.4%

Private Industry	Employment		Real Earnings ($000)		Average Earnings Per Job	
	1995	% Chg. 90-95	1995	Real % Chg. 90-95	1995	Real % Chg. 90-95
Ag. Services	72	-11.1%	695	-30.2%	9,653	-21.5%
Mining	11	-57.7%	274	-28.3%	24,909	69.6%
Construction	507	15.2%	11,528	-23.5%	22,738	-33.6%
Manufacturing	442	-30.3%	14,166	-19.2%	32,050	16.0%
Transportation, Public Utilities	367	38.5%	11,762	76.2%	32,049	27.2%
Wholesale Trade	160	29.0%	3,760	37.4%	23,500	6.5%
Retail Trade	1,130	42.3%	12,211	34.3%	10,806	-5.6%
Finance, Insurance, Real Estate	242	-5.8%	4,622	19.6%	19,099	27.0%
Services	1,389	40.6%	23,073	87.0%	16,611	33.0%

FULTON COUNTY

Population 1997 (Est.)	20,351	# Households 1995 (Projection)	7,300	Personal Income 1995 ($000)	$208,875
Land Area (Sq. Mi.)	368.5	% Family	72.2%	Avg. Wage Per Job 1995	$20,013
Population Density 1997	55.2	% Non-Family	27.4%	Employed in 1996	9,810
% Under 20 1996	28.1%	% Living Alone	24.4%	Unemployed in 1996	430
% 65 & Over 1996	16.2%	Births 1995	277	Unemployment Rate 1996	4.2%
% White 1996	98.6%	Births to Teens 1995	48	Avg. Covered Payroll 1996 ($000)	$40,048
% African-Amer. 1996	0.8%	Deaths 1995	223	Average Weekly Earnings in Manufacturing 1996	$478.75
% Hispanic* 1996	0.9%	Marriages 1995	161	Registered Vehicles 1996	21,253

*May be of any race.

Percent of Total Population By Sex and Age

Male — 2010 — Female

(Population pyramid chart with age groups from 0-4 to 95+, scaled 8% to 0% to 8%)

Population Projections

Age Groups	2000	2010	% Change
0-17	4,890	4,850	-0.8%
18-24	1,970	1,830	-7.1%
25-39	3,340	3,920	17.4%
40-59	4,860	4,640	-4.5%
60-74	2,440	2,610	7.0%
75 +	1,500	1,490	-0.7%
Total	19,000	19,400	2.1%

Personal Income
Real 1995 Dollars ($000)

	1990	1995	% Chg.
Total Earnings by Place of Work	195,274	208,875	7.0%
Less Personal Contributions for Social Insurance	12,531	15,143	20.8%
Net Income by Place of Work	182,742	193,732	6.0%
Plus Residence Adjustment	27,023	32,825	21.5%
Net Income by Place of Residence	209,765	226,557	8.0%
Plus Dividends, Rent and Interest	58,383	55,154	-5.5%
Plus Transfer Payments	52,325	63,483	21.3%
Personal Income by Place of Residence	320,473	345,194	7.7%
Per Capita Income ($)	16,975	17,349	2.2%
Rank	61	65	82

Educational Attainment 1990

(Chart showing categories: Graduate or Prof. Degree, Bachelor's Degree, Associate Degree, Some College No Degree, High School Graduate, 9th-12th No Diploma, Less than 9th Grade; x-axis 0 to 6,000)

High School Grad or Higher
Percent: 75%
Rank in State: 36

Population Change by Decade
(1990-2000 projected)

(Area chart with y-axis -2,000 to 3,000; x-axis decades 1900-10, 1930-40, 1960-70, 90-2000)

For EDIN tables, sources and footnotes, see page 380.

Occupation of Employed Persons Age 16 & Over		
	1990	% Chg. 80-90
Managerial & Professional	1,263	0.8
Technical, Sales & Admin. Support	2,034	5.2
Service Occupations	1,052	15.9
Farming, Forestry and Fishing	561	-23.6
Precision Production, Craft & Repair	1,365	13.4
Operators, Fabricators	2,479	-9.5

Top 5 Counties Commuting in 1990			
From Fulton Into:		Into Fulton From:	
Marshall	658	Miami	493
Kosciusko	528	Pulaski	197
Cass	203	Cass	194
Wabash	192	Marshall	176
Miami	178	Kosciusko	115

6,137 persons lived and worked in this county.

2,475 lived in the county but worked elsewhere.

Number of Establishments
(% Change 1990-1995)

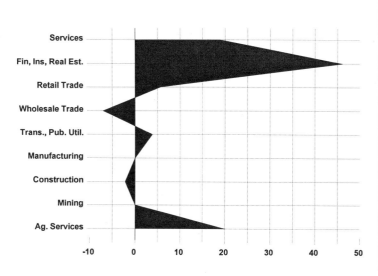

Establishments by Sector 1995		
Industry	Number of Establishments	% with fewer than 10 employees
Ag. Services	6	83.3%
Mining	0	NA
Construction	44	90.9%
Manufacturing	55	30.9%
Transportation, Public Utilities	27	70.4%
Wholesale Trade	40	85.0%
Retail Trade	131	68.7%
Finance, Insurance, Real Estate	38	86.8%
Services	145	90.3%

Private Industry	Employment		Real Earnings ($000)		Average Earnings Per Job	
	1995	% Chg. 90-95	1995	Real % Chg. 90-95	1995	Real % Chg. 90-95
Ag. Services	209	77.1%	4,193	34.5%	20,062	-24.1%
Mining	12	9.1%	369	9.6%	30,750	0.5%
Construction	569	-2.1%	18,164	15.0%	31,923	17.5%
Manufacturing	3,254	10.0%	91,767	8.2%	28,201	-1.6%
Transportation, Public Utilities	369	17.1%	10,034	23.2%	27,192	5.1%
Wholesale Trade	241	-14.2%	5,733	-3.5%	23,788	12.5%
Retail Trade	1,877	29.2%	21,655	29.8%	11,537	0.5%
Finance, Insurance, Real Estate	403	5.2%	5,902	13.0%	14,645	7.4%
Services	1,849	12.7%	27,395	33.4%	14,816	18.4%

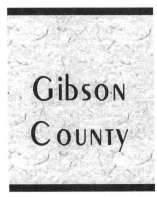

Gibson County

Population 1997 (Est.)	31,948	# Households 1995 (Projection)	12,100	Personal Income 1995 ($000)	$274,987
Land Area (Sq. Mi.)	488.9	% Family	73.5%	Avg. Wage Per Job 1995	$19,864
Population Density 1997	65.3	% Non-Family	26.5%	Employed in 1996	14,920
% Under 20 1996	27.2%	% Living Alone	24.3%	Unemployed in 1996	810
% 65 & Over 1996	16.0%	Births 1995	411	Unemployment Rate 1996	5.2%
% White 1996	97.4%	Births to Teens 1995	59	Avg. Covered Payroll 1996 ($000)	$52,615
% African-Amer. 1996	2.0%	Deaths 1995	337	Average Weekly Earnings in Manufacturing 1996	$510.50
% Hispanic* 1996	0.5%	Marriages 1995	218	Registered Vehicles 1996	32,322

*May be of any race.

Percent of Total Population By Sex and Age

Male 2010 Female

Population Projections

Age Groups	2000	2010	% Change
0-17	7,510	7,130	-5.1%
18-24	3,220	2,880	-10.6%
25-39	5,920	6,550	10.6%
40-59	8,440	8,430	-0.1%
60-74	4,010	4,290	7.0%
75 +	2,210	2,150	-2.7%
Total	31,300	31,400	0.3%

Personal Income
Real 1995 Dollars ($000)

	1990	1995	% Chg.
Total Earnings by Place of Work	290,906	274,987	-5.5%
Less Personal Contributions for Social Insurance	19,755	20,564	4.1%
Net Income by Place of Work	271,151	254,423	-6.2%
Plus Residence Adjustment	87,805	108,750	23.9%
Net Income by Place of Residence	358,957	363,173	1.2%
Plus Dividends, Rent and Interest	121,920	108,043	-11.4%
Plus Transfer Payments	98,824	115,580	17.0%
Personal Income by Place of Residence	579,701	586,796	1.2%
Per Capita Income ($)	18,184	18,345	0.9%
Rank	42	55	85

Educational Attainment 1990

Graduate or Prof. Degree
Bachelor's Degree
Associate Degree
Some College No Degree
High School Graduate
9th-12th No Diploma
Less than 9th Grade

0   3,000   6,000   9,000

High School Grad or Higher
Percent: 73%
Rank in State: 54

Population Change by Decade
(1990-2000 projected)

3,000
2,000
1,000
0
-1,000
-2,000

1900-10   1930-40   1960-70   90-2000

For EDIN tables, sources and footnotes, see page 380.

Occupation of Employed Persons Age 16 & Over		
	1990	% Chg. 80-90
Managerial & Professional	2,519	8.7
Technical, Sales & Admin. Support	3,438	14.8
Service Occupations	1,924	17.2
Farming, Forestry and Fishing	657	-20.3
Precision Production, Craft & Repair	2,481	3.3
Operators, Fabricators	3,655	-3.8

Top 5 Counties Commuting in 1990			
From Gibson Into:		Into Gibson From:	
Vanderburgh	2,729	Vanderburgh	565
Outside Indiana	680	Outside Indiana	530
Pike	380	Pike	351
Warrick	277	Knox	176
Dubois	221	Posey	137

9,599 persons lived and worked in this county.
4,803 lived in the county but worked elsewhere.

Number of Establishments
(% Change 1990-1995)

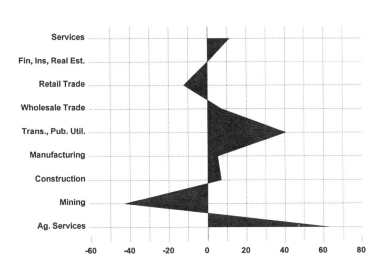

Establishments by Sector 1995		
Industry	Number of Establishments	% with fewer than 10 employees
Ag. Services	13	84.6%
Mining	12	83.3%
Construction	76	89.5%
Manufacturing	41	46.3%
Transportation, Public Utilities	52	78.8%
Wholesale Trade	44	65.9%
Retail Trade	186	68.8%
Finance, Insurance, Real Estate	56	83.9%
Services	244	86.5%

Private Industry	Employment		Real Earnings ($000)		Average Earnings Per Job	
	1995	% Chg. 90-95	1995	Real % Chg. 90-95	1995	Real % Chg. 90-95
Ag. Services	182	11.7%	2,437	17.4%	13,390	5.1%
Mining	291	-41.1%	3,458	-69.6%	11,883	-48.4%
Construction	539	0.6%	12,556	-5.7%	23,295	-6.2%
Manufacturing	2,480	-8.6%	73,702	-10.7%	29,719	-2.3%
Transportation, Public Utilities	1,067	-9.9%	46,809	-2.7%	43,870	7.9%
Wholesale Trade	413	-38.9%	9,095	-33.1%	22,022	9.5%
Retail Trade	3,111	21.8%	36,109	28.8%	11,607	5.8%
Finance, Insurance, Real Estate	600	8.3%	7,354	4.6%	12,257	-3.4%
Services	3,257	10.4%	47,915	16.8%	14,711	5.7%

GRANT COUNTY

Population 1997 (Est.)	72,818	# Households 1995 (Projection)	27,400	Personal Income 1995 ($000)	$1,069,399
Land Area (Sq. Mi.)	414.0	% Family	72.7%	Avg. Wage Per Job 1995	$25,208
Population Density 1997	175.9	% Non-Family	27.2%	Employed in 1996	33,620
% Under 20 1996	27.7%	% Living Alone	23.8%	Unemployed in 1996	2,060
% 65 & Over 1996	13.7%	Births 1995	984	Unemployment Rate 1996	5.8%
% White 1996	91.5%	Births to Teens 1995	210	Avg. Covered Payroll 1996 ($000)	$196,967
% African-Amer. 1996	7.4%	Deaths 1995	825	Average Weekly Earnings in Manufacturing 1996	$780.75
% Hispanic* 1996	2.6%	Marriages 1995	731	Registered Vehicles 1996	68,508

*May be of any race.

Percent of Total Population By Sex and Age

■ Male   2010   ■ Female

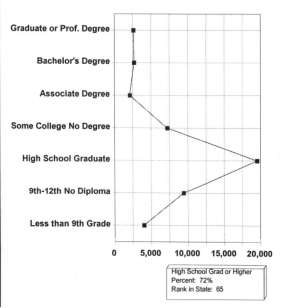

Population Projections

Age Groups	2000	2010	% Change
0-17	17,300	15,600	-9.8%
18-24	7,420	6,840	-7.8%
25-39	13,720	13,520	-1.5%
40-59	19,100	18,080	-5.3%
60-74	9,500	10,720	12.8%
75 +	4,620	4,780	3.5%
Total	71,700	69,500	-3.1%

Personal Income
Real 1995 Dollars ($000)

	1990	1995	% Chg.
Total Earnings by Place of Work	1,088,897	1,069,399	-1.8%
Less Personal Contributions for Social Insurance	71,187	73,146	2.8%
Net Income by Place of Work	1,017,710	996,253	-2.1%
Plus Residence Adjustment	-89,750	-57,723	-35.7%
Net Income by Place of Residence	927,960	938,530	1.1%
Plus Dividends, Rent and Interest	194,178	202,657	4.4%
Plus Transfer Payments	235,108	287,993	22.5%
Personal Income by Place of Residence	1,357,246	1,429,180	5.3%
Per Capita Income ($)	18,298	19,388	6.0%
Rank	39	42	61

Educational Attainment 1990

Graduate or Prof. Degree
Bachelor's Degree
Associate Degree
Some College No Degree
High School Graduate
9th-12th No Diploma
Less than 9th Grade

0   5,000   10,000   15,000   20,000

High School Grad or Higher
Percent: 72%
Rank in State: 65

Population Change by Decade
(1990-2000 projected)

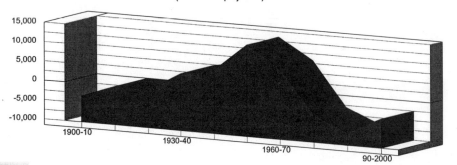

15,000
10,000
5,000
0
-5,000
-10,000

1900-10   1930-40   1960-70   90-2000

For EDIN tables, sources and footnotes, see page 380.

Occupation of Employed Persons Age 16 & Over

	1990	% Chg. 80-90
Managerial & Professional	6,546	16.6
Technical, Sales & Admin. Support	8,626	7.2
Service Occupations	4,824	-4.3
Farming, Forestry and Fishing	595	-23.7
Precision Production, Craft & Repair	4,771	6.7
Operators, Fabricators	8,448	-11.4

Top 5 Counties Commuting in 1990

From Grant Into:		Into Grant From:	
Howard	651	Madison	969
Huntington	591	Wabash	715
Madison	448	Blackford	614
Wabash	418	Miami	525
Miami	385	Huntington	503

28,382 persons lived and worked in this county.

4,488 lived in the county but worked elsewhere.

Number of Establishments
(% Change 1990-1995)

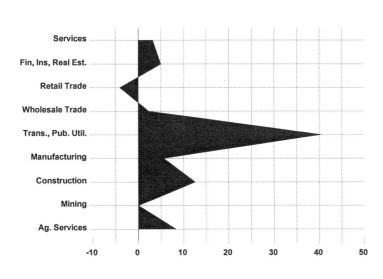

Establishments by Sector 1995

Industry	Number of Establishments	% with fewer than 10 employees
Ag. Services	13	76.9%
Mining	3	0.0%
Construction	134	81.3%
Manufacturing	94	36.2%
Transportation, Public Utilities	66	65.2%
Wholesale Trade	88	72.7%
Retail Trade	454	66.5%
Finance, Insurance, Real Estate	147	79.6%
Services	546	77.3%

Private Industry	Employment		Real Earnings ($000)		Average Earnings Per Job	
	1995	% Chg. 90-95	1995	Real % Chg. 90-95	1995	Real % Chg. 90-95
Ag. Services	NA	NA	NA	NA	NA	NA
Mining	NA	NA	NA	NA	NA	NA
Construction	1,342	-0.2%	35,756	9.4%	26,644	9.6%
Manufacturing	10,407	-12.6%	486,353	-11.6%	46,733	1.1%
Transportation, Public Utilities	1,229	-11.8%	37,330	-11.1%	30,374	0.8%
Wholesale Trade	842	1.2%	21,088	2.4%	25,045	1.2%
Retail Trade	7,586	9.8%	97,717	12.9%	12,881	2.9%
Finance, Insurance, Real Estate	1,717	-0.6%	33,327	12.9%	19,410	13.6%
Services	10,446	15.4%	208,770	21.2%	19,986	5.0%

GREENE COUNTY

Population 1997 (Est.)	33,074	# Households 1995 (Projection)	12,000	Personal Income 1995 ($000)	$219,128
Land Area (Sq. Mi.)	542.1	% Family	73.1%	Avg. Wage Per Job 1995	$18,561
Population Density 1997	61.0	% Non-Family	26.7%	Employed in 1996	14,060
% Under 20 1996	26.8%	% Living Alone	24.5%	Unemployed in 1996	1,210
% 65 & Over 1996	16.6%	Births 1995	414	Unemployment Rate 1996	7.9%
% White 1996	99.5%	Births to Teens 1995	68	Avg. Covered Payroll 1996 ($000)	$37,966
% African-Amer. 1996	0.0%	Deaths 1995	324	Average Weekly Earnings in Manufacturing 1996	$316.50
% Hispanic* 1996	0.7%	Marriages 1995	305	Registered Vehicles 1996	32,569

*May be of any race.

Percent of Total Population By Sex and Age

■ Male   2010   ■ Female

(Population pyramid chart showing age groups from 0-4 to 95+, with male on left and female on right, scale 8% to 0% to 8%)

Population Projections

Age Groups	2000	2010	% Change
0-17	7,110	6,800	-4.4%
18-24	3,190	2,750	-13.8%
25-39	5,820	6,300	8.2%
40-59	8,070	7,960	-1.4%
60-74	3,890	4,360	12.1%
75 +	2,350	2,260	-3.8%
Total	30,400	30,400	0.0%

Personal Income
Real 1995 Dollars ($000)

	1990	1995	% Chg.
Total Earnings by Place of Work	193,733	219,128	13.1%
Less Personal Contributions for Social Insurance	13,435	16,554	23.2%
Net Income by Place of Work	180,298	202,574	12.4%
Plus Residence Adjustment	123,695	121,068	-2.1%
Net Income by Place of Residence	303,994	323,642	6.5%
Plus Dividends, Rent and Interest	88,590	87,552	-1.2%
Plus Transfer Payments	103,900	121,427	16.9%
Personal Income by Place of Residence	496,484	532,621	7.3%
Per Capita Income ($)	16,283	16,303	0.1%
Rank	71	83	86

Educational Attainment 1990

(Chart showing educational attainment categories from Less than 9th Grade to Graduate or Prof. Degree, scale 0 to 9,000)

High School Grad or Higher
Percent: 72%
Rank in State: 66

Population Change by Decade
(1990-2000 projected)

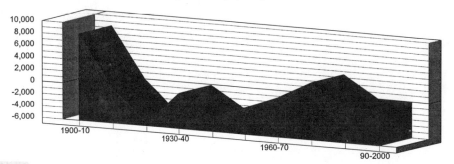

(Area chart showing population change from 1900-10 to 90-2000, scale -6,000 to 10,000)

Occupation of Employed Persons Age 16 & Over				Top 5 Counties Commuting in 1990			
	1990	% Chg. 80-90	From Greene Into:		Into Greene From:		
Managerial & Professional	2,451	47.3	Monroe	2,558	Sullivan	474
Technical, Sales & Admin. Support	3,173	16.1	Martin	1,351	Clay	276
Service Occupations	1,905	36.9	Vigo	417	Knox	166
Farming, Forestry and Fishing	567	-13.7	Sullivan	360	Daviess	151
Precision Production, Craft & Repair	2,070	4.2	Daviess	164	Monroe	138
Operators, Fabricators	2,754	-13.1	6,934	persons lived and worked in this county.		
			5,711	lived in the county but worked elsewhere.		

Number of Establishments
(% Change 1990-1995)

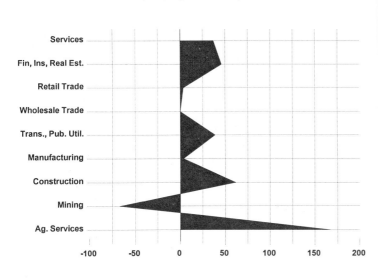

Establishments by Sector 1995		
Industry	Number of Establishments	% with fewer than 10 employees
Ag. Services	8	100.0%
Mining	3	66.7%
Construction	105	83.8%
Manufacturing	29	55.2%
Transportation, Public Utilities	43	90.7%
Wholesale Trade	39	76.9%
Retail Trade	180	69.4%
Finance, Insurance, Real Estate	57	82.5%
Services	230	91.7%

Private Industry	Employment		Real Earnings ($000)		Average Earnings Per Job	
	1995	% Chg. 90-95	1995	Real % Chg. 90-95	1995	Real % Chg. 90-95
Ag. Services	120	17.6%	1,407	59.5%	11,725	35.5%
Mining	681	31.7%	36,337	22.1%	53,358	-7.3%
Construction	910	39.1%	18,439	51.7%	20,263	9.0%
Manufacturing	1,553	-0.7%	28,075	-14.1%	18,078	-13.5%
Transportation, Public Utilities	460	-7.4%	11,666	3.3%	25,361	11.6%
Wholesale Trade	287	-2.4%	14,895	20.4%	51,899	23.3%
Retail Trade	2,318	18.1%	24,934	27.7%	10,757	8.1%
Finance, Insurance, Real Estate	498	2.3%	6,985	11.9%	14,026	9.4%
Services	2,475	1.1%	36,373	24.1%	14,696	22.7%

Hamilton County

Population 1997 (Est.)	154,785	# Households 1995 (Projection)	43,400	Personal Income 1995 ($000)	$2,446,233
Land Area (Sq. Mi.)	398.0	% Family	80.1%	Avg. Wage Per Job 1995	$27,920
Population Density 1997	388.9	% Non-Family	19.8%	Employed in 1996	79,570
% Under 20 1996	30.0%	% Living Alone	16.6%	Unemployed in 1996	1,370
% 65 & Over 1996	8.1%	Births 1995	2,316	Unemployment Rate 1996	1.7%
% White 1996	97.7%	Births to Teens 1995	86	Avg. Covered Payroll 1996 ($000)	$464,753
% African-Amer. 1996	0.7%	Deaths 1995	729	Average Weekly Earnings in Manufacturing 1996	$712.25
% Hispanic* 1996	0.9%	Marriages 1995	953	Registered Vehicles 1996	134,564

*May be of any race.

Percent of Total Population By Sex and Age

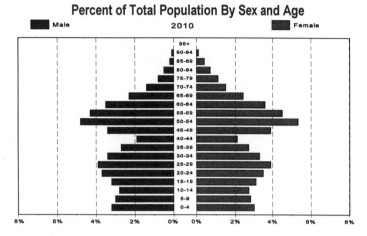

■ Male 2010 ■ Female

Population Projections

Age Groups	2000	2010	% Change
0-17	32,000	29,240	-8.6%
18-24	13,700	13,350	-2.6%
25-39	22,190	27,290	23.0%
40-59	43,810	41,440	-5.4%
60-74	11,740	20,050	70.8%
75 +	4,380	5,510	25.8%
Total	127,800	136,900	7.1%

Personal Income
Real 1995 Dollars ($000)

	1990	1995	% Chg.
Total Earnings by Place of Work	1,555,099	2,446,233	57.3%
Less Personal Contributions for Social Insurance	101,805	167,326	64.4%
Net Income by Place of Work	1,453,294	2,278,907	56.8%
Plus Residence Adjustment	1,079,774	1,306,331	21.0%
Net Income by Place of Residence	2,533,068	3,585,238	41.5%
Plus Dividends, Rent and Interest	640,004	797,608	24.6%
Plus Transfer Payments	215,332	290,507	34.9%
Personal Income by Place of Residence	3,388,404	4,673,353	37.9%
Per Capita Income ($)	30,723	33,163	7.9%
Rank	1	1	41

Educational Attainment 1990

Graduate or Prof. Degree
Bachelor's Degree
Associate Degree
Some College No Degree
High School Graduate
9th-12th No Diploma
Less than 9th Grade

0   5,000   10,000   15,000   20,000

High School Grad or Higher
Percent: 89%
Rank in State: 1

Population Change by Decade
(1990-2000 projected)

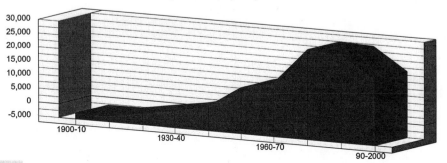

30,000
25,000
20,000
15,000
10,000
5,000
0
-5,000

1900-10   1930-40   1960-70   90-2000

For EDIN tables, sources and footnotes, see page 380.

Occupation of Employed Persons Age 16 & Over

	1990	% Chg. 80-90
Managerial & Professional	20,743	87.7
Technical, Sales & Admin. Support	20,466	63.3
Service Occupations	5,237	32.5
Farming, Forestry and Fishing	941	35.0
Precision Production, Craft & Repair	5,166	15.8
Operators, Fabricators	5,432	-4.6

Top 5 Counties Commuting in 1990

From Hamilton Into:		Into Hamilton From:	
Marion	26,255	Marion	11,202
Howard	1,156	Madison	2,302
Madison	1,133	Boone	1,297
Outside Indiana	556	Tipton	811
Boone	481	Hendricks	547

26,041 persons lived and worked in this county.

31,237 lived in the county but worked elsewhere.

Number of Establishments
(% Change 1990-1995)

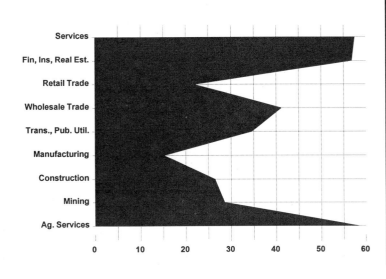

Establishments by Sector 1995

Industry	Number of Establishments	% with fewer than 10 employees
Ag. Services	114	84.2%
Mining	9	22.2%
Construction	550	80.9%
Manufacturing	182	47.8%
Transportation, Public Utilities	140	69.3%
Wholesale Trade	521	79.3%
Retail Trade	739	64.4%
Finance, Insurance, Real Estate	483	77.0%
Services	1,493	79.2%

Private Industry	Employment		Real Earnings ($000)		Average Earnings Per Job	
	1995	% Chg. 90-95	1995	Real % Chg. 90-95	1995	Real % Chg. 90-95
Ag. Services	1,493	35.2%	27,238	36.5%	18,244	0.9%
Mining	414	31.8%	10,126	55.5%	24,459	18.0%
Construction	6,106	16.5%	228,796	33.2%	37,471	14.3%
Manufacturing	9,509	63.3%	381,050	94.1%	40,073	18.9%
Transportation, Public Utilities	3,394	0.9%	133,139	-0.1%	39,228	-1.0%
Wholesale Trade	5,951	30.6%	286,197	43.9%	48,092	10.2%
Retail Trade	15,661	57.5%	254,995	63.8%	16,282	4.0%
Finance, Insurance, Real Estate	12,401	68.7%	348,146	139.7%	28,074	42.0%
Services	21,188	49.6%	593,640	56.4%	28,018	4.6%

For EDIN tables, sources and footnotes, see page 380.

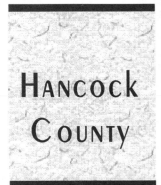

Hancock County

Population 1997 (Est.)	53,071	# Households 1995 (Projection)	16,500	Personal Income 1995 ($000)	$470,738
Land Area (Sq. Mi.)	306.2	% Family	80.9%	Avg. Wage Per Job 1995	$23,235
Population Density 1997	173.3	% Non-Family	19.3%	Employed in 1996	27,390
% Under 20 1996	29.1%	% Living Alone	17.2%	Unemployed in 1996	800
% 65 & Over 1996	10.4%	Births 1995	687	Unemployment Rate 1996	2.8%
% White 1996	99.2%	Births to Teens 1995	68	Avg. Covered Payroll 1996 ($000)	$87,324
% African-Amer. 1996	0.1%	Deaths 1995	391	Average Weekly Earnings in Manufacturing 1996	$820.50
% Hispanic* 1996	1.0%	Marriages 1995	436	Registered Vehicles 1996	54,850

*May be of any race.

Percent of Total Population By Sex and Age

■ Male 2010 ■ Female

Population Projections

Age Groups	2000	2010	% Change
0-17	11,200	10,680	-4.6%
18-24	5,370	4,310	-19.7%
25-39	8,430	10,570	25.4%
40-59	14,900	12,830	-13.9%
60-74	5,390	7,950	47.5%
75 +	2,190	2,550	16.4%
Total	47,500	48,900	2.9%

Personal Income
Real 1995 Dollars ($000)

	1990	1995	% Chg.
Total Earnings by Place of Work	388,885	470,738	21.0%
Less Personal Contributions for Social Insurance	24,316	31,786	30.7%
Net Income by Place of Work	364,569	438,952	20.4%
Plus Residence Adjustment	381,245	461,283	21.0%
Net Income by Place of Residence	745,813	900,235	20.7%
Plus Dividends, Rent and Interest	136,660	150,415	10.1%
Plus Transfer Payments	106,699	137,097	28.5%
Personal Income by Place of Residence	989,172	1,187,747	20.1%
Per Capita Income ($)	21,644	23,325	7.8%
Rank	8	9	44

Educational Attainment 1990

High School Grad or Higher
Percent: 80%
Rank in State: 9

Population Change by Decade
(1990-2000 projected)

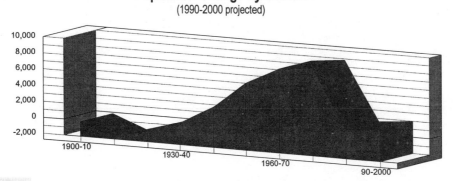

For EDIN tables, sources and footnotes, see page 380.

Occupation of Employed Persons Age 16 & Over

	1990	% Chg. 80-90
Managerial & Professional	5,365	43.6
Technical, Sales & Admin. Support	7,853	39.9
Service Occupations	2,148	0.8
Farming, Forestry and Fishing	498	-20.6
Precision Production, Craft & Repair	3,392	13.4
Operators, Fabricators	3,856	-15.4

Top 5 Counties Commuting in 1990

From Hancock Into:		Into Hancock From:	
Marion	12,026	Marion	1,477
Madison	491	Henry	805
Hamilton	374	Madison	616
Shelby	368	Shelby	501
Henry	194	Rush	303

8,396 persons lived and worked in this county.
14,161 lived in the county but worked elsewhere.

Number of Establishments
(% Change 1990-1995)

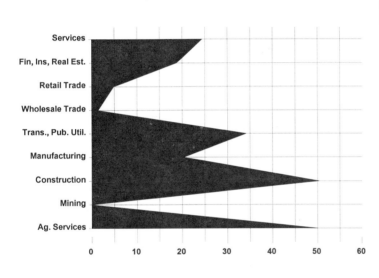

Establishments by Sector 1995

Industry	Number of Establishments	% with fewer than 10 employees
Ag. Services	27	85.2%
Mining	2	50.0%
Construction	221	80.5%
Manufacturing	71	53.5%
Transportation, Public Utilities	55	72.7%
Wholesale Trade	72	70.8%
Retail Trade	215	63.7%
Finance, Insurance, Real Estate	76	89.5%
Services	357	85.7%

Private Industry	Employment		Real Earnings ($000)		Average Earnings Per Job	
	1995	% Chg. 90-95	1995	Real % Chg. 90-95	1995	Real % Chg. 90-95
Ag. Services	NA	NA	NA	NA	NA	NA
Mining	NA	NA	NA	NA	NA	NA
Construction	2,015	42.9%	62,054	59.3%	30,796	11.5%
Manufacturing	3,167	7.3%	142,111	18.7%	44,872	10.6%
Transportation, Public Utilities	615	12.0%	18,392	25.2%	29,906	11.8%
Wholesale Trade	716	21.4%	24,750	33.5%	34,567	10.0%
Retail Trade	3,992	19.7%	49,699	22.5%	12,450	2.4%
Finance, Insurance, Real Estate	1,138	9.2%	15,999	30.9%	14,059	19.9%
Services	4,509	15.1%	78,185	21.7%	17,340	5.8%

HARRISON COUNTY

Population 1997 (Est.)	33,999	# Households 1995 (Projection)	11,100	Personal Income 1995 ($000)	$223,715
Land Area (Sq. Mi.)	485.3	% Family	79.0%	Avg. Wage Per Job 1995	$18,964
Population Density 1997	70.1	% Non-Family	20.6%	Employed in 1996	16,520
% Under 20 1996	29.8%	% Living Alone	18.3%	Unemployed in 1996	740
% 65 & Over 1996	11.5%	Births 1995	390	Unemployment Rate 1996	4.3%
% White 1996	99.2%	Births to Teens 1995	51	Avg. Covered Payroll 1996 ($000)	$40,089
% African-Amer. 1996	0.4%	Deaths 1995	271	Average Weekly Earnings in Manufacturing 1996	$470.25
% Hispanic* 1996	0.6%	Marriages 1995	241	Registered Vehicles 1996	36,562

*May be of any race.

Percent of Total Population By Sex and Age

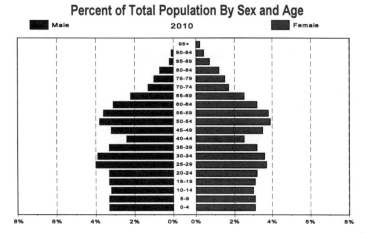

Population Projections

Age Groups	2000	2010	% Change
0-17	7,680	7,350	-4.3%
18-24	3,580	2,930	-18.2%
25-39	5,950	7,070	18.8%
40-59	9,190	8,680	-5.5%
60-74	3,400	4,540	33.5%
75 +	1,670	1,910	14.4%
Total	31,500	32,500	3.2%

Personal Income
Real 1995 Dollars ($000)

	1990	1995	% Chg.
Total Earnings by Place of Work	178,268	223,715	25.5%
Less Personal Contributions for Social Insurance	11,785	15,959	35.4%
Net Income by Place of Work	166,483	207,756	24.8%
Plus Residence Adjustment	182,838	225,228	23.2%
Net Income by Place of Residence	349,320	432,984	24.0%
Plus Dividends, Rent and Interest	81,816	83,343	1.9%
Plus Transfer Payments	72,970	93,158	27.7%
Personal Income by Place of Residence	504,107	609,485	20.9%
Per Capita Income ($)	16,839	18,692	11.0%
Rank	62	52	15

Educational Attainment 1990

High School Grad or Higher
Percent: 71%
Rank in State: 71

Population Change by Decade
(1990-2000 projected)

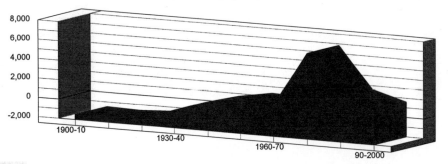

For EDIN tables, sources and footnotes, see page 380.

Occupation of Employed Persons Age 16 & Over			Top 5 Counties Commuting in 1990				
	1990	% Chg. 80-90	From Harrison Into:		Into Harrison From:		
Managerial & Professional	2,208	39.5	Outside Indiana	3,991	Floyd	436	
Technical, Sales & Admin. Support	3,991	55.9	Floyd	1,765	Crawford	424	
Service Occupations	1,722	48.2	Clark	1,069	Outside Indiana	377	
Farming, Forestry and Fishing	539	-14.6	Washington	167	Washington	168	
Precision Production, Craft & Repair	2,117	25.0	Crawford	141	Clark	163	
Operators, Fabricators	3,357	-2.3					

6,295 persons lived and worked in this county.

7,333 lived in the county but worked elsewhere.

Number of Establishments
(% Change 1990-1995)

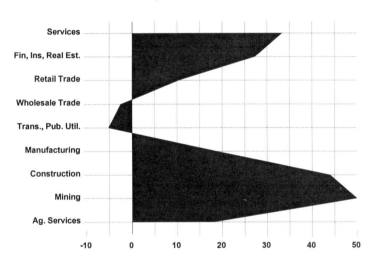

Establishments by Sector 1995		
Industry	Number of Establishments	% with fewer than 10 employees
Ag. Services	13	84.6%
Mining	6	33.3%
Construction	95	92.6%
Manufacturing	38	39.5%
Transportation, Public Utilities	37	70.3%
Wholesale Trade	39	79.5%
Retail Trade	161	72.7%
Finance, Insurance, Real Estate	42	73.8%
Services	180	86.7%

Private Industry	Employment		Real Earnings ($000)		Average Earnings Per Job	
	1995	% Chg. 90-95	1995	Real % Chg. 90-95	1995	Real % Chg. 90-95
Ag. Services	207	NA	3,673	NA	17,744	NA
Mining	78	NA	2,139	NA	27,423	NA
Construction	774	17.6%	14,950	31.1%	19,315	11.5%
Manufacturing	2,226	35.3%	66,963	40.9%	30,082	4.1%
Transportation, Public Utilities	584	3.0%	17,150	18.7%	29,366	15.2%
Wholesale Trade	361	0.0%	8,910	-4.7%	24,681	-4.7%
Retail Trade	2,616	33.2%	28,787	41.8%	11,004	6.5%
Finance, Insurance, Real Estate	451	8.9%	7,305	31.3%	16,197	20.6%
Services	2,488	3.7%	34,273	35.0%	13,775	30.2%

HENDRICKS COUNTY

Population 1997 (Est.)	92,291	# Households 1995 (Projection)	27,500	Personal Income 1995 ($000)	$750,152
Land Area (Sq. Mi.)	408.4	% Family	81.4%	Avg. Wage Per Job 1995	$22,846
Population Density 1997	226.0	% Non-Family	18.5%	Employed in 1996	47,060
% Under 20 1996	29.3%	% Living Alone	16.3%	Unemployed in 1996	980
% 65 & Over 1996	9.6%	Births 1995	1,067	Unemployment Rate 1996	2.0%
% White 1996	98.2%	Births to Teens 1995	93	Avg. Covered Payroll 1996 ($000)	$136,112
% African-Amer. 1996	1.1%	Deaths 1995	604	Average Weekly Earnings in Manufacturing 1996	$536.50
% Hispanic* 1996	0.6%	Marriages 1995	644	Registered Vehicles 1996	91,256

*May be of any race.

Percent of Total Population By Sex and Age

Male — 2010 — Female

(Population pyramid chart: age groups from 0-4 up to 95+, horizontal axis from 8% to 0% (male, left) and 0% to 8% (female, right))

Population Projections

Age Groups	2000	2010	% Change
0-17	19,260	17,760	-7.8%
18-24	8,880	7,820	-11.9%
25-39	14,810	17,300	16.8%
40-59	25,320	23,430	-7.5%
60-74	8,450	12,510	48.0%
75 +	3,340	3,830	14.7%
Total	80,100	82,700	3.2%

Personal Income
Real 1995 Dollars ($000)

	1990	1995	% Chg.
Total Earnings by Place of Work	614,088	750,152	22.2%
Less Personal Contributions for Social Insurance	39,911	50,673	27.0%
Net Income by Place of Work	574,177	699,479	21.8%
Plus Residence Adjustment	700,449	878,785	25.5%
Net Income by Place of Residence	1,274,626	1,578,264	23.8%
Plus Dividends, Rent and Interest	214,076	287,676	34.4%
Plus Transfer Payments	151,897	197,749	30.2%
Personal Income by Place of Residence	1,640,598	2,063,689	25.8%
Per Capita Income ($)	21,567	23,819	10.4%
Rank	9	7	16

Educational Attainment 1990

(Line chart with categories: Graduate or Prof. Degree, Bachelor's Degree, Associate Degree, Some College No Degree, High School Graduate, 9th-12th No Diploma, Less than 9th Grade; horizontal axis 0 to 20,000)

High School Grad or Higher
Percent: 84%
Rank in State: 3

Population Change by Decade
(1990-2000 projected)

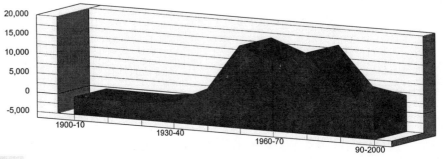

(Chart with vertical axis -5,000 to 20,000; horizontal axis decades from 1900-10, 1930-40, 1960-70, 90-2000)

For EDIN tables, sources and footnotes, see page 380.

Occupation of Employed Persons Age 16 & Over

	1990	% Chg. 80-90
Managerial & Professional	10,158	51.6
Technical, Sales & Admin. Support	12,919	27.8
Service Occupations	3,647	4.9
Farming, Forestry and Fishing	740	2.9
Precision Production, Craft & Repair	5,727	18.4
Operators, Fabricators	5,511	-3.7

Top 5 Counties Commuting in 1990

From Hendricks Into:		Into Hendricks From:	
Marion	21,811	Marion	3,461
Hamilton	547	Morgan	982
Morgan	400	Putnam	865
Boone	301	Boone	313
Putnam	214	Johnson	190

13,709 persons lived and worked in this county.

24,326 lived in the county but worked elsewhere.

Number of Establishments
(% Change 1990-1995)

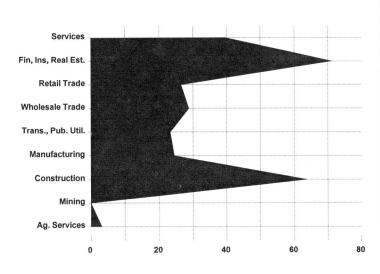

Establishments by Sector 1995

Industry	Number of Establishments	% with fewer than 10 employees
Ag. Services	32	87.5%
Mining	2	50.0%
Construction	326	85.9%
Manufacturing	66	60.6%
Transportation, Public Utilities	90	71.1%
Wholesale Trade	94	80.9%
Retail Trade	382	62.3%
Finance, Insurance, Real Estate	161	89.4%
Services	557	82.9%

Private Industry	Employment		Real Earnings ($000)		Average Earnings Per Job	
	1995	% Chg. 90-95	1995	Real % Chg. 90-95	1995	Real % Chg. 90-95
Ag. Services	NA	NA	NA	NA	NA	NA
Mining	NA	NA	NA	NA	NA	NA
Construction	3,164	28.9%	88,088	23.8%	27,841	-3.9%
Manufacturing	1,381	0.6%	39,814	5.8%	28,830	5.2%
Transportation, Public Utilities	3,116	-2.5%	155,287	5.4%	49,835	8.2%
Wholesale Trade	955	19.2%	34,856	35.3%	36,498	13.5%
Retail Trade	7,334	29.9%	95,050	30.0%	12,960	0.0%
Finance, Insurance, Real Estate	1,882	11.7%	27,918	39.5%	14,834	24.9%
Services	8,986	34.4%	156,149	48.6%	17,377	10.5%

HENRY COUNTY

Population 1997 (Est.)	48,867	# Households 1995 (Projection)	18,300	Personal Income 1995 ($000)	$487,126
Land Area (Sq. Mi.)	393.0	% Family	74.9%	Avg. Wage Per Job 1995	$24,599
Population Density 1997	124.3	% Non-Family	25.2%	Employed in 1996	23,860
% Under 20 1996	26.2%	% Living Alone	23.0%	Unemployed in 1996	1,290
% 65 & Over 1996	14.9%	Births 1995	611	Unemployment Rate 1996	5.1%
% White 1996	98.5%	Births to Teens 1995	101	Avg. Covered Payroll 1996 ($000)	$92,517
% African-Amer. 1996	1.1%	Deaths 1995	527	Average Weekly Earnings in Manufacturing 1996	$894.75
% Hispanic* 1996	0.6%	Marriages 1995	451	Registered Vehicles 1996	51,091

*May be of any race.

Percent of Total Population By Sex and Age

Male — 2010 — Female

Population Projections

Age Groups	2000	2010	% Change
0-17	10,620	9,680	-8.9%
18-24	4,500	4,100	-8.9%
25-39	8,900	9,190	3.3%
40-59	13,030	12,020	-7.8%
60-74	6,190	7,200	16.3%
75 +	3,270	3,300	0.9%
Total	46,500	45,500	-2.2%

Personal Income
Real 1995 Dollars ($000)

	1990	1995	% Chg.
Total Earnings by Place of Work	400,833	487,126	21.5%
Less Personal Contributions for Social Insurance	25,751	33,454	29.9%
Net Income by Place of Work	375,081	453,672	21.0%
Plus Residence Adjustment	191,265	201,679	5.4%
Net Income by Place of Residence	566,346	655,351	15.7%
Plus Dividends, Rent and Interest	136,984	121,995	-10.9%
Plus Transfer Payments	161,749	191,168	18.2%
Personal Income by Place of Residence	865,079	968,514	12.0%
Per Capita Income ($)	17,964	19,704	9.7%
Rank	45	35	23

Educational Attainment 1990

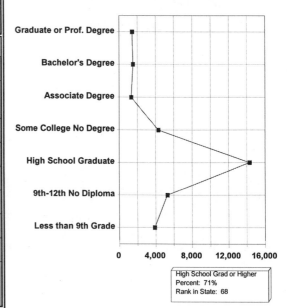

High School Grad or Higher
Percent: 71%
Rank in State: 68

Population Change by Decade
(1990-2000 projected)

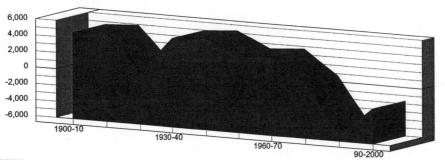

Occupation of Employed Persons Age 16 & Over

	1990	% Chg. 80-90
Managerial & Professional	3,886	26.5
Technical, Sales & Admin. Support	5,509	13.1
Service Occupations	3,445	27.5
Farming, Forestry and Fishing	571	-17.6
Precision Production, Craft & Repair	3,012	6.8
Operators, Fabricators	4,792	-13.7

Top 5 Counties Commuting in 1990

From Henry Into:		Into Henry From:	
Madison	1,991	Delaware	458
Marion	1,800	Wayne	292
Delaware	1,682	Rush	291
Hancock	805	Madison	212
Wayne	682	Hancock	194

12,581 persons lived and worked in this county.
8,356 lived in the county but worked elsewhere.

Number of Establishments
(% Change 1990-1995)

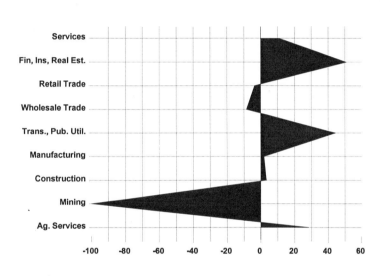

Establishments by Sector 1995

Industry	Number of Establishments	% with fewer than 10 employees
Ag. Services	18	88.9%
Mining	0	NA
Construction	94	83.0%
Manufacturing	54	44.4%
Transportation, Public Utilities	52	71.2%
Wholesale Trade	54	74.1%
Retail Trade	267	68.9%
Finance, Insurance, Real Estate	77	81.8%
Services	323	81.4%

Private Industry	Employment		Real Earnings ($000)		Average Earnings Per Job	
	1995	% Chg. 90-95	1995	Real % Chg. 90-95	1995	Real % Chg. 90-95
Ag. Services	232	34.9%	2,630	-23.2%	11,336	-43.0%
Mining	16	33.3%	686	121.3%	42,875	66.0%
Construction	1,051	0.2%	23,414	0.1%	22,278	-0.1%
Manufacturing	3,653	10.7%	216,505	50.4%	59,268	35.9%
Transportation, Public Utilities	573	19.6%	13,598	10.7%	23,731	-7.4%
Wholesale Trade	439	1.9%	11,471	-0.2%	26,130	-2.0%
Retail Trade	4,272	17.9%	54,860	22.2%	12,842	3.6%
Finance, Insurance, Real Estate	904	6.0%	14,009	17.9%	15,497	11.2%
Services	4,126	4.8%	68,631	17.0%	16,634	11.6%

HOWARD COUNTY

Population 1997 (Est.)	83,586	# Households 1995 (Projection)	31,500	Personal Income 1995 ($000)	$2,207,375
Land Area (Sq. Mi.)	293.1	% Family	71.7%	Avg. Wage Per Job 1995	$33,976
Population Density 1997	285.2	% Non-Family	28.2%	Employed in 1996	41,730
% Under 20 1996	28.3%	% Living Alone	25.3%	Unemployed in 1996	1,590
% 65 & Over 1996	11.7%	Births 1995	1,207	Unemployment Rate 1996	3.7%
% White 1996	93.0%	Births to Teens 1995	227	Avg. Covered Payroll 1996 ($000)	$423,193
% African-Amer. 1996	6.0%	Deaths 1995	699	Average Weekly Earnings in Manufacturing 1996	$1,080.50
% Hispanic* 1996	1.7%	Marriages 1995	852	Registered Vehicles 1996	79,325

*May be of any race.

Percent of Total Population By Sex and Age

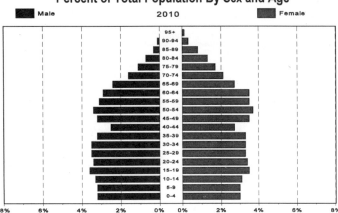

Population Projections

Age Groups	2000	2010	% Change
0-17	20,150	18,680	-7.3%
18-24	8,030	7,820	-2.6%
25-39	15,560	16,320	4.9%
40-59	22,430	20,940	-6.6%
60-74	9,840	12,300	25.0%
75 +	4,540	5,100	12.3%
Total	80,500	81,200	0.9%

Personal Income
Real 1995 Dollars ($000)

	1990	1995	% Chg.
Total Earnings by Place of Work	1,679,223	2,207,375	31.5%
Less Personal Contributions for Social Insurance	109,027	137,515	26.1%
Net Income by Place of Work	1,570,197	2,069,860	31.8%
Plus Residence Adjustment	-353,276	-581,856	64.7%
Net Income by Place of Residence	1,216,921	1,488,004	22.3%
Plus Dividends, Rent and Interest	244,486	234,276	-4.2%
Plus Transfer Payments	234,235	280,110	19.6%
Personal Income by Place of Residence	1,695,642	2,002,390	18.1%
Per Capita Income ($)	20,947	24,013	14.6%
Rank	12	6	2

Educational Attainment 1990

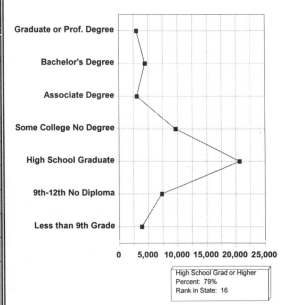

High School Grad or Higher
Percent: 79%
Rank in State: 16

Population Change by Decade
(1990-2000 projected)

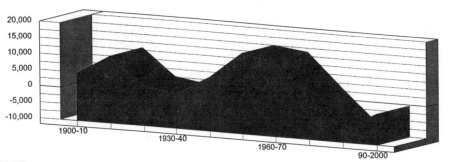

For EDIN tables, sources and footnotes, see page 380.

Occupation of Employed Persons Age 16 & Over

	1990	% Chg. 80-90
Managerial & Professional	7,601	23.9
Technical, Sales & Admin. Support	10,162	12.2
Service Occupations	5,279	13.8
Farming, Forestry and Fishing	542	-16.5
Precision Production, Craft & Repair	5,946	8.1
Operators, Fabricators	7,511	-24.6

Top 5 Counties Commuting in 1990

From Howard Into:		Into Howard From:	
Miami	693	Tipton	2,159
Marion	587	Miami	2,101
Grant	359	Cass	1,651
Tipton	338	Hamilton	1,156
Hamilton	314	Clinton	715

33,020 persons lived and worked in this county.

3,683 lived in the county but worked elsewhere.

Number of Establishments
(% Change 1990-1995)

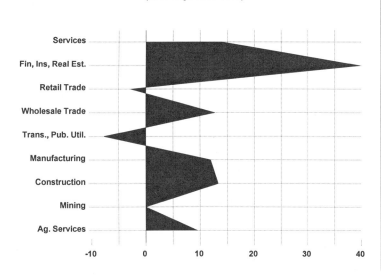

Establishments by Sector 1995

Industry	Number of Establishments	% with fewer than 10 employees
Ag. Services	23	91.3%
Mining	4	75.0%
Construction	170	84.1%
Manufacturing	75	42.7%
Transportation, Public Utilities	59	55.9%
Wholesale Trade	124	70.2%
Retail Trade	576	62.8%
Finance, Insurance, Real Estate	186	83.9%
Services	708	76.1%

Private Industry	Employment		Real Earnings ($000)		Average Earnings Per Job	
	1995	% Chg. 90-95	1995	Real % Chg. 90-95	1995	Real % Chg. 90-95
Ag. Services	377	10.6%	4,755	-4.5%	12,613	-13.6%
Mining	103	19.8%	2,179	76.1%	21,155	47.0%
Construction	2,014	7.3%	51,916	8.6%	25,778	1.2%
Manufacturing	20,286	13.1%	1,475,395	45.0%	72,730	28.3%
Transportation, Public Utilities	1,418	-9.0%	49,361	-8.7%	34,810	0.3%
Wholesale Trade	1,084	3.8%	33,896	15.1%	31,269	10.9%
Retail Trade	11,030	14.9%	142,389	16.0%	12,909	1.0%
Finance, Insurance, Real Estate	2,200	2.9%	44,607	26.3%	20,276	22.7%
Services	11,843	19.4%	242,899	13.9%	20,510	-4.6%

HUNTINGTON COUNTY

Population 1997 (Est.)	37,144	# Households 1995 (Projection)	13,000	Personal Income 1995 ($000)	$464,938
Land Area (Sq. Mi.)	382.6	% Family	75.6%	Avg. Wage Per Job 1995	$20,623
Population Density 1997	97.1	% Non-Family	24.2%	Employed in 1996	19,640
% Under 20 1996	29.7%	% Living Alone	21.2%	Unemployed in 1996	790
% 65 & Over 1996	14.4%	Births 1995	523	Unemployment Rate 1996	3.9%
% White 1996	98.9%	Births to Teens 1995	85	Avg. Covered Payroll 1996 ($000)	$94,678
% African-Amer. 1996	0.2%	Deaths 1995	363	Average Weekly Earnings in Manufacturing 1996	$498.00
% Hispanic* 1996	1.0%	Marriages 1995	378	Registered Vehicles 1996	36,033

*May be of any race.

Percent of Total Population By Sex and Age

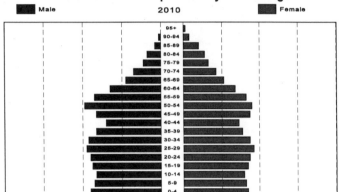

Population Projections

Age Groups	2000	2010	% Change
0-17	9,440	9,130	-3.3%
18-24	3,920	3,690	-5.9%
25-39	7,220	7,870	9.0%
40-59	9,380	9,970	6.3%
60-74	3,830	4,630	20.9%
75 +	2,270	2,080	-8.4%
Total	36,100	37,400	3.6%

Personal Income
Real 1995 Dollars ($000)

	1990	1995	% Chg.
Total Earnings by Place of Work	387,650	464,938	19.9%
Less Personal Contributions for Social Insurance	25,253	32,546	28.9%
Net Income by Place of Work	362,396	432,392	19.3%
Plus Residence Adjustment	98,732	89,330	-9.5%
Net Income by Place of Residence	461,129	521,722	13.1%
Plus Dividends, Rent and Interest	114,345	113,702	-0.6%
Plus Transfer Payments	91,369	109,138	19.4%
Personal Income by Place of Residence	666,843	744,562	11.7%
Per Capita Income ($)	18,793	20,244	7.7%
Rank	26	27	47

Educational Attainment 1990

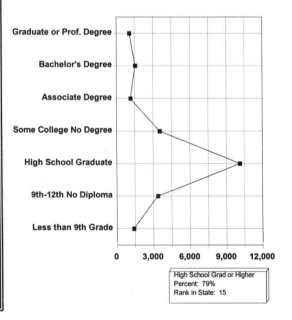

High School Grad or Higher
Percent: 79%
Rank in State: 15

Population Change by Decade
(1990-2000 projected)

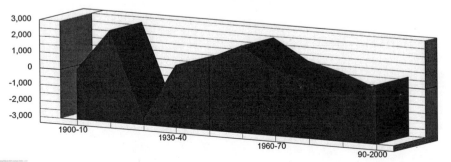

For EDIN tables, sources and footnotes, see page 380.

Occupation of Employed Persons Age 16 & Over				Top 5 Counties Commuting in 1990			

Occupation of Employed Persons Age 16 & Over	1990	% Chg. 80-90	From Huntington Into:		Into Huntington From:	
Managerial & Professional	3,174	20.8	Allen	2,485	Allen	2,047
Technical, Sales & Admin. Support	3,988	12.8	Grant	503	Wabash	695
Service Occupations	2,570	35.8	Wells	423	Wells	639
Farming, Forestry and Fishing	627	-8.7	Whitley	307	Grant	591
Precision Production, Craft & Repair	2,592	18.8	Wabash	286	Whitley	325
Operators, Fabricators	4,670	-2.7	12,810	persons lived and worked in this county.		
			4,509	lived in the county but worked elsewhere.		

Number of Establishments
(% Change 1990-1995)

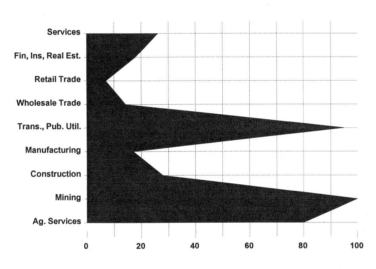

Establishments by Sector 1995		
Industry	Number of Establishments	% with fewer than 10 employees
Ag. Services	18	88.9%
Mining	2	0.0%
Construction	96	90.6%
Manufacturing	89	39.3%
Transportation, Public Utilities	39	69.2%
Wholesale Trade	72	72.2%
Retail Trade	229	67.7%
Finance, Insurance, Real Estate	79	86.1%
Services	265	80.8%

Private Industry	Employment		Real Earnings ($000)		Average Earnings Per Job	
	1995	% Chg. 90-95	1995	Real % Chg. 90-95	1995	Real % Chg. 90-95
Ag. Services	153	20.5%	1,629	-3.6%	10,647	-20.0%
Mining	67	0.0%	2,862	-3.3%	42,716	-3.3%
Construction	931	18.4%	22,870	9.4%	24,565	-7.6%
Manufacturing	7,761	22.8%	226,917	30.3%	29,238	6.1%
Transportation, Public Utilities	503	0.4%	17,079	18.6%	33,954	18.1%
Wholesale Trade	624	7.2%	16,728	25.8%	26,808	17.3%
Retail Trade	3,607	16.9%	44,014	19.1%	12,202	1.9%
Finance, Insurance, Real Estate	757	4.6%	12,210	36.9%	16,129	30.9%
Services	4,407	18.3%	66,299	26.0%	15,044	6.6%

JACKSON COUNTY

Population 1997 (Est.)	40,884	# Households 1995 (Projection)	14,300	Personal Income 1995 ($000)	$561,068
Land Area (Sq. Mi.)	509.3	% Family	76.6%	Avg. Wage Per Job 1995	$21,971
Population Density 1997	80.3	% Non-Family	23.6%	Employed in 1996	20,130
% Under 20 1996	28.5%	% Living Alone	21.1%	Unemployed in 1996	850
% 65 & Over 1996	13.7%	Births 1995	576	Unemployment Rate 1996	4.0%
% White 1996	98.8%	Births to Teens 1995	99	Avg. Covered Payroll 1996 ($000)	$107,010
% African-Amer. 1996	0.4%	Deaths 1995	390	Average Weekly Earnings in Manufacturing 1996	$551.50
% Hispanic* 1996	0.4%	Marriages 1995	392	Registered Vehicles 1996	41,310

*May be of any race.

Percent of Total Population By Sex and Age

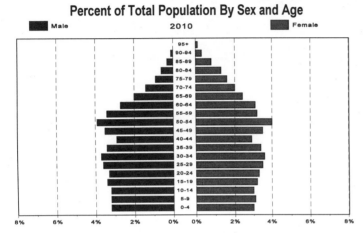

Male 2010 Female

Population Projections

Age Groups	2000	2010	% Change
0-17	9,380	8,920	-4.9%
18-24	4,070	3,630	-10.8%
25-39	7,790	8,300	6.5%
40-59	10,410	10,660	2.4%
60-74	4,510	5,330	18.2%
75 +	2,400	2,450	2.1%
Total	38,600	39,300	1.8%

Personal Income
Real 1995 Dollars ($000)

	1990	1995	% Chg.
Total Earnings by Place of Work	454,149	561,068	23.5%
Less Personal Contributions for Social Insurance	29,786	38,683	29.9%
Net Income by Place of Work	424,363	522,385	23.1%
Plus Residence Adjustment	707	7,462	955.4%
Net Income by Place of Residence	425,070	529,847	24.6%
Plus Dividends, Rent and Interest	114,886	111,868	-2.6%
Plus Transfer Payments	105,042	124,369	18.4%
Personal Income by Place of Residence	644,998	766,084	18.8%
Per Capita Income ($)	17,044	19,021	11.6%
Rank	58	47	13

Educational Attainment 1990

Graduate or Prof. Degree
Bachelor's Degree
Associate Degree
Some College No Degree
High School Graduate
9th-12th No Diploma
Less than 9th Grade

0   3,000   6,000   9,000   12,000

High School Grad or Higher
Percent: 69%
Rank in State: 74

Population Change by Decade
(1990-2000 projected)

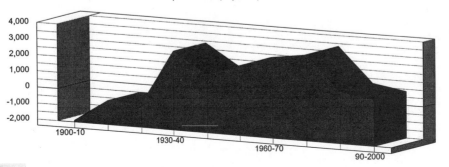

4,000
3,000
2,000
1,000
0
-1,000
-2,000

1900-10   1930-40   1960-70   90-2000

For EDIN tables, sources and footnotes, see page 380.

Occupation of Employed Persons Age 16 & Over		
	1990	% Chg. 80-90
Managerial & Professional	2,880	20.3
Technical, Sales & Admin. Support	4,646	29.0
Service Occupations	2,174	27.6
Farming, Forestry and Fishing	738	-13.5
Precision Production, Craft & Repair	2,223	1.5
Operators, Fabricators	4,670	2.1

Top 5 Counties Commuting in 1990			
From Jackson Into:		Into Jackson From:	
Bartholomew	1,950	Jennings	1,299
Scott	260	Scott	922
Jennings	234	Bartholomew	577
Lawrence	176	Washington	270
Outside Indiana	170	Lawrence	204

13,626   persons lived and worked in this county.

3,448   lived in the county but worked elsewhere.

Number of Establishments
(% Change 1990-1995)

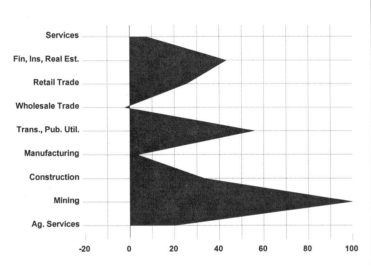

Establishments by Sector 1995		
Industry	Number of Establishments	% with fewer than 10 employees
Ag. Services	12	100.0%
Mining	2	100.0%
Construction	112	83.9%
Manufacturing	90	42.2%
Transportation, Public Utilities	53	71.7%
Wholesale Trade	46	52.2%
Retail Trade	305	68.2%
Finance, Insurance, Real Estate	86	87.2%
Services	287	79.1%

Private Industry	Employment		Real Earnings ($000)		Average Earnings Per Job	
	1995	% Chg. 90-95	1995	Real % Chg. 90-95	1995	Real % Chg. 90-95
Ag. Services	NA	NA	NA	NA	NA	NA
Mining	NA	NA	NA	NA	NA	NA
Construction	1,216	17.9%	29,216	22.9%	24,026	4.2%
Manufacturing	6,577	13.3%	232,198	28.6%	35,305	13.5%
Transportation, Public Utilities	928	10.3%	37,445	19.3%	40,350	8.1%
Wholesale Trade	1,245	39.3%	30,592	35.9%	24,572	-2.4%
Retail Trade	5,751	30.1%	85,577	28.6%	14,880	-1.1%
Finance, Insurance, Real Estate	1,013	17.0%	15,606	34.3%	15,406	14.8%
Services	3,956	20.5%	64,874	25.1%	16,399	3.8%

For EDIN tables, sources and footnotes, see page 380.

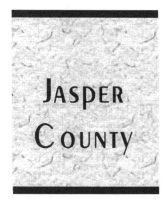

JASPER COUNTY

Population 1997 (Est.)	28,697	# Households 1995 (Projection)	8,800	Personal Income 1995 ($000)	$276,117
Land Area (Sq. Mi.)	559.9	% Family	79.3%	Avg. Wage Per Job 1995	$20,786
Population Density 1997	51.3	% Non-Family	21.1%	Employed in 1996	13,560
% Under 20 1996	31.2%	% Living Alone	19.1%	Unemployed in 1996	820
% 65 & Over 1996	12.5%	Births 1995	365	Unemployment Rate 1996	5.7%
% White 1996	99.1%	Births to Teens 1995	51	Avg. Covered Payroll 1996 ($000)	$54,490
% African-Amer. 1996	0.4%	Deaths 1995	240	Average Weekly Earnings in Manufacturing 1996	$491.75
% Hispanic* 1996	1.6%	Marriages 1995	210	Registered Vehicles 1996	31,250

*May be of any race.

Percent of Total Population By Sex and Age

■ Male   2010   ■ Female

(95+, 90-94, 85-89, 80-84, 75-79, 70-74, 65-69, 60-64, 55-59, 50-54, 45-49, 40-44, 35-39, 30-34, 25-29, 20-24, 15-19, 10-14, 5-9, 0-4)

8% 6% 4% 2% 0% 0% 2% 4% 6% 8%

Population Projections

Age Groups	2000	2010	% Change
0-17	6,670	6,580	-1.3%
18-24	3,050	2,610	-14.4%
25-39	5,270	5,760	9.3%
40-59	6,560	6,760	3.0%
60-74	2,680	3,480	29.9%
75 +	1,430	1,380	-3.5%
Total	25,700	26,600	3.5%

Personal Income
Real 1995 Dollars ($000)

	1990	1995	% Chg.
Total Earnings by Place of Work	247,422	276,117	11.6%
Less Personal Contributions for Social Insurance	15,354	19,485	26.9%
Net Income by Place of Work	232,068	256,632	10.6%
Plus Residence Adjustment	53,365	48,418	-9.3%
Net Income by Place of Residence	285,434	305,050	6.9%
Plus Dividends, Rent and Interest	81,333	81,762	0.5%
Plus Transfer Payments	62,128	76,203	22.7%
Personal Income by Place of Residence	428,894	463,015	8.0%
Per Capita Income ($)	17,127	16,619	-3.0%
Rank	56	78	89

Educational Attainment 1990

(Graduate or Prof. Degree, Bachelor's Degree, Associate Degree, Some College No Degree, High School Graduate, 9th-12th No Diploma, Less than 9th Grade)

0 2,000 4,000 6,000 8,000

High School Grad or Higher
Percent: 76%
Rank in State: 35

Population Change by Decade
(1990-2000 projected)

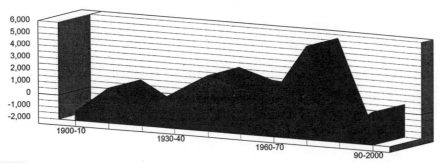

6,000 / 5,000 / 4,000 / 3,000 / 2,000 / 1,000 / 0 / -1,000 / -2,000

1900-10   1930-40   1960-70   90-2000

Occupation of Employed Persons Age 16 & Over

	1990	% Chg. 80-90
Managerial & Professional	1,929	28.7
Technical, Sales & Admin. Support	2,782	12.2
Service Occupations	1,415	14.6
Farming, Forestry and Fishing	682	-30.7
Precision Production, Craft & Repair	1,773	-7.1
Operators, Fabricators	2,636	1.0

Top 5 Counties Commuting in 1990

From Jasper Into:		Into Jasper From:	
Lake	1,498	Newton	776
Porter	758	Porter	330
Outside Indiana	500	White	329
Newton	323	Lake	221
White	297	Pulaski	210

7,063 persons lived and worked in this county.

3,914 lived in the county but worked elsewhere.

Number of Establishments
(% Change 1990-1995)

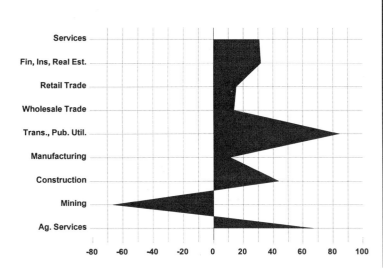

Establishments by Sector 1995

Industry	Number of Establishments	% with fewer than 10 employees
Ag. Services	20	90.0%
Mining	2	50.0%
Construction	118	94.1%
Manufacturing	30	46.7%
Transportation, Public Utilities	70	78.6%
Wholesale Trade	58	75.9%
Retail Trade	189	66.1%
Finance, Insurance, Real Estate	62	91.9%
Services	187	83.4%

Private Industry	Employment		Real Earnings ($000)		Average Earnings Per Job	
	1995	% Chg. 90-95	1995	Real % Chg. 90-95	1995	Real % Chg. 90-95
Ag. Services	198	34.7%	1,598	2.5%	8,071	-23.9%
Mining	23	-17.9%	665	13.4%	28,913	38.1%
Construction	1,105	21.0%	30,300	27.5%	27,421	5.4%
Manufacturing	1,406	9.6%	42,028	24.0%	29,892	13.2%
Transportation, Public Utilities	1,731	32.5%	68,476	19.8%	39,559	-9.6%
Wholesale Trade	376	-7.4%	11,655	-1.4%	30,997	6.5%
Retail Trade	2,819	32.4%	36,528	38.1%	12,958	4.3%
Finance, Insurance, Real Estate	620	6.0%	8,396	24.5%	13,542	17.5%
Services	2,533	12.3%	39,839	19.3%	15,728	6.2%

For EDIN tables, sources and footnotes, see page 380.

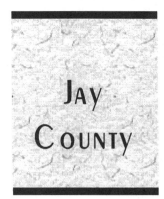

JAY COUNTY

Population 1997 (Est.)	21,692	# Households 1995 (Projection)	8,100	Personal Income 1995 ($000)	$211,989
Land Area (Sq. Mi.)	383.7	% Family	73.5%	Avg. Wage Per Job 1995	$19,637
Population Density 1997	56.5	% Non-Family	26.0%	Employed in 1996	11,450
% Under 20 1996	28.0%	% Living Alone	23.7%	Unemployed in 1996	590
% 65 & Over 1996	15.5%	Births 1995	310	Unemployment Rate 1996	4.9%
% White 1996	99.3%	Births to Teens 1995	48	Avg. Covered Payroll 1996 ($000)	$40,439
% African-Amer. 1996	0.1%	Deaths 1995	234	Average Weekly Earnings in Manufacturing 1996	$466.00
% Hispanic* 1996	0.9%	Marriages 1995	231	Registered Vehicles 1996	21,304

*May be of any race.

Percent of Total Population By Sex and Age

■ Male   2010   ■ Female

(Population pyramid chart, age groups from 0-4 to 95+, horizontal axis from 8% to 8%)

Population Projections

Age Groups	2000	2010	% Change
0-17	5,620	5,510	-2.0%
18-24	2,180	2,120	-2.8%
25-39	3,950	4,330	9.6%
40-59	5,460	5,280	-3.3%
60-74	2,660	2,980	12.0%
75 +	1,530	1,420	-7.2%
Total	21,400	21,600	0.9%

Personal Income
Real 1995 Dollars ($000)

	1990	1995	% Chg.
Total Earnings by Place of Work	191,467	211,989	10.7%
Less Personal Contributions for Social Insurance	12,261	15,018	22.5%
Net Income by Place of Work	179,206	196,971	9.9%
Plus Residence Adjustment	29,442	30,706	4.3%
Net Income by Place of Residence	208,648	227,677	9.1%
Plus Dividends, Rent and Interest	57,128	47,138	-17.5%
Plus Transfer Payments	62,209	74,719	20.1%
Personal Income by Place of Residence	327,985	349,534	6.6%
Per Capita Income ($)	15,231	16,058	5.4%
Rank	84	85	65

Educational Attainment 1990

(Line chart with categories: Graduate or Prof. Degree, Bachelor's Degree, Associate Degree, Some College No Degree, High School Graduate, 9th-12th No Diploma, Less than 9th Grade; horizontal axis 0 to 8,000)

High School Grad or Higher
Percent: 69%
Rank in State: 75

Population Change by Decade
(1990-2000 projected)

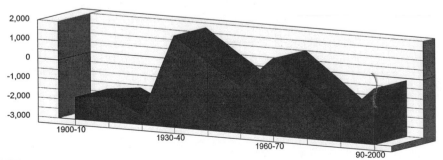

(Area chart, vertical axis from -3,000 to 2,000, horizontal axis decades from 1900-10 to 90-2000)

For EDIN tables, sources and footnotes, see page 380.

Occupation of Employed Persons Age 16 & Over		
	1990	% Chg. 80-90
Managerial & Professional	1,365	13.5
Technical, Sales & Admin. Support	2,031	4.6
Service Occupations	1,248	19.3
Farming, Forestry and Fishing	424	-27.6
Precision Production, Craft & Repair	1,559	14.1
Operators, Fabricators	3,372	-6.6

Top 5 Counties Commuting in 1990			
From Jay Into:		Into Jay From:	
Adams	1,298	Delaware	586
Delaware	565	Randolph	409
Outside Indiana	399	Outside Indiana	256
Blackford	210	Blackford	234
Randolph	203	Adams	182

6,544 persons lived and worked in this county.
3,235 lived in the county but worked elsewhere.

Number of Establishments
(% Change 1990-1995)

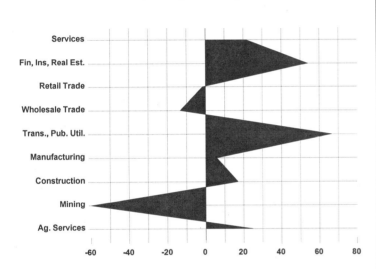

Establishments by Sector 1995		
Industry	Number of Establishments	% with fewer than 10 employees
Ag. Services	5	80.0%
Mining	2	50.0%
Construction	41	92.7%
Manufacturing	36	27.8%
Transportation, Public Utilities	20	60.0%
Wholesale Trade	26	69.2%
Retail Trade	124	67.7%
Finance, Insurance, Real Estate	40	87.5%
Services	158	78.5%

Private Industry	Employment		Real Earnings ($000)		Average Earnings Per Job	
	1995	% Chg. 90-95	1995	Real % Chg. 90-95	1995	Real % Chg. 90-95
Ag. Services	NA	NA	NA	NA	NA	NA
Mining	NA	NA	NA	NA	NA	NA
Construction	393	9.8%	5,938	6.5%	15,109	-3.0%
Manufacturing	3,538	11.7%	107,323	20.3%	30,334	7.7%
Transportation, Public Utilities	259	0.0%	6,929	2.0%	26,753	2.0%
Wholesale Trade	202	41.3%	4,176	20.6%	20,673	-14.6%
Retail Trade	1,569	-2.5%	19,024	-0.1%	12,125	2.5%
Finance, Insurance, Real Estate	309	-1.6%	4,809	12.4%	15,563	14.2%
Services	2,211	32.7%	28,918	31.4%	13,079	-1.0%

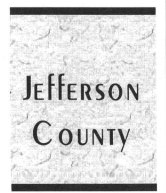

JEFFERSON COUNTY

Population 1997 (Est.)	31,292	# Households 1995 (Projection)	11,000	Personal Income 1995 ($000)	$379,940
Land Area (Sq. Mi.)	361.4	% Family	73.5%	Avg. Wage Per Job 1995	$21,223
Population Density 1997	86.6	% Non-Family	26.1%	Employed in 1996	14,030
% Under 20 1996	27.6%	% Living Alone	23.1%	Unemployed in 1996	790
% 65 & Over 1996	13.6%	Births 1995	398	Unemployment Rate 1996	5.3%
% White 1996	97.9%	Births to Teens 1995	67	Avg. Covered Payroll 1996 ($000)	$72,411
% African-Amer. 1996	1.4%	Deaths 1995	310	Average Weekly Earnings in Manufacturing 1996	$570.00
% Hispanic* 1996	0.5%	Marriages 1995	239	Registered Vehicles 1996	28,176

*May be of any race.

Percent of Total Population By Sex and Age

Male ■ 2010 ■ **Female**

(Population pyramid chart showing age groups from 0-4 to 95+, with X-axis from 8% to 0% on left and 0% to 8% on right)

Population Projections

Age Groups	2000	2010	% Change
0-17	6,960	6,200	-10.9%
18-24	3,270	2,910	-11.0%
25-39	6,210	6,160	-0.8%
40-59	7,860	7,980	1.5%
60-74	3,420	4,090	19.6%
75 +	1,760	1,680	-4.5%
Total	29,500	29,000	-1.7%

Personal Income
Real 1995 Dollars ($000)

	1990	1995	% Chg.
Total Earnings by Place of Work	344,066	379,940	10.4%
Less Personal Contributions for Social Insurance	21,992	25,872	17.6%
Net Income by Place of Work	322,074	354,068	9.9%
Plus Residence Adjustment	-29,215	-20,370	-30.3%
Net Income by Place of Residence	292,859	333,698	13.9%
Plus Dividends, Rent and Interest	85,062	85,274	0.2%
Plus Transfer Payments	95,667	109,300	14.3%
Personal Income by Place of Residence	473,588	528,272	11.5%
Per Capita Income ($)	15,874	17,126	7.9%
Rank	80	72	42

Educational Attainment 1990

(Line chart with categories: Graduate or Prof. Degree, Bachelor's Degree, Associate Degree, Some College No Degree, High School Graduate, 9th-12th No Diploma, Less than 9th Grade; X-axis from 0 to 8,000)

High School Grad or Higher
Percent: 70%
Rank in State: 72

Population Change by Decade
(1990-2000 projected)

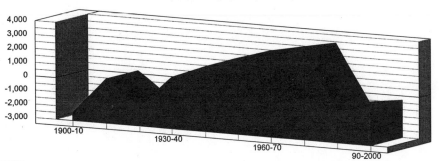

(Area chart with Y-axis from -3,000 to 4,000 and X-axis labels: 1900-10, 1930-40, 1960-70, 90-2000)

For EDIN tables, sources and footnotes, see page 380.

Occupation of Employed Persons Age 16 & Over		
	1990	% Chg. 80-90
Managerial & Professional	2,877	26.6
Technical, Sales & Admin. Support	3,295	11.2
Service Occupations	2,061	11.6
Farming, Forestry and Fishing	509	8.5
Precision Production, Craft & Repair	1,968	3.9
Operators, Fabricators	3,000	8.2

Top 5 Counties Commuting in 1990			
From Jefferson Into:		Into Jefferson From:	
Outside Indiana	852	Outside Indiana	951
Jennings	303	Switzerland	411
Clark	275	Jennings	357
Scott	171	Ripley	304
Switzerland	112	Scott	303

11,302 persons lived and worked in this county.

2,205 lived in the county but worked elsewhere.

Number of Establishments
(% Change 1990-1995)

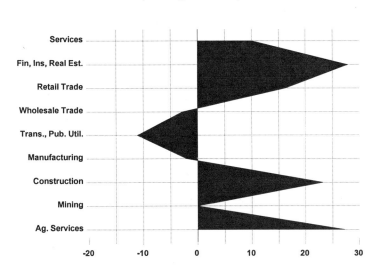

Establishments by Sector 1995		
Industry	Number of Establishments	% with fewer than 10 employees
Ag. Services	14	92.9%
Mining	0	NA
Construction	69	84.1%
Manufacturing	47	46.8%
Transportation, Public Utilities	24	66.7%
Wholesale Trade	34	79.4%
Retail Trade	228	71.9%
Finance, Insurance, Real Estate	55	87.3%
Services	220	82.3%

Private Industry	Employment		Real Earnings ($000)		Average Earnings Per Job	
	1995	% Chg. 90-95	1995	Real % Chg. 90-95	1995	Real % Chg. 90-95
Ag. Services	135	12.5%	1,433	1.2%	10,615	-10.1%
Mining	NA	NA	86	NA	NA	NA
Construction	NA	NA	NA	NA	NA	NA
Manufacturing	4,274	7.3%	142,497	20.2%	33,340	12.1%
Transportation, Public Utilities	NA	NA	NA	NA	NA	NA
Wholesale Trade	245	8.9%	5,674	11.8%	23,159	2.7%
Retail Trade	3,272	22.5%	40,618	31.6%	12,414	7.4%
Finance, Insurance, Real Estate	585	-0.3%	7,740	19.3%	13,231	19.7%
Services	3,901	NA	79,197	NA	20,302	NA

JENNINGS COUNTY

Population 1997 (Est.)	27,217	# Households 1995 (Projection)	8,600	Personal Income 1995 ($000)	$205,905
Land Area (Sq. Mi.)	377.3	% Family	77.0%	Avg. Wage Per Job 1995	$18,835
Population Density 1997	72.1	% Non-Family	23.3%	Employed in 1996	13,590
% Under 20 1996	29.2%	% Living Alone	20.3%	Unemployed in 1996	460
% 65 & Over 1996	11.7%	Births 1995	374	Unemployment Rate 1996	3.3%
% White 1996	98.6%	Births to Teens 1995	67	Avg. Covered Payroll 1996 ($000)	$40,981
% African-Amer. 1996	0.9%	Deaths 1995	210	Average Weekly Earnings in Manufacturing 1996	$449.00
% Hispanic* 1996	0.5%	Marriages 1995	289	Registered Vehicles 1996	26,396

*May be of any race.

Percent of Total Population By Sex and Age

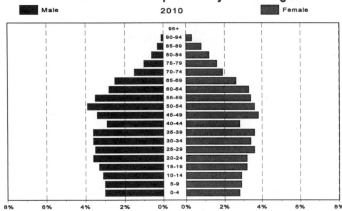

Population Projections

Age Groups	2000	2010	% Change
0-17	5,850	5,360	-8.4%
18-24	2,500	2,320	-7.2%
25-39	5,050	5,240	3.8%
40-59	6,800	6,720	-1.2%
60-74	2,830	3,590	26.9%
75 +	1,300	1,450	11.5%
Total	24,300	24,700	1.6%

Personal Income
Real 1995 Dollars ($000)

	1990	1995	% Chg.
Total Earnings by Place of Work	164,736	205,905	25.0%
Less Personal Contributions for Social Insurance	9,838	13,944	41.7%
Net Income by Place of Work	154,898	191,961	23.9%
Plus Residence Adjustment	81,629	120,385	47.5%
Net Income by Place of Residence	236,527	312,346	32.1%
Plus Dividends, Rent and Interest	47,776	45,404	-5.0%
Plus Transfer Payments	85,811	109,013	27.0%
Personal Income by Place of Residence	370,113	466,763	26.1%
Per Capita Income ($)	15,622	17,875	14.4%
Rank	81	59	3

Educational Attainment 1990

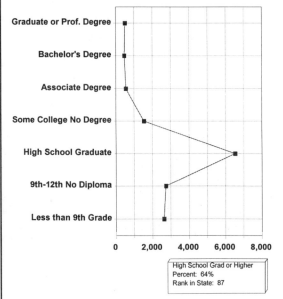

High School Grad or Higher
Percent: 64%
Rank in State: 87

Population Change by Decade
(1990-2000 projected)

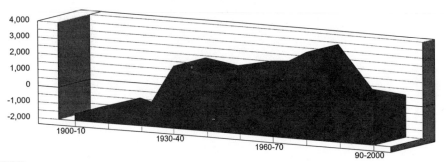

Occupation of Employed Persons Age 16 & Over		
	1990	% Chg. 80-90
Managerial & Professional	1,516	20.0
Technical, Sales & Admin. Support	2,341	34.1
Service Occupations	1,725	24.3
Farming, Forestry and Fishing	461	4.3
Precision Production, Craft & Repair	1,842	54.0
Operators, Fabricators	2,880	8.6

Top 5 Counties Commuting in 1990				
From Jennings Into:		Into Jennings From:		
Bartholomew	2,193	Jefferson	303
Jackson	1,299	Ripley	251
Jefferson	357	Bartholomew	240
Marion	191	Jackson	234
Decatur	171	Scott	162

5,793 persons lived and worked in this county.
4,655 lived in the county but worked elsewhere.

Number of Establishments
(% Change 1990-1995)

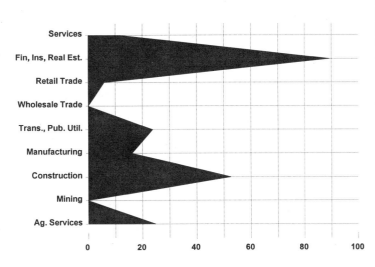

Establishments by Sector 1995		
Industry	Number of Establishments	% with fewer than 10 employees
Ag. Services	5	100.0%
Mining	3	33.3%
Construction	55	76.4%
Manufacturing	43	30.2%
Transportation, Public Utilities	26	84.6%
Wholesale Trade	20	75.0%
Retail Trade	106	70.8%
Finance, Insurance, Real Estate	36	88.9%
Services	103	87.4%

Private Industry	Employment		Real Earnings ($000)		Average Earnings Per Job	
	1995	% Chg. 90-95	1995	Real % Chg. 90-95	1995	Real % Chg. 90-95
Ag. Services	NA	NA	NA	NA	NA	NA
Mining	NA	NA	NA	NA	NA	NA
Construction	835	NA	21,657	NA	25,937	NA
Manufacturing	2,134	23.6%	56,723	30.3%	26,581	5.5%
Transportation, Public Utilities	278	-10.6%	5,798	14.3%	20,856	27.9%
Wholesale Trade	196	28.9%	4,208	50.0%	21,469	16.3%
Retail Trade	1,945	56.6%	26,042	80.3%	13,389	15.1%
Finance, Insurance, Real Estate	337	14.6%	4,350	29.5%	12,908	13.0%
Services	1,916	30.1%	34,946	42.9%	18,239	9.8%

JOHNSON COUNTY

Population 1997 (Est.)	106,888	# Households 1995 (Projection)	33,200	Personal Income 1995 ($000)	$999,343
Land Area (Sq. Mi.)	320.2	% Family	77.9%	Avg. Wage Per Job 1995	$20,390
Population Density 1997	333.8	% Non-Family	22.2%	Employed in 1996	55,890
% Under 20 1996	29.2%	% Living Alone	19.0%	Unemployed in 1996	1,410
% 65 & Over 1996	10.5%	Births 1995	1,456	Unemployment Rate 1996	2.5%
% White 1996	98.1%	Births to Teens 1995	160	Avg. Covered Payroll 1996 ($000)	$189,028
% African-Amer. 1996	0.9%	Deaths 1995	825	Average Weekly Earnings in Manufacturing 1996	$584.25
% Hispanic* 1996	0.9%	Marriages 1995	914	Registered Vehicles 1996	96,393

*May be of any race.

Percent of Total Population By Sex and Age

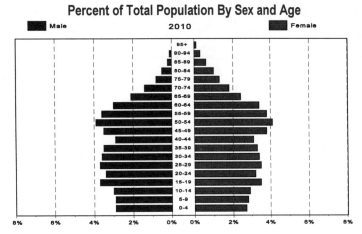

Male   2010   Female

Population Projections

Age Groups	2000	2010	% Change
0-17	22,960	20,890	-9.0%
18-24	10,020	9,200	-8.2%
25-39	19,450	20,240	4.1%
40-59	27,620	27,770	0.5%
60-74	9,510	13,690	44.0%
75 +	4,550	4,910	7.9%
Total	94,100	96,700	2.8%

Personal Income
Real 1995 Dollars ($000)

	1990	1995	% Chg.
Total Earnings by Place of Work	775,121	999,343	28.9%
Less Personal Contributions for Social Insurance	51,003	69,203	35.7%
Net Income by Place of Work	724,118	930,140	28.5%
Plus Residence Adjustment	705,294	814,382	15.5%
Net Income by Place of Residence	1,429,413	1,744,522	22.0%
Plus Dividends, Rent and Interest	306,656	327,100	6.7%
Plus Transfer Payments	204,805	259,945	26.9%
Personal Income by Place of Residence	1,940,874	2,331,567	20.1%
Per Capita Income ($)	21,904	22,934	4.7%
Rank	6	11	69

Educational Attainment 1990

(chart with categories from top to bottom: Graduate or Prof. Degree, Bachelor's Degree, Associate Degree, Some College No Degree, High School Graduate, 9th-12th No Diploma, Less than 9th Grade; horizontal axis 0 to 25,000)

High School Grad or Higher
Percent: 80%
Rank in State: 8

Population Change by Decade
(1990-2000 projected)

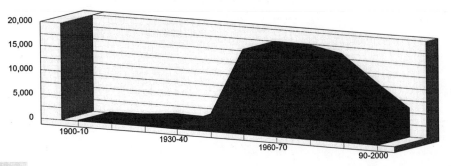

For EDIN tables, sources and footnotes, see page 380.

Occupation of Employed Persons Age 16 & Over

	1990	% Chg. 80-90
Managerial & Professional	10,604	46.1
Technical, Sales & Admin. Support	15,683	44.5
Service Occupations	5,575	39.5
Farming, Forestry and Fishing	758	-9.9
Precision Production, Craft & Repair	6,317	27.4
Operators, Fabricators	6,633	-7.2

Top 5 Counties Commuting in 1990

From Johnson Into:		Into Johnson From:	
Marion	22,370	Marion	5,929
Bartholomew	898	Bartholomew	1,402
Morgan	419	Morgan	1,011
Outside Indiana	328	Shelby	714
Hamilton	224	Brown	619

19,655 persons lived and worked in this county.

25,273 lived in the county but worked elsewhere.

Number of Establishments
(% Change 1990-1995)

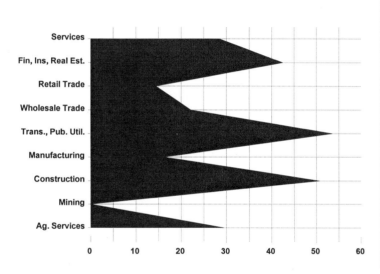

Establishments by Sector 1995

	Number of Establishments	% with fewer than 10 employees
Ag. Services	44	88.6%
Mining	4	100.0%
Construction	366	81.7%
Manufacturing	136	45.6%
Transportation, Public Utilities	86	70.9%
Wholesale Trade	138	82.6%
Retail Trade	689	62.3%
Finance, Insurance, Real Estate	238	83.2%
Services	803	79.5%

Private Industry	Employment		Real Earnings ($000)		Average Earnings Per Job	
	1995	% Chg. 90-95	1995	Real % Chg. 90-95	1995	Real % Chg. 90-95
Ag. Services	NA	NA	NA	NA	NA	NA
Mining	NA	NA	NA	NA	NA	NA
Construction	3,909	43.0%	104,709	51.8%	26,787	6.1%
Manufacturing	6,348	15.1%	218,631	30.3%	34,441	13.2%
Transportation, Public Utilities	1,188	24.5%	35,576	-27.6%	29,946	-41.9%
Wholesale Trade	1,138	22.5%	35,778	28.7%	31,439	5.1%
Retail Trade	13,504	33.7%	171,382	33.5%	12,691	-0.2%
Finance, Insurance, Real Estate	2,773	8.2%	45,378	30.3%	16,364	20.5%
Services	11,844	24.1%	246,244	39.4%	20,791	12.3%

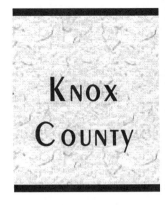

KNOX COUNTY

Population 1997 (Est.)	39,686	# Households 1995 (Projection)	15,100	Personal Income 1995 ($000)	$493,393
Land Area (Sq. Mi.)	515.9	% Family	68.3%	Avg. Wage Per Job 1995	$19,544
Population Density 1997	76.9	% Non-Family	31.5%	Employed in 1996	20,260
% Under 20 1996	28.7%	% Living Alone	27.0%	Unemployed in 1996	1,000
% 65 & Over 1996	16.3%	Births 1995	483	Unemployment Rate 1996	4.7%
% White 1996	98.0%	Births to Teens 1995	79	Avg. Covered Payroll 1996 ($000)	$87,266
% African-Amer. 1996	1.3%	Deaths 1995	516	Average Weekly Earnings in Manufacturing 1996	$467.00
% Hispanic* 1996	0.6%	Marriages 1995	329	Registered Vehicles 1996	36,922

*May be of any race.

Percent of Total Population By Sex and Age

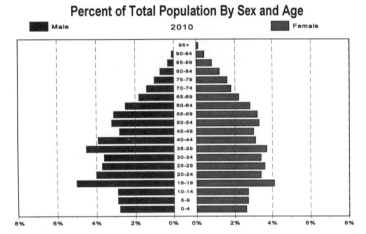

Male   2010   Female

Population Projections

Age Groups	2000	2010	% Change
0-17	9,190	8,490	-7.6%
18-24	4,750	4,240	-10.7%
25-39	8,460	8,660	2.4%
40-59	9,310	9,810	5.4%
60-74	4,520	4,840	7.1%
75 +	2,720	2,430	-10.7%
Total	39,000	38,500	-1.3%

Personal Income
Real 1995 Dollars ($000)

	1990	1995	% Chg.
Total Earnings by Place of Work	417,078	493,393	18.3%
Less Personal Contributions for Social Insurance	24,893	31,440	26.3%
Net Income by Place of Work	392,185	461,953	17.8%
Plus Residence Adjustment	9,936	-129	-101.3%
Net Income by Place of Residence	402,120	461,824	14.8%
Plus Dividends, Rent and Interest	133,413	121,401	-9.0%
Plus Transfer Payments	143,334	163,087	13.8%
Personal Income by Place of Residence	678,867	746,312	9.9%
Per Capita Income ($)	17,070	18,778	10.0%
Rank	57	50	20

Educational Attainment 1990

Graduate or Prof. Degree
Bachelor's Degree
Associate Degree
Some College No Degree
High School Graduate
9th-12th No Diploma
Less than 9th Grade

0 2,000 4,000 6,000 8,000 10,000

High School Grad or Higher
Percent: 75%
Rank in State: 38

Population Change by Decade
(1990-2000 projected)

8,000
6,000
4,000
2,000
0
-2,000
-4,000

1900-10   1930-40   1960-70   90-2000

For EDIN tables, sources and footnotes, see page 380.

Occupation of Employed Persons Age 16 & Over

	1990	% Chg. 80-90
Managerial & Professional	3,514	4.9
Technical, Sales & Admin. Support	5,127	20.9
Service Occupations	2,859	8.1
Farming, Forestry and Fishing	1,024	-16.6
Precision Production, Craft & Repair	1,895	-14.0
Operators, Fabricators	2,748	-11.2

Top 5 Counties Commuting in 1990

From Knox Into:		Into Knox From:	
Daviess	504	Outside Indiana	1,087
Outside Indiana	481	Daviess	307
Gibson	176	Gibson	178
Greene	166	Sullivan	165
Vanderburgh	157	Pike	135

14,658 persons lived and worked in this county.
2,353 lived in the county but worked elsewhere.

Number of Establishments
(% Change 1990-1995)

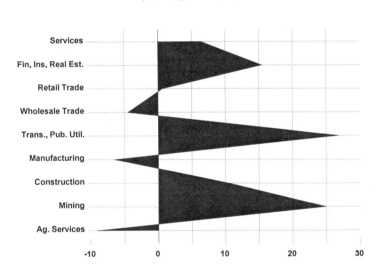

Establishments by Sector 1995

Industry	Number of Establishments	% with fewer than 10 employees
Ag. Services	10	60.0%
Mining	10	70.0%
Construction	84	85.7%
Manufacturing	43	37.2%
Transportation, Public Utilities	85	63.5%
Wholesale Trade	85	67.1%
Retail Trade	303	68.0%
Finance, Insurance, Real Estate	82	84.1%
Services	333	78.4%

Private Industry	Employment		Real Earnings ($000)		Average Earnings Per Job	
	1995	% Chg. 90-95	1995	Real % Chg. 90-95	1995	Real % Chg. 90-95
Ag. Services	278	50.3%	3,025	47.4%	10,881	-1.9%
Mining	451	96.9%	17,845	250.8%	39,568	78.1%
Construction	835	4.2%	19,547	14.6%	23,410	9.9%
Manufacturing	2,319	45.7%	66,601	35.9%	28,720	-6.7%
Transportation, Public Utilities	1,258	15.6%	38,322	-4.7%	30,463	-17.6%
Wholesale Trade	1,082	1.3%	30,446	9.5%	28,139	8.1%
Retail Trade	4,552	14.6%	52,728	16.3%	11,583	1.5%
Finance, Insurance, Real Estate	1,235	4.7%	25,588	18.9%	20,719	13.7%
Services	5,034	9.2%	99,213	25.6%	19,709	15.0%

Kosciusko County

Population 1997 (Est.)	70,363	# Households 1995 (Projection)	24,500	Personal Income 1995 ($000)	$1,115,072
Land Area (Sq. Mi.)	537.5	% Family	76.4%	Avg. Wage Per Job 1995	$25,458
Population Density 1997	130.9	% Non-Family	23.5%	Employed in 1996	37,840
% Under 20 1996	30.6%	% Living Alone	20.1%	Unemployed in 1996	1,290
% 65 & Over 1996	11.9%	Births 1995	1,040	Unemployment Rate 1996	3.3%
% White 1996	98.6%	Births to Teens 1995	153	Avg. Covered Payroll 1996 ($000)	$219,305
% African-Amer. 1996	0.6%	Deaths 1995	560	Average Weekly Earnings in Manufacturing 1996	$679.75
% Hispanic* 1996	2.5%	Marriages 1995	698	Registered Vehicles 1996	71,227

*May be of any race.

Percent of Total Population By Sex and Age

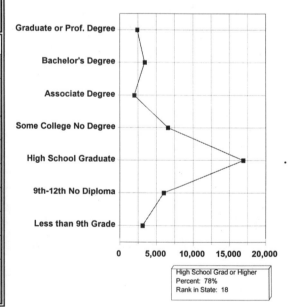

2010   ■ Male   ■ Female

Population Projections

Age Groups	2000	2010	% Change
0-17	19,620	19,460	-0.8%
18-24	7,290	7,510	3.0%
25-39	13,910	14,970	7.6%
40-59	18,120	19,140	5.6%
60-74	7,630	9,420	23.5%
75 +	3,790	4,110	8.4%
Total	70,300	74,600	6.1%

Personal Income
Real 1995 Dollars ($000)

	1990	1995	% Chg.
Total Earnings by Place of Work	970,895	1,115,072	14.8%
Less Personal Contributions for Social Insurance	63,852	76,925	20.5%
Net Income by Place of Work	907,043	1,038,147	14.5%
Plus Residence Adjustment	23,576	30,685	30.2%
Net Income by Place of Residence	930,619	1,068,832	14.9%
Plus Dividends, Rent and Interest	250,284	265,278	6.0%
Plus Transfer Payments	141,378	179,153	26.7%
Personal Income by Place of Residence	1,322,281	1,513,263	14.4%
Per Capita Income ($)	20,226	21,893	8.2%
Rank	17	17	37

Educational Attainment 1990

```
Graduate or Prof. Degree
Bachelor's Degree
Associate Degree
Some College No Degree
High School Graduate
9th-12th No Diploma
Less than 9th Grade
          0    5,000  10,000  15,000  20,000
```

High School Grad or Higher
Percent: 78%
Rank in State: 18

Population Change by Decade
(1990-2000 projected)

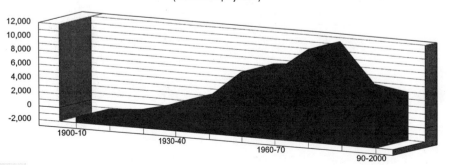

Occupation of Employed Persons Age 16 & Over

	1990	% Chg. 80-90
Managerial & Professional	6,210	31.7
Technical, Sales & Admin. Support	8,136	23.5
Service Occupations	3,551	24.4
Farming, Forestry and Fishing	1,109	-8.1
Precision Production, Craft & Repair	4,692	16.5
Operators, Fabricators	9,091	15.0

Top 5 Counties Commuting in 1990

From Kosciusko Into:		Into Kosciusko From:	
Elkhart	3,437	Marshall	1,075
Whitley	503	Elkhart	808
Wabash	477	Wabash	669
Noble	464	Whitley	657
Allen	425	Fulton	528

25,617 persons lived and worked in this county.

6,653 lived in the county but worked elsewhere.

Number of Establishments
(% Change 1990-1995)

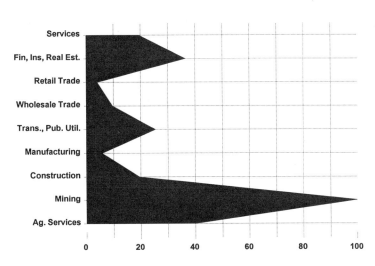

Establishments by Sector 1995

Industry	Number of Establishments	% with fewer than 10 employees
Ag. Services	28	89.3%
Mining	2	50.0%
Construction	202	89.1%
Manufacturing	182	36.8%
Transportation, Public Utilities	69	78.3%
Wholesale Trade	136	80.1%
Retail Trade	437	67.3%
Finance, Insurance, Real Estate	131	92.4%
Services	578	80.8%

Private Industry	Employment		Real Earnings ($000)		Average Earnings Per Job	
	1995	% Chg. 90-95	1995	Real % Chg. 90-95	1995	Real % Chg. 90-95
Ag. Services	NA	NA	NA	NA	NA	NA
Mining	NA	NA	NA	NA	NA	NA
Construction	1,764	10.0%	44,349	12.3%	25,141	2.1%
Manufacturing	16,142	16.1%	659,903	18.1%	40,881	1.7%
Transportation, Public Utilities	1,323	9.7%	44,546	1.5%	33,670	-7.5%
Wholesale Trade	1,092	10.3%	32,551	24.6%	29,809	13.0%
Retail Trade	6,563	12.3%	83,502	10.6%	12,723	-1.5%
Finance, Insurance, Real Estate	1,647	1.0%	25,900	28.4%	15,726	27.2%
Services	8,930	26.0%	150,550	29.6%	16,859	2.8%

For EDIN tables, sources and footnotes, see page 380.

LAGRANGE COUNTY

Population 1997 (Est.)	32,719	# Households 1995 (Projection)	9,900	Personal Income 1995 ($000)	$416,252
Land Area (Sq. Mi.)	379.6	% Family	80.3%	Avg. Wage Per Job 1995	$22,111
Population Density 1997	86.2	% Non-Family	19.6%	Employed in 1996	16,260
% Under 20 1996	36.7%	% Living Alone	16.7%	Unemployed in 1996	690
% 65 & Over 1996	10.5%	Births 1995	662	Unemployment Rate 1996	4.1%
% White 1996	99.2%	Births to Teens 1995	59	Avg. Covered Payroll 1996 ($000)	$70,850
% African-Amer. 1996	0.1%	Deaths 1995	220	Average Weekly Earnings in Manufacturing 1996	$570.50
% Hispanic* 1996	1.7%	Marriages 1995	325	Registered Vehicles 1996	26,166

*May be of any race.

Percent of Total Population By Sex and Age

Male 2010 Female

(age groups 0-4 through 95+, population pyramid, scale 8% to 0% to 8%)

Population Projections

Age Groups	2000	2010	% Change
0-17	11,170	12,430	11.3%
18-24	4,030	4,200	4.2%
25-39	6,680	8,270	23.8%
40-59	7,330	7,990	9.0%
60-74	3,090	3,820	23.6%
75 +	1,480	1,680	13.5%
Total	33,800	38,400	13.6%

Personal Income
Real 1995 Dollars ($000)

	1990	1995	% Chg.
Total Earnings by Place of Work	293,368	416,252	41.9%
Less Personal Contributions for Social Insurance	17,339	27,619	59.3%
Net Income by Place of Work	276,029	388,633	40.8%
Plus Residence Adjustment	42,080	19,055	-54.7%
Net Income by Place of Residence	318,109	407,688	28.2%
Plus Dividends, Rent and Interest	76,245	77,738	2.0%
Plus Transfer Payments	51,556	66,239	28.5%
Personal Income by Place of Residence	445,911	551,665	23.7%
Per Capita Income ($) Rank	15,096 85	17,370 64	15.1% 1

Educational Attainment 1990

(chart: Graduate or Prof. Degree, Bachelor's Degree, Associate Degree, Some College No Degree, High School Graduate, 9th-12th No Diploma, Less than 9th Grade; scale 0 to 6,000)

High School Grad or Higher
Percent: 57%
Rank in State: 92

Population Change by Decade
(1990-2000 projected)

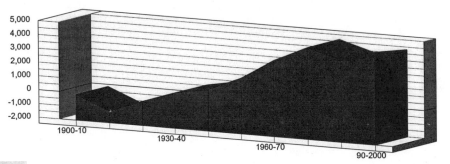

(chart: scale -2,000 to 5,000; decades 1900-10, 1930-40, 1960-70, 90-2000)

For EDIN tables, sources and footnotes, see page 380.

Occupation of Employed Persons Age 16 & Over

	1990	% Chg. 80-90
Managerial & Professional	1,606	21.7
Technical, Sales & Admin. Support	2,444	26.1
Service Occupations	1,476	41.7
Farming, Forestry and Fishing	1,338	-5.2
Precision Production, Craft & Repair	2,130	45.4
Operators, Fabricators	4,206	47.8

Top 5 Counties Commuting in 1990

From Lagrange Into:		Into Lagrange From:	
Elkhart	2,182	Outside Indiana	1,023
Noble	1,123	Noble	935
Outside Indiana	784	Elkhart	856
Allen	380	Steuben	411
Steuben	268	Allen	131

8,041 persons lived and worked in this county.

5,017 lived in the county but worked elsewhere.

Number of Establishments
(% Change 1990-1995)

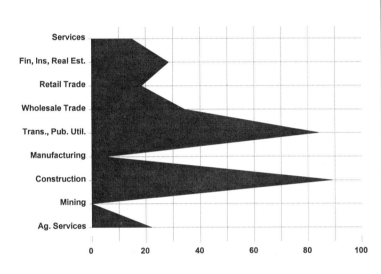

Establishments by Sector 1995

Industry	Number of Establishments	% with fewer than 10 employees
Ag. Services	11	72.7%
Mining	1	100.0%
Construction	70	92.9%
Manufacturing	81	44.4%
Transportation, Public Utilities	35	85.7%
Wholesale Trade	47	72.3%
Retail Trade	192	69.8%
Finance, Insurance, Real Estate	36	80.6%
Services	169	85.8%

Private Industry	Employment		Real Earnings ($000)		Average Earnings Per Job	
	1995	% Chg. 90-95	1995	Real % Chg. 90-95	1995	Real % Chg. 90-95
Ag. Services	230	37.7%	4,964	12.7%	21,583	-18.2%
Mining	NA	NA	221	-16.5%	NA	NA
Construction	840	44.3%	16,644	51.9%	19,814	5.3%
Manufacturing	7,145	53.8%	247,246	78.7%	34,604	16.2%
Transportation, Public Utilities	406	18.0%	10,762	32.7%	26,507	12.4%
Wholesale Trade	608	-10.1%	11,461	-8.4%	18,850	1.8%
Retail Trade	2,534	31.9%	28,507	25.7%	11,250	-4.7%
Finance, Insurance, Real Estate	484	1.5%	7,000	5.9%	14,463	4.4%
Services	2,885	30.0%	44,944	55.5%	15,579	19.6%

For EDIN tables, sources and footnotes, see page 380.

LAKE COUNTY

Population 1997 (Est.)	479,339	# Households 1995 (Projection)	168,800	Personal Income 1995 ($000)	$6,885,307
Land Area (Sq. Mi.)	497.0	% Family	73.4%	Avg. Wage Per Job 1995	$26,899
Population Density 1997	964.5	% Non-Family	26.6%	Employed in 1996	214,370
% Under 20 1996	29.9%	% Living Alone	23.5%	Unemployed in 1996	12,810
% 65 & Over 1996	12.2%	Births 1995	7,339	Unemployment Rate 1996	5.6%
% White 1996	73.0%	Births to Teens 1995	1,296	Avg. Covered Payroll 1996 ($000)	$1,368,411
% African-Amer. 1996	26.0%	Deaths 1995	4,784	Average Weekly Earnings in Manufacturing 1996	$898.25
% Hispanic* 1996	11.5%	Marriages 1995	3,604	Registered Vehicles 1996	356,457

*May be of any race.

Percent of Total Population By Sex and Age

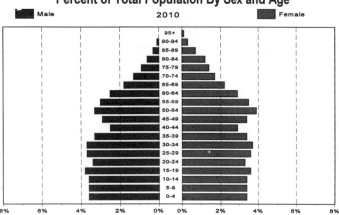

Population Projections

Age Groups	2000	2010	% Change
0-17	124,500	122,050	-2.0%
18-24	51,060	46,450	-9.0%
25-39	91,770	101,400	10.5%
40-59	123,590	121,690	-1.5%
60-74	52,440	59,580	13.6%
75 +	27,050	27,290	0.9%
Total	470,400	478,500	1.7%

Personal Income
Real 1995 Dollars ($000)

	1990	1995	% Chg.
Total Earnings by Place of Work	6,729,325	6,885,307	2.3%
Less Personal Contributions for Social Insurance	446,681	475,590	6.5%
Net Income by Place of Work	6,282,644	6,409,717	2.0%
Plus Residence Adjustment	195,009	507,353	160.2%
Net Income by Place of Residence	6,477,653	6,917,070	6.8%
Plus Dividends, Rent and Interest	1,389,802	1,389,352	-0.0%
Plus Transfer Payments	1,486,716	1,748,039	17.6%
Personal Income by Place of Residence	9,354,171	10,054,461	7.5%
Per Capita Income ($)	19,638	20,923	6.5%
Rank	20	23	57

Educational Attainment 1990

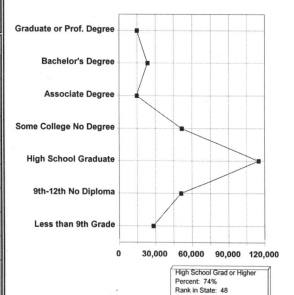

High School Grad or Higher
Percent: 74%
Rank in State: 48

Population Change by Decade
(1990-2000 projected)

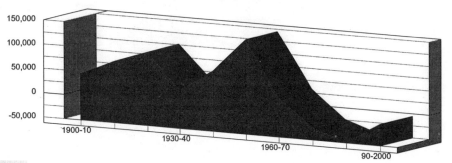

For EDIN tables, sources and footnotes, see page 380.

Occupation of Employed Persons Age 16 & Over		
	1990	% Chg. 80-90
Managerial & Professional	42,985	24.3
Technical, Sales & Admin. Support	64,336	14.0
Service Occupations	28,531	0.1
Farming, Forestry and Fishing	1,264	5.2
Precision Production, Craft & Repair	28,528	-21.0
Operators, Fabricators	38,322	-30.3

Top 5 Counties Commuting in 1990			
From Lake Into:		Into Lake From:	
Outside Indiana	39,501	Porter	18,056
Porter	6,505	Outside Indiana	14,313
Laporte	1,411	Jasper	1,498
St. Joseph	232	Laporte	1,422
Jasper	221	Newton	1,124

150,858 persons lived and worked in this county.
48,842 lived in the county but worked elsewhere.

Number of Establishments
(% Change 1990-1995)

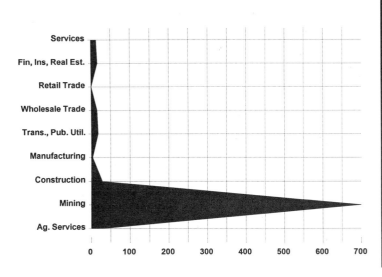

Establishments by Sector 1995		
Industry	Number of Establishments	% with fewer than 10 employees
Ag. Services	116	81.9%
Mining	8	100.0%
Construction	1,061	77.6%
Manufacturing	422	37.7%
Transportation, Public Utilities	451	67.6%
Wholesale Trade	624	63.8%
Retail Trade	2,627	64.1%
Finance, Insurance, Real Estate	851	79.2%
Services	3,722	76.8%

Private Industry	Employment		Real Earnings ($000)		Average Earnings Per Job	
	1995	% Chg. 90-95	1995	Real % Chg. 90-95	1995	Real % Chg. 90-95
Ag. Services	1,527	31.9%	24,044	38.7%	15,746	5.2%
Mining	149	53.6%	2,897	82.7%	19,443	18.9%
Construction	15,392	-1.6%	560,802	-5.0%	36,435	-3.5%
Manufacturing	40,925	-9.6%	2,170,457	-5.3%	53,035	4.8%
Transportation, Public Utilities	13,663	-8.9%	518,303	-6.8%	37,935	2.3%
Wholesale Trade	9,287	2.0%	327,463	5.4%	35,260	3.4%
Retail Trade	45,922	4.3%	630,123	6.7%	13,722	2.4%
Finance, Insurance, Real Estate	12,327	4.6%	238,970	21.6%	19,386	16.2%
Services	66,513	10.8%	1,669,819	14.5%	25,105	3.3%

LaPorte County

Population 1997 (Est.)	109,080	# Households 1995 (Projection)	39,200	Personal Income 1995 ($000)	$1,395,071
Land Area (Sq. Mi.)	598.3	% Family	72.4%	Avg. Wage Per Job 1995	$22,496
Population Density 1997	182.3	% Non-Family	27.6%	Employed in 1996	51,290
% Under 20 1996	27.0%	% Living Alone	23.7%	Unemployed in 1996	2,740
% 65 & Over 1996	13.2%	Births 1995	1,325	Unemployment Rate 1996	5.1%
% White 1996	89.4%	Births to Teens 1995	219	Avg. Covered Payroll 1996 ($000)	$267,394
% African-Amer. 1996	9.8%	Deaths 1995	994	Average Weekly Earnings in Manufacturing 1996	$610.50
% Hispanic* 1996	1.9%	Marriages 1995	1,053	Registered Vehicles 1996	100,992

*May be of any race.

Percent of Total Population By Sex and Age

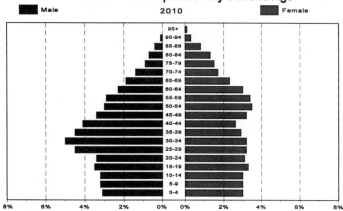

Population Projections

Age Groups	2000	2010	% Change
0-17	25,920	24,780	-4.4%
18-24	10,620	10,090	-5.0%
25-39	24,780	25,650	3.5%
40-59	28,050	28,570	1.9%
60-74	12,140	13,900	14.5%
75 +	6,650	6,620	-0.5%
Total	108,200	109,600	1.3%

Personal Income
Real 1995 Dollars ($000)

	1990	1995	% Chg.
Total Earnings by Place of Work	1,293,939	1,395,071	7.8%
Less Personal Contributions for Social Insurance	83,592	94,916	13.5%
Net Income by Place of Work	1,210,347	1,300,155	7.4%
Plus Residence Adjustment	141,060	165,480	17.3%
Net Income by Place of Residence	1,351,407	1,465,635	8.5%
Plus Dividends, Rent and Interest	347,180	337,566	-2.8%
Plus Transfer Payments	293,796	353,588	20.4%
Personal Income by Place of Residence	1,992,383	2,156,789	8.3%
Per Capita Income ($)	18,577	19,673	5.9%
Rank	28	36	62

Educational Attainment 1990

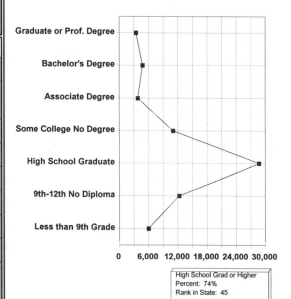

High School Grad or Higher
Percent: 74%
Rank in State: 45

Population Change by Decade
(1990-2000 projected)

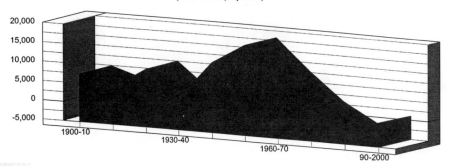

For EDIN tables, sources and footnotes, see page 380.

Occupation of Employed Persons Age 16 & Over

	1990	% Chg. 80-90
Managerial & Professional	9,239	15.2
Technical, Sales & Admin. Support	13,389	9.0
Service Occupations	6,783	11.8
Farming, Forestry and Fishing	1,030	-14.4
Precision Production, Craft & Repair	6,614	-4.9
Operators, Fabricators	11,251	-8.5

Top 5 Counties Commuting in 1990

From Laporte Into:		Into Laporte From:	
Porter	3,580	Porter	3,244
St. Joseph	2,456	Lake	1,411
Outside Indiana	2,064	Outside Indiana	1,266
Lake	1,422	St. Joseph	760
Marshall	168	Starke	639

36,971 persons lived and worked in this county.
10,357 lived in the county but worked elsewhere.

Number of Establishments
(% Change 1990-1995)

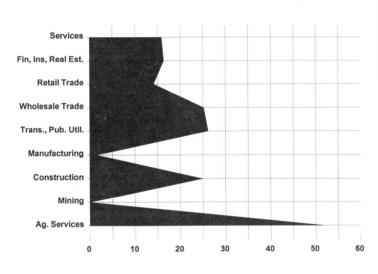

Establishments by Sector 1995

Industry	Number of Establishments	% with fewer than 10 employees
Ag. Services	47	83.0%
Mining	3	100.0%
Construction	271	84.1%
Manufacturing	203	30.0%
Transportation, Public Utilities	111	68.5%
Wholesale Trade	174	75.9%
Retail Trade	727	65.7%
Finance, Insurance, Real Estate	192	89.6%
Services	861	79.8%

Private Industry	Employment		Real Earnings ($000)		Average Earnings Per Job	
	1995	% Chg. 90-95	1995	Real % Chg. 90-95	1995	Real % Chg. 90-95
Ag. Services	657	18.8%	9,485	16.6%	14,437	-1.8%
Mining	82	10.8%	1,437	10.8%	17,524	0.0%
Construction	2,847	23.0%	81,571	19.6%	28,652	-2.7%
Manufacturing	12,701	-3.9%	451,870	1.3%	35,578	5.4%
Transportation, Public Utilities	2,462	4.7%	101,620	1.2%	41,275	-3.4%
Wholesale Trade	2,330	17.6%	69,601	17.5%	29,872	-0.1%
Retail Trade	11,282	11.8%	148,430	15.5%	13,156	3.3%
Finance, Insurance, Real Estate	2,488	-2.5%	38,961	15.1%	15,660	18.1%
Services	13,873	13.1%	283,971	17.8%	20,469	4.2%

LAWRENCE COUNTY

Population 1997 (Est.)	45,539	# Households 1995 (Projection)	16,400	Personal Income 1995 ($000)	$528,741
Land Area (Sq. Mi.)	448.9	% Family	75.0%	Avg. Wage Per Job 1995	$23,564
Population Density 1997	101.4	% Non-Family	24.9%	Employed in 1996	22,590
% Under 20 1996	27.2%	% Living Alone	22.4%	Unemployed in 1996	1,720
% 65 & Over 1996	14.5%	Births 1995	562	Unemployment Rate 1996	7.1%
% White 1996	99.3%	Births to Teens 1995	112	Avg. Covered Payroll 1996 ($000)	$96,571
% African-Amer. 1996	0.3%	Deaths 1995	503	Average Weekly Earnings in Manufacturing 1996	$720.25
% Hispanic* 1996	0.4%	Marriages 1995	493	Registered Vehicles 1996	44,645

*May be of any race.

Percent of Total Population By Sex and Age

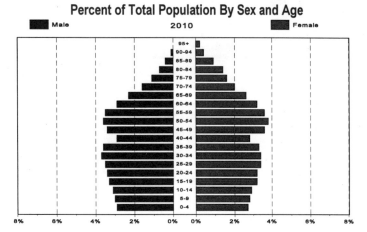

■ Male 2010 ■ Female

Population Projections

Age Groups	2000	2010	% Change
0-17	9,940	9,050	-9.0%
18-24	4,330	3,900	-9.9%
25-39	8,440	8,880	5.2%
40-59	11,920	11,570	-2.9%
60-74	5,310	6,220	17.1%
75 +	2,880	2,870	-0.3%
Total	42,800	42,500	-0.7%

Personal Income
Real 1995 Dollars ($000)

	1990	1995	% Chg.
Total Earnings by Place of Work	426,749	528,741	23.9%
Less Personal Contributions for Social Insurance	28,427	36,755	29.3%
Net Income by Place of Work	398,322	491,986	23.5%
Plus Residence Adjustment	83,772	80,399	-4.0%
Net Income by Place of Residence	482,094	572,385	18.7%
Plus Dividends, Rent and Interest	110,054	102,135	-7.2%
Plus Transfer Payments	136,549	164,619	20.6%
Personal Income by Place of Residence	728,696	839,139	15.2%
Per Capita Income ($)	16,976	18,607	9.6%
Rank	60	53	24

Educational Attainment 1990

Graduate or Prof. Degree
Bachelor's Degree
Associate Degree
Some College No Degree
High School Graduate
9th-12th No Diploma
Less than 9th Grade

0   3,000   6,000   9,000   12,000 15,000

High School Grad or Higher
Percent: 70%
Rank in State: 73

Population Change by Decade
(1990-2000 projected)

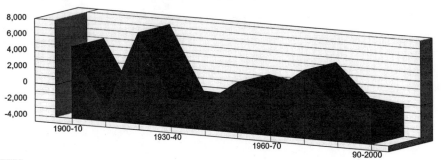

8,000
6,000
4,000
2,000
0
-2,000
-4,000

1900-10   1930-40   1960-70   90-2000

For EDIN tables, sources and footnotes, see page 380.

Occupation of Employed Persons Age 16 & Over		
	1990	% Chg. 80-90
Managerial & Professional	3,655	50.8
Technical, Sales & Admin. Support	4,615	22.0
Service Occupations	2,621	34.4
Farming, Forestry and Fishing	484	7.6
Precision Production, Craft & Repair	2,936	8.3
Operators, Fabricators	4,882	-6.5

Top 5 Counties Commuting in 1990			
From Lawrence Into:		Into Lawrence From:	
Monroe	2,675	Monroe	658
Martin	922	Orange	644
Orange	439	Jackson	176
Jackson	204	Martin	112
Marion	182	Greene	92

13,831 persons lived and worked in this county.
5,011 lived in the county but worked elsewhere.

Number of Establishments
(% Change 1990-1995)

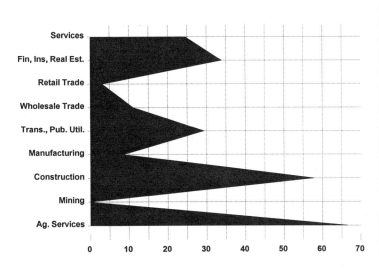

Establishments by Sector 1995		
Industry	Number of Establishments	% with fewer than 10 employees
Ag. Services	10	90.0%
Mining	4	25.0%
Construction	90	83.3%
Manufacturing	76	39.5%
Transportation, Public Utilities	44	77.3%
Wholesale Trade	40	67.5%
Retail Trade	262	66.8%
Finance, Insurance, Real Estate	71	83.1%
Services	279	85.3%

Private Industry	Employment		Real Earnings ($000)		Average Earnings Per Job	
	1995	% Chg. 90-95	1995	Real % Chg. 90-95	1995	Real % Chg. 90-95
Ag. Services	135	-2.2%	1,535	3.9%	11,370	6.2%
Mining	120	-22.1%	3,767	-10.2%	31,392	15.2%
Construction	1,121	12.0%	24,214	2.3%	21,600	-8.6%
Manufacturing	5,858	25.8%	257,735	35.0%	43,997	7.3%
Transportation, Public Utilities	641	4.4%	19,103	19.6%	29,802	14.6%
Wholesale Trade	533	51.9%	11,458	16.0%	21,497	-23.6%
Retail Trade	4,471	22.7%	54,112	19.5%	12,103	-2.6%
Finance, Insurance, Real Estate	803	7.8%	10,806	7.9%	13,457	0.1%
Services	4,508	12.1%	86,653	27.9%	19,222	14.1%

Madison County

Population 1997 (Est.)	131,840	# Households 1995 (Projection)	49,700	Personal Income 1995 ($000)	$1,772,605
Land Area (Sq. Mi.)	452.2	% Family	71.7%	Avg. Wage Per Job 1995	$27,750
Population Density 1997	291.6	% Non-Family	28.2%	Employed in 1996	63,780
% Under 20 1996	26.9%	% Living Alone	25.0%	Unemployed in 1996	2,960
% 65 & Over 1996	14.1%	Births 1995	1,660	Unemployment Rate 1996	4.4%
% White 1996	91.1%	Births to Teens 1995	306	Avg. Covered Payroll 1996 ($000)	$341,256
% African-Amer. 1996	8.3%	Deaths 1995	1,385	Average Weekly Earnings in Manufacturing 1996	$968.50
% Hispanic* 1996	0.9%	Marriages 1995	1,296	Registered Vehicles 1996	124,464

*May be of any race.

Percent of Total Population By Sex and Age

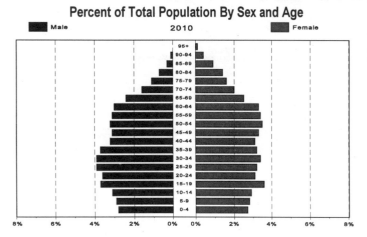

Male — 2010 — Female

Population Projections

Age Groups	2000	2010	% Change
0-17	30,260	27,520	-9.1%
18-24	13,050	12,250	-6.1%
25-39	26,470	26,940	1.8%
40-59	34,030	32,770	-3.7%
60-74	15,750	18,710	18.8%
75 +	8,590	8,470	-1.4%
Total	128,200	126,700	-1.2%

Personal Income
Real 1995 Dollars ($000)

	1990	1995	% Chg.
Total Earnings by Place of Work	1,731,963	1,772,605	2.3%
Less Personal Contributions for Social Insurance	115,763	124,652	7.7%
Net Income by Place of Work	1,616,200	1,647,953	2.0%
Plus Residence Adjustment	7,694	176,813	2198.1%
Net Income by Place of Residence	1,623,894	1,824,766	12.4%
Plus Dividends, Rent and Interest	392,233	347,722	-11.3%
Plus Transfer Payments	395,726	470,522	18.9%
Personal Income by Place of Residence	2,411,853	2,643,010	9.6%
Per Capita Income ($)	18,430	19,928	8.1%
Rank	33	31	39

Educational Attainment 1990

Graduate or Prof. Degree
Bachelor's Degree
Associate Degree
Some College No Degree
High School Graduate
9th-12th No Diploma
Less than 9th Grade

0 8,000 16,000 24,000 32,000 40,000

High School Grad or Higher
Percent: 74%
Rank in State: 48

Population Change by Decade
(1990-2000 projected)

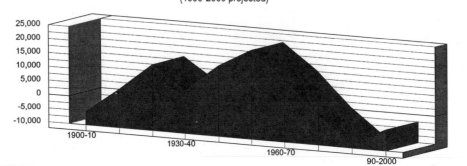

25,000
20,000
15,000
10,000
5,000
0
-5,000
-10,000

1900-10   1930-40   1960-70   90-2000

For EDIN tables, sources and footnotes, see page 380.

Occupation of Employed Persons Age 16 & Over		
	1990	% Chg. 80-90
Managerial & Professional	10,830	19.6
Technical, Sales & Admin. Support	17,380	29.5
Service Occupations	8,584	13.8
Farming, Forestry and Fishing	1,016	13.6
Precision Production, Craft & Repair	7,921	-5.4
Operators, Fabricators	13,315	-14.2

Top 5 Counties Commuting in 1990			
From Madison Into:		Into Madison From:	
Marion	5,815	Delaware	2,238
Hamilton	2,302	Henry	1,991
Delaware	1,855	Hamilton	1,133
Grant	969	Marion	913
Hancock	616	Hancock	491
44,461	persons lived and worked in this county.		
13,575	lived in the county but worked elsewhere.		

Number of Establishments
(% Change 1990-1995)

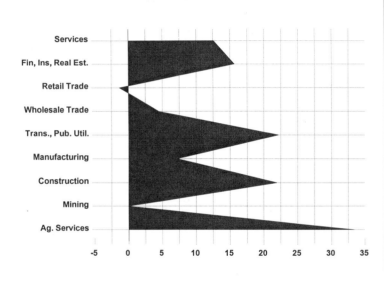

Establishments by Sector 1995		
Industry	Number of Establishments	% with fewer than 10 employees
Ag. Services	40	87.5%
Mining	4	50.0%
Construction	261	85.4%
Manufacturing	133	49.6%
Transportation, Public Utilities	99	76.8%
Wholesale Trade	116	69.0%
Retail Trade	740	65.1%
Finance, Insurance, Real Estate	251	86.5%
Services	1,039	79.4%

Private Industry	Employment		Real Earnings ($000)		Average Earnings Per Job	
	1995	% Chg. 90-95	1995	Real % Chg. 90-95	1995	Real % Chg. 90-95
Ag. Services	541	17.1%	8,200	10.4%	15,157	-5.7%
Mining	82	17.1%	2,554	81.8%	31,146	55.2%
Construction	2,938	27.0%	69,954	41.5%	23,810	11.4%
Manufacturing	14,255	-13.3%	839,696	-6.6%	58,905	7.7%
Transportation, Public Utilities	1,827	17.2%	45,574	8.8%	24,945	-7.1%
Wholesale Trade	1,497	3.2%	41,397	-1.5%	27,653	-4.5%
Retail Trade	13,161	8.1%	165,586	6.5%	12,582	-1.5%
Finance, Insurance, Real Estate	2,530	-2.6%	48,841	16.1%	19,305	19.2%
Services	17,630	14.7%	359,233	22.8%	20,376	7.1%

MARION COUNTY

Population 1997 (Est.)	813,670	# Households 1995 (Projection)	328,000	Personal Income 1995 ($000)	$20,976,027
Land Area (Sq. Mi.)	396.4	% Family	64.8%	Avg. Wage Per Job 1995	$28,815
Population Density 1997	2,052.6	% Non-Family	35.2%	Employed in 1996	437,270
% Under 20 1996	27.4%	% Living Alone	29.0%	Unemployed in 1996	16,360
% 65 & Over 1996	11.7%	Births 1995	13,920	Unemployment Rate 1996	3.6%
% White 1996	75.5%	Births to Teens 1995	2,096	Avg. Covered Payroll 1996 ($000)	$4,091,895
% African-Amer. 1996	23.0%	Deaths 1995	7,582	Average Weekly Earnings in Manufacturing 1996	$900.75
% Hispanic* 1996	1.4%	Marriages 1995	7,281	Registered Vehicles 1996	699,785

*May be of any race.

Percent of Total Population By Sex and Age

■ Male   2010   ■ Female

Population Projections

Age Groups	2000	2010	% Change
0-17	220,080	212,770	-3.3%
18-24	79,210	81,290	2.6%
25-39	227,680	200,610	-11.9%
40-59	198,310	241,970	22.0%
60-74	76,160	89,400	17.4%
75 +	39,830	39,140	-1.7%
Total	841,300	865,200	2.8%

Personal Income
Real 1995 Dollars ($000)

	1990	1995	% Chg.
Total Earnings by Place of Work	18,502,244	20,976,027	13.4%
Less Personal Contributions for Social Insurance	1,190,220	1,380,085	16.0%
Net Income by Place of Work	17,312,024	19,595,942	13.2%
Plus Residence Adjustment	-4,486,669	-5,417,474	20.7%
Net Income by Place of Residence	12,825,355	14,178,468	10.6%
Plus Dividends, Rent and Interest	3,249,687	3,190,320	-1.8%
Plus Transfer Payments	2,427,406	2,902,899	19.6%
Personal Income by Place of Residence	18,502,448	20,271,687	9.6%
Per Capita Income ($)	23,158	24,826	7.2%
Rank	3	3	53

Educational Attainment 1990

Graduate or Prof. Degree
Bachelor's Degree
Associate Degree
Some College No Degree
High School Graduate
9th-12th No Diploma
Less than 9th Grade

0   50,000   100,000   150,000   200,000

High School Grad or Higher
Percent: 77%
Rank in State: 23

Population Change by Decade
(1990-2000 projected)

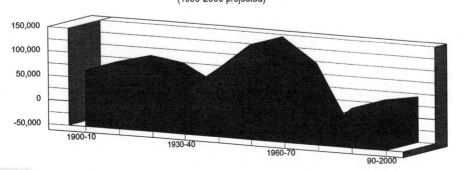

150,000
100,000
50,000
0
-50,000

1900-10   1930-40   1960-70   90-2000

For EDIN tables, sources and footnotes, see page 380.

Occupation of Employed Persons Age 16 & Over		
	1990	% Chg. 80-90
Managerial & Professional	108,137	36.8
Technical, Sales & Admin. Support	140,813	15.5
Service Occupations	54,242	13.5
Farming, Forestry and Fishing	2,859	48.3
Precision Production, Craft & Repair	39,662	3.5
Operators, Fabricators	55,411	-15.1

Top 5 Counties Commuting in 1990			
From Marion Into:		Into Marion From:	
Hamilton	11,202	Hamilton	26,255
Johnson	5,929	Johnson	22,370
Hendricks	3,461	Hendricks	21,811
Outside Indiana	2,600	Morgan	12,036
Hancock	1,477	Hancock	12,026

363,631 persons lived and worked in this county.
32,953 lived in the county but worked elsewhere.

Number of Establishments
(% Change 1990-1995)

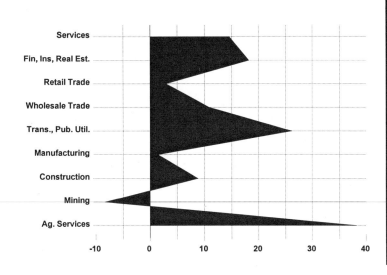

Establishments by Sector 1995		
Industry	Number of Establishments	% with fewer than 10 employees
Ag. Services	293	80.5%
Mining	22	45.5%
Construction	1,956	69.1%
Manufacturing	1,318	45.4%
Transportation, Public Utilities	872	58.3%
Wholesale Trade	2,309	62.0%
Retail Trade	5,453	59.9%
Finance, Insurance, Real Estate	2,544	74.4%
Services	8,982	72.3%

Private Industry	Employment		Real Earnings ($000)		Average Earnings Per Job	
	1995	% Chg. 90-95	1995	Real % Chg. 90-95	1995	Real % Chg. 90-95
Ag. Services	3,252	28.0%	56,786	36.6%	17,462	6.7%
Mining	775	-22.3%	16,147	-55.8%	20,835	-43.1%
Construction	33,314	1.8%	1,101,738	0.7%	33,071	-1.1%
Manufacturing	83,700	-2.9%	4,644,284	14.2%	55,487	17.6%
Transportation, Public Utilities	41,037	10.6%	1,461,284	6.9%	35,609	-3.3%
Wholesale Trade	43,106	14.3%	1,752,711	20.5%	40,660	5.4%
Retail Trade	115,354	10.2%	1,824,798	9.5%	15,819	-0.7%
Finance, Insurance, Real Estate	57,078	2.4%	1,787,905	16.6%	31,324	13.8%
Services	197,113	17.0%	5,549,155	21.2%	28,152	3.6%

Marshall County

Population 1997 (Est.)	45,337	# Households 1995 (Projection)	15,600	Personal Income 1995 ($000)	$567,169
Land Area (Sq. Mi.)	444.3	% Family	76.3%	Avg. Wage Per Job 1995	$20,929
Population Density 1997	102.0	% Non-Family	23.7%	Employed in 1996	25,220
% Under 20 1996	30.0%	% Living Alone	20.8%	Unemployed in 1996	950
% 65 & Over 1996	13.5%	Births 1995	606	Unemployment Rate 1996	3.6%
% White 1996	99.1%	Births to Teens 1995	86	Avg. Covered Payroll 1996 ($000)	$113,986
% African-Amer. 1996	0.2%	Deaths 1995	418	Average Weekly Earnings in Manufacturing 1996	$514.00
% Hispanic* 1996	2.6%	Marriages 1995	448	Registered Vehicles 1996	44,236

*May be of any race.

Percent of Total Population By Sex and Age

■ Male   2010   ■ Female

(Population pyramid chart showing age groups 0-4 through 95+ with Male on left and Female on right, scale 8% to 0% to 8%)

Population Projections

Age Groups	2000	2010	% Change
0-17	11,550	11,260	-2.5%
18-24	4,820	4,520	-6.2%
25-39	8,330	9,670	16.1%
40-59	11,940	12,030	0.8%
60-74	4,920	6,040	22.8%
75 +	2,740	2,830	3.3%
Total	44,300	46,400	4.7%

Personal Income
Real 1995 Dollars ($000)

	1990	1995	% Chg.
Total Earnings by Place of Work	471,554	567,169	20.3%
Less Personal Contributions for Social Insurance	30,924	39,328	27.2%
Net Income by Place of Work	440,631	527,841	19.8%
Plus Residence Adjustment	92,399	94,232	2.0%
Net Income by Place of Residence	533,030	622,073	16.7%
Plus Dividends, Rent and Interest	135,049	136,465	1.0%
Plus Transfer Payments	93,752	115,406	23.1%
Personal Income by Place of Residence	761,830	873,944	14.7%
Per Capita Income ($)	18,030	19,536	8.4%
Rank	44	39	35

Educational Attainment 1990

(Line chart with categories: Graduate or Prof. Degree, Bachelor's Degree, Associate Degree, Some College No Degree, High School Graduate, 9th-12th No Diploma, Less than 9th Grade; x-axis 0 to 12,000)

High School Grad or Higher
Percent: 74%
Rank in State: 44

Population Change by Decade
(1990-2000 projected)

(Area chart from 1900-10 to 90-2000, y-axis -1,000 to 5,000)

For EDIN tables, sources and footnotes, see page 380.

Occupation of Employed Persons Age 16 & Over

	1990	% Chg. 80-90
Managerial & Professional	3,920	39.4
Technical, Sales & Admin. Support	4,768	26.7
Service Occupations	2,482	25.1
Farming, Forestry and Fishing	904	-8.7
Precision Production, Craft & Repair	2,776	11.1
Operators, Fabricators	5,974	24.5

Top 5 Counties Commuting in 1990

From Marshall Into:		Into Marshall From:	
St. Joseph	2,356	Starke	1,442
Elkhart	1,692	St. Joseph	1,045
Kosciusko	1,075	Fulton	658
Starke	227	Kosciusko	314
Outside Indiana	192	Elkhart	310

14,368 persons lived and worked in this county.
6,147 lived in the county but worked elsewhere.

Number of Establishments
(% Change 1990-1995)

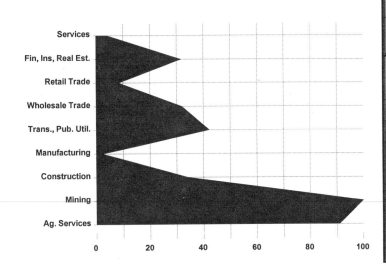

Establishments by Sector 1995

Industry	Number of Establishments	% with fewer than 10 employees
Ag. Services	21	90.5%
Mining	2	100.0%
Construction	122	93.4%
Manufacturing	128	27.3%
Transportation, Public Utilities	64	76.6%
Wholesale Trade	95	73.7%
Retail Trade	283	69.3%
Finance, Insurance, Real Estate	79	81.0%
Services	301	81.4%

Private Industry	Employment		Real Earnings ($000)		Average Earnings Per Job	
	1995	% Chg. 90-95	1995	Real % Chg. 90-95	1995	Real % Chg. 90-95
Ag. Services	200	24.2%	2,704	62.6%	13,520	30.9%
Mining	NA	NA	189	-35.4%	NA	NA
Construction	1,041	3.5%	22,506	0.0%	21,620	-3.3%
Manufacturing	9,082	23.4%	270,355	30.2%	29,768	5.5%
Transportation, Public Utilities	980	1.1%	30,827	1.6%	31,456	0.4%
Wholesale Trade	733	21.8%	21,893	2.1%	29,868	-16.1%
Retail Trade	4,071	16.0%	49,829	17.0%	12,240	0.9%
Finance, Insurance, Real Estate	1,057	-10.7%	22,456	6.5%	21,245	19.2%
Services	5,478	28.7%	88,338	39.6%	16,126	8.5%

MARTIN COUNTY

Population 1997 (Est.)	10,510	# Households 1995 (Projection)	3,800	Personal Income 1995 ($000)	$279,725
Land Area (Sq. Mi.)	336.2	% Family	74.5%	Avg. Wage Per Job 1995	$31,156
Population Density 1997	31.3	% Non-Family	26.6%	Employed in 1996	4,955
% Under 20 1996	28.5%	% Living Alone	24.5%	Unemployed in 1996	305
% 65 & Over 1996	13.9%	Births 1995	149	Unemployment Rate 1996	5.8%
% White 1996	99.6%	Births to Teens 1995	20	Avg. Covered Payroll 1996 ($000)	$16,213
% African-Amer. 1996	0.1%	Deaths 1995	108	Average Weekly Earnings in Manufacturing 1996	$471.25
% Hispanic* 1996	0.2%	Marriages 1995	114	Registered Vehicles 1996	10,737

*May be of any race.

Percent of Total Population By Sex and Age

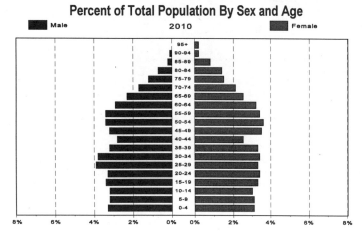

Population Projections

Age Groups	2000	2010	% Change
0-17	2,540	2,400	-5.5%
18-24	1,080	980	-9.3%
25-39	1,980	2,170	9.6%
40-59	2,740	2,690	-1.8%
60-74	1,290	1,530	18.6%
75 +	660	670	1.5%
Total	10,300	10,400	1.0%

Personal Income
Real 1995 Dollars ($000)

	1990	1995	% Chg.
Total Earnings by Place of Work	291,699	279,725	-4.1%
Less Personal Contributions for Social Insurance	13,641	12,759	-6.5%
Net Income by Place of Work	278,058	266,966	-4.0%
Plus Residence Adjustment	-173,667	-153,115	-11.8%
Net Income by Place of Residence	104,391	113,851	9.1%
Plus Dividends, Rent and Interest	27,131	26,270	-3.2%
Plus Transfer Payments	33,140	39,845	20.2%
Personal Income by Place of Residence	164,661	179,966	9.3%
Per Capita Income ($)	15,884	17,117	7.8%
Rank	79	73	46

Educational Attainment 1990

Graduate or Prof. Degree
Bachelor's Degree
Associate Degree
Some College No Degree
High School Graduate
9th-12th No Diploma
Less than 9th Grade

0 500 1,000 1,500 2,000 2,500 3,000

High School Grad or Higher
Percent: 64%
Rank in State: 86

Population Change by Decade
(1990-2000 projected)

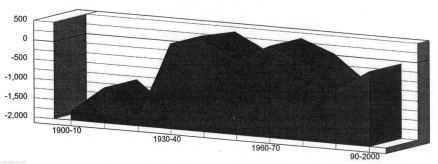

For EDIN tables, sources and footnotes, see page 380.

Occupation of Employed Persons Age 16 & Over

	1990	% Chg. 80-90
Managerial & Professional	779	18.9
Technical, Sales & Admin. Support	916	-1.4
Service Occupations	599	40.6
Farming, Forestry and Fishing	263	5.6
Precision Production, Craft & Repair	724	13.7
Operators, Fabricators	1,291	0.7

Top 5 Counties Commuting in 1990

From Martin Into:		Into Martin From:	
Dubois	717	Greene	1,351
Daviess	307	Daviess	1,114
Orange	202	Lawrence	922
Lawrence	112	Monroe	862
Monroe	63	Orange	203

3,004 persons lived and worked in this county.

1,563 lived in the county but worked elsewhere.

Number of Establishments
(% Change 1990-1995)

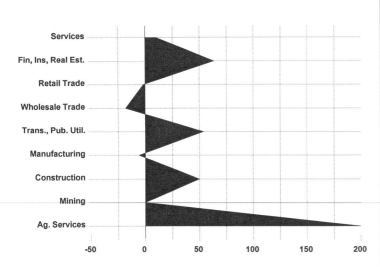

Establishments by Sector 1995

Industry	Number of Establishments	% with fewer than 10 employees
Ag. Services	2	100.0%
Mining	0	NA
Construction	28	85.7%
Manufacturing	16	56.2%
Transportation, Public Utilities	19	78.9%
Wholesale Trade	9	77.8%
Retail Trade	59	72.9%
Finance, Insurance, Real Estate	16	75.0%
Services	76	84.2%

Private Industry	Employment		Real Earnings ($000)		Average Earnings Per Job	
	1995	% Chg. 90-95	1995	Real % Chg. 90-95	1995	Real % Chg. 90-95
Ag. Services	54	NA	1,931	NA	35,759	NA
Mining	NA	NA	NA	NA	NA	NA
Construction	NA	NA	NA	NA	NA	NA
Manufacturing	743	24.0%	21,946	14.1%	29,537	-8.1%
Transportation, Public Utilities	550	90.3%	15,934	96.7%	28,971	3.3%
Wholesale Trade	100	-68.2%	2,941	-52.0%	29,410	50.6%
Retail Trade	724	14.0%	7,633	20.3%	10,543	5.5%
Finance, Insurance, Real Estate	164	1.9%	2,490	22.0%	15,183	19.8%
Services	780	-1.3%	11,975	14.3%	15,353	15.8%

MIAMI COUNTY

Population 1997 (Est.)	33,199	# Households 1995 (Projection)	11,500	Personal Income 1995 ($000)	$274,136
Land Area (Sq. Mi.)	375.8	% Family	75.6%	Avg. Wage Per Job 1995	$20,950
Population Density 1997	88.3	% Non-Family	24.7%	Employed in 1996	14,030
% Under 20 1996	30.4%	% Living Alone	22.3%	Unemployed in 1996	900
% 65 & Over 1996	12.0%	Births 1995	424	Unemployment Rate 1996	6.1%
% White 1996	94.5%	Births to Teens 1995	74	Avg. Covered Payroll 1996 ($000)	$46,041
% African-Amer. 1996	3.1%	Deaths 1995	292	Average Weekly Earnings in Manufacturing 1996	$479.00
% Hispanic* 1996	1.9%	Marriages 1995	338	Registered Vehicles 1996	34,635

*May be of any race.

Percent of Total Population By Sex and Age

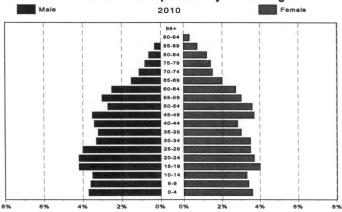

Population Projections

Age Groups	2000	2010	% Change
0-17	9,350	8,840	-5.5%
18-24	3,340	3,800	13.8%
25-39	6,820	6,950	1.9%
40-59	7,750	8,760	13.0%
60-74	3,310	3,890	17.5%
75 +	1,880	1,810	-3.7%
Total	32,400	34,000	4.9%

Personal Income
Real 1995 Dollars ($000)

	1990	1995	% Chg.
Total Earnings by Place of Work	358,375	274,136	-23.5%
Less Personal Contributions for Social Insurance	21,363	18,921	-11.4%
Net Income by Place of Work	337,012	255,215	-24.3%
Plus Residence Adjustment	76,473	119,585	56.4%
Net Income by Place of Residence	413,485	374,800	-9.4%
Plus Dividends, Rent and Interest	87,900	81,281	-7.5%
Plus Transfer Payments	98,721	115,915	17.4%
Personal Income by Place of Residence	600,106	571,996	-4.7%
Per Capita Income ($)	16,276	17,637	8.4%
Rank	72	62	34

Educational Attainment 1990

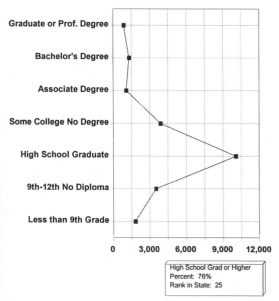

High School Grad or Higher
Percent: 76%
Rank in State: 25

Population Change by Decade
(1990-2000 projected)

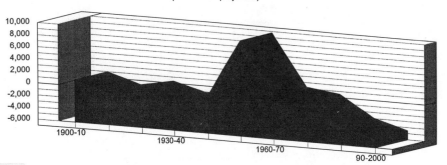

For EDIN tables, sources and footnotes, see page 380.

Occupation of Employed Persons Age 16 & Over		
	1990	% Chg. 80-90
Managerial & Professional	2,269	3.1
Technical, Sales & Admin. Support	3,761	10.3
Service Occupations	2,198	12.8
Farming, Forestry and Fishing	560	-18.0
Precision Production, Craft & Repair	2,334	8.8
Operators, Fabricators	3,771	-19.4

Top 5 Counties Commuting in 1990			
From Miami Into:		Into Miami From:	
Howard	2,101	Howard	693
Wabash	845	Cass	450
Grant	525	Grant	385
Fulton	493	Wabash	206
Cass	452	Fulton	178

11,479 persons lived and worked in this county.
5,208 lived in the county but worked elsewhere.

Number of Establishments
(% Change 1990-1995)

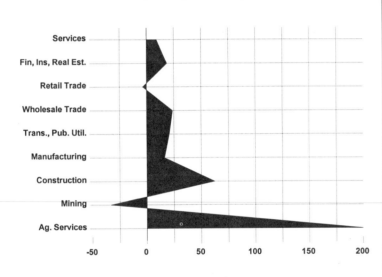

Establishments by Sector 1995		
Industry	Number of Establishments	% with fewer than 10 employees
Ag. Services	6	100.0%
Mining	2	0.0%
Construction	86	90.7%
Manufacturing	43	37.2%
Transportation, Public Utilities	35	60.0%
Wholesale Trade	47	76.6%
Retail Trade	170	67.6%
Finance, Insurance, Real Estate	57	89.5%
Services	201	87.6%

Private Industry	Employment		Real Earnings ($000)		Average Earnings Per Job	
	1995	% Chg. 90-95	1995	Real % Chg. 90-95	1995	Real % Chg. 90-95
Ag. Services	NA	NA	NA	NA	NA	NA
Mining	NA	NA	NA	NA	NA	NA
Construction	741	-0.5%	15,308	-8.9%	20,659	-8.4%
Manufacturing	2,940	-3.1%	84,794	-1.9%	28,841	1.2%
Transportation, Public Utilities	550	10.2%	17,982	8.1%	32,695	-1.9%
Wholesale Trade	373	9.7%	11,808	25.6%	31,657	14.5%
Retail Trade	2,376	4.8%	27,042	1.5%	11,381	-3.1%
Finance, Insurance, Real Estate	580	-19.2%	7,789	-7.4%	13,429	14.7%
Services	2,401	1.6%	33,549	18.8%	13,973	16.9%

For EDIN tables, sources and footnotes, see page 380.

MONROE COUNTY

Population 1997 (Est.)	116,653	# Households 1995 (Projection)	41,900	Personal Income 1995 ($000)	$1,698,795
Land Area (Sq. Mi.)	394.4	% Family	58.9%	Avg. Wage Per Job 1995	$21,228
Population Density 1997	295.8	% Non-Family	41.2%	Employed in 1996	59,210
% Under 20 1996	27.4%	% Living Alone	28.4%	Unemployed in 1996	1,670
% 65 & Over 1996	8.8%	Births 1995	1,162	Unemployment Rate 1996	2.7%
% White 1996	93.8%	Births to Teens 1995	107	Avg. Covered Payroll 1996 ($000)	$328,749
% African-Amer. 1996	2.9%	Deaths 1995	662	Average Weekly Earnings in Manufacturing 1996	$573.50
% Hispanic* 1996	1.7%	Marriages 1995	909	Registered Vehicles 1996	87,382

*May be of any race.

Percent of Total Population By Sex and Age

Male 2010 Female

(Age pyramid chart with age groups from 0-4 to 95+, scale 8% to 0% to 8%)

Population Projections

Age Groups	2000	2010	% Change
0-17	26,350	26,880	2.0%
18-24	26,710	28,240	5.7%
25-39	27,830	27,060	-2.8%
40-59	23,970	26,950	12.4%
60-74	9,410	12,410	31.9%
75 +	4,670	5,380	15.2%
Total	118,900	126,900	6.7%

Personal Income
Real 1995 Dollars ($000)

	1990	1995	% Chg.
Total Earnings by Place of Work	1,477,309	1,698,795	15.0%
Less Personal Contributions for Social Insurance	83,479	100,752	20.7%
Net Income by Place of Work	1,393,829	1,598,043	14.7%
Plus Residence Adjustment	-75,906	-89,267	17.6%
Net Income by Place of Residence	1,317,923	1,508,776	14.5%
Plus Dividends, Rent and Interest	350,628	369,971	5.5%
Plus Transfer Payments	218,216	268,227	22.9%
Personal Income by Place of Residence	1,886,766	2,146,974	13.8%
Per Capita Income ($)	17,262	18,603	7.8%
Rank	54	54	45

Educational Attainment 1990

(Line chart with categories: Graduate or Prof. Degree, Bachelor's Degree, Associate Degree, Some College No Degree, High School Graduate, 9th-12th No Diploma, Less than 9th Grade; scale 0 to 20,000)

High School Grad or Higher
Percent: 82%
Rank in State: 6

Population Change by Decade
(1990-2000 projected)

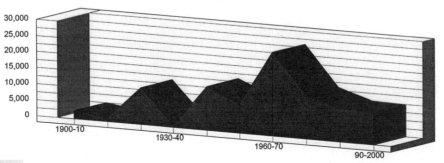

(Area chart, scale 0 to 30,000; decades 1900-10, 1930-40, 1960-70, 90-2000)

For EDIN tables, sources and footnotes, see page 380.

Occupation of Employed Persons Age 16 & Over

	1990	% Chg. 80-90
Managerial & Professional	16,879	30.3
Technical, Sales & Admin. Support	16,278	20.5
Service Occupations	7,813	12.7
Farming, Forestry and Fishing	626	4.3
Precision Production, Craft & Repair	4,830	14.8
Operators, Fabricators	6,138	-0.8

Top 5 Counties Commuting in 1990

From Monroe Into:		Into Monroe From:	
Marion	1,560	Lawrence	2,675
Martin	862	Greene	2,558
Lawrence	658	Owen	2,047
Morgan	420	Morgan	818
Owen	398	Brown	642

46,142 persons lived and worked in this county.

5,395 lived in the county but worked elsewhere.

Number of Establishments
(% Change 1990-1995)

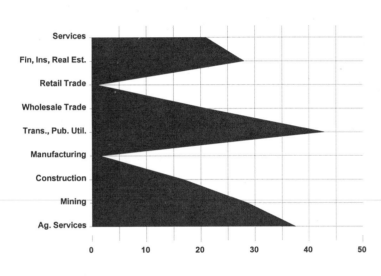

Establishments by Sector 1995

Industry	Number of Establishments	% with fewer than 10 employees
Ag. Services	44	81.8%
Mining	9	0.0%
Construction	313	80.5%
Manufacturing	131	56.5%
Transportation, Public Utilities	100	64.0%
Wholesale Trade	138	73.9%
Retail Trade	730	59.9%
Finance, Insurance, Real Estate	274	83.6%
Services	1,040	76.0%

Private Industry	Employment		Real Earnings ($000)		Average Earnings Per Job	
	1995	% Chg. 90-95	1995	Real % Chg. 90-95	1995	Real % Chg. 90-95
Ag. Services	586	21.3%	7,721	28.3%	13,176	5.7%
Mining	255	-13.0%	8,532	2.0%	33,459	17.2%
Construction	3,820	20.3%	120,557	15.9%	31,559	-3.7%
Manufacturing	10,060	3.8%	349,086	10.6%	34,700	6.6%
Transportation, Public Utilities	2,048	2.0%	68,335	3.1%	33,367	1.0%
Wholesale Trade	1,641	-3.2%	46,346	-6.7%	28,243	-3.7%
Retail Trade	14,692	19.4%	179,545	20.0%	12,221	0.5%
Finance, Insurance, Real Estate	3,880	12.9%	73,189	45.1%	18,863	28.5%
Services	16,568	13.7%	357,351	30.6%	21,569	14.9%

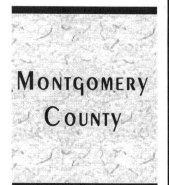

MONTGOMERY COUNTY

Population 1997 (Est.)	36,285	# Households 1995 (Projection)	13,400	Personal Income 1995 ($000)	$571,016
Land Area (Sq. Mi.)	504.6	% Family	72.5%	Avg. Wage Per Job 1995	$23,368
Population Density 1997	71.9	% Non-Family	27.2%	Employed in 1996	19,080
% Under 20 1996	27.4%	% Living Alone	24.0%	Unemployed in 1996	590
% 65 & Over 1996	14.4%	Births 1995	494	Unemployment Rate 1996	3.0%
% White 1996	98.6%	Births to Teens 1995	69	Avg. Covered Payroll 1996 ($000)	$115,410
% African-Amer. 1996	0.7%	Deaths 1995	368	Average Weekly Earnings in Manufacturing 1996	$633.75
% Hispanic* 1996	0.6%	Marriages 1995	356	Registered Vehicles 1996	35,793

*May be of any race.

Percent of Total Population By Sex and Age

■ Male   2010   ■ Female

Population Projections

Age Groups	2000	2010	% Change
0-17	8,750	8,180	-6.5%
18-24	3,490	3,540	1.4%
25-39	7,090	6,900	-2.7%
40-59	8,890	9,500	6.9%
60-74	4,230	4,750	12.3%
75 +	2,260	2,230	-1.3%
Total	34,700	35,100	1.2%

Personal Income
Real 1995 Dollars ($000)

	1990	1995	% Chg.
Total Earnings by Place of Work	505,019	571,016	13.1%
Less Personal Contributions for Social Insurance	32,707	39,570	21.0%
Net Income by Place of Work	472,312	531,446	12.5%
Plus Residence Adjustment	-39,366	-46,103	17.1%
Net Income by Place of Residence	432,946	485,343	12.1%
Plus Dividends, Rent and Interest	119,046	122,871	3.2%
Plus Transfer Payments	97,642	115,136	17.9%
Personal Income by Place of Residence	649,634	723,350	11.3%
Per Capita Income ($)	18,851	20,011	6.2%
Rank	25	30	59

Educational Attainment 1990

High School Grad or Higher
Percent: 80%
Rank in State: 11

Population Change by Decade
(1990-2000 projected)

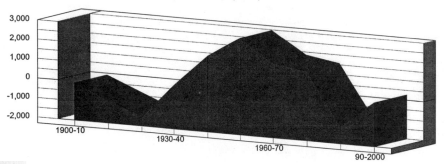

Occupation of Employed Persons Age 16 & Over

	1990	% Chg. 80-90
Managerial & Professional	2,947	6.0
Technical, Sales & Admin. Support	4,366	6.2
Service Occupations	2,095	9.7
Farming, Forestry and Fishing	804	-21.7
Precision Production, Craft & Repair	2,299	1.8
Operators, Fabricators	4,171	10.9

Top 5 Counties Commuting in 1990

From Montgomery Into:		Into Montgomery From:	
Tippecanoe	772	Fountain	780
Marion	599	Putnam	560
Boone	243	Parke	429
Outside Indiana	163	Tippecanoe	355
Putnam	120	Boone	291

14,276 persons lived and worked in this county.

2,237 lived in the county but worked elsewhere.

Number of Establishments
(% Change 1990-1995)

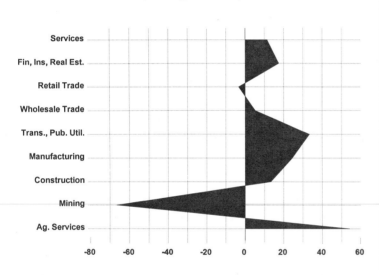

Establishments by Sector 1995

Industry	Number of Establishments	% with fewer than 10 employees
Ag. Services	17	94.1%
Mining	1	0.0%
Construction	94	87.2%
Manufacturing	61	39.3%
Transportation, Public Utilities	60	83.3%
Wholesale Trade	60	78.3%
Retail Trade	228	65.8%
Finance, Insurance, Real Estate	74	85.1%
Services	296	84.5%

Private Industry	Employment		Real Earnings ($000)		Average Earnings Per Job	
	1995	% Chg. 90-95	1995	Real % Chg. 90-95	1995	Real % Chg. 90-95
Ag. Services	279	74.4%	2,553	103.2%	9,151	16.6%
Mining	NA	NA	396	-41.3%	NA	NA
Construction	767	3.1%	18,193	9.5%	23,720	6.2%
Manufacturing	8,340	16.6%	300,736	17.3%	36,059	0.6%
Transportation, Public Utilities	726	2.0%	20,078	1.0%	27,656	-0.9%
Wholesale Trade	477	-32.3%	15,259	-26.4%	31,990	8.9%
Retail Trade	4,101	30.6%	55,086	34.7%	13,432	3.1%
Finance, Insurance, Real Estate	836	0.8%	12,625	13.1%	15,102	12.1%
Services	5,147	18.7%	92,382	33.4%	17,949	12.4%

MORGAN COUNTY

Population 1997 (Est.)	64,787	# Households 1995 (Projection)	20,400	Personal Income 1995 ($000)	$390,485
Land Area (Sq. Mi.)	406.5	% Family	81.1%	Avg. Wage Per Job 1995	$19,768
Population Density 1997	159.4	% Non-Family	19.1%	Employed in 1996	32,360
% Under 20 1996	29.6%	% Living Alone	16.4%	Unemployed in 1996	1,120
% 65 & Over 1996	10.4%	Births 1995	909	Unemployment Rate 1996	3.4%
% White 1996	99.5%	Births to Teens 1995	128	Avg. Covered Payroll 1996 ($000)	$72,632
% African-Amer. 1996	0.0%	Deaths 1995	520	Average Weekly Earnings in Manufacturing 1996	$527.75
% Hispanic* 1996	0.5%	Marriages 1995	556	Registered Vehicles 1996	65,079

*May be of any race.

Percent of Total Population By Sex and Age

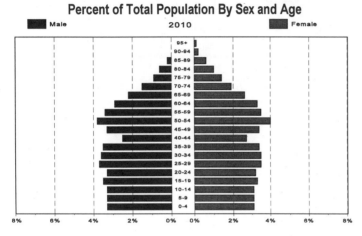

Male   2010   Female

Population Projections

Age Groups	2000	2010	% Change
0-17	14,920	14,400	-3.5%
18-24	6,390	5,740	-10.2%
25-39	11,710	13,090	11.8%
40-59	17,130	16,460	-3.9%
60-74	6,580	8,890	35.1%
75 +	2,710	3,170	17.0%
Total	59,400	61,700	3.9%

Personal Income
Real 1995 Dollars ($000)

	1990	1995	% Chg.
Total Earnings by Place of Work	343,061	390,485	13.8%
Less Personal Contributions for Social Insurance	22,884	27,982	22.3%
Net Income by Place of Work	320,177	362,503	13.2%
Plus Residence Adjustment	455,900	564,966	23.9%
Net Income by Place of Residence	776,076	927,469	19.5%
Plus Dividends, Rent and Interest	128,700	135,358	5.2%
Plus Transfer Payments	131,205	164,419	25.3%
Personal Income by Place of Residence	1,035,981	1,227,246	18.5%
Per Capita Income ($)	18,425	19,792	7.4%
Rank	34	33	49

Educational Attainment 1990

Graduate or Prof. Degree
Bachelor's Degree
Associate Degree
Some College No Degree
High School Graduate
9th-12th No Diploma
Less than 9th Grade

0   4,000   8,000   12,000   16,000

High School Grad or Higher
Percent: 74%
Rank in State: 46

Population Change by Decade
(1990-2000 projected)

12,000
10,000
8,000
6,000
4,000
2,000
0
-2,000

1900-10   1930-40   1960-70   90-2000

Occupation of Employed Persons Age 16 & Over

	1990	% Chg. 80-90
Managerial & Professional	4,833	48.2
Technical, Sales & Admin. Support	8,007	35.9
Service Occupations	3,285	31.3
Farming, Forestry and Fishing	538	-5.1
Precision Production, Craft & Repair	5,054	32.2
Operators, Fabricators	5,692	-0.7

Top 5 Counties Commuting in 1990

From Morgan Into:		Into Morgan From:	
Marion	12,036	Marion	1,026
Johnson	1,011	Monroe	420
Hendricks	982	Johnson	419
Monroe	818	Hendricks	400
Outside Indiana	144	Owen	262

11,185 persons lived and worked in this county.
15,729 lived in the county but worked elsewhere.

Number of Establishments
(% Change 1990-1995)

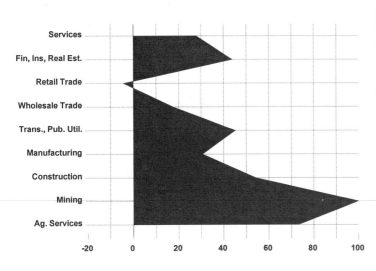

Establishments by Sector 1995

Industry	Number of Establishments	% with fewer than 10 employees
Ag. Services	26	88.5%
Mining	6	33.3%
Construction	216	88.9%
Manufacturing	77	64.9%
Transportation, Public Utilities	61	70.5%
Wholesale Trade	67	83.6%
Retail Trade	265	59.6%
Finance, Insurance, Real Estate	95	86.3%
Services	372	85.2%

Private Industry	Employment		Real Earnings ($000)		Average Earnings Per Job	
	1995	% Chg. 90-95		Real % Chg. 90-95	1995	Real % Chg. 90-95
Ag. Services	313	38.5%	3,325	24.3%	10,623	-10.2%
Mining	110	52.8%	3,466	73.7%	31,509	13.7%
Construction	1,959	36.0%	44,454	36.3%	22,692	0.2%
Manufacturing	2,609	-16.8%	77,629	-0.1%	29,754	20.1%
Transportation, Public Utilities	874	17.6%	29,744	17.9%	34,032	0.2%
Wholesale Trade	435	23.2%	12,810	36.7%	29,448	10.9%
Retail Trade	4,524	12.2%	53,720	8.8%	11,874	-3.0%
Finance, Insurance, Real Estate	976	2.2%	14,011	20.5%	14,356	17.9%
Services	4,677	22.3%	82,735	22.0%	17,690	-0.2%

NEWTON COUNTY

Population 1997 (Est.)	14,683	# Households 1995 (Projection)	4,800	Personal Income 1995 ($000)	$93,277
Land Area (Sq. Mi.)	401.9	% Family	75.8%	Avg. Wage Per Job 1995	$19,297
Population Density 1997	36.5	% Non-Family	23.1%	Employed in 1996	6,060
% Under 20 1996	30.6%	% Living Alone	20.4%	Unemployed in 1996	360
% 65 & Over 1996	13.5%	Births 1995	151	Unemployment Rate 1996	5.6%
% White 1996	99.4%	Births to Teens 1995	20	Avg. Covered Payroll 1996 ($000)	$19,262
% African-Amer. 1996	0.1%	Deaths 1995	147	Average Weekly Earnings in Manufacturing 1996	$465.50
% Hispanic* 1996	1.7%	Marriages 1995	96	Registered Vehicles 1996	15,368

*May be of any race.

Percent of Total Population By Sex and Age

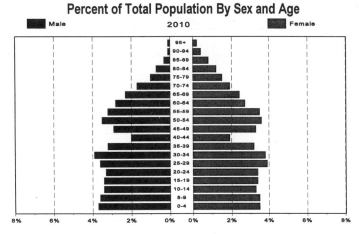

Male   2010   Female

Population Projections

Age Groups	2000	2010	% Change
0-17	3,510	3,480	-0.9%
18-24	1,570	1,310	-16.6%
25-39	2,380	3,000	26.1%
40-59	3,610	3,310	-8.3%
60-74	1,600	1,910	19.4%
75 +	840	880	4.8%
Total	13,500	13,900	3.0%

Personal Income
Real 1995 Dollars ($000)

	1990	1995	% Chg.
Total Earnings by Place of Work	106,344	93,277	-12.3%
Less Personal Contributions for Social Insurance	6,687	7,626	14.0%
Net Income by Place of Work	99,656	85,651	-14.1%
Plus Residence Adjustment	54,712	58,206	6.4%
Net Income by Place of Residence	154,368	143,857	-6.8%
Plus Dividends, Rent and Interest	41,166	37,734	-8.3%
Plus Transfer Payments	35,177	40,041	13.8%
Personal Income by Place of Residence	230,711	221,632	-3.9%
Per Capita Income ($)	16,995	15,394	-9.4%
Rank	59	88	92

Educational Attainment 1990

Graduate or Prof. Degree
Bachelor's Degree
Associate Degree
Some College No Degree
High School Graduate
9th-12th No Diploma
Less than 9th Grade

0   1,000   2,000   3,000   4,000   5,000

High School Grad or Higher
Percent: 72%
Rank in State: 57

Population Change by Decade
(1990-2000 projected)

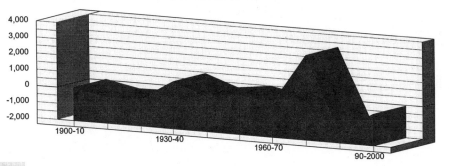

4,000
3,000
2,000
1,000
0
-1,000
-2,000

1900-10   1930-40   1960-70   90-2000

For EDIN tables, sources and footnotes, see page 380.

Occupation of Employed Persons Age 16 & Over

	1990	% Chg. 80-90
Managerial & Professional	975	15.2
Technical, Sales & Admin. Support	1,451	23.7
Service Occupations	813	9.1
Farming, Forestry and Fishing	440	-29.9
Precision Production, Craft & Repair	946	-15.5
Operators, Fabricators	1,448	-7.7

Top 5 Counties Commuting in 1990

From Newton Into:		Into Newton From:	
Lake	1,124	Jasper	323
Jasper	776	Benton	309
Outside Indiana	662	Outside Indiana	251
Porter	89	Lake	164
Tippecanoe	48	White	32

3,115 persons lived and worked in this county.
2,849 lived in the county but worked elsewhere.

Number of Establishments
(% Change 1990-1995)

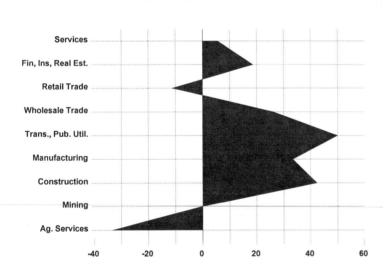

Establishments by Sector 1995

Industry	Number of Establishments	% with fewer than 10 employees
Ag. Services	2	50.0%
Mining	1	0.0%
Construction	37	86.5%
Manufacturing	24	50.0%
Transportation, Public Utilities	24	95.8%
Wholesale Trade	29	75.9%
Retail Trade	71	76.1%
Finance, Insurance, Real Estate	19	89.5%
Services	57	93.0%

Private Industry	Employment		Real Earnings ($000)		Average Earnings Per Job	
	1995	% Chg. 90-95	1995	Real % Chg. 90-95	1995	Real % Chg. 90-95
Ag. Services	78	13.0%	697	59.2%	8,936	40.9%
Mining	33	-13.2%	1,302	-2.6%	39,455	12.2%
Construction	370	6.3%	7,846	-14.2%	21,205	-19.3%
Manufacturing	1,453	14.6%	40,195	21.1%	27,663	5.7%
Transportation, Public Utilities	165	3.1%	5,263	39.2%	31,897	35.0%
Wholesale Trade	272	6.7%	8,292	12.2%	30,485	5.2%
Retail Trade	712	-5.2%	8,695	-9.6%	12,212	-4.7%
Finance, Insurance, Real Estate	265	10.4%	3,613	26.2%	13,634	14.3%
Services	926	-10.8%	13,909	-8.9%	15,021	2.1%

Noble County

Population 1997 (Est.)	41,918	# Households 1995 (Projection)	13,900	Personal Income 1995 ($000)		$574,810
Land Area (Sq. Mi.)	411.1	% Family	77.1%	Avg. Wage Per Job 1995		$22,242
Population Density 1997	102.0	% Non-Family	22.9%	Employed in 1996		23,880
% Under 20 1996	31.2%	% Living Alone	19.6%	Unemployed in 1996		930
% 65 & Over 1996	12.1%	Births 1995	692	Unemployment Rate 1996		3.8%
% White 1996	99.3%	Births to Teens 1995	106	Avg. Covered Payroll 1996 ($000)		$122,289
% African-Amer. 1996	0.2%	Deaths 1995	304	Average Weekly Earnings in Manufacturing 1996		$536.75
% Hispanic* 1996	2.1%	Marriages 1995	446	Registered Vehicles 1996		41,414

*May be of any race.

Percent of Total Population By Sex and Age

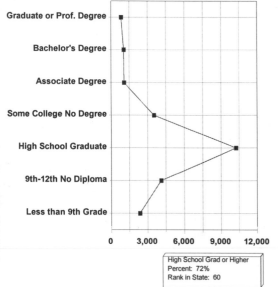

■ Male   2010   ■ Female

Population Projections

Age Groups	2000	2010	% Change
0-17	11,170	10,910	-2.3%
18-24	4,250	4,300	1.2%
25-39	8,180	8,830	7.9%
40-59	10,410	10,980	5.5%
60-74	4,040	5,130	27.0%
75 +	2,140	2,180	1.9%
Total	40,200	42,300	5.2%

Personal Income
Real 1995 Dollars ($000)

	1990	1995	% Chg.
Total Earnings by Place of Work	426,288	574,810	34.8%
Less Personal Contributions for Social Insurance	27,457	38,348	39.7%
Net Income by Place of Work	398,831	536,462	34.5%
Plus Residence Adjustment	77,084	73,148	-5.1%
Net Income by Place of Residence	475,915	609,610	28.1%
Plus Dividends, Rent and Interest	96,759	90,779	-6.2%
Plus Transfer Payments	83,495	104,613	25.3%
Personal Income by Place of Residence	656,168	805,002	22.7%
Per Capita Income ($)	17,265	19,710	14.2%
Rank	53	34	5

Educational Attainment 1990

Graduate or Prof. Degree
Bachelor's Degree
Associate Degree
Some College No Degree
High School Graduate
9th-12th No Diploma
Less than 9th Grade

0   3,000   6,000   9,000   12,000

High School Grad or Higher
Percent: 72%
Rank in State: 60

Population Change by Decade
(1990-2000 projected)

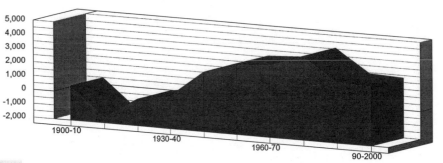

5,000
4,000
3,000
2,000
1,000
0
-1,000
-2,000

1900-10   1930-40   1960-70   90-2000

For EDIN tables, sources and footnotes, see page 380.

Occupation of Employed Persons Age 16 & Over

	1990	% Chg. 80-90
Managerial & Professional	2,838	48.4
Technical, Sales & Admin. Support	4,001	25.1
Service Occupations	1,844	32.2
Farming, Forestry and Fishing	725	-21.6
Precision Production, Craft & Repair	2,952	29.5
Operators, Fabricators	6,144	11.2

Top 5 Counties Commuting in 1990

From Noble Into:		Into Noble From:	
Allen	2,129	Dekalb	1,326
Elkhart	1,144	Lagrange	1,123
Lagrange	935	Allen	784
Dekalb	711	Kosciusko	464
Whitley	660	Steuben	273

11,679 persons lived and worked in this county.
6,449 lived in the county but worked elsewhere.

Number of Establishments
(% Change 1990-1995)

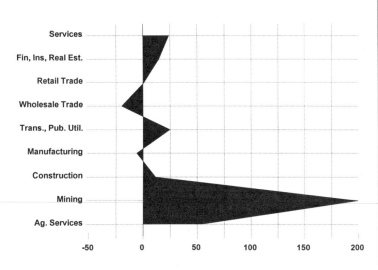

Establishments by Sector 1995

Industry	Number of Establishments	% with fewer than 10 employees
Ag. Services	20	95.0%
Mining	3	66.7%
Construction	96	86.5%
Manufacturing	144	29.9%
Transportation, Public Utilities	35	71.4%
Wholesale Trade	56	69.6%
Retail Trade	205	65.4%
Finance, Insurance, Real Estate	62	91.9%
Services	280	83.2%

Private Industry	Employment		Real Earnings ($000)		Average Earnings Per Job	
	1995	% Chg. 90-95	1995	Real % Chg. 90-95	1995	Real % Chg. 90-95
Ag. Services	204	33.3%	1,874	9.4%	9,186	-18.0%
Mining	27	-41.3%	736	-47.3%	27,259	-10.3%
Construction	1,065	23.8%	25,475	24.1%	23,920	0.2%
Manufacturing	11,231	30.6%	351,750	48.7%	31,320	13.9%
Transportation, Public Utilities	565	18.4%	15,105	30.3%	26,735	10.0%
Wholesale Trade	493	-1.0%	16,091	-6.7%	32,639	-5.7%
Retail Trade	2,916	8.4%	33,736	10.4%	11,569	1.8%
Finance, Insurance, Real Estate	676	-3.6%	7,426	-1.3%	10,985	2.3%
Services	3,742	39.6%	58,761	50.0%	15,703	7.5%

OHIO
COUNTY

Population 1997 (Est.)	5,458	# Households 1995 (Projection)	2,000	Personal Income 1995 ($000)	$15,682
Land Area (Sq. Mi.)	86.7	% Family	77.0%	Avg. Wage Per Job 1995	$14,971
Population Density 1997	63.0	% Non-Family	24.5%	Employed in 1996	2,525
% Under 20 1996	27.8%	% Living Alone	22.0%	Unemployed in 1996	140
% 65 & Over 1996	14.1%	Births 1995	57	Unemployment Rate 1996	5.3%
% White 1996	98.9%	Births to Teens 1995	9	Avg. Covered Payroll 1996 ($000)	$4,728
% African-Amer. 1996	0.8%	Deaths 1995	53	Average Weekly Earnings in Manufacturing 1996	NA
% Hispanic* 1996	0.2%	Marriages 1995	24	Registered Vehicles 1996	5,626

*May be of any race.

Percent of Total Population By Sex and Age

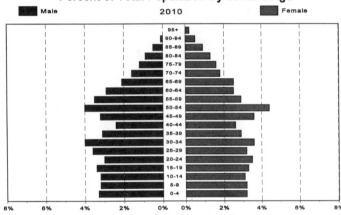

Population Projections

Age Groups	2000	2010	% Change
0-17	1,350	1,330	-1.5%
18-24	610	520	-14.8%
25-39	1,030	1,170	13.6%
40-59	1,530	1,530	0.0%
60-74	660	780	18.2%
75 +	380	410	7.9%
Total	5,600	5,700	1.8%

Personal Income
Real 1995 Dollars ($000)

	1990	1995	% Chg.
Total Earnings by Place of Work	13,904	15,682	12.8%
Less Personal Contributions for Social Insurance	1,054	1,378	30.7%
Net Income by Place of Work	12,850	14,304	11.3%
Plus Residence Adjustment	43,722	52,644	20.4%
Net Income by Place of Residence	56,572	66,948	18.3%
Plus Dividends, Rent and Interest	11,166	10,653	-4.6%
Plus Transfer Payments	14,788	15,356	3.8%
Personal Income by Place of Residence	82,526	92,957	12.6%
Per Capita Income ($)	15,486	17,085	10.3%
Rank	82	74	17

Educational Attainment 1990

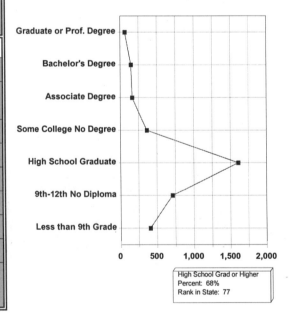

High School Grad or Higher
Percent: 68%
Rank in State: 77

Population Change by Decade
(1990-2000 projected)

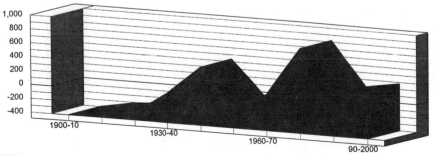

For EDIN tables, sources and footnotes, see page 380.

Occupation of Employed Persons Age 16 & Over

	1990	% Chg. 80-90
Managerial & Professional	291	-2.3
Technical, Sales & Admin. Support	586	49.5
Service Occupations	261	13.0
Farming, Forestry and Fishing	115	-10.9
Precision Production, Craft & Repair	499	66.9
Operators, Fabricators	633	-2.9

Top 5 Counties Commuting in 1990

From Ohio Into:		Into Ohio From:	
Dearborn	809	Switzerland	56
Outside Indiana	755	Dearborn	32
Switzerland	70	Ripley	13
Ripley	56	NA	—
Jefferson	19	NA	—

588 persons lived and worked in this county.
1,744 lived in the county but worked elsewhere.

Number of Establishments
(% Change 1990-1995)

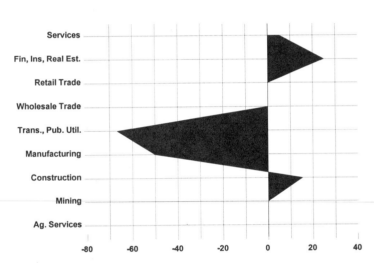

Establishments by Sector 1995

Industry	Number of Establishments	% with fewer than 10 employees
Ag. Services	2	100.0%
Mining	0	NA
Construction	15	93.3%
Manufacturing	1	100.0%
Transportation, Public Utilities	1	100.0%
Wholesale Trade	2	100.0%
Retail Trade	14	85.7%
Finance, Insurance, Real Estate	5	80.0%
Services	20	85.0%

Private Industry	Employment		Real Earnings ($000)		Average Earnings Per Job	
	1995	% Chg. 90-95	1995	Real % Chg. 90-95	1995	Real % Chg. 90-95
Ag. Services	33	43.5%	124	27.2%	3,758	-11.4%
Mining	0	NA	0	NA	NA	NA
Construction	86	8.9%	1,472	20.0%	17,116	10.2%
Manufacturing	14	-44.0%	2,353	66.4%	NA	NA
Transportation, Public Utilities	23	-39.5%	647	-34.5%	28,130	8.2%
Wholesale Trade	11	10.0%	211	12.9%	19,182	2.6%
Retail Trade	198	-0.5%	2,248	0.9%	11,354	1.4%
Finance, Insurance, Real Estate	24	-54.7%	151	-72.0%	6,292	-38.1%
Services	280	14.3%	4,307	41.0%	15,382	23.3%

ORANGE COUNTY

Population 1997 (Est.)	19,378	# Households 1995 (Projection)	6,900	Personal Income 1995 ($000)	$180,592
Land Area (Sq. Mi.)	399.6	% Family	74.5%	Avg. Wage Per Job 1995	$18,534
Population Density 1997	48.5	% Non-Family	25.7%	Employed in 1996	8,140
% Under 20 1996	28.5%	% Living Alone	22.9%	Unemployed in 1996	865
% 65 & Over 1996	15.5%	Births 1995	236	Unemployment Rate 1996	9.6%
% White 1996	99.0%	Births to Teens 1995	47	Avg. Covered Payroll 1996 ($000)	$31,982
% African-Amer. 1996	0.7%	Deaths 1995	199	Average Weekly Earnings in Manufacturing 1996	$396.50
% Hispanic* 1996	0.4%	Marriages 1995	209	Registered Vehicles 1996	19,303

*May be of any race.

Percent of Total Population By Sex and Age

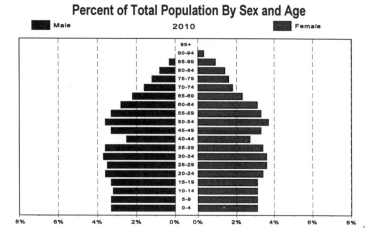

■ Male   2010   ■ Female

Population Projections

Age Groups	2000	2010	% Change
0-17	4,440	4,220	-5.0%
18-24	1,930	1,770	-8.3%
25-39	3,560	3,970	11.5%
40-59	4,880	4,750	-2.7%
60-74	2,270	2,560	12.8%
75 +	1,240	1,200	-3.2%
Total	18,300	18,500	1.1%

Personal Income
Real 1995 Dollars ($000)

	1990	1995	% Chg.
Total Earnings by Place of Work	165,476	180,592	9.1%
Less Personal Contributions for Social Insurance	11,059	13,185	19.2%
Net Income by Place of Work	154,417	167,407	8.4%
Plus Residence Adjustment	20,598	24,564	19.3%
Net Income by Place of Residence	175,015	191,971	9.7%
Plus Dividends, Rent and Interest	41,327	39,636	-4.1%
Plus Transfer Payments	52,607	65,738	25.0%
Personal Income by Place of Residence	268,949	297,345	10.6%
Per Capita Income ($)	14,595	15,651	7.2%
Rank	89	87	51

Educational Attainment 1990

Graduate or Prof. Degree
Bachelor's Degree
Associate Degree
Some College No Degree
High School Graduate
9th-12th No Diploma
Less than 9th Grade

0   1,500   3,000   4,500   6,000

High School Grad or Higher
Percent: 65%
Rank in State: 85

Population Change by Decade
(1990-2000 projected)

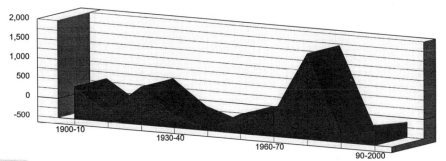

2,000
1,500
1,000
500
0
-500

1900-10   1930-40   1960-70   90-2000

For EDIN tables, sources and footnotes, see page 380.

Occupation of Employed Persons Age 16 & Over

	1990	% Chg. 80-90
Managerial & Professional	1,182	22.0
Technical, Sales & Admin. Support	1,569	7.6
Service Occupations	1,192	17.2
Farming, Forestry and Fishing	359	-20.8
Precision Production, Craft & Repair	1,121	8.5
Operators, Fabricators	2,360	-2.5

Top 5 Counties Commuting in 1990

From Orange Into:		Into Orange From:	
Lawrence	644	Lawrence	439
Dubois	291	Washington	237
Washington	283	Crawford	228
Outside Indiana	253	Martin	202
Martin	203	Dubois	164

5,346 persons lived and worked in this county.
2,292 lived in the county but worked elsewhere.

Number of Establishments
(% Change 1990-1995)

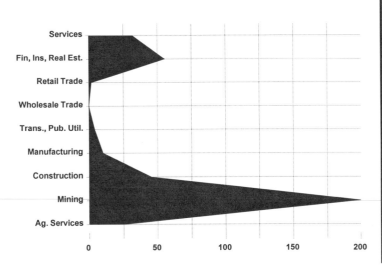

Establishments by Sector 1995

Industry	Number of Establishments	% with fewer than 10 employees
Ag. Services	5	100.0%
Mining	3	66.7%
Construction	48	81.2%
Manufacturing	32	40.6%
Transportation, Public Utilities	25	76.0%
Wholesale Trade	22	77.3%
Retail Trade	111	74.8%
Finance, Insurance, Real Estate	28	78.6%
Services	116	82.8%

Private Industry	Employment		Real Earnings ($000)		Average Earnings Per Job	
	1995	% Chg. 90-95	1995	Real % Chg. 90-95	1995	Real % Chg. 90-95
Ag. Services	179	40.9%	3,359	245.7%	18,765	145.3%
Mining	NA	NA	NA	NA	NA	NA
Construction	734	19.7%	20,978	28.7%	28,580	7.5%
Manufacturing	2,880	14.6%	68,227	12.0%	23,690	-2.3%
Transportation, Public Utilities	NA	NA	NA	NA	NA	NA
Wholesale Trade	116	-7.9%	3,555	17.6%	30,647	27.8%
Retail Trade	1,190	2.0%	14,767	-3.9%	12,409	-5.7%
Finance, Insurance, Real Estate	309	-9.9%	5,182	4.9%	16,770	16.4%
Services	1,986	3.7%	28,446	8.6%	14,323	4.7%

OWEN COUNTY

Population 1997 (Est.)	20,257	# Households 1995 (Projection)	6,600	Personal Income 1995 ($000)	$100,086
Land Area (Sq. Mi.)	385.2	% Family	77.7%	Avg. Wage Per Job 1995	$17,690
Population Density 1997	52.6	% Non-Family	22.9%	Employed in 1996	9,930
% Under 20 1996	28.3%	% Living Alone	19.7%	Unemployed in 1996	490
% 65 & Over 1996	13.5%	Births 1995	238	Unemployment Rate 1996	4.7%
% White 1996	99.2%	Births to Teens 1995	47	Avg. Covered Payroll 1996 ($000)	$17,541
% African-Amer. 1996	0.3%	Deaths 1995	177	Average Weekly Earnings in Manufacturing 1996	$458.00
% Hispanic* 1996	0.4%	Marriages 1995	220	Registered Vehicles 1996	20,588

*May be of any race.

Percent of Total Population By Sex and Age

Male — 2010 — Female

Age groups (bottom to top): 0-4, 5-9, 10-14, 15-19, 20-24, 25-29, 30-34, 35-39, 40-44, 45-49, 50-54, 55-59, 60-64, 65-69, 70-74, 75-79, 80-84, 85-89, 90-94, 95+

X-axis: 8% 6% 4% 2% 0% 0% 2% 4% 6% 8%

Population Projections

Age Groups	2000	2010	% Change
0-17	4,600	4,550	-1.1%
18-24	2,010	1,790	-10.9%
25-39	3,330	3,960	18.9%
40-59	5,040	4,800	-4.8%
60-74	2,430	2,830	16.5%
75 +	1,120	1,320	17.9%
Total	18,500	19,300	4.3%

Personal Income
Real 1995 Dollars ($000)

	1990	1995	% Chg.
Total Earnings by Place of Work	76,268	100,086	31.2%
Less Personal Contributions for Social Insurance	5,345	7,638	42.9%
Net Income by Place of Work	70,922	92,448	30.4%
Plus Residence Adjustment	98,306	108,402	10.3%
Net Income by Place of Residence	169,229	200,850	18.7%
Plus Dividends, Rent and Interest	43,403	44,860	3.4%
Plus Transfer Payments	43,979	54,878	24.8%
Personal Income by Place of Residence	256,610	300,588	17.1%
Per Capita Income ($)	14,776	15,306	3.6%
Rank	88	89	75

Educational Attainment 1990

Categories (top to bottom): Graduate or Prof. Degree, Bachelor's Degree, Associate Degree, Some College No Degree, High School Graduate, 9th-12th No Diploma, Less than 9th Grade

X-axis: 0, 1,000, 2,000, 3,000, 4,000, 5,000

High School Grad or Higher
Percent: 66%
Rank in State: 78

Population Change by Decade
(1990-2000 projected)

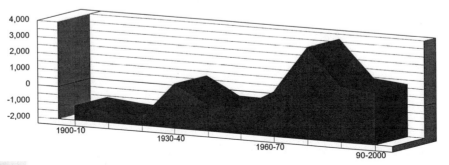

Y-axis: 4,000 / 3,000 / 2,000 / 1,000 / 0 / -1,000 / -2,000

X-axis: 1900-10, 1930-40, 1960-70, 90-2000

Occupation of Employed Persons Age 16 & Over			Top 5 Counties Commuting in 1990			
	1990	% Chg. 80-90	From Owen Into:		Into Owen From:	
Managerial & Professional	1,158	74.9	Monroe	2,047	Monroe	398
Technical, Sales & Admin. Support	1,689	18.2	Marion	1,052	Greene	119
Service Occupations	1,036	44.5	Putnam	343	Clay	72
Farming, Forestry and Fishing	241	-38.8	Morgan	262	Vigo	51
Precision Production, Craft & Repair	1,474	48.4	Clay	92	Outside Indiana	36
Operators, Fabricators	1,989	6.9	3,150	persons lived and worked in this county.		
			4,249	lived in the county but worked elsewhere.		

Number of Establishments
(% Change 1990-1995)

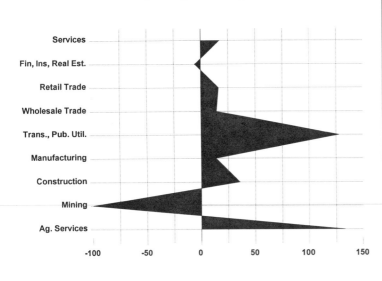

Establishments by Sector 1995		
Industry	Number of Establishments	% with fewer than 10 employees
Ag. Services	7	100.0%
Mining	0	NA
Construction	38	86.8%
Manufacturing	25	52.0%
Transportation, Public Utilities	41	95.1%
Wholesale Trade	16	81.2%
Retail Trade	64	73.4%
Finance, Insurance, Real Estate	17	88.2%
Services	75	86.7%

Private Industry	Employment		Real Earnings ($000)		Average Earnings Per Job	
	1995	% Chg. 90-95	1995	Real % Chg. 90-95	1995	Real % Chg. 90-95
Ag. Services	104	4.0%	1,413	9.2%	13,587	5.0%
Mining	11	-21.4%	372	12.4%	33,818	43.1%
Construction	463	44.7%	7,338	40.2%	15,849	-3.1%
Manufacturing	1,071	22.7%	31,722	62.7%	29,619	32.7%
Transportation, Public Utilities	373	41.3%	10,974	36.7%	29,421	-3.2%
Wholesale Trade	98	42.0%	2,338	29.8%	23,857	-8.6%
Retail Trade	999	11.1%	10,688	10.8%	10,699	-0.3%
Finance, Insurance, Real Estate	318	3.2%	3,478	28.0%	10,937	24.0%
Services	1,055	7.5%	15,548	28.4%	14,737	19.4%

PARKE COUNTY

Population 1997 (Est.)	16,446	# Households 1995 (Projection)	5,800	Personal Income 1995 ($000)	$83,601
Land Area (Sq. Mi.)	444.8	% Family	73.3%	Avg. Wage Per Job 1995	$16,518
Population Density 1997	37.0	% Non-Family	25.9%	Employed in 1996	7,300
% Under 20 1996	26.1%	% Living Alone	23.8%	Unemployed in 1996	400
% 65 & Over 1996	15.9%	Births 1995	187	Unemployment Rate 1996	5.2%
% White 1996	98.4%	Births to Teens 1995	28	Avg. Covered Payroll 1996 ($000)	$14,566
% African-Amer. 1996	1.2%	Deaths 1995	180	Average Weekly Earnings in Manufacturing 1996	$390.75
% Hispanic* 1996	0.7%	Marriages 1995	179	Registered Vehicles 1996	16,068

*May be of any race.

Percent of Total Population By Sex and Age

■ Male   2010   ■ Female

Population Projections

Age Groups	2000	2010	% Change
0-17	3,590	3,320	-7.5%
18-24	1,550	1,460	-5.8%
25-39	2,700	3,050	13.0%
40-59	4,010	3,630	-9.5%
60-74	2,100	2,240	6.7%
75 +	1,180	1,230	4.2%
Total	15,100	14,900	-1.3%

Personal Income
Real 1995 Dollars ($000)

	1990	1995	% Chg.
Total Earnings by Place of Work	88,064	83,601	-5.1%
Less Personal Contributions for Social Insurance	5,510	6,312	14.6%
Net Income by Place of Work	82,554	77,289	-6.4%
Plus Residence Adjustment	81,553	103,861	27.4%
Net Income by Place of Residence	164,108	181,150	10.4%
Plus Dividends, Rent and Interest	45,844	43,393	-5.3%
Plus Transfer Payments	47,494	52,548	10.6%
Personal Income by Place of Residence	257,446	277,091	7.6%
Per Capita Income ($)	16,710	17,188	2.9%
Rank	65	69	78

Educational Attainment 1990

High School Grad or Higher
Percent: 77%
Rank in State: 24

Population Change by Decade
(1990-2000 projected)

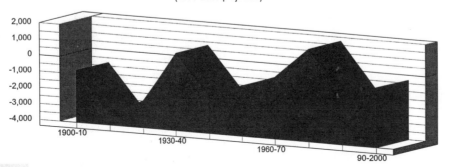

For EDIN tables, sources and footnotes, see page 380.

Occupation of Employed Persons Age 16 & Over		
	1990	% Chg. 80-90
Managerial & Professional	1,064	21.7
Technical, Sales & Admin. Support	1,461	4.8
Service Occupations	1,013	31.6
Farming, Forestry and Fishing	556	-9.9
Precision Production, Craft & Repair	944	-9.4
Operators, Fabricators	1,556	-8.6

Top 5 Counties Commuting in 1990			
From Parke Into:		Into Parke From:	
Vigo	1,076	Vermillion	220
Vermillion	668	Vigo	149
Montgomery	429	Fountain	67
Marion	263	Clay	61
Clay	230	Outside Indiana	48

3,155 persons lived and worked in this county.

3,267 lived in the county but worked elsewhere.

Number of Establishments
(% Change 1990-1995)

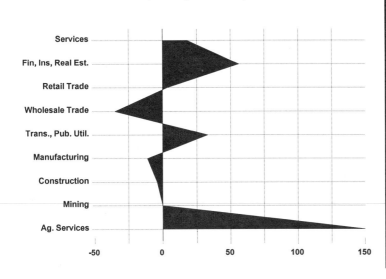

Establishments by Sector 1995		
Industry	Number of Establishments	% with fewer than 10 employees
Ag. Services	5	80.0%
Mining	1	100.0%
Construction	24	100.0%
Manufacturing	16	37.5%
Transportation, Public Utilities	24	83.3%
Wholesale Trade	13	69.2%
Retail Trade	87	74.7%
Finance, Insurance, Real Estate	25	92.0%
Services	98	87.8%

Private Industry	Employment		Real Earnings ($000)		Average Earnings Per Job	
	1995	% Chg. 90-95	1995	Real % Chg. 90-95	1995	Real % Chg. 90-95
Ag. Services	69	-2.8%	692	-43.8%	10,029	-42.1%
Mining	NA	NA	85	-4.9%	NA	NA
Construction	230	-38.7%	3,488	-51.8%	15,165	-21.4%
Manufacturing	597	20.6%	14,992	7.1%	25,112	-11.2%
Transportation, Public Utilities	250	-1.2%	7,072	-9.8%	28,288	-8.7%
Wholesale Trade	97	0.0%	2,436	4.1%	25,113	4.1%
Retail Trade	816	6.5%	9,120	5.9%	11,176	-0.6%
Finance, Insurance, Real Estate	269	52.8%	4,190	73.5%	15,576	13.5%
Services	1,101	0.3%	17,963	21.5%	16,315	21.2%

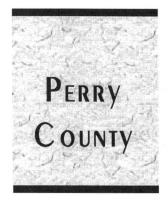

PERRY COUNTY

Population 1997 (Est.)	19,306	# Households 1995 (Projection)	6,900	Personal Income 1995 ($000)	$150,060
Land Area (Sq. Mi.)	381.4	% Family	74.6%	Avg. Wage Per Job 1995	$19,058
Population Density 1997	50.6	% Non-Family	25.1%	Employed in 1996	8,445
% Under 20 1996	27.5%	% Living Alone	23.0%	Unemployed in 1996	690
% 65 & Over 1996	14.8%	Births 1995	206	Unemployment Rate 1996	7.6%
% White 1996	98.2%	Births to Teens 1995	41	Avg. Covered Payroll 1996 ($000)	$27,776
% African-Amer. 1996	1.4%	Deaths 1995	192	Average Weekly Earnings in Manufacturing 1996	$488.00
% Hispanic* 1996	0.5%	Marriages 1995	151	Registered Vehicles 1996	18,687

*May be of any race.

Percent of Total Population By Sex and Age

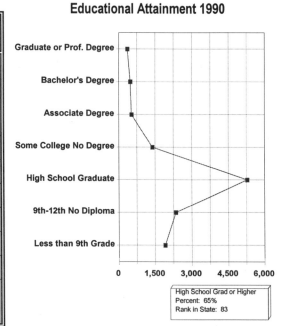

Population Projections

Age Groups	2000	2010	% Change
0-17	4,350	4,060	-6.7%
18-24	2,260	1,910	-15.5%
25-39	4,000	4,450	11.2%
40-59	4,900	4,960	1.2%
60-74	2,140	2,360	10.3%
75 +	1,320	1,280	-3.0%
Total	19,000	19,000	0.0%

Personal Income
Real 1995 Dollars ($000)

	1990	1995	% Chg.
Total Earnings by Place of Work	139,420	150,060	7.6%
Less Personal Contributions for Social Insurance	9,248	10,732	16.0%
Net Income by Place of Work	130,171	139,328	7.0%
Plus Residence Adjustment	48,388	50,550	4.5%
Net Income by Place of Residence	178,559	189,878	6.3%
Plus Dividends, Rent and Interest	53,660	52,643	-1.9%
Plus Transfer Payments	53,987	61,347	13.6%
Personal Income by Place of Residence	286,207	303,868	6.2%
Per Capita Income ($)	14,975	15,874	6.0%
Rank	86	86	60

Educational Attainment 1990

High School Grad or Higher
Percent: 65%
Rank in State: 83

Population Change by Decade
(1990-2000 projected)

For EDIN tables, sources and footnotes, see page 380.

Occupation of Employed Persons Age 16 & Over

	1990	% Chg. 80-90
Managerial & Professional	988	-10.8
Technical, Sales & Admin. Support	1,558	2.8
Service Occupations	1,039	17.4
Farming, Forestry and Fishing	333	0.9
Precision Production, Craft & Repair	1,257	-1.4
Operators, Fabricators	2,634	-5.7

Top 5 Counties Commuting in 1990

From Perry Into:		Into Perry From:	
Dubois	840	Spencer	436
Spencer	705	Outside Indiana	377
Outside Indiana	617	Crawford	75
Warrick	154	Floyd	41
Vanderburgh	115	Dubois	35

5,093 persons lived and worked in this county.
2,588 lived in the county but worked elsewhere.

Number of Establishments
(% Change 1990-1995)

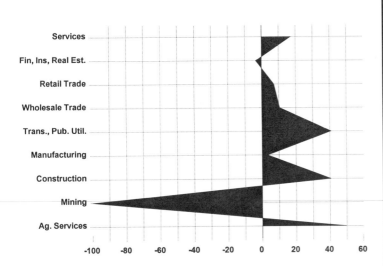

Establishments by Sector 1995

Industry	Number of Establishments	% with fewer than 10 employees
Ag. Services	6	100.0%
Mining	0	NA
Construction	45	82.2%
Manufacturing	31	48.4%
Transportation, Public Utilities	31	87.1%
Wholesale Trade	21	71.4%
Retail Trade	118	68.6%
Finance, Insurance, Real Estate	28	78.6%
Services	109	88.1%

Private Industry	Employment		Real Earnings ($000)		Average Earnings Per Job	
	1995	% Chg. 90-95	1995	Real % Chg. 90-95	1995	Real % Chg. 90-95
Ag. Services	NA	NA	NA	NA	NA	NA
Mining	NA	NA	NA	NA	NA	NA
Construction	409	21.0%	10,119	17.1%	24,741	-3.2%
Manufacturing	1,669	-6.6%	45,501	-7.0%	27,262	-0.4%
Transportation, Public Utilities	231	7.9%	7,044	23.5%	30,494	14.4%
Wholesale Trade	119	NA	3,138	NA	26,370	NA
Retail Trade	1,546	21.4%	17,224	8.7%	11,141	-10.4%
Finance, Insurance, Real Estate	355	5.7%	8,196	47.3%	23,087	39.4%
Services	1,338	11.5%	22,288	25.5%	16,658	12.6%

PikE CouNtY

Population 1997 (Est.)	12,758	# Households 1995 (Projection)	4,800	Personal Income 1995 ($000)	$101,595
Land Area (Sq. Mi.)	336.2	% Family	74.4%	Avg. Wage Per Job 1995	$25,940
Population Density 1997	37.9	% Non-Family	25.8%	Employed in 1996	5,880
% Under 20 1996	25.8%	% Living Alone	23.8%	Unemployed in 1996	330
% 65 & Over 1996	16.0%	Births 1995	125	Unemployment Rate 1996	5.3%
% White 1996	99.7%	Births to Teens 1995	18	Avg. Covered Payroll 1996 ($000)	$20,273
% African-Amer. 1996	0.0%	Deaths 1995	149	Average Weekly Earnings in Manufacturing 1996	$436.50
% Hispanic* 1996	0.3%	Marriages 1995	92	Registered Vehicles 1996	13,535

*May be of any race.

Percent of Total Population By Sex and Age

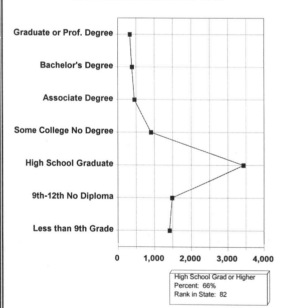

Population Projections

Age Groups	2000	2010	% Change
0-17	2,830	2,620	-7.4%
18-24	1,150	1,100	-4.3%
25-39	2,320	2,440	5.2%
40-59	3,320	3,170	-4.5%
60-74	1,660	1,780	7.2%
75 +	870	870	0.0%
Total	12,100	12,000	-0.8%

Personal Income
Real 1995 Dollars ($000)

	1990	1995	% Chg.
Total Earnings by Place of Work	126,871	101,595	-19.9%
Less Personal Contributions for Social Insurance	8,677	7,653	-11.8%
Net Income by Place of Work	118,194	93,942	-20.5%
Plus Residence Adjustment	25,536	47,644	86.6%
Net Income by Place of Residence	143,729	141,586	-1.5%
Plus Dividends, Rent and Interest	38,386	34,612	-9.8%
Plus Transfer Payments	38,926	48,388	24.3%
Personal Income by Place of Residence	221,042	224,586	1.6%
Per Capita Income ($)	17,706	17,921	1.2%
Rank	49	58	84

Educational Attainment 1990

High School Grad or Higher
Percent: 66%
Rank in State: 82

Population Change by Decade
(1990-2000 projected)

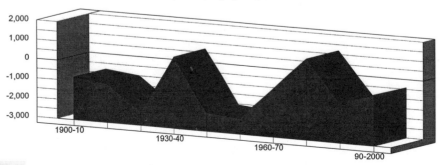

For EDIN tables, sources and footnotes, see page 380.

Occupation of Employed Persons Age 16 & Over

	1990	% Chg. 80-90
Managerial & Professional	884	40.1
Technical, Sales & Admin. Support	1,093	17.4
Service Occupations	841	19.8
Farming, Forestry and Fishing	262	0.0
Precision Production, Craft & Repair	908	-16.6
Operators, Fabricators	1,489	3.9

Top 5 Counties Commuting in 1990

From Pike Into:		Into Pike From:	
Dubois	1,346	Gibson	380
Gibson	351	Daviess	227
Daviess	248	Dubois	149
Vanderburgh	246	Knox	111
Outside Indiana	135	Vanderburgh	86

2,576 persons lived and worked in this county.

2,801 lived in the county but worked elsewhere.

Number of Establishments
(% Change 1990-1995)

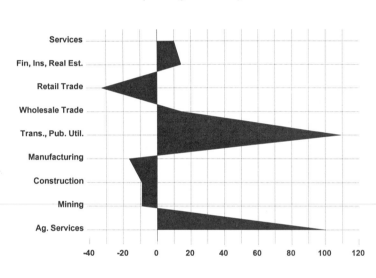

Establishments by Sector 1995

Industry	Number of Establishments	% with fewer than 10 employees
Ag. Services	2	100.0%
Mining	10	60.0%
Construction	10	90.0%
Manufacturing	10	50.0%
Transportation, Public Utilities	23	56.5%
Wholesale Trade	16	81.2%
Retail Trade	39	79.5%
Finance, Insurance, Real Estate	16	75.0%
Services	66	84.8%

Private Industry	Employment		Real Earnings ($000)		Average Earnings Per Job	
	1995	% Chg. 90-95	1995	Real % Chg. 90-95	1995	Real % Chg. 90-95
Ag. Services	29	11.5%	326	410.5%	11,241	357.7%
Mining	392	-52.3%	20,009	-54.4%	51,043	-4.3%
Construction	134	-43.2%	2,247	-64.3%	16,769	-37.2%
Manufacturing	230	23.7%	7,933	25.5%	34,491	1.5%
Transportation, Public Utilities	772	9.5%	35,155	13.9%	45,538	4.0%
Wholesale Trade	85	-39.3%	3,067	-43.0%	36,082	-6.2%
Retail Trade	481	-2.6%	6,111	1.2%	12,705	3.9%
Finance, Insurance, Real Estate	174	-2.8%	3,079	6.5%	17,695	9.6%
Services	815	4.9%	11,575	19.9%	14,202	14.3%

PORTER COUNTY

Population 1997 (Est.)	144,084	# Households 1995 (Projection)	47,400	Personal Income 1995 ($000)	$1,915,775
Land Area (Sq. Mi.)	418.2	% Family	76.5%	Avg. Wage Per Job 1995	$27,003
Population Density 1997	344.5	% Non-Family	23.5%	Employed in 1996	69,760
% Under 20 1996	29.7%	% Living Alone	19.9%	Unemployed in 1996	2,760
% 65 & Over 1996	9.9%	Births 1995	1,724	Unemployment Rate 1996	3.8%
% White 1996	98.4%	Births to Teens 1995	182	Avg. Covered Payroll 1996 ($000)	$383,494
% African-Amer. 1996	0.4%	Deaths 1995	1,064	Average Weekly Earnings in Manufacturing 1996	$1,004.00
% Hispanic* 1996	3.8%	Marriages 1995	1,023	Registered Vehicles 1996	125,044

*May be of any race.

Percent of Total Population By Sex and Age

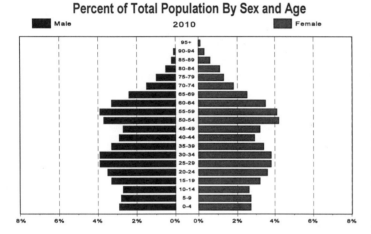

Population Projections

Age Groups	2000	2010	% Change
0-17	30,850	27,600	-10.5%
18-24	16,150	13,150	-18.6%
25-39	25,340	29,800	17.6%
40-59	40,410	37,430	-7.4%
60-74	13,980	20,260	44.9%
75 +	6,270	7,020	12.0%
Total	133,000	135,300	1.7%

Personal Income
Real 1995 Dollars ($000)

	1990	1995	% Chg.
Total Earnings by Place of Work	1,599,830	1,915,775	19.7%
Less Personal Contributions for Social Insurance	103,091	128,291	24.4%
Net Income by Place of Work	1,496,740	1,787,484	19.4%
Plus Residence Adjustment	660,449	718,769	8.8%
Net Income by Place of Residence	2,157,188	2,506,253	16.2%
Plus Dividends, Rent and Interest	418,443	454,205	8.5%
Plus Transfer Payments	280,872	353,836	26.0%
Personal Income by Place of Residence	2,856,504	3,314,294	16.0%
Per Capita Income ($)	22,083	23,627	7.0%
Rank	5	8	55

Educational Attainment 1990

High School Grad or Higher
Percent: 82%
Rank in State: 5

Population Change by Decade
(1990-2000 projected)

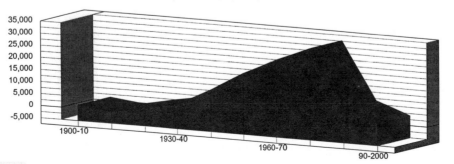

For EDIN tables, sources and footnotes, see page 380.

Occupation of Employed Persons Age 16 & Over

	1990	% Chg. 80-90
Managerial & Professional	15,898	57.2
Technical, Sales & Admin. Support	18,021	24.6
Service Occupations	7,216	15.8
Farming, Forestry and Fishing	600	-16.4
Precision Production, Craft & Repair	9,954	-4.9
Operators, Fabricators	10,134	-4.4

Top 5 Counties Commuting in 1990

From Porter Into:		Into Porter From:	
Lake	18,056	Lake	6,505
Outside Indiana	4,428	Laporte	3,580
Laporte	3,244	Jasper	758
Jasper	330	Outside Indiana	754
St. Joseph	201	Starke	397

33,913 persons lived and worked in this county.
26,658 lived in the county but worked elsewhere.

Number of Establishments
(% Change 1990-1995)

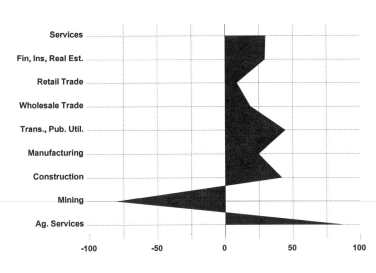

Establishments by Sector 1995

Industry	Number of Establishments	% with fewer than 10 employees
Ag. Services	54	87.0%
Mining	1	100.0%
Construction	431	82.6%
Manufacturing	147	50.3%
Transportation, Public Utilities	156	73.1%
Wholesale Trade	184	73.9%
Retail Trade	658	62.2%
Finance, Insurance, Real Estate	242	83.5%
Services	1,065	78.2%

Private Industry	Employment		Real Earnings ($000)		Average Earnings Per Job	
	1995	% Chg. 90-95	1995	Real % Chg. 90-95	1995	Real % Chg. 90-95
Ag. Services	671	88.5%	9,486	68.6%	14,137	-10.6%
Mining	34	-56.4%	208	-86.9%	6,118	-70.0%
Construction	5,161	53.5%	177,877	74.8%	34,466	13.8%
Manufacturing	12,257	2.1%	687,768	8.3%	56,112	6.1%
Transportation, Public Utilities	3,855	11.4%	137,518	22.9%	35,673	10.3%
Wholesale Trade	2,723	25.0%	100,253	12.6%	36,817	-9.9%
Retail Trade	12,572	23.8%	164,657	28.4%	13,097	3.7%
Finance, Insurance, Real Estate	3,188	6.0%	50,332	37.2%	15,788	29.4%
Services	17,355	14.0%	366,219	25.1%	21,102	9.7%

POSEY COUNTY

Population 1997 (Est.)	26,640	# Households 1995 (Projection)	9,600	Personal Income 1995 ($000)	$369,641
Land Area (Sq. Mi.)	408.5	% Family	77.0%	Avg. Wage Per Job 1995	$29,206
Population Density 1997	65.2	% Non-Family	22.9%	Employed in 1996	13,340
% Under 20 1996	29.4%	% Living Alone	20.5%	Unemployed in 1996	510
% 65 & Over 1996	12.2%	Births 1995	327	Unemployment Rate 1996	3.7%
% White 1996	98.5%	Births to Teens 1995	33	Avg. Covered Payroll 1996 ($000)	$69,536
% African-Amer. 1996	1.2%	Deaths 1995	181	Average Weekly Earnings in Manufacturing 1996	$921.25
% Hispanic* 1996	0.5%	Marriages 1995	200	Registered Vehicles 1996	27,935

*May be of any race.

Percent of Total Population By Sex and Age

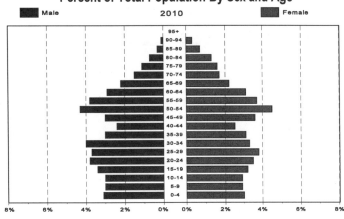

Population Projections

Age Groups	2000	2010	% Change
0-17	6,550	5,830	-11.0%
18-24	2,840	2,660	-6.3%
25-39	4,760	5,560	16.8%
40-59	7,710	7,400	-4.0%
60-74	2,910	3,670	26.1%
75 +	1,470	1,600	8.8%
Total	26,200	26,700	1.9%

Personal Income
Real 1995 Dollars ($000)

	1990	1995	% Chg.
Total Earnings by Place of Work	303,388	369,641	21.8%
Less Personal Contributions for Social Insurance	20,203	25,516	26.3%
Net Income by Place of Work	283,185	344,125	21.5%
Plus Residence Adjustment	61,034	54,528	-10.7%
Net Income by Place of Residence	344,219	398,653	15.8%
Plus Dividends, Rent and Interest	92,391	88,754	-3.9%
Plus Transfer Payments	63,957	77,061	20.5%
Personal Income by Place of Residence	500,567	564,468	12.8%
Per Capita Income ($)	19,258	21,402	11.1%
Rank	22	20	14

Educational Attainment 1990

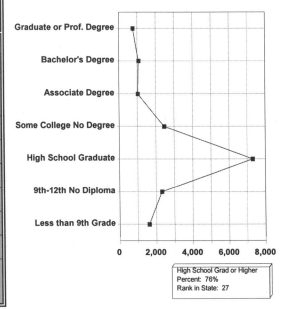

High School Grad or Higher
Percent: 76%
Rank in State: 27

Population Change by Decade
(1990-2000 projected)

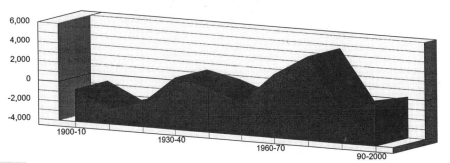

For EDIN tables, sources and footnotes, see page 380.

Occupation of Employed Persons Age 16 & Over

	1990	% Chg. 80-90
Managerial & Professional	2,267	33.8
Technical, Sales & Admin. Support	3,582	28.5
Service Occupations	1,568	6.5
Farming, Forestry and Fishing	499	-28.9
Precision Production, Craft & Repair	1,790	-8.9
Operators, Fabricators	2,352	-8.9

Top 5 Counties Commuting in 1990

From Posey Into:		Into Posey From:	
Vanderburgh	4,510	Vanderburgh	1,516
Outside Indiana	300	Outside Indiana	546
Gibson	137	Gibson	147
Warrick	83	Warrick	107
Knox	15	Lake	55

6,779 persons lived and worked in this county.

5,100 lived in the county but worked elsewhere.

Number of Establishments
(% Change 1990-1995)

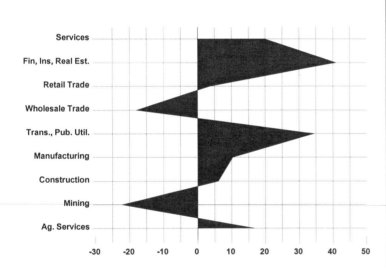

Establishments by Sector 1995

Industry	Number of Establishments	% with fewer than 10 employees
Ag. Services	7	100.0%
Mining	14	100.0%
Construction	88	80.7%
Manufacturing	32	40.6%
Transportation, Public Utilities	39	56.4%
Wholesale Trade	32	62.5%
Retail Trade	115	68.7%
Finance, Insurance, Real Estate	31	80.6%
Services	157	80.9%

Private Industry	Employment		Real Earnings ($000)		Average Earnings Per Job	
	1995	% Chg. 90-95	1995	Real % Chg. 90-95	1995	Real % Chg. 90-95
Ag. Services	140	62.8%	1,271	78.9%	9,079	9.9%
Mining	268	-12.4%	2,595	-22.0%	9,683	-10.9%
Construction	1,151	56.2%	36,969	75.6%	32,119	12.4%
Manufacturing	3,118	0.1%	195,779	24.5%	62,790	24.4%
Transportation, Public Utilities	800	17.6%	27,355	19.9%	34,194	1.9%
Wholesale Trade	426	1.7%	10,884	-5.0%	25,549	-6.6%
Retail Trade	1,394	16.7%	16,472	14.3%	11,816	-2.0%
Finance, Insurance, Real Estate	376	-14.0%	5,244	-0.2%	13,947	16.0%
Services	2,258	-2.3%	41,135	5.4%	18,217	7.9%

Pulaski County

Population 1997 (Est.)	13,212	# Households 1995 (Projection)	4,600	Personal Income 1995 ($000)	$132,072
Land Area (Sq. Mi.)	433.7	% Family	74.6%	Avg. Wage Per Job 1995	$21,033
Population Density 1997	30.5	% Non-Family	26.1%	Employed in 1996	5,825
% Under 20 1996	30.0%	% Living Alone	23.7%	Unemployed in 1996	350
% 65 & Over 1996	15.8%	Births 1995	174	Unemployment Rate 1996	5.6%
% White 1996	99.1%	Births to Teens 1995	23	Avg. Covered Payroll 1996 ($000)	$25,380
% African-Amer. 1996	0.5%	Deaths 1995	153	Average Weekly Earnings in Manufacturing 1996	$574.00
% Hispanic* 1996	1.0%	Marriages 1995	107	Registered Vehicles 1996	15,015

*May be of any race.

Percent of Total Population By Sex and Age

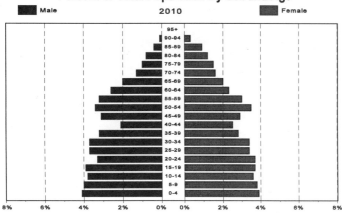

Population Projections

Age Groups	2000	2010	% Change
0-17	3,550	3,670	3.4%
18-24	1,400	1,320	-5.7%
25-39	2,260	2,680	18.6%
40-59	3,170	3,120	-1.6%
60-74	1,460	1,570	7.5%
75 +	890	830	-6.7%
Total	12,700	13,200	3.9%

Personal Income
Real 1995 Dollars ($000)

	1990	1995	% Chg.
Total Earnings by Place of Work	143,784	132,072	-8.1%
Less Personal Contributions for Social Insurance	7,997	9,128	14.1%
Net Income by Place of Work	135,787	122,944	-9.5%
Plus Residence Adjustment	12,527	17,393	38.8%
Net Income by Place of Residence	148,314	140,337	-5.4%
Plus Dividends, Rent and Interest	52,773	45,449	-13.9%
Plus Transfer Payments	33,001	40,001	21.2%
Personal Income by Place of Residence	234,087	225,787	-3.5%
Per Capita Income ($)	18,492	17,217	-6.9%
Rank	31	68	91

Educational Attainment 1990

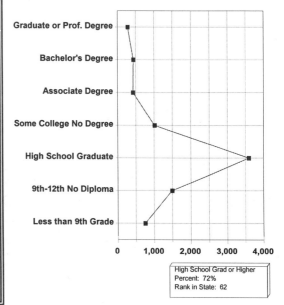

High School Grad or Higher
Percent: 72%
Rank in State: 62

Population Change by Decade
(1990-2000 projected)

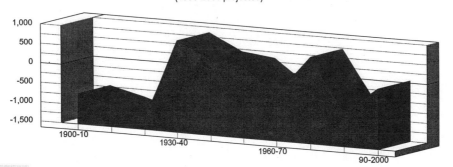

For EDIN tables, sources and footnotes, see page 380.

Occupation of Employed Persons Age 16 & Over

	1990	% Chg. 80-90
Managerial & Professional	761	-0.7
Technical, Sales & Admin. Support	1,182	7.7
Service Occupations	673	-0.1
Farming, Forestry and Fishing	560	-6.2
Precision Production, Craft & Repair	744	8.0
Operators, Fabricators	1,580	4.3

Top 5 Counties Commuting in 1990

From Pulaski Into:		Into Pulaski From:	
Starke	302	Starke	235
Cass	238	Fulton	158
Jasper	210	Jasper	146
White	203	White	145
Fulton	197	Cass	122

3,809 persons lived and worked in this county.
1,628 lived in the county but worked elsewhere.

Number of Establishments
(% Change 1990-1995)

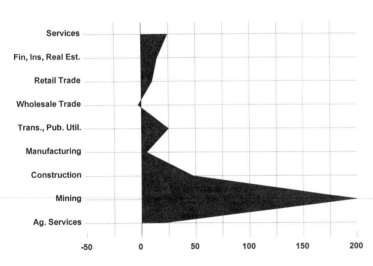

Establishments by Sector 1995

Industry	Number of Establishments	% with fewer than 10 employees
Ag. Services	6	100.0%
Mining	3	33.3%
Construction	31	93.5%
Manufacturing	22	27.3%
Transportation, Public Utilities	20	90.0%
Wholesale Trade	33	54.5%
Retail Trade	76	69.7%
Finance, Insurance, Real Estate	31	83.9%
Services	97	88.7%

Private Industry	Employment		Real Earnings ($000)		Average Earnings Per Job	
	1995	% Chg. 90-95	1995	Real % Chg. 90-95	1995	Real % Chg. 90-95
Ag. Services	86	-8.5%	898	-6.1%	10,442	2.6%
Mining	38	-11.6%	1,572	5.4%	41,368	19.2%
Construction	220	24.3%	5,162	34.3%	23,464	8.1%
Manufacturing	1,466	0.8%	51,389	2.4%	35,054	1.6%
Transportation, Public Utilities	235	3.5%	6,179	16.4%	26,294	12.5%
Wholesale Trade	380	-3.6%	9,798	-6.8%	25,784	-3.4%
Retail Trade	936	17.7%	11,377	22.1%	12,155	3.7%
Finance, Insurance, Real Estate	267	14.1%	4,566	43.0%	17,101	25.3%
Services	1,056	6.0%	16,250	8.6%	15,388	2.5%

PUTNAM COUNTY

Population 1997 (Est.)	33,706	# Households 1995 (Projection)	10,400	Personal Income 1995 ($000)	$316,751
Land Area (Sq. Mi.)	480.3	% Family	76.1%	Avg. Wage Per Job 1995	$18,940
Population Density 1997	70.2	% Non-Family	23.8%	Employed in 1996	16,060
% Under 20 1996	27.4%	% Living Alone	21.1%	Unemployed in 1996	610
% 65 & Over 1996	13.1%	Births 1995	461	Unemployment Rate 1996	3.7%
% White 1996	96.2%	Births to Teens 1995	73	Avg. Covered Payroll 1996 ($000)	$58,654
% African-Amer. 1996	2.8%	Deaths 1995	286	Average Weekly Earnings in Manufacturing 1996	$494.00
% Hispanic* 1996	0.8%	Marriages 1995	291	Registered Vehicles 1996	31,790

*May be of any race.

Percent of Total Population By Sex and Age

■ Male   2010   ■ Female

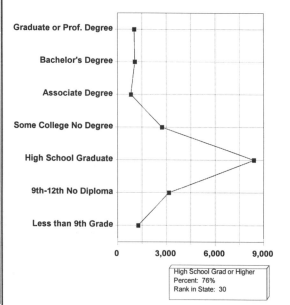

Population Projections

Age Groups	2000	2010	% Change
0-17	7,120	6,570	-7.7%
18-24	4,360	3,940	-9.6%
25-39	7,420	7,720	4.0%
40-59	7,320	7,870	7.5%
60-74	3,520	3,840	9.1%
75 +	1,680	1,750	4.2%
Total	31,400	31,700	1.0%

Personal Income
Real 1995 Dollars ($000)

	1990	1995	% Chg.
Total Earnings by Place of Work	250,169	316,751	26.6%
Less Personal Contributions for Social Insurance	15,574	21,332	37.0%
Net Income by Place of Work	234,595	295,419	25.9%
Plus Residence Adjustment	91,141	97,132	6.6%
Net Income by Place of Residence	325,735	392,551	20.5%
Plus Dividends, Rent and Interest	87,810	88,341	0.6%
Plus Transfer Payments	72,550	88,742	22.3%
Personal Income by Place of Residence	486,095	569,634	17.2%
Per Capita Income ($)	15,968	17,295	8.3%
Rank	77	66	36

Educational Attainment 1990

High School Grad or Higher
Percent: 76%
Rank in State: 30

Population Change by Decade
(1990-2000 projected)

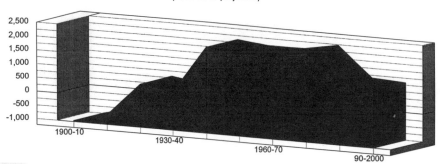

Occupation of Employed Persons Age 16 & Over			Top 5 Counties Commuting in 1990			
	1990	% Chg. 80-90	From Putnam Into:		Into Putnam From:	
Managerial & Professional	2,574	26.3	Marion	2,113	Clay	560
Technical, Sales & Admin. Support	3,612	19.2	Hendricks	865	Owen	343
Service Occupations	2,131	23.5	Montgomery	560	Vigo	230
Farming, Forestry and Fishing	523	-33.7	Vigo	278	Parke	219
Precision Production, Craft & Repair	1,729	11.6	Clay	193	Hendricks	214
Operators, Fabricators	2,419	-9.3	8,167 persons lived and worked in this county.			
			4,470 lived in the county but worked elsewhere.			

Number of Establishments
(% Change 1990-1995)

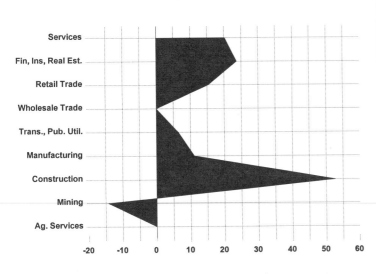

Establishments by Sector 1995

Industry	Number of Establishments	% with fewer than 10 employees
Ag. Services	10	100.0%
Mining	6	50.0%
Construction	81	85.2%
Manufacturing	30	50.0%
Transportation, Public Utilities	33	72.7%
Wholesale Trade	33	84.8%
Retail Trade	173	68.8%
Finance, Insurance, Real Estate	47	87.2%
Services	232	80.6%

Private Industry	Employment		Real Earnings ($000)		Average Earnings Per Job	
	1995	% Chg. 90-95	1995	Real % Chg. 90-95	1995	Real % Chg. 90-95
Ag. Services	144	4.3%	1,220	-10.6%	8,472	-14.4%
Mining	51	-38.6%	1,821	-43.8%	35,706	-8.5%
Construction	767	14.6%	15,493	10.7%	20,199	-3.4%
Manufacturing	2,780	46.3%	84,003	58.3%	30,217	8.2%
Transportation, Public Utilities	509	11.4%	20,250	63.0%	39,784	46.3%
Wholesale Trade	246	2.1%	6,734	-8.6%	27,374	-10.4%
Retail Trade	3,693	61.5%	49,144	64.5%	13,307	1.9%
Finance, Insurance, Real Estate	659	16.2%	9,124	27.9%	13,845	10.0%
Services	4,004	5.2%	65,269	11.3%	16,301	5.8%

RANDOLPH COUNTY

Population 1997 (Est.)	27,480	# Households 1995 (Projection)	10,200	Personal Income 1995 ($000)	$255,094
Land Area (Sq. Mi.)	452.9	% Family	74.1%	Avg. Wage Per Job 1995	$20,749
Population Density 1997	60.7	% Non-Family	25.7%	Employed in 1996	11,670
% Under 20 1996	27.8%	% Living Alone	23.0%	Unemployed in 1996	1,030
% 65 & Over 1996	15.5%	Births 1995	369	Unemployment Rate 1996	8.1%
% White 1996	99.4%	Births to Teens 1995	62	Avg. Covered Payroll 1996 ($000)	$43,932
% African-Amer. 1996	0.2%	Deaths 1995	275	Average Weekly Earnings in Manufacturing 1996	$538.50
% Hispanic* 1996	0.9%	Marriages 1995	223	Registered Vehicles 1996	28,085

*May be of any race.

Percent of Total Population By Sex and Age

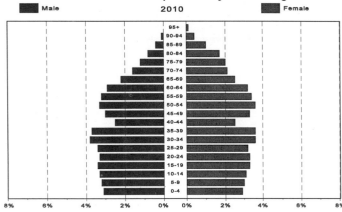

Population Projections

Age Groups	2000	2010	% Change
0-17	6,240	5,890	-5.6%
18-24	2,730	2,410	-11.7%
25-39	5,020	5,540	10.4%
40-59	6,890	6,460	-6.2%
60-74	3,480	3,790	8.9%
75 +	1,920	1,940	1.0%
Total	26,300	26,000	-1.1%

Personal Income
Real 1995 Dollars ($000)

	1990	1995	% Chg.
Total Earnings by Place of Work	267,163	255,094	-4.5%
Less Personal Contributions for Social Insurance	17,598	18,224	3.6%
Net Income by Place of Work	249,565	236,870	-5.1%
Plus Residence Adjustment	56,477	88,089	56.0%
Net Income by Place of Residence	306,042	324,959	6.2%
Plus Dividends, Rent and Interest	80,992	68,372	-15.6%
Plus Transfer Payments	77,608	94,761	22.1%
Personal Income by Place of Residence	464,642	488,092	5.0%
Per Capita Income ($)	17,139	17,788	3.8%
Rank	55	60	73

Educational Attainment 1990

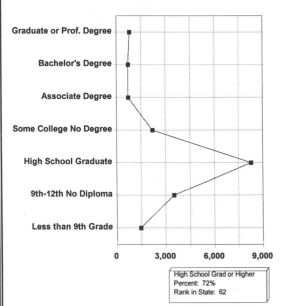

High School Grad or Higher
Percent: 72%
Rank in State: 62

Population Change by Decade
(1990-2000 projected)

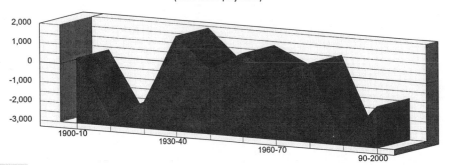

For EDIN tables, sources and footnotes, see page 380.

Occupation of Employed Persons Age 16 & Over		
	1990	% Chg. 80-90
Managerial & Professional	1,974	22.4
Technical, Sales & Admin. Support	2,774	0.1
Service Occupations	1,751	18.4
Farming, Forestry and Fishing	669	-13.2
Precision Production, Craft & Repair	1,727	-7.9
Operators, Fabricators	3,128	-19.2

Top 5 Counties Commuting in 1990			
From Randolph Into:		Into Randolph From:	
Delaware	1,572	Outside Indiana	1,198
Wayne	770	Delaware	471
Outside Indiana	726	Wayne	330
Jay	409	Jay	203
Henry	88	Henry	93

7,824 persons lived and worked in this county.
3,942 lived in the county but worked elsewhere.

Number of Establishments
(% Change 1990-1995)

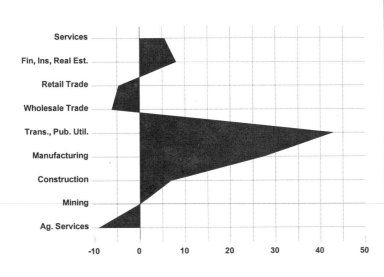

Establishments by Sector 1995		
Industry	Number of Establishments	% with fewer than 10 employees
Ag. Services	10	100.0%
Mining	1	100.0%
Construction	62	93.5%
Manufacturing	65	43.1%
Transportation, Public Utilities	40	60.0%
Wholesale Trade	46	76.1%
Retail Trade	145	73.8%
Finance, Insurance, Real Estate	40	85.0%
Services	171	87.1%

Private Industry	Employment		Real Earnings ($000)		Average Earnings Per Job	
	1995	% Chg. 90-95	1995	Real % Chg. 90-95	1995	Real % Chg. 90-95
Ag. Services	122	11.9%	3,046	-26.3%	24,967	-34.1%
Mining	18	0.0%	572	29.3%	31,778	29.3%
Construction	504	5.9%	10,782	17.6%	21,393	11.1%
Manufacturing	3,562	-7.1%	118,273	-7.9%	33,204	-0.9%
Transportation, Public Utilities	452	-0.9%	13,568	-3.1%	30,018	-2.2%
Wholesale Trade	369	-8.9%	19,102	-11.2%	51,767	-2.5%
Retail Trade	1,787	7.4%	19,522	3.7%	10,924	-3.4%
Finance, Insurance, Real Estate	374	-8.1%	5,999	3.8%	16,040	12.9%
Services	1,907	-3.7%	26,316	11.9%	13,800	16.3%

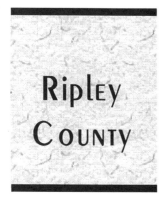

Ripley County

Population 1997 (Est.)	27,177	# Households 1995 (Projection)	8,800	Personal Income 1995 ($000)	$385,796
Land Area (Sq. Mi.)	446.4	% Family	76.7%	Avg. Wage Per Job 1995	$24,181
Population Density 1997	60.9	% Non-Family	23.9%	Employed in 1996	13,060
% Under 20 1996	30.0%	% Living Alone	21.8%	Unemployed in 1996	610
% 65 & Over 1996	14.3%	Births 1995	420	Unemployment Rate 1996	4.4%
% White 1996	99.5%	Births to Teens 1995	61	Avg. Covered Payroll 1996 ($000)	$73,321
% African-Amer. 1996	0.1%	Deaths 1995	260	Average Weekly Earnings in Manufacturing 1996	$678.50
% Hispanic* 1996	0.3%	Marriages 1995	220	Registered Vehicles 1996	28,001

*May be of any race.

Percent of Total Population By Sex and Age

2010

Male ■   Female ■

Age groups (top to bottom): 95+, 90-94, 85-89, 80-84, 75-79, 70-74, 65-69, 60-64, 55-59, 50-54, 45-49, 40-44, 35-39, 30-34, 25-29, 20-24, 15-19, 10-14, 5-9, 0-4

Axis: 8% 6% 4% 2% 0%   0% 2% 4% 6% 8%

Population Projections

Age Groups	2000	2010	% Change
0-17	6,910	6,840	-1.0%
18-24	2,750	2,620	-4.7%
25-39	4,960	5,570	12.3%
40-59	6,610	6,690	1.2%
60-74	2,710	3,360	24.0%
75 +	1,560	1,480	-5.1%
Total	25,500	26,600	4.3%

Personal Income
Real 1995 Dollars ($000)

	1990	1995	% Chg.
Total Earnings by Place of Work	330,908	385,796	16.6%
Less Personal Contributions for Social Insurance	22,531	27,442	21.8%
Net Income by Place of Work	308,377	358,354	16.2%
Plus Residence Adjustment	-6,757	23,185	-443.1%
Net Income by Place of Residence	301,620	381,539	26.5%
Plus Dividends, Rent and Interest	82,325	96,857	17.7%
Plus Transfer Payments	70,553	82,932	17.5%
Personal Income by Place of Residence	454,498	561,328	23.5%
Per Capita Income ($)	18,389	21,019	14.3%
Rank	36	22	4

Educational Attainment 1990

Categories (top to bottom): Graduate or Prof. Degree, Bachelor's Degree, Associate Degree, Some College No Degree, High School Graduate, 9th-12th No Diploma, Less than 9th Grade

Axis: 0 2,000 4,000 6,000 8,000

High School Grad or Higher
Percent: 69%
Rank in State: 76

Population Change by Decade
(1990-2000 projected)

Axis: 4,000 3,000 2,000 1,000 0 -1,000

Decades: 1900-10, 1930-40, 1960-70, 90-2000

For EDIN tables, sources and footnotes, see page 380.

Occupation of Employed Persons Age 16 & Over

	1990	% Chg. 80-90
Managerial & Professional	1,816	28.4
Technical, Sales & Admin. Support	2,483	26.9
Service Occupations	1,412	27.2
Farming, Forestry and Fishing	471	-37.9
Precision Production, Craft & Repair	1,734	20.8
Operators, Fabricators	3,123	0.9

Top 5 Counties Commuting in 1990

From Ripley Into:		Into Ripley From:	
Outside Indiana	1,047	Franklin	1,469
Decatur	657	Dearborn	1,109
Dearborn	614	Decatur	465
Jefferson	304	Outside Indiana	322
Jennings	251	Jefferson	109

7,385 persons lived and worked in this county.

3,474 lived in the county but worked elsewhere.

Number of Establishments
(% Change 1990-1995)

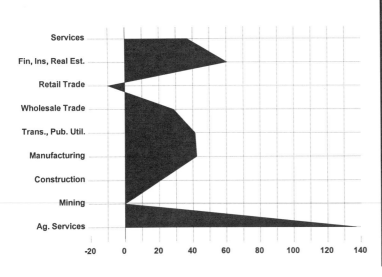

Establishments by Sector 1995		
Industry	Number of Establishments	% with fewer than 10 employees
Ag. Services	19	94.7%
Mining	4	50.0%
Construction	87	90.8%
Manufacturing	47	51.1%
Transportation, Public Utilities	41	78.0%
Wholesale Trade	45	82.2%
Retail Trade	160	68.1%
Finance, Insurance, Real Estate	53	81.1%
Services	215	83.3%

Private Industry	Employment		Real Earnings ($000)		Average Earnings Per Job	
	1995	% Chg. 90-95	1995	Real % Chg. 90-95	1995	Real % Chg. 90-95
Ag. Services	NA	NA	NA	NA	NA	NA
Mining	NA	NA	NA	NA	NA	NA
Construction	748	24.9%	17,954	34.7%	24,003	7.9%
Manufacturing	5,045	6.8%	198,542	10.4%	39,354	3.4%
Transportation, Public Utilities	752	13.6%	20,768	20.3%	27,617	5.9%
Wholesale Trade	320	-35.4%	6,209	-65.4%	19,403	-46.5%
Retail Trade	2,231	8.3%	27,649	12.8%	12,393	4.1%
Finance, Insurance, Real Estate	659	36.4%	15,939	154.5%	24,187	86.5%
Services	2,929	17.3%	61,806	69.7%	21,101	44.6%

RUSH COUNTY

Population 1997 (Est.)	18,236	# Households 1995 (Projection)	6,400	Personal Income 1995 ($000)	$148,814
Land Area (Sq. Mi.)	408.3	% Family	76.9%	Avg. Wage Per Job 1995	$18,960
Population Density 1997	44.7	% Non-Family	23.4%	Employed in 1996	9,850
% Under 20 1996	29.5%	% Living Alone	21.2%	Unemployed in 1996	390
% 65 & Over 1996	15.1%	Births 1995	264	Unemployment Rate 1996	3.8%
% White 1996	98.7%	Births to Teens 1995	41	Avg. Covered Payroll 1996 ($000)	$28,957
% African-Amer. 1996	0.8%	Deaths 1995	190	Average Weekly Earnings in Manufacturing 1996	$539.00
% Hispanic* 1996	0.4%	Marriages 1995	150	Registered Vehicles 1996	18,789

*May be of any race.

Percent of Total Population By Sex and Age

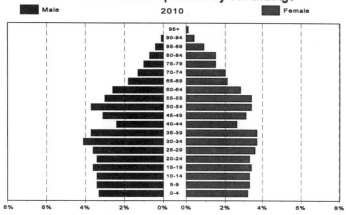

Population Projections

Age Groups	2000	2010	% Change
0-17	4,570	4,410	-3.5%
18-24	2,020	1,750	-13.4%
25-39	3,520	4,090	16.2%
40-59	4,570	4,510	-1.3%
60-74	2,090	2,290	9.6%
75 +	1,260	1,220	-3.2%
Total	18,000	18,300	1.7%

Personal Income
Real 1995 Dollars ($000)

	1990	1995	% Chg.
Total Earnings by Place of Work	138,317	148,814	7.6%
Less Personal Contributions for Social Insurance	8,486	10,846	27.8%
Net Income by Place of Work	129,831	137,968	6.3%
Plus Residence Adjustment	68,179	79,596	16.7%
Net Income by Place of Residence	198,010	217,564	9.9%
Plus Dividends, Rent and Interest	55,727	51,624	-7.4%
Plus Transfer Payments	50,502	60,386	19.6%
Personal Income by Place of Residence	304,239	329,574	8.3%
Per Capita Income ($)	16,760	17,971	7.2%
Rank	64	57	52

Educational Attainment 1990

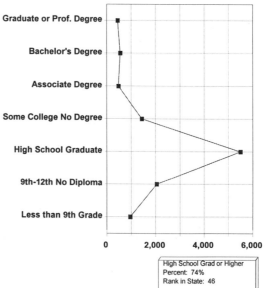

High School Grad or Higher
Percent: 74%
Rank in State: 46

Population Change by Decade
(1990-2000 projected)

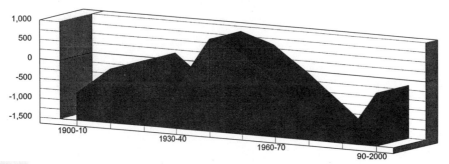

Occupation of Employed Persons Age 16 & Over

	1990	% Chg. 80-90
Managerial & Professional	1,277	19.3
Technical, Sales & Admin. Support	2,025	20.8
Service Occupations	1,068	15.8
Farming, Forestry and Fishing	900	-5.6
Precision Production, Craft & Repair	1,074	7.6
Operators, Fabricators	1,970	-4.3

Top 5 Counties Commuting in 1990

From Rush Into:		Into Rush From:	
Shelby	931	Henry	337
Marion	914	Fayette	310
Hancock	303	Decatur	109
Fayette	301	Shelby	96
Henry	291	Franklin	82

4,946 persons lived and worked in this county.
3,250 lived in the county but worked elsewhere.

Number of Establishments
(% Change 1990-1995)

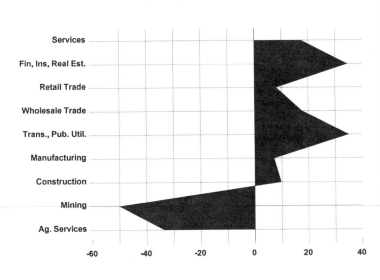

Establishments by Sector 1995

Industry	Number of Establishments	% with fewer than 10 employees
Ag. Services	4	100.0%
Mining	1	0.0%
Construction	45	82.2%
Manufacturing	30	40.0%
Transportation, Public Utilities	27	81.5%
Wholesale Trade	40	75.0%
Retail Trade	94	66.0%
Finance, Insurance, Real Estate	35	88.6%
Services	115	88.7%

Private Industry	Employment		Real Earnings ($000)		Average Earnings Per Job	
	1995	% Chg. 90-95	1995	Real % Chg. 90-95	1995	Real % Chg. 90-95
Ag. Services	NA	NA	NA	NA	NA	NA
Mining	NA	NA	NA	NA	NA	NA
Construction	468	28.2%	8,759	31.6%	18,716	2.6%
Manufacturing	1,634	26.8%	51,215	22.8%	31,343	-3.2%
Transportation, Public Utilities	333	8.8%	8,236	22.2%	24,733	12.3%
Wholesale Trade	302	-17.5%	8,493	3.4%	28,123	25.3%
Retail Trade	1,287	13.8%	15,511	6.3%	12,052	-6.6%
Finance, Insurance, Real Estate	318	-8.1%	4,040	7.8%	12,704	17.3%
Services	1,675	33.9%	26,302	53.7%	15,703	14.8%

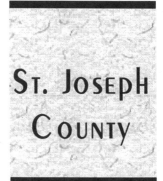

ST. JOSEPH COUNTY

Population 1997 (Est.)	258,056	# Households 1995 (Projection)	94,300	Personal Income 1995 ($000)	$4,210,145
Land Area (Sq. Mi.)	457.3	% Family	69.2%	Avg. Wage Per Job 1995	$24,363
Population Density 1997	564.3	% Non-Family	30.7%	Employed in 1996	130,440
% Under 20 1996	28.2%	% Living Alone	26.2%	Unemployed in 1996	5,400
% 65 & Over 1996	14.2%	Births 1995	3,762	Unemployment Rate 1996	4.0%
% White 1996	87.7%	Births to Teens 1995	539	Avg. Covered Payroll 1996 ($000)	$784,384
% African-Amer. 1996	10.7%	Deaths 1995	2,350	Average Weekly Earnings in Manufacturing 1996	$664.00
% Hispanic* 1996	2.7%	Marriages 1995	2,073	Registered Vehicles 1996	221,807

*May be of any race.

Percent of Total Population By Sex and Age

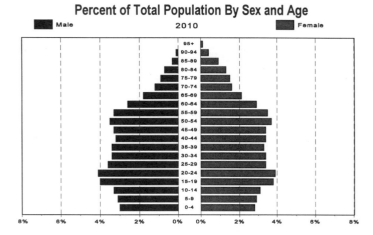

Population Projections

Age Groups	2000	2010	% Change
0-17	64,700	59,270	-8.4%
18-24	28,510	28,730	0.8%
25-39	53,300	52,690	-1.1%
40-59	65,170	70,570	8.3%
60-74	26,400	31,280	18.5%
75 +	16,450	15,730	-4.4%
Total	254,500	258,300	1.5%

Personal Income
Real 1995 Dollars ($000)

	1990	1995	% Chg.
Total Earnings by Place of Work	3,679,457	4,210,145	14.4%
Less Personal Contributions for Social Insurance	247,845	296,011	19.4%
Net Income by Place of Work	3,431,612	3,914,134	14.1%
Plus Residence Adjustment	17,403	42,580	144.7%
Net Income by Place of Residence	3,449,015	3,956,714	14.7%
Plus Dividends, Rent and Interest	909,581	930,224	2.3%
Plus Transfer Payments	713,885	853,767	19.6%
Personal Income by Place of Residence	5,072,480	5,740,705	13.2%
Per Capita Income ($)	20,495	22,350	9.1%
Rank	15	14	28

Educational Attainment 1990

Graduate or Prof. Degree
Bachelor's Degree
Associate Degree
Some College No Degree
High School Graduate
9th-12th No Diploma
Less than 9th Grade

0   15,000   30,000   45,000   60,000

High School Grad or Higher
Percent: 76%
Rank in State: 30

Population Change by Decade
(1990-2000 projected)

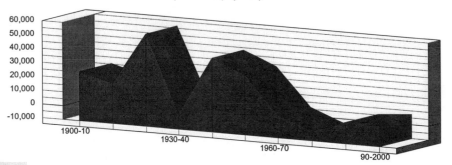

60,000
50,000
40,000
30,000
20,000
10,000
0
-10,000

1900-10   1930-40   1960-70   90-2000

For EDIN tables, sources and footnotes, see page 380.

Occupation of Employed Persons Age 16 & Over

	1990	% Chg. 80-90
Managerial & Professional	29,974	28.6
Technical, Sales & Admin. Support	37,235	13.2
Service Occupations	15,563	5.2
Farming, Forestry and Fishing	1,164	12.0
Precision Production, Craft & Repair	12,686	-6.2
Operators, Fabricators	20,510	-2.8

Top 5 Counties Commuting in 1990

From St. Joseph Into:		Into St. Joseph From:	
Elkhart	10,742	Outside Indiana	9,183
Outside Indiana	3,167	Elkhart	3,601
Marshall	1,045	Laporte	2,456
Laporte	760	Marshall	2,356
Kosciusko	233	Starke	714

98,792   persons lived and worked in this county.

16,821   lived in the county but worked elsewhere.

Number of Establishments
(% Change 1990-1995)

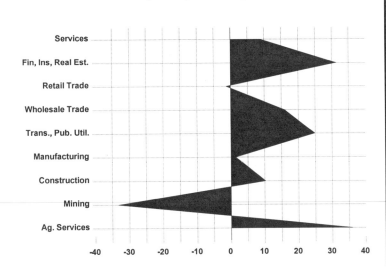

Establishments by Sector 1995

Industry	Number of Establishments	% with fewer than 10 employees
Ag. Services	94	80.9%
Mining	4	75.0%
Construction	644	76.9%
Manufacturing	498	44.4%
Transportation, Public Utilities	231	59.7%
Wholesale Trade	575	63.5%
Retail Trade	1,570	62.0%
Finance, Insurance, Real Estate	578	80.6%
Services	2,363	75.0%

Private Industry	Employment		Real Earnings ($000)		Average Earnings Per Job	
	1995	% Chg. 90-95	1995	Real % Chg. 90-95	1995	Real % Chg. 90-95
Ag. Services	1,069	21.8%	15,758	20.4%	14,741	-1.1%
Mining	71	-28.3%	1,180	9.5%	16,620	52.7%
Construction	8,520	9.4%	264,204	12.8%	31,010	3.1%
Manufacturing	23,904	8.8%	1,153,203	16.6%	48,243	7.1%
Transportation, Public Utilities	6,394	0.5%	213,051	-1.1%	33,320	-1.6%
Wholesale Trade	8,783	10.1%	305,640	9.7%	34,799	-0.4%
Retail Trade	29,859	13.5%	402,085	16.7%	13,466	2.8%
Finance, Insurance, Real Estate	9,677	-1.7%	218,581	12.4%	22,588	14.3%
Services	52,037	15.6%	1,280,915	22.1%	24,615	5.6%

SCOTT COUNTY

Population 1997 (Est.)	22,818	# Households 1995 (Projection)	7,800	Personal Income 1995 ($000)	$173,261
Land Area (Sq. Mi.)	190.4	% Family	77.3%	Avg. Wage Per Job 1995	$18,832
Population Density 1997	119.8	% Non-Family	22.3%	Employed in 1996	10,110
% Under 20 1996	29.6%	% Living Alone	20.0%	Unemployed in 1996	540
% 65 & Over 1996	12.0%	Births 1995	301	Unemployment Rate 1996	5.1%
% White 1996	99.4%	Births to Teens 1995	67	Avg. Covered Payroll 1996 ($000)	$34,712
% African-Amer. 1996	0.1%	Deaths 1995	245	Average Weekly Earnings in Manufacturing 1996	$506.50
% Hispanic* 1996	0.9%	Marriages 1995	227	Registered Vehicles 1996	22,099

*May be of any race.

Percent of Total Population By Sex and Age

Male — 2010 — Female

Population Projections

Age Groups	2000	2010	% Change
0-17	5,580	5,340	-4.3%
18-24	2,330	2,140	-8.2%
25-39	4,560	4,760	4.4%
40-59	5,760	5,870	1.9%
60-74	2,380	2,930	23.1%
75 +	1,130	1,150	1.8%
Total	21,700	22,200	2.3%

Personal Income
Real 1995 Dollars ($000)

	1990	1995	% Chg.
Total Earnings by Place of Work	131,547	173,261	31.7%
Less Personal Contributions for Social Insurance	8,879	12,591	41.8%
Net Income by Place of Work	122,668	160,670	31.0%
Plus Residence Adjustment	86,543	98,290	13.6%
Net Income by Place of Residence	209,211	258,960	23.8%
Plus Dividends, Rent and Interest	40,794	39,003	-4.4%
Plus Transfer Payments	63,491	76,053	19.8%
Personal Income by Place of Residence	313,496	374,016	19.3%
Per Capita Income ($)	14,910	16,691	11.9%
Rank	87	77	12

Educational Attainment 1990

High School Grad or Higher
Percent: 60%
Rank in State: 89

Population Change by Decade
(1990-2000 projected)

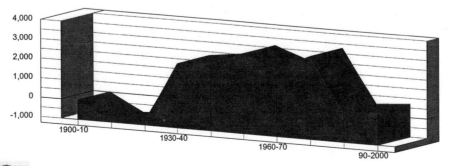

Occupation of Employed Persons Age 16 & Over		
	1990	% Chg. 80-90
Managerial & Professional	1,137	18.9
Technical, Sales & Admin. Support	2,043	56.3
Service Occupations	1,159	44.2
Farming, Forestry and Fishing	186	12.0
Precision Production, Craft & Repair	1,274	19.1
Operators, Fabricators	2,849	-0.3

Top 5 Counties Commuting in 1990			
From Scott Into:		Into Scott From:	
Jackson	922	Jackson	260
Clark	654	Washington	251
Outside Indiana	636	Clark	189
Bartholomew	361	Jefferson	171
Jefferson	303	Outside Indiana	89

5,072 persons lived and worked in this county.
3,436 lived in the county but worked elsewhere.

Number of Establishments
(% Change 1990-1995)

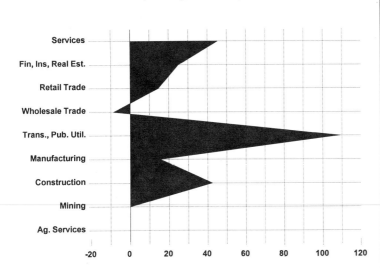

Establishments by Sector 1995		
Industry	Number of Establishments	% with fewer than 10 employees
Ag. Services	5	100.0%
Mining	1	0.0%
Construction	47	93.6%
Manufacturing	37	45.9%
Transportation, Public Utilities	23	87.0%
Wholesale Trade	21	81.0%
Retail Trade	125	72.0%
Finance, Insurance, Real Estate	30	90.0%
Services	141	85.1%

Private Industry	Employment		Real Earnings ($000)		Average Earnings Per Job	
	1995	% Chg. 90-95	1995	Real % Chg. 90-95	1995	Real % Chg. 90-95
Ag. Services	NA	NA	NA	NA	NA	NA
Mining	NA	NA	NA	NA	NA	NA
Construction	401	9.0%	8,401	15.9%	20,950	6.4%
Manufacturing	2,435	39.0%	69,036	40.2%	28,352	0.9%
Transportation, Public Utilities	224	8.2%	8,630	74.3%	38,527	61.1%
Wholesale Trade	118	-16.3%	2,651	14.6%	22,466	36.9%
Retail Trade	1,903	28.1%	23,316	34.8%	12,252	5.3%
Finance, Insurance, Real Estate	287	19.1%	4,894	40.8%	17,052	18.3%
Services	1,617	23.1%	24,588	37.4%	15,206	11.7%

For EDIN tables, sources and footnotes, see page 380.

Shelby County

Population 1997 (Est.)	43,151	# Households 1995 (Projection)	15,000	Personal Income 1995 ($000)	$495,144
Land Area (Sq. Mi.)	412.7	% Family	75.9%	Avg. Wage Per Job 1995	$23,458
Population Density 1997	104.6	% Non-Family	24.0%	Employed in 1996	22,370
% Under 20 1996	29.0%	% Living Alone	20.7%	Unemployed in 1996	860
% 65 & Over 1996	12.3%	Births 1995	550	Unemployment Rate 1996	3.7%
% White 1996	98.5%	Births to Teens 1995	89	Avg. Covered Payroll 1996 ($000)	$95,545
% African-Amer. 1996	0.9%	Deaths 1995	410	Average Weekly Earnings in Manufacturing 1996	$615.50
% Hispanic* 1996	0.4%	Marriages 1995	364	Registered Vehicles 1996	43,051

*May be of any race.

Percent of Total Population By Sex and Age

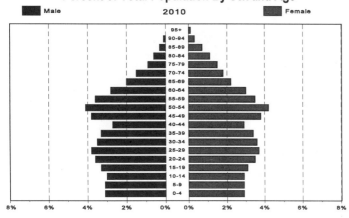

Population Projections

Age Groups	2000	2010	% Change
0-17	9,970	8,990	-9.8%
18-24	4,260	4,000	-6.1%
25-39	8,320	8,760	5.3%
40-59	11,450	11,750	2.6%
60-74	4,590	5,530	20.5%
75 +	2,210	2,310	4.5%
Total	40,800	41,300	1.2%

Personal Income
Real 1995 Dollars ($000)

	1990	1995	% Chg.
Total Earnings by Place of Work	425,010	495,144	16.5%
Less Personal Contributions for Social Insurance	27,262	33,832	24.1%
Net Income by Place of Work	397,748	461,312	16.0%
Plus Residence Adjustment	170,789	183,934	7.7%
Net Income by Place of Residence	568,537	645,246	13.5%
Plus Dividends, Rent and Interest	115,484	109,896	-4.8%
Plus Transfer Payments	98,576	122,572	24.3%
Personal Income by Place of Residence	782,596	877,714	12.2%
Per Capita Income ($)	19,374	20,492	5.8%
Rank	21	26	64

Educational Attainment 1990

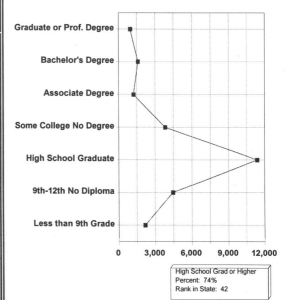

High School Grad or Higher
Percent: 74%
Rank in State: 42

Population Change by Decade
(1990-2000 projected)

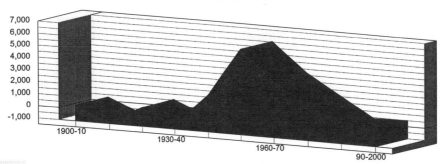

Occupation of Employed Persons Age 16 & Over			Top 5 Counties Commuting in 1990			
	1990	% Chg. 80-90	From Shelby Into:		Into Shelby From:	
Managerial & Professional	3,319	21.8	Marion	5,207	Rush	931
Technical, Sales & Admin. Support	5,498	18.3	Johnson	714	Marion	648
Service Occupations	2,374	20.5	Hancock	501	Decatur	440
Farming, Forestry and Fishing	806	-5.6	Bartholomew	292	Hancock	368
Precision Production, Craft & Repair	3,008	13.9	Decatur	231	Johnson	222
Operators, Fabricators	4,820	0.8	11,928	persons lived and worked in this county.		
			7,519	lived in the county but worked elsewhere.		

Number of Establishments
(% Change 1990-1995)

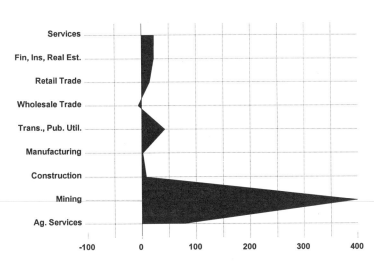

Establishments by Sector 1995		
Industry	Number of Establishments	% with fewer than 10 employees
Ag. Services	16	93.8%
Mining	5	40.0%
Construction	125	80.8%
Manufacturing	80	33.8%
Transportation, Public Utilities	50	80.0%
Wholesale Trade	60	80.0%
Retail Trade	205	63.9%
Finance, Insurance, Real Estate	81	92.6%
Services	281	82.6%

Private Industry	Employment		Real Earnings ($000)		Average Earnings Per Job	
	1995	% Chg. 90-95	1995	Real % Chg. 90-95	1995	Real % Chg. 90-95
Ag. Services	181	0.6%	2,287	-23.5%	12,635	-23.9%
Mining	133	60.2%	4,565	84.3%	34,323	15.0%
Construction	1,509	15.5%	34,289	-0.7%	22,723	-14.0%
Manufacturing	6,484	10.3%	230,981	24.3%	35,623	12.7%
Transportation, Public Utilities	544	6.0%	15,492	14.1%	28,478	7.6%
Wholesale Trade	888	30.4%	27,945	30.5%	31,470	0.1%
Retail Trade	3,075	8.8%	37,453	10.6%	12,180	1.6%
Finance, Insurance, Real Estate	869	-6.1%	9,841	12.5%	11,325	19.7%
Services	4,180	6.2%	70,905	26.8%	16,963	19.4%

SPENCER COUNTY

Population 1997 (Est.)	20,690	# Households 1995 (Projection)	7,000	Personal Income 1995 ($000)	$205,672
Land Area (Sq. Mi.)	398.7	% Family	77.6%	Avg. Wage Per Job 1995	$21,225
Population Density 1997	51.9	% Non-Family	22.1%	Employed in 1996	10,520
% Under 20 1996	28.8%	% Living Alone	20.4%	Unemployed in 1996	540
% 65 & Over 1996	13.3%	Births 1995	257	Unemployment Rate 1996	4.9%
% White 1996	99.0%	Births to Teens 1995	35	Avg. Covered Payroll 1996 ($000)	$38,910
% African-Amer. 1996	0.6%	Deaths 1995	195	Average Weekly Earnings in Manufacturing 1996	$484.25
% Hispanic* 1996	0.6%	Marriages 1995	153	Registered Vehicles 1996	21,226

*May be of any race.

Percent of Total Population By Sex and Age

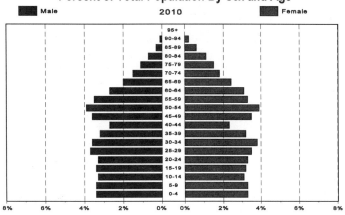

■ Male   2010   ■ Female

Population Projections

Age Groups	2000	2010	% Change
0-17	4,840	4,760	-1.7%
18-24	2,130	1,840	-13.6%
25-39	3,780	4,230	11.9%
40-59	5,480	5,360	-2.2%
60-74	2,310	2,710	17.3%
75 +	1,070	1,120	4.7%
Total	19,600	20,000	2.0%

Personal Income
Real 1995 Dollars ($000)

	1990	1995	% Chg.
Total Earnings by Place of Work	184,843	205,672	11.3%
Less Personal Contributions for Social Insurance	12,203	14,540	19.2%
Net Income by Place of Work	172,640	191,132	10.7%
Plus Residence Adjustment	50,414	48,857	-3.1%
Net Income by Place of Residence	223,053	239,989	7.6%
Plus Dividends, Rent and Interest	56,489	53,754	-4.8%
Plus Transfer Payments	47,948	58,284	21.6%
Personal Income by Place of Residence	327,491	352,027	7.5%
Per Capita Income ($)	16,771	17,291	3.1%
Rank	63	67	77

Educational Attainment 1990

Graduate or Prof. Degree
Bachelor's Degree
Associate Degree
Some College No Degree
High School Graduate
9th-12th No Diploma
Less than 9th Grade

0   1,500   3,000   4,500   6,000

High School Grad or Higher
Percent: 72%
Rank in State: 62

Population Change by Decade
(1990-2000 projected)

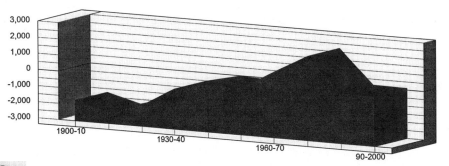

For EDIN tables, sources and footnotes, see page 380.

Occupation of Employed Persons Age 16 & Over

	1990	% Chg. 80-90
Managerial & Professional	1,271	13.5
Technical, Sales & Admin. Support	2,064	42.7
Service Occupations	1,156	31.2
Farming, Forestry and Fishing	544	-13.4
Precision Production, Craft & Repair	1,433	5.8
Operators, Fabricators	2,390	6.7

Top 5 Counties Commuting in 1990

From Spencer Into:		Into Spencer From:	
Dubois	1,245	Perry	705
Vanderburgh	850	Outside Indiana	671
Warrick	794	Dubois	475
Outside Indiana	564	Warrick	378
Perry	436	Vanderburgh	139

4,675 persons lived and worked in this county.
3,992 lived in the county but worked elsewhere.

Number of Establishments
(% Change 1990-1995)

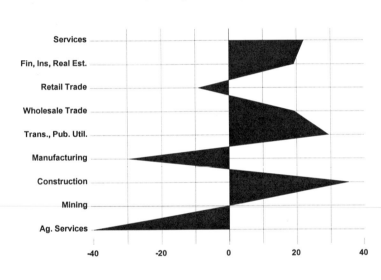

Establishments by Sector 1995

Industry	Number of Establishments	% with fewer than 10 employees
Ag. Services	3	100.0%
Mining	13	69.2%
Construction	46	95.7%
Manufacturing	19	36.8%
Transportation, Public Utilities	44	72.7%
Wholesale Trade	37	81.1%
Retail Trade	91	75.8%
Finance, Insurance, Real Estate	31	80.6%
Services	110	90.0%

Private Industry	Employment		Real Earnings ($000)		Average Earnings Per Job	
	1995	% Chg. 90-95	1995	Real % Chg. 90-95	1995	Real % Chg. 90-95
Ag. Services	93	106.7%	1,648	158.1%	17,720	24.9%
Mining	281	-4.7%	8,723	-7.7%	31,043	-3.1%
Construction	321	21.6%	6,279	42.6%	19,561	17.3%
Manufacturing	1,511	-3.7%	44,465	-9.2%	29,428	-5.7%
Transportation, Public Utilities	1,572	57.0%	56,672	51.2%	36,051	-3.7%
Wholesale Trade	444	26.5%	11,992	19.5%	27,009	-5.6%
Retail Trade	1,132	9.5%	13,382	11.8%	11,822	2.1%
Finance, Insurance, Real Estate	269	-9.7%	3,678	6.0%	13,673	17.4%
Services	2,503	12.5%	35,507	9.6%	14,186	-2.5%

Starke County

Population 1997 (Est.)	23,759	# Households 1995 (Projection)	8,300	Personal Income 1995 ($000)	$123,805
Land Area (Sq. Mi.)	309.3	% Family	75.5%	Avg. Wage Per Job 1995	$17,811
Population Density 1997	76.8	% Non-Family	24.2%	Employed in 1996	10,580
% Under 20 1996	29.9%	% Living Alone	21.3%	Unemployed in 1996	680
% 65 & Over 1996	14.6%	Births 1995	340	Unemployment Rate 1996	6.0%
% White 1996	99.0%	Births to Teens 1995	71	Avg. Covered Payroll 1996 ($000)	$21,079
% African-Amer. 1996	0.3%	Deaths 1995	254	Average Weekly Earnings in Manufacturing 1996	$422.75
% Hispanic* 1996	2.1%	Marriages 1995	206	Registered Vehicles 1996	22,984

*May be of any race.

Percent of Total Population By Sex and Age

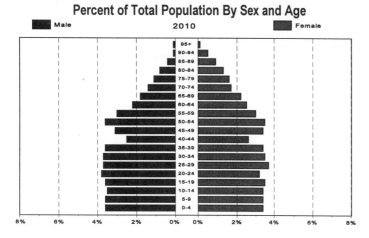

■ Male   2010   ■ Female

Population Projections

Age Groups	2000	2010	% Change
0-17	6,110	6,040	-1.1%
18-24	2,530	2,360	-6.7%
25-39	4,610	5,200	12.8%
40-59	5,740	5,920	3.1%
60-74	2,830	2,870	1.4%
75 +	1,590	1,620	1.9%
Total	23,400	24,000	2.6%

Personal Income
Real 1995 Dollars ($000)

	1990	1995	% Chg.
Total Earnings by Place of Work	111,955	123,805	10.6%
Less Personal Contributions for Social Insurance	7,141	9,016	26.3%
Net Income by Place of Work	104,813	114,789	9.5%
Plus Residence Adjustment	87,712	98,552	12.4%
Net Income by Place of Residence	192,526	213,341	10.8%
Plus Dividends, Rent and Interest	49,652	41,165	-17.1%
Plus Transfer Payments	59,689	71,208	19.3%
Personal Income by Place of Residence	301,867	325,714	7.9%
Per Capita Income ($)	13,214	14,427	9.2%
Rank	90	90	25

Educational Attainment 1990

Graduate or Prof. Degree
Bachelor's Degree
Associate Degree
Some College No Degree
High School Graduate
9th-12th No Diploma
Less than 9th Grade

0   1,500   3,000   4,500   6,000

High School Grad or Higher
Percent: 60%
Rank in State: 90

Population Change by Decade
(1990-2000 projected)

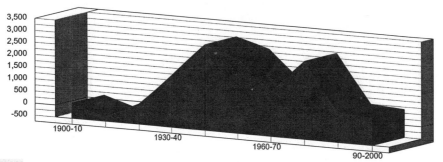

3,500
3,000
2,500
2,000
1,500
1,000
500
0
-500

1900-10   1930-40   1960-70   90-2000

Occupation of Employed Persons Age 16 & Over		
	1990	% Chg. 80-90
Managerial & Professional	1,334	30.7
Technical, Sales & Admin. Support	1,988	36.6
Service Occupations	1,342	18.4
Farming, Forestry and Fishing	505	11.0
Precision Production, Craft & Repair	1,462	25.4
Operators, Fabricators	2,715	3.1

Top 5 Counties Commuting in 1990			
From Starke Into:		Into Starke From:	
Marshall	1,442	Pulaski	302
St. Joseph	714	Marshall	227
Laporte	639	Laporte	156
Porter	397	St. Joseph	82
Outside Indiana	286	Porter	71

4,850 persons lived and worked in this county.
4,288 lived in the county but worked elsewhere.

Number of Establishments
(% Change 1990-1995)

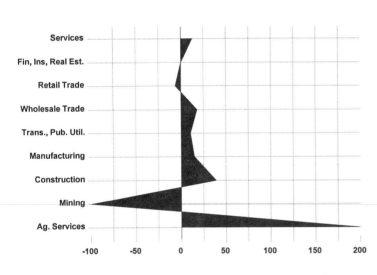

Establishments by Sector 1995		
Industry	Number of Establishments	% with fewer than 10 employees
Ag. Services	3	66.7%
Mining	0	NA
Construction	32	96.9%
Manufacturing	23	26.1%
Transportation, Public Utilities	21	85.7%
Wholesale Trade	33	84.8%
Retail Trade	104	65.4%
Finance, Insurance, Real Estate	21	95.2%
Services	89	89.9%

Private Industry	Employment		Real Earnings ($000)		Average Earnings Per Job	
	1995	% Chg. 90-95	1995	Real % Chg. 90-95	1995	Real % Chg. 90-95
Ag. Services	95	13.1%	905	18.8%	9,526	5.1%
Mining	NA	NA	55	-31.3%	NA	NA
Construction	282	5.2%	6,127	16.2%	21,727	10.4%
Manufacturing	1,295	29.6%	33,949	43.3%	26,215	10.5%
Transportation, Public Utilities	279	2.6%	7,070	24.7%	25,341	21.5%
Wholesale Trade	183	-18.7%	3,856	-21.4%	21,071	-3.3%
Retail Trade	1,348	-2.0%	16,118	-0.1%	11,957	1.9%
Finance, Insurance, Real Estate	225	-12.1%	2,562	-15.0%	11,387	-3.2%
Services	1,282	-6.8%	20,648	19.1%	16,106	27.8%

STEUBEN COUNTY

Population 1997 (Est.)	31,102	# Households 1995 (Projection)	10,600	Personal Income 1995 ($000)	$474,165
Land Area (Sq. Mi.)	308.7	% Family	72.7%	Avg. Wage Per Job 1995	$20,750
Population Density 1997	100.8	% Non-Family	27.1%	Employed in 1996	16,420
% Under 20 1996	28.4%	% Living Alone	23.0%	Unemployed in 1996	630
% 65 & Over 1996	13.3%	Births 1995	415	Unemployment Rate 1996	3.7%
% White 1996	98.9%	Births to Teens 1995	57	Avg. Covered Payroll 1996 ($000)	$90,334
% African-Amer. 1996	0.2%	Deaths 1995	236	Average Weekly Earnings in Manufacturing 1996	$501.00
% Hispanic* 1996	0.9%	Marriages 1995	482	Registered Vehicles 1996	32,742

*May be of any race.

Percent of Total Population By Sex and Age

■ Male   2010   ■ Female

Age groups (top to bottom): 95+, 90-94, 85-89, 80-84, 75-79, 70-74, 65-69, 60-64, 55-59, 50-54, 45-49, 40-44, 35-39, 30-34, 25-29, 20-24, 15-19, 10-14, 5-9, 0-4

Axis: 8% 6% 4% 2% 0% 0% 2% 4% 6% 8%

Population Projections

Age Groups	2000	2010	% Change
0-17	7,170	6,580	-8.2%
18-24	3,300	3,190	-3.3%
25-39	5,450	5,860	7.5%
40-59	7,770	7,610	-2.1%
60-74	3,420	4,170	21.9%
75 +	1,790	1,980	10.6%
Total	28,900	29,400	1.7%

Personal Income
Real 1995 Dollars ($000)

	1990	1995	% Chg.
Total Earnings by Place of Work	380,316	474,165	24.7%
Less Personal Contributions for Social Insurance	25,113	32,535	29.6%
Net Income by Place of Work	355,203	441,630	24.3%
Plus Residence Adjustment	-2,439	-3,168	29.9%
Net Income by Place of Residence	352,764	438,462	24.3%
Plus Dividends, Rent and Interest	90,434	88,569	-2.1%
Plus Transfer Payments	70,582	92,787	31.5%
Personal Income by Place of Residence	513,780	619,818	20.6%
Per Capita Income ($)	18,704	20,536	9.8%
Rank	27	25	22

Educational Attainment 1990

Categories (top to bottom): Graduate or Prof. Degree, Bachelor's Degree, Associate Degree, Some College No Degree, High School Graduate, 9th-12th No Diploma, Less than 9th Grade

Axis: 0 2,000 4,000 6,000 8,000

High School Grad or Higher
Percent: 79%
Rank in State: 12

Population Change by Decade
(1990-2000 projected)

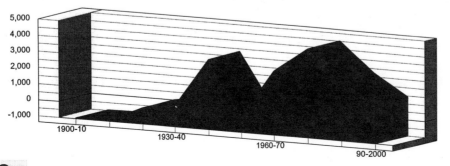

Axis values: 5,000 4,000 3,000 2,000 1,000 0 -1,000

Decades: 1900-10, 1930-40, 1960-70, 90-2000

Occupation of Employed Persons Age 16 & Over		
	1990	% Chg. 80-90
Managerial & Professional	2,501	52.5
Technical, Sales & Admin. Support	3,353	37.1
Service Occupations	1,674	24.6
Farming, Forestry and Fishing	467	-27.5
Precision Production, Craft & Repair	1,732	22.2
Operators, Fabricators	3,915	24.6

Top 5 Counties Commuting in 1990			
From Steuben Into:		Into Steuben From:	
Dekalb	1,065	Outside Indiana	2,194
Allen	810	Dekalb	827
Outside Indiana	452	Lagrange	268
Lagrange	411	Allen	252
Noble	273	Noble	106

10,126 persons lived and worked in this county.
3,228 lived in the county but worked elsewhere.

Number of Establishments
(% Change 1990-1995)

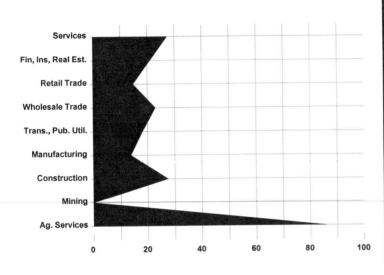

Establishments by Sector 1995		
Industry	Number of Establishments	% with fewer than 10 employees
Ag. Services	13	100.0%
Mining	2	100.0%
Construction	102	88.2%
Manufacturing	107	29.0%
Transportation, Public Utilities	39	71.8%
Wholesale Trade	59	76.3%
Retail Trade	280	64.3%
Finance, Insurance, Real Estate	52	90.4%
Services	252	80.6%

Private Industry	Employment		Real Earnings ($000)		Average Earnings Per Job	
	1995	% Chg. 90-95	1995	Real % Chg. 90-95	1995	Real % Chg. 90-95
Ag. Services	127	30.9%	1,397	36.6%	11,000	4.3%
Mining	NA	NA	NA	NA	NA	NA
Construction	837	24.0%	20,379	35.7%	24,348	9.4%
Manufacturing	8,047	29.4%	245,252	36.8%	30,477	5.7%
Transportation, Public Utilities	940	-20.7%	33,622	-25.1%	35,768	-5.5%
Wholesale Trade	573	42.2%	13,289	26.1%	23,192	-11.3%
Retail Trade	4,095	25.1%	51,942	36.7%	12,684	9.2%
Finance, Insurance, Real Estate	603	-9.7%	9,986	53.7%	16,561	70.2%
Services	3,705	18.9%	63,200	30.5%	17,058	9.8%

SULLIVAN COUNTY

Population 1997 (Est.)	20,280	# Households 1995 (Projection)	7,100	Personal Income 1995 ($000)	$147,291
Land Area (Sq. Mi.)	447.2	% Family	73.8%	Avg. Wage Per Job 1995	$18,922
Population Density 1997	45.3	% Non-Family	26.8%	Employed in 1996	9,220
% Under 20 1996	25.8%	% Living Alone	24.8%	Unemployed in 1996	830
% 65 & Over 1996	17.4%	Births 1995	247	Unemployment Rate 1996	8.2%
% White 1996	99.7%	Births to Teens 1995	39	Avg. Covered Payroll 1996 ($000)	$29,247
% African-Amer. 1996	0.1%	Deaths 1995	256	Average Weekly Earnings in Manufacturing 1996	$384.75
% Hispanic* 1996	0.3%	Marriages 1995	214	Registered Vehicles 1996	20,567

*May be of any race.

Percent of Total Population By Sex and Age

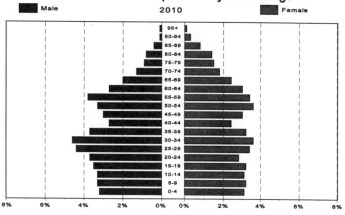

Population Projections

Age Groups	2000	2010	% Change
0-17	4,340	4,250	-2.1%
18-24	2,040	1,690	-17.2%
25-39	3,620	4,220	16.6%
40-59	5,050	4,610	-8.7%
60-74	2,180	2,420	11.0%
75 +	1,400	1,170	-16.4%
Total	18,600	18,300	-1.6%

Personal Income
Real 1995 Dollars ($000)

	1990	1995	% Chg.
Total Earnings by Place of Work	137,419	147,291	7.2%
Less Personal Contributions for Social Insurance	9,321	10,541	13.1%
Net Income by Place of Work	128,098	136,750	6.8%
Plus Residence Adjustment	58,863	75,937	29.0%
Net Income by Place of Residence	186,961	212,687	13.8%
Plus Dividends, Rent and Interest	58,364	52,094	-10.7%
Plus Transfer Payments	67,825	83,426	23.0%
Personal Income by Place of Residence	313,151	348,207	11.2%
Per Capita Income ($)	16,489	17,145	4.0%
Rank	69	70	71

Educational Attainment 1990

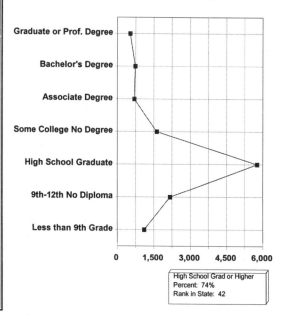

High School Grad or Higher
Percent: 74%
Rank in State: 42

Population Change by Decade
(1990-2000 projected)

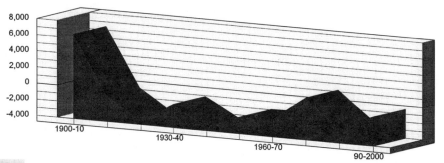

For EDIN tables, sources and footnotes, see page 380.

Occupation of Employed Persons Age 16 & Over	1990	% Chg. 80-90
Managerial & Professional	1,423	15.0
Technical, Sales & Admin. Support	1,777	2.4
Service Occupations	1,246	25.6
Farming, Forestry and Fishing	396	-12.8
Precision Production, Craft & Repair	1,315	-1.9
Operators, Fabricators	1,653	-19.3

Top 5 Counties Commuting in 1990			
From Sullivan Into:		Into Sullivan From:	
Vigo	1,909	Greene	360
Greene	474	Vigo	271
Knox	165	Knox	104
Outside Indiana	133	Outside Indiana	81
Vermillion	110	Daviess	36

4,513 persons lived and worked in this county.
3,182 lived in the county but worked elsewhere.

Number of Establishments
(% Change 1990-1995)

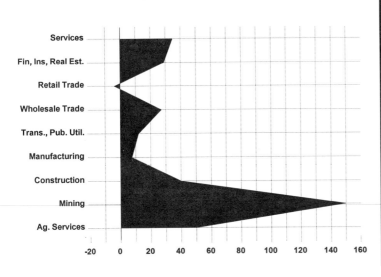

Establishments by Sector 1995		
Industry	Number of Establishments	% with fewer than 10 employees
Ag. Services	3	100.0%
Mining	10	60.0%
Construction	35	97.1%
Manufacturing	28	57.1%
Transportation, Public Utilities	37	70.3%
Wholesale Trade	28	82.1%
Retail Trade	98	71.4%
Finance, Insurance, Real Estate	40	90.0%
Services	128	87.5%

Private Industry	Employment		Real Earnings ($000)		Average Earnings Per Job	
	1995	% Chg. 90-95	1995	Real % Chg. 90-95	1995	Real % Chg. 90-95
Ag. Services	74	27.6%	725	22.2%	9,797	-4.2%
Mining	273	-25.6%	9,397	-47.8%	34,421	-29.9%
Construction	312	11.8%	4,246	-23.1%	13,609	-31.2%
Manufacturing	644	10.3%	15,038	19.7%	23,351	8.6%
Transportation, Public Utilities	669	-23.9%	25,664	-15.5%	38,362	11.0%
Wholesale Trade	248	15.3%	5,434	-2.4%	21,911	-15.4%
Retail Trade	1,416	8.9%	14,735	1.7%	10,406	-6.6%
Finance, Insurance, Real Estate	377	18.9%	6,192	49.2%	16,424	25.4%
Services	1,601	30.3%	26,353	60.6%	16,460	23.3%

Switzerland County

Population 1997 (Est.)	8,636	# Households 1995 (Projection)	2,900	Personal Income 1995 ($000)	$40,669
Land Area (Sq. Mi.)	221.2	% Family	74.1%	Avg. Wage Per Job 1995	$16,334
Population Density 1997	39.0	% Non-Family	25.9%	Employed in 1996	3,685
% Under 20 1996	28.4%	% Living Alone	22.8%	Unemployed in 1996	280
% 65 & Over 1996	15.4%	Births 1995	101	Unemployment Rate 1996	7.1%
% White 1996	99.3%	Births to Teens 1995	15	Avg. Covered Payroll 1996 ($000)	$6,870
% African-Amer. 1996	0.2%	Deaths 1995	117	Average Weekly Earnings in Manufacturing 1996	$366.50
% Hispanic* 1996	0.3%	Marriages 1995	53	Registered Vehicles 1996	8,018

*May be of any race.

Percent of Total Population By Sex and Age

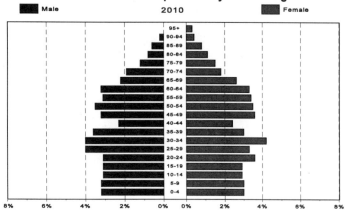

Population Projections

Age Groups	2000	2010	% Change
0-17	1,840	1,770	-3.8%
18-24	920	720	-21.7%
25-39	1,460	1,770	21.2%
40-59	2,140	2,000	-6.5%
60-74	1,010	1,210	19.8%
75 +	570	560	-1.8%
Total	7,900	8,000	1.3%

Personal Income
Real 1995 Dollars ($000)

	1990	1995	% Chg.
Total Earnings by Place of Work	34,019	40,669	19.5%
Less Personal Contributions for Social Insurance	2,390	3,342	39.8%
Net Income by Place of Work	31,628	37,327	18.0%
Plus Residence Adjustment	34,257	39,465	15.2%
Net Income by Place of Residence	65,885	76,792	16.6%
Plus Dividends, Rent and Interest	13,803	13,007	-5.8%
Plus Transfer Payments	22,312	27,167	21.8%
Personal Income by Place of Residence	101,999	116,966	14.7%
Per Capita income ($)	13,138	14,164	7.8%
Rank	91	91	43

Educational Attainment 1990

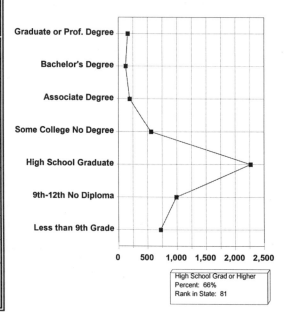

High School Grad or Higher
Percent: 66%
Rank in State: 81

Population Change by Decade
(1990-2000 projected)

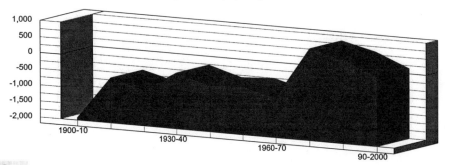

For EDIN tables, sources and footnotes, see page 380.

Occupation of Employed Persons Age 16 & Over

	1990	% Chg. 80-90
Managerial & Professional	394	17.3
Technical, Sales & Admin. Support	613	58.8
Service Occupations	400	39.9
Farming, Forestry and Fishing	161	-44.9
Precision Production, Craft & Repair	614	63.7
Operators, Fabricators	1,167	24.3

Top 5 Counties Commuting in 1990

From Switzerland Into:		Into Switzerland From:	
Outside Indiana	681	Jefferson	112
Jefferson	411	Outside Indiana	104
Dearborn	347	Ohio	70
Ripley	90	Bartholomew	17
Ohio	56	Ripley	16

1,660	persons lived and worked in this county.
1,626	lived in the county but worked elsewhere.

Number of Establishments
(% Change 1990-1995)

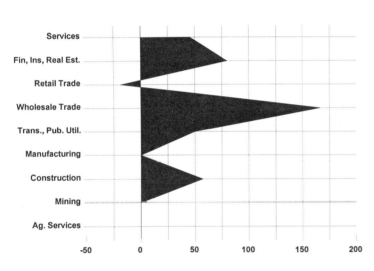

Establishments by Sector 1995

Industry	Number of Establishments	% with fewer than 10 employees
Ag. Services	2	100.0%
Mining	1	0.0%
Construction	11	90.9%
Manufacturing	8	50.0%
Transportation, Public Utilities	12	91.7%
Wholesale Trade	8	75.0%
Retail Trade	26	88.5%
Finance, Insurance, Real Estate	9	88.9%
Services	32	90.6%

Private Industry	Employment		Real Earnings ($000)		Average Earnings Per Job	
	1995	% Chg. 90-95	1995	Real % Chg. 90-95	1995	Real % Chg. 90-95
Ag. Services	25	8.7%	120	3.4%	4,800	-4.9%
Mining	NA	NA	NA	NA	NA	NA
Construction	151	51.0%	2,888	105.1%	19,126	35.8%
Manufacturing	708	23.1%	16,816	40.1%	23,751	13.7%
Transportation, Public Utilities	NA	NA	NA	NA	NA	NA
Wholesale Trade	39	44.4%	651	79.1%	16,692	24.0%
Retail Trade	210	6.1%	3,249	14.9%	15,471	8.4%
Finance, Insurance, Real Estate	94	22.1%	1,398	44.6%	14,872	18.4%
Services	512	22.2%	6,144	29.1%	12,000	5.7%

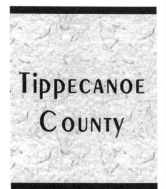

TIPPECANOE COUNTY

Population 1997 (Est.)	138,307	# Households 1995 (Projection)	47,600	Personal Income 1995 ($000)	$2,361,634
Land Area (Sq. Mi.)	499.8	% Family	63.7%	Avg. Wage Per Job 1995	$24,380
Population Density 1997	276.7	% Non-Family	36.3%	Employed in 1996	69,930
% Under 20 1996	28.3%	% Living Alone	25.0%	Unemployed in 1996	1,980
% 65 & Over 1996	9.7%	Births 1995	1,740	Unemployment Rate 1996	2.7%
% White 1996	93.0%	Births to Teens 1995	172	Avg. Covered Payroll 1996 ($000)	$469,325
% African-Amer. 1996	2.2%	Deaths 1995	980	Average Weekly Earnings in Manufacturing 1996	$738.25
% Hispanic* 1996	2.1%	Marriages 1995	1,121	Registered Vehicles 1996	106,810

*May be of any race.

Percent of Total Population By Sex and Age

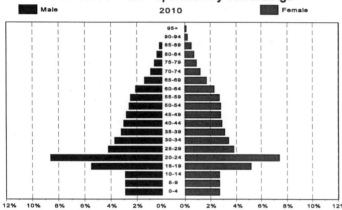

■ Male 2010 ■ Female

Population Projections

Age Groups	2000	2010	% Change
0-17	34,570	34,350	-0.6%
18-24	29,380	30,030	2.2%
25-39	30,920	31,610	2.2%
40-59	29,240	32,660	11.7%
60-74	10,820	14,370	32.8%
75 +	5,460	5,360	-1.8%
Total	140,400	148,400	5.7%

Personal Income
Real 1995 Dollars ($000)

	1990	1995	% Chg.
Total Earnings by Place of Work	2,018,851	2,361,634	17.0%
Less Personal Contributions for Social Insurance	116,989	142,138	21.5%
Net Income by Place of Work	1,901,862	2,219,496	16.7%
Plus Residence Adjustment	-233,242	-283,403	21.5%
Net Income by Place of Residence	1,668,620	1,936,093	16.0%
Plus Dividends, Rent and Interest	434,064	461,079	6.2%
Plus Transfer Payments	277,998	329,587	18.6%
Personal Income by Place of Residence	2,380,682	2,726,759	14.5%
Per Capita Income ($)	18,232	19,842	8.8%
Rank	40	32	30

Educational Attainment 1990

Graduate or Prof. Degree
Bachelor's Degree
Associate Degree
Some College No Degree
High School Graduate
9th-12th No Diploma
Less than 9th Grade

0   7,000   14,000   21,000   28,000

High School Grad or Higher
Percent: 85%
Rank in State: 2

Population Change by Decade
(1990-2000 projected)

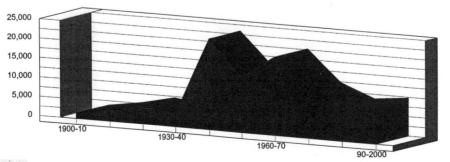

25,000
20,000
15,000
10,000
5,000
0

1900-10   1930-40   1960-70   90-2000

Occupation of Employed Persons Age 16 & Over		
	1990	% Chg. 80-90
Managerial & Professional	19,053	30.9
Technical, Sales & Admin. Support	19,442	12.7
Service Occupations	10,204	11.9
Farming, Forestry and Fishing	1,195	-7.4
Precision Production, Craft & Repair	5,856	0.6
Operators, Fabricators	8,332	1.2

Top 5 Counties Commuting in 1990			
From Tippecanoe Into:		Into Tippecanoe From:	
Outside Indiana	530	Clinton	2,156
Marion	498	White	2,009
White	495	Carroll	1,969
Clinton	424	Benton	1,284
Montgomery	355	Fountain	792

59,310 persons lived and worked in this county.
3,771 lived in the county but worked elsewhere.

Number of Establishments
(% Change 1990-1995)

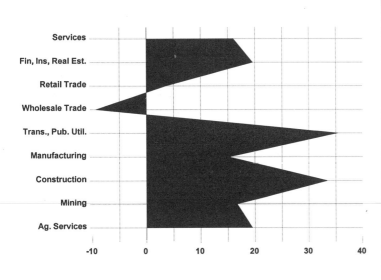

Establishments by Sector 1995		
Industry	Number of Establishments	% with fewer than 10 employees
Ag. Services	49	75.5%
Mining	7	57.1%
Construction	327	76.1%
Manufacturing	129	46.5%
Transportation, Public Utilities	134	64.9%
Wholesale Trade	136	68.4%
Retail Trade	787	58.4%
Finance, Insurance, Real Estate	305	82.3%
Services	1,094	73.9%

Private Industry	Employment		Real Earnings ($000)		Average Earnings Per Job	
	1995	% Chg. 90-95	1995	Real % Chg. 90-95	1995	Real % Chg. 90-95
Ag. Services	NA	NA	NA	NA	NA	NA
Mining	NA	NA	NA	NA	NA	NA
Construction	4,246	15.3%	130,504	18.3%	30,736	2.6%
Manufacturing	16,947	19.8%	750,829	26.1%	44,305	5.3%
Transportation, Public Utilities	2,302	0.1%	73,746	0.5%	32,036	0.4%
Wholesale Trade	1,849	6.8%	57,001	11.7%	30,828	4.5%
Retail Trade	16,225	13.2%	204,099	12.3%	12,579	-0.8%
Finance, Insurance, Real Estate	5,042	7.8%	118,274	16.9%	23,458	8.4%
Services	21,502	13.6%	464,044	29.1%	21,581	13.7%

TIPTON COUNTY

Population 1997 (Est.)	16,395	# Households 1995 (Projection)	6,000	Personal Income 1995 ($000)	$119,442
Land Area (Sq. Mi.)	260.4	% Family	75.3%	Avg. Wage Per Job 1995	$20,668
Population Density 1997	63.0	% Non-Family	24.3%	Employed in 1996	8,635
% Under 20 1996	27.7%	% Living Alone	21.8%	Unemployed in 1996	305
% 65 & Over 1996	15.0%	Births 1995	187	Unemployment Rate 1996	3.4%
% White 1996	99.5%	Births to Teens 1995	19	Avg. Covered Payroll 1996 ($000)	$23,008
% African-Amer. 1996	0.1%	Deaths 1995	172	Average Weekly Earnings in Manufacturing 1996	$588.50
% Hispanic* 1996	0.9%	Marriages 1995	160	Registered Vehicles 1996	18,605

*May be of any race.

Percent of Total Population By Sex and Age

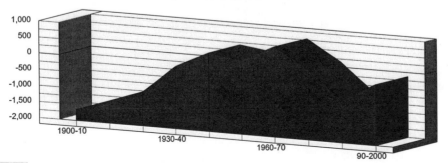

Male 2010 Female

Population Projections

Age Groups	2000	2010	% Change
0-17	3,710	3,550	-4.3%
18-24	1,740	1,420	-18.4%
25-39	2,920	3,460	18.5%
40-59	4,560	4,120	-9.6%
60-74	1,870	2,400	28.3%
75 +	1,150	1,080	-6.1%
Total	16,000	16,000	0.0%

Personal Income
Real 1995 Dollars ($000)

	1990	1995	% Chg.
Total Earnings by Place of Work	118,549	119,442	0.8%
Less Personal Contributions for Social Insurance	6,692	8,016	19.8%
Net Income by Place of Work	111,857	111,426	-0.4%
Plus Residence Adjustment	108,823	153,071	40.7%
Net Income by Place of Residence	220,680	264,497	19.9%
Plus Dividends, Rent and Interest	54,624	50,786	-7.0%
Plus Transfer Payments	44,816	50,507	12.7%
Personal Income by Place of Residence	320,120	365,790	14.3%
Per Capita Income ($)	19,831	22,208	12.0%
Rank	19	15	11

Educational Attainment 1990

Graduate or Prof. Degree
Bachelor's Degree
Associate Degree
Some College No Degree
High School Graduate
9th-12th No Diploma
Less than 9th Grade

0   1,000   2,000   3,000   4,000   5,000

High School Grad or Higher
Percent: 77%
Rank in State: 21

Population Change by Decade
(1990-2000 projected)

1,000
500
0
-500
-1,000
-1,500
-2,000

1900-10   1930-40   1960-70   90-2000

For EDIN tables, sources and footnotes, see page 380.

Occupation of Employed Persons Age 16 & Over

	1990	% Chg. 80-90
Managerial & Professional	1,514	47.3
Technical, Sales & Admin. Support	2,048	29.0
Service Occupations	917	10.5
Farming, Forestry and Fishing	398	-25.6
Precision Production, Craft & Repair	1,195	19.0
Operators, Fabricators	1,708	-16.4

Top 5 Counties Commuting in 1990

From Tipton Into:		Into Tipton From:	
Howard	2,159	Madison	343
Hamilton	811	Howard	338
Madison	377	Hamilton	195
Marion	349	Clinton	117
Grant	75	Marion	64

3,521 persons lived and worked in this county.
4,093 lived in the county but worked elsewhere.

Number of Establishments
(% Change 1990-1995)

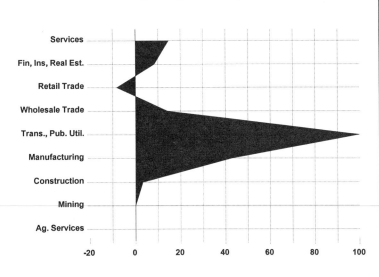

Establishments by Sector 1995

Industry	Number of Establishments	% with fewer than 10 employees
Ag. Services	6	100.0%
Mining	0	NA
Construction	32	81.2%
Manufacturing	20	35.0%
Transportation, Public Utilities	22	86.4%
Wholesale Trade	24	58.3%
Retail Trade	78	67.9%
Finance, Insurance, Real Estate	26	80.8%
Services	109	88.1%

Private Industry	Employment		Real Earnings ($000)		Average Earnings Per Job	
	1995	% Chg. 90-95	1995	Real % Chg. 90-95	1995	Real % Chg. 90-95
Ag. Services	168	13.5%	1,524	31.8%	9,071	16.1%
Mining	NA	NA	93	NA	NA	NA
Construction	363	23.1%	6,938	35.4%	19,113	10.0%
Manufacturing	813	52.5%	28,555	39.4%	35,123	-8.6%
Transportation, Public Utilities	208	-1.9%	4,686	2.2%	22,529	4.1%
Wholesale Trade	281	-1.7%	8,776	1.7%	31,231	3.5%
Retail Trade	1,145	8.1%	14,220	-3.3%	12,419	-10.6%
Finance, Insurance, Real Estate	278	-15.0%	3,662	-6.5%	13,173	9.9%
Services	1,099	-3.1%	18,079	5.0%	16,450	8.3%

UNION COUNTY

Population 1997 (Est.)	7,272	# Households 1995 (Projection)	2,600	Personal Income 1995 ($000)	$36,491
Land Area (Sq. Mi.)	161.6	% Family	76.5%	Avg. Wage Per Job 1995	$15,767
Population Density 1997	45.0	% Non-Family	23.8%	Employed in 1996	3,735
% Under 20 1996	29.5%	% Living Alone	21.2%	Unemployed in 1996	185
% 65 & Over 1996	14.1%	Births 1995	96	Unemployment Rate 1996	4.7%
% White 1996	99.2%	Births to Teens 1995	18	Avg. Covered Payroll 1996 ($000)	$5,654
% African-Amer. 1996	0.3%	Deaths 1995	86	Average Weekly Earnings in Manufacturing 1996	$450.75
% Hispanic* 1996	0.4%	Marriages 1995	55	Registered Vehicles 1996	7,839

*May be of any race.

Percent of Total Population By Sex and Age

■ Male   2010   ■ Female

| 95+ |
| 90-94 |
| 85-89 |
| 80-84 |
| 75-79 |
| 70-74 |
| 65-69 |
| 60-64 |
| 55-59 |
| 50-54 |
| 45-49 |
| 40-44 |
| 35-39 |
| 30-34 |
| 25-29 |
| 20-24 |
| 15-19 |
| 10-14 |
| 5-9 |
| 0-4 |

8% 6% 4% 2% 0% 0% 2% 4% 6% 8%

Population Projections

Age Groups	2000	2010	% Change
0-17	1,690	1,590	-5.9%
18-24	780	650	-16.7%
25-39	1,410	1,610	14.2%
40-59	1,940	1,900	-2.1%
60-74	830	1,060	27.7%
75 +	460	450	-2.2%
Total	7,100	7,300	2.8%

Personal Income
Real 1995 Dollars ($000)

	1990	1995	% Chg.
Total Earnings by Place of Work	35,280	36,491	3.4%
Less Personal Contributions for Social Insurance	2,133	2,806	31.6%
Net Income by Place of Work	33,147	33,685	1.6%
Plus Residence Adjustment	39,525	49,260	24.6%
Net Income by Place of Residence	72,672	82,945	14.1%
Plus Dividends, Rent and Interest	20,215	16,844	-16.7%
Plus Transfer Payments	18,515	22,041	19.0%
Personal Income by Place of Residence	111,402	121,830	9.4%
Per Capita Income ($)	15,946	16,555	3.8%
Rank	78	79	72

Educational Attainment 1990

Graduate or Prof. Degree
Bachelor's Degree
Associate Degree
Some College No Degree
High School Graduate
9th-12th No Diploma
Less than 9th Grade

0   500   1,000   1,500   2,000

High School Grad or Higher
Percent: 71%
Rank in State: 69

Population Change by Decade
(1990-2000 projected)

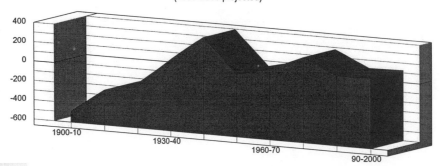

400
200
0
-200
-400
-600

1900-10   1930-40   1960-70   90-2000

For EDIN tables, sources and footnotes, see page 380.

Occupation of Employed Persons Age 16 & Over		
	1990	% Chg. 80-90
Managerial & Professional	547	20.0
Technical, Sales & Admin. Support	729	12.0
Service Occupations	541	35.2
Farming, Forestry and Fishing	305	-18.0
Precision Production, Craft & Repair	433	17.3
Operators, Fabricators	643	1.9

Top 5 Counties Commuting in 1990			
From Union Into:		Into Union From:	
Outside Indiana	711	Outside Indiana	97
Wayne	565	Wayne	83
Fayette	429	Fayette	78
Franklin	109	Franklin	70
Rush	19	Carroll	5

1,235 persons lived and worked in this county.
1,909 lived in the county but worked elsewhere.

Number of Establishments
(% Change 1990-1995)

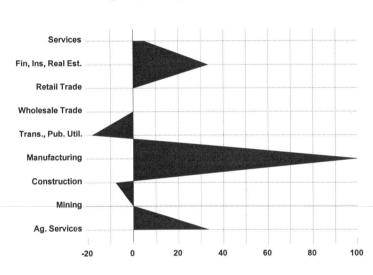

Establishments by Sector 1995		
Industry	Number of Establishments	% with fewer than 10 employees
Ag. Services	4	100.0%
Mining	0	NA
Construction	12	91.7%
Manufacturing	6	50.0%
Transportation, Public Utilities	9	88.9%
Wholesale Trade	11	72.7%
Retail Trade	41	75.6%
Finance, Insurance, Real Estate	12	75.0%
Services	42	90.5%

Private Industry	Employment		Real Earnings ($000)		Average Earnings Per Job	
	1995	% Chg. 90-95	1995	Real % Chg. 90-95	1995	Real % Chg. 90-95
Ag. Services	49	25.6%	1,285	39.6%	26,224	11.1%
Mining	NA	NA	55	-69.8%	NA	NA
Construction	94	2.2%	1,849	10.3%	19,670	7.9%
Manufacturing	102	45.7%	4,924	52.2%	48,275	4.5%
Transportation, Public Utilities	125	-1.6%	3,968	4.9%	31,744	6.6%
Wholesale Trade	48	-12.7%	1,292	-23.6%	26,917	-12.4%
Retail Trade	478	10.1%	6,513	17.0%	13,626	6.2%
Finance, Insurance, Real Estate	189	46.5%	2,686	41.8%	14,212	-3.2%
Services	469	15.2%	6,413	43.7%	13,674	24.7%

For EDIN tables, sources and footnotes, see page 380.

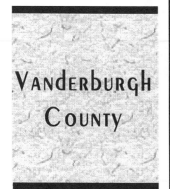

VANDERBURGH COUNTY

Population 1997 (Est.)	166,837	# Households 1995 (Projection)	66,700	Personal Income 1995 ($000)	$3,254,278
Land Area (Sq. Mi.)	234.6	% Family	66.8%	Avg. Wage Per Job 1995	$23,512
Population Density 1997	711.2	% Non-Family	33.1%	Employed in 1996	86,670
% Under 20 1996	26.0%	% Living Alone	28.9%	Unemployed in 1996	3,710
% 65 & Over 1996	15.8%	Births 1995	2,203	Unemployment Rate 1996	4.1%
% White 1996	90.9%	Births to Teens 1995	384	Avg. Covered Payroll 1996 ($000)	$643,547
% African-Amer. 1996	8.2%	Deaths 1995	1,822	Average Weekly Earnings in Manufacturing 1996	$656.00
% Hispanic* 1996	0.7%	Marriages 1995	1,063	Registered Vehicles 1996	150,555

*May be of any race.

Percent of Total Population By Sex and Age

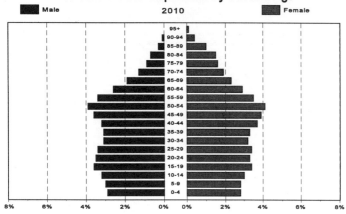

Population Projections

Age Groups	2000	2010	% Change
0-17	39,540	35,680	-9.8%
18-24	14,780	15,560	5.3%
25-39	34,850	31,700	-9.0%
40-59	43,610	47,610	9.2%
60-74	19,110	21,000	9.9%
75 +	11,990	10,960	-8.6%
Total	163,900	162,500	-0.9%

Personal Income
Real 1995 Dollars ($000)

	1990	1995	% Chg.
Total Earnings by Place of Work	2,894,533	3,254,278	12.4%
Less Personal Contributions for Social Insurance	197,100	229,593	16.5%
Net Income by Place of Work	2,697,433	3,024,685	12.1%
Plus Residence Adjustment	-470,789	-630,195	33.9%
Net Income by Place of Residence	2,226,643	2,394,490	7.5%
Plus Dividends, Rent and Interest	826,315	805,078	-2.6%
Plus Transfer Payments	561,902	654,166	16.4%
Personal Income by Place of Residence	3,614,861	3,853,734	6.6%
Per Capita Income ($)	21,887	23,008	5.1%
Rank	7	10	67

Educational Attainment 1990

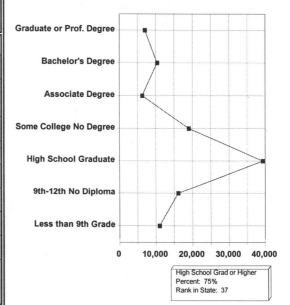

High School Grad or Higher
Percent: 75%
Rank in State: 37

Population Change by Decade
(1990-2000 projected)

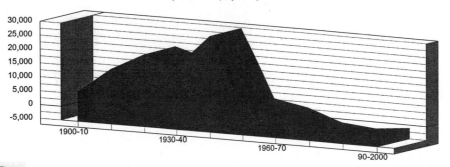

For EDIN tables, sources and footnotes, see page 380.

Occupation of Employed Persons Age 16 & Over		
	1990	% Chg. 80-90
Managerial & Professional	18,465	23.2
Technical, Sales & Admin. Support	25,690	15.2
Service Occupations	11,405	1.1
Farming, Forestry and Fishing	771	17.5
Precision Production, Craft & Repair	8,701	-15.9
Operators, Fabricators	13,462	-19.9

Top 5 Counties Commuting in 1990			
From Vanderburgh Into:		Into Vanderburgh From:	
Warrick	2,494	Warrick	10,608
Outside Indiana	2,142	Outside Indiana	5,238
Posey	1,516	Posey	4,510
Gibson	565	Gibson	2,729
Spencer	139	Spencer	850

69,527 persons lived and worked in this county.
7,392 lived in the county but worked elsewhere.

Number of Establishments
(% Change 1990-1995)

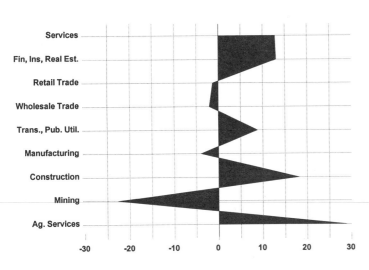

Establishments by Sector 1995		
Industry	Number of Establishments	% with fewer than 10 employees
Ag. Services	58	74.1%
Mining	48	70.8%
Construction	514	73.5%
Manufacturing	266	43.2%
Transportation, Public Utilities	209	56.0%
Wholesale Trade	434	57.6%
Retail Trade	1,250	59.4%
Finance, Insurance, Real Estate	485	77.5%
Services	1,901	71.1%

Private Industry	Employment		Real Earnings ($000)		Average Earnings Per Job	
	1995	% Chg. 90-95	1995	Real % Chg. 90-95	1995	Real % Chg. 90-95
Ag. Services	619	18.8%	7,195	3.8%	11,624	-12.6%
Mining	886	-20.1%	38,523	-25.7%	43,480	-7.0%
Construction	7,931	17.1%	308,305	14.2%	38,873	-2.5%
Manufacturing	19,376	4.0%	718,128	2.5%	37,063	-1.5%
Transportation, Public Utilities	5,788	14.6%	198,143	8.2%	34,233	-5.6%
Wholesale Trade	7,210	10.5%	235,152	11.6%	32,615	1.0%
Retail Trade	25,335	6.3%	334,002	4.6%	13,183	-1.6%
Finance, Insurance, Real Estate	8,002	24.2%	194,995	52.4%	24,368	22.7%
Services	38,754	17.4%	940,340	22.2%	24,264	4.1%

VERMILLION COUNTY

Population 1997 (Est.)	16,997	# Households 1995 (Projection)	6,300	Personal Income 1995 ($000)	$173,733
Land Area (Sq. Mi.)	256.9	% Family	71.3%	Avg. Wage Per Job 1995	$26,778
Population Density 1997	66.2	% Non-Family	29.5%	Employed in 1996	7,505
% Under 20 1996	26.7%	% Living Alone	26.7%	Unemployed in 1996	610
% 65 & Over 1996	17.5%	Births 1995	221	Unemployment Rate 1996	7.5%
% White 1996	99.5%	Births to Teens 1995	33	Avg. Covered Payroll 1996 ($000)	$35,871
% African-Amer. 1996	0.1%	Deaths 1995	199	Average Weekly Earnings in Manufacturing 1996	NA
% Hispanic* 1996	0.4%	Marriages 1995	148	Registered Vehicles 1996	17,573

*May be of any race.

Percent of Total Population By Sex and Age

2010 — Male / Female

Population Projections

Age Groups	2000	2010	% Change
0-17	3,590	3,350	-6.7%
18-24	1,700	1,380	-18.8%
25-39	2,970	3,430	15.5%
40-59	4,470	4,080	-8.7%
60-74	1,920	2,280	18.8%
75 +	1,180	950	-19.5%
Total	15,800	15,500	-1.9%

Personal Income
Real 1995 Dollars ($000)

	1990	1995	% Chg.
Total Earnings by Place of Work	183,849	173,733	-5.5%
Less Personal Contributions for Social Insurance	12,389	12,702	2.5%
Net Income by Place of Work	171,460	161,031	-6.1%
Plus Residence Adjustment	7,038	30,133	328.2%
Net Income by Place of Residence	178,498	191,164	7.1%
Plus Dividends, Rent and Interest	44,202	40,372	-8.7%
Plus Transfer Payments	54,198	56,644	4.5%
Personal Income by Place of Residence	276,897	288,180	4.1%
Per Capita Income ($)	16,523	17,134	3.7%
Rank	68	71	74

Educational Attainment 1990

High School Grad or Higher
Percent: 72%
Rank in State: 60

Population Change by Decade
(1990-2000 projected)

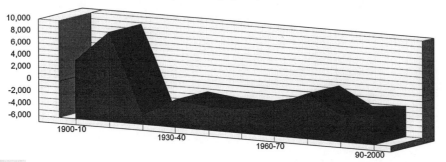

For EDIN tables, sources and footnotes, see page 380.

Occupation of Employed Persons Age 16 & Over

	1990	% Chg. 80-90
Managerial & Professional	1,185	22.9
Technical, Sales & Admin. Support	1,860	11.4
Service Occupations	1,001	15.2
Farming, Forestry and Fishing	191	-33.2
Precision Production, Craft & Repair	1,011	-18.1
Operators, Fabricators	1,704	-11.3

Top 5 Counties Commuting in 1990

From Vermillion Into:		Into Vermillion From:	
Vigo	1,730	Vigo	947
Outside Indiana	971	Parke	668
Parke	220	Outside Indiana	430
Fountain	175	Fountain	135
Clay	48	Sullivan	110

3,453 persons lived and worked in this county.

3,373 lived in the county but worked elsewhere.

Number of Establishments
(% Change 1990-1995)

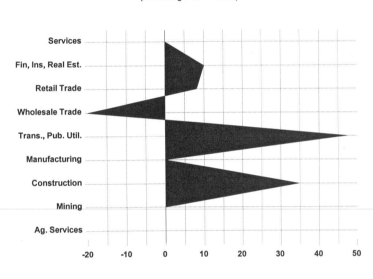

Establishments by Sector 1995

Industry	Number of Establishments	% with fewer than 10 employees
Ag. Services	2	100.0%
Mining	3	100.0%
Construction	31	90.3%
Manufacturing	12	50.0%
Transportation, Public Utilities	28	71.4%
Wholesale Trade	12	91.7%
Retail Trade	93	75.3%
Finance, Insurance, Real Estate	22	86.4%
Services	77	88.3%

Private Industry	Employment		Real Earnings ($000)		Average Earnings Per Job	
	1995	% Chg. 90-95	1995	Real % Chg. 90-95	1995	Real % Chg. 90-95
Ag. Services	43	-20.4%	2,072	185.6%	48,186	258.6%
Mining	23	-90.2%	815	-93.8%	35,435	-37.0%
Construction	383	21.6%	11,289	14.2%	29,475	-6.1%
Manufacturing	1,413	-20.5%	77,094	-11.2%	54,561	11.7%
Transportation, Public Utilities	441	-0.9%	15,811	3.5%	35,853	4.5%
Wholesale Trade	91	-25.4%	1,994	-24.7%	21,912	1.0%
Retail Trade	1,332	16.9%	17,611	20.4%	13,221	2.9%
Finance, Insurance, Real Estate	191	2.1%	3,165	22.0%	16,571	19.5%
Services	1,326	19.8%	23,410	67.8%	17,655	40.1%

For EDIN tables, sources and footnotes, see page 380.

Vigo County

Population 1997 (Est.)	104,940	# Households 1995 (Projection)	39,400	Personal Income 1995 ($000)	$1,600,977
Land Area (Sq. Mi.)	403.3	% Family	67.3%	Avg. Wage Per Job 1995	$21,858
Population Density 1997	260.2	% Non-Family	32.7%	Employed in 1996	49,920
% Under 20 1996	27.0%	% Living Alone	27.9%	Unemployed in 1996	3,410
% 65 & Over 1996	15.4%	Births 1995	1,413	Unemployment Rate 1996	6.4%
% White 1996	92.4%	Births to Teens 1995	236	Avg. Covered Payroll 1996 ($000)	$291,467
% African-Amer. 1996	5.9%	Deaths 1995	1,181	Average Weekly Earnings in Manufacturing 1996	$641.00
% Hispanic* 1996	1.1%	Marriages 1995	920	Registered Vehicles 1996	90,440

*May be of any race.

Percent of Total Population By Sex and Age

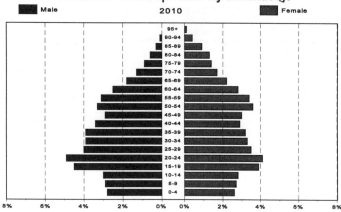

Population Projections

Age Groups	2000	2010	% Change
0-17	24,380	22,420	-8.0%
18-24	13,790	12,730	-7.7%
25-39	21,440	22,440	4.7%
40-59	25,810	26,410	2.3%
60-74	11,180	12,600	12.7%
75 +	7,220	6,330	-12.3%
Total	103,800	102,900	-0.9%

Personal Income
Real 1995 Dollars ($000)

	1990	1995	% Chg.
Total Earnings by Place of Work	1,417,883	1,600,977	12.9%
Less Personal Contributions for Social Insurance	92,860	109,866	18.3%
Net Income by Place of Work	1,325,023	1,491,111	12.5%
Plus Residence Adjustment	-163,915	-211,610	29.1%
Net Income by Place of Residence	1,161,108	1,279,501	10.2%
Plus Dividends, Rent and Interest	369,812	359,893	-2.7%
Plus Transfer Payments	335,779	393,926	17.3%
Personal Income by Place of Residence	1,866,699	2,033,320	8.9%
Per Capita Income ($)	17,598	19,093	8.5%
Rank	50	45	33

Educational Attainment 1990

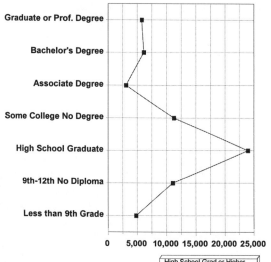

High School Grad or Higher
Percent: 76%
Rank in State: 32

Population Change by Decade
(1990-2000 projected)

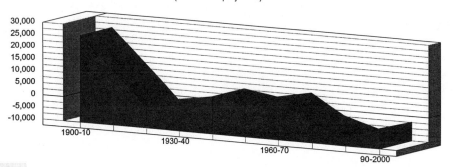

Occupation of Employed Persons Age 16 & Over			Top 5 Counties Commuting in 1990			
	1990	% Chg. 80-90	From Vigo Into:		Into Vigo From:	
Managerial & Professional	11,253	15.0	Vermillion	947	Clay	2,652
Technical, Sales & Admin. Support	14,776	-0.1	Clay	632	Outside Indiana	1,951
Service Occupations	7,036	-5.3	Outside Indiana	570	Sullivan	1,909
Farming, Forestry and Fishing	665	0.8	Marion	320	Vermillion	1,730
Precision Production, Craft & Repair	5,138	-13.1	Sullivan	271	Parke	1,076
Operators, Fabricators	7,330	-27.4	41,245 persons lived and worked in this county.			
			3,977 lived in the county but worked elsewhere.			

Number of Establishments
(% Change 1990-1995)

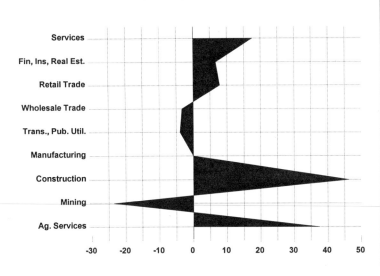

Establishments by Sector 1995		
Industry	Number of Establishments	% with fewer than 10 employees
Ag. Services	33	81.8%
Mining	13	61.5%
Construction	259	75.3%
Manufacturing	142	44.4%
Transportation, Public Utilities	98	62.2%
Wholesale Trade	172	59.3%
Retail Trade	741	62.9%
Finance, Insurance, Real Estate	207	82.6%
Services	992	78.7%

Private Industry	Employment		Real Earnings ($000)		Average Earnings Per Job	
	1995	% Chg. 90-95	1995	Real % Chg. 90-95	1995	Real % Chg. 90-95
Ag. Services	347	11.9%	4,189	8.3%	12,072	-3.3%
Mining	128	-37.6%	1,726	-59.0%	13,484	-34.3%
Construction	4,006	23.9%	132,851	36.0%	33,163	9.8%
Manufacturing	8,931	-7.5%	338,808	-4.3%	37,936	3.5%
Transportation, Public Utilities	2,796	10.1%	90,656	6.0%	32,423	-3.7%
Wholesale Trade	2,363	0.5%	71,248	2.9%	30,152	2.4%
Retail Trade	16,962	27.5%	241,868	27.8%	14,259	0.3%
Finance, Insurance, Real Estate	2,844	4.4%	55,993	13.2%	19,688	8.4%
Services	18,372	19.1%	413,288	29.3%	22,496	8.6%

WABASH COUNTY

Population 1997 (Est.)	34,525	# Households 1995 (Projection)	12,500	Personal Income 1995 ($000)	$426,741
Land Area (Sq. Mi.)	413.2	% Family	74.9%	Avg. Wage Per Job 1995	$21,700
Population Density 1997	83.6	% Non-Family	24.8%	Employed in 1996	16,920
% Under 20 1996	28.5%	% Living Alone	22.1%	Unemployed in 1996	740
% 65 & Over 1996	15.2%	Births 1995	445	Unemployment Rate 1996	4.2%
% White 1996	98.4%	Births to Teens 1995	65	Avg. Covered Payroll 1996 ($000)	$82,634
% African-Amer. 1996	0.4%	Deaths 1995	393	Average Weekly Earnings in Manufacturing 1996	$592.25
% Hispanic* 1996	1.1%	Marriages 1995	319	Registered Vehicles 1996	35,741

*May be of any race.

Percent of Total Population By Sex and Age

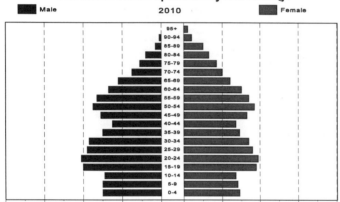

Population Projections

Age Groups	2000	2010	% Change
0-17	8,250	7,460	-9.6%
18-24	4,220	3,760	-10.9%
25-39	6,180	6,960	12.6%
40-59	8,900	8,650	-2.8%
60-74	4,090	4,670	14.2%
75 +	2,450	2,390	-2.4%
Total	34,100	33,900	-0.6%

Personal Income
Real 1995 Dollars ($000)

	1990	1995	% Chg.
Total Earnings by Place of Work	420,894	426,741	1.4%
Less Personal Contributions for Social Insurance	26,843	29,911	11.4%
Net Income by Place of Work	394,051	396,830	0.7%
Plus Residence Adjustment	23,268	29,581	27.1%
Net Income by Place of Residence	417,320	426,411	2.2%
Plus Dividends, Rent and Interest	119,135	118,783	-0.3%
Plus Transfer Payments	99,301	117,283	18.1%
Personal Income by Place of Residence	635,756	662,477	4.2%
Per Capita Income ($)	18,111	19,045	5.2%
Rank	43	46	66

Educational Attainment 1990

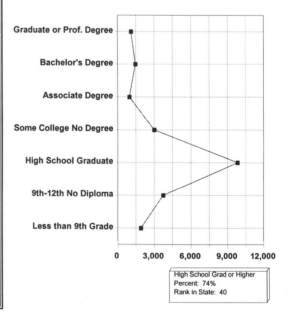

High School Grad or Higher
Percent: 74%
Rank in State: 40

Population Change by Decade
(1990-2000 projected)

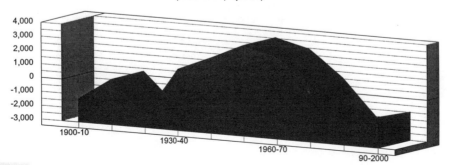

For EDIN tables, sources and footnotes, see page 380.

Occupation of Employed Persons Age 16 & Over		
	1990	% Chg. 80-90
Managerial & Professional	2,731	3.9
Technical, Sales & Admin. Support	3,838	8.6
Service Occupations	2,335	7.5
Farming, Forestry and Fishing	842	-1.1
Precision Production, Craft & Repair	2,339	-0.3
Operators, Fabricators	4,797	-8.9

Top 5 Counties Commuting in 1990			
From Wabash Into:		Into Wabash From:	
Grant	715	Miami	845
Huntington	695	Kosciusko	477
Kosciusko	669	Grant	418
Allen	286	Huntington	286
Miami	206	Fulton	192

13,383 persons lived and worked in this county.
3,200 lived in the county but worked elsewhere.

Number of Establishments
(% Change 1990-1995)

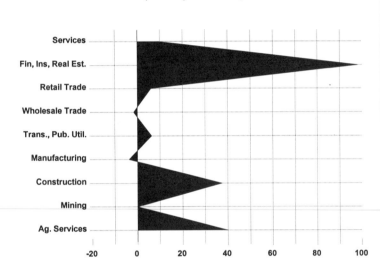

Establishments by Sector 1995		
Industry	Number of Establishments	% with fewer than 10 employees
Ag. Services	14	85.7%
Mining	0	NA
Construction	66	86.4%
Manufacturing	77	36.4%
Transportation, Public Utilities	50	74.0%
Wholesale Trade	63	76.2%
Retail Trade	226	71.2%
Finance, Insurance, Real Estate	117	91.5%
Services	252	83.7%

Private Industry	Employment		Real Earnings ($000)		Average Earnings Per Job	
	1995	% Chg. 90-95	1995	Real % Chg. 90-95	1995	Real % Chg. 90-95
Ag. Services	204	32.5%	2,894	21.2%	14,186	-8.5%
Mining	76	65.2%	226	126.4%	2,974	37.0%
Construction	994	26.0%	23,636	25.7%	23,779	-0.3%
Manufacturing	5,947	-4.5%	196,315	1.9%	33,011	6.7%
Transportation, Public Utilities	608	3.8%	16,072	-8.2%	26,434	-11.6%
Wholesale Trade	615	14.5%	15,730	12.2%	25,577	-2.0%
Retail Trade	3,266	10.2%	37,556	7.3%	11,499	-2.6%
Finance, Insurance, Real Estate	877	13.2%	12,121	23.2%	13,821	8.9%
Services	4,383	7.8%	68,043	11.5%	15,524	3.4%

For EDIN tables, sources and footnotes, see page 380.

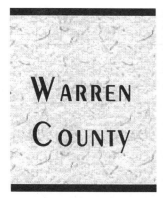

WARREN COUNTY

Population 1997 (Est.)	8,170	# Households 1995 (Projection)	3,000	Personal Income 1995 ($000)	$54,933
Land Area (Sq. Mi.)	364.9	% Family	77.7%	Avg. Wage Per Job 1995	$20,594
Population Density 1997	22.4	% Non-Family	20.7%	Employed in 1996	3,790
% Under 20 1996	27.5%	% Living Alone	19.0%	Unemployed in 1996	140
% 65 & Over 1996	15.0%	Births 1995	85	Unemployment Rate 1996	3.5%
% White 1996	99.5%	Births to Teens 1995	14	Avg. Covered Payroll 1996 ($000)	$9,298
% African-Amer. 1996	0.0%	Deaths 1995	87	Average Weekly Earnings in Manufacturing 1996	$525.25
% Hispanic* 1996	0.3%	Marriages 1995	66	Registered Vehicles 1996	9,667

*May be of any race.

Percent of Total Population By Sex and Age

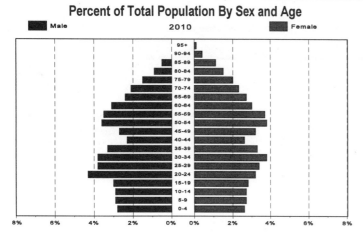

Population Projections

Age Groups	2000	2010	% Change
0-17	1,780	1,520	-14.6%
18-24	840	740	-11.9%
25-39	1,370	1,640	19.7%
40-59	2,180	1,940	-11.0%
60-74	1,080	1,200	11.1%
75 +	590	600	1.7%
Total	7,800	7,600	-2.6%

Personal Income
Real 1995 Dollars ($000)

	1990	1995	% Chg.
Total Earnings by Place of Work	66,534	54,933	-17.4%
Less Personal Contributions for Social Insurance	3,471	3,823	10.1%
Net Income by Place of Work	63,063	51,110	-19.0%
Plus Residence Adjustment	29,249	35,909	22.8%
Net Income by Place of Residence	92,312	87,019	-5.7%
Plus Dividends, Rent and Interest	23,204	22,408	-3.4%
Plus Transfer Payments	19,759	23,536	19.1%
Personal Income by Place of Residence	135,275	132,963	-1.7%
Per Capita Income ($)	16,555	16,132	-2.6%
Rank	67	84	88

Educational Attainment 1990

High School Grad or Higher
Percent: 72%
Rank in State: 66

Population Change by Decade
(1990-2000 projected)

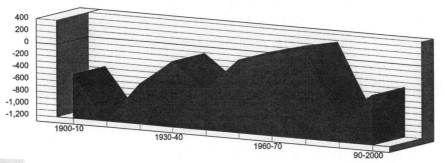

Occupation of Employed Persons Age 16 & Over		
	1990	% Chg. 80-90
Managerial & Professional	517	-1.5
Technical, Sales & Admin. Support	924	20.0
Service Occupations	471	-19.6
Farming, Forestry and Fishing	386	-10.4
Precision Production, Craft & Repair	537	-0.2
Operators, Fabricators	820	-20.7

Top 5 Counties Commuting in 1990			
From Warren Into:		Into Warren From:	
Tippecanoe	752	Fountain	192
Fountain	691	Outside Indiana	110
Outside Indiana	594	Vermillion	44
Benton	153	Tippecanoe	28
Vermillion	28	Parke	8

1,270 persons lived and worked in this county.
2,324 lived in the county but worked elsewhere.

Number of Establishments
(% Change 1990-1995)

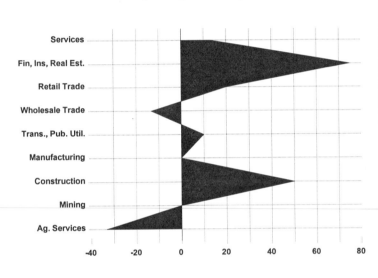

Establishments by Sector 1995		
Industry	Number of Establishments	% with fewer than 10 employees
Ag. Services	2	100.0%
Mining	1	0.0%
Construction	12	91.7%
Manufacturing	10	20.0%
Transportation, Public Utilities	11	81.8%
Wholesale Trade	13	53.8%
Retail Trade	18	88.9%
Finance, Insurance, Real Estate	14	78.6%
Services	26	88.5%

Private Industry	Employment		Real Earnings ($000)		Average Earnings Per Job	
	1995	% Chg. 90-95	1995	Real % Chg. 90-95	1995	Real % Chg. 90-95
Ag. Services	NA	NA	NA	NA	NA	NA
Mining	NA	NA	NA	NA	NA	NA
Construction	129	19.4%	2,326	19.8%	18,031	0.3%
Manufacturing	600	7.9%	18,689	-5.4%	31,148	-12.4%
Transportation, Public Utilities	87	-19.4%	3,480	38.7%	40,000	72.2%
Wholesale Trade	159	37.1%	4,481	22.5%	28,182	-10.6%
Retail Trade	345	-11.8%	4,107	-8.4%	11,904	3.8%
Finance, Insurance, Real Estate	86	14.7%	860	-22.7%	10,000	-32.6%
Services	557	-7.3%	8,141	-2.2%	14,616	5.5%

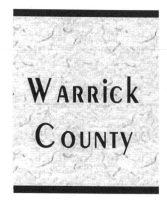

WARRICK COUNTY

Population 1997 (Est.)	50,831	# Households 1995 (Projection)	16,400	Personal Income 1995 ($000)	$461,263
Land Area (Sq. Mi.)	384.1	% Family	80.7%	Avg. Wage Per Job 1995	$26,336
Population Density 1997	132.3	% Non-Family	19.3%	Employed in 1996	26,220
% Under 20 1996	29.9%	% Living Alone	16.7%	Unemployed in 1996	1,030
% 65 & Over 1996	10.2%	Births 1995	621	Unemployment Rate 1996	3.8%
% White 1996	98.4%	Births to Teens 1995	71	Avg. Covered Payroll 1996 ($000)	$86,328
% African-Amer. 1996	0.9%	Deaths 1995	357	Average Weekly Earnings in Manufacturing 1996	NA
% Hispanic* 1996	0.5%	Marriages 1995	286	Registered Vehicles 1996	49,517

*May be of any race.

Percent of Total Population By Sex and Age

Male — 2010 — Female

Population Projections

Age Groups	2000	2010	% Change
0-17	11,310	10,640	-5.9%
18-24	5,320	4,430	-16.7%
25-39	8,750	10,570	20.8%
40-59	14,910	13,360	-10.4%
60-74	4,730	7,380	56.0%
75 +	2,190	2,360	7.8%
Total	47,200	48,700	3.2%

Personal Income
Real 1995 Dollars ($000)

	1990	1995	% Chg.
Total Earnings by Place of Work	523,653	461,263	-11.9%
Less Personal Contributions for Social Insurance	34,661	32,292	-6.8%
Net Income by Place of Work	488,992	428,971	-12.3%
Plus Residence Adjustment	189,463	335,989	77.3%
Net Income by Place of Residence	678,455	764,960	12.8%
Plus Dividends, Rent and Interest	144,902	159,403	10.0%
Plus Transfer Payments	102,831	131,541	27.9%
Personal Income by Place of Residence	926,187	1,055,904	14.0%
Per Capita Income ($)	20,586	21,428	4.1%
Rank	13	19	70

Educational Attainment 1990

High School Grad or Higher
Percent: 80%
Rank in State: 9

Population Change by Decade
(1990-2000 projected)

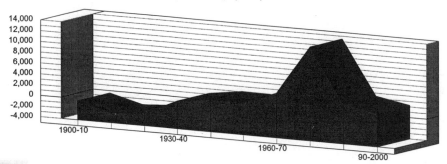

For EDIN tables, sources and footnotes, see page 380.

Occupation of Employed Persons Age 16 & Over		
	1990	% Chg. 80-90
Managerial & Professional	4,774	34.8
Technical, Sales & Admin. Support	6,729	52.3
Service Occupations	2,431	22.8
Farming, Forestry and Fishing	363	-24.5
Precision Production, Craft & Repair	3,375	4.5
Operators, Fabricators	4,326	6.0

Top 5 Counties Commuting in 1990			
From Warrick Into:		Into Warrick From:	
Vanderburgh	10,608	Vanderburgh	2,494
Outside Indiana	586	Outside Indiana	807
Spencer	378	Spencer	794
Dubois	230	Gibson	277
Gibson	120	Perry	154

9,298 persons lived and worked in this county.
12,268 lived in the county but worked elsewhere.

Number of Establishments
(% Change 1990-1995)

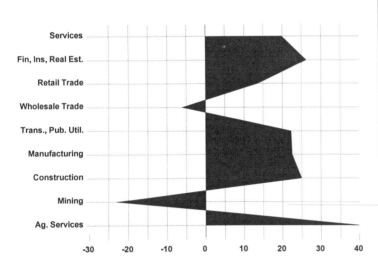

Establishments by Sector 1995		
Industry	Number of Establishments	% with fewer than 10 employees
Ag. Services	21	90.5%
Mining	10	40.0%
Construction	175	87.4%
Manufacturing	49	59.2%
Transportation, Public Utilities	55	76.4%
Wholesale Trade	46	87.0%
Retail Trade	218	71.6%
Finance, Insurance, Real Estate	77	85.7%
Services	309	85.1%

Private Industry	Employment		Real Earnings ($000)		Average Earnings Per Job	
	1995	% Chg. 90-95	1995	Real % Chg. 90-95	1995	Real % Chg. 90-95
Ag. Services	206	43.1%	3,512	28.1%	17,049	-10.5%
Mining	729	-38.3%	35,963	-43.4%	49,332	-8.3%
Construction	1,403	8.6%	33,772	5.5%	24,071	-2.9%
Manufacturing	3,368	-19.3%	174,500	-25.3%	51,811	-7.4%
Transportation, Public Utilities	813	-4.7%	28,044	-6.1%	34,494	-1.5%
Wholesale Trade	628	35.9%	17,902	4.5%	28,506	-23.1%
Retail Trade	2,985	9.3%	33,688	6.4%	11,286	-2.6%
Finance, Insurance, Real Estate	913	10.5%	13,535	41.8%	14,825	28.3%
Services	4,431	19.6%	75,419	27.8%	17,021	6.8%

WASHINGTON COUNTY

Population 1997 (Est.)	27,143	# Households 1995 (Projection)	9,000	Personal Income 1995 ($000)	$172,294
Land Area (Sq. Mi.)	514.5	% Family	76.8%	Avg. Wage Per Job 1995	$18,558
Population Density 1997	52.8	% Non-Family	23.8%	Employed in 1996	10,910
% Under 20 1996	29.2%	% Living Alone	21.1%	Unemployed in 1996	810
% 65 & Over 1996	13.6%	Births 1995	335	Unemployment Rate 1996	6.9%
% White 1996	99.6%	Births to Teens 1995	60	Avg. Covered Payroll 1996 ($000)	$31,311
% African-Amer. 1996	0.1%	Deaths 1995	246	Average Weekly Earnings in Manufacturing 1996	$441.75
% Hispanic* 1996	0.6%	Marriages 1995	257	Registered Vehicles 1996	26,159

*May be of any race.

Percent of Total Population By Sex and Age

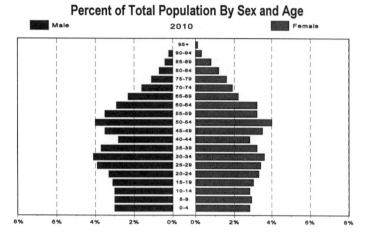

Male   2010   Female

Population Projections

Age Groups	2000	2010	% Change
0-17	5,740	5,320	-7.3%
18-24	2,750	2,260	-17.8%
25-39	4,930	5,500	11.6%
40-59	6,800	6,860	0.9%
60-74	2,810	3,520	25.3%
75 +	1,570	1,600	1.9%
Total	24,600	25,100	2.0%

Personal Income
Real 1995 Dollars ($000)

	1990	1995	% Chg.
Total Earnings by Place of Work	155,616	172,294	10.7%
Less Personal Contributions for Social Insurance	10,208	12,394	21.4%
Net Income by Place of Work	145,408	159,900	10.0%
Plus Residence Adjustment	99,078	137,829	39.1%
Net Income by Place of Residence	244,486	297,729	21.8%
Plus Dividends, Rent and Interest	57,309	50,391	-12.1%
Plus Transfer Payments	60,046	79,123	31.8%
Personal Income by Place of Residence	361,842	427,243	18.1%
Per Capita Income ($)	15,242	16,385	7.5%
Rank	83	81	48

Educational Attainment 1990

Graduate or Prof. Degree
Bachelor's Degree
Associate Degree
Some College No Degree
High School Graduate
9th-12th No Diploma
Less than 9th Grade

0   2,000   4,000   6,000   8,000

High School Grad or Higher
Percent: 66%
Rank in State: 79

Population Change by Decade
(1990-2000 projected)

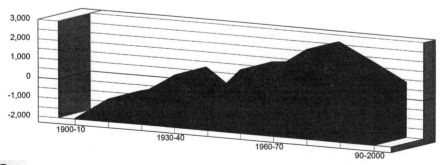

3,000
2,000
1,000
0
-1,000
-2,000

1900-10   1930-40   1960-70   90-2000

Occupation of Employed Persons Age 16 & Over

	1990	% Chg. 80-90
Managerial & Professional	1,295	24.6
Technical, Sales & Admin. Support	2,353	45.8
Service Occupations	1,119	24.6
Farming, Forestry and Fishing	616	-17.2
Precision Production, Craft & Repair	1,605	21.3
Operators, Fabricators	3,663	35.0

Top 5 Counties Commuting in 1990

From Washington Into:		Into Washington From:	
Outside Indiana	1,131	Orange	283
Clark	993	Clark	181
Floyd	492	Harrison	167
Jackson	270	Scott	156
Scott	251	Outside Indiana	87

6,594 persons lived and worked in this county.

3,879 lived in the county but worked elsewhere.

Number of Establishments
(% Change 1990-1995)

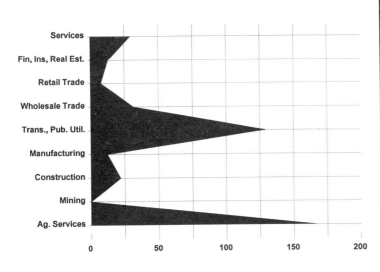

Establishments by Sector 1995

Industry	Number of Establishments	% with fewer than 10 employees
Ag. Services	8	100.0%
Mining	2	50.0%
Construction	39	89.7%
Manufacturing	46	47.8%
Transportation, Public Utilities	39	87.2%
Wholesale Trade	25	80.0%
Retail Trade	111	75.7%
Finance, Insurance, Real Estate	35	88.6%
Services	123	90.2%

Private Industry	Employment		Real Earnings ($000)		Average Earnings Per Job	
	1995	% Chg. 90-95	1995	Real % Chg. 90-95	1995	Real % Chg. 90-95
Ag. Services	93	34.8%	1,036	33.8%	11,140	-0.7%
Mining	17	-22.7%	692	12.0%	40,706	45.0%
Construction	483	27.1%	10,529	41.8%	21,799	11.5%
Manufacturing	2,780	0.4%	72,606	9.2%	26,117	8.8%
Transportation, Public Utilities	347	27.6%	9,500	31.4%	27,378	3.0%
Wholesale Trade	148	-27.5%	2,914	-35.8%	19,689	-11.5%
Retail Trade	1,450	12.9%	18,589	21.7%	12,820	7.8%
Finance, Insurance, Real Estate	351	-2.0%	4,369	6.9%	12,447	9.0%
Services	1,638	17.2%	21,892	31.1%	13,365	11.9%

For EDIN tables, sources and footnotes, see page 380.

WAYNE COUNTY

Population 1997 (Est.)	71,800	# Households 1995 (Projection)	27,200	Personal Income 1995 ($000)	$1,055,552
Land Area (Sq. Mi.)	403.6	% Family	71.7%	Avg. Wage Per Job 1995	$21,793
Population Density 1997	177.9	% Non-Family	28.3%	Employed in 1996	36,930
% Under 20 1996	27.5%	% Living Alone	25.0%	Unemployed in 1996	1,780
% 65 & Over 1996	15.3%	Births 1995	903	Unemployment Rate 1996	4.6%
% White 1996	93.4%	Births to Teens 1995	161	Avg. Covered Payroll 1996 ($000)	$204,277
% African-Amer. 1996	5.8%	Deaths 1995	772	Average Weekly Earnings in Manufacturing 1996	$602.50
% Hispanic* 1996	0.7%	Marriages 1995	651	Registered Vehicles 1996	64,783

*May be of any race.

Percent of Total Population By Sex and Age

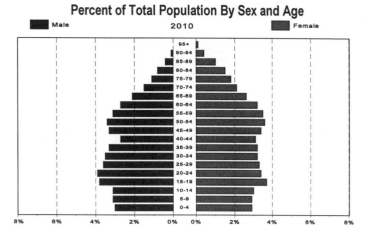

Population Projections

Age Groups	2000	2010	% Change
0-17	16,940	15,620	-7.8%
18-24	7,400	7,110	-3.9%
25-39	13,610	13,980	2.7%
40-59	18,360	18,170	-1.0%
60-74	8,920	9,850	10.4%
75 +	5,010	4,960	-1.0%
Total.	70,200	69,700	-0.7%

Personal Income
Real 1995 Dollars ($000)

	1990	1995	% Chg.
Total Earnings by Place of Work	943,458	1,055,552	11.9%
Less Personal Contributions for Social Insurance	62,471	74,451	19.2%
Net Income by Place of Work	880,987	981,101	11.4%
Plus Residence Adjustment	-43,240	-56,108	29.8%
Net Income by Place of Residence	837,747	924,993	10.4%
Plus Dividends, Rent and Interest	229,979	224,655	-2.3%
Plus Transfer Payments	224,869	267,172	18.8%
Personal Income by Place of Residence	1,292,595	1,416,820	9.6%
Per Capita Income ($)	17,954	19,593	9.1%
Rank	46	38	26

Educational Attainment 1990

High School Grad or Higher
Percent: 71%
Rank in State: 70

Population Change by Decade
(1990-2000 projected)

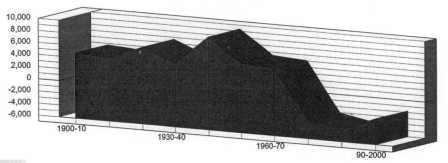

For EDIN tables, sources and footnotes, see page 380.

Occupation of Employed Persons Age 16 & Over

	1990	% Chg. 80-90
Managerial & Professional	6,968	19.5
Technical, Sales & Admin. Support	8,830	4.7
Service Occupations	4,842	10.3
Farming, Forestry and Fishing	929	-13.4
Precision Production, Craft & Repair	4,003	3.7
Operators, Fabricators	7,078	-7.7

Top 5 Counties Commuting in 1990

From Wayne Into:		Into Wayne From:	
Outside Indiana	1,241	Outside Indiana	2,502
Fayette	890	Randolph	770
Randolph	330	Henry	682
Marion	302	Fayette	622
Henry	292	Union	565

28,346 persons lived and worked in this county.
3,600 lived in the county but worked elsewhere.

Number of Establishments
(% Change 1990-1995)

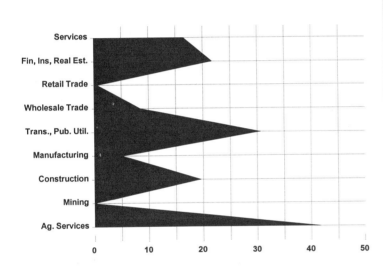

Establishments by Sector 1995

Industry	Number of Establishments	% with fewer than 10 employees
Ag. Services	17	100.0%
Mining	4	25.0%
Construction	159	84.3%
Manufacturing	142	39.4%
Transportation, Public Utilities	81	63.0%
Wholesale Trade	115	60.9%
Retail Trade	466	62.7%
Finance, Insurance, Real Estate	157	86.0%
Services	623	81.2%

Private Industry	Employment		Real Earnings ($000)		Average Earnings Per Job	
	1995	% Chg. 90-95	1995	Real % Chg. 90-95	1995	Real % Chg. 90-95
Ag. Services	227	2.7%	1,899	-24.0%	8,366	-26.0%
Mining	80	17.6%	1,369	46.7%	17,112	24.7%
Construction	1,950	9.0%	56,547	23.6%	28,998	13.4%
Manufacturing	9,323	1.4%	337,675	5.2%	36,220	3.7%
Transportation, Public Utilities	2,500	56.9%	66,195	49.7%	26,478	-4.6%
Wholesale Trade	1,842	9.3%	101,331	23.3%	55,011	12.8%
Retail Trade	8,419	12.4%	109,708	7.0%	13,031	-4.8%
Finance, Insurance, Real Estate	1,860	-3.9%	33,680	5.7%	18,108	10.0%
Services	12,249	23.7%	228,683	21.5%	18,670	-1.8%

For EDIN tables, sources and footnotes, see page 380.

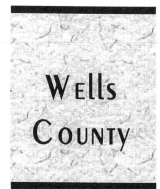

Wells County

Population 1997 (Est.)	26,773	# Households 1995 (Projection)	9,600	Personal Income 1995 ($000)	$314,932
Land Area (Sq. Mi.)	370.0	% Family	76.8%	Avg. Wage Per Job 1995	$22,098
Population Density 1997	72.4	% Non-Family	23.2%	Employed in 1996	14,180
% Under 20 1996	29.8%	% Living Alone	20.9%	Unemployed in 1996	490
% 65 & Over 1996	13.7%	Births 1995	360	Unemployment Rate 1996	3.3%
% White 1996	99.6%	Births to Teens 1995	54	Avg. Covered Payroll 1996 ($000)	$61,436
% African-Amer. 1996	0.0%	Deaths 1995	245	Average Weekly Earnings in Manufacturing 1996	$567.50
% Hispanic* 1996	1.3%	Marriages 1995	234	Registered Vehicles 1996	28,223

*May be of any race.

Percent of Total Population By Sex and Age

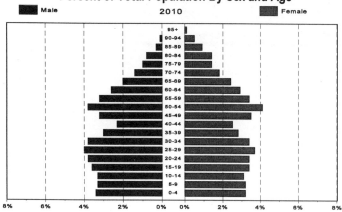

Population Projections

Age Groups	2000	2010	% Change
0-17	7,050	6,630	-6.0%
18-24	2,940	2,780	-5.4%
25-39	4,950	5,770	16.6%
40-59	7,220	7,280	0.8%
60-74	2,890	3,620	25.3%
75 +	1,760	1,790	1.7%
Total	26,800	27,900	4.1%

Personal Income
Real 1995 Dollars ($000)

	1990	1995	% Chg.
Total Earnings by Place of Work	266,178	314,932	18.3%
Less Personal Contributions for Social Insurance	17,261	21,726	25.9%
Net Income by Place of Work	248,916	293,206	17.8%
Plus Residence Adjustment	100,091	112,912	12.8%
Net Income by Place of Residence	349,007	406,118	16.4%
Plus Dividends, Rent and Interest	105,676	91,205	-13.7%
Plus Transfer Payments	61,355	75,609	23.2%
Personal Income by Place of Residence	516,038	572,932	11.0%
Per Capita Income ($)	19,891	21,633	8.8%
Rank	18	18	31

Educational Attainment 1990

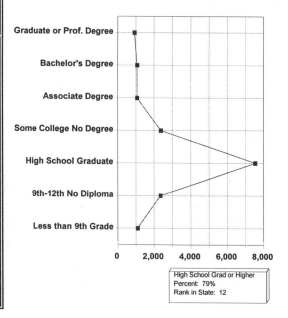

High School Grad or Higher
Percent: 79%
Rank in State: 12

Population Change by Decade
(1990-2000 projected)

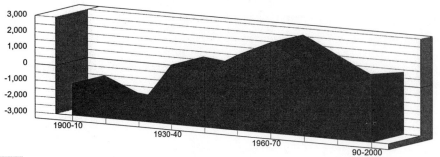

For EDIN tables, sources and footnotes, see page 380.

Occupation of Employed Persons Age 16 & Over

	1990	% Chg. 80-90
Managerial & Professional	2,305	33.1
Technical, Sales & Admin. Support	3,371	22.3
Service Occupations	1,738	21.0
Farming, Forestry and Fishing	588	-20.4
Precision Production, Craft & Repair	1,755	7.5
Operators, Fabricators	3,184	-4.2

Top 5 Counties Commuting in 1990

From Wells Into:		Into Wells From:	
Allen	3,218	Adams	599
Huntington	639	Huntington	423
Adams	434	Allen	403
Grant	191	Blackford	392
Blackford	138	Jay	193

7,696 persons lived and worked in this county.
4,949 lived in the county but worked elsewhere.

Number of Establishments
(% Change 1990-1995)

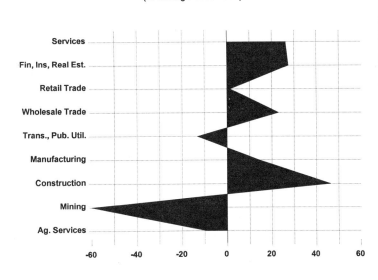

Establishments by Sector 1995

Industry	Number of Establishments	% with fewer than 10 employees
Ag. Services	10	90.0%
Mining	2	100.0%
Construction	82	89.0%
Manufacturing	48	35.4%
Transportation, Public Utilities	26	84.6%
Wholesale Trade	48	72.9%
Retail Trade	153	68.0%
Finance, Insurance, Real Estate	51	92.2%
Services	202	84.2%

Private Industry	Employment		Real Earnings ($000)		Average Earnings Per Job	
	1995	% Chg. 90-95	1995	Real % Chg. 90-95	1995	Real % Chg. 90-95
Ag. Services	NA	NA	NA	NA	NA	NA
Mining	NA	NA	NA	NA	NA	NA
Construction	601	13.4%	13,733	9.0%	22,850	-3.9%
Manufacturing	3,503	15.1%	125,260	30.7%	35,758	13.6%
Transportation, Public Utilities	469	19.3%	13,362	28.4%	28,490	7.6%
Wholesale Trade	450	23.3%	13,553	30.0%	30,118	5.5%
Retail Trade	2,747	8.0%	39,502	16.3%	14,380	7.7%
Finance, Insurance, Real Estate	511	1.4%	6,444	20.4%	12,611	18.7%
Services	3,179	5.3%	60,143	12.1%	18,919	6.4%

White County

Population 1997 (Est.)	25,041	# Households 1995 (Projection)	8,800	Personal Income 1995 ($000)	$302,026
Land Area (Sq. Mi.)	505.3	% Family	73.2%	Avg. Wage Per Job 1995	$19,579
Population Density 1997	49.6	% Non-Family	26.9%	Employed in 1996	13,540
% Under 20 1996	28.5%	% Living Alone	24.2%	Unemployed in 1996	950
% 65 & Over 1996	15.9%	Births 1995	336	Unemployment Rate 1996	6.5%
% White 1996	99.5%	Births to Teens 1995	56	Avg. Covered Payroll 1996 ($000)	$51,543
% African-Amer. 1996	0.0%	Deaths 1995	252	Average Weekly Earnings in Manufacturing 1996	$441.50
% Hispanic* 1996	1.0%	Marriages 1995	246	Registered Vehicles 1996	27,513

*May be of any race.

Percent of Total Population By Sex and Age

Male   2010   Female

(Population pyramid chart showing age groups from 0-4 to 95+ on vertical axis, with percentages from 8% to 8% on horizontal axis)

Population Projections

Age Groups	2000	2010	% Change
0-17	5,930	5,870	-1.0%
18-24	2,530	2,220	-12.3%
25-39	4,130	4,960	20.1%
40-59	6,210	5,940	-4.3%
60-74	2,860	3,060	7.0%
75 +	1,750	1,710	-2.3%
Total	23,400	23,800	1.7%

Personal Income
Real 1995 Dollars ($000)

	1990	1995	% Chg.
Total Earnings by Place of Work	250,178	302,026	20.7%
Less Personal Contributions for Social Insurance	15,757	20,670	31.2%
Net Income by Place of Work	234,422	281,356	20.0%
Plus Residence Adjustment	37,034	35,367	-4.5%
Net Income by Place of Residence	271,455	316,723	16.7%
Plus Dividends, Rent and Interest	85,706	79,492	-7.3%
Plus Transfer Payments	71,501	87,554	22.5%
Personal Income by Place of Residence	428,662	483,769	12.9%
Per Capita Income ($)	18,408	19,655	6.8%
Rank	35	37	56

Educational Attainment 1990

(Chart showing educational attainment levels: Graduate or Prof. Degree, Bachelor's Degree, Associate Degree, Some College No Degree, High School Graduate, 9th-12th No Diploma, Less than 9th Grade; horizontal axis from 0 to 8,000)

High School Grad or Higher
Percent: 78%
Rank in State: 17

Population Change by Decade
(1990-2000 projected)

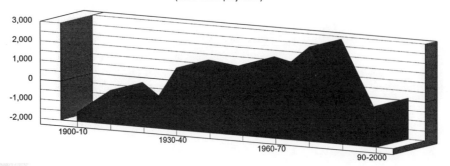

(Chart with vertical axis from -2,000 to 3,000 and horizontal axis with decades 1900-10, 1930-40, 1960-70, 90-2000)

For EDIN tables, sources and footnotes, see page 380.

Occupation of Employed Persons Age 16 & Over

	1990	% Chg. 80-90
Managerial & Professional	2,048	31.1
Technical, Sales & Admin. Support	2,743	29.4
Service Occupations	1,335	25.8
Farming, Forestry and Fishing	739	-15.7
Precision Production, Craft & Repair	1,533	-2.4
Operators, Fabricators	2,571	-11.3

Top 5 Counties Commuting in 1990

From White Into:		Into White From:	
Tippecanoe	2,009	Carroll	829
Cass	383	Tippecanoe	495
Jasper	329	Jasper	297
Carroll	247	Cass	289
Pulaski	145	Pulaski	203

7,305 persons lived and worked in this county.

3,549 lived in the county but worked elsewhere.

Number of Establishments
(% Change 1990-1995)

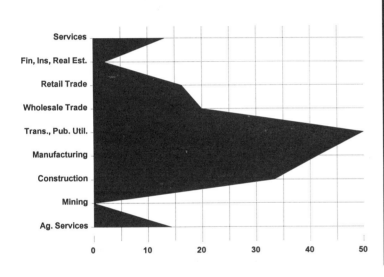

Establishments by Sector 1995

Industry	Number of Establishments	% with fewer than 10 employees
Ag. Services	16	87.5%
Mining	1	0.0%
Construction	64	90.6%
Manufacturing	58	50.0%
Transportation, Public Utilities	48	68.8%
Wholesale Trade	60	70.0%
Retail Trade	186	71.0%
Finance, Insurance, Real Estate	52	82.7%
Services	198	90.4%

Private Industry	Employment		Real Earnings ($000)		Average Earnings Per Job	
	1995	% Chg. 90-95	1995	Real % Chg. 90-95	1995	Real % Chg. 90-95
Ag. Services	172	37.6%	1,816	32.2%	10,558	-3.9%
Mining	14	7.7%	546	50.3%	39,000	39.5%
Construction	555	19.1%	11,466	22.6%	20,659	3.0%
Manufacturing	4,860	53.1%	138,696	48.3%	28,538	-3.1%
Transportation, Public Utilities	700	4.5%	22,145	2.7%	31,636	-1.7%
Wholesale Trade	639	35.1%	16,942	32.2%	26,513	-2.1%
Retail Trade	2,410	22.6%	29,279	21.9%	12,149	-0.6%
Finance, Insurance, Real Estate	440	-14.9%	8,166	-2.3%	18,559	14.8%
Services	2,410	14.7%	33,435	16.1%	13,873	1.2%

For EDIN tables, sources and footnotes, see page 380.

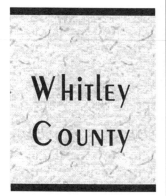

Whitley County

Population 1997 (Est.)	29,969	# Households 1995 (Projection)	10,300	Personal Income 1995 ($000)	$354,518
Land Area (Sq. Mi.)	335.5	% Family	76.8%	Avg. Wage Per Job 1995	$21,722
Population Density 1997	89.3	% Non-Family	22.9%	Employed in 1996	15,650
% Under 20 1996	30.0%	% Living Alone	19.9%	Unemployed in 1996	490
% 65 & Over 1996	13.2%	Births 1995	409	Unemployment Rate 1996	3.0%
% White 1996	99.4%	Births to Teens 1995	48	Avg. Covered Payroll 1996 ($000)	$69,816
% African-Amer. 1996	0.1%	Deaths 1995	282	Average Weekly Earnings in Manufacturing 1996	$534.50
% Hispanic* 1996	0.6%	Marriages 1995	236	Registered Vehicles 1996	31,385

*May be of any race.

Percent of Total Population By Sex and Age

■ Male 2010 ■ Female

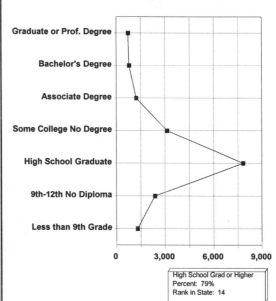

Population Projections

Age Groups	2000	2010	% Change
0-17	7,580	7,300	-3.7%
18-24	3,120	2,950	-5.4%
25-39	5,400	6,300	16.7%
40-59	8,080	7,980	-1.2%
60-74	3,160	3,840	21.5%
75 +	1,680	1,790	6.5%
Total	29,000	30,200	4.1%

Personal Income
Real 1995 Dollars ($000)

	1990	1995	% Chg.
Total Earnings by Place of Work	324,384	354,518	9.3%
Less Personal Contributions for Social Insurance	20,767	24,010	15.6%
Net Income by Place of Work	303,617	330,508	8.9%
Plus Residence Adjustment	73,665	122,232	65.9%
Net Income by Place of Residence	377,281	452,740	20.0%
Plus Dividends, Rent and Interest	84,746	83,487	-1.5%
Plus Transfer Payments	69,997	84,200	20.3%
Personal Income by Place of Residence	532,025	620,427	16.6%
Per Capita Income ($)	19,179	21,059	9.8%
Rank	23	21	21

Educational Attainment 1990

Graduate or Prof. Degree
Bachelor's Degree
Associate Degree
Some College No Degree
High School Graduate
9th-12th No Diploma
Less than 9th Grade

0   3,000   6,000   9,000

High School Grad or Higher
Percent: 79%
Rank in State: 14

Population Change by Decade
(1990-2000 projected)

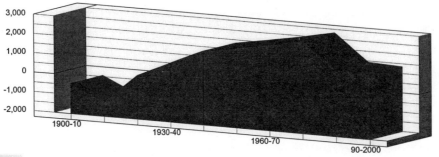

For EDIN tables, sources and footnotes, see page 380.

Occupation of Employed Persons Age 16 & Over		
	1990	% Chg. 80-90
Managerial & Professional	2,262	42.0
Technical, Sales & Admin. Support	3,443	29.8
Service Occupations	1,693	21.9
Farming, Forestry and Fishing	318	-49.4
Precision Production, Craft & Repair	2,259	28.0
Operators, Fabricators	3,733	6.4

Top 5 Counties Commuting in 1990			
From Whitley Into:		Into Whitley From:	
Allen	3,970	Allen	1,691
Kosciusko	657	Noble	660
Huntington	325	Kosciusko	503
Noble	259	Huntington	307
Wabash	112	Dekalb	119

7,639 persons lived and worked in this county.
5,878 lived in the county but worked elsewhere.

Number of Establishments
(% Change 1990-1995)

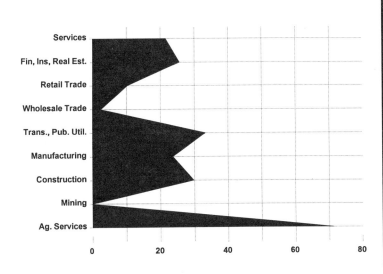

Establishments by Sector 1995		
Industry	Number of Establishments	% with fewer than 10 employees
Ag. Services	12	91.7%
Mining	0	NA
Construction	87	87.4%
Manufacturing	68	42.6%
Transportation, Public Utilities	20	60.0%
Wholesale Trade	42	69.0%
Retail Trade	161	66.5%
Finance, Insurance, Real Estate	49	85.7%
Services	209	79.4%

Private Industry	Employment		Real Earnings ($000)		Average Earnings Per Job	
	1995	% Chg. 90-95	1995	Real % Chg. 90-95	1995	Real % Chg. 90-95
Ag. Services	148	28.7%	2,645	41.6%	17,872	10.0%
Mining	NA	NA	90	-32.6%	NA	NA
Construction	767	11.6%	18,041	15.1%	23,522	3.1%
Manufacturing	5,379	10.2%	172,543	3.1%	32,077	-6.5%
Transportation, Public Utilities	478	15.2%	14,585	25.3%	30,513	8.8%
Wholesale Trade	395	26.2%	9,876	30.3%	25,003	3.3%
Retail Trade	2,568	12.4%	28,912	18.6%	11,259	5.5%
Finance, Insurance, Real Estate	523	-10.6%	7,974	10.4%	15,247	23.5%
Services	2,868	29.9%	49,865	32.8%	17,387	2.3%

For EDIN tables, sources and footnotes, see page 380.

Data Sources for the Indiana Counties in Profile

Population
> Source: U.S. Bureau of the Census
> EDIN table: POPE

Land Area
> Source: U.S. Bureau of the Census
> EDIN table: POPD

Population Density
> Source: U.S. Bureau of the Census
> EDIN table: POPE, POPD

% Under 20
> Source: U.S. Bureau of the Census
> EDIN table: PAGE

% 65 and Over
> Source: U.S. Bureau of the Census
> EDIN table: PAGE

% White
> Source: U.S. Bureau of the Census
> EDIN table: PORE

% African-American
> Source: U.S. Bureau of the Census
> EDIN table: PORE

% Hispanic
> Source: U.S. Bureau of the Census
> EDIN table: PORE

Number of Households
> Source: U.S. Bureau of the Census
> EDIN table: HHPP

% Family
> Source: U.S. Bureau of the Census
> EDIN table: HHPP

% Non-family
> Source: U.S. Bureau of the Census
> EDIN table: HHPP

% Living Alone
> Source: U.S. Bureau of the Census
> EDIN table: HHPP

Births
> Source: Indiana Department of Health
> EDIN table: VITB

Births to Teens
> Source: Indiana Department of Health
> EDIN table: KIDS

Deaths
> Source: Indiana Department of Health
> EDIN table: VITD

Marriages
> Source: Indiana Department of Health
> EDIN table: VIMR

Personal Income
> Source: U.S. Bureau of Economic Analysis
> EDIN table: PIRE

Average Wage Per Job
> Source: U.S. Bureau of Economic Analysis
> EDIN table: WAGE

Employed
> Source: Indiana Department of Workforce Development
> EDIN table: LFAA

Unemployed
> Source: Indiana Department of Workforce Development
> EDIN table: LFAA

Unemployment Rate
> Source: Indiana Department of Workforce Development
> EDIN table: LFAA

Average Covered Payroll
> Source: Indiana Department of Workforce Development
> EDIN table: PAYC

Average Weekly Earnings in Manufacturing
> Source: Indiana Department of Workforce Development
> EDIN table: PAYE

Registered Vehicles
> Source: Indiana Bureau of Motor Vehicles
> EDIN table: REGT

Total Population by Sex and Age
> Source: U.S. Bureau of the Census
> EDIN table: PPAF, PPAM

Population Projections
> Source: Indiana University Kelley School of Business, 1993 edition
> EDIN table: PPTA

Personal Income
> Source: U.S. Bureau of Economic Analysis
> EDIN table: PIRE

Educational Attainment
> Source: U.S. Bureau of the Census
> EDIN table: EDAT

Population Change by Decade
> Source: U.S. Bureau of the Census
> EDIN table: POPU

Occupation of Employed Persons Age 16 and Over
> Source: U.S. Bureau of the Census
> EDIN table: OCCS

Top 5 Counties Commuting
> Source: U.S. Bureau of the Census
> EDIN table: CPAT, CPAF

Number of Establishments
> Source: U.S. Bureau of the Census
> EDIN table: EMIE

Establishments by Sector
> Source: U.S. Bureau of the Census
> EDIN table: EMIC

Private Industry Employment
> Source: U.S. Bureau of Economic Analysis
> EDIN table: EMPT

Private Industry Earnings
> Source: U.S. Bureau of Economic Analysis
> EDIN table: PITE

Private Industry Average Earnings Per Job
> Source: U.S. Bureau of Economic Analysis
> EDIN table: PITE

Further Sources of Information

Federal	Indiana

Federal

U.S. Bureau of the Census
Customer Services
Washington, DC 20233
P: 301.457.4100
F: 301.457.3842
Web: www.census.gov

U.S. Bureau of Economic Analysis
Public Information Office
Washington, D.C. 20230
P: 202.606.9900
F: 202.606-5310
Web: www.bea.doc.gov

U.S. Bureau of Labor Statistics
Division of Information Services
2 Massachusetts Avenue, N.E. Room 2860
Washington, D. C. 20212
P: 202.606.5886
F: 202.606.7890
Web: www.bls.gov

U.S. Bureau of Justice Statistics
810 Seventh Street, NW
Washington, DC 20253
P: 202.307.0765
Web: www.ojp.usdoj.gov

Bureau of Transportation Statistics,
400 Seventh Street, S.W.
Washington, D.C. 20590
P: 202.554.3564; 800.853.1351
F: 202.366.3640
Web: www.bts.gov

U.S. Department of Agriculture
14th St. and Independence Avenue S.W.
Washington, DC 20250
P: 202.720.2791
Web: www.usda.gov

For a more complete list of federal agencies with statistical information, go to:
www.fedstats.gov

Indiana

Indiana Business Research Center
Indiana University, Kelley School of Business
801 W. Michigan St. - Suite 4000
Indianapolis, IN 46202-5151
P: 317.274.2979
F: 317.274.3312
Web: www.iupui.edu/it/ibrc

Indiana Department of Commerce
One North Capitol Ave.
Indianapolis, IN 46204
P: 317.232.8800
F: 317.232.5123
Web: www.ai.org/doc/

Indiana Family & Social Services Administration
Indiana Government Center
Indianapolis, IN 46204
P: 317.233.4453
F: 317.232-6467
Web: www.ai.org/fssa

Indiana State Department of Health
2 N. Meridian St.
Indianapolis, IN 46204
P: 317.233.1325
F: 317.233.7210
Web: www.ai.org/doh

Indiana State Library
State Data Center
140 North Senate Ave.
Indianapolis, IN 46204
P: 317.232.3733
F: 317.232.3728
Web: www.statelib.lib.in.us

Indiana Department of Workforce Development
Labor Market Information
10 North Senate Ave.
P: 317.232.7670
F: 317.233.0317
Web: www.dwd.state.in.us/

For a more complete list of state agencies, go to:
www.ai.org

DATE DUE